American Politics & Government Today

AP® Edition

VOTE
HERE
City of Milwaukee
WARNING
$100 to $500 fine or
imprisonment for removing
or tampering with this sign
4057

AP® Edition

American Politics & Government Today

William T. Bianco
Indiana University, Bloomington

Kimberly A. Owens
Shaker Heights High School

David T. Canon
University of Wisconsin, Madison

James Wehrli
American School of Paris

Julie U. Strong
Albemarle High School

W. W. NORTON & COMPANY
Independent Publishers Since 1923

W. W. Norton & Company has been independent since its founding in 1923, when William Warder Norton and Mary D. Herter Norton first published lectures delivered at the People's Institute, the adult education division of New York City's Cooper Union. The firm soon expanded its program beyond the Institute, publishing books by celebrated academics from America and abroad. By midcentury, the two major pillars of Norton's publishing program—trade books and college texts—were firmly established. In the 1950s, the Norton family transferred control of the company to its employees, and today—with a staff of five hundred and hundreds of trade, college, and professional titles published each year—W. W. Norton & Company stands as the largest and oldest publishing house owned wholly by its employees.

Director of High School Publishing: Jenna Bookin Barry
College Editor: Laura Wilk
Project Editor: Thea Goodrich
College Assistant Editor: Catherine Lillie
High School Editorial Assistant: Rose Paulson
Managing Editor, College: Marian Johnson
Managing Editor, College Digital Media: Kim Yi
Associate Director of Production, College: Eric Pier-Hocking
Ebook Production Assistant: Emily Schwoyer
College Media Editor: Spencer Richardson-Jones
High School Media Editor: Alicia Jimenez
Media Project Editor: Marcus Van Harpen
College Associate Media Editor: Michael Jaoui
College Assistant Media Editor: Lena Nowak-Laird
College Marketing Manager, Political Science: Ashley Sherwood
High School Marketing Manager: Anna Marie Anastasi
Design Director: Jillian Burr
Text Designer: Open, NY
Photo Editor: Catherine Abelman
Photo Researcher: Lynn Gadson
Director of College Permissions: Megan Schindel
Permissions Consultant: Elizabeth Trammell
Composition: KnowledgeWorks Global Ltd.
Manufacturing: Transcontinental Interglobe, Inc.

AP® is a trademark registered and/or owned by the College Board, which was not involved in the production of, and does not endorse, this product.

Permission to use copyrighted material is included on p. A197.

Library of Congress Cataloging-in-Publication Data

Names: Bianco, William T., 1960– author.
Title: American politics & government today / William T. Bianco, David T. Canon,
    Kimberly A. Owens, James Wehrli, Julie U. Strong.
Other titles: American politics and government today
Description: AP edition. | New York : W.W. Norton & Company, 2021. |
    Includes bibliographical references and index.
Identifiers: LCCN 2021033638 | ISBN **9780393887402** (hardcover) | ISBN
    9780393887457 (epub)
Subjects: LCSH: United States--Politics and government--Textbooks. |
    Advanced placement programs (Education)
Classification: LCC JK275 .B529 2013 | DDC 320.473--dc23
LC record available at https://lccn.loc.gov/2021033638

W. W. Norton & Company, Inc., 500 Fifth Avenue, New York, N.Y. 10110
        www.wwnorton.com
W. W. Norton & Company Ltd., 15 Carlisle Street, London W1D 3BS

234567890

About the Authors

William T. Bianco

is professor of political science at Indiana University, Bloomington, where he is also Director of the Indiana Political Analysis Workshop (IPAW). His research focuses on congressional institutions, representation, and science policy. He received his undergraduate degree from SUNY Stony Brook and his MA and PhD from the University of Rochester. He is the author of *Trust: Representatives and Constituents*; *American Politics: Strategy and Choice*; and numerous articles on American politics. His research and graduate students have received funding from the National Science Foundation and the National Council for Eurasian and East European Research. He has also served as a consultant to congressional candidates and party campaign committees, as well as to the U.S. Department of Energy, the U.S. Department of Health and Human Services, and other state and local government agencies. He was also a Fulbright Senior Scholar in Moscow, Russia, during 2011–2012.

David T. Canon

is professor of political science at the University of Wisconsin, Madison. His teaching and research interests focus on American political institutions, especially Congress, and racial representation. He is the author of *Actors, Athletes, and Astronauts: Political Amateurs in the U.S. Congress*; *Race, Redistricting, and Representation: The Unintended Consequences of Black Majority Districts* (winner of the Richard F. Fenno Prize); *The Dysfunctional Congress?* (with Kenneth Mayer); and various articles and book chapters. He is the editor of the *Election Law Journal* and previously served as the Congress editor of *Legislative Studies Quarterly*. He is an AP® consultant and has taught in the University of Wisconsin Summer AP® Institute for U.S. Government and Politics since 1997. Professor Canon is the recipient of a University of Wisconsin Chancellor's Distinguished Teaching Award.

Kimberly A. Owens

is a veteran AP* U.S. Government and Politics teacher at Shaker Heights High School, in an inner-ring suburb of Cleveland, Ohio. She has taught in a variety of settings, both domestic and international, since 1998. She has been involved with AP* Reading for the AP* U.S. Government and Politics exam since 2003, serving as a Reader, Table Leader, Question Leader, Exam Leader, and, for the last six years, as Assistant to the Chief Reader. Previously, she served as the College Board Advisor and on the Course Audit Committee for the AP* U.S. Government and Politics course. Additionally, as a member of the Curriculum Design and Assessment Committee, she contributed to the development of the new Course and Exam Description. She is the former co-chair of the Development Committee, writing and evaluating questions for the AP* exam for the redesigned course. She currently provides support to AP* teachers as the moderator of the online AP* U.S. Government and Politics Teacher Community and as an endorsed consultant for the College Board.

James Wehrli

is a teacher of economics and political science at the American School of Paris, where he also serves on the school's Work Council, the *Comité Social et Economique*. He has taught at the high school and college levels in New York, South Carolina, North Carolina, and Tennessee. As an AP* consultant he has conducted workshops in the United States and abroad for AP* U.S. Government and Politics, AP* Comparative Government and Politics, AP* Microeconomics, and AP* Macroeconomics. He has been an AP* Table Leader and served on the Test Development Committee, during which time he was also the College Board Advisor for AP* Comparative Government and Politics. He holds a PhD and MA in political science, and an MA and BA in economics, all from Binghamton University. In addition to writing and editing several publications for the College Board, he has also been the editor and author of a variety of AP* review books and teachers' guides.

Julie U. Strong

is a veteran AP* U.S. Government and Politics teacher at Albemarle High School in Charlottesville, Virginia. She holds BS and EdM degrees from the University of Virginia. She is the former co-chair of the AP* U.S. Government and Politics Development Committee, as a member of which she designed assessments, contributed to College Board outreach events, and provided mentorship and support to AP* teachers and their students. She serves as an AP* U.S. Government and Politics exam Table Leader and AP* workshop consultant. She also worked as a Curriculum Specialist at the Youth Leadership Initiative, a program of the University of Virginia Center for Politics responsible for developing instructional resources for high school social studies teachers.

Contents in Brief

Contents

Unit I: Foundations of American Democracy

Unit 2: Interactions among Branches of Government

4. Congress   128

5. The Presidency 182

6. The Courts 224

7. The Bureaucracy   272

Unit 3: Civil Liberties and Civil Rights

8. Civil Liberties   314

Unit 4: American Political Ideologies and Beliefs

10. Public Opinion   428

11. Political Parties   472

Unit 5: Political Participation

12. Interest Groups   514

13. Elections   556

14. The Media — 610

Appendix

Preface

American Politics & Government Today, AP® Edition, teaches students of AP® U.S. Government and Politics exactly what they need to know to succeed in the course and become informed citizens. The part structure and chapter organization clearly mirror the five AP® U.S. Government and Politics units, for close alignment with the course framework. The overarching goals of the AP® Edition are to describe what happens in American politics and to explain behavior and outcomes. In part we wish to counter the widespread belief among students that politics is too complicated, too chaotic, or too secretive to make sense of. More than that, we want to empower our students, by demonstrating that American politics is relevant to their lives. This emphasis is also a response to the typical complaints about government textbooks: that they are full of facts but devoid of useful information, and that after students finish reading, they are no better able to answer "why" questions than they were before they cracked open the book.

For this reason, this textbook is also based on three simple premises: politics is conflictual, political process matters, and politics is everywhere. It reflects our belief that politics is explainable, that political outcomes can be understood in terms of decisions made by individuals—and that high school students can make sense of the political world in these terms. It focuses on contemporary American politics, the events and outcomes that our students have lived through and know something about. The result, we believe, is a book that provides an accessible but rigorous account of the American political system.

We focus on conflict and compromise in American politics—identifying what Americans agree and disagree about and assessing how conflict shapes American politics, from campaign platforms to policy outcomes. Though this emphasis seems especially timely given recent elections and the social movements and dynamic global events that preceded them, our aim is to go beyond these events to identify a fundamental constant in American politics: the reality that much of politics is driven by disagreements over the scope and form of government policy, and that compromise is an essential component of virtually all significant changes in government policy. Indeed, it is impossible to imagine politics without conflict. Conflict was embedded in the American political system by the Founders, who set up a system of checks and balances to make sure that no single group could dominate. The Constitution's division of power guarantees that enacting and implementing laws will involve conflict and compromise. Furthermore, the Constitution itself was constructed as one long series of compromises. Accordingly, despite the general dislike people have for conflict, our students must recognize that conflict and compromise lie at the heart of politics.

Throughout the text, we emphasize common sense, showing students that politics inside the Beltway is often strikingly similar to the students' own everyday interactions. For example, what sustains policy compromises made by members of Congress? The fact that the members typically have long careers, that they interact frequently with each other, and that they only deal with colleagues who have kept their word in the past. These strategies are not unique to the political world. Rather, they embody rules of thumb that most people follow (or are at least aware of) in their everyday interactions. In short, we try to help students understand American politics by emphasizing how it is not all that different from the world they know.

This focus on common sense is coupled with many references to the political science literature. We believe that contemporary research has something to say about prediction and explanation of events that students care about—and that these insights can be taught without turning students into game theorists or statisticians. Our text presents the essential insights of contemporary research, motivated by real-world political phenomena and explained using text or simple diagrams. This approach gives students a set of tools for understanding politics, provides an introduction to the political science literature, and matches up well with students' commonsense intuitions about everyday life.

In addition, an AP® U.S. Government and Politics Skills Handbook at the beginning of the book prepares students to master the skills they need for the course by presenting key close-reading strategies, discussing the necessary Reasoning Processes and Disciplinary Practices, and guiding them about how to respond to each type of free-response question. Throughout the chapters, marginal definitions of important terms ensure that students are familiar with the key content assessed in the AP® U.S. Government and Politics exam. These definitions also cover every required foundational document and Supreme Court case.

In the back of the book, you'll find more coverage of both those elements that are necessary knowledge for the AP® course and exam. Each foundational document reprinted in the appendix includes an introduction, the full primary text annotated with clarifications for archaic words and explications of difficult sentences, and a set of "Making Connections" questions that move from ones ensuring comprehension to ones that compare the text to other foundational documents. Callouts to these full documents appear throughout the chapters to provide historical context where relevant. Following the required foundational documents is "Supreme Court Case Clusters," a collection of twelve clusters—each comprised of three or four cases that integrate the Supreme Court cases required for the course with related important ones—on topics such as freedom of speech and the press, privacy and due process, and the powers of Congress. The discussion of each case includes background information, the portions of the Constitution that were contested, a summary of significant facts, key constitutional questions, summaries of and quotations from the majority and dissenting opinions, and implications of the case as it relates to subsequent judicial and policy decisions. The required cases are similarly flagged in the margins of the book to provide context for and examples of their enduring impact. We thank Bob Baker for his work on these clusters.

In accordance with the AP® U.S. Government and Politics Course and Exam Description (CED), we integrate policy into every chapter via "AP® Policy in Practice" sections, which explore the issues behind legislation such as the Affordable Care Act, the DREAM Act, and the Federal Election Campaign Act. This integrated policy coverage allows students to see how social, economic, and foreign policy all relate to real life. Several of the big ideas and units in the CED refer to policy, so it is important that policy topics are woven throughout the entire textbook.

Information literacy is also key to being an informed citizen. The "How it Works" infographics in each chapter—starting with the "Media Checklist for Assessing Reporting on Politics," which provides a framework for evaluating sources of political information—help students hone this skill. This theme is carried throughout the "What Do the Facts Say?" sections, where we apply the five-step framework from the checklist to help evaluate news articles, tweets, and quotations. Additionally, chapter openers use contemporary stories and examples and offer quotations from people on both sides of an issue (from the debate over federal funds for COVID-19 relief to the impeachment of President Trump) to highlight the conflict and compromise theme. We refer to these openers throughout the chapters to illustrate and extend our discussion. Lastly, "Take a Stand" sections explicitly argue both sides of policy questions.

The text is contemporary, but also places recent events in context. Although we do not ignore American history, our stress is on contemporary politics—on the debates, actions, and outcomes that most high school students are aware of. Focusing on recent events emphasizes the utility of the concepts and insights that we develop in the text. It also goes a long way toward establishing the relevance of the AP® class.

Finally, our book offers an individual-level perspective on America's government. The essential message is that politics—elections, legislative proceedings, regulatory choices, and everything else we see—is a product of the decisions made by real flesh-and-blood people. This approach grounds our discussion of politics in the real world. Many texts focus on abstractions such as "the eternal debate," "the great questions," or "the pulse of democracy." We believe that these constructs don't explain where the debate, the questions, or even democracy come from. Nor do they help students understand what's going on in Washington, D.C., and elsewhere, as it's not obvious that the participants themselves care much about these sorts of abstractions—quite the opposite, in fact.

We replace these constructs with a focus on real people and actual choices. The primary goal is to make sense of American politics by understanding why politicians, bureaucrats, judges, and citizens act as they do. That is, we are grounding our description of American politics at the most fundamental level—an individual facing a decision. How, for example, does a voter choose among candidates? Stated that way, it is reasonably easy to talk about where the choice came from, how the individual might evaluate different options, and why one choice might look better than the others. Voters' decisions may be understood by examining the different feasible strategies they employ (issue voting, retrospective evaluations, stereotyping, and so on) and by asking why some voters use one strategy while others use a different one.

By focusing on individuals and choices, we can place students in the shoes of the decision makers, and in so doing, give them insight into why people act as they do. We can discuss, for example, why a House member might favor enacting wasteful pork-barrel spending, even though a proposal full of such projects will make his constituents economically worse off—and why constituents might reward such behavior, even if they suspect the truth. By taking this approach, we are not trying to let legislators off the hook. Rather, we believe that any real understanding of the political process must begin with a sense of the decisions the participants make and why they make them. Focusing on individuals also segues naturally into a discussion of consequences, allowing us to move from examining decisions to describing and evaluating outcomes. In this way, we can show students how large-scale outcomes in politics, such as inefficient programs, don't happen by accident or because of malfeasance. Rather, they are the predictable results of choices made by individuals (here, politicians and voters).

Ultimately, this book reflects our experience as practicing scholars and teachers, as well as interactions with more than 20,000 students. We believe the AP® U.S. Government and Politics Course offers a unique opportunity for giving students the tools they need to behave as knowledgeable citizens. We hope that it works for you as well as it does for us.

Features of the Text and Media Package

The book's "three key ideas"
are fully integrated throughout the text.

- **Politics Is Conflictual** and conflict and compromise are a normal, healthy part of politics. The questions debated in elections and the policy options considered by people in government are generally marked by disagreement at all levels. Making policy typically involves important issues on which people disagree, sometimes strongly, so compromise, bargaining, and tough choices about trade-offs are often necessary.
- **Political Process Matters** because it is the mechanism we have established to resolve conflicts and achieve compromise. Governmental actions result from conscious choices made by voters, elected officials, and bureaucrats. The media often cover political issues in the same way they do sporting events, and though this makes for entertaining news, it also leads citizens to overlook the institutions, rules, and procedures that have a decisive influence on American life. Politics really is not just a game.
- **Politics Is Everywhere** in that the results of the political process affect all aspects of Americans' everyday lives. Politics governs what people can and cannot do, their quality of life, and how they think about events, other people, and situations.

Chapter openers and conclusions

present two sides of a controversy that has dominated media headlines—and about which people have passionate, emotion-driven opinions from both points of view—framed by quotes from politicians, pundits, and everyday people who hold these views. These include the impeachment of President Trump (The Constitution and the Founding), the use of excessive force by the police (Civil Rights), and the CARES legislation (Interest Groups). The "Unpacking the Conflict" sections toward the end of each chapter show how the nuts and bolts of the chapter topic can be applied to help students understand both sides of these debates.

Coverage of the 2020 elections and Trump presidency

provides more than 20 pages and numerous graphics analyzing the 2018 and 2020 elections and the Trump presidency, including coverage of current issues such as the failure to pass "Trumpcare," executive actions around immigration, the governmental response to COVID-19, tax reform, impeachment, the escalation of the trade war with China, and President Trump's use of social media.

Organization around chapter goals

stresses learning objectives and mastery of core material.

- **Chapter Goals** appear at the beginning of the chapter and then recur at the start of the relevant sections throughout the chapter to create a more active reading experience that emphasizes important learning objectives.
- **Extensive end-of-chapter study guides** include summaries, key terms, and practice exam questions. Students have everything they need to master the material in each chapter.

Special features for critical thinking

reinforce the three key ideas while introducing other important ways to think about American politics.

- **The "Media Checklist for Assessing Reporting on Politics" infographic** in Chapter 1 provides a five-step framework of best practices for assessing media sources ranging from tweets to news articles.
- **"How It Works: In Theory/How It Works: In Practice" graphics** highlight key political processes and structures and build graphical literacy. Discussions include the 2020 Democratic primary (Political Parties) and gerrymandering decisions in the court system (The Courts).
- **"What Do the Facts Say?" features** develop quantitative reasoning skills by teaching students to read and interpret data on important political issues and current events. Of particular note are five features focused on honing students' media literacy skills by breaking down various media sources, including tweets, articles, and quotations, using the framework introduced in the Media Checklist for Assessing Reporting on Politics.
- **"Why Should I Care?" sections** draw explicit connections between the chapter material and students' lives. These have also been added to the "Nuts & Bolts" features mentioned below to provide students with a big-picture perspective.
- **"Did You Know?" features and pull quotes** give students tidbits of information that may induce questions and even inspire students to get involved.
- **"Take a Stand" features** address contemporary issues in a pro/con format and invite students to consider how they would argue their own position on the topic. Each feature concludes with critical-thinking questions.
- **"Nuts & Bolts" features** provide students with concise explanations of key concepts, like the difference between civil liberties and civil rights, different kinds of gerrymanders, and brief summaries of campaign finance rules. These features provide an easy way to quickly study and review.

AP® features and tools

- **The AP® U.S. Government and Politics Skills Handbook** provides critical reading strategies, detailed instruction on all of the Reasoning Processes and Disciplinary Practices, and tips for responding to each of the exam's four free-response questions, with suggested exercises throughout.
- **Marginal definitions of key AP® terms** ensure students are familiar with the content assessed in the exam.

- **"AP® Policy in Practice" sections** at the end of each chapter integrate a relevant piece of legislation and walk students through the bill-making process and outcomes.
- **End-of-chapter AP® multiple-choice and free-response questions** offer students a full range of questions types to practice for the exam.
- **Annotated foundational documents and detailed overviews of the required Supreme Court cases,** all referenced throughout the text, are included in the back of the book with additional guidance and pedagogy.
- **The AP® test bank** features over 1,800 questions, securely delivered to teachers in Norton Testmaker, and covers every AP® question type as well as content mastery questions in order to check student understanding.
- **An AP® Course Planning and Pacing Guide (CPPG)** provides recommendations for how to teach the course, whether it is a semester or a full year, with suggestions for lessons and timing, activities, assessments, and further sources for students to explore.

Tools for a dynamic classroom

- **InQuizitive, Norton's adaptive learning tool,** reinforces reading comprehension with a focus on the foundations of government and major political science concepts. Guiding feedback helps students understand why their answers were right or wrong and steers them back to the text. Norton recently conducted a within-subjects efficacy study, and among the students who did not earn a perfect score on the pre-test, we saw an average InQuizitive Effect of 17 percentage points. To try it out, go to https://digital.wwnorton.com/amerpolgovap.
- **The "Evaluating Sources" InQuizitive module,** like the "How to Read Charts and Graphs" tutorial, walks students step by step through identifying and understanding what a source is, how it is used in an argument, and whether it is a valid source or not (such as fake news). Paired with the Media Checklist and Weekly News Quizzes, this module will help students be better prepared than ever to understand and evaluate the news.
- **Weekly News Quizzes** prompt students to engage with the major stories of the day and see their connection to American government. Using a variety of media (print, video, and podcast), each quiz takes a major news story from the previous week and pairs it with assessment for students and a suggested class activity for instructors to use.
- **Features for your Learning Management System (LMS)** allow you to easily bring Norton's high-quality digital content into your existing LMS. The content is fully editable and adaptable to your course needs and contains the following activities and quizzes:
  - **"How to Read Charts and Graphs" tutorial** that provides students with extra practice and guidance interpreting common representations of data that they will encounter in this textbook and in the world,
  - **Simulations** tied to each chapter that allow students to inhabit the role of various political actors to help them better understand political decision making,
  - **"How It Works: In Theory/How It Works: In Practice" animated graphics,** with assessment, that guide students through understanding political processes and institutions,

- **"What Do the Facts Say?" activities** that give students more practice with quantitative skills and more familiarity with how political scientists know what they know, and
- **"Take a Stand" exercises** that present students with multiple sides of contemporary debates and ask them to consider and refine their own views based on what they've learned.
- **An Interactive Instructor's Guide (IIG)** includes chapter outlines, class activities, and discussion questions, and suggestions for additional resources to engage students.
- **Instructor PowerPoints** contain fully customizable lecture slides with clicker questions and "How It Works: In Theory" and "How It Works: In Practice" animated PowerPoint slides for optimal classroom presentation.

Reviewers

Audrey Ambrosino, *Middlesex Community College*
Brent Andersen, *University of Maine, Presque Isle*
Sean Anderson, *California State University, Stanislaus*
John Aughenbaugh, *Virginia Commonwealth University*
Manuel Avalos, *University of Southern Maine*
Bruce Brady, *Norfolk Public Schools*
Cynthia Breneman, *Erie Community College, City Campus*
Kizmet Chandler, *Nitro High School*
Anne Comiskey, *St. Mary's Dominican High School*
Mark Drake, *West Bend West High School*
Denise Dupas, *Del Norte High School*
Erin Engels, *Indiana University–Purdue University Indianapolis*
John C. Evans, *Century College*
Frank Franz, *James Madison High School*
Annika Hagley, *Roger Williams University*
Rick Henderson, *Texas State University*
Josh Herring, *Jones County High School*
Mark Jendrysik, *University of North Dakota*
Jerrod Kelly, *North Carolina Wesleyan College*
Daniel Kirsch, *California State University, Sacramento*
Ronald Kuykendall, *Trident Technical College*
Denise Lutz, *East Meadow High School*

Thomas Marshall, *University of Texas at Arlington*
Laura Matthews, *Rochester High School*
Markie McBrayer, *University of Idaho*
Dylan McLean, *University of West Georgia*
Peter Meinberg, *Hartford Union High School*
Wendel Morden, *Shadow Hills High School*
Anthony Nownes, *University of Tennessee*
Anthony Peek, *Baton Rouge Magnet High School*
Joseph Pelletier, *Bangor High School*
Curt Portzel, *Pepperdine University*
Christina Rice, *Thomas M. Wootton High School*
Heather M. Rice, *Slippery Rock University of Pennsylvania*
Suzanne Robbins, *University of Florida*
Michael Romano, *Shenandoah University*
Marc Schwarz, *Pflugerville Independent School District*
Jeffrey Sher, *McKinney North High School*
Rebecca Small, *Fairfax County Public Schools*
Christine Soderquist, *Kenowa Hills High School*
Bob Turner, *Skidmore College*
Greg Wall, *Amador High School*
Paul Weizer, *Fitchburg State University*
Dave Wells, *Arizona State University*
Adam Wemmer, *Pacifica High School*

AP® U.S. Government and Politics Skills Handbook

An Introduction

Kim Owens
AP® U.S. Government and Politics Teacher
Shaker Heights High School, Shaker Heights, OH

Whether you want to be an attorney, work on Capitol Hill, or be a political consultant trying to help a candidate get elected to office, you need the strong analytic and critical thinking skills that are the hallmark of a political scientist. Political science is a social science that uses scientific methods to understand how individuals and groups behave and how political institutions interact. This introduction aims to provide you with the tools necessary to think like a political scientist and to be successful on the AP® U.S. Government and Politics exam. The goal of this handbook is also to help improve your critical reading, writing, and thinking skills—all of which will be useful in your future endeavors, whether college or career. This handbook will use examples and illustrations from political science and from sections found in this textbook, *American Politics & Government Today*, AP® Edition. However, you can and should use these methods in all your AP® social science courses—and in other subjects, too.

The AP® U.S. Government and Politics course is organized into five units that are commonly taught in college courses. The course is also structured around five themes, known as the big ideas. These themes are the foundation of the course and weave throughout the five units to help enable students to connect concepts in a meaningful way. The following description is taken from the College Board AP® U.S. Government and Politics Course and Exam Description:[1]

"Below are the big ideas of the course and a brief description of each.

- **Big Idea 1: Constitutionalism (CON)**—The U.S. Constitution establishes a system of checks and balances among branches of government and allocates power between federal and state governments. This system is based on the rule of law and the balance between majority rule and minority rights.
- **Big Idea 2: Liberty and Order (LOR)**—Governmental laws and policies balancing order and liberty are based on the U.S. Constitution and have been interpreted differently over time.
- **Big Idea 3: Civic Participation in a Representative Democracy (PRD)**—Popular sovereignty, individualism, and republicanism are important considerations of U.S. laws and policy making and assume citizens will engage and participate.
- **Big Idea 4: Competing Policy-Making Interests (PMI)**—Multiple actors and institutions interact to produce and implement possible policies.
- **Big Idea 5: Methods of Political Analysis (MPA)**—Using various types of analyses, political scientists measure how U.S. political behavior, attitudes, ideologies, and institutions are shaped by a number of factors over time."

---

1. College Board, "AP® U.S. Government and Politics Course and Exam Description," https://apcentral.collegeboard.org/pdf/ap-us-government-and-politics-course-and-exam-description.pdf (accessed 1/15/21).

The AP® U.S. Government and Politics course content is assessed in a three-hour long exam that is divided into two sections with each section worth 50 percent of the overall exam score. Section 1 consists of 55 multiple-choice questions to be completed in 80 minutes and Section 2 consists of four unique free-response question (FRQ) types to be completed in 100 minutes. Details on the free-response question types and recommended timing for each question will be discussed later in the handbook.

To be successful on the exam, you will need to be able to apply the reasoning processes and disciplinary practices that are central to the study and practice of government and politics. These practices and processes were designed by committees of college faculty and expert teachers to ensure that the AP® course reflects and measures college-level expectations for studying political science. Data collected from a range of colleges and universities ensure that the AP® courses and exams represent current scholarship and developments in the discipline of political science.

American Politics & Government Today provides you with opportunities to learn the four reasoning processes:

1. definition/classification
2. process
3. causation
4. comparison

You will also learn five disciplinary practices, along with their associated skills, identified by the experts:

1. concept application
2. SCOTUS (Supreme Court of the United States) application
3. data analysis
4. source analysis
5. argumentation

Skills 1–4 will be evaluated on both the multiple-choice questions and free-response questions. However, the last skill, argumentation, will be assessed only through the free-response questions.

As with any activity, whether playing an instrument or perfecting a free throw or learning a new language, habits of mind must be practiced. However, once you master them, they will help you become a better critical reader, thinker, and writer—and, by extension, a more effective student, worker, and citizen.

This introductory handbook also addresses critical reading strategies that will help you study political science. You already know how to read, but can you do so *critically*? Do you know how to take notes *efficiently* as part of your critical reading process? The first section of this handbook addresses some techniques that will help improve your reading and note-taking skills.

CRITICAL READING STRATEGIES FOR AP® U.S. GOVERNMENT AND POLITICS

When you pick up a novel to read by the pool or before bed, it's likely you're reading passively and for pleasure. You aren't necessarily concentrating for deeper meaning or understanding; your mind may even wander as you read. There might be sections that you find boring and skip altogether. When reading a textbook or a primary or secondary document, you cannot read passively. You must read *actively* for understanding and meaning. The following strategies are skills to help you read more quickly and effectively for comprehension.

Unlike other forms of reading, critical reading requires that you complete multiple passes through the text so that you can get the most out of the material. Don't worry.

This does not mean reading word for word, as you might expect. Instead, you do a preliminary scan to familiarize yourself with the overall structure of the book, a skim of the chapter to get the big picture, a deep-dive reading for understanding and learning, and finally, a reflective review to condense your knowledge by summarizing. Fully engaged active reading will involve note-taking to reinforce learning.

READING STRATEGY #1—KNOW YOUR TEXTBOOK

Special Note: You need to do this initial reading only the first time you encounter a textbook.

1. Examine the title page:
   - Who are the authors and what are their qualifications?
   - Who is the publisher and when was the text published? What does that information tell you about the book?
2. Examine the preface or introduction:
   - What is the purpose of the preface?
   - Do the authors introduce any unusual features of the book in the preface and prepare you to be on the lookout for them?
3. Examine the table of contents:
   - What does the table of contents tell you about the content covered?
   - How is this textbook organized? What are the main divisions?
4. Examine the index, glossary, and other material at the back of the book:
   - What sort of topics should be looked up in the index instead of in the table of contents?
   - Is there a glossary in your textbook? Are accent markings provided to help you pronounce the words?
   - Is there an appendix in your book? Why isn't this information included in the body of the book?
5. Examine the study questions, guides, and other learning aids:
   - Are the study aids in the form of questions, exercises, or activities? Where are they located throughout the chapter?
   - If the text uses questions, do they merely require finding the answers, or must you perform some critical problem-type thinking to arrive at answers?
   - Does the text provide suggestions for other readings or materials designed to help you understand the chapter?
6. Examine the chapter headings, section headings, margin guides, and graphics features:
   - How do the chapter headings and the section headings help you structure your thinking?
   - How do headings and different type fonts help you when skimming a chapter for specific information?
   - How can you use topic sentences, photo captions, artwork (such as maps, charts, diagrams, and tables), and summaries to extend and organize your reading?

READING STRATEGY #2—SURVEY THE CHAPTER (No need to take notes.)

Before your in-depth reading of each textbook chapter, it is helpful to spend a few minutes surveying the material. This survey is similar to knowing the overall plot of a movie before watching it. During the second reading stage, you are merely getting primed. Skim through the chapter and see how the headings and subheadings are organized. Read any chapter summaries. Briefly survey the chapter introduction by reading the topic sentences in each paragraph.

As you complete this quick survey, you will want to ask the following questions:

- What is the overall topic of this chapter?
- What are the political principles, institutions, processes, policies, or behaviors covered in this chapter?
- Which of the five big ideas is most prevalent in this chapter?
- Can you make any connections or comparisons of items in the text to your prior knowledge or a preceding chapter?

The point of this step is to get the big picture the chapter is trying to impart and to understand the overall view before you take a deep dive into the material. At this point, you haven't written any notes and likely have spent around five minutes in your survey of the material. Nevertheless, you have a good preview of what you will be reading and have saved yourself time since you will complete the next step more efficiently.

READING STRATEGY #3—DEEP-DIVE READING FOR UNDERSTANDING (Take notes.)

As your instructor will tell you, reading the assigned material *before* a class lecture or lesson is crucial to understanding the material presented in class. As you do this, remember that you must read actively and maintain focus. The best way to stay focused is to take notes, but first you must understand what you have read. A brief online search of active reading strategies will result in tips touting techniques with five, six, or even ten steps to improve your active reading. But nearly all of these resources share four main components:

1. asking questions while you read
2. identifying or defining any unfamiliar words
3. taking well-organized notes
4. writing a summary of the material

The actions do not always need to take place in this order. Over time, they will develop into a habit—a "habit of mind"—that will come naturally. These four actions are the most significant strategies for successful active reading.

Ask Questions

Continually asking questions is at the heart of critical thinking and reading. *American Politics & Government Today* models this throughout but also provides opportunities for you to create your own questions. For example, let's look at Chapter 1, "Understanding American Politics," on p. 2. The title of the chapter, "Understanding American Politics," is followed by a question, "How does politics work and why does politics matter?" Using this technique as an example, try changing all the titles, subtitles, and section and paragraph headings into questions, as you're reading the textbook. On p. 21 of the textbook, the section heading "Resolving Conflict: Democracy and American Political Values" might become "How does democracy and other American political values help to resolve conflict?" Also notice that each section heading employs a task verb, such as "identify," "describe," or "explain," to help guide your reading. In this case, readers are asked to "Explain how the American values of democracy, liberty, and equality work to resolve political conflict." Using the task verbs will also help prepare you to answer the free-response questions, which are part of the AP® exam. Task verbs and how they apply to the free-response questions will be discussed in detail later in this handbook. These task verbs can also help you formulate questions for not only the section headings but the paragraph headings as well. As you continue reading, on p. 22 (which falls under the same section heading) the paragraph heading is simply "Liberty." Rather than just asking, What is liberty? refer back to the section heading and the task verb and ask yourself, What is liberty and how does this American political value work to resolve political conflict? This method will focus your attention on the concept of liberty being a political principle, rather than just a random term related to the chapter.

These are suggestions for *American Politics & Government Today*, given the design of the textbook and the subject matter. However, they can be used with other textbooks, even those that are not scaffolded in the same way. No one way or set of questions is right for everyone, so you might try different questioning techniques to determine what works best for you. Over time, you may develop your own set of questions based on the type of textbook or subject that you're studying.

Identify Unfamiliar Words

Comprehending what you are reading begins by fully understanding the words found in the text. Studying political science can be similar to studying a foreign language. As you read, are there any words you don't understand? If so, it is imperative that you clarify or define those words so that you can more clearly understand the passage or section.

Typically, the first step readers take is to try to understand the word based on the context (how the term is used in a sentence, paragraph, or section). Does the word become clearer as you reread the words preceding it or as you read further into the text? While context clues are frequently a solid way to decipher meaning, looking words up in a dictionary, glossary, or other source is an important technique used by active readers. Adding new terms to your notes can expand your political science vocabulary and enrich your writing.

If you encounter a confusing or difficult passage, defining any unfamiliar terms will typically ease the confusion. However, there are times when knowing the terms does not help you completely understand the material. The final step to fully identify what you're reading is to *slowly reread* a sentence, paragraph, or section—even aloud. Varying your reading rate and slowing down for tough passages is often necessary for understanding. Slow down enough to enable yourself to untangle tough sections and get an accurate idea of the essential concepts in the passage.

Take Notes

As you complete the deep-dive reading for understanding, you will want to take notes. Reading the text alone is not adequate. Good note-taking is a key component of learning the material and remembering the most important points. Note-taking may seem like a simple task, yet students often experience difficulties with it. The first thing you should remember is that highlighting is not the same as note-taking (especially if you find yourself highlighting nearly everything!). Actively writing out your ideas will help reinforce learning, but you should take notes only after you comprehend the passage. Ask questions, identify words and concepts, and summarize the material as you read each chapter, then use an outline to guide your note-taking. The easiest outline is one based on the textbook chapter headings, subheadings, and subsections. Using your outline, go back through the text and take notes of the items that signify the main ideas and supporting details of that section.

Another difficulty that students often face is taking too many notes. If your notes include most of the text in the book, there's a good chance you aren't differentiating between the author's main points and the material used to tie these points together, which are often composed of multiple examples. Remember that in political science, the focus is on process. You don't need to write everything; the main idea and an example that demonstrates the process will suffice. As an early part of your note-taking, you might consider making comments in the margins of the book if you own it. If you don't, write your comments on sticky notes and place them in the margins. Once you have completed this, add these comments and a summary to your notes for that section.

Write a Summary

When you write a summary, you should precisely and briefly account for the most significant parts of a text. If you can write an effective overview, it is a decent sign that you read the text carefully and comprehended its major arguments and supporting points. Your summary should explain the main idea of each chapter and answer each of the questions that you originally posed. Your summary should also identify which of the five big ideas best relates to the content of the chapter. For most people, this is the final step of the note-taking process. For your purposes, a summary does not need to be too long; between 35 and 50 words should be sufficient.

Practice: Read the first chapter in the textbook, on pp. 2–39. Using the strategies above, complete the steps for "Readings" 2 and 3 and then take notes and write a summary of the chapter.

AP® U.S. GOVERNMENT AND POLITICS REASONING PROCESSES

Once you have learned the content through a careful reading of the textbook and supporting documents, you will use political science reasoning to define, interpret, and evaluate this material. The following four political science reasoning processes identified by the College Board will help you think like a political scientist as you develop arguments that you can support in your written work.

REASONING PROCESS 1: DEFINITION/CLASSIFICATION

Reasoning Process 1 is definition/classification. Students will be expected to demonstrate this by completing the following:[2]

- "Describe characteristics, attributes, traits, and elements in defining terms and concepts
- Classify concepts
- Describe structures and functions
- Describe patterns and/or trends
- Describe the perspective of a source or author
- Describe assumptions and/or reasoning of a source or author"

One aspect of learning political science is akin to learning a new language. Just like when learning a new language, you need to go beyond just identifying the word and be able to give a definition of the term, or describe the term or concept, in order to be able to use it in a meaningful way. Using the cognitive process of describing, whether describing characteristics, elements, structures, or functions, you can learn to talk like a political scientist. Classification is another part of this reasoning process. Continuing with the cognitive process of describing and building on that process by focusing on patterns, trends, perspectives, and assumptions being made by the source or an author can enable you to make connections across content areas.

For example, Figure 13.2 on p. 588 of the textbook is a bar graph that shows turnout of registered voters in both presidential and midterm elections. In order to effectively analyze this data, you will need to use Reasoning Process 1. As part of the curriculum, midterm and presidential elections are important to understand. Most students can define a presidential election and understand that they occur every four years to align with the term of a president. Many students also understand that elections are held

---

2. College Board, "AP® U.S. Government and Politics Course and Exam Description," https://apcentral.collegeboard.org/pdf/ap-us-government-and-politics-course-and-exam-description.pdf (accessed 1/15/21).

more than once every four years. A midterm election is an election that falls on the even years between presidential election years. But just knowing the definition is not enough. Being able to take that definition and describe the concept in relation to other types of elections is essential. Why do political scientists study both midterm and presidential elections? First of all, the entire House of Representatives and one-third of the U.S. Senate is up for election during the midterms. Secondly, the president's party tends to gain seats during a presidential election and lose seats the following midterm election. So when classifying elections, one might think that voter turnout is similar during both midterm and presidential elections. Looking at the graph, you can see that turnout varies both over time and between presidential and midterm elections. The next question to ask is why? This is another reasoning process, causation, that will be discussed later in the handbook.

Practice: To practice, look at Figure 1.2 on p. 19 in Chapter 1. Choose one of the self-identified categories of race and ethnicity. How would you describe this category relative to the overall population? Describe the projected growth trend of your chosen category of the population between 2020 and 2060.

REASONING PROCESS 2: PROCESS

The second reasoning process is process. Students will be expected to demonstrate this by completing the following:[3]

- "Identify steps and/or stages in a process
- Explain how the steps or stages in a process relate to each other
- Explain challenges with processes and/or interactions
- Explain the relevance or significance of processes and/or interactions"

The general definition of a process is "a series of actions or steps taken in order to achieve a particular end."[4] It involves the relationship between cause and effect, or causality. This cognitive operation represents how political scientists think about concepts in the discipline. Rather than focusing on facts and dates, political science is all about process. Its approach to process is one of the ways the discipline separates itself from the study of history.

For instance, look at the How It Works: Passing Legislation infographic (see p. 162 in Chapter 4, "Congress"). What do you notice about the process of how a bill becomes a law? Can you identify the distinct stages in the process? Can you explain how the steps in the bill-making process relate to one another? Where can a bill be amended or where can it die? Does understanding the stages in the process give you enough information to understand how a bill actually becomes a law?

Now look at the How It Works: Passing the Tax Cuts and Jobs Act infographic also in Chapter 4 (see p. 163). What do you notice? By looking at the process that an actual bill took to become law, you can see the challenges involved and the interactions between the committees and political parties. If you are thinking like a political scientist, you see that mastering Reasoning Process 2 requires you to go beyond just identifying the steps and being able to explain the relevance or significance of the process and the interactions within that process.

Practice: This textbook follows the AP® U.S. Government and Politics Course and Exam Description by integrating policy into each content area. To practice Reasoning Process 2, read about the policy-making process on pp. 27–28 in Chapter 1. What are

---

3. College Board, "AP® U.S. Government and Politics Course and Exam Description," https://apcentral.collegeboard.org/pdf/ap-us-government-and-politics-course-and-exam-description.pdf (accessed 1/15/21).
4. Oxford Lexico, "Process," www.lexico.com/definition/process (accessed 1/15/21).

the seven stages in policy making? Now read about the implementation of the Afford-able Care Act of 2010 (see p. 118 in Chapter 3, "Federalism"). Explain how health care policy is part of an ongoing debate between the states and the federal government over who is responsible for providing and helping to pay for health care for citizens.

REASONING PROCESS 3: CAUSATION

The third reasoning process is causation. Students will be expected to demonstrate this by completing the following:[5]

- "Identify causes and/or effects
- Explain the reasons for causes and/or effects
- Explain change over time
- Explain the significance of causes and/or effects
- Explain the implications of change over time"

Causation has to do with determining how or why changes take place. It involves the relationship between cause and effect, or causality. While it is often easy to identify the causes or effects of a relationship, understanding the reasons for the change or the implications of the change over time is often more complicated. This complexity makes it necessary to think like a political scientist when analyzing causation.

Throughout the curriculum, you will encounter opportunities to use this reasoning process. One area in particular is when studying decisions made by the Supreme Court. When the Court accepts a case for review and makes a decision, it is setting precedent that will be used to help evaluate future cases wrestling with the same constitutional issue.

For example, the Supreme Court upheld students' constitutional right to use symbolic speech as a form of protest in the case of *Tinker v. Des Moines Independent Community School District* (1969). The Court noted that since the students "were not disruptive and did not impinge upon the rights of others" their conduct was protected under the First and Fourteenth Amendments. (See p. 333 in Chapter 8, "Civil Liberties.") After reading about the Court's decision, political science students who practice this reasoning process would ask about its significance and implications. Would it enable a student to wear a Black Lives Matter T-shirt to school to protest a series of recent police shootings? How about if the protest was disruptive, as in the case of what some schools classify as inappropriate dress? Does this case also restrict students' rights by serving as a precedent to uphold a dress code?

This example illustrates that you must be mindful of not only the reasons for the change but also the significance and implications of the change. To master this cogni-tive process, you need to ask yourself not only to identify the causes but also to explain the significance and implications of those causes. This reasoning process applies to content beyond Court decisions. It is also used to help you take a deeper dive into analyzing data sources. Earlier in the practice for Reasoning Process 1, you were asked to make observations about information provided in stimulus material. Now using the reasoning process of causation, you build on that skill to figure out the significance and implications of the data. This is how you start thinking like a political scientist!

Practice: To practice, look back at Figure 1.2 on p. 19 in Chapter 1. You already picked one of the self-identified categories of race and ethnicity and described that category relative to the overall population. You also described the projected growth trend of that category of the population between 2020 and 2060. Now use the reasoning

---

5. College Board, "AP® U.S. Government and Politics Course and Exam Description," https://apcentral.collegeboard.org/pdf/ap-us-government-and-politics-course-and-exam-description.pdf (accessed 1/15/21).

process of causation and explain the significance of the data in relation to government and politics. What changes would you expect in American politics and federal policy if the actual population in 2060 matches the projections?

REASONING PROCESS 4: COMPARISON

The final reasoning process is comparison. Students will be expected to demonstrate this by completing the following:[6]

- "Identify relevant categories of comparison
- Identify similarities and/or differences
- Explain the reasons for similarities and/or differences
- Explain the relevance, implications, and/or significance of similarities and differences"

One way you can examine events/processes and their significance is through comparison. **Comparison** (sometimes called compare and contrast) helps political scientists understand how one political concept or institution is similar to or different from another one. Through this reasoning process, political scientists explain not only the reasons for those similarities or differences but also the significance behind those comparisons.

For example, through comparative study, political scientists have determined that Republicans and Democrats share some fundamental similarities. Both political parties seek to control the government by nominating candidates to office. Additionally, they both are decentralized entities composed of a loose network of organizations, groups, and individuals who share a party label but are under no obligation to work together. (See p. 474 in Chapter 11, "Political Parties.")

While the initial comparisons hold true, the two party coalitions differ systematically in terms of their policy preferences. When asked what the top priorities of the Republican Party were, the party coalition responded with terrorism, the economy, and immigration as among the top three. In contrast, the top three priorities of the Democratic Party coalition were environment, education, and health care costs. (See Figure 11.1 on p. 482 in Chapter 11.)

To fully address this reasoning process, you need to go beyond the comparison and explain either the reasons for the similarities and/or differences or the significance of those differences. For example, while Republicans and Democrats are both political parties with the intent of controlling government from within, they differ systematically on their policy preferences, or what they want the government to do. The significance of this is that these data demonstrate that party labels are meaningful and knowing a person's individual party preference tells you something about what that person probably wants the government to do. (See p. 482 in Chapter 11.)

In the end, be sure that the items you are comparing are similar enough to provide some resulting information. If the issues are too different, the comparison will not make sense.

Practice: Both the multiple-choice section and the free-response section of the AP° exam will require you to analyze government and politics using comparisons. To practice, look at the comparison-based multiple-choice question on p. 512 in Chapter 11. When you approach this question type, look at each column and identify the correct answers relative to the heading. There will more than likely be multiple

---

6. College Board, "AP® U.S. Government and Politics Course and Exam Description," https://apcentral.collegeboard.org/pdf/ap-us-government-and-politics-course-and-exam-description.pdf (accessed 1/15/21).

correct answers in each column. Then look across the rows and choose the letter that has a correct answer for both columns in that row. Each chapter has a multiple-choice question formatted in this manner for you to practice.

AP® DISCIPLINARY PRACTICES

In addition to the four reasoning skills identified by the College Board, there are five disciplinary practices that you should learn in order to critically think and write like a political scientist. These disciplinary practices, along with their associated skills (represented by each bullet under the practice and later labeled Skill 1.A, 1.B, and so on), will teach you how to interpret both quantitative and qualitative sources as well as write an effective argument, using foundational documents as evidence to write about political principles, institutions, processes, policies, or behaviors. By using these various discipline-based practices, you are learning more than just the content taught in a traditional high school civics course, as you are continuing on your journey to learn how to think like a political scientist. Not only will these practices and skills prepare you for sequent courses in college but they are also the abilities that you will need to display in both the multiple-choice and the written portion of the AP® U.S. Government and Politics exam.

DISCIPLINARY PRACTICE 1: CONCEPT APPLICATION: Apply political concepts and processes to scenarios in context.

The first disciplinary practice is concept application. Students will be expected to demonstrate this practice, along with the associated skills, by completing the following:[7]

- "Describe political principles, institutions, processes, policies, and behaviors.
- Explain political principles, institutions, processes, policies, and behaviors.
- Compare political principles, institutions, processes, policies, and behaviors.
- Describe political principles, institutions, processes, policies, and behaviors illustrated in different scenarios in context.
- Explain how political principles, institutions, processes, policies, and behaviors apply to different scenarios in context."

The purpose of this practice is to enable you to go beyond rote memorization of political science terminology and instead to demonstrate a deep understanding of the concepts in which these terms exist. In order to achieve this, Practice 1 is scaffolded to prepare you by the end of the course to be able to apply the knowledge that you have learned to different contexts and scenarios. For example, in the associated Skill 1.A, students are asked to demonstrate understanding by describing characteristics of a term or a concept. So prior to a discussion on the extent to which the Electoral College (which is the indirect method used to elect the president of the United States) promotes or impedes democracy, you would first describe the winner-take-all method used by most states to allocate electoral votes. To build on this practice, you would then need to explain the significance of the Electoral College process, which is the focus of Skill 1.B, by explaining how minor parties are affected by the winner-take-all system.

Another associated skill within this practice is Skill 1.C, which focuses on identifying similarities and differences between two different categories and explaining the relevance or significance of those similarities and/or differences. This associated

---

7. College Board, "AP® U.S. Government and Politics Course and Exam Description," https://apcentral.collegeboard.org/pdf/ap-us-government-and-politics-course-and-exam-description.pdf (accessed 1/15/21).

skill is essential in political science, which is why it is also a reasoning process. An example of the application of this skill would be to demonstrate an understanding of the cross-section, in terms of views on issues, among and between the ideologies of liberals, conservatives, and libertarians.

Upon mastery of the associated Skills 1.D and 1.E, you should be able to expand on just providing an explanation of a political concept or process and continue the progression by relating that political concept to a given scenario and explaining the implications. For example, the Founders were concerned with the role that factions (basically, groups with similar interests) would play in the new government. Given a series of quotes, you would need to demonstrate which quote best exemplifies that concern. You would need to understand not only that a faction is a group with similar interests but also which historical quote best represents the Founders' concern about the new government as related to that concept.

In the "Writing for AP® U.S. Government and Politics" section below, the manner in which this practice is applied to Free-Response Question 1 is specifically addressed. However, this practice is also assessed in the multiple-choice section of the AP® exam. Individual and set-based multiple-choice questions require mastery of all of the skills associated with Practice 1.

Practice: The end of Chapter 1 focuses on how the practices are assessed on the multiple-choice section of the AP® exam. For Practice 1, see Questions 1–3 on p. 36.

DISCIPLINARY PRACTICE 2: SCOTUS APPLICATION: Apply Supreme Court decisions.
Disciplinary Practice 2 is Supreme Court of the United States (SCOTUS) application. Students will be expected to demonstrate this practice, along with the associated skills, by completing the following:[8]

- "Describe the facts, reasoning, decision, and majority opinion of required Supreme Court cases.
- Explain how a required Supreme Court case relates to a foundational document or to other primary or secondary sources.
- Compare the reasoning, decision, and majority opinion of a required Supreme Court case to a non-required Supreme Court case.
- Explain how required Supreme Court cases apply to scenarios in context."

The Course and Exam Description has identified 15 required Supreme Court cases. This practice is focused on the SCOTUS and helping you understand the implications of the decisions in those cases. The first associated skill within this practice, Skill 2.A, models the format of how to organize a SCOTUS case by describing the facts, reasoning, decision, and majority opinion of the case.

By understanding the key components of the case, you are then able to compare the case with a primary or secondary source (Skill 2.B). For example, you could compare the decision in *Marbury v. Madison* (1803), which established the principle of judicial review (the Court's ability to declare a law passed by Congress unconstitutional), with the principle of checks and balances, which was a key argument in *Federalist 51*.

You are also asked to compare one of the components in the required case with a component in a nonrequired Supreme Court case (Skill 2.C). While this skill is assessed on the multiple-choice section of the AP® exam, it is one of the key parts of Free-Response Question 3. Strategies on how to apply this skill for that purpose are explicitly detailed in the "Writing for AP® U.S. Government and Politics" section below.

---

8. College Board, "AP® U.S. Government and Politics Course and Exam Description," https://apcentral.collegeboard.org/pdf/ap-us-government-and-politics-course-and-exam-description.pdf (accessed 1/15/21).

Similar to the practice above, the last associated skill in Practice 2 is applying a required Supreme Court case to a scenario in context. For example, after you describe the constitutional right of students to use symbolic speech to protest, as ruled in *Tinker v. Des Moines Independent Community School District* (1969), which allowed students to wear armbands to protest the Vietnam War, related scenarios are then presented. You would then need to identify the scenario that addressed the same constitutional issue of symbolic speech (for example, a group of students is suspended for protesting a series of recent police shootings by wearing Black Lives Matter T-shirts to school). Notice that this scenario was also discussed earlier in the handbook (see Reasoning Process 3: Causation on p. xxxiv). This demonstrates how the reasoning processes are applied to the disciplinary practices.

Practice: The end of Chapter 1 focuses on how the practices are assessed on the multiple-choice section of the AP° exam. For Practice 2, see Question 4 on p. 36.

DISCIPLINARY PRACTICE 3: DATA ANALYSIS: Analyze and interpret quantitative data represented in tables, charts, graphs, maps, and infographics.
The third disciplinary practice is data analysis. Students will be expected to demonstrate this practice, along with the associated skills, by completing the following:[9]
- "Describe the data presented.
- Describe patterns and trends in data.
- Explain patterns and trends in data to draw conclusions.
- Explain what the data implies or illustrates about political principles, institutions, processes, policies, and behaviors.
- Explain possible limitations of the data provided.
- Explain possible limitations of the visual representation of the data provided."

Being able to analyze and interpret quantitative data is fundamental to the work of a political scientist. Political scientists rely on facts and data to understand how political institutions function and individuals behave. The associated skills related to this practice are scaffolded to serve as building blocks to provide the tools needed to interpret tables, charts, graphs, and other visual representations and apply that information to the content being addressed. When Practice 3 is assessed on the AP° exam, multiple-choice questions are presented in sets. The first question will ask you to interpret the data using information found in the stimulus provided and the second question will ask you to analyze that information in terms of how it relates to the content. When you're asked to analyze quantitative stimuli, here are some guidelines that should aid your understanding.

Questions for Interpreting Quantitative Data
- How are the data presented? If the data are supplemented by written material (for example, a caption, heading, map key/legend, or citation), read everything carefully to gain a clearer understanding of the source.
- What do you notice about the data? Are the data displaying more than one piece of information? Can you find similarities and differences between the various data presented? Is there a pattern or a trend? Remember that a trend usually occurs over a period of time rather than at a point in time.
- In which context was the source created? Why is the data displayed in this manner? What is the author trying to tell us and why? Look at the patterns or trends that you noticed. Can you draw a conclusion and how would you support that conclusion?

9. College Board, "AP° U.S. Government and Politics Course and Exam Description," https://apcentral.collegeboard.org/pdf/ap-us-government-and-politics-course-and-exam-description.pdf (accessed 1/15/21).

- What is the purpose of the data? How do the data illustrate, or relate to, the content being portrayed?
- What is missing? Are there possible limitations of the data? Does the way in which the data are presented limit their use?

Here is an example:

- Look at the line graph in the What Do the Facts Say? feature on p. 484 in Chapter 11. Read the supplemental material. What are the data displaying? What is the author trying to tell us about political parties? Do you notice a pattern or a trend? Can you answer the question in the title, "Are the Parties More Polarized than Ever?" What do the data illustrate about how likely it is for members of the contemporary Congress to enact major changes in government policy?

Demonstrating Disciplinary Practice 3 means being able to explain possible limitations of the provided data or limitations in how the provided data are presented. For instance, a data source could be biased, misleading, or inaccurate. The first area to focus on when approached with visual-based material is the source. Reliable data are more likely to come from a reliable source. If you are uncertain of the source, pay attention to how the data are presented. How are the axes labeled? If the baseline for a bar graph isn't zero, it can skew how the data are perceived. Look at the scale of the y axis. If it is expanded or compressed, the data may appear more or less significant than they actually are. Pay attention to the type of graph that is being used. If you want to accurately depict differences between groups, a bar graph is a better visualization. On the other hand, pie charts are used to compare the parts of a whole rather than differences between groups, and the total percentage should equal 100 percent minus any rounding error.

Now let's look at data visualizations that are accurate but still have limitations because they don't tell the whole story. This is more likely what you are going to find in a textbook or other secondary source. For example, look at the line graph again on p. 484 in Chapter 11. The data are presented with visual accuracy. However, after your study of Congress, you will learn that representatives may vote against a bill even if they align with the bill ideologically because an amendment was added to the bill that they do not support. Since the data in the line graph are based upon the congressional roll call votes, consider how knowing that information demonstrates a limitation in the visual display of the data.

Practice: The end of Chapter 1 focuses on how the practices are assessed on the multiple-choice section of the AP° exam. For Practice 3, see Questions 5–6 on p. 37. The application of this practice to the free-response section is detailed in the "Writing for AP° U.S. Government and Politics" section below.

DISCIPLINARY PRACTICE 4: SOURCE ANALYSIS: Read, analyze, and interpret foundational documents and other text-based and visual sources.

Disciplinary Practice 4 is source analysis. Students will be expected to demonstrate this practice, along with the associated skills, by completing the following:[10]

- "Describe the author's claim(s), perspective, evidence, and reasoning.
- Explain how the author's argument or perspective relates to political principles, institutions, processes, policies, and behaviors.
- Explain how the implications of the author's argument or perspective may affect political principles, institutions, processes, policies, and behaviors.
- Explain how the visual elements of a cartoon, map, or infographic illustrate or relate to political principles, institutions, processes, policies, and behaviors."

---

10. College Board, "AP® U.S. Government and Politics Course and Exam Description," https://apcentral.collegeboard.org/pdf/ap-us-government-and-politics-course-and-exam-description.pdf (accessed 1/15/21).

Closely reading and analyzing foundational documents and other text-based and visual sources are an important task for both political scientists and students of AP® U.S. Government and Politics. Consider this skill as being akin to the way police use evidence to solve a crime. In this case, you are the detective solving a political science mystery. To crack the case on the multiple-choice section and on the free-response questions, you must display the ability to analyze evidence. Foundational documents and other text-based and visual sources are the evidence that scholars use to make arguments about government and politics. Foundational documents, for our purpose, are the nine documents identified by the College Board as instrumental to the study of political science. Other text-based sources are items such as books, articles, and essays written by political scientists, and visual sources are maps, political cartoons, and infographics. Foundational documents are not formally assessed using Disciplinary Practice 4. Rather, they are a key component of the final disciplinary practice. However, since the skills required to understand and analyze the foundational documents are similar to those for other text-based sources, the strategies for both are addressed here.

Foundational Documents

In order to understand the philosophical underpinnings and political values of the U.S. political system, you will need to have a working knowledge of the nine required foundational documents. You may find reading the foundational documents to be challenging. For the most part, textbooks and other secondary sources will inform you early on about what is essential in the text. Authors may include the main ideas in an introduction and will organize the material with the reader in mind. In comparison, because the vast majority of the foundational documents are primary sources, the authors did not have current-day students in mind when they created them, and they may not have designed a road map to help you navigate the documents. The language of primary sources may be antiquated, and the references may be difficult to understand. Therefore, when reading primary sources, you bear more of the responsibility to identify what is essential—a skill you can practice.

How should you approach the examination of primary sources? Approach the foundational documents similarly to how you would approach a primary source in a history course. Before starting to read or write, ask yourself the following:

- What do I already know about this subject/historical event?
- What do I hope to achieve by reading this source?

Since you will need the documents either to answer multiple-choice questions or to support an essay response, it helps to have a structure in place to enable you to decipher them. Mnemonic devices are techniques that improve your ability to remember things. There are many mnemonic devices used to help students remember the ways in which to analyze sources. **SOAPSTone** is one popular mnemonic for analyzing historical primary sources. The following steps will help you begin the process of formulating an argument by understanding your sources:

- **S = Speaker/Author**
  - Who is the speaker (author)? What is the author's age? Class? Gender? Ethnicity? Level of education? Religion?
  - How does knowledge about the author's place in society (job, access to power or freedom, and so on) help you understand the person's point of view or outlook?
  - Is the author an expert about the topic in the document?
  - How does the author's point of view influence your understanding of the document?

- **O = Occasion/Context**
  - How does knowing the occasion (context) of location, period, or surrounding historical events help you understand the document?
  - What events could the document relate to?
  - What belief systems were in place that could shed light on the document?
- **A = Audience**
  - Who was the intended audience for the document?
  - How and why might the author have wanted to persuade this particular audience?
  - Based on the audience, can you determine whether the document setting is informal or formal?
- **P = Purpose**
  - What inferences can you make about why the author produced the document? Was the purpose to persuade? Was it a call to action? Was it to discredit an opponent?
  - Can you read between the lines to determine any useful information?
  - Was the document available to the public, or was it private correspondence?
- **S = Significance of the Subject**
  - Can you explain the subject in a few words?
  - How does the document's subject matter help you answer the question at hand?
  - How significant is this source?
  - Does the document provide detail on the significance of a larger historical event or person?
- **T = Tone**
  - What is the author's attitude about the subject?
  - What clues can you get from the word choice, sentence construction, or use of figurative language (simile, metaphor, and allusions)?

Other Text-Based Sources

Other text-based sources, for the purpose of this course, are sources that are not on the list of the required nine foundational documents. For example, both *Federalist 51* and *Federalist 68* are historical primary sources, but since only *Federalist 51* is on the required foundational document list, *Federalist 68* is considered a text-based source. Regardless of the particular categorization of a source, using the SOAPSTone strategy above to analyze any historical primary source can be very effective.

The SOAPSTone strategy is most effective when reading primary or secondary sources provided in the AP® Foundational Documents section of the appendix (pp. A1–A70) of the textbook or given to you in class. However, it is more likely that on the AP® exam, you will receive an excerpt. While reading an excerpt will save you time, it may make answering some of the SOAPSTone questions a little more difficult. So you may need to fill in the gaps. The more you practice, the easier your work will be!

Analyzing a text-based source is only the first half of Practice 4. This is a distinction between how analyzing a *Federalist Paper* is different in a political science course versus a history course. Political scientists go beyond theory and incorporate qualitative sources to help explain the interaction between institutions and the policy process, for instance. Therefore, you need to go beyond just understanding the author's argument or point of view; you also need to be able to relate that argument to a political principle, institution, process, policy, or behavior. Similar to how Practice 3 is assessed, Practice 4 is also assessed using multiple-choice question sets with the first question relating to analyzing a text-based or visual source and the second question tying that analysis to content.

Here is an example:
- Read the first six paragraphs of *Federalist 10* on pp. A11–A12 in the AP® Foundational Documents in the appendix of this textbook. Use the SOAPSTone strategy as you read the excerpt. After reading, can you describe Madison's view on the purpose of government? As you continue learning content related to government and politics, you will be able to use this strategy to explain how the role of the elite model in policy making is evidence of how Madison's view on factions is still evident in the U.S. political system today.

Visual Sources

In political science, visual representations such as maps, infographics, and political cartoons of a political concept can have a greater impact than textual sources. Thus, it is important for students to learn how to interpret and analyze both textual and visual sources. When analyzing visual sources, you will use skills that relate to analyzing quantitative sources as well as text-based sources. Here are some guidelines that should aid your understanding.

Questions for Interpreting Visual Sources
- How is the visual presented? If it is a map, what is being shown? Is there a key/legend or any other written material? If it is an infographic, what is it about? Who created the infographic and why? If it is a political cartoon, how are the characters or objects portrayed? What is it about? What message is the cartoonist trying to convey?
- What is the author's or artist's implication and how does that implication affect a political principle, institution, process, policy, or behavior? How do the images in the infographic, or the perspectives in the cartoon, shape what you are learning related to government and politics?
- Focusing on the visual elements, how do those elements relate to what you are learning in this course?

Here is an example:
- Examine the map in Nuts & Bolts 4.1 on p. 147 titled "Types of Gerrymanders," found in Chapter 4. What is being shown in the map on the left (definition)? Who created this map and why (process)? What effect does drawing districts in this manner have on the party not in power (causation)? Is this a short-term or long-term advantage for the majority party (comparison)? Notice that in order to effectively master this disciplinary practice and analyze this visual source like a political scientist, you need to use the reasoning processes discussed earlier in the handbook.

Practice: The end of Chapter 1 focuses on how the practices are assessed on the multiple-choice section of the AP® exam. For Practice 4, analyzing visual sources, see Questions 7–8 on p. 38. For Practice 4, analyzing text-based sources, see Questions 9–10 on p. 38.

DISCIPLINARY PRACTICE 5: ARGUMENTATION: Develop an argument in essay format.
The final disciplinary practice is argumentation. Students will be expected to demonstrate this practice, along with the associated skills, by completing the following:[11]
- "Articulate a defensible claim/thesis.
- Support the argument using relevant evidence.

11. College Board, "AP® U.S. Government and Politics Course and Exam Description," https://apcentral.collegeboard.org/pdf/ap-us-government-and-politics-course-and-exam-description.pdf (accessed 1/15/21).

- Use reasoning to organize and analyze evidence, explaining its significance to justify the claim or thesis.
- Use refutation, concession, and rebuttal in responding to opposing or alternate perspectives."

This disciplinary practice, argumentation, is assessed solely on the AP® exam in the free-response section. It is also the only question that is required to be written in essay form. Political science courses often use essays as part of a midterm or final exam. Professors need to evaluate both your writing and critical thinking skills, while also providing a chance to reflect on the content of the course.

Throughout the AP® U.S. Government and Politics course, your instructor should provide you with various opportunities to practice argumentation, whether through class discussions or informal writing activities. It is a difficult skill that you can develop with practice over time. You will master it if you put in the effort.

Like many of the other skills addressed here, the art of argumentation is based on a multi-step process. You can condense the maneuvers necessary for a solid argument into three actions: (1) understanding the question, (2) formulating a solid thesis, and (3) skillfully using evidence.

Political science arguments always respond to a question, usually posed by your instructor or possibly the College Board. Therefore, first understand the question by following these simple steps: (1) Read The Full Question (RTFQ) and (2) Answer The Full Question (ATFQ). Any time you see a new prompt, remember RTFQ and ATFQ. You might be surprised how often students possess political science knowledge but do poorly addressing a question because they fail to respond clearly to the actual prompt.

For example, read this prompt (Question 4) from the 2019 exam:[12] "The United States Constitution establishes a federal system of government. Under federalism, policy making is shared between national and state governments. Over time, the powers of the national government have increased relative to those of the state governments. Develop an argument about whether the expanded powers of the national government benefit or hinder policy making." Understanding that this is the argument essay question, if you were to circle the critical components of the question, you would focus on "federalism," "policy making is shared," "powers of the national government have increased," "expanded powers of the national government," "benefit or hinder," and the time period. RTFQ so you can ATFQ.

Next, look at the foundational documents provided. In the 2019 exam, they were the Articles of Confederation, Brutus 1, and *Federalist 10*. Examine how each one relates to the prompt. Does one particular document fit best with one particular argument or does a single document cover both possible arguments?

Then, you'll need to formulate a claim or a thesis that will be the heart of your argument. You should place this brief yet clear statement of your main assertion at the beginning of your essay and you should also include a line of reasoning, which is the initial justification for your claim. Since you are required to use at least one of the provided foundational documents as evidence, write a thesis that is supported by one of the documents that you are the most comfortable describing as evidence. You will draw your secondary evidence and reasoning from a different foundational document or from content learned in the course and from this textbook, so keep that in mind when writing the thesis as well.

This remainder of the essay is fairly prescribed; thus, the best way to organize your essay is to follow the order of the skills outlined in Practice 5. Once you have created

12. College Board, "AP® United States Government and Politics Sample Student Responses and Scoring Commentary," https://ap-central.collegeboard.org/pdf/ap19-apc-us-go-po-q4.pdf (accessed 1/15/21).

your thesis, you will support your claim with two pieces of relevant evidence, one piece from the provided list of foundational documents and a second piece from a different document on the list or from course knowledge. You need to describe each piece of evidence and explain how it relates to the claim made in the introduction. Additionally, for each piece of evidence, you need to demonstrate why that evidence supports your thesis. Basically, explain how or why the evidence supports the line of reasoning presented with your claim. (Remember ATFQ!)

Finally, you will need to respond to an opposing point of view. If you argued that expanded power of the national government hindered policy making, then you would respond to the argument that it benefited policy making by explaining the alternative perspective and then responding to that perspective.

As with all the other skills presented here, writing an argument essay is challenging and requires practice. You must use evidence effectively, demonstrate logical thinking, and convey ideas to the reader in a convincing way. For AP® U.S. Government and Politics essays, it is crucial to be both clear and concise since the time constraints require you to write a full argument essay in 40 minutes. The next section of this handbook explains each of the question types and suggests steps to help you answer the free-response questions.

Practice: Since Practice 5 is assessed only in the free-response section, you will find examples of Question 4 throughout *American Politics & Government Today*.

WRITING FOR AP® U.S. GOVERNMENT AND POLITICS

So far in this handbook, you have learned about critical reading, note-taking, and political science reasoning processes and disciplinary practices. We now turn to what many students feel is the most challenging portion of the AP® U.S. Government and Politics exam: writing. The components of the writing portion of the exam are four free-response questions with each FRQ focusing on one of the disciplinary practices.

As discussed earlier, the disciplinary practices are scaffolded, as they are divided into sub-practices or associated skills. For example, within each practice you will need to master a describe-based skill before advancing to an explain-based skill. This skill progression is also evident in the writing section of the AP® exam. Each task verb serves a specific purpose in the assessment of the application of the disciplinary practices to the content in the course. The following description of each task verb is taken from the College Board AP® U.S. Government and Politics Course and Exam Description:[13]

"The following task verbs are commonly used in the free-response questions:
- Compare: Provide a description or explanation of similarities and/or differences.
- Define: Provide a specific meaning for a word or concept.
- Describe: Provide the relevant characteristics of a specified topic.
- Develop an argument: Articulate a claim and support it with evidence.
- Draw a conclusion: Use available information to formulate an accurate statement that demonstrates understanding based on evidence.
- Explain: Provide information about how or why a relationship, process, pattern, position, situation, or outcome occurs, using evidence and/or reasoning. Explain 'how' typically requires analyzing the relationship, process, pattern, position, situation, or outcome, whereas explain 'why' typically

13. College Board, "AP® U.S. Government and Politics Course and Exam Description," https://apcentral.collegeboard.org/pdf/ap-us-government-and-politics-course-and-exam-description.pdf (accessed 1/15/21).

requires analysis of motivations or reasons for the relationship, process, pattern, position, situation, or outcome.

- Identify: Indicate or provide information about a specified topic, without elaboration or explanation."

Understanding these task verbs and how they relate to the four different free-response question types will enable you to fully address the prompt. There are three key elements to successful writing on the AP® U.S. Government and Politics exam: (1) know the format of the exam questions and scoring guidelines, (2) use time wisely for both planning and writing, and (3) remain calm enough that you remember what you studied. With that in mind, here are some guidelines for writing AP® U.S. Government and Politics free-response questions.

General Rules for AP® U.S. Government and Politics Writing

- Before you take the exam, check out the most recently released questions, scoring guidelines, and sample student responses at AP® Central. You can also search online for previous years' questions and practice quizzes. Then practice taking the exam several times.
- Don't panic. Read through all of the prompts slowly. Focus on the instructions. (Remember RTFQ.)
- Determine how you will address the prompt and establish your central points. Don't write the first thing that comes into your head. Re-read the prompt to make sure you understand what it is asking.
- Organize your response around the specific reasoning process that aligns to what the question is asking.
- Model your response on the prompt by using the language of the prompt in your answer. If the prompt asks you to "identify," "describe," or "explain," be sure that is what you do *and*, whenever possible, include those terms in your response.
- Plan your response with an outline or short list of central points to guide your answer.
- For the argumentation question, include a clear thesis statement or claim at the beginning of the essay and choose one of the given documents to use as evidence to support that claim or thesis. The other FRQs do not require this.
- If you have additional time at the end, re-read your work and edit any unclear ideas or sentences.

QUESTION 1: CONCEPT APPLICATION

Question 1 is the first activity of the written portion of the AP® U.S. Government and Politics exam and focuses exclusively on Disciplinary Practice 1. This question and the next two free-response questions are short-answer-style questions. They are not written in essay form and do not require a thesis. While 100 minutes are allocated for this section of the exam, given that these questions are short-answer, the recommendation is to spend 20 minutes each on Questions 1–3 and 40 minutes on Question 4, the argument essay.

The following description is taken from the College Board AP® U.S. Government and Politics Course and Exam Description:[14]

"Free-response question 1: Concept Application presents students with an authentic scenario. This question assesses student ability to describe and explain

14. College Board, "AP® U.S. Government and Politics Course and Exam Description," https://apcentral.collegeboard.org/pdf/ap-us-government-and-politics-course-and-exam-description.pdf (accessed 1/15/21).

the effects of a political institution, behavior, or process. Additionally, this question assesses student ability to transfer understanding of course concepts and apply them in a new situation or scenario."

In order to receive the highest scores, students must go beyond just a description of key vocabulary and demonstrate a deep understanding of concepts. Understanding the task verbs, mentioned earlier, is essential to answering the question. This FRQ type will focus on the task verbs "describe" and "explain."

Included below are a sample Question 1: Concept Application and sample student responses from the AP® U.S. Government and Politics Course and Exam Description.[15] See AP® Central online for the complete free-response and scoring guidelines.

Sample Question 1: Concept Application

The National Association of Home Builders, a national interest group that represents over 140,000 members in the home construction industry, has endorsed David Valadao (R) for reelection in California's Twenty-First Congressional District in the 2018 midterm election.

"Rep. Valadao has made housing and home ownership a top national priority and understands that expanding housing opportunities for all Americans is essential to the economic and social well-being of our nation," said Randy Noel, chairman of the National Association of Home Builders.

"We are proud to endorse Rep. Valadao for reelection in November because he helped to shepherd the landmark tax reform bill through Congress that will put more money into the pockets of hard-working families, reduce the tax burden for small businesses and promote job and economic growth," Noel said.

Recent polls show Valadao holding an 11-point lead over Democratic challenger T. J. Cox.

Source: "Valadao Picks Up Several Endorsements," *Hanford Sentinel* (Hanford, CA), October 19, 2018.

After reading the scenario, respond to A, B, and C below:

(A) Describe an action being taken by the National Association of Home Builders in the scenario.

(B) Explain how the action described in Part A affects policy making in Congress.

(C) Another group interested in conserving land in California supports the Democratic candidate in the election. Rather than having 140,000 members, the group is led by a few very wealthy families. Explain how this difference will likely affect the conservationist group's strategy in the election.

Sample Responses That Would Earn Credit

- One point is earned for describing an action being taken by the National Association of Home Builders in the scenario. An example might include the following: *"By releasing a statement supporting Representative Valadao, the Home Builders Association is educating voters about the candidate in the upcoming election."*

- One point for explaining how the action described in Part A affects policy making in Congress. An example might include the following: *"By publicly supporting candidates in elections, interest groups demonstrate to members of Congress their ability to affect elections, which could lead to members of Congress supporting the legislation promoted by the Home Builders Association."*

15. College Board, "AP® U.S. Government and Politics Course and Exam Description," https://apcentral.collegeboard.org/pdf/ap-us-government-and-politics-course-and-exam-description.pdf (accessed 1/15/21).

- One point for explaining how this difference will likely affect the conservationist group's strategy in the election. An example might include the following: "*Groups with more members, such as the Home Builders Association, are generally more active in endorsing and publicly supporting candidates because they have strength in numbers with their memberships. A group that does not have many members but has funding, such as the conservationist group described in the scenario, will need to consider a different strategy, such as forming a political action committee or a super PAC.*"

Key Points to Remember When Answering Question 1: Concept Application

Read all three parts of the question before you start writing your answer. There may be multiple possible answers to Part A; however, one specific answer might make it easier to answer Part B. In Part A, make sure you explicitly address the scenario. This is more than just repeating the question. Part A uses the task verb "describe," not "identify." Make sure that you are describing. For example, instead of writing, "the First Amendment," write, "the First Amendment's establishment clause, which restricts the government from establishing a national religion."

In Part B, make sure that you are addressing the answer that you wrote in Part A. These two parts of the question will always go together. When you read the question, insert what you wrote in Part A where the question asks, ". . . described in Part A." For example, the instructions to "explain how the use of congressional power described in Part A can be affected by its interaction with the presidency" become "explain how Congress's power to pass a law can be affected by its interaction with the presidency." In Part B, you will be asked to explain how or explain why. An "explain how/why" question will have two parts: a description of how the terms or concepts relate and an explanation of how/why that relationship answers the question. This is the "therefore" response, or basically an explicit reference back to the scenario.

In Part C, you will be asked for more general knowledge about the course related to the issue in the scenario. You will again be asked to explain how or explain why. Follow the tips above for answering an "explain how/why" part of the question.

Practice: You will find practice Question 1: Concept Application free-response questions throughout *American Politics & Government Today*. Use the tips above when answering these questions.

QUESTION 2: QUANTITATIVE ANALYSIS

Question 2 is another short-answer question. This question focuses exclusively on Practice 3. Similar to Question 1, the recommendation is to spend 20 minutes answering this prompt.

The following description is taken from the College Board AP® U.S. Government and Politics Course and Exam Description:[16]

"Free-response question 2: Quantitative Analysis presents students with quantitative data in the form of a table, graph, map, or infographic. This question assesses students' ability to perform the following:

- Describe the data presented
- Describe a pattern, trend, similarity, or difference in the data presented
- Draw a conclusion based on the data
- Explain how the data demonstrate a political principle, institution, process, policy, or behavior"

---

16. College Board, "AP® U.S. Government and Politics Course and Exam Description," https://apcentral.collegeboard.org/pdf/ap-us-government-and-politics-course-and-exam-description.pdf (accessed 1/15/21).

In order to receive the highest scores, you will need to not only interpret the quantitative stimulus provided but also apply that knowledge to what you have been learning about U.S. government and politics. As with Question 1, understanding the task verbs is essential to answering the question.

Included below are a sample Question 2: Quantitative Analysis and sample student responses from the AP® U.S. Government and Politics Course and Exam Description.[17] See AP® Central online for the complete free-response and scoring guidelines.

Sample Question 2: Quantitative Analysis

State Public Education Spending per Pupil, 2014

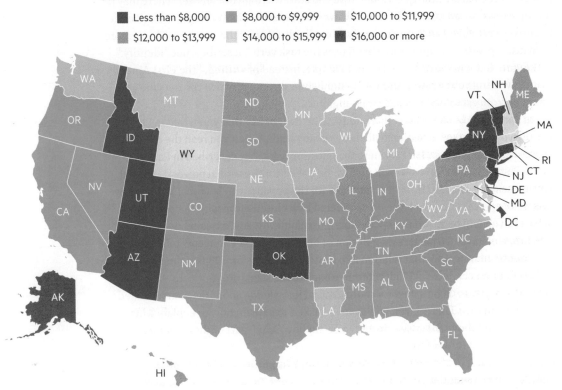

Source: U.S. Census Bureau, Educational Finance Branch, "Public Education Finances: 2014," June 2016, www2.census.gov/govs/school/14f33pub.pdf (accessed 11/11/20).

Use the information graphic to answer the questions.

(A) Identify the most common level of education spending by states in the Southeast.

(B) Describe a similarity or difference in public education spending by state or region, as illustrated in the information graphic.

(C) Draw a conclusion about that similarity or difference in public education spending by state or region illustrated in the information graphic.

(D) Explain how public education spending as shown in the information graphic demonstrates the principle of federalism.

Sample Responses That Would Earn Credit

- One point is earned for identifying the most common level of education spending by states in the Southeast as "*$8,000–$9,999.*"
- One point for describing a similarity or difference in public education spending by state or region, as illustrated in the information graphic. An example

17. College Board, "AP® U.S. Government and Politics Course and Exam Description," https://apcentral.collegeboard.org/pdf/ap-us-government-and-politics-course-and-exam-description.pdf (accessed 1/15/21).

might include the following: *"The Northeast region of the United States spends the highest amount of money on public education than any other region in the U.S."*
- One point for drawing a conclusion about that similarity or difference in public education spending by state or region illustrated in the information graphic. An example might include the following: *"One possible conclusion is that Northern states are wealthier and thus can afford to spend more."*
- One point for explaining how public education spending as shown in the information graphic demonstrates the principle of federalism. An example might include the following: *"While the national government requires states to provide education, states are permitted to create and organize their own education systems. Thus, as shown in the map all states spend money on education, but each spends a different amount per pupil."*

Key Points to Remember When Answering Question 2: Quantitative Analysis
Prior to writing your answer, use the techniques suggested for Practice 3 on how to effectively analyze data. Look at the stimulus and ask yourself, What information is being provided? Look at the features of the information graphic, such as the labels, the title, and the axes. Are the numbers raw numbers or a percentage? What is being represented? What is missing?

In Part A, you will be asked for information directly from the provided stimulus. If you are asked to identify, you need to provide very specific information. Even though this is not an essay question, and while it is not required, your answer needs to be at least a full sentence. It should incorporate the terminology of the question. This guideline helps make sure that you are ATFQ.

Prior to answering Part B, look at Part C. There may be multiple possible answers to Part B; however, one specific answer might make it easier to answer Part C. Part B is going to ask you to describe one of the following:
- Pattern: This is an observation of what is happening in the data. It is not a singular point on the stimulus.
- Trend: This often occurs over time or is a line that is used to represent the behavior of a set of data to determine if there is a certain pattern. It is also not a singular point on the stimulus.
- Similarity/Difference: Make sure that you explicitly reference both of the components that you are asked to compare.

Part B uses the task verb "describe," not "identify." Refer to the task verbs in the previous section to delineate between the two.

In Part C, you will be asked to either draw a conclusion about what you described in Part B or explain how or why. If you are asked to draw a conclusion, you need to explain how or why the data in the stimulus led to the similarity/difference that you described in Part B. You need to include specific examples using data from the stimulus in your response. Similar to Question 1, if you are asked to explain how or why, you will provide a description of how the terms or concepts relate and an explanation of how/why that relationship answers the question. This is the "therefore" response, or basically an explicit reference back to the data provided in the stimulus.

Part D is very similar to Part C. You will be asked to use different course knowledge to explain how or why the content relates to the stimulus provided. Follow the tips above for answering an "explain how/why" part of the question.

Practice: You will find practice Question 2: Quantitative Analysis free-response questions throughout *American Politics & Government Today*. Use the tips above when answering these questions.

QUESTION 3: SCOTUS COMPARISON

Question 3 is the last of the short-answer questions. This question focuses primarily on Practice 2. Similar to the two questions above, the recommendation is to spend 20 minutes answering this prompt.

The following description is taken from the College Board AP® U.S. Government and Politics Course and Exam Description:[18]

"Free-response question 3: SCOTUS Comparison presents students with a description of a non-required Supreme Court Case and its holding. This question assesses students' ability to do the following:

- Identify a similarity or difference between the non-required Supreme Court case and a specified Supreme Court case required in the course
- Describe the details, reasoning, or holding of the required Supreme Court case specified in the question
- Explain a similarity or difference in the reasoning or holding of the two Supreme Court cases
- Explain how the reasoning or holding in the non-required Supreme Court case demonstrates a political principle, institution, process, policy, or behavior"

In order to receive the highest scores, you must go beyond just a description of key vocabulary and demonstrate a deep understanding of concepts. Understanding the task verbs is essential to answering the question.

Included below are a sample question for Question 3: SCOTUS Comparison and sample student responses from the AP® U.S. Government and Politics Course and Exam Description.[19] See AP® Central online for the complete free-response and scoring guidelines.

Sample Question 3: SCOTUS Comparison

In 1935, Congress passed the National Labor Relations Act (NLRA), which among other things guaranteed workers the right to join a labor union and collectively bargain with employers. The law also established the National Labor Relations Board (NLRB), an independent agency responsible for enforcing the law.

The Jones and Laughlin Steel Corporation fired ten workers attempting to unionize its plant located in Aliquippa, Pennsylvania. When the National Labor Relations Board determined this to be in violation of the recently passed NLRA, the company sued claiming that labor relations had only an indirect effect on commerce, and thus Congress did not have the constitutional power to regulate it.

In the subsequent case, *National Labor Relations Board v. Jones and Laughlin Steel Corporation* (1937), the Supreme Court ruled in favor of the National Labor Relations Board by a 5–4 vote, holding that the Jones and Laughlin Steel Corporation conducted interstate commerce and that industrial labor relations affects that commerce.

(A) Identify the constitutional clause that is common in both *United States v. Lopez* (1995) and *National Labor Relations Board v. Jones and Laughlin Steel Corporation* (1937).

(B) Explain how the facts in *United States v. Lopez* led to a different holding than in *National Labor Relations Board v. Jones and Laughlin Steel Corporation*.

(C) Explain how the holding in *National Labor Relations Board v. Jones and Laughlin Steel Corporation* affected the balance of power between the states and the national government.

18. College Board, "AP® U.S. Government and Politics Course and Exam Description," https://apcentral.collegeboard.org/pdf/ap-us-government-and-politics-course-and-exam-description.pdf (accessed 1/15/21).

19. College Board, "AP® U.S. Government and Politics Course and Exam Description," https://apcentral.collegeboard.org/pdf/ap-us-government-and-politics-course-and-exam-description.pdf (accessed 1/15/21).

Sample Responses That Would Earn Credit

- One point is earned for identifying the constitutional clause that is common in both *United States v. Lopez* (1995) and *National Labor Relations Board v. Jones* (1937) as *"the commerce clause."*
- One point for describing relevant information about the required case of *United States v. Lopez*. An example might include the following: *"In United States v. Lopez, the court ruled that the commerce clause did not extend to creating gun free school zones."*
- One point for explaining how the facts of both cases led to a different holding. An example might include the following: *"In United States v. Lopez, gun possession was not an economic activity that could be considered interstate commerce under the commerce clause. In the NLRB v. Jones case, Congress determined that labor disputes were related to interstate commerce and, thus, could be regulated by the federal government."*
- One point for explaining how the holding in *National Labor Relations Board v. Jones and Laughlin Steel Corporation* affected the balance of power between the states and the national government. An example might include the following: *"By granting Congress more authority to make laws under the commerce clause, and also to establish a regulatory agency to rule in labor disputes, it substantially increased the power of the federal government."*

Key Points to Remember When Answering Question 3: SCOTUS Comparison

Since this question requires you to compare one of the fifteen required SCOTUS cases with a provided case, Part A will ask you to identify how one of the following is similar in the two cases:

- Clause: commerce clause, national supremacy clause, equal protection clause, due process clause, and so on
- Amendment: First (free exercise or establishment), Second, Sixth, and so on
- Civil liberty: any one of the Bill of Rights
- Principle or provision: selective incorporation, judicial review, equal protection, and so on

Since this is an identification, you need to be specific in your answer. For example, instead of responding with, "the First Amendment," write, "the establishment clause of the First Amendment."

In Part B, you will be asked about how the case that you are given is similar to or different from one of the required cases. In order to earn full credit for this part, you will need to provide specific information about the required case, focusing on what type of information is requested in the prompt, such as facts, reasoning, decision, or majority opinion. You will then need to relate the given case to the required case using the same focus as above. For example, if the question asks you to explain how the facts of the two cases led to a different holding, you need to focus on the facts in the two cases, and not another part of the case, to explain the different holdings in the two cases.

In Part C, you will be asked to explain how or why the given case is related to other content in the curriculum. Use the same strategy from Questions 1–2 to answer the "explain how/why" part of the question.

Practice: You will find practice Question 3: SCOTUS Comparison free-response questions throughout *American Politics & Government Today*. Use the tips above when answering these questions.

QUESTION 4: ARGUMENT ESSAY

Question 4 is the final activity of the AP® U.S. Government and Politics exam and is the most traditional of the writing activities in terms of being in the form of an essay. The question requires you to develop an argument, use two pieces of evidence to support that argument, and respond to a different perspective. This question is focused exclusively on Practice 5: Argumentation as this practice is not explicitly assessed in the multiple-choice section of the exam.

The following description is taken from the College Board AP® U.S. Government and Politics Course and Exam Description:[20]

"Free-response question 4: Argument Essay assesses students' ability to do the following:

- Articulate a defensible claim or thesis that responds to the question and establishes a line of reasoning
- Provide evidence from one of the foundational documents listed in the question to support the claim
- Provide evidence from a second foundational document or from knowledge of course concepts to support the claim
- Use reasoning to explain why the evidence supports the claim
- Respond to an opposing or alternate perspective using refutation, concession, or rebuttal"

In order to receive the highest scores, you must develop an argument by taking a position and establishing a line of reasoning to support that position or claim. Variations of this question ask about large-scale topics specifically mentioned in the concept outline, but they are framed to allow you to provide in-depth discussion of specific examples drawn from a provided list of required foundational documents and from content covered in the course.

Included below are a sample Question 4: Argument Essay and sample student responses from the 2019 AP® U.S. Government and Politics exam.[21] See AP® Central online for the complete free-response and scoring guidelines.

Sample Question 4: Argument Essay
Develop an argument that explains which of the three models of representative democracy—participatory, pluralist, or elite—best achieves the founders' intent for American democracy in terms of ensuring a stable government run by the people. Use at least one piece of evidence from one of the following foundational documents:

- Brutus 1
- *Federalist 10*
- U.S. Constitution

In your response, you should do the following:

- Respond to the prompt with a defensible claim or thesis that establishes a line of reasoning.
- Support your claim with at least *two* pieces of specific and relevant evidence.
  - One piece of evidence must come from one of the foundational documents listed above.
  - A second piece of evidence can come from any other foundational document not used as your first piece of evidence, or it may be from your knowledge of course concepts.
- Use reasoning to explain why your evidence supports your claim or thesis.
- Respond to an opposing or alternate perspective using refutation, concession, or rebuttal.

20. College Board, "AP® U.S. Government and Politics Course and Exam Description," https://apcentral.collegeboard.org/pdf/ap-us-government-and-politics-course-and-exam-description.pdf (accessed 1/15/21).
21. College Board, "AP® United States Government and Politics Sample Student Responses and Scoring Commentary," https://ap-central.collegeboard.org/pdf/ap19-apc-us-go-po-q4.pdf (accessed 1/15/21).

Sample Student Responses to the Above Sample Question 4: Argument Essay

- Example of an acceptable claim: "It is clear that the main intent of the founders best aligns with the model of elite representative democracy. The rules crafted for appointment of Congress members and the president demonstrate an elitist model of democracy for the nation." *(Responds to the prompt with a defensive claim that establishes a line of reasoning.)*

- Example of supporting the claim with evidence from a listed foundational document: "The elitist model intentions of the founders are further seen in the electoral college system. In this system, the people are allowed the initial vote for president, or the 'popular vote,' which determines the composition of the electorate." *(Provides relevant evidence to the claim using one of the provided foundational documents. This would need to be done a second time with a different foundational document or evidence from the student's knowledge of course concepts in order to earn all of the evidence points.)*

- Example of using reasoning to explain why the evidence supports the claim: "However the actual vote for president is left to a small number of individuals (electors) who cast the final ballots rather than just using the popular vote, mirroring the philosophies of the elite model." *(Explains why the evidence provided supports the claim.)*

- Example of a response to an opposing perspective: "Advocates of the participatory theory may argue that citizens have the power to participate by voting in elections in the United States. However, the founders designed a government which allowed for representation of the people, while leaving the more complex and important decisions to a well-educated few, as demonstrated by the systems of elections for both senators and the president." *(Describes the opposing perspective and then responds with a rebuttal.)*

Key Points to Remember When Answering Question 4: Argument Essay

For the first paragraph, you need to address the prompt by taking a position. You need to pick a side in order to earn a point for your thesis. After you take a position, provide two supporting reasons as to why you took that position. This is considered your line of reasoning. Consider which document and additional evidence you are going to use to support your thesis before you write your line of reasoning. You will need to refer back to your line of reasoning in order to earn the reasoning points below. Avoid talking about a foundational document in your introduction. Save that discussion for your next paragraph.

For the second paragraph, choose a foundational document from the list. Identify the document and write a few sentences to demonstrate that you understand the main points of the document and how it relates to your claim/thesis (your argument). After considering your line of reasoning in your thesis, write a few more sentences that explain *how* or *why* the evidence provided from the foundational document supports the line of reasoning in your thesis.

For the third paragraph, choose a different foundational document from the list or other knowledge learned in the course. Repeat the process above with the new evidence. Identify the document, or specifically describe the other knowledge, and write a few sentences to demonstrate that you understand the main points as they relate to your argument. Explain *how* or *why* the second piece of evidence supports the line of reasoning in your claim/thesis.

For the final paragraph, you will present a counterargument, which is a perspective that contrasts with your main argument. If, in response to the question presented above, you argued that an elite model best achieves the Founders' intent, then a different perspective would be that one of the other models (participatory or pluralist) best achieves that goal. You want the alternate perspective to relate to the intent of the question. Next you need to describe this alternate point of view. It is not necessary to explain how a foundational document supports this point of view; rather just give one or two reasons why someone might support that view. Follow your description of the counterargument with a discussion of either why that view is incorrect or why even though that view may have merits, those merits are outweighed by additional evidence that you are providing.

Practice: Throughout the textbook in the study guides, you will find Question 4: Argument Essay prompts to help you practice your skills even more.

You may feel apprehensive about writing for the AP® U.S. Government and Politics exam. However, once you become accustomed to the four unique free-response question types and practice addressing these questions successfully, you'll soon realize you have no reason to be anxious about this task. Actually, you should look at this portion of the exam as an opportunity. The free-response section is your chance to show what you know about government and politics in a more flexible way than you could demonstrate in the multiple-choice section of the exam.

If, over your time in this course, you have learned to think like a political scientist, have read critically, analyzed text-based and visual stimuli, and practiced writing using the methods above, not only will you relish the chance to put your political science critical thinking and writing skills on display—you will be proud to earn a top score on the AP® U.S. Government and Politics exam.

WORKS CONSULTED

Books

Svinicki, Marilla D., and Wilbert J. McKeachie. *McKeachie's Teaching Tips: Strategies, Research, and Theory for College and University Teachers*, 14th ed. Belmont, CA: Wadsworth, 2014.

Writing-Based Teaching: Essential Practices and Enduring Questions. Edited by Teresa Vilardi and Mary Chang. Albany, NY: State University of New York Press, 2009.

Online Sources

King, Charles. "Writing a Political Science Essay." Georgetown University, 1997. https://faculty.georgetown.edu/kingch/Writing_PolSci_Essay.htm.

Oxford Lexico. "Process." 2021. www.lexico.com/definition/process.

Manuals and Resources from AP® Central

College Board. *AP® United States Government and Politics Sample Student Responses and Scoring Commentary*. 2019. https://apcentral.collegeboard.org/pdf/ap19-apc-us-go-po-q4.pdf.

College Board. *AP® U.S. Government and Politics Course and Exam Description*. 2020. https://apcentral.collegeboard.org/pdf/ap-us-government-and-politics-course-and-exam-description.pdf.

Morse, Ogden. "SOAPSTone: A Strategy for Reading and Writing." *College Board*. 2021. https://apcentral.collegeboard.org/courses/resources/soapstone-strategy-reading-and-writing.

ADDITIONAL SUGGESTED RESOURCES

Dartmouth College Academic Skills Center. "Learning Strategies." 2021. https://
students.dartmouth.edu/academic-skills/learning-resources/learning-
strategies.

Princeton University McGraw Center for Teaching and Learning. "Active
Reading Strategies: Remember and Analyze What You Read." 2021. https://
mcgraw.princeton.edu/active-reading-strategies.

American Politics & Government Today

AP® Edition

In a democracy, oftentimes other people win.

—C. J. Cregg, *The West Wing*

1
Understanding American Politics

How does politics work and why does politics matter?

» "America is indebted as a democratic nation to the free press for truths it has uncovered, for truth it has disseminated, and for falsehoods it has repudiated. The press uncovered the government's lies about the war in Vietnam; it exposed Watergate; it opened our eyes to the sexual abuse of children by priests; and, most recently, it shed a light on the sexual assault by numerous men in power.... The work of a free press is essential."[1]
Senator Mitt Romney (R-UT)

« "Fake news, fake news. They're scum, many of them are scum. You have some good reporters but not many, I'll be honest with you. And that's one of the things we battle.... But they're total—just terrible dishonest people—and they couldn't figure out—'What do we say bad about this conversation?'"[2]
President Donald Trump

Fake news extends beyond print media. Political pundits on cable news channels have also been responsible for the spread of false information. Using his personal Twitter account, President Trump quoted one such pundit, further disseminating the false claim that the Obama administration had spied on his presidential campaign.

One of Donald Trump's favorite responses to unfavorable media coverage of his presidency is to label the accounts as "FAKE NEWS!" From stories detailing Russian involvement in the 2016 election to accounts of the federal government's response to the COVID-19 pandemic, Trump argued that mainstream media outlets (aided by leaks from "deep state" career bureaucrats) were deliberately slanting coverage to build public opposition and ensure Trump's defeat in 2020. The media outlets argued in turn that they were simply reporting facts as facts.

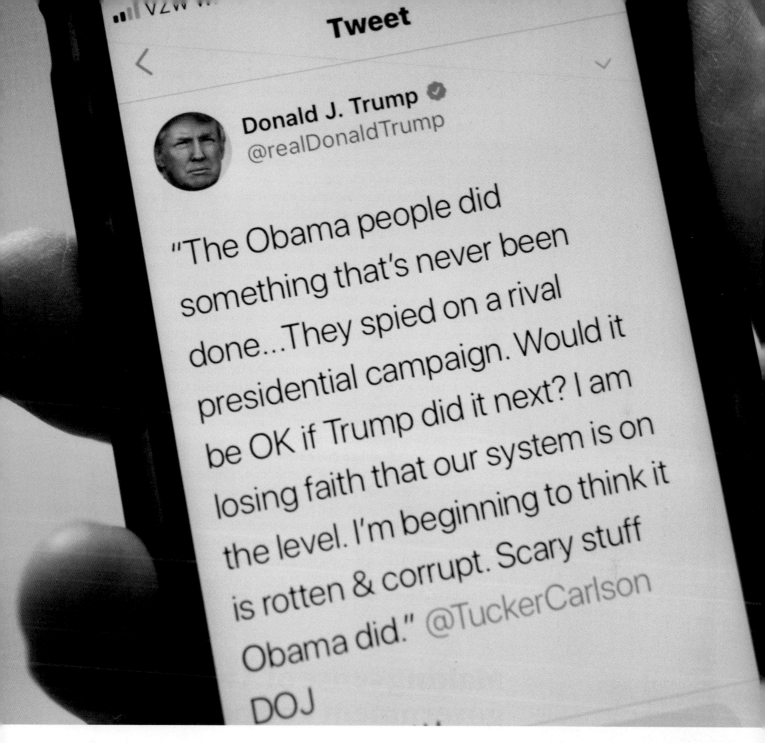

Tweet

Donald J. Trump ✔
@realDonaldTrump

"The Obama people did something that's never been done...They spied on a rival presidential campaign. Would it be OK if Trump did it next? I am losing faith that our system is on the level. I'm beginning to think it is rotten & corrupt. Scary stuff Obama did." @TuckerCarlson DOJ

CHAPTER GOALS

Describe the basic functions of government. pages 4–9

Define *politics* and identify three key ideas that help explain politics. pages 9–15

Identify major sources of conflict in American politics. pages 16–21

Explain how the American values of democracy, liberty, and equality work to resolve political conflict. pages 21–24

Understand how to interpret, evaluate, and use political information. pages 24–26

While Trump's defeat in the 2020 elections means that he will likely fade from public view, his protracted conflict with the media illustrates one of the key ideas in this book—that conflict in American politics reflects real disagreements about government policy. While some of Trump's policy goals (such as his support for tax cuts) reflected conventional Republican ideas, others, such as his imposition of punitive tariffs, skepticism about American engagement abroad, proposals for immigration restrictions, and his support for reopening American society in the case of COVID-19, were controversial even among Republican lawmakers and voters. It's not surprising that Trump wanted more positive coverage as a way of building public support. It's also not surprising that reporters and editors were unwilling to comply, as their goal is to inform a broad audience, and not all of them are Trump supporters. And from the perspective of sustaining a functioning democracy, skeptical and even negative news coverage of political leaders is essential.

Trump's complaints also illustrate a deeper issue in contemporary American politics: while there are many information sources, it is often hard to determine which are reliable. Americans' propensity to share information through social media means that outlandishly false stories can get widespread attention. In 2019 and 2020, stories circulated that House Speaker Nancy Pelosi had diverted Social Security funds to pay for impeachment hearings, that Representative Alexandria Ocasio-Cortez had proposed a ban on motorcycles, that President Trump's father had been a member of the Ku Klux Klan, and that fireworks were being distributed in American cities to increase tensions and create a rationale for law enforcement to crack down on protests against the murder of George Floyd, who died in police custody in Minneapolis.[3] None of these stories are true—but in a world where the public is bombarded with political information, it is easy to see why some truly fake news gets taken seriously. If Americans can't even agree on which news is "fake," how can we know what to trust? In a complex world, how do Americans understand, evaluate, and act on the political information that they encounter? In part, we will explore these questions throughout the book because the answers can tell us a lot about important political outcomes, including how people vote, what kinds of candidates win elections, and why some policies get enacted in Congress while others are defeated. At the same time, we hope to give you some ideas about how to find the information you need to make up your own mind about political debates.

DESCRIBE THE BASIC FUNCTIONS OF GOVERNMENT

Making sense of American government and politics

The premise of this book is simple: *American politics makes sense*. What happens in elections, in Washington, D.C., and everywhere else has a logical and often simple explanation. By the end of this book, we hope you get really good at analyzing the politics you see everywhere—in the news and in your own life.

This claim may seem unrealistic or even naive. On the surface, American politics often makes no sense. Polls show strong support for extreme, unconstitutional, or downright silly proposals. Candidates put more time into insulting their opponents than into making credible campaign promises. Members of Congress seem more interested in beating their political opponents than in getting something done, and the Democratic and Republican caucuses agree on virtually nothing. As we've just described, information from historically trusted national sources is labeled "fake news." The last year has also revealed the limits of government power, showing its inability to prevent a nationwide pandemic or stop the racially biased exercise of police force.

You are also living through an unusual period in American politics. President Trump broke many well-established norms, such as threatening to initiate Justice Department probes of prominent Democrats (including his 2020 opponent for the presidency, Joe Biden), and asked several foreign governments to investigate Biden's family. This last event led to Trump's first impeachment proceedings. Trump also told attendees at a rally in Washington, D.C., on January 6, 2021 to "fight hard" against congressional certification of the 2020 election, leading to an insurrection at the Capitol and, ultimately, his second impeachment. Trump's agenda on trade, international alliances, and other issues conflicted with the long-held consensus in both political parties. He refused to place his business holdings in a blind trust or to make his tax returns public, both things that all modern presidents have done.

Whether you approve or disapprove of Trump's behavior in office or his impeachment by the House, it is important to remember two things. First, Trump's presidency has shown that some things we believed about how American politics works were in fact wrong. Four years ago, few political scientists would have believed that presidential candidates could win election (or remain in office) if they were found to have paid hush money to someone with whom they had had an affair, if they were accused of sexual assault by multiple individuals, if they offhandedly used Twitter to criticize and insult political opponents and members of their own party, or if they used a combination of threats, bluffs, and bluster to manage domestic and foreign policy. Trump's presidency revealed new things about how politicians win and hold political support and how presidents can use their official and unofficial powers to shape policy outcomes.

However, for all of Trump's successes, much of what we understood about American politics still holds. It is true that Trump unexpectedly won the 2016 presidential election, breaking down the "blue wall" of reliably Democratic states and constituencies. But Trump received a minority of the popular vote in 2016, his party suffered severe losses in the 2018 midterms, and he lost the 2020 election even as Republican congressional candidates did better than predicted in their contests. Many of his policy priorities were blocked by Congress or the courts. One of our central goals in this book is to explain why Trump succeeded in some areas but not others, and to use his performance in office to understand how American politics works.

Conflicts within the government—say, over immigration policy—often reflect real divisions among American citizens about what government should do about certain issues. Groups on all sides of controversial issues pressure the government to enact their preferred policies.

The second thing to keep in mind is that the polarization, distrust, anger, and worries about the survival of democracy that seem to be core features of contemporary American politics are actually nothing new. Many people, we believe, are hostile toward American politics because they don't understand the political process, feel helpless to influence election outcomes or policy making, and believe that it is impossible to work within the system to change things (even deeply flawed practices such as racially biased policing). A surprisingly high percentage of Americans dislike both political parties and their candidates and see the conflict between Republicans and Democrats as more evidence that American politics does not work well. Here again, while these beliefs might be somewhat stronger than they were a generation ago, Americans have been skeptical of politicians and political parties since the Founding.

To be clear, it is *not* our goal to turn you into a political junkie or policy wonk (or a Democrat, a Republican, or anything else). You don't need to like politics to make sense of it, but we hope that after finishing this book you will have a basic understanding of how the political process works and why it matters.

One of our goals is to help you take an active role in the political process, if you want to. A functioning democracy allows citizens to defer complicated policy decisions to their elected leaders, but a democracy works better when citizens organize to make demands of government, monitor what politicians do, and hold them accountable at the voting booth. This book will help you be an effective participant by providing the analytical skills you need to make sense of politics, even when it initially appears to make no sense at all.

We are not going to spend time talking about how American politics should be. Rather, our focus will be on explaining American politics as it is. Here are some other questions we will examine:

- Why don't people vote? Why *do* people vote? How do they decide whom to vote for?
- Why do so many people mistrust politicians and the political system?
- Why can't Congress get things done?
- Why is the Supreme Court so political?
- Can presidents do whatever they want? Why can't they do more?
- How much power do bureaucrats have?
- Is the media biased?

We will answer these questions and many others by applying three key ideas about the nature of politics: politics is conflictual, political process matters, and politics is everywhere. But first, we begin with an even more basic question: Why do we have a government?

Why do we have a government?

government
The system for implementing decisions made through the political process.

As we prepare to address this question, let's agree on a definition: government is the system for implementing decisions made through the political process. All countries have some form of government, which in general serves two broad purposes: to provide order and to promote the general welfare.

To Provide Order At a basic level, the answer to the question "Why do we have a government?" seems obvious: without government there would be chaos. As the seventeenth-century British philosopher Thomas Hobbes said, life in the "state of nature" (that is, without government) would be "solitary, poor, nasty, brutish, and short."[4] Without government there would be no laws—people could do whatever they wanted. Even if people tried to develop informal rules, there would be no way to guarantee enforcement of those rules. Accordingly, some of the most important roles of government are policing and providing national security.

The Founders of the United States noted this crucial role in the Constitution's preamble: two of the central goals of government are to "provide for the common defense" and to "insure domestic Tranquility." The former refers to military protection against foreign invasion and the defense of our nation's common security interests. The latter refers to policing and law enforcement within the nation, which today includes the National Guard, the Federal Bureau of Investigation (FBI), the Department of Homeland Security, state and local police, and the courts. So at a minimal level, government is necessary to provide security.

However, there's more to it than that. The Founders cited the desire to "establish Justice . . . and secure the Blessings of Liberty to ourselves and our Posterity." But do we need government to do these things? It may be obvious that the police power of the nation is required to prevent anarchy, but can't people have justice and liberty without government? In a perfect world, maybe, but the Founders had a more realistic view of human nature. As James Madison, one of the founding fathers (and the fourth president of the United States), said in *Federalist 51*, "But what is government itself, but the greatest of all reflections on human nature? If men were angels, no government would be necessary. If angels were to govern men, neither external nor internal controls on government would be necessary."[5] Furthermore, Madison continued, people have a variety of interests that have "divided mankind into parties, inflamed them with mutual animosity, and rendered them much more disposed to vex and oppress each other than to co-operate for their common good."[6] That is, without government, we would quickly be headed toward Hobbes's nasty and brutish state of nature because of differences in opinion about what society should look like. Having a government means that people cannot act unilaterally against each other, but it also creates a new problem: people will try to use the government and its powers to impose their views on the rest of society.

Madison's view of human nature might sound pessimistic, but it was also realistic. He assumed that people were self-interested: we want what is best for ourselves and for our families, and to satisfy those interests we tend to form groups with like-minded people. Madison saw these groups, which he called **factions**, as being opposed to the public good, and his greatest fear was of tyranny by a faction imposing its will on the rest of the nation. For example, if one group took power and established an official state religion, that faction would be tyrannizing people who practiced a different religion. This type of oppression is precisely why many of the early American colonists fled Europe in the first place.

As we will discuss in Chapters 2 and 3, America's government seeks to control the effects of factions by dividing government power in three main ways. First, the **separation of powers** divides the government into three branches—judicial, executive, and legislative—and assigns distinct duties to each branch. Second, the system of **checks and balances** gives each branch some power over the other two. (For example, the president can veto legislation passed by Congress; Congress can impeach the president; and the Supreme Court has the power to interpret laws written by Congress to determine whether they are constitutional.) Third, **federalism** divides power yet again by allotting different responsibilities to local, state, and national government. With power divided in this fashion, Madison reasoned, no single faction could dominate the government.

To Promote the General Welfare The preamble to the Constitution also states that the federal government exists to "promote the general Welfare." This means tackling the hard problems that Americans cannot solve on their own, such as taking care of the poor, the sick, and the aged and dealing with global issues like climate change, pandemics, terrorist threats, and poverty in other countries. However, government

AP®
FOUNDATIONAL
DOCUMENT

AP®
FOUNDATIONAL
DOCUMENT

factions
Groups of like-minded people who try to influence the government. American government is set up to avoid domination by any one of these groups.

separation of powers
The division of government power across the judicial, executive, and legislative branches.

checks and balances
A system in which each branch of government has some power over the others.

federalism
The division of power across the local, state, and national levels of government.

Two important government functions described in the Constitution are to "provide for the common defense" and "insure domestic Tranquility." The military and local police are two of the most commonly used forces the government maintains to fulfill those roles.

intervention is not inevitable—people can decide that these problems aren't worth solving. But if people *do* want to address these large problems, government action is necessary because public goods such as environmental protection or national defense are not efficiently provided by the free market, either because of collective action problems or for other reasons.

It is easy for two people or even a small group to tackle a common problem without the help of government, but 1,000 people (to say nothing of the more than 334 million in the United States today) would have a very difficult time. They would suffer from the free rider problem—that is, because it is in everyone's own interest to let someone else do the work, the danger is that no one will contribute, even though everyone wants the outcome that collective contributions would create. A government representing more than 334 million people can provide public goods that all those people acting on their own would be unable to provide, so people elect leaders and pay taxes to provide those public goods.

Collective action problems are common in modern society. Education provides a great example. You benefit personally from your primary, secondary, and college education in terms of the knowledge and experience you gain, and from the higher salary and better job you will earn because of your college degree. However, society also benefits from your education. Your employer will benefit from your knowledge and skills, as will people you interact with. If education were provided solely by the free market, those who could afford schooling would be educated, but the rest would not, leaving a large segment of society with little or no education and therefore unemployable. So public education, like many important services, benefits all levels of society and must be provided by the government for the general welfare.

Now that we understand *why* we have a government, the next question is, *What* does the government do to "insure domestic Tranquility" and "promote the general Welfare"? Many visible components of the government promote these goals, from the police and armed services to the Internal Revenue Service, Federal Reserve, Postal Service, Social Security Administration, National Aeronautics and Space Administration, Department of Education, and Food and Drug Administration. In fact, it is hard to find an aspect of everyday life that does not involve the government in some way, either as a provider of public goods, as a protector of civil liberties, as an enforcer of laws and property rights, or as a regulator of individual or corporate behavior. What makes politics both interesting and important is that in most of these cases, Americans disagree on what kinds of public goods the government should provide, or whether government should be involved at all.

Forms of government

While all governments must provide order and promote the general welfare, different types of governments accomplish this in various ways. Greek political philosopher Aristotle, writing in the fourth century BC, developed a classification scheme for governments that is still surprisingly useful. Aristotle distinguished three pure types of government based on the number of rulers versus the number of people ruled: monarchy (rule by one), aristocracy (rule by the few), and polity (rule by the many, such as the general population—this is the most general description of a democracy).

There are many ways to implement democracy. In its purest form, a democracy is a system in which citizens make policy choices directly, such as through referenda. However, all current democracies, including America's national government, are organized as republics, in which elected representatives make policy decisions on behalf of citizens. Republics throughout the world are organized very differently. For example, they allocate power differently among the executive, legislative, and judicial branches. Presidential systems such as the one we have in the United States tend to follow a separation of power among the three branches, while parliamentary systems such as the one in the United Kingdom elect the chief executive from the legislature, resulting in much closer coordination between those two branches. An additional distinction is the relationship among different levels of government. In a federal system (such as the United States), power is shared among the local, state, and national levels of government. In a unitary system (such as France or Japan), all power is held at the national level, and local governments must comply with orders from the central government. The final type, a confederation, is a less common form of government in which states retain their sovereignty and autonomy but form a loose association at the national level.

DID YOU KNOW?

63%

of the world's population lives in countries considered to be free or partly free. Most countries considered not free are in Asia or Africa.
Source: Freedom House

What is politics?

We define **politics** as the process that determines what government does—whether and how it provides different public and private goods. You may consider politics the same thing as government, but we see government as the institutions that carry out the decisions that are a result of the political process. Many aspects of our discussion of politics will probably sound familiar because your life involves politics on a regular basis. This may sound a little abstract, but it should become clear in light of the three key ideas of this book (see the How It Works graphic in this chapter).

First, *politics is conflictual*. The questions debated in election campaigns and in Washington and the options considered by policy makers generally involve disagreement at all levels. The federal government does not spend much time resolving questions that everyone agrees on the answers to. Rather, making government policy involves issues on which people disagree, sometimes strongly, which makes compromise difficult—and this is a normal, healthy part of politics. Although compromise may be difficult to achieve, it is often necessary to produce outcomes that can be enacted and implemented.

Second, *political process matters*. Governmental actions don't happen by accident—they result from conscious choices made by elected officials and bureaucrats. Politics puts certain individuals into positions of power and makes the rules that structure their choices. The media often cover political campaigns the way they would report on a boxing match or the Super Bowl, focusing on the competition, rivalries, and

DEFINE *POLITICS* AND IDENTIFY THREE KEY IDEAS THAT HELP EXPLAIN POLITICS

politics
The process that determines what government does.

entertaining stories, which can lead people to overlook the institutions, rules, and procedures that have a decisive influence on politics. Indeed, the political process is in part a mechanism for resolving conflict. The most obvious example of the political process at work is elections, which democracies use to resolve a fundamental conflict: deciding who should lead the country and make policy choices.

Third, *politics is everywhere*. Decisions about what government should do or who should be in charge are integral to society, and they influence the everyday lives of all Americans. Politics helps determine what people can and cannot do, their quality of life, and how they think about events, people, and situations. Moreover, people's political thought and behavior are driven by the same types of calculations and decision-making rules that shape beliefs and actions in other parts of life. For example, deciding which presidential candidate to vote for is not so different from deciding which college to attend. For candidates, you might consider issue positions, character, and leadership ability, while for college you would weigh how schools fit your academic goals, how much tuition you can afford, and where different schools are located. In both cases you are consciously making a decision that will satisfy the criteria most important to you, given known budgetary and academic constraints.

Politics is conflictual

Political scientists have long recognized the central role of conflict in politics. In fact, one prominent theory in the mid-twentieth century saw conflict between interest groups as explaining most outcomes in American politics. The political scientist E. E. Schattschneider argued that the scope of political conflict—that is, how many people are involved in the fight—determines who wins in politics.[7] Others have argued that some conflict is helpful for group decision making: if nobody challenges a widely shared but flawed view, people may convince themselves that the obvious flaws are not a problem.[8] Bureaucratic politics, congressional politics, elections, and even Supreme Court decision making have all been studied through the lens of political conflict.[9]

Despite the consensus that conflict in politics is inevitable, most people do not like conflict, either in their personal lives or in politics. You probably have heard people

Conflict is inherent in American politics. Here, supporters and opponents of same-sex marriage argue in front of the Supreme Court building in Washington on the day the Court heard arguments in *Obergefell v. Hodges*, the 2015 case that legalized same-sex marriage throughout the nation.

Three Key Ideas for Understanding Politics

Politics Is Conflictual

Conflict and compromise are natural parts of politics. Political conflict over issues like the national debt, abortion, and health care **reflects disagreements among the American people** and often requires compromises within government.

Vote aquí

Political Process Matters

How political conflicts are resolved is important. Elections determine who represents citizens in government. **Rules and procedures determine who has power** in Congress and other branches of government.

Politics Is Everywhere

What happens in government affects our lives in countless ways. Policies related to jobs and the economy, food safety and nutrition, student loans, and many other areas shape **our everyday lives**. We see political information in the news and encounter political situations in many areas of our lives.

? Critical Thinking

1. **One implication of the idea that politics is conflictual is that politicians** may not want to negotiate compromises on important policy questions. Why do you think politicians sometimes refuse to compromise rather than work together to get things done?

2. **Think back to the discussion** of fake news at the beginning of this chapter. In what ways do disagreements over what constitutes "fake" news illustrate the three key ideas described here?

say that the three topics one should not discuss in polite company are money, religion, and politics. Indeed, political scientists have found strong evidence that people avoid discussing politics in order to maintain social harmony.[10]

Many people apply their disdain for conflict to politicians as well. "Why is there so much partisan bickering?" our students frequently ask. "Why can't they just get along?" This dislike of conflict, and of politics more generally, produces a desire for what political scientists John R. Hibbing and Elizabeth Theiss-Morse call "stealth democracy"—that is, nondemocratic practices such as running government like a business or taking action without political debate. In essence, this idea reflects the hope that everything would be better if we could just take the politics out of politics. Hibbing and Theiss-Morse argue that, to combat this belief, we need to do a better job of educating people about conflict and policy differences and that the failure to do so "is encouraging students to conclude that real democracy is unnecessary and stealth democracy will do just fine."[11] Conflict cannot be avoided in politics; ignoring fundamental disagreements will not make conflict go away.

The argument over abortion is a good example. Abortion rights have been a perennial topic of debate since a 1973 Supreme Court decision held that state laws banning abortion were unconstitutional. Surveys about abortion rights show that public opinion spans a wide range of policy options, with little agreement about which policy is best. (In Chapter 10, we will examine the political implications of this kind of broad disagreement.) Such conflicts reflect intense differences of opinion that are rooted in self-interest, ideology, and personal beliefs. Moreover, in such situations, no matter what Congress does, many people will be unhappy with the result. You might expect that politicians will ultimately find a compromise that satisfies everyone, but this is not always true. In many cases (abortion rights are a good example), no single policy choice satisfies even a slight majority of elected officials or citizens.

The idea that conflict is nearly always a part of politics should be no surprise. Situations in which everyone (or almost everyone) agrees about what government should be doing are easy to resolve: either a popular new policy is enacted or an unpopular issue is avoided, and the debate moves off the political agenda. Although issues where there is consensus resolve quickly and disappear, conflictual issues remain on the agenda as the winners try to extend their gains and the losers work to roll back policies. Thus, one reason that abortion rights is a perennial issue in campaigns and congressional debates is that there is no national consensus on when to allow abortions, no indication that the issue is becoming less important to citizens or elected officials, and no sign of a compromise policy that would attract widespread support.

An important consequence of the inevitable conflicts in American politics is that compromise and bargaining are essential to getting things done. Politicians who bargain with opponents are not necessarily abandoning their principles; striking a deal may be the only way to make some of the policy changes they want. Moreover, agreement sometimes exists even in the midst of controversy. For example, surveys that measure attitudes about abortion find widespread support for measures such as prohibiting government funding for abortions, requiring parental notification when a minor has an abortion, or requiring doctors who perform the procedure to present their patients with information on alternatives such as adoption, while only 15–25 percent (depending on the survey) think that abortion should always be illegal.[12]

Another consequence of conflict is that it is almost impossible to get exactly what you want from the political process. Even when a significant percentage of the population is united behind common goals—such as supporters of Donald Trump after the 2016 election, who demanded the repeal of Obamacare—these individuals

One consequence of political conflict is that one party's policy victories last only until the other party wins control of government. Here, President Trump signs a law repealing most of Dodd-Frank, an Obama-era measure that imposed new regulations on the banking industry in the wake of the 2008 financial crisis.

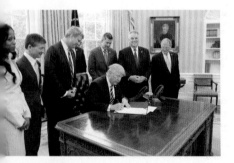

As long as the reason of man continues fallible, and he is at liberty to exercise it, different opinions will be formed.

—**James Madison,** founding father

almost always find that translating these demands into policy change requires them to accept something short of their ideal. Even with Democratic gains in the 2020 election, supporters of initiatives such as free college tuition or Medicare for All are likely to find that they must accept more modest changes or risk winning nothing at all. The need for compromise does not mean that change is impossible, but rather means that what is achievable often falls short of individuals' demands.

Political process matters

The political process is often described like a sporting event. Election coverage often emphasizes the "horse race" (who's ahead in the latest poll), and accounts of negotiations between the president and Congress often make the process sound like a poker game. This emphasis overlooks an important point: politics is the process that determines what government does, none of which is inevitable. Public policy—everything from defending the nation to spending on Medicare—is up for grabs. Changes in federal policy can have profound consequences for large swaths of the population. Politics is not just a game.

Elections are an excellent example. Elections allow voters to give fellow citizens the power to enact laws, write budgets, and appoint senior bureaucrats and federal judges. It matters who gets elected. In the first two years after the 2016 election produced unified Republican control of the presidency and Congress, many Obama-era environmental and employment regulations were repealed, conservatives were appointed to the Supreme Court and other federal courts, corporate tax rates were cut, and the United States withdrew from the Paris Agreement on climate change. Even after Democrats gained majority control of the House in 2018, Senate Republicans continued to confirm conservative federal judges, and the Trump administration continued to revise federal regulations. Clearly, political process matters: if the 2016 election had gone the other way, outcomes in all these important areas would have been significantly different.

Yet politics is more than elections. As you will see, many unelected members of the federal bureaucracy have influence over what government does by virtue of their roles in developing and implementing government policies. The same is true for federal judges, who review government actions to see if they are consistent with the Constitution and other federal laws. These individuals' decisions are part of the political process, even though they are not elected to their positions.

Ordinary citizens are also part of politics. They can vote; donate time or money to interest groups, party organizations, or individual candidates; or demand action from

The political process mattered in the 2020 election, from determining who the candidates were to affecting which states received the most attention from campaigns. Both Joe Biden and Donald Trump spent a lot of time campaigning in Florida in a bid to win the state's Electoral College votes.

these groups or individuals by writing letters, sending e-mails, or participating in public protest. Such actions can influence government policy, either by determining who holds the power to directly change policy or by signaling to policy makers which options have public support.

Another important element of politics is the web of rules and procedures that determines who has the power to make choices about government policy. These rules range from the requirement that the president must be born a U.S. citizen, to the rules that structure debates and voting in the House and the Senate, to the procedures for approving new federal regulations. Seemingly innocuous rules can have an enormous impact on what can or does happen, which means that choices about these rules are actually choices about outcomes. The ability to determine political rules empowers the people who make those choices.

Politics is everywhere

Even though most Americans have little interest in politics, most of us encounter it every day. When you read the newspaper, watch television, go online, or listen to the radio, you'll almost surely encounter a political story. When you are walking down the street, you may see billboards, bumper stickers, or T-shirts advertising a candidate, a political party, an interest group, or an issue position. Someone may ask you to sign a petition. You may walk past a homeless person and wonder whether a winning candidate followed through on her promise to help. You may glance at a headline about a Black Lives Matter protest and wonder why the protection of civil rights is such an enduring problem in America.

Many people have an interest in putting politics in front of us on a daily basis. Interest groups, political parties, and candidates work to raise public awareness of the political process and to shape what people know and want. Moreover, the news media offer extensive coverage of elections, governing, and how government policies affect ordinary Americans. Through efforts like these, politics really is everywhere.

Politics is also a fundamental part of how Americans think about themselves. Virtually all of us can name our party identification (Democrat, Republican, or Independent)[13] and can place our views on a continuum between liberal and conservative.[14]

Politics is everywhere in another important way, too: actions by the federal government touch virtually every aspect of your life. Figure 1.1 shows a time line for a typical college student on a typical day. As you can see, from the moment this student wakes up until

FIGURE 1.1

Government in a Student's Daily Life

On a typical day, the government plays a critical role in a student's daily life through federal programs, regulation, and spending. In addition to what is listed here, in what other aspects of your life does government play a part?

7:30	Wake up in dorm funded by federal program.
8:00	Eat cereal regulated by Food and Drug Administration.
8:15	Get dressed in clothing subject to import tariffs and regulations.
8:30	Read weather reports that use data from the National Weather Service.
9:00	Check e-mail using Internet developed with federal funding.
10:00	Drive to school in car whose design is shaped by federal regulations.
10:30	Drive past post office, military recruitment office, and environmental cleanup site.
11:00	Attend lecture by professor whose research receives federal funding.
4:00	Ride home from school on federally subsidized mass transit.
7:30	Pay bursar bill using federally funded student loan.
8:00	Call friend on cellular network regulated by the Federal Communications Commission.
10:00	Watch TV program on station that has federal license.

the end of the day, his or her actions are influenced by federal programs, spending, and regulations. Moreover, this chart omits actions by state and local governments, which are very active in areas such as education policy and law enforcement. As you will see in later chapters, it's not surprising that the federal government touches your everyday life in many ways. The federal government is extraordinarily large regardless of whether you measure it in terms of spending (more than $4.4 trillion a year), number of employees (over 2 million, not including contract workers and Postal Service employees), or regulations (over 180,000 pages in the *Code of Federal Regulations*).[15]

Moreover, the idea that politics is everywhere has a deeper meaning: people's political behavior is similar to their behavior in the rest of their lives. For example, collective action problems occur when you live with roommates and need to keep common areas neat and clean. Everyone has an interest in a clean area, but each person is inclined to let someone else do the work. The same principles help us understand campus protests over tuition hikes, alcohol bans, or changes in graduation requirements in terms of which kinds of issues and circumstances foster cooperation. In each case, individual free riders acting in their own self-interest may undermine the outcome that most people prefer.

Similarly, convincing like-minded individuals to contribute to a political group's lobbying efforts is no easy task. Each would-be contributor of time or money also has the opportunity to be a free rider who refuses to participate yet reaps the benefits of others' participation. Because of these difficulties, some groups of people with common goals remain unorganized. College students are a good example: many want more student aid and lower interest rates on government-subsidized student loans, but they fail to organize politically toward those ends.

This similarity between behavior in political situations and in the rest of life is no surprise; everything that happens in politics is the result of individuals' choices. And the connections between politics and everyday life mean you already know more about politics than you realize.

The idea that "politics is everywhere" means that government actions touch virtually all aspects of our lives, from regulating the business of Internet service providers to maintain net neutrality to mandating equal funding for men's and women's sports in high schools and colleges. Moreover, everyday life often helps us make sense of politics and politicians; for example, U.S. senator Ted Cruz joked that "The Democrats are the party of Lisa Simpson and Republicans are happily the party of Homer, Bart, Maggie and Marge," riffing on the perceived elitism of Lisa in comparison to the rest of her down-to-earth and highly relatable (and amusing) family members.

Just because you do not take an interest in politics does not mean that politics will not take an interest in you.

—Pericles, ancient Greek lawmaker

When you are trying to make sense of a political situation, think first of the three key ideas that we have just discussed. Focusing on conflict helps you understand what is at stake. Focusing on rules helps explain the strategies that participants use to achieve their goals. And the idea that politics is everywhere is there to remind you that conflicts over government policy are not things that happen only to other people—for better or worse, the outcome of political conflicts can touch virtually all aspects of our lives.

"Why Should I Care?"

Sources of conflict in American politics

Where does political conflict come from? The reality is that conflict must be addressed in order to find compromise and enact policy. Sometimes, however, disagreements resist resolution because of inherent differences among people and their opinions about government and politics.

Economic interests

People's economic interests today vary widely, and they constitute a source of conflict in politics. In contrast, relative economic equality was a defining characteristic of our nation's early history—at least among White men—since small landowners, businessmen, craftsmen, and their families constituted a large majority of the nation's population. Compared with our European counterparts, the United States has, historically, been relatively free from class-based politics. Over time, our nation has become more stratified by class, to the point that the United States now has one of the highest levels of income inequality among developed nations. Nonetheless, a broad commitment to the **free market** (an economic system based on competition among businesses without government interference) and to *economic individualism* (the autonomy of individuals to manage their own financial decisions without government interference) remains central to our national identity.

Despite this basic consensus on economic principles and a history relatively free of class-based politics, there are important differences among American citizens, interest groups, and political parties in terms of their economic interests and favored economic policies. Democratic politicians and activists tend to favor more **redistributive tax policies** (that is, tax policies that attempt to create greater social equality, such as taxing the rich at higher rates than the middle class or the poor, as in the wealth tax proposed by a 2020 Democratic presidential candidate, Senator Elizabeth Warren) and social spending on programs for the poor. Democrats are also more inclined to regulate industry to protect the environment and ensure worker and product safety, but they tend to favor fewer restrictions on the personal behavior of individuals. Republicans favor lower taxes and less spending on social policies. They are also more supportive than Democrats of the free market and less inclined to interfere with business interests, although many Republicans favor regulation of individual behaviors, such as abortion, same-sex marriage, and marijuana consumption.

Cultural values

Another source of conflict in American politics is differing cultural values. For example, political analysts often focus attention on the **culture wars** in the United States between "red-state" Americans, who tend to have strong religious beliefs, and "blue-state" Americans, who tend to be more secular. (The color coding of the states comes from the election-night maps on television that show the states carried by Republican candidates in red and those won by Democrats in blue—but see the What Do the Facts Say? feature for a more nuanced take on this.)

Although the precise makeup and impact of "values voters" is still debated, there is no doubt that many Americans disagree on cultural and moral issues. These

free market
An economic system based on competition among businesses without government interference.

redistributive tax policies
Policies, generally favored by Democratic politicians, that use taxation to attempt to create social equality (for example, higher taxation of the rich to provide programs for the poor).

culture wars
Political conflict in the United States between "red-state" Americans, who tend to have strong religious beliefs, and "blue-state" Americans, who tend to be more secular.

Purple America: The 2020 Presidential Election

The media create maps of the country on election night with red states indicating where Republicans win and blue states where Democrats win, like the top map here. But what do we see if we look beyond the state level to the county level? And what if we look not just at who won and who lost, but which party was stronger relative to the other? This is what the bottom map, created by Robert Vanderbei at Princeton University, shows. The simple view of two Americas—Republican versus Democrat, red versus blue—starts to look a lot more purple.

Think about it

- **Which sections of the country** were the strongest for Biden, and which were strongest for Trump?
- **In the bottom map,** which areas are the most mixed (purple)?
- **Over the next 20 years,** the nation will become more racially and ethnically diverse. How do you think these maps will change in light of this growing diversity?

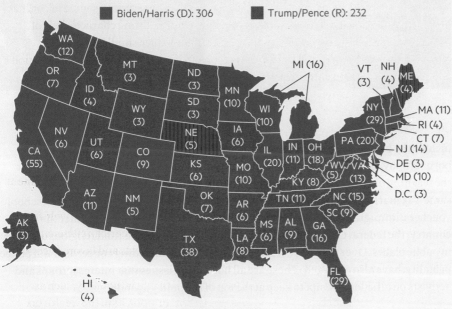

Biden/Harris (D): 306   Trump/Pence (R): 232

Note: 2020 Electoral map represents the authors' estimates as of 11/13/20. Two states split their electoral votes: in Maine, Trump received 1 vote and Biden 3; in Nebraska, Trump received 4 votes and Biden 1.

Democrat

Other

Republican

© Robert J. Vanderbei

Source: Provided by Robert J. Vanderbei, Princeton University, "2020 Presidential Election, Purple America," https://vanderbei.princeton.edu/JAVA/election2020/ (accessed 11/12/20).

Differing cultural values are a significant source of conflict among groups of voters in the United States. Pictured here are students in Odessa, Texas, protesting a school district policy that changed the names of the "invocation" and "benediction" to "opening" and "closing" at their graduation ceremony.

Civil and voting rights contributed to the realignment of the South in the second half of the twentieth century, as more Whites began supporting the Republican Party, and the Democratic Party came to be seen as the champion of minority rights. Here, Blacks and Whites in Alabama wait in line together to vote at a city hall after the enactment of the 1965 Voting Rights Act.

include the broad category of "family values" (such as whether and how to regulate pornography, gambling, and media obscenity and violence); whether to supplement the teaching of evolution in public schools with intelligent design and creationism; same-sex marriage; abortion; school prayer; legalization of drugs; gun control; school vouchers; immigration policy, including allowing political refugees to enter the country; the federal Common Core curriculum for K–12 schools; and religious displays in public places. Over the last several years, new topics, including concerns about police brutality, have also emerged. These are all hot-button issues that interest groups and activists on all sides attempt to keep at the top of the policy agenda.

Identity politics: racial, gender, and ethnic differences

Many political differences are correlated with racial, gender, and ethnic differences. For example, over the last generation about 90 percent of African Americans have been strong supporters of Democratic candidates. Other racial and ethnic groups have been less cohesive in their voting, with their support for a particular party ranging from 55 to 70 percent. Whites tend to vote Republican; Latinos tend to vote Democratic, with the exception of Cuban Americans, who tend to vote Republican; and Asian Americans tend to support Democrats with about 70 percent of the vote. A gender gap in national politics has also been evident in recent elections, with women being more likely to vote for Democrats and men for Republicans. Because these tendencies are not fixed, however, the political implications of racial, gender, and ethnic differences can change over time.

One of the enduring debates in American politics concerns whether ethnic and racial differences *should* be tied to political interests. One perspective reflects the melting pot image of America, which holds that as different racial and ethnic groups come to this country, they should mostly leave their native languages and customs behind. This perspective focuses on assimilation into American culture, with the belief that while immigrant groups will maintain some traditions from their native country, our common bonds as Americans are more important. Supporters of this view usually advocate making English the country's official language, oppose bilingual public education, and, if they favor immigration at all, prefer that it be restricted to well-off people from English-speaking countries.

However, there are varied alternatives to the melting pot view. These range from racial separatists such as the Nation of Islam, whose members see White-dominated society as oppressive and discriminatory, to multiculturalists, who argue that there is strength in diversity and embrace a "tossed salad" version of assimilation (that is, each ingredient remains distinct but contributes to the overall quality of the salad).[16] In general, people holding this viewpoint favor less restrictive immigration laws and oppose policies that encourage immigrants to assimilate. Given that immigrant groups also differ from the population in terms of education levels, occupation, family size, and other factors, it should not be surprising that members of these groups have their own ideas about what government should and should not do.

This debate over culture is one reason why recent discussions about immigration law have been so conflictual—the two sides start from very different premises about the value of diversity. But regardless of how this debate is resolved, our multiracial makeup is clear, as Figure 1.2 shows. In fact, trends in population growth suggest that by 2060 or so, Whites will no longer constitute a majority of the U.S. population. The extent to which this diversity continues to be a source of political conflict depends on the broader role of race in our society. As long as there are racial differences in employment, education, health, housing, and crime, and as long as racial discrimination is present in our society, race will continue to be a source of political conflict, as the Black Lives Matter protests in 2020 illustrate.

Many of the same observations apply to gender and politics. The women's movement is usually viewed as beginning in 1848 at the first Women's Rights Convention in Seneca Falls, New York. The fight for women's suffrage and legal rights dominated the movement through the late nineteenth and early twentieth centuries, with women gaining the right to vote in 1920 after passage of the Nineteenth Amendment to the Constitution. Beginning in the 1960s and 1970s, feminism and the

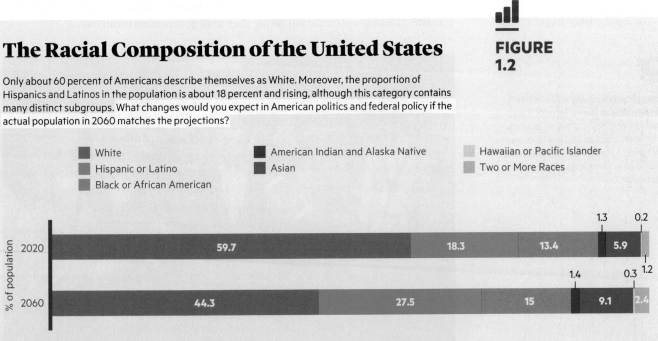

The Racial Composition of the United States

FIGURE 1.2

Only about 60 percent of Americans describe themselves as White. Moreover, the proportion of Hispanics and Latinos in the population is about 18 percent and rising, although this category contains many distinct subgroups. What changes would you expect in American politics and federal policy if the actual population in 2060 matches the projections?

Legend:
- White
- Hispanic or Latino
- Black or African American
- American Indian and Alaska Native
- Asian
- Hawaiian or Pacific Islander
- Two or More Races

% of population

2020: 59.7 | 18.3 | 13.4 | 1.3 | 5.9 | 0.2

2060: 44.3 | 27.5 | 15 | 1.4 | 9.1 | 0.3 | 1.2 | 2.4

Source: Census data aggregated by author. Raw data available at www.census.gov/programs-surveys/popproj/data/tables.html (accessed 12/2/19).

women's liberation movement highlighted a broad range of issues: workplace issues such as maternity leave, equal pay, and sexual harassment; reproductive rights and abortion; domestic violence; and sexual violence.

While progress has occurred on many fronts, including electing women to political office, gender remains an important source of political disagreement and identity politics. While the Congress elected in 2020 has more than 100 female House members and more than 20 female senators, these percentages are far lower than in the general population, and many other nations have a higher percentage of women in elected office. Gender politics became even more central during President Trump's presidency, starting with the January 2017 Women's March, which drew between 3.3 and 4.6 million people in more than 500 U.S. cities, and continuing with the #MeToo movement that has drawn attention to sexual assault (see Chapter 9 for additional details on contemporary civil rights politics).

Ideology

ideology
A cohesive set of ideas and beliefs used to organize and evaluate the political world.

conservative
The side of the ideological spectrum defined by support for lower taxes, a free market, and a more limited government; generally associated with Republicans.

liberal
The side of the ideological spectrum defined by support for stronger government programs and more market regulation; generally associated with Democrats.

libertarians
Those who prefer very limited government and therefore tend to be conservative on issues such as social welfare policy, environmental policy, and government funding for education but liberal on issues involving personal liberty such as free speech, abortion, and the legalization of drugs.

Another source of differences in interests is **ideology**: a cohesive set of ideas and beliefs that allows an individual to organize and evaluate the political world. Ideology may seem most obviously related to political interests through political parties, since Republicans tend to be **conservative** and Democrats tend to be **liberal**. While this is true in a relative sense (most Republicans are more conservative than most Democrats), few Americans consider their own views ideologically extreme.[17]

Ideology shapes beliefs about more specific policies. Conservatives promote traditional social practices and favor lower taxes, a free market, and a more limited government, whereas liberals support social tolerance, stronger government programs, and more market regulation. However, the picture gets cloudy if we look more closely. **Libertarians**, for example, prefer very limited government—they believe government should provide for the national defense and should have only a few other narrowly defined responsibilities. Because they are at the extreme end of the ideological continuum on this issue, libertarians are generally conservative in areas such as social welfare policy, environmental policy, and government funding for education and generally liberal on issues involving personal liberty such as free speech, abortion, and the legalization of drugs. For libertarians, the consistent ideological theme is limiting the role of government in our lives.

Though he is formally affiliated with the Republican party, Senator Rand Paul of Kentucky is often associated with libertarianism and is well known for taking a libertarian conservative stance on economic issues, in particular.

Personal ideologies are not always consistent. Someone can be both a fiscal conservative (favoring balanced budgets) and a social liberal (favoring the pro-choice position on abortion and marital rights for gay men and lesbians), or a liberal on foreign policy issues (supporting humanitarian aid and opposing military intervention overseas) and a conservative on moral issues (being pro-life on abortion and opposing stem-cell research). Ideology is a significant source of conflict in politics, and it does not always operate in a straightforward manner. In Chapter 10, we explore whether America is becoming more ideological and polarized, deepening our conflicts and making compromise more difficult.

Even so, there are clear areas of agreement in American politics, even on issues that once divided us. For example, while there is still considerable disagreement over same-sex marriage, public opinion has clearly shifted toward accepting these unions. Along the same lines, two generations ago Americans were divided on the legality of mixed-race marriage, while today very few people would object. Thus, even though conflict is a constant in American politics, it is wrong to say that we are divided into two groups, red and blue, that oppose each other on all issues of significance.

The first step in understanding any political conflict is to determine who wants what. Who is involved? What do they, or their side, want? In modern American politics, citizens' demands are often connected to their economic interests, values, race, gender, ethnicity, and ideology. As a result, the group affiliations of individuals often tell us a lot about what they want from candidates and the government, and why they want it.

"Why Should I Care?"

EXPLAIN HOW THE AMERICAN VALUES OF DEMOCRACY, LIBERTY, AND EQUALITY WORK TO RESOLVE POLITICAL CONFLICT

Resolving conflict: democracy and American political values

When we say that rules shape how conflicts are worked out in American politics, most of the time we are referring to formal (written-down) constraints that describe how the actions taken by each participant shape the ultimate outcome. For example, most American House and Senate elections are decided using plurality rule (whichever candidate gets the most votes wins), while a few states require winners to receive an absolute majority (50 percent + 1) of votes cast. However, some of the most important rules are not written down—these **norms** constitute America's political culture, or a collective idea of how a government and society should operate, including democracy, equality, and liberty, and more specific ideas about everyday political interactions.[18]

norms
Unwritten rules and informal agreements among citizens and elected officials about how government and society should operate.

Democracy

The idea of democracy means that policy disagreements are ultimately resolved through decisions made by citizens, such as their votes in elections. In the simplest terms, "**democracy**" means government by the people. As put into practice, this typically means representative democracy rather than direct democracy—that is, the people elect representatives who decide policies and pass laws rather than determining those things directly. There are some examples of direct democracy in the United States, such as the New England town meeting and the referendum process, through

democracy
Government by the people. In most contexts, this means representative democracy in which the people elect leaders to enact policies. Democracies must have fair elections with at least two options.

which people in a state directly determine policy.[19] But for the most part, Americans elect politicians to represent us, from school board and city council members at the local level, to state legislators and governors at the state level, to U.S. House members, senators, and the president at the national level.

Democracy is not the only way to resolve conflict, nor do all societies have as strong a belief in democracy as in America. One mechanism used by authoritarian governments is to suppress conflict though violence and limitations on freedom. Some governments, such as those of China and Russia, control political outcomes while allowing relatively free markets. The Iranian government is a theocracy, in which religious leaders have a veto over the government's policy choices. And some countries, such as the oil sheikdoms in the Middle East, like the United Arab Emirates, have a monarchy, in which rulers are determined by heredity. While nondemocratic systems vary widely in terms of their structure and their popularity, the common thread is that some individual or group is in charge of the country and the policy-making process and cannot be removed except by revolution.

In contrast, democracies select rulers and resolve conflict through voting and elections. When the second president of the United States, John Adams, turned over power to his bitter rival, Thomas Jefferson, after losing a hotly contested election in 1800, his departure demonstrated that democratic government by the people had real meaning—electoral winners get to exercise power, while losers go home to strategize about how to increase their popularity and win the next election. Democracy depends on the consent of the governed: if the views of the people change, then the government must eventually be responsive to those views or the people will choose new leaders. It also means that citizens must accept election results as authoritative—you have to obey the laws passed by a new Congress, even if you voted for the other party's candidates.

Liberty

To the Founders, **liberty** was a central principle for their new government: they believed that people must have the freedom to express their political views, with the understanding that conflict may arise between different views expressed by different people. The Bill of Rights of the Constitution (discussed in Chapter 8) outlines the nature of those liberties: the freedom of speech, press, assembly, and religion, as well as many legal and due process rights protecting individuals from government control.

Liberty also means that within broad limits, people are free to determine what they want from government and to organize themselves to demand their preferred policies from elected officials. Thus, in the case of immigration policy, it is acceptable to hold the view that America should have open borders, and it is also acceptable to demand (and lobby Congress to enact) a complete ban on immigration—or to hold any view in between these extremes.

A system in which individuals are free to form their own views about what government should do virtually guarantees conflict over government policy. James Madison recognized this essential trade-off between liberty and conflict. He argued that suppressing conflict by limiting freedom was "worse than the disease" (worse than conflict). To put it another way, any political system that prioritizes liberty will have conflict.

Another consequence of valuing liberty (and the inevitable conflict over policy that results) is the need for compromise in the policy-making process. In most policy areas, Americans and their elected officials hold a wide range of views, with no consensus on what government should do. Getting something done requires fashioning an agreement that gives no one what he or she really wants, but is nevertheless better than nothing. Standing on principle and refusing to compromise may sound like a noble strategy, but it often results in getting none of what you want, as other individuals or groups work to change policy without your involvement.

**AP®
FOUNDATIONAL
DOCUMENT**

liberty
Political freedom, such as the freedom of speech, press, assembly, and religion. These and other legal and due process rights protecting individuals from government control are outlined in the Bill of Rights of the U.S. Constitution.

Equality

Another principle of democracy is **equality**. Even though the Declaration of Independence boldly declared that "all men are created equal," this did not mean that all people were entitled to the same income or even the same social status (and the Founders obviously ignored slavery as well). Instead, the most widely embraced notion of equality in the United States today is the equality of opportunity—that is, everyone should have the same chance to realize his or her potential. Political equality also means that people are treated the same in the political system. Everyone has one vote in an election, and everyone is equal in the eyes of the law—that is, we are all subject to the same rules that limit how we can lobby, contribute, work for a candidate, or express our opinions. In practice, political equality has not always existed in America. In our early history, only White men could vote and in many states those men needed to be property owners in order to vote. Slowly, political equality expanded as property requirements were dropped; Black men (in 1870), women (in 1920)—though restrictions for people of color persisted into the 1960s—and 18- to 20-year-olds (in 1971) got the right to vote. (For more on the expansion of the right to vote, see Chapter 9.) Today, although wealthy people clearly can have their voices heard more easily than poor people can (through campaign contributions or independent expenditures on political ads), the notion of political equality is central to our democracy.

Like democracy, political equality also contributes to resolving conflict. First, if people know that they will be treated equally by the political system, they are more likely to respect the system. Indeed, one of the triggers for revolutions around the world is reaction against rigged elections or policies that benefit only the supporters of winning candidates. Political equality also gives us cues about how to get involved in politics. Most fundamentally, it suggests that the way to change policy is to elect candidates who share your views, rather than appealing to a friend or relative who works in the government or offering a bribe to a bureaucrat.

While America's political culture has many other aspects, the concepts of democracy, liberty, and equality are central to understanding how American politics works. Agreement on these principles helps lessen conflicts and limit their scope. For example, when Democratic senators lost the battle to prevent Trump's Supreme Court nominee Amy Coney Barrett from being appointed, they didn't have to worry that Trump would remove

AP®
FOUNDATIONAL
DOCUMENT

equality
In the context of American politics, "equality" means equality before the law, political equality (one person, one vote), and equality of opportunity (the equal chance for everyone to realize his or her potential), but not material equality (equal income or wealth).

In democracies like the United States, voting is one of the most visible ways citizens use the political process to express their opinions and resolve conflict.

them from office or throw them in jail for opposing her. Moreover, Democrats had a clear path to preventing Trump from appointing more justices like Barrett: regain control of the Senate or win the presidency. Americans and their elected officials have been willing to grant one another political equality and to take political defeats in stride because there is agreement on the basic boundaries of political debate. Again, this consensus does not imply there is no conflict—quite the contrary. However, conflict is easier to resolve if it is over a narrower range of options.

Not surprisingly, many aspects of America's political culture will come up throughout this book. You also might want to look out for them when you are watching the news or reading about national politics. When Democrats in Congress talk about the need to provide health insurance for all Americans, they are emphasizing equality—and when Trump and his Republican allies argue that minimizing government involvement and allowing people more choice (even if it means some people cannot afford insurance) will lead to a better system, they are emphasizing liberty. Moreover, as this example suggests, part of the conflict in American politics is over which aspect of political culture should carry the day. The fact that issues such as health care have been central in recent elections is a reminder of the importance of elections in a democracy and our belief that elections are one venue where conflicts are debated and resolved.

"Why Should I Care?"

To truly understand American politics, you must understand America's core values: democracy, liberty, and equality. These values set broad limits on how political conflicts will be resolved. Democracy implies that the people are the ultimate authority over political outcomes. Liberty implies that people are able to express whatever demands they want and to choose among a wide range of strategies in trying to shape the outcomes of political decisions. And equality means that everyone has an equal share of decision-making power. Despite conflicts over their interpretations, most Americans believe in these core values, and reminding ourselves of this can help us work toward resolving political conflicts.

UNDERSTAND HOW TO INTERPRET, EVALUATE, AND USE POLITICAL INFORMATION

The further a society drifts from the truth, the more it will hate those who speak it.

—George Orwell, novelist

How to be a critical consumer of politics

One of the biggest problems in understanding American politics today is deciding whom you should believe. If you want to justify a particular policy solution or point of view on any political issue, you can find a source that will help you do just that. Would free college tuition for all create a well-informed American citizenry? There are people who think so—and who have spent a great deal of time making this argument on free and paid media. Alternatively, would making college free do nothing except increase enrollments? There are plenty of easily accessible arguments for this position as well.

In one sense, the mountain of available information is an amazing asset. If you want to learn about politics, there are many more sources available now compared to generations ago, from mainstream media to a large number of political observers who put together websites, podcasts, Twitter feeds, or other social media sites. The problem is, if two sources disagree, who should you believe? If a source makes an extraordinary claim ("Space aliens control Congress!"), when should you take it seriously—at least seriously enough to research the claim? What rules should you follow to become well informed without being misled?

The Media Checklist for Assessing Reporting on Politics on p. 27 provides some general guidelines for learning about politics. We will be referring to these rules throughout the text, to help you understand how to put them into practice.

Consider the Author While it is true that the rise of the Internet and social media allows virtually anyone to report on politics, authors are not created alike. Some reporters have covered American politics for several decades and have a track record for cultivating sources, uncovering information, or analyzing and interpreting events. Other reporters essentially come out of nowhere, offering insights on a brand-new blog or website. Other things being equal, who should you believe—someone who has produced reliable reporting in the past or someone whose abilities can't be evaluated? Think about it this way: Whom do you want to fix your car—someone who's been fixing cars for 30 years and has thousands of satisfied customers (including your best friend, once a mechanic herself) or the newbie who just opened a shop last week? The answer is easy: unless the newbie has some identifiable edge, go with the track record.

Look for Verifiable Evidence Another important criterion for evaluating political reports is to see if they provide evidence to back up their claims. Anyone can say that free tuition will create a well-informed citizenry. However, this argument is more credible if it comes with supporting data, such as a study showing that college graduates are better informed than people who never attended. As engineer David Akin once put it, "Analysis without numbers is only an opinion." It's also important for the article to include enough information about the source so that it can be found without too much searching. That way, readers can examine the source themselves to verify that evidence was reported fairly. Of course, many reports on American politics rely on anonymous sources—in these cases, the author's reputation looms especially large in the decision of whether to take the story seriously.

Think about the Size of the Claim Evidence should also match the claims being made by a reporter. If someone claims that space aliens control Congress, we need more than his or her word to believe the report. In fact, in an era when everyone has access to Photoshop, pictures would not be enough. We'd probably want a news conference with a space alien and congressional leaders in which the full plot is revealed in detail. As the astronomer Carl Sagan often said, "Extraordinary claims require extraordinary evidence." The problem, of course, is that in many cases available evidence is fragmentary, contradictory, or even nonexistent. For example, one persistent rumor over the last few years was that the Russian government has some sort of embarrassing information about President Trump and that it was controlling his actions by threatening to release it. However, there is no hard evidence to back up these claims or many other possible explanations for Trump's allegedly pro-Russia actions. Which is to say, some of the time, it makes sense to disregard a potentially explosive story because those reporting it cannot prove what they claim to be true.

Read Multiple Reports A story about a political event or outcome is more credible if it is consistent with other reports. For example, on June 16, 2017, Trump tweeted about a Rasmussen Reports poll that showed his approval rate at 50 percent. However, the Rasmussen poll was an outlier; all the other polls taken at the same time showed Trump's approval rating to be significantly lower. In fact, FiveThirtyEight's aggregated estimate that same day was 38.7 percent. Moreover, past Rasmussen polls had also showed higher approval ratings for Trump. We'll talk more about polling and how to interpret poll results in Chapter 10. For now, these numbers illustrate the dangers of relying on a single information source.

Some sources are also better than others. For example, even though pollsters cannot measure public opinion with perfect certainty, they know some techniques are better than others. Accordingly, most public opinion scholars criticize the polling techniques used by Rasmussen Reports, on the grounds that they produce less accurate (and more pro-Republican) findings than the techniques used by other pollsters. Of course, pollsters don't know which techniques are the best in all circumstances—but they can still distinguish better from worse.

Beware of Simple Explanations In general, you should be skeptical about simple explanations for political outcomes. For example, one explanation for Hillary Clinton's defeat in 2016 (or the failure of the presidential campaigns of Senators Elizabeth Warren, Amy Klobuchar, and Kirsten Gillibrand during the 2020 Democratic nomination process) was that Americans were not ready to elect a female president. However, this account ignores the fact that throughout America women are routinely elected as mayors, governors, and members of Congress—and, after Kamala Harris's win in the 2020 election, as vice president. This is not to say that attitudes about gender did not play a role in Clinton's defeat (or that of the others), but rather to note that this outcome was the result of many factors working together. Complex outcomes are rarely explained by a single factor.

Finally, you might ask, If I'm supposed to be skeptical, why should I believe anything in this book? The answer is that throughout this book we've strived to follow all the rules presented here. Our aim is to describe how American politics works, rather than to make an argument about how it *should* work. We are social scientists, not cheerleaders. Rather than shaping your preferences, our goal is to give you the tools to understand, evaluate, and interpret political information and to help you be an informed, effective participant in the political process. As we always tell our students, "My goal is not to tell you *what* to think, but to help you learn *how* to think about politics." We emphasize facts and data (often from multiple sources, with citations and references) because the first step in understanding why things happen is to learn the details of actual events. And while we believe that American politics makes sense and that you can learn to make sense of it, we avoid simple explanations, as these generally do not provide much insight into political behavior or policy outcomes.

"Why Should I Care?"

Which reports about American politics should we take seriously? Those whose authors have reputations for insight and reliability, those that present appropriate evidence given their claims, those that are consistent with what other reporters are saying, and those that reflect the complexity of America's society and its government.

**AP®
POLICY IN
PRACTICE**

Policy introduction

The beginning of this chapter introduced three key ideas for understanding politics: politics is conflictual, political process matters, and politics is everywhere. At the end of this and each subsequent chapter, a specific policy is examined in detail that will bring these three themes to life. Of course, many different policies are discussed throughout this book, but what makes these end-of-chapter explorations different is that they delve into the dynamics of policy making by looking through the lens of seven policy stages, outlined below. This approach may be familiar to students who have learned about the

Media Checklist for Assessing Reporting on Politics

① Says who?

✓ **Evaluate the author's reputation**
The Internet and social media allow virtually anyone to report on politics, but authors are not created alike. Trust reporters who have experience covering American politics.

② Fact or "fake news"?

✓ **Verify the information**
Good reporting is the result of good sources, and you should always be able to identify and find the source without too much searching. Take a look at the source yourself—whether it is data, polling results, or even a journal article —to verify that evidence was reported fairly.

③ What's the impact?

✓ **Assess the extent of the claim**
As the astronomer Carl Sagan once put it, "Extraordinary claims require extraordinary evidence." Evidence should also match the claims being made by reporters. We need more than their word to believe what they are saying.

④ Who agrees?

✓ **Corroborate the report**
A story about a political event or outcome is more credible if it is consistent with other reports. Make sure you verify that other credible sources of news and reporters are saying the same thing.

⑤ Tell me more!

1+1=3

✓ **Assess if the explanation is too simple**
Be skeptical about simple explanations for political outcomes. Complex outcomes are rarely explained by a single factor.

scientific method, the process that scientists use when doing experiments. Scientists propose a hypothesis, test that theory, assess the results, revise the hypothesis, perform another experiment, and so on.

The procedure is very similar when making policies in the United States and studying them in the AP® U.S. Government and Politics course. The policy process starts with the recognition of a problem in a society (stage 1). There are numerous segments of society, which social scientists call stakeholders, that might recognize the problem and bring it to the attention of political leaders in hopes that it will be prioritized on the policy agenda (stage 2). That allows the problem to be discussed and debated with the goal of articulating a policy, a set of proposals to deal with the issues at hand. After the policy is deliberated and formulated (stage 3), it is then formally enacted and announced to the public (stage 4). It is then time for the policy to be put into practice (stage 5). After the policy is implemented, its consequences, intended and otherwise, will start to come to light and the various stakeholders will begin to evaluate how effective the policy is (stage 6). In light of these considerations, the policy might be modified, expanded, or terminated (stage 7)—and the process starts all over again.

Policy making resembles the scientific method in that both procedures feature steps done in sequence and both are continual processes whose goals, though not always achieved, are to keep refining and improving (and in some cases, rejecting) the initial proposals. Most of the policies discussed in this book take the form of bills, which if passed by Congress and signed by the president are turned into laws. Some of the policies considered, however, circumvent the legislative process because they are enacted by the president through executive actions. Both cases follow those seven policy stages. As you read the AP® Policy in Practice sections at the end of each chapter or consider any other policies, think about these stages as a template for understanding how political leaders and various stakeholders identify what they perceive as problems, the actions those groups take to address and to eliminate (or at least to improve) the circumstances stemming from those problems, and all of the challenges they face during the ongoing policy-making process. Below is the general outline of the policy stages that will be expanded with details of a different policy at the end of each chapter and that can be applied to any other policy you study.

Policy Stages
1. Problem Recognition
2. Agenda Setting
3. Deliberation and Formulation
4. Enactment
5. Implementation
6. Evaluation
7. Possible Modifications, Expansion, or Termination of Policy

Social Security

Social Security was part of Franklin Delano Roosevelt's New Deal programs, which were formulated as a result of the 1930s worldwide economic devastation known as the Great Depression. Although the United States was deeply committed to capitalism, there was a growing consensus that a stronger safety net was needed to protect American workers from the unpredictable nature of the market economy. Charles E. Townsend, a physician, developed such a plan, which was an impetus and inspiration for what became known as Social Security. As with all policies, there were proponents and opponents, though the latter group was in the distinct minority consisting mostly of pro-market advocates who did not like the involuntary nature of the program and the cost to employers who had to contribute to their employees' Social Security retirement accounts. One very vocal and popular opponent, Governor Huey Long of Louisiana, believed Roosevelt's plan did not go far enough.

Social Security is the most popular social program in the United States. Consequently, it has developed a reputation as the "third rail" of politics—like the dangerous, power-conducting rail on electrified train tracks—because a politician who dares to oppose Social Security risks political death. Despite serious problems concerning its long-term solvency, Social Security has proven remarkably immune to any steps that could be taken to shore up its financial health, such as cutting benefits or raising taxes. The third-rail quality of the program has been especially evident to those who would like to privatize part of Social Security. President George W. Bush made a serious push for personal savings accounts that would replace some Social Security benefits, but Congress rebuffed him when his appeals fell flat with the American public. The outline below highlights some of the changes Social Security has undergone over the years. Most of these amendments have favored the recipients, though some amendments to the original legislation—such as increasing Social Security taxes and increasing the age of eligibility—have been less beneficial, at least in the short run. But even with all these changes, President Roosevelt's original plan is essentially still intact as he had planned. By linking payments to earnings, he wanted to give workers a sense of ownership of their retirement plan so "no damn politician can ever scrap my social security program."[20]

Why else is Social Security so popular? One reason is Social Security's universal quality—that is, nearly every working American participates in the program, from the president to the teenager flipping burgers at McDonald's. Once people reach a certain age, they are all entitled to Social Security checks without regard to how much income they have from other sources, such as dividends, interest, or other pensions. So, unlike many social programs that develop an "us against them" mentality ("Why should we have to support other people?"), Social Security does not pit citizens from different classes or ethnic groups against one another.

This story is ongoing. Every president and every Congress is very likely to want to make changes either to prolong or to end the system. For many years, economists, politicians, and pundits have warned that unless changes are made, Social Security funds will run out. Thus far, this has not happened, either because the fears were unfounded or because the necessary changes were made to keep the system solvent. The latter situation is known as a self-defeating prophecy, in which actions are taken to prevent an expected outcome, which, as a result of the actions, does not occur. Time, the economy, elections, public will, and demographics will tell how Social Security evolves in the future.

Policy Stages

1. Problem Recognition
   - The average lifespan increased by 10 years in the 1900–1930 period.
   - For the first time in American history, more people were living in cities than in the country starting in the 1920s.[21]
   - The increase in the number of nuclear families meant less family support than when there were more extended families.
   - With more people working in factories, as opposed to working on farms, unemployment became more of a concern since workers relied on money to buy their necessities to a much greater degree than before.

- . The Great Depression had numerous social effects, such as:
  - · A large proportion of elderly people fell into poverty.
  - · A large percentage of the population was unemployed.
  - · Two million unemployed people became hoboes, itinerant homeless people who traveled across the United States looking for food, lodging, and jobs, often having to move frequently so as not to overstay their welcome and to avoid arrest for vagrancy.
- · A precedent had been set by 34 nations that already had some sort of social security or safety-net system in place.

2. Agenda Setting
- · Governor Huey Long announced the Share Our Wealth plan in a national radio address on February 23, 1934.
- · The Townsend Plan of Old Age Revolving Pensions was in place between September 1933 and February 1978 and stipulated the following:
  - · Those retiring at age 60 received a $200 monthly payment.
  - · Recipients had to have no habitual criminal tendencies.
  - · Recipients had to spend money within the month to stimulate the economy.
- · Social Security became a priority for FDR, who sent a message to Congress on June 8, 1934.
- · FDR issued an executive order to create the Committee on Economic Security with these goals:
  - · Everyone—rich and poor—would benefit to create universal buy-in.
  - · The system would be set up like retirement bank accounts, allowing recipients to track potential benefits.
  - · Workers would contribute through a payroll tax, which would link payments to earnings.

3. Deliberation and Formulation
- · Bill H.R. 7260 was introduced in the House of Representatives by Robert Doughton (D-NC) and David Lewis (D-MD) on January 17, 1935.
- · The House Ways and Means Committee held hearings from January 12, 1935 to February 12, 1935.
- · The House Ways and Means Committee renamed the Economic Security Bill as the Social Security Act.
- · Debate in the House began on April 4, 1935.
- · Bill H.R. 7260 was introduced in the Senate by Robert Wagner (D-NY) on January 17, 1935.
- · The Senate Finance Committee held hearings from January 22, 1935 to February 20, 1935.
- · Debate in the Senate began on June 12, 1935.
- · Fiscal conservatives fought back against the bill in both houses, arguing these points:
  - · It would unfairly compete with many private pensions, which were more generous.
  - · It would cost too much for firms since they had to match employee contributions.

4. Enactment
- · The House of Representatives passed the bill on April 19, 1935: **372 YEAs:** 284 Democrats, 81 Republicans, 7 others; **33 NAYs:** 15 Democrats, 15 Republicans,

3 others; **2 Present:** 2 Republicans, 0 Democrats, 0 others; **25 Not Voting:** 20 Democrats, 4 Republicans, 1 other.
- The Senate passed an alternative form of the bill on June 19, 1935: **77 YEAs:** 60 Democrats, 16 Republicans, 1 other; **6 NAYs:** 1 Democrat, 5 Republicans, 0 others; **12 Not Voting:** 8 Democrats, 4 Republicans, 0 others.
- The conference committee met in July 1935.
- The Social Security Act of 1935 was signed into law by President Franklin Delano Roosevelt on August 14, 1935.

5. Implementation
   - The Social Security Board (later known as the Social Security Administration) was established to oversee first three and then four different categories of beneficiaries, initially protecting over 30 million people, including
     - Workers aged 65 and older
     - Survivors, including widowers and children
     - Blind people
     - People receiving disability before retirement (the law was amended in 1956 to also provide disability benefits)
   - A system would be established by January 1, 1937, that would assign Social Security numbers and register employees and employers.
   - A payroll tax of 1 percent (now 6.2 percent) was imposed on incomes up to $3,000 ($142,800 in 2021); employers also paid 1 percent (now they pay 6.2 percent).
   - Recipients began to receive payments in January 1944 if they contributed for at least five years.
   - Self-employed workers were originally excluded; they now can participate but have to pay the full 12.4 percent.
   - A pay-as-you-go (not a self-funded) system emerged, in which today's workers support today's retirees through the payroll tax.

6. Evaluation
   - The program initially excluded many categories of minority workers, such as agricultural and domestic workers.
   - Social Security is a very efficient government program: only 0.8 percent goes to administration expenses compared with the average mutual fund that spends more than 1 percent for most privately managed pensions.
   - There is a low return on investment, but Social Security is more stable and predictable than investments in the stock market.
   - The program is highly regressive: lower-income workers pay a greater percentage of their income in Social Security contributions than higher-income workers because the maximum a worker can pay regardless of income is $137,700 (as of 2020).
   - Benefits are progressive: poorer people receive back in benefits a larger share of their lifetime payroll taxes than wealthy people receive.
   - Poorer and younger workers have found it difficult to give up so much of their income now for benefits received so many years later.
   - Fewer than 10 percent of the elderly are in poverty today, which is a lower rate than for the general public and significantly lower than the 35 percent of the elderly who were in poverty in 1960.
   - Nearly half of the elderly (44 percent) would be in poverty today without their Social Security payments.

- President Reagan's National Commission on Social Security Reform (also known as the Greenspan Commission) issued its report in 1983, making the following claims:
  - Funds could run out in the foreseeable future unless changes were made.
  - The retirement eligibility age should be increased.
- President George W. Bush's 2001 President's Commission to Strengthen Social Security made the following points:
  - The number of workers per beneficiary decreased over the years due to the retirement of baby boomers (people born between 1946 and 1964).
  - Minorities have a shorter lifespan and some receive fewer, if any, retirement payments.
  - Divorced women do not receive adequate benefits from their former spouses.
  - Beneficiaries actually receive a poor return on their investment.
  - Workers would benefit if they had more say over how their retirement money is invested.

7. Possible Modifications, Expansion, or Termination of Policy
   - The program extended disability coverage beyond blind people to others receiving disability before retirement.
   - Survivors' benefits afforded payments to the spouse of a retired worker in case of premature death.
   - Dependents' benefits afforded payments to minor children of a retired worker in case of premature death.
   - Medicare was established in 1965, introducing hospital and medical insurance.
   - Over the years, coverage was extended to an increasing number of workers, including agricultural workers, domestic workers, federal employees, the self-employed, and nonprofit employees.
   - The Social Security Amendments of 1961 lowered the minimum age from 65 to 62 for retirement benefits, which decreased to 80 percent of the amount otherwise payable at age 65.
   - The Social Security Amendments of 1972 made the following changes:
     - The automatic cost-of-living adjustment (COLA) benefits were increased to reflect inflation in 1972.
     - Benefit payment levels were raised beyond COLA.
   - The Social Security Reform Act of 1983 made the following changes:
     - Between 2003 and 2027 the retirement age would increase gradually from 65 to 67 for full retirement benefits.
     - Payroll taxes were increased to create a surplus ("trust fund").
   - "Trust fund" revenues that were supposed to increase Social Security revenues were redirected toward general government spending (for example, the war in Afghanistan, food stamps, school loans, and funding the FBI).
   - President George W. Bush suggested privatizing Social Security and creating personal savings accounts in which workers could invest their contributions as they see fit, but his effort failed to gain traction.
   - President Obama initially wanted to make several changes to the Social Security system:
     - Employee contribution payments would be reduced.
     - A less generous COLA index would be used for annual Social Security payment increases.
     - The retirement age would be increased.
   - He then reversed course and pushed for increasing Social Security payments.
   - President Trump proposed Social Security payroll tax cuts.

Questions for Discussion

1. Social Security is one of the most popular social programs in the United States. Under what kind of conditions might it be modified or changed?

2. Identify what groups are most likely to support or oppose reductions in Social Security benefits. In what ways might either one of these groups have influence over Social Security policy?

3. If people were allowed to invest their Social Security money as they see fit, they might have more money when they retire, but they might have less. Should people be allowed to make this decision themselves, even though they might be worse off? Why or why not?

Unpacking the Conflict

As we consider the three key ideas about politics that we've discussed in this chapter—politics is conflictual, political process matters, and politics is everywhere—let's return to the problem of defining "fake news" discussed at the beginning of the chapter. If Americans can't even agree on which news is "fake," how can we know what to trust?

Understanding that politics is conflictual reveals important details about the fight between Trump and the mainstream media. Because media coverage shapes public support, Trump wanted stories that said good things about his performance in office. But the job of a reporter is not to support the president—it's to provide a combination of facts and analysis that captures the situation. Virtually all presidents have felt at times that they were being treated unfairly by the media. But those feelings reflect the different goals held by presidents and the people who report on their performance. It's all about conflict, not fake news.

Understanding that process matters also provides insight into fake news. One reason why presidents complain about press coverage (although rarely in as blunt terms as Trump) is that there is very little they can do to stop the media from publishing critical stories. This is because of the First Amendment to our Constitution, which guarantees a free press. Trump can fume in private and publish critical tweets, but he has only marginal influence over what is written about him.

Finally, the media's coverage of Trump illustrates the fact that politics is everywhere. Trump's actions got attention because they affect our lives directly and indirectly. You might prefer that all the stories about Trump were replaced by additional coverage of your hobbies, favorite sports team, or other interests. But even if you ignore politics, politics does not ignore you. Decisions made in Washington have a profound impact on your life, whether you want them to or not.

As you read this book, we hope you will learn important "nuts and bolts" of the American political process as well as some political history that will help you gauge the likely accuracy of what you learn from news reports and help you determine if there might be more to the story than the narratives that are being presented. In general, your reading in this book will focus on contemporary questions, debates, and examples—the kinds of stories that constitute a lot of political news coverage—to illustrate broader points about our nation's political system.

Although you will no doubt disagree with—or even be angry about—some aspects of American politics and some media coverage, our goal is to provide you with the tools to understand *why* government operates as it does. We are not arguing that the federal government is perfect, that one party's agenda (or leadership) is better than the other's, or that imperfect responses to policy problems are inevitable. Rather, we believe that any attempt to explain these outcomes, or to devise ways to prevent similar problems, requires an understanding of why they happened in the first place. After reading this book, you will have a better sense of how American politics really works, and why it matters.

"What's Your Take?"

Is the media the "watchdog" that protects democracy, or is it an out-of-control, self-serving, biased group of partisans?

And if Americans can't even agree on which news is "fake," how can we know what to trust?

AP® STUDY GUIDE

Summary

Forms of government can be characterized by the number of people who hold power (many versus few) and the different levels over which power is distributed (national versus state versus local). Government exists primarily to provide order, although it must do so while avoiding oppression by the rulers. Government also needs to provide public goods because they will be under-provided by the free market.

Conflict in politics cannot be avoided: the American people disagree on nearly every issue on which politicians make policy decisions. Compromise and bargaining are essential to enacting policy, but this means that it is almost impossible to get exactly what you want from the political process. Policy outcomes are also influenced by the policy process itself—different procedures of making policy can lead to different outcomes. Whether it is on the news or influencing most aspects of your life, politics is all around us.

Although Americans generally agree on a free market system, there is considerable conflict over how much the government should support tax policies that redistribute wealth. Conflict also arises on cultural grounds, pitting religious "red-state" Americans against more secular "blue-state" Americans. There is also disagreement on the extent to which racial, gender, and ethnic diversity should be celebrated or minimized.

Democracy, liberty, and equality are American political values that are essential for understanding how conflict is resolved. Representative democracies resolve conflict through elections rather than through violence. Additionally, the various models of representative democracy (participatory, pluralist, and elite) are evident throughout the American political system. Although liberty ensures that people will have the freedom to express differing views, democracy is the best system for resolving those conflicts. Political equality ensures that everyone is treated the same before the law and that all votes are equal, and the equality of opportunity means that all people have an equal chance to realize their potential.

One of the biggest problems in understanding American politics today is deciding whom you should believe. In one sense, the mountain of available information is an amazing asset. If you want to learn about politics, there are many more sources and much more content available now compared

Key Terms

checks and balances (p. 7)
collective action problems (p. 8)
conservative (p. 20)
culture wars (p. 16)
democracy (p. 21)
elite democracy (p. 37)
equality (p. 23)

factions (p. 7)
federalism (p. 7)
free market (p. 16)
free rider problem (p. 8)
government (p. 6)
ideology (p. 20)
liberal (p. 20)
libertarians (p. 20)
liberty (p. 22)

norms (p. 21)
participatory democracy (p. 37)
pluralist democracy (p. 37)
politics (p. 9)
public goods (p. 8)
redistributive tax policies (p. 16)
representative democracy (p. 37)
separation of powers (p. 7)

with generations ago. But if sources disagree, whom should you believe? One answer is to focus on sources that provide evidence to back up their claims. It also helps to gather information from multiple sources, especially if the sources have different ideological or other biases. You should also be skeptical about simple explanations for political outcomes. Complex outcomes are rarely explained by a single factor.

Multiple-Choice Questions (Arranged by Practice)

Practice 1: Concept Application

1. **Which of the following constitutional principles best describes the division of government into three branches with each branch having distinct duties?**
   - (A) checks and balances
   - (B) separation of powers
   - (C) federalism
   - (D) free rider problem

2. **Which of the following is an accurate comparison of liberal and conservative ideologies?**

	Liberal	Conservative
(A)	favors market regulation	supports lower taxes
(B)	supports humanitarian aid abroad	opposes military intervention overseas
(C)	generally associated with Republicans	generally associated with Democrats
(D)	supports traditional social practices	supports a limited government

3. **Which of the following quotes best describes a concern of the Founders about the role that factions would play in new government?**
   - (A) "If men were angels, no government would be necessary. If angels were to govern men, neither external nor internal controls on government would be necessary." —James Madison
   - (B) "No arts; no letters; no society; and which is worst of all, continual fear, and danger of violent death: and the life of man, solitary, poor, nasty, brutish, and short." —Thomas Hobbes
   - (C) "[A variety of interests] divided mankind into parties, inflamed them with mutual animosity, and rendered them much more disposed to vex and oppress each other than to co-operate for their common good." —James Madison
   - (D) "Just because you do not take an interest in politics does not mean that politics will not take an interest in you." —Pericles

Practice 2: SCOTUS Application

4. **In the case of *Marbury v. Madison* (1803), the Supreme Court established the principle of judicial review, which gave the Court the power to interpret laws written by Congress to determine whether they are constitutional. This is an example of which of the following constitutional principles?**
   - (A) checks and balances
   - (B) separation of powers
   - (C) federalism
   - (D) popular sovereignty

Practice 3: Data Analysis

Questions 5–6 refer to the graph.

Racial Composition of the United States (Self-Identified)

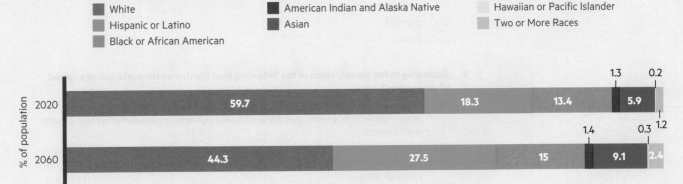

Legend:
- White
- Hispanic or Latino
- Black or African American
- American Indian and Alaska Native
- Asian
- Hawaiian or Pacific Islander
- Two or More Races

2020: 59.7 | 18.3 | 13.4 | 5.9 | 1.3 | 0.2

2060: 44.3 | 27.5 | 15 | 9.1 | 2.4 | 1.4 | 0.3 | 1.2

y-axis: % of population

Source: Census data aggregated by author. Raw data available at www.census.gov/programs-surveys/popproj/data/tables.html (accessed 12/2/19).

5. Based on the information in the graph, which of the following statements is true?

(A) In 2020, 18.3 million people self-identified as Hispanic or Latino.

(B) In 2020, the percentage of those identifying as two or more races was higher than the percentage of those identifying as Asian.

(C) In 2060, fewer people are expected to identify as Black or African-American than in 2020.

(D) In 2060, those identifying as White will no longer constitute a majority of the U.S. population.

6. Which of the following is a likely consequence of the trend presented in the data displayed in the graph?

(A) Issues related to immigration are likely to continue to be a source of conflict in American politics.

(B) The growth in population will lead to an increase in the number of representatives in Congress.

(C) There will be a push toward less redistributive tax policies and a greater commitment to the free market system.

(D) The population growth in red states will increase significantly compared with the population growth in blue states.

Practice 4: Source Analysis (Visual and Text)

Questions 7–8 refer to the visual.

Models of Representative Democracy

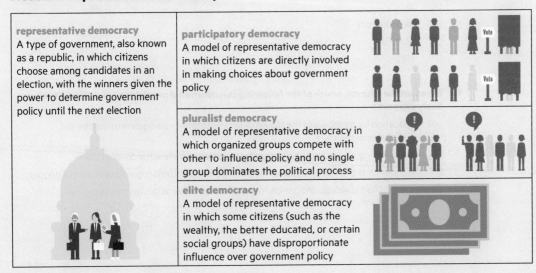

representative democracy
A type of government, also known as a republic, in which citizens choose among candidates in an election, with the winners given the power to determine government policy until the next election

participatory democracy
A model of representative democracy in which citizens are directly involved in making choices about government policy

pluralist democracy
A model of representative democracy in which organized groups compete with other to influence policy and no single group dominates the political process

elite democracy
A model of representative democracy in which some citizens (such as the wealthy, the better educated, or certain social groups) have disproportionate influence over government policy

7. In the 1950s, lawyers for the National Association for the Advancement of Colored People (NAACP) brought a series of class-action lawsuits on behalf of Black families seeking court orders to require segregated schools to allow Black children to attend. According to the visual, this process represents which of the following models of democracy?

   (A) direct

   (B) participatory

   (C) pluralist

   (D) elite

8. According to the visual, which of the following best illustrates the participatory model of democracy?

   (A) When Congress was reconsidering the ban on importing medication, the CEOs of large pharmaceutical companies donated money indirectly to candidates that aligned with their position.

   (B) In 2012, Ohio voters turned down a ballot initiative that would have created a 12-person commission rather than using the state legislature to redraw congressional district maps every 10 years.

   (C) In the 1980s, organizations like Mothers Against Drunk Driving (MADD) lobbied President Reagan to support a law to create a 21-year-old minimum drinking age.

   (D) Delegates to the Democratic convention used the votes of superdelegates, who are elected party officials, to steer the nomination in the direction they preferred.

Questions 9–10 refer to the excerpt.

To the People of the State of New York: . . . the election of the President is pretty well guarded. I venture somewhat further, and hesitate not to affirm, that if the manner of it be not perfect, it is at least excellent. It unites in an eminent degree all the advantages, the union of which was to be wished for.

It was desirable that the sense of the people should operate in the choice of the person to whom so important a trust was to be confided. This end will be answered by committing the right of making it, not to any preestablished body, but to men chosen by the people for the special purpose, and at the particular conjuncture.

It was equally desirable, that the immediate election should be made by men most capable of analyzing the qualities adapted to the station, and acting under circumstances favorable to deliberation, and to a judicious combination of all the reasons and inducements which were proper to govern their choice. A small number of persons, selected by their fellow-citizens from the general mass, will be most likely to possess the information and discernment requisite to such complicated investigations.

—Alexander Hamilton, *Federalist 68*, March 14, 1788

9. Which of the following models of democracy best supports Hamilton's argument in the excerpt?

   (A) direct

   (B) participatory

   (C) pluralist

   (D) elite

10. Based on the excerpt, which of the following constitutional provisions would Hamilton most likely support?

   (A) allocation for members of the House of Representatives being determined by the population of the state

   (B) the choosing of U.S. senators by the state legislatures of each individual state

   (C) amendments providing for universal suffrage for all citizens regardless of race or gender

   (D) the right for individuals and groups to peacefully assemble as designated by the First Amendment

Free-Response Questions

Concept Application

America is indebted as a democratic nation to the free press for truths it has uncovered, for truth it has disseminated, and for falsehoods it has repudiated. The press uncovered the government's lies about the war in Vietnam; it exposed Watergate; it opened our eyes to the sexual abuse of children by priests; and, most recently, it shed a light on the sexual assault by numerous men in power.... The work of a free press is essential.[a]

—Senator Mitt Romney (R-UT)

After reading the quotation, respond to A and B below:

(A) Referencing the scenario, describe the amendment that is discussed in the scenario.

(B) In the context of the scenario, explain how the government's attempt to balance liberty and order might be affected by the interpretation of the amendment described in Part A.

Quantitative Analysis

Top Priorities

Percent of Republicans and Democrats saying that each of the following should be a top priority for the federal government

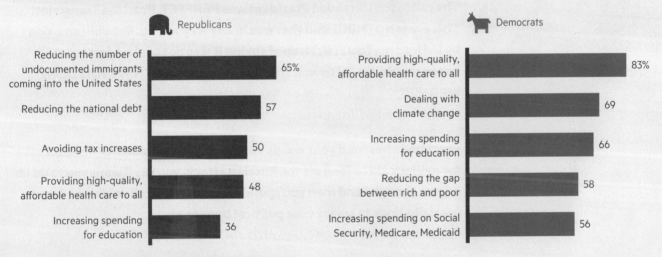

Republicans	
Reducing the number of undocumented immigrants coming into the United States	65%
Reducing the national debt	57
Avoiding tax increases	50
Providing high-quality, affordable health care to all	48
Increasing spending for education	36

Democrats	
Providing high-quality, affordable health care to all	83%
Dealing with climate change	69
Increasing spending for education	66
Reducing the gap between rich and poor	58
Increasing spending on Social Security, Medicare, Medicaid	56

Source: Pew Research Center, "Worries, Priorities and Potential Problem-Solvers," March 21, 2019, www.pewsocialtrends.org/2019/03/21/worries-priorities-and-potential-problem-solvers/ (accessed 7/28/20).

Use the bar graphs to answer the questions.

(A) Identify the political affiliation of people who are most likely to believe that in order to improve the quality of life for future generations, the top priority of the federal government should be to reduce the number of undocumented immigrants coming into the United States.

(B) Describe the difference between Republicans and Democrats on their attitudes of the priority level of increasing spending for education in order to improve the quality of life for future generations, as illustrated in the bar graphs.

2

The Constitution and the Founding

What are the rules of the political game?

 "The call to the Ukrainian President was PERFECT. Read the Transcript! There was NOTHING said that was in any way wrong. Republicans, don't be led into the fools [*sic*] trap of saying it was not perfect, but is not impeachable. No, it is much stronger than that. NOTHING WAS DONE WRONG!"[1]
President Donald Trump

"Everybody has read your words on the call. The Ukrainian President asks for military aid to fend off the Russian attack, you say 'I want you to do us a favor though,' and then you spend the rest of the call asking for bogus investigations to smear your political opponents."[2]
Speaker of the House Nancy Pelosi (D-CA)

In 2019, Donald Trump became the third president in U.S. history to be impeached by the House of Representatives, led by Speaker Pelosi. After several months of House investigations and a brief Senate trial, the president was acquitted almost along party lines. Speaking from the East Room of the White House after the conclusion of the trial, President Trump holds up a copy of the *Washington Post* announcing his acquittal.

In August 2019, a "whistleblower" filed a complaint alleging that President Trump had asked the president of Ukraine, Volodymyr Zelensky, to investigate Joe Biden, who at that point appeared to be Trump's chief rival in the 2020 campaign. The House started investigating the matter in early September and later that month it began an impeachment inquiry. Three different House committees heard testimony from more than a dozen witnesses over the next two months, first in private interviews and then in public hearings. In December, the House impeached the president, passing two articles of impeachment on nearly straight party votes. Article I alleged that Trump had abused his power by threatening to withhold $391 million in military and security assistance and a White House meeting until Ukraine agreed to two demands: (1) announce that it had opened investigations into the Bidens and (2) state that it, rather than Russia, had interfered in the 2016 presidential election. Article II alleged that Trump had obstructed Congress by directing executive branch officials not to testify before Congress and to withhold documents and records concerning the impeachment inquiry.

CHAPTER GOALS

Describe the historical circumstances that led to the Constitutional Convention of 1787. pages 42–49

Analyze the major issues debated by the framers of the Constitution. pages 50–59

Contrast the arguments of the Federalists with those of the Antifederalists. pages 59–62

Outline the major provisions of the Constitution. pages 62–70

Explore how the meaning of the Constitution has evolved. pages 71–77

Although substantial evidence was presented in the impeachment trial to support the allegations, the Senate voted to acquit the president, again on a party-line vote, with the exception of a vote from Republican Mitt Romney of Utah to convict on Article I.

Why was the president acquitted if the evidence was clear? The answer lies in the sparseness of the **Constitution**'s language concerning impeachment and the Senate's interpretation of these words: "The President, Vice President and all civil Officers of the United States, shall be removed from Office on Impeachment for, and Conviction of, Treason, Bribery, or other High Crimes and Misdemeanors" (Article II, Section 4). Treason and bribery are pretty clear, but what is a "high crime and misdemeanor"? When the words of the Constitution are unclear, scholars first look to two sources to figure out the framers' intent: James Madison's notes to the Constitutional Convention and the *Federalist Papers* (which we will talk about in more detail later in the chapter). Madison's notes reveal that initially the framers planned to limit impeachment to treason and bribery, but George Mason objected that the narrowness of those terms would excuse some impeachable behavior and "will not reach many great and dangerous offenses." So the framers added "high crimes and misdemeanors." At the time, misdemeanor meant "misconduct or misbehavior," so the term would have applied to a general abuse of power.

The president's expert on constitutional law in the impeachment trial, Alan Dershowitz, argued that an impeachable offense had to be a crime or "criminal-like behavior." But most constitutional scholars agree with Alexander Hamilton, who argued that impeachment is for "offenses which proceed from the misconduct of public men, or, in other words, from the abuse or violation of public trust. They are of a nature which may with peculiar propriety be denominated POLITICAL, as they relate chiefly to injuries done immediately to the society itself."[3] However, because impeachment is inherently a political process, not a legal process, impeachment means whatever a given House and Senate say that it means. So, when a majority of the Senate decided that President Trump's behavior did not warrant removal from office, many senators explicitly said that the voters should be able to decide, given that an election was coming up in less than a year. Well, the voters *did* decide and elected Joe Biden by extremely thin margins in a handful of states. President Trump claimed the election was stolen and for the first time in U.S. history, a peaceful transition of power was in doubt.

What would have happened if President Trump refused to leave office? Was American democracy in danger? Does the American political system as laid out in the Constitution work to keep conflicts between politicians and branches of government in check, or does it allow space for these conflicts to spiral out of control?

Constitution
A document that embodies the fundamental laws and principles by which the United States is governed. It was drafted at the Constitutional Convention and later supplemented by the Bill of Rights and other amendments.

DESCRIBE THE HISTORICAL CIRCUMSTANCES THAT LED TO THE CONSTITUTIONAL CONVENTION OF 1787

The historical context of the Constitution

The Constitution was created through conflict and compromise, and understanding its historical context can help clarify *why* the framers made the specific choices they did and how those choices influence our understanding of the Constitution today. The first event that led many American colonists to question the fairness of British rule and shape their ideas about self-governance was the Stamp Act of 1765, which imposed a tax on many publications and legal documents in the colonies. The British Parliament enacted the tax to help pay for the French and Indian War (1754–1763), which those lawmakers thought was only reasonable because the American colonies had benefited from the protection of British troops during the war. However, many colonists saw this

Under the Articles of Confederation, the weak national government was unable to raise enough money from the states to support American troops in the Revolutionary War. General George Washington's men lacked food, clothing, and sufficient arms and munitions until they were assisted by the French.

as unfair "taxation without representation," because they had no representation in British Parliament and thus had no say in the passage of the act. A series of escalating events moved the colonies closer to their inevitable break with Great Britain. These included the British-imposed Tea Act (1773) and the resulting Boston Tea Party later that year, in which colonists dumped tea from the British East India Company into the harbor rather than pay the new tax on tea. The British Parliament responded to the Tea Party with the Coercive Acts (or Intolerable Acts) of 1774 in a series of moves aimed at making sure the colonists paid for the tea they had destroyed, and designed to break the pattern of the colonists' resistance to British rule. Attempts at a political solution failed, so the Continental Congress declared independence from Britain on July 4, 1776.[4]

The Articles of Confederation: the first attempt at government

Throughout the Revolutionary (1775–1783) and early post-Revolutionary era (1783–1787), the future of the American colonies was very much in doubt. While many Americans were eager to sever ties with the oppressive British government and establish a new nation that rejected the trappings of royalty, there was still a large contingent of Tories (supporters of the British monarchy) and probably an even larger group of Americans who wished the conflict would just go away. Although public opinion on the matter is impossible to know, John Adams, the second president of the United States, estimated that the Second Continental Congress was about equally divided between Tories, "true blue" revolutionaries, and "those too cautious or timid to take a position one way or the other."[5] This context of uncertainty and conflict made the Founders' task of creating a lasting republic extremely difficult.

The first attempt to structure an American government, the **Articles of Confederation**, swung too far in the direction of decentralized and **limited government**. The Articles were written in the summer of 1776 during the Second Continental Congress, which had also authorized and approved the **Declaration of Independence**. They were submitted to all 13 states in 1777 for approval, but they did not take effect until the last state ratified them in 1781. However, in the absence of any alternative, the Articles of Confederation served as the basis for organizing the government during the Revolutionary War (see Figure 2.1).

Articles of Confederation
Sent to the states for ratification in 1777, these were the first attempt at a new American government. It was later decided that the Articles restricted national government too much, and they were replaced by the Constitution.

limited government
A political system in which the powers of the government are restricted to prevent tyranny by protecting property and individual rights.

Declaration of Independence
Adopted by Congress on July 4, 1776, this foundational document declared the colonies' independence from Britain. Its bold statement "all men are created equal" gave a limited conception of equality.

AP® FOUNDATIONAL DOCUMENT

AP® FOUNDATIONAL DOCUMENT

FIGURE 2.1

Constitutional Time Line

The sequence of important events leading to independence and the writing and ratification of the Constitution.

September
First Continental Congress

May
Second Continental Congress

January
First publication of Thomas Paine's *Common Sense*

July
Congress adopts the Declaration of Independence

November 15
Articles of Confederation adopted by Congress, sent to the states for ratification

February 6
Treaty of Alliance with France

October 19
Cornwallis surrenders the British army at Yorktown

March 1
Articles of Confederation are ratified by the requisite number of states

1774   1775   1776   1777   1778   1779   1780   1781

1775–1783 Revolutionary War

Source: Compiled by the authors.

monarchy
A form of government in which power is held by a single person, or monarch, who comes to power through inheritance rather than election.

In their zeal to reject monarchy, the authors of the Articles did not even include provisions for a president or any other executive leader. Instead, they assigned all national power to a Congress in which each state had a single vote. Members of Congress were elected by state legislatures rather than directly by the people. There was no judicial branch; all legal matters were left to the states, with the exception of disputes among the states, which would be resolved by special panels of judges appointed on an as-needed basis by Congress. To limit the power of government, the authors of the Articles gave each state veto power over any changes to the Articles and required approval from 9 of the 13 states on any legislation. Even more important, the states maintained autonomy and did not sacrifice any significant power to the national government; thus, government power was decentralized in the states, rather than centralized in the national government. For example, both the national government and the states could make treaties and coin money.

Congress also lacked any real authority over the states. For example, Congress could suggest the amount of money each state owed to support the Revolutionary army but could not enforce payment. This meant that General George Washington's troops were in dire straits, lacking basic food and clothing—to say nothing about the arms and munitions they needed to defeat the British. At first, Congress tried to compel the states to support their own troops, but this appeal failed. Desperate for funds, Congress tried in 1781 to give itself the power to raise taxes, but the measure was vetoed by Rhode Island, which represented less than 2 percent of the nation's population! If France had not come to the aid of the American army with much-needed funds and troops, the weakness of the national government could have led to defeat.[6]

After the Revolutionary War ended with the Treaty of Paris in September 1783, the inability to raise revenue through taxes continued to plague Congress. The new government owed millions of dollars in war debts to foreign governments and domestic creditors. Because it had no way to make the states pay their share, Congress proposed

October 27
Federalist Papers
begin appearing
in New York
newspapers

September 14
Annapolis
delegates
decide that
Articles need
to be fixed

September 17
Constitution
signed

June 21
Constitution
ratified when
New Hampshire
is the ninth
state to ratify

March 4
Constitution
takes effect

September 3
Treaty of Paris signed,
ending the Revolutionary War

**August 1786–
January 1787**
Shays's Rebellion

May 25
Constitutional
Convention
begins in
Philadelphia

'82   1783   1784   1785   1786   1787   1788   1789

81–1789 Articles of Confederation period

an amendment to the Articles that would allow the national government to collect import duties to put toward paying off the debt. However, New York, the busiest seaport in the nation, did not want to share its revenue and vetoed the amendment. Foreign trade also suffered because of the weak national government. If a foreign government negotiated a trade arrangement with Congress, it could be vetoed or amended by a state government, so a foreign country wanting to conduct business with the United States might have to negotiate separate agreements with Congress and each state legislature. Even trade among the states was complicated and inefficient: each state could make its own currency, exchange rates varied, and many states charged tolls and fees to export goods across state lines. (Just imagine how difficult interstate commerce would be today if you had to exchange currency at every state line and if the value of your currency varied depending on which state you were in.)

A small group of leaders decided that something had to be done. A group from Virginia urged state legislatures to send delegates to a convention on interstate commerce in Annapolis, Maryland, in September 1786. Only five states sent delegates. However, Alexander Hamilton and James Madison salvaged success from the convention by getting those delegates to agree to convene again in Philadelphia the following May. Delegates to the Annapolis Convention also agreed that the next convention would examine the defects of the current government and "devise such further provisions as shall appear to them necessary to render the Constitution of the Federal Government adequate to the exigencies of the Union."[7]

The issues that motivated the Annapolis Convention gained new urgency as events unfolded over the next several months. Economic chaos and depression in the years after the war had caused many farmers to lose their land because they could not pay their debts or state taxes. Frustration mounted throughout the latter half of 1786, and early in 1787 a former captain in the Revolutionary army, Daniel Shays, led a force of 1,500 men in an attempt to take over the Massachusetts state government arsenal in

The Founders wanted to create a constitution that was general enough to stand the test of time. Their approach succeeded, and the U.S. Constitution is the oldest written constitution still in use today. However, by leaving some passages open to interpretation, they also set the stage for conflict over the meaning of the Constitution. This painting depicts the signing of the document at the Constitutional Convention of 1787.

Shays's Rebellion
An uprising of about 1,500 men in Massachusetts in 1786 and 1787 to protest oppressive laws and gain payment of war debts. The unrest prompted calls for a new constitution.

Springfield. Their goal was to force the state courts to stop prosecuting debtors and taking their land, but the rebels were repelled by a state militia. Similar protests on a smaller scale took place in Pennsylvania and Virginia. Some state legislatures gave in to the debtors' demands, causing national leaders to fear that Shays's Rebellion had exposed fundamental discontent with the new government. The very future of the fledgling nation was at risk.

The rebellion exposed the central flaws of the government under the Articles of Confederation. If its leaders could not build a political system that addressed the problems of state sovereignty, redundant or conflicting responsibilities (such as coining money, foreign policy and trade, and taxing power), and the resulting political and economic chaos, then the United States would not be able to unite. Something clearly needed to be done.

Political theories of the framers

Although the leaders who gathered in Philadelphia in the summer of 1787 to write the Constitution were chastened by the failure of the Articles of Confederation, these men still shared many of the principles that had motivated the Revolution. There continued to be broad consensus on three key principles: (1) popular control of government through a republican democracy, (2) a rejection of monarchy, and (3) limitations on government power that would protect individual rights and personal property (that is, protect against tyranny).

republicanism
As understood by James Madison and the framers, the belief that a form of government in which the interests of the people are represented through elected leaders is the best form of government. Our form of government is known as a republican democracy.

Republicanism First among these principles was rejection of monarchy in favor of a form of government based on self-rule. Republicanism as understood by the framers is a government in which elected leaders represent the views of the people. Thomas Paine, an influential political writer of the Revolutionary era, wrote a pamphlet titled *Common Sense* in 1776 that was a widely read indictment of monarchy and an endorsement of the principles that fueled the Revolution and underpinned the framers' thinking.[8] Paine wrote that monarchy was the "most bare-faced falsity ever imposed on mankind" and that the common interests of the community should be served by elected representatives.

The Founders' views of republicanism, together with liberal principles of liberty and individual rights, shaped their vision of the proper form of government. The best expression of these principles is found in Thomas Jefferson's inspirational words in the Declaration of Independence:

We hold these truths to be self-evident, that all men are created equal, that they are endowed by their Creator with certain unalienable Rights, that among these are Life, Liberty, and the pursuit of Happiness. That to secure these rights, Governments are instituted among Men, deriving their just powers from the consent of the governed. That whenever any Form of Government becomes destructive of these ends, it is the Right of the People to alter or to abolish it, and to institute new Government.

Three crucial ideas are packed into this passage: equality, self-rule, and natural rights. Equality was not given much attention in the Constitution (later in this chapter we discuss how the problem of slavery was handled), but the notion that a government gains its legitimacy from the "consent of the governed" (the idea of **popular sovereignty**) and that its central purpose is to uphold the "unalienable" or **natural rights** of the people was central to the framers. The "right of the people to alter or abolish" a government that did not protect these rights served both to justify the revolt against the British and to remind the framers of their continuing obligation to make sure that those rights were maintained. The leaders who met in Philadelphia thought the Articles of Confederation had become "destructive to those ends" and therefore needed to be altered.

Paine, Jefferson, Madison, and other political thinkers of the American Founding broke new ground in laying out the principles of republican democracy, but they also built on the ideas of political philosophers of their era. As mentioned in Chapter 1, Thomas Hobbes argued that government was necessary to prevent people from living in an anarchic "state of nature" in which life would be "nasty, brutish, and short."[9] However, Hobbes's central conclusion was undemocratic: he believed that a single king must rule because any other form of government would produce warring factions. Another influential seventeenth-century philosopher, John Locke, took the notion of the consent of the governed in determining a government's legitimacy in a more democratic direction. He discussed many of the ideas that later appeared in the Declaration of Independence and the Constitution, including natural rights, property rights, the need for a vigorous executive branch that would be checked by a legislative branch, and self-rule through elections.[10] Baron de Montesquieu, an eighteenth-century political thinker, also influenced the framers. Although he did not use the term "separation of powers," Montesquieu argued in *The Spirit of the Laws* (1748) that no two, let alone three, functions of government (judicial, legislative, and executive) should be controlled by one branch. He also argued that in order to preserve liberty, one branch of government should be able to check the excesses of the other branches.

Human Nature and Its Implications for Democracy The most comprehensive statement of the framers' political philosophy and democratic theory was a series of essays written by James Madison, Alexander Hamilton, and John Jay titled the *Federalist Papers*. These essays explained and justified the framework of government created by the Constitution; they also revealed the framers' view of human nature and its implications for democracy. The framers' view of human nature as basically being driven by self-interest led to Madison's assessment that "[i]n framing a government which is to be administered by men over men, the great difficulty lies in this: you must first enable the government to control the governed; and in the next place oblige it to control itself." This analysis, which comes from *Federalist 51*, is often considered the clearest articulation of the need for republican government and a system of separated powers.

Seventeenth-century political philosopher John Locke greatly influenced the Founders. Many ideas discussed in Locke's writing appear in the Declaration of Independence and the Constitution.

popular sovereignty
The idea that government gains its legitimacy through regular elections in which the people living under that government participate to elect their leaders.

natural rights
Also known as "unalienable rights," these rights are defined in the Declaration of Independence as "Life, Liberty, and the pursuit of Happiness." The Founders believed that upholding these rights should be the government's central purpose.

Federalist 51
A foundational document written by James Madison in 1788 and titled *The Structure of the Government Must Furnish the Proper Checks and Balances between the Different Departments.*

AP®
FOUNDATIONAL
DOCUMENT

Federalist 10
A foundational document written by James Madison in 1787 and titled *The Union as a Safeguard against Domestic Faction and Insurrection.*

The economic context of the American Founding had an important impact on the framing of the Constitution. Most Americans worked on small farms or as artisans or business owners, which meant that economic power was broadly distributed. This woodcut shows New York City around the time the Constitution was written, viewed from upper Manhattan.

Federalists
Those at the Constitutional Convention who favored a strong national government and a system of separated powers.

In *Federalist 10*, Madison described the central problem for government as the need to control factions. He argued that governments cannot control the causes of factions because differences of opinion—based on the fallibility of reason; differences in wealth, property, and native abilities; and attachments to different leaders—are part of human nature. The only way to eliminate factions would be to either curtail liberty or try to make everyone the same. The first remedy Madison called "worse than the disease" of factions themselves, and the second he found "as impracticable as the first would be unwise." Because people are driven by self-interest, which sometimes conflicts with the common good, government must, however, try to control the effects of factions. This was the task facing the framers at the Constitutional Convention.

Economic interests

Political ideas were central to the framers' thinking at the Constitutional Convention, but economic context and interests were equally important. First, while there were certainly class differences among Americans in the late eighteenth century, they were insignificant compared with the inequalities found in Europe. America did not have the history of feudalism that had created tremendous inequality in Europe between landowners and propertyless serfs who worked the land. In contrast, most Americans owned small farms or worked as middle-class artisans and craftsmen. Thus, while political equality did not figure prominently in the Constitution, citizens' relative economic equality did influence the context of debates at the Constitutional Convention.

Second, despite Americans' general economic equality, there were significant regional economic differences. The South was largely agricultural, with cotton and tobacco plantations that depended on the labor of enslaved people. The region favored free trade because of its export-based economy (bolstered by westward expansion) and the trading of enslaved people. The middle Atlantic and northern states, however, had smaller farms and a broad economic base of manufacturing, fishing, and trade. These states favored government-managed trade and commercial development.

Despite these different interests, people in many sectors of the economy favored a stronger national government and reform of the Articles of Confederation (see Nuts & Bolts 2.1). Creditors wanted a government that could pay off its debts to them, southern farmers wanted free trade that could be efficiently promoted only by a central government, and manufacturers and traders wanted a single national currency and uniform interstate commerce regulations. However, there was a deep division between those who supported empowering the national government and those who still favored strong state governments and a weak national government. These two groups became known as the **Federalists** and the **Antifederalists**. Now the stage was set for a productive but contentious convention.

"Why Should I Care?"

The historical context and political ideas that shaped the thinking of the framers still resonate today. While we are centuries removed from the oppressive rule of the British monarchy, most Americans still support the ideas of representative democracy and limited government that replaced it. The division between the Federalists and Antifederalists on how to best create a representative government that protected our freedom is evident today in ongoing debates about the proper role of the government in our everyday lives.

Comparing the Articles of Confederation and the Constitution

NUTS & BOLTS 2.1

Issue	Articles of Confederation	Constitution
Legislature	Unicameral Congress	Bicameral Congress divided into the House of Representatives and the Senate
Members of Congress	Between two and seven per state (the number was determined by each state)	Two senators per state; representatives apportioned according to population of each state
Voting in Congress	One vote per state	One vote per representative or senator
Selection of members	Appointed by state legislatures	Representatives elected by popular vote; senators appointed by state legislatures
Chief executive	None (there was an Executive Council within Congress, but it had limited executive power)	President
National judiciary	No general federal courts	Supreme Court; Congress authorized to establish national judiciary
Amendments to the document	When approved by all states	When approved by two-thirds of each house of Congress and three-fourths of the states
Power to coin money	Federal government and the states	Federal government only
Taxes	Apportioned by Congress, collected by the states	Apportioned and collected by Congress
Ratification	Unanimous consent required	Consent of nine states required

Source: Compiled by the authors.

"Why Should I Care?"

The Constitution, which to this day outlines the rules for American government, provides for a strong federal government. This resolved many of the challenges that handicapped the early republic under the Articles of Confederation.

The politics of compromise at the Constitutional Convention

The central players at the Constitutional Convention were James Madison, Gouverneur Morris, Edmund Randolph, James Wilson, Benjamin Franklin, and George Washington, who was the unanimous choice to preside over the convention (despite his initial decision not to attend). Several of the important leaders of the Revolution were not present. Patrick "Give me Liberty, or give me Death!" Henry was selected to attend but declined to do so, as he opposed any changes in the Articles, saying he "smelled a rat." Indeed, those who were opposed to a stronger national government largely avoided the convention. Other prominent leaders who did not attend included Thomas Jefferson and John Adams, who were working overseas as U.S. diplomats, and Thomas Paine, who was back in England. Moreover, John Hancock and Samuel Adams were not selected to attend. The delegates met in secret to encourage open, uncensored debate.

Although there was broad consensus among the delegates that the Articles of Confederation needed to be changed, there were many tensions over the issues that required political compromise (see Nuts & Bolts 2.2). Among them were the following:

- majority rule versus minority rights
- large states versus small states
- legislative power versus executive power (and how to elect the executive)
- national power versus state and local power
- slave states versus nonslave states

These complex competing interests meant that the delegates had to focus on pragmatic, achievable solutions rather than on proposals that represented particular groups' ideals but that could not gain majority support. Robert A. Dahl, a leading democratic theorist of the twentieth century, argues that it was impossible for the Constitution to "reflect a coherent, unified theory of government" because so much compromising and vote trading was required to find common ground.[11] The delegates tackled the problems one at a time, holding lengthy debates and multiple votes on most issues. The most important initial decision they made was to give up on the original plan to revise the Articles of Confederation; instead, they decided to start from scratch with a new blueprint for government.

Majority rule versus minority rights

A central problem for any representative democracy is protecting minority rights within a system ruled by the majority. The framers thought of this issue not in terms of racial and ethnic minorities (as we might today), but in terms of regional and economic minorities. How could the framers be sure that small landowners and poorer people would not impose onerous taxes on the wealthier minority? How could they guarantee that dominant agricultural interests would not impose punitive tariffs on manufacturing while allowing free export of farmed commodities? The answers to these questions can be found in Madison's writings on the problem of factions in *Federalist 10*.

Madison defined a "faction" as a group motivated by selfish interests against the common good. If these interests prevailed, it could produce the very kind of tyranny

DID YOU KNOW?

The average age of the delegates to the Constitutional Convention was

42

Four of the delegates were in their 20s, and 14 were in their 30s.

Source: teachingamericanhistory.org

Major Compromises at the Constitutional Convention

Conflict	Position of the Large States	Position of the Small States	Compromise
Apportionment in Congress	By population	State equality	Great Compromise created the Senate and House
Method of election to Congress	By the people	By the states	House elected by the people; Senate elected by the state legislatures*
Electing the executive (president)	By Congress	By the states	By the Electoral College
Who decides federal–state conflicts?	Some federal authority	State courts	State courts to decide†
	Position of the Slave States	**Position of the Nonslave States**	**Compromise**
Control over commerce	By the states	By Congress	By Congress, but with 20-year exemption for the importation of enslaved people
Counting enslaved people toward apportionment	Counted 1:1 like citizens	Not counted	Three-Fifths Compromise
	Position of the Federalists	**Position of the Antifederalists**	**Compromise**
Protection for individual rights‡	Secured by state constitutions; national Bill of Rights not needed	National Bill of Rights needed	Bill of Rights passed by the 1st Congress; ratified by all states as of December 1791

*This was changed by the Seventeenth Amendment in 1913, which allowed for the direct election by the people of two senators from each state.
†This was changed by the Judiciary Act of 1789, which provided for appeals from state to federal courts.
‡This issue was raised but not resolved until after the convention.

Source: Compiled by the authors.

"Why Should I Care?" As we noted in Chapter 1, politics is conflictual. People will always have different goals and objectives. Adhering to one's principles is admirable, but unless one is willing to compromise, no one will get anything he or she wants in politics—or in life. The success of the Constitution is a result of compromises outlined above.

that the Americans had fought to escape during the Revolutionary War. Madison was especially concerned about tyranny by majority factions because, in a democracy, minority tyranny would be controlled by the republican principle: the majority could simply vote out the minority faction. If, however, the majority always rules, majority tyranny could be a real problem. Given the understanding of selfish human nature that Madison so clearly outlined, a populist, majoritarian democracy would not necessarily promote the common good. John Jay expressed his concern about popular majorities in strong terms: "The wise and the good never form the majority of any large society, and it seldom happens that their measures are uniformly adopted; or that they can always prevent being overborne themselves by the strong and almost never-ceasing union of the wicked and the weak."[12] However, if too many protections

James Madison argued that it is beneficial to put the interests of one group in competition with the interests of other groups, so that no one group can dominate government. He hoped to achieve this through the separation of powers across different branches of the national government and across the national, state, and local levels.

pluralism
The idea that having a variety of parties and interests within a government will strengthen the system, ensuring that no group possesses total control.

Virginia Plan
A plan proposed by the larger states during the Constitutional Convention that based representation in the national legislature on population. The plan also included a variety of other proposals to strengthen the national government.

New Jersey Plan
A plan that was suggested in response to the Virginia Plan; smaller states at the Constitutional Convention proposed that each state should receive equal representation in the national legislature, regardless of size.

were provided to minority and regional interests, the collective interest would not be served because constructive changes could be vetoed too easily, as under the Articles of Confederation.

Madison's solution to this problem provided the justification for our form of government. He argued that to control majority tyranny, factions must be set against one another to counter each other's ambitions and prevent the tyranny of any single majority faction. This was to be accomplished through the "double protection" of the separation of powers within the national government in the form of checks and balances, and by further dividing power across the levels of state and local governments through the system of federalism (which we will discuss in detail in the next chapter).

Popular majorities were also controlled, as we discuss below, by the indirect election of the president through the Electoral College and senators by state legislatures.

Madison also argued that additional protection against majority tyranny would come from the "size principle." That is, the new nation would be a large and diverse republic in which majority interests would be less likely to organize and therefore less able to dominate. According to Madison in *Federalist 10*, "Extend the sphere, and you take in a greater variety of parties and interests; you make it less probable that a majority of the whole will have a common motive to invade the rights of other citizens; or if such a common motive exists, it will be more difficult for all who feel it to discover their own strength, and to act in unison with each other."[13] This insight provides the basis for modern **pluralism**, a political theory that makes the same argument about the crosscutting interests of groups today.

The precise contours of Madison's solution still had to be hammered out at the convention, but the general principle pleased both the Antifederalists and the Federalists. State governments would maintain some autonomy, but the national government would become stronger than it had been under the Articles. The issue was striking the appropriate balance: none of the framers favored a pure populist majoritarian democracy, and few wanted to protect minority rights to the extent that the Articles had.

Small states versus large states

The question of the appropriate balance came to an immediate head in a debate between small-population and large-population states over representation in the national legislature. Under the Articles, every state had a single vote, but this did not seem fair to large states. They pushed for representation based on population. This proposal, along with others that would strengthen the national government, was the **Virginia Plan**. The small states countered with the **New Jersey Plan**, which proposed maintaining equal representation for every state. Rhode Island, the smallest state, was so concerned about small-state power that it boycotted the convention. Tensions were running high; this issue appeared to have all the elements of a deal breaker, and there seemed to be no way to resolve the impasse.

Just as it appeared that the convention might grind to a halt before it really got started, Connecticut proposed what became known as the **Great Compromise**, or Connecticut Compromise. The plan suggested establishing a Congress with two houses: the Senate would have two senators from each state, and in the House of Representatives each state's number of representatives would be based on its population. At first glance, the Connecticut Compromise seems to make perfect sense: as the seventh of 13 states in terms of population, Connecticut was positioned to offer a compromise that would appeal to both large and small states. But the situation was actually much more complicated. First, Rhode Island did not attend the convention, so there was no true median state (with only 12 states at the convention, no one stood alone at the center).

**FIGURE
2.2**

Connecticut's Pivotal Place at the Constitutional Convention

Though there were many disagreements over the details of America's new constitution, one of the most intense focused on how states would be represented in Congress, either allocating representatives equally or based on population. After other plans were considered and rejected, the Connecticut Compromise won out. Why do you think Connecticut was well positioned to find a compromise? How do these graphs help us understand why the Virginia and New Jersey Plans were in conflict and ultimately rejected?

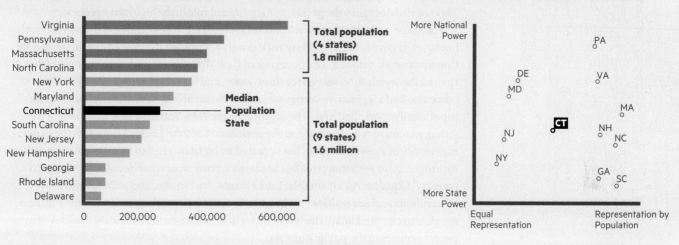

State Populations at the Time of the Constitutional Convention

Votes at the Constitutional Convention

Source: Keith L. Dougherty and Jac C. Heckelman, "A Pivotal Voter from a Pivotal State: Roger Sherman at the Constitutional Convention," *American Political Science Review* 100:2 (May 2006): 298.

Second, given that each state had one vote at the convention, the smallest states could have easily outvoted the biggest ones and insisted on equal representation for each state.

Why didn't the smaller states impose their view? Two of the smaller states, Georgia and South Carolina, focused on their future growth, so they supported representation based on population, the Virginia Plan. But when other smaller states balked at their loss of power, the Connecticut Compromise was able to win the support of North Carolina (and Massachusetts's delegates were divided), so the compromise passed 5-4-1.

Despite this more complex picture, an analysis of all 569 votes at the Constitutional Convention clearly shows that Connecticut occupied a pivotal place at the convention. As the graphs in Figure 2.2 illustrate, Connecticut was in the middle in terms of desire for representation based on population and in terms of desire for more state power. Connecticut is right in the center of these graphs—no wonder it could broker a compromise!

Legislative power versus executive power

An equally difficult challenge was how to divide power at the national level. Here the central issues revolved around the executive: the president. How much power should the president have relative to the legislative branch? (The courts also figured here, but they were less central to the discussions.) And how would the president be elected?

Limiting Presidential Power The delegates knew what they did not want: the king of England and his colonial governors were viewed as tramplers of liberty. But many delegates rejected outright the idea of a single executive because they believed it was

Great Compromise
A compromise between the large and small states, proposed by Connecticut, in which Congress would have two houses: a Senate with two legislators per state and a House of Representatives in which each state's representation would be based on population (also known as the Connecticut Compromise).

impossible to have an executive who would not be oppressive. Edmund Randolph proposed a three-person executive for this reason, arguing that a single executive would be the "fetus of monarchy." The Virginia Plan envisioned a single executive who would share some legislative power with federal judges in a Council of Revision with the power to veto legislation passed by Congress (however, the veto could be overridden by a simple majority vote in Congress). The delegates finally agreed on the single executive because he would have the most "energy, dispatch, and responsibility for the office" (as explained in *Federalist 70*), but they constrained the president's power through the system of checks and balances. One significant power they granted to the executive was the veto. It could be overridden by Congress, but only with the support of two-thirds of both chambers. This requirement gave the president a significant role in the legislative process.

Hamilton and the other New Yorkers favored a strong executive. This was probably because the governorship of New York closely resembled the type of executive that the Constitution envisioned. The governor of New York was elected by the people rather than by the legislature, served for three years, and was eligible for reelection. The office also had a legislative veto power and considerable control over appointments to politically controlled jobs. The arguments the New Yorkers made on behalf of the strong executive relied heavily on the philosophy of John Locke. Locke saw the general superiority of a government of laws created by legislatures, but he also saw the need for an executive with more flexible leadership powers, or what he called "prerogative powers." Legislatures are unable, Locke wrote, "to foresee, and so by laws to provide for all accidents and necessities."[14] They also are, by virtue of their size and unwieldiness, too slow to alter and adapt the law in times of crisis, when the executive could step in to pursue policies in the public's interest.

Although there was support for this view, the Antifederalists were concerned that if such powers were viewed as open-ended they could give rise to the type of oppressive leader the framers were trying to avoid. Madison attempted to reassure the opponents of executive power, arguing that any prerogative powers would have to be clearly enumerated in the Constitution. In fact, the Constitution explicitly provides only one extraordinary executive power: the right to grant reprieves and pardons, which means that the president can forgive any crimes against the federal government.

Selecting the President Another contentious issue concerning the executive was the method of selecting a president. The way the president was elected involved the issues of majority rule and minority rights, state versus national power, and the nature of executive power itself. Would the president be elected by the nation as a whole, by the states, or by coalitions within Congress? If the state-level governments played a central role, would this mean that the president could not speak for national interests? If Congress elected the president, could the executive still provide a check on the legislative branch?

Most Americans do not realize that (1) our presidential system is unique and (2) we came close to having a parliamentary system, which is the form of government that exists in most other established democracies. In a parliamentary system, the executive branch depends on the support of the legislative branch. The Virginia Plan proposed that Congress elect the president, just as Parliament elects the British prime minister. However, facing lingering concerns that a congressionally elected president would be too beholden to that body, a committee of framers subsequently made the following recommendations: (1) that the president be selected by an Electoral College, representation in which would be based on the number of representatives and senators each state has in Congress, and (2) that members of each state's legislature would determine the method for choosing their state's electors.[15] The delegates ultimately approved this recommendation.

Why did the delegates favor this complicated, indirect way of electing the president? As with good compromises, all sides could claim victory to some extent. Advocates of

parliamentary system
A system of government in which legislative and executive power are closely joined. The legislature (parliament) selects the chief executive (prime minister), who forms the cabinet from members of the parliament.

state power were happy because state legislatures played a central role in presidential elections; those who worried about the direct influence of the people liked the indirect manner of election; and proponents of strong executive power were satisfied that the president would not simply be an agent of Congress.

However, the solution had its flaws and did not work out the way the framers intended. First, if the Electoral College was supposed to provide an independent check on the voters, it never played this role because of the quick emergence of political parties (which the framers did not anticipate). Electors became agents of the parties, as they remain today, rather than independent actors who would use their judgment to pick the most qualified candidate for president. Second, the emergence of parties created a serious technical error in the Constitution: the provision that gave each elector two votes and elected the candidate with the most votes as president and the second-place finisher as vice president. With electors acting as agents of parties, they ended up casting one vote each for the presidential and vice-presidential candidate of their own party. This created a tie in the 1800 presidential election when Thomas Jefferson and Aaron Burr each received 73 electoral votes. The problem was fixed by the Twelfth Amendment, which required that electors cast separate ballots for president and vice president.

National power versus state and local power

Tensions over the balance of power cut across virtually every debate at the convention. The issues included presidential versus legislative power, whether the national government could supersede state laws, apportionment in the legislature, slavery, regulation of commerce and taxation, and the amendment process. The overall compromise that addressed these tensions was the second of Madison's "double protections," the system of federalism, which divided power between autonomous levels of government that controlled different areas of policy.

Federalism is such an important topic that we devote the entire next chapter to it, but two brief points about it are important here. First, the Tenth Amendment, which was added as part of the Bill of Rights shortly after ratification, was a concession to the Antifederalists, who were concerned that the national government would gain too much power in the new political system. The Tenth Amendment says: "The powers not delegated to the United States by the Constitution, nor prohibited by it to the States, are reserved to the States respectively, or to the people." This definition of reserved powers was viewed as setting outer limits on the reach of national power.

Between 1918 and 1937 and then again starting in the 1990s, the Supreme Court has frequently invoked the Tenth Amendment to nullify various laws passed by Congress as unconstitutional intrusions on the reserved powers of the states (see the discussion in Chapter 3 of the Supreme Court's recent preference for state-centered federalism). The Tenth Amendment continues to play an important role in current debates about the proper level of national power. For example, conservative Republicans argue that the states and the private sector, not the national government, should have the primary responsibility for health care policy, while Democrats in state and local government have served as a check on President Trump's policy agenda concerning immigration and climate change (among other issues).

Second, the national supremacy clause of the Constitution (Article VI) says that any national law is the supreme law of the land and takes precedence over any state law that conflicts with it. This is especially important in areas where the national and state governments have overlapping responsibilities for policy.

Jefferson: You hear this guy? Man openly campaigns against me, talking 'bout "I look forward to our partnership!"

Madison: It is crazy that the guy who comes in second gets to be vice president.

Jefferson: OOOH! Y'know what, we can change that! Y'know why?

Madison: Why?

Jefferson: 'Cause I'm the president!

—*Hamilton,* the musical

**AP®
FOUNDATIONAL
DOCUMENT**

reserved powers
As defined in the Tenth Amendment, powers that are not given to the national government by the Constitution, or not prohibited to the states, are reserved by the states or the people.

national supremacy clause
The part of Article VI, Section 2, of the Constitution stating that the Constitution and the laws and treaties of the United States are the "supreme Law of the Land," meaning national laws take precedence over state laws if the two conflict.

Slave states versus nonslave states

Slavery was another nearly insurmountable issue for the delegates. Southern states would not agree to any provisions limiting slavery; indeed, about 25 of the 55 delegates to the Constitutional Convention owned enslaved people.[16] Although the nonslave states opposed the practice, they were not willing to scuttle the entire Constitution by taking a principled stand. Even after these basic positions had been recognized, many unresolved issues remained. Could the importation of enslaved people be restricted in the future? How would northern states deal with enslaved people who had escaped to freedom? Most important in terms of the politics of the issue, how would the enslaved population be counted for the purpose of slave states' representation in Congress? The deals that the convention delegates cut on the issue of slavery illustrate the two most common forms of compromise: splitting the difference and logrolling (trading votes). Splitting the difference is familiar to anyone who has haggled over the price of a car or bargained for something at a flea market; you end up meeting halfway, or splitting the difference. Logrolling occurs when politicians trade votes for one another's pet projects, for example, support for dairy subsidies in one district in exchange for opening up more federal lands for mining in another.

The delegates went through similar negotiations over how enslaved people would be counted for purposes of states' congressional representation. The states had been through this debate once before, when they addressed the issue of taxation under the Articles of Confederation. At that point, the slave states had argued that enslaved people should not be counted because they did not receive the same benefits as citizens and were not the same burden to the government. Nonslave states had countered that enslaved people should be counted the same way as citizens when determining a state's fair share of the tax burden. The sides had reached a compromise by agreeing that each enslaved person would count as three-fifths of a person for purposes of taxation. The arguments over the issue of representation became even more contentious at the Constitutional Convention, where the positions were reversed, with slave states arguing that enslaved people should be counted like everyone else for the purposes of determining the number of House representatives for each state. Once again, both sides managed to agree on the Three-Fifths Compromise (see the What Do the Facts Say? feature).

Three-Fifths Compromise
The states' decision during the Constitutional Convention to count each enslaved person as three-fifths of a person in a state's population for the purposes of determining the number of House members and the distribution of taxes.

This advertisement from a slave-trading company appeared in a Richmond, Virginia, newspaper shortly after the Constitution was signed. Slavery is often referred to as the "original sin" of our nation and proved to be very problematic at the Constitutional Convention: Would there be limits on the importation of enslaved people? How would enslaved people who had escaped to freedom be dealt with by nonslave states? And how would enslaved people be counted for the purposes of congressional representation?

WANTED, ONE HUNDRED NEGROES, From 12 to 30 years old, for which a good price will be given. THEY are to be sent out of the state, therefore we shall not be particular respecting the character of any of them—Hearty and well made is all that is necessary. Moses Austin & Co. Richmond, Dec. 15, 1787.

The Three-Fifths Compromise

The Three-Fifths Compromise is often described as the "original sin" of the Constitution, but less recognized is the impact that it had on the Electoral College. The figure shows the number of each state's House members in the 1790s based on the Three-Fifths Compromise, and then how many representatives they would have had if only the free population had been counted or if the total population, including enslaved people, had been counted.

Think about it

- **How many additional seats in the House did southern states get** as a result of the Three-Fifths Compromise, relative to the number of seats they would have had if enslaved people had not been counted at all?
- **How many additional seats in the House would southern states have gotten** if enslaved people had been counted as full members of the population?
- **How did the Three-Fifths Compromise** have an impact on the Electoral College? (Remember: each state's number of electors is equal in number to its combined total of representatives in the House and senators.)

Number of House Members

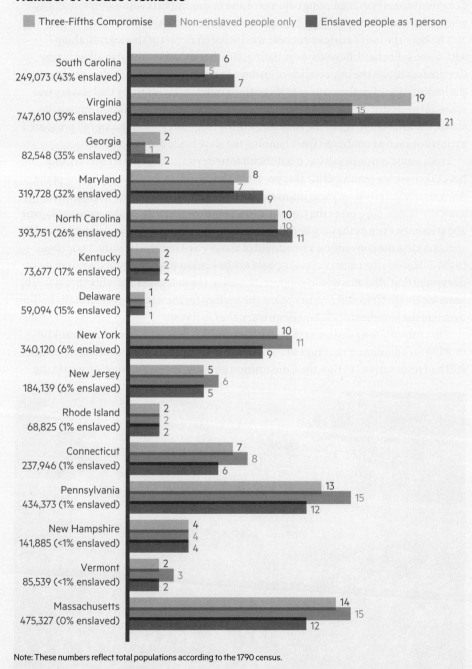

Legend: Three-Fifths Compromise / Non-enslaved people only / Enslaved people as 1 person

- South Carolina — 249,073 (43% enslaved): 6, 5, 7
- Virginia — 747,610 (39% enslaved): 19, 15, 21
- Georgia — 82,548 (35% enslaved): 2, 1, 2
- Maryland — 319,728 (32% enslaved): 8, 7, 9
- North Carolina — 393,751 (26% enslaved): 10, 10, 11
- Kentucky — 73,677 (17% enslaved): 2, 2, 2
- Delaware — 59,094 (15% enslaved): 1, 1, 1
- New York — 340,120 (6% enslaved): 10, 11, 9
- New Jersey — 184,139 (6% enslaved): 5, 6, 5
- Rhode Island — 68,825 (1% enslaved): 2, 2, 2
- Connecticut — 237,946 (1% enslaved): 7, 8, 6
- Pennsylvania — 434,373 (1% enslaved): 13, 15, 12
- New Hampshire — 141,885 (<1% enslaved): 4, 4, 4
- Vermont — 85,539 (<1% enslaved): 2, 3, 2
- Massachusetts — 475,327 (0% enslaved): 14, 15, 12

Note: These numbers reflect total populations according to the 1790 census.

Source: U.S. Census Bureau, "Return of the Whole Number of Persons within the Several Districts of the United States," www2.census.gov/library/publications/decennial/1790/number_of_persons/1790a-02.pdf (accessed 10/2/20); calculations are by the authors.

Union and Confederate troops clash in close combat in the Battle of Cold Harbor, Virginia, in June 1864. The inability of the framers to resolve the issue of slavery allowed tensions over the issue to grow throughout the early nineteenth century, culminating in the Civil War.

The other two issues, the importation of enslaved people and dealing with enslaved people who had escaped to freedom, were handled by logrolling combined with an element of splitting the difference. Logrolling is more likely to occur than splitting the difference when the issue cannot be neatly divided. For example, northern states either would be obligated to return freedom seekers to their southern owners or would not; there was no way to split the difference. On issues like this with no clear middle ground, opposing sides will look for other issues on which they can trade votes. In this case, the nonslave states saw an opportunity to push for more national government control over commerce and trade than was provided under the Articles, a change that the slave states opposed. A logroll—or vote trade—developed as a way to compromise the competing regional interests of slavery and regulation of commerce. Northern states agreed to return freedom seekers (the Fugitive Slave Clause), and southern states agreed to allow Congress to pass laws regulating commerce and taxing imports with a simple majority vote (rather than the supermajority required under the Articles).

The importation of enslaved people was included as part of this logroll, along with some split-the-difference negotiating. Northern states wanted to allow future Congresses to ban the importation of enslaved people; southern states wanted to allow the importation of enslaved people to continue indefinitely, arguing that slavery was essential to produce their labor-intensive crops. After much negotiation among the states, the final language of the Article resulting from this part of the logroll prevented a constitutional amendment from banning the slave trade until 1808.[17]

From a modern perspective, it is difficult to understand how the framers could have taken such a purely political approach to the moral issue of slavery. Many of the delegates believed slavery was immoral, yet they were willing to negotiate for the southern states' support of the Constitution. Some southern delegates were apologetic about slavery, even as they argued for protecting their interests. Many constitutional scholars view the convention's treatment of slavery as its central failure. In fairness to the delegates, the issue of slavery could not be settled since the goal was to create a document that all states would support. However, the delegates' inability to resolve this issue meant that it would simmer below the surface for the next 70 years, finally boiling over into the bloodiest of all American wars: the Civil War.

The convention ended on a relatively harmonious note with Benjamin Franklin moving for adoption. Franklin's motion was worded ambiguously to allow those who still had reservations to sign the Constitution anyway. Franklin's motion was in the

"following convenient form": "Done in Convention by the unanimous consent of the States present the 17th of September.... In Witness whereof we have hereunto subscribed our names." His clever wording meant that the signers were only bearing witness to the approval by the states and therefore could still, in good faith, oppose substantial parts of the document. Franklin's motion passed with 10 ayes, no nays, and one delegation divided. All but three of the remaining delegates signed.

Politicians today have a very difficult time compromising on issues like gun control, abortion rights, and even the proper levels of taxation and spending. At the Constitutional Convention, the framers had to struggle with fundamental issues such as executive power and state versus national power as well as incredibly divisive issues like slavery. The framers were facing uncertainty about the very survival of their new nation and the nearly impossible task of creating a new framework that would allow our nation to not only survive but also flourish. Yet the framers were able to arrive at workable compromises on all of these issues. Without compromise, our nation would not exist. When you hear a politician today say, "I am going to stick to my principles; I am not going to compromise," reflect on the fact that governing is not possible without compromise. "Compromise" is not a dirty word; it is an essential feature of politics.

"Why Should I Care?"

Ratification

Article VII of the Constitution, which described the process for ratifying the document, was also designed to maximize its chance of success. Only nine states were needed to ratify, unlike under the unanimity rule that had applied to changing the Articles of Confederation. Equally important, ratification votes would be taken in state conventions set up specifically for that purpose, bypassing the state legislatures, which would be more likely to resist some of the Constitution's state–federal power-sharing arrangements.

The near-unanimous approval at the Constitutional Convention's end masked the very strong opposition that remained. Many delegates simply left the convention when it became clear that things were not going their way (overall, 74 delegates were elected to go, 55 attended, and 39 signed the Constitution). Rhode Island sent no delegates and refused to appoint a ratification convention. More ominously, New York seemed dead set against the Constitution, and Pennsylvania, Virginia, and Massachusetts were split. The ratifying conventions in each state subjected the Constitution to intense scrutiny, as attendees examined every sentence for possible objections. A national debate raged over the next nine months.

The Antifederalists' concerns

The Antifederalists were most worried about the role of the president, the transfer of power from the states to the national government, and the lack of specific guarantees of civil liberties. In short, they feared that a strong, centralized national government would become tyrannical and they favored a small, decentralized republic. This concern was summarized in **Brutus 1**, an Antifederalist paper believed to have

CONTRAST THE ARGUMENTS OF THE FEDERALISTS WITH THOSE OF THE ANTIFEDERALISTS

Brutus 1
Antifederalist writing that advocated for a a small, decentralized republic, arguing that the Constitution gave too much power to the federal government at the expense of the states.

AP® FOUNDATIONAL DOCUMENT

This engraving by Amos Doolittle titled *The Looking Glass for 1787* satirizes some of the issues raised in the debate over the ratification of the Constitution. The wagon in the center is carrying Connecticut and sinking into the mud under the weight of debts and paper money as "Federalists" and "Antifederalists" try to pull it out.

A lady asked Dr. [Benjamin] Franklin, "Well, Doctor, what have we got—a republic or a monarchy?"

"A republic," replied the Doctor, "if you can keep it."

—**James McHenry,** *The Records of the Federal Convention of 1787*

been written by Robert Yates, a New York judge and delegate to the Constitutional Convention: the Constitution would create a federal government that would "possess absolute and uncontrollable power."[18] The doubts about the single central executive were expressed by Patrick Henry, a leading Antifederalist. Speaking to the Virginia ratifying convention, Henry was mocking in his indictment: "Your president may easily become a king.... There will be no checks, no real balances in this government."[19] Even Thomas Jefferson complained that the president would control the armed forces and could be reelected indefinitely.[20] State power and the ability to regulate commerce were also central concerns. States such as New York would lose substantial revenue if they could no longer charge tariffs on goods that came into their ports. Other states were concerned that they would pay a disproportionate share of national taxes.

The Antifederalists' foremost objection was to the lack of protections for civil liberties in the new political system. During the last week of the convention, Elbridge Gerry and George Mason offered a resolution "to prepare a Bill of Rights." However, the resolution was unanimously defeated by the state delegations. Some believed that the national government posed no threat to liberties, such as freedom of the press, because it did not have the power to restrict them in the first place. Others thought that because it would be impossible to enumerate all rights, it was better to list none at all. Federalists such as Roger Sherman argued that state constitutions, most of which protected freedom of speech, freedom of the press, right to a trial by jury, and other civil liberties, would be sufficient to protect liberty. However, many Antifederalists still wanted assurances that the *national* government would not trample their rights.

The Federalists' strategies

The Antifederalists had many strong arguments and there was no denying that the Constitution was really a "leap in the dark"—many of the ideas of the document had never been tested, so the experiment in government had high risks and no guarantee of success. To try to reassure opponents of the Constitution, the Federalists counterattacked on several fronts. First, supporters of the Constitution gained the upper hand in the debate by claiming the term "federalist." It is a common tactic in debates to co-opt a strong point of the opposing side as a positive for your side. The opponents of the Constitution probably had a stronger claim than its supporters to being federalists—that is, those who favor and emphasize the autonomous power of the state governments. Today, for example, the Federalist Society is a conservative group organized around the principles of states' rights and limited government. By calling themselves Federalists, the supporters of the Constitution asserted that they were the true protectors of states' interests, which irritated the Antifederalists to no end. The Antifederalists also had the rhetorical disadvantage of having "anti" attached to their name, thereby being defined in terms of their opponents' position rather than their own. But the problem was more than just rhetorical: the Federalists pointed out that the Antifederalists did not have their own plan to solve the problems created by the Articles and therefore were cast as defenders of the status quo, which the Federalists viewed as unsustainable.

Second, as we mentioned earlier, the Federalists published the *Federalist Papers*. Although originally published in New York newspapers, they were widely read throughout the nation. The *Federalist Papers* were essentially one-sided arguments aimed at changing public opinion. The authors downplayed potentially unpopular aspects of the new system, such as the power of the president, while emphasizing points they knew would appeal to the opposition. Despite the authors' biased arguments, the *Federalist Papers* are considered the best comprehensive discussion of the political theory underlying the Constitution, such as the framers' views of self-interested human nature and the dangers of factions, and their interpretations of many of the document's key provisions, such as the meaning of impeachment, as noted in the chapter opener.

Third, the Federalists agreed that the new Congress's first order of business would be to add a **Bill of Rights** to the Constitution to protect individual rights and liberties. This promise was essential for securing the support of New York, Massachusetts, and Virginia. The ninth state, New Hampshire, ratified the Constitution on June 21, 1788, but New York and Virginia were still dragging their heels, and their support was viewed as necessary for the legitimacy of the United States, even if it technically was not needed. By the end of the summer, both Virginia

Alexander Hamilton authored a majority of the *Federalist Papers* and was a strong advocate for ratification of the Constitution.

Bill of Rights
The first 10 amendments to the Constitution; they protect individual rights and liberties.

This political cartoon from 1788 depicts the erection of the "eleventh pillar of the great national dome" when New York became the eleventh state to ratify the Constitution, leaving only North Carolina and Rhode Island (shown as still wobbling in this cartoon) to ratify the document.

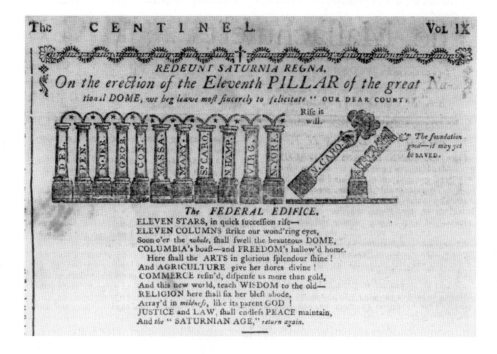

and New York finally voted for ratification. Rhode Island and North Carolina refused to ratify until Congress made good on its promise of a Bill of Rights (our civil liberties, which are guaranteed in the Bill of Rights, will be examined in Chapter 8). The 1st Congress submitted 12 amendments to the states, and 10 were ratified by all the states as of December 15, 1791.

The ratifying conventions in each state subjected the Constitution to intense scrutiny, as attendees examined every sentence for possible objections. A national debate raged over the next nine months, framed by the arguments of the Federalists and the Antifederalists. As we explained in Chapter 1, all politics is conflictual, but ultimately compromise is necessary in order to move forward. The resulting compromise between these two groups was the addition of the Bill of Rights, securing the civil liberties we hold as central American values to this day.

★

OUTLINE THE MAJOR PROVISIONS OF THE CONSTITUTION

The Constitution: a framework for government

The Constitution certainly has its flaws (some of which have been corrected through amendments), primarily its undemocratic qualities: the indirect election of senators and the president, the compromises that suppressed the issue of slavery (indeed, the words "slave" and "slavery" do not appear in the Constitution), the overrepresentation of small states in the Senate, and the absence of any general statement about citizens' right to vote. However, given the delegates' political context and the various factions that had to be satisfied, the Constitution's accomplishments are substantial.

The document's longevity is testimony to the framers' foresight in crafting a flexible framework for government. Perhaps its most important feature is the system of separation of powers and checks and balances that prevents majority tyranny while maintaining sufficient flexibility for decisive leadership during times of crisis (such as the Civil War, the Great Depression, and World War II). The system of checks and balances means that each branch of national government has certain exclusive powers, some shared powers, and the ability to check the other two branches (see How It Works: Checks and Balances).

The Constitution is the guide which I never will abandon.

—President George Washington

Exclusive powers

The framers viewed Congress as the "first branch" of government and granted it significant exclusive powers. With the House of Representatives elected by popular vote and the Senate indirectly elected by state legislatures, Congress was designed to be both the voice of the people and an institution more removed from the people, with an important role in domestic and foreign policy. Congress was given the specific **enumerated powers** to raise revenue for the federal government through taxes and borrowing, regulate interstate and foreign commerce, coin money, establish post offices and roads, grant patents and copyrights, create the system of federal courts,

enumerated powers
Powers explicitly granted to Congress, the president, or the Supreme Court in the first three articles of the Constitution. Examples include Congress's power to "raise and support Armies" and the president's power as commander in chief.

Congress alone has "the power of the purse" to fund government programs. Although Congress appropriated $11 billion to fund the construction of 500 miles of new barriers at the southern U.S. border, President Trump reallocated several billion dollars in Pentagon funds as well to the border wall project, drawing sharp bipartisan criticism from lawmakers who say that this move infringed upon the appropriations power granted solely to Congress by the Constitution.

declare war, "raise and support armies," make rules for the military, and create and maintain a navy. Most important is the so-called **power of the purse**—control over taxation and spending—given to Congress in Article I, Section 8, of the Constitution: "No money shall be drawn from the Treasury, but in consequence of appropriations made by law." Or, as Madison put it, "the legislative department alone has access to the pockets of the people." One other exclusive congressional power that received new attention during the first years of the Trump presidency is the "emoluments clause," which gives Congress the sole power to consent to any government official's receipt of anything of value from a foreign state. Lawsuits filed in federal court contend that the Trump family's ownership of hotels that are frequented by foreign officials in business with the federal government constitutes a violation of the emoluments clause. Two of these cases, in the Second and Fourth Circuit Courts of Appeals, have been permitted to proceed. A third case, which was brought by 215 Democratic members of Congress, was thrown out by the D.C. Court of Appeals early in 2020, and the Supreme Court declined to hear the case in October.[21]

Congress's exclusive powers take on additional significance through the **necessary and proper clause**, also known as the elastic clause. It gives Congress the flexibility to "make all Laws which shall be necessary and proper for carrying into Execution the foregoing Powers, and all other Powers vested by this Constitution in the Government of the United States, or in any Department or Officer thereof." This broad grant of power meant that Congress could pass laws related to any of its exclusive powers. For example, although the Constitution did not explicitly mention Congress's right to compel people to serve in the military, its power to enact a draft was clearly given by the necessary and proper clause, in conjunction with its power to "raise and support Armies."

power of the purse
The constitutional power of Congress to raise and spend money. Congress can use this as a negative or checking power over the other branches by freezing or cutting their funding.

necessary and proper clause
The part of Article I, Section 8, of the Constitution that grants Congress the power to pass all laws related to its expressed powers; also known as the elastic clause.

Checks and Balances

The Constitution stipulates that if one branch tries to assert too much power, the other branches have certain key powers that allow them to fight back and restore the balance. (In addition to the powers noted in the diagram, Congress can impeach the president and remove him or her from office.)

The president nominates judges.

The president can veto congressional legislation.

The Senate confirms the president's judicial nominations. Congress can impeach and remove judges from office.

Executive

Legislative

Judicial

The Senate approves presidential nominations, and Congress can override the president's veto and pass laws.

The Court interprets the laws passed by Congress.

The Court interprets actions by the executive branch.

Checks and Balances in the War on Terror

Shortly after the attacks of September 11, 2001, President George W. Bush, acting on his power as commander in chief, authorized the Guantánamo Bay detention center in Cuba to be used as a place to detain, interrogate, and try prisoners related to the War on Terror. President Obama tried to close the facility, but President Trump advocated keeping it open. At the same time, Trump called for a broad ban restricting travel to the U.S. from several Muslim countries. The controversies and policies surrounding these efforts in the War on Terror show how checks and balances work in practice.

He said...

First prisoners are taken to Guantánamo on January 11, 2002. President George W. Bush asserts that Guantánamo is outside legal U.S. jurisdiction and that prisoners held there do not have protections guaranteed to prisoners of war under the Geneva Convention.

But then...

The Supreme Court disagrees in *Hamdan v. Rumsfeld* on June 29, 2006, ruling that the detainees were entitled to basic legal rights and that the Geneva Convention did apply.

Shut it down?

The detention center is increasingly controversial. Two days after taking office in 2009, President Obama **signs an order to close the center** by the end of the year and to suspend all Guantánamo military commission hearings for 120 days.

Nope.

A week later, a military court judge **overturns the order** to suspend hearings at Guantánamo.

Another plan.

President Obama **wants to move Guantánamo prisoners** to a federal prison in Illinois.

Plan blocked.

A few months later, **Congress votes to block funds** needed for the transfer or release of prisoners held at the facility.

Sigh.

By the end of Obama's presidency, **41 prisoners remained**. President Trump vows to keep the facility open.

New strategy.

In 2017, President Trump tries a new approach by **issuing a ban on travel** from several mostly Muslim countries.

Is this okay?

Several district courts **strike down the ban as religious profiling**, but the Supreme Court reinstates a more limited version of the ban, citing the president's powers over national security and immigration policy.

?

Critical Thinking

1. **Why do you think it has been so difficult for presidents** to have their way in fighting terrorism, with regard to the travel ban and Guantánamo? Is it because of the issue of terrorism and national security? Or is it because of our system of checks and balances? Why?

2. **Do you think our system of checks and balances creates** too much gridlock, or is it an essential check on potential tyranny?

In contrast to Congress's numerous and specific exclusive powers, the Constitution grants very limited exclusive powers to the president. The president is the commander in chief of the armed forces, has power to receive ambassadors and foreign ministers, and may issue pardons. While these powers are fewer in number than those of Congress, they are consequential. For example, President Trump pulled out of the Paris Agreement on climate change, the Trans-Pacific Partnership, the Iran nuclear agreement, and the Intermediate-Range Nuclear Forces (INF) Treaty, and imposed (and then expanded) an extensive travel ban for national security reasons. He pulled U.S. troops out of northern Syria, engaged in a lengthy trade war with China, moved the U.S. embassy in Israel to Jerusalem, and threatened war with North Korea and then attempted to get it to stop its nuclear weapons program.

Trump also created a stir in 2017 when he explored the possibility of preemptively granting pardons to everyone, including himself, targeted by the Justice Department's Russia investigation.[22] Another controversy exploded when he pardoned three army officers accused of war crimes and granted clemency to a navy SEAL. His supporters saw these acts as sticking up for the nation's warriors, but many military leaders saw them as undermining military justice and the Law of Armed Conflict.[23] The president's most important powers are contained in the executive powers clause that says, "The executive power shall be vested in a President of the United States of America," and in the directive to ensure "that the laws are faithfully executed." As we see later in the chapter, these Article II clauses impart most of the president's power.

The courts did not receive nearly as much attention in the Constitution as either Congress or the president. Alexander Hamilton argued in *Federalist 78* that the Supreme Court would be the "least dangerous branch," because it had "neither the power of the purse nor the sword." The most important positive powers that the framers gave the Supreme Court were lifetime tenure for justices "during good behaviour" and relative independence from the other two branches. The critical negative power of judicial review, the ability to strike down the laws and actions of other branches, will be discussed later in this chapter.

AP®
FOUNDATIONAL
DOCUMENT

Shared powers

Along with dividing the exclusive powers between branches, the Constitution's system of checks and balances designates some shared powers. These are areas where no branch has exclusive control. For example, the president has the power to negotiate treaties and make appointments to the federal courts and other government offices, but these executive actions are to be undertaken with the "advice and consent" of the Senate, which means they were intended to be shared powers. In the twentieth century, these particular powers became executive centered, with the Senate providing almost no advice to the president and routinely giving its consent (often disapprovingly called rubber-stamping). However, the Senate can assert its shared power, as shown by the Senate's blocking of several of President George W. Bush's and President Barack Obama's lower-court nominees and Obama's nomination of Merrick Garland to the Supreme Court in 2016.

The war powers, which include decisions about when and how to use military force, were also intended to be shared. After serious disagreements, the ultimate compromise that the framers reached shows checks and balances at work, with the president serving as the commander in chief of the armed forces and Congress having the power

to declare war and to appropriate the funds to conduct a war. One other goal of the Founders in making the war powers a shared power was to ensure civilian control of the military. By providing a role for both Congress and the president, the Constitution made it more likely that this important democratic principle would be maintained. George Washington set a critical precedent for this before the Constitution was written when he resigned his commission as commander in chief of the Continental Army. Congress had given Washington complete authority over conduct of the Revolutionary War, and many in Congress wanted him to continue to rule, almost as a king. Washington knew that it was essential for the new nation to have democratically elected leaders control the military. By resigning his commission, he made it clear that any future leadership role he would play (and it was widely assumed by the Founders that he would be the first president) would be as a civilian rather than a general.

Since very early in our nation's history, the president has taken a lead role in the war powers, often making the decision to use military force. Presidents have authorized the use of American troops on hundreds of occasions, but Congress has declared war only five times. Of these, Congress debated the merits of entering only one war, the War of 1812. The other "declarations" recognized a state of war that already existed. (For example, after Japan bombed Pearl Harbor, Hawaii, in 1941, Congress's subsequent declaration of war formally recognized what everyone already knew.) As the 2003 invasion of Iraq demonstrated, if a president is intent on going to war, Congress must go along or get out of the way. President Trump's authorization of strikes against ISIS in Syria and subsequent removal of troops from the Turkish border demonstrate that the president has substantial power in situations that are short of full-scale war.

Because the president's war powers have grown significantly, some fear that the president could lead us into a full-scale war on his or her own. But the president's war powers are not unlimited. Since the Vietnam War, Congress has tried to redress the imbalance in the war powers in a variety of ways. In 1970, Congress passed a resolution that prevented any funds from supporting ground troops in Laos or Cambodia (nations that bordered Vietnam). Congress passed the War Powers Resolution in 1973 to further

This painting, which hangs in the Capitol rotunda, shows General George Washington resigning his commission as commander in chief of the Continental Army. This set the precedent that democratically elected officials would control the U.S. military.

limit the president's war powers. In 2013, Congress was strongly opposed to a military strike against Syria in response to its use of chemical weapons against its own people. A showdown with President Obama, who favored a strike, was averted when Syria agreed to allow weapons inspectors to destroy its chemical weapons stockpile. These examples show that although the president continues to dominate the war powers, Congress can assert its power when it has the will—just as it can by advising the president in treaty negotiations or by withholding approval of the president's nominees for appointed positions. Congress can also express its displeasure when the president acts unilaterally against its will, as it did when the House voted 354–60 to condemn Trump's withdrawal of American forces from northern Syria.[24]

Negative or checking powers

The last part of the system of checks and balances is the negative power that the branches have over one another. These powers are especially important to ensure that no single branch dominates the national government.

Congressional Checks Congress has two important negative checks on the other branches: impeachment and the power of the purse. The impeachment power allows Congress to remove the president, vice president, or other "officers of the United States" (including federal judges) for abuses of power—specifically, "Treason, Bribery, or other High Crimes or Misdemeanors." The framers placed this central check with Congress as part of the overall system of checks and balances.

Through the power of the purse, Congress can punish executive agencies by freezing or cutting their funding or holding hearings on, investigations of, or audits of their operations to make sure money is being spent properly. Congress can also freeze judges' salaries to show displeasure with court decisions, and it has the power to limit the issues that federal courts can consider. Congress can also limit the discretion of judges in other ways, such as by setting federal sentencing guidelines that recommend

impeachment
A negative or checking power over the other branches that allows Congress to remove the president, the vice president, or other "officers of the United States" (including federal judges) for abuses of power.

a range of years in prison that should be served for various crimes. Even today, the system of checks and balances is not fixed in stone but evolves according to the changing political climate.

In addition to these two formal constitutional checks, Congress may limit presidential power through its legislative powers of lawmaking and oversight. When Congress is controlled by a different party than the president, such checking is common; for example, in the last six years of Obama's presidency, Republicans in Congress tried to stop much of his agenda. But even under unified government, as in the first two years of Trump's presidency, Congress can check presidential power. Republicans passed stronger sanctions against Russia, investigated Russian interference in our elections, failed to provide full funding for the wall at the U.S.-Mexico border, and failed to "repeal and replace" the Affordable Care Act (Obamacare), all in the face of Trump's opposition.

Presidential Checks The framers placed important checks on congressional power as well, and the president's most important check on Congress is the veto. Again, there was very little agreement on this topic. The Antifederalists argued that it was "a political error of the greatest magnitude, to allow the executive power a negative, or in fact any kind of control over the proceedings of the legislature." But the Federalists worried that Congress would slowly strip away presidential powers and leave the president too weak. In the end, the Federalist view that the president needed some protections against the "depredations" of the legislature won the day. However, the veto has developed into a major policy-making tool for the president, which is probably broader than the check against "depredations" envisioned by the framers.

The president does not have any formal check on the courts other than the power to appoint judges. However, presidents have, at various times, found unconventional ways to try to influence the courts. For example, Franklin Delano Roosevelt tried to "pack the Court" by expanding the size of the Supreme Court with justices who would be sympathetic to his New Deal policies. More recently, George W. Bush attempted to expand the reach of executive power in the War on Terror by taking over some functions within the executive branch that the courts had previously performed,

The Constitution attempts to strike a balance between protecting our civil liberties from government intrusion and providing for a government strong enough to protect our national security. In this photo, a security officer is using facial recognition technology to identify a woman before she boards a plane at Dulles International Airport. Although this technology poses several benefits for law enforcement, critics argue that it could be misused in ways that infringe upon the basic civil rights of U.S. citizens. For example, in China facial recognition technology is used to identify and arrest citizens for jaywalking.

such as defining which suspected terrorists would have legal rights. However, the Supreme Court struck down some of these policies as unconstitutional violations of defendants' due process rights.[25] President Obama changed many of Bush's policies, such as harsh interrogation methods and excessive secrecy. But other Bush-era policies were either more difficult to change than Obama anticipated, such as the detainment of enemy combatants in the prison at Guantánamo Bay, or deemed necessary to fight terrorism, such as indefinite detention without trial for suspected terrorists who were arrested outside combat areas.[26] President Trump continued these policies and created other new ones, such as the travel ban aimed at specific countries that are viewed as terrorist threats (see the How It Works graphic in this chapter). Critics claim that the expansion of executive power in order to fight terrorism has threatened the institutional balance of power by giving the president too much control over functions previously carried out by the courts.[27]

Judicial Review The Constitution did not provide the Supreme Court with any negative checks on the other two branches. Instead, the Court itself (in the landmark decision of *Marbury v. Madison* in 1803) established the practice of judicial review, the ability of the Supreme Court to strike down a law or an executive branch action as unconstitutional. For example, early in Trump's first year, federal courts struck down the initial versions of his travel ban because they were viewed as discriminatory against Muslims. According to Madison's notes, nine of the eleven framers who spoke on the topic clearly favored explicitly granting the Supreme Court the power of judicial review, but the issue was not resolved at the convention. In several states assertive courts had struck down state laws, and delegates from those states resisted giving an unelected national court similar power over the entire country.

Although judicial review is not explicitly mentioned in the Constitution, supporters of the practice justify it by pointing to the supremacy clause, which states that the "Constitution, and the Laws of the United States which shall be made in Pursuance thereof . . . shall be the supreme Law of the Land." As Chief Justice John Marshall argued in *Marbury v. Madison,* to enforce the Constitution as the supreme law of the land, the Court must determine which laws are "in pursuance thereof." Critics of judicial review argue that the Constitution is supreme because it gains its legitimacy from the people and that therefore elected officials—Congress and the president—should be the primary interpreters of the Constitution rather than the courts. This dispute may never be fully resolved, but Marshall's bold assertion of judicial review made the Supreme Court an equal partner in the system of separate powers and checks and balances rather than "the least dangerous branch" that the framers described.

AP®
SUPREME
COURT CASE

Marbury v. Madison
The landmark case in which the Supreme Court for the first time declared that part of a law passed by Congress was unconstitutional. This case helped establish judicial review.

judicial review
The Supreme Court's power to strike down a law or executive branch action that it finds unconstitutional.

"Why Should I Care?"

If you remember anything from your elementary civics class, it is probably some foggy notion of the system of checks and balances and separation of powers. But why is this system so important? This institutional framework provides the basis for our government and explains the nature of political conflict and outcomes. When the government shuts down because of a dispute over spending or the Senate blocks the president's court nominees, this is because the president and Congress have different roles but can check each other's powers. Understanding checks and balances and separation of powers helps us be realistic about what government can do and shows us that all parts of the government are critical, but none are dominant, in making policy and enforcing laws.

Is the Constitution a "living" document?

Polls suggest that many Americans are unfamiliar with the Constitution's basic provisions. Indeed, a national poll found that only 26 percent could name all three branches of the U.S. government, while 31 percent could not identify even one; 12 percent believed there was a constitutional right to own a pet, and 34 percent thought there was a right to own a home.[28] Even more disconcerting, another poll showed that 52 percent could name at least two members of Bart Simpson's family, while only 28 percent could list more than one of their five First Amendment rights.[29] In the face of such public ignorance, can the Constitution provide the blueprint for modern democratic governance? If so, how has it remained relevant after more than 230 years? The answer to the first question, in our opinion, is clearly yes. Although the United States falls short on many measures of an ideal democracy, the Constitution remains relevant in part because it embodies many of the central values of American citizens: liberty and freedom, majority rule and minority rights, equal protection for all citizens under the laws, and a division of power across and within levels of government. The Constitution presents a list of substantive values, largely within the Bill of Rights, aimed at legally protecting certain individual rights that we still consider basic and necessary. The Constitution also sets out the institutional framework within which the government operates.

But these observations beg the question of *why* the Constitution remains relevant today. Why does this framework of government still work? How can the framers' values still be meaningful to us? There are at least three components of the Constitution that allow it to continue as a "living" document: the ambiguity in central passages that permits flexible interpretation, the amending process, and the document's own designation of multiple interpreters of the Constitution. These factors have allowed the Constitution to evolve with the changing values and norms of the nation (see the Take a Stand feature).

EXPLORE HOW THE MEANING OF THE CONSTITUTION HAS EVOLVED

The people made the Constitution, and the people can unmake it. It is the creature of their will, and lives only by their will.

—**John Marshall,** chief justice, 1801–1835

Ambiguity

The Constitution's inherent ambiguity is a characteristic that has kept the document relevant to this day. Key passages were written in very general language, which has allowed the Constitution to evolve along with changing norms, values, and political contexts. This ambiguity was a political necessity: not only were the framers aware that the document would need to survive for generations, but in many instances the language that they chose was simply the only wording that all the framers could agree on.

Three of the most important parts of the Constitution are also among its most ambiguous: the necessary and proper (or elastic) clause, the **executive powers clause**, and the **commerce clause**. As discussed earlier, the necessary and proper clause gives Congress the power to enact laws that are related to its enumerated powers, or those that are explicitly granted. But what does "necessary and proper" mean? For the most part, Congress gets to answer that question.

The executive powers clause is even more vague: Article II begins with the words "The executive Power shall be vested in a President of the United States of America." This sentence has served to justify a broad range of presidential actions because it does not define any boundaries for the "executive powers" it grants. The vague wording was necessary because the Constitutional Convention delegates could not agree on a definition of executive power. The wording also had the desirable consequence of making the clause flexible enough to serve the country both in times that require strong

executive powers clause
The part of Article II, Section 1, of the Constitution that states: "The executive Power shall be vested in a President of the United States of America." This broad statement has been used to justify many assertions of presidential power.

commerce clause
The part of Article I, Section 8, of the Constitution that gives Congress "the power to regulate Commerce … among the several States." The Supreme Court's interpretation of this clause has varied, but today it serves as the basis for much of Congress's legislation.

presidential action (such as the Civil War, the Great Depression, or World War II) and in times when the president was not as central (such as the "golden age of Congress" in the late nineteenth century).

Perhaps the best illustration of the importance of ambiguity in the Constitution is the commerce clause, which gives Congress "the power to regulate commerce ... among the several States." What is "commerce" and what exactly does "among the states" mean? Different interpretations have reflected prevailing norms of the time. In the nineteenth century, when the national government was relatively weak and more power was held at the state level, the Supreme Court interpreted the clause to mean that Congress could not regulate commerce that was entirely within the boundaries of a single state (*intra*state, as opposed to *inter*state, commerce). Because manufacturing typically occurred within the boundaries of a given state, this ruling led to a distinction between manufacturing and commerce, which had significant implications. For example, Congress could not regulate working hours, worker safety, or child labor given that these were defined as part of manufacturing rather than commerce. In the New Deal era of the mid-1930s, the Court adopted a more expansive interpretation of the commerce clause that largely obliterated the distinction between intrastate and interstate commerce. This view was strengthened in the 1960s when the Supreme Court upheld a civil rights law that, among other things, prevented owners of hotels and restaurants from discriminating against African Americans. For nearly 60 years this interpretation held. More recently the Supreme Court has tightened the scope of Congress's powers to regulate commerce,[30] but the clause still serves as the basis for most important national legislation. The commerce clause has been unchanged since 1789, but its ambiguous wording has been used to justify or restrict a varying array of legislation.

One consequence of this ambiguity is that both sides of every major political debate in our history have claimed to ground their views in the Constitution. Proslavery and antislavery factions during the pre–Civil War period, New Deal supporters and opponents during the Great Depression, and civil rights activists and segregationists all claimed to have the Constitution on their side, whether the dispute was over a broad or narrow interpretation of the commerce clause, the Fourteenth Amendment, or the Tenth Amendment. Today's vigorous debate about the proper scope of the national government's powers on issues such as health care, immigration, and economic policy is only the most recent chapter in this perpetual conflict.

Changing the Constitution

The most obvious way that the Constitution keeps up with the times is by allowing for changes to its language. The framers broadly supported the idea behind Article V, which lays out the formal process for amending the Constitution: the people must control their own political system, which includes the ability to change it through a regular, nonviolent process. George Washington called constitutional amendments "explicit and authentic acts," and Thomas Jefferson was adamant that each generation needed to have the power to change the Constitution. Toward the end of his life, he wrote in a letter to James Madison:

Some men look at constitutions with sanctimonious reverence, and deem them like the ark of the covenant, too sacred to be touched. They ascribe to the men of the preceding age a wisdom more than human, and suppose what they did to be beyond amendment. I knew that age well; I belonged to it and labored with it. . . . It was very like the present. . . . Let us not weakly believe that one generation is not as capable as another of taking care of itself.[31]

A Living Constitution?

Should the Constitution be viewed as a flexible framework or a document that has fixed meaning? The public is fairly split on this issue, with 55 percent saying that constitutional interpretation should be based on "what it means in current time" (the living Constitution approach) and 41 percent saying that it should be based on "what it originally meant" (originalism). However, there is a deep partisan divide on this issue, with 78 percent of Democrats taking the living Constitution approach and 77 percent of Republicans supporting originalism.[a]

The meaning of the Constitution doesn't change.
Justice Clarence Thomas is perhaps the strongest advocate of the originalist view. He wrote: "Let me put it this way; there are really only two ways to interpret the Constitution—try to discern as best we can what the framers intended or make it up."[b] Former chief justice William Rehnquist, although generally adhering to the originalist view, took a more nuanced approach. He favorably cited a 1920 Supreme Court opinion by Oliver Wendell Holmes: "When we are dealing with words that also are a constituent act, like the Constitution of the United States, we must realize that they have called into life a being the development of which could not have been foreseen completely by the most gifted of its begetters."[c] John Marshall in *McCulloch v. Maryland* also endorsed this view, saying the Constitution was "intended to endure for ages to come, and consequently to be adapted to the various crises of human affairs." Rehnquist said that "scarcely anyone would disagree" with the idea that the Constitution was written broadly enough to allow principles such as the prohibition against illegal searches and seizures to apply to technologies, such as the telephone or the Internet, that could not have been envisioned by the framers.[d]

However, according to this view, the *meaning* of the Constitution cannot change with the times. Rehnquist wrote that "mere change in public opinion since the adoption of the Constitution, unaccompanied by a constitutional amendment, should not change the meaning of the Constitution. A merely temporary majoritarian groundswell should not abrogate some individual liberty truly protected by the Constitution."[e] Therefore, recent rulings restricting the death penalty (which is clearly endorsed by the Constitution), expanding gay rights, or allowing children to testify remotely against their sexual abusers rather than having to confront them directly in court (as guaranteed by the Sixth Amendment) would all be inconsistent with the originalist view. This view would also hold that anything other than relying on the meaning of the words of the Constitution allows justices to "legislate from the bench," which is undemocratic given that the judges are not elected.

There is a vigorous debate among justices of the Supreme Court as to whether the Constitution is a living document or should be interpreted more strictly according to the original intent of the framers.

The meaning of the Constitution changes with the times.
Proponents of a living Constitution argue for a more flexible view. Justice Thurgood Marshall advocated a living Constitution, noting that the framers "could not have imagined, nor would they have accepted, that the document they were drafting would one day be construed by a Supreme Court to which had been appointed a woman and the descendent of an African slave."[f] If the meaning of the Constitution is fixed, then the Court would have to uphold a state law allowing the death penalty for horse stealing, which was common during the Founding era. Executing horse thieves, or, more realistically, children and the mentally impaired (which was allowed in many states until 2005), is unacceptable in a modern society, even if it would be allowed by a strict reading of the Constitution.

The answer to the question about how justices should interpret the Constitution ultimately depends on one's broader views of the proper role of the Court within a representative democracy. Should justices be constrained by the original meaning of the Constitution, or should that meaning evolve over time?

take a stand

1. If you were on the Supreme Court, would you adopt an originalist or a living Constitution approach? Justify your position.

2. Based on the originalist view, should a state be allowed to execute whomever it wants to, including minors (or horse thieves)? Based on the living Constitution approach, should limits be placed on justices to prevent them from "legislating from the bench"?

Amending the Constitution

This flowchart shows how amendments to the Constitution can be proposed and ratified and the frequency with which each method has been used. Interestingly, the president is not a part of the formal process of amending the Constitution.

Source: Compiled by the authors.

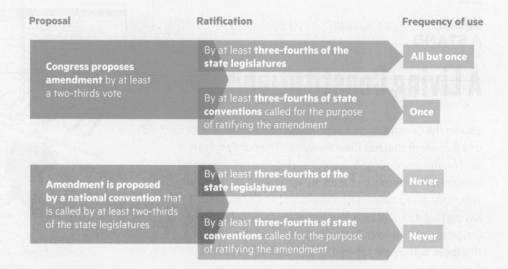

Proposal	Ratification	Frequency of use
Congress proposes amendment by at least a two-thirds vote	By at least **three-fourths of the state legislatures**	All but once
	By at least **three-fourths of state conventions** called for the purpose of ratifying the amendment	Once
Amendment is proposed by a national convention that is called by at least two-thirds of the state legislatures	By at least **three-fourths of the state legislatures**	Never
	By at least **three-fourths of state conventions** called for the purpose of ratifying the amendment	Never

"Why Should I Care?"

The amendment process reflects the idea that the people must control their own political system, which includes the ability to change it through a regular, nonviolent process. Would the country have survived the Civil War if not for the ability to amend the Constitution? Would the Senate be as representative as it is now? How does this process serve as a safeguard for the future?

Proposal and Ratification Although there was strong consensus on including in the Constitution a set of provisions for amending it, there was no agreement on how this should be done. The Virginia Plan envisioned a relatively easy process of changing the Constitution "whensoever it shall seem necessary" by means of ratification by the people, whereas the New Jersey Plan proposed a central role for state governments. Madison suggested the plan that was eventually adopted, which once again accommodated both those who wanted a stronger national government and those who favored the states.

Article V describes the two steps necessary to change the Constitution: proposal and ratification. Congress may *propose* an amendment that has the approval of two-thirds of the members in both houses, or an amendment may be proposed by a national convention that has been called by two-thirds of the states' legislatures. In either case, the amendment must be *ratified* by three-fourths of the states' legislatures or state conventions (see Nuts & Bolts 2.3). A national convention has never been used to propose an amendment, and every amendment except for the Twenty-First, which repealed Prohibition, has been ratified by state legislatures rather than state conventions.

A Range of Amendments Amendments have ranged from fairly narrow, technical corrections of errors in the original document (Eleventh and Twelfth Amendments) to important topics such as abolishing slavery (Thirteenth Amendment), mandating equal protection of the laws for all citizens (Fourteenth Amendment), providing for the popular election of senators (Seventeenth Amendment), giving Black men and then women the right to vote (Fifteenth and Nineteenth Amendments), and allowing a national income tax (Sixteenth Amendment). Potential constitutional amendments have addressed

Recent Amendments Introduced in Congress That Did Not Pass

TABLE 2.1

Many proposed constitutional amendments have almost no chance of passing. Indeed, most of those listed here did not even make it to the floor of the House or Senate for a vote. Why do you think a member of Congress would propose an amendment that he or she knew would fail?

116th Congress (2019–2020)	Limit the pardon power of the president.
	Provide equal rights for men and women.
	Extend the right to vote to citizens 16 and 17 years of age.
	Limit the number of terms a representative or senator may serve.
115th Congress (2017–2018)	Require that the federal budget be balanced.
	Abolish the Electoral College to provide for the direct election of the president and vice president.
	Protect the voting rights of the citizens of the United States.
	Amend the First Amendment to allow limitations on federal campaign contributions and expenditures.
114th Congress (2015–2016)	Require that the rights extended by the Constitution be granted only to natural persons (not corporations).
	Repeal the Sixteenth Amendment (income tax).

Source: Compiled by the authors from www.congress.gov (accessed 12/6/19).

many other issues, with more than 10,000 proposed; of those, 33 were sent to the states and 27 have made it through the amending process (the first 10 came at once in the Bill of Rights). Table 2.1 shows several amendments that were introduced but not ratified.

Multiple interpreters

The final way that the Constitution maintains its relevance is through changing views of the document by multiple interpreters. As we pointed out in the previous discussion of the commerce clause, there have been significant changes in the way the Constitution structures the policy-making process, even though the pertinent text of the Constitution has not changed.[32] This point is best understood by examining

Amending the Constitution is difficult and can be controversial. Some amendments that are widely accepted today, like the Nineteenth Amendment giving women the right to vote, were intensely debated prior to their ratification.

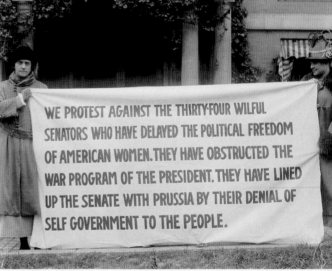

implied powers
Powers supported by the Constitution that are not expressly stated in it.

**AP®
SUPREME
COURT CASE**

The Eighth Amendment's ban on "cruel and unusual punishments" is generally viewed as excluding capital punishment, but the execution of juveniles and the mentally impaired has been found unconstitutional. This picture shows the lethal injection chamber at the Arizona State Prison in Florence.

the concept of **implied powers**—that is, powers that are not explicitly stated in the Constitution but can be inferred from an enumerated power. The Supreme Court often defines the boundaries of implied powers, but Congress, the president, and the public can also play key roles.

Three of the earliest examples of implied powers show the president, the Supreme Court, and Congress each interpreting the Constitution and contributing to its evolving meaning. The first involved the question of how active the president should be in stating national foreign policy principles. In issuing his famous proclamation of neutrality in 1793, George Washington unilaterally set forth a national foreign policy, even though the president's power to do so is not explicitly stated in the Constitution. Alexander Hamilton defended the presidential power to make such a proclamation as implied in both the executive powers clause and the president's explicitly granted powers in the area of foreign policy (receiving ambassadors, negotiating treaties, and serving as commander in chief). Thomas Jefferson, in contrast, thought it was a terrible idea for presidents to have that kind of power. He preferred that such general policy statements be left to Congress.

The Supreme Court first made its mark on the notion of implied powers in a landmark case involving the creation of a national bank. In *McCulloch v. Maryland* (1819), the Court ruled that the federal government had the power to create a national bank and denied the state of Maryland the right to tax a branch of that bank. The Court said it was not necessary for the Constitution to expressly grant Congress the power to create the bank; rather, it was implied in Congress's power over financial matters and from the necessary and proper clause of the Constitution.

Congress got into the act with an early debate over the president's implied power to remove appointed officials. The Constitution clearly gives the president the power to make appointments to cabinet positions and other top executive branch offices, but it is silent on how these people can be removed. This was one of the most difficult issues that faced the 1st Congress, and members spent more than a month debating the topic. The record of the debate is the most thorough examination of implied powers ever conducted in Congress. However, Congress ended up not taking any action on the issue, which left the president's removal power implicit in the Constitution.

Issues concerning implied powers continue to surface. The president's appointment powers have recently evolved as the Senate has played a much more aggressive role in providing its "advice and consent" on presidential nominations to the federal courts. As we explore in Chapter 6, in the past 20 years the Senate has blocked court appointments at a significantly higher rate than it did in the first half of the twentieth century. The relevant language in the Constitution is the same, yet the Senate's understanding of its role in this important process has changed. The president's power to remove appointees also recently came into play in May 2017 when President Trump fired FBI Director James Comey, who was investigating the Trump campaign's connections to Russia. This situation raised the constitutional question of when (or whether) the president's removal of one of his or her appointees constitutes an obstruction of justice. Presidential use of executive powers to go around Congress when it declines to act on issues the president deems important also demonstrates the ambiguous nature of constitutional powers. For example, Obama's executive actions on immigration policy and EPA rules concerning carbon emissions and Trump's use of executive orders to impose a travel ban on specific countries to limit the threat of terrorism were viewed as either appropriate and necessary executive action or "constitutional overreach," depending on whom you ask.

Public opinion and social norms also influence the prevailing interpretation of the Constitution, as is evident in the evolving meanings of capital punishment (the death penalty) and freedom of speech. When the Constitution was written, capital punishment was broadly accepted, even for horse thieves. The framers were concerned only that people not be "deprived of life, liberty, or property without the due process of law." Therefore, the prohibition in the Eighth Amendment against "cruel and unusual punishments" certainly did not mean to the framers that the death penalty was unconstitutional. However, in 1972 the Supreme Court struck down capital punishment as unconstitutional because it was being applied arbitrarily.[33] Subsequently, after procedural changes were made, the Court once again upheld the practice. However, the Court has since decided that capital punishment for minors and mentally impaired people constitutes cruel and unusual punishment—decisions that reflect modern sensibilities but not the thinking of the framers.[34] Similarly, the text of the First Amendment protections for freedom of speech has never changed, but the Supreme Court has been willing to uphold significant limitations on free speech, especially in wartime. When external threats are less severe, the Court has been more tolerant of controversial speech.

The line between a new interpretation of the Constitution and constitutional change is difficult to define. Clearly, not every new direction taken by the Supreme Court or new interpretation of the constitutional roles of the president or Congress is comparable to a constitutional amendment. In one respect, a constitutional amendment is much more permanent than a new interpretation by the Court. For example, the Court could not unilaterally decide that 18- to 20-year-olds, women, and African Americans no longer have the right to vote. Constitutional amendments expanded the right to vote to include these groups, and only further amendments could either expand or restrict the right to vote. However, gradual changes in constitutional interpretation are probably just as important as the amending process in explaining the Constitution's ability to keep pace with the times. For example, although the Civil War amendments produced lasting and significant changes in the Constitution, during the New Deal shifts in constitutional interpretation helped establish a huge growth in national power without changing a single word of the document.

"Why Should I Care?"

One of the most remarkable things about the Constitution is its longevity. While there are intense debates about whether a "living Constitution" is a good thing, there is no doubt that its ability to change with the times, whether because of its amending process, multiple interpreters, or ambiguity, has helped make it the oldest constitution in the world. People may joke that the Constitution isn't relevant anymore, but it shapes the boundaries for all of today's policy debates and institutional struggles.

The USA PATRIOT Act

The policy process often takes many years, from problem recognition to implementation (stages one through five), and can also be extended due to possible modifications, expansion, or termination of the policy (stages six and seven). But due to the circumstances, the policy process for the USA PATRIOT Act (2001) was entirely different. Though there were several preceding domestic terrorist events in the United States that made Americans aware of the potential threat, it was clearly the September 11, 2001, attacks on the World Trade Center and the Pentagon that led to the relatively quick passage of the USA PATRIOT Act, an acronym for "Uniting and Strengthening America by Providing Appropriate Tools Required to Intercept and Obstruct Terrorism."

Foreign terrorists hijacked four commercial airplanes in order to fly them into buildings that held significant meaning for the United States. Two airplanes crashed into the Twin Towers of the World Trade Center, which, in addition to being a New York City landmark, represented for the terrorists a symbol of the harmful effects of globalization for much of the developing, non-Western world. Striking the Pentagon, the headquarters for the Department of Defense, would show Americans how vulnerable they were to attacks. Passengers on the fourth plane were able to bring it down before it reached its probable destination of Washington, D.C., though its intended target is unknown. In total, there were 2,977 victims of this multipronged, coordinated attack, and Americans were understandably afraid that more attacks were forthcoming—when and where were the questions that law enforcement agencies, if Congress and the president gave them more power and resources, might be able to answer.

There was a sense of urgency among the public and political leaders and across party lines to do what was necessary to ensure that future attacks were prevented. In less than two weeks (September 24, 2001), the Bush administration put together its own bill to be introduced in Congress, and Attorney General Ashcroft urged the two houses to pass the bill without any changes within one week. While there was general consensus about the need for such wide-ranging legislation, some members of the House and Senate were concerned that the different bill proposals went too far and infringed on the public's civil liberties. As predicted, the bill passed very quickly with little debate and few changes, less than two months after the September 11 attacks. As indicated in the outline of the policy process, each section of the USA PATRIOT Act had an expiration date that could be renewed. Most sections of the law were eventually made permanent, but the most controversial sections still have to be renewed and still cause debate and controversy to this day. The USA PATRIOT Act is the perfect example of how the tension between liberty and safety is debated and constantly reconsidered in the public and political arenas.

Policy Stages

1. Problem Recognition
   - The World Trade Center was attacked by terrorists on February 26, 1993.
   - A domestic terrorist attack destroyed the Alfred P. Murrah Federal Building in Oklahoma City, Oklahoma, on April 19, 1995.
   - Legislation, such as the Antiterrorism and Effective Death Penalty Act of 1996, was a precedent for using more extreme measures to combat terrorism.
   - Concerns about terrorism were mentioned in the Democratic and Republican platforms for the 2000 presidential election (Osama bin Laden, the September 11 mastermind, was even mentioned by name in the Democratic platform), but the topic was barely discussed by either candidate during the campaign.
   - Terrorist attacks on the World Trade Center and Pentagon on September 11, 2001 ("9/11" attacks), were the main impetus for the legislation.
   - Anthrax, a poisonous powder, was sent to news outlets and two Senate leaders from September 18 to October 12, 2001.

2. Agenda Setting
   - The Bush administration wrote the Anti-Terrorism Act of 2001 (also known as the Combating Terrorism Act of 2001) soon after the September 11 attacks and wanted Congress to pass the bill very quickly and without amendments.
   - Several other bills were also introduced in Congress, including:
     - The Public Safety and Cyber Security Enhancement Act
     - The Intelligence to Prevent Terrorism Act
     - The Financial Anti-Terrorism Act
   - President Bush declared "war on terrorism" to a joint session of Congress on September 20, 2001.
   - President Bush launched Operation Enduring Freedom attacking Al Qaeda and the Taliban in Afghanistan on October 7, 2001.

3. Deliberation and Formulation
   - The bill was initially introduced in the House of Representatives on October 2, 2001, as the Provide Appropriate Tools Required to Intercept and Obstruct Terrorism (PATRIOT) Act of 2001.
   - Bill H.R. 3162 was introduced in the House of Representatives by Frank J. Sensenbrenner Jr. (R-WI) on October 23, 2001.
   - The bill was referred to many committees.
   - Bill S. 1510 was introduced in the Senate as the USA Act of 2001 by Tom Daschle (D-SD) on October 24, 2001.
   - Members of both houses criticized how quickly the bill was being passed with almost no debate.
   - Issues were raised about how intrusive this legislation was on the privacy rights of American citizens, especially with the extensive use of wiretapping.
   - Issues were also raised that this legislation would allow illegal searches and seizures by circumventing the requirements of probable cause.

4. Enactment
   - The House of Representatives passed a compromise bill on October 24, 2001: **357 YEAs**: 145 Democrats, 211 Republicans, 1 other; **66 NAYs**: 62 Democrats, 3 Republicans, 1 other; **9 Not Voting**: 4 Democrats, 5 Republicans, 0 others.
   - The compromise bill consisted mostly of the Senate USA Act of 2001.
   - A two-thirds majority was required since the House rules were suspended to cut off debate.
   - The Senate passed the compromise bill on October 25, 2001: **98 YEAs**: 48 Democrats, 49 Republicans, 1 other; **1 NAY**: 1 Democrat, 0 Republicans, 0 others; **1 Not Voting**: 1 Democrat, 0 Republicans, 0 others.
   - The Uniting and Strengthening America by Providing Appropriate Tools Required to Intercept and Obstruct Terrorism (USA PATRIOT) Act of 2001 was signed into law by President George W. Bush on October 26, 2001.

5. Implementation
   - **Title I: Enhancing Domestic Security against Terrorism**
     - More money and human resources were devoted to seeking out potential terrorist threats.
     - Military would be employed, when necessary, to help find weapons of mass destruction (WMD).
   - **Title II: Enhanced Surveillance Procedures**
     - The Foreign Intelligence Surveillance Act of 1977 (FISA) and the Electronic Communications Privacy Act of 1986 (ECPA) were amended.
     - The use of wiretaps and other forms of surveillance was extended.
   - **Title III: International Money Laundering Abatement and Anti-terrorist Financing Act of 2001**
     - The Money Laundering Control Act of 1986 was amended.
     - Money launderers had a harder time using domestic and international banks.
     - Attempts were made to better coordinate the investigations and the sharing of evidence and information between government agencies and the banking system.
   - **Title IV: Protecting the Border**
     - The Immigration and Nationality Act of 1952 was amended to make it more difficult for terrorists to enter the United States.

- **Title V: Removing Obstacles to Investigating Terrorism**
  - The power of the U.S. attorney general, U.S. Secret Service, and Federal Bureau of Investigation (FBI) was enhanced.
  - The use of national security letters increased: government could issue search warrants without seeing a judge ahead of time.
- **Title VI: Providing for Victims of Terrorism, Public Safety Officers and Their Families**
  - Funding increased.
  - Payments were expedited.
- **Title VII: Increased Information Sharing for Critical Infrastructure Protection**
  - Collaboration between local-, state-, and federal-level law enforcement agencies increased.
- **Title VIII: Strengthening the Criminal Laws against Terrorism**
  - The definition of terrorism broadened.
  - The penalties and the number of offenses for what constitutes terrorism increased.
- **Title IX: Improved Intelligence**
  - More power centralized in the office of the Central Intelligence Agency (CIA) director.
  - Intelligence agencies were allowed to withhold information from Congress.
  - The Foreign Terrorist Asset Tracking Center was established to thwart the finances of terrorist organizations.
  - Written and oral communications and other documents would be translated quickly and accurately.
- **Title X: Miscellaneous**

6. Evaluation
   - Groups, such as the American Civil Liberties Union (ACLU), the Electronic Frontier Foundation (EFF), the Electronic Privacy Information Center (EPIC), and the Center for Democracy and Technology (CDT), were concerned that the balance between safety, privacy, and civil rights had tipped too far in the wrong direction:
     - Too much power was given to law enforcement agencies to search telephones, financial records, and e-mail without court orders.
   - The American Library Association (ALA) and the American Booksellers Foundation for Free Expression (ABFFE) were concerned about threats to intellectual freedom.
   - *Holder v. Humanitarian Law Project* (2010) supported the government's power to stop aid to groups that might be construed as aiding terrorism even if the overt purpose is some form of training.
   - In 2012, the Heritage Foundation issued a report titled *Fifty Terror Plots Foiled Since 9/11: The Homegrown Threat and the Long War on Terrorism*.
   - The *Washington Times* published an article on May 21, 2015, titled "FBI Admits No Major Cases Cracked with Patriot Act Snooping Powers."
   - Officials of legitimate banks were upset they were being unfairly linked with banks connected to terrorism.

7. Possible Modifications, Expansion, or Termination of Policy
   - **The USA PATRIOT Improvement and Reauthorization Act of 2005 was signed on March 9, 2006.**
     - The act strengthened some aspects of the original law but also provided more oversight on other sections.
     - Most sections of the original law were made permanent.

- Gag orders were eliminated so the accused could notify their lawyers, but they had to tell the FBI whom they notified.
- Several sections had an expiration ("sunset") date of December 31, 2009.
- **The USA PATRIOT Act Additional Reauthorizing Amendments Act of 2006** was signed on March 9, 2006.
  - The act included more privacy and confidentiality provisions for those who receive Foreign Intelligence Surveillance Act (FISA) orders.
  - The accused no longer had to identify their lawyers to the FBI.
- **The Protect America Act** amended FISA on August 5, 2007.
  - The act made it easier to surveil suspects in foreign countries.
  - Aspects of FISA had been incorporated and modified in the Patriot Act.
- **The PATRIOT Sunsets Extension Act of 2011** (enacted on May 11, 2012) amended the USA PATRIOT Improvement and Reauthorization Act of 2005 to make it effective until June 1, 2015. It renewed the following provisions:
  - Roving wiretaps became connected to the suspect, not the device.
  - Section 215 (the business records provision) allowed the government to request records from third parties.
  - The lone wolf provision allowed the government to track terrorists who are possibly acting on their own and are not associated with a known terrorist group.
- **The USA Freedom Act** (Uniting and Strengthening America by Fulfilling Rights and Ensuring Effective Discipline Over Monitoring) renewed the roving wiretaps and lone wolf provisions and curbed the extent of some of the data collection. It was enacted on June 2, 2015, and renewed until 2019.
  - The USA PATRIOT Act was renewed by Congress as part of a spending bill in November 2019.
  - The Senate voted to extend the act for 77 days, but the House of Representatives went on recess on March 27, 2020, before passing a similar extension.
- **The USA FREEDOM Reauthorization Act of 2020** allows the government to look at Internet searches and Web browsing data without warrants.

Questions for Discussion

1. In what ways might the USA PATRIOT Act have been an overreaction that infringed too much on people's liberty? In what ways might it have been justified?
2. Should the government be allowed to subpoena patrons' library records if they are suspected of terrorist activity? Why or why not?
3. When George W. Bush campaigned for the presidency, he promised to reduce the size of the federal government, but after the September 11 attacks, he created the Department of Homeland Security. Did he break his promise? Explain your answer.

Unpacking the Conflict

As we discussed at the beginning of this chapter, the presidency of Donald Trump raises many questions about the strength and resilience of our Constitution. Considering all that we know about how the Constitution works, was American democracy in danger? Is our system of checks and balances working?

While this presidency raised other new, important constitutional questions such as "Can the president pardon himself?" and "How does the emoluments clause apply to the complex real estate holdings of the Trump family?" a look at the facts indicates that the Constitution is working just as the Founders intended. The Trump presidency illustrates many of the themes of this chapter: the conflictual nature of politics established by the Constitution (there has been plenty of conflict!) and the fact that multiple interpreters and ambiguous language provide the flexibility for our political system to respond to challenging times. Most significantly, elections served their function of imposing accountability, and there was a peaceful transition of power.

To protect against majority tyranny, the separation of powers and the system of checks and balances in our political system divide power by giving each branch of government the power to check the others (and the additional check of divided power across levels of government). Therefore, when the presidency starts to drift out of the mainstream of American politics, Congress, the courts, and state governments can reel it back in. We've seen throughout the chapter how our constitutional system has allowed the courts and Congress to effectively check the more extreme aspects of Trump's agenda that have alarmed pundits on the left, from Trump's proposed immigration and environmental policies, to the failure to "repeal and replace" Obamacare, to the early versions of his travel bans, to his relationship with Russia. This self-corrective feature of our constitutional system means that no branch of government will attain disproportionate power for very long, and it has kept the political system stable.

Even more fundamentally, the Constitution promotes long-term stability by providing the basis for resolving conflict through elections and representative government rather than by taking up arms. Losers of one round of elections know that they have an opportunity to compete in the next election and that their voices can be heard in another part of the government. Indeed, after heavy losses in 2016, Democrats were especially energized for the competitive 2018 midterms and taking back the presidency two years later.

Congress, the president, and the Supreme Court all must interpret the Constitution in the normal course of fulfilling their institutional roles, which also helps preserve an institutional balance of power. Having multiple interpreters of the Constitution is built into our system. The Trump presidency also compelled the general public to become more interested in the Constitution.[35] Maybe with enough attention, those public-opinion polls showing that Americans are more familiar with *The Simpsons* than with the three branches of government can be reversed. If Americans are more informed about the Constitution, they can become even more significant interpreters of the Constitution.

Finally, the general and ambiguous language of the Constitution means that both supporters and opponents of the president can find evidence for their views. It is impossible to know exactly how the emoluments clause should apply to foreign officials staying in a Trump-owned property or whether the president can pardon himself, because these constitutional questions have never come up before. Therefore, answers to these questions, and the broader health of our American democracy, will continue to be determined by the outcome of the political process and democratic elections as established by the Constitution. While there is no guarantee that our nation will be around for another 230 years, these past four years have demonstrated the Constitution's resilience and strength once again.

A leading constitutional scholar, Walter Murphy, addressed the relevance of the Constitution this way: "The ideals it enshrines, the processes it prescribes, and the actions it legitimizes must either help to change its citizenry or at a minimum reflect their current values. If a constitution does not articulate, at least in general terms, the ideals that form or will re-form its people and express the political character they have . . . , it will soon be replaced or atrophy."[36] The Constitution's ability to change with the times and reflect its citizens' values has enabled it to remain relevant and important today. Its flexibility and general language mean that there will never be definitive answers to the conflict over its meaning, but they ensure that these debates will be enduring and meaningful.

"What's Your Take?"

Did Trump's actions as president threaten democracy?

Or did our system of government as laid out in the Constitution work to keep conflicts over Trump's policies in check?

AP® STUDY GUIDE

Summary

The U.S. Constitution was shaped by historical events preceding its creation, particularly the period of British rule over the colonies, the Revolutionary War, and the states' experience under the Articles of Confederation. Under British rule, the colonies were relatively independent of one another, and the framers sought to create a strong nation while still maintaining the autonomy of the states in the system. The Declaration of Independence, reflecting the ideas of the social contract **and an individual's natural rights, provided a foundation for popular sovereignty. The Constitution, drafted by the framers, was designed with three key principles: the rejection of a monarchy, popular control of the government, and a limited government that protected against tyranny.**

Key weaknesses in the Articles of Confederation were brought to light by the inability of the state to address Shays's Rebellion. Although the framers of the Constitution agreed that the Articles of Confederation needed to be changed, there was little consensus otherwise. The Federalists and Antifederalists clashed on several issues, though the most important were (1) balancing majority rule with minority rights, (2) allocating power between large and small states, (3) allocating power between the legislature and executive, (4) allocating power between the national government and the states, and (5) determining how to handle slavery.

After the Constitution was written and approved at the Constitutional Convention, it still needed to be ratified by nine states. The Constitution was primarily criticized by the Antifederalists, launching a lengthy public debate over the merits of the proposed framework, as seen in the writings of Brutus. Ultimately, to win over the necessary support in the states, the framers had to include the Bill of Rights, which was tailored to protect the rights of states and individuals from the national government.

The defining feature of the Constitution, which was discussed in *Federalist 10* and *Federalist 51*, is its separation of powers while still maintaining flexibility for leadership in times of crisis. The system of checks and balances gives each branch of the federal government some explicit powers, some shared powers, and some ability to limit the power of the other two branches of government.

social contract
A concept developed by political philosophers of the eighteenth century that defined the legitimacy of the state. The people recognize the authority of the state to govern over them, and, in turn, the government protects the rights and freedoms of the people.

Key Terms

Antifederalists (p. 49)

Articles of Confederation (p. 43)

Bill of Rights (p. 61)

Brutus I (p. 59)

commerce clause (p. 71)

Constitution (p. 42)

Declaration of Independence (p. 43)

enumerated powers (p. 62)

executive powers clause (p. 71)

Federalist 10 (p. 48)

Federalist 51 (p. 47)

Federalists (p. 48)

Great Compromise (p. 53)

impeachment (p. 68)

implied powers (p. 76)

judicial review (p. 70)

limited government (p. 43)

Marbury v. Madison (p. 70)

monarchy (p. 44)

national supremacy clause (p. 55)

natural rights (p. 47)

necessary and proper clause (p. 63)

New Jersey Plan (p. 52)

parliamentary system (p. 54)

pluralism (p. 52)

popular sovereignty (p. 47)

power of the purse (p. 63)

republicanism (p. 46)

reserved powers (p. 55)

Shays's Rebellion (p. 46)

social contract (p. 83)

Three-Fifths Compromise (p. 56)

Virginia Plan (p. 52)

The Constitution is more than 230 years old, yet it still provides a blueprint for modern governance. It has maintained its relevance due to its ambiguity in several key passages, its ability to be amended rather than entirely rewritten, and its designation of multiple interpreters of the Constitution.

Enduring Understandings

LOR-1: "A balance between governmental power and individual rights has been a hallmark of American political development." (AP® U.S. Government and Politics Course and Exam Description)

CON-1: "The Constitution emerged from the debate about the weaknesses in the Articles of Confederation as a blueprint for limited government." (AP® U.S. Government and Politics Course and Exam Description)

PMI-1: "The Constitution created a competitive policy-making process to ensure the people's will is represented and that freedom is preserved." (AP® U.S. Government and Politics Course and Exam Description)

Multiple-Choice Questions (Arranged by Topic)

Topic 1.1: Ideals of Democracy (LOR-1)

1. The use of "We the People . . ." in the first line of the Preamble to the Constitution of the United States best reflects which of the following democratic ideals?
   (A) limited government
   (B) popular sovereignty
   (C) republicanism
   (D) natural rights

Topic 1.2: Types of Democracy and Topic 1.3 – Government Power and Individual Rights (LOR-1)

Questions 2–3 refer to the excerpt.

In so extensive a republic, the great officers of government would soon become above the control of the people, and abuse their power to the purpose of aggrandizing themselves, and oppressing them. . . . The command of all the troops and navy of the republic, the appointment of officers, the power of pardoning offences, the collecting of all the public revenues, and the power of expending them, with a number of other powers, must be lodged and exercised in every state, in the hands of a few. When these are attended with great honor and emolument, as they always will be in large states, so as greatly to interest men to pursue them, and to be proper objects for ambitious and designing men, such men will be ever restless in their pursuit after them. They will use the power, when they have acquired it, to the purposes of gratifying their own interest and ambition, and it is scarcely possible, in a very large republic, to call them to account for their misconduct, or to prevent their abuse of power.

—Brutus 1, October 17, 1787

2. Which of the following statements best describes the point of view of the author in the excerpt?
   (A) The power of the office will attract ambitious and self-interested men who are likely to abuse their authority.
   (B) America will suffer if this new government leads to a loss of liberty, and future generations will blame and despise us.
   (C) The new Constitution places so much power in a central government that the state governments may no longer be able to function as republics under the control of their citizens.
   (D) While the Constitution will reserve some minor power for the states, all the important powers are delegated to the central government.

3. **Which of the following models of democracy best supports the argument in the excerpt?**

   (A) elite

   (B) monarchical

   (C) participatory

   (D) pluralist

4. **Which of the following best describes the central argument in *Federalist 10*?**

   (A) A small decentralized republic that divides power between the state and national governments has far-reaching benefits.

   (B) It is beneficial to put the interests of one group in competition with the interests of other groups to prevent any one group from dominating government.

   (C) A powerful and centralized government is too far removed from individuals to meet the needs of all citizens.

   (D) Each branch of government is checked by the power of the other two branches and each branch of government is dependent on the people, who are the source of legitimate authority.

Topic 1.4: Challenges of the Articles of Confederation (CON-1)

5. **Which of the following best describes the impact of Shays's Rebellion?**

   (A) It led to the Great Compromise, which created a bicameral legislature with two distinct houses.

   (B) It led to the landmark decision of judicial review, which set the precedent for the Supreme Court to declare a law unconstitutional.

   (C) It exposed a central flaw of the government under the Articles of Confederation, leading to the Constitutional Convention.

   (D) It settled a compromise that resulted in enslaved people being counted as three-fifths of a person for representation in the House.

6. **Which of the following is an accurate comparison of the Articles of Confederation and the U.S. Constitution?**

	Articles of Confederation	Constitution
(A)	one vote per state in Congress	amendments require unanimous consent
(B)	unicameral Congress	established the Supreme Court
(C)	established a federal court system	established a single executive (president)
(D)	representatives appointed by state legislatures	both state and federal governments could coin money

Topic 1.5: Ratification of the U.S. Constitution (CON-1)

Questions 7–8 refer to the graphs.

State Populations at the Time of the Constitutional Convention

Total population (4 states) 1.8 million

Median Population State

Total population (9 states) 1.6 million

Votes at the Constitutional Convention

More National Power

More State Power

Equal Representation

Representation by Population

Source: Keith L. Dougherty and Jac C. Heckelman, "A Pivotal Voter from a Pivotal State: Roger Sherman at the Constitutional Convention," *American Political Science Review* 100:2 (May 2006): 298.

7. **Based on the information in the graphs, which of the following states wanted both more state power and representation by population?**
   - **(A)** Delaware (DE)
   - **(B)** Virginia (VA)
   - **(C)** Connecticut (CT)
   - **(D)** South Carolina (SC)

8. **Based on the information in the graphs, which of the following states would be more likely to support the New Jersey Plan?**
   - **(A)** Virginia (VA)
   - **(B)** Pennsylvania (PA)
   - **(C)** Delaware (DE)
   - **(D)** Georgia (GA)

9. **Which of the following was a consequence of the passage of the Three-Fifths Compromise?**
   - **(A)** Southern states had greater influence in the Electoral College.
   - **(B)** Northern states were less likely to support a ban on the importation of enslaved people.
   - **(C)** Southern states had an increase in their number of representatives in the Senate.
   - **(D)** Northern states were more likely to elect a Democrat for president.

Topic 1.6: Principles of American Government (PMI-1)

10. **Which of the following best describes the impeachment process for the president?**
    - **(A)** The Senate votes to impeach and the Supreme Court votes to remove.
    - **(B)** The House votes to impeach and the Senate votes to remove.
    - **(C)** Congress votes to impeach and the state legislatures vote to remove.
    - **(D)** The Supreme Court determines both impeachment and removal.

Free-Response Questions

Concept Application

In 2019, Steve Cohen, a Democrat and representative from Tennessee's 9th congressional district, proposed H.J.Res. 8, an amendment that would redefine the power of the pardon for the president of the United States. A president can pardon anyone—even a family member and him- or herself—who has committed a federal crime. A pardon can happen prior to a trial or even before an individual has been accused of a crime. If passed, this amendment would prevent the current and any future presidents from pardoning themselves, family members, paid campaign staff, and current and past members of the president's administration. In order to go into effect, the bill would need to pass the House and Senate with a two-thirds vote and then be ratified either by three-fourths of state legislatures or by conventions in three-fourths of the states.[a]

After reading the scenario, respond to A, B, and C below:
   - **(A)** Referencing the scenario, describe the two-part process, outlined in the Constitution, that would be used to address the situation in the scenario.
   - **(B)** In the context of the scenario, explain how the constitutional principle described in Part A may be one of the reasons the process has only happened 27 times in over 200 years.
   - **(C)** If the Constitution were changed to choose a president similar to that in a parliamentary system, explain how the constitutional principle of separation of powers would be affected.

Argument Essay

Take a position on whether the justices of the Supreme Court should adopt an originalist or a living Constitution approach when making decisions.

Use at least one piece of evidence from the following foundational document:
- U.S. Constitution

In your response, you should do the following:

✓ Respond to the prompt with a defensible claim or thesis that establishes a line of reasoning.

✓ Support your claim with at least *one* piece of specific and relevant evidence.

- The evidence must come from the foundational document listed above.

3

Federalism

States or the federal government: who's got the power?

 "While the White House clings to the past, automakers and American families embrace cleaner cars. The evidence is irrefutable: today's clean car standards are achievable, science-based, and a boon for hardworking American families and public health. It's time to remove your blinders, President Trump, and acknowledge that the only person standing in the way of progress is you. You have no basis and no authority to pull this waiver. We're ready to fight for a future that you seem unable to comprehend; we'll see you in court if you stand in our way."

Xavier Becerra, California attorney general

 "We embrace federalism and the role of the states, but federalism does not mean that one state can dictate standards for the nation."

Andrew Wheeler, administrator of the Environmental Protection Agency

Since passage of the Clean Air Act of 1970, the state of California has required auto manufacturers to meet higher fuel economy standards for cars and light trucks sold in the state than are required by federal law. This policy was one way that the state met the Clean Air Act's mandates to reduce auto pollution. More recently, California had agreed with auto manufacturers to increase fuel economy standards and tighten emissions limits as a way of fighting climate change. Because California is such a large market, auto companies often implement the changes needed to satisfy California's requirements to all the cars they produce, meaning that California's policies influence the design of cars sold throughout America.

In September 2019, however, the Trump administration revoked California's authority to set its own fuel economy and pollution standards. President Trump argued that revocation would reduce car prices and increase safety. As the quote from California's attorney general shows, California's response was to fight the administration's move in federal court, a case that is likely to be dropped given the Biden presidency.[1]

How strictly should the government regulate automobile fuel emissions? While individual Americans disagree about this question, the states and the federal government also disagree about the states' role in determining fuel economy standards. EPA Administrator Andrew Wheeler sees California's aggressive regulation as overstepping its bounds.

CHAPTER GOALS

Define *federalism* **and explain its significance.**
pages 90–93

Explain what the Constitution says about federalism. pages 93–97

Trace the major shifts in state and federal government power over time. pages 97–103

Describe the major trends and debates in federalism today. pages 103–113

Analyze the arguments for and against a strong federal government. pages 114–118

This conflict over fuel economy standards reflects a fundamental feature of America's government: federalism. In areas such as education, law enforcement, and environmental policy, the federal government has limited power to affect policy at the state and local level. Because of federalism, your experiences with government, including the services you receive, the laws you are supposed to obey, and the regulations that constrain your actions, differ depending on where you live.

As we discussed in Chapter 2, one of the reasons we have a federal system is the desire to limit the power of the national government. Federalism also enables state and local governments to take account of citizens' demands or local conditions—information that might not be available to decision makers in Washington. By giving power to state and local governments, federalism can increase citizen satisfaction and governmental efficiency.

However, as the fight over emissions standards suggests, federalism is more than a way to increase responsiveness and efficiency. In many policy areas, federalism sets up conflicts between different levels of government over who gets to make policy choices. In the case of fuel economy standards, while California's policies are designed in part to address local pollution issues, it is also true that a substantial majority of California's citizens would like the federal government to do more to fight climate change. Because auto companies often implement California standards throughout their production line, the state can impose these standards on people elsewhere, whether they like it or not—a concept with which EPA administrator Andrew Wheeler strongly disagrees.[2]

The conflict triggered by fuel economy standards is a great example of the tensions created by a federal system. Joe Biden's victory in the 2020 election means that the conflict is moot—but the potential for disagreement between federal and state governments remains. When local and federal officials disagree about fuel economy and global warming, who wins? What are the responsibilities of the states and what is the domain of the national government? What happens when levels of government disagree? How have the answers to these questions changed over the course of American history—and how does federalism work today?

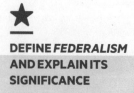

DEFINE *FEDERALISM* AND EXPLAIN ITS SIGNIFICANCE

federalism
The division of power across the local, state, and national governments.

sovereign power
The supreme power of an independent state to regulate its internal affairs without foreign interference.

What is federalism and why does it matter?

Federalism is a form of government that divides sovereign power across at least two political units. Dividing **sovereign power** simply means that each unit of government (in the United States, national, state, and local governments) has some degree of authority and autonomy. As discussed in Chapter 2, this division of power across levels of government is central to the system of separated powers in the United States. Dividing power across levels of government seems like a simple concept, but as we will see later in this chapter, the political battles over *how* that power is divided have been intense. (One important note on terminology: while the national government in Washington, D.C., is referred to as the federal government, it is only one part of the federal system that combines national, state, and local governments.)

In practical terms, federalism is about intergovernmental relations: How do the different levels of government interact, and how is power divided? But even that may seem a little abstract. Why does federalism matter? On a broad range of issues, the level of government that dictates policy can make a real difference, simply because preferences vary across these levels. Sometimes these disagreements reflect different beliefs about what citizens want from government. But more commonly, conflicts result from differences of opinion about what government should be doing. In the case of fuel economy standards, for example, the national government, represented by President Trump and the Environmental Protection Agency, wants to roll back many current environmental regulations, believing that they provide little benefit and cost too much. While some state and local politicians (as well as their supporters) hold similar feelings, others, such as California's attorney general and many of his constituents, disagree. This divergence between the policies desired by politicians at different levels of government means that decisions about federalism (which level of government does what) affect how environmental laws are ultimately interpreted and enforced.

The fact that many policies are administered by multiple levels of government provides multiple access points for citizens and groups who want to influence the details of these policies. Finally, conflicts over federalism create a key role for the federal courts, as their power to interpret the Constitution makes them the ultimate arbiter of conflicts between federal and state governments. As we will see, at various points in American history (including recent years), changes in the composition of the Supreme Court have had important consequences for the balance of power between different levels of government.

AP®
FOUNDATIONAL
DOCUMENT

The relationship between the national government and states and territories involves cooperation as well as competition. During the COVID-19 pandemic, FEMA partnered with local officials to provide emergency support, including the construction of a temporary hospital in New York City.

Levels of government and their degrees of autonomy

A distinguishing feature of federalism is that each level of government has some degree of autonomy from the other levels—that is, each level can carry out some policies without interference from the others. In the United States, this means that the national and state governments have distinct powers and responsibilities (see Nuts & Bolts 3.1). The national government, for example, has **exclusive powers** for national defense and foreign policy. State and local governments have primary responsibility for conducting elections and promoting public safety, or **police powers**. In other areas, such as transportation, the different levels of government have **concurrent powers**— they share responsibilities. The national government has also taken on additional responsibilities through implied powers that are inferred from the powers explicitly granted in the Constitution (see Chapter 2 and later in this chapter).

exclusive powers
Policy-making responsibilities that are exercised only by the national government.

police powers
The power to enforce laws and provide for public safety.

concurrent powers
Responsibilities for particular policy areas, such as transportation, that are shared by federal, state, and local governments.

Local governments—cities, towns, school districts, and counties—are not autonomous units of government: they are creatures of state governments. State governments create local governments and control the types of activities they can engage in by specifying in the state charter what local governments can do and cannot do.

A comparative perspective

It is useful to compare U.S. federalism with forms of government in other countries. Just because a nation is composed of states does not mean that it is a federal system: the key factor in determining whether a system is federal or not is the autonomy of the political subunits. The United Kingdom, for example, is made up of England, Scotland,

NUTS & BOLTS 3.1

National and State Responsibilities

National Government Powers	State Government Powers	Concurrent Powers
Print money	Issue licenses	Collect taxes
Regulate interstate commerce and international trade	Regulate intrastate (within the state) businesses	Build roads
Make treaties and conduct foreign policy	Conduct elections	Borrow money
Declare war	Establish local governments	Establish courts
Provide an army and navy	Ratify amendments to the Constitution	Make and enforce laws
Establish post offices	Promote public health and safety	Charter banks and corporations
Make laws necessary and proper to carry out these powers	May exert powers the Constitution does not delegate to the national government or does not prohibit the states from using	Spend money for the general welfare; take private property for public purposes, with just compensation

Powers Denied to the National Government	Powers Denied to State Governments
May not violate the Bill of Rights	May not enter into treaties with other countries
May not impose export taxes among states	May not print money
May not use money from the Treasury without an appropriation from Congress	May not tax imports or exports
May not change state boundaries	May not interfere with contracts
	May not suspend a person's rights without due process

Source: Compiled by the authors.

"Why Should I Care?" These provisions of the Constitution define the scope of policy conflict between the state and federal governments—which powers are given exclusively to one level, which are shared, and, most important, which are left unallocated. Modern fights over federalism start with these provisions and how they should be interpreted.

Wales, and Northern Ireland. In 1998, the British Parliament created a new Scottish government and gave it authority in a broad range of areas. However, Parliament retained the right to unilaterally dissolve the Scottish government; therefore, the subunit (Scotland) is not fully autonomous. This type of government, in which power is centralized at the national level, is a **unitary government**. Unitary governments are the most common in the modern world (about 80 percent); other examples include Israel, Italy, France, Japan, and Sweden. Although U.S.-style federalism is not as common, Australia, Canada, and Germany, among others, share this form of government. At the opposite end of the spectrum is a **confederal government**, in which the states have most of the power. This was the first type of government in the United States under the Articles of Confederation, but there are very few modern examples. One was the Commonwealth of Independent States, which formed from former Soviet Republics after the dissolution of the Soviet Union in 1991, but exists today only as a forum for discussion and coordination between Russia, Belarus, and a few central Asian republics.

unitary government
A system in which the national, centralized government holds ultimate authority. It is the most common form of government in the world.

confederal government
A form of government in which states hold power over a limited national government.

**AP®
FOUNDATIONAL
DOCUMENT**

Federalism explains why laws and regulations may differ from state to state; it allows for differences of opinion across regions. For example, how do your state's opinions on fuel efficiency differ from California's? How does federalism allow your state to respond differently to address issues of climate change? This is federalism in action.

"Why Should I Care?"

**EXPLAIN WHAT THE
CONSTITUTION SAYS
ABOUT FEDERALISM**

Balancing national and state power in the Constitution

Although the Founders wanted a national government that was stronger than it had been under the Articles of Confederation, they also wanted to preserve states' autonomy. These goals are reflected in different parts of the Constitution, which provides ample support for advocates of both strong state governments and a strong national government. The nation-centered position has its roots in the document's preamble, which begins: "We the People of the United States." The Articles of Confederation, by contrast, began: "We the undersigned delegates of the States." The Constitution's phrasing emphasizes the nation as a whole over the separate states—although as we will see, it also allocates significant powers to the states.

A strong national government

Most of the Founders wanted a strong national government to provide national security and a healthy and efficient economy, so they included various powers in the Constitution for the federal government. In terms of national security, as we saw in Chapter 2, Congress was granted the power to raise and support armies, declare war, and "suppress Insurrections and repel Invasion," while the president, as commander in chief of the armed forces, would oversee the conduct of war. Congress's power to regulate interstate commerce promoted economic efficiency and centralized an important economic power at the national level. The Constitution outlines restrictions on state power that contribute to the centralization of national military and economic power: states were *prohibited* from entering into "any Treaty, Alliance, or Confederation" or keeping troops or "Ships of War" during peacetime. They also could not coin money or impose duties on imports or exports (see Article I, Section 10).

The necessary and proper clause (Article I, Section 8) was another broad grant of power to the national government: it gave Congress the power "[t]o make all Laws which shall be necessary and proper for carrying into Execution the foregoing Powers." Similarly, the national supremacy clause (Article VI) says that the Constitution and all laws and treaties that are made under the Constitution shall be the "supreme Law of the Land" and that "the Judges in every State shall be bound thereby, any Thing in the Constitution or Laws of any State to the Contrary notwithstanding." This is perhaps the clearest statement of the nation-centered focus of the Constitution. If any state law or constitution conflicts with national law or the Constitution, the national perspective wins. Thus, in the case of same-sex marriages, once the Supreme Court ruled that all laws prohibiting same-sex marriage were unconstitutional, elected officials at all levels knew that if they enacted new prohibitions, the laws would be immediately invalidated by the courts.

You might be thinking, "Wait a minute, if the Constitution and the federal government always win, how can California set fuel economy standards even though the Trump administration opposes them?" The answer is not simple. (See the What Do the Facts Say? feature.) For one thing, there is no constitutional provision that gives the federal government control over fuel economy standards. Congress set national standards beginning with the Clean Air Act of 1970—these have been increased several times by subsequent EPA regulations. However, as part of negotiations between the states and the federal government over how to implement the Clean Air Act, California received a waiver that allowed it to impose stricter standards. It is not clear whether the Trump administration could have revoked this waiver. Federal courts will ultimately decide. The controversy illustrates that even after 230 years, there still is disagreement over how the Constitution divides power between the federal government and the states. As we will see, when conflicts between the federal and local governments arise, the federal government can try to persuade local governments by offering grants or other forms of aid to induce cooperation, but it often cannot simply order local governments to comply with its wishes.

Jim Obergefell, the plaintiff in the *Obergefell v. Hodges* Supreme Court case that legalized same-sex marriage nationwide, is backed by supporters of the ruling on the steps of the Texas capitol during a rally on June 29, 2015, in Austin. This ruling shows the power of the supremacy clause, as it struck down laws in 14 states.

Will New Regulations Save "a Million Lives"?

One of the most important rules when reading a news story about a controversial issue is to look for sources and documentation. We all want media coverage that gives "just the facts"—but a good article also tells readers where the facts came from, so that they can be checked and verified. This is particularly true when a story relies on quotes from participants in a political conflict, as their comments may be designed to persuade rather than inform.

Let's look at an example from Breitbart News' coverage of the Trump administration's fight with the state of California over fuel economy standards. A March 2019 story on the Breitbart site featured an interview with EPA Administrator Andrew Wheeler, who was quoted as follows:

> **B BREITBART**

> "We were hoping to work something out with California, but it just didn't take place. We are moving forward with our own regulation; it's going to reduce the price of a new car by about $2,300. Right now, people are holding on to their cars longer," the EPA chief said. "The average lifespan for a car is about 12 years; it used to be about eight years. The older cars are less safe, less environmentally friendly, so by getting the older cars off, by reducing the price of a car, hopefully more people will buy newer cars, safer cars that will also save lives. I believe the number is that a million lives will be saved by this proposal as opposed to the Obama proposal, and we get there by reducing the cost of a new car. And we're still reducing pollutants at the same time."

Source: Sean Moran, "Exclusive—EPA's Andrew Wheeler: Green New Deal Activists Don't Want American 'Energy Domination,'" Breitbart, March 2, 2019, www.breitbart.com/politics/2019/03/02/exclusive-epa-administrator-andrew-wheeler-green-new-deal-activists-dont-want-american-energy-domination/ (accessed 11/18/19).

Wheeler's quote gives two of the central arguments for taking away California's waiver: that it will reduce the price of a new car by $2,300, and that it will save a million lives. But he doesn't provide any documentation for these numbers, and the article doesn't question the claims.

A Google search on "EPA $2,300" finds several stories with well-documented critiques of Wheeler's claims.[a] It turns out that the $2,300 figure refers to increased costs over the lifetime of owning a car, which is 12 years—so the actual increase is only about $200 per year, which does not take into account decreased fuel costs from California's higher mileage standards. There is also no formal study or report to justify the claim about saving a million lives—in fact, some internal e-mails sent by EPA analysts to the Office of Management and Budget argued that revoking California's waiver would actually increase deaths from auto accidents.

The point is not that you should think every story on Breitbart is fake or that a source such as Vox can always be trusted. Rather, when trying to make sense of American politics, you should look for stories that give you a way to assess the reliability of the information they provide, whether it is the story's account of political issues and events or information contained in a quote. A lack of sources or documentation is a red flag.

Think about it

- **What are some credible sources** of news you go to for "just the facts"? What do you do when you can't validate the information in a second source?

- **What are the dangers** of spreading misleading or incorrect information? How might these errors lead people to make uninformed decisions?

State powers and limits on national power

Despite the Founders' nation-centered bias, many parts of the Constitution also address state powers and set limits on national power. Article II gives the states the power to choose electors for the Electoral College, and Article V grants the states a central role in the process of amending the Constitution. Three-fourths of the states must ratify any constitutional amendment (either through conventions or their state legislatures, as specified by Congress), but the states can also bypass Congress in proposing amendments if two-thirds of the states call for a Constitutional Convention (this route to amending the Constitution has never been used).

There are also limitations on Congress's authority over the states. For example, although Congress was given the power to regulate interstate commerce (this was the power used to justify the Clean Air Act), it cannot regulate commerce that occurs entirely within a state. Moreover, Congress cannot favor one state over another in regulating commerce, and it cannot impose a tax on any good that is shipped from one state to another.

While Article I of the Constitution enumerates many specific powers for Congress, the list of state powers is much shorter. One could interpret this as more evidence for the nation-centered perspective, but at the time of the Founding the expectation was that most power would be exercised at the state level. Therefore, the federal powers that were exceptions to this rule had to be clearly specified, and state governments received authority over all other matters. The **Tenth Amendment** supports this view: "The powers not delegated to the United States by the Constitution, nor prohibited by it to the states, are reserved to the states respectively, or to the people."

Tenth Amendment
"The powers not delegated to the United States by the Constitution, nor prohibited by it to the states, are reserved to the states respectively, or to the people." The Court has interpreted this language to protect state power and limit the reach of the national government in areas such as environmental policy, gun control, and workplace regulations.

Clauses that favor both perspectives

Article IV of the Constitution includes provisions that favor both the state-centered and the nation-centered perspectives. For example, its **full faith and credit clause** specifies that states must respect one another's laws, granting citizens the "Full Faith and Credit" of their home state's laws if they go to another state. At the same time, however, the article's **privileges and immunities clause** says that citizens of each state are "entitled to all Privileges and Immunities" of citizens in the other states, which means that states must treat visitors from other states the same as their own residents.

There are many examples of the full faith and credit clause and privileges and immunities clause at work today. If you have a Michigan driver's license and are traveling to Texas, you do not need to stop at every state line to get a new license; each state will honor your Michigan license. Similarly, a legal marriage in one state (even a same-sex marriage) must be honored by another state. But not all state licenses are subject to full faith and credit: if you have an open or concealed-carry gun permit in one state, that does not automatically give you the right to carry a firearm in another state. Similarly, states do not have to permit nonresidents to vote in state elections, and public colleges and universities may charge out-of-state residents higher tuition than in-state residents. Therefore, the privileges and immunities clause cuts both ways on the question of the balance of power: it allows the states to determine and uphold their own laws autonomously, but it also emphasizes that national citizenship is more important than state citizenship.

full faith and credit clause
The part of Article IV of the Constitution requiring that each state's laws be honored by the other states. For example, a legal marriage in one state must be recognized across state lines.

privileges and immunities clause
The part of Article IV of the Constitution requiring that states must treat nonstate residents within their borders as they would treat their own residents. This was meant to promote commerce and travel between states.

Why is it important to understand the Constitution's role in federalism? The Constitution sets the boundaries for the battles over state and federal power. For example, no state can decide to print its own currency, and the U.S. government cannot take over the public schools. But within those broad boundaries, the balance between national and state power at any given point in history is a political decision, the product of choices made by elected leaders and the courts. The struggle over fuel economy standards is a perfect example: the Trump administration wanted to weaken standards and California's government wanted to increase them.

The evolving concept of federalism

The nature of federalism has changed as the size and functions of the national and state governments have evolved. In the first century of our nation's history, the national government played a relatively limited role and the boundaries between the levels of government were distinct. As the national government took on more power in the twentieth century, intergovernmental relations became more cooperative and the boundaries less distinct. Even within this more cooperative framework, federalism remains a source of conflict within our political system, both because the levels of government share lawmaking authority and because they may disagree over the details of government policy.

The early years

As the United States gained its footing, clashes between the advocates of state-centered and nation-centered federalism turned into a partisan struggle. The Federalists—the party of George Washington, John Adams, and Alexander Hamilton—controlled the new government for its first 12 years and favored strong national power. One of their strongest allies was Chief Justice John Marshall, who wrote several landmark Supreme Court decisions that enhanced the power of the national government. The Federalists' opponents, the Democratic-Republicans, led by Thomas Jefferson and James Madison, favored state power, or, as it came to be known, **dual federalism**. Dual federalism, as we will discuss, was the guiding principle of Marshall's successor as chief justice, Roger Taney. Table 3.1 highlights several important decisions resolved during Marshall's and Taney's tenures on the Court.

Establishing National Supremacy The first confrontation came when the Federalists established a national bank in 1791, followed by a second national bank in 1816. At that time, the state of Maryland, which was controlled by the Democratic-Republicans, tried to tax the National Bank's Baltimore branch out of existence. However, the bank refused to pay the tax, creating a conflict that sent the case to the Supreme Court. In the landmark decision *McCulloch v. Maryland* (1819), Marshall's Court held that even though the word "bank" does not appear in the Constitution, Congress's power to create one is implied through its relevant enumerated powers—such as the power to coin money, levy taxes, and borrow money. The Court also ruled that Maryland did not have the right to tax the bank because of the Constitution's national supremacy clause.

"Why Should I Care?"

★

TRACE THE MAJOR SHIFTS IN STATE AND FEDERAL GOVERNMENT POWER OVER TIME

dual federalism
The form of federalism favored by Chief Justice Roger Taney, in which national and state governments are seen as distinct entities providing separate services. This model limits the power of the national government.

**AP®
SUPREME
COURT CASE**

McCulloch v. Maryland
A landmark Supreme Court ruling in 1819 that Maryland did not have the power to tax the Second Bank of the United States and that Congress did have the power to create the Bank under the necessary and proper clause and the national supremacy clause.

TABLE 3.1

Early Landmark Supreme Court Decisions on Federalism

Case	Holding and Significance for States' Rights	Direction of the Decision
Chisholm v. Georgia (1793)	Held that citizens of one state could sue another state; led to the Eleventh Amendment, which prohibited such lawsuits.	Less state power
McCulloch v. Maryland (1819)	Upheld the national government's right to create a bank and reaffirmed the idea of "national supremacy."	Less state power
Gibbons v. Ogden (1824)	Held that Congress, rather than the states, has broad power to regulate interstate commerce.	Less state power
Barron v. Baltimore (1833)	Endorsed a notion of "dual federalism" in which the rights of a U.S. citizen under the Bill of Rights did not apply to that same person under state law.	More state power
Dred Scott v. Sandford (1857)	Sided with southern states' view that enslaved people were property and ruled that the Missouri Compromise violated the Fifth Amendment, because making slavery illegal in some states deprived owners of enslaved people of property. Contributed to the start of the Civil War.	More state power

Source: Compiled by the authors.

A few years later, Marshall's Court held in *Gibbons v. Ogden* (1824) that Congress has broad power to regulate interstate commerce. The ruling struck down a New York law that had granted a monopoly to a private company that was operating steamboats on the Hudson River between New York and New Jersey. By granting this monopoly, New York was interfering with interstate commerce, a power reserved to Congress by the Constitution. Even in the modern era, this ruling underlies many of the federal government's regulations on businesses, which are based on the expectation that virtually any commercial activity will involve buying and selling across state lines.

In the early 1800s, the Supreme Court confirmed the national government's right to regulate commerce between the states. The state of New York granted a monopoly to a ferry company serving ports in New York and New Jersey, but this was found to interfere with interstate commerce and was therefore subject to federal intervention.

The emergence of states' rights and dual federalism

Under Marshall's successor, Chief Justice Roger Taney, Court decisions involving federalism shifted to reflect a new concept: dual federalism. According to the system of dual federalism, the national and state governments are considered distinct, with little overlap in their activities or the services they provide. In this view, the national government's activities are confined to powers strictly enumerated in the Constitution.

Dual federalism was expressed most consequentially in the *Dred Scott v. Sandford* decision of 1857. Dred Scott was an enslaved man who had lived for many years with his owner in the free state of Illinois and the free Wisconsin Territory but was living in Missouri, a slave state, when his master died. Scott petitioned for his freedom under the Missouri Compromise, which had made slavery illegal in any free state. The Court did not grant Scott his freedom. Its majority decision held that enslaved people were not citizens but private property; therefore, the Missouri Compromise's ban on slavery in certain territories violated the Fifth Amendment because it deprived citizens (owners of enslaved people) of their property without the due process of law. Put another way, the *Dred Scott* decision said that state law, not federal, determined the legal status of enslaved people.

Contrasting Marshall's decisions in favor of national power with Taney's decisions in favor of state power highlights the policy consequences of judicial decisions. The Taney Court's decision that the Missouri Compromise was unconstitutional is consistent with a dual federalism interpretation of the Constitution—but it also sustained the legality of slavery in southern states and halted attempts by representatives from the North to limit the spread of slavery into the western territories. There is little doubt that Taney favored this outcome on policy grounds. In this sense, debates about dual federalism during this time were really about the legality of slavery, its expansion into new states, and the rights of formerly enslaved people in free states.

Arguments about dual federalism are sometimes framed using the concept of **states' rights**: the idea that states retain some powers under the Constitution (specifically those reserved by the Tenth Amendment) and can ignore federal policies that encroach on these powers. The key question is, where does federal authority end and state authority begin? As this chapter demonstrates, the lines are not always easy to define and are still being debated today. Some people argue that southern states fought the Civil War to preserve the concept of states' rights, but this argument tells only a fraction of the whole story. Southern secessionists were not interested in states' rights per se; what they wanted was to continue slavery without federal intervention. States' rights was a convenient rationale for their proslavery position.

After the Civil War, constitutional amendments banned slavery (Thirteenth Amendment), prohibited states from denying citizens due process or the equal protection of the laws (Fourteenth Amendment), and gave newly freed men the right to vote (Fifteenth Amendment). Congress also passed the 1875 Civil Rights Act (although it was later overturned by the Supreme Court). The Fourteenth Amendment was the most important in terms of federalism because it was the constitutional basis for many of the civil rights laws passed by the federal government during Reconstruction. The Civil War fundamentally changed the way Americans thought about the relationship between the national government and the states: before the war people said "the United States *are* . . . ," but after the war they said "the United States *is* . . . "

states' rights
The idea that states are entitled to a certain amount of self-government, free of federal government intervention. This became a central issue in the period leading up to the Civil War.

The *Dred Scott* decision, covered here in *Frank Leslie's Illustrated Newspaper*, was the subject of much public interest when it was handed down in 1857. The decision inflamed tensions between slave states and nonslave states and vindicated those who saw state law as superior to federal law.

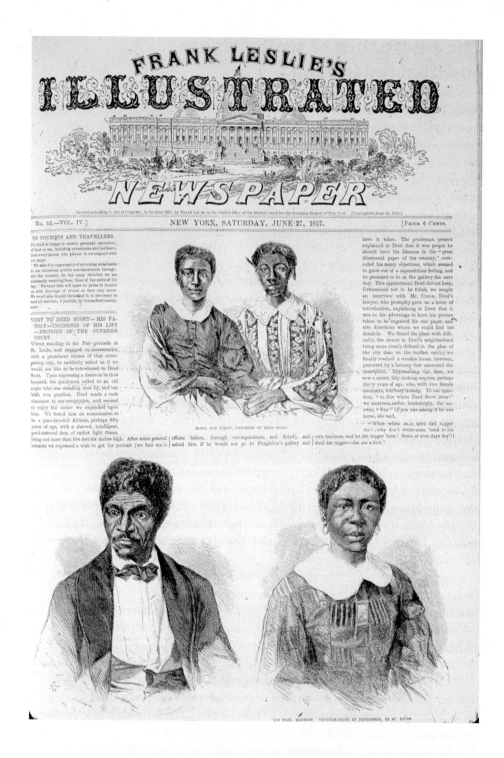

The Supreme Court and Limited National Government The assertion of power by Congress during Reconstruction was short-lived, as the Supreme Court soon stepped in again to limit the power of the national government. In 1873, the Court reinforced the notion of dual federalism, ruling that the Fourteenth Amendment did not change the balance of power between the national and state governments. Specifically, the Court ruled that the Fourteenth Amendment right to due process and equal treatment under the law applied to individuals' rights only as citizens of the United States, not to their state citizenship.[3] By extension, freedom of speech, freedom of the press, and the other liberties protected in the Bill of Rights applied only to laws passed by Congress, not to state laws. Here again, these decisions can be read as an articulation of a theoretical interpretation of the Constitution, but they are also part of a broader, more concrete debate over how much the government should regulate interactions between individuals, or between individuals and corporations.

In 1883, the Court overturned the 1875 Civil Rights Act, which had guaranteed equal treatment in public accommodations. The Court argued that the Fourteenth Amendment did not give Congress the power to regulate private conduct, such as whether a White restaurant owner had to serve a Black customer; it affected only the conduct of state governments, not individuals in these states.[4] This narrow view of the Fourteenth Amendment left the national government powerless to prevent southern states from implementing state and local laws that led to complete segregation of Blacks and Whites in the South (called Jim Crow laws) and the denial of many basic rights to Blacks after northern troops left the South at the end of Reconstruction.

The Supreme Court also limited the reach of the national government by curtailing Congress's authority to regulate the economy through its commerce clause powers. In a series of cases in the late nineteenth and early twentieth centuries, the Supreme Court endorsed a view of laissez-faire—French for "leave alone"—capitalism aimed at protecting business from regulation by the national government. To this end, the Court defined clear boundaries between *inter*state and *intra*state commerce, ruling that Congress could not regulate any economic activity that occurred *within* a state (intrastate). The Supreme Court let some national legislation that was connected to interstate commerce stand, such as the Sherman Antitrust Act (1890), which placed limits on monopolies. However, when the national government tried to use this act to break up a cartel of four sugar companies that controlled 98 percent of the nation's sugar production, the Court ruled that Congress did not have this power. The Court's decision argued that the commerce clause allowed Congress to regulate the transportation of goods, not their manufacture, and the sugar in question was made within a single state. Even if the sugar was sold throughout the country, this was "incidental" to its manufacture.[5] On the same grounds, the Court struck down attempts by Congress to regulate child labor.[6]

After the Supreme Court struck down the 1875 Civil Rights Act, southern states were free to impose Jim Crow laws. These state and local laws led to complete racial segregation, even for public drinking fountains.

Cooperative federalism

From the early years of the twentieth century through the 1930s, a new era of American federalism emerged in which the national government became much more involved in activities that were formerly reserved for the states, such as transportation, civil rights, agriculture, social welfare, and management–labor relations. At first, the Supreme Court resisted this broader reach of national power, clinging to its nineteenth-century conception of dual federalism.[7] But as commerce became more national, the distinctions between interstate and intrastate commerce, and between manufacture and transportation, became increasingly difficult to sustain. Starting in 1937 with the landmark ruling *National Labor Relations Board v. Jones and Laughlin Steel Corporation*, the Supreme Court largely discarded these distinctions and gave Congress far more latitude to shape economic and social policy for the nation.[8]

Shifting National–State Relations The type of federalism that emerged in this era is called cooperative federalism, or "marble cake" federalism, as opposed to the "layer cake" model of dual federalism.[9] As the image of a marble cake suggests, the boundaries of state and national responsibilities are less well defined than they are under dual federalism. With the increasing industrialization and urbanization of the late 1930s and 1940s, along with the Great Depression, more complex problems arose that could not be solved at one level of government. Cooperative federalism adopted a more practical focus on intergovernmental relations and the efficient delivery of services. State and local governments maintained a level of influence as the implementers of national programs, but the national government played an enhanced role as the initiator, director, and funder of key policies.

"Cooperative federalism" accurately describes this important shift in national–state relations in the first half of the twentieth century, but it only partially captures the complexity of modern federalism. The marble cake metaphor falls short in one important way: the lines of authority and patterns of cooperation are not as messy as implied by the gooey flow of chocolate through white cake. Instead, the 1960s metaphor of picket fence federalism is a better description of cooperative federalism in action. As the How It Works: Versions of Federalism graphic shows, each picket of the fence represents a different policy area and the horizontal boards that hold the pickets together represent the different levels of government. This is a much more orderly image than the marble cake provides, and it illustrates important implications about how policy is made across levels of government.

The most important point to be drawn from this analogy is that activity in the cooperative federal system occurs *within* pickets of the fence—that is, within policy areas. Policy makers within a given policy area will have more in common with others in that area (even if they are at different levels of government) than they do with people who work in different areas (even if they are at the same level of government). For example, someone working in a state's Department of Natural Resources will have more contact with people working in local park programs and the national Department of the Interior than with people who also work at the state level but who focus on, say, law enforcement.

Cooperative federalism, then, is likely to emerge within policy areas rather than across them. This may create problems for the chief executives who are trying to run the show (mayors, governors, the president), as rivalries develop among policy agencies competing for funds. Also, contact within policy areas

Franklin Delano Roosevelt's New Deal shifted more power than ever to the national government. Through major new programs to address the Great Depression, such as the Works Progress Administration construction projects pictured here, the federal government expanded its reach into areas that had been primarily the responsibility of state and local governments.

is not always cooperative. (Think of detective shows in which the FBI arrives to investigate a local crime and pulls rank on the town sheriff, provoking resentment from local law-enforcement officials.) This is the inefficient side of picket fence federalism in action.

Why is it important to understand the history of federalism? You might think that the Civil War ended the debates over nation-centered versus state-centered federalism (in favor of the national government), but disputes today over immigration, health care, welfare, and education policy all revolve around the balance of power between the levels of government. State legislatures that talk about ignoring federal criticisms of their policy choices are invoking the same arguments used by advocates of states' rights in the 1830s and 1840s concerning tariffs and slavery.

"Why Should I Care?"

★

DESCRIBE THE MAJOR TRENDS AND DEBATES IN FEDERALISM TODAY

Federalism today

Federalism today is a complex mix of all the types of federalism that our nation's political system has experienced in the past. Our current system is predominantly characterized by cooperative federalism, but it has retained strong elements of national supremacy, dual federalism, and states' rights (see Nuts & Bolts 3.2). Debates over the appropriate role of the federal and state governments continue to occur in areas such as government surveillance of individuals (especially after September 11) and funding of social-welfare programs like public school education and health care. And the courts continue to play a key role in deciding the constitutionality of new laws and regulations.

The Evolution of Federalism

Type of Federalism	Period	Characteristics
Dual federalism (layer cake)	1789–1937	The national and state governments were viewed as very distinct with little overlap in their activities or the services they provided. Within this period, federalism could have been state centered or nation centered, but relations between levels of government were limited.
Cooperative federalism (marble cake)	1937–present	This indicates greater cooperation and collaboration between the levels of government.
Fiscal federalism	1937–present	This system of transfer payments or grants from the national government to lower-level governments involves varying degrees of national control over how the money is spent: categorical grants give the national government a great deal of control whereas block grants involve less national control.
Picket fence federalism	1960–present	This version of cooperative federalism emphasizes that policy makers within a given policy area have more in common with others in their area at different levels of government than with people at the same level of government who work on different issues.
Coercive federalism	1970s–present	This involves federal preemptions of state and local authority and unfunded mandates on state and local governments to force the states to change their policies to match national goals or policies established by Congress.

Source: Compiled by the authors.

"Why Should I Care?"

Over the 240 years of American history, shifts in citizen demands and the expansion of the federal government have changed the nature of policy conflicts between state and federal governments. Even so, the fact that many policy responsibilities are shared or left undetermined, coupled with the fact that politics is conflictual, means that the federal government and the states will always be arguing over who gets to do what.

Cooperative federalism lives on: fiscal federalism

Cooperative federalism refers to situations in which federal and state governments share responsibility for delivering a policy. In the case of the Medicaid program that provides health coverage for low-income adults (and the equivalent Medicare program for senior citizens), programs in each state are administered by state agencies operating under federal guidelines, sometimes with waivers. In the modern era, the federal government has also become involved in funding and setting requirements for K–12 education as well as paying for welfare benefits and food stamps for poor people, policies that were long considered local responsibilities. And in other cases like fuel economy standards, the federal government can issue waivers that transfer some policy-making power to state and local governments.

Most examples of cooperative federalism involve some element of **fiscal federalism**, a system whereby the federal government provides some of the funds needed to sustain the state programs that deliver services to citizens. For example, the federal government pays a large share of state Medicaid costs and a portion of

fiscal federalism
A form of federalism in which federal funds are allocated to the lower levels of government through transfer payments or grants.

the funding for local school districts. At one level, fiscal federalism is a way for the federal government to help states deal with responsibilities that outstrip their financial resources. However, fiscal federalism also gives the federal government a way to influence the kinds of policies implemented at the state level. In theory, states have large amounts of discretion in terms of determining who is eligible for Medicaid or the fees paid to doctors. However, the promise of federal Medicaid funds comes with program requirements that state agencies must meet in order to receive these funds. This type of relationship may sound familiar. When your parents let you use the car or lent you $50, was it "no strings attached"? Or did they expect something in return—such as help with yard work or other chores? Fiscal federalism works the same way, as the federal government tries to use its resources to gain control over state policies.

An extreme version of fiscal federalism is **coercive federalism**, which is the use of federal mandates or conditions to force or entice the states to change their policies to match national goals or policies established by Congress. A related concept, **federal preemption**, occurs when the federal government passes a law that overrides state law or makes it impossible for a state to enact its own statute. The Clean Air and Clean Water Acts, the Americans with Disabilities Act (ADA) (which promotes making public buildings and commercial facilities more accessible to those with disabilities), and the Motor Voter Act (which requires states to provide voter registration services at motor vehicle departments) are all laws that forced states to change their policies. The laws most objectionable to the states are **unfunded mandates**, which require states to do certain things but carry no federal money to pay for them. Republican criticism of unfunded mandates in the 1990s led to passage of the Unfunded Mandate Reform Act of 1995. This act made it more difficult for Congress to impose these mandates on the states; it required a separate vote on mandates that imposed costs of more than $50 million, and it required a Congressional Budget Office estimate of exactly how much such mandates would cost the states. Although this law could not prevent unfunded mandates, Republicans hoped that bringing more attention to the practice would create political pressure against such policies.

Types of Federal Aid to States The method used to transfer resources from the federal government to states and localities often determines the effectiveness of fiscal federalism. Today, most federal aid comes in two forms. **Categorical grants** are for specific purposes—they have strings attached. Funds that help states run their Medicaid programs, for example, are delivered as categorical grants. **Block grants** are financial aid to states for use within a specific policy area, but within that area the states have discretion on how to spend the money. An example of a block grant is TANF (Temporary Assistance for Needy Families), which is federal money given to states to help fund their welfare programs. However, in contrast to Medicaid, federal welfare funds are given without restrictions about how the states determine benefits or the eligibility of welfare recipients. As a result, both of these factors vary across states. Since the 1970s, grants to the states as a proportion of the size of the national economy (gross domestic product, or GDP) have been relatively constant, whereas the rate of state and local spending has continued to inch up.

Advocates of cooperative federalism often promote block grants as the best way for the levels of government to work together to solve problems: the national government identifies problem areas and then provides money to the states to help solve them. The problem is that state governments may disagree with the president or Congress on how these programs should be implemented, which creates a temptation for the federal government to move to categorical grants as a way to shape state policy.

A separate argument for block grants is made by people who believe that state governments are better informed about local conditions—as well as people who prefer the results of state-led policies to a situation wherein states must obey federal directives.

coercive federalism
A form of federalism in which the federal government pressures the states to change their policies by using regulations, mandates, or conditions (often involving threats to withdraw federal funding).

federal preemption
Imposition of national priorities on the states through national legislation that is based on the Constitution's supremacy clause.

unfunded mandates
Federal laws that require the states to do certain things but do not provide state governments with funding to implement these policies.

categorical grants
Federal aid to state or local governments that is provided for a specific purpose, such as a mass-transit program within the transportation budget or a school lunch program within the education budget.

block grants
Federal aid provided to a state government to be spent within a certain policy area, but the state can decide how to spend the money within that area.

Versions of Federalism

Version 1:
Layer Cake Federalism

1789–1937
No interactions between the levels
of government.

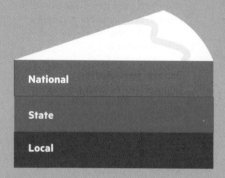

Version 2:
Marble Cake Federalism

1937–today
Interactions between the levels
of government are common.

Version 3:
Picket Fence Federalism

1960s–today
Horizontal boards represent different
levels of government, and the pickets are
policy areas within which coordination
happens across those levels.

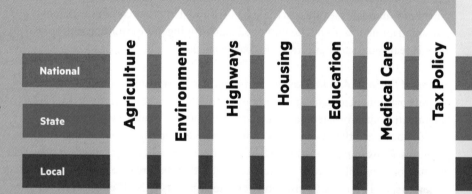

National

State

Local

Agriculture Environment Highways Housing Education Medical Care Tax Policy

Version 4:
Coercive Federalism

1970s–today
National government uses
regulations, mandates, and conditions
to pressure states to fall into line with
national policy goals.

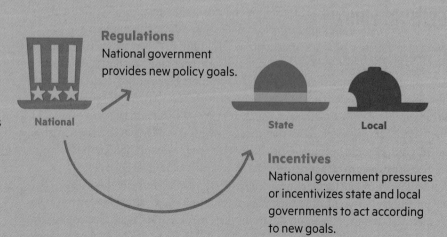

National

Regulations
National government
provides new policy goals.

State   Local

Incentives
National government pressures
or incentivizes state and local
governments to act according
to new goals.

Federalism and Environmental Policy

This is who carries out environmental policy in...

The National Government:
Environmental Protection Agency (EPA), Department of the Interior, Department of Energy

The State Government:
State Department of Natural Resources, State Park Service, State Environmental Protection Agencies

The Local Government:
City park system, city and county oversight boards for land use policy and zoning

Environmental policy shows contemporary federalism in action. As you can see on the right, all levels of government combine to effect environmental policy (exemplifying picket fence federalism). Also, the national government provides both rules and incentives for state and local governments to change their environmental policies (exemplifying coercive federalism).

Congress passed new acts.

Over the last several decades, Congress has passed the **Coastal Zone Management Act**, the **Clean Water Act**, the **Endangered Species Act**, and the **Clean Air Act**.

What does that mean?

This legislation has provided states and localities with **federal regulations and mandates**.

Stricter rules...

During the Obama administration, **the EPA set tougher limits on ozone and water pollution** and proposed stricter limits on carbon emissions.

But also incentives.

Other federal programs **provided grants and tax incentives** to encourage use of renewable energy technologies.

Change happens.

Beginning in 2017, the Trump administration **repealed many of the new EPA regulations** but left the tax credits and grant programs largely intact.

The states fight back.

Fifteen states **sued the federal government**, claiming that the regulatory rollbacks violated the Clean Air Act. Litigation is currently underway and will likely end up in the Supreme Court.

❓ Critical Thinking

1. **Which do you think is a more effective tool** to change environmental policy—the "stick" of regulation or the "carrot" of incentives? Why?

2. **Should the government provide tax credits and other incentives** for things like renewable energy, or leave such things up to the free market?

In short:

The national government **imposes new rules** on **state and local governments** and **provides incentives** to follow these new rules and goals. However, the content of these rules, as well as whether they stay in place over time, **depends on who is elected to federal office and decisions made by federal courts**.

For example, Republican attempts to repeal the Affordable Care Act (the ACA, or "Obamacare") have proposed transforming the program into a block grant to state governments, arguing along the lines of the quote from Nobel Laureate Elinor Ostrom—that local decision makers are often better informed about citizen needs. While Ostrom's work shows that decentralization can lead to more efficient, effective policies, it appears that these efforts by Republicans are more about saving money and reducing services, as the block grants they propose would not cover predicted increases in health care costs.

Expanding national power

Despite the overall shift toward cooperative federalism, strong overtones of national government supremacy remain. Three important characteristics of American politics in the past 60 years have reinforced the role of the national government: (1) reliance on the national government in times of crisis and war; (2) the "rights revolution" of the 1950s and 1960s, as well as the Great Society programs of the 1960s; and (3) the rise of coercive federalism.

Crisis and War Reliance on the national government in times of crisis and war has always been a characteristic of American politics. Even in the 1800s, during the period of dual federalism and strong state power, the national government's strong actions were needed during the Civil War to hold the nation together. More recently, during the COVID-19 pandemic that spread across the country, most people looked to the federal government to deliver emergency supplies, aid in emergency medical operations, and allocate funds for affected communities. Policy responses to the major crises of the twentieth century (the Great Depression's New Deal policies, the massive mobilization for World War II), as well as the response to the banking meltdown of 2008–2009, also dramatically shifted the balance of power toward Washington.

The "Rights Revolution" and Great Society Programs The "rights revolution" initiated by the Supreme Court, as well as Lyndon Johnson's Great Society programs, contributed to increased national control over state policies. Landmark Court decisions thrust the national government into policy areas that had typically been reserved to the states. In the school desegregation and busing cases of the 1950s and 1960s, for example, the Court upheld the national goal of promoting racial equality and fighting discrimination over the earlier norm of local control of school districts.[10] The "one person, one vote" decisions, which required that the populations of legislative districts be equalized when district lines were redrawn, put the federal courts at the center of another policy area that had always been left to the states.[11] The rights revolution also applied to police powers, another area of traditional state control, including protection against self-incrimination and preventing illegally obtained evidence from being used in a criminal trial.[12]

These Court actions were paralleled by a burst of legislation that tackled civil rights, education, the environment, medical care for the poor, and housing. These so-called Great Society policies made the national government much more active in policy areas previously controlled by state and local governments. For example, after passage of the 1965 Voting Rights Act, federal marshals were sent to the South to make sure that African Americans were allowed to vote.

In the 1960s, the national government also expanded its reach through a large increase in categorical grants, although most of these funds came with strings attached. For example, the 1964 Civil Rights Act required nondiscrimination as a condition for receiving any kind of federal grants. The Elementary and Secondary Education Act of 1965 gave the federal government heightened control over public education by attaching conditions to federal grant money.

Bureaucrats sometimes do not have the correct information, while citizens and users of resources do.

—**Elinor Ostrom,** Nobel Laureate

More Unfunded Mandates Despite the legislation enacted by Congress designed to curb unfunded mandates, the practice has continued. President George W. Bush imposed significant mandates related to education testing, sales tax collection, emergency management, infrastructure, and election administration. President Barack Obama's administration required state governments to adopt policies preventing discrimination against the disabled and mandated reforms to local school lunch menus. More recently, the Trump administration's crackdown on undocumented immigrants has an unfunded mandate: if local police arrest someone suspected of being undocumented, they are expected to keep these suspects in custody until federal authorities can arrange for a transfer, even though the federal government does not reimburse them for the cost of the detention.

The fact that members of Congress enact unfunded mandates makes sense given the themes of this textbook. First, politics is about conflict, and when there is disagreement between the federal and state government over what policies should look like, we should expect each side to do whatever it can to advance its own priorities. Second, the rules matter. The fact that the Constitution prioritizes federal law over state law, coupled with increased federal aid to state and local governments, gives the federal government considerable leverage to get its way when conflicts arise. In the case of suspected undocumented immigrants, the Trump administration threatened to withhold various forms of federal aid to communities that refuse to hold suspects for transfer, although it never actually did so, and it is questionable whether aid cutoffs would survive a court challenge.

The states fight back

Most Americans support some of the policies that have been imposed on the states: racial equality, clean air and water, a fair legal process, safer highways, and equal access to the voting booth. At the same time, there has always been considerable opposition in some states to federal mandates, whether unfunded or otherwise. For example, about 20 states have refused to accept federal funds to expand

State governments, including Washington D.C., have taken up the mantle of meeting the United States' commitments to the climate goals set by the Paris Agreement. Muriel Bowser, mayor of Washington, D.C., reaffirmed her administration's commitment to fighting climate change.

competitive federalism
A form of federalism in which states compete to attract businesses and jobs through the policies they adopt.

Crucial to understanding federalism in modern day America is the concept of mobility, or "the ability to vote with your feet." If you don't support the death penalty and citizens packing a pistol—don't come to Texas. If you don't like medicinal marijuana and gay marriage, don't move to California.

—**Rick Perry,** former Texas governor

Medicaid as outlined in the Affordable Care Act. While the law initially did not give states the flexibility to opt out of the expansion, the Supreme Court found that mandating that states expand their Medicaid programs to receive these funds was unconstitutional.

States appear to be reversing their traditional role of resisting change and protecting the status quo. In recent years, states have followed California's lead on environmental policy, refusing to accept national pollution standards that are too lenient or the lack of national action on issues such as global warming. Many policies to address climate change—including the development of renewable energy sources, carbon emissions limits, and carbon cap and trade programs—have been advocated or enacted at the state level, and some governors have announced that their states will comply with the Paris Agreement on climate change regardless of what the federal government does. States have been out in front on fighting electronic waste, mercury emissions, and air pollution more generally.[13] Similarly, during the COVID-19 pandemic, many states implemented mandatory mask regulations despite the absence of federal action. To take another example, Kansas and Montana passed laws holding that federal gun laws do not apply to guns manufactured in their states (and making it a felony to try to enforce those laws).[14] Many such state laws will not stand up in federal court; the Montana gun law has already been struck down. But the laws are clearly a reflection of state frustration with assertions of federal power and with the policy goals that underlie these assertions. Simply put, local elected officials and their constituents often disagree with federal directives. From this perspective, federalism provides a way for state and local officials to shape public policy in ways that favor their own policy goals.

States have one important advantage over the national government when it comes to experimenting with new policies: their numbers. There are 50 states potentially trying a mix of different policies—another reason that advocates of state-centered federalism see the states as the proper repository of government power. In this view, such a mix of policies produces **competitive federalism**—competition among states to provide the best policies to attract businesses, create jobs, and maintain a healthy social fabric.[15] For example, one of the arguments in favor of repealing Obamacare and giving the program's funds to states as a block grant was that state governments might develop better, more efficient ways to deliver health care without having to meet federal requirements.

Fighting for states' rights: the role of the modern Supreme Court

Just as the Supreme Court played a central role in defining dual federalism in the nineteenth and early twentieth centuries and in opening the door to a more nation-centered cooperative federalism in the late 1930s, today's Court is once again reshaping federalism. But this time the move is decidedly in the direction of state power (see Table 3.2).

The Tenth Amendment On paper, it seems that the Tenth Amendment would be at the center of any resurgence of state power because it ensures that all powers not delegated to the national government are reserved to the states or to the people. Until recent years, this amendment had been overshadowed by federal supremacy—state laws contradicting the Constitution or federal laws and regulations were generally found to be unconstitutional. For example, state laws enforcing racial segregation were deemed unconstitutional because they conflicted with the equal protection clause of the Fourteenth Amendment. Similarly, a state law concerning public education,

Recent Important Supreme Court Decisions on Federalism

TABLE
3.2

Case	Holding and Significance for States' Rights	Direction of the Decision
Gregory v. Ashcroft (1991)	The Missouri constitution's requirement that state judges retire by age 70 did not violate the Age Discrimination in Employment Act.	More state power
United States v. Lopez (1995)	Carrying a gun in a school did not fall within "interstate commerce"; thus, Congress could not prohibit the possession of guns on school property.	More state power
Seminole Tribe v. Florida (1996)	The Court used the Eleventh Amendment to strengthen states' sovereign immunity, ruling that Congress could not compel a state to negotiate with Native American tribes about gaming and casinos.	More state power
City of Boerne v. Flores (1997)	The Court struck down the Religious Freedom Restoration Act as an overly broad attempt to curtail the state-sponsored harassment of religion, saying that national legislation aimed at remedying states' discrimination must be "congruent and proportional" to the harm.	More state power
United States v. Morrison (2000)	The Court struck down part of the Violence Against Women Act, saying that Congress did not have the power under the commerce clause to provide a national remedy for gender-based crimes.	More state power
Alabama v. Garrett (2001)	The Court struck down the portion of the ADA that applied to the states, saying that state governments are not required to make special accommodations for the disabled.	More state power
Nevada Department of Human Resources v. Hibbs (2003)	The Court upheld Congress's power to apply the 1993 Family Leave Act to state employees as "appropriate legislation" under Section 5 of the Fourteenth Amendment.	Less state power
United States v. Bond (2011)	The Court upheld an individual's right to challenge the constitutionality of a federal law under the Tenth Amendment.	More state power
National Federation of Independent Business v. Sebelius (2012)	The Court upheld most provisions of the ACA but struck down the expansion of Medicaid as an unconstitutional use of coercive federalism (states could voluntarily take the additional funding to cover the expansion, but they would not lose existing funds if they opted out).	Mixed
United States v. Windsor (2013)	The Court held that Section 3 of DOMA was unconstitutional because it denied federal benefits to same-sex couples who were legally married under state law.	More state power
Shelby County v. Holder (2013)	The Court struck down Section 4 of the Voting Rights Act on the grounds that it violated the "equal sovereignty" of the states.	More state power

Source: Compiled by the authors.

traditionally a state power, is void if it conflicts with the Constitution or with a national law that is based on an enumerated power. For example, a state could not compel an 18-year-old to attend school if the student had been drafted to serve in the army. Under the Tenth Amendment, the constitutionally enumerated national power to "raise and support armies" would override the reserved state power to support public education.

However, with the appointment of three conservative justices between 1986 and 1991 who favored a stronger role for the states, the Court started to limit the national government's reach. One common thread in these decisions was to require that Congress provide an unambiguous statement of its intent for a particular law to overrule state authority. For example, the Court ruled that the Missouri constitution, which requires state judges to retire by age 70, did not violate the Age Discrimination in Employment Act because Congress did not make its intentions "unmistakably clear in the language of the statute."[16]

The Fourteenth Amendment The Supreme Court has also empowered states by limiting the applicability of the Constitution's Fourteenth Amendment to state laws. The Fourteenth Amendment was intended to give the national government broad control

> The immense size and power of the Government of the United States ought not obscure its fundamental character. It remains a Government of enumerated powers.
>
> **—Sandra Day O'Connor,**
> former Supreme Court justice

remedial legislation
National laws that address discriminatory state laws. Authority for such legislation comes from Section 5 of the Fourteenth Amendment.

states' sovereign immunity
Based on the Eleventh Amendment, immunity that prevents state governments from being sued by private parties in federal court unless the state consents to the suit.

**AP®
SUPREME
COURT CASE**

United States v. Lopez
A 1995 Supreme Court case that struck down a federal law regulating the possession of firearms around schools. It was the first time that the Court had restricted Congress's power to pass legislation under the commerce clause since the New Deal in the 1930s.

over the potentially discriminatory laws of southern states after the Civil War. Section 1 guarantees that no state shall make or enforce any law depriving any person of "life, liberty, or property, without due process of law" or denying any person the "equal protection of the laws," and Section 5 empowers Congress "to enforce" those guarantees by "appropriate legislation." Throughout most of the twentieth century, the Court interpreted Section 5 to give Congress broad discretion to pass legislation to remedy bad state laws. For example, discriminatory application of literacy tests prevented millions of African Americans from voting in the South before the Voting Rights Act was passed in 1965.

As part of the federalism revolution of the 1990s, the Court started to chip away at Congress's Fourteenth Amendment powers. In one important case in 1997, the Supreme Court struck down the Religious Freedom Restoration Act as an overly broad attempt to curtail state-sponsored harassment based on religion. This case established a new standard to justify remedial legislation—that is, national legislation that fixes discriminatory state law—under Section 5 of the Fourteenth Amendment, saying: "There must be a congruence and proportionality between the injury to be prevented or remedied and the means adopted to that end."[17] In one application of the new standard for remedial legislation, the Court ruled that the Age Discrimination in Employment Act of 1967 could not be applied to state employees because it was not "appropriate legislation."[18] Two applications of this logic also applied to the Eleventh Amendment, which originally was interpreted to mean that residents of one state could not sue other (non-home-state) state governments. More recently, the Supreme Court has expanded the reach of the Eleventh Amendment through the concept of states' sovereign immunity. States are now immune from a much broader range of lawsuits in state and federal court.

The Commerce Clause Another category of cases that have been decided in favor of more state power concerns the commerce clause of the Constitution. The first Court case to limit Congress's commerce powers since the New Deal of the 1930s came in 1995. The case involved the Gun-Free School Zones Act of 1990, which Congress passed in response to the increase in school shootings around the nation. The law made it a federal offense to have a gun within 1,000 feet of a school. Congress assumed that it had the power to pass this legislation, given the Court's expansive interpretation of the commerce clause over the previous 55 years, even though it concerned a traditional area of state power. Although it was a stretch to claim that carrying a gun in or around a school was related to interstate commerce, Congress might have been able to demonstrate the point by showing that (1) most guns are made in one state and sold in another (thus commercially crossing state lines); (2) crime affects the economy and commerce; and (3) the quality of education, which is also crucial to the economy, is harmed if students and teachers are worrying about guns in their schools. However, members of Congress did not present this evidence.

Alfonso Lopez, a senior at Edison High School in San Antonio, Texas, was arrested for carrying a concealed .38-caliber handgun with five bullets in it, in violation of the Gun-Free School Zone Act. Attorneys for Lopez moved to dismiss the charges, arguing that the law was unconstitutional because carrying a gun in a school could not be regulated as "interstate commerce." The Court agreed in *United States v. Lopez*,[19] and the ruling was widely viewed as a warning shot over Congress's bow. If Congress wanted to encroach on the states' turf in the future, it would have to demonstrate that the law in question was a legitimate exercise of the commerce clause powers.

Congress learned its lesson. The next time it passed legislation that affected law enforcement at the state level, it was careful to document the impact on interstate commerce. The Violence Against Women Act was passed in 1994 with strong bipartisan support after testimony and evidence were entered into the record showing the links between violence against women and commerce. Despite the evidence Congress presented,

The *Lopez* decision struck down the 1990 Gun-Free School Zones Act, ruling that Congress did not have the power to forbid people to carry guns near schools. After the shooting of 34 people at Marjory Stoneman Douglas High School in Parkland, Florida, on February 14, 2018, students led renewed calls nationwide for strengthening gun control laws.

the Supreme Court ruled that Congress did not have the power under the commerce clause to make a national law that gave victims of gender-motivated violence the right to sue their attackers in federal court (the Court struck down only that part of the law, however; the program funding remained unaffected and was reauthorized in 2013 and again in 2019).[20]

The impact of these cases goes well beyond setting limits on the federal government's ability to regulate commerce. Not only has the Supreme Court set new limits on Congress's ability to address national problems, but it has also clearly stated that the Court alone will determine which rights warrant protection by Congress. However, it is important to recognize that the Court does not consistently rule against Congress; it often rules against the states because of broader constitutional principles or general public consensus behind a specific issue. For example, the Court has struck down state laws limiting gay rights as a violation of the equal protection clause of the Fourteenth Amendment.[21] And although the Court rejected the commerce clause as the constitutional justification for national health care reform, it did uphold the ACA based on Congress's taxing power.[22]

It's also important to keep in mind that the national government still has the upper hand in the balance of power and has many tools at its disposal to blunt the impact of any Court decision. Congress can pass new laws to clarify its legislative intent and overturn any of the Court cases that involved statutory interpretation. Congress can also use its financial power to impose its will on the states, although this power is not unlimited. For example, in a 2012 case dealing with Obamacare's requirement that states expand Medicaid coverage in order to receive federal subsidies for the program, the Court ruled that the threat embodied in this requirement was a "gun to the head,"[23] meaning states did not have a real choice: without the subsidies, no state could afford to provide Medicaid coverage on its own, even without the expansion in coverage. This was the first time the Court limited Congress's coercive budgetary power over the states, and the boundaries of the new limits will have to be decided in future cases.

Why is it important to understand federalism today? More than at any time in U.S. history, the question of which branch of government has power over a particular policy is up for grabs. This change gives elected officials new opportunities to influence policy—rather than changing the policy itself, they can influence decisions about which level of government implements the policy.

"Why Should I Care?"

Assessing federalism

There is much to recommend federalism as a cornerstone of our political system. However, there are disadvantages as well, such as inefficiency in the policy process and inequality in policy outcomes. This section will assess the advantages, disadvantages, and ideological complexities of federalism.

Policy preferences

Issues concerning federalism often seem to break down along traditional liberal and conservative lines. Liberals generally favor strong national power to fight discrimination against women, minorities, disabled people, the LGBTQ community, and the elderly, and they push for progressive national policies on issues such as protecting the environment, providing national health care, and supporting the poor. Conservatives, in contrast, tend to favor limiting intrusion from the national government and allowing the states to decide their own mix of social welfare and regulatory policies, including how aggressively they will protect various groups from discrimination. In this way, individuals' feelings about federalism are connected to their policy preferences and their judgments about what kinds of policies should emerge from different levels of government.

However, assessing the implications of having policies carried out by one level of government or another is not always so simple. In recent years the tables have turned, and in many cases liberals are suddenly arguing for states' rights while conservatives are advocating the virtues of uniform national laws. On a broad range of new issues, such as gay rights, aid in dying, and the recreational use of marijuana (see the Take a Stand feature), some state governments have enacted socially liberal legislation in recent years. As a result, liberals who might have favored a strong national government as a way of implementing their policy goals have found themselves arguing for states' rights, and conservatives have ended up arguing for the virtues of centralizing power.

Advantages of a strong role for the states

In addition to pointing out the policy implications of federalism, any assessment of federalism today must consider the advantages and disadvantages for our political system. The advantages of a strong role for the states can be summarized in four main points: (1) states can be laboratories of democracy, (2) state and local governments are closer to the people, (3) states provide more access to the political system, and (4) states provide an important check on national power.

The first point refers to the role that states can play as the source of policy diversity and innovation. If many states are trying to solve problems creatively, their efforts can complement those of the national government. Successful policies first adopted at the state level often percolate up to the national level. Consider health care. Many provisions of Obamacare were taken from the highly successful state-level program in Massachusetts. Similarly, climate change initiatives emerging in California and other states may provide templates for federal action in the future. (Of course, as the case of auto fuel economy standards illustrate, state-level innovations may be opposed by the president or majorities in Congress.)

> [A] state may, if its citizens choose, serve as a laboratory; and try novel social and economic experiments without risk to the rest of the country.
>
> —Louis Brandeis,
> former Supreme Court justice

Recreational Marijuana and Federalism

Should the federal government be able to tell a state that it cannot allow the recreational use of marijuana? While the use and possession of marijuana is illegal under federal law, 11 states (Alaska, California, Colorado, Illinois, Maine, Massachusetts, Michigan, Nevada, Oregon, Vermont, and Washington) have legalized nonmedical use. In most of these states, commercial activity (growing and sales) has also been legalized. Over 30 states have legalized marijuana use for medical purposes. And in most other states, possession of small amounts of marijuana is no longer treated as a crime. In the coming years, several other states are likely to move toward partial or complete legalization.

The federal government should be "hands off." Up until recently, the federal government responded to these changes in state law by adopting a "hands off" policy. The so-called Cole Memo (named after Deputy Associate Attorney General James Cole, who served during the Obama administration) stated that the federal government would not prosecute marijuana cases unless there had been a violation of both state and federal law. This policy reflected an attitude within the Obama Justice Department that prosecution of marijuana cases was not a high priority. Moreover, some Justice Department staff members (and perhaps President Obama) probably favored federal legalization. However, this step would have required congressional approval, which would have been unlikely during Obama's administration given the Republican majority in the House (and, after January 2015, in the Senate). Thus, deferring to state law helped move parts of the country toward decriminalization without requiring additional legislative action and allowed public support for legalization to build. Opponents of marijuana legalization in Congress may eventually be forced to reconsider their position based on the tides of public opinion.

The federal government should be "hands on." The situation changed after the election of Donald Trump. Throughout 2017, Trump's first Attorney General Jeff Sessions argued that the federal government needed to be more aggressive in its enforcement of marijuana laws as a means of reducing drug abuse, fighting criminal organizations, and decreasing violent crime. In January 2018, Sessions formally

Federal drug enforcement agents raid a medical marijuana club.

rescinded the Cole Memo, although his new guidelines did not order U.S. attorneys to give marijuana prosecutions a higher priority, distinguish between medical or recreational use, or provide additional resources for anti-marijuana efforts. Sessions did not order states to change their laws or compel local law-enforcement agencies to enforce federal law.

Sessions's successor as attorney general, William Barr, has the option of proposing new federal legislation to increase the penalties for possession or sale of marijuana or providing local governments with funds or other assistance to enforce anti-marijuana laws. However, many Republican legislators, particularly from states that have relaxed marijuana laws, might oppose higher penalties. Similarly, law-enforcement agencies in communities that have decriminalized marijuana would likely decline federal help in prosecuting activities that they no longer consider a crime. On the other hand, insofar as Barr's responsibility is to enforce the laws as written, these steps are reasonable options for increased federal involvement in deterring marijuana production, sale, and consumption.

take a stand

1. As a matter of policy, should marijuana be legalized in all cases or just some cases—ranging from complete legalization to legalization only for medical use when prescribed by a doctor? If some possession is legal, what should policies be for growth and sale?

2. Do you tend to support a state-centered or a nation-centered perspective on federalism? Now revisit your answers to question 1. Are your positions more consistent with your views on federalism or with your policy concerns?

Second, government that is closer to the people can encourage participation in the political process and may be more responsive to local needs. Local politicians know better what their constituents want than further-removed national politicians do. On the one hand, if voters want higher taxes to pay for more public benefits, such as public parks and better schools, they can enact these changes at the state and local levels. On the other hand, if they prefer lower taxes and fewer services, local politicians can be responsive to those desires. In addition, local government provides a broad range of opportunities for direct involvement in politics, from working on local political campaigns to attending school board or city council meetings, which may increase the input that citizens have in the establishment of new policies.

Third, our federalist system provides more access points for interested parties (stakeholders) to influence government policy. For example, the court system allows citizens to pursue complaints under state or federal law. If a group, such as anti-abortion activists, loses at the federal level, it can try to enact similar legislation at the state level. Likewise, cooperative federalism can draw on the strengths of different levels of government to solve problems. A local government may recognize a need and respond to it more quickly than the national government can, but if additional resources are needed to address the problem, the municipality may be able to turn to the state or national government for help—as in the cases of Hurricanes Harvey, Irma, and Maria, when local governments were assisted by the U.S. military and Federal Emergency Management Agency (FEMA) and received supplemental federal aid for rebuilding efforts.

Finally, federalism can provide a check on national tyranny. Competitive federalism ensures that Americans have a broad range of social policies, levels of taxation and regulation, and public services to choose from (see Figure 3.1). When people "vote with their feet" by deciding whether to move and where to live, they encourage healthy competition among states that would be impossible under a unitary government.

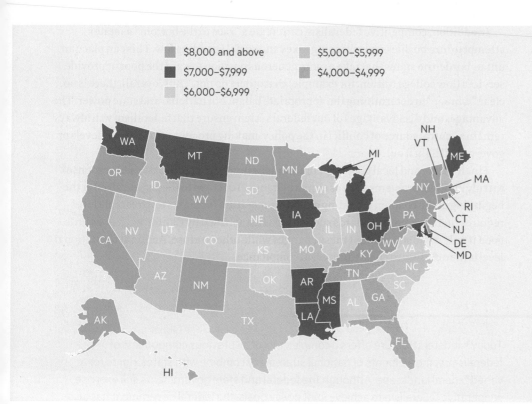

FIGURE 3.1

State Spending per Person

Spending per person varies dramatically by state. What are some of the advantages and disadvantages of living in a low-spending state or in a high-spending state? What type of state would you rather live in? Why?

Source: State and Local Government Finance Data Query System, http://slfdqs.taxpolicycenter.org (accessed 2/13/20).

Map legend:
- $8,000 and above
- $7,000–$7,999
- $6,000–$6,999
- $5,000–$5,999
- $4,000–$4,999

Disadvantages of too much state power

A balanced assessment of federalism must acknowledge that there are problems with a system that gives too much power to the states. The disadvantages include unequal distribution of resources across the states, unequal protection for civil rights, competition that produces a "race to the bottom," and the problem of coordinating local responses to truly national problems.

The resource problem becomes more acute when dealing with national-level problems that affect different areas differently. For example, many communities across the United States are faced with deteriorating public infrastructure, including highways, bridges, and mass transit. Paying for these repairs can outstrip the resources of state and local governments, particularly for a small number of localities that have a disproportionate number of bridges and roads needing repairs.

Another problem, unequal civil rights protection, is evident in various federalism cases that have passed before the Supreme Court. These clearly show that states are not uniformly willing to protect the civil liberties and civil rights of their citizens. This was critically important during the 1950s and 1960s when the national government forced southern states to end segregation and passed laws outlawing discrimination in housing, employment, transportation, and voting. The Supreme Court recently stepped in to provide equal rights to marry, but states still vary a great deal in terms of antidiscrimination laws based on sexual orientation. Without national laws, there will be large differences in the levels of protection against discrimination based on age, disability, and sexual orientation. More generally, insofar as we give power to states, we create a situation whereby individuals' rights, as well as the benefits they are entitled to, depend on which state they happen to live in.

In addition, competitive federalism can create a "race to the bottom" as states attempt to lure businesses by keeping taxes and social spending low. This can place an unfair burden on states that take a more generous position toward the poor or provide services (low college tuition, for example) that others do not. Thus, overall, there is no clear "winner" in determining the appropriate balance of national and state power. The advantages and disadvantages of our federal system ensure that federalism will always remain a central source of conflict in the policy-making process as the various levels of government fight it out.

Finally, state and local governments might be unable to coordinate their response to truly national problems such as climate change. To return to the issues raised at the beginning of the chapter, if holding global temperature increases to a tolerable level requires fuel economy standards such as those established by California, it does little good if only some states adopt these changes while others refuse. Action at the national level is the only way to ensure universal compliance.

"Why Should I Care?"

Today's federal structure offers a complex mix of all previous components of federalism: some elements of national supremacy combine with states' rights for a varied federal landscape. Although the federal and state governments still exercise cooperative federalism to achieve joint policy goals, the federal government has also utilized coercive federalism to impose federal priorities on the states without offering compensation.

**AP®
POLICY IN
PRACTICE**

The Affordable Care Act of 2010

Attempts to reform the overall health care system in the United States have failed since the presidency of Theodore Roosevelt in the early 1900s. Whereas all other industrialized countries, in this same time period, have overhauled their health care systems and moved toward some version of universal health care, the United States has always been resistant to moving in that direction. Much of the leadership and many citizens have feared that universal health care would mean a loss of health care quality, higher taxes, and fewer choices regarding physicians, hospitals, and treatments.

When Senator Barack Obama ran for president the first time, one of his campaign promises concerned tackling health care reform. Though many were skeptical that this could be accomplished, and there are still ongoing debates about its positives and negatives, the Patient Protection and Affordable Care Act of 2010 was passed only 14 months after President Obama took office. Obviously, there are many more details and nuances to the actual events that occurred in the months leading up to the official announcement in July 2009 by the Democratic House leadership all the way through the present, when Obamacare (as the law came to be known) is still being criticized, supported, and implemented, but this gives you a good idea of the challenges that face policy makers regardless of the issue.

You might wonder why this issue is addressed in the Federalism chapter rather than in the Congress or President chapters (Chapters 4-5). A good argument could be made for including it in either place or even in the Courts chapter (Chapter 6), but it also applies here because of the ongoing debate between the states and the federal government about where responsibility lies for providing and helping to pay for citizens' health care coverage. Pay particular attention to the Supreme Court decision mentioned in the Evaluation section to see how the Roberts Court has viewed the balance of responsibilities and power between the states and national government on the subject of the Affordable Care Act.

Policy Stages

1. Problem Recognition
   - Too many Americans did not have health care because they could not afford it.
   - About 50 million Americans had no health insurance.
   - Attempts for capitalism and competition to drive down costs had not worked.
   - The overwhelming majority of other industrialized countries have universal health care.
   - The United States pays more for health care than any other industrialized country.
   - Many U.S. citizens, political leaders, and policy specialists felt that health care is a basic right, and that it was time to act.
   - It has been discussed since the presidency of Theodore Roosevelt.

2. Agenda Setting
   - Health care reform was announced by House leadership on July 14, 2009.
   - It emphasized choice of quality and affordable health care coverage for all Americans.
   - It would build on the current system.
   - It would allow people to keep their current insurance.
   - It would offer competitive options, to keep costs down, for those who did not have health insurance.
   - It aimed to improve Medicare and Medicaid.

3. Deliberation and Formulation
   - Bill H.R. 3962 was introduced in the House of Representatives by Charles Rangel (D-NY) on September 17, 2009.
   - Three House committees worked on the bill and five Senate committees worked on their version.
   - The bill was debated in Congress (in subcommittees and public and private hearings).
   - House Speaker Pelosi and Senate Majority Leader Reid added things that were not in their respective committee versions.
   - The White House held daily meetings with committees from both houses.
   - No conference committee was established to reconcile differences between each house's version.
   - Committee leaders, White House staff, and party leadership negotiated details of the bills.

4. Enactment
   - The House of Representatives passed the bill on November 7, 2009: **220 YEAs**: 219 Democrats, 1 Republican, 0 others; **215 NAYs**: 39 Democrats, 176 Republicans, 0 others; **0 Not Voting**.
   - The Senate passed an alternative form of the bill on December 24, 2009: **60 YEAs**: 60 Democrats, 0 Republicans, 0 others; **39 NAYs**: 0 Democrats, 39 Republicans, 0 others; **1 Not Voting**: 0 Democrats, 1 Republican, 0 others.

- The House passed the Senate form of the bill on March 21, 2010: **219 YEAs**: 219 Democrats, 0 Republicans, 0 others; **212 NAYs**: 34 Democrats, 178 Republicans, 0 others; **0 Not Voting**.
- The House also passed a separate reconciliation bill that had many amendments to the Senate bill.
- The Senate amended the reconciliation bill, which was passed by the House.
- The Patient Protection and Affordable Care Act of 2010: both bills were signed into law by President Barack Obama on March 23, 2010.

5. Implementation
   - The website (http://healthcare.gov) was put up for enrollment starting on October 1, 2013.
   - The Affordable Care Act was publicized and advertised.
   - All health care exchanges were put online to drive competition in order to keep prices down.
   - The goal was to cover 20–22 million people.
   - People would have to pay a tax if they did not buy health insurance.

6. Evaluation
   - The website did not work—it had major glitches.
   - People could not always get the doctors they wanted.
   - For many, coverage was expensive.
   - Public debate surrounded the site.
   - *National Federation of Independent Business v. Sebelius*, 567 U.S. 519 (2012): The Supreme Court ruled that the individual mandate is constitutional and limited the expansion of Medicaid; states that do not want to expand Medicaid cannot be penalized; the decision was based not on commerce clause and necessary and proper clause powers but on Congress's power to tax.
   - The Supreme Court decision "strikes a balance between principles of federalism and judicial restraint."[24]
   - Twenty million more were insured from 2010 to 2016.
   - Medicaid was expanded to cover more people.
   - People could not be denied coverage due to preexisting conditions.
   - Firms were required to offer health insurance.
   - Taxes were raised for some groups.
   - Medicare payments to hospitals and insurance companies were reduced and incentives were put in place to make doctors and hospitals more efficient.
   - Insurance companies were required to disclose payments made to doctors.
   - Chain restaurants were required to inform customers of how many calories are in each meal.
   - Employers of a certain size had to provide a place for nursing mothers.

7. Possible Modifications, Expansion, or Termination of Policy
   - Republicans pushed for "repeal and replace" of the Affordable Care Act at least 70 times.
   - The American Health Care Act of 2017 (AHCA) was passed by the House: **217 YEAs:** 0 Democrats, 217 Republicans, 0 others; **213 NAYs:** 193 Democrats, 20 Republicans, 0 others; **1 Not Voting:** 0 Democrats, 1 Republican, 0 others.
   - The Senate's version, the Better Care Reconciliation Act of 2017 ("Repeal and Replace"), failed to pass on July 25, 2017: **43 YEAs:** 0 Democrats, 43 Republicans, 0 others; **57 NAYs:** 46 Democrats, 9 Republicans, 2 others; **0 Not Voting**.

- If AHCA had become law, 23 million people would have lost coverage over the next 10 years, and budget deficits would have decreased by $119 billion over the same 10 years.[25]
- The Senate's Partial Repeal Amendment (the Obamacare Repeal and Reconciliation Act) failed to pass on July 26, 2017.
- The Senate's Skinny Repeal Amendment (Health Care Freedom) failed to pass on July 28, 2017.

Questions for Discussion

1. Do you think health care is a right or a privilege?

2. What impact will the COVID-19 virus have on the American public's perception of national health care?

Unpacking the Conflict

Considering all that we've discussed in this chapter, let's apply what we know about how federalism works to the example of competing federal and state-level automobile standards from the beginning of the chapter. When local and federal officials disagree about fuel economy standards and global warming, who wins? How can we explain this conflict, or conflicts between federal and state authorities over other policies?

As we have seen, one issue is that even after 230 years, the boundaries between federal authority and state authority are not always clear, particularly given the rise of cooperative federalism and the use of unfunded mandates. In other areas, such as laws governing the legality of marijuana, federal authority and state authority are genuinely overlapping. Thus, at least some of the time, the question of whether the federal government can tell states what to do (or whether states have the right to ignore federal directives) has no clear answer. In these situations, politicians' (or citizens') judgments about federalism probably reflect their ideas about which level of government is more likely to give them an outcome they want.

In other policy areas, the lines of authority between federal and state governments are relatively clear, but federalism can be justified as a way to deliver policies more effectively or efficiently. Like many other regulatory initiatives over the last generation, the Clean Air Act was designed with the idea that some states and communities would implement policies that deviated from federal standards—and that allowing such flexibility would ensure consideration of local needs or conditions. However, nothing in the Constitution mandates that the federal government allow local discretion. You can disagree on policy grounds with the Trump administration's revocation of California's fuel economy waiver, but the decision itself is entirely consistent with how the courts have interpreted the federal government's regulatory powers.

The fight over fuel economy standards also highlights the idea that Americans are citizens of several levels of government simultaneously. Martha Derthick, a leading scholar of American federalism, says that the basic question of federalism involves choices about how many communities we will be.[26] If you asked most people in our nation about their primary geopolitical community, they would probably not say, "I am a Montanan" or "I am an Arizonan." Most people would likely say, "I am an American." Yet we have strong attachments to our local communities and state identities. We are members of multiple communities and subject to several different sets of overlapping laws, a fact that has had an indelible impact on our political system and the policy choices that affect our everyday life.

"What's Your Take?"

Should the federal government be able to force states to comply with national auto fuel efficiency standards?

Or should state and local officials be able to conduct their business without federal interference?

AP® STUDY GUIDE

Summary

In a unitary government power is given only to the national government, whereas a confederal system gives power only to the states. However, a federal system simultaneously allocates power to both the states and the federal government. These exclusive powers to the national government and concurrent, or shared, powers between the national and state governments help explain the ongoing negotiations over the balance of power between the two levels.

Although the state governments have considerable power in our system, the Founders disproportionately favored the federal government in the Constitution so that the federal government's interests superseded those of the states in the event of a conflict. This preference is evident in the U.S. Supreme Court's interpretation of cases such as *McCulloch v. Maryland* (1819), which declared that Congress has implied powers necessary to implement its enumerated powers and established supremacy of the Constitution and federal laws over state laws.

The relationship between the state and federal governments has changed dramatically over time. Whereas the federal and state governments traditionally operated with little interaction under the era of dual federalism, the trend over the past 80 years has been one of increasing federal interaction with state governments to address particular policy areas.

Today's federal structure offers a complex mix of all previous components of federalism: some elements of national supremacy combine with states' rights for a varied federal landscape. Federal and state governments exercise cooperative federalism (with block grants, categorical grants, and federal revenue sharing), while the federal government also coerces states to abide by federal policy with the use of unfunded mandates. The ongoing interpretation of the Tenth and Fourteenth Amendments, and other enumerated and implied powers, continues to fuel the debates over the balance of power between the national and state governments. This balance of power continues to devolve, as evident in cases such as *United States v. Lopez* (1995), which determined that Congress stretched the commerce clause too far by trying to use its implied powers to make possession of a gun in a school zone a federal crime. This introduced a new phase of federalism with a focus on state sovereignty and local control.

Although conservatives have traditionally advocated for states' rights and liberals generally prefer a stronger national government, contemporary issues do not always fit neatly in this scheme.

Key Terms

block grants (p. 105)

categorical grants (p. 105)

coercive federalism (p. 105)

competitive federalism (p. 110)

concurrent powers (p. 91)

confederal government (p. 93)

cooperative federalism (p. 102)

dual federalism (p. 97)

exclusive powers (p. 91)

federal preemption (p. 105)

federalism (p. 90)

fiscal federalism (p. 104)

full faith and credit clause (p. 96)

McCulloch v. Maryland (p. 97)

picket fence federalism (p. 102)

police powers (p. 91)

privileges and immunities clause (p. 96)

remedial legislation (p. 112)

sovereign power (p. 90)

states' rights (p. 99)

states' sovereign immunity (p. 112)

Tenth Amendment (p. 96)

unfunded mandates (p. 105)

unitary government (p. 93)

United States v. Lopez (p. 112)

There are several reasons that strong state governments are beneficial for our country, such as the proximity of state and local governments to the citizens, providing multiple access points to help influence public policy; however, there are also some drawbacks to the federal system, such as the vastly disproportionate distribution of resources across states. Overall, national policy making is limited by the division of power between the levels of government and the distribution of power among the three branches of government.

Enduring Understanding

CON-2: "Federalism reflects the dynamic distribution of power between national and state governments." (AP® U.S. Government and Politics Course and Exam Description)

Multiple-Choice Questions (Arranged by Topic)

Topic 1.7: Relationship between the States and Federal Government (CON-2)

1. Which of the following clauses in the U.S. Constitution best explains why a legal marriage in one state must be recognized across state lines?

    (A) privileges and immunities

    (B) necessary and proper

    (C) full faith and credit

    (D) commerce

2. Which of the following is an accurate comparison of exclusive and concurrent powers?

	Exclusive Powers	Concurrent Powers
(A)	make treaties	establish post offices
(B)	charter banks	establish courts
(C)	print money	tax exports
(D)	declare war	collect taxes

3. Which of the following scenarios best describes a block grant?

    (A) a federal law that requires state motor vehicle departments to provide voter registration services

    (B) federal money given to states to help fund their welfare programs without specific restrictions on how the states determine eligibility

    (C) federal aid given to a state to help repair highways provided that the state raises the minimum drinking age

    (D) a state law that requires auto manufacturers to meet higher fuel economy standards for cars in the state than are required by federal law

Topic 1.8: Constitutional Interpretations of Federalism (CON-2)

Questions 4–5 refer to the excerpt.

The powers reserved to the several States will extend to all the objects which, in the ordinary course of affairs, concern the lives, liberties, and properties of the people, and the internal order, improvement, and prosperity of the State. The operations of the federal government will be most extensive and important in times of war and danger; those of the State governments, in times of peace and security.

—James Madison, *Federalist 45*, January 26, 1788

4. **Which of the following statements best describes the author's view on the role of the two levels of government?**

   (A) The federal government has reserved powers to protect the life, liberty, and property of the people.

   (B) The power of the federal government should expand during times of conflict.

   (C) Federal and state government should be equal in power and strength.

   (D) The state government is best able to defend the nation from an attack.

5. **Which of the following amendments is most likely related to the topic in the excerpt?**

   (A) First Amendment

   (B) Fourth Amendment

   (C) Eighth Amendment

   (D) Tenth Amendment

6. **Which of the following best describes the significance of the decision in *McCulloch v. Maryland* (1819)?**

   (A) When both levels of government share the power, the state law is supreme over the federal law.

   (B) States have the broad power to regulate interstate commerce.

   (C) Congress has implied powers necessary to implement enumerated powers.

   (D) Citizens of one state could sue another state, leading to the prohibition of such lawsuits by the Eleventh Amendment.

7. **The Fourteenth Amendment has both increased and limited the power of the state government. Which of the following is the best example of how the courts interpreted the Fourteenth Amendment to give Congress broad discretion to pass legislation to override state laws?**

   (A) elimination of literacy tests

   (B) elimination of poll taxes

   (C) suffrage for women

   (D) suffrage for African-American men

Topic 1.9: Federalism in Action (CON-2)

Questions 8–9 refer to the map.

State Spending per Person

$8,000 and above	$5,000–$5,999
$7,000–$7,999	$4,000–$4,999
$6,000–$6,999	

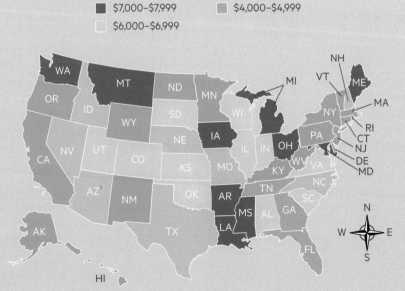

Source: State and Local Government Finance Data Query System, http://slfdqs.taxpolicycenter.org (accessed 2/13/20).

8. **Which of the following statements is true based on the information in the map?**

   (A) States in the Southeast tend to spend more money per person than states in the Northwest.

   (B) States with Republican governors spend more money per person than states with Democratic governors.

   (C) The amount of state spending per person varies by state and region.

   (D) State taxes are higher in Texas (TX) than they are in Ohio (OH).

9. **Which of the following is a consequence of the system of government represented in the map?**

   (A) Multiple access points for stakeholders allow individuals to draw on the strengths of different levels of government to solve problems.

   (B) When the government is closer to the people, they can become disengaged in the political process because the government may be less responsive to local needs.

   (C) Since states usually create uniform policies, their efforts can complement those of the national government.

   (D) Healthy competition among states is discouraged, making it difficult to provide a check on national power.

10. **Which of the following best describes the first stage of the policy-making process as it relates to the coronavirus pandemic (COVID-19)?**

    (A) Families making under $75,000 a year begin receiving direct payments of $1,200 per adult and $500 per child.

    (B) H.R. 748, the Coronavirus Aid, Relief, and Economic Security (CARES) Act, is signed into law by President Trump.

    (C) Shelter-in-place orders, which were created to limit disease transmission, cause businesses to close and unemployment to rise.

    (D) An amendment to the economic relief bill is proposed, providing emergency assistance for individuals, families, and businesses affected by the pandemic.

Free-Response Questions

SCOTUS Comparison

This question requires you to compare a Supreme Court case you studied in class with one you have not studied in class. A summary of the Supreme Court case you did not study in class is presented below and provides all of the information you need to know about this case to answer the prompt.

California voters legalized marijuana for medicinal use with the passage of the Compassionate Use Act in 1996. The Drug Enforcement Administration (DEA) seized marijuana that was prescribed by a doctor because the possession of marijuana violated the Controlled Substances Act (CSA). The CSA classifies marijuana as a Schedule I drug, meaning it is considered unsafe even under medical supervision. A group of medicinal marijuana users sued, arguing that Congress had exceeded its powers.

In the ensuing case, *Gonzales v. Raich* (2005), the Supreme Court held in a 6–3 decision that Congress did not exceed its powers, ruling that Congress could ban marijuana production because it was part of a national marijuana market that crossed state lines.

Based on the information above, respond to the following questions.

   (A) Identify the constitutional clause that was used as the basis for the decision in both *United States v. Lopez* (1995) and *Gonzales v. Raich* (2005).

   (B) Explain how the facts in *United States v. Lopez* led to a different holding than in *Gonzales v. Raich*.

Argument Essay

The distribution of powers among three federal branches and between national and state governments impacts policy making. Develop an argument that explains which level of government—federal or state—should be the primary responder for a major disaster, such as the coronavirus pandemic (COVID-19).

Use at least one piece of evidence from one of the following foundational documents:

- Articles of Confederation
- Brutus 1
- Tenth Amendment of the U.S. Constitution

In your response, you should do the following:

✓ Respond to the prompt with a defensible claim or thesis that establishes a line of reasoning.

✓ Support your claim with at least *two* pieces of specific and relevant evidence.

- One piece of evidence must come from one of the foundational documents listed above.
- A second piece of evidence can come from any other foundational document not used as your first piece of evidence, or it may be from your knowledge of course concepts.

4

Congress

Who does Congress represent?

>> **"As President of the United States, I am asking for a legal solution on DACA, not a political one, consistent with the rule of law. The Supreme Court is not willing to give us one, so now we have to start this process all over again."[1]**
President Donald Trump

<< **"I do not believe we should be granting a path to citizenship to anybody here illegally."[2]**
Senator Ted Cruz (R-TX)

>> **"We can't allow these young people to continue to live in fear, to be at risk."[3]**
Representative Joe Neguse (D-CO)

Late in the first year of his presidency, Donald Trump announced that he would end President Obama's Deferred Action for Childhood Arrivals (DACA) program on March 5, 2018. The program allowed residents who were brought illegally to the United States as children to remain in the country if they had graduated from high school, were currently in school, or had served in the military, and had not committed a felony. President Trump expressed strong support for the program, calling the 700,000 people enrolled "incredible kids." However, Trump believed that President Obama had overstepped his authority by creating the program through executive action, so Trump asked Congress to create a legislative solution.[4] In a meeting with congressional leaders early in 2018, President Trump said that he would sign whatever compromise on DACA that Congress could agree to. Polls showed that between 73 and 87 percent of Americans favored allowing the Dreamers, as program participants are called, to stay and have a path to citizenship.[5]

One would think that enacting a policy that is supported by more than three-fourths of Americans, the president, and both parties in Congress would be a no-brainer. But shortly before the March 5 deadline, the wheels came off. Democrats initially tried to

Representatives Nydia Velázquez (D-NY) and Adriano Espaillat (D-NY) announce the Dream and Promise Act, a bill designed to provide DACA recipients, known as "Dreamers," with a path to U.S. citizenship.

CHAPTER GOALS

Explain how members of Congress represent their constituents and how elections hold members accountable. pages 131–150

Examine how parties, the committee system, and staffers enable Congress to function. pages 150–160

Trace the steps in the legislative process. pages 160–169

Describe how Congress ensures that the bureaucracy implements policies correctly. pages 169–171

attach the DACA bill to a must-pass budget bill, but this effort failed after a three-day government shutdown. Democrats agreed to a two-year budget bill three weeks later, but without a resolution to the DACA issue. In a reversal of his earlier position that he would sign any DACA bill that Congress put forward, President Trump took a hard line against bills that did not include $25 billion in funding for the border wall with Mexico and that did not replace the lottery program for legal immigration and family-based immigration with a merit-based system. Critics on the far right, such as Senator Ted Cruz, called it amnesty for illegal immigrants, while those on the far left called for a "clean bill" that addressed only the Dreamers. After Democrats took control of the House in 2019, they passed a bill that would have provided a path to citizenship for 2.3 million undocumented immigrants, including the Dreamers, but the bill was not taken up in the Senate. (See What Do the Facts Say? on p. 132.)

Given Congress's inability to solve the problem, DACA supporters turned to the courts, which stopped the deportation of the Dreamers. Then, in June 2020 the Supreme Court ruled in a 5–4 decision that President Trump had not provided legal justification for ending the program, and as a result he could not disassemble it. The ruling granted a reprieve to the close to 650,000 people in the program who had been brought to the United States as children.

On a basic level, this appears to be an example of congressional incompetence and dysfunction. How could a policy with such broad support and positive consequences for the economy not be passed? But it is not unusual for congressional leaders to use a consensual policy such as DACA to help pass more controversial legislation such as building the wall with Mexico. Some would argue that it is an essential feature of the legislative process.

The essential nature of conflict and compromise in the legislative process is not very well understood by the general public. Americans often view the type of wheeling and dealing that is necessary to reach compromises as improper and wonder why there is so much conflict. A typical sentiment is "Why does there have to be so much partisan bickering? Can't they just implement the best solutions to our problems?"

In this chapter, we argue that Congress members' behavior is driven by their desire to respond to constituent interests (and the closely related goal of reelection) and constrained by the institutional structures within which they operate (such as the committee system, parties, and leadership). At the same time, members try to be responsible for broader national interests, which are often at odds with their constituents' interests and, consequently, the goal of reelection.

This tension between being responsible and responsive is a source of conflict and requires members of Congress to make tough decisions, often involving political trade-offs and compromises. Should a House member vote for dairy price supports for her local farmers even if it means higher milk prices for families around the nation? Should a senator vote to subsidize the production of tobacco, the biggest cash crop in his state, despite the tremendous health costs it imposes on millions of Americans? Should a member vote to close a military base, as requested by the Pentagon, even if it means the loss of thousands of jobs back home? These are difficult questions. On a complex issue, such as immigration, there is no obvious "responsible" solution and fair-minded people can disagree. These disagreements take on a partisan edge, as most Republicans favor building a stronger border with more limits on legal immigration while most Democrats do not, which obviously leads to conflict. Why is it so hard for Congress to compromise on issues that appear to be consensual, like protecting the Dreamers? How can members of Congress best serve the collective interests of the nation while also representing their local constituents?

Congress and the people

Congress and the Constitution

Congress was the "first branch" in the early decades of our nation's history. The Constitution specified for Congress a vast array of enumerated powers, including regulating commerce, coining money, raising and supporting armies, creating the courts, establishing post offices and roads, declaring war, and levying taxes (see Article I, Section 8, of the Constitution in the appendix). In contrast, the president was given few explicit powers and played a much less prominent role early in our history. Furthermore, much of Congress's authority came from its implicit powers, which were rooted in the elastic clause of Article I of the Constitution, which gives Congress the power "to make all Laws which shall be necessary and proper for carrying into Execution the foregoing Powers."

As noted in Chapter 2, the compromises that gave rise to Congress's initial structure reflected an attempt to reconcile the competing interests of the day (large versus small states, northern versus southern interests, and proponents of strong national power versus state power). These compromises included establishing a system of **bicameralism**, that is, a bicameral (two-chambered) institution made up of a popularly elected House reflecting the relative populations of the states and a Senate chosen by state legislatures, representing each state equally; allowing each enslaved person to count as three-fifths of a person for purposes of apportionment for the House; and setting longer terms for senators (six years) than for House members (two years).

But these compromises also laid the foundation for the split loyalties that members of Congress have: they must respond to both their local constituencies and the nation's interests. Although the Founders hoped that Congress would pass legislation that emphasized the national good over local interests, they also recognized the importance of local constituencies. Thus, the relatively short two-year House term was intended to tie legislators to public sentiment.

At the same time, the *Federalist Papers* made it clear that the new government was by no means a direct democracy that would put all policy questions to the public. In *Federalist 57*, Madison asserted that "the aim of every political constitution is, or ought to be, first to obtain for rulers men who possess most wisdom to discern, and most virtue to pursue, the common good of the society." This common good may often conflict with local concerns, such that members are expected to both "refine and enlarge the debate" to encompass the common good *and* represent their local constituents.

In general, the Founders viewed the Senate as the more likely institution to enlarge the debate and speak for the national interests; it was intended to check the more responsive and passionate House. Because senators were indirectly elected and served longer terms than House members, the Senate was more insulated from the people. A famous (although perhaps fictional) story of an argument between George Washington and Thomas Jefferson points out the differences between the House and Senate. Jefferson did not think the Senate was necessary, while Washington supported having two chambers. During the argument, Jefferson poured some coffee he was drinking into his saucer. Washington asked him why he had done so. "To cool it," replied Jefferson. "Even so," said Washington, "we pour legislation into the senatorial saucer to cool it." This idea of a more responsible Senate survived well into the twentieth century, even after the Seventeenth Amendment in 1913 allowed the direct, popular election of senators.

EXPLAIN HOW MEMBERS OF CONGRESS REPRESENT THEIR CONSTITUENTS AND HOW ELECTIONS HOLD MEMBERS ACCOUNTABLE

AP® FOUNDATIONAL DOCUMENT

bicameralism
The system of having two chambers within one legislative body, like the House and Senate in the U.S. Congress.

Are the DACA Dreamers "Hardened Criminals"?

While Twitter became the preferred method for President Trump to communicate his thoughts on policy issues, the medium has raised some questions. How do we fact-check a tweet? What safeguards are in place to ensure accuracy? The day that the Supreme Court heard oral arguments in the DACA case, the president tweeted his thoughts, presenting an excellent example of this challenge: How do we assess the claim that some DACA recipients have become "hardened criminals"?

It is well known that President Trump often played fast-and-loose with the facts—the *Washington Post* documented 22,247 "false or misleading claims" the president uttered from his first day in office through August 27, 2020.[a] To figure out how to wrestle with this, think about the size of the claim.

Big claims need to be investigated with multiple sources and more extensive reading, but smaller claims can usually be settled by the various media fact-checkers. The claim made by the president is that some DACA recipients are "hardened criminals." This is a very specific claim that can be checked pretty easily with a credible source. For example, FactCheck.org, part of the Annenberg Public Policy Center, provides an excellent analysis. An article on the site points out that on its face, the claim doesn't make sense because "DACA applicants have to meet several eligibility criteria, including not having been convicted of a felony, significant misdemeanor or three or more other misdemeanors." That is, they can't be in the program if they are "hardened criminals."

However, there is something to the president's claim. First, 2,130 DACA recipients from fiscal years 2013–2017 had their status revoked because of criminal or gang activity (this is less than 0.5 percent), so they are no longer in the program. Second, in 2018 the U.S. Citizen and Immigration Services found that of the "770,628 approved DACA applications from 2012 to 2018, 53,792 had a prior arrest or apprehension, and 7,814 had a later arrest or apprehension, after approval and before renewal." This is a much larger number (about 7 percent) and these are people who were in the program. However, on closer inspection most of the arrests were for driving or immigration violations, and there was no indication that any of the DACA recipients were convicted of any crimes (or they would not have been allowed in the program). Also, the article points out that the *Wall Street Journal* reports an average arrest rate of 30 percent for the U.S. adult population, so the DACA participants have an arrest rate that is less than one-fourth the rate of the general public.

Source: Lori Robertson, "The Data on DACA and Crime," FactCheck.org, November 13, 2019, www.factcheck.org/2019/11/the-data-on-daca-and-crime/ (accessed 6/10/20).

Donald J. Trump ✓
@realDonaldTrump

Many of the people in DACA, no longer very young, are far from "angels." Some are very tough, hardened criminals. President Obama said he had no legal right to sign order, but would anyway. If Supreme Court remedies with overturn, a deal will be made with Dems for them to stay!

6:45 AM · Nov 12, 2019 · Twitter for iPhone

30.5K Retweets **77.3K** Likes

Think about it

- **When you read something** in a news story or in a tweet, do you have a favorite fact-checker you consult? This can be a very useful tool for being a good consumer of the news.
- **How do you decide** about the size of the claim that is being made? When would you need to consult more sources to get to the bottom of a story?

Today the Senate is still more insulated than the House. Because of the six-year terms of senators, only one-third of the 100 Senate seats are contested in each election, while all 435 House members are elected every two years. However, differences between the representational roles of the House and the Senate have become muted as senators seem to campaign for reelection 365 days a year, every year, just like House members.[6] This "permanent campaign" means that senators are now less insulated from electoral forces than they were in the past.

The relationship between the president and Congress has also evolved significantly. In the nineteenth century, Congress's roots in geographic constituencies made it well suited for the politics of the time. Although several great presidents left their mark on national politics early in U.S. history (George Washington and Abraham Lincoln, among others), Congress dominated much of the day-to-day politics, which revolved around issues such as the tariff (taxes on imported or exported goods), slavery, and internal improvements such as building roads and canals. Given the tendency to address these issues with patronage and the pork barrel—that is, jobs and policies targeted to benefit specific constituents—Congress was better suited for the daily task of governing than the president was.

Beginning around the turn of the twentieth century and accelerating with the New Deal of the 1930s (which established modern social welfare and regulatory policies), the scope of national policy expanded and politics became more centered in Washington. With this nationalization of politics and the increasing importance of national security issues from World War II through the War on Terror, the president has assumed a more central policy-making role. Nonetheless, the central tensions between representing local and national interests remain essential in understanding the legislative process and the relationship between members of Congress and their constituents.

Congress represents the people (or tries to)

Americans have a love–hate relationship with Congress; that is, we generally love our own member of Congress, but we hate Congress as a whole. Well, "hate" is a strong word, but as we show later in this section, individual members of Congress routinely have approval ratings 30 to 40 points higher than the institution's. One poll found that members of Congress landed third from the bottom in a ranking of 22 professions in terms of perceived honesty and ethical standards, narrowly ahead of car salespeople and lobbyists (nurses and military officers were at the top).[7] A more whimsical poll by Public Policy Polling asked respondents questions such as "What do you have a higher opinion of, Congress or root canals?" Root canals won handily, 56 percent to 32 percent. Congress was also less popular than head lice, traffic jams, and cockroaches, but narrowly beat out telemarketers and had a comfortable margin over North Korea, the Kardashians, and meth labs.[8] Why is Congress so unpopular? How do members of Congress try to represent their constituents? And how do elections influence this important dynamic?

Types of Representation The relationships between constituents and their member of Congress can be characterized in two basic ways: as both descriptive and substantive. Descriptive representation occurs when members of Congress "look like" their constituents in demographic or socioeconomic terms. For example, are members African American, Latino, or White; male or female; Catholic, Protestant, or some other religion; middle-class or upper-class? Many people believe that this kind of representation is a distinct value in itself. Having positive role models for various demographic groups helps

A ROW IN CONGRESS.

The Founders viewed the House as more passionate than the Senate, or as the "hot coffee" that needed to be cooled in the "saucer" of the Senate. This perception probably did not include coming to blows over differences in policy as Congressmen Albert G. Brown and John A. Wilcox did in 1851 about whether Mississippi should secede from the Union.

permanent campaign
The continual quest for reelection that is rooted in high-cost professional campaigns that are increasingly reliant on consultants and expensive media campaigns.

pork barrel
Legislative appropriations that benefit specific constituents, created with the aim of helping local representatives win reelection.

The American Republic will endure until the day Congress discovers that it can bribe the public with the public's money.

—Alexis de Tocqueville,
French diplomat and author

descriptive representation
Representation in which a member of Congress shares the characteristics (such as gender, race, religion, or ethnicity) of his or her constituents.

Descriptive Representation in the 116th Congress

Compared with a generation ago, the number of women and racial and ethnic minorities in Congress has increased. But on these dimensions, how representative of the people is Congress? How close does Congress come to "looking like us"? What do the facts say?

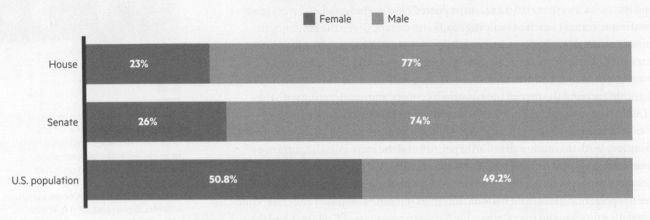

Gender in Congress

- Female
- Male

	Female	Male
House	23%	77%
Senate	26%	74%
U.S. population	50.8%	49.2%

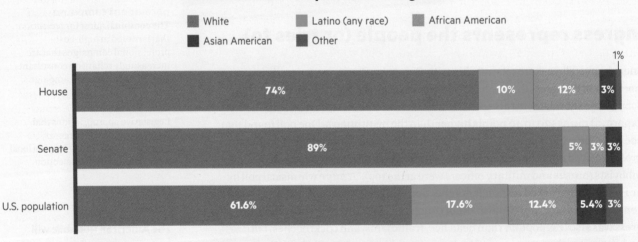

Racial and Ethnic Composition of Congress

- White
- Asian American
- Latino (any race)
- Other
- African American

	White	Latino (any race)	African American	Asian American	Other
House	74%	10%	12%	3%	1%
Senate	89%	5%	3%	3%	
U.S. population	61.6%	17.6%	12.4%	5.4%	3%

Sources: Congressional data from Jennifer Manning, "Membership of the 116th Congress: A Profile," Congressional Research Service, June 1, 2020, https://fas.org/sgp/crs/misc/R45583.pdf; population data from U.S. Census Bureau, "Quick Facts: United States," July 1, 2019, www.census.gov/quickfacts/fact/table/US/PST045219 (both accessed 6/11/20).

Think about it

- **Which comes closer to "looking like us,"** the House or the Senate?
- **How could having more women or racial and ethnic minorities** in Congress affect legislation and policy decisions?
- **Latinos now make up the largest ethnic minority** in the United States, yet they still lag behind African Americans in terms of representation in the House. Why do you think this is?

create greater trust in the system. Moreover, constituents benefit from being represented by someone who shares something as basic as their skin color.

Descriptive representation is also related to the perceived responsiveness of a member of Congress. In general, constituents report higher levels of satisfaction with representatives who are of their same racial or ethnic background. Thus, descriptively represented constituents are more likely than those who are not to assume that their interests are being represented.[9] If you doubt that descriptive representation makes a difference, ask yourself whether it would be fair if all 435 House members and 100 senators were White male Protestants. Although the demographics of Congress are considerably more diverse than this, the legislature does not come close to "looking like us" on a nationwide scale (see the What Do the Facts Say? feature on p. 134). This is especially true in the Senate, where only ten African Americans and nine Latinos have served in the history of the institution (in the 116th Congress, 2019–2021, there were three African Americans and five Latinos in the Senate).[10]

Although descriptive representation is important, it goes only so far. More important than a member's race, gender, or religion, many argue, is the *substance* of what that person does. The fact that a representative shares some characteristics with you does not necessarily mean that he or she will represent your interests. However, extensive research demonstrates a link between descriptive representation and how our elected leaders represent us: minority members of Congress are more likely to pay attention to racial issues than White members are, and female members are more committed to women's issues than male members are. For example, political scientist Michele Swers finds that women senators are more active than male senators on women's issues, playing a key role on fair pay, abortion, women's rights, and representation on the Supreme Court.[11]

Substantive representation involves *how* the member serves constituents' interests. Two long-standing models of this kind of representation are (1) the **trustee**, who represents the interests of constituents from a distance, weighing numerous national, collective, local, and moral concerns; and (2) the **delegate**, who carries out the direct desires of the voters. In a sense, trustees are more concerned with being responsible and delegates are more interested in being responsive.

One of the most famous examples of a representative acting as a trustee was Marjorie Margolies-Mezvinsky (D-PA) in a crucial 1993 vote on President Clinton's budget, which included controversial tax increases and spending cuts to balance the budget. Hours before the vote, she told reporters that she would vote against the budget, in accordance with her constituents' wishes. But she had also promised Clinton she would support the bill if her vote was needed. As she cast the critical vote in the 218–216 cliff-hanger (in which she fulfilled her promise to the president), she did what she thought was in the best long-term interests of her constituents and the nation, even though it meant voting against their wishes, which led to her defeat in the next election. More recently, in 2008 bipartisan majorities in the House and Senate voted for the hugely unpopular Troubled Asset Relief Program (TARP or, as its critics called it, the Wall Street bailout) because President Bush and congressional leaders convinced them it was necessary to prevent a complete economic meltdown.

In contrast, a delegate does not have to worry about angering voters because he or she simply does what voters want. Examples are so numerous it is pointless to single out one member for attention: when it comes to tax cuts, agricultural subsidies, increases in Medicare payments, or new highway projects, hundreds of representatives act as delegates for their districts' interests.

Truth be told, nearly all members act like trustees in some circumstances and like delegates in others. The third model of representation captures this reality: the **politico** is more likely to act as a delegate on issues that are highly salient to his or her constituency

Suppose you were an idiot. And suppose you were a member of Congress. But I repeat myself.

—**Mark Twain,** author

DID YOU KNOW?

$1 million

was the average net worth of the 116th Congress (2019–2021). More than half of all members of Congress are millionaires.
Source: Center for Responsive Politics

substantive representation
Representation in which a member of Congress serves constituents' interests and shares their policy concerns.

trustee
A member of Congress who represents constituents' interests while also taking into account national, collective, and moral concerns that sometimes cause the member to vote against the preference of a majority of constituents.

delegate
A member of Congress who loyally represents constituents' direct interests.

politico
A member of Congress who acts as a delegate on issues that constituents care about (such as immigration reform) and as a trustee on more complex or less salient issues (such as some foreign policy or regulatory matters).

Members of Congress spend a good deal of time in their districts, developing relationships with constituents. Here, Representative Elise Stefanik (R-NY) speaks with constituents at a community open house at the Fort Drum Youth Center in Fort Drum, New York.

(such as immigration reform or farm subsidies) but as a trustee on less salient or very complex issues (such as some foreign policies). Therefore, the crucial component of representation is the nature of the constituency and how the member of Congress attempts to balance and represent constituents' conflicting needs and desires.

The Role of the Constituency Most voters do not monitor their representatives' behavior closely. Can representation work if voters are not paying attention?

Members of Congress behave as if voters were paying attention, even when constituents are inattentive. Incumbents know that at election time challengers may raise issues that become salient after the public thinks about them, so they try to deter challengers by anticipating what the constituents would want *if* they were fully informed.[12] For example, the public hadn't thought much about voting by mail, but it became an issue in the 2020 elections when the COVID-19 pandemic forced many states to cut down on in-person voting. President Trump claimed that voting by mail was an effort by Democrats to steal the election, while many states argued that it was a way to protect voters from being exposed to the virus. Savvy incumbents would have tried to stake out a position consistent with what the voters would want *before* a strong challenger raised the issue in a campaign. Richard F. Fenno, one of the leading congressional scholars of the twentieth century, points out that some segments of the constituency are more attentive and more important for a member's reelection than others (see Figure 4.1).[13] For example, the "primary constituency" probably had a well-formed view about voting by mail early in the election season because they are more politically engaged, while many in the "geographic constituency" may have become aware of the issue only when it was raised by a challenger.

Another way to examine the representative–constituency relationship is to look at differences across districts. How do districts vary? First, they differ in size: Senate "districts" (that is, states) vary in terms of area and population. House districts all have about 760,000 people, but they vary tremendously in geographic size, from Alaska's 663,000 square miles to New York's 13th district with 10.25 square miles. Second, districts differ in terms of who lives there and what they want from government. Some districts are located in poor city neighborhoods, where voters' concerns are

FIGURE
4.1

How Do Representatives See Their Constituents?

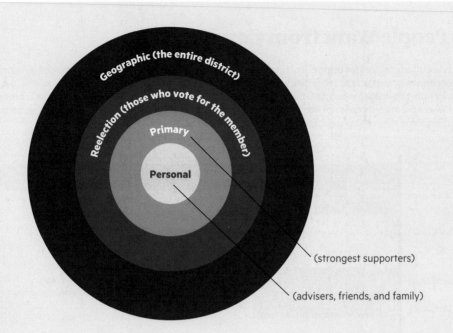

The concentric circles of a congressional constituency illustrate the various parts of a district that a member represents. Can you think of an issue on which House members would be more responsive to their reelection constituency than to their geographic constituency?

Source: Based on Richard F. Fenno, *Home Style: House Members in Their Districts* (Boston: Little, Brown, 1978).

economic development, crime control, antipoverty programs, and looser immigration regulations. Some are wealthy and urban, where citizens are more supportive of foreign aid and higher taxes to support social programs. Some are suburban, where funding for education and transportation is critical. Some are conservative and rural, where agricultural policies, gun rights, and support for tax cuts dominate. Districts vary from the religious to the secular, from domination by one industry to a diversified corporate base to no industry at all. Some consider government a force for good, while others argue that government should get off people's backs. And some districts are a mixture of all these things.

Because districts are so multifaceted, the legislators they elect differ from one another as well. Regardless of the office, most voters want to elect someone whose policy positions are close to theirs. As a result, legislators tend to reflect the central tendencies of their districts. At one level, electing a legislature that "thinks like America" sounds good: if legislators act and think like their districts, then the legislature will contain a good mixture of the interests representing the country or state. But this often makes finding compromise difficult. We elect legislators to get things done, but they may be unable to agree on anything because their disagreements are too fundamental to bridge. Consider abortion rights. The country is sharply divided on this issue, as are the House, the Senate, and most state legislatures. The fact that legislators have not come to a decision on this issue is no surprise: just as citizens disagree, so do their elected representatives.

Despite the vast differences between congressional constituencies, voters want many of the same things: a healthy economy, a safe country (in terms of national defense and local crime), good schools, and effective health care. Figure 4.2 reports responses to a survey about how citizens feel that legislators should do their jobs. The survey shows tensions between being a delegate and a trustee. Respondents want their representatives to "vote for what the people they represent want" and "spend more time at home," and they show little interest in having the representatives "spend more time in Washington." Thus, responsibilities for national interests may be more difficult for members of Congress to explain to their constituents.

FIGURE 4.2

What Do People Want from Congress?

Members of Congress are often criticized for being out of touch with their constituents. Based on a *USA Today* poll, Americans seem to want their congressional members to vote in line with their constituents' views, to work across party lines, and to spend more time in the district rather than Washington, D.C. But what happens if these goals conflict? What if the member represents a very partisan district where the majority does not want him or her to work with the other party? Also, is there no room for trustees who follow their conscience and stick to their principles?

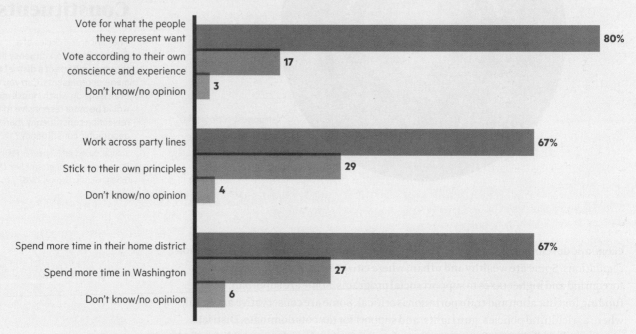

Vote for what the people they represent want — 80%
Vote according to their own conscience and experience — 17
Don't know/no opinion — 3

Work across party lines — 67%
Stick to their own principles — 29
Don't know/no opinion — 4

Spend more time in their home district — 67%
Spend more time in Washington — 27
Don't know/no opinion — 6

Source: Susan Page and Kendall Breitman, "Divided We Still Stand—and Getting Used to It," *USA Today*, March 23, 2014, www.usatoday.com/story/news/politics/2014/03/23/congress-divided-poll/6792585/ (accessed 6/10/20).

Members of Congress want to keep their jobs

Members' relationships to their constituents also must be understood within the context of their desire to be reelected. Political scientist David R. Mayhew argues in *Congress: The Electoral Connection* that members of Congress are "single-minded seekers of reelection."[14] Members certainly hold multiple goals, including making good policy, but if they cannot maintain their seats, then they cannot attain other goals in office.

After assuming that reelection is central, Mayhew asks this question: "Members of Congress may be electorally motivated, but are they in a position to do anything about it?"[15] Although individual members of Congress cannot do much to alter national economic or political forces that may affect voters' choices, they can control their own activities in the House or Senate. The importance of the **electoral connection** in explaining the behavior of members of Congress seems especially clear for marginal incumbents who are constantly trying to shore up their electoral base. But for those from safe districts, why should they worry?

Incumbents Work toward Reelection While objectively it looks as though about 90 percent of House members (and a large proportion of senators) are absolutely safe (see Figure 4.3), incumbents realize that this security is not guaranteed. Even in elections with relatively low turnover overall, many incumbents are "running scared";

electoral connection
The idea that congressional behavior is centrally motivated by members' desire for reelection.

House and Senate Reelection Rates, 1956–2020

FIGURE
4.3

The whole House is up for reelection every two years, so the line showing the reelection of House members in a given election year represents the percentage of the entire House. Since senators are up for reelection every six years, only one-third of the members are seeking reelection every two years. The line for the Senate represents the percentage of those who won who were up for reelection in that election year. Why do you think that House members have an easier time getting reelected than senators?

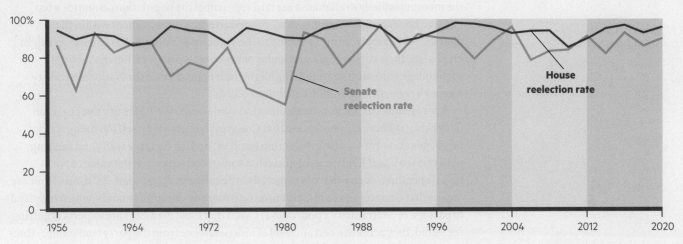

Sources: 1956–2012 percentages were compiled from Norman J. Ornstein, Thomas E. Mann, Michael J. Malbin, and Andrew Rugg, "Vital Statistics on Congress," www.brookings.edu/vitalstats, pp. 49–50 (accessed 7/26/20); 2014–2018 percentages were calculated from OpenSecrets.org (accessed 11/7/18) and 2020 percentages from CNN Politics, www.cnn.com/election/2020/results (accessed 11/8/20).

in every election, a few supposedly safe incumbents are unexpectedly defeated, and members tend to think that it could happen to them the next time around. Mayhew warns: "When we say 'Congressman Smith is unbeatable,' we do not mean that there is nothing he could do that would lose him his seat." This actually means: "Congressman Smith is unbeatable as long as he continues to do the things that he is doing."[16] Members recognize that becoming inattentive to their district, being on the wrong side of a key string of votes, or failing to bring home the district's share of federal benefits could cost them their seats. A potential challenger is always waiting in the wings.

Mayhew outlines three ways that members promote their chances for reelection: advertising, credit claiming, and position taking. Each approach shapes the way members relate to their constituents. "Advertising" in this context refers to appeals or appearances without issue content that get the member's name in front of the public in a favorable way. Advertising includes activities associated with "working the district," such as attending town meetings; appearing in a parade; going to a local Rotary Club lunch; or sending letters of congratulation for graduations, birthdays, or anniversaries. Members of Congress also spend a fair amount of time meeting with their constituents in Washington, D.C., including seeing school groups, tourists, and interest groups from their districts.

In "credit claiming," the member of Congress takes credit for something of value to voters—most commonly, pork-barrel policies targeted to benefit specific constituents or the district as a whole. The goods must be specific and small enough in scale that the member of Congress may believably claim credit. In other words, it is far less credible to take credit for a national drop in violent crime or an increase in SAT scores than for the renovations at a local veterans' hospital or a highway improvement grant. The other main source of credit claiming is casework for individual constituents who request help with tasks such as tracking down a lost Social Security check or expediting the processing of a passport. This activity, like advertising, has both district-based and Washington-based components.

"Position taking" refers to any public statement—such as a roll call vote, speech, editorial, or position paper—about a topic of interest to constituents or interest groups. This may be the toughest aspect of a member's job, because, on many issues, the member is likely to alienate a certain segment of the population no matter what position he or she takes. Members try to appeal to specific audiences within their district. For example, while speaking to the Veterans of Foreign Wars members might emphasize their support for a particular new weapons program, but in meetings with college students they might highlight their opposition to the National Security Agency's collection of millions of phone records.

Representatives' focus on reelection has some costs. We'll identify five common ones here: (1) There is a perception that Congress has granted itself too many special privileges aimed at securing reelection (such as funding for large staffs and sending mail at no cost). (2) Evidence suggests that some voters question the value of pork-barrel spending, even when it is targeted to their district.[17] (3) Members' desire to please means that Congress has a difficult time refusing any group's demands, which may lead to passage of contradictory policies. (4) Given that most members are experts at getting reelected, they achieve a certain level of independence from the party leadership—that is, they do not depend on party leaders for their reelection. This fact contributes to the fragmentation of Congress and creates difficulties for congressional leaders as they attempt to shepherd policies through the legislative maze. (5) Time spent actively campaigning takes time away from the responsibilities of enacting laws and overseeing their implementation.

The desire to be reelected influences House members' and senators' behavior both in their districts and in Congress. Consider the early career of Senator Tammy Baldwin (D-WI), who served as the representative of Wisconsin's 2nd congressional district from 1999 to 2013. Initially elected in 1998, she was Wisconsin's first female representative and the first openly gay person ever elected to a freshman term in Congress.[18] In her first two elections, she won with the overwhelming support of liberal voters in Madison, but she lost the surrounding rural areas and suburbs, narrowly winning districtwide. Baldwin recognized that she needed to shore up support outside Madison, and she spent time over the next several years meeting with constituents in the rural and suburban parts of her district. She also explored issues important to these voters, such as the dairy price support program and the problem of chronic wasting disease in Wisconsin deer. Having built up her electoral base (and having benefited from favorable redistricting in 2002), she cruised to victories in her next two elections, winning nearly two-thirds of the vote. After winning reelection to the House four more times, she became the first lesbian elected to the Senate in 2012 and was reelected in 2018.

The Incumbency Advantage Members' success at pleasing constituents produces large election rewards. As Figure 4.3 shows, very few members are defeated in their reelection races. One way that political scientists have documented the growth of the incumbency advantage is to examine the electoral margins in House elections. If a member is elected with less than 55 percent of the vote, he or she is said to hold a marginal seat. Since the late 1960s, the number of marginal districts has been declining. Having fewer marginal districts does not necessarily translate into fewer incumbent defeats, but in the past two decades incumbent reelection rates have been near record high levels, with 95–98 percent of House incumbents winning in many years.[19]

In 2008, in an election that many called transformational, 94 percent of House incumbents were still reelected. Even in the "tsunami" election of 2010, in which Republicans made the largest gains in the House since 1948, picking up 63 seats, 86 percent of all incumbents were reelected. In the 2018 midterm, in which Democrats picked up 41 seats and regained control of the House, 91 percent of incumbents were reelected. Why are incumbents so successful? Scholars have offered several reasons for this increase in incumbency advantage.

In the District: Home Style One explanation for the increasing incumbency advantage is rooted in the diversity of congressional districts and states. Members typically respond to the diversity in their districts by developing an appropriate home style: a way of relating to the district.[20] A home style shapes the way members allocate resources, the way incumbents present themselves to their district, and the way they explain their policy positions.

Given the variation among districts, members' home styles vary as well. In some rural districts it is important for representatives to have local roots and voters expect extensive contact with members. Urban districts expect a different kind of style. They have a more mobile population, so it is not crucial to be homegrown. Voters expect less direct contact and place more emphasis on how members explain their policy positions. Incumbency advantage may be explained in part by the skill with which members have cultivated their individual home styles in the last two decades. Members are spending more time at home and less time in Washington than was true a generation ago. This familiarity with the voters has helped them remain in office.

Table 4.1 shows how one member, Senator Tammy Baldwin, spent her time in Washington and in her district as a House member. In general, a legislator's workday in the Capitol is split among committee meetings, briefings, staff meetings, meetings with constituents, and various dinners and fund-raisers with interest groups and other organizations, punctuated by dashes to the floor of the House or Senate to vote. Days in the district are spent meeting with constituents to explain what is happening in Washington and to listen to voters' concerns.

Campaign Fund-Raising Raising money is also key to staying in office. Incumbents need money to pay for campaign staff, travel, and advertising. It takes at least $1 million to make a credible challenge to an incumbent in most districts, and in many areas with expensive media markets the minimum price tag is $2 million or more. Few challengers can raise that much money. The gap between incumbent and challenger spending has grown dramatically in the past decade, and incumbents now spend about three times as much, on average, as challengers.[21] However, for the first time ever, Senate challengers outspent incumbents in 2020. (For more on campaign finance, see Chapters 12 and 13.)

Money also functions as a deterrent to potential challengers. A sizable reelection fund signals that an incumbent knows how to raise money and will run a strong campaign. The aim is to convince would-be challengers that they have only a slim chance of beating the incumbent—and to convince contributors and party organizations that there's no point in trying to find or support a challenger. This last point is crucial in explaining incumbency advantage, because it is nearly impossible for a weak challenger to beat an incumbent. Consider that only 10–15 percent of challengers in a typical election year have any previous elective experience; when such a high proportion of challengers are amateurs, it is not surprising that so many incumbents win.

Constituency Service Another thing incumbents do to get reelected is "work their districts," taking every opportunity to meet with constituents, listen to their concerns,

DID YOU KNOW?

On average, House incumbents raised

$1,870,700

for their campaigns in 2020. The average Senate incumbent raised $17,083,000. This is compared with $626,411 and $18,497,000 for the average House and Senate challengers.

Source: OpenSecrets.org

TABLE
4.1

Typical Workdays for a Congressional Representative

Members of Congress are generally busy from morning until late at night, both in Washington, D.C., and in their districts, attending meetings and events. This is the actual schedule for Tammy Baldwin when she represented Wisconsin's 2nd congressional district in the House.

In Washington, D.C. (votes scheduled throughout the day)

9:15–9:45	Office time
9:45–10:00	Caucus, Democratic members, Subcommittee on Energy and Environment on markup legislation
10:00–12:00	Markup H.R. 3276, H.R. 3258, H.R. 2868, Subcommittee on Energy and Environment
11:30–11:45	Step outside markup to meet with constituents on specifics of health care reform legislation
12:00–12:15	Travel to Department of Justice
12:15–1:15	Lunch with Attorney General Eric Holder
1:30–1:45	Meet with health care CEO on specifics of health care reform legislation
2:00–3:00	Meet with members who support single-payer health care amendment
3:00–4:30	Markup H.R. 3792, Subcommittee on Health
4:30–5:30	Office time
5:30–6:00	Caucus, Democratic members, Energy and Commerce Committee on financial services bill
6:00–6:30	Meet with legislative staff
6:30–7:00	Meet with chief of staff
7:00–7:50	Office time
8:00–10:00	Dinner with chief of staff and political adviser

In the District

7:00 ET–8:00 CT	Fly from Washington, D.C., to Madison, WI
8:15–10:30	Free time at home
10:30–10:40	Phone interview with area radio station on constituent survey, health care reform, and upcoming listening session
12:15–12:25	Travel to office
12:25–1:00	Office time, edit/sign correspondence
1:00–1:20	Travel to Madison West High School
1:30–1:55	Remarks at school plaza dedication ceremony
2:00–2:30	Travel to Stoughton, WI
2:45–5:00	Listening session (originally scheduled for one hour but continued until all present could speak)
5:00–5:40	Travel home
5:15–5:20	Phone interview with University of Wisconsin student radio station
6:15–6:45	Travel to Middleton, WI
7:00–8:00	Attend and give brief remarks at NAACP annual banquet
8:05–8:25	Travel home

Note: The authors would like to thank then-representative Tammy Baldwin and her press secretary, Jerilyn Goodman, for sharing this information. Ms. Goodman emphasized that there really isn't a "typical day" for a member but said that these two days illustrate the workload. Baldwin was reelected to the U.S. Senate in 2018 (having won her first Senate term in 2012).

Representative Lauren Underwood (D-IL, center) speaks to constituents at the 2019 Fox Valley Women's March in Geneva, Illinois. "Position taking," such as in this speech, is an important way representatives show they are responsive to their constituents' interests.

and perform casework (helping constituents interact with government programs or agencies). Most legislators travel around their districts or states with several staffers whose job is to follow up with people who meet the incumbent, write down their contact information, and note what the incumbent has promised to do for them. High levels of constituency service may help explain why some incumbents have become electorally secure.

Members of Congress love doing constituency service because it is an easy way to make voters happy. If a member can help a constituent solve a problem, that person will be more likely to support the member in the future.[22] Many voters might give the incumbent some credit simply for being willing to listen. Therefore, most members devote a significant portion of their staff to constituency service, publish newsletters that tout their good deeds on behalf of constituents, and solicit citizens' requests for help through their newsletters and websites. Most House members have a "How can I help?" type of link on their home page that connects to information on government agencies, grants, internships, service academies, and visiting Washington, D.C.

Most House members work their districts to an extreme; they are said to be in the "Tuesday to Thursday Club," meaning they are in Washington only during the middle of the week and spend the rest of their time at home in their districts. These members go to diners and coffee shops on Saturday mornings to chat, spend the day at public events in their "Meet Your Representative" RV, then hit the bowling alleys at night to meet a few more people. One member has even joked that his wife has given up sending him out for groceries because he spends three hours talking with people while getting a loaf of bread.

This combination of factors gives incumbents substantial advantages over candidates who might run against them. By virtue of their position, they can help constituents who have problems with an agency or a program. They attract media attention because of their actions in office; small local newspapers will even reprint members' press releases verbatim. Members can use the money and other resources associated with their position for casework and contact with voters (trips home to their district and the salaries of their staffers who do constituency service are taxpayer funded). And they use their official position as a platform for raising campaign cash. A contributor who donates as a way to gain access to the policy-making process will be inclined to give to someone already in office. Finally, most incumbents represent states

House reelection rates have been upwards of 90 percent for decades, but incumbents still campaign vigorously. Congressman Steve King (R-IA), a nine-term incumbent, lost his 2020 primary bid to Iowa state senator Randy Feenstra following widespread scrutiny over King's history of racist remarks.

or districts whose partisan balance (the number of likely supporters of their party versus the number likely to prefer the other party) is skewed in their favor—if it weren't, they probably wouldn't have won the seat in the first place.

National Forces in Congressional Elections There is also another consequence of the electoral connection. Because congressional politics tends to be local, voters generally are not strongly influenced by the president or the national parties. Because most incumbents can insulate themselves from national forces, it is more difficult to hold members of Congress accountable. For example, in the 2020 elections 63 percent of voters believed the nation was "on the wrong track." Yet 96 percent of House incumbents won reelection.

Many House and Senate candidates distance themselves from the national party. For example, in a 2018 House race in suburban Philadelphia, Republican nominee Dan David was asked if he wanted President Trump to campaign for him and he replied, "I would like the president to do his job and I'll do mine."[23] (He lost by nearly 27 points.) In fact, 2018 was an example of nationalized "wave" elections in which national issues overwhelmed incumbents' attempts to insulate themselves. As Democrats regained control of the House, 29 Republican incumbents were defeated but no Democratic incumbents were. In the 2010 midterms, the same thing happened to moderate Democrats, who were ousted by voters who believed the government had gone too far in responding to the recession and providing access to health care. These national forces led the Democrats to lose 63 House seats (and 6 Senate seats), with the result that the Republicans regained control of the House.

National forces in congressional elections also may be evident in presidential years. In 2008, Republicans faced a backlash against Bush, whose approval ratings had hit record lows. Republican members of Congress avoided being seen with the president, Democrats highlighted their opponents' earlier support for him, and Democrats gained unified control of government. The 2016 presidential election featured two nominees, Hillary Clinton and Donald Trump, who had the highest negative ratings of any pair of major-party candidates. Republican congressional candidates were especially likely to distance themselves from their party's nominee. President Trump won a tight race, but Democrats picked up two seats in the Senate and six in the House (but Republicans retained majorities in both chambers). In 2020, Joe Biden defeated Trump, but it was a status quo election, rather than the blue wave Democrats were hoping for. Democrats picked up only one Senate seat and Republicans gained about eight House seats, but neither chamber changed party control.

Overall, the localized nature of congressional elections and the incumbency advantage promote congressional stability in the face of presidential change. This dynamic has profound implications for governance because it increases the likelihood that different parties will control the presidency and Congress. Divided government complicates accountability. Because the president and Congress have become adept at blaming each other when things go wrong, voters do not always know who to vote out of office when they're unhappy with the status quo.

Redistricting connects representation and elections

The shape and makeup of congressional districts are critical to understanding representation in Congress and the electoral connection. District boundaries determine who is eligible to vote in any given congressional race, and these boundaries are re-drawn every 10 years, after each national census. **Redistricting** is usually the task of state legislatures. Its official purpose is to ensure that districts are roughly equal in population, which in turn ensures that every vote counts equally in determining the composition of the legislature. This decennial process placed additional significance on state elections in 2020, as control over redistricting was at stake. Final results were not available as this edition went to press, but it appears that Republicans picked up control of a net of two state legislative chambers and two governorships and now have unified control in 23 states. Democrats control 15 state governments and 12 states have split control.

District populations vary over time as people move from state to state or from one part of a state to another. At the national level, states gain or lose legislative seats after each census through **apportionment**, which is the process of dividing the fixed number of House seats (435) among the states based on increases and decreases in state populations. Thus, states growing the fastest gain seats, and states that are not growing as fast or that are losing population lose seats (for example, after the 2010 census Texas gained four seats in Congress while Ohio lost two). After the 2020 census, Texas is projected to pick up three seats, Florida will gain two seats, and at least 15 more states will gain or lose a single seat.[24] The one legislature in America that is not redistricted is the U.S. Senate, which has two legislators elected per state. Voters in small states thus have proportionally more influence than those in large states when it comes to the Senate.

In theory, redistricting proceeds from a set of principles that define what districts should look like. One criterion is that districts should be roughly equal in population based on the principles of "one-person, one-vote" established by the Supreme Court with *Baker v. Carr* in the 1960s.[25] They should also reflect "communities of interest," grouping like-minded voters into the same district. There are also technical criteria, including compactness (districts should not have extremely bizarre shapes) and contiguity (one part of a district cannot be completely separated from the rest of the district). Mapmakers also try to respect traditional natural boundaries, avoid splitting municipalities, preserve existing districts, and avoid diluting the voting power of racial minorities.

redistricting
Re-drawing the geographic boundaries of legislative districts. This happens every 10 years to ensure that districts remain roughly equal in population.

apportionment
The process of assigning the 435 seats in the House to the states based on increases or decreases in state population.

**AP®
SUPREME
COURT CASE**

Baker v. Carr
The 1962 Supreme Court case that established the doctrine of "one-person, one-vote" and held that challenges to redistricting were protected by the equal protection clause of the Fourteenth Amendment and could be heard by federal courts.

Partisan Redistricting Although the preceding principles are important, they are not the driving force in the redistricting process. Suppose a Democrat holds a House seat from an urban district populated mainly by citizens with strong Democratic Party ties. After a census, the Republican-dominated state legislature develops a new plan that extends the representative's district into the suburbs, claiming that the change counteracts population declines within the city by adding suburban voters. However, these suburban voters will likely be Republicans, increasing the chance that the Democrat will face strong opposition in future elections and lose his or her seat. Such changes have an important impact on voters as well. Voters who are "shifted" to a new district by a change in boundaries may be unable to vote for the incumbent they have supported for years and may instead get a representative who doesn't share their views.

In congressional redistricting, a reduction in the number of seats allocated to a state can lead to districting plans that put two incumbents in the same district, forcing them to run against each other. Incumbents from one party use these opportunities to defeat incumbents from the other party. Both parties use this technique and other tools of creative cartography to gain partisan advantage.

These attempts to use the redistricting process for political advantage are called **gerrymandering**. The term is named after Elbridge Gerry, a Massachusetts House member and governor, vice president under James Madison, and author of the original partisan redistricting plan in 1812 (including a district with a thin, winding shape resembling a salamander). While partisan motivations have produced some funny-looking districts (see Nuts & Bolts 4.1 for examples of a partisan gerrymander and redistricting strategies), the courts have allowed the practice to continue until recently. More than 30 years ago, the Supreme Court ruled that partisan gerrymandering *may* be unconstitutional, but over the next three decades the Court struggled to find a standard that allowed it to distinguish between partisan bias so extreme that it violated the Constitution and normal partisan politics.[26]

Then, from 2016 through 2018, a flood of litigation in federal and state courts showed judges' increasing willingness to rule that parties had gone too far in their redistricting plans. Increasingly sophisticated mapping programs and access to detailed political data allowed parties to slice and dice districts with increasing precision, yielding partisan maps that were no longer acceptable to the courts. In Wisconsin, North Carolina, Maryland, and Pennsylvania, federal and state courts struck down state legislative and congressional maps that they ruled to be unfairly partisan (see the Take a Stand feature for more on the debate on this topic). However, in June 2019 the Supreme Court took up cases from North Carolina and Maryland and concluded that "partisan gerrymandering claims present political questions beyond the reach of the federal courts" because they lacked a "limited and precise standard" for evaluating the extent of partisan bias. While recognizing that partisan gerrymandering may "reasonably seem unjust" and is "incompatible with democratic principles," the Court left it up to states to resolve this problem. Justice Kagan issued a scathing dissent, writing, "For the first time ever, this Court refuses to remedy a constitutional violation because it thinks the task beyond judicial capabilities. . . . Of all times to abandon the Court's duty to declare the law, this was not the one. The practices challenged in these cases imperil our system of government. Part of the Court's role in that system is to defend its foundations. None is more important than free and fair elections."[27]

Racial Redistricting Redistricting may yield boundaries that look highly unusual. During the 1992 redistricting process in North Carolina, the Justice Department told state legislators that they needed to create two districts with majority populations of

gerrymandering
Attempting to use the process of re-drawing district boundaries to benefit a political party, protect incumbents, or change the proportion of minority voters in a district.

Types of Gerrymanders

We have learned that the redistricting process is a powerful tool politicians can use to help their party, or individual members, win and maintain seats in Congress. Let's look at two key types of gerrymandering.

Partisan gerrymanders

Elected officials from one party draw district lines that benefit candidates from their party and hurt candidates from other parties. This usually occurs when one party has majorities in both houses of the state legislature and occupies the governorship and can therefore enact redistricting legislation without input from the minority party.

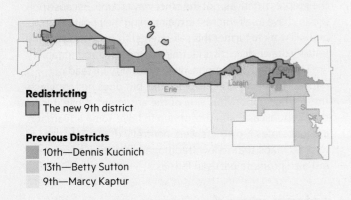

Redistricting

■ The new 9th district

Previous Districts

■ 10th—Dennis Kucinich
■ 13th—Betty Sutton
□ 9th—Marcy Kaptur

After the 2010 census, Ohio lost two seats in Congress (see our discussion of apportionment on p. 145). Republicans controlled the redistricting process and wanted the loss of seats to come from the Democrats. So the Republicans drew a new 9th congressional district that cut across the districts of three existing Democratic members of Congress. Obviously only one could win the Democratic primary—that happened to be Marcy Kaptur. Democrats Kucinich and Sutton had to leave Congress.

Racial gerrymanders

Redistricting is used to help or hurt the chances of minority legislative candidates. The Voting Rights Act (VRA) of 1965 mandated that districting plans for many parts of the South be approved by the U.S. Department of Justice or a Washington, D.C., district court. Subsequent interpretations of the 1982 VRA amendments and Supreme Court decisions led to the creation of districts in which racial minorities are in the majority. The aim of these majority-minority districts was to raise the percentage of African-American and Latino elected officials.

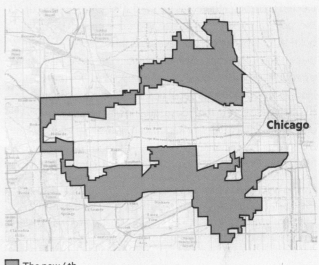

Chicago

■ The new 4th congressional district

Illinois's 4th congressional district is a clear example of racial gerrymandering. The district has a very odd shape, but it incorporates two heavily Latino areas. (The northern part has a high Puerto Rican population and the southern part is largely Mexican; both areas are heavily Democratic.) This district was a stronghold of Democrat Luis Gutiérrez, who is of Puerto Rican descent, and is currently held by Chuy García, who is of Mexican descent. It is seen as a safe district for Democrats.

"Why Should I Care?" Many people question whether or not their vote "counts." While all votes count, actions like gerrymandering are attempts to manipulate the results to ensure particular geographic areas are overwhelmingly Republican or Democratic, thus diluting the influence of minority-party voters in those regions.

Partisan Redistricting

Partisan redistricting is the re-drawing of legislative district lines in a way that gives one party an advantage. As we have noted, until recently the courts allowed the practice as a normal part of politics: of course, the majority party that controls the redistricting process has tried to stack the deck in its favor. When combined with the reluctance of the Supreme Court to address "political questions"—those that are better left to the elected branches—there was a powerful incentive to stay out of the "political thicket."[78] But as mapping software and "big data" political tools became readily available, the extent of partisan bias in redistricting became more pronounced. In Pennsylvania, a Republican gerrymander gave the party 13 of the state's 18 U.S. House seats, despite the Republicans' failure to win a majority of the statewide vote in the House races. In Maryland, a Democratic gerrymander turned a safe Republican House seat into a Democratic seat. Should this practice be reined in by the Court? Is it fair that some votes seem to count more than others?

Redistricting is always partisan. Those who say that the courts should stay out of redistricting argue that the practice is inherently partisan. The majority party will always try to solidify or expand its power when it has the opportunity. This has been true since the earliest years of our nation. Furthermore, those on this side of the argument say that courts are not well suited to draw legislative maps; this responsibility should remain with the state legislatures.

A second line of argument concedes that the process has gotten a little out of hand, but contends that the standard for redistricting should be partisan *neutrality* rather than partisan *fairness*. That is, rather than trying to make sure that the votes for candidates of one party have the same collective impact on the outcome of elections as the votes for the other party (fairness), the redistricting process should simply ignore partisanship (neutrality). Another perspective, adopted by the Supreme Court when it deemed partisan gerrymandering to be a political question, is that there are no objective standards to identify partisan fairness, so the problem cannot be resolved by the courts.

Partisan redistricting undermines democracy. The other side of the debate counters that just because we have always had partisan gerrymandering doesn't make it right. Indeed, democracy means that voters should be able to choose their representatives, not the other way around. Because politicians have a self-interest in maintaining their political power and will work to further this self-interest through redistricting, unfairly drawn districts undermine democratic accountability.

The strategy of emphasizing neutrality instead of fairness in redistricting is plausible, but does not convince those who support this side of the argument. While it is true that Republicans would continue to have some advantage in most states if districts were neutrally drawn, it is possible to draw maps that follow traditional districting principles but also promote partisan fairness.

take a stand

1. If you were a Supreme Court justice, how would you have ruled in the Pennsylvania and Maryland cases? Should partisan redistricting be limited?

2. Is the appropriate standard for evaluating a legislative map partisan neutrality or partisan fairness? Or should the courts stay out of redistricting entirely?

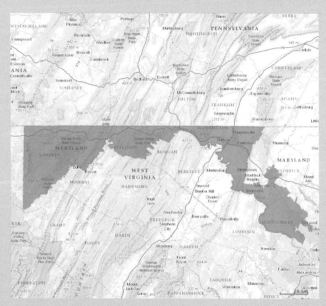

Maryland's 6th congressional district from 2011 map.

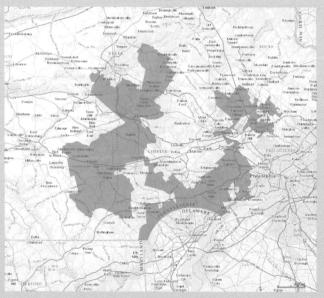

Pennsylvania's 7th congressional district from 2011 map.

minority voters (called majority-minority districts). Figure 4.4 shows the plan the legislature enacted, in which the district boundaries look like a pattern of spiderwebs and ink blots. Moreover, one of the districts had parts that ended up being only as wide as I-85, following the highway off an exit ramp, over a bridge, and down the entrance ramp on the other side. This move prevented the I-85 district from bisecting the district it was traveling through, which would have violated the state law requiring contiguous districts.

The North Carolina example shows how convoluted redistricting plans can become. Part of the complexity is due to the availability of census databases that allow line drawers to divide voters as closely as they want, moving neighborhood by neighborhood, even house by house. Why bother with this level of detail? Because redistricting influences who gets elected. It is active politicking in its most fundamental form. The North Carolina plan was ultimately declared unconstitutional by the U.S. Supreme Court in *Shaw v. Reno*—a ruling that opened the door for dozens of lawsuits about racial redistricting. (See the discussion in Chapter 9 of the Voting Rights Act of 1965 and more recent Supreme Court rulings on racial redistricting, especially the 2013 case in which the Court struck down the part of the law that identified states that needed to have their redistricting plans preapproved by the Justice Department.[28]) The current legal standard is that race cannot be the *predominant* factor in drawing congressional district lines, but it can be one of the factors. Nonetheless, there is still plenty of room to create districts that will be composed of voters who will vote in ways that will have profound political consequences. The obvious political implications of redistricting often lead to demands that district plans be prepared or approved by nonpartisan committees or by a state agency (as in Iowa) who are theoretically immune from political pressure. Such a process, as used in 17 states, often produces more competitive districts. Political support for a nonpartisan process has surged in recent years, with voters in four states approving redistricting commissions in 2018 and two more in 2020.

AP® SUPREME COURT CASE

Shaw v. Reno
The 1993 Supreme Court case that held that congressional districts created to help elect racial minorities violate White plaintiffs' equal protection of the laws under the Fourteenth Amendment unless there is a compelling governmental interest.

FIGURE 4.4

North Carolina Redistricting, 1992

This set of House districts was the subject of the landmark Supreme Court ruling *Shaw v. Reno* (1993), in which the Court said that "appearances matter" when drawing district lines. Do you agree? Should other factors such as race, party, and competitiveness play a greater role than district shape?

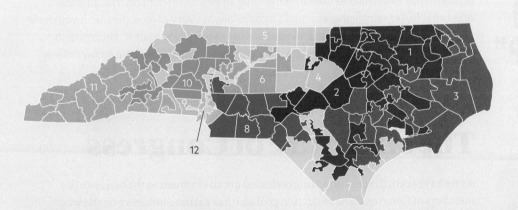

Source: North Carolina General Assembly, 1992 Congressional Base Plan No. 10, www.ncleg.gov/Files/GIS/ReferenceDocs/2011/NC%20Congressional%20Districts%20-%20Historical%20Plans%20-%201941-1992.pdf (accessed 7/26/20).

The responsibility–responsiveness dilemma

As mentioned earlier, polls show that despite generally approving of their own member of Congress, people hold Congress itself in very low esteem. This is rooted in the conflicts that arise from Congress's dual roles: responsibility for national policy making and responsiveness to local constituencies.[29] This duality may make members of Congress appear to be simultaneously great leaders who debate important issues and locally oriented representatives who work hard to deliver benefits for the district (which may not be good for the country as a whole). Indeed, the range of issues that Congress must address is vast, from debating tax and health care reform to overseeing the classification of black-eyed peas, from debating the war on terror and expanding free trade to declaring a National Cholesterol Education Month. Part of the national frustration with Congress arises because we want our representatives to be responsible *and* responsive; we want them to be great national leaders *and* to take care of our local and, at times, personal concerns.

Difficult choices have to be made between being responsive and being responsible. Rather than understanding these issues as inherent in the legislative process, we often accuse members of gridlock and partisan bickering when our conflicting demands are not met. For example, public-opinion polls routinely show that the public wants lower taxes; more spending on education, the environment, and health care; and balanced budgets. But those three things cannot happen simultaneously. We often expect the impossible from Congress and then are frustrated when it doesn't happen.

The responsibility–responsiveness dilemma brings us back to the puzzle we posed at the beginning of this section: Why is there a persistent 30–40 percent gap between approval ratings for individual members and for the institution? As Richard Fenno put it, "If Congress is the 'broken branch,' how come we love our congressman so much?"[30] The answer may simply be that members of Congress tend to respond more to their constituents' demands than to take on the responsibility of solving national problems. And when Congress becomes embroiled in debates about constituencies' conflicting demands, the institution may appear ineffectual. But as long as members keep the "folks back home" happy, their individual popularity will remain high.

gridlock
An inability to enact legislation because of partisan conflict within Congress or between Congress and the president.

"Why Should I Care?"

How would you like your member of Congress to represent you? Should members represent the interests of just their district or the broader nation? Should they be responsive or responsible? Constituents have an interest in holding their members accountable, yet most congressional elections are not very competitive. So if you don't like how your member is representing you, what can you do about it? Understanding the nature of representation and the incumbency advantage can help answer these important questions.

EXAMINE HOW PARTIES, THE COMMITTEE SYSTEM, AND STAFFERS ENABLE CONGRESS TO FUNCTION

The structure of Congress

As we have seen, the goal of getting reelected greatly influences the behavior of members of Congress. The reelection goal also has a strong influence on the way that Congress is structured, both formally (staff, the committee system, parties, and leadership roles) and informally (norms). Despite the importance of the electoral connection, the goal of being reelected cannot explain everything about members' behavior and the congressional structure. This section examines some other explanations that underlie the informal and formal structures of Congress: the policy motivations of members, the partisan basis for congressional institutions, and the importance of the committee system.

Informal structures

Various norms provide an informal structure for the way Congress works. *Universalism* is the norm that when benefits are divided up, they should be awarded to as many districts and states as possible. Thus, when it comes to handing out federal highway dollars or expenditures for the Pentagon's weapons programs, the benefits are broadly distributed across the entire country, which means that votes in support of these bills tend to be very lopsided (as some areas of the country need the federal funds more urgently than others). For example, the $86.2 billion 2020 transportation bill contained some spending in every part of the country and passed by strong bipartisan votes, even though it was introduced in the middle of the contentious impeachment process.[31]

Another norm, **logrolling**, reinforces universalism with the idea that "if you scratch my back, I'll scratch yours." This norm leads members of Congress to support bills that they otherwise might not vote for in exchange for other members' votes on bills that are very important to them. For example, House members from a dairy state might vote for tobacco price supports even if their state has no tobacco farmers, and in return they would expect a member from the tobacco state to vote for the dairy price support bill. This norm can produce wasteful pork-barrel spending. For example, in the 2011 budget a $1.1 trillion omnibus appropriations bill contained more than 6,488 **earmarks** worth $8.3 billion, so nearly everyone gained something by passing it. The $1.4 trillion 2020 omnibus appropriations bill did not include any traditional earmarks (or "pork," as they are informally known), following the ban on formal earmarks in both the House and Senate in 2011, but there were still billions of dollars in targeted spending as members of Congress found ways to secure funding for their district or state. Representative Jim Banks (R-IN) complained about the wasteful spending in the sprawling bill, saying, "Like 'mystery meat,' you don't want to know what's in it. Also like 'mystery meat'—you can bet at least one ingredient is a whole lot of pork."[32]

logrolling
A form of reciprocity in which members of Congress support bills that they otherwise might not vote for in exchange for other members' votes on bills that are very important to them.

earmarks
Federally funded local projects attached to bills passed through Congress.

Representative Bill Flores (R-TX) poses with Faye, a potbellied pig, after a news conference held by Citizens Against Government Waste at the Phoenix Park Hotel to release the "2017 Congressional Pig Book," which identifies pork-barrel spending in Congress.

The norm of *specialization* is also important, both for the efficient operation of Congress and for members' reelection. By specializing and becoming an expert on a given issue, members provide valuable information to the institution as a whole and also create a basis for credit claiming. This norm is stronger in the House, where members often develop a few areas of expertise, whereas senators tend to be policy generalists. For example, Representative John Lewis (D-GA), who passed away in 2020 after serving 17 terms, dedicated much of his decades-long House career to the issue of civil rights, while Senator Lisa Murkowski (R-AK) has her hand in a variety of issues, especially energy and public lands, but also Native American issues, health care, and women's issues.

The **seniority** norm also serves individual and institutional purposes. This norm holds that the member with the longest service on a given committee will chair that committee. Although there have been numerous violations of this norm in the past 30 years, whereby the most senior member has been passed over for someone whom the party leaders favored, the norm benefits the institution by ensuring orderly succession in committee leadership.[33] The norm also benefits members by providing a tangible reason why voters should return them to Congress year after year. Many members of Congress make this point when campaigning, and the issue is more than just posturing. Committee chairs *are* better able to "bring home the bacon" than a junior member who is still learning the ropes.

Formal structures

Formal structures also shape members' behavior in Congress. Political parties, party leadership, the committee system, and staff provide the context within which members of Congress make policy and represent their constituents (see Nuts & Bolts 4.2).

Parties and Party Leaders Political parties are important for allocating power in Congress. Party leaders are always elected on straight party-line votes, with the majority party determining committee leadership, the division of seats on committees, and the allocation of committee resources. Parties in Congress also become more important when opposing parties control the two chambers. This was the case in 1981–1986 and in 2019–2022, when Republicans controlled the Senate and Democrats controlled the House, and in part of 2001 and 2002 and 2011–2014, when the opposite was true.

A leading theory of congressional organization points to the importance of parties in solving collective action problems in Congress. Without parties, the legislative process would be much more fractured and decentralized because members would be autonomous agents in battle with one another. Parties provide a team framework that allows members to work together for broadly beneficial goals. Just think how difficult it would be for a member of Congress to get a bill passed if he or she had to build a coalition from scratch every time. Instead, parties provide a solid base from which coalition building may begin. As discussed in Chapter 11, political parties provide brand name recognition for members.

The top party leader in the House—and the only House leader mentioned in the Constitution—is the **Speaker of the House**, who is the head of the majority party and influences the legislative agenda, committee assignments, scheduling, and overall party strategy. The Democratic Party made history in January 2007 when its representatives elected Nancy Pelosi as the first woman to serve as Speaker. John Boehner was elected Speaker in 2011 after Republicans regained control of the House in the 2010 midterm elections and was replaced by Paul Ryan in 2015. Ryan, who was only 48 years old and at the peak of his career, shocked the Washington establishment when he announced his retirement early in 2018. Nancy Pelosi then reassumed the role in 2019 when the Democrats took control of the House.

Majority-Party Structure in the House of Representatives and the Senate

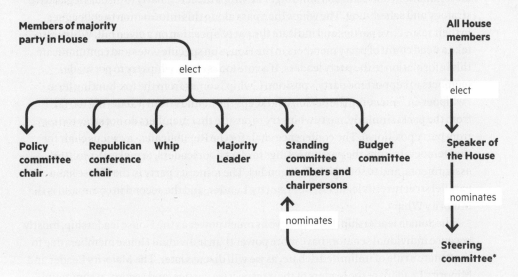

Members of majority party in House — elect → Policy committee chair, Republican conference chair, Whip, Majority Leader, Standing committee members and chairpersons, Budget committee

All House members — elect → Speaker of the House — nominates → Steering committee*

Steering committee* — nominates → Standing committee members and chairpersons

*Steering committee includes the Speaker, Majority Leader, and whip, and some members who are appointed by the Speaker and some who are elected by the conference.

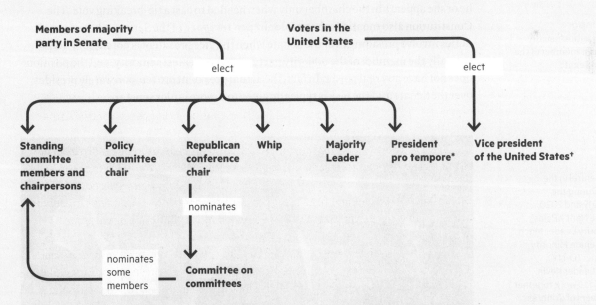

Members of majority party in Senate — elect → Standing committee members and chairpersons, Policy committee chair, Republican conference chair, Whip, Majority Leader, President pro tempore*

Voters in the United States — elect → Vice president of the United States†

Republican conference chair — nominates → Committee on committees — nominates some members → Standing committee members and chairpersons

*The president pro tempore is elected by the majority-party members, but by custom is the most senior member of the majority party.
†The vice president of the United States is the president of the Senate, but rarely presides over the floor. The vice president's most important role is to break tie votes.

Source: Compiled by the authors.

Majority Leader
The elected head of the party holding the majority of seats in the House or Senate.

whip system
An organization of House leaders who work to disseminate information and promote party unity in voting on legislation.

Minority Leader
The elected head of the party holding the minority of seats in the House or Senate.

president pro tempore
A largely symbolic position usually held by the most senior member of the majority party in the Senate.

Party leadership is central in the legislative process. During the 116th Congress, in 2019 and 2020, Speaker of the House Nancy Pelosi (D-CA), Senate Majority Leader Mitch McConnell (R-KY), Senate Minority Leader Chuck Schumer (D-NY), and House Minority Leader Kevin McCarthy (R-CA) had to work together and with other members of Congress to pass legislation.

The Speaker is aided by the **Majority Leader**, the Majority Whip, and the conference or caucus chair (in addition to many others in lower-level party positions). The Majority Leader is one of the national spokespersons for the party and also helps with the day-to-day operation of the legislative process. The Majority Whip oversees the extensive **whip system**, which has three functions: information gathering, information dissemination, and coalition building. The whips meet regularly to discuss legislative strategy and scheduling. The whips then pass along this information to colleagues in their respective parties and indicate the party's position on a given bill. Whips also take a head count of party members in the House on specific votes and communicate this information to the party leaders. If a vote looks close, whips try to persuade members to support the party's position ("whip" comes from the fox-hunting term "whipper-in," meaning the person who keeps the hounds from wandering too far from the pack; similarly, party whips try to ensure that members do not stray too far from party positions). The conference chair for the Republicans, or caucus chair for the Democrats, runs the party meetings to elect floor leaders, to make committee assignments, and to set legislative agendas. The minority party in the House has a parallel structure: its leader is the **Minority Leader**, and the second in command is the Minority Whip.

The Senate leadership does not have as much power as the House leadership, mostly because individual senators have more power than individual House members due to the Senate's rule of unlimited debate, as we will discuss later. The Majority Leader and Minority Leader are the leaders of their respective parties, and second in command to them are the Assistant Majority and Minority Leaders. The Senate also has a whip system, but it is not as developed as the House system. Republicans have a separate position for the conference chair, while the Democratic leader also serves as the caucus chair. Officially, the country's vice president is also the president of the Senate, but he or she appears in the chamber only when needed to cast a tie-breaking vote. The Constitution also mentions the **president pro tempore** of the Senate, whose formal duties involve presiding over the Senate when the vice president is not there. This is typically the member of the majority party with the greatest seniority, and the position does not have any real power. In fact, the actual president pro tempore rarely presides over the Senate and the task is typically given to a more junior senator.

The Role of Parties and Conditional Party Government Political parties in Congress also reflect the individualism of the institution. Compared with parties in parliamentary systems, U.S. congressional parties are very weak. They do not impose a party line or penalize members who vote against the party. Indeed, they have virtually no ability to impose electoral restrictions (such as denying the party's nomination) on renegade members.

Although still weaker than their overseas counterparts, parties in Congress have greatly strengthened since the 1960s (see Figure 4.5). Partisanship—evident when party members stick together in opposition to the other party—reached its highest levels

Party Votes and Unity in Congress, 1962–2019

FIGURE 4.5

Party votes are said to occur when a majority of one party opposes a majority of the other party, and party unity refers to the percentage of the party members who vote together on party votes. These two graphs make two important points. First, partisanship has increased in the last two decades, in terms of both the proportion of party votes and the level of party unity. Second, despite these increased levels of partisanship, only about two-thirds of all votes in the House and Senate divide the two parties. Given these potentially conflicting observations, how would you assess the argument that partisanship in Congress is far too intense?

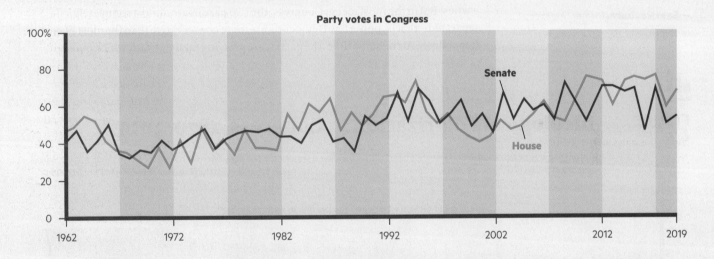

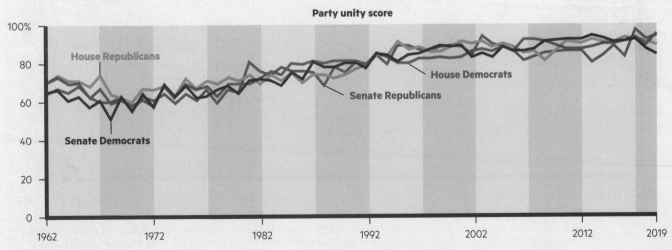

Source: Congressional Quarterly, "CQ Federal Congressional Bill Tracker," https://info.cq.com/legislative-tracking/cq-federal/ (accessed 8/1/20).

If you want to get along, go along.

—**Sam Rayburn,** former Speaker of the House

of the post–World War II era in recent years. About 70 percent of all **roll call votes** were **party votes**, in which a majority of one party opposed a majority of the other party. The proportion of party votes fell to between 50 and 60 percent between 1996 and 2008 but recently has hit new highs. The highest proportions were 72 percent in the Senate in 2009 and 76 percent in the House in 2017; the numbers fell in both the House and Senate in 2019 to 68 percent and 54 percent, respectively. **Party unity**, the percentage of party members voting together on party votes, soared during this period as well, especially in the House. Party unity hit an all-time high for House Democrats in 2019, with 95 percent of them voting together on party votes. House Republicans were almost as unified at 89 percent.[34]

Party-line votes have become more common as the Democratic Party has become more cohesive: southern Democrats now vote more like their northern counterparts, partly because of the importance of African-American voters, who tend to vote for Democrats in the South. Moreover, increasing Republican strength in the South means that the remaining Democratic districts are more liberal, because Republicans defeat the more moderate Democrats. Similarly, there are fewer moderates within the Republican Party, as most regions of the country that used to elect moderate Republicans are now electing Democrats.[35]

Another way to examine changes in the composition of the parties is to examine the ideological distribution of members of Congress (see Figure 4.6). The parties in Congress are now more polarized than they have been at any point in U.S. history. In the 1970s, there was considerable overlap between the Democratic and Republican parties. But in the most recent Congress, the two parties are almost completely separated—that is, only a few Democrats are more conservative than the most liberal Republican. At the same time, the parties are growing farther apart, which makes it

FIGURE 4.6

Ideological Polarization in Congress, 1879–2019

Although party polarization in Congress has been high in the past, it lessened in the early twentieth century. Polarization has increased steadily in the last 70 years, and today's Congress is more polarized than ever. What do you think causes this extreme polarization?

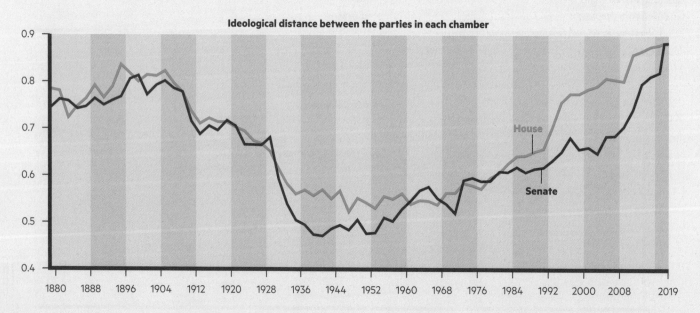

Source: Polarization in Congress, "Liberal-Conservative Partisan Polarization by Chamber," Jeff Lewis, March 11, 2018, https://voteview.com/articles/party_polarization (accessed 7/29/20); updated with Realtime NOMINATE Ideology and Related Data, which track the ideological distance between each party's average vote, voteview.com (accessed 6/3/20).

even harder for the Republicans and the Democrats to work together and compromise to pass legislation.

This greater cohesiveness within parties and separation across parties means that conditional party government may be in play—that is, strong party leadership is possible in Congress, but it is conditional on the consent of party members.[36] That consent is more likely if there are strong differences between the parties but unity within parties. Leaders' chief responsibility is to get their party's legislative agenda through Congress, but they primarily have to rely on persuasion and control over the timing of when bills come up for a vote rather than telling members what to do. Leaders' success largely depends on their personal skills, communicative abilities, and trustworthiness. Some of the most successful leaders, such as Lyndon Johnson (D-TX), Majority Leader of the Senate from 1955 to 1961, and Sam Rayburn (D-TX), Speaker of the House for more than 17 years, kept in touch with key members on a daily basis. Another important tool of the leadership is agenda control: both positive (getting bills to the floor that are favored by the party) and negative (preventing votes on bills that would divide the majority party).

Leaders must also have the ability to bargain and compromise. One observer noted, "To Senator Johnson, public policy evidently was an inexhaustibly bargainable product."[37] Such leaders find solutions where none appear possible. Leaders also do favors for members (such as making campaign appearances, helping with fund-raising, contributing to campaigns, helping them get desired committee assignments, or guiding pet projects through the legislative process) to engender a feeling of personal obligation to the leadership when it needs a key vote.

The party's most powerful positive incentives are in the area of campaign finance. In recent years the congressional campaign committees of both parties and the national party organizations have been supplying candidates with money and resources in an attempt to gain more influence in the electoral process. Party leaders may also help arrange a campaign stop or a fund-raiser for a candidate with party leaders or the president. For example, President Obama held dozens of fund-raisers for Democrats in 2014, earning him the label of "Fundraiser-in-Chief" from CNN.[38] Such events

A sitting president can be a powerful ally in a campaign. Here, President Trump uses his Twitter account to endorse Representative Mo Brooks (R-AL), who was reelected to the House in 2020.

typically raise $500,000 to more than $1 million. President Trump campaigned actively for congressional Republicans during the 2018 midterms. Despite headlining a record-breaking fund-raiser, he held fewer for other candidates than any president since Ronald Reagan.[39]

Despite these positive reinforcements, members' desire for reelection always comes before party concerns, and leadership rarely tries to force a member to vote against his or her constituents' interests. For example, Democrats from rural areas, where most constituents support gun ownership and many are hunters, would not be expected to vote the party line favoring a gun control bill. But if a member of Congress did something much more extreme that crossed the party's leadership—for example, supporting the opposing party's candidate for Speaker or passing strategic information to the opposition—he or she could expect to be disciplined by the party's leaders.

The most difficult challenge for party leadership in recent years in terms of party cohesion has been the Freedom Caucus within the House Republicans. This group of conservative members forced several government shutdowns during the Obama years over funding for Obamacare and tax increases. Most significantly, they forced John Boehner to resign as Speaker of the House in September 2015 and then rejected the heir apparent, Majority Leader Kevin McCarthy, because he was too moderate. Finally, they agreed to accept Paul Ryan as Speaker, but nine Freedom Caucus members voted against him.[40] When President Trump was elected, many Republicans believed that they would finally be able to enact a conservative policy agenda, but in his first two years it was difficult to pass legislation that both the Freedom Caucus in the House and moderate Republicans in the Senate could agree to. The deadlock over DACA, discussed in the chapter opener, is a prime example. After Democrats retook control of the House in the 2018 midterms, Speaker Pelosi faced similar challenges from the liberal wing of her party led by Alexandria Ocasio-Cortez (D-NY) and "the Squad" (a group of first-term representatives composed of Ocasio-Cortez, Ilhan Omar [MN], Rashida Tlaib [MI], and Ayanna Pressley [MA]), but Pelosi was able to maintain a tight grip on her party.

The Committee System The committee system in the House and Senate is another crucial part of the legislative structure. There are four types of committees: standing, select, joint, and conference. Standing committees, which have ongoing membership and jurisdictions, are where most of Congress's work gets done. These committees draft legislation and oversee the implementation of the laws they pass. For example, the Agriculture Committees in the House and Senate have jurisdiction over farm programs such as commodity price supports, crop insurance, and soil conservation. But they also create and oversee policy for rural electrification and development; nutrition programs like the Supplemental Nutrition Assistance Program (SNAP); and the inspection of livestock, poultry, seafood, and meat products. Many committees share jurisdiction on policy—for example, the House Natural Resources Committee oversees the U.S. Forest Service and forests on federally owned lands, and the Agriculture Committee oversees policy for forests on privately owned lands. There are 21 standing committees in the House and 20 in the Senate.

Select committees typically address a specific topic for one or two terms, such as the House Select Committee on the Climate Crisis. These committees do not have the same legislative authority as standing committees; rather, they mostly serve to collect information, provide policy options, and draw attention to a given issue.

There are four joint committees made up of members of both the House and the Senate, and they rarely have legislative authority. The Joint Committee on Taxation, for example, does not have authority to send legislation concerning tax policy to the

standing committees
Committees that are a permanent part of the House or Senate structure, holding more importance and authority than other committees.

select committees
Committees in the House or Senate created to address a specific issue for one or two terms.

joint committees
Committees that contain members of both the House and Senate but have limited authority.

floor of the House or Senate. Instead, it gathers information and provides estimates of the consequences of proposed tax legislation. Joint committees may also be temporary, such as the "Supercommittee" (officially the Joint Select Committee on Deficit Reduction) that was formed in 2011 to try to reach bipartisan agreement on a deficit reduction plan. The committee failed to reach agreement and was disbanded in 2012.

Conference committees are formed as needed to resolve specific differences between House and Senate versions of legislation that are passed in each chamber. These committees mostly comprise standing committee members from each chamber who worked on the bill in question.

The committee system creates a division of labor that helps members get reelected by facilitating specialization and credit claiming. For example, a chair of the Agriculture Committee or of a key agricultural subcommittee may reasonably take credit for passing an important bill for the farmers back home, such as the Cottonseed Payment Program that provides assistance to cottonseed farmers who lost crops due to hurricanes.[41]

The number of members who could make these credible claims expanded dramatically in the 1970s with the proliferation of subcommittees (there are 102 in the House and 67 in the Senate). Speaking about the House, one observer said, with some exaggeration, that if you ever forget a member's name, you can simply refer to him or her as "Mr. or Ms. Chairman" and you will be right about half the time. This view of congressional committees is based on the **distributive theory**, which is rooted in the norm of reciprocity and representatives' incentives to provide benefits for their districts. The theory holds that members will seek committee assignments to best serve their district's interests, the leadership will accommodate those requests, and the floor will respect the views of the committees in a big institution-level logroll— that is, committee members will support one another's legislation. This means that members tend to have an interest in and to support the policies produced by the committees they serve on. For example, members from farm states would want to serve on the Agriculture Committee, and members with a lot of military bases or defense contractors in their districts would want to be on the Armed Services Committee.

Nonetheless, the committee system does not exist simply to further members' electoral goals. According to **informational theory**, it also provides collective benefits to the rest of the members through committee members' expertise on policy, which helps reduce uncertainty about policy outcomes.[42] By deferring to expert committees, members are able to achieve beneficial outcomes while using their time more efficiently. This informational theory is also consistent with the argument made by Richard Fenno 45 years ago that members will serve on committees for reasons other than simply trying to achieve reelection (which is implied by the distributive theory). Fenno argued that members also were interested in achieving power within the institution and in making good policy.[43] Others argue that goals vary from bill to bill and all members pursue reelection advantage, institutional power, and effective policy in different circumstances.[44] Thus, the committee system does not exist only to further members' electoral goals, but it often serves that purpose.

Committees also serve the policy needs of the majority party, largely because the party in power controls a majority of seats on every committee. The party ratios on each committee generally reflect the partisan distribution in the overall chamber, but the majority party gives itself somewhat larger majorities on the important committees such as Ways and Means (which controls tax policy), Appropriations, and Rules. This is especially true for the Rules Committee (in which the majority party controls 9 of the 13 seats). The Rules Committee is important to the majority party because it structures the nature of debate in the House: it sets the length of debate and the type and number of amendments to a bill that will be allowed. These decisions are called *rules* and must

conference committees
Temporary committees created to negotiate differences between the House and Senate versions of a piece of legislation that has passed through both chambers.

distributive theory
The idea that members of Congress will join committees that best serve the interests of their district and that committee members will support one another's legislation.

informational theory
The idea that having committees in Congress made up of experts on specific policy areas helps ensure well-informed policy decisions.

be approved by a majority of the House members. The Rules Committee has become an arm of the majority-party leadership, and in many instances it provides rules that support the party's policy agenda or that protect its members from having to take controversial positions. For example, the Rules Committee prevented amendments on the articles of impeachment brought against President Trump in December 2019, fearing that amendments could have divided the Democratic Party.[45] Majority members are expected to support their party on votes on rules, even if they end up voting against the related legislation.

Congressional Staff The final component of the formal structure of Congress is congressional staff. The size of personal and committee staff exploded in the 1970s and 1980s but has since leveled off. The total number of congressional staff is more than four times as large as it was 50 years ago. Part of the motivation for this growth was to reduce the gap between the policy-making capability of Congress and the president, especially with regard to fiscal policy. The other primary motivation was electoral. By increasing the size of their personal staff, members were able to open multiple district offices and expand opportunities for helping constituents. When the Republicans took control of Congress in 1994, they vowed to cut the waste in the internal operation of the institution, in part by cutting committee staff. However, although they reduced committee staff by nearly a third, they made no cuts in personal staff.

"Why Should I Care?"

The Constitution says very little about the internal structure of Congress, so the institution is largely the creation of its members. The norms of the institution and its formal structure facilitate members' electoral and policy goals, so if they don't like the way something works, they can change it. While this may sound very self-serving, members of Congress also work to serve broader collective and policy goals—or else they would be booted out of office. Understanding this fundamental point provides great insight into why Congress is structured the way that it is.

★

TRACE THE STEPS IN THE LEGISLATIVE PROCESS

How a bill becomes a law

Every introductory textbook on American politics has an obligatory section including a neat little diagram that describes how a bill becomes a law (see How It Works: Passing Legislation). But we provide an important truth-in-advertising disclosure: many important laws do not follow this orderly path. In fact, Barbara Sinclair's book *Unorthodox Lawmaking* argues that "the legislative process for major legislation is now less likely to conform to the textbook model than to unorthodox lawmaking."[46] After presenting the standard view, we describe the most important deviations from that path.

The conventional process

The details of the legislative process can be incredibly complex, but its basic aspects are fairly simple. The most important thing to understand about the process is that before a piece of legislation can become a law it must be passed *in identical form* by both the House and the Senate and signed by the president. If the president vetoes the bill, it can still be passed with a two-thirds vote in each chamber. Note, however, that all legislation that is signed by the president (or for which Congress overrides a veto) carries the weight of law; legislation that is not signed by the president has only internal legislative or symbolic purposes (see Nuts & Bolts 4.3 for a description of different types of legislation). Here are the basic steps of the process to pass a bill:

1. A member of Congress introduces the bill.
2. A subcommittee and committee craft the bill.
3. Floor action on the bill takes place in the first chamber (House or Senate).
4. Committee and floor action takes place in the second chamber.
5. The conference committee works out any differences between the House and Senate versions of the bill. (If the two chambers pass the same version, steps 5 and 6 are not necessary.)
6. The conference committee version is given final approval on the floor of each chamber.
7. The president either signs or vetoes the final version.
8. If the bill is vetoed, both chambers can attempt to override the veto with a two-thirds vote in both chambers.

The first part of the process, unchanged from the earliest Congresses, is the introduction of the bill. Only members of Congress can introduce the bill, either by dropping it into the "hopper," a wooden box at the front of the chamber in the House, or by presenting it to one of the clerks at the presiding officer's desk in the Senate. Even the president would need to have a House member or senator introduce his or her bill. Each bill has one or more sponsors and often many co-sponsors. Members may introduce bills on any topic they choose, but often the bills are related to a specific constituency interest. For example, Senator Roy Blunt (R-MO) introduced Senate Resolution 490, "Congratulating the Kansas City Chiefs on

Types of Legislation

NUTS & BOLTS 4.3

- **Bill:** A legislative proposal that becomes law if it is passed by both the House and the Senate in identical form and approved by the president. Each is assigned a bill number, with "H.R." indicating bills that originated in the House and "S.R." denoting bills that originated in the Senate. Private bills are concerned with a specific individual or organization and often address immigration or naturalization issues. Public bills affect the general public if enacted into law.
- **Simple resolution:** Legislation used to express the sense of the House or Senate, designated by "H.Res." or "S.Res." Simple resolutions affect only the chamber passing the resolution, are not signed by the president, and cannot become public law. Resolutions are often used for symbolic legislation, such as congratulating sports teams or naming a post office after a famous person (see Figure 4.7).

- **Concurrent resolution:** Legislation used to express the position of both chambers on a nonlegislative matter to set the annual budget or to fix adjournment dates, designated by "H.Con.Res" or "S.Con.Res." Concurrent resolutions are not signed by the president and therefore do not carry the weight of law.
- **Joint resolution:** Legislation that has few practical differences from a bill (passes both chambers in identical form, signed by the president) unless it proposes a constitutional amendment. In that case, a two-thirds majority of those present and voting in both the House and the Senate, and ratification by three-fourths of the states, are required for the amendment to be adopted and it does not require the president's signature.

How it works: in theory
Passing Legislation

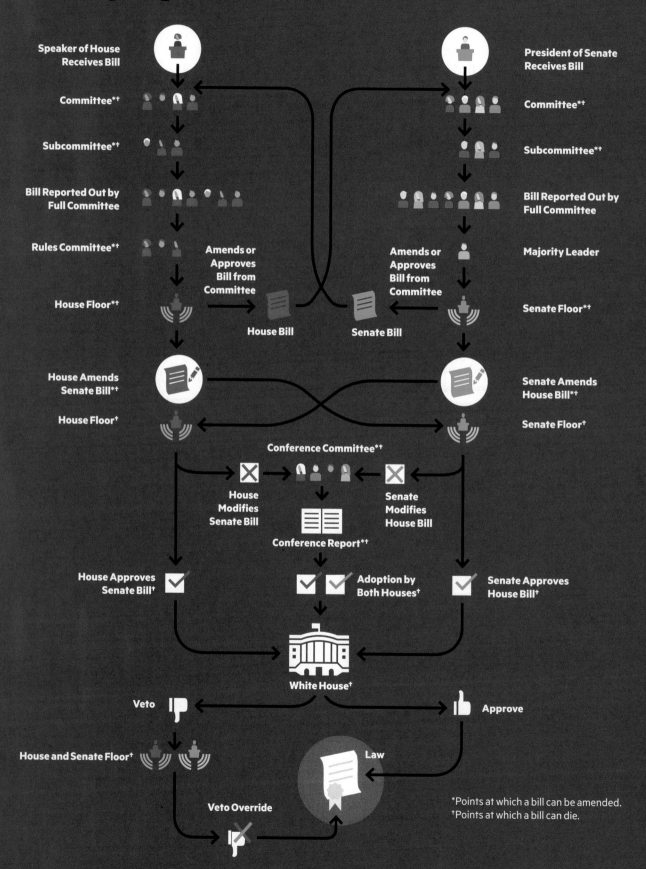

Speaker of House Receives Bill

President of Senate Receives Bill

Committee*†

Committee*†

Subcommittee*†

Subcommittee*†

Bill Reported Out by Full Committee

Bill Reported Out by Full Committee

Rules Committee*†

Amends or Approves Bill from Committee

Amends or Approves Bill from Committee

Majority Leader

House Floor*†

Senate Floor*†

House Bill

Senate Bill

House Amends Senate Bill*†

Senate Amends House Bill*†

House Floor†

Senate Floor†

Conference Committee*†

House Modifies Senate Bill

Senate Modifies House Bill

Conference Report*†

House Approves Senate Bill†

Adoption by Both Houses†

Senate Approves House Bill†

White House†

Veto

Approve

House and Senate Floor†

Law

Veto Override

*Points at which a bill can be amended.
†Points at which a bill can die.

Passing the Tax Cuts and Jobs Act

The 2017 Tax Cuts and Jobs Act provides an example of how passing legislation often deviates from the conventional method.

In the House...

The House Ways and Means Committee crafted H.R. 1, the House version of the Tax Bill. **All tax bills must originate in the House**.

House passes its version.

In the Senate...

The Senate Finance Committee **crafted the initial Senate version**.

Not so fast.

Republicans **cannot pass the Finance Committee's version** without the 60 votes needed to break a filibuster.

So the Budget Committee saves the day.

The Senate Budget Committee packages the Finance Committee's bill with a bill on drilling for oil as a reconciliation bill (which only needs 51 votes, rather than a filibuster-proof 60, to be approved). **It keeps the title of the House bill, H.R. 1, on this new bill to preserve the fiction that it originated in the House** and then submits it in the Senate.

Meanwhile, on the Left...

10 Democratic senators **try to slow the bill down** by sending it to the Finance Committee.

Meanwhile, on the Right...

Several Republican senators say **they will vote against the bill if changes are not made**, so Majority Leader Mitch McConnell cuts some deals.

Vote-a-rama!

After 355 amendments to the reconciliation bill are proposed, key provisions ratifying McConnell's deals are approved and the **Democrats' efforts are defeated** in a marathon of overnight voting.

Senate passes its version.

Conference committee **works out the differences** in the House version of H.R. 1 and the revamped Senate version of H.R. 1.

Passed!

House passes the conference report.

Passed!

Passed!

House passes the Senate's amendments.

Senate passes the conference report—with amendments.

Signed into law.

President Trump signs the **bill into law**.

❓ Critical Thinking

1. **What are the most significant ways in which** the process to pass the 2017 Tax Cuts and Jobs Act deviated from the conventional method?

2. **Do you think the 2017 Tax Cuts and Jobs Act could have been** passed without this unconventional process? Why or why not?

their victory in Super Bowl LIV" (see Figure 4.7). Obviously, most legislation is more substantive, but members of Congress are always attentive to issues their constituents care about.

The next step is to send the bill to the relevant committee. House and Senate rules specify committee jurisdictions (there are more than 200 categories), and the bill is matched with the committee that best fits its subject matter. In the House, major legislation may be sent to more than one committee in a practice known as multiple referral, but one of the committees is designated the primary committee and the bill is reviewed by the other committees sequentially or in parts. The practice is less common in the Senate, partly because senators have more opportunities to amend legislation on the floor. However, there were three committees in the House and five in the Senate that simultaneously worked on health care reform in 2009.

Once the bill goes to a committee, the chair refers it to the relevant subcommittee, where much of the legislative work is done. One important point: 80–90 percent of bills die at this stage of the process; they never make it out of the subcommittee or committee. For bills that see some action, the subcommittee holds hearings, calls witnesses, and gathers the information necessary to rewrite, amend, and edit the

FIGURE 4.7

Taking Care of the Fans

The congratulatory resolution here is symbolic and commends the Kansas City Chiefs for winning the Super Bowl in 2020. Why do you think members of Congress spend time passing seemingly trivial resolutions like this?

S. RES. 490

In the Senate of the United States
February 13, 2020

Congratulating the Kansas City Chiefs on their victory in Super Bowl LIV in the successful 100th season of the National Football League.

Whereas, on Sunday, February 2, 2020, the Kansas City Chiefs (in this preamble referred to as the "Chiefs") defeated the San Francisco 49ers by a score of 31 to 20 to win Super Bowl LIV in Miami, Florida . . .

Whereas Super Bowl LIV was the culmination of the 100th season of the NFL, a season in which the league has promoted stars both past and present, served the community, and looked toward the next 100 years of football;

Whereas the Chiefs overcame a 10-point deficit in the fourth quarter and scored 21 straight points in the final 6 minutes and 13 seconds of gameplay to earn the victory;

Whereas the victory in Super Bowl LIV earned the Chiefs their second Super Bowl victory, ending their 50-year Super Bowl drought that had lasted since the team last won Super Bowl IV on January 11, 1970 . . .

Whereas head coach Andy Reid earned his 222nd career win, placing him sixth on the all-time wins list of the NFL and earning his first Super Bowl title in his 21-year tenure as a head coach in the NFL . . .

Whereas quarterback Patrick Mahomes completed 26 of 42 pass attempts for 286 yards and 2 touchdowns, rushed 9 times for 29 yards and 1 touchdown, and was named Most Valuable Player of Super Bowl LIV . . .

Whereas people all over the world are asking, "How 'bout those Chiefs?": Now, therefore, be it *Resolved,*

That the Senate—

(1) congratulates the Kansas City Chiefs and their entire staff, Mayor of Kansas City Quinton Lucas, Governor of Missouri Mike Parson, and loyal fans of the Kansas City Chiefs for their victory in Super Bowl LIV . . .

Source: Congress.gov, www.congress.gov/bill/116th-congress/senate-resolution/490/text?q=%7B"search"%3A%5B"super+bowl"%5D%7D&r=2&s=1 (accessed 6/3/20).

bill. The final language of the bill is determined in a collaborative process known as the **markup**. During this meeting, members debate aspects of the issue and offer amendments to change the language or content of the bill. After all amendments have been considered, a final vote is taken on whether to send the bill to the full committee. If it is sent, the full committee then considers whether to pass it along to the floor. This committee also has the option of amending the bill, passing it as is, or tabling it (which kills the bill). Every bill sent to the floor by a committee is accompanied by a report and full documentation of all the hearings. These documents constitute the bill's legislative history, which the courts, executive departments, and the public use to determine the purpose and meaning of the law.

When the bill makes it to the floor, it is placed on one of the various legislative calendars. Bills are removed from the calendar to be considered by the floor under a broad range of possible rules. When the bill reaches the floor, the majority party and minority party each designate a bill manager who is responsible for guiding the debate on the floor. In the House, debate proceeds according to tight time limits and rules governing the nature of amendments. Senate debate is much more open and unlimited in most circumstances (unless all the senators agree to a limit). If you have ever watched C-SPAN, you know that often there are very few people on the floor during debates. Typically only the small number of people who are most interested in the bill (usually members of the committee that produced it) actively participate and offer amendments.

When debate is completed and all amendments have been considered, the presiding officer calls for a voice vote, with those in favor saying "aye" and those opposed "no." If it is unclear which side has won, any member may call for a "division vote," which requires members on each side to stand and be counted. At that point, any member may call for a recorded vote (there is no way of recording members' positions on voice votes and division votes). If at least 25 members agree that a recorded vote is desired, buzzers go off in the office buildings and committee rooms, calling members to the floor for the vote. Once they reach the floor, members vote by an electronic system in which they insert ATM-like cards into slots and each vote is recorded on a big board at the front of the House or Senate chamber. In late May 2020, the House approved proxy voting and virtual hearings to allow members to participate in the legislative process during the COVID-19 pandemic. Members could vote for up to 10 of their colleagues if they had written authorization filed with the clerk of the House and specific instructions (that would be publicly announced) on each vote. Republicans were strongly opposed to the measure, saying that members should be required to vote in person, despite the pandemic.[47]

If the bill passes the House and the Senate in different forms, the discrepancies have to be resolved. On many minor bills, one chamber may simply accept the other chamber's version to solve the problem. On other minor bills and some major bills, differences are resolved through a process known as amendments between the chambers. In this case, one chamber modifies a bill passed by the other chamber and sends it back. These modifications can go back and forth several times before both houses agree on an identical bill. A complicated version of this approach was used to pass health care reform in 2010.

The most common way to resolve differences on major legislation is through a conference committee made up of key players in the House and the Senate. A majority of major bills go to a conference committee, but minor bills rarely do.[48] Sometimes the conferees split the difference between the House and Senate versions, but at other times the House and Senate approaches are so different that one must be chosen—an especially tricky prospect when different parties control the two chambers. Sometimes the conference cannot resolve differences and the bill dies. If the conference

markup
One of the steps through which a bill becomes a law, in which the final wording of the bill is determined.

veto

The president's rejection of a bill that has been passed by Congress. A veto can be overridden by a two-thirds vote in both the House and Senate.

pocket veto

The automatic death of a bill passed by the House and Senate when the president fails to sign the bill in the last 10 days of a legislative session.

discharge petition

A mechanism for forcing a standing committee to report a bill to the floor in the U.S. House (and some state legislatures). A majority of members must sign the petition to force a bill out of committee.

committee can agree on changes, each chamber must pass the final version, the conference report, by a majority vote and neither chamber is allowed to amend it.

The bill is then sent to the president. If the president approves and signs the measure within 10 days (not counting Sundays), it becomes law. If the president objects to the bill, he or she may **veto** it within 10 days, sending it back to the chamber where it originated, along with a statement of objections. Unless both the House and the Senate vote to override the veto by a two-thirds majority, the bill dies. If the president does not act within 10 days and Congress is in session, the bill becomes law without the president's approval. If Congress is not in session, the measure dies through what is known as a **pocket veto**.

One final point on how a bill becomes a law is important: any bill that appropriates money must pass through the two-step process of authorization and appropriation. In the authorization process, members debate the merits of the bill, determine its language, and limit the amount that can be spent on the bill. The appropriations process involves the Budget Committees in both the House and the Senate, which set the overall guidelines for the national budget, and the Appropriations Committees in the two chambers, which determine the actual amounts of money that will be spent. In recent years, Congress has been unable to pass its appropriations bills in time for the start of the new fiscal year, so it ends up having to pass "continuing resolutions" that spend money at the last year's levels in order to keep the government open. Congress passed eight continuing resolutions for the 2019 fiscal year (but only two for 2020). That may sound like a lot, but the record is 21 for the 2001 fiscal year.[49]

Deviations from the conventional process

There are many ways in which legislation may not follow the typical path. First, in some Congresses up to 20 percent of *major* bills bypass the committee system. This may be done by a **discharge petition**, in which a majority of the members force a bill out of its assigned committee, or by a special rule in the House. In some cases, a bill may go to the relevant committee, but then party leadership may impose its version of the bill later in the process. For example, in the wake of the terrorist attacks of September 11, the House Judiciary Committee, after hard bipartisan work, quickly approved a version of the Patriot Act to be considered by the full House to give the government stronger surveillance powers. But a few days later, according to committee member Representative Jerrold Nadler (D-NY), "[t]hen the bill just disappeared. And we had a new several hundred-page bill revealed from the Rules Committee" that had to be voted on the next day. Most members of Congress did not have a chance to read it.[50] The Affordable Care Act (ACA) also deviated from the standard path.

Second, about one-third of major bills are adjusted post-committee and before the legislation reaches the floor by supporters of the bills to increase their chances of passage. Sometimes the bill goes back to the committee after these changes, and sometimes it does not. One good example of this approach was the ACA, which was altered by House and Senate leadership after the committees deadlocked on different versions of the bill. The legislation also bypassed the conference committee; party leadership worked out the differences between the House and Senate versions directly. Thus, although most of the legislative work is accomplished in committees, a significant amount of legislation bypasses committee review.

Third, summit meetings between the president and congressional leaders may bypass or jump-start the normal legislative process. For example, rather than going through the Budget Committees to set budgetary targets, the president may meet with top leaders from both parties and hammer out a compromise that is presented to Congress as a done deal. This technique is especially important on delicate budget negotiations or when the president is threatening to use the veto. Often the congressional rank and file go along with the end product of the summit meeting, but occasionally they reject it—as happened in February 2014, when all but 28 House Republicans voted against their leadership on the extension of the debt ceiling that had been agreed to by President Obama and House and Senate leaders.

Fourth, **omnibus legislation**—massive bills that run hundreds of pages long and cover many different subjects and programs—often requires creative approaches by the leadership to guide the bill through the legislative maze. In addition, the massive legislation often carries riders—extraneous legislation attached to the "must pass" bill to secure approval for pet projects that would otherwise fail. This is a form of pork-barrel legislation and another mechanism used in the quest for reelection. One example was the 2,232-page 2018 omnibus spending legislation that combined all 12 appropriation bills and authorized more than $1.3 trillion in spending. Some of the "extras" in the bill included $1.6 billion for the border wall (Trump had asked for $25 billion), $4.65 billion to help address the opioid crisis, and $380 million to the federal Election Assistance Commission to improve election security and technology.[51] The COVID-19 relief bills were also packed with billions of dollars in spending that were not directly related to the pandemic.[52]

Differences in the House and Senate legislative processes

There are three central differences in the legislative processes of the House and the Senate: (1) the continuity of the membership and the impact this has on the rules, (2) the way in which bills get to the floor, and (3) the structure of the floor process, including debate and amendments. As discussed earlier, the Senate is a continuing body, with two-thirds of its members returning to the next session without facing reelection (because of the six-year term), whereas all House members are up for reelection every two years. This has an important impact on the rules of the two chambers: there has been much greater stability in the rules of the Senate than in those of the House. Whereas the House adopts its rules anew at the start of each new session (sometimes with major changes, sometimes with only minor modifications), the Senate has not had a general reaffirmation of its rules since 1789. However, the Senate rules can be changed at the beginning of a session to meet the needs of the new members.

The floor process is much simpler and less structured in the Senate than in the House. In part, this is due to the relative size of the two chambers: the House with its 435 members needs to have more rules than the Senate with its 100 members. Ironically, however, the floor process is actually much easier to navigate in the House because of its structure. Since the adoption of Reed's Rules in 1890, the House has been a very majoritarian body—that is, a majority of House members can almost always have their way. Named after Speaker Thomas Reed, the rules were an implementation of his view that "the best system is to have one party govern and the other party watch."[53] In contrast, the Senate has always been a much more individualistic body. Former Majority Leader Howard Baker compared leading the Senate to "herding cats," saying it was difficult "trying to make ninety-nine independent souls act in concert under rules that encourage polite anarchy and embolden people who find majority rule a dubious proposition at best."[54]

The Filibuster Part of the challenge in getting the Senate to act collectively is rooted in the Senate's unlimited debate and very open amendment process. Unless restricted

unanimous consent agreement
Agreement reached by party leaders in the Senate to limit debate and the consideration of amendments on legislation.

cloture
A procedure through which the Senate can limit the amount of time spent debating a bill (cutting off a filibuster) if a supermajority of 60 senators agree.

filibuster
A tactic used by senators to block a bill by continuing to hold the floor and speak—under the Senate rule of unlimited debate—until the bill's supporters back down.

hold
An objection to considering a measure on the Senate floor.

reconciliation
Reconciliation allows for expedited consideration of certain tax, spending, and debt limit legislation. The main advantage of the procedure is that reconciliation legislation is not subject to filibusters in the Senate, and therefore may be passed with simple majorities in the House and Senate.

House Rules Committee
Resolutions (or "rules") governing the amending process and length of debate come from this committee. These rules must be adopted by a majority vote of the entire House.

closed rules
Conditions placed on a legislative debate by the House Rules Committee prohibiting amendments to a bill.

open rules
Conditions placed on a legislative debate by the House Rules Committee allowing relevant amendments to a bill.

modified rules
Conditions placed on a legislative debate by the House Rules Committee allowing certain amendments to a bill while barring others.

by a **unanimous consent agreement**, senators can speak as long as they want and offer any amendment to a bill, even if it isn't directly related to the underlying bill. Debate may be cut off only if a supermajority of 60 senators agree in a process known as invoking **cloture**. Therefore, one senator can stop any bill by threatening to talk the bill to death if 40 of his or her colleagues agree. This practice is known as a **filibuster**. The filibuster strengthens the hand of the minority party in the Senate, giving it veto power over legislation unless the majority party has 60 senators who support a bill.

Before the 1960s, senators really did hold the floor for hours by reading from the phone book or reciting recipes. The late senator Strom Thurmond of South Carolina holds the record of 24 hours and 18 minutes of continuous talking. Today it is rare for a filibuster to tie up Senate business, since a senator's threat to filibuster a bill is usually enough to take the bill off the legislative agenda. If the bill is actually filibustered, it goes on a separate legislative track so that it does not bring the rest of the business of the Senate to a halt. Alternatively, if supporters of the bill think they have enough votes, they can invoke cloture to stop the filibuster and bring the bill to the floor for a vote. Frustrated over repeated Republican filibusters on President Obama's nominations to federal courts and agencies, Senate Democrats in November 2013 removed the filibuster for all presidential nominations, except those to the Supreme Court.[55] When Democrats filibustered Trump's nomination of Neil Gorsuch to the Supreme Court in April 2017, the Senate changed the rules again to allow Supreme Court nominees to be confirmed by a simple majority vote.[56]

Because of the practice of unlimited debate in the Senate, much of its business is conducted under unanimous consent agreements by which senators agree to adhere to time limits on debate and amendments. However, because these are literally *unanimous* agreements, a single senator can obstruct the business of the chamber by issuing a **hold** on the bill or presidential nomination. This practice is often a bargaining tool to extract concessions from the bill's supporters, but sometimes, especially late in a session when time gets tight, a hold can actually kill a bill by removing it from the active agenda.

One way that the Senate has circumvented the filibuster is through the **reconciliation** process, which was established in 1974 to make the budget process more efficient. If reconciliation legislation is related to budget matters and does not increase the deficit outside the specified time period (and satisfies several other rules), it may be passed with a simple majority vote in the House and Senate. The process was initially used for budget items, but in recent years it has been used to pass other controversial bills that threatened to be derailed by a filibuster. For example, the ACA was passed in 2010 through reconciliation, and the process was also used for various attempts to repeal the ACA (the most recent attempt, in 2017, failed in the Senate by a single vote). It was also used to pass the 2017 Tax Cuts and Jobs Act.

House Rules In contrast to the Senate, the House is a more orderly, although complex, institution. The **House Rules Committee** exerts great control over the legislative process, especially on major legislation, through special rules that govern the nature of debate on a bill. There are three general types of rules: **closed rules** do not allow any amendments to the bill, **open rules** allow any germane amendments, and **modified rules** allow some specific amendments but not others. House leadership has used closed and modified rules much more aggressively in recent years. Twenty-five years ago, as many as two-thirds of bills would come to the floor under an open rule. Since 2017, there has not been a single bill considered under an open rule.[57] Once a special rule is adopted, general debate is tightly controlled by the floor managers. Amendments are considered under a five-minute rule, but this rule is routinely bent as members offer phantom "pro forma" amendments to, for example, "strike the last word" or "strike the requisite number of words." This means that the member is not really offering an amendment but simply going through the formal procedure of offering one in order to get an additional five minutes to talk about the amendment.

These descriptions of the two chambers show that although the Senate is formally committed to unlimited debate, senators often voluntarily place limits on themselves through unanimous consent, which makes the Senate operate much more like the House. Similarly, although the House has very strict rules concerning debate and amendments, there are ways of bending those rules to make the House operate a bit more like the potentially freewheeling Senate.

Otto von Bismarck, the Prussian statesman of the late nineteenth century, famously said, "Laws are like sausages; it is better not to see them being made." Indeed, the legislative process may be messy, but knowledge of how laws are made is important both for being an effective legislator and for being a good democratic citizen. Understanding how a bill becomes a law, seeing the various stages of the process, and recognizing the various veto points at which a bill may die all help put into context the simplistic complaints about gridlock and conflict. Now that you have a better understanding of the legislative process, you should have a stronger basis for evaluating what Congress is doing.

Oversight

DESCRIBE HOW CONGRESS ENSURES THAT THE BUREAUCRACY IMPLEMENTS POLICIES CORRECTLY

Once a bill becomes a law, Congress plays another crucial role by overseeing the implementation of the law to make sure the bureaucracy interprets it as Congress intended. Other motivations drive the oversight process as well, such as the desire to gain publicity that may help in the reelection quest or to embarrass the president if he or she is of the opposite party. For example, in 2015 Republicans used their oversight powers to call attention to Hillary Clinton's use of private servers for her work-related e-mail as secretary of state and the way that she handled the attack on the U.S. embassy in Benghazi. Similarly, when Democrats investigated President Trump's withholding of funds to Ukraine until its president promised to investigate the Bidens (see Chapter 2), there were serious concerns about an abuse of executive power that undermined national security. While these hearings were, at least in part, politically motivated, the most important motivation for oversight is to ensure that laws are implemented properly.[58]

There are several mechanisms that Congress may use to accomplish this goal (see also Chapter 7). First, the bluntest instrument is the **power of the purse**. If members of Congress think an agency is not properly implementing their programs, they can simply cut off the funds to that agency. However, this approach to punishment is rarely used because it often eliminates good aspects of the agency along with the bad.

Second, Congress can hold hearings and investigations. By summoning administration officials and agency heads to a public hearing, Congress can use the media spotlight to focus attention on problems within the bureaucracy or on issues that have been overlooked. For example, the House Oversight Committee has investigated Russian interference in the 2016 election, violations of the emoluments clause by President Trump (with a focus on his hotel in Washington, D.C.), the process for providing security clearances, immigration policy, and voting rights.[59] This type of oversight is known as "fire alarm oversight"—that is, members wait until there

power of the purse
(1) The constitutional power of Congress to raise and spend money. Congress can use this as a negative or checking power over the other branches by freezing or cutting their funding. (2) The power of Congress to control fiscal policy, the taxing and spending power that is the basis for most government programs.

is a crisis before they spring to action.[60] It is in contrast to "police patrol" oversight, which involves constant vigilance in overseeing the bureaucracy. For example, House Democrats were very concerned about the executive branch interfering with the Justice Department, dating back to President Trump's firing of FBI Director James Comey in 2017 and Attorney General William Barr's handling of the Mueller report, which documented Russian interference in the 2016 election and possible obstruction of justice by the White House. Tensions between Democrats in Congress and the Justice Department continued throughout Trump's impeachment trial into the summer of 2020, with congressional hearings on prosecutorial independence.[61] Of the two, fire alarm oversight is far more common because Congress does not have the resources to constantly monitor the entire bureaucracy.

Finally, the Senate exercises specific control over other executive functions through its constitutional responsibilities to provide "advice and consent" on presidential appointments and approval of treaties. The Senate typically defers to the president on these matters, but it may assert its power, especially when constituent interests are involved. Two current examples would be the Senate's increasing skepticism about free-trade agreements negotiated by the president's trade representatives and the Senate's holds on presidential nominations (however, those holds were less effective as Majority Leader Mitch McConnell [R-KY] was quite successful in getting President Trump's executive branch and court nominations approved).

The ultimate in congressional oversight is the process of removing the president, vice president, other civil officers, or federal judges through impeachment. The House and Senate share this power: the House issues articles of impeachment, which outline the charges against the official, and the Senate conducts the trial of the impeached officials. Three presidents have been impeached: Andrew Johnson in the controversy over Reconstruction after the Civil War, Bill Clinton over the scandal involving White House intern Monica Lewinsky, and Donald Trump for the abuse of power and obstruction of Congress concerning his interactions with Ukraine. However, none of them were convicted and removed by the Senate.

As should be clear from this summary, one important aspect of congressional oversight is to serve as a check on the executive branch. The boundaries of the system of checks and balances may be fundamentally altered, depending on the outcome of three cases concerning President Trump's claims of absolute executive immunity from congressional subpoenas. The first case concerns a House subpoena requiring White House Counsel Donald McGahn to testify in the impeachment inquiry. President Trump refused to allow McGahn to testify, so the House sued in federal court to enforce the subpoena. An appeals court ruled in Congress's favor, but it was unlikely that McGahn would testify before the elections.[62] The other two cases involve President Trump's financial records and tax returns, to which Congress is attempting to gain access.[63] Most presidents have claimed immunity against some congressional requests for information, but no previous president has claimed absolute immunity. In June 2020, the Supreme Court ruled 7–2 against the president in both cases. Chief Justice John Roberts wrote the majority opinions, concluding, "In our system, the public has a right to every man's evidence ... since the founding of the Republic, every man has included the President of the United States."[64] However, as in the McGahn case, the White House was able to delay the release of any documents until after the election.

An even more far-reaching erosion of congressional oversight is playing out in the context of the COVID-19 relief bills. One of the key provisions of the laws was to provide oversight to make sure that the trillions of dollars were being properly spent. However, President Trump refused to allow executive branch officials to testify before the Democrat-controlled House, while those same officials were routinely appearing before Senate

The director of the National Institute of Allergy and Infectious Diseases, Dr. Anthony Fauci, testified via video before the Senate Health Committee in May 2020 in the midst of the COVID-19 outbreak. Hearings such as this are an important tool used in congressional oversight.

committees. The *Washington Post* reported, "Since the virus outbreak in early March, House Democrats have sent at least 203 letters to agencies, 173 directly related to the pandemic, and almost all have been rejected or have yet to receive a response. President Trump explained he didn't want his people to appear before Speaker Nancy Pelosi's committees because they are 'a bunch of Trump haters.'"[65] Congress can't do its job if executive branch officials refuse to testify.

The CARES Act

AP®
POLICY IN
PRACTICE

The coronavirus disease (COVID-19) started infecting humans in 2019 and became a worldwide pandemic in early 2020. Throughout that year, it raged in the United States and affected almost every area of the world to different degrees in terms of infection rates, hospitalizations, and deaths. Partly due to the federalist system in the United States, states have large control over how they deal with such issues, and they have each handled coronavirus differently. Moreover, the Trump administration, in large part, decided not to formulate an overall national policy to mitigate the health and safety dangers of the disease and left it up to the states to make their own decisions. While the lack of a national strategy could be leveled as a criticism, one could also argue that it is a by-product and strength of federalism that states are allowed to come up with their own creative solutions. As a counterexample, in France, a unitary government whose power emanates from the national government, decisions about how to combat the disease were made by the president and prime minister for the entire country. This approach has its advantages and disadvantages.

When the disease started to spread at alarming rates, the reaction of most governments was to close down all nonessential businesses and either encourage or legally compel people to quarantine themselves as much as possible, leaving the house only when necessary. Even though the disease hit the United States later than it hit Asia and Europe, the United States did not react as quickly with business closings and self-quarantine measures as other countries. But even had the United States acted more quickly, the interconnectedness and interdependence of every economy meant that American businesses and workers were affected especially by disruptions in the supply chain. The United States imports a great deal of goods and raw materials, so slowed-down or stopped factory production in other countries directly affected the transport and sales of goods in the United States. The problem was compounded when American businesses were forced to close their doors in many states for an uncertain period of time. The closing of countless businesses led to high levels of unemployment not seen since the Great Depression of the 1930s, and the CARES (Coronavirus Aid, Relief, and Economic Security) Act of 2020 was one of several bills passed in order to improve the economy.

The CARES Act was the third phase in a series of spending bills related to the COVID-19 pandemic, but it was the first bill that dealt exclusively with improving the economy. Since the Great Depression, there has been an ongoing debate in economics about how to fight unemployment. Should there be a supply-side or a demand-side approach? Those who follow the supply-side approach believe that the government should give money to businesses or reduce their taxes so they can continue to operate or to grow. This approach will allow businesses to maintain or increase employment. In the demand-side approach, sometimes referred to as Keynesian theory (named after the British economist John Maynard Keynes), the quickest way to stimulate the economy is to use a bottom-up method, in which the government gives money directly to people, reduces income taxes, and/or creates jobs, such as public works projects (for example, building bridges and schools). If people have more money, so the thinking goes, they will spend it, and this behavior will have a ripple (or more technically, a multiplier) effect throughout the economy: as spending increases, firms will have to hire more people, which means more workers will have more money to spend and so on. While no one can be sure of the correct option, these views have become associated with right-wing (supply-side) and left-wing (demand-side) ideologies.

As often happens in politics, a middle ground was reached with the CARES Act. Republican legislators pushed for more spending for businesses (and less for workers), and the Democrats wanted more spending for workers (and less for businesses). President Trump, a Republican, was a proponent of not only business relief but also direct cash payments to Americans. The effectiveness of these policies will be debated for years. After all, economists still debate if Keynesian economics actually got the United States out of the Great Depression, prolonged it, or had no effect at all.

Policy Stages

1. Problem Recognition
   - COVID-19 emerged as a worldwide pandemic with no known cure that affected thousands of Americans and the economy.
   - Unemployment rapidly increased in the United States and the rest of the world.
   - The health care industry became overburdened with too many patients needing hospitalization in the absence of enough equipment and beds.
   - Voluntary and state-directed confinement measures placed additional strains on the economy and the health care industry.

2. Agenda Setting
   - Phase One: Coronavirus Preparedness and Response Supplemental Appropriation Act of 2020
     - Funding in the amount of $8.3 billion would be applied to medical supplies, treatment, and vaccines.
   - Phase Two: Families First Coronavirus Response Act
     - Free testing became available and paid leave became an option for workers.

- Presidential candidate Andrew Yang's proposal of universal basic income (UBI) of $1,000 per month was back on the public's radar as a (temporary) solution.
- Other prominent politicians, such as Alexandria Ocasio-Cortez and Tulsi Gabbard, supported similar UBI packages.

3. Deliberation and Formulation
   - Bill H.R. 748 (originally titled the Middle Class Health Benefits Tax Repeal Act of 2019) was initially introduced in the House of Representatives by Joe Courtney (D-CT) on January 24, 2019.
   - Bill S. 3548 was introduced in the Senate by Mitch McConnell (R-KY) on March 19, 2020, as a shell bill (an amendment to an unrelated existing bill) since revenue-raising bills need to start in the House.
   - Senate Republicans and President Trump crafted the Senate version and then negotiated with Senate Democrats before sending it to the House of Representatives.
   - Some Senate Republicans thought the stimulus check funds should be given instead to businesses as loans and grants so they would not go out of business, leading to significant unemployment.
   - House Democrats were critical of the amount of money devoted to bailing out corporations and believed that not enough money was being allocated to workers.
   - Bill H.R. 6379 introduced the Take Responsibility for Workers and Family Act in the House of Representatives by Nita M. Lowey (D-NY) on March 23, 2020.
   - The House bill put pressure on Senate Republicans to make compromises.

4. Enactment
   - The House of Representatives passed the bill on July 17, 2019: **419 YEAs**: 230 Democrats, 189 Republicans, 0 others; **6 NAYs**: 3 Democrats, 2 Republicans, 1 other; **8 Not Voting**: 2 Democrats, 6 Republicans, 0 others.
   - The Senate passed the bill with amendment on March 25, 2020: **96 YEAs**: 45 Democrats, 49 Republicans, 2 others; **0 NAYs**; **4 Not Voting**: 0 Democrats, 4 Republicans, 0 others.
   - The House of Representatives agreed to the Senate amendment on March 27, 2020 (voice vote).
   - The Coronavirus Aid, Relief, and Economic Security (CARES) Act of 2020 was signed into law by President Donald Trump on March 27, 2020.
   - The CARES Act became Public Law 116-136, launching phase three.

5. Implementation
   - Individuals and families received 30 percent of funding.
     - Americans received $1,200 per adult and $500 per child ("helicopter money") up to a certain level of income.
     - Federal student loans were temporarily suspended.
     - Mortgage payments on federally funded loans were temporarily suspended.
     - Workers in more job categories (including freelancers and furloughed employees) became eligible for unemployment benefits.
     - The length of time benefits would be available was extended four more months.
   - Big business received 25 percent of funding.
     - Loan money could not be used to buy back stocks.
   - Small business received 19 percent of funding.
     - Loans were for paying rent and paying employees.

- State and local governments received 17 percent of funding to address these areas of need:
    - Issues related to COVID-19
    - Schools
    - Childcare
- Public and health responses received 9 percent of funding.
    - The health care industry benefitted by, among other things, offsetting lost revenue from delayed elective surgeries.
    - Additional payments went toward treating Medicare patients.

6. Evaluation
- Criticism and praise mostly fell along party lines.
- Some Democrats believed that not enough money was given to workers and too much money was given to businesses.
- Some Republicans believed that the unemployment benefits were too generous in amount and duration.
- Many Democrats believed that too much money was given to corporations and not enough to smaller businesses.
- Many were concerned that the benefits would expire too soon before the pandemic ended.
    - Firms might go out of business.
    - Workers would remain unemployed.
    - Firms would open too soon, leading to a rise in illnesses and deaths, which would hurt the economy even more.
- Many believed this policy should be considered relief rather than stimulus since it will just tide workers and businesses over until the economy can open up again.
- It was difficult to reach all eligible recipients.
- State and local governments needed more money to cover their budget deficits.
- Of the stimulus payments that were made, $1.4 billion in checks were sent to dead people.

7. Possible Modifications, Expansion, or Termination of Policy
- The House of Representatives passed the HEROES (Health and Economic Recovery Omnibus Emergency Solutions) Act on May 15, 2020, with the following provisions:
    - An aid package totaling $3 trillion
    - State and local government funding
    - Stimulus checks for individuals and families
    - Hazard pay for essential workers
    - Extended unemployment insurance until February 2021
    - Money for COVID-19 testing
    - Subsidies for housing and utility payments
    - Money to help bail out the U.S. Postal Service
    - Grants for small businesses
    - Allowances for workers who lost health insurance to sign up for the Affordable Care Act (ACA) outside of the normal enrollment period
- Senate Majority Leader Mitch McConnell indicated that the Senate would not consider the HEROES Act.
- Senate leaders said that their proposal would have been closer to $1 trillion.
- President Trump promised to veto the HEROES Act if it crossed his desk.

- President Trump announced a phase four stimulus package with the following provisions:
  - Funding totaling $2 trillion
  - A supply-side focus on creating more manufacturing jobs
  - Money also devoted to rebuilding infrastructure
  - The Explore America tax credit, which would subsidize Americans who want to travel for pleasure in the United States before 2022
  - Payroll tax cuts, which may replace stimulus checks for workers
- Both houses of Congress passed their own stimulus package in mid-December 2020, which included $600 direct payments to individuals, $300 billion in business compensation, and a temporary $300 increase in weekly federal unemployment payments. President Trump signed this bill (the Coronavirus Response and Relief Supplemental Appropriations Act of 2021) into law on December 27, 2020.

Questions for Discussion

1. Is a demand-side or a supply-side approach more effective in improving the economy? Explain your answer.
2. What are the advantages and disadvantages of the federalist structure of the U.S. government in dealing with the COVID-19 pandemic? Would a unitary structure have been more or less effective? Why or why not?
3. Since there are so many factors involved, explain whether or not it is fair to criticize the president if the economy is not doing well. Should the president get credit for a good economy? Explain your answer.

Unpacking the Conflict

Considering all that we've learned in this chapter about how Congress works, let's return to our discussion of DACA. Why is it so hard for Congress to compromise on issues that appear to be consensual, like protecting the Dreamers? How can members of Congress best serve the collective interests of the nation while also representing their local constituents?

Although the details of the legislative process and the institutions of Congress can be complicated, the basic explanations for members' behavior are quite straightforward when viewed in terms of the trade-off between responsiveness and responsibility. Members of Congress want to be reelected, so they are generally quite responsive to constituents' interests. They spend considerable time on casework—meeting with people in their district and delivering benefits for their district. At the same time, members are motivated to be responsible—to rise above local interests and attend to the nation's best interests. The conflict between these two impulses can create contradictory policies that contribute to Congress's image problem. For example, the chapter opener discussed the difficulty of reaching a compromise on DACA. Both parties and the president appeared to want to help the Dreamers, but conservatives in the Republican Party were strongly opposed to providing any path to citizenship. Clearly, the country as a whole benefits from the economic and social

I have seen in the Halls of Congress more idealism, more humanness, more compassion, more profiles of courage than in any other institution that I have ever known.

—**Hubert Humphrey,** former senator and vice president

contributions of the Dreamers, but some members of Congress responded to their political base by opposing a compromise. The tension between responsible lawmaking and responsiveness to constituents is evident on many issues.

Considering members' motivations is crucial to understanding how Congress functions, but their behavior is also constrained by the institutions in which they operate. When moderate House Republicans were on the verge of forcing a vote on the Dreamers, the Senate Republican Leader stood firm in his opposition, saying he would not bring a bill to a vote in the Senate that did not have President Trump's approval. So ultimately, it did not matter that the House was able to find a compromise solution. In this instance, party leadership served as a constraint, but the committee system can provide a positive vehicle for lawmaking as an important source of expertise and information, and it provides a platform from which members can take positions and claim credit. When they aren't obstructing legislation, parties in Congress can provide coherence to the legislative agenda and help structure voting patterns on bills. Rules and norms constrain the nature of debate and the legislative process. Although these institutions shape members' behavior, it is important to remember that members can also change those rules and institutions. Therefore, Congress has the ability to evolve with changing national conditions and demands from voters, groups, and the president.

In this context, much of what Congress does can be understood in terms of the conflicts inherent in politics. As we have seen, even on consensual issues like DACA, conflict and political strategy may doom the common ground that is within reach. The extremes on the right and left did not want to compromise on DACA: the former viewed any path to citizenship as amnesty and the latter wanted a "clean bill" with no money for the wall or other changes to immigration policy. There was a huge majority in the middle that could have passed a DACA bill with some money for border security and the wall, but President Trump and Republicans wanted to leverage the consensual issue of DACA to enact the broader immigration policies they favored. Their approach did not work, and we got deadlock instead. Congress does not always live up to the expectations of being the "first branch" of government, but it tries to do the best it can to balance the conflicting pressures it faces.

"What's Your Take?"

Does Congress do a reasonable job of representing both national and local interests?

If not, how should Congress change?

AP®
STUDY
GUIDE

Summary

The Constitution gave Congress vast enumerated powers, such as raising revenue, declaring war, and maintaining the armed forces, making it the "first branch" of government. While Congress has long dominated day-to-day politics, the president has become considerably more powerful over time. Despite the low approval ratings for Congress itself, most voters like their members of Congress. Members of Congress work hard to strike a balance between responding to what constituents want and doing what is in the nation's best interest. In the balance, however, they prioritize district interests over national policy.

Many aspects of Congress are set up to meet the needs of its members. The norms of universalism and reciprocity still dominate, meaning that members of Congress share resources more broadly than partisan politics would dictate.

Congressional behavior is also influenced by the manner in which members of Congress are elected, with the Senate designed to represent the states while the House is designed to represent the population. House members have constituencies created through redistricting, which sometimes results in gerrymandered districts. Elections resulting in a divided government may lead a contentious confirmation process, especially with the appointments of lame-duck presidents of the opposite party. Constituency accountability varies based on whether the member is behaving as a trustee, delegate, or politico.

Most bills become law in a conventional manner, but major pieces of legislation generally deviate considerably from this path. The legislative process differs for the House, with the use of a Rules Committee, the **Committee of the Whole**, and discharge petitions, and for the Senate, with the

Committee of the Whole
The parliamentary mechanism for initial consideration of legislation and expediting debate and voting on amendments in the U.S. House. The Committee of the Whole is comprised of all members of the House but has a smaller quorum (100 members instead of 218) and amendments are considered under a five-minute rule.

Key Terms

apportionment (p. 145)

Baker v. Carr (p. 145)

bicameralism (p. 131)

casework (p. 140)

closed rules (p. 168)

cloture (p. 168)

Committee of the Whole (p. 177)

conference committees (p. 159)

delegate (p. 135)

descriptive representation (p. 133)

discharge petition (p. 166)

distributive theory (p. 159)

earmarks (p. 151)

electoral connection (p. 138)

filibuster (p. 168)

gerrymandering (p. 146)

gridlock (p. 150)

hold (p. 168)

House Rules Committee (p. 168)

incumbency advantage (p. 140)

informational theory (p. 159)

joint committees (p. 158)

logrolling (p. 151)

Majority Leader (p. 154)

markup (p. 165)

Minority Leader (p. 154)

modified rules (p. 168)

omnibus legislation (p. 167)

open rules (p. 168)

party unity (p. 156)

party vote (p. 156)

permanent campaign (p. 133)

pocket veto (p. 166)

politico (p. 135)

pork barrel (p. 133)

power of the purse (p. 169)

president pro tempore (p. 154)

reconciliation (p. 168)

redistricting (p. 145)

roll call vote (p. 156)

select committees (p. 158)

seniority (p. 152)

Shaw v. Reno (p. 149)

Speaker of the House (p. 152)

standing committees (p. 158)

substantive representation (p. 135)

trustee (p. 135)

unanimous consent agreement (p. 168)

veto (p. 166)

whip system (p. 154)

use of the filibuster, holds, and unanimous consent agreements, sometimes making it difficult to reconcile differences between bills. The formality of debate is influenced by the difference in size and constituencies of the two chambers.

After passing bills into law, Congress oversees the bureaucracy in its implementation of the law, making sure it fits Congress's intentions. Although controlling funding is the most powerful mechanism for this purpose, Congress has a number of other mechanisms for achieving bureaucratic fidelity. Generally, Congress does not actively patrol the bureaucracy but waits until a crisis emerges to act.

Enduring Understanding

CON-3: "The republican ideal in the U.S. is manifested in the structure and operation of the legislative branch." (AP® U.S. Government and Politics Course and Exam Description)

Multiple-Choice Questions (Arranged by Topic)

Topic 2.1: Congress: The Senate and House of Representatives (CON-3)

1. **Which of the following is an accurate comparison of the House of Representatives and the Senate?**

	House of Representatives	Senate
(A)	designed to represent the population	designed to represent the states equally
(B)	members are elected to represent districts within a state	has 435 members
(C)	has 100 members	members are elected to represent the state as a whole
(D)	members serve six-year terms	members serve two-year terms

2. **Which of the following best describes where Congress's enumerated powers are listed in the Constitution?**
   - **(A)** Article I, Section 4
   - **(B)** Article I, Section 8
   - **(C)** Article I, Section 9
   - **(D)** Article I, Section 10

Topic 2.2: Structure, Powers, and Functions of Congress (CON-3)

Questions 3–4 refer to the excerpt.

In the third place, those ties which bind the representative to his constituents are strengthened by motives of a more selfish nature. His pride and vanity attach him to a form of government which favors his pretensions and gives him a share in its honors and distinctions. Whatever hopes or projects might be entertained by a few aspiring characters, it must generally happen that a great proportion of the men deriving their advancement from their influence with the people, would have more to hope from a preservation of the favor, than from innovations in the government subversive of the authority of the people. All these securities, however, would be found very insufficient without the restraint of frequent elections.

—James Madison, *Federalist 58*, February 20, 1788

3. **Which of the following best describes Madison's response to the argument that representatives will consist of people who are too ambitious and unsympathetic to the majority of the population?**

   (A) Since representatives are appointed by state legislatures, those with the heightened ability to make decisions will be able to control them.

   (B) The fear of impeachment will persuade representatives to follow the will of the majority.

   (C) Representatives will have a sense of duty, gratitude, interest, and ambition that will ensure they serve the people well.

   (D) The use of filibusters and holds will enable representatives to support those that elect them to office.

4. **The inclusion of which of the following constitutional provisions best responds to Madison's point of view?**

   (A) requiring the entire House of Representatives to run for election every two years

   (B) providing lifetime appointments for justices of the Supreme Court

   (C) amending the Constitution to allow a president to serve only two terms in office

   (D) requiring the Senate to confirm most presidential appointments

5. **Which of the following best describes a step in the process of how a bill becomes a law?**

   (A) The bill is introduced by the president at the start of a new session of Congress.

   (B) A veto by the president can be overridden with a majority vote by both houses.

   (C) The Senate can pass a discharge petition with a majority vote to force a bill out of its assigned committee.

   (D) A conference committee works out any differences between the House and Senate versions of a bill.

6. **Which of the following best explains how committees are created in terms of party representation?**

   (A) Committee membership is divided equally between the two major parties.

   (B) Committee members are assigned based on seniority regardless of their political affiliation.

   (C) Committee assignments are proportional to the numbers of seats each party holds in their respective houses in Congress.

   (D) Committee assignments are allocated so that each committee has a majority of their members from the same party as the president.

Topic 2.3: Congressional Behavior (CON-3)

7. **In which of the following scenarios would the Supreme Court most likely use *Baker v. Carr* (1962) as a precedent when making its decision?**

   (A) A member of Congress is prevented from running for a third term due to the passage of a law restricting members of Congress from serving more than 10 years.

   (B) A woman living in a large city claims that her congressional district has over a million people, when other districts in the state have fewer than 750,000.

   (C) A parent sues because her child is required to recite a prayer in public school after Congress passed a law declaring Christianity the national religion.

   (D) A state re-draws its congressional district lines to create a district of primarily minority voters in an attempt to have more minority members elected to Congress.

8. **Which of the following best describes the concept of logrolling?**

   (A) federally funded local projects attached to bills passed through Congress

   (B) when members of Congress support bills that they otherwise might not vote for in exchange for other members' votes on bills that are very important to them

   (C) the inability to enact legislation because of partisan conflict within Congress or between Congress and the president

   (D) the re-drawing of district boundaries to benefit a political party, protect incumbents, or change the proportion of minority voters in a district

Types of Gerrymanders

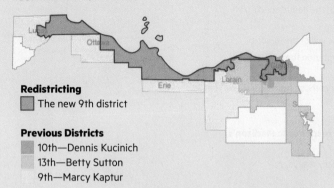

Redistricting
[ ] The new 9th district

Previous Districts
[ ] 10th—Dennis Kucinich
[ ] 13th—Betty Sutton
[ ] 9th—Marcy Kaptur

After the 2010 census, Ohio lost two seats in Congress (see our discussion of apportionment on p. 145). Republicans controlled the redistricting process and wanted the loss of seats to come from the Democrats. So the Republicans drew a new 9th congressional district that cut across the districts of three existing Democratic members of Congress. Obviously only one could win the Democratic primary—that happened to be Marcy Kaptur. Democrats Kucinich and Sutton had to leave Congress.

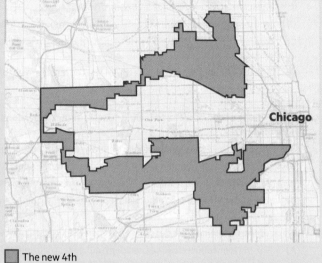

[ ] The new 4th congressional district

Illinois's 4th congressional district is a clear example of racial gerrymandering. The district has a very odd shape, but it incorporates two heavily Latino areas. (The northern part has a high Puerto Rican population and the southern part is largely Mexican; both areas are heavily Democratic.) This district was a stronghold of Democrat Luis Gutiérrez, who is of Puerto Rican descent, and is currently held by Chuy García, who is of Mexican descent. It is seen as a safe district for Democrats.

9. **Using the information shown in the maps, which of the following statements is the most accurate?**

(A) Ohio's new 9th congressional district has three representatives in the House.

(B) Ohio's new 9th congressional district likely violates the Supreme Court's ruling in *Baker v. Carr* (1962).

(C) Illinois's new 4th congressional district was most likely gerrymandered by Republicans.

(D) Illinois's new 4th congressional district is likely to continue to elect a Latino to the House of Representatives.

10. **Which of the following best explains how the drawing of districts, like those in the maps, can impact congressional elections?**

(A) When districts are gerrymandered to create overwhelmingly Democratic areas, the influence of minority-party voters is increased.

(B) Drawing districts in this way reduces incumbency advantage over time.

(C) Since these types of districts create safe seats, the incumbent is less likely to have a viable challenger in the general election.

(D) Districts drawn in this way are more likely to elect senators that support issues that are important to minority voters.

Free-Response Questions

Concept Application

In 2018, Michael Allman ran for Congress as a Republican. But he ran his campaign stating that if his constituents lean left of him on a particular issue before Congress, that's how Allman will vote. For every issue, voters in his district will be able to use a blockchain-enabled website to securely log their opinions, and Allman will follow the will of the people.

Allman has no background in politics but has worked in the tech industry, and he realized that the technology exists to make direct representation possible. Working with a tech company that had an existing platform, he created a custom website that will outline both sides of a general issue—for example, whether or not there should be more gun control laws—or a specific bill. Voters can read the arguments on both sides and selected op-eds. The site can verify that voters are in a particular district and that they're registered to vote and then register their opinions confidentially.[a]

After reading the scenario, respond to A, B, and C below:

(A) Referencing the scenario, describe the congressional role (trustee, delegate, or politico) exhibited by Mr. Allman in the scenario.

(B) In the context of the scenario, explain how the role described in Part A could affect the policy-making process.

(C) Michael Allman ended up losing the race to the incumbent. Explain why an incumbent often has an advantage over a challenger in an election for a seat in the U.S. House of Representatives.

SCOTUS Comparison

This question requires you to compare a Supreme Court case you studied in class with one you have not studied in class. A summary of the Supreme Court case you did not study in class is presented below and provides all of the information you need to know about this case to answer the prompt.

In 2010, the Texas legislature created a redistricting plan based on new census data. This plan was challenged and subsequently re-drawn by a federal appellate court and adopted into law by the legislature. The plaintiffs and registered voters, Evenwel and Pfenniger, argued that the new map violated the Constitution because the map provided roughly equal districts based on total population, but these districts were unequal in population when only the population of registered voters was taken into account.

In the ensuing case, *Evenwel v. Abbott* (2016), the Supreme Court ruled in a unanimous decision that the Texas redistricting plan was constitutional and did not violate the "one-person, one-vote" test. Arguing constitutional wording on apportionment of House seats based on total population as well as past practice by the states, the Court found that redistricting based solely on total population was constitutional.

Based on the information above, respond to the following questions.

(A) Identify the constitutional clause that is common in both *Evenwel v. Abbott* (2016) and *Baker v. Carr* (1962).

(B) Based on the constitutional clause identified in Part A, explain how the facts in *Evenwel v. Abbott* led to a different holding than in *Baker v. Carr*.

(C) Explain how a citizen group upset with the *Evenwel v. Abbott* ruling might try to limit the impact of the decision.

5

The Presidency

Are there limits on presidential power?

» **"This is when somebody is the President of the United States, the authority is total and that's the way it's got to be. It's total, it's total—and that's the way it's got to be. And the governors know that."**[1]
President Donald Trump, in a COVID-19 briefing, April 13, 2020

« **"I will be speaking to all 50 governors very shortly and I will then be authorizing each individual governor of each individual state to implement a reopening and a very powerful reopening plan of their state at a time and in a manner as most appropriate."**[2]
President Donald Trump, in a COVID-19 briefing, April 14, 2020

Outlining the major achievements of Donald Trump's four years in office illustrates the immense power of the presidency. Trump commanded the most powerful military forces on earth—and pushed through budget increases that will make them even stronger. Working with Republicans in Congress, Trump enacted the largest tax cut in American history. His directives transformed federal policy in areas such as immigration, the environment, and federal regulations.[3] And he placed himself at the center of the government's response to COVID-19, personally fielding calls from state and local officials for allocations of federal medical supplies.

A look at the personal style that Trump brought to the office, too, seems to underline its power. Trump behaved very differently compared to his predecessors. He hired and fired people working at the highest levels of government, seemingly at whim. Anything he said—even an offhand comment or tweet—became the focus of public attention. He relied on social media to communicate directly with the American people; responded to criticism with strong, personal attacks; made abrupt, radical changes in America's domestic and foreign policy; routinely ignored many presidential traditions and norms; pushed the boundaries of formal and informal limits on presidential authority; and made personal loyalty a dominant criterion for his appointees.

Yet the two quotes at the beginning of this chapter illustrate that there are fundamental limits to presidential power. One day, Trump claimed the authority to determine when states would ease COVID-19 lockdown and social-distancing

President Trump placed himself at the center of the government's response to the coronavirus pandemic in 2020, often butting heads with his advisers, as well as state-level officials. The crisis raised many questions about the power of the presidency. Is the power of the president "total"? What powers does the Constitution grant the president? How do the other branches of the government "check" these powers?

CHAPTER GOALS

Trace the evolution of presidential power.
pages 184–188

Describe the constitutional and statutory powers of the president today. pages 188–201

Explain how the Executive Office of the President, the vice president, and the Cabinet help the president. pages 202–205

Explain how modern presidents have become even more powerful. pages 205–214

regulations. The very next day, Trump said he would authorize governors to act as they thought best—a face-saving way to acknowledge the constitutional reality that this decision lies with the states. Other events during Trump's presidency illustrate limits on presidential power. While Trump frequently threatened to end the Justice Department's investigation into Russian collusion with the 2016 Trump campaign, he did not intervene. His attempts to force other nations to lower tariffs on American goods were largely unsuccessful. Although Trump campaigned on promises to repeal Obamacare and build a wall on the Mexican border, he did not succeed. He is one of only three presidents to be impeached by the House of Representatives (and the only one to have been impeached twice), although in both cases he was later acquitted by the Senate. And the COVID-19 pandemic illustrates that the awesome power of the presidency does not always translate into the ability to prevent disaster.

Just like the other 43 individuals who served as president before him—and like his successor, Joe Biden—Trump was often constrained by factors that were out of his control, from disagreements with other members of the federal government to the sometimes-fickle opinions of the American public. The fact is that the president is but one actor in a complex political system tasked with achieving often-impossible goals. This truth has constrained all presidents, not just Trump.

Trump's at times unorthodox approach to the office of the presidency raised questions about where presidential power comes from and what limits there are on its exercise. Did Trump redefine what makes a successful president—or a failed one? What factors distinguish presidential successes from presidential failures?

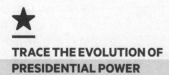

TRACE THE EVOLUTION OF PRESIDENTIAL POWER

AP® FOUNDATIONAL DOCUMENT

The development of presidential power

As we consider the history of America's 46 presidencies, four facts stand out: (1) Presidents matter. Their actions have had profound consequences for the nation, in both domestic and foreign policy. (2) Presidents get their power from a variety of sources, from provisions of the Constitution to their management of the actions taken by the executive branch of government. (3) Presidential power has increased over time, not because of changes in the Constitution but because of America's growth as a nation, its emergence as a dominant actor in international politics, the expansion of the federal government, and various acts of legislation that have given new authority to the president. (4) There are sharp limits to presidential power. Presidents are often forced to compromise or abandon their plans in the face of public, congressional, or foreign opposition. It is also important to note that while all 46 presidencies have been held by men, and almost all of them have been White, breaking this regularity is only a matter of time. In recent years, in addition to the election of Barack Obama in 2008 and 2012, the groundbreaking presidential campaign of Hillary Clinton in 2016, and the election of Kamala Harris as vice president in 2020, more women as well as minorities—including Senator Cory Booker (D-NJ), surgeon Ben Carson, and entrepreneur Andrew Yang—have been credible contenders for their party's presidential nominations.[4] In 2020, Pete Buttigieg, the mayor of South Bend, Indiana, became the first openly gay presidential candidate.

These lessons are particularly important as we consider the presidency of Donald Trump. Trump's background and behavior in office were often described as being radically different from those of past presidents. Even so, Trump had to contend with the same limits on presidential power faced by his predecessors, including voters' high expectations; unexpected events such as pandemics, natural disasters, or military actions by other countries; conflicts within his own party as well as between Republicans and Democrats in Congress; and differences between his goals and those held by federal bureaucrats who implement his decisions. Understanding how the accomplishments of past presidents were shaped by these constraints can help us begin to analyze and understand the Trump presidency.

Early years through World War I

Since the early years of the republic, presidents' actions have had profound consequences for the nation. Presidents George Washington, John Adams, and Thomas Jefferson forged compromises on domestic issues such as choosing a permanent location for the nation's capital, establishing the federal courts, and financing the government. Presidents Andrew Jackson and Martin Van Buren were instrumental in forming the Democratic Party and its local party organizations.[5]

In addition, early presidents made important foreign policy decisions. For example, the Monroe Doctrine issued by President James Monroe in 1823 stated that America would remain neutral in wars involving European nations and that these nations must cease attempts to colonize or occupy areas in North and South America.[6] Presidents John Tyler and James Polk oversaw the admission of the huge territory of Texas into the Union following the Mexican-American War, as well as the acquisition of land that later became Oregon, Washington, Idaho, and parts of Montana and Wyoming.[7]

Presidents also played key roles in the conflict over slavery. President Millard Fillmore's support helped enact the Compromise of 1850, which limited slavery in California, and Franklin Pierce supported the Kansas-Nebraska Act, which regulated slavery in those territories. And, of course, Abraham Lincoln, who helped form the Republican Party in the 1850s, played a transformative role during the Civil War. His orders raised the huge Union army, and as commander in chief he directed the conduct of the bloody war that ultimately ended slavery and brought the southern states back into the Union.[8]

During the late 1800s and early 1900s, presidents were instrumental in federal responses to the nation's rapid expansion and industrialization.[9] The country's growing size and economy generated conflict over which services the federal government should provide to citizens and the extent to which the government should regulate individual and corporate behavior.[10] Various acts of legislation created new federal agencies as well as new presidential powers and responsibilities. For example, Republican president Theodore Roosevelt used the Sherman Antitrust Act to break up the Northern Securities Company, a mammoth nationwide railroad trust. Roosevelt also expanded federal conservation programs and increased the power of the Interstate Commerce Commission to regulate businesses. Democratic president Woodrow Wilson further increased the government's role in managing the economy through his support of the Clayton Antitrust Act, the Federal Reserve Act, the first federal income tax, and legislation banning child labor.[11]

As these examples illustrate, presidential power has grown over time as the federal government has expanded. The president and members of the executive branch have obtained new regulatory powers over corporations and individual Americans. Presidents have also proposed new policies in response to shifts in public opinion. Moreover, the power of the presidency grew around the turn of the century and thereafter due to the actions of presidents, particularly Roosevelt and Wilson, who firmly believed that the presidency was the most important federal office.

George Washington remains, for many Americans, the presidential ideal—a leader whose crucial domestic and foreign policy decisions shaped the growth of America's democracy.

Yet the limits of presidential power were also evident during this era—for example, in Wilson's foreign policy initiatives. Although he campaigned in the 1916 election on a promise to keep America out of World War I, Wilson ultimately ordered American troops to fight on the side of the Allies. After the war, Wilson offered a peace plan that proposed (1) reshaping the borders of European countries in order to mitigate future conflicts; (2) creating an international organization, the League of Nations, to prevent future conflicts; and (3) taking other measures to encourage free trade and democracy.[12] However, America's allies rejected most of Wilson's proposals and the Senate refused to allow American participation in the League of Nations.

The Great Depression through the present

Presidential actions defined the government's response to the Great Depression—the worldwide economic collapse in the late 1920s and 1930s marked by high unemployment, huge stock market declines, and many bank failures. After winning the 1932 presidential election, Democrat Franklin Roosevelt and his staff began reshaping American government in an effort to pull the country out of the Depression. Roosevelt's New Deal reforms created many federal agencies that helped individual Americans and imposed many new corporate regulations.[13] This expansion continued under Roosevelt's successors. Even Republican Dwight Eisenhower, whose party had initially opposed many New Deal reforms, presided over the creation of new agencies and the building of the interstate highway system.[14]

Presidential power also grew as the United States became more involved in the international arena. America was a key player in the Allied coalition against Germany and Japan in World War II, with President Roosevelt leading the negotiation of key agreements with American allies over war aims and the establishment of the United Nations. After the war, through the beginning of the Cold War with the Soviet Union, America's military might, dominant nuclear forces, and overwhelming economic power made it the leader of the free world. Because of this position, postwar presidents such as Harry Truman had enormous influence over the lives of people everywhere.

Presidents were instrumental in the civil rights reforms and expansion of the federal government in the 1960s. With congressional approval, President Lyndon Johnson's

Presidents throughout the twentieth century expanded the power of the office in terms of both domestic and foreign policy making. President Franklin Delano Roosevelt (left) called on the public to support his New Deal social programs through his signature "fireside chat" radio broadcasts. President Ronald Reagan (right) was instrumental in negotiating and executing numerous arms reduction agreements with the Soviet Union, then led by Mikhail Gorbachev.

administration created a wide range of domestic programs, such as the Department of Housing and Urban Development, Medicare, Medicaid, and federal funding for schools. The job of enacting voting rights and civil rights legislation also took place during Johnson's presidency.

Both Johnson and his successor, Richard Nixon, directed America's involvement in the Vietnam War, with the goal of forcing the North Vietnamese to abandon their plans to unify North and South Vietnam. But presidential efforts in Vietnam did not meet with success. Despite enormous deployments of American forces and the deaths of more than 58,000 American soldiers, Nixon eventually signed an agreement that allowed American troops to leave but did not end the conflict, which concluded only after a North Vietnamese victory in 1975.

The two presidents immediately after Nixon, Republican Gerald Ford and Democrat Jimmy Carter, faced the worst economic conditions since the Great Depression, largely due to increased energy prices. Both presidents offered plans to reduce unemployment and inflation, restore economic growth, and enhance domestic energy sources. However, their efforts were largely unsuccessful, which became a critical factor in their failed reelection bids. The experiences of Ford and Carter highlight that presidents often face situations for which there are no good solutions. Given the realities of the American economy in the 1970s, it is hard to imagine policies that would have improved on Ford and Carter's performance.

The political and policy importance of presidential actions continued to increase during the presidency of Republican Ronald Reagan, despite the fact that he ran on a platform of tax cuts, fewer regulations, and smaller government. Reagan and his staff also negotiated important arms control agreements with the Soviet Union. Reagan's successor, Republican George H. W. Bush, led American and international participation in the Persian Gulf War during 1990 and 1991, which succeeded in removing Iraqi forces from Kuwait with minimal American casualties.

Democrat Bill Clinton's presidency was marked by passage of the North American Free Trade Agreement, welfare reform, arms control agreements, and successful peacekeeping efforts by U.S. troops in Haiti and the Balkans. His presidency also was distinguished by having one of the longest periods of economic growth in U.S. history and the first balanced budgets since the 1960s. President George W. Bush won congressional approval of his tax cuts and education reforms, but he is remembered for managing America's response to the September 11 attacks, including the wars in Iraq and Afghanistan.

President Obama secured several notable changes in domestic and foreign policy, including the enactment of health care reform, economic stimulus legislation, and new financial regulations and the appointment of two Supreme Court justices. However, Obama had to compromise in enacting many of these new policies, and in areas such as immigration reform and gun control he was largely unsuccessful. Obama's experience highlights a fundamental limit on presidential power: in many areas, presidents require congressional support in order to achieve their policy goals.

Despite the ways Donald Trump differed from past presidents (his personal wealth, life outside politics, and willingness to deviate from established norms), the Trump presidency still illustrates both the exercise of presidential power and the limits on presidential action. Trump had considerable success in forcing policy and regulatory changes though administrative actions. However, in many cases (and particularly after Democrats regained a House majority in 2019), his plans were blocked by lack of public support, the failure to build majorities in the House and Senate, his unwillingness to fully staff the executive branch because of concerns over disloyalty, and congressional investigations prompted by leaks and whistleblower reports. Thus, Trump sometimes looked decisive and influential—but at other times he appeared relatively constrained and weak.

After presidents leave office, their performance is often evaluated as though their powers and foresight during their term had been unlimited. The history of presidential successes and failures reminds us that, in fact, presidents are often constrained by circumstances. Many of the problems past presidents have faced were totally unanticipated or had no good solutions. Other times, attempts to address national needs failed because of congressional resistance. Thus, before we make judgments about presidential performance, we need to understand the president's job and the resources available to accomplish it.

DESCRIBE THE CONSTITUTIONAL AND STATUTORY POWERS OF THE PRESIDENT TODAY

constitutional authority (presidential)
Powers derived from the provisions of the Constitution that outline the president's role in government.

statutory authority (presidential)
Powers derived from laws enacted by Congress that add to the powers given to the president in the Constitution.

The president's job description

This section describes the president's **constitutional authority** (powers derived from the provisions of the Constitution) and **statutory authority** (powers that come from laws), as well as the additional capabilities that presidents derive from their position as the head of the executive branch of government. Nuts & Bolts 5.1 summarizes the president's constitutional and statutory powers. As the box indicates, some presidential powers arise from the Constitution only, and others derive from a combination of constitutional and statutory authority. Questions about the sources and limits of presidential authority have bedeviled political scientists for several generations. In fact, one very influential book, Richard Neustadt's *Presidential Power*, argued that the main source was a president's power to persuade people to do what the president wanted.[15] Building on more recent research, our aim is to show how the provisions that define presidential authority operate in modern-day American politics: what kinds of opportunities and constraints they create for the current president and future holders of the office.

Head of the executive branch

vesting clause
Article II, Section 1, of the Constitution, which states: "The executive Power shall be vested in a President of the United States of America," making the president both the head of government and the head of state.

head of government
One role of the president, through which he or she has authority over the executive branch.

head of state
One role of the president, through which he or she represents the country symbolically and politically.

A president's responsibilities and the source of presidential power begin with the constitutional responsibilities of the office. The Constitution's **vesting clause**—"The executive Power shall be vested in a President of the United States of America"—makes the president the **head of government**, or the leader of the executive branch, as well as the **head of state**, or the symbolic and political representative of the country. The precise meaning of the vesting clause has been debated for more than 200 years. Presidents and their supporters argue for an expansive meaning, while their opponents counter that the clause is so vague as to be meaningless. These debates are an important clue that presidential power is only partially due to specific constitutional grants of authority—some of it comes from how each president interprets less concrete statements such as the vesting clause.

The Constitution also places the president in charge of the implementation of laws, saying "he shall take Care that the Laws be faithfully executed." Sometimes the implementation of a law is nearly automatic, as was the case with the part of the 2020 COVID-19 stimulus package that provided $1,200 payments to most Americans. In this case, all the president needed to do to implement the directive was to ask Treasury bureaucrats to send the payments, either by direct deposit or mail.

More commonly, the president's authority to implement the law requires using judgment to translate legislative goals into programs, budgets, and regulations. For example, another part of the stimulus package directed the secretary of the Treasury to make grants and loans to firms in order to prevent layoffs and bankruptcies. However, the law did not specify which firms should get these funds or whether any conditions would be applied (repayment terms, guarantees about no layoffs, and so on). All of these provisions were left up to the Treasury bureaucrats, giving them and the president considerable discretion to set the terms of these bailouts.

Appointments

The president appoints ambassadors, senior bureaucrats, and members of the federal judiciary, including Supreme Court justices.[16] As the head of the executive branch, the president can appoint individuals to about 8,000 positions, ranging from high-profile jobs such as secretary of state to mundane administrative and secretarial positions. About 1,200 of these appointments—generally high-level positions such as cabinet secretaries—require Senate confirmation. These individuals "serve at the pleasure of the president," meaning that the president can remove them from their positions whenever he or she likes. Thus, when Donald Trump fired National Security Advisor John Bolton in November 2019, this action

Millions of Americans found themselves unemployed in the wake of the coronavirus pandemic, and small businesses especially suffered, scrambling to find loans and grants to stay in business throughout the crisis. As a temporary solution, the president approved a stimulus package that provided $1,200 payments to most Americans, and the secretary of the Treasury made grants and loans to firms to prevent additional layoffs and bankruptcies.

NUTS & BOLTS 5.1

Presidential Powers

Power	Source of Power
Head of government, head of state (vesting clause)	Constitutional authority
Implementation of laws ("faithful execution")	Constitutional and statutory authority
Executive orders and similar directives (rare)	Constitutional and statutory authority
Administration of executive branch	Constitutional authority
Nominations and appointments to executive branch and judiciary	Constitutional and statutory authority
Commander in chief of armed forces	Constitutional authority
Negotiation of treaties and executive agreements	Constitutional and statutory authority
Veto of congressional actions	Constitutional authority
Presidential pardons	Constitutional authority
Other ceremonial powers	Constitutional authority
Executive privilege	Other
Recommendation of spending levels and other legislative initiatives	Other

Source: Compiled by the authors.

"Why Should I Care?"

The question of where a president's power comes from matters because it affects the extent of the power, and whether it can be taken away or blocked by other actors in American politics.

was a legitimate exercise of presidential appointment power, as was Trump's nomination of Robert O'Brien to succeed Bolton.

The president also nominates individuals to fill federal judgeships, including Supreme Court justices, although these nominations require Senate approval in order to take effect. Because these positions are lifetime appointments, they enable the president to put people into positions of power who will remain after he or she leaves office. For example, President Trump nominated many young conservative justices to federal judgeships during his presidency, including Supreme Court associate justices Neil Gorsuch, Brett Kavanaugh, and Amy Coney Barrett. The full effects of these and future judicial appointments by Trump will not be completely apparent for years to come.

The need for Senate confirmation of the president's appointments is one of the fundamental limits on presidential power. Historically, the Senate has approved virtually all nominees without much debate or controversy, although in recent years senators (particularly Republicans during Obama's presidency) have blocked votes on judicial and agency nominees. Some of Trump's cabinet appointees, including Secretary of Education Betsy DeVos, were approved only because Vice President Mike Pence (who is the president of the Senate under the Constitution) voted to break a tie. In several cases, Trump has named individuals to serve as acting cabinet secretaries; these positions do not require Senate confirmation, but the officeholders can serve only for a limited time.

If the Senate is in recess (adjourned for more than three days), the president can make a recess appointment, whereby an appointee is temporarily given a position without a Senate vote and holds the office until the beginning of the next congressional session. All presidents make recess appointments, but typically for relatively minor offices and for noncontroversial nominees. For example, when the Republican-controlled Senate refused to vote on President Obama's 2016 Supreme Court nominee, Merrick Garland, it would have been highly unusual (and perhaps unconstitutional) for President Obama to appoint Garland to the Supreme Court via a recess appointment. In any case, the Senate can (and sometimes does) eliminate the possibility of recess appointments by holding brief working sessions as often as needed to ensure that no recess lasts more than three days.

Executive orders

Presidents have the power to issue executive orders—that is, proclamations that unilaterally change government policy without subsequent congressional consent—as well as other kinds of orders that change policy, such as National Security Presidential Directives and Presidential Findings (see the How It Works feature). For example, one of President Trump's orders in April 2020 put strict limits on immigration for 60 days. Another order used Trump's authority under the Defense Production Act to order companies to increase production of face masks during the coronavirus pandemic.

As the What Do the Facts Say? feature shows, all presidents issue many executive orders. Most are not consequential, like the annual order that gives federal employees an early dismissal on the last working day before Christmas. But some executive orders implement large changes in federal policy. Lincoln's Emancipation Proclamation was issued as an executive order. Similarly, President Trump issued a series of executive orders that have reduced the number of refugees admitted to the United States each year, from about 70,000 per year during the Obama administration to only about 18,000 in 2019.

Executive orders may appear to give the president authority to do whatever he or she wants, even in the face of strong opposition from Congress. However, particularly during the Trump administration, executive orders have been used to signal intentions

The public sees presidents as speechmakers, but it's mostly butt-in-seat work, a continuous cycle of meetings, decisions, and preparation for meetings and decisions. Governing is a lot harder than tweeting.

—**Michael Grunwald,** Politico reporter

rather than directly change policy. For example, one of Trump's executive orders directed the Border Patrol to end its "catch and release" policy whereby people caught trying to enter the United States from Mexico illegally were simply escorted back to a border checkpoint and set free. However, the order did not command the Border Patrol to hold all illegal immigrants for trial; rather, it instructed the agency to determine what changes would be needed to implement this practice.

In the main, when the president issues an order that makes real policy changes and Congress does not respond, it means that congressional majorities agree with the president's actions or there is already a law giving the president the authority that he or she is exercising in the order. That said, presidents often turn to executive orders and other directives when they know they cannot secure congressional support for the policy changes they want to implement—as was likely the case for Trump's executive orders restricting immigration and Obama's executive orders limiting deportations of so-called Dreamers, who are undocumented individuals brought to the United States as children. While members of Congress can overrule the president, they may be too busy with other matters to do so, or simply not care enough about the change to take the steps needed to undo it.

Commander in chief

The Constitution makes the president the commander in chief of America's military forces but gives Congress the power to declare war. These provisions are potentially contradictory, and the Constitution leaves open the broader question of who controls the military.[18] In practice, however, the president controls day-to-day military operations through the Department of Defense and has the power to order troops into action without explicit congressional approval. For example, both the Trump and Obama administrations joined over a dozen other nations to aid rebel forces in the Syrian civil war. They provided arms and training to rebel fighters and conducted air strikes against ISIS and Syrian government forces. Even today, some American group forces remain in Syrian territory and limited air strikes continue. Similarly, the 2011 attack on Osama bin Laden's compound and the 2020 drone strike that killed Iranian general Qasem Soleimani were carried out without prior congressional approval. In fact, even though the United States has been involved in hundreds of military conflicts, there have been only five declarations of war: the War of 1812, the Mexican-American War (1846), the Spanish-American War (1898), World War I (1917), and World War II (1941).

As a way of restraining presidential war-making power, Congress enacted the War Powers Resolution of 1973 (Nuts & Bolts 5.2 lists the specific provisions of the resolution). However, a 2019 study found that the War Powers Resolution has been formally used by Congress to limit presidential authority only once, to limit the duration of a deployment of Marines in Lebanon on a peacekeeping mission.[19] Moreover, although it has been in effect for nearly 40 years, it has never faced Supreme Court review. Some scholars have even argued that the resolution actually expands presidential power because it gives the president essentially unlimited control for the first 90 days of a military operation—and in many cases, 90 days is more than enough time to complete military action without getting Congress involved.[20]

Even with its limitations, the War Powers Resolution has had some impact on presidential decisions regarding the use of force. Threats by members of Congress to invoke the War Powers Resolution were one factor in President Obama's 2011 decision to curtail American involvement in the NATO-led mission to end the Libyan civil war. The impact of the War Powers Resolution is also evident in the fact that presidents often consult with congressional leaders or try to gain congressional approval before committing troops to battle. It is important to remember, too, that the act is not the

reduce
in extent/quantity
impose restriction

How Presidents Make Policy Outside the Legislative Process

The Constitution describes the president's influence over new policy initiatives in terms of the power to sign or veto acts of Congress. But what can the president do when Congress fails to act how he or she wants?

President + White House staff develop proposals—they talk to the public, members of Congress, interest groups, union and corporation heads, party leaders, and others. Some of these groups initiate contact and submit their own ideas or even fully drafted plans.

President + Congress sometimes find compromise proposals—but other times negotiations reveal that the president's plans will not receive majority support in the House and Senate.

President + White House staff investigate whether some or all of the president's goals can be achieved through executive order or other means.

President issues appropriate orders and directives.

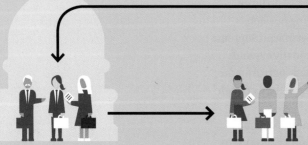

Congress decides whether to enact legislation reversing the president's actions. They need a two-thirds majority in both houses to override an expected presidential veto.

Presidential appointees, assuming congressional attempts to reverse the new policies are unsuccessful, administer implementation of the new policies.

Presidential Action and the Paris Agreement on Climate Change

The United States' involvement in the Paris Agreement on climate change illustrates how a president can bypass Congress and initiate meaningful policy change. Members of President Obama's executive branch participated in the initial talks to develop the accord, and Obama announced that the United States would comply with the agreement in late 2015. However, Donald Trump opposed the agreement during his 2016 campaign, and although he said he was open to keeping the United States in the accord if some of its provisions were renegotiated, the United States government ultimately submitted its formal notice to withdraw from the Paris Agreement on November 4, 2019.

❓ Critical Thinking

1. **Why do you think President Obama decided to treat the accord as an executive agreement** rather than a treaty? Would the situation be different if Democrats were the majority party in the Senate?

2. **Candidate Trump campaigned against the Paris Agreement—** but President Trump did show some willingness to remain in a renegotiated accord. Why might he have reconsidered his initial position once he was in office?

President + staff + other nations

This is important.

During both of President Obama's campaigns for office, **he argued in favor** of new international agreements to fight climate change.

Let's talk.

Obama, White House staff, and others in the executive branch **discussed policy options** and negotiation strategies. **American diplomats were deeply involved** in negotiating the United Nations Framework Convention on Climate Change.

We have a deal.

Building on the Framework Convention, representatives from **196 nations developed the Paris Agreement on climate change**. U.S. Secretary of State John Kerry signed the accord in November 2015.

President + Congress

We want a say!

Many Republican senators who opposed the accord **demanded that President Obama submit the agreement** for ratification as a treaty.

You don't get one.

The Obama administration announced it would implement the accord as an executive agreement, so a **congressional vote was not required**.

This is a risk.

Although making the accord an executive agreement removed the risk that the Senate would reject the treaty, it also meant that **any future president** could end the United States' participation without further action by Congress.

A new president

We're out!

In August 2017, President Trump announced that the **United States intended to withdraw** from the agreement, though he did concede that he might be willing to remain if the terms of the agreement were renegotiated.

Not so fast.

Under the terms of the agreement, a country cannot submit a notice to withdraw **until the agreement has been in effect for four years, and it must then wait one year for the withdrawal to take effect**.

A formal withdrawal.

Renegotiation did not take place, and on November 4, 2019, **President Trump announced the United States' formal withdrawal from the Paris Agreement**, which would officially take place one year later, on November 4, 2020.

President Trump's Executive Orders

Many critics (including then–presidential candidate Donald Trump) argued that President Obama issued an unprecedented number of executive orders in order to bypass a Republican Congress that was unsympathetic to his policy proposals. Was Obama an outlier? How has Trump behaved in office?

Executive Orders Issued by Recent Presidents

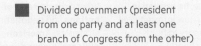

Divided government (president from one party and at least one branch of Congress from the other)

Unified government (president and both branches of Congress from the same party)

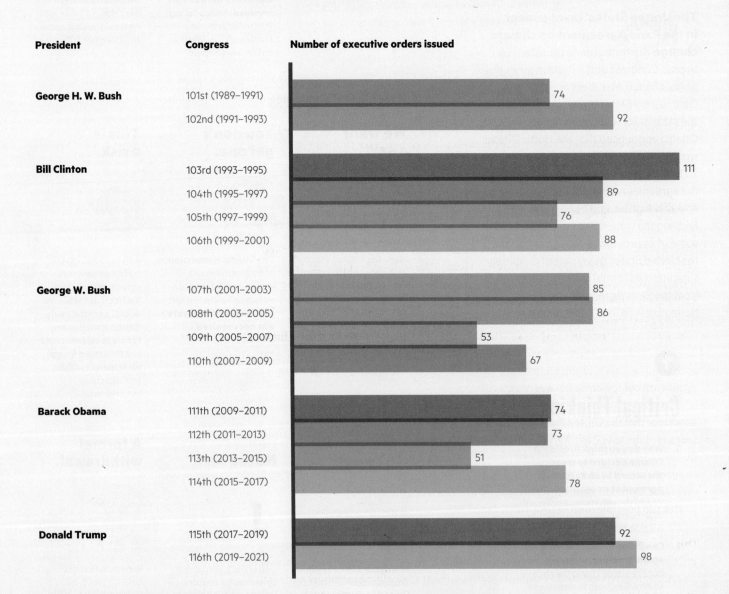

President	Congress	Number of executive orders issued
George H. W. Bush	101st (1989–1991)	74
	102nd (1991–1993)	92
Bill Clinton	103rd (1993–1995)	111
	104th (1995–1997)	89
	105th (1997–1999)	76
	106th (1999–2001)	88
George W. Bush	107th (2001–2003)	85
	108th (2003–2005)	86
	109th (2005–2007)	53
	110th (2007–2009)	67
Barack Obama	111th (2009–2011)	74
	112th (2011–2013)	73
	113th (2013–2015)	51
	114th (2015–2017)	78
Donald Trump	115th (2017–2019)	92
	116th (2019–2021)	98

Note: Data current as of October 10, 2020.

Source: "Executive Orders Disposition Tables Index," *Federal Register*, www.federalregister. gov/presidential-documents/executive-orders (accessed 10/10/20).

Think about it

- **Is there any evidence** that Obama issued more executive orders than his predecessors?
- **How does Trump's behavior** compare to that of Obama and other presidents?

1. The president is required to report to Congress any introduction of U.S. forces into hostilities or imminent hostilities.
2. The use of force must be terminated within 60 days unless Congress approves of the deployment. The time limit can be extended to 90 days if the president certifies that additional time is needed to safely withdraw American forces.
3. The president is required whenever possible to consult with Congress before introducing American forces into hostilities or imminent hostilities.
4. Any congressional resolution authorizing the continued deployment of American forces will be considered under expedited procedures.

The War Powers Resolution of 1973

Source: Richard F. Grimmett, "The War Powers Resolution: After Thirty Years," Congressional Research Service Report RL32267, March 11, 2004, www.hsdl.org/?view&did=446200 (accessed 6/20/20).

"Why Should I Care?" While the War Powers Resolution is often described as a way for Congress to limit the president's control over America's armed forces, the reality is that the procedures do not address the vast majority of military operations.

only tool available to members of Congress who disagree with a president's policy: they can curb a president's war-making powers through budget restrictions, legislative prohibitions, public appeals, and, ultimately, impeachment.[21]

Treaty making and foreign policy

Treaty-making power is shared between Congress and the president: presidents and their staff negotiate treaties, which are then sent to the Senate for approval. (Many need the support of a two-thirds majority of senators to be approved, but some need only a simple majority.) However, the president has a first-mover advantage in the treaty-making process. Congress considers treaties only after negotiations have ended; there is no way for members of Congress to force the president to negotiate a treaty or limit its scope. That said, the need for congressional approval often leads presidents to take account of senators' preferences when negotiating treaties, which often results in significant compromise between the two branches.

Presidents have two strategies for avoiding a congressional treaty vote. One is to announce that the United States will voluntarily abide by a treaty without ratifying it. In the case of the 2015 Paris Agreement on climate change, one of the reasons why President Obama supported voluntary targets for reductions in greenhouse gases was that such an agreement did not require Senate approval. Of course, this strategy allowed Obama's successor, Donald Trump, to unilaterally withdraw from the agreement in 2017.

It is also possible to structure a deal as an [executive agreement] between the executive branch and a foreign government, which does not require Senate approval. This strategy was followed in the case of the deal between the United States, its allies, and the Iranian government to curtail Iran's nuclear weapons research program. In this case, Congress passed (and President Obama signed) a law giving members 30 days to review the deal and the opportunity to pass a resolution rejecting it. The deal ultimately went into effect, although Donald Trump ended U.S. participation in early 2018.

The president also serves as the principal representative of the United States in foreign affairs other than treaty negotiations. Presidential duties include communicating with

[executive agreement]
An agreement between the executive branch and a foreign government, which acts as a treaty but does not require Senate approval.

The president often meets with foreign leaders in both formal and informal settings. For example, in March 2016 President Obama watched a baseball game with Cuban leader Raúl Castro in Havana, Cuba, and in June 2018 President Trump met with Kim Jong-un, the supreme leader of North Korea, in Singapore. Such meetings provide a venue for the president not only to present American views and mediate disagreements but also to act as a visible symbol of America's position as a world superpower.

foreign leaders, nongovernmental organizations, and even ordinary citizens to persuade them to act in ways that the president believes are in the best interest of the United States. For example, in February 2020 President Trump attended the World Economic Forum in Davos, Switzerland, where he met with leaders of the European Union as well as the prime minister and other officials from Iraq. While such meetings generally have no direct effect on policy, they signal presidential interest and highlight the importance of ongoing negotiations and joint efforts to address issues of mutual concern.

The amount of time the administration devotes to foreign policy is subject to domestic and world events and therefore not entirely under presidential control. While President Trump promised to limit overseas military operations, he largely continued his predecessor's policies. In the case of North Korea, Trump's public pressure on the North Korean regime (including threats to respond with "fire and fury" if North Korea were to attack the United States) was a departure from the Obama administration in terms of tone, as was Trump's willingness to hold two meetings with North Korean leader Kim Jong-un. Even so, there were a few observable policy differences between Trump's and Obama's policies toward North Korea, as well as toward Syria, as Trump ultimately removed U.S. troops from the conflict there.

Legislative power

The Constitution establishes lawmaking as a shared power between the president and Congress, and compromise between the two branches is fundamental to passing laws that satisfy both.[22] The president recommends policies and legislative priorities to Congress, notably in the annual **State of the Union** address. Presidents and their legislative staff also work with Congress to develop legislative proposals: they spend considerable time lobbying members of Congress to support their proposals and negotiating with legislative leaders over policy details. Although the president cannot formally introduce legislation, it is typically easy to find a member of Congress willing to sponsor a presidential proposal.[23]

The president's legislative power also stems from the ability to veto legislation (see Nuts & Bolts 5.3). Once both chambers of Congress have passed a bill by simple majority, the president must decide within two weeks of congressional action whether to sign it or issue a veto. Signed bills become law, but vetoed bills return to the House and Senate for a vote to override the veto. If both chambers enact the bill again with at least two-thirds majorities, the bill becomes law; otherwise, it is defeated. If Congress adjourns before the president has made a decision, the president can **pocket veto** the proposal by not responding to it. Pocket vetoes cannot be overridden, but as has

State of the Union
An annual speech in which the president addresses Congress to report on the condition of the country and to recommend policies.

pocket veto
The automatic death of a bill passed by the House and Senate when the president fails to sign the bill in the last 10 days of a legislative session.

happened in recent years, congressional leaders can avoid them by keeping Congress in session for two weeks after a bill is enacted.

Figure 5.1 shows the number of vetoes issued by recent presidents—and the number overridden by Congress. In general, vetoes are most likely to occur under divided

FIGURE 5.1

Presidential Vetoes from H. W. Bush to Trump

The figure shows the number of vetoes issued by recent presidents in each congressional term they held office, along with whether the term involved unified or divided government. Do the data support the argument that vetoes are less likely given unified government? Compared with other presidents, did Presidents Trump and Obama issue an inordinately high or low number of vetoes?

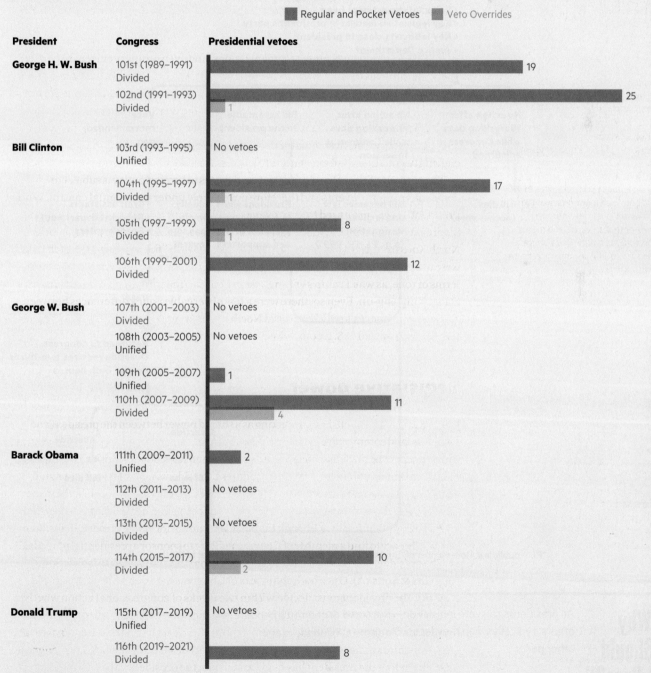

Note: Data current as of October 1, 2020.

Source: United States House of Representatives, History, Art, & Archives, "Presidential Vetoes," https://history.house.gov/Institution/Presidential-Vetoes/Presidential-Vetoes (accessed 10/1/20); data aggregated by the authors.

The Veto Process

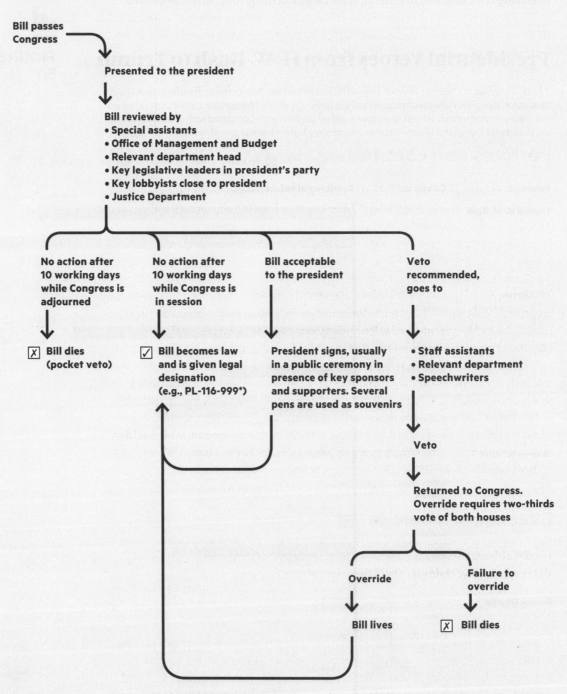

Bill passes Congress

Presented to the president

Bill reviewed by
- Special assistants
- Office of Management and Budget
- Relevant department head
- Key legislative leaders in president's party
- Key lobbyists close to president
- Justice Department

No action after 10 working days while Congress is adjourned

[X] Bill dies (pocket veto)

No action after 10 working days while Congress is in session

[✓] Bill becomes law and is given legal designation (e.g., PL-116-999*)

Bill acceptable to the president

President signs, usually in a public ceremony in presence of key sponsors and supporters. Several pens are used as souvenirs

Veto recommended, goes to

- Staff assistants
- Relevant department
- Speechwriters

Veto

Returned to Congress. Override requires two-thirds vote of both houses

Override

Bill lives

Failure to override

[X] Bill dies

*PL = public law; 116 = number of Congress (116th was 2019–2021); 999 = number of the law.

Source: Compiled by the authors.

"Why Should I Care?"

All presidents can veto legislation—but some do it more than others, typically when they face a Congress controlled by the other party.

government, when a president from one party faces a House and Senate controlled by the other party (in the case of Obama, the relatively small number of vetoes reflects a sharp reduction in the number of laws enacted by Congress).[24] Vetoes are much less likely under unified government, when one party controls both Congress and the presidency, because the chances are much higher that the president and legislators from his or her party hold similar policy priorities. Thus, in the first two years of the Trump administration, when a Republican president faced a Republican Congress, the president did not veto any legislation. A president's veto threats also allow the president to specify what kinds of proposals he or she is willing or unwilling to accept from Congress. Legislators then know that they need to write a proposal that attracts two-thirds support in both houses or accede to a president's demands.

Pardons and commutations

The Constitution gives the president several additional powers, including the authority to pardon people convicted of federal crimes or to commute (reduce) their sentences. The only limit on this power is that a president cannot pardon anyone who has been impeached and convicted by Congress. (Thus, if a president is removed from office via impeachment, he or she can neither pardon himself or herself nor be pardoned when the vice president assumes the presidency.)

Although most presidential pardons attract little attention, some have been extremely controversial. Many of Obama's pardons involved individuals with no prior criminal record who had been sentenced to long prison terms for nonviolent drug offenses. Obama also pardoned army private Chelsea Manning, who had been convicted of leaking classified information to the WikiLeaks organization. Donald Trump issued relatively few pardons. Notably, in 2017 President Trump pardoned former Arizona sheriff Joe Arpaio, who had been convicted of contempt of court for refusing a judge's order to stop racial profiling in police traffic stops. In 2020 Trump pardoned financier Michael Milken for securities fraud crimes committed in the 1980s and, in his final days in office, pardoned many of his former campaign aides, including his campaign manager Paul Manafort and two senior advisers, Steve Bannon and Roger Stone.

Executive privilege

Finally, although this power is not formally set out in the Constitution or a statute, all presidents have claimed to hold the power of executive privilege. This refers to the ability to shield themselves and their subordinates from revealing White House discussions, decisions, or documents (including e-mails) to members of the legislative or judicial branches of government.[25]

Although claims of executive privilege have been made since the ratification of the Constitution in 1789, it is still not clear exactly what falls under the privilege and what does not. In the 1974 case *United States v. Nixon*, a special prosecutor appointed by the Justice Department to investigate the Watergate scandal challenged President Nixon's claims of executive privilege to force him to hand over tapes of potentially incriminating Oval Office conversations involving Nixon and his senior aides. The Supreme Court ruled unanimously that executive privilege does exist but that the privilege is not absolute. The Court's decision required Nixon to release the tapes, which proved his involvement with attempts to cover up the scandal, but the ruling did not clearly state the conditions under which a future president could withhold such information.[26]

All presidents have claimed executive privilege, although the circumstances have differed. President Trump argued for a very strong version of executive privilege,

DID YOU KNOW?

Between January 20, 2017 and Election Day 2020, President Trump pardoned or commuted the sentences of

44

individuals convicted of federal crimes.

Source: U.S. Department of Justice

executive privilege
The right of the president to keep executive branch conversations and correspondence confidential from the legislative and judicial branches.

During the Congressional impeachment hearings, Trump claimed executive privilege in order to prevent his aides from testifying in the Ukraine investigation. Numerous expert witnesses, as seen being sworn in here, testified on constitutional issues raised by these proceedings, including executive privilege.

including limits on congressional investigation of Russian interference in the 2016 election and a blanket refusal to allow aides to testify in House impeachment hearings in 2019. Trump's decisions are currently under review by federal courts, and it is unclear whether they will be upheld. President Obama invoked executive privilege several times, in cases ranging from demands by congressional Republicans for documents related to a Justice Department sting operation, to requests by both Republicans and Democrats for information on drone strikes against terrorist groups (see the Take a Stand feature). In the former case, federal courts rejected Obama's claim, forcing release of the documents; in the latter, members of Congress did not pursue their claims in the courts.

Claims of executive privilege present a dilemma. On the one hand, members of Congress need to know what is happening in the executive branch. In the case of President Nixon and the Watergate scandal, claims of executive privilege allowed the Watergate cover-up to continue for more than a year and would have kept this information secret permanently if the Supreme Court had ruled in Nixon's favor.[27] Exercising executive privilege can also weaken accountability to the public, as restricting information may leave the average voter unaware of what an administration is doing. On the other hand, the president and his or her staff need to be able to communicate freely and discuss alternative strategies, hypothetical situations, or national security secrets without fear that they will be forced to reveal conversations that could become politically embarrassing or costly.

"Why Should I Care?"

Criticisms of presidents often center on cases of inaction or failure, in which they do nothing to address a national problem or they try to change policy but are unsuccessful. The underlying expectation is that presidents are powerful and can do anything. The reality is that presidents are more powerful in some areas than others. For example, they are more powerful when they negotiate with foreign leaders than when they propose changes in spending, which require congressional approval. Thus, when we judge presidents' performance, we must consider whether achieving their goals required the assistance of others to make their proposals a reality.

The Limits of Executive Privilege

Deciding what information a president can be compelled to release to the public or to other branches of government and what information can be kept confidential requires confronting fundamentally political questions. There are no right answers, and the limits of executive privilege remain unclear. On the one hand, members of Congress need facts, predictions, and estimates from the executive branch to make good public policy. On the other hand, the president and his or her staff have a right to keep their deliberations confidential, as well as a practical need to keep some things secret.

Consider the controversy over the practice (begun during the Bush administration and continued under Presidents Obama and Trump) of targeting terrorists using attacks by unmanned drone aircraft. Compared with deployments of other military forces, drone attacks have the advantages of surprise (drones are small and fly high enough to be invisible), low cost (drones are cheaper than fighters or bombers), and lower risk (the drones can be controlled from anywhere, so there is no risk of American casualties in an attack). Nonetheless, drone attacks carry the risk of collateral damage—an attack may also hurt or kill innocent civilians. Moreover, because drone attacks are conducted in secret, there is little to no congressional oversight of who gets targeted by drone strikes or the potential for collateral damage. Should drone attacks fall under executive privilege?

Keep the attacks secret. Clearly, revealing the targets of drone strikes in advance of the actual attacks would destroy the secrecy that makes these strikes so effective—terrorists could stop using cell phones, stay indoors as much as possible, travel only at night, and take other actions to make themselves hard to spot from the air. But there would be danger even in forcing an administration to release information after an attack, as such documents would reveal the criteria used to decide which terrorists to target, the limits of the drone technology, and what factors made it easier to carry out a successful attack. All of this information would help terror targets evade future drone attacks and perhaps require a return to using Special Forces to attack terror targets, which would place American lives at risk.

Reveal the information. The problem with imposing a high level of secrecy on drone attacks is that it is an exception to the rule of keeping Congress informed about the use of military force. In the end, a drone is simply a different way of attacking terrorists or their organization. While the need for secrecy in advance of an attack makes sense, it is not obvious why it should continue after an attack has been carried out. In general, presidents are required to give Congress (in the case of secret operations, the chairs and ranking members of the Intelligence Committees) "prompt notification" of all secret operations. This rule was intended to govern reporting of all covert operations. Should drone attacks be given a higher level of secrecy, or should presidents be forced to keep members of Congress informed?

 The president's role as commander in chief of America's armed forces gives him or her a tremendous amount of power—power that often can be exercised secretly. What should be the limits on presidential secrecy?

take a stand

1. One argument for using drones to attack terrorist targets highlights their greater effectiveness and lower costs than other options. But drone attacks also involve lower political risks to the president. Explain why this is so.

2. Under current law, the president has to inform only a few members of Congress about covert operations and can wait until an operation is in progress before releasing information. Why would members of Congress want expanded notification requirements, such as informing more members or requiring disclosure during the planning of an operation?

The presidency as an institution

As head of the executive branch, the president runs a huge, complex organization with hundreds of thousands of employees. We speak of this organization as an "institution" to emphasize that both the *structure* of the executive branch (the division of responsibilities across different agencies and offices) and the *individuals* who serve in different positions (their experience, skills, and ideological leanings) can have a profound impact on government policies. This section describes the organizations and staff who help the president exercise his or her vast responsibilities, from managing disaster-response efforts to implementing policy changes.[28] Among these employees are appointees who hold senior positions in the government. These individuals serve as the president's eyes and ears in the bureaucracy, making sure that bureaucrats are following presidential directives.

The Executive Office of the President

Executive Office of the President (EOP)
The group of policy-related offices that serve as support staff to the president.

The executive branch's organizational chart begins with the **Executive Office of the President (EOP)**, which has employed several thousand people in recent administrations, divided between policy-making positions and administrating personnel. About a third of these employees are concentrated in two offices: the Office of Management and Budget, which develops the president's budget proposals and monitors spending by government agencies, and the Office of the United States Trade Representative, which negotiates trade agreements with other nations. Nuts & Bolts 5.4 lists the organizations that make up the EOP.

NUTS & BOLTS 5.4

The Executive Office of the President

Source: Compiled by the authors from whitehouse.gov.

Council of Economic Advisers	Office of National Drug Control Policy
Council on Environmental Quality	Office of Science and Technology Policy
Domestic Policy Council	Office of the First Lady
Homeland Security Council	Office of the United States Trade Representative
National Economic Council	President's Foreign Intelligence Advisory Board
National Security Council	Privacy and Civil Liberties Oversight Board
Office of Administration	White House Fellows Office
Office of Faith-Based and Community Initiatives	White House Military Office
Office of Management and Budget	White House Office
Office of National AIDS Policy	

"Why Should I Care?" Organizations in the EOP play a major role in bringing information to the president and executing his or her directives. They are a reflection of presidential priorities and policy goals.

One of the most important duties of EOP staff is helping presidents achieve their policy goals and get reelected. In the Trump White House, for example, Senior Adviser Stephen Miller focused on domestic policy (especially immigration policy) but also helped write Trump's speeches, including his State of the Union addresses. Trump's daughter Ivanka and her spouse, Jared Kushner, also played important advisory roles. These three individuals, as well as other influential EOP staff, occupied offices in the West Wing of the White House. The West Wing contains the president's office, known as the Oval Office, and space for the president's chief aide and personal secretary, as well as senior aides such as the vice president, the president's press secretary, and the chief of staff (for Trump, former congressman Mark Meadows), who manages all aspects of White House operations—including, as former Reagan chief of staff James Baker put it, who gets to play tennis on the White House courts. Some recent chiefs of staff have been central in the development of policy proposals and negotiations with members of Congress. However, the chief of staff serves as the agent of the president—what matters is what the president wants, not a chief of staff's policy preferences.

Most EOP staff members are presidential appointees who retain their positions only as long as the president who appointed them remains in office. These individuals are often drawn to government service out of loyalty to the president or because they share the president's policy goals. However, most leave their positions after two or three years to escape the pressures of the job, the long hours, and the relatively low government salaries.[29] Some EOP offices—such as the Office of Management and Budget, the Office of the United States Trade Representative, and the National Security Council (NSC)—also have a significant number of permanent staff analysts and experts.[30] The emphasis on loyalty in presidential appointments has obvious drawbacks: appointees may not know much about the jobs they are given, and they may not be very effective at managing the agencies they are supposed to control. For example, Trump's son-in-law, Jared Kushner, was given responsibility for American efforts to negotiate a peace deal between Israel and the Palestinian Authority, even though his prior experience was as a real estate developer and he had never served in government.

Trump's EOP appointments were a departure from previous practice in several respects. First, while all presidents must balance expertise and loyalty in their appointments, Trump appears to have placed a very high weight on personal loyalty. Second, Trump appointed significantly fewer individuals to EOP positions, keeping many positions empty even after several years in office and appointing many individuals to serve in an acting capacity. Third, turnover in Trump's EOP was much higher than in previous administrations. Finally, throughout his term but particularly after the end of congressional impeachment hearings in early 2020, Trump removed many long-serving individuals from positions on the EOP and throughout the executive branch because of concerns than they were not sufficiently loyal and supportive of him.[31]

The vice president

As set out in the Constitution, the vice president's job is to preside over Senate proceedings. This largely ceremonial job is, in practice, usually delegated to the president pro tempore of the Senate, who in turn typically gives the duty to a more junior member. The vice president also has the power to cast tie-breaking votes in the Senate. Mike Pence, for example, cast several such votes in 2018 to break ties on presidential nominees. The vice president's other formal responsibility is to become president if the current president dies, becomes incapacitated, resigns, or is impeached, convicted, and ultimately removed from office. Of the 46 presidencies, 9 were instances in which vice presidents became president in midterm.

You don't need to know who's playing on the White House tennis court to be a good president.

—**James Baker,** former White House chief of staff

The president's closest advisers are chosen for their loyalty to the president and his or her policy goals. President Trump's closest advisers include his daughter Ivanka Trump and his son-in-law, Jared Kushner (center), who are seen here meeting with Japanese prime minister Shinzō Abe.

While many people perceive the vice president's position to be ceremonial and relatively powerless, recently the vice president's role has expanded significantly. President Trump's vice president, Mike Pence, served as a trusted policy adviser and directed several initiatives such as the Coronavirus Task Force.

Cabinet
The group of 15 executive department heads who implement the president's agenda in their respective positions.

These rather limited official duties of the vice president pale in comparison with the influential role played by recent vice presidents. Vice President Dick Cheney, who served with President George W. Bush, exerted a significant influence over many policy areas, including the rights of terror suspects, tax and spending policy, environmental decisions, and the writing of new government regulations.[32] Although Cheney's level of influence was unique, other recent vice presidents have also had real power, and it is likely that Kamala Harris will play a similar role, particularly given the possibility that President Biden will opt for a single term in office.

The president's Cabinet

The president's **Cabinet** is composed of the heads of the 15 executive departments in the federal government, along with other appointees given cabinet rank by the president. Nuts & Bolts 5.5 lists the Cabinet and cabinet-level positions. The cabinet members' principal job is to be the frontline implementers of the president's agenda in their executive departments. As we discuss in Chapter 7, these appointees monitor the actions of the lower-level bureaucrats who retain their jobs regardless of who is president and are not necessarily sympathetic to the president's priorities.

Like other presidential appointees, cabinet members are chosen for a combination of loyalty to the president and expertise. Trump's second secretary of state, Mike Pompeo, served as a member of Congress from Kansas and as director of the Central Intelligence Agency. Trump's secretary of the Treasury, Steven Mnuchin, was a former hedge fund manager and investor who held a senior position in the 2016 Trump campaign.

"Why Should I Care?"

Having read the job description for America's president, you might reasonably ask, How does any one person handle all of these responsibilities? The answer is that presidents have help: trusted advisers and people chosen for policy knowledge, political skills, and loyalty. Put another way, if you want to know whether someone will make a good president, don't look at his or her experience or campaign promises—look at the people he or she picks to help run the government.

Cabinet and Cabinet-Level Positions

The president's Cabinet is composed of the heads of the 15 executive departments along with other appointees given cabinet rank by the president.

Secretary of Agriculture	Secretary of Transportation
Secretary of Commerce	Secretary of the Treasury
Secretary of Defense	Secretary of Veterans Affairs
Secretary of Education	Vice President
Secretary of Energy	White House Chief of Staff
Secretary of Health and Human Services	Attorney General
Secretary of Homeland Security	Head of the Environmental Protection Agency
Secretary of Housing and Urban Development	Head of the Office of Management and Budget
Secretary of the Interior	Head of the Office of National Drug Control Policy
Secretary of Labor	United States Trade Representative
Secretary of State	

Source: Compiled by the authors from whitehouse.gov.

"Why Should I Care?" Cabinet secretaries are the president's eyes and ears in the executive branch, carrying out the president's wishes and serving as the public faces of the departments they lead.

Presidential power today

EXPLAIN HOW MODERN PRESIDENTS HAVE BECOME EVEN MORE POWERFUL

As we have discussed, presidential authority comes from two sources, on paper: the limited powers granted by the Constitution, and laws that have expanded the president's power. Even so, assessing presidential power requires expanding our notions of where this power actually comes from. Saying that presidents have become more powerful over time because of the expansion of the United States or the increased size of the federal budget or bureaucracy tells only part of the story. What about these circumstances made presidents more powerful?

One important clue about where presidential power comes from is that, after more than two centuries, many of the limits to these powers are not well defined. It is unclear, for example, which executive actions require congressional approval and which ones can be reversed by Congress. The very ambiguity of the Constitution and most statutes also creates opportunities for the exercise of presidential power. As we have seen, the Constitution makes the president military commander in chief but gives Congress the power to declare war and to raise and support armies, without specifying which branch of government is in charge of the military. Thus, at least part of presidential authority must be derived or assumed from what the Constitution and statutes *do not say*—the ways in which they fail to define or delineate presidential power—and how presidents use this ambiguity to pursue their goals.

In addition to these ambiguities, presidents also gain real power from other, more informal aspects of their office. Recall our discussion of the president's ability to influence the legislative process. In the Constitution, the president's powers in this realm are limited to advising Congress on the state of the union and to vetoing legislation (subject to congressional override). But presidents often have very real influence at all points in the legislative process: they can offer a variety of small inducements, such as visits to the Oval Office and campaign assistance, and they can draw on the natural respect that most people (including members of Congress) feel for the presidency regardless of who holds the office, thereby securing compromises that achieve the president's policy goals. [33]

Donald Trump made no secret of his willingness to push the boundaries of presidential authority in areas such as executive privilege, to keep key executive branch positions open or rely on acting appointments, and to build relationships with the leaders of nondemocratic regimes such as Vladimir Putin of Russia, Xi Jinping of China, and Kim Jong-un of North Korea. He also removed individuals from high-level jobs in the executive branch because they advised against these actions or informed Congress about them (as they were obligated to do under law). Regardless of whether or not you support these moves, they are not clearly in violation of the Constitution or established law. In fact, what is notable about Trump's behavior in office is that despite his strong rhetoric, he backed off threats when challenged by the courts or Congress. For example, during negotiations over additional funding for small businesses during the 2020 COVID-19 pandemic, Trump administration officials originally said they would not approve any bill that gave funding to hospitals and an expanded testing effort, only to reverse course when it was clear that both provisions had support among congressional Republicans.[34] While Joe Biden is unlikely to follow these strategies, he will, like all other presidents, use his informal authority to pursue policy and political goals.

Presidents, unilateral action, and policy making

unilateral action (presidential)
Any policy decision made and acted upon by the president and presidential staff without the explicit approval or consent of Congress.

Political scientists Terry M. Moe and William G. Howell argue that constitutional and statutory ambiguities in some cases enable presidents to take **unilateral action**, changing policy on their own without consulting Congress or anyone else.[35] Although Congress can, in theory, undo unilateral actions through legislation, court proceedings, or impeachment, Moe and Howell maintain that the costs of doing so, in terms of time, effort, and public perceptions, are often prohibitive. The result is that presidents can take unilateral action despite congressional opposition, knowing that their actions stand little chance of being reversed.

The 2018 debate over U.S. attacks on suspected chemical weapons facilities in Syria provides a good example of how constitutional ambiguities create opportunities for unilateral action. The Trump administration argued that because the operation involved only air strikes, it did not trigger the "hostilities or imminent hostilities" provisions of the War Powers Resolution. While some in Congress disagreed and wanted to vote on whether to authorize the operation, no such vote was ever taken.

This example is far from the first time that a president has argued that military operations were not subject to congressional review. For example, the arguments advanced by the Trump administration were very similar to those made by the Obama administration when it sent military aid and advisers to Syria in 2011. Even during the Iraq War, when some Democrats in Congress wanted to cut off war funding to force the withdrawal of American forces, supporters of the Bush administration cited the **unitary executive theory** to argue that the Constitution's description of the president as commander in chief of America's armed forces meant that, even if Congress refused to appropriate funds for the war, the president could (1) order American forces to stay in Iraq and (2) order the Department of the Treasury to spend any funds necessary to continue operations. Ultimately, members of Congress approved a funding resolution. (The unitary executive theory was also cited during the investigation of possible collusion between the Russian government and the 2016 Trump presidential campaign, when President Trump's lawyers used it to justify their claim that, since the Constitution made Trump the head of the executive branch, including the Justice Department, he could not be indicted for committing a crime.)

In both cases, the positions of the Obama and Bush administrations left members of Congress with a single unattractive option: invoking the War Powers Resolution to force the end of combat operations. This option would take time, as it would require building majority support in the House and the Senate for the resolution. It would also trigger Supreme Court review of the War Powers Resolution, which is a significant risk—if the Court were to rule in favor of the president and to hold that the resolution was unconstitutional, it would sharply reduce Congress's control over future military operations.

Presidents act unilaterally to make domestic policy as well. President Trump, for example, issued orders to limit the admission of refugees into the United States and to move toward adding work requirements for recipients of federal welfare benefits. Similarly, during President Obama's second term in office, Obama gave several directives to the Justice Department that limited deportations of undocumented immigrants. And while President Trump reversed some of Obama's executive orders (particularly those dealing with deportations), the others will remain in place until a future president, Congress, or federal court acts to rescind them.

It is important to understand that throughout the nation's history, there have been many other examples of unilateral presidential actions, such as the annexation of Texas, the freeing of enslaved people in the Emancipation Proclamation, the desegregation of the U.S. military, the initiation of affirmative action programs, and the creation of agencies such as the Peace Corps.[36] In part, unilateral actions are the product of the president's constitutional and statutory authority, which gives the president the right to act unilaterally under some circumstances. Additional opportunities are created by the ambiguities in the president's authority that we discussed earlier. Finally, because no one becomes president without a strong, broad vision of what he or she would like government to do, it should be no surprise that presidents are continually testing the bounds of their authority by taking unilateral actions as a way of translating their policy ideas into reality.

unitary executive theory
The idea that the vesting clause of the Constitution gives the president the authority to issue orders and policy directives that cannot be undone by Congress.

Constitutional ambiguities create opportunities for unilateral action. The 2018 debate over U.S. attacks on suspected chemical weapons facilities in Syria provides a good example. The Trump administration argued that because the operation involved only air strikes, it did not trigger the "hostilities or imminent hostilities" provisions of the War Powers Resolution.

Control over the interpretation and implementation of laws

By virtue of their control over the executive branch, presidents are sometimes in a position to shape policy outcomes by influencing how a law is implemented. For example, after Congress passed a law in 2017 that mandated sanctions on Russians who had participated in efforts to interfere in the 2016 American presidential election, the Trump administration took over six months to identify which individuals would be subject to sanctions. Besides missing a deadline laid out in the bill, the administration's actions targeted only a small number of individuals—significantly fewer than supporters of the law had expected. However, because the law did not specify how extensive the sanctions had to be, the administration's actions, while unilateral, were in fact legal.

Other presidents have found and exploited loopholes in laws that were initially designed to restrict presidential power. For example, current law requires the president to give congressional leaders "timely notification" of secret intelligence operations. However, during the Reagan administration, senior officials did not reveal the existence of ongoing operations for several months. When these operations were eventually discovered, officials claimed they were within the letter of the law because it did not specify a time limit within which Congress must be notified.[37]

Most presidents have tried to control the implementation of laws by issuing **signing statements** when signing bills into law. These documents, which explain the president's interpretation of a new law, are issued most often when the president wishes to approve a bill but disagrees with the way that supporters of the bill in Congress interpret the legislation. Presidents issue signing statements so that if the courts have to resolve uncertainties about the bill's intent, judges can take into account not only the views expressed during congressional debates about the bill but also the president's interpretation of it.[38]

Congressional responses to unilateral action

In theory, members of Congress can undo a president's unilateral action by enacting a law to overturn it, but this is harder than it may sound.[39] Some members of Congress may approve of what the president has done or be indifferent to it, or they may give a higher priority to enacting other laws, making it hard to assemble a majority of legislators who are motivated enough to pass a law overturning the president's action. For example, the Trump administration went far enough on its implementation of the Russia sanctions that only a minority of House members and senators were willing to invest the time to enact a new bill that went further. Still, reversals do happen: Congress enacted a Russia sanctions bill in the first place in a reversal of the Trump administration's refusal to agree that Russians actually interfered in the 2016 election or that America should impose sanctions as a response. And the impeachment of Donald Trump can be seen as a response to claims that Trump had pressured the government of Ukraine to investigate his 2020 political rival, Democrat Joe Biden.

Members of Congress can also write laws in a way that limits the president's authority over their implementation.[40] However, this strategy has drawbacks. The problem is that members of Congress delegate authority to the president or the executive branch bureaucracy for good reasons—either because it is difficult for legislators to predict how a policy should be implemented or because they cannot agree among themselves on an implementation plan.[41] In the case of Russia sanctions, for example, members of Congress may have been unsure of whom to sanction or what appropriate punishments would look like. Members of Congress from the president's party may also want to grant authority to the president because they hold policy goals similar to the president's and would therefore benefit from the exercise of unilateral power.

Aside from legislation, the only option for members of Congress to overturn a president's unilateral action is to take the president to court (probably all the way to the Supreme Court) to demonstrate that he or she has overstepped his or her authority. In the case of the Trump administration's travel ban barring people from several countries, including five with large Muslim populations, from entering the United States, some

signing statement
A document issued by the president when signing a bill into law explaining his or her interpretation of the law, which often differs from the interpretation of Congress, in an attempt to influence how the law will be implemented.

President Trump's closeness to Russian president Vladimir Putin led to speculation about the nature of their relationship. After President Trump refused to agree that Russians actually interfered in the 2016 election, Congress enacted a Russia sanctions bill. This is an example of members of Congress undoing a president's unilateral action by enacting a law to overturn it.

members of Congress were involved in court cases intended to suspend or reverse the ban. The problem with pursuing this option is the time required for judicial proceedings—and the fact that the courts may uphold the president's right to act unilaterally. In the case of the travel ban, for example, a later version was upheld by the Supreme Court in June 2018.

Congress also has the power to remove the president or vice president from office through the impeachment process. However, removing a president is much more difficult than passing a law to undo a unilateral action. First, House members must impeach (indict) the president by majority vote, which accuses him or her of a crime or breach of his or her sworn duties. Then senators hold a trial, followed by a vote in which a two-thirds majority is required to remove the president from office. Only three presidents have faced an impeachment vote: Andrew Johnson in 1866, Bill Clinton in 1999, and Donald Trump in 2019 and 2021 (a fourth president, Richard Nixon, resigned from office to prevent an impeachment vote). Johnson was involved in a political dispute over administration of the southern states after the Civil War; Clinton was alleged to have lied under oath in a sexual harassment lawsuit. Although both of these presidents were impeached by the House, they were not convicted by the Senate, so they stayed in office.

Donald Trump's first impeachment focused on Trump's request to the prime minister of Ukraine to open an investigation into Democratic presidential candidate Joe Biden's son, Hunter Biden, who had been appointed as a director of Burisma, a Ukrainian energy company. At about the same time, the Trump administration had suspended military aid to Ukraine, which was vital given the ongoing Russian-sponsored separatist movement in Eastern Ukraine. A whistleblower (whose name has not been made public) used established procedures to reveal these developments to senior Inspector General staff in the National Security Council, who then forwarded the complaint to Congress, as they were obligated to do under the law.

Hearings in the House of Representatives documented both Trump's request and the freeze on military aid. As Lieutenant Colonel Alexander Vindman, a senior White House official who knew about the conversations, put it, "I did not think it was proper to demand that a foreign government investigate a U.S. citizen, and I was worried about the implications for the U.S. Government's support of Ukraine."[42] Trump's defenders argued that the aid freeze was coincidental, and that Trump was trying to reduce corruption in Ukraine. Ultimately, the House of Representatives voted to impeach Trump in December 2019 almost completely along party lines. The Senate held an abbreviated trial; it voted on largely partisan lines against calling witnesses and acquitted Trump by majority vote, with only one Republican, Senator Mitt Romney (R-UT), voting to convict on one of the articles of impeachment.

Trump's second impeachment focused on a speech he gave near the White House on January 6, 2021, in which he allegedly encouraged protestors to "fight" against congressional certification of Joe Biden's victory in the 2020 election, which was concurrently taking place in the Capitol. Members of the crowd stormed and temporarily occupied the Capitol, interrupting, but not preventing, certification. Again, the House and Senate voted on impeachment largely along party lines (although some prominent Republicans, including Romney and House Republican Conference Chair Liz Cheney [R-WI], voted against Trump).

The Trump impeachments illustrate how impeachment is at best of limited use in curbing unilateral action by a president. Members of Congress who are upset about presidential actions might nevertheless oppose removing the president from office—this was exactly the argument used by several Republican senators and House members. They might approve of the president's other initiatives, want to prevent the vice president from becoming president, have concerns about the political backlash that impeachment could generate against them or their party, or believe that the president's actions did not rise to the level needed to remove him or her from office. Thus, even though Democrats took over the House in the 2018 midterms, in both impeachments they still lacked the plurality in the Senate (let alone the 67-vote supermajority) that was necessary to remove Trump from office.

In sum, ambiguities in the Constitution create opportunities for unilateral presidential action. These actions are subject to reversal through legislation, court decisions, and impeachment, but members of Congress face significant costs if they undertake any of these options. As long as presidents are careful to limit their exercise of unilateral power to actions that do not generate intense opposition in Congress, they can implement a wide range of policy goals without official congressional consent—provided that bureaucrats go along with the president's wishes, a question we take up in Chapter 7.

Presidents as politicians

Aside from situations in which the president has (or has been given) the authority to act unilaterally, the reality of presidential power is that much of what presidents do (or want to do) requires support from others, including legislators, bureaucrats, and citizens. As a result, the presidency is an inherently political office—something that all presidents learn is true, regardless of their expectations when they take office.[43] Presidents have to take into account the political consequences of their decisions: the effects on their political support, reelection prospects, and party. A president must also contend with the reality that achieving his or her personal policy goals often requires bargaining and compromising with others, both inside and outside government. Many accounts of Trump's presidency have emphasized that his experience as a CEO, the head of an organization in which his word was law, did not prepare him for being president, a role in which he faced members of Congress and bureaucrats who often had the power to reject presidential initiatives.

In part, presidents must keep their eyes on the political implications of their actions in office because they want to be reelected to a second term. One important indicator of presidential performance is the **presidential approval rating**, the percentage of the public who think the president is doing a good job in office. Figure 5.2, which shows the presidential approval ratings for the last ten presidents who ran for reelection, reveals that first-term presidents with less than 50 percent approval are in real trouble.

He'll sit here, and he'll say, "Do this! Do that!" And nothing will happen. Poor Ike—it won't be a bit like the Army. He'll find it very frustrating.

—President Harry Truman, describing incoming president Dwight Eisenhower

presidential approval rating
The percentage of Americans who think that the president is doing a good job in office.

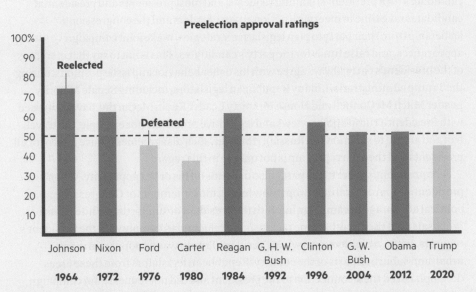

Preelection approval ratings

Source: Approval data from the Roper Center for Public Opinion Research, Cornell University, "Presidential Approval," https://presidential.roper.center (accessed 11/2/20).

**FIGURE
5.2**

Presidential Popularity and Reelection

This figure shows the preelection-year average approval ratings for recent presidents who ran for reelection. It shows that a president's chances of winning reelection are related to his or her popularity. At what level of approval would you say that an incumbent president is likely to be reelected?

No recent president has been reelected with less than a 50 percent approval rating. Donald Trump's approval rating in reputable polls never moved higher than the mid-40s despite a strong economy. Criticism of his mismanagement of the COVID-19 pandemic did not reduce his popularity by much, but it likely prevented any increase in his rating—and his chance of reelection.

Of course, it would be wrong to say that presidents are single-mindedly focused on keeping their approval rating as high as possible. For one thing, as we discuss in Chapter 10, presidential approval is shaped by factors that they have only limited control over, such as the state of the economy. And all presidents have taken actions that were politically costly because they believed that the policies were worthwhile. For example, many of President Trump's decisions (such as the travel ban) and legislative initiatives (such as the tax cuts enacted in 2017) were opposed by a majority of Americans. Even so, presidents and their advisers are keenly aware of the political consequences of their actions, and there is no doubt that these consequences shape both their decisions and how they explain these actions to American citizens. This was probably one reason why Donald Trump appeared at daily press conferences during the COVID-19 pandemic.

The President as Party Leader The president is the unofficial head of his or her political party and generally picks the party's day-to-day leaders (or at least has considerable influence over their selection). This process begins when a presidential candidate captures the party's nomination and continues through the president's time in office. For example, while many members of the Republican National Committee (RNC) opposed Donald Trump's nomination in 2016, the party organized to help Trump get elected and ran countless campaign ads on his behalf. After the election, Trump supporters, including the chair of the RNC at the time, Ronna McDaniel, moved into positions within the party organization.

The connection between the president and the party reflects their intertwining interests. The president needs support from members of his or her party in Congress to enact legislation, and the party and its candidates need the president to compile a record of policy achievements that reflect well on the organization and to help raise the funds needed for the next election. Therefore, party leaders generally defer to a presidential candidate's (or a president's) staffing requests, and most presidents and presidential candidates take time to meet with national party leaders and the congressional leadership from their party to plan legislative strategies, make joint campaign appearances, and raise funds for the party's candidates. This is not to say that members of the president's party always agree with his or her behavior and issue positions: during the Trump administration, many Republican legislators, including Senate Majority Leader Mitch McConnell and House Minority Leader Kevin McCarthy, have disagreed with President Trump's policy views and legislative proposals (for example, the travel ban and an end to sanctions on Russia). However, such disagreements have arisen for all presidents and their party; Trump is not unique in this regard.

The president's value to the party also depends on his or her popularity. When presidential approval ratings drop to low levels, most members of Congress see no political advantage in campaigning with the president or supporting White House proposals, and they may become increasingly reluctant to comply with the president's requests. In the 2020 elections, when President Trump was unpopular in many urban and suburban parts of the country, Republican legislators from these areas de-emphasized their connection to the president and did not request joint campaign appearances. On the other hand, Trump appeared at many rallies for Republicans campaigning in rural areas, and many candidates appeared with Vice President Mike Pence, whose popularity was significantly higher than Trump's.

Going Public and Public Opinion Presidents are in an excellent position to communicate with the American people because of their prominent role and the extensive media coverage devoted to anything they say to the nation. Broadcast and cable networks even give the president prime-time slots for the State of the Union speech and other major addresses. The media attention that comes with the presidency provides the president with a unique strategy for shaping government policy: **going public**, that is, appealing directly to American citizens.[44] Presidential appeals are designed partly to persuade and partly to motivate the president's supporters, in the hope that they will pressure members of the House and Senate to support the president's requests.

Going public sometimes works—but more often it is ineffectual or even counterproductive. A president's appeals may energize supporters, but they may also have a similar effect on opponents.[45] Thus, rather than facilitating compromise (or a wholesale presidential victory), publicizing an issue may deepen existing conflicts. More generally, studies suggest that most Americans ignore or reject a president's attempts to go public. As presidency scholar George C. Edwards III notes, people who disapprove of a president's time in office are not going to change their minds just because of a presidential speech.[46] Other times, presidential efforts to shape opinion fail spectacularly, such as President Trump's use of a Sharpie to alter a National Oceanographic and Atmospheric Administration (NOAA) hurricane prediction map to justify his tweeted assertion that the storm might hit Alabama.[47] While few Americans are political experts, most citizens are not gullible.

George C. Edwards's findings explain why most recent presidents have had little success with their efforts to go public. President George W. Bush gave many speeches to build support for his Iraq War policies and for his proposal to privatize Social Security. President Barack Obama did the same in an effort to enact gun control legislation. And while President Trump used a broader range of media outlets compared to his predecessors (most notably, Twitter and his campaign rallies), his efforts to shape public opinion on issues such as the travel ban, the border wall, or immigration reform have not significantly changed public opinion (see Figure 5.3). Thus, while presidents have a unique platform from which to deliver their arguments directly to the American people, in practice they are often frustrated in their ability to shape public opinion.

DID YOU KNOW?

Since becoming president in 2017, President Trump held over

300

rallies (often televised) calling for enactment of his policy priorities.
Source: *New York Times*

going public
A president's use of speeches and other public communications to appeal directly to citizens about issues the president would like the House and Senate to act on.

After mistakenly tweeting that Alabama was under threat from Hurricane Dorian in September 2019, President Donald Trump appeared during a briefing by federal agencies with a map that seems to have been updated with a Sharpie marker to extend the range of at-risk areas into Alabama. The National Weather Service never included Alabama in its projected path for Dorian, leaving many Americans confused about whom to trust.

FIGURE 5.3

Presidential Approval Ratings for Donald Trump

Donald Trump's approval ratings were remarkably stable throughout his presidency, which is what we would expect given steady economic growth and high levels of partisan polarization. Many Democrats argued that Trump should be blamed for mismanagement of the COVID-19 pandemic as well as statements and actions that damaged America's relations with other nations. Does the trend in Trump's approval ratings suggest these attacks had much effect?

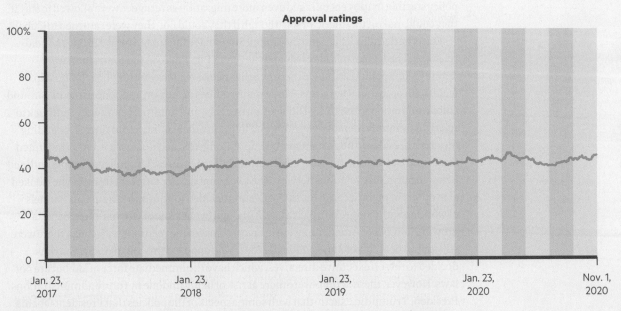

Source: FiveThirtyEight, "How Popular Is Donald Trump?," https://projects.fivethirtyeight.com/trump-approval-ratings (accessed 11/4/20).

The difficulty presidents have in shaping public opinion is another reason why some presidents seem to accomplish more than others. Political scientist Stephen Skowronek argues that presidents are constrained by the era in which they govern.[48] Some presidents (such as Ronald Reagan in 1981) take office when public opinion is strongly behind their policy agenda, making it easier for them to persuade Congress and bureaucrats to comply with their requests. Other presidents have the misfortune to hold office when public opinion is not supportive of significant policy change in the form of new laws or changes in regulations. Under these conditions, presidents are limited in what they can do, even with all their powers and capability for unilateral action. Even though President Donald Trump held office with unified Republican control of the House and Senate, there was only modest public support for many Republican initiatives, such as repealing Obamacare, cutting entitlement programs, or curtailing government regulations. This political climate contributed to the difficulties Trump faced in trying to enact these parts of his agenda.

AP®
POLICY IN
PRACTICE

The Cuban Thaw

Before its revolution (1953–1959), Cuba was a favorite destination in the Caribbean for American tourists and as a source of investment for businesses. When Fidel Castro assumed power after the Cuban Revolution, he initiated a communist state and nationalized many businesses that were once American-owned. In response, the United States extensively strengthened an embargo that had been initially imposed on arms sales in 1958. The goal was to end the Castro regime by shattering its economy, but no other countries joined the embargo. Cuba found trading partners elsewhere and became allies with the Soviet Union. Fidel Castro formally left all leadership positions of his own accord in 2011 and handed over power to his brother Raúl, who stayed in power until 2018. Cuba is a poor country characterized by a history of significant human rights abuses. As a result, many Cubans have attempted to escape to the United States over the past decades. During a downturn in the Cuban economy in the late 1970s and early 1980s, Castro even allowed many people to leave Cuba (the Mariel boatlift), though it turns out some of these people had been prisoners or mental health facilities residents. The so-called wet foot, dry foot policy starting in 1995 encouraged even more migration as refugees were allowed to stay if they could make it to American soil (though if they could not, they were returned to Cuba).

Over the decades, Cuba and the United States have fluctuated between hot and cold relations. The Cuban missile crisis and the Bay of Pigs fiasco in the 1960s (hot) were definitely low points, and since then there has been an uneasy status quo relationship (cold) with occasional flare-ups. Three main sources of tension and concern center around Cuban migration to the United States, family visits, and remittances (money sent back to relatives by family members working and living in other countries) to Cuba. Depending on who is president, the particular makeup of Congress, and domestic events, the United States and Cuba either relax or tighten up on these measures. The policy attempts outlined below to normalize relations between the two countries are different from policies looked at in other chapters because President Obama decided to go around the usual channels of working with Congress to pass a law. Although by the time of Obama's presidency a growing number of Americans were in favor of improving relations with Cuba, there were still many vocal citizens and political leaders who opposed this alliance. Obama thus decided to rely on executive directives, which have the immediate force of law but are not laws. However, these actions were more at risk of being undone by future administrations. President Trump did exactly that with some aspects of the policies that President Obama enacted. The ultimate goal of what came to be known as the Cuban thaw was the lifting of the embargo; however, this has not yet been accomplished.

Policy Stages

1. Problem Recognition
   - Long-term hostilities between the United States and Cuba are due to the following events:
     - Cuban Revolution (1953–1959)
     - The Cuban nationalization of U.S. assets in 1960
     - A series of U.S. embargoes against Cuba starting in 1958 and most extensively in 1962
     - The end of U.S. diplomatic recognition of Cuba in 1961
   - Extensive poverty gripped Cuba.
   - Cubans in the United States wanted to assist relatives and friends living in Cuba, especially through remittances.
   - Cuban and American remittance and travel policies became more relaxed over the decades.
   - Embargo did not work; no other country joined the United States.
   - The United States had already resumed relations with other communist countries (China and Vietnam).
   - Younger generations in the United States did not have the same negative memories of the Cuban regime.
   - Cuba's advances in the medical field provided great opportunities for sharing ideas between the two countries.
   - There were several humanitarian issues at stake:
     - Many people are living in poverty in Cuba, and they would greatly benefit from increased tourism and trade with the United States.
     - Cubans would also benefit if they knew they could rely on remittances from American relatives.
     - Easing travel restrictions would make it easier for families to reconnect and stay in touch.
   - Public opinion about Cuba and the embargo was changing.
   - Fidel Castro stepped down as president of Cuba on February 18, 2008.

2. Agenda Setting
   - During the 2008 presidential election, Senator Obama met with prominent Cuban leaders, such as the Cuban American National Foundation, to discuss improving relations.
   - President Obama and White House staff spoke to different stakeholders—including the public, Congress members, interest groups, union and corporate heads, and party leaders—about improving relations between the United States and Cuba.
   - Starting in 2009, President Raúl Castro made some transitions away from a command economy and toward a market economy by encouraging the development of these important economic sectors:
     - Agriculture
     - Small business
     - Real estate
     - Self-employment
   - With Public Law 111-8, President Obama lifted all restrictions on family travel and remittances in March 2009.
   - President Obama announced he wanted to improve economic, political, and diplomatic relations with Cuba at the Fifth Summit of the Americas on April 17–19, 2009.
   - Restrictions were eased in 2011 on other types of travel (religious, educational, and people-to-people exchanges).

- President Obama met Pope Francis, who raised the issue of Cuban-American relations, on March 27, 2014.
- Pope Francis sent letters to President Castro and President Obama in the early summer of 2014, encouraging them to better their relations.
- Some interest groups, such as the Cuba Study Group, argued that it would be in the economic interest of both countries to normalize relations.
- Other interest groups, such as the Cuban-American lobby, have consistently opposed the Castro regime and want to continue all measures, such as the embargo, until Cuba reforms its authoritarian, non-humanitarian, anti-capitalist regime.

3. Deliberation and Formulation
   - Eighteen months of secret negotiations between Cuban and American representatives started in June 2013 in Canada.
     - President Obama was concerned that Congress and other stakeholders would hinder the process, so talks were conducted in secret.
   - Details were finalized at Vatican City.
     - Some restrictions on travels and remittances were lifted.
     - U.S. banks gained access to the Cuban financial system.
     - An embassy was established.
   - The handshake seen 'round the world: President Barack Obama shook hands with President Raúl Castro as Obama was walking up to the podium to make a speech at a memorial service for Nelson Mandela in Johannesburg, South Africa, on December 10, 2013.

4. Enactment
   - After 18 months of secret talks, President Obama and President Castro gave simultaneous speeches on December 17, 2014, announcing the Cuban thaw, which led to these developments:
     - Economic ties were expanded.
     - Secretary of State John Kerry revisited and reviewed Cuba's state-sponsored terrorism status.
     - Family visits were allowed.
     - Business visits were allowed.
     - Educational activities and visits to Cuba were permitted.
     - Tourism was not initially allowed.
     - Prisoners were released from both countries.

5. Implementation
   - Alan Gross was released on December 17, 2014, after being sentenced in 2009 for 15 years for smuggling satellites and other communication equipment into Cuba.
   - A spy/agent exchange between Cuba and the United States took place on December 17, 2017.
   - U.S. Assistant Secretary of State Roberta S. Jacobson and Josefina Vidal Ferreiro, Cuba's head of North American affairs, met in Havana on January 21, 2015, to discuss migration policy.
   - Cuba requested an end to the wet foot, dry foot policy, which allowed Cuban refugees who made it to American soil to claim residency status one year later.
   - The wet foot, dry foot policy ended on January 12, 2017.
   - Cuba also allowed Cuban nationals to return without reprisals.
   - Two more rounds of meetings took place in Washington, D.C., and Havana in February and March 2015.
   - The Obama administration announced on April 14, 2015, that Cuba would be removed from the U.S. State Sponsors of Terrorism list.
   - Cuba was officially removed from the list on May 29, 2015.

- The United States restored diplomatic relations with Cuba by reopening the U.S. Embassy on July 20, 2015.
- Secretary of State John Kerry visited Cuba on August 14, 2015.
- Kerry canceled his mid-March visit to Cuba on March 3, 2016 due to American and Cuban diplomats arguing over which dissidents President Obama would be allowed to meet during his own visit.
- President Obama visited Cuba on March 20–22, 2016.
  - President Calvin Coolidge had been the last president to visit, in 1928.
  - Obama met with over 10 dissidents, including a journalist, a gay rights advocate, a rapper, and a Catholic Church leader.
  - Some of the dissidents were not in favor of renewed relations with Cuba.
- President Obama issued a Presidential Policy Directive (United States-Cuba Normalization) on October 14, 2016, which led to these developments:
  - Americans were allowed to travel to Cuba.
  - American business investment in Cuba was encouraged.
  - Sharing medical information between the two countries was encouraged.
  - Bilateral cooperation allowed the countries to take on a wide range of issues, including environmental, migration, economic, disaster prevention, and defense issues.
  - Transportation for the purposes of personal and business travel and commerce was coordinated and developed.
  - The U.S. government worked with the Cuban financial system to strengthen it.

6. Evaluation
   - President Obama asked Congress to end the embargo against Cuba in his 2015 and 2016 State of the Union addresses to Congress.
   - Private enterprise grew considerably in Cuba.
   - Increased tourism improved the Cuban economy.
     - Travel to Cuba by foreigners increased by 30 percent from 2015 to 2016.
     - Airline flights increased, as did hotel construction and occupancy.
   - Opinion polls indicated that Americans have increasingly favorable views about Cuba over the years.
   - Senator Marco Rubio criticized various aspects of Obama's Cuba policies, believing:
     - The wet foot, dry foot policy should not have been ended.
     - The Cuban Medical Professional Parole Program should not have been terminated.
     - Migration to the United States has increased as a result.
   - Senator Ted Cruz asserted that Obama's policies enabled the Cuban government to continue its antidemocratic regime.
   - Senator Bob Menendez condemned President Obama's visit to Cuba as lending support and legitimacy to the Castro brothers' dictatorship.
   - Pope Francis praised the Cuban thaw.
   - Human rights violations have not improved, and may have worsened, according to organizations such as Human Rights Watch and the U.S. State Department.
   - Relaxed policies toward Cuba have enabled repressive measures and indicate that the embargo should not be ended, according to some pro-democratic leaders such as Jorge Luis Garcia Perez (Antunez) and Antonio Rodiles.

7. Possible Modifications, Expansion, or Termination of Policy
   - President Trump suspended the policy of unconditional sanctions relief on June 16, 2017.
   - President Trump suggested a different plan in the future, but no specific plans were discussed.

- Business and travel restrictions were reinstated on November 9, 2017.
- National Security Adviser John Bolton announced a rollback of many of Obama's policies:
  - The 1996 Helms-Burton Act was reinstated on April 17, 2019.
    - Citizens could sue business partners connected to the nationalization of foreign assets after the Cuban Revolution.
    - Citizens could sue for lost property stemming from the Cuban Revolution.
  - Remittance amounts were reduced.
  - Nonfamily travel to Cuba was limited and more closely monitored.
    - Cuban firms could no longer work with other countries to attain hard currency and evade the U.S. embargo.
  - Additional restrictions on remittances were imposed on November 9, 2017.
  - On June 4, 2019, further travel restrictions were placed on Americans traveling to Cuba.

Questions for Discussion

1. Should the United States lift the embargo against Cuba? Why or why not?
2. Was the Obama administration justified in keeping its early meetings with Cuba secret? Explain your answer.
3. Under what circumstances, if any, is it justified for a president to circumvent Congress by issuing executive orders?

Unpacking the Conflict

Considering all that we've discussed in this chapter, let's apply what we know about how the office of the president works to the questions we presented at the beginning of this chapter. Did Trump redefine what makes a successful president—or a failed one? What factors distinguish presidential successes from presidential failures?

The president occupies an office whose power is derived from constitutional authority, statutory authority, and ambiguities that enable unilateral action. While Trump promised during the 2016 campaign to transform America, his presidency highlights the difficulties that any president would face in trying to deliver on this promise. Although presidents are given considerable powers, big policy changes generally require congressional consent. And as we have seen, even with unified government, Trump was no more successful than his predecessors at persuading members of Congress to accept his policy plans such as the building of a border wall. Trump also faced opposition from within the bureaucracy and from citizens pursuing their claims through the federal judicial system.

Even so, Trump had some notable successes, particularly in areas where he could act unilaterally using executive orders or directives, as well as in shaping American foreign policy. Trump's appointees to posts in cabinet departments and federal agencies made significant progress in implementing his agenda in the form of regulatory changes and new interpretations of existing laws. Considering these successes along with the failures that we've noted, we should not conclude that President Trump had some special powers that his predecessors lacked or that he was deficient in some crucial talent. While his day-to-day behavior was sometimes different from what we have come to expect from our presidents, Trump's overall performance was not surprising. Rather, it illustrates both the possibilities and the limitations of the presidency in contemporary American politics.

"What's Your Take?"

Did Trump's presidency represent a departure from the norm?

How do the results he achieved in office compare with those of previous presidents?

AP® STUDY GUIDE

Summary

Justification for a single executive is outlined by Hamilton in *Federalist 70*. Presidents get their powers from a variety of sources: some powers are from the Constitution, such as vetoes and powers associated with being commander in chief; others have more informal origins, such as executive agreements and signing statements. Although the president's constitutional powers have not changed, presidential power has grown substantially over time. Nonetheless, even presidents' power is still limited in a number of contexts.

The president's formal powers arise from a combination of constitutional provisions and additional laws that give him or her increased responsibilities. The president has many duties, but the primary responsibilities of the office are to oversee the executive branch and implement laws passed by Congress. Although some presidents might prefer to focus on either domestic or foreign policy, most find that their priorities are determined by domestic and world events. Presidential power is also limited by the passage of the Twenty-Second Amendment.

The executive branch is a huge, complex organization that helps the president exercise vast responsibilities. Appointees to the branch serve as the president's eyes and ears on the bureaucracy. Almost all appointees are replaced when a new administration begins.

While presidents have gained power over time, the Constitution grants the president rather limited powers. The growth of presidential power is closely related to the fact that most limits on it are not well-defined and presidents have succeeded in taking advantage of these ambiguities. Presidents have always used the State of the Union address and the bully pulpit to influence the national agenda. Changes in communication technology, such as the use of social media, have led to an increased response to public policy issues.

Federalist 70
A foundational document written by Alexander Hamilton in 1788 and titled *The Executive Department Further Considered.*

Twenty-Second Amendment
"No person shall be elected to the office of the President more than twice, and no person who has held the office of President, or acted as President, for more than two years of a term to which some other person was elected President shall be elected to the office of the President more than once." This constitutional amendment limits presidential power.

bully pulpit
The president's ability to speak directly to the American public in support of his policy agenda and decisions.

Enduring Understanding

CON-4: "The presidency has been enhanced beyond its expressed constitutional powers." (AP® U.S. Government and Politics Course and Exam Description)

Key Terms

appointment power (p. 190)

bully pulpit (p. 219)

Cabinet (p. 204)

constitutional authority (presidential) (p. 188)

executive agreement (p. 195)

Executive Office of the President (EOP) (p. 202)

executive orders (p. 190)

executive privilege (p. 199)

Federalist 70 (p. 219)

going public (p. 212)

head of government (p. 188)

head of state (p. 188)

pocket veto (p. 196)

presidential approval rating (p. 210)

recess appointment (p. 190)

signing statement (p. 208)

State of the Union (p. 196)

statutory authority (presidential) (p. 188)

Twenty-Second Amendment (p. 219)

unilateral action (presidential) (p. 206)

unitary executive theory (p. 207)

vesting clause (p. 188)

Multiple-Choice Questions (Arranged by Topic)

Topic 2.4: Roles and Powers of the President (CON-4)

1. Which of the following is an accurate comparison of the formal and informal powers of the president?

	Formal Powers	Informal Powers
(A)	ratifying treaties	serving as commander in chief
(B)	making executive agreements	granting executive orders
(C)	vetoing legislation	adding signing statements
(D)	appointing ambassadors	confirming ambassadors

2. Which of the following best explains why a president would use a signing statement?

   (A) The president wants to use his or her formal power of commander in chief to send troops abroad.

   (B) The president has a different interpretation of a law than Congress and wants to attempt to influence how the law will be implemented.

   (C) The president needs to appoint a new ambassador, but the Senate is not in session.

   (D) The president wants general protection from revealing White House discussions to members of the other branches of government.

3. Which of the following best describes the fundamental difference between an executive agreement and a treaty?

   (A) Unlike an executive agreement, a treaty requires Senate approval.

   (B) Treaties are approved by the House and executive agreements are approved by the Senate.

   (C) Treaties last the length of a president's term, while executive agreements last indefinitely.

   (D) Unlike a treaty, an executive agreement requires ratification by three-quarters of the state legislatures.

Topic 2.5: Checks on the Presidency (CON-4)

Questions 4–5 refer to the graph.

Female Federal Judges from Carter to Trump

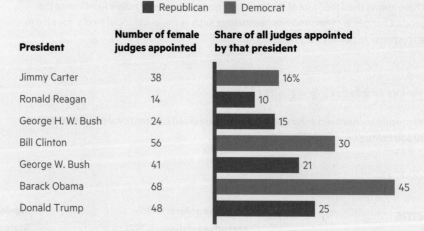

President	Number of female judges appointed	Share of all judges appointed by that president
Jimmy Carter	38	16%
Ronald Reagan	14	10
George H. W. Bush	24	15
Bill Clinton	56	30
George W. Bush	41	21
Barack Obama	68	45
Donald Trump	48	25

Note: Data current as of 7/7/20. Excludes judges confirmed to certain specialized or territorial courts.
Source: John Gramlich, "How Trump Compares with Other Recent Presidents in Appointing Federal Judges," Pew Research Center, July 15, 2020, www.pewresearch.org/fact-tank/2020/07/15/how-trump-compares-with-other-recent-presidents-in-appointing-federal-judges/ (accessed 9/11/20).

4. Which of the following statements is the most accurate based on the graph?

   (A) The majority of federal judges appointed by Donald Trump have been women.

   (B) Donald Trump appointed a higher share of women judges than any other Republican president at the same point in their presidencies.

   (C) Barack Obama appointed more women justices to the Supreme Court than Bill Clinton.

   (D) Bill Clinton and Barack Obama appointed a higher number of women as federal judges because they each served eight years in office.

5. **Which of the following best explains how the power used by the president, as shown in the graph, can be limited?**

   (A) Since federal judges serve set terms, the impact of the presidential appointment is reduced.

   (B) Federal judges are usually recess appointments and thus can only serve until the end of the congressional term.

   (C) Two-thirds of the House of Representatives are required to confirm federal judicial appointments.

   (D) A majority vote in the Senate is required to confirm federal judicial appointments.

Topic 2.6: Expansion of Presidential Powers (CON-4)

Questions 6–7 refer to the excerpt.

The idea of a council to the Executive, which has so generally obtained in the State constitutions, has been derived from that maxim of republican jealousy which considers power as safer in the hands of a number of men than of a single man. If the maxim should be admitted to be applicable to the case, I should contend that the advantage on that side would not counterbalance the numerous disadvantages on the opposite side. But I do not think the rule at all applicable to the executive power. I clearly concur in opinion, in this particular, with a writer whom the celebrated Junius pronounces to be "deep, solid, and ingenious," that "the executive power is more easily confined when it is ONE"; that it is far more safe there should be a single object for the jealousy and watchfulness of the people; and, in a word, that all multiplication of the Executive is rather dangerous than friendly to liberty.

—Alexander Hamilton, *Federalist 70*, March 15, 1788

6. **Which of the following best describes Hamilton's view in the excerpt?**

   (A) A single executive would give too much power to one person and cause jealousy between the other branches of government.

   (B) A single executive would be watched more narrowly and vigilantly by the people than an executive comprised of a group of people.

   (C) An executive council would be safer than a single executive because a group could better represent a diverse republic.

   (D) An executive comprised of a group of people would be much more friendly to liberty than a single executive.

7. **Which of the following best explains how Hamilton's argument in the excerpt was manifested in the Constitution?**

   (A) The executive branch is formally divided with the president and the heads of the cabinet departments having equal power.

   (B) Lawmaking power is shared between the president, who has the power to introduce bills and veto laws, and Congress, which has the power to pass laws.

   (C) The executive branch is formally divided with the president focusing on foreign policy issues and the vice president focusing on domestic policy issues.

   (D) The president serves in multiple roles including commander in chief of the armed forces and chief legislator with the power to check Congress with a veto.

8. **Which of the following amendments was passed in an attempt to rein in the power of the president?**

   (A) Twelfth Amendment

   (B) Seventeenth Amendment

   (C) Twenty-Second Amendment

   (D) Twenty-Third Amendment

9. **Which of the following best explains how the Supreme Court ruled in *United States v. Nixon* (1974)?**

   (A) Executive privilege is granted to both the president and leadership positions in Congress.

   (B) Executive privilege does not exist in the courts but does exist for the purpose of congressional hearings.

   (C) Executive privilege does exist, but that privilege can only be used once the president is out of office.

   (D) Executive privilege was ruled unconstitutional and communications between the president and his or her staff are no longer protected.

10. **Which of following best describes the State of the Union address?**

    (A) a monthly meeting between the president and Congress to review bills awaiting the president's signature

    (B) a monthly speech given by the president to the public to report on the condition of the country and to recommend policies

    (C) an annual event used by the president to formally introduce legislation into Congress

    (D) an annual speech in which the president addresses Congress to report on the condition of the country and to recommend policies

Free-Response Questions

Quantitative Analysis

Presidential Vetoes from H. W. Bush to Trump

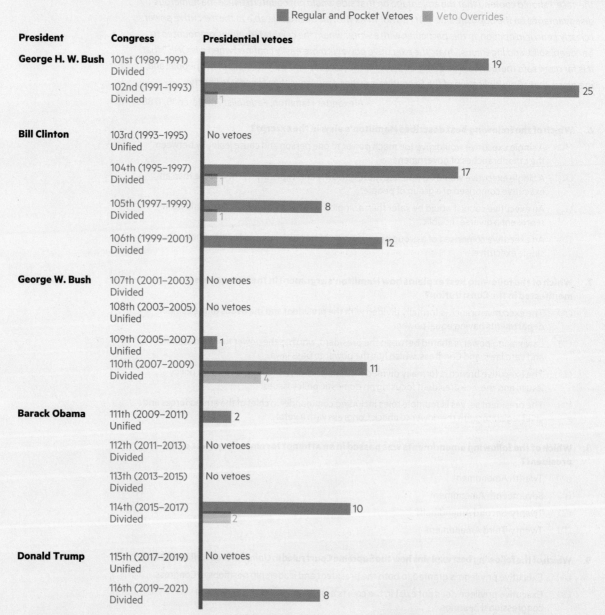

Note: The figure shows the number of vetoes issued by recent presidents in each congressional term they held office, along with whether the term involved unified or divided government. Data current as of 10/1/20.

Source: Data aggregated by the author from U.S. House of Representatives, History, Art, & Archives, "Presidential Vetoes," https://history.house.gov/Institution/Presidential-Vetoes/Presidential-Vetoes/ (accessed 10/1/20).

Use the bar graph to answer the questions.

(A) Identify the president that had the most regular and pocket vetoes during a single congressional term.

(B) Describe a similarity or difference in the number of vetoes during a congressional term with unified versus divided government, as illustrated in the bar graph.

(C) Explain a possible limitation of the visual representation of the data provided.

(D) Explain how the president could attempt to influence the lawmaking process prior to a bill being passed by Congress rather than through the strategy shown in the bar graph.

Argument Essay

Develop an argument that explains which branch of government—executive or legislative—the Founders intended to be the most powerful.

Use at least one piece of evidence from one of the following foundational documents:

- Article I of the U.S. Constitution
- Article II of the U.S. Constitution
- *Federalist 70*

In your response, you should do the following:

✓ Respond to the prompt with a defensible claim or thesis that establishes a line of reasoning.

✓ Support your claim with at least *two* pieces of specific and relevant evidence.

- One piece of evidence must come from one of the foundational documents listed above.
- A second piece of evidence can come from any other foundational document not used as your first piece of evidence, or it may be from your knowledge of course concepts.

✓ Use reasoning to explain why your evidence supports your claim or thesis.

✓ Respond to an opposing or alternative perspective using refutation, concession, or rebuttal.

6

The Courts

What is the role of courts in our political system?

 "He is a faker. He has no consistency about him. He says whatever comes into his head at the moment."

Justice Ruth Bader Ginsburg, commenting on Donald Trump

"Justice Ginsburg of the U.S. Supreme Court has embarrassed all by making very dumb political statements about me. Her mind is shot—resign!"[1]

President Donald Trump

In the heat of the 2016 presidential campaign, the late Justice Ruth Bader Ginsburg cut loose with a series of comments about a possible Trump presidency. In addition to labeling Trump a "faker" in an interview conducted by CNN,[2] Ginsburg told the *New York Times*, "I can't imagine what this place would be—I can't imagine what the country would be—with Donald Trump as our president."[3]

These comments set off a firestorm, not just from Trump and his supporters but also from left-leaning editorial boards such as that of the *Washington Post*. It called her observations "inappropriate," noting that the Code of Conduct for United States Judges "flatly states" that a "judge should not . . . publicly endorse or oppose a candidate for public office."[4] Under the headline "Donald Trump Is Right about Justice Ruth Bader Ginsburg," the *New York Times* was even more critical, saying, "Justice Ruth Bader Ginsburg needs to drop the political punditry and the name-calling."[5] We have come to expect such personal attacks from politicians, but not from Supreme Court justices, which is why Ginsburg's words were so jarring.

Bowing to the public pressure, Justice Ginsburg backed off, saying, "On reflection, my recent remarks in response to press inquiries were ill-advised and I regret making them. Judges should avoid commenting on a candidate for public office. In the future I will be more circumspect."[6]

Chief Justice John G. Roberts Jr. also weighed in on the topic of judicial independence, rebuking the president for complaining about an "Obama judge" who ruled against him in a political asylum case. "We do not have Obama judges or Trump judges, Bush judges or Clinton judges," Roberts said. "What we have is an extraordinary group of dedicated judges doing their level best to do equal right to

Justice Ginsburg broke from the image of the blindfolded Lady Justice when she expressed her opinions on a Trump presidency. Here, Justice Ginsburg (left), along with other Supreme Court justices, looks on as President Trump makes a speech during the swearing-in ceremony for Justice Brett Kavanaugh.

those appearing before them. That independent judiciary is something we should all be thankful for."[7]

Why all the fuss? Why should a sitting justice's political comments or a president's remark about something that is obviously true (judges do have political biases) be so controversial? The simple answer is that our political system is strongly committed to the image of the blindfolded Lady Justice, holding the scales, neutrally applying the law. As Chief Justice Roberts famously said, justices are like baseball umpires, just calling the balls and strikes within the constitutional system. After all, the guiding principles of the "rule of law" in the American political system—embodied in the words carved above the entrance to the Supreme Court ("Equal Justice under Law") and the image of Lady Justice—seem to contradict the view of a political Supreme Court. We normally think of the courts as objectively applying the law and interpreting the Constitution for each case. Indeed, there is often consensus among the justices on how to rule in a given case. In the 2019–2020 term, 36 percent of the cases decided were unanimous (22 of 61) and 6 more had only one dissenting vote.[8]

However, a massive body of political science research shows that the Supreme Court can be quite political and divided ideologically. In the most recent term, 23 percent of cases were decided by a 5–4 vote, including controversial cases concerning the Deferred Action for Childhood Arrivals program, hospital admitting privileges for abortion providers, and the counting of absentee ballots in the Wisconsin primary. As justices interpret the Constitution, they also play one of two roles in our political system: either asserting their own policy-making authority or deferring to the decisions of others (Congress, the president, or the people). The Court's decision about which path to take in a given case is often political, involving conflict, trade-offs, and compromise, much like decision making in Congress.

For those who resist the view that the courts are a policy-making institution, the theme "political process matters" may not seem to apply in this chapter. However, the courts often *do* make policy, and the way they make decisions has an impact on outcomes. To see how political process matters for the courts, it is important to answer the following questions: What are the different roles of the courts and the structure of the judicial system? How do court decisions shape policy? In a nutshell, what is the nature of judicial decision making? With this context in mind, we can reexamine the controversy over Justice Ginsburg's comments. Did Justice Ginsburg overstep her boundaries with her remarks on Donald Trump, or was it appropriate for her to express her opinions? Was Justice Roberts overreacting to Trump's comments about political judges? What is the proper place of the courts within our political system? Should judges attempt to neutrally apply the law, or should their political views play a role?

AP®
FOUNDATIONAL
DOCUMENT

The Supreme Court building features the words "Equal Justice under Law" across the facade, as well as a statue titled *The Contemplation of Justice*.

EXPLAIN HOW THE POWER OF JUDICIAL REVIEW WAS ESTABLISHED

The development of an independent and powerful federal judiciary

The Constitution did not definitively establish the role of the courts in American politics or the Supreme Court's authority as the ultimate interpreter of the Constitution. The powers of the Supreme Court evolved over time, and debates about its proper role continue to this day.

The Founders' views of the courts: the weakest branch?

AP®
FOUNDATIONAL
DOCUMENT

The Federalists and Antifederalists did not see eye to eye on much, and the judiciary was no exception. Alexander Hamilton, writing in *Federalist 78*, said that the Supreme Court would be "beyond comparison the weakest of the three departments of power." In contrast, one of the authors of the *Antifederalist Papers* wrote: "The supreme court under this constitution would be exalted above all other power in the government and subject to no control."[9] Hmmm, which is it: weakest or strongest? Although the framers could not agree on how powerful the Court was likely to be relative to the other branches of government, there was surprisingly little debate at the Constitutional Convention about the judiciary. Article III of the Constitution, which concerns the judicial branch of government, created one Supreme Court and gave the courts independence by providing federal judges with lifetime terms (assuming "good behavior").

The main disagreements about the judiciary had to do with how independent the courts should be vis-à-vis the other branches of government and how much power to give to the courts. Some of the framers feared a tyrannical Congress and wanted to create judicial and executive branches that could check this power. Others argued for making the executive and judicial branches more closely related so they would be better able to balance Congress. A central debate was whether to give the judiciary some "revisionary power" over Congress, similar to the president's veto power. This idea of judicial review would have given the Supreme Court the power to strike down laws passed by Congress that violated the Constitution. The framers could not agree on judicial review, so the Constitution remained silent on the matter.

While the Constitution clearly specified the kinds of cases over which the Court would have **original jurisdiction** (see Nuts & Bolts 6.1), many details about the Supreme Court were left up to Congress, including its size, the time and place it would meet, and its internal organization. These details, and the system of lower federal courts, were outlined in the **Judiciary Act of 1789**. This law set the number of justices at six (one chief justice and five associates). The number of justices gradually increased to ten by the end of the Civil War and was then restricted to seven under Reconstruction policies. In 1869 the number was set at nine, where it has remained ever since.[10] The 1789 act also created a system of federal courts, which included 13 **district courts** and 3 circuit courts—the intermediate-level courts with **appellate jurisdiction**. Since the circuit courts hear cases on appeal from lower courts, they are now more commonly called appeals courts. The district courts each had one judge, while the circuit courts were each staffed by two Supreme Court justices and one district judge. This odd arrangement in which Supreme Court justices had to preside over both cases in Washington and cases in their assigned circuit remained in place for more than 100 years, over the objections of the justices who resented having to "ride circuit" in difficult traveling conditions.[11] Today separate judges are appointed to fill the appeals courts.

The Supreme Court had a rough start. Indeed, it seemed determined to prove Alexander Hamilton right, that it was the weakest branch. Of the six original justices appointed by George Washington, one declined to serve and another never showed up for a formal session. The Court's first sessions lasted only a few days because it did not have much business. In fact, the Court did not decide a single case in 1791 or 1792. When Justice Rutledge resigned in 1791 to take a state court position, two potential appointees turned down the job in order to keep their positions in their state legislatures! Such career decisions would be unimaginable today, when serving on the Supreme Court is considered the pinnacle of a legal career.[12]

original jurisdiction
The authority of a court to handle a case first, as in the Supreme Court's authority to initially hear disputes between two states. However, original jurisdiction for the Supreme Court is not exclusive; it may assign such a case to a lower court.

Judiciary Act of 1789
The law in which Congress laid out the organization of the federal judiciary. The law refined and clarified federal court jurisdiction and set the original number of justices at six. It also created the office of the attorney general and established the lower federal courts.

district courts
Lower-level trial courts of the federal judicial system that handle most U.S. federal cases.

appellate jurisdiction
The authority of a court to hear appeals from lower courts and change or uphold the decision.

Jurisdiction of the Federal Courts

Source: Lee Epstein and Thomas G. Walker, *Constitutional Law for a Changing America: Institutional Powers and Constraints*, 5th ed. (Washington, DC: CQ Press, 2004), p. 65.

Jurisdiction of Lower Federal Courts

- Cases involving the U.S. Constitution, federal laws, and treaties.
- Controversies between two or more states. (Congress passed a law giving the Supreme Court exclusive jurisdiction over these cases.)
- Controversies between citizens of different states.
- Controversies between a state and citizens of another state. (The Eleventh Amendment removed federal jurisdiction in these cases.)
- Controversies between a state or its citizens and any foreign states, citizens, or subjects.
- Cases affecting ambassadors, public ministers, and consuls.
- Cases of admiralty and maritime jurisdictions.
- Controversies between citizens of the same state claiming lands under grants of different states.

Jurisdiction of the Supreme Court
Original Jurisdiction*

- Cases involving ambassadors, public ministers, and consuls.
- Cases that involve a state.

Appellate Jurisdiction

- Cases falling under the jurisdiction of the lower federal courts, "with such exceptions, and under such Regulations as the Congress shall make."

* This does not imply exclusive jurisdiction. For example, the Supreme Court may refer to a district court for a case involving an ambassador (the more likely outcome).

"Why Should I Care?" Understanding the type of cases that are heard by the federal courts is essential for recognizing their role in the system of checks and balances. Congress has some power to limit the jurisdiction of the federal courts.

judicial review
The Supreme Court's power to strike down a law or an executive branch action that it finds unconstitutional.

Judicial review and *Marbury v. Madison*

The Court started to gain more power when John Marshall was appointed chief justice in 1801. Marshall single-handedly transformed the Court into an equal partner in the system of checks and balances. The most important step was the decision *Marbury v. Madison* (1803), which gave the Supreme Court the power of judicial review. As noted earlier, the framers were split on the wisdom of giving the Court the power to strike down laws passed by Congress, and the Constitution does not explicitly address the issue. However, historians have established that a majority of the framers, including the most influential ones, favored judicial review (Hamilton endorsed it in some detail in *Federalist 78*). Given that the Constitution did not address the issue of judicial review, Marshall simply asserted that the Supreme Court had the power to determine when a law was unconstitutional. As the power of judicial review has evolved, it has become a central part of the system of checks and balances (see Chapter 2).

The facts and legal reasoning behind *Marbury* are worth explaining because it is one of the most important court cases in American history. The Federalists had just lost the election of 1800 to Thomas Jefferson and the Democratic-Republicans. In a last-minute power grab, the Federalist-controlled lame-duck Congress gave outgoing President Adams an opportunity to appoint 42 new justices of the peace for the

District of Columbia and Alexandria, Virginia. Adams made the appointments, and the Senate confirmed them, but not before time ran out and the new administration took over. The secretary of state, John Marshall (the same Marshall who had just been confirmed as chief justice before President Adams left office), failed to ensure that all the commissions for the new judges were delivered by midnight. When President Jefferson assumed office, he ordered his new secretary of state, James Madison, not to deliver the remaining commissions that had been issued by the outgoing Federalist administration. William Marbury was one of the people who did not receive his commission, and he asked the Supreme Court to issue an order giving him the position.

As leading figures in opposing parties, Chief Justice Marshall and President Jefferson did not like each other. This put Marshall in a difficult position. He was concerned that if he issued the order that Marbury wanted, giving Marbury his job, Jefferson probably would ignore it. (Though Secretary of State Madison was technically the other party in the lawsuit, Jefferson was calling the shots.) Given the weakness of the Court, having such an order disregarded by the president could have been a final blow to its position in the national government. However, if the Court did not issue the order, it would be giving in to Jefferson despite the merits of Marbury's case—he really had been cheated out of his job. It appeared that the Court would lose whether it issued the order or not.

To get out of the predicament, Marshall applied the idea of judicial review. Although the idea was not original to Marshall, the Court had never before exercised its authority to rule on the constitutionality of a federal law. Marshall's reasoning was quite clever: the Court's opinion said that Marbury was due his commission, but the Court could not give him his job because the part of the Judiciary Act of 1789 that gave it the power to do so was unconstitutional! The portion of the act in question was Section 13, which gave the Court the power to issue orders (writs of mandamus) to anyone holding federal office. Because this section expanded the original jurisdiction of the Supreme Court, Marshall ruled that Congress had overstepped its bounds in passing it. The original jurisdiction of the Court is clearly specified in the Constitution, so any attempt by Congress to change that jurisdiction through legislation would be unconstitutional; the only way to change original jurisdiction would be through a constitutional amendment.[13] Marshall wrote: "It is emphatically the province and duty of the judicial department to say what the law is.... If two laws conflict with each other, the courts must decide on the operation of each. So if a law be in opposition to the Constitution ... the court must determine which of these conflicting rules governs the case. This is of the very essence of judicial duty."[14]

Chief Justice John Marshall favored the idea of judicial review and claimed this power for the Court in the *Marbury v. Madison* decision.

Judicial review in practice

Chief Justice Marshall and the Federalists lost the battle—poor Mr. Marbury never did get his job, and Jefferson appointed the people he wanted to be justices of the peace—but the Supreme Court won the war. By asserting its power to review the constitutionality of laws passed by Congress, the Court became an equal partner in the institutional balance of power. Although it would be more than 50 years until the Court would use judicial review again to strike down a law passed by Congress (in the unfortunate 1857 *Dred Scott* case, which concerned slavery and effectively led to the Civil War), the reasoning behind *Marbury* has never been challenged by subsequent presidents or Congresses.[15]

Interpreting federal laws may seem like a logical responsibility for the Supreme Court, but what about state laws? Should the Supreme Court have final say over them as well? The Constitution does not answer this question. But the supremacy clause requires that the Constitution and national laws take precedence over state constitutions and state laws when they conflict. The Judiciary Act of 1789 made it clear that the Supreme Court would rule on these matters.

constitutional interpretation
The process of determining whether a piece of legislation or governmental action is supported by the Constitution.

statutory interpretation
The various methods and tests used by the courts for determining the meaning of a law and applying it to specific situations. Congress may overturn the courts' interpretation by writing a new law; thus, it also engages in statutory interpretation.

The contours of the relationship between the national government and the states have been largely defined by the Supreme Court's assertion of judicial review and its willingness to intervene in matters of state law. For much of the nineteenth century, the Court embraced dual federalism, in which the national government and the states operated on two separate levels (see Chapter 3). Later the Court involved itself more in state law as it moved toward a more active role for the national government in regulating interstate commerce and using the Fourteenth Amendment to selectively incorporate the amendments that constitute the Bill of Rights (see Chapter 8).

All in all, the Court has struck down more than 205 acts of Congress (and about 1,400 state laws). This sounds like a lot, but Congress passed more than 60,000 laws in its first 230 years. Over time, the Court has ruled on state laws in many important areas, including civil liberties, desegregation and civil rights, abortion, privacy, redistricting, labor laws, employment and discrimination, and business and environmental regulation.

When the Supreme Court strikes down a congressional or state law, it engages in **constitutional interpretation**—that is, it determines that the law is unconstitutional. But the Supreme Court also engages in **statutory interpretation**—that is, it applies national and state laws to particular cases (statutes are laws that are passed by legislatures). Often the language of a statute may be unclear and the Court must interpret how to apply the law. For example, should the protection of endangered species prevent economic development that may destroy the species' habitat? How does one determine if an employer is responsible for punishing sexual harassment in the workplace? How should the voting rights of minorities be protected? In each case, the Court must interpret the relevant statutes to determine what Congress really meant. In addition, in the third main area of the law—administrative law—the Court is sometimes required to assess how federal agencies have interpreted and implemented laws passed by Congress. Often this involves the controversial practice of consulting legislative histories—floor debates, congressional hearings, and so on—to determine how the legislature intended the laws to be interpreted. But the late justice Antonin Scalia argued that such searches are inherently subjective and that justices should interpret only the actual text of the laws in question.

Although politicians and other political actors accept judicial review as a central part of the political system, critics are concerned about its antidemocratic nature. Why, for example, do we give nine unelected justices such extraordinary power over our elected representatives? Debates about the proper role for the Court will continue as long as it is involved in controversial decisions. We will take up this question later in the chapter when we address the concepts of judicial activism and judicial restraint.

"Why Should I Care?"

Judicial review may seem like "inside baseball" that doesn't really matter for most Americans. However, the power to strike down laws and government actions means that the Court may act against political majorities to strike down unconstitutional actions such as segregating schools by race and discriminating against same-sex marriage. Judicial review may also be used, however, to frustrate popular majorities during times of political change, such as during the New Deal of the 1930s. Recently, the Court has done some of both—requiring the government to have a court order to search cell phone records but also deciding that states must collect sales taxes on Internet sales, despite public opposition to the practice. In either case, this is an awesome political power that puts the Supreme Court on an equal institutional footing with Congress and the president.

The American legal and judicial system

Two sets of considerations are necessary to understand the overall nature of our judicial system: the fundamentals of the legal system that apply to all courts in the United States, and the structure of the court system within our system of federalism. You may have some understanding of the legal system from watching *Law & Order* or *Better Call Saul,* but a refresher on the basics never hurts.

Court fundamentals

The general characteristics of the court system begin with the people who are in the courtroom. The **plaintiff** brings the case, and the **defendant** is the person or party who is being sued or charged with a crime. If the case is appealed, the petitioner is the person bringing the appeal and the respondent is on the other side of the case. In a civil case, the plaintiff sues to determine who is right or wrong and to gain something of value, such as monetary damages, the right to vote, or admission to a university. For example, imagine that your neighbor accidentally backs his car into the fence that divides your property, destroying a large section of it. The neighbor does not have adequate insurance to cover the damages and refuses to pay for the repairs. You do not want to pay the $1,000 deductible on your insurance policy, so you (the plaintiff) sue your neighbor (the defendant) to see whether your neighbor has to pay for the repairs. In a criminal case, the plaintiff is the government and the prosecutor attempts to prove the guilt of the defendant (the person accused of the crime).

Many, but not all, civil and criminal cases are heard before a jury that decides the outcome in the case, which is called the verdict. Often cases get settled before they go to trial (or even in the middle of the trial) using **plea bargains** in criminal cases and **settlement agreements** in civil cases. In a civil case, this would mean that the plaintiff and the defendant agree on a monetary settlement and admission of guilt (or not; in some cases the defendant may agree to pay a fine or damages but not to admit guilt). In a criminal case, the defendant may agree to plead guilty in exchange for receiving

plaintiff
The person or party who brings a case to court.

defendant
The person or party against whom a case is brought.

plea bargains and **settlement agreements**
Agreements between a plaintiff and a defendant to settle a case before it goes to trial or the verdict is decided. In a civil case, this usually involves an admission of guilt and an agreement on monetary damages; in a criminal case, this often involves an admission of guilt in return for a reduced charge or sentence.

In 2019, several celebrities were accused of participating in a college admissions scandal that involved using their wealth and influence to improve the odds of their children being admitted to selective colleges; the scheme included falsifying SAT scores and academic records. Actress and producer Lori Loughlin, center, was accused of bribing an athletic coach to get her two daughters admitted to the University of Southern California. She ultimately accepted a plea bargain to reduce her prison sentence and fine.

a shorter sentence or being charged with a lesser crime. More than 95 percent of federal felony cases that result in a conviction are settled in this way.[16] Plea bargains and settlement agreements are excellent examples of how legal conflict between two parties can be resolved through compromise.

Differences between Civil and Criminal Cases There are important differences between civil and criminal cases. One is the standard of proof that serves to determine the outcome of the case. In civil cases, the jury has to determine whether the "preponderance of evidence"—that is, a majority of the evidence—proves that the plaintiff wins. In criminal cases, a much stiffer standard must be met: the defendant must be found guilty "beyond a reasonable doubt."

Another difference is where the burden of proof lies. In criminal cases, there is a presumption of "innocent until proven guilty"—that is, the state must prove the guilt of the defendant. However, in civil cases the burden of proof may be on either the plaintiff or the defendant, depending on the law that governs the case. Even more complicated, in civil cases the plaintiff may have to prove certain points and the defendant other points. For example, in certain race-based voting rights cases plaintiffs would have to prove that race was the predominant motivation for creating a Black-majority congressional district to support their complaint that their interests were not being served in the district. If that point is demonstrated, then the burden of proof shifts to the defendants to show that there was some "compelling state interest" to justify the use of race as a predominant factor.

class-action lawsuit
A case brought by a group of individuals on behalf of themselves and others in the general public who are in similar circumstances.

One type of civil suit is the **class-action lawsuit**, a case brought by a group of individuals on behalf of themselves and others in similar circumstances. Their target may be a corporation that produced hazardous or defective products or that harmed a particular group through illegal behavior. For example, 1.5 million current and former female Walmart employees sued the retailing giant for sex discrimination in 2011, claiming that the store had paid women less than men for the same work and had promoted fewer women than men.[17] Suits are often filed on behalf of shareholders of companies that have lost value because of fraud committed by corporate leaders. Cases like these are an important mechanism for providing accountability and justice in our economic system. Federal regulators do not have the ability to ensure the complete safety of food, drugs, and consumer products or to continually monitor all potential business fraud. Therefore, consumers rely on the legal system and class-action lawsuits to ensure that businesses act fairly and produce safe products.

Common Elements of the Judicial System Several characteristics of the judicial system apply to all cases. First, ours is an adversarial system in which lawyers on both sides have an opportunity to present their case, challenge the testimony of the opposing side, and try to convince the court that their version of the events is true. The process of "discovery," in which both sides share the information that will be presented in court before the trial begins, ensures a fair process and few last-minute surprises. Second, 49 of the 50 states and the federal courts operate under a system of **common law**, which means that legal decisions build from precedents established in previous cases and apply commonly throughout the jurisdiction of the court. The alternative, which is practiced only in Louisiana, is the civil law tradition, which is based on a detailed codification of the law that is applied to each specific case.

common law
Law based on the precedent of previous court rulings rather than on legislation. It is used in all federal courts and 49 of the 50 state courts.

precedent
A legal norm established in court cases that is then applied to future cases dealing with the same legal questions.

The notion of **precedent** (or stare decisis: "let the decision stand") deserves special attention. Precedent is a previously decided case or set of cases that serves as a guide for future cases on the same topic. Lower courts are bound by Supreme Court decisions when there is a clear precedent that is relevant for a given case. In many cases, following precedent is not clear-cut because several precedents may seem relevant. The lower courts have considerable discretion in sorting out which precedents are the most important. The Supreme Court tries to follow its own precedents, but in the past 70 years justices have been willing to deviate from earlier decisions when they think that the precedent is flawed. The Court has overruled more than five times as many decisions since 1950 as it overturned in the previous 161 years.[18] Part of this can be explained by the relatively small number of precedents that *could* have been overturned in the first few decades of our nation's history. But even when accounting for the natural accumulation of more precedents to potentially overturn, recent Courts have been much more willing to deviate from precedent than previous Courts. The Court has developed four factors that it uses to decide if a case should be overturned: the quality of the past decision's reasoning, its consistency with related decisions, legal developments since the past decision, and reliance on the decision throughout the legal system and society. But in some cases, the Court overturns a precedent simply because the ideological composition of the Court has changed. For example, in a case concerning states' immunity from lawsuits in another state's courts, the Court overturned a 40-year precedent even though none of the four factors were met.[19] As this record indicates, precedent is not a rule the Court must follow but a norm that constrains its behavior.

Another characteristic common to all cases is that the person bringing the case must have **standing** to sue in a civil case, which means that the person has a legitimate basis for bringing the case. This usually means that the individual has suffered some direct and personal harm from the action addressed in the court case. Standing is easy to establish for private parties; in our earlier example, if your neighbor destroys your fence, you have been harmed. However, determining who has standing gets more interesting when the government is the one being sued. For example, when an environmental group challenged the Interior Department's interpretation of the Endangered Species Act, the Supreme Court ruled that the group did not have standing to sue because it had not demonstrated that the government's policy would cause it "imminent" injury.[20] Similarly, federal courts have ruled that 10 members of Congress did not have standing to challenge American bombing in Libya and that taxpayers do not have standing to sue the government if they disagree with a specific policy.[21] Depending on your politics, you may not want your hard-earned cash going to buy school lunches for poor children or to fund various wars. However, your status as a taxpayer does not give you enough of a personal stake in these policies to challenge them in court, so you do not have standing. Later, in the section discussing how cases get to the Supreme Court, we will see that justices have some leeway in defining standing.

The final general characteristic of the legal system is the **jurisdiction** of the court. When bringing a case before the court, you must choose a court that actually has the power to hear your case. For example, if you wanted to contest a speeding ticket, you would not file your case in the state supreme court or in the federal district court; you would file it in your local traffic court. What if you believed you were the victim of discrimination in the workplace? Would you sue in state or federal court? You probably could do either, but the decision would be based on which set of laws would provide you with more protection from discrimination. This varies by state, so the proper jurisdiction for a given case is often a judgment call based on specific legal questions. (This practice of seeking the best court for your case is called *venue shopping*.)

Structure of the court system and federalism

The structure of the court system is like the rest of the political system: it is divided within and across levels of government. Across the levels of government, the court system operates on two parallel tracks within (1) the state and local courts and (2) the federal courts. Within each level of government, both tracks include courts of original jurisdiction, appeals courts, and courts of special jurisdiction. As shown in the How It Works graphic, the state courts are entirely separate from the federal courts, with the exception of the small proportion of cases that are appealed from a state supreme court to

standing
Legitimate justification for bringing a civil case to court.

jurisdiction
The sphere of a court's legal authority to hear and decide cases.

How it works: in theory
The Court System

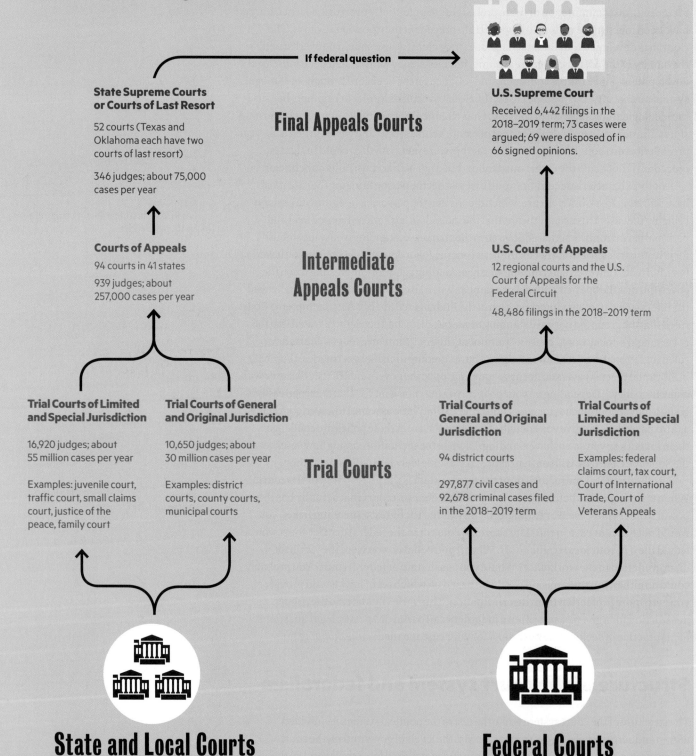

If federal question

Final Appeals Courts

State Supreme Courts or Courts of Last Resort

52 courts (Texas and Oklahoma each have two courts of last resort)

346 judges; about 75,000 cases per year

U.S. Supreme Court

Received 6,442 filings in the 2018–2019 term; 73 cases were argued; 69 were disposed of in 66 signed opinions.

Intermediate Appeals Courts

Courts of Appeals

94 courts in 41 states

939 judges; about 257,000 cases per year

U.S. Courts of Appeals

12 regional courts and the U.S. Court of Appeals for the Federal Circuit

48,486 filings in the 2018–2019 term

Trial Courts

Trial Courts of Limited and Special Jurisdiction

16,920 judges; about 55 million cases per year

Examples: juvenile court, traffic court, small claims court, justice of the peace, family court

Trial Courts of General and Original Jurisdiction

10,650 judges; about 30 million cases per year

Examples: district courts, county courts, municipal courts

Trial Courts of General and Original Jurisdiction

94 district courts

297,877 civil cases and 92,678 criminal cases filed in the 2018–2019 term

Trial Courts of Limited and Special Jurisdiction

Examples: federal claims court, tax court, Court of International Trade, Court of Veterans Appeals

State and Local Courts

Federal Courts

Sources: Data on federal courts are from U.S. Supreme Court, "2019 Year-End Report on the Federal Judiciary," www.supremecourt.gov/publicinfo/year-end/2019year-endreport.pdf (accessed 6/12/20). Data on state courts are from National Center for State Courts, www.ncsc.org; Ballotpedia.org, "Intermediate Appellate Courts," https://ballotpedia.org/Intermediate_appellate_courts; and Ron Malega and Thomas H. Cohen, "State Court Organization, 2011," U.S. Department of Justice, Bureau of Justice Statistics, www.bjs.gov/content/pub/pdf/sco11.pdf (all accessed 6/12/20).

Partisan Gerrymandering through the Court System

Partisan gerrymandering has been addressed in dozens of state and federal court cases in the past 30 years. A landmark case decided in June 2019 illustrates how cases make their way through the court system and how the Supreme Court may decide *not* to resolve a conflict.

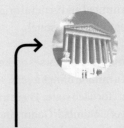
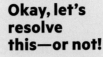

We *still* don't like it!

North Carolina and Maryland stuck to their guns and **struck down their maps again**. Michigan and Ohio agreed.

Okay, let's resolve this—or not!

Supreme Court: In a landmark ruling in June 2019, the Supreme Court got out of the partisan gerrymandering business, saying it is a "non-justiciable political question." The majority opinion **recognized it as a problem but said the Court does not have a measure to determine when a set of districts is unconstitutional**. The dissenters feared for the future of democracy.

We will just leave this sticky problem to the states.

The majority opinion noted that **states would still be free to address partisan gerrymandering**, but this path would not be open to states where politicians don't want to reform the process and voters don't have the initiative and referendum process to impose the change.

It's unconstitutional.

Hang on, don't get too excited...

In June 2018, the Court punted in cases from Wisconsin and Maryland, **sending the cases back to the lower courts**.

The states don't like it either!

Federal courts:
In Ohio, North Carolina, Maryland, and Wisconsin, federal courts **struck down state legislative or congressional maps as unconstitutional**.

State courts:
In Pennsylvania and Florida, state courts **struck down partisan gerrymanders, and voters in more than a dozen states took the control over redistricting out of the hands of politicians** and gave it to nonpartisan commissions.

Well, maybe, maybe not...

Over the next decade, state and federal courts struggled with various issues concerning redistricting, but **conflicting decisions left the issue unresolved**.

It's okay to do this, right?

State and Federal Trial Courts:
From 1986 to 2004, the Supreme Court **upheld partisan gerrymanders but left the door open for proving they were unconstitutional** if the right evidence was presented.

❓

Critical Thinking

1. **What are the advantages and disadvantages** of having such a complex court system?

2. **When is it appropriate for the Supreme Court to decide** an issue is a "political question"? Do you think it was appropriate in this case? Can you think of an issue other than partisan gerrymandering for which this is likely to occur?

the U.S. Supreme Court. There is much variation between the states in terms of how they structure their court systems. However, they all follow the same general pattern of trial courts with limited and general original jurisdiction and appeals courts (either one or two levels, depending on the state).

District Courts Workhorses of the federal system, the district courts handle more than a quarter of a million filings a year. There are 89 districts in the 50 states, with at least one district court for each state. There are also district courts in Puerto Rico, the Virgin Islands, the District of Columbia, Guam, and the Northern Mariana Islands to bring the total to 94 districts with 677 judges.[22] There are two limited-jurisdiction district courts: the Court of International Trade, which addresses cases involving international trade and customs issues, and the U.S. Court of Federal Claims, which handles most claims for money damages against the United States, disputes over federal contracts, unlawful "takings" of private property by the federal government, and other claims against the United States.

Appeals Courts The appeals courts (officially called circuit courts until 1948)[23] are the intermediate courts of appeals, but in practice they are the final court for most federal cases that are appealed from the district courts. The losing side in a federal case can appeal to the Supreme Court, but given that the highest court in the land hears so few cases, the appeals courts usually get the final word. Appeals courts did not always have this much power; in fact, through much of the nineteenth century they had very limited appellate jurisdiction and did not hear many significant cases.

The number of appeals courts in the nation slowly expanded as the workload of these courts grew. Currently, there are 12 regional courts and the Court of Appeals for the Federal Circuit, which handles specialized cases from all over the country. The smallest of the regional appeals courts is the First Circuit, which has 6 judges, and the largest is the Ninth Circuit, which has 29 judges. In 2019, there were 179 appeals court judges and about 85 "senior judges" (these numbers include the appeals court for the federal circuit).[24] Senior judges are semi-retired judges who hear certain cases to help out with the overall federal court system workload; they typically handle about 25 percent of the workload for the federal court system (there are also nearly 400 senior judges in the district courts who handle about a quarter of the workload).[25]

The Supreme Court The Supreme Court sits at the top of the federal court system. The Supreme Court is the "court of last resort" for cases coming from both the state and the federal courts. One important function of the Court is to ensure that the application and interpretation of the Constitution are consistent nationwide by resolving conflicts between lower courts, or between state law and federal law, or between laws in different states. A district court or appeals court ruling is applicable only within the specific region of that court, whereas Supreme Court rulings apply to the entire country.

Although the Supreme Court is the most important interpreter of the Constitution, the president and Congress also interpret the Constitution on a regular basis. This means that the Supreme Court does not always have the final say. For example, if the Court strikes down a federal law for being overly vague, Congress can rewrite the law to clarify the offending passage. When this happens, Congress may have the final word. For example, Congress overturned *Ledbetter v. Goodyear Tire & Rubber Co.* (2007) when it passed the Lilly Ledbetter Fair Pay Act in 2009. The law explicitly states that the Supreme Court had misinterpreted the 1964 Civil Rights Act when it ruled in 2007 that Ledbetter would have had to file her pay discrimination suit within 180 days of being hired.[26]

Even on matters of constitutional interpretation rather than statutory interpretation, Congress can fight back by passing a constitutional amendment. However, this is a difficult and time-consuming process (see Chapter 2). Nevertheless, that option is available as a way of overturning an unpopular Court decision. Perhaps the best example of this is the very first major case ever decided by the Supreme Court—*Chisholm v. Georgia* (1793). This case upheld the right of a citizen of one state to sue another state in federal court. The states were shocked by this challenge to their sovereignty, and a constitutional amendment to overturn the decision quickly made its way through Congress. By 1795, the Eleventh Amendment had been ratified and citizens could no longer sue a state (in federal court) in which they did not live.[27]

How judges are selected

Although the Constitution provides detailed stipulations for serving in Congress and as president, it does not specify requirements for serving on the federal courts. Federal judges don't even have to have a law degree! (This is probably due to the limited number of law schools at the time of the Founding; when the Constitution was written, someone who wanted to be a lawyer generally would serve as an apprentice in a law office to learn the trade.) The president appoints federal judges with the "advice and consent" of the Senate, which in practice means that the Senate must approve the nominees with a majority vote.

Nomination battles for federal judges can be intense, because the stakes are high: the Supreme Court plays a central role in the policy process, and because justices have life tenure, a justice's impact can outlive the president and Senate who put him or her on the Court. Justices often serve for decades, much longer than the people who appoint them.

The Role of the President Given the Constitution's silence on the qualifications of federal judges, presidents have broad discretion over whom to nominate. Presidents have always tried to influence the direction of the federal courts, especially the Supreme Court, by picking people who share their views. Because the Senate often has different ideas about the proper direction for the Court, nomination disputes end up being a combination of debates over the merit of a nominee and partisan battles about the ideological composition of the Court.

Although presidents would *like* to influence the direction of the Court, it is not always possible to predict how judges will behave once they are on the bench. Earl Warren is a good example. He was appointed by Republican president Dwight Eisenhower and

DID YOU KNOW?

49

of the 115 people to serve on the Supreme Court have had law degrees. However, all since 1957 have had law degrees, and all but one of the current Court justices attended either Harvard or Yale law school (the newest justice, Amy Coney Barrett, attended Notre Dame).

Source: SupremeCourt.gov

President Trump, who nominated Judge Neil Gorsuch to the Supreme Court, watches as Supreme Court Justice Anthony Kennedy swears him in during a ceremony in the Rose Garden of the White House.

had been the Republican governor of California, yet he turned out to be one of the most liberal chief justices of the last century. Eisenhower called Warren's nomination the biggest mistake he ever made.[28]

Nonetheless, the president can make a good guess about how a justice is likely to vote based on the nominee's party affiliation and the nature of his or her legal writings and decisions (if the nominee has prior judicial experience). Not surprisingly, 105 of the 115 justices who have served on the Court have shared the nominating president's party (91 percent). Overall, more than 90 percent of the lower-court judges appointed by presidents in the twentieth and twenty-first centuries have also belonged to the same party as the president.

The most partisan move to influence the Court was President Franklin Delano Roosevelt's infamous plan to pack the Court. FDR was frustrated because the Court had struck down several pieces of important New Deal legislation, so to get a more sympathetic Court, he proposed nominating a new justice for every justice who was over 70 years old. At the time, six justices were over 70, so this would have increased the size of the Court to 15 justices. Roosevelt's effort to disguise the partisan power play as a humanitarian gesture (to help the old-timers with their workload) didn't fool anyone. The plan to pack the Court ran into opposition, but once the Court started ruling in favor of the New Deal legislation, the plan was dropped.

In addition to the ideological considerations about whom to nominate, the president also considers the individual's reputation as a legal scholar and his or her personal relationship to the candidate. Further considerations are the candidate's ethical standards, religion, gender, and race (see Figure 6.1). The religion of justices has

FIGURE 6.1

Race and Gender on Federal Courts

Since the 1980s, the proportion of women on the federal bench has gone up fivefold while the percentage of White men has plummeted by more than half. Do you think that descriptive representation in the judicial branch is important?

Percentage and number of U.S. Circuit Court nominees by gender in president's first year in office

■ Male ■ Female

Trump — 79% (15) — 21% (4)
Obama — 67% (8) — 33% (4)
Bush — 76% (22) — 24% (7)
Clinton — 40% (2) — 60% (3)

Percentage and number of U.S. Circuit Court nominees by race in president's first year in office

■ White ■ Black ■ Hispanic ■ Asian

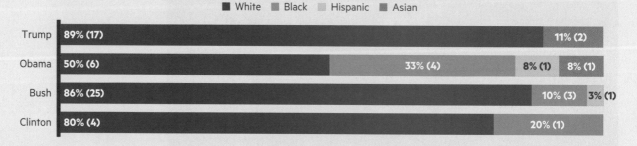

Trump — 89% (17) — 11% (2)
Obama — 50% (6) — 33% (4) — 8% (1) — 8% (1)
Bush — 86% (25) — 10% (3) — 3% (1)
Clinton — 80% (4) — 20% (1)

Source: Barry J. McMillion, "U.S. Circuit and District Court Nominations during President Trump's First Year in Office: Comparative Analysis with Recent Presidents," Congressional Research Service, May 2, 2018, https://fas.org/sgp/crs/misc/R45189.pdf (accessed 8/19/20). Data may not add up to 100 percent due to rounding.

undergone a complete transformation: for the nation's first 125 years, nearly all justices were Protestants. Now there are six Catholic justices, two Jewish justices, and one unknown (Gorsuch was raised Catholic but most recently attended an Episcopal church).[29] Over time, the federal courts have steadily become more diverse in terms of race and gender. However, Donald Trump reversed this trend. Of his first 87 nominees to the federal courts, only one was African American and only one was Latino. Judges' demographic backgrounds also became an issue in the 2016 campaign when Trump said that federal district judge Gonzalo P. Curiel could not be objective in the lawsuit concerning Trump University because Curiel was a Mexican (the judge was born in Indiana and his parents are from Mexico).

The Role of the Senate The Senate is the other half of the equation that determines the composition of the federal courts. The Senate has shifted from a very active role in providing "advice and consent" on court appointments to a passive role and then back to an active role. One constant is that the Senate rarely rejects nominees because of their qualifications; rather, it tends to reject them for political reasons. Of 28 Supreme Court nominees rejected by the Senate in the history of the United States, only 2 were turned down because they were seen as unqualified. Serious questions were also raised about a third justice, Clarence Thomas, who had served for only 18 months as a federal judge before being nominated to the Court. Thomas also was accused of sexual harassment by former colleague Anita Hill. Hill's testimony in 1991 predates the #MeToo movement by 26 years and brought sexual harassment into the public limelight for the first time. There were only two women in the Senate at the time and the unsympathetic hearing she received before the all-male Senate Judiciary Committee helped produce the "Year of the Woman" in House and Senate races the next year (as of 2020, there are now 26 women in the Senate, an all-time high). Nonetheless, Thomas ultimately won confirmation by a 52–48 vote. The other 26 nominees were rejected for political reasons. Most commonly, when a president makes a nomination close to an election and the Senate is controlled by the opposing party, the Senate will kill the nomination, hoping that its party will win the presidency and nominate a justice more to its liking.

Throughout the nineteenth century, the Senate was very willing to turn down Court nominations for political reasons. In fact, between 1793 and 1894 the Senate did not confirm 21 nominees to the Court, which was about a third of the total number nominated. In contrast, between 1894 and 1968 the Senate did not even require nominees to testify and during that period only 4 nominees were rejected.

A rethinking of this passive role occurred in the late 1960s. President Nixon vowed to pull the Court back from the "liberal excesses" of the Warren Court, but the Senate stiffened its spine and rejected two conservative nominees in a row: Clement Haynsworth (in 1969) and G. Harrold Carswell (in 1970). With Haynsworth, there were ethical problems involving his participation in cases in which he had a financial interest. Carswell had a mediocre judicial record, and civil rights groups raised questions about his commitment to enforcing antidiscrimination laws. Nixon must have thought that the Senate wouldn't reject his choice twice in a row! The most recent Senate rejection took place in 1987. Judge Robert Bork was a brilliant, very conservative, and controversial figure. Liberal interest groups mobilized against him in part for following Nixon's order to fire the special prosecutor in the Watergate investigation after two attorneys general refused to do so and resigned in protest. The Senate rejected him by the widest margin of any nominee since 1846 (the vote was 42–58). The Senate's unwillingness to even consider President Obama's nomination of Merrick Garland to the Supreme Court to fill the vacancy left by Justice Antonin Scalia's death in February 2016 may signal a return to the more politicized era of Supreme Court nominations in the nineteenth century, especially given that the strategy worked: Trump won the presidency and nominated Neil Gorsuch, who was approved by a 54–45 vote in the Senate. Brett Kavanaugh, whose confirmation was more contentious due to sexual assault allegations, was ultimately confirmed in a 50–48 vote, the second-closest positive vote in history. Partisan tensions were even higher when liberal icon Ruth Bader Ginsburg passed away in September 2020 and the Senate rushed through confirmation of Amy Coney Barrett by a 52–48 vote. The 46 days between Ginsburg's death and Election Day marked the shortest period in U.S. history during which a justice was confirmed before a presidential election (the second shortest span between a vacancy and the election was 149 days in 1916).

Yet not all recent Supreme Court nominations have been controversial. President Bill Clinton's two Supreme Court picks were judicial moderates who were overwhelmingly confirmed—Ginsburg by a 96–3 vote and Stephen Breyer by an 87–9 vote. George W. Bush's nominees, John G. Roberts Jr. and Samuel Alito Jr., were confirmed by comfortable margins. President Obama appointed the first Latina to serve on the Supreme Court, Sonia Sotomayor, who was confirmed by a 68–31 vote. Elena Kagan's confirmation by a 63–37 vote in 2010 meant that three women were serving on the Court for the first time (and there are still three in 2021, with Barrett replacing the late Ginsburg).

Battles over Lower-Court Judges The contentious battles between the president and the Senate over nominees to the federal bench and the Supreme Court have recently expanded to include nominees to the district and appeals courts. For much of the nation's history, the president did not play a very active role in the nomination process for district courts, instead deferring to the home-state senators of the president's party to suggest candidates—a norm called **senatorial courtesy**. If neither senator from the state was from the president's party, he would consult House members from his party and other high-ranking party members from the state for district court nominees. The president typically has shown more interest in appeals court nominations. The Justice Department plays a key role in screening candidates, but the local senators of the president's party remain active as well through the "blue slip" process: home-state senators record their support or opposition to nominees on blue slips of paper. Some committee chairs have allowed a single home-state senator to use the blue slip to veto a nominee, but others have not followed the process so strictly (in the current Senate, blue slips are generally used for district court, but not appeals court, nominations).

Recently the process has become much more contentious. While the confirmation rate for federal judges has been relatively stable in the past 35 years (between 80 and 90 percent), the average time to confirm nominees has increased dramatically. The average length of delay from nomination to confirmation has increased from a little over 50 days in the 1980s to over 200 days in recent years (see Figure 6.2), and the situation has intensified. Democrats blocked 39 of President Bush's nominees between 2001 and 2009,[30] and Republicans returned the favor during Obama's presidency by blocking dozens of his nominees, which included employing a record number of filibusters of lower-court nominees. After the Senate blocked three nominees to the D.C. Court of Appeals, the second-most-important court in the nation, Democrats responded in November 2013 by eliminating the filibuster on lower-court and executive branch nominations but not Supreme Court nominations.[31] This move was originally labeled the "nuclear option" by Democrats who had threatened to shut down the Senate if the Republican leadership got rid of the filibuster during the George W. Bush presidency. In response to the detonation of the nuclear option, the confirmation process slowed to a trickle in President Obama's last year, which produced a near-record level of vacancies (more than 10 percent of all federal judgeships). With unified control of government for the first time since 2009, Republicans moved quickly to fill many of those vacancies and approve Trump's nominations. To approve Neil Gorsuch's nomination, Senate

senatorial courtesy
A norm in the nomination of district court judges in which the president consults with his or her party's senators from the relevant state in choosing the nominee.

President Obama nominated Judge Merrick Garland (right) to the Supreme Court. Here, the nominee meets with Senator Cory Booker (D-NJ). Judge Garland, however, was not confirmed prior to the end of Obama's term, and in 2017 President Trump nominated Judge Gorsuch to fill the vacancy left by Justice Scalia's death.

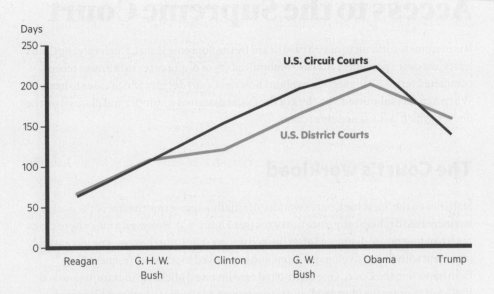

FIGURE 6.2

Average Confirmation Delay for Federal Court Nominations, 1981–2018

Since the 1980s, the length of time needed to confirm federal court nominations has increased dramatically. Why do you think this happened? Why does it matter?

Sources: Reagan–Obama: Barry J. McMillion, "Length of Time from Nomination to Confirmation for 'Uncontroversial' U.S. Circuit and District Court Nominees: Detailed Analysis," *Congressional Research Service*, September 18, 2012, http://fas.org (accessed 8/21/20); Trump: Rory Spill Solberg and Eric N. Waltenburg, "Are Trump's Judicial Nominees Being Confirmed at a Record Pace? The Answer is Complicated," *Washington Post*, June 14, 2018, www.washingtonpost.com/news/monkey-cage/wp/2018/06/14/are-trumps-judicial-nominees-really-being-confirmed-at-a-record-pace-the-answer-is-complicated (accessed 8/19/20).

Republicans eliminated the filibuster on Supreme Court nominations. With the process still not moving as quickly as they wanted, the Senate also changed Senate rules to limit floor debate on nominations to 2 hours instead of 30 hours. They also approved a record number of appeals court nominees in Trump's first term (51). However, there are still 79 vacancies on the federal bench.[32]

Although there is no definitive answer as to how active the Senate should be in giving "advice and consent," it is clear that the Founders intended the Senate to play an active role. The first draft of the Constitution gave the Senate the sole power to appoint Supreme Court justices. However, the final version made appointment a shared power with the president. It was not expected that the Senate would compete with the president over whom to nominate, but it *was* assumed that the Senate would exercise independent judgment as to the suitability of the president's nominees.

It is safe to assume that most Americans do not follow the details of battles over court nominations. However, these battles are every bit as important as the elections that *do* capture much attention. Unelected judges often serve for 20 or 30 years, much longer than the average member of Congress, and have the power to strike down laws that Congress passes. Confirmation battles also support our argument that politics is conflictual and that we should expect it to be that way. The Founders certainly did not expect that the process would be free of politics or that the Senate would be an essentially passive and subordinate player in a nominally joint enterprise. Even George Washington had two of his nominations turned down by the Senate for political reasons. Therefore, politics will continue to play an important role in deciding who serves on the federal bench.

"Why Should I Care?"

Access to the Supreme Court

It is extremely difficult to have a case heard by the Supreme Court. Currently the Court hears just over 1 percent of the cases submitted (73 of 6,442 cases in the most recent completed term).[33] This section explains how the Court decides which cases to hear. When a case is submitted, the clerk of the Court assigns it a number and places it on the docket, which is the schedule of cases.

The Court's workload

Statistics on the Supreme Court's workload initially suggest that the size of the docket has increased dramatically since the 1970s (see Figure 6.3). However, a majority of cases are frivolous and are dismissed after limited review. The Court has become increasingly impatient with these frivolous petitions and has moved to prevent "frequent filers" from harassing the Court. One often-cited case involved Michael Sindram, who asked the Court to order the Maryland courts to remove a $35 traffic ticket from his record. Our favorite example concerned a wealthy drug dealer, Frederick W. Bauer, who was convicted on 10 counts of dealing drugs and petitioned the Court 12 times on various issues. The justices finally had enough and directed "the Clerk not to accept any further petitions for *certiorari* or petitions for extraordinary writs from Bauer in noncriminal matters" unless he paid his docketing fees. They concluded that the order would allow the Court to focus on "petitioners who have not abused our processes."[34]

FIGURE 6.3

The Court Sees More Opportunities ... but Hears Fewer Cases

The Supreme Court's workload appears to be headed in two directions: the Court is receiving more cases but hearing fewer of them. What are the implications of having the Supreme Court hear fewer cases? Should something be done to try to get the Court to hear more cases?

Source: Data compiled from John Roberts, "2019 Year-End Reports on the Federal Judiciary," U.S. Supreme Court, December 31, 2019, www.supremecourt.gov/publicinfo/year-end/2019year-endreport.pdf (accessed 3/21/20).

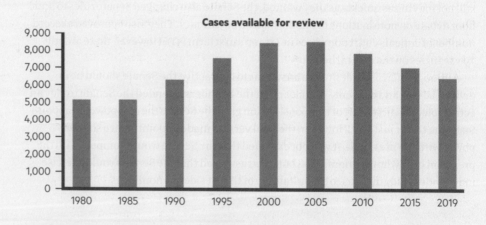

Cases available for review

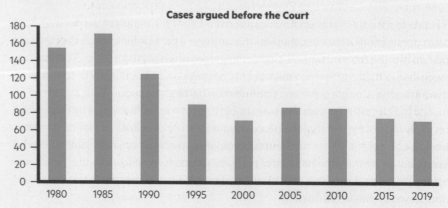

Cases argued before the Court

Although the increase in workload is not as significant as it appears due to the high number of frivolous cases, another change is more important: the number of opinions issued by the Court has fallen by more than half in the past 35 years. The Court heard roughly 150 cases a year through the 1980s, but this number has fallen to only 65 to 95 cases in recent years (see Figure 6.3).[35] The change is even more dramatic when one considers that the Court has reduced the number of "summary decisions" it issues (cases that do not receive a full hearing but on which the Court issues a decision anyway) from 150 a year in the 1970s to a handful today. The number of summary judgments declined when Congress gave the Court more control over its docket and dramatically reduced the number of cases that it was *required* to hear on appeal. However, there is no good explanation for why the Court issues half as many opinions as it used to, other than that the chief justices have decided that the Court shouldn't issue so many opinions.

Rules of access

With the smaller number of cases being heard, it is even more important to understand how the Court decides which cases to consider. There are four paths that a case may take to get to the Supreme Court.

First, Article III of the Constitution specifies that the Court has original jurisdiction in cases involving a foreign ambassador or foreign countries or cases in which a state is a party. As a practical matter, the Court shares jurisdiction with the lower courts on these issues. In recent years, the Court has invoked original jurisdiction only in cases involving disputes between two or more states over territorial or natural resource issues. For example, New Jersey and New York had a disagreement about which state should control 24 acres of filled land that the federal government had added around Ellis Island. Another case involved a dispute between Texas and New Mexico over access to water from the Rio Grande river (recent disputes often concern water rights).[36] One water dispute between Texas and New Mexico over the Pecos River Compact has been going on since 1960! If original jurisdiction is granted and there are factual issues to be resolved, the Court will appoint a "special master" (usually a retired federal judge) to hold a hearing, gather evidence, and make a recommendation to the Court. This process is necessary because the Supreme Court is not a trial court. In the history of our nation, only about 190 cases have made it to the Court through this path, an average of less than 1 per year, and typically these cases do not have any broader significance beyond the parties involved.[37]

The other three routes to the Court are all on appeal: as a matter of right (usually called "on appeal"), through certification (a process that has been used only five times since 1982),[38] or through a writ of *certiorari*. Cases on appeal are those that Congress has determined to be so important that the Supreme Court must hear them. Before 1988, these cases constituted a larger share of the Court's docket and they included (1) cases in which a lower court declared a state or federal law unconstitutional and (2) cases in which a state court upheld a state law that had been challenged as unconstitutional under the U.S. Constitution. The Court currently has much more discretion on these cases, however; the only ones that the Court is still compelled to take on appeal are some voting rights and redistricting cases.

The fourth path is the most common: at least 95 percent of the cases in most sessions arrive through a **writ of *certiorari*** (from the Latin "to be informed"). In these cases, a litigant who lost in a lower court can file a petition to the Supreme Court explaining why it should hear the case. If four justices agree, the case will get a full hearing (this is called, reasonably enough, the Rule of Four). This process may sound simple, but sifting through the 6,500 or so cases that the Court receives every year and deciding which 70 to 75 of them

On rare occasions the Supreme Court serves as a court of original jurisdiction. One of those unusual times is when there is a dispute between two states, such as when the Court had to settle a disagreement between Texas and New Mexico over the Pecos River.

writ of *certiorari*
The most common way for a case to reach the Supreme Court, in which at least four of the nine justices agree to hear a case that has reached them via an appeal from the losing party in a lower court's ruling.

will be heard is daunting. Former justice William O. Douglas said that this winnowing process is "in many respects the most important and interesting of all our functions."[39]

The Court's criteria

How does the Court decide which cases to hear? Several factors come into play, including the specific characteristics of the case and the broader politics surrounding it. Although several criteria generally must be met before the Court will hear the case, justices still have leeway in defining the boundaries of these conditions.

Collusion, Standing, and Mootness First, there are the constitutional guidelines, which are sparse. The Constitution limits the Court to hearing actual "cases and controversies," which has been interpreted to mean that the Court cannot offer advisory opinions about hypothetical situations but must deal with actual cases. The term "actual controversy" also includes several other concepts that limit whether a case will be heard: collusion, standing, and mootness. *Collusion* simply means that the litigants in the case cannot want the same outcome and cannot be testing the law without an actual dispute between the two parties.[40]

Standing, as we noted earlier, means that the party bringing the case must have a personal stake in the outcome. The Court has discretion in defining standing: it may hear cases that it thinks are important even when the plaintiff may not have standing as traditionally understood, or it may avoid hearing cases that may be politically sensitive on the grounds that there is no standing. In an example of the former, the Court decided several important racial redistricting cases even when the White plaintiffs had not suffered any personal harm by being in the Black-majority districts.[41] In an example of the latter, the Court decided not to hear a politically sensitive case involving the Pledge of Allegiance and the First Amendment, saying that the father of the student who brought the case did not have standing because he did not have sufficient custody over his daughter (he was divorced and the mother had primary custody).[42] Clearly, the Court was more eager to voice its views on redistricting than on the Pledge of Allegiance, because it could have just as easily avoided hearing the former case by saying the plaintiffs did not have standing and taken up the latter case despite the concern over custody (it was his daughter after all, which should have given him some stake!). This is an important point to consider: the Court often avoids hearing a controversial case based on a "threshold" issue like standing and then does not have to decide on the merits of the case.

mootness
The irrelevance of a case by the time it is received by a federal court, causing the Supreme Court to decline to hear the case.

A controversy must still be relevant when the Court hears the case; **mootness** occurs when a case is irrelevant by the time it is brought before a federal court. Nonetheless, there are exceptions to this principle, because some types of cases are necessarily moot by the time they get to the Supreme Court. For example, exceptions have been made for abortion cases because a pregnancy lasts only nine months, and it always takes longer than that for a case to get from district court to the appeals court to the Supreme Court.

Thousands of cases every year meet these basic criteria. One very simple guideline eliminates the largest number of cases: if a case does not involve a "substantial federal question," it will not be heard. This essentially means that the Court does not have to hear a case if the justices do not think it is important enough. Of course, the "federal" part of this standard is also important: if a case is governed by state law rather than federal law, the Court will decline to hear the case unless there are constitutional implications. The "political question doctrine" is another basis upon which the Court may decide not to hear a case (as we'll discuss in more detail later, these are cases that the Court thinks are better handled by the elected branches of government). After considering all of these criteria, 20–30 percent of the cases originally submitted for the

Deciding to Hear
a Case in the
Supreme Court

Rule 10 of the *Rules of the Supreme Court of the United States* says that a case is more likely to be heard when

- there is conflict between appeals court opinions or between a state supreme court opinion and another state supreme court on an important federal question,
- there is conflict between a federal appeals court and a state supreme court on an important federal question,
- a lower-court decision has "departed from the accepted and usual course of judicial proceedings,"
- a state supreme court or appeals court has ruled on a substantial federal question that has not yet been addressed by the Court, or
- a state supreme court or appeals court ruling conflicts with Supreme Court precedent.

Rule 10 also states that *certiorari* is unlikely to be granted when "the asserted error consists of erroneous factual findings or the misapplication of a properly stated rule of law."

Source: U.S. Supreme Court, *Rules of the Supreme Court of the United States*, adopted April 8, 2019, effective July 1, 2019, www.supremecourt.gov/ctrules/2019RulesoftheCourt.pdf (accessed 3/21/20).

"Why Should I Care?" Rule 10 helps explain how the Supreme Court decides which cases it will hear of the 6,500 it receives every year. However, the Court still has great discretion, with the only firm rule being that four justices have to agree to hear a case to put it on the docket.

Court's consideration are left. These cases are then winnowed to the final list with the more specific guidance of Rule 10 in the Supreme Court rules (see Nuts & Bolts 6.2). Of the criteria listed in Rule 10, conflict between appeals court decisions is most likely to produce a Supreme Court hearing.

Internal politics

Not much is known about the actual discussions that determine which cases will be heard by the Court. The justices meet in conference with no staff or clerks. Leaks are rare, but a few insider accounts and the papers of retired justices provide some insights to the process. First, since the late 1970s most justices have used a **cert pool**, whereby their law clerks take a first cut at the cases. Law clerks to the justices are top graduates of elite law schools who help justices with background research at several stages of the process. Clerks write joint memos about groups of cases, providing their recommendations about which cases should be heard. The ultimate decisions are up to the justices, but clerks have significant power to help shape the agenda.

Second, the chief justice has an important agenda-setting power: he or she decides the "discuss list" for a given day. Any justice can add a case to the list, but there is no systematic evidence on how often this happens. Only 20–30 percent of the cases are discussed in conference, which means that about three-quarters of the cases that are submitted to the Supreme Court are never even discussed by the justices. The decision not to discuss certain cases is often justified because of the high proportion of frivolous suits submitted to the Court.[43]

Many factors outside the legal requirements or internal processes of the Court influence access to the Court and which cases will be heard. Cases that have generated a lot of activity from interest groups or other governmental parties, such as the solicitor

cert pool
A system initiated in the Supreme Court in the 1970s in which law clerks screen cases that come to the Supreme Court and recommend to the justices which cases should be heard.

Law clerks, such as those seen here with Justice Clarence Thomas, often take a first cut at the cases and help justices with background research.

general, are more likely to be heard. The solicitor general is a presidential appointee who works in the Justice Department and supervises the litigation of the executive branch. In cases in which the federal government is a party, the solicitor general or someone else from that office will represent the government in court. The Court accepts about 70–80 percent of cases in which the U.S. government is a party, compared with about 1 percent overall.[44]

Even with these influences, the Court has a great deal of discretion as to which cases it hears. Well-established practices such as standing and mootness may be ignored (or modified) if the Court wants to hear a specific case. However, one final point is important: although the justices may pick and choose their cases, they cannot completely set their own agenda. They can select only from the cases that come to them.

Hearing cases before the Supreme Court

A surprisingly small proportion of the Court's time—only about 37 days per term—is actually spent hearing cases. The Court's term extends from the first Monday in October through the end of June. It hears cases on Mondays through Wednesdays in alternating two-week cycles in which it is in session from 10 A.M. to 3 P.M., with a one-hour break for lunch. In the two weeks of the cycle when it is not in session, justices review briefs, write opinions, and sift through the next batch of petitions. On most Fridays during the Court's term, the justices meet in conference to discuss cases that have been argued and decide which cases they will hear. Opinions are released throughout the term, but the bulk of them come in May and June.[45]

The Court is in recess from July through September. Justices may take some vacation, but they mostly use the time for studying, reading, writing, and preparing for the next term. During the summer, the Court also considers emergency petitions (such as stays of execution) and occasionally hears important cases. For example, on September 9, 2009 (nearly a month before the fall session started), the Court heard a challenge to the Bipartisan Campaign Reform Act, more commonly known as the McCain–Feingold Act after its two principal sponsors. Congress urged the Court to give the law a speedy review, given its importance for the upcoming 2010 elections. In the blockbuster case *Citizens United v. Federal Election Commission (FEC)*, the Supreme Court decided that independent spending in campaigns by corporations and labor unions is protected by the First Amendment.

Briefs

During its regular sessions, the Court follows rigidly set routines. The justices prepare for a case by reading the briefs submitted by both parties. Because the Supreme Court hears only appeals, it does not call witnesses or gather new evidence. Instead, in structured briefs of no more than 50 pages the parties present their arguments about why they either support the lower-court decision or believe the case was improperly decided. Interest groups often submit amicus curiae ("friend of the court") briefs that convey their opinions to the Court; in fact, 85 percent of cases before the Supreme Court have at least one amicus brief.[46] The federal government also files amicus briefs on important issues such as school busing, school prayer, abortion, reapportionment of legislative districts, job discrimination against women and minorities, and affirmative action in higher education.

It is difficult to determine the impact of amicus briefs on the outcome of a case, but those that are filed early in the process increase the chances that the case will be heard.[47] Given the limited information that justices have about any given case, interest group involvement can be a strong signal about the importance of a case. There is also some evidence that briefs from the solicitor general have an impact on the outcome of a case.[48]

Oral argument

Once the briefs are filed and have been reviewed by the justices, cases are scheduled for oral arguments. Except in unusual circumstances, each case gets one hour, which is divided evenly between the two parties. In especially important cases, extra time may be granted (for example, the case challenging Obamacare had six hours of oral argument, which was the most since a Voting Rights Act case in 1966).[49] Usually there is only one lawyer for each side who presents the case, but parties who have filed amicus briefs may participate if their arguments "would provide assistance to the Court not otherwise available." Given the tight time pressures, the Court is usually unwilling to extend the allotted time to allow "friends of the court" to testify.[50]

The Court is strict about its time limits and uses a system of three lights to show the lawyers how much of their allotted 30 minutes is left. A green light goes on when the speaker's time begins, a white light provides a five-minute warning, and a red light means to stop. Most textbooks cite well-known examples of justices cutting people off in midsentence or walking out of the courtroom as the lawyer drones on. One source implies that these anecdotes are generally revealing of Court procedure, saying, "Anecdotes probably tell as much about the proceeding of the Court during oral argument as does any careful study of the rules and procedures."[51]

However, having a preference for "careful study" over anecdotes, we were curious about how common it was for justices to strictly impose the time limits. Initially, we

oral arguments
Spoken presentations made in person by the lawyers of each party to a judge or an appellate court outlining the legal reasons their side should prevail.

Cameras are not allowed in the Supreme Court, so artists' sketches are the only available images of oral arguments. Depicted here is the first round of oral arguments that Justice Kavanaugh participated in following his confirmation by the Senate.

examined 42 cases from the 2004–2005 term, using the online transcripts on the Court's website.[52] We found that most lawyers did not use all their allotted time, with 62 percent of the cases coming in under 60 minutes, 17 percent at exactly an hour, and 21 percent at over an hour. One-sixth of the lawyers still had at least five minutes left on the clock. We found only two instances in which a justice cut someone off in midsentence after the person had gone over the half-hour limit. We updated the analysis for the Roberts Court, examining all 61 cases argued in the 2019–2020 term. Roberts was not much of a stickler for adhering to the time limits: nearly 60 percent of oral arguments went past their allotted time (most by only a minute or two), 16 percent were exactly one hour, and 25 percent were under an hour. However, things changed dramatically when the Court moved to teleconference on May 3, 2020, because of the COVID-19 pandemic. All 10 of the oral arguments went over time, most of them substantially so. However, even with the new format, only 2 of the 10 oral arguments ended with an attorney being cut off in midsentence by the chief justice (none of the 47 regular oral arguments ended with an interruption). Thus, while the Court tries to encourage attorneys to stay within the time limits, it is not as draconian as some anecdotes imply.

Some lawyers may not use all their time because their train of thought is interrupted by aggressive questioning. Transcripts reveal that justices jump in with questions almost immediately and some attorneys never regain their footing. The frequency and pointedness of the questions vary by justice, with Justices Breyer, Kagan, Roberts, and Sotomayor being the most aggressive on the current Court in terms of the number of words spoken. In recent years, Sotomayor and Ginsburg have been the most likely to ask the first question, with Sotomayor asking nearly a third of the first questions and waiting an average of only 39 seconds before she jumps in.[53] Justice Thomas went more than 10 years without asking a single question but broke his streak in 2016, perhaps feeling the need to fill the void created by the death of Justice Scalia.[54] The new teleconference format was much more structured, with the questions being asked in order of seniority and the chief justice serving as a timekeeper to allocate time more evenly. Thus, while Thomas still participated less than the other justices, he did ask questions in all 10 of the teleconference oral arguments.[55] Cameras are not allowed in the courtroom, so most Americans have never seen the Court in action—although a small live audience is admitted every morning the Court is in session, and live audio was streamed online for the first time ever as a result of the Supreme Court's move to teleconferencing in the midst of the COVID-19 pandemic. If you are curious about oral arguments, audio recordings of every case since 1995 are available at www.oyez.org.

Conference

After oral arguments, the justices meet in conference to discuss and then vote on the cases. As with the initial conferences, these meetings are conducted in secret. We know, based on notes in the personal papers of retired justices, that the conferences are orderly and structured but can become quite heated. The justices take turns discussing the cases and outlining the reasons for their positions. Justice Thurgood Marshall described the decision-making process in conference as

a continuing conversation among nine distinct individuals on dozens of issues simultaneously. The exchanges are serious, sometimes scholarly, occasionally brash and personalized, but generally well-reasoned and most often cast in understated, genteel language.... In other cases, a majority of justices start down one path, only to reverse direction.[56]

Opinion writing

After the justices indicate how they are likely to vote on a case, if the chief justice is in the majority (which is most of the time), the chief justice decides who will write the **majority opinion**. Otherwise, the most senior justice in the majority assigns the opinion. Several considerations determine how an opinion will be assigned. First, the chief justice will try to ensure the smooth operation of the Court by trying to equalize the number of cases across the nine justices. John Roberts has been especially careful to spread out the workload evenly.[57] A second factor is the justices' individual areas of expertise. For example, Justice Harry Blackmun had developed expertise in medical law when he was in private practice. This experience played a role in Chief Justice Burger's decision to assign Blackmun the majority opinion in the landmark abortion decision *Roe v. Wade* (1973). Likewise, Justice Sandra Day O'Connor developed expertise in racial redistricting cases and authored most of those decisions in the 1990s, while Justice Samuel Alito has specialized in criminal justice cases in recent years.[58]

Strategy on the Court Other factors in how opinions are assigned are more strategic, taking into account the Court's external relations, internal relations, and the personal policy goals of the opinion assigner. The Court must be sensitive to how others might respond to its decisions because it must rely on the other branches of government to enforce them. One famous example of this consideration in an opinion assignment came in a case from the 1940s that struck down a practice that had prevented African Americans from voting in Democratic primaries.[59] Originally, the opinion was assigned to Justice Felix Frankfurter, but Justice Robert Jackson wrote a memo suggesting that it might be unwise to have a liberal, politically independent Jew from the Northeast write an opinion that was sure to be controversial in the South. Chief Justice Harlan Fiske Stone agreed and reassigned the opinion to Justice Stanley Reed, a Protestant and Democrat from Kentucky.[60] It may not seem that the Court is sensitive to public opinion, but these kinds of considerations happen fairly frequently in important cases. Internal considerations occasionally cause justices to vote strategically—differently from their sincere preferences—so they can put themselves in the majority. If they are the most senior justice in the majority, they then have the power to assign the opinion, and they often assign it to themselves.

Justices may also assign opinions to further their own personal policy goals. The most obvious strategy is for the chief justice to assign opinions to justices who are closest to his or her position. This practice is constrained by the chief justice's responsibility to ensure the smooth operation of the Court. If the chief justice assigned all the opinions to the justices who are closest to him or her ideologically, then justices with other ideological leanings would get a chance to write opinions only in the 15–20 percent of cases in which the chief is in the minority. However, Chief Justice Roberts has allocated the most important cases to his ideological allies and has taken about twice as many of the most important cases for himself (compared to what would have been expected by chance).[61] Charles Hughes, chief justice from 1930 to 1941, sometimes assigned opinions on liberal decisions to conservative justices and cases with conservative outcomes to liberal justices in order to downplay the importance of ideology on the Court.[62]

After the opinions are assigned, the justices work on writing a draft opinion. Law clerks typically help with this process. Some justices insist on writing all of their opinions, whereas others allow a clerk to write the first draft. The drafts are circulated to the other justices for comments and reactions. Some bargaining may occur, in which a justice says he or she will withdraw support unless a provision of the opinion is changed. Justices may join the majority opinion, may write a separate **concurring opinion**, or may write a **dissenting opinion** (see Nuts & Bolts 6.3 for details on the types of opinions).

majority opinion
A court ruling on which more than half of the members agree. The ruling will present the decision of the court and explain the reasoning behind the decision.

**AP®
SUPREME
COURT CASE**

Chief Justice John Roberts (left foreground) stands with Associate Justices Elena Kagan, Neil Gorsuch, and Brett Kavanaugh as they await the arrival of President Trump before his 2020 State of the Union address.

concurring opinion
An opinion of the court that agrees with the majority decision but disagrees on at least part of the rationale for the decision.

dissenting opinion
An opinion of the court that disagrees with the majority decision in a case.

Types of Supreme Court Decisions

- **Majority opinion:** The core decision of the Court that must be agreed upon by at least five justices. The majority opinion presents the legal reasoning for the Court's decision.
- **Concurring opinion:** Written by a justice who agrees with the outcome of the case but not with part of the legal reasoning. Concurring opinions may be joined by other justices. A justice may sign on to the majority opinion and write a separate concurring opinion.
- **Plurality opinion:** Occurs when a majority cannot agree on the legal reasoning in a case. The plurality opinion is the one that has the most agreement (usually three or four justices). Because of the fractured nature of these opinions, they typically are not viewed as having as much clout as majority opinions.

- **Dissent:** Submitted by a justice who disagrees with the outcome of the case. Other justices can sign on to a dissent or write their own, so there can be as many as four dissents. Justices can also sign on to part of a dissent but not the entire opinion.
- **Per curiam (Latin for "by the court") opinion:** An unsigned opinion of the Court or a decision written by the entire Court. However, this is not the same as a unanimous decision that is signed by the entire Court. Per curiam opinions are usually very short opinions on noncontroversial issues, but not always. For example, *Bush v. Gore*, which decided the outcome of the 2000 presidential election, was a per curiam opinion. Per curiam decisions may also have dissents.

Source: Compiled by the authors.

"Why Should I Care?" The type of decision influences how to interpret the impact of the decision. Majority opinions generally carry more weight than plurality opinions, concurring opinions are important for developing some of the nuances on the winning side, and dissent may lay the groundwork for future shifts in the opinions of the Court.

So that's the dissenter's hope: that they are writing not for today but for tomorrow.

—Justice Ruth Bader Ginsburg

Dissents Two final points about the process of writing and issuing opinions are important. First, until 1940, there was a premium placed on unanimous decisions. John Marshall, who was chief justice from 1800 to 1835, started this practice. Through the 1930s, about 80–90 percent of decisions were unanimous. This changed dramatically in the 1940s, when most cases had at least one dissent. In recent decades, about two-thirds of cases have had a dissent.[63] However, in the 2013–2014 term two-thirds of the cases were unanimous, the highest proportion since at least 1946. That proportion fell to 36 percent in the 2019–2020 term.[64] Second, dissents serve an important purpose. Not only do they allow the minority view to be expressed, but they also often provide the basis later on for reversing a poorly reasoned case. When justices strongly oppose the majority opinion, they may take the unusual step of reading a portion of the dissent from the bench.

"Why Should I Care?" The process of hearing cases before the Court, including the written briefs, oral arguments, discussions in conference, and opinion assignment, is a very political one. As discussed in the chapter opener, it may be disturbing to think of the Court as a political institution that bargains and considers external forces like public opinion. Although justices do not have to answer to voters, they are still sensitive to a broad range of considerations in hearing cases.

Supreme Court decision making

Judicial decision making is influenced by many different factors, but the two main categories are *legal* and *political*. Legal factors include the precedents of earlier cases and the norm that justices must follow the language of the Constitution. Political influences include the justices' preferences or ideologies, their stances on whether the Court should take a restrained or activist role with respect to the elected branches, and external factors such as public opinion and interest group involvement. Most observers of the Court recognize that both legal and political factors are important in explaining judicial decision making, but some stake out a view more strongly on one side or the other. Some scholars argue, for example, that all Court behavior is political and that the use of legal factors is just a smoke screen for hiding personal preferences. The fact that there are differences of opinion as to which factors are most important can often make empirical arguments (those that describe the way decisions are made) evolve into normative arguments (those about the way that justices *should* behave). These different perspectives about how justices make decisions may also lead to arguments about the proper role of the Court within our political system, which we will explore in the next section.

Legal factors

Legal factors embody the image we cited at the beginning of the chapter of Lady Justice neutrally applying the law while fairly balancing various interests. While this ideal image is incomplete, legal factors do independently influence judicial decision making on a broad range of cases.

Precedent The most basic legal factor is precedent, discussed earlier. Precedent does not determine the outcome of any given case, because every case has a range of precedents that can serve to justify a justice's decision. The "easy" cases, in which settled law makes the outcome obvious, are less likely to be heard by the Court because of the justices' desire to focus on the more controversial areas of unsettled law or cases in which there is conflict between lower courts' decisions. However, in some areas of the law—such as free speech, the death penalty, and search and seizure—precedent is an important explanation for how the justices decide a case.

The Language of the Constitution The Constitution is the obvious starting point for any Supreme Court case that involves a Constitutional right.[65] However, there are various perspectives on exactly how, and to what degree, the language of the Constitution can and should influence judicial decision making today.

People in one camp argue that the *language* used in the Constitution is the most important guiding factor. Their perspectives fall under the heading of  strict construction. The most basic of these is the literalist view of the Constitution. Sometimes this view is called a textualist position because it sees the text of the document as determining the outcome of any given case. Literalists argue that justices need to look no further than the actual words of the Constitution.

Justice Hugo Black was one of the most famous advocates of the literalist position. When the First Amendment says that "Congress shall make no law . . . abridging

strict construction
A way of interpreting the Constitution based on its language alone.

the freedom of speech," that literally means *no* law. Justice Black said, "My view is, without deviation, without exception, without any ifs, buts, or whereases, that freedom of speech means that government shall not do anything to people … either for the views they have or the views they express or the words they speak or write."[66] While that may be clear enough with regard to political speech, how about pornography, Internet speech, or symbolic speech, such as burning an American flag or wearing an armband to protest the Vietnam War? A literal interpretation of the Constitution does not necessarily help determine whether these forms of speech should be restricted. (Indeed, Black was one of the two dissenters in a case that upheld students' right to wear armbands as a form of symbolic speech. Black believed that school officials should be allowed to decide whether a symbolic protest would be too disruptive in the classroom and argued that only spoken and written speech should be afforded the strongest protection of the First Amendment. So much for "without deviation, without exception" concerning restricting expression of the "views … [people] have"!)

On the current Court, Neil Gorsuch is the most well-known for the textualist position. A recent example involves statutory rather than Constitutional interpretation, but the concept is the same: justices should follow the plain language of the law. When the Court in 2020 ruled that Title VII of the 1964 Civil Rights Act prohibits employers from discriminating based on sexual orientation (gays and lesbians) or gender identity (transgender people) Gorsuch wrote, "When the express terms of a statute give us one answer and extratextual considerations suggest another, it's no contest. Only the written word is the law, and all persons are entitled to benefit."[67]

Critics of strict construction also point out that the Constitution is silent on many important points (such as a right to privacy) and could not have anticipated the many legal implications of changes in technology in the twentieth and twenty-first centuries, such as eavesdropping devices, cloning, and the Internet. Also, although the language of the First Amendment is relatively clear when it comes to political speech, other equally important words of the Constitution such as "necessary and proper," "executive power," "equal protection," and "due process" are open-ended and vague.

Some strict constructionists respond by arguing that, if the words of the Constitution are not clear, the justices should be guided by what the Founders *intended* by the words, a perspective called the original intent or originalist perspective. Clarence Thomas is the current justice who is most influenced by this view, especially on issues of federalism.

Those in the other camp are often described as supporting a living Constitution perspective on the document (see Chapter 2). They argue that originalism or other versions of strict construction can "make a nation the prisoner of its past, and reject any constitutional development save constitutional amendment."[68] If the justices are bound to follow the literal words of the Constitution, *with the meaning they had when the document was written,* we certainly could be legally frozen in time. The option of amending the Constitution is a long and difficult process, so that is not always a viable way for the Constitution to reflect changing norms and values. Justice William Brennan, a critic of originalism, also argued it was "arrogance cloaked in humility" to presume to know what the framers intended. According to this view, interpreting the Constitution is always somewhat subjective and it is misleading to claim otherwise.[69]

Political factors

The living Constitution perspective points to the second set of influences on Supreme Court decision making: political factors. Indeed, many people are uncomfortable thinking about the Court in political terms and prefer to think of the image of "blind

---

original intent
The theory that justices should surmise the intentions of the Founders when the language of the Constitution is unclear.

living Constitution
A way of interpreting the Constitution that takes into account evolving national attitudes and circumstances rather than the text alone.

Mary Beth Tinker and two other students in the Des Moines, Iowa, public schools were suspended for wearing armbands to protest the Vietnam War. The Supreme Court ruled in *Tinker v. Des Moines Independent Community School District* (1969) that the First Amendment protected symbolic political speech, even in public schools. Mary Beth is shown here with her mother and brother.

**AP®
SUPREME
COURT CASE**

justice," in which constitutional principles are fairly applied. However, political influences are clearly evident in the Court—maybe less than in Congress or the presidency, but they are certainly present. This means that the courts respond to and shape politics in ways that often involve compromise, both within the courts themselves and in the broader political system.

Political Ideology and Attitudes There is evidence that justices' ideology or attitudes about various issues influence their decisions. Those who argue that this is the most important factor in understanding Supreme Court decision making are said to take an **attitudinalist approach**. Liberal judges are strong defenders of individual civil liberties (including defendants' rights), tend to be pro-choice on abortion, support regulatory policy to protect the environment and workers, support national intervention in the states, and favor race-conscious policies such as affirmative action. Conservative judges favor state regulation of private conduct (especially on moral issues), support prosecutors over defendants, tend to be pro-life on abortion, and support the free market and property rights over the environment and workers, states' rights over national intervention, and a color-blind policy on race. See the What Do the Facts Say? feature for more on how the balance between liberal and conservative judges has shifted.

These are, of course, just general tendencies. However, they do provide a strong basis for explaining patterns of decisions, especially on some types of cases. For example, there were dramatic differences in the chief justices' rulings on civil liberties cases from 1953 to 2001: Earl Warren took the liberal position on 79 percent of the 771 cases he participated in, Warren Burger took the liberal position on 30 percent of 1,429 cases, and William Rehnquist took the liberal position on only 22 percent of his 2,127 cases.[70] If justices were neutrally applying the law, there would not be such dramatic differences. Returning to President Trump's reference to an "Obama judge" from the chapter opener, while there are plenty of deviations from ideological consistency, there are substantial differences in the behavior of Democrat- and Republican-appointed judges.

Proponents of the attitudinalist view also argue that justices who *claim* to be strict constructionists or originalists are really driven by ideology because they selectively

attitudinalist approach
A way of understanding decisions of the Supreme Court based on the political ideologies of the justices.

WHAT DO THE FACTS SAY?

Think about it

- **Look at where Scalia is on the ideological scale.** If the Democratic candidate, Hillary Clinton, had been elected in 2016 and all but ensured Garland joining the Court, where would Scalia's dot have likely moved?
- **Did the median justice change** with the addition of Neil Gorsuch and Brett Kavanaugh to the Court?
- **What happened when John Roberts replaced Kennedy** as the median justice for the 2018 term?

The Shifting Ideological Balance of the Court

After Justice Antonin Scalia died in early 2016, the open seat on the Supreme Court became a major issue in the presidential election. Why? As this figure shows, when justices are replaced, the ideological shifts can be quite large (as when Thurgood Marshall, a very liberal justice, was replaced by a strong conservative, Clarence Thomas) or nonexistent (as when Sonia Sotomayor replaced David Souter—they both were moderate liberals). Many people said that replacing Scalia with Merrick Garland would have drastically altered the ideological makeup of the Court, given the 4–4 split on the Court between liberal and conservative justices. When Scalia was replaced by Neil Gorsuch instead of Garland, what happened to the ideological balance of the Court? Then, when Kennedy retired in 2018, he was replaced by conservative Brett Kavanaugh and the center of the Court was kept in about the same place. What do you think will happen now that Amy Coney Barrett has replaced Ruth Bader Ginsburg? What do the facts say?

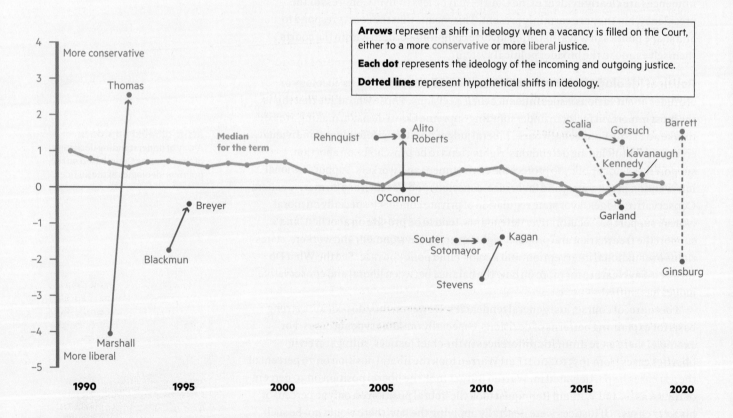

Sources: Alicia Parlapiano and Margot Sanger-Katz, "A Supreme Court with Merrick Garland Would Be the Most Liberal in Decades," *New York Times*, March 16, 2016, www.nytimes.com/interactive/2016/02/18/upshot/potential-for-the-most-liberal-supreme-court-in-decades.html; data for Scalia, Gorsuch, Kennedy, and Kavanaugh are from Martin Quinn Scores, "Measures," http://mqscores.lsa.umich.edu/measures.php; estimate for Garland is from Adam Bonica et al., "New Data Show How Liberal Merrick Garland Really Is," *Washington Post*, March 30, 2016, www.washingtonpost.com/news/monkey-cage/wp/2016/03/30/new-data-show-how-liberal-merrick-garland-really-is/ (all accessed 6/24/20); estimate for Barrett is from "The Supreme Court May Be About to Take a Hard Right Turn," *The Economist*, September 21, 2020, www.economist.com/graphic-detail/2020/09/21/the-supreme-court-may-be-about-to-take-a-hard-right-turn (accessed 11/10/20).

use the text of the Constitution. For example, Justice Thomas voted against the University of Michigan's affirmative action program without considering whether the authors of the Fourteenth Amendment supported the practice (the historical record shows that they supported similar policies for the newly freed enslaved people). Therefore, if Justice Thomas had been true to his originalist perspective, he would have supported affirmative action, but his ideology led him to oppose the policy. The example of Hugo Black's contradictory position on free speech rights cited earlier demonstrates that a liberal textualist view may also be inconsistently applied.

Other Justices' and Politicians' Preferences Another approach to understanding Supreme Court decision making, known as the strategic model, focuses on justices' calculations about the preferences of the other justices, the president, and Congress; the choices that other justices are likely to make; and the institutional context within which they operate. After all, justices do not operate alone: at a minimum, they need the votes of four of their colleagues if they want their position to prevail. Therefore, it makes sense to focus on the strategic interactions that take place to build coalitions.

The median voter on the Court—the one in the middle when the justices are arrayed from the most liberal to the most conservative—has an especially influential role in the strategic model. For many years, the median justice was Anthony M. Kennedy. The four conservatives to his right (Thomas, Scalia, Roberts, and Alito) and the four liberals to his left (Breyer, Ginsburg, Souter, and Stevens) all wanted to attract his vote. When Justice Sotomayor replaced Justice Souter, Justice Kagan replaced Justice Stevens, and Justice Gorsuch replaced Justice Scalia, Kennedy remained the median voter on the Court (because Souter, Sotomayor, Stevens, and Kagan were all to his left and Gorsuch and Scalia were both to his right). When Kennedy retired and Brett Kavanaugh took his place, Roberts became the median and the center of the Court stayed in roughly the same place. With Justice Barrett replacing Ginsburg, Kavanaugh is the new median, with the center moving slightly to the right. Research shows that at least one justice switches his or her vote at some stage in the process (from the initial conference to oral arguments to the final vote) on at least half the cases, so strategic bargaining appears to be fairly common.[71] Our earlier discussion of opinion assignment and writing opinions to attract the support of a specific justice is more evidence in support of the strategic model.

Separation of Powers Another political influence on justices' decision making is their view of the place of the Court with respect to the democratically elected institutions (Congress and the president). Specifically, do they favor an activist or a restrained role for the Court? Advocates of judicial restraint argue that judges should defer to the elected branches and not strike down their laws or other actions. In contrast, advocates of judicial activism argue that the Court must play an active role in interpreting the Constitution to protect minority rights even if it means overturning the actions of the elected branches. (We will discuss these views in more detail later in the chapter.)

Outside Influences: Interest Groups and Public Opinion Finally, there are external influences on the Court, such as public opinion and interest groups. We have already talked about the role of interest groups in filing amicus briefs. This is the only avenue of influence open to interest groups; other tactics such as lobbying and fund-raising are either inappropriate or irrelevant (because justices are not elected). The role of public opinion is more complex. Obviously, justices do not consult public-opinion polls the way elected officials do. However, the Court expresses the public's preferences in several indirect ways.

The Supreme Court, of course, has the responsibility of ensuring that our government never oversteps its proper bounds or violates the rights of individuals. But the Court must also recognize the limits on itself and respect the choices made by the American people.

—**Justice Elena Kagan**

judicial restraint
The idea that the Supreme Court should defer to the democratically elected executive and legislative branches of government rather than contradicting existing laws.

judicial activism
The idea that the Supreme Court should assert its interpretation of the law even if it overrules the elected executive and legislative branches of government.

The first was most colorfully expressed by Mr. Dooley, a fictional Irish-American bartender whom newspaper satirist Finley Peter Dunne created in 1898. Mr. Dooley offered keen insights on politics and general social criticism, including this gem on the relationship between the Supreme Court and the public: "th' supreme coort always follows th' iliction returns."[72] That is, the public elects the president and the Senate, who nominate and confirm the justices. Therefore, sooner or later, the Court should reflect the views of the public. Subsequent work by political scientists has confirmed this to be largely the case,[73] especially in recent years, when Supreme Court nominations have become more political and more important to the public.[74]

The second mechanism through which public opinion may influence the Court is somewhat more direct: when the public has a clear position on an issue that is before the Court, the Court tends to agree with the public. One study found that the "public mood" and Court opinions correlated very highly between 1956 and 1981, but their association was weaker through the rest of the 1980s.[75] One scholar found that three-fifths to two-thirds of Supreme Court decisions are consistent with public opinion when the public has a clear preference on an issue.[76] More recent work demonstrates that the Court is constrained by public opinion, in part because it may fear resistance to implementing an unpopular decision.[77]

Several high-profile examples support the idea that the Court is sensitive to public opinion: the Court switched during the New Deal in the 1930s to support Roosevelt's policy agenda after standing in the way for four years, gave in to wartime opinion to support the internment of Japanese Americans during World War II, limited an accused child molester's right to confront his or her accuser in a courtroom, and supported same-sex marriage. In each of these cases, the justices reflected the current public opinion of the nation rather than a strict reading of the Constitution or the Founders' intent. On the other hand, there are plenty of decisions in which the Court has stood up for unpopular views, such as banning prayer in schools, allowing flag burning, and protecting criminal defendants' rights.

Sometimes the Court may shift its views to reflect *international* opinion. The most recent example struck down the death penalty for minors in 12 states. Ruling by a 5–4 vote that the execution of 16- or 17-year-olds violated the Eighth Amendment's prohibition against "cruel and unusual punishments," the majority opinion overturned a 1989 case and said that the new decision was necessary to reflect the "evolving standards of decency" concerning the definition of "cruel and unusual punishments." Justice Kennedy, who had voted on the other side of this issue 16 years earlier, wrote: "It is fair to say that the United States now stands alone in a world that has turned its face against the juvenile death penalty." Justice Kennedy said that although the Court was not obligated to follow foreign developments, "it is proper that we acknowledge the overwhelming weight of international opinion" for its "respected and significant confirmation for our own conclusions."[78] This explicit recognition of the role of public opinion firmly placed a majority of the Court on the side of the "living Constitution" perspective on this issue, while rejecting the strict constructionist view of the dissenters.

Another way that the Court may consider the public mood is to shift the timing of a decision. The best example here is the landmark school desegregation case, *Brown v. Board of Education* (1954), that the Court sat on for more than two years—until after the 1952 presidential election—because it didn't think the public was ready for its bombshell ruling.[79] Others have argued that the Court rarely *changes* its views to reflect public opinion,[80] but at a minimum the evidence supports the notion that the Court is usually in step with the public.[81]

**AP®
SUPREME
COURT CASE**

Shouldn't the Court be neutrally applying the words of the Constitution to the cases it hears? While a normatively appealing view, this textualist view ignores many of the realities of how the Court actually operates. Justices often let their own political views shape their decisions, but more neutral forces such as precedent and deferring to the elected branches also play important roles. A realistic perception of the various factors that go into a justice's decision can help you understand why the Court strikes down some laws and upholds others.

"Why Should I Care?"

ASSESS THE SUPREME COURT'S POWER IN THE POLITICAL SYSTEM

The role of the Court in our political system

We conclude with the topic addressed early in the chapter—the place of the Court within the political system. Is the Court the "weakest branch"? As Alexander Hamilton pointed out, the Court has "neither the power of the purse nor the sword." Therefore, it is not clear how it can enforce decisions. In some instances, the Court can force its views on the other branches; in other cases, it needs their support to enforce its decisions.

Compliance and implementation

To gain compliance with its decisions, the Court can rely only on its reputation and on the actions of Congress and the president to back it up. If the other branches don't support the Court, there isn't much it can do. The Court's lack of enforcement power is especially evident when a ruling applies broadly to millions of people who care deeply about the issue. Consider school prayer, which still exists in hundreds of public schools nationwide despite having been ruled unconstitutional nearly 60 years ago. It is impossible to enforce the ban unless someone in a school complains and is willing to bring a lawsuit.

In most cases that involve a broad policy, the Court depends on the president for enforcement. After *Brown v. Board of Education* (1954), the landmark school desegregation case, Presidents Eisenhower and Kennedy had to send in federal troops to desegregate public schools and universities. However, presidential foot-dragging can have a big impact on how the law is enforced. President Nixon attempted to lessen the impact of a school busing decision in 1971 that forced the integration of public schools by interpreting it very narrowly. Republican presidents who oppose abortion have limited the scope of *Roe v. Wade*, which legalized abortion in 1973, by denying federal support for abortions for Medicaid recipients, banning abortions on military bases, and preventing doctors from mentioning abortion as an option during pregnancy counseling. The Court must rely on its reputation and prestige to compel the president and Congress not to stray too far from its decisions.

Relations with the other branches

Relations with the other branches of government may become strained when the Court rules on fundamental questions about institutional power. In some cases, the other branches may fight back; in others, the Court may exercise self-restraint and not get involved.

Students at a middle school in Alton, Illinois, gather around a flagpole for prayers before the start of the school day. Unless someone complains, it is difficult to enforce the ban on prayer in public schools.

Judicial Activism and Restraint A central question concerning the role of the Court within our political system revolves around judicial review: Should the Court strike down laws passed by Congress and actions of the executive (activism) or defer to the elected branches (restraint)? Often the answer to this question varies when considered in light of specific lines of cases. A political conservative may favor activist decisions striking down environmental laws or workplace regulations but oppose activist decisions that defend flag burning or defendants' rights. Political liberals may do the opposite—calling for judicial restraint on the first set of cases but for judicial activism to protect civil liberties.

The term "activist judges" often appears in the media. Sometimes the media mistakenly assert that liberal justices are more activist than conservative justices. In fact, though, that is not always the case. The current Court is quite conservative, but it is also activist.[82] Two conservative justices, Roberts and Thomas, have voted to overturn laws passed by Congress 71 percent and 76 percent of the time, respectively, whereas two of the most liberal justices in the 2020 session, Breyer and Ginsburg, have taken the activist position in only 58 percent and 56 percent of the cases.[83] The 1930s Court that struck down much of the New Deal legislation was also conservative and activist, but the Warren Court of the late 1950s and early 1960s was liberal and activist.

A prominent legal journalist observed that the way the popular media describe activism and restraint typically boils down to ideology: if you like a decision, it is restrained; if you do not like a decision, it is activist. For example, *Bush v. Gore*, the decision that decided the outcome of the 2000 presidential election, shows that "most conservatives tie themselves in knots to defend judicial activism when they like the results and to denounce it when they do not. As the reactions to *Lawrence* (the gay sodomy case discussed in Chapter 8) and, earlier, *Roe* (the landmark abortion case) have shown, liberals have been no less selective in their outrage at judicial adventurousness."[84] However, there are instances in which restraint reflects more than ideology and preferences. Justice O'Connor, for example, took restrained positions on abortion and affirmative action, despite her personal views against these policies. Another prominent example of judicial restraint being more important than ideology is Chief Justice Roberts's position in the health care reform case; he said that some decisions "are entrusted to our nation's elected leaders, who can be thrown out of

In a survey taken about the judicial branch, most respondents were unable to name any Supreme Court justices. Just so you are not in danger of falling into that category, for much of 2020 the justices were (front row, left to right) Stephen Breyer, Clarence Thomas, John G. Roberts Jr. (chief justice), Ruth Bader Ginsburg, Samuel Alito Jr., (standing, left to right) Neil Gorsuch, Sonia Sotomayor, Elena Kagan, and Brett Kavanaugh. Justice Ginsburg died shortly before the 2020 elections, in September 2020, and was replaced by Amy Coney Barrett.

office if the people disagree with them." However, despite providing the pivotal vote to uphold central provisions of the law, he made his personal views against the law clear. "It is not our job," he said, "to protect the people from the consequences of their political choices."[85]

It is important to define activism and restraint in terms of the Court's role in our nation's system of separated powers: Does the Court check the elected branches by overturning their decisions through judicial review? If so, the Court has taken an activist position.

Resistance from the Other Branches The president and Congress often fight back when they think the Court is exerting too much influence, which can limit the Court's power as a policy-making institution. For the president, this can escalate to open conflict. In the Take a Stand feature, we discuss President Obama's criticism of the Court's ruling in *Citizens United v. Federal Election Commission* (2010) in his State of the Union message and President Trump's conflict with the federal courts over their decisions on LGBTQ rights and the status of DACA recipients. Such open conflict with the Court is often criticized as inappropriate. For example, during his confirmation process, Neil Gorsuch told Senator Richard Blumenthal (D-CT) that Trump's criticisms were "disheartening" and "demoralizing" to independent federal courts.[86] The president can counter the Court's influence in a more restrained way by failing to enforce a decision vigorously.

Congress can try to control the Court by blocking appointments it disagrees with (however, this often involves a disagreement with the president more than the Court), limiting the jurisdiction of the federal courts, changing the size of the Court, or even impeaching a judge. The latter three options are rarely used, but Congress often threatens to take these drastic steps. The most common way for Congress to respond to a Court decision that it disagrees with is simply to pass legislation that overturns the decision (if the case concerns the interpretation of a law).

Self-Imposed Restraint In general, the Court avoids stepping on the toes of the other branches unless it is absolutely necessary. The Court often exercises self-imposed restraint and refuses to act on "political questions"—issues that are outside the judicial domain and should be decided by elected officials. The practice dates back to an 1804 dispute over whether a piece of land next to the Mississippi River belonged to Spain or the United States. The Court observed: "A question like this, respecting the boundaries of nations, is . . . more a political than a legal question, and in its discussion, the courts of every country must respect the pronounced will of the legislature."[87]

A more recent application of the doctrine came when the Washington, D.C., district court dismissed a lawsuit from Representative Charles Rangel (D-NY) against former Speaker John A. Boehner (R-OH) concerning the House of Representatives' censure of Rangel for tax evasion and other unethical behavior. The district court dismissed the suit, in part on the grounds that this was a political question that should be decided by Congress, not the Court: "The House has wide discretion to discipline its Members under the Discipline Clause, and this Court may not lightly intrude upon that discretion."[88] The Court is generally reluctant to get involved in internal congressional disputes.

Although this self-imposed limitation on judicial power is important, one must also recognize that the Court reserves the right to decide what a political question is. Therefore, one could argue that this is not much of a limit on judicial power after all. For example, for many decades the Court avoided the topic of legislative redistricting, saying that it did not want to enter that "political thicket." However, it changed its position in the 1960s in a series of cases that imposed the idea of "one-person, one-vote" on the redistricting process, and it has been intimately involved in redistricting ever since. The Court's ability to define the boundaries of political questions is an important source of its policy-making power.

The Independence of the Courts

Many presidents have been frustrated by federal court decisions that they perceived to be unreasonable. Some have responded by lashing out at the courts—an action that never fails to stir controversy. Recently, both Presidents Obama and Trump have criticized high-profile Court decisions. In Obama's 2010 State of the Union address, he noted his disagreement with the Court's ruling in *Citizens United v. Federal Election Commission* (2010) and stated that he believed the decision had opened the floodgates for corporate spending—including by foreign corporations—in elections. Justice Alito was caught on camera mouthing the words "not true" in response. Washington was abuzz for days about whether the president's comment or Alito's response was out of line.[a] President Trump, for his part, was incensed with the Supreme Court's "horrible and politically charged decisions" on LGBTQ rights and the Dreamers, calling them "shotgun blasts into the face of people that are proud to call themselves Republicans or Conservatives."[b] Though it is not very common for presidents to openly criticize the federal courts, they routinely try to influence the courts through nominations to the federal bench. As we discussed earlier, all presidents try to pick justices who share their political views. Is this kind of influence different from that of presidents who directly express their opinions on Court decisions? Is either kind of influence acceptable?

Presidents should be able to influence the courts.

Some argue that whether it is President Obama criticizing the Court's ruling on campaign finance or President Trump expressing his views on its decisions on LGBTQ rights and DACA, presidents should be able to express their views on the important issues of the day. Furthermore, presidents are not obligated to nominate centrist judges. If a Republican president can nominate conservative judges, that is certainly his or her right. Trump exercised this right, to the dismay of some observers who believe that he picked extremely conservative judges to push his policy agenda.

Trump's appointees, like those of any other president, had to be confirmed by the Senate. If people don't like the ideological makeup of the judges the president selects, they can vote out the president and their senator in the next election. Besides, the president speaks for the people who elected him or her, while the courts are less democratic because they are not elected.

 President Barack Obama was criticized during his 2010 State of the Union address for his comments on *Citizens United v. Federal Election Commission*, a federal court decision that he perceived to be unreasonable.

The independence of the courts is crucial: the president needs to back off.

Others argue that while it is fine for presidents to express their policy views on issues that come before the Court, they should refrain from direct criticism of specific cases or judges. Just as it was improper for Justice Ginsburg to criticize Trump during the campaign, presidents should not interject politics into the Court.

And though it is true that all presidents try to influence the Court through their nominations, moderation here would also serve the long-term interests of the country better than wild swings between ideological extremes.

The ballot box is the ultimate recourse for accountability, but even the mighty power of the vote is limited when it comes to holding judges responsible: many judges will serve on the bench for 25 years or more, much longer than the president or most senators.

take a stand

1. Where would you draw the line on presidents' criticizing the courts?

2. Does it bother you that courts are not accountable to the people and yet make important policy decisions? If so, how should presidents be able to influence the courts?

3. Should presidents be able to nominate whomever they want to the courts (subject to Senate approval, of course), or should the process be less partisan and less ideological?

The Court has been an important protector of minority rights, including in the civil rights era. This picture from 1953 shows people waiting in line at the Supreme Court to hear oral arguments in *Brown v. Board of Education*. But at other times, the Court has supported the will of the majority.

The Court's Multifaceted Role This "big picture" question about the relationship of the Court to the other branches boils down to this: Does the judiciary constrain the other branches, or does it defer to their wishes? Given the responsiveness of the elected branches to the will of the people, this question can alternatively be stated: Does the Court operate against the political majority to protect minority interests, or does it defer to the popular will? The evidence on this is mixed.

The judicial branch as a whole contains a basic paradox: it may be simultaneously seen as the least democratic and most democratic branch.[89] The least democratic part is obvious: federal judges and many state and local judges are unelected and are not accountable to the voters (except indirectly through the elected leaders who appoint them). But the judiciary can also be seen as the most democratic branch. Cases that are brought to the courts come from the people and, as long as the legal criteria for bringing a case are met, the courts must hear those cases. Although people have the right to petition "the government for a redress of grievances," there is no guarantee that Congress or the executive branch will listen to them. Of course, only a small fraction of the cases brought to the Supreme Court are heard, so the antidemocratic charge carries more weight at the top. However, the court system as a whole may be seen as providing an important outlet for participation in our political system.

Whether the Supreme Court goes against our elected leaders—that is, is the Court a countermajoritarian force in our political system?—is also a complicated question to sort out. The Court is activist on many issues, exercising judicial review, but on many other issues it defers to the elected institutions. Sometimes an activist Court defends minority interests on issues such as criminal defendants' rights, school prayer, gay rights (which initially were not supported by the majority, but are now), and flag burning, but that is not always the case. Is the Court acting undemocratically when it exercises its power of judicial review (or, as critics would say, "legislates from the bench")? Or is it playing its vital role in our constitutional system as a check on the other branches, as with some of its recent cases concerning the legal rights of enemy combatants in the War on Terror and the attempt by President Trump to end DACA?

The answers depend somewhat on one's political views. Conservatives would generally applaud the activism of the Rehnquist and Roberts Courts, while liberals would see it as an unwarranted check on the elected branches. Moreover, the Court's role has varied throughout history: in some instances, it defended unpopular views and strongly protected minority rights; in other cases, it followed majority opinion and declined to play that important role. But clearly, the Court has the *potential* to play an important policy-making role in our system of checks and balances; whether it actually plays that role depends on the political, personal, and legal factors outlined in this chapter.

The Defense of Marriage Act

After reading several of the policies discussed in different chapters, you might think that policy stages could just as accurately be called the policy cycle. In most cases, it is an ongoing process that is constantly being modified to reflect possible ways that policies can be improved. The perpetuity of the process is a reflection of the changing times and the changing perceptions held by society, or at least held by the people in office who are in a direct position to modify policies. Sometimes these include attempts to undo the original intent of the policy. The Defense of Marriage Act (DOMA), a law defining marriage to apply only to the legal union of a man and a woman, is outlined below; there does not seem to be any middle ground on what improvement means for this issue. Either heterosexual marriage is the only type that should be legal, or same-sex marriage should also be legal in the eyes of the law.

When studying most policies, students of government and politics are entering in the middle of the conversation, so to speak. DOMA is no exception. It was signed into law in 1996, but its history in many ways can be traced back to the 1960s during the civil rights movement, whose primary focus was to give equal rights to African Americans. At that time, it is fair to say that very few people were thinking about equal rights for the LGBTQ community, and very few people were thinking of the necessity of writing a law to define marriage in such a way as to exclude this community. But the civil rights movement inspired other types of minority groups to take notice that they too deserved equal rights and protection under the law. As the policy for legalizing same-sex marriage started to evolve, so too did the policy for making same-sex marriage illegal. The formulation of one policy, therefore, led another group to formulate an opposing policy. Such is the nature of politics and the dynamics of the policy-making process.

As you will also note when specifically looking at stage seven, DOMA essentially ended almost 20 years after its enactment when the Supreme Court overturned it in *Obergefell v. Hodges* (2015). This radical change/termination of the policy was an improvement for gay rights advocates of whom President Obama, a Democrat, could be counted, and those who saw this as a step backward were mostly Republicans. A lot happened in 15 years. The president who signed DOMA into law, Bill Clinton, was also a Democrat, and at different times Barack Obama, before and during his presidency, supported and also opposed DOMA. From the first legal same-sex marriage attempt in the early 1970s to the *Obergefell* case, this process has played out over 50 years. It is ironic that the very policy those who promoted DOMA were trying to prevent eventually came to pass, but this Supreme Court case is not necessarily the end of the story since future presidents, future Congresses, and future leaders will most assuredly make attempts to modify it or reverse it, just as DOMA was eventually reversed.

Policy Stages

1. Problem Recognition
   - The population was divided between those who believe that the LGBTQ community should have the right to marry and those who believe that marriages only between men and women should be legally recognized.

- Civil rights campaigning for gay rights began in earnest in the 1970s, sparked in part by the Stonewall riots in 1969, which were a reaction to a violent police raid of the Stonewall Inn, a gay bar in Greenwich Village, New York City.
- Opposition, especially among Christian leaders and their followers, grew more vocal since the 1970s.
- Since the 1970s, more and more politicians have either been outed or declared they are part of the LGBTQ community while in office, running for office, or running for reelection.
- Surveys showed that a growing number of Americans are more accepting of the LGBTQ community since the 1970s, though some of this acceptance is attributed to generational difference and does not include a steadfast, vocal opposition to discrimination based on sexual orientation.

2. Agenda Setting
   - *Richard John Baker v. Gerald R. Nelson* (1971)
     - This case involved the first gay couple to apply for a marriage license.
     - The Minnesota Supreme Court denied the legality of the union.
     - The couple appealed to the Supreme Court.
   - *Baker v. Nelson* (1972)
     - The Supreme Court dismissed the case, upholding the Minnesota decision.
     - Before the ruling was handed down, the couple's second application for a marriage was approved because of the confusion intentionally created by Baker's new, gender-neutral name, Pat Lyn McConnell.
     - The union became the first same-sex marriage in the United States, though the couple encountered decades of legal problems and challenges.
   - The AIDS epidemic, starting in 1981 with the first reported case, made the gay community more aware of inheritance and hospital visitation rights afforded to married couples but denied to them.
   - *Baehr v. Miike* (originally *Baehr v. Lewin,* 1999)
     - Although not decided outright in favor of same-sex marriage, the Hawaii Supreme Court opened the door to the possibility of same-sex marriage in a series of court cases and appeals from 1993 to 1999.
     - Groups opposed to same-sex marriage started worrying that legislation or an amendment was needed to prevent it from becoming a reality.
   - On February 28, 1994, President Clinton implemented "don't ask, don't tell," a policy regarding the right for members of the LGBTQ community to serve in the military.
     - Gay rights opponents saw this as another step toward making same-sex marriage a possibility.
   - President Obama's position on same-sex marriage evolved over the decades.
     - Illinois state senator Obama was in favor of same-sex marriage in the late 1990s.
     - Senator (and President) Obama was in favor of civil unions and certain civil rights for LGBTQ couples (such as hospital visits, inheritance, property transfer, and non-discrimination in the workplace) but did not believe that marriage is a basic civil right.

3. Deliberation and Formulation
   - A majority of states, some before and some after the passage of DOMA, made laws, enacted executive orders, or added amendments defining only heterosexual marriage as legal, or they explicitly banned same-sex marriage.
   - Those in favor of same-sex marriage said that homosexuality is natural and normal.
   - Some opponents believed homosexuality is unnatural and that children should be raised only by heterosexual parents.

- DOMA
  - It was introduced in the House of Representatives by Bob Barr (R-GA) on May 7, 1996.
  - It was introduced in the Senate by Don Nickles (R-OK) on May 8, 1996.
4. Enactment
   - The House of Representatives passed the bill on July 12, 1996: **342 YEAs:** 118 Democrats, 224 Republicans, 0 others; **67 NAYs:** 65 Democrats, 1 Republican, 1 other; **22 Not Voting:** 13 Democrats, 9 Republicans, 0 others.
   - The Senate passed the bill on September 10, 1996: **85 YEAs:** 32 Democrats, 53 Republicans, 0 others; **14 NAYs:** 14 Democrats, 0 Republicans, 0 others; **1 Not Voting:** 1 Democrat, 0 Republicans, 0 others.
   - The Defense of Marriage Act of 1996 was signed into law by President Bill Clinton on September 21, 1996.
5. Implementation
   - DOMA defined marriage as only occurring between a man and a woman.
   - Section 2 specified that the full faith and credit clause does not apply. That is, if an LGBTQ couple got married in a state where same-sex marriage is legal, this marriage would not be recognized in states where it is illegal.
   - Section 3 denied federal recognition of certain financial and legal rights connected to insurance benefits, inheritance, and tax filing, including those enjoyed by straight married couples.
6. Evaluation
   - Although President Clinton signed DOMA, he said that it was "unnecessary and divisive."[90]
   - Seeing a connection between their struggles and the fight for gay rights, the following prominent Black civil rights leaders and organizations made statements of support for same-sex marriage:
     - Coretta Scott King, widow of Martin Luther King Jr. and founder of the Martin Luther King Jr. Center for Nonviolent Social Change, in 2004
     - Richard Loving of the Supreme Court case *Loving v. Virginia* (1967), which legalized interracial marriage, in 2007
     - Julian Bond, first president of the Southern Poverty Law Center, in 2009
     - The National Association for the Advancement of Colored People (NAACP) in 2013
     - John Lewis, U.S. Representative for Georgia, in 2015
   - Obama's position continued to change.
     - As a U.S. senate candidate in 2004, he was against DOMA.
     - As a 2008 presidential candidate, Obama promised to repeal DOMA and "don't ask, don't tell."
   - President Obama said the LGBTQ community should be able to marry, but he believed the legality of same-sex marriage is up to each state to decide (allowing a proposed amendment to North Carolina's state constitution that would ban same-sex marriage to pass on May 8, 2012, for instance).
7. Possible Modifications, Expansion, or Termination of Policy
   - Some states, particularly in the Northeast and on the West Coast, began legalizing same-sex marriage.
     - Maine, Maryland, and Washington were the first states to legalize same-sex marriage starting on November 6, 2012.
   - Starting in the 1970s, some states passed laws specifically limiting marriage to heterosexual couples, but many states did this after the passage of DOMA.

- President Obama signed the Matthew Shepard (killed because of his sexual identity) and James Byrd Jr. (killed because of the color of his skin) Hate Crimes Act in 2009.
  - This act extended the coverage of hate crimes to include those related to gender identity and sexual orientation as well as color, gender, and disability.
- President Obama signed the Don't Ask, Don't Tell Repeal Act of 2010 (which did not apply to transgender military personnel) on December 22, 2010.
- The Respect for Marriage Act was introduced in several congressional terms from 2009 to 2015 as an attempt to essentially repeal DOMA.
- President Obama instructed the Justice Department to stop defending DOMA in February 2011.
- President Obama changed his position again and announced his support for gay marriage in 2012, moving up the date of his announcement due to Vice President Joe Biden's own announcement supporting gay marriage.
- *United States v. Windsor* (2013)
  - This case struck down Section 3 of DOMA, which denied federal recognition for certain legal benefits connected to marriage between a man and a woman.
- *Hollingsworth v. Perry* (2013)
  - This case legalized same-sex marriage in California.
- *Obergefell v. Hodges* (2015)
  - A 5-4 vote overturned DOMA.
  - Same-sex marriage was deemed a basic civil right.

Questions for Discussion

1. President Obama changed his mind regarding same-sex marriage and was criticized for doing so. Do you think it is fair to voters if they elect officials who change their mind about major issues after they are in office?
2. How do proponents and opponents of same-sex marriage support their respective positions?
3. Why was it important to get civil rights leaders to support same-sex marriage? How might this support have played a role in changing people's minds about this issue?

Unpacking the Conflict

Considering all that we've discussed in this chapter, let's apply what we know about how the courts work to the events introduced at the beginning of this chapter: Justice Ginsburg's comments about Donald Trump during the 2016 presidential campaign and Chief Justice Roberts's defense of the independence of the courts in rebutting Trump's complaint about an "Obama judge." Did Justice Ginsburg overstep her boundaries with her remarks on Donald Trump, or was it appropriate for her to express her opinions? Was Justice Roberts overreacting to Trump's comments about political judges? What is the proper place of the courts within our political system? Should judges attempt to neutrally apply the law, or should their political views play a role?

The chapter-opening examples demonstrate that we often have a difficult time coming to grips with the political nature of the Supreme Court and prefer the comforting image of the neutral and fair Lady Justice: that is why there was such a strong reaction to Justice Ginsburg's comments about Trump. We *want* our courts to be politically neutral, but the reality is very different.

Politics is indeed everywhere, even in the courts, where you would least expect to see it. Politics affects everything from the selection of judges to the decisions they make. Some characteristics of the federal courts (the most important of which is judges' lifetime tenure) insulate the system from politics. However, courts are subject to influence by judges' ideologies, interest groups, and the president and Senate, who try to shape the courts' composition through the nomination process.

While many recoil from a politicized Court, we also value its independence and don't want the president and Congress stepping on its toes. Thus, if the federal courts are allowed to play their proper role, they can serve as a referee between the other branches of government, and between the national and state governments, by defining the boundaries of permissible conduct.

The courts demonstrate that politics is conflictual. And many conflicts demonstrate that the courts are political. Although plenty of unanimous Supreme Court decisions do not involve much conflict among the justices, many landmark cases deeply divide the Court on constitutional interpretation and how to balance those competing interpretations against other values and interests. These conflicts in the Court often reveal deeper fault lines in the broader political system.

"What's Your Take?"

What should the proper place of the courts be in our political system?

How much influence should the executive and legislative branches have over the courts, and vice versa?

AP® STUDY GUIDE

Summary

In *Federalist 78*, Hamilton argued that the judiciary is designed to be the weakest of the three branches of government. Article III of the Constitution offers few specifics on the organization of the judiciary, in contrast to other branches of government. In fact, most of the details on the arrangement of the judiciary do not come from the Constitution at all, but from congressional action. In addition, the Supreme Court's strongest power—judicial review—is not even mentioned in the Constitution but was established in the *Marbury v. Madison* decision.

Federalist 78
A foundational document written by Alexander Hamilton in 1788 and titled *The Judiciary Department*.

All courts within the United States have a similar set of fundamental attributes, such as the distinction between civil and criminal cases and the reliance on legal precedent. The judicial system is divided between state and federal courts, and within each level of government there are courts of original jurisdiction and appeals courts.

The Supreme Court hears only about 1 percent of the cases that are brought to it. To help decide which cases to hear, the Court generally uses three factors: collusion, standing, and mootness. Ultimately, the justices have a great deal of discretion in deciding to hear a case, but they can hear only cases that come to them.

When hearing a case, the justices prepare by reading briefs before they hear the oral arguments. After oral arguments, the justices meet in conference to discuss and vote on the cases. The majority opinion explains the rationale for how a decision is reached, although justices can also write dissenting and concurring opinions.

The Court makes decisions based on legal factors such as precedent and informal norms, and political factors such as the justices' own ideologies and positions on the role that the Court plays in government. The Court's power can be restricted by congressional legislation, the appointment and confirmation process, or the president's ignoring a decision. Although the Court does not consider public opinion the way elected officials do, most decisions generally stay in step with the views of the public.

Key Terms

amicus curiae (p. 246)

appeals courts (p. 236)

appellate jurisdiction (p. 227)

attitudinalist approach (p. 253)

Brown v. Board of Education (p. 376)

cert pool (p. 245)

Citizens United v. Federal Election Commission (p. 246)

class-action lawsuit (p. 232)

common law (p. 232)

concurring opinion (p. 249)

constitutional interpretation (p. 230)

defendant (p. 231)

dissenting opinion (p. 249)

district courts (p. 227)

Federalist 78 (p. 267)

judicial activism (p. 255)

judicial restraint (p. 255)

judicial review (p. 228)

Judiciary Act of 1789 (p. 227)

jurisdiction (p. 233)

living Constitution (p. 252)

majority opinion (p. 249)

mootness (p. 244)

oral arguments (p. 247)

original intent (p. 252)

original jurisdiction (p. 227)

plaintiff (p. 231)

plea bargains and settlement agreements (p. 231)

precedent (p. 232)

Roe v. Wade (p. 355)

senatorial courtesy (p. 240)

solicitor general (p. 246)

standing (p. 233)

statutory interpretation (p. 230)

strict construction (p. 251)

Tinker v. Des Moines Independent Community School District (p. 333)

writ of *certiorari* (p. 243)

Enduring Understanding

CON-5: "The design of the judicial branch protects the Supreme Court's independence as a branch of government, and the emergence and use of judicial review remains a powerful judicial practice." (AP® U.S. Government and Politics Course and Exam Description)

Multiple-Choice Questions (Arranged by Topic)

Topic 2.8: The Judicial Branch (CON-5)

Questions 1–2 refer to the excerpt.

This simple view of the matter suggests several important consequences. It proves incontestably that the judiciary is beyond comparison the weakest of the three departments of power; that it can never attack with success either of the other two; and that all possible care is requisite to enable it to defend itself against their attacks. It equally proves that though individual oppression may now and then proceed from the courts of justice, the general liberty of the people can never be endangered from that quarter: I mean, so long as the judiciary remains truly distinct from both the legislative and executive. For I agree that "there is no liberty if the power of judging be not separated from the legislative and executive powers." And it proves, in the last place, that as liberty can have nothing to fear from the judiciary alone, but would have everything to fear from its union with either of the other departments; that as all the effects of such a union must ensue from a dependence of the former on the latter, notwithstanding a nominal and apparent separation; that as, from the natural feebleness of the judiciary, it is in continual jeopardy of being overpowered, awed or influenced by its coordinate branches; and that as nothing can contribute so much to its firmness and independence as permanency in office, this quality may therefore be justly regarded as an indispensable ingredient in its constitution, and in a great measure as the citadel of the public justice and the public security.

The complete independence of the courts of justice is peculiarly essential in a limited Constitution. By a limited Constitution, I understand one which contains certain specified exceptions to the legislative authority; such, for instance, as that it shall pass no bills of attainder, no ex post facto laws, and the like. Limitations of this kind can be preserved in practice no other way than through the medium of the courts of justice, whose duty it must be to declare all acts contrary to the manifest tenor of the Constitution void. Without this, all the reservations of particular rights or privileges would amount to nothing.

—Alexander Hamilton, *Federalist 78*, May 28, 1788

1. **Which of the following best describes Hamilton's point of view in the excerpt?**
   - **(A)** Federal judges should be directly elected to prevent undue influence from the other branches of government.
   - **(B)** As one of three coequal branches, the judicial branch will not be overpowered by the other two.
   - **(C)** If the judicial branch creates a union with either of the other departments, individual liberty will be protected.
   - **(D)** Since the judicial branch is the weakest of the three branches, it will not endanger individual liberty.

2. **Which of the following arguments, made by Hamilton, best relates to the Supreme Court's decision in *Marbury v. Madison* (1803)?**
   - **(A)** "...the courts of justice, whose duty it must be to declare all acts contrary to the manifest tenor of the Constitution void."
   - **(B)** "It proves incontestably that the judiciary is beyond comparison the weakest of the three departments of power ...."
   - **(C)** "By a limited Constitution, I understand one which contains certain specified exceptions to the legislative authority ..., as that it shall pass no bills of attainder ...."
   - **(D)** "The complete independence of the courts of justice is peculiarly essential in a limited Constitution."

3. **Which of the following best describes how the majority of federal courts were created?**

   (A) They were outlined in the Constitution.

   (B) They were created from congressional legislation.

   (C) They were established by an executive order.

   (D) They are a by-product of the courts themselves.

4. **Which of the following best explains why the Founders gave federal judges the term of "good behavior"?**

   (A) to insulate the Supreme Court from politics

   (B) to hold the Supreme Court accountable to the public through regular elections

   (C) to provide a check against the appointment power of the Senate

   (D) to prevent Supreme Court justices from being impeached

Topic 2.9: Legitimacy of the Judicial Branch (CON-5)

5. **Which of the following scenarios best describes the doctrine of stare decisis?**

   (A) the overruling of the decision in *Plessy v. Ferguson* (1896) with the decision in *Brown v. Board of Education* (1954)

   (B) the Court's refusal to hear a case about a public school's requirement to pledge allegiance to the flag because the petitioner did not have standing

   (C) the shift in the Court from making decisions based on the judicial philosophy of judicial restraint to that of judicial activism

   (D) the Court deciding a case using a precedent that was established when the same legal issue was in question

Questions 6–7 refer to the graphs.

The Court's Workload

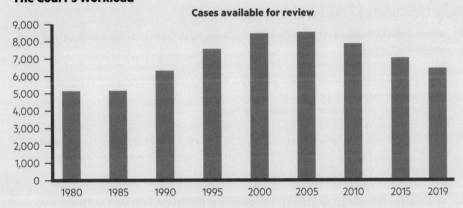

Cases available for review

Cases argued before the Court

Source: Data compiled from John Roberts, "2019 Year-End Reports on the Federal Judiciary," U.S. Supreme Court, December 31, 2019, www.supremecourt. gov/publicinfo/year-end/2019year-endreport.pdf (accessed 3/21/20).

6. **Which of the following best describes a trend in the graphs?**

   (A) The Supreme Court is both receiving more cases and hearing more cases.

   (B) The Supreme Court is receiving more cases but hearing fewer of them.

   (C) In 1985, the Supreme Court had over 5,000 cases for review, but fewer than 180 were argued before the Court.

   (D) In 2000, the Supreme Court received the lowest number of cases and heard the lowest number of cases.

7. **Which of the following is an implication of the trend in the graphs?**

   (A) Since the Supreme Court is required to hear all cases, the justices will need to increase the number of hours they work.

   (B) The majority of cases argued before the Supreme Court are those with original jurisdiction, so the Court will need to move those cases to the next term.

   (C) Cases the Supreme Court doesn't hear will be retried in state courts.

   (D) Conflicting decisions made by district and circuit courts are left unsettled.

Topic 2.10: The Court in Action (CON-5)

8. **Which of the following best explains how the legitimacy of the Supreme Court can come into question?**

   (A) when the Court practices stare decisis when hearing a controversial case

   (B) when the Senate appoints a conservative justice to replace a liberal justice due to a controversial ruling

   (C) when the Court makes a controversial decision that the president refuses to implement

   (D) when the president proposes an amendment to try to overturn a controversial decision

Topic 2.11: Checks on the Judicial Branch (CON-5)

9. **Which of the following best describes the fundamental difference between judicial activism and judicial restraint?**

   (A) Judicial activism aligns exclusively with liberal justices and judicial restraint aligns exclusively with conservative justices.

   (B) Judicial activism is the role played by the majority opinion writer and judicial restraint is the role played by the dissenting opinion writer.

   (C) Judicial activism advocates that the Court should assert its interpretation of the law and judicial restraint believes the Court should defer to the elected branches of government.

   (D) Judicial activism actively pursues cases that have been heard at the state level and judicial restraint focuses on cases of original jurisdiction.

10. **Which of the following is an accurate comparison of the executive branch and legislative branch checks on the Supreme Court?**

	Executive Checks	Legislative Checks
(A)	ignoring Supreme Court decisions	confirming judicial appointments
(B)	making judicial appointments	refusing to enforce a ruling
(C)	proposing a constitutional amendment to circumvent a ruling	passing legislation to modify the impact of a decision
(D)	passing legislation impacting the Court's jurisdiction	ratifying a constitutional amendment to circumvent a ruling

Free-Response Questions

SCOTUS Comparison

This question requires you to compare a Supreme Court case you studied in class with one you have not studied in class. A summary of the Supreme Court case you did not study in class is presented below and provides all of the information you need to know about this case to answer the prompt.

In 2006, Congress passed the Adam Walsh Child Protection and Safety Act in an effort to keep dangerous sexual predators off the street following the completion of their federal prison sentences. A provision in this law gives the Department of Justice the authority to detain a mentally ill, sexually dangerous federal prisoner beyond the date the prisoner would be otherwise released. An extensive process determines which federal prisoners should be a part of the civil commitment program following the end of their sentences. Four men who were confined two years past the end of their federal prison sentences challenged this law. They claimed that their constitutional rights were violated based on the grounds of double jeopardy, the ex post facto clause, and the Sixth and Eighth Amendments.

In the ensuing case, *United States v. Comstock* (2010), the Supreme Court ruled in a 7–2 decision that Congress could expand its authority to enact the Adam Walsh Child Protection and Safety Act provision that allowed for the continued confinement of prisoners that the Department of Justice found "sexually dangerous." The Court recognized that Congress had good reason to pass the statute as it has the power to protect nearby communities from dangerous prisoners.[a]

Based on the information above, respond to the following questions.

(A) Identify the constitutional principle that is common in both *United States v. Comstock* (2010) and *Marbury v. Madison* (1803).

(B) Based on the constitutional principle identified in Part A, explain how the facts in *Marbury v. Madison* led to a different holding than in *United States v. Comstock*.

(C) Explain how the decision in *United States v. Comstock* could affect the balance between liberty and order.

Argument Essay

Develop an argument that explains if a Supreme Court justice should take the role of judicial activism or judicial restraint when deciding a case.

Use at least one piece of evidence from one of the following foundational documents:

- Article I of the U.S. Constitution
- Article V of the U.S. Constitution
- *Federalist 78*

In your response, you should do the following:

✓ Respond to the prompt with a defensible claim or thesis that establishes a line of reasoning.

✓ Support your claim with at least two pieces of specific and relevant evidence.

- One piece of evidence must come from one of the foundational documents listed above.
- A second piece of evidence can come from any other foundational document not used as your first piece of evidence, or it may be from your knowledge of course concepts.

✓ Use reasoning to explain why your evidence supports your claim or thesis.

✓ Respond to an opposing or alternative perspective using refutation, concession, or rebuttal.

7
The Bureaucracy
What's with all this red tape?

 "Government! Three-fourths parasitic and the rest stupid fumbling."[1]
Robert A. Heinlein, American writer

 "Bureaucracy is not an obstacle to democracy but an inevitable complement to it."[2]
Joseph A. Schumpeter, American economist

Throughout the COVID-19 pandemic, one of the most important pieces of information was the number of people who died each day from the disease. Death statistics captured not only changes in how many people were suffering from the virus but also our success at treating these cases. At the same time, death statistics were politically significant, as they were a visible indicator of the government's effectiveness at dealing with the pandemic. Particularly in the earliest-affected states, sharp increases in the number of daily COVID-related deaths highlighted gaps in state and local government preparedness, including a lack of protective equipment and other medical supplies, a reluctance to impose lockdown measures, and an overall unwillingness to take the problem seriously.

The political significance of death statistics was one reason for an ongoing debate within the federal government over measuring COVID-related deaths. For example, if a patient with a compromised immune system caught the virus and died, was the death due to COVID-19 or the underlying condition that increased that person's vulnerability? Scientists at the federal Centers for Disease Control and Prevention wanted to ignore underlying conditions, while members of President Trump's staff favored excluding cases from the pandemic's mortality statistics if an underlying condition could be identified.

This example highlights three essential features of the federal bureaucracy. First, bureaucrats are often engaged in highly technical tasks that require expertise and judgment. Second, these tasks have political consequences—for President Trump, a reduction in death statistics would have helped him argue during the 2020 election campaign that his administration had responded effectively to the pandemic. Third, while Trump wields considerable power as president, he cannot simply order bureaucrats to do whatever he wants. Throughout his time as president, Trump described the bureaucracy as a more or less autonomous "deep state," raising the question of whether bureaucratic actions reflect expertise or a political agenda (in this case, opposition to Trump's reelection).

In the midst of the coronavirus outbreak, the White House Coronavirus Task Force held daily television briefings to disseminate information to the public. Here, Dr. Anthony Fauci, director of the National Institute of Allergy and Infectious Diseases, can be seen placing his hand over his face in dismay as President Trump makes a comment about "deep state" conspiracies during a briefing, demonstrating the often-contentious relationship between President Trump and the federal bureaucracy.

CHAPTER GOALS

Define *bureaucracy* and explain its major functions. pages 274–283

Trace the expansion of the federal bureaucracy over time. pages 284–287

Describe the size and structure of the executive branch today. pages 288–294

Describe who bureaucrats are and the regulations that govern their employment. pages 294–297

Explain how Congress and the president oversee the executive branch. pages 297–303

Up to now, we've described the policy-making process in terms of three steps: (1) citizens elect representatives, (2) these representatives go to Washington and enact laws, and (3) bureaucrats are given these laws to implement. The reality in our system is that the responsibility for implementing laws conveys policy-making power. When bureaucrats write regulations, sign contracts with private corporations, deliver services to citizens, or make judgments about how to measure things like deaths due to COVID-19, they are translating often-vague statutes into concrete decisions. Moreover, because of their training and experience, bureaucrats are often better informed than elected officials about the details of government policy. Bureaucratic expertise creates a new problem for elected officials: if they ignore what bureaucrats tell them or force bureaucrats to implement laws and directives as written, the result may be policy failures. However, if elected officials acknowledge that bureaucrats are experts and allow them to make as well as implement government policy, elected officials in effect give up all their power to the bureaucracy—something that the Trump administration was unwilling to risk. Were bureaucrats really obstructing the Trump agenda, or were they just doing their jobs? How do elected officials control a bureaucracy of experts, in the midst of a pandemic or in more routine times?

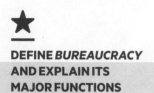

DEFINE *BUREAUCRACY* AND EXPLAIN ITS MAJOR FUNCTIONS

bureaucracy
The system of civil servants and political appointees who implement congressional or presidential decisions; also known as the *administrative state*.

civil servants
Employees of bureaucratic agencies within the government.

political appointees
People selected by an elected leader, such as the president, to hold a government position.

What is the federal bureaucracy?

The federal **bureaucracy** is the vast network of agencies that makes up the government's executive branch. It is composed of millions of **civil servants**, who work for the government in permanent positions, and thousands of **political appointees**, who hold short-term, usually senior positions and are appointed by an elected leader such as the president. Another name for the bureaucracy is the *administrative state*, which refers to the role bureaucrats play in administering government policies.[3] Most constitutional scholars agree that the president is nominally in charge of the bureaucracy—although generally the president shares this power with members of Congress.

In general, the job of the federal bureaucracy includes a wide range of tasks, from regulating the behavior of individuals and corporations to buying pencils, jet fighters, vaccines, and everything in between. At one level, these actions implement policy decisions made by others, including presidential directives or legislation enacted by Congress. But as we will see, implementation often involves giving bureaucrats considerable discretion over the details of policy decisions. Moreover, these activities are inherently political and often conflictual: ordinary citizens, elected officials, and bureaucrats themselves often disagree about aspects of these activities, and they work to influence bureaucratic actions to suit their policy goals.

What do bureaucrats do?

The task of the bureaucracy is to develop and implement policies established by congressional acts or presidential decisions. Sometimes the tasks associated with putting these laws and resolutions into effect are very specific. For example, in the appropriations bill for fiscal year 2020, Congress mandated that the navy purchase 98 F-35 attack jets from defense contractor Lockheed Martin. This provision required no discretion on the part of the bureaucrats tasked to implement it—all they needed to do was sign the contract, make sure the jets were delivered, and pay Lockheed Martin.

More commonly, however, legislation provides only general guidelines for meeting governmental goals. Bureaucrats thus have considerable latitude to develop particular policies and programs. For example, the 1938 Federal Food, Drug, and Cosmetic Act gave the Food and Drug Administration (FDA) the job of determining which drugs are safe and effective (including drugs to treat COVID-19 symptoms and vaccines to prevent people from getting the disease), but it allowed FDA bureaucrats to develop their own procedures for making these determinations.[4] Currently, the FDA requires that drug manufacturers first test new drugs for safety and then conduct further trials to determine their effectiveness. An FDA advisory board of scientists and doctors reviews the results of these tests, and FDA bureaucrats decide whether to allow the manufacturer to market the drug. While members of Congress and the president created this procedure, they have no way to intervene in the process except by enacting a new bill that makes an exception to the FDA's normal procedures or revamps these procedures entirely.

Developing Regulations A regulation is a rule that allows the government to exercise control over individuals and corporations by allowing or prohibiting behavior, setting out the conditions under which certain behaviors can occur, or assessing costs or granting benefits based on behavior. Bureaucrats gain the authority to write regulations from acts passed by Congress, either through the statute that initially set up their agency or through subsequent laws. For example, the Environmental Protection Agency (EPA) has many regulations that limit the amount of various pollutants that can be emitted from factories, automobiles, and electrical power plants. The EPA's authority to develop these regulations, as well as limits on other power plant emissions, comes from the Clean Air Act legislation of 1970 as well as subsequent reauthorizations (newer versions) of this legislation (for more details, see How It Works: Legislation).

Regulations are developed according to the **notice-and-comment procedure**.[5] Before most proposed regulations can take effect, they are published in the *Federal Register*, an official journal that includes rules, proposed rules, and other types of government documents. Individuals and companies potentially affected by the regulation can then comment, or respond to the agency that proposed it, either supporting or opposing the regulation or offering different versions for consideration.

regulation
A rule that allows the government to exercise control over individuals and corporations by restricting certain behaviors.

notice-and-comment procedure
A step in the rule-making process in which proposed rules are published in the *Federal Register* and made available for debate by the general public.

Although the term "bureaucracy" may suggest workers shuffling papers in cubicles, the agencies of the federal bureaucracy perform a wide range of tasks. The Centers for Disease Control and Prevention—a federal agency—contributed in many ways during the coronavirus pandemic in 2020, including tracking the spread of the virus, launching campaigns to educate people on how to protect themselves from the virus, and helping distribute lifesaving equipment to affected areas.

Bureaucracy and Legislation

After Congress passes legislation and the president signs it, the transition from legislation to regulation begins. Input from local government officials, interest groups, and others helps to refine the regulations as they are developed, and has a strong influence on how regulations will affect people "on the ground."

Congress passes legislation.

The president signs the bill into law.

Bureaucrats interpret the law and design appropriate regulations.

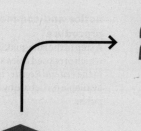

Courts respond to challenges to the law, and they can provide guidelines for implementation.

Other bureaucrats disseminate regulations to state and local governments, corporations, and individuals, and they monitor compliance.

Citizens and interest groups provide information and proposals to bureaucrats, and they lobby for their preferred implementation of the legislation.

Regulations can be revised in light of changing circumstances, different political climates, or unanticipated consequences.

Regulating Greenhouse Gas Emissions

In November 2017, the Trump administration announced a plan to repeal and replace the Environmental Protection Agency (EPA)'s Clean Power Plan regulations that limited CO_2 emissions from fossil fuel power plants, and in May 2019 announced further plans to issue new regulations dealing with CO_2 emissions. These actions were some of the latest steps in a 20-year process of court cases, presidential directives, and actions by EPA bureaucrats.

New Acts!

Congressional Action: Congress enacts two Clean Air Acts, in 1963 and 1970 respectively, with amendments in 1977 and 1990, authorizing the government to monitor and limit emissions of harmful chemicals into the atmosphere.

Although... maybe not?

Bureaucratic Action (2003): The EPA announces that the **Clean Air Act does not give it the authority to regulate CO_2** and other greenhouse gases.

Actually... yes.

Judicial Action (2007): In response to a case brought by 12 states, the Supreme Court rules that **greenhouse gases are covered by the Clean Air Act**.

Obama weighs in.

Presidential Directive (June 2013): President Obama **directs the EPA to develop additional regulations** for limiting CO_2 emissions from new and existing power plants.

Results?

September 2013: The EPA modifies its draft regulations to place **CO_2 standards** on new power plants and issues a revised proposal.

June 2014: The EPA proposes an additional rule that aims to **cut CO_2 emissions from existing power plants**.

Third try!

New Regulations Finalized (August 2015): After receiving over 6 million comments, the EPA **announces its Clean Power Plan**, which will regulate CO_2 emissions from both new and existing power plants.

Stand by.

February 2016: The Supreme Court **puts implementation of the Clean Power Plan for existing plants on hold**, pending litigation. Moreover, these regulations are subject to change by the Trump administration.

Up in the air?

November 2017: Under the Trump administration, **the EPA announces a plan to repeal and replace the Clean Power Plan**.

More to come.

May 2019: Following President Trump's directive, **the EPA announces plans to issue a new set of regulations** dealing with CO_2 emissions, beginning the entire process over again.

? Critical Thinking

1. **Critics of the regulatory process complain that unelected** bureaucrats make most of the decisions while elected officials sit on the sidelines. Is this complaint supported by the case of the Clean Power Plan?

2. **The Clean Power Plan illustrates how acts of legislation are often** reinterpreted years after their passage. Why don't members of Congress write legislation in ways that prevent this from happening?

They can also appeal to members of Congress or to the president's staff for help in lobbying bureaucrats to revise the proposal. The agency then issues a final regulation that incorporates changes based on the comments. This final regulation is also published in the *Federal Register* and then put into effect. The process is time-consuming. For example, an ongoing effort of the Federal Aviation Administration (FAA) to develop regulations on the use of drone aircraft began with a congressional mandate issued in 2012. Current regulations limit the size and weight of drones that can be flown without registering with the agency, but the FAA is still developing rules to govern larger package-delivery drones that must fly over populated areas. Many regulations can take even longer to craft from beginning to end.

This process of devising or modifying regulations is often political. Members of Congress and the president usually have strong opinions about how new regulations should look—and even when they don't, they may still get involved on behalf of a constituent or an interest group. Bureaucrats take account of these pressures from elected officials for two reasons: (1) the bureaucrats' policy-making power may derive from a statute that members of Congress could overturn; and (2) bureaucrats need congressional support to get larger budgets and to expand their agency's mission. Thus, despite bureaucrats' power to develop and implement policies, their agencies' budgets, appointed leaders, and overall missions are subject to elected officials' oversight.

Many regulations are issued each year. In 2019, the *Federal Register* had more than 70,000 pages containing thousands of new regulations.[6] Although nearly all government agencies issue regulations, most come from a few agencies, including the Federal Trade Commission (FTC), which regulates commerce; the Federal Communications Commission (FCC), which regulates media companies that create content as well as telecommunications companies that transmit information; and the Food and Drug Administration (FDA), which regulates drugs, medical products, food, and cosmetics.

Federal regulations affect most aspects of everyday life. They influence the gas mileage of cars sold in the United States, the materials used to build roads, and the

Federal regulations influence many aspects of everyday life that would seem unlikely to be affected by government actions. The increase in the number of women's intercollegiate athletic teams is partly due to regulations that require equal funding for men's and women's teams. Pictured here is Baylor University's 2019 NCAA women's basketball championship team.

price of gasoline. They determine the amounts that doctors can charge senior citizens for medical procedures; the hours that medical residents can work; the criteria used to determine who gets a heart, lung, or kidney transplant; and the allowable emissions from power plants. Regulations set the eligibility criteria for student loans, limit how the military can recruit on college campuses, determine who can get a home mortgage and what the interest rate will be, and describe what constitutes equal funding for men's and women's college sports teams. Regulations also shape contribution limits and spending decisions in political campaigns.

Regulations are often controversial because they involve trade-offs between incompatible goals, as well as decisions made under uncertain circumstances. For example, the regulations that guide the FDA drug-approval process prioritize the goal of preventing harmful drugs from coming to market.[7] As a result, patients sometimes cannot get access to experimental treatments because FDA approval has not been granted, even when those treatments are the patients' only remaining option.[8] Advocates for patients have argued that people with dire prognoses should be allowed to use these treatments as a potentially lifesaving last resort.[9] However, current FDA regulations prevent patients from doing so except under very special circumstances. In the case of COVID-19, exceptions were made for the drugs hydroxychloroquine and remdesivir, both of which had been tested for safety and approved for treatment of other diseases. However, follow-up studies found that hydroxychloroquine did not improve survival rates and also caused severe side effects for some patients, illustrating the risks associated with bypassing the FDA review process.

President Trump campaigned in 2016, and again in his reelection campaign in 2020, on a platform of reducing government regulations, and he issued many directives to bureaucrats to reduce the number and scope of regulations. You may wonder if the number of regulations was, in fact, reduced during the Trump administration. The short answer is no. Though federal agencies issued fewer new regulations during the Trump administration, much of this decline can be attributed to the delay or cancellation of proposed rules that Trump inherited from the Obama administration. In 2017, Republican majorities in Congress also took advantage of a law that allows the House and Senate to repeal regulations issued during the last months of a presidential term. However, Trump had only limited success in eliminating regulations that were already in force when he entered office. The problem is that once regulations are in place, changing or repealing them is a lengthy process that often requires Congress to pass new laws. For example, while Trump and his appointees at the EPA proposed repealing some environmental regulations, the process can take several years and can be delayed further or even stopped by court challenges. Thus, while reducing the number of government regulations was one of the central promises of Trump's campaign, his administration made very little progress toward this goal.

Bringing Expertise to Policy Making Bureaucrats are also an important source of new government policies. For example, Congress and the president give civilian and military personnel in the Department of Defense the job of revising military doctrines—broad directives on how our armed forces should go about accomplishing specific tasks such as protecting civilian freighters from attacks by Somali pirates, deploying troops to rescue American civilians in hostile territory, or running military training operations in Africa. While military doctrines reflect input from members of Congress, the State Department and the president's appointees, and groups outside government (including lobbyists, think tanks, and defense contractors), they also reflect the preferences of the bureaucrats assigned to the task. Thus, as in the case of regulations, when it comes to government policy, bureaucrats are not just implementers: they have a significant influence on what government does and does not do.

The nine most terrifying words in the English language are: I'm from the government, and I'm here to help.

—President Ronald Reagan

Delivering Services Some bureaucrats are the face of the federal government, interacting directly with citizens to provide services and other benefits. People working in the Department of Agriculture assist farmers by processing crop loans and providing advice on new technologies and techniques. Members of the Park Service operate the network of national parks and wilderness areas. And the Transportation Security Administration staffs the security checkpoints at American airports. These and other jobs are a reminder of how intertwined the federal government is with the lives of ordinary Americans. We may like to think of the federal government as something that exists only in Washington, D.C., but the reality is that bureaucrats are spread out across the country and are deeply involved with all elements of American society.

Bureaucratic expertise and its consequences

Bureaucrats are experts. Even compared with most members of Congress or presidential appointees, the average bureaucrat is a specialist in a certain policy area (often holding an advanced degree), with a good grasp of his or her agency's mission. For example, people who hold scientific or management positions in the FDA usually know more about the benefits and risks of new drugs than people outside the agency do. Their decision to deny unapproved drugs to seriously ill patients may seem cruel, but it may also reflect a thoughtful balancing of two incompatible goals: preventing harmful drugs from reaching the market and allowing people who have exhausted all other treatments access to risky, experimental products. A bureaucracy of experts is an important part of what political scientists call state capacity—the knowledge, personnel, and institutions needed to effectively implement policies.[10] It is an important check on elected officials, helping to ensure that government policies are effective and efficient.

While having an expert bureaucracy seems like an obvious good idea, it creates a new problem for elected officials. Bureaucrats can bring expertise to their policy choices only if elected officials stop ordering bureaucrats around and instead allow them to act as they think best. But when elected officials allow such discretion, they risk losing control over the policy-making process and having to live with policy choices that serve bureaucratic interests without satisfying the elected officials or their constituents.

The Problem of Control: Principals and Agents Political scientists refer to the difficulty that elected officials and their staff face when they try to interpret or influence bureaucratic actions as the problem of control.[11] A classic illustration of this situation is the principal–agent game. The principal–agent game describes an interaction in which an individual or a group (an "agent") acts on behalf of another (the "principal"). In the federal government, the president and Congress are principals and bureaucrats are agents. An agent in the bureaucracy may not want to work (because he or she is lazy) or may prefer outcomes that the principal does not like. Moreover, because the agent is an expert at the task he or she has been given, he or she has additional knowledge and experience that is inaccessible to the principal. The conundrum for the principal, then, is this: giving the agent very specific orders prevents the agent from acting based on expertise, but if the principal gives the agent the freedom to make decisions based on expertise, the principal has less control over the agent's actions.

For example, suppose Congress and the president directed the FDA to shorten its drug-approval process to approve new drugs or vaccines to fight COVID-19. FDA officials might have mandated a lengthy process based on their expert assessment of the best way to screen out harmful drugs. By giving orders that superseded the FDA officials' screening process, elected officials would be sacrificing the valuable

state capacity
The knowledge, personnel, and institutions that the government requires to effectively implement policies.

problem of control
A difficulty faced by elected officials in ensuring that when bureaucrats implement policies they follow these officials' intentions but still have enough discretion to use their expertise.

principal–agent game
The interaction between a principal (such as the president or Congress), who needs something done, and an agent (such as a bureaucrat), who is responsible for carrying out the principal's orders.

bureaucratic expertise behind the policy and risking the hasty approval of unsafe drugs. On the other hand, if Congress and the president allowed FDA bureaucrats to devise their own procedures and regulations, there would be a chance that the FDA could use this freedom to pursue goals that have nothing to do with drug safety. For example, critics of the FDA's procedures have asserted that a drawn-out approval process is designed to favor large companies that already have drugs on the market over smaller companies trying to get approval for drugs that would compete with existing products.

The principal–agent game can also be framed in terms of citizens. Figure 7.1 shows that a majority of survey respondents agreed that the federal government is typically inefficient and wasteful—although the percentage agreeing with this assessment declined from its peak in 1994 until more recent years, when it again increased. Such opinions give citizens a strong motivation to demand that elected officials control the bureaucracy—to reduce the waste and inefficiency or, as the earlier quote from Ronald Reagan suggests, to prevent bureaucrats from overly intruding into American society.

Members of Congress and citizens are sometimes right to question the motives of members of the bureaucracy. Sometimes bureaucratic actions are the result of **regulatory capture**, which occurs when bureaucrats cater to a small group of individuals or corporations, regardless of the impact of these actions on public welfare. For example, until very recently the FCC allowed telecommunications companies to charge very high rates for phone calls made by individuals in federal prisons to their families, friends, or legal counsel. The companies have long argued to the FCC that these rates were justified by the cost of special hardware needed to monitor prison calls—but no one was lobbying the FCC in favor of federal prisoners, who have no alternative but to pay what the companies charge.[12] One mechanism for capture occurs

regulatory capture
A situation in which bureaucrats favor the interests of the groups or corporations they are supposed to regulate at the expense of the general public.

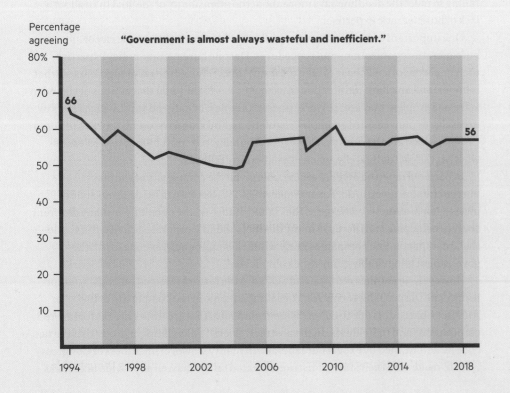

Percentage agreeing

"Government is almost always wasteful and inefficient."

FIGURE 7.1

How Americans View the Federal Bureaucracy

Many Americans believe the bureaucracy is wasteful and inefficient. Note, however, that the magnitude of negative feelings varies over time. Consider the time frame represented in the graph. What happened during these years that might explain the changes in citizens' opinions about the government?

Source: Pew Research Center, "In a Politically Polarized Era, Sharp Divides in Both Partisan Coalitions," December 17, 2019, www.pewresearch.org/politics/2019/12/17/views-of-government-and-the-nation/ (accessed 5/20/20).

During the coronavirus pandemic, government was divided on the best way to get the country back to work and reopen the economy after the shutdown. John Howard, MD, the director of the National Institute for Occupational Safety and Health, testified on how to protect workers from COVID-19 at a U.S. House Committee on Education and Labor Subcommittee on Workforce Protections hearing.

red tape
Excessive or unnecessarily complex regulations imposed by the bureaucracy.

standard operating procedures (SOPs)
Rules that lower-level bureaucrats must follow when implementing policies.

when short-term political appointees come from (and will return to) the very industries they are supposed to regulate, a phenomena known as the revolving door (as discussed in Chapter 12). For example, in 2019 an appointee in the Department of the Interior who had pushed for expanded oil drilling in Alaska left the government to work for one of the companies that would benefit from this expansion.[13]

You might think that the problem of control isn't too difficult to solve as long as bureaucrats act as impartial experts and set aside their own policy goals. Many studies of bureaucracies, beginning with the work of the early political theorist Max Weber, argue that bureaucrats should provide information and expertise and avoid taking sides on policy questions or being swayed by elected officials, people outside government, or their own policy goals.[14] However, bureaucrats' behavior doesn't always fit Weber's vision. Many enter the bureaucracy with their own ideas about what government should do, and they make decisions in line with those goals. For example, during the coronavirus pandemic, scientists in the federal Centers for Disease Control and Prevention (CDC) were forced to change their guidelines for reopening the country in response to comments from senior political appointees, who believed that a more rapid reopening would minimize economic damage. In the end, our system places experts in positions of power, but the ultimate power is in the hands of elected officials and their appointees. Thus, even if bureaucrats wanted to remain completely dispassionate, they would still face a government in which many other people with their own policy goals would attempt to influence their behavior.[15] And of course, the fact is that bureaucrats have their own ideas of what government should be doing. In the case of COVID-19, the CDC scientists' initial guidelines may have reflected their personal feelings (which are no better than anyone else's) about what the right trade-off was between economic harm and deaths from the pandemic.

Even expert bureaucrats have their limits. The federal government often takes on problems that have no known solution—and may be unsolvable.[16] For example, the National Aeronautics and Space Administration (NASA) is currently tasked with landing American astronauts on the moon by the end of 2024 but has not been given significant additional resources to accomplish this goal. Under these conditions, failing to meet the deadline says more about the infeasibility of the goal than about a lack of bureaucratic expertise.

One important consequence of the problem of control is the complexity of bureaucratic organizations and procedures. Despite bureaucrats' policy expertise, their decisions often appear to take too much time, rely on arbitrary judgments of what is important, and have unintended consequences—to the point that actions designed to solve one problem may create worse ones. Examples include **red tape**, which refers to excessive or unnecessarily complex regulations, and **standard operating procedures (SOPs)**, which are the rules that lower-level bureaucrats must follow, regardless of whether they actually apply, when implementing policies.

In part, red tape and SOPs are inevitable given the complexity of the tasks bureaucrats are given to do. For example, the U.S. Tax Code takes up thousands of pages—but in a country as large as the United States, where people have many different sources of income and there are many distinct kinds of corporate activity, a tax code that treats people and companies fairly while raising enough revenue to run the government is inevitably going to be complicated.

However, sometimes red tape and SOPs are the result of elected officials' attempts to mitigate the problem of control. For example, some of the complexity of the American tax code is due to congressional mandates that create tax breaks for favored corporations and individuals. In the abstract, elected officials might prefer that the tax code be determined by expert bureaucrats. In reality, however, members of Congress want to make sure their state or district is treated fairly—as well as provide tax breaks

Despite their policy expertise, bureaucrats still make mistakes. When the Medicare program implemented the Prescription Drug Benefit in 2006, information about the coverage was available on an easy-to-read website, but the agency soon learned that many seniors who needed the information did not own a computer or even know how to use a Web browser.

in order to increase their chances of getting reelected—and are willing to sacrifice expertise in favor of these other benefits, even if it makes the tax code more complex.

In other ways, such as the notice-and-comment procedure described earlier, elected officials require bureaucrats to inform them in advance about proposed policy decisions before they are implemented. Other congressional mandates define who can work in different jobs at an agency, where agency offices are located, and many other specifics of agency structure and process. Very few of these mandates contribute to bureaucratic nimbleness, but that is not their intent. What they are designed to do is give elected officials ways to mitigate the problems of control.

The problem of control has existed throughout the history of the federal government. It affects both the kinds of policies that bureaucrats implement and the structure of the federal bureaucracy, including the number of agencies and their missions, staff, and tasks. Moreover, elected officials use a variety of methods to solve the problem of control, including making it easier for people outside government to learn about agency actions before they take effect. However, all these tactics are, at best, partial solutions to the problem of control. The trade-off between expertise and control remains.

Bureaucrats aren't mindless paper pushers. Rather, they are experts who have considerable power to shape what government does. The way many elected officials talk, it's easy to think that once they pass a piece of legislation or issue an executive order, government policy automatically changes. In most cases, however, these directives are only the first step. To bring these changes to life, bureaucrats must step in to translate often-vague goals into concrete regulations, budgets, and actions. In other words, while you might not think much about bureaucrats, they can have a profound effect on your daily life.

"Why Should I Care?"

AP® FOUNDATIONAL DOCUMENT

This cartoon of a monument depicting President Andrew Jackson riding a pig decries his involvement in the spoils system, which allowed politicians to dole out government service jobs in return for political support.

How has the American bureaucracy grown?

The evolution of America's federal bureaucracy was not steady or smooth. Most of its important developments occurred during three short periods: the late 1890s and early 1900s, the 1930s, and the 1960s.[17] In all three, the driving force was a combination of citizens' demands for enhanced government services and government officials' desires to either respond to these demands or increase the size and scope of the federal government to be more in line with their own policy goals.

The beginning of America's bureaucracy

From the Founding of the United States until the election of Andrew Jackson in 1828, the staff of the entire federal bureaucracy numbered at most in the low thousands. The small size of the federal government during these years reflected Americans' deep suspicion of government, especially unelected officials. In the Declaration of Independence, in fact, one of the charges against George III was that he had "erected a multitude of new offices and sent hither swarms of officers to harass our people and eat out their substance."[18]

In these early years, there were only three executive departments (State, Treasury, and War), along with a postmaster general,[19] and executive branch offices were formed only when absolutely necessary. This small bureaucracy performed a very narrow range of tasks. It collected taxes on imports and exports and delivered the mail. The national army consisted of a small Corps of Engineers and a few frontier patrols. The attorney general was a private attorney who had the federal government as one of his clients. Members of Congress outnumbered civil servants in Washington, and the president had very little staff at all.[20]

Despite its small size, conflicts soon arose around control of the bureaucracy. The legislation that established the departments of State, Treasury, and War allowed the president to nominate the people in charge of these departments but made these appointments subject to Senate approval. The same is true today for the heads of all executive departments and many other presidential appointments.

The election of Andrew Jackson in 1828 brought the first large-scale use of the spoils system: people who had worked for Jackson's campaign were rewarded with new positions in the federal government (usually as local postmasters).[21] The spoils system was extremely useful to party organizations, as it gave them a powerful incentive with which to convince people to work for the party, and it was a particularly important tool for Jackson. His campaign organization was at that time the largest ever organized.

The challenge facing the spoils system was ensuring that these government employees, who often lacked experience in their new fields, could actually carry out their jobs. The solution was to develop procedures for these employees that guided them on exactly what to do even if they had little or no experience or training.[22] These instructions became one of the earliest uses of standard operating procedures. They ensured that the government could function even if large numbers of employees had been hired in reward for political work rather than because of their qualifications.[23]

As America expanded in size, so did the federal government, which saw an almost eightfold increase in the bureaucracy between 1816 and the beginning of the Civil War in 1861. This growth did not reflect fundamental changes in what the government did; in fact, much of the increase came in areas such as the Post Office, which needed to serve a geographically larger nation—and, of course, to provide "spoils" for party workers in the form of government jobs.[24] Even by the end of the Civil War, the federal government still had very little involvement in the lives of ordinary Americans. State and local governments provided services such as education, public works, and welfare benefits, if they were provided at all. The federal government's role in daily life was limited to mail delivery, the collection of import and export taxes, and work in a few other sectors.

Building a new American state: the Progressive Era

Political developments in the second half of the nineteenth century transformed America's bureaucracy.[25] While the transformation began after the Civil War, the most significant changes occurred during the Progressive Era, from 1890 to 1920. Many laws and executive actions increased the government's regulatory power during this period, including the Sherman Antitrust Act of 1890, the Pure Food and Drug Act of 1906, the Federal Meat Inspection Act of 1906, expansion of the Interstate Commerce Commission, and various conservation measures.[26] Now the federal government was no longer simply a deliverer of mail and a defender of borders; rather, it had an indirect impact on several aspects of everyday life. When Americans bought food or other products, went to work, or traveled on vacation, the choices available to them were shaped by the actions of federal bureaucrats in Washington and elsewhere.

These developments were matched by a fundamental change in the federal bureaucracy following passage of the 1883 Pendleton Civil Service Act. This measure created the federal civil service, in which the merit system (qualifications, not political connections) would be the basis for hiring and promoting bureaucrats.[27] In other words, when new presidents took office they could not replace government workers with their own campaign workers. Initially, only about 13,000 federal jobs acquired civil service protections, but over the next two decades many additional positions were incorporated into the civil service. In some cases, presidents gave civil service protections to people who had been hired under the spoils system to prevent the next president from replacing these bureaucrats with his or her own loyalists. Over time, these reforms created a bureaucracy in which people were hired for their expertise and allowed to build a career in government without having to fear being fired when a new president or Congress took office.[28] In the modern era, virtually all full-time, permanent government employees have civil service protections—although many individuals lack these protections because they work for a company that contracts services to the government, or because they are senior political appointees.

federal civil service
A system created by the 1883 Pendleton Civil Service Act in which bureaucrats are hired on the basis of merit rather than political connections.

The New Deal, the Great Society, and the Reagan Revolution

Dramatic expansion of the federal bureaucracy occurred during the New Deal period in the 1930s and during the mid-1960s Great Society era. In both cases, the changes were driven by a combination of citizen demands and the preferences of elected officials who favored an increased role of government in society. These expansion trends were only marginally curtailed during the Reagan Revolution of the 1980s.

The New Deal "The New Deal" refers to the government programs implemented during Franklin Roosevelt's first term as president in the 1930s. At one level, these programs were a response to the Great Depression and the inability of local governments and private charities to provide adequate support to Americans during this economic crisis. Many advocates of the New Deal also favored an expanded role for

Franklin Roosevelt's New Deal programs greatly expanded the power of the federal government and the bureaucracy. As this cartoon shows, these changes were controversial, with some seeing them as moving too much power from Congress to the president and bureaucracy.

government in American society, regardless of the immediate need for intervention.[29] Roosevelt's programs included reforms to the financial industry as well as efforts to help people directly, including the stimulation of employment and economic growth, and the formation of labor unions. The Social Security Act, the first federally funded pension program for all Americans, was also passed as part of the New Deal.[30]

These reforms resulted in a vast increase in the size, responsibilities, and capacity of the bureaucracy, as well as a large transfer of power to bureaucrats and to the president.[31] While the Progressive Era reforms created an independent bureaucracy and increased its state capacity, the New Deal reforms broadened the range of policy areas in which this capacity could be applied. Before the New Deal, the federal government influenced citizens' choices through activities such as regulating industries and workplace conditions. After the New Deal, the federal government took on the role of directly delivering a wide range of benefits and services to its citizens—ranging from jobs to electricity. It also increased regulations on many industries, including those in the banking and financial sectors.

The expansion of the federal government and the subsequent delegation of power to bureaucrats and to the president were controversial changes, both when they were enacted and as they were implemented in subsequent years.[32] Many Republicans opposed New Deal reforms because they believed that the federal government could not deliver services efficiently and that an expanded federal bureaucracy would create a modern spoils system. Many southerners worried that the federal government's increased involvement in everyday life would endanger the system of racial segregation in southern states.[33] Even so, Democratic supporters of the New Deal, aided by public support, carried the day.

The Great Society The Great Society was a series of federal programs enacted during Lyndon Johnson's presidency (1963–1969) that further expanded the size, capacity, and activities of the bureaucracy. During these years, Johnson proposed and Congress passed programs that funded bilingual education, loans and grants for college students, special education, preschools, construction of elementary and secondary schools, mass-transit programs in many cities, health care for seniors and poor people, job training and urban renewal, enhanced voting rights and civil rights for minorities, environmental protection, funding for the arts and cultural activities, and space exploration.[34]

The Great Society programs had mixed success. Voting rights and civil rights reforms ended the "separate but equal" system of social order in southern states and dramatically increased political participation by African Americans.[35] But many of the antipoverty programs were dismal failures. During the 1960s and 1970s, poverty rates among most groups remained relatively constant, and other indicators, such as the rate of teen pregnancy, actually increased.[36] In retrospect, the people who designed and implemented these programs did not realize the complexities of the problems they were trying to address.[37] For example, many antipoverty programs were built on the assumption that most people receiving welfare needed job training programs in order to transition from welfare to permanent, paid employment. However, additional data that became available a decade after these laws were passed showed that most people receiving welfare do so for short periods because of medical or family crises—problems that the Great Society programs did not address.[38] Despite these shortcomings, the expansion of the federal government during the New Deal and Great Society has remained in place well into the twenty-first century.

The Reagan Revolution and Afterward The election of Ronald Reagan to the presidency in 1980, along with a Republican takeover of the Senate and Republican gains in the House of Representatives, created an opportunity for conservatives to roll back the size and scope of the federal government. These efforts were largely unsuccessful. In the years since Reagan, members of Congress and presidents from both parties have fought for large expansions in government policy. For example, while Democrat Barack Obama's administration issued many new environmental regulations and profoundly changed the American health care system, these changes are not too different in magnitude from the reforms championed by Republican George W. Bush, including education policies that increased federal control over local school districts, new drug financing benefits for seniors, and changes to financial regulations that increased financial reporting requirements for corporations. After four years in office, the Trump administration had little success in cutting overall federal spending or in reducing the size of specific agencies. For example, the administration initially proposed a one-third cut in the budget of the State Department for fiscal year 2018, only to ultimately accept a congressional budget that kept spending levels constant.

Under President George W. Bush, the federal bureaucracy continued to expand. Programs like No Child Left Behind increased the role of government in society.

Though sometimes their rhetoric seems to tell a different story, the difference between Republicans' and Democrats' philosophies about the bureaucracy is not over the size of the federal government but over what government should do. While Republicans often argue for making government smaller and Democrats respond by highlighting the consequences of even a small cut in services, the truth is that most people on both sides accept the fact that a large federal government is here to stay. Knowing how the federal bureaucracy has grown, as well as evaluating whether this growth has caused problems or created benefits, is central to building your own ideas about what government should do.

"Why Should I Care?"

The modern federal bureaucracy

The size and scope of the modern federal bureaucracy reflect the expansion of the federal government over the last half century and its increased role in the lives of everyday Americans. The structure of the bureaucracy also reflects ongoing attempts by presidents, members of Congress, and others to control bureaucratic actions in line with their policy goals.

The structure of the federal government

Nuts & Bolts 7.1 shows the structure of the executive branch of the federal government. As discussed in Chapter 5, the Executive Office of the President (EOP) contains organizations that support the president and implement presidential policy initiatives. Individuals working in these organizations aim to ensure that bureaucrats (agents) act appropriately to implement the president's (principal's) policy priorities and preferences.[39] Among its many offices, the EOP contains the Office of Management and Budget, which prepares the president's annual budget proposal to Congress and monitors government spending and the development of new regulations. Below the EOP are the 15 executive departments, from the Department of Agriculture to the Department of Veterans Affairs, which constitute the major divisions within the executive branch. The heads of these 15 organizations (plus others added by presidential order) make up the president's Cabinet. One thing to remember: while the diagram places the EOP above the cabinet departments and all other government agencies, the president's authority to direct agency decisions is not absolute, as it is limited by statute, regulations, and the Constitution, as well as by the pressure of business and a lack of information. These limits are discussed later in this chapter as well as in Chapter 5.

Each executive department contains many smaller, sometimes diverse organizations. Nuts & Bolts 7.2 shows the organizational chart for the Department of Agriculture, for example. As you can see, the Department of Agriculture includes offices that help farmers produce and sell their crops and offices that ensure food safety, but it also houses the Forest Service and offices that manage issues related to housing and utilities in rural areas. The Department of Agriculture also administers the Supplemental Nutritional Assistance Program (SNAP; formerly known as food stamps), even though the program has no direct connection to farming or food safety.

In addition to executive departments, the government contains a group of agencies, commissions, and government corporations that are called independent agencies to highlight that they are not part of an executive department. Most of these agencies carry out specialized functions, such as regulating a particular activity (these are called independent regulatory agencies) or carrying out policy in a narrow area. The Federal Reserve System, for example, manages the money supply, banking system, and interest rates, while NASA directs aviation research and space exploration. Nuts & Bolts 7.1 includes only some noteworthy or well-known agencies; there are many more.

There are two important lessons to draw from these charts. First, the federal government handles an enormous range of functions. Second, the division of activities among executive departments and independent agencies does not always have an obvious logic. Why, for example, does the Department of Agriculture administer rural utilities programs and SNAP? Similarly, it is not always clear why certain tasks are handled by an independent agency whereas others fall within the scope of an executive department.[40]

Office of Management and Budget
An office within the EOP that is responsible for creating the president's annual budget proposal to Congress, reviewing proposed rules, and performing other budget-related tasks.

**AP®
FOUNDATIONAL
DOCUMENT**

independent agencies
Government offices or organizations that provide government services and are not part of an executive department.

The Executive Branch of the Federal Government

The executive branch includes the 15 cabinet offices, as well as several independent agencies, commissions, and government corporations.

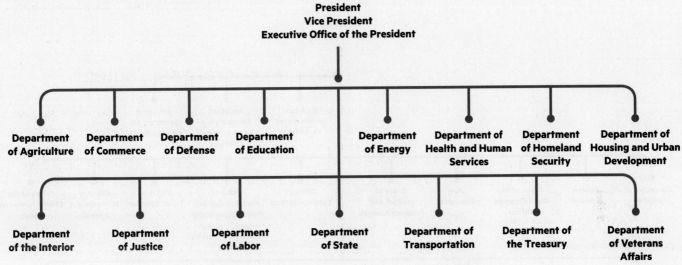

Selected Independent Establishments and Government Corporations

Central Intelligence Agency
Consumer Financial Protection Bureau
Consumer Product Safety Commission
Environmental Protection Agency
Equal Employment Opportunity Commission
Federal Communications Commission
Federal Deposit Insurance Corporation
Federal Election Commission

Federal Reserve System
Federal Trade Commission
General Services Administration
National Aeronautics and Space Administration
National Foundation on the Arts and the Humanities
National Labor Relations Board
National Railroad Passenger Corporation (Amtrak)
National Science Foundation

Occupational Safety and Health Review Commission
Peace Corps
Securities and Exchange Commission
Selective Service System
Small Business Administration
Social Security Administration
U.S. Agency for International Development
U.S. Postal Service

Source: United States General Services Administration, "Government Organizational Chart," www.usgovernmentmanual.gov/ReadLibraryItem.ashx?SFN=Myz95sTyO4rJRM/nhIRwSw==&SF=VHhnJrOeEAnGaa/rtk/JOg== (accessed 6/19/20).

The list of cabinet departments and agencies illustrates the priorities of the federal government—the issues that are a high enough priority to be given an agency to address them.

Why is the Food and Drug Administration (FDA) an independent agency rather than part of the Department of Commerce—and why is the Federal Aviation Administration (FAA) located within the Department of Transportation rather than being independent?

Organizational decisions like these often reflect elected officials' attempts to shape agency behavior—and the extent to which political process matters. Part of the difference between independent agencies and the organizations contained within executive departments has to do with the president's ability to control these organizations' activities. Organizations that fall within an executive department, such as the FAA or the

The Structure of the Department of Agriculture

The Department of Agriculture is headed by the secretary of agriculture and the deputy secretary of agriculture and includes various assistant secretaries and undersecretaries for specific areas, such as natural resources and the environment, farm services, rural development, and food safety.

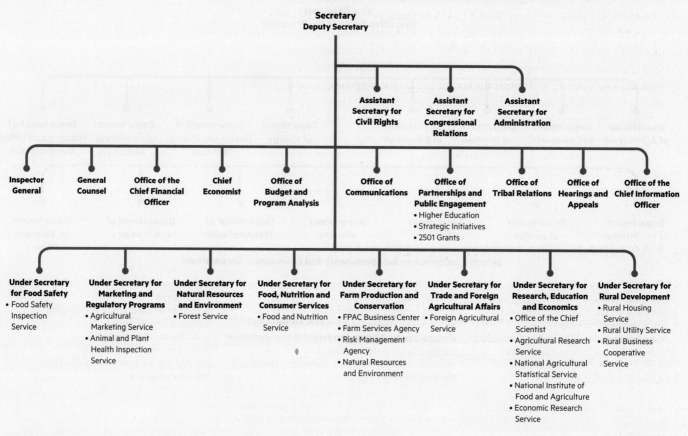

Source: U.S. Department of Agriculture, "USDA Organization Chart," www.usda.gov/sites/default/files/documents/usda-organization-chart.pdf (accessed 6/15/20).

"Why Should I Care?" Organizational charts illustrate both governmental priorities and which agencies are subordinate to others. For example, if the Forest Service were in the Department of the Interior instead of Agriculture, America would likely have different policies concerning the management of forests and timber.

Federal Highway Administration (FHA) (both within the Department of Transportation), can be controlled by the president (to some extent) through his or her appointees.[41] In contrast, independent agencies are often designed to have more freedom from oversight and control by the president and Congress. For example, governors of the Federal Reserve, though nominated by the president and confirmed by the Senate, serve for 14 years—outlasting the administration that nominated them. Outside the nomination and confirmation process, the president and Congress have very little control over the

Federal Reserve's policies; the organization is self-financing, and its governors can be removed from office only if Congress takes the extreme step of impeaching them.

In contrast, appointees to executive departments and the EOP serve "at the pleasure of the president," meaning the president can remove them from office at any time. Such removals happen in all presidential administrations because of scandal, complaints about performance, or concerns about leaks to the media or disloyalty to the president. President Trump placed a high priority on loyalty and appeared to prioritize having bureaucrats who would execute his directives without question. For example, in April 2020 Trump removed Dr. Rick Bright from his position as head of the Department of Health and Human Services' Biomedical Advanced Research and Development Authority. Bright had pressed for further review of the drug hydroxychloroquine before allowing it to be used to treat COVID-19 patients and had continued to raise objections even after President Trump made strong statements in favor of prescribing the drug.[42] Whether it was ethical and politically wise to fire Bright is a good question—but there is no doubt that Trump had the authority to remove him from office.

These details about the hiring and firing of bureaucrats and the location of agencies in the structure of the federal government matter because they determine the amount of political control that other parts of the government can exercise over an agency, as well as which individuals (the president or members of Congress) get to exercise this power. As political scientist Terry M. Moe puts it, "The bureaucracy rises out of politics, and its design reflects the interests, strategies, and compromises of those who exercise political power."[43]

The size of the federal government

The federal government employs millions of people. Table 7.1 shows the number of employees in each executive department. The Department of Defense is the largest cabinet department, with more than 700,000 civilian personnel. The Department of Education is the smallest, with only 3,600 employees. Many departments are on the small side: four cabinet departments have fewer than 20,000 employees. The same is

TABLE 7.1

Employment in Cabinet Departments

Source: Office of Management and Budget, "A Budget for America's Future: Analytical Perspectives, Fiscal Year 2021," 2020, www.whitehouse.gov/wp-content/uploads/2020/02/spec_fy21.pdf (accessed 5/22/20).

Organization	Total Employees
Defense (civilian only)	741,500
Veterans Affairs	375,800
Homeland Security	192,400
Justice	111,900
Treasury	88,000
Agriculture	81,400
Health and Human Services	73,000
Interior	70,000
Transportation	53,100
Commerce	45,000
State	27,100
Labor	14,800
Energy	14,000
Housing and Urban Development	7,400
Education	3,600

true for many independent agencies and organizations within the EOP. The General Services Administration (GSA), for example, has only about 12,000 employees. Millions of additional people work for the government as members of the armed forces, as employees of the Postal Service, as employees of civilian companies that contract with the government, or as recipients of federal grant money.

The What Do the Facts Say? feature in this chapter shows the number of civilian federal employees from 1961 to 2020. Clearly, the federal workforce has steadily increased over time, although it has declined from its peak in the 1990s and remained steady in recent years. Some observers argue that growth in employment was driven by the fact that bureaucrats are **budget maximizers** who never pass up a chance to increase the size of their organization regardless of whether the increase is worthwhile.[44] Of course, the fact that federal employment has remained steady in recent years suggests that something besides budget maximization is at work. The best explanation for the overall size of the federal government is the size of America itself—nearly 330 million people spread out over an area more than twice the size of the European Union—combined with America's position as the most powerful nation in the world with the largest military, and the increased costs associated with some government services, such as health care.

Those who blame bureaucrats for the increasing size of the federal government miss some important points. First, the increase in total federal spending masks the fact that many agencies see their budgets shrink.[45] Particularly in recent administrations, one of the principal missions of presidential appointees, both in agencies and in the EOP, has been to scrutinize budget requests with an eye to cutting spending as much as possible.[46] And in most years, some government agencies are eliminated (in fact, most of the executive department head counts in Table 7.1 have grown smaller in recent editions of this text).[47]

Public-opinion data also provide an explanation for the overall growth in government: the American public's demand for services.[48] Despite complaints about the federal bureaucracy, polls find little evidence of demands for less government. When the Pew Research Center asked people in 2019 to name programs that should have their spending cut as a way of reducing the budget deficit, the only program that was named by more than a quarter of respondents was foreign aid (see Figure 7.2). Far fewer people favored cuts in

budget maximizers
Bureaucrats who seek to increase funding for their agency whether or not that additional spending is worthwhile.

DID YOU KNOW?

In the first two years of the Trump presidency, 12 of 15 Cabinet Departments reduced their number of employees, some by almost

10%

Source: Office of Personnel Management

FIGURE
7.2

Public Opinion on Spending Cuts

Many Americans complain about the size of the federal government. However, their complaints do not translate into support for reductions in policy areas or cuts in specific programs that could significantly reduce spending. Based on these data, are there any kinds of proposals for significantly reducing the size of the federal government that might attract widespread support?

Source: Pew Research Center, "Little Public Support for Reductions in Federal Spending," April 11, 2019, www.people-press.org/2019/04/11/little-public-support-for-reductions-in-federal-spending/ (accessed 5/22/20).

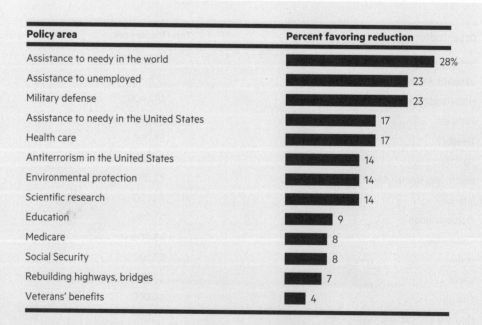

Policy area	Percent favoring reduction
Assistance to needy in the world	28%
Assistance to unemployed	23
Military defense	23
Assistance to needy in the United States	17
Health care	17
Antiterrorism in the United States	14
Environmental protection	14
Scientific research	14
Education	9
Medicare	8
Social Security	8
Rebuilding highways, bridges	7
Veterans' benefits	4

Is the Federal Bureaucracy Too Big?

One of the most intense conflicts in American political life is over the size of the federal government. Generally, Republicans say that the size of the federal bureaucracy should be reduced, while Democrats tend to favor increasing the size of government programs, including adding more employees if needed. Has the size of government increased over time?

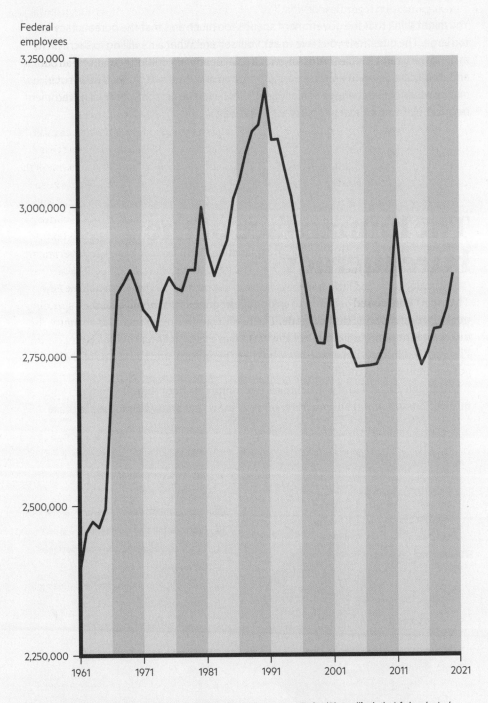

Think about it

- **During the 2016 presidential campaign,** candidate Donald Trump claimed that the size of the bureaucracy had significantly increased under President Obama. Do the data support this assertion?

- **The size of the federal bureaucracy** increased significantly during the 1960s and 1970s, then declined after about 1990. What political or historical events explain these changes?

Source: Based on Federal Reserve Bank, St. Louis, "All Employees: Government: Federal," https://fred.stlouisfed.org/series/CES9091000001#0 (accessed 5/21/20).

the programs that account for the overwhelming majority of federal spending: defense, health care spending, and Social Security. In other words, while in the abstract Americans might want a smaller government that is less involved in everyday life, they do not support the large-scale budget cuts that would be necessary to achieve this goal. The public's desire for more government services is often encouraged by elected officials, who create new government programs (and expand existing ones in response to constituent demands) as a way of building support and improving their chances of reelection.

"Why Should I Care?"

You might think that the government spends too much and that the bureaucracy is too large. The questions you have to ask yourself are: What am I willing to sacrifice to make government smaller? Am I OK with a smaller military, fewer regulations on banks and credit card companies, less oversight of food and drug safety? And how much money would these changes actually save? We have a large, costly federal government because, in the end, most people want it that way.

DESCRIBE WHO BUREAUCRATS ARE AND THE REGULATIONS THAT GOVERN THEIR EMPLOYMENT

The human face of the bureaucracy

The term "bureaucrat" applies to a wide range of people with different qualifications and job descriptions. The federal government includes so many different kinds of jobs because of the vast array of services it provides (see Figure 7.3). This section describes who these people are and the terms of their government employment.

Although citizens and politicians often complain about the efficiency or motivations of federal bureaucrats, surveys show that many employees in these

FIGURE 7.3

Types of Federal Workers

Source: Bureau of Labor Statistics, "Occupational Employment Statistics," www.bls.gov/oes/current/naics4_999100.htm#00-0000 (accessed 5/22/20).

Note: Data may not total 100 percent due to rounding.

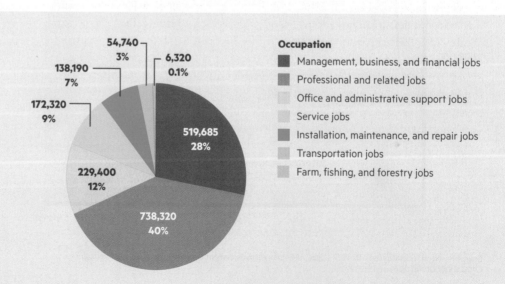

positions have a strong interest in public service or the implementation of good public policy. In fact, these motivations are often strong enough that scholars such as James L. Perry have argued against attempts to motivate federal workers with monetary incentives—bureaucrats who work hard because they feel it is the right thing to do may resent incentive schemes that presume they are lazy or only interested in money.[49]

Civil service regulations

Most jobs in the federal bureaucracy are subject to the civil service regulations that we described earlier.[50] The current civil service system sets out job descriptions and pay ranges for all federal jobs.[51] The system also establishes tests that determine who is hired for low-level clerical and secretarial positions. People with less than a college degree are generally eligible for entry-level jobs, and, as in the private sector, a college degree or an advanced degree and work experience qualify an individual for higher-level positions. Federal salaries are supposed to be comparable to what people earn in similar, private-sector positions, and salaries are somewhat higher for federal employees who work in areas with a high cost of living.

Civil service regulations provide job security. After three years of satisfactory performance, employees cannot be fired except "for cause," meaning that the firing agency must cite a reason. Civil service regulations set out a multistep procedure for firing someone, beginning with low performance evaluations, then warning letters given to the employee, followed by a lengthy appeals process before a firing takes place.[52] It is hard to get exact data, but most estimates are that about 10,000 federal employees are fired every year—out of a total workforce of over 2 million. A subpar performer may be assigned other duties, transferred to another office, or even given nothing to do in the hope that the person will leave voluntarily out of boredom or embarrassment.

If you think civil service regulations sound cumbersome, you're right.[53] The hiring criteria remove a manager's discretion to hire someone who would do an excellent job but lacks the education or work experience that the regulations specify as necessary for the position. The firing requirements make it extremely difficult to remove poor performers. The salary and promotion restrictions create problems with rewarding excellent performance or promoting the best employees rather than those with the most seniority.

Why do these requirements exist? Recall that the aim of civil service regulations was to separate politics from policy. The mechanism for achieving this goal was a set of rules and requirements that made it hard for elected officials to control the hiring and firing of government employees to further their own political goals. In effect, even though civil service regulations have obvious drawbacks, they also provide this less apparent but very important benefit. For example, without civil service protections, members of Congress might pressure employees in the Office of Personnel Management to increase pensions for retiring federal workers in the representatives' constituencies.

Although loyalty to the president is a widely accepted criterion for hiring agency heads and other presidential appointees, professionals with permanent civil service positions are supposed to be hired on the basis of their qualifications, not their political beliefs. In fact, it is illegal to bring politics into these hiring decisions. However, there is no doubt that all presidential administrations worry about the political loyalties of midlevel bureaucrats because of the problem of control, as we discussed earlier.

Limits on political activity

Legislation places limits on the political activities that federal employees can undertake. The Hatch Act, enacted in 1939 and amended in 1940, prohibited federal employees from engaging in organized political activities.[54] Under the act, employees could vote and contribute to candidates but could not work for candidates or for political parties. These restrictions were modified in the 1993 Federal Employees Political Activities Act, which allows federal employees to participate in a wider range of political activities, including fund-raising and serving as an officer of a political party. Senior members of the president's White House staff and political appointees are exempt from most of these restrictions, although they cannot use government resources for political activities.

While the Hatch Act is often invoked when government employees express controversial views, it technically restricts only activities that directly help a particular political candidate. For example, in 2019 a Department of Energy (DOE) employee was disciplined for giving a tour of the Hanford Nuclear Waste Site to a congressional candidate and allowing the candidate to take pictures that would be used in the candidate's campaign. (The DOE employee had also been warned that giving the tour would constitute a violation of the Hatch Act.)[55]

The Hatch Act makes life especially difficult for presidential appointees whose job duties, such as helping the president they work for get reelected, often mix government service with politics. In order to comply with Hatch Act restrictions, these officials need to carry separate cell phones to make calls related to their political activities and maintain separate e-mail accounts—usually provided by the party or campaign committee—for their political communications.

Federal employees must be careful that their comments to the media comply with Hatch Act restrictions. Kellyanne Conway, former counselor to President Trump, violated the Hatch Act when she advocated for and against candidates in the 2017 Senate special election in Alabama on CNN and Fox News programs.

turkey farms
Agencies to which campaign workers and donors can be appointed in reward for their service because it is unlikely that their lack of qualifications will lead to bad policy.

Political appointees and the Senior Executive Service

Not every federal employee is a member of the civil service. About 3,000 senior positions in the executive branch—such as the leaders of executive departments and independent agencies like NASA, as well as members of the EOP—are not subject to civil service regulations. The president appoints individuals to these positions, and, in some cases, the Senate must confirm them. The majority of a president's appointees act as the president's eyes, ears, and hands throughout the executive branch. They hold positions of power within government agencies, serving as secretaries of executive departments, agency heads, or senior deputies. Their jobs involve finding out what the president wants from their agency and ordering, persuading, or cajoling their subordinates to implement presidential directives.

Some appointees get their jobs as a reward for working on the president's campaign staff, contributing substantial funds to the campaign, or raising money from other donors. These individuals are not always given positions with real decision-making power. Some government agencies have the reputation of being **turkey farms**, places where campaign stalwarts can be appointed without the risk that their lack of experience will lead to bad policy.[56] In many agencies, people in the top positions are members of the Senior Executive Service (SES), who are also exempt from civil service restrictions.[57] As of 2020, there are about 8,000 SES members, most of whom were career government employees who held relatively high-level agency positions before moving to the SES. This change of employment status costs them their civil service protections but allows them to apply for senior leadership positions in the bureaucracy. Some political appointees are also given SES positions, although most do not have the experience or expertise held by career bureaucrats who typically move to the SES.

President Trump's use of political appointments raises a puzzle. At one level, his 2016 campaign promises to undertake large-scale changes in government policy suggested that Trump would make appointments as rapidly as possible, so that he would have people in each agency who were loyal to him and would implement his reform efforts. However, the pace of Trump's appointments was slow compared to that of previous presidents, and even after four years in office many senior-level positions in the bureaucracy were vacant or filled by a series of acting appointees.[58] In part, appointments were slowed by Senate Democrats who opposed Trump's nominees. In addition, however, some potential appointees did not want to work in a Trump-led administration. Others were dropped from consideration because they had opposed Trump during the 2016 campaign or had spoken publicly against Trump's actions in office. Whatever the reason, the slow pace of appointments complicated Trump's reform efforts.

Perhaps because of the difficulties in appointing senior-level officials, many relatively young individuals who had worked for the Trump campaign during 2016 and thereafter were appointed to positions in various executive departments and independent agencies.[59] These individuals were chosen for their loyalty to Trump rather than their knowledge of the agency they were assigned to—some of them were even finishing their college degrees while working in the executive branch. Their primary job seemed to be monitoring agency operations and reporting how agency staff were responding to Trump's directives. However, because these individuals knew little about their agencies, and because they had no authority to issue policy directives on their own, they were relatively ineffective in implementing the Trump agenda.

"Why Should I Care?"

The problem of control shapes the kinds of people who are hired as bureaucrats as well as their job protections. Political appointees and members of the SES are supposed to ride herd on the rest of the bureaucracy. Civil service protections exist to ensure that bureaucrats' decisions reflect expertise rather than political considerations.

Controlling the bureaucracy

EXPLAIN HOW CONGRESS AND THE PRESIDENT OVERSEE THE EXECUTIVE BRANCH

As the expert implementers of legislation and presidential directives, bureaucrats hold significant power to influence government policy. This situation creates the problem of control illustrated by the principal–agent game, as we discussed earlier: elected officials must figure out how to reap the benefits of bureaucratic expertise without simply giving bureaucrats free rein to do whatever they want.

One strategy is to take away discretion entirely and give bureaucrats simple, direct orders. For example, from 1996 to 2015 a law passed by Congress forbade the CDC from conducting research that would "advocate or promote gun control"—which was interpreted by the CDC as limiting all gun-related research by agency scientists or by outside researchers who received agency funds.[60] (The ban was repealed after a series of mass shootings in 2013, although to this day the CDC conducts very little gun-related research.) Similarly, the Trump administration banned the use of the words "climate change" and "global warming" from the EPA's websites and documents and abolished scientific advisory panels dealing with this topic.[61] Trump appointees in the Department of Agriculture also buried studies by agency staff and outside researchers that warned how climate change could affect crop yields.[62]

The problem with eliminating bureaucrats' discretion in this way is that it limits the positive influence of their expertise. Particularly when new policies are being developed, taking away bureaucratic discretion is costly for legislators or presidential appointees because it forces them to work out the policy details themselves—and may produce less effective policies than those constructed by bureaucrats with specialized knowledge.[63] Moreover, preventing bureaucrats from using their judgment makes it impossible for them to craft policies that take into account new developments or unforeseen circumstances.[64]

For all these reasons, elected officials must find other ways to reduce or eliminate **bureaucratic drift**—that is, bureaucrats' pursuit of their own goals rather than their assignments from officeholders or appointees—while still reaping the benefits of bureaucratic expertise. This section describes two common strategies: changing the way agencies are organized and staffed and using standardized procedures for monitoring agency actions. In both cases, the aim is to set up agencies so that bureaucrats can use their expertise, while making sure their actions are consistent with elected officials' wishes.[65] These measures mitigate—but do not eliminate—the problem of control (see the Take a Stand feature).

bureaucratic drift
Bureaucrats' tendency to implement policies in a way that favors their own political objectives rather than following the original intentions of the legislation.

Agency organization

Over the last 20 years, political scientists have shown how agencies can be organized to minimize bureaucratic drift.[66] Specifically, when an agency is set up or given new responsibilities, the officials who initiate the change don't simply tell the new agency what to do. To make sure that the agency pursues the policies officials want, they also determine where the agency is located within the federal government structure and who runs it. These efforts may occur solely within Congress, may involve both Congress and the president, or may be arranged by presidential actions.[67]

For example, one of the Obama administration's responses to the 2008 financial crisis was to form a new agency, the Consumer Financial Protection Bureau (CFPB), which would help enforce new bank regulations and investigate consumer complaints about financial firms. However, Republican senators opposed Obama's initial nominee to run the agency, Elizabeth Warren, believing she would encourage her subordinates to be excessively pro-consumer. Similarly, in 2017 President Trump appointed Michael Mulvaney (a former Republican congressman and the head of the Office of Management and Budget and chief of staff in the Trump administration) to run the agency, even though Mulvaney was a longtime opponent of the CFPB who as a member of Congress had sought to abolish the agency. Both Trump and Obama's appointments were intended to shape agency operations by appointing an individual who was expected to act in line with the then-president's preferences.

Is Political Control of the Bureaucracy Beneficial?

When working with bureaucrats, elected officials (the president or members of Congress) face the problem of political control: Should they allow bureaucrats to exercise judgment when implementing policies or give them specific, narrow directives? Compounding this problem is the fact that most bureaucrats are civil service employees, meaning they cannot be fired except under very extreme circumstances. As a result, even when elected officials give very specific directives to an agency, they may find that bureaucrats essentially ignore the directives and that very little can be done to force compliance (after all, regardless of what bureaucrats do or don't do, they will still have a job). Civil service protections also mean that members of Congress or a new presidential administration cannot clean house in an agency, replacing untrustworthy bureaucrats with individuals who will do what they are told. Should civil service protections be abolished?

Get rid of civil service protections. The civil service system began in an era when few government jobs required specialized knowledge, expertise, or an advanced degree.

The modern federal bureaucracy is exactly the opposite: most jobs, particularly those that involve real policy-making power, require expertise to be done effectively. Under these conditions, civil service protections are to some extent unnecessary, as bureaucrats have considerable job security because of their expertise and experience. Getting rid of recalcitrant bureaucrats involves significant costs: by removing their knowledge of the policies being decided and the procedures by which decisions are made, it may become impossible for an agency to function at all. Moreover, a bureaucrat's reluctance to behave as ordered may be a sign that something is wrong—that the directive makes no sense or that there are easier ways of accomplishing the task.

Consider the U.S. Environmental Protection Agency. There is little doubt that most EPA scientists believe that climate change is real and that it is the result of human actions. Both of these views were in opposition to President Trump's stated positions. Were civil service protections the only thing preventing Trump from firing these scientists? Firing the scientists would have decimated the EPA and made it impossible for the agency to carry out many of its functions, some of which (like cleaning up Superfund sites) were things Trump favored. Trump may not have liked having EPA scientists that disagree with him, but he would probably have liked the consequences of a mass firing even less. Moreover, the replacements would have operated

Civil service protections help ensure that agency scientists will continue to do cutting-edge research and report their findings, even if their conclusions conflict with the views of their political superiors.

within existing resource, regulatory, and legal constraints, so their actions might not have looked different from those of their predecessors.

Civil service protections are still needed. The fact that firing bureaucrats costs the government the benefit of their experience and expertise does not mean that elected officials will never threaten to do so, or even carry out their threats. Removing civil service protections—making bureaucrats vulnerable to threats about their future employment—could easily lead to bad policy outcomes. Eliminating civil service protections would also change the kinds of people who undertake careers in government service. Civil service protections enable policy experts to work for the government without fearing that they will be fired for simply voicing their concerns or because a new administration places a high value on loyalty. Without the protections afforded by civil service regulations, these individuals might choose a different career, depriving the federal government (and the American people) of the benefits of their knowledge and training.

In the case of the EPA, civil service protections helped ensure that agency scientists continued to do cutting-edge research and report their findings—even if their conclusions conflicted with the views of their political superiors—and that these scientists work for the agency in the first place.

take a stand

1. In general, contemporary Democratic politicians tend to favor civil service protections, while Republicans want to weaken them. Does this preference make sense in light of what we know about the differences between the parties in their beliefs about the size and scope of government?

2. Not all jobs in the federal bureaucracy require specialized knowledge and expertise. Would it make sense to abandon civil service protections for low-level jobs such as clerical positions? Why or why not?

Monitoring

One of the most important ways elected officials prevent bureaucratic drift is by keeping an eye on what bureaucrats are doing or planning to do. Information gathering by members of Congress about bureaucratic actions is termed oversight. Congressional committees often hold hearings to question agency heads, secretaries of executive departments, or senior agency staff. Similarly, one of the primary responsibilities of presidential appointees is to monitor how lower-level bureaucrats are responding to presidential directives. The problem is that appointees may be unable to fulfill this role. Because they are chosen for their loyalty to the president, they may lack the experience needed to fully understand what bureaucrats in their agency are doing (as discussed earlier, this was especially true for some of Trump's lower-level appointees). Moreover, given that appointees typically hold their position for only a year or two, they have little time to learn the details of agency operations.

Advance Warning Members of Congress, the president, and his or her staff gain advance knowledge of planned bureaucratic actions through the notice-and-comment procedure described earlier in the chapter, which requires bureaucrats to disclose proposed regulations before they take effect.[68] This delay gives opponents the opportunity to register complaints with their congressional representatives, and it allows these legislators time either to pressure the agency to revise the regulation or to even enact another law undoing or modifying the agency action. Members of Congress also pressure bureaucrats to release memos, working drafts, and other documents as a way of keeping track of what bureaucrats are doing. For example, in 2020 members of Congress requested documents from the State Department in the wake of the removal of Inspector General Steve Linick—the concern was that Linick was fired because he was investigating complaints that Secretary of State Mike Pompeo had used State Department staff to run personal errands.[69]

Investigations: Police Patrols and Fire Alarms Congress, legislative staff, or presidential appointees may initiate investigations of government programs or offices to scrutinize the organizations, their expenditures, and their activities. There are two types of investigation: police patrol oversight and fire alarm oversight. Ideally, every agency would be investigated on a consistent basis, with agencies that have large budgets or carry out important functions being investigated more

oversight
Congressional efforts to make sure that laws are implemented correctly by the bureaucracy after they have been passed.

The Senate's power over the confirmation of senior agency officials is often used as a tool to shape agency policy and operations. Richard Cordray (left), the first head of the Consumer Financial Protection Bureau, was nominated after some senators objected to President Obama's first nominee, Elizabeth Warren, who was a Harvard law professor at the time. Some senators also opposed the nomination of the current head, Kathy Kraninger (right), who worked for Republicans on Capitol Hill and in the Office of Management and Budget in the Trump administration.

frequently. These investigations may involve fact-finding trips to local offices, interviews with senior personnel, audits of agency accounts, and calls to the agency to see how it responds to citizens' requests. This method of investigation is called **police patrol oversight**.[70] Think of a police officer walking his or her beat, rattling doors to see if they are locked, checking out broken windows, and looking down alleys for suspicious behavior.

The disadvantage of police patrol oversight is that it is costly in terms of money and staff time. Moreover, these investigations often find that agencies are doing what they should be doing. Because of these problems, Congress and the president often follow a different strategy. Rather than undertaking a series of investigations, they wait until they receive a complaint about bureaucratic actions, then focus investigative efforts on those cases. This practice is labeled **fire alarm oversight**.[71] The so-called fire alarm that sets off an investigation can take many different forms. Constituents may let their congressional representatives or their staff know of a problem with the bureaucracy. Similarly, lobbyists, corporate executives, and ordinary citizens often contact the president and his or her staff with complaints. Newspaper reporters and Internet bloggers also provide information on what bureaucrats are doing. In addition, some agencies have advisory committees that not only help make agency decisions but also keep Congress and the president informed about their agencies' actions.[72]

The case of the COVID-19 death statistics mentioned at the beginning of this chapter is a clear example of fire alarm oversight. After major media outlets reported on the debate between the White House and the CDC over which deaths should be included (and some members of Congress then came out in support of the CDC), the White House quietly ended its effort to intervene in the CDC's reporting process. These fire alarms provide exactly the sort of information that Congress and the president often lack about how bureaucrats are implementing laws and directives, including cases in which bureaucrats are doing (or planning to do) something that contradicts their mandate. Such communications tell Congress and the president where to focus their efforts to monitor the bureaucracy, drawing their attention to agencies or programs in which problems have been reported and removing the need to try to oversee the entire government at once.

While we have talked a lot in this chapter about the efforts of Republicans, including President Trump, to control the bureaucracy, an interest in bureaucratic actions is a bipartisan phenomenon in Washington. Democratic elected officials may prefer a larger, more active government, but they are just as unwilling as Republicans to remove all checks on bureaucratic actions. Democrats often take the position of protecting bureaucrats against executive branch interference. At the same time, though, Democratic elected officials use their control over budgets to push bureaucrats toward decisions they prefer. For example, in the case of NASA's moon landing plans discussed earlier, Texas Democrats have worked to ensure that the project is controlled by the Johnson Space Center in Houston rather than another NASA center located elsewhere.

Correcting violations

When the president or members of Congress find a case of bureaucratic drift, they can take steps to influence the bureaucrats' actions. Many tactics can be used to bring a wayward agency into line. Legislation or an executive order can send a clear directive to an agency or remove its discretion, tasks and programs can be moved to an agency that is more closely aligned with elected officials' goals, political appointees at an agency can be replaced, and agencies can be reorganized. For example, one consequence of the

police patrol oversight
A method of oversight in which members of Congress constantly monitor the bureaucracy to make sure that laws are implemented correctly.

fire alarm oversight
A method of oversight in which members of Congress respond to complaints about the bureaucracy or problems of implementation only as they arise rather than exercising constant vigilance.

One reason that attempts to pass legislation forcing the FDA to alter its drug-approval process have had little success is that the FDA's process is considered to have worked mostly as intended, approving new drugs that are safe and effective and keeping ineffective or unsafe drugs off the market. This was especially important as drug manufacturers raced to find a cure for COVID-19.

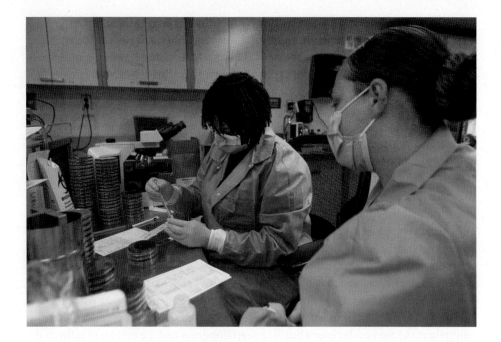

Trump administration's slow process of making political appointments and its reliance on acting positions, particularly for the State Department, was a shift in policy-making power to individuals in the White House.

One of the most significant difficulties in dealing with bureaucratic drift is disagreement between members of Congress and the president about whether an agency is doing the right thing—regardless of whether the agency is following its original orders. Many strategies for influencing an agency's behavior require joint action by the president and congressional majorities. Without presidential support, members of Congress need a two-thirds majority to impose corrections. Without congressional support, the president can only threaten to cut an agency's proposed budget, change its home within the federal bureaucracy, or set up a new agency to do what the errant agency refuses to do. Actually carrying out these threats requires congressional approval. As a result, disagreements between the president and Congress can give an agency significant freedom, as long as it retains the support of at least one branch of government.

An agency may also be able to fend off elected officials' attempts to take political control if it has a reputation for expertise. For example, one reason that attempts to pass legislation forcing the FDA to alter its drug-approval process have had little success is that the FDA's process is thought to have worked mostly as intended, approving new drugs that are safe and effective and keeping ineffective or unsafe drugs off the market. At the same time, the FDA has responded to pressure from Congress and the president to revise some rules on its own.[73]

Finally, agencies can sometimes combat attempts to control their behavior by appealing to groups that benefit from agency actions.[74] For example, since the 1980s the Occupational Safety and Health Administration (OSHA) has resisted attempts by Republican presidents and Republican members of Congress to eliminate the agency or limit its operations.[75] One element of its strategy has been to build strong ties to labor unions. As a result, OSHA is much more likely to receive complaints about workplace safety from companies with strong unions. The second prong of the strategy has involved building cooperative arrangements with large companies to prevent workplace accidents, an approach that not only protects workers but can save companies a lot of money over the long term. Moreover, when OSHA levies fines against companies that violate safety regulations, the fines are generally much less than the maximum fines that would be allowed by law. As a result, when proposals to limit or eliminate OSHA are debated in Congress, members hear from unions as well as many large corporations in support of keeping the agency in place. Over time, this strategy has generated support for the agency from Democrats and Republicans in the House and Senate.

The consequences of control

Elected officials' competing desires to both control what bureaucrats do and tap their expertise explain many of the seemingly dysfunctional aspects of the bureaucracy. Part of the problem is the nature of the tasks given to bureaucrats. Even when members of Congress and the president agree on which problems deserve attention, bureaucrats often face the much harder task of translating these officials' lofty problem-solving goals into concrete policies. Given the magnitude of this job, it is no surprise that even the best efforts of government agencies do not always succeed.

Most important, the use of standard operating procedures is rooted partly in the complexity of bureaucrats' tasks—but also in the desire of agency heads and elected officials to control the actions of lower-level staff. In some disaster relief efforts, government agencies have found that preset plans and procedures worked against the need to respond quickly to alleviate human suffering. And while the FDA's drug-approval process succeeds for the most part at preventing harmful drugs from coming to market, the delays imposed by the process do prevent some patients from receiving lifesaving treatments. However, in all these cases the decisions do not reflect incompetence or malice. Rules and procedures are needed in any organization to ensure that decisions are made fairly and that they reflect the goals of the organization. But it is impossible to find procedures that will work well in all cases, particularly for the kinds of policy decisions made by bureaucrats.

Cases of bureaucratic failure (poorly conceived policies or regulations, inaction, red tape) are often cited to "prove" that bureaucrats are incompetent, lazy, or dumb. The real story is that bureaucrats are often given nearly impossible tasks or political mandates that limit their authority. In this sense, complaints about bureaucrats have more to do with what we want them to do than with their unwillingness or inability to execute these missions.

"Why Should I Care?"

**AP®
POLICY IN
PRACTICE**

The Clean Power Plan

Many of the policies covered in this book have culminated in legislation passed by both houses of Congress and signed by the president of the United States (or sometimes vetoed by the president and then overridden by a 2–3 vote in the House of Representatives and the Senate). This is the normal path, but sometimes presidents have felt that Congress is not acting in accord with their wishes and, in turn, with the common good. If presidents feel this way, there are other ways that they can implement policy by circumventing Congress. One such tool at a president's disposal is the executive order, which is defined in Chapter 5 (The Presidency) as a proclamation that unilaterally changes government policy without subsequent congressional consent.

Executive orders are often controversial, especially for opponents of the actions, for the very fact that they do not go through the normal legislative process. Furthermore, it is supposed to be the legislative branch and not the executive who makes laws. As pointed out in Chapter 5, executive orders usually concern administrative/bureaucratic issues because Congress passed a law giving the president specific authority on some aspects of the policy. But sometimes there is a belief (or a Supreme Court judgment) that presidents have overstepped their authority. Despite these possible drawbacks to a well-functioning democracy, as some would define it, all presidents from George Washington to the present have used executive orders, some more than others.

As outlined in more detail in the Policy in Practice section on the Endangered Species Act in Chapter 8 (pp. 358–62), environmental damage caused by pollution has been on the minds of many Americans since at least the height of the industrial revolution in the late 1800s and early 1900s. Major antipollution laws were passed in the early 1970s under President Nixon, who also started the Environmental Protection Agency (EPA) through an executive order (though this use is more in line with the powers of the executive branch as viewed by the Supreme Court). Throughout most of the twentieth century, concern for the environment was a nonpartisan issue, something agreed upon by both Democrats and Republicans. The Republican Party started parting ways with the Democrats in the 1980s under President Reagan, but the schism between the two parties grew most pronounced in the twenty-first century when global warming and climate change became major components of the environmental conservation vocabulary. Roughly speaking, across the political divide, both parties initially agreed that climate change was real, but its extent was debated as well as the costs to businesses and the economy of doing anything to reverse the changes. As the twenty-first century progressed, the terms "climate change denial" and "global warming denial" entered the vocabulary as well. Climate change deniers, in short, either do not believe there is a significant warming of the planet or do not believe that the primary cause is human activity or rising levels of carbon dioxide. Those who support this view tend to identify more as Republicans than Democrats, though this view is by no means held by a majority of Republicans.

When Barack Obama was sworn in as the 44th president in January 2008, this was the political environment into which he entered. With the support of almost the entire scientific community, a significant portion of Americans, many environmental groups, and state leaders from around the world, he pledged that his administration would combat global warming. In his inaugural address, he talked about utilizing alternative forms of energy, such as solar and wind. Just a month later, he ensured that fighting climate change would be on the political agenda by proposing $15 billion a year to invest in renewable energy sources. He raised the issue again in the 2010 State of the Union address, and three years later, when he saw that Congress was still not willing to act, he warned he would use other means at his disposal, such as executive orders "to reduce pollution, prepare our communities for the consequences of climate change, and speed the transition to more sustainable sources of energy."[76] The result of these executive orders is the Clean Power Plan (CPP), which was hailed by its supporters as the most aggressive and ambitious plan of its kind in the United States for pollution abatement. Opponents agreed, and since this plan is not a duly passed law, a weakness of an executive order, it was relatively easy for President Trump to effectively dismantle the CPP and replace it with the Affordable Clean Energy rule (ACE). As mentioned repeatedly, the policy process is a cycle, and with this new policy the next cycle has begun, which will most likely be criticized and modified in future administrations.

Policy Stages

1. Problem Recognition
    -   Global warming, a major aspect of climate change, is a human-made problem that must be reversed, according to a growing number of scientists, environmental organizations, and governments.
    -   Global warming is caused primarily by the burning of fossil fuels, such as coal, oil, and natural gas, which emit so-called greenhouse gases.
    -   Global warming leads to droughts, famine, storms, receding coastlines, melting icebergs, and, in general, unpredictable weather patterns.
    -   Reducing pollution from power plants, which use fossil fuels, is key to reversing global warming.
    -   There is a growing concern in countries around the world about global warming and its effects.
    -   Developing countries feel the burden of reducing emissions should be shared by all countries, most of all by the countries that produce the most pollution, such as advanced, industrialized countries like the United States.

2. Agenda Setting
    -   The United Nations Framework Convention on Climate Change was adopted in May 1992 and went into effect on March 21, 1994.
        -   It made a worldwide commitment to reduce the harmful effects of global warming by reducing carbon emissions.
        -   It meets annually.
        -   Kyoto Protocol was adopted on December 11, 1997, and went into effect on February 16, 2005.
            -   It established targets for reducing emissions of six greenhouse gases.
        -   COP 21 (Conference of the Parties 21), also known as the Paris Agreement, was adopted on December 12, 2015, and went into effect on November 4, 2016.
            -   Signatory countries agreed to keep global temperatures below 2°C and possibly no more than 1.5°C by 2100.
    -   President Obama promised to tackle this pollution issue in major speeches:
        -   Inaugural address on January 21, 2009
        -   First address to a joint session of Congress on February 24, 2009
        -   State of the Union speeches on January 27, 2010, and February 12, 2013
    -   On June 18, 2014, the EPA made a proposal that became the framework for the CPP.

3. Deliberation and Formulation
    -   President Obama tried to introduce cap-and-trade legislation, which sets limits on the amount of pollution each firm can emit and allows firms to then buy permits from other firms polluting below the limit. However, this legislation died in the Senate in 2010 because of opposition from the Republican Party (especially Tea Party members) and the coal industry.
        -   The system is viewed as a tax on the energy industry.
        -   Opponents of the legislation speculated that it would increase electricity costs and the price of energy and decrease jobs and the gross domestic product (GDP).

- President Obama decided to address climate change by introducing new rules through existing laws, such as the Clean Air Act of 1970, which gives the EPA the authority to reduce any pollutants that can cause health problems.
  - Finding new uses of existing antipollution laws meant that the president could enact this policy without the approval of Congress.
- Over 300 major businesses signed a letter supporting the plan.
- Opposition came from Republican states, which made the following claims:
  - Unemployment would increase in the coal industry due to lower demand and higher costs.
  - Electricity prices would increase due to higher costs.

4. Enactment
   - President Obama presented the CPP to the public on August 3, 2015.
   - It was the first policy ever proposed by the EPA to reduce CO_2 emissions from power plants.
   - It claimed that it would decrease health issues and create jobs by decreasing greenhouse emissions by almost one-third in 15 years.

5. Implementation
   - The EPA determined the Best System of Emissions Reduction (BSER) consisting of three building blocks:
     - Building block 1 improved the efficiency of coal-fired power plants.
     - Building block 2 shifted away from coal-fired plants (more pollution) to natural gas plants (less pollution) as much as possible.
     - Building block 3 moved more toward wind, water, and solar power, all of which use renewable energy resources.
   - Each state was allowed to design its own plan to meet its particular targets with regard to regulating its power plants.
   - If states did not design their own plans, the federal government would work directly with the power plants in those states.
   - Carbon pollution limits would start to be phased in beginning in 2022 and gradually reach the 32 percent reduction level (compared with 2005 levels) by 2030.

6. Evaluation
   - The EPA projected that carbon emissions from electricity would decrease significantly by 2030 compared with 2005.
   - It projected health and cost benefits by predicting reduced premature deaths, asthma-related illnesses, heart attacks, and absences from work and school.
   - Since minorities and poorer people disproportionately live near power plants, they would benefit a great deal if carbon emissions were reduced.
   - Many members of the Republican Party claimed that there would be a series of negative effects on the economy, including higher costs, lower profits, and less employment.
     - The latitude given to states for reducing pollution meant that many might make the decision to close many coal plants, which would reduce pollution but increase unemployment in that sector.
   - Circumventing Congress is unconstitutional according to some members of Congress and legal experts.

7. Possible Modifications, Expansion, or Termination of Policy
   - Both houses used the Congressional Review Act (1996) to pass a "resolution of disapproval" in late 2015 in an attempt to strike down the CPP because of its overreach.
     - The act was vetoed by President Obama on December 18, 2015.

- The Supreme Court "stayed" (stopped implementation of) the CPP on February 9, 2016, until all legal battles against it were resolved.
- President Trump withdrew from the Paris Agreement on climate change on June 11, 2017.
- President Trump and other members of his administration, such as EPA administrator Scott Pruitt, did not believe that CO_2 emissions are a major source of climate change.
- Senate Majority Leader Mitch McConnell sent a letter to all governors telling them to ignore the directives outlined in the CPP.
- The EPA implemented ACE on June 19, 2019.
  - It replaced the CPP.
  - It reduced efficiency standards for coal-powered plants, which would make it cheaper to produce electricity using coal.
  - It increased pollution from coal, according to the EPA.
  - The EPA lowered the health cost rubric used to calculate coal's harmful effects.
  - It was praised by many states that have a large coal industry; Republican members of Congress; and various organizations, such as the Heritage Foundation, Americans for Tax Reform, the Edison Electric Institute, and the U.S. Chamber's Global Energy Institute.
  - It was opposed by many states; Democratic politicians; legal experts; and health advocacy organizations, such as the American Lung Association, the Allergy & Asthma Network, the American Heart Association, and the Center for Climate Change and Health.

Questions for Discussion

1. Economists and political leaders often consider costs and benefits when deciding whether or not a policy should be enacted. What are the costs and benefits of implementing the CPP?
2. Identify the stakeholders who would most likely be in favor of implementing the CPP and the stakeholders who would most likely be against it. What are the reasons behind each of their positions?
3. There are many different definitions of democracy. Is it democratic for a president to issue an executive order rather than going through the normal legislative process? Why or why not?

Unpacking the Conflict

Considering all that we've discussed in this chapter, let's return to President Trump's often-contentious relationship with members of the federal bureaucracy. Were bureaucrats really obstructing the Trump agenda, or were they just doing their jobs? How do elected officials control a bureaucracy of experts, in the midst of a pandemic or in more routine times?

A deeper look shows that some of the time, conflicts between President Trump and bureaucratic officials reflected real disagreements. In the case of counting deaths from COVID-19, for example, it is not hard to see why Trump or the politically minded people around him preferred a definition that minimized casualties. However, the fact

that many bureaucrats are policy experts suggests an alternative explanation for their preference for a different accounting scheme. Rather than trying to embarrass Trump or ensure his defeat, bureaucrats may have been acting from expertise, working to account for the pandemic in a way that facilitated an effective governmental response.

Bureaucratic expertise and the resulting problem of control also explain the cumbersome procedures for hiring, firing, and decision making that are a feature of operations in many government agencies. Sometimes bureaucrats simply make mistakes, choosing the wrong policy because they—and, in some cases, all the people involved—lack information about the tasks they were given. Bureaucrats may drag their feet when they oppose their tasks on policy grounds. But in many cases, cumbersome procedures are the result of a fundamental trade-off faced by elected officials between wanting to exercise control over the bureaucracy and wanting to ensure that changes in policy produce their intended effect. Put another way, conflict over public policy often translates into conflicting ideas about what bureaucrats should do, resulting in complex, often-contradictory mandates and directions imposed on bureaucrats. In this way, politics shapes virtually all aspects of the bureaucracy and of the choices bureaucrats make, even in places where it is hard to discern political motivations.

"What's Your Take?"

Should elected officials defer to bureaucratic expertise?

Or should the president's agenda override other concerns?

AP® STUDY GUIDE

Summary

The bureaucracy is composed of both civil servants and political appointees who use their bureaucratic discretion to interpret and implement a wide range of government policies. While bureaucrats are policy experts, most members of Congress are not. Nonetheless, Congress tries to control how the bureaucracy operates, which can result in inefficiencies.

The bureaucracy has grown substantially since the turn of the twentieth century, largely in response to citizens' demands that the government do more for the people. The federal government had a very limited role in daily life for much of the nineteenth century, but it expanded during the Progressive Era, when regulatory activity increased and the spoils system was replaced by the federal civil service. The bureaucracy expanded again with the New Deal and Great Society programs, which increased the number of services the government provided.

The modern bureaucracy serves a wide range of functions, but the division of labor within the bureaucracy does not always have an obvious logic. Overlapping or confusing jurisdictions can be the result of elected officials' attempts to shape the agency behavior by assigning a task to an executive department rather than an independent agency. The overall size of the bureaucracy reflects the demands of constituents but also fits the needs of elected officials to improve their chances of reelection.

The regulations within the civil service system were established to separate politics from policy. Rather than getting and retaining a job for political reasons, individuals are hired based on merit and are quite difficult to fire. However, the president makes senior-level appointments that are not protected by civil service regulations and are more political in nature. These appointments are instrumental in helping the president control the bureaucracy.

With their expertise, bureaucrats have the power to significantly influence government policy. This creates a dilemma for elected officials, who want to enjoy the benefits of the expertise while retaining control of the bureaucracy. Lawmakers can generally organize agencies and monitor their behavior to reduce, but not eliminate, bureaucratic drift.

Enduring Understanding

PMI-2: "The federal bureaucracy implements federal policies." (AP® U.S. Government and Politics Course and Exam Description)

Key Terms

budget maximizers (p. 292)
bureaucracy (p. 274)
bureaucratic drift (p. 298)
civil servants (p. 274)
federal civil service (p. 285)
fire alarm oversight (p. 301)

independent agencies (p. 288)
notice-and-comment procedure (p. 275)
Office of Management and Budget (p. 288)
oversight (p. 300)
police patrol oversight (p. 301)
political appointees (p. 274)
principal–agent game (p. 280)
problem of control (p. 280)

red tape (p. 282)
regulation (p. 275)
regulatory capture (p. 281)
standard operating procedures (SOPs) (p. 282)
state capacity (p. 280)
turkey farms (p. 296)

Multiple-Choice Questions (Arranged by Topic)

Topic 2.12: The Bureaucracy (PMI-2)

Questions 1–3 refer to the table.

Employment in Cabinet Departments

Organization	Total Employees
Defense (civilian only)	741,500
Veterans Affairs	375,800
Homeland Security	192,400
Justice	111,900
Treasury	88,000
Agriculture	81,400
Health and Human Services	73,000
Interior	70,000
Transportation	53,100
Commerce	45,000
State	27,100
Labor	14,800
Energy	14,000
Housing and Urban Development	7,400
Education	3,600

Source: Office of Management and Budget, "A Budget for America's Future: Analytical Perspectives, Fiscal Year 2021," 2020, www.whitehouse.gov/wp-content/uploads/2020/02/spec_fy21.pdf (accessed 5/22/20).

1. **Which of the following accurately describes the information presented in the table?**
    (A) The Department of Defense has the largest number of employees because of the high number of individuals enlisted in the military.
    (B) The department with the lowest number of employees is the Department of Education.
    (C) There are more bureaucrats working for independent agencies than for cabinet departments.
    (D) Congress has allocated more money to the Department of Labor than to the Department of Energy.

2. **Which of the following best explains how the majority of the employees in the table get their jobs?**
    (A) They are hired for their expertise through the merit system.
    (B) They are hired as a reward for helping the president get elected.
    (C) They are appointed by the president and confirmed by the Senate.
    (D) They are appointed by the president and confirmed by the House.

3. **Which of the following best explains how the heads of most of the cabinet departments in the table would be addressed?**
    (A) attorney general
    (B) inspector general
    (C) secretary
    (D) deputy

Topic 2.13: Discretionary and Rule-Making Authority (PMI-2)

Questions 4–5 refer to the political cartoon.

4. **Which of the following best describes the cartoonist's point of view in the political cartoon?**

   (A) One role of the bureaucracy is to teach senior citizens how to read a diagram.

   (B) The ins and outs of the Medicare Prescription Drug Benefit is easy to follow if you just look at the provided diagram.

   (C) Bureaucratic agencies often neglect to consider the needs of their customers when making policy decisions.

   (D) The Medicare Prescription Drug Benefit will put senior citizens on the road to good health.

5. **Which of the following best describes the unnecessarily complex regulations demonstrated in the political cartoon?**

   (A) power of the purse

   (B) red tape

   (C) merit system

   (D) turkey farms

6. **Which of the following statements best explains how the Environmental Protection Agency (EPA) decides on the limits to the amount of various pollutants that can be emitted from factories, automobiles, and electrical power plants?**

   (A) The EPA relies on the Supreme Court to determine the allowable limits.

   (B) The amounts of pollutants that are allowed are explicitly spelled out in the Clean Air Act of 1970 and must be followed by the EPA.

   (C) The EPA uses rule-making authority from the Clean Air Act of 1970 to use its discretion to decide on the appropriate levels of pollution.

   (D) The president dictates in a signing statement the exact limits that the EPA must in turn follow.

Topic 2.14: Holding the Bureaucracy Accountable (PMI-2)

7. Which of the following scenarios best explains how the bureaucracy is affected by the power of the purse?

   (A) An appointee in the Department of the Interior who had pushed for expanded oil drilling in Alaska left the government to work for one of the companies that would benefit from this expansion.

   (B) Richard Cordray, the first head of the Consumer Financial Protection Bureau, was nominated after some senators objected to President Obama's first nominee, Elizabeth Warren.

   (C) The Federal Food, Drug, and Cosmetic Act gave the Food and Drug Administration (FDA) the job of determining which drugs are safe and effective.

   (D) In an attempt to refocus the Centers for Disease Control and Prevention (CDC) on its core mission of preventing and controlling infectious diseases, Congress trims the budget for the agency by 8 percent.

8. In 2017, President Trump appointed Michael Mulvaney, who was a former Republican congressman and the head of the Office of Management and Budget and chief of staff in the Trump administration, to run the Consumer Financial Protection Bureau (CFPB), even though Mulvaney was a longtime opponent of the CFPB and sought, as a member of Congress, to abolish the agency. Which of the following best explains why President Trump appointed Mulvaney?

   (A) A majority in the House of Representatives belonged to the same party as President Trump and therefore he knew Mulvaney would more than likely be confirmed.

   (B) Since Mulvaney had served previously in both the executive and legislative branches, he was automatically part of an iron triangle and would be easily confirmed.

   (C) To avoid future instances of congressional oversight, Trump appointed an expert in the area of finance.

   (D) Trump's appointment of an individual who was likely to act in line with the president's policy preferences was made to try to shape the agency's operations.

Topic 2.15: Policy and the Branches of Government (PMI-2)

9. Which of the following best explains why bureaucrats often respond to pressure from elected officials?

   (A) Bureaucrats are appointed by Congress and their continuation in office is dependent on pleasing members of Congress.

   (B) Bureaucrats need the support of Congress in order to fund their departments and agencies.

   (C) Elected officials are experts and bureaucrats look up to them for guidance.

   (D) Federal law requires bureaucrats to implement the law as passed by Congress.

10. Which of the following is an accurate comparison of the executive branch and legislative branch checks on the federal bureaucracy?

	Executive Checks	Legislative Checks
(A)	firing the head of an agency	conducting committee hearings about an agency's actions
(B)	confirming nominations for the head of an agency	nominating the head of an agency
(C)	impeaching the head of an agency	controlling the funding for an agency
(D)	eliminating an agency and distributing its functions to another agency	declaring bureaucratic law unconstitutional

Free-Response Questions

Concept Application

The regulations that guide the FDA drug-approval process prioritize the goal of preventing harmful drugs from coming to market. As a result, patients sometimes cannot get access to experimental treatments because FDA approval has not been granted, even when those treatments are the patients' only remaining option. Advocates for patients have argued that people with dire prognoses should be allowed to use these treatments as a potentially lifesaving last resort. However, current FDA regulations prevent patients from doing so except under very special circumstances.

After reading the scenario, respond to A, B, and C below:

(A) Referencing the scenario, describe a power Congress could use to encourage the agency to speed up the process that is discussed in the scenario.

(B) In the context of the scenario, explain how the use of congressional power described in Part A impacts Congress's relationship with the executive branch.

(C) There has been a lot of pressure to approve new drugs or vaccines to fight COVID-19. Explain why Congress gives agencies discretion rather than outlining the specifics when writing the original law.

Quantitative Analysis

Employment in Cabinet Departments

Organization	Total Employees
Defense (civilian only)	741,500
Veterans Affairs	375,800
Homeland Security	192,400
Justice	111,900
Treasury	88,000
Agriculture	81,400
Health and Human Services	73,000
Interior	70,000
Transportation	53,100
Commerce	45,000
State	27,100
Labor	14,800
Energy	14,000
Housing and Urban Development	7,400
Education	3,600

Source: Office of Management and Budget, "A Budget for America's Future: Analytical Perspectives, Fiscal Year 2021," 2020, www.whitehouse.gov/wp-content/uploads/2020/02/spec_fy21.pdf (accessed 5/22/20).

Use the table to answer the questions.

(A) Identify the number of individuals employed by the Department of Homeland Security.

(B) Describe a difference between the number of individuals employed by the Department of Education and the Department of Homeland Security, as shown in the table.

(C) Explain how the difference in the number of individuals employed by the Department of Education and the Department of Homeland Security shown in the table is reflective of the concept of federalism.

(D) Explain why, despite being appointed by the president, heads of the cabinet departments might not always follow the will of the president.

8

Civil Liberties
It's a free country...right?

» **"Under the guise of 'speech codes' and 'safe spaces' and 'trigger warnings,' these universities have tried to restrict free thought, impose total conformity, and shut down the voices of great young Americans.... All of that changes starting right now."**[1]
President Donald Trump

« **"If I were president of a university and I had some hate speech person coming, I wouldn't let them come. I just wouldn't."**[2]
John Kasich, former Ohio governor

The constitutional protection for speech is clear and strong: "Congress shall make no law...abridging the freedom of speech." However, recent protests against controversial speakers booked to speak on college campuses are calling into question the scope of those protections. Must college campuses allow talks by right-wing provocateur Milo Yiannopoulos, who has said child sexual abuse "really is not that big of a deal," or White nationalist Richard Spencer, who has called for a White ethno-state?[3] Must they embrace conservative speakers like political commentator Ann Coulter and political scientist Charles Murray? All of these speakers met strong and sometimes violent protests at campuses around the country.[4] A CNN headline described the situation as "War on Campus."[5] A speech by Richard Spencer at the University of Florida caused Governor Rick Scott to declare a state of emergency, and the university had to spend nearly $600,000 to provide security for the event. Despite these efforts, three men shouting "Heil Hitler" fired a shot at students demonstrating against Spencer's speech (but nobody was hurt).[6]

Many are calling for limits on the kind of hate speech that some claim speakers like Yiannopoulos and Spencer promote and for the creation of "safe spaces" on campus where students would be protected from hurtful speech within a broader effort to promote social justice. Others see such efforts as "political correctness" run amok and are concerned that free speech is under attack as conservative speakers are prevented from talking. When announcing his executive order on free speech on campus, President Trump said, "We will not stand idly by and allow public institutions to violate their students' constitutional rights. If a college or university doesn't allow you to speak, we will not give them money."[7]

Should controversial figures like Milo Yiannopoulos be allowed to speak on public college campuses in the face of popular opposition to their views? In February 2017, Berkeley students organized protests in response to a planned appearance by Yiannopoulos. Although the speech was eventually canceled, that didn't stop protests from getting violent. Students and supporters of Yiannopoulos clashed on campus.

CHAPTER GOALS

The controversy over free speech on campus does not divide neatly along partisan or ideological lines. While strongly disagreeing with the conservative speakers' views, recently President Obama has expressed support for the free speech side, saying college students shouldn't be "coddled and protected from different points of view.... Feel free to disagree with somebody, but don't try to shut them up."[8] The left-leaning American Civil Liberties Union has also defended free speech on campus, arguing, "Speech that deeply offends our morality or is hostile to our way of life warrants the same constitutional protection as other speech because the right of free speech is indivisible: when we grant the government the power to suppress controversial ideas, we are all subject to censorship by the state."[9]

Some have argued that the controversy is overblown, pointing to evidence that there is more support for the First Amendment on college campuses than in the public at large[10] and that the number of disinvited conservative speakers is down from a high of 24 in 2016 to 5 in 2019.[11] However, others argue that the swastikas and nooses, historically symbols of hate and aggression, that have recently been portrayed on campuses are not free speech and that the real question is where to draw the line.

Defining the boundaries of our liberties and freedoms, like freedom of speech, is messy and complicated. Can controversial speech on college campuses be limited? When we say America is a free country, what does this really mean? Are there limits to those freedoms? If so, how should political actors draw the lines between protected behavior and actions that may be regulated?

DEFINE WHAT WE MEAN BY CIVIL LIBERTIES

**AP®
FOUNDATIONAL
DOCUMENT**

civil liberties
Constitutionally established guarantees and freedoms that protect citizens, opinions, and property against arbitrary government interference.

Defining civil liberties

The terms "civil rights" and "civil liberties" are often used interchangeably, but there are important differences (see Nuts & Bolts 8.1). To oversimplify a bit, civil liberties are about freedom and civil rights are about equality. Given that civil liberties are rooted in the Bill of Rights, it might have been less confusing if it had been called the "Bill of Liberties." (This distinction is discussed further in Chapter 9.)

Civil liberties are deeply rooted in our key idea that politics is conflictual and involves trade-offs. When the Supreme Court rules on civil liberties cases, it must balance an individual's freedom with government interests and the public good. In some cases, the Court must not only balance these interests but also "draw a line" between permissible and illegal conduct concerning a specific liberty.

Balancing interests

Civil liberties must be balanced against competing interests, because when it comes to our freedoms there are no absolutes. The trade-off between civil liberties and national security in the war on terrorism illustrates this point. Many Americans were concerned that civil liberties were being eroded upon discovering that the government was arresting suspected terrorists in the United States and taking them to foreign countries that are less protective of civil liberties—Egypt, Syria, Jordan, and Morocco—to be interrogated through torture.[12] Despite these concerns, even the strongest critic of state-sponsored torture would have to admit that, in some instances, it might be justified. For example, if a nuclear device were set to detonate in

Distinguishing Civil Liberties from Civil Rights

NUTS & BOLTS 8.1

Civil Liberties	Civil Rights
Basic freedoms and liberties	Protection from discrimination
Rooted in the Bill of Rights and the "due process" protection of the Fourteenth Amendment	Rooted in laws and the "equal protection" clause of the Fourteenth Amendment
Primarily restrict what the government can do to you ("*Congress* shall make no law . . . abridging the freedom of speech")	Protect you from discrimination both by the government and by individuals

Source: Compiled by the authors.

"Why Should I Care?" One easy way to remember the difference between the two is that civil liberties are about freedom and civil rights concern equality. Also, civil liberties *limit* the actions government can take against you, while civil rights *expand* the actions that you can take as a citizen while also protecting you from discrimination from the government and other citizens.

Manhattan in three hours, few would insist on protecting the civil liberties of someone who knew where the bomb was hidden. Once we recognize that our freedoms are not absolute, it becomes a question of how they are balanced against other interests, such as national security.

Other interests that compete with civil liberties include public safety and public health. For example, members of some Christian fundamentalist churches regularly handle dangerous snakes in their services, though many states and cities have laws prohibiting the practice. The courts have upheld those laws, saying that "public safety is superior to religious practice."[13] But despite the laws, snake handling in churches continues to be a problem. In 2013, Tennessee Wildlife Resource Agency officials cited Reverend Andrew Hamblin, co-star of the National Geographic Channel reality show *Snake Salvation*, for keeping 53 poisonous snakes and using them in services (an estimated 125 churches still handle snakes). Hamblin was eventually acquitted by a grand jury. A couple of months later, his co-star Reverend Jamie Coots died after being bitten by a rattlesnake in his church and refusing treatment.[14] Similarly, in some states the Amish are forced to place reflective "slow-moving vehicle" triangles on their horse-drawn carriages, even if it violates their religious beliefs, because of the paramount concern for public safety (see the How It Works graphic in this chapter, pp. 324–25).[15] Yet the Amish are not forced to send their children to public schools despite a state law requiring all children to attend school through age 16. In *Wisconsin v. Yoder* (1972), the Court said this law presented "a very real threat of undermining the Amish community and religious practice as it exists today."[16]

Wisconsin v. Yoder
A 1972 case in which the Supreme Court held that compelling Amish students to attend school past the eighth grade violates the free exercise clause. The ruling opened the door to homeschooling, which is a common practice today.

AP® SUPREME COURT CASE

How can conflicts be resolved between civil liberties and other legitimate interests, such as public safety and public health? Sometimes freedom is forced to give way. Courts have upheld bans on the religious practice of snake handling (though several churches have been undeterred by these bans) and laws requiring the Amish to display reflective triangles when driving slow-moving buggies on public roads, despite religious objections to doing so.

These decisions show that balancing interests is never a simple process and involves deciding whether a specific civil liberty or some competing public interest is more compelling in a specific case.

Drawing lines

Along with balancing competing interests, court rulings draw the lines defining the limits of permissible conduct by the government or an individual in the context of a specific civil liberty. For example, despite the First Amendment protection of freedom of speech, it is obvious that some speech cannot be permitted. The classic example is falsely yelling "fire!" in a crowded theater. Therefore, the courts must interpret the law to draw the line between protected speech and impermissible speech.

The same applies to other civil liberties, such as the establishment of religion, freedom of the press, freedom from illegal searches, or other due process rights. For example, the First Amendment prohibits the government from establishing an official religion, which the Court has carefully interpreted over the years to avoid "excessive entanglement" between any religion and the government. On these grounds, government-sponsored prayer in public schools has been banned since the early 1960s. But sometimes it is difficult to draw the line between acceptable and impermissible government involvement concerning religion in schools. One such ruling allowed taxpayer subsidies to fund parochial schools for buying books but not maps. (This odd hairsplitting led the late senator Daniel Patrick Moynihan to quip, "What about atlases?"[17]) Another difficult issue is the Fourth Amendment prohibition against "unreasonable searches and seizures" and the role of drug-sniffing dogs. Here the line drawing involves deciding whether a sniff is a search and, if so, under what circumstances it is reasonable (see the Take a Stand feature in this chapter). Search and seizure cases also involve balancing interests: in this case, the individual freedoms of the target of police action and the broader interests in public order and security.

Drug-Sniffing Dogs: An Illegal Search?

In 2013, the Supreme Court was presented with the case of Joelis Jardines, whom police suspected of growing marijuana inside his Miami home based on an anonymous tip. Police went to the home with a trained drug-detection dog. On the front porch, the dog gave a positive signal indicating the presence of drugs. The police returned with a search warrant, found a marijuana-growing operation, and arrested Jardines. However, the Florida Supreme Court threw out the evidence, arguing it was an illegal search. The case then made its way to the U.S. Supreme Court, which was faced with this question: Should drug-sniffing dogs be allowed outside a home without a warrant? More broadly, in the context of rapidly changing technology, what is the public's "reasonable expectation" for privacy?

A drug-sniffing dog is no more invasive than the surveillance technologies we encounter every day. The Court has ruled that police do not need a search warrant to have drug-sniffing dogs search luggage at an airport or a car that has been stopped for a traffic violation unrelated to drugs. Lower courts have also ruled that sniffs are not considered searches in a hotel hallway, at a school locker, outside a passenger train's sleeper compartments, or outside an apartment door. Is a sniff outside someone's home any more invasive?

It might not seem that way, especially when you consider the reach of new surveillance methods that are on the horizon. Other technologies that are becoming more common or will be used soon include RFIDs (radio frequency identifications), which are the size of a grain of rice and transmit information wirelessly through radio waves; facial recognition software and iris scanners; "smart dust devices"—tiny wireless micromechanical sensors—that can detect light and movement; and drones, which have primarily been used for military purposes but also have vast potential for tracking suspects in any situation.

Warrantless surveillance of somebody's home crosses a line. Lower courts have been split on whether drug-sniffing dogs may be used outside a home without a warrant, due, in part, to a Supreme Court precedent giving homes stronger Fourth Amendment protection than cars, lockers, or other areas. For example, in 2001 the Court ruled that police needed a warrant to use a thermal-imaging device outside a home when trying to detect marijuana that was believed to be growing under heat lamps inside.

The U.S. Supreme Court ultimately agreed in the Jardines case, saying that there is a general expectation that anyone may come onto a front porch as long as the uninvited person simply knocks and then leaves if there is no answer. The majority opinion wryly noted: "Complying with the terms of that traditional invitation does not require fine-grained legal knowledge; it is generally managed without incident by the Nation's Girl Scouts and trick-or-treaters." But, they continued, "introducing a trained police dog to explore the area around the home in hopes of discovering incriminating evidence is something else. There is no customary invitation to do *that*."[a]

A U.S. Customs and Border Patrol agent in Florida uses a drug-sniffing dog to inspect incoming mail at a sorting facility.

New and future technologies continue to complicate the question of just what is "reasonable." Justice Alito raised this question in oral arguments in a Supreme Court case involving a GPS tracking device. He said, "Technology is changing people's expectations of privacy. . . . Maybe 10 years from now 90 percent of the population will be using social networking sites and they will have on average 500 friends and they will have allowed their friends to monitor their location 24 hours a day, 365 days a year, through the use of their cell phones. Then—what would the expectation of privacy be then?"[b]

take a stand

1. If you had to decide the case of the drug-sniffing dog, how would you have ruled? Do you think that homes should have stronger privacy expectations than cars or school lockers? Even when it concerns illegal drugs?

2. How would you answer Justice Alito's question about the expectation of privacy in an era of rapidly changing technology? When should law-enforcement officials have to get a warrant to monitor our behavior?

EXPLAIN WHY THE BILL OF RIGHTS WAS ADDED TO THE CONSTITUTION AND HOW IT CAME TO APPLY TO THE STATES

**AP®
FOUNDATIONAL
DOCUMENT**

**AP®
FOUNDATIONAL
DOCUMENT**

The origins of civil liberties

Courts define the boundaries of civil liberties, but the other branches of government and the public often get involved as well. The earliest debates during the American Founding illustrate the broad public involvement concerning the basic questions of how our civil liberties would be defined: Should government be limited by an explicit statement of individual liberties? Would these limitations apply to the state governments or just the national government? How should these freedoms evolve as our society changes?

Origins of the Bill of Rights

The original Constitution provided only limited protection of civil liberties: it guaranteed habeas corpus rights (a protection against illegal incarceration) and prohibited bills of attainder (legislation punishing someone for a crime without the benefit of a trial) and ex post facto laws (laws that retroactively change the legal consequences of some behavior). Delegates to the Constitutional Convention made a few attempts to include a broader statement of civil liberties, including one by George Mason and Elbridge Gerry five days before the convention adjourned. But their motion to appoint a committee to draft a bill of rights was rejected. Charles Pinckney and Gerry also tried to add a provision to protect the freedom of the press, but that too was rejected.[18]

Mason and Gerry opposed ratification of the Constitution, partly because it did not include a bill of rights, and many Antifederalists echoed this view, including in the influential Brutus essays, which were written to encourage New Yorkers to reject the Constitution (see especially Brutus 1). In a letter to James Madison, Thomas Jefferson predicted that four states would withhold ratification until a bill of rights was added.[19] Some states ratified the Constitution but urged Congress to draft specific protections for individuals' and states' rights from federal action (they believed protection of civil liberties from state actions should reside in state constitutions). In other states, the Antifederalists who lost the ratification battle continued making their case to the public and Congress. One of the most famous arguments came from the Antifederalists of Pennsylvania, who claimed that a bill of rights was needed to "fundamentally establish those unalienable and personal rights of men, without the full, free, and secure enjoyment of which there can be no liberty, and over which it is not necessary for a good government to have the control."[20] Their statement went on to outline many of those civil liberties that ultimately became the basis for the Bill of Rights.

Madison and other supporters of the Constitution agreed that the 1st Congress would take up the issue, despite their reservations that a Bill of Rights could lead the people into falsely believing that it was an exhaustive list of all their rights. State conventions submitted 124 amendments for consideration. That list was whittled down to 17 by the House and then to 12 by the Senate. This even dozen was approved by the House and sent to the states, which in 1791 ratified the 10 amendments that became the Bill of Rights (see Nuts & Bolts 8.2).[21]

Despite the profound significance of the Bill of Rights, one point limited its reach: it applied only to the laws and actions of the national government and not to those of the states. For example, the First Amendment says that "*Congress* shall make no law" infringing on freedom of religion, speech, and the press, among others. Madison submitted another amendment, which he characterized as "the most valuable of

The Bill of Rights: A Statement of Our Civil Liberties

First Amendment	Freedom of religion, speech, press, and assembly; the separation of church and state; and the right to petition the government.
Second Amendment	Right to bear arms.
Third Amendment	Protection against the forced quartering of troops in one's home.
Fourth Amendment	Protection from unreasonable searches and seizures; "probable cause" is required for search warrants, which must specifically describe the "place to be searched, and the persons or things to be seized."
Fifth Amendment	Protection from forced self-incrimination or double jeopardy (being tried twice for the same crime); no person can be deprived of life, liberty, or property without due process of law; private property cannot be taken for public use without just compensation; and no person can be tried for a serious crime without the indictment of a grand jury.
Sixth Amendment	Right of the accused to a speedy and public trial by an impartial jury, to an attorney, to confront witnesses, to a compulsory process for obtaining witnesses in his or her favor, and to counsel in all felony cases.
Seventh Amendment	Right to a trial by jury in civil cases involving common law.
Eighth Amendment	Protection from excessive bail, excessive fines, and cruel and unusual punishment.
Ninth Amendment	The enumeration of specific rights in the Constitution shall not be construed to deny other rights retained by the people. This has been interpreted to include a general right to privacy and other fundamental rights.
Tenth Amendment	Powers not delegated by the Constitution to the national government, nor prohibited by it to the states, are reserved to the states or to the people.

Source: Compiled by the authors.

"Why Should I Care?" Many of the rights and liberties Americans think of as core American values weren't originally outlined in the Constitution. These first 10 amendments, outlined in the Bill of Rights, affect your daily life: you can practice the religion you choose, you can express your opinions on government actions, and you can choose to carry a gun. Additionally, if you are accused of a crime, the Bill of Rights guarantees your right to a trial by jury and various due process rights.

the whole list," requiring states to protect some civil liberties: "The equal rights of conscience, the freedom of speech or of the press, and the right of trial by jury in criminal cases shall not be infringed by any State."[22] But Antifederalists feared another power grab by the Federalists in limiting states' rights, so the proposed amendment was voted down in Congress. This decision proved consequential, because the national government was quite weak for the first half of our nation's history. Because states exercised as much power over people's lives as the national government did, if not more, it would have been more important for the Bill of Rights to limit the reach of the state governments than to limit that of the federal government. Thus, the Bill of Rights played a surprisingly small role for more than a century. The Supreme Court used it only once before 1866 to invalidate a federal action—in the infamous *Dred Scott* case that contributed to the Civil War (see Chapter 3).

Selective incorporation and the Fourteenth Amendment

The significance of the Bill of Rights increased somewhat with the ratification of the Fourteenth Amendment in 1868. It was one of the three **Civil War amendments** that attempted to guarantee equal rights to the newly freed, formerly enslaved people. (The other two Civil War amendments were the Thirteenth, which abolished slavery, and the Fifteenth, which gave formerly enslaved men the right to vote.) Northern politicians were concerned that southerners would deny basic rights to the formerly enslaved people, so the sweeping language of the Fourteenth Amendment was adopted. Section 1 of the Fourteenth Amendment says:

All persons born or naturalized in the United States, and subject to the jurisdiction thereof, are citizens of the United States and of the State wherein they reside. No State shall make or enforce any law which shall abridge the privileges or immunities of citizens of the United States; nor shall any State deprive any person of life, liberty, or property, without due process of law; nor deny to any person within its jurisdiction the equal protection of the laws.

This language was intended to make sure that states would not deny newly freed people the full protection of the law.[23] The **due process clause**, which forbids any state from denying "life, liberty, or property, without due process of law," led to an especially important expansion of civil liberties because the similar clause in the Fifth Amendment had previously been interpreted by the Court to apply only to the federal government.

Evolving Interpretations by the Supreme Court Despite the amendment's clear statement that "no State shall make or enforce any law," in the Supreme Court's first opportunity to interpret the Fourteenth Amendment in 1873 it continued to rule in favor of protecting states from national government actions only, embracing the "dual citizenship" idea set forth in *Barron v. Baltimore* (the 1833 case ruling that the Fifth Amendment's protection of property from being taken by the government without compensation applied only to the federal government, not to state governments; see Chapter 3).[24] Over the next 50 years, a minority of justices tried mightily to strengthen the power of the Fourteenth Amendment and use it to protect civil liberties against state government action. In two early cases involving property rights and self-incrimination, the Supreme Court started to use the Fourteenth Amendment to prohibit state governments from violating individual rights—but stopped short of invoking amendments in the Bill of Rights itself to support their decisions.[25]

This progression culminated in the 1925 case *Gitlow v. New York*. Here the Court said for the first time that the Fourteenth Amendment incorporated one of the amendments in the Bill of Rights (provisions protecting freedom of speech and freedom of the press) and applied it to the states. The case involved Benjamin Gitlow, a radical socialist convicted under New York's Criminal Anarchy Act of 1902 for advocating the overthrow of the government. The Court upheld his conviction, arguing that his writings were the "language of direct incitement," but it also warned state governments that there were limits on such suppression of speech. This decision marked the first time that the Court ruled that a state law could be challenged because it violated an amendment in the Bill of Rights.[26]

Applying Civil Liberties to the States Slowly over the next 50 years, most civil liberties covered in the Bill of Rights were applied to the states on a right-by-right, case-by-case basis through the Fourteenth Amendment. However, this process of **selective incorporation** was not smooth and incremental. Rather, it progressed in surges with flurries of activity in the 1930s and the 1960s (see Table 8.1). As a result, the

---

Civil War amendments
The Thirteenth, Fourteenth, and Fifteenth Amendments to the Constitution, which abolished slavery and granted civil liberties and voting rights to newly freed people after the Civil War.

due process clause
Part of the Fourteenth Amendment that forbids states from denying "life, liberty, or property" to any person without due process of law. (A nearly identical clause in the Fifth Amendment applies only to the national government.)

Gitlow v. New York
The 1925 Supreme Court ruling that the free speech protections of the First Amendment apply to the states because of the due process clause of the Fourteenth Amendment. However, states could still restrict speech if it had a "dangerous tendency" (that standard is not applied today).

selective incorporation
The process through which most of the civil liberties granted in the Bill of Rights were applied to the states on a case-by-case basis through the Fourteenth Amendment.

Selective Incorporation

TABLE
8.1

The process of applying most of the Bill of Rights to the states progressed in two stages. The first, coming in the 1920s and 1930s, applied the First Amendment to the states; the second came a few decades later and involved criminal defendants' rights.

Amendment	Issue	Case
First Amendment	Freedom of speech	*Gitlow v. New York* (1925)
	Freedom of the press	*Near v. Minnesota* (1931)
	Freedom of assembly	*De Jonge v. Oregon* (1937)
	Right to petition the government	*Hague v. CIO* (1939)
	Free exercise of religion	*Hamilton v. Regents of the University of California* (1934); *Cantwell v. Connecticut* (1940)
	Separation of church and state	*Everson v. Board of Education of Ewing Township* (1947)
Second Amendment	Right to bear arms	*McDonald v. Chicago* (2010)
Fourth Amendment	Protection from unreasonable search and seizure	*Wolf v. Colorado* (1949); *Mapp v. Ohio* (1961)*
Fifth Amendment	Protection from forced self-incrimination	*Malloy v. Hogan* (1964)
	Protection from double jeopardy	*Benton v. Maryland* (1969)
Sixth Amendment	Right to a public trial	*In re Oliver* 333 U.S. 257 (1948)
	Right to a fair trial and an attorney in death-penalty cases	*Powell v. Alabama* (1932)
	Right to an attorney in all felony cases	*Gideon v. Wainwright* (1963)
	Right to an attorney in cases involving jail time	*Argersinger v. Hamlin* (1972)
	Right to a jury trial in a criminal case	*Duncan v. Louisiana* (1968)
	Right to cross-examine a witness	*Pointer v. Texas* (1965)
	Right to compel the testimony of witnesses who are vital for the defendant's case	*Washington v. Texas* (1967)
	Right to a unanimous jury verdict	*Ramos v. Louisiana* (2020)
Eighth Amendment	Protection from cruel and unusual punishment	*Robinson v. California* (1962)†
	Protection from excessive bail	*Schilb v. Kuebel* (1971)‡
	Protection from excessive fines	*Timbs v. Indiana* (2019)
Ninth Amendment	Right to privacy and other nonenumerated, fundamental rights	*Griswold v. Connecticut* (1965)§

Not Incorporated

Third Amendment	Prohibition against the quartering of troops in private homes	
Fifth Amendment	Right to indictment by a grand jury	
Seventh Amendment	Right to a jury trial in a civil case	

* *Wolf v. Colorado* applied the Fourth Amendment to the states (which meant that states could not engage in unreasonable searches and seizures); *Mapp v. Ohio* applied the exclusionary rule to the states (which excludes the use in a trial of illegally obtained evidence).

† Some sources list *Louisiana ex rel. Francis v. Resweber* (1947) as the first case that incorporated the Eighth Amendment. While the decision mentioned the Fifth and Eighth Amendments in the context of the due process clause of the Fourteenth Amendment, this argument was not included in the majority opinion that upheld as constitutional the bizarre double electrocution of prisoner Willie Francis (the electric chair malfunctioned on the first attempt but was successful on the second attempt; see Henry J. Abraham and Barbara A. Perry, *Freedom and the Court: Civil Rights and Civil Liberties in the United States*, 8th ed. [Lawrence: University Press of Kansas, 2003], pp. 71–72).

‡ Justice Blackmun "assumed" in this case that "the Eighth Amendment's proscription of excessive bail [applies] to the states through the Fourteenth Amendment," but later decisions did not seem to share this view. However, Justices Stevens and O'Connor agreed with Blackmun's view in *Browning-Ferris v. Kelco Disposal* (1989). Some sources argue that the excessive bail clause of the Eighth Amendment is unincorporated.

§ Justice Goldberg argued for explicit incorporation of the Ninth Amendment in a concurring opinion joined by Justices Warren and Brennan. The opinion of the Court referred more generally to a privacy right rooted in five amendments, including the Ninth, but did not explicitly argue for incorporation.

Source: Compiled by the authors.

The First Amendment

The First Amendment states:

"Congress shall make no law respecting an establishment of religion, or prohibiting the free exercise thereof; or abridging the freedom of speech, or of the press; or the right of the people peaceably to assemble, and to petition the government for a redress of grievances."

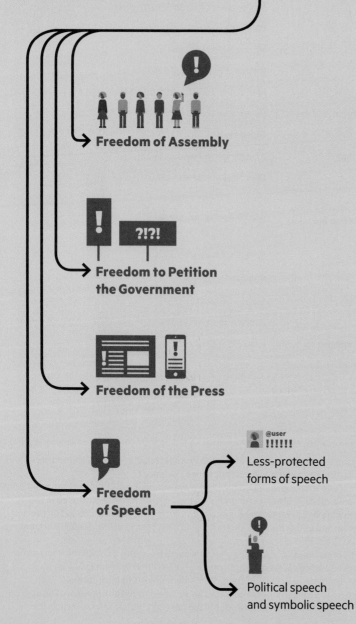

Freedom of Expression

Freedom of Assembly

Freedom to Petition the Government

?!?!

Freedom of the Press

Freedom of Speech

@user
!!!!!!
Less-protected forms of speech

Political speech and symbolic speech

Freedom of Religion

Establishment
The government cannot establish an official state religion or favor one religion over others.

Free Exercise
The government cannot prevent people from practicing their religion.

Balancing Interests and Drawing Lines: Government and Religion

While the different branches of the First Amendment on the opposite page are an accurate representation of the various aspects of our religious and expressive freedoms, in practice, the implementation of these civil liberties is more complicated.

Free Exercise:

When they refused...

When Masterpiece Cakeshop **refused to make a wedding cake** for a same-sex couple...

They said...

The baker didn't have to bake the cake... for now (postponing a decision on the broader question).

Here's why.

In cases like these, **courts must balance religious freedom against other state interests**, such as freedom from discrimination.

Establishment Clause:

Banned.

Since 1962 the Supreme Court has **banned school prayer as a violation of the establishment clause**.

What about...?

But does the separation of church and state also apply to town board members who **start their meetings with a prayer**? In 2014, the Court decided by a 5–4 vote that it did not.

It's tough.

The establishment clause often asks courts to **draw lines between what type of religious conduct is allowed** and what would be considered an "excessive entanglement" between church and state.

❓ Critical Thinking

1. **Balancing interests can be tricky.** Consider these two scenarios in which competing interests are in play: Company policy restricts employees from wearing political T-shirts or buttons at work. A pharmacist denies birth control pills to a customer for religious reasons. Which (if either) do you think should be allowed? Why did you select the one(s) you did?

2. **Drawing lines for a given civil liberty** can also be difficult. What if a high school football coach knelt in a private prayer on the field after a game? Should that be allowed? Or, consider a different scenario: Should Congress be able to start its sessions with a prayer? Reference the First Amendment and its interpretations in your answer.

In some cases,

the free exercise and establishment clauses are in tension with one another. For example, while the establishment clause prohibits school-sponsored prayer, the free exercise clause guarantees that any student can pray at any time in school on his or her own, **as long as he or she is not bothering others**.

Bill of Rights has evolved from a narrow range of protections for people from national government actions during the early nineteenth century to a robust set of protections for freedom and liberty that limit national, state, and local government actions today.

"Why Should I Care?"

Today the Bill of Rights is one of the most revered and important parts of the Constitution. But it didn't start out that way. Initially, the Bill of Rights applied to only the national government, not the states. But through the Fourteenth Amendment and the process of selective incorporation, the Supreme Court has gradually applied most of the Bill of Rights to the states. While all levels of government must respect our civil liberties today, there are many unresolved areas in terms of balancing interests and drawing lines. The next time you feel strongly about an issue concerning civil liberties, take some time to consider the other side—these questions are often not as black-and-white as they seem. Should speakers who hold extreme, even racist, views be allowed to speak on campus? How do we balance our freedom of speech or freedom from illegal searches with the need for national security?

DESCRIBE THE FIRST AMENDMENT LIBERTIES RELATED TO FREEDOM OF RELIGION

establishment clause
Part of the First Amendment that states, "Congress shall make no law respecting an establishment of religion," which has been interpreted to mean that Congress cannot sponsor or favor any religion.

free exercise clause
Part of the First Amendment that states that Congress cannot prohibit or interfere with the practice of religion unless there are important secular reasons for doing so.

Freedom of religion

The First Amendment's ringing words are the most famous statement of personal freedoms in the Constitution: "Congress shall make no law respecting an establishment of religion, or prohibiting the free exercise thereof; or abridging the freedom of speech, or of the press; or the right of the people peaceably to assemble, and to petition the Government for a redress of grievances." (The How It Works graphic illustrates how much is packed into this one amendment.)

The First Amendment has two parts that deal with religion: the **establishment clause**, which has been interpreted to mean that Congress cannot sponsor or endorse any particular religion, and the **free exercise clause**, which has been interpreted to mean that Congress cannot interfere with the practice of religion unless there are important secular reasons for doing so. To simplify only slightly, the former says that Congress should not *help* religion and the latter that it should not *hurt* religion. The establishment clause is primarily concerned with drawing lines. For example, does a prayer at a public high school football game or a Nativity scene on government property constitute state sponsorship of religion? The free exercise clause has more to do with balancing interests. Recall the earlier examples of balancing public safety concerns against snake handling in religious services and the use of Amish buggies on highways.

The combination of the establishment and free exercise clauses results in a general policy of noninterference and government neutrality toward religion. As Thomas Jefferson put it in 1802, the First Amendment provides a "wall of eternal separation between church and state." This language continues to be cited in Court cases in which religion and politics intersect.[27] Since both areas carry great moral weight and emotional charge, it's no wonder that vehement debates continue over the appropriateness of the saying "In God We Trust" on our currency, the White House Christmas tree, and whether evolution and "intelligent design" should be taught in public schools. The boundaries of religious expression remain difficult to draw.

The establishment clause and separation of church and state

Determining the boundaries between church and state—the central issue of the establishment clause—is very difficult. As a leading text on civil liberties puts it, the words of the establishment clause—"Congress shall make no law respecting an establishment of religion"—are commanding and clear, but their meaning is entirely unclear. What does the clause allow or forbid?[28] We know that the Founders did not want an official state religion and did not want the government to favor one religion over another, but beyond that it's hard to say. Jefferson's "wall of eternal separation" comment has been used in Court decisions that prohibit state aid for religious activities, but lately the Court has been moving toward a more "accommodationist" perspective that sometimes allows religious activity in public institutions.

Public Prayer The prohibition of prayer in public schools has become the most controversial establishment clause issue. It exploded onto the political scene in 1962 when the Court ruled in *Engel v. Vitale* that the following prayer, written by the New York State Board of Regents and read every day in the state's public schools, violated the establishment clause and the separation of church and state: "Almighty God, we acknowledge our dependence upon Thee, and we beg Thy blessing upon us, our parents, our teachers, and our country."[29] Banning the prayer caused a huge public outcry protesting the perceived attack on religion.

Over the next 50 years, Congress repeatedly tried, unsuccessfully, to amend the Constitution to allow school prayer. Meanwhile, the Court continued to take a hard line on school-sponsored prayer. In 1985, the Court struck down the practice of observing a one-minute moment of silence for "meditation or voluntary prayer" in the Alabama public schools, showing that it isn't the *words* of the prayer that are the problem, but the idea of prayer itself.[30] More recently, the Court said that benedictions or prayers at public school graduations and a school policy that allowed an elected student representative to lead a prayer at a high school football game also violated the establishment clause. The former established a strong "coercion test" that prohibited prayers that may appear to be voluntary (students are not required to attend their high school graduation) but in effect are compulsory.[31] Yet the Court has upheld the practice of opening every session of Congress with a prayer, has let stand without comment a lower-court ruling that allowed a prayer that was planned and led by students (rather than recited as school policy) at a high school graduation, and, most recently, in 2014 upheld prayers by voluntary chaplains for town board meetings in Greece, New York.[32] The latter case was especially significant because the legislative prayers were offered at town meetings that included residents, unlike the previously approved prayers that were intended for the elected leaders only.

Aid to Religious Organizations and Religious Symbols The Court has had an even more difficult time coming up with principles to govern government aid to religious organizations, either directly, through tax dollars, or indirectly, through the use of public space for religious symbols. One early attempt was known as the Lemon test, after one of the parties in a 1971 case involving government support for religious schools (*Lemon v. Kurtzman*). This case said that a practice violated the establishment clause if it (1) did not have a "secular legislative purpose," (2) either advanced or inhibited religion, or (3) fostered "an excessive government entanglement with religion."[33] The third part of the test was later found open to interpretation by lower courts and therefore led to conflicting rulings.

The number, the industry, and the morality of the Priesthood, & the devotion of the people have been manifestly increased by the total separation of the Church from the State.

—President James Madison

AP®
SUPREME
COURT CASE

Engel v. Vitale
The 1962 Supreme Court ruling that prayer in public schools was a violation of the First Amendment's establishment clause.

Lemon test
The Supreme Court uses this test, established in *Lemon v. Kurtzman*, to determine whether a practice violates the First Amendment's establishment clause.

Can a cross be displayed on federal land? This 40-foot cross in Bladensburg, Maryland, is on state property, but serves as a World War I memorial. The Court allowed it to remain in place, stating that though the cross is a Christian symbol, removing the Bladensburg Cross would be a disservice to all that it has come to represent.

The Court started to move away from the Lemon test in a 1984 case involving a crèche owned by the city of Pawtucket, Rhode Island, and displayed in a park owned by a nonprofit corporation. The Court allowed the Nativity display, saying: "The Constitution does not require complete separation of church and state; it affirmatively mandates accommodation, not merely tolerance, of all religions, and forbids hostility toward any."[34] This "endorsement test" simply says that government action is unconstitutional if a "reasonable observer" would think that the action either endorses or disapproves of religion. Later rulings upheld similar religious displays, especially if they conformed to what observers have labeled the "three plastic animals rule"—if the baby Jesus is surrounded by Rudolph the red-nosed reindeer and other secular symbols, the overall display is considered sufficiently nonreligious to pass constitutional muster.[35]

More recently, in a 2019 case the Court upheld the American Legion's right to display a 40-foot cross at a World War I memorial on state property in Bladensburg, Maryland, saying that Lemon should not apply in cases that "involve the use, for ceremonial, celebratory, or commemorative purposes, of words or symbols with religious associations." Instead, the Court ruled, "The cross is undoubtedly a Christian symbol, but that fact should not blind us to everything else that the Bladensburg Cross has come to represent.... [D]estroying or defacing the Cross that has stood undisturbed for nearly a century would not be neutral and would not further the ideals of respect and tolerance embodied in the First Amendment."[36] Three justices wanted to completely overturn Lemon; Justice Gorsuch called it a "dog's breakfast"—a confusing mess. But it still has application to direct government support for religious schools.

In cases involving funding for religious schools, the Court has applied the accommodationist perspective by looking more favorably on providing tax dollars to students' families to subsidize tuition costs at religious schools than on funding parochial schools directly. For example, the Court upheld an Ohio school voucher program that distributed scholarships to needy students so they could attend the Cleveland school of their choice, including private religious schools. The Court said the program did not violate the establishment clause because it allowed students and their families "to exercise genuine choice among options public and private, secular and religious."[37] Critics of the decision pointed out that 96 percent of the students participating in the scholarship program were enrolled in religiously affiliated schools, which amounted to state sponsorship of religious education, something that the Court had not previously allowed. In 2011, the Court expanded taxpayer support for religious education when it upheld an Arizona law that provides state tax credits for contributions to organizations that provide tuition for religious schools.[38] The Court has also ruled that it is acceptable to use federal funds to buy computers and other educational equipment to be used in public and private schools for "secular, neutral, and nonideological programs"[39] and tax dollars for a sign language interpreter for a deaf student who attended a parochial school.[40]

In a landmark 2020 decision, *Espinoza v. Montana Department of Revenue*, the Supreme Court ruled 5–4 that under the free exercise clause, a state could not prevent the use of state-based, publicly-funded scholarship funds meant for private school tuition from being applied toward religious school tuition. The case was brought by Montana parents who qualified for these income-based scholarships, and whose children attended a Christian school. They were informed that the scholarship funds could not be applied toward the religious school tuition because of a Montana state rule barring the use of "any direct or indirect appropriations or payment" to any religious organizations or schools affiliated with religious organizations. The case went to the Montana Supreme Court, which in 2018 found the entire scholarship program

Cake shop owner Jack Phillips did not want to bake a wedding cake for Charlie Craig and David Mullins because it would have violated his religious beliefs. In a narrow ruling that did not settle the broader free exercise question, the Court sided with the baker because he had not been treated fairly by the commission that heard his case.

unconstitutional, as it unfairly benefited religious schools. As a result, the public scholarship program was terminated, so the parents appealed to the U.S. Supreme Court. In the majority opinion, Chief Justice Roberts wrote that the program violated the free exercise clause, as it "bars religious schools from public benefits solely because of the religious character of the schools" and "also bars parents who wish to send their children to a religious school from those same benefits, again solely because of the religious character of the school."[41]

The free exercise clause

While the freedom of belief is absolute, freedom of religious conduct cannot be unrestricted. That is, you can believe whatever you want without government interference, but if you *act* on those beliefs, the government may regulate your behavior. And while the government has restricted religious conduct in dozens of cases, the freedom of religion has been among the most consistently protected civil liberties.

Hundreds of cases have come before the Court in the area of the free exercise of religion.[42] Here are some examples of the questions they addressed: May Amish parents be forced to send their children to schools beyond the eighth grade? (No, as established in *Wisconsin v. Yoder* in 1972.) May religion serve as the basis for attaining "conscientious objector" status and avoiding the draft? (Generally yes, but with many qualifications.) Is animal sacrifice as part of a religious ceremony protected by the First Amendment? (Generally yes.) May Mormons have multiple wives? (No.) May people be forced to work on Friday night and Saturday if those are their days of worship? (No.) Does the First Amendment protect distribution of religious leaflets on public streets? And religious meetings in public parks? (Yes, for both, but the latter is subject to **"time, manner, and place" restrictions**.) May religious dress be regulated? (Generally not, but in some contexts, such as the military, yes.) Are all prison inmates entitled to hold religious services (apparently yes, but this is still an open question) and grow short beards? (Yes.) Are religious organizations subject to child labor laws? (Yes.) Whew! Keep in mind that this list is by no means exhaustive.

"time, manner, and place" restrictions
Reasonable and content-neutral limits imposed by the government to regulate the context of expression.

One particular case, brought by plaintiffs who had been fired for using peyote as part of a religious ceremony and then denied unemployment benefits because they had broken the law, had broad implications that defined the general basis for government restrictions of religious expression. The Court ultimately ruled that the state of Oregon had not violated the free exercise clause in denying the plaintiffs unemployment benefits. More significantly, with this ruling the Court announced a new interpretation of the free exercise clause: the government does not need a "compelling interest" in regulating a particular behavior to justify a law that limits a religious practice; it only needs a demonstration that the law in question was a "neutral law of general applicability."[43] In other words, after this decision it would be easier for the government to limit the exercise of religion because the Court would no longer require a "compelling" reason for the restrictions.

Congress responded by passing the Religious Freedom Restoration Act (RFRA) in 1993, reinstating the need to demonstrate a "compelling state interest" before limiting religious freedoms; the act also specified exceptions to the Controlled Substances Act to allow the use of peyote in religious ceremonies. After several cases and congressional actions, the Court made it clear that it would have the final word in deciding when a compelling interest is required in order to limit religious practice.[44] The Court relied on this standard in the controversial 2014 case involving the family-owned Hobby Lobby stores, ruling that a "closely held" private corporation could not be forced to provide contraception to women under the Affordable Care Act if there was a "less restrictive" means available to have the insurance provide it.[45] This was the first time that a corporation was given First Amendment protections based on the religious beliefs of the owners of the corporation. In 2020, the Court extended the opt-out options to private employers on religious or moral grounds. The Court also expanded religious freedom when it approved, for the first time in 2017, direct government payments to a church in support of a secular purpose (in this case, funds for a playground in a church-run day-care center). The Court ruled that churches should have equal access to state grants made available to fund neutral, secular programs.[46]

In a highly anticipated case, the Court was faced with a difficult question concerning the civil rights of a same-sex couple and the religious beliefs of a cake shop owner. The baker had refused to bake a cake for the couple, saying that doing so would violate his religious beliefs. The Court avoided ruling on this central question because the Colorado Civil Rights Commission, which initially heard the case, did not treat religion in a neutral manner and did not give the baker a fair hearing. While concluding that the baker did not have to bake the cake because of the commission's biased behavior, the Court affirmed that the free exercise clause will not provide a basis for such refusals of service when there is not the expression of hostility to religion and that LGBTQ people have the right to "equal access to goods and services under a neutral and generally applicable public accommodations law."[47]

"Why Should I Care?"

Being familiar with these freedoms and the controversies around them is important because they concern the most deeply personal freedoms debated today. Would you, or do you, send your children to religious schools? Should the government pay for it? If you attend a public college or university, should it be allowed to organize a prayer before a football or basketball game? Should business owners be able to deny equal access to a service (baking a wedding cake) or a public program (health insurance) because of their religious beliefs?

Freedom of speech, assembly, and the press

As we noted earlier, defining the scope of our civil liberties depends on balancing interests and drawing lines. This is especially true of the First Amendment's freedom of speech, which can be envisioned on a continuum from most to least protected types of speech based on the Supreme Court cases that have tested their limits.

Generally protected expression

Any time you attend a religious service or a political rally, post a tweet, write a blog post or letter to the editor, or express a political idea, you are protected by the First Amendment. However, the nature of this protection is continually evolving due to political forces and shifting constitutional interpretations. For much of our nation's history, freedom of speech and freedom of the press were not strongly protected. Only recently have the courts developed a complex continuum ranging from strongly protected political speech to less protected speech.

Standards for Protection The basis for the continuum of protected speech is rooted in the content of the speech. The Supreme Court has interpreted the law to mean that content-based regulation of speech is not permissible (unless it falls into one of the categories of exceptions we outline later). For example, the Court struck down a local ordinance that banned picketing outside schools except for labor picketing.[48] This ordinance was deemed to be content-based regulation because it favored one form of speech (from labor unions) over others. Such regulation is subject to the **strict scrutiny** standard of judicial review, which means the regulation must be narrowly tailored so that it is the least restrictive on an individual's fundamental right to free speech and the government must demonstrate a compelling state interest to curtail the speech. In most cases, such strict scrutiny by the courts means that the speech will be protected and the regulation will be struck down. If a regulation is content neutral and does not favor any given viewpoint over another, then it is subject to the less demanding **intermediate scrutiny** standard. This means that the government must demonstrate only a substantial interest in curtailing the speech, the interest must be unrelated to the content of the speech, and there must be alternative opportunities for communication.[49]

Political Speech Freedom of speech got off to a rocky start when Congress passed the Alien and Sedition Acts in 1798. The controversial Sedition Act made it a crime to "write, print, utter or publish . . . any false, scandalous and malicious writing or writings against the government of the United States." Supporters of the acts claimed they were necessary to strengthen the national government in response to the French Revolution, but in reality they were an attempt by the governing Federalist Party to neutralize the opposition—the Democratic-Republican Party. As many as 25 people, mostly newspaper editors, were tried under the law and 10 were jailed, including Benjamin Franklin's grandson. The outcry against the laws helped Thomas Jefferson win the presidential election in 1800. Jefferson pardoned the convicted editors, Congress repealed one of the acts in 1802, and the other acts were allowed to expire before the Supreme Court had a chance to rule that they were unconstitutional.

World War I prompted the harshest crackdowns on free speech since the Sedition Act of 1798. The most important case from this period involved the general secretary of the Socialist Party, Charles Schenck, who opposed U.S. involvement in the war. He had

strict scrutiny
The highest level of scrutiny the courts can use when determining whether a law is constitutional. To meet this standard, the law or policy must be shown to serve a "compelling state interest" or goal, it must be narrowly tailored to achieve that goal, and it must be the least restrictive means of achieving that goal.

intermediate scrutiny
The middle level of scrutiny the courts can use when determining whether a law is constitutional. To meet this standard, the law or policy must be "content neutral," must further an important government interest in a way that is "substantially related" to that interest, and must use means that are a close fit to the government's goal and not substantially broader than is necessary to accomplish that goal.

printed a leaflet urging young men to resist the draft. Schenck was arrested under the Espionage Act of 1917, which prohibited "interfering with military or naval operations," including the draft. He appealed all the way to the Supreme Court, arguing that the First Amendment permitted him to protest the war and to urge others to resist the draft. But the Court sustained his conviction, noting that free speech is not an absolute right:

> *The most stringent protection of free speech would not protect a man in falsely shouting fire in a theatre and causing a panic. . . . The question in every case is whether the words used are used in such circumstances and are of such a nature as to create a clear and present danger that they will bring about the substantive evils that Congress has a right to prevent.*[50]

This clear and present danger test meant that the government could suppress speech it deemed dangerous (in this instance, preventing the government from fighting the war). However, critics of the decision argue that Schenck's actions were not dangerous for the country and should have been allowed.[51]

Justice Oliver Wendell Holmes, author of the *Schenck v. United States* (1919) decision and the clear and present danger test, had a change of heart and dissented in a case later that year that upheld the conviction of six anarchists who supported the cause of the Bolsheviks in Russia. In one of the most famous statements of the importance of the freedom of speech, he touted the "free trade in ideas," saying, "The best test of truth is the power of the thought to get itself accepted in the competition of the market. . . . [W]e should be eternally vigilant against attempts to check the expression of opinion that we loathe and believe to be fraught with death."[52] This notion of the marketplace of ideas in which good ideas triumph over bad is still central to modern defenses of the First Amendment.

Over the next several decades, the Court struggled to draw the line between dangerous speech and words that were simply unpopular. During the Red Scare of the late 1940s and early 1950s the hunt for communists in government was led by Senator Joe McCarthy, and the Court had many opportunities to defend unpopular speech, but for the most part it declined to do so. For example, in 1951 the Court upheld the conviction of 11 members of the Communist Party under the Smith Act, which banned the advocacy of force or violence against the United States.[53]

Then, in 1969, the Court established a strong protection for free speech, superseding the clear and present danger test, that still holds today. This case involved a leader of the Ku Klux Klan who made a threatening speech at a cross-burning rally that was subsequently shown on television. Twelve hooded figures were shown, many with weapons. The speech said that "revengence [*sic*]" might be taken if "our president, our Congress, our Supreme Court continues to suppress the white, Caucasian race." It continued, "We are marching on Congress July the Fourth, four hundred thousand strong." The Klan leader was convicted under the Ohio law banning "sabotage, violence, or unlawful methods of terrorism as a means of accomplishing industrial or political reform," but the Court unanimously reversed his conviction, arguing that threatening speech could not be suppressed just because it sounded dangerous. Specifically, the direct incitement test holds that speech is protected "except where such advocacy is directed to inciting or producing imminent lawless action and is likely to incite or produce such action."[54] Under this standard, most, if not all, of the sedition convictions and limitations on speech during World War I and the Red Scare would have been overturned.

Perhaps the strongest example of protecting unpopular speech comes from the case of the Westboro Baptist Church (WBC). Since 2005, members of the WBC have protested at hundreds of funerals of members of the armed services who were killed in Iraq and Afghanistan. However, these are not typical antiwar protests. Instead, the protesters claim that the troops' deaths were God's punishment for "the homosexual lifestyle

---

clear and present danger test
Established in *Schenck v. United States*, this test allowed the government to restrict certain types of speech deemed dangerous.

**AP®
SUPREME
COURT CASE**

Schenck v. United States
The 1919 Supreme Court ruling that Charles Schenck's protests against World War I were not protected by the First Amendment because they posed a "clear and present danger . . . that Congress has a right to prevent."

Restriction of free thought and free speech is the most dangerous of all subversions. It is the one un-American act that could most easily defeat us.

—William O. Douglas, former Supreme Court justice

direct incitement test
Established in *Brandenburg v. Ohio*, this test protects threatening speech under the First Amendment unless that speech aims to and is likely to cause imminent "lawless action."

Should free speech be protected even when the ideas are offensive? The Supreme Court ruled that the Westboro Baptist Church had a right to protest at military funerals, even though many Americans found the arguments and approach of the church members deeply offensive.

of soul-damning, nation-destroying filth." The church and its members have drawn strong reactions and counterprotests for their confrontational approach at the military funerals, including their use of signs that say "God Hates Fags," "Thank God for Dead Soldiers," "God Killed Your Sons," and "God Hates America." Critics, including many veterans groups and attorneys general from 48 states, argue that the protests should not be considered protected speech under the First Amendment. The Veterans of Foreign Wars issued a statement saying, "In a time of profound grief and emotional vulnerability, these personal attacks are an affront of the most egregious kind." However, in 2011 the Supreme Court ruled 8-1 that the WBC's protests were protected speech.[55]

Symbolic Speech The use of signs, symbols, or other unspoken acts or methods to communicate in a political manner—symbolic speech—enjoys many of the same protections as regular speech. For example, during the Vietnam War the Court protected the right of a war protester to wear an American flag patch sewn on the seat of his pants,[56] high school students' right to wear an armband to protest the war (*Tinker v. Des Moines School District*, 1969),[57] and an individual's right to tape a peace symbol on the flag and fly it upside down outside an apartment window.[58] Lower courts had convicted these protesters under state laws that protected the American flag or under a school policy that prohibited wearing armbands to protest the Vietnam War. In the flag desecration case involving the peace symbol, the Court stated that protected "speech" need not be verbal: "[T]here can be little doubt that appellant communicated through the use of symbols."[59]

A 1989 case provided the strongest protection for symbolic speech yet. The case involved a man who burned a flag outside the 1984 Republican National Convention in Texas, chanting along with other protesters, "America the red, white, and blue, we spit on you. You stand for plunder, you will go under." The Court refrained from critiquing the jingle, but its 5–4 decision overturned the man's conviction under Texas's flag desecration law on the grounds that symbolic political speech is protected by the First Amendment.[60] In response to this unpopular decision, Congress passed the Flag Protection Act of 1989, which the Court also struck down as an unconstitutional infringement on political expression.[61] Congress then attempted to pass a constitutional amendment to overturn the Court decision; the House passed

symbolic speech
Nonverbal expression, such as the use of signs or symbols. It benefits from many of the same constitutional protections as verbal speech because of its expressive value.

**AP®
SUPREME
COURT CASE**

Tinker v. Des Moines School District
In 1969, the Supreme Court ruled that students may wear armbands to protest the Vietnam War. The Court noted that the students "were not disruptive and did not impinge upon the rights of others" and therefore their conduct was protected by the First and Fourteenth Amendments.

The American flag is a popular target for protesters: it has been spat upon, shredded, turned into underwear, and burned. Here, protesters burn a U.S. flag as they march through downtown Washington, D.C., following the Ferguson, Missouri, grand jury's decision not to indict Officer Darren Wilson for the shooting death of Michael Brown.

DID YOU KNOW?

73%

of college-educated Black Americans and 45 percent of college-educated White Americans view the Confederate battle flag primarily as a symbol of racism.

Source: YouGov

the amendment six times between 1995 and 2005 with the necessary two-thirds vote, but each time the measure failed by a narrow margin in the Senate (by just one vote in 2006). President Trump reignited this debate shortly after he was elected, tweeting, "Nobody should be allowed to burn the American flag—if they do, there must be consequences—perhaps loss of citizenship or year in jail!" However, Republican leaders in Congress have not been interested in revisiting this fight.[62]

Although the Court has protected flag burning and other forms of symbolic speech, there are limits, especially when the symbolic speech conflicts with another substantial governmental interest. Here the critical test is whether the action can be regulated for important reasons unrelated to ideas. If so, then the "intermediate scrutiny" standard will apply. For example, Vietnam War protesters who burned their draft cards were not protected by the First Amendment because their actions interfered with Congress's constitutional authority to "raise and support" armies, and the purpose of the draft was not to suppress speech.[63] The Court also ruled in 2015 that states may ban the use of the Confederate battle flag on state vanity plates. The Sons of Confederate Veterans argued that the battle flag honored their southern heritage, but the state of Texas said it was offensive.[64] The debate over the flag intensified after a "Unite the Right" rally in Charlottesville, Virginia, in which a White supremacist killed a woman and injured 19 others, and demonstrators prominently displayed the Confederate battle flag. According to the Southern Poverty Law Center, at least 114 statues and memorials to Confederate leaders were removed in response to the violence in Charlottesville.[65]

Money as Speech Spending money in political campaigns may also be protected by the First Amendment since it provides the means for more conventional types of political speech. Here the central question is whether the government can control campaign contributions and spending for a broader public purpose such as lessening the potential for corruption, or whether such laws violate the First Amendment rights of candidates or their supporters. You probably have heard the old saying "Money talks," which implies that money is speech. Given the importance of advertising in modern campaigns, limitations on raising and spending money could limit the ability of candidates and groups to reach voters with their message. The Court has walked a tightrope on this one, balancing the public interest in honest and ethical elections and the First Amendment rights of candidates and their advocates. The Court has upheld individual candidates' right to spend their own money in federal elections, but presidential candidates give up that right if they accept federal campaign funds (taxpayers' money) in a presidential election. Also, candidates in federal elections are subject to limits on the types and size of contributions they can receive, and they must report all contributions and spending to the Federal Election Commission.[66]

The Bipartisan Campaign Reform Act, which went into effect for the 2004 elections, included a "Millionaires' Amendment" that lifted restrictions on campaign contributions for candidates whose opponents spent more than $350,000 of their own money in the election. This attempt to level the campaign finance playing field was struck down by the Supreme Court in 2008 as a violation of wealthy candidates' First Amendment rights.[67] In 2010 the Court also extended First Amendment rights to corporations and labor unions that want to spend money on campaign ads, and in 2014 it struck down the aggregate (collective) limits placed on individual contributions to candidates and parties (these cases are discussed in more detail in Chapter 13).[68] However, the Court upheld a ban on unlimited "soft money" contributions because they were seen by the Court as the type of contribution with the most potential for corruption.[69]

Student fees as a form of symbolic speech came up in a case in 2000 involving student activity fees at the University of Wisconsin. A group of students argued that they should not have to pay fees to fund groups whose activities they opposed, including a student environmental group, a gay and bisexual student center, a community legal office, an AIDS support network, a campus women's center, and the Wisconsin Student Public Interest Research Group. The Court ruled that mandatory student fees could continue to support the full range of groups as long as the process for allocating money was "viewpoint neutral." The Court also said that student referendums that could add or cut money for specific groups violated viewpoint neutrality. The potential for the majority to censor unpopular views was unacceptable to the Court, since "the whole theory of viewpoint neutrality is that minority views are treated with the same respect as are majority views."[70]

Hate Speech Whether or not freedom of speech should apply to hate speech has been a controversial issue both on college campuses and in society generally. Do people have a right to say things that are offensive or abusive, especially in terms of race, gender, and sexual orientation? By the mid-1990s, more than 350 public colleges and universities said no by regulating some forms of hate speech.[71]

Many of these speech codes were struck down in federal court, but in the last few years the issue has resurfaced on many college campuses. In addition to the controversial speakers discussed in the chapter opener, a variety of "campus climate" issues consumed dozens of schools. At Yale University in 2015, controversy erupted over the response of a residential college faculty administrator, Erika Christakis, to an e-mail students received cautioning them not to wear Halloween costumes that could be racially or culturally insensitive. Christakis wrote that universities no longer allowed students to be "a little bit inappropriate or provocative or, yes, offensive."[72] She resigned a few weeks later, saying, "[T]he current climate at Yale is not, in my view, conducive to the civil dialogue and open inquiry required to solve our urgent societal problems."[73] The president of the University of Missouri also resigned in 2015 after students, including the football team, said that he was racially insensitive and not open to their demands for a more inclusive and supportive environment on campus. In 2017, Indiana University students petitioned to remove part of a mural that depicts the history of the state using imagery of a burning cross and white-hooded Klansmen.

hate speech
Expression that is offensive or abusive, particularly in terms of race, gender, or sexual orientation. It is currently protected under the First Amendment.

University leaders compromised by leaving the artwork but saying that classes would no longer be held in the lecture hall with the mural.[74]

Another significant issue combines the topics of symbolic speech and hate speech. Can a person who burned a cross on a Black family's lawn be convicted under a city ordinance that prohibits conduct in St. Paul, Minnesota, that "arouses anger, alarm, or resentment in others on the basis of race, color, creed, religion, or gender"? Or is the ordinance an unconstitutional limit on First Amendment rights? The Court said the cross burner could be punished for arson, terrorism, trespassing, or other violations of the law, but he could not be convicted under this ordinance because it was overly broad and vague. The Court said: "Let there be no mistake about our belief that burning a cross in someone's front yard is reprehensible. But St. Paul has sufficient means at its disposal to prevent such behavior without adding the First Amendment to the fire."[75] The city ordinance was unconstitutional because it took selective aim at a disfavored message; it constituted "viewpoint discrimination." However, the Court has since upheld more carefully worded bans of cross burning. Eleven years after the St. Paul case, the Court ruled that Virginia could prohibit cross burning if there was intent to intimidate. The Court also noted that the law was content neutral because it did not engage in viewpoint discrimination: any burning of a cross in a threatening context was illegal.[76]

Speech on the Internet Internet hate speech has become increasingly controversial in recent years. Cyberbullying through social media like Instagram, Twitter, Facebook, and Reddit precipitated several suicides. In 2013, Facebook cracked down on offensive content that glorified violence against women, such as pages with headlines like "Violently Raping Your Friend Just for Laughs."[77] Facebook's "community standards" have a more restrictive definition of hate speech than is allowed by the direct incitement test. While Facebook makes a distinction between humor and serious speech, it "do[es] not permit individuals or groups to attack others based on their race, ethnicity, national origin, religion, sex, gender, sexual orientation, disability or medical condition."[78] This led law professor Jeff Rosen to conclude that "today, lawyers at Google, YouTube, Facebook, and Twitter have more power over who can speak and who can be heard than any president, judge, or monarch."[79] This may sound like hyperbole, but he is right: corporations are not restricted by the First Amendment (which, after all, says "*Congress* shall make no law . . ."). So if Facebook and

A historic mural illustrating a member of the Ku Klux Klan provoked controversy at Indiana University in 2017, with many students calling for the removal of the offensive imagery.

other social media want to restrict hate speech, they can. Although free speech advocates are concerned about restrictions on Internet hate speech, civil rights groups such as the Anti-Defamation League, the Leadership Conference on Civil and Human Rights, and the National Organization for Women all support the move. Another controversial area of speech on the Internet is political ads. Late in 2019, Twitter announced that it was banning all political ads for the 2020 elections, while Google restricted "micro-targeting" based on ideology, party, or voting history. Facebook, on the other hand, still allows political ads, but with warnings if they are deemed untrue.[80]

While social media companies have great latitude in what they permit online, the government has limited power to regulate access to social media. In 2017, the Court struck down a North Carolina law that prohibited sex offenders from accessing or using social media sites, saying that these sites are the "principal sources for knowing current events, checking ads for employment, speaking and listening in the modern public square, and otherwise exploring the vast realms of human thought and knowledge." Therefore, limiting access to social media would prevent the "legitimate exercise of First Amendment rights."[81]

Freedom of Assembly The right to assemble peaceably has been consistently protected by the Supreme Court.[82] Perhaps the most famous freedom of assembly case involved a neo-Nazi group that wanted to march in Skokie, a suburb of Chicago that had 70,000 residents, nearly 60 percent of whom were Jewish, including many Holocaust survivors. The village passed ordinances that effectively banned the group from marching, arguing that residents would be so upset by the Nazi marchers that they might become violent. But the lower courts did not accept this argument, ruling that if "the audience is so offended by the ideas being expressed that it becomes disorderly and attempts to silence the speaker, it is the duty of the police to attempt to protect the speaker, not to silence his speech."[83] Otherwise, the right to assemble would be restricted by a "heckler's veto." The Court elaborated on this responsibility to protect expressions of unpopular views by striking down another town's ordinance that allowed it to charge a higher permit fee to groups whose march would likely require more police protection.[84] But in many cases, permit fees do not come close to covering the actual costs of security. When White supremacist Richard Spencer came to speak at the University of Florida, as noted in the chapter opener, his group, the National Policy Institute, was charged only $10,564 while the actual costs for security paid by the university and the state were estimated at nearly $600,000.[85]

The August 2017 "Unite the Right" rally in Charlottesville, Virginia—initially organized in opposition to the removal of a statue of Confederate general Robert E. Lee from a public park—raised issues of symbolic speech and freedom of assembly. Can the use of symbols that some deem offensive, such as the Confederate battle flag, be regulated by the government? Should groups promoting hate speech be permitted to peaceably assemble in public areas?

While broad protection is provided for peaceable assemblies, governments may regulate the time, manner, and place of expression as long as these regulations do not favor certain groups or messages over others. For example, the Court ruled that anti-abortion protesters were not allowed to picket a doctor's home in Brookfield, Wisconsin, on the grounds that the ordinance banning all residential picketing was content neutral; there was a government interest in preserving the "sanctity of the home, the one retreat to which men and women can repair to escape from the tribulations of their daily pursuits."[86] "Time, manner, and place" restrictions also may be invoked for practical reasons. For instance, if the Ku Klux Klan planned to hold a march around a football stadium on the day of a game, the city council could deny it a permit and could suggest that it choose another day that would not interfere with game day activities. In the case of Spencer's speech at the University of Florida, the school initially turned down Spencer's request to speak on campus just a month after the tragic events in Charlottesville, saying that it would not have time to provide adequate security for the event. However, it approved the talk for a date a month later.[87]

The legal standard for "time, manner, and place" regulations is that they must be "reasonable." This standard came into play in a 2014 case in which the Court ruled that a Massachusetts state law creating a 35-foot buffer zone around entrances to abortion clinics violated the First Amendment. While the buffer zone was content neutral, it was unreasonable because it was more restrictive than necessary to allow access to the clinics.[88] While the "reasonableness" standard is vague, it allows the courts to balance the right to assemble against other practical considerations.

Freedom of the Press The task of balancing interests is central to many First Amendment cases involving freedom of the press. Which is more important, the First Amendment freedom of the press to disclose details about current events or the Sixth Amendment right to a fair trial, which may require keeping important information out of the public eye? When do national security concerns prevail over journalists' right to keep citizens informed? The general issue here is prior restraint, the government's right to prevent the media from publishing something.

Prior restraint has never been clearly defined by the Court, but several landmark cases have set a very high bar for applying it. In 1971, the Pentagon Papers case (*New York Times Co. v. United States*) involved disclosure of parts of the top-secret report on internal planning for the Vietnam War. This incredibly divided case had nine separate written opinions! In a 6–3 decision the Court said that the government could not prevent the publication of the Pentagon Papers, but at least five justices supported the view that, under some circumstances, the government could use prior restraint—although they could not agree on the standard.[89] For some of the justices, a crucial consideration was the Pentagon Papers' revelation that the U.S. government had lied about its involvement in and the progress of the Vietnam War. Justice Hugo Black noted the importance of this point, saying, "Only a free and unrestrained press can effectively expose deception in government."[90]

The debate over restraining the media heated up in 2010, when WikiLeaks released a classified video of an air strike in Baghdad showing U.S. pilots mistakenly firing on two Reuters reporters and more than 91,000 classified battlefield incident reports from Iraq and Afghanistan and U.S. State Department cables. All of these documents had been leaked by U.S. Army Private First Class Chelsea Manning. This sensational leaking ratcheted up the stakes, and some members of Congress called the leaks treason and urged for prosecution (Manning was tried and convicted in a military court for violations of the Espionage Act and for copying and releasing classified information; she served seven years in prison before President Obama pardoned her, commuting the rest of Manning's 35-year sentence).

President Trump has frequently expressed frustration about leaks to the media and has aggressively used the Espionage Act to try to stop leaks. Prosecuting government employees for leaking information to the press had been relatively rare until recently; President Obama did it a few times and President Trump pursued eight prosecutions under the law from 2017 to 2020. While it is illegal to leak classified information, the law doesn't allow a balancing test to assess whether the leak was in the public's interest (as was true in the Pentagon Papers case). First Amendment advocates, such as former *New York Times* reporter James Risen, worry that this "gives the government enormous leverage over journalists and, in the United States, provides them with a detour around First Amendment concerns."[91]

The forms of expression discussed in this section—speech, assembly, and press—all have strong protections based on the First Amendment. The strongest protections

prior restraint
A limit on freedom of the press that allows the government to prohibit the media from publishing certain materials.

**AP®
SUPREME
COURT CASE**

New York Times Co. v. United States
The Supreme Court ruled in 1971 that the government could not prevent the publication of the Pentagon Papers, which revealed lies about the progress of the war in Vietnam.

The freedom of the press is one of the greatest bulwarks of liberty, and can never be restrained but by despotic governments.

—**George Mason,** politician and father of the Bill of Rights

are for content-based expression—that is, if a regulation is trying to limit *what* can be said, the Court applies the strict scrutiny standard and usually strikes down the regulation. However, there are exceptions, such as speech that directly incites an imminent danger. If the regulation is content neutral and does not favor one viewpoint over another, then it is easier to uphold. But even then, the government must have a substantial reason for limiting expression.

Less protected speech and publications

Some forms of speech do not warrant the same level of protection as political speech because they do not contribute to public debate or express ideas that have important social value. Four categories of speech may be more easily regulated by the government than political speech: fighting words, slander and libel, commercial speech, and obscenity. The first two categories may be prevented by the state if certain conditions are met, and the second two receive some protection, but not as much as political speech.

Fighting Words Governments may regulate fighting words, "which by their very utterance inflict injury or tend to incite an immediate breach of the peace."[92] Such laws must be narrowly written; it is not acceptable to ban all foul language, and the prohibited speech must target a single person rather than a group. Moreover, the question of whether certain words provoke a backlash depends on the reaction of the targeted person. Inflammatory words directed at Pope Francis would not be fighting words because he would turn the other cheek, whereas the same words yelled at musician Kanye West or actor Alec Baldwin *would* be fighting words because he would probably deck you. The Court clarified the test based on "what persons of common intelligence would understand to be words likely to cause an average addressee to fight."[93] While this provides a somewhat objective test, the fighting words doctrine has still been difficult to apply.

Slander and Libel A more extensive line of cases prohibiting speech concerns slander, spoken false statements that damage someone's reputation (defamation), and libel, written statements that do the same thing. As in many areas of First Amendment

fighting words
Forms of expression that "by their very utterance" can incite violence. These can be regulated by the government but are often difficult to define.

slander
Spoken false statements that damage a person's reputation. They can be regulated by the government but are often difficult to distinguish from permissible speech.

libel
Written false statements that damage a person's reputation. They can be regulated by the government but are often difficult to distinguish from permissible speech.

law, it is difficult to draw the line between permissible speech and slander or libel. The current legal standard distinguishes between speech about a public figure, such as a politician or celebrity, and about a regular person. In short, it is much more difficult for public figures to prove libel. A public figure has to demonstrate that the defamatory statement was made with "actual malice" and "with knowledge that it was false or with reckless disregard of whether it was false or not."[94]

One of the most famous libel cases was brought against *Hustler* magazine by the Reverend Jerry Falwell, a famous televangelist and political activist. Falwell sued *Hustler* for libel and emotional distress after the magazine published a parody of a liquor advertisement depicting him in a "drunken incestuous rendezvous with his mother in an outhouse" (this quote is from the Supreme Court case).[95] The lower court said that the parody wasn't believable, so *Hustler* couldn't be sued for libel, but they awarded Falwell damages for emotional distress. The Court overturned the damages, saying that public figures and public officials must put up with such things, comparing the parody to outrageous political cartoons, which have always been protected by the First Amendment.

While it is extremely difficult to win a slander or libel case, Hulk Hogan's 2016 case against the website Gawker shows that it is not impossible. Hogan sued Gawker—and won a $140 million verdict—for posting a sex tape of him with his friend's wife, Heather Clem, that had been recorded without his knowledge. He ultimately settled with Gawker for $31 million, and the website declared bankruptcy because of the case. The case has broader political implications because it shows that public figures may be able to win damages even when the defamatory content is *true*.[96] Melania Trump also reached a settlement with the *Daily Mail*, a British tabloid, for articles that the outlet published in 2016 falsely claiming that she had once worked for an escort service (the paper printed a retraction, apologized, and paid damages).[97] President Trump has vowed to "open up our libel laws" to deter what he claimed were false "fake news" stories. Libel law, however, is controlled by the states, subject to limits from the U.S. Supreme Court, so it is not something that the president can change.[98] Trump is also facing a lawsuit in New York state court from *Apprentice* contestant Summer Zervos, who alleges that he groped her. Her suit claims that Trump slandered her by calling her a liar. In November 2019, a New York judge allowed the case to move forward and ruled that Trump has to testify. An appeal of that decision is still working its way through the courts.[99]

Hulk Hogan testifies in court against Gawker Media, which he sued on charges of defamation and emotional distress. In a rare victory against the press, Hogan won his case.

Commercial Speech Commercial speech, which mostly refers to advertising, has evolved from having almost no protection under the First Amendment to enjoying quite strong protection. One early case involved a business owner who distributed leaflets to advertise rides on his submarine, which was docked in New York City. Under city ordinances, leafleting was permitted only if it was devoted to "information or a public protest," but not for a commercial purpose. The plaintiff changed the leaflet to have his advertisement on one side and a statement protesting a city policy on the other side (clever guy!). He was arrested anyway, and the Supreme Court upheld his conviction, saying that the city council had the right to regulate the distribution of leaflets.[100]

The Court became much more sympathetic to commercial speech in the 1970s when it struck down a law against advertising prescription drug prices and a law prohibiting placing newspaper racks on city streets to distribute commercial publications such as real estate guides.[101] The key decision in 1980 established a test that is still central today: the government may regulate commercial speech if it concerns an illegal activity, if the advertisement is misleading, or if regulating speech directly advances a substantial government interest and the regulation is not excessive. In practice, this test means that commercial speech can be regulated, but the government must have a very good reason to do it.[102]

Commercial speech is protected even when it could be considered offensive. In 2017, the Court sided with the Slants, an Asian-American rock band, in overturning a provision of U.S. patent and trademark law that prohibited the registration of trademarks that "disparage" or "bring . . . into contempt or disrepute" any "persons, living or dead." The Slants, whose application to trademark their band name had been denied, argued that their goal was to reclaim the racial slur against Asian Americans, in the same way that the LGBTQ community over time redefined the use of "queer." The Court agreed, saying, "A law that can be directed against speech found offensive to some portion of the public can be turned against minority and dissenting views to the detriment of all." This ruling also means that the Washington Redskins football team will be able to keep its nickname, despite the fact that many find it offensive.[103]

An even stronger protection for potentially offensive commercial speech came with the 2019 ruling that struck down bans on trademarking words and symbols that are "immoral" or "scandalous." A clothing designer wanted to trademark the phrase FUCT, which the majority opinion wryly noted was "the equivalent of [the] past participle form of a well-known word of profanity." The Court said that the law banning the trademark was overly broad and violates the First Amendment guarantee of free speech because "it disfavors certain ideas." The dissenters worried that it would lead to more "obscene, vulgar, and profane modes of expression."[104]

Obscenity One area in which the press has never experienced complete freedom involves the publication of pornography and material considered obscene. The difficulty arises in deciding where to draw the line. Nearly everyone would agree that child pornography should not be published[105] and that pornography should not be available to minors. However, beyond these points there is not much consensus. For example, some

commercial speech
Public expression with the aim of making a profit. It has received greater protection under the First Amendment in recent years but remains less protected than political speech.

Commercial speech may be protected even if some consider its content offensive. The rock band the Slants won the right to trademark their band name even though it refers to a racial slur against the Asian-American community.

people are offended by nude paintings in art museums, while others enjoy watching hard-core X-rated movies.

Defining obscenity has proven difficult for the courts. In an often-quoted moment of frustration, Justice Potter Stewart wrote that he could not define obscenity, but "I know it when I see it."[106] In its first attempt, the Court ruled that a particular publication could be banned if an "average person, applying contemporary community standards," would find that the material appeals to prurient interests and is "utterly without redeeming social importance."[107] This standard proved unworkable because lower courts differed in their interpretation. The Court took another stab at it in 1973 in a case that gave rise to the **Miller test**, which is still applied today.[108] The test has three standards that must all be met in order for material to be banned as obscene: (1) it appeals to prurient interests, (2) it is "patently offensive," and (3) the work as a whole lacks serious literary, artistic, political, or scientific value. The Court also clarified that *local* community standards were to apply rather than a single national standard, reasoning that what passes for obscenity in Sioux City, Iowa, probably would be considered pretty tame in Las Vegas.

In 2009, the Supreme Court addressed an area of the law that it had not touched for more than 30 years: regulating vulgar language that does not rise to the level of obscenity on broadcast television and radio (but not on cable or other paid-subscription services, which are not regulated as to language). In 1978, the Court ruled that the Federal Communications Commission (FCC) had the power to regulate indecent language, but the FCC had always interpreted that power to cover only repeated use of vulgar words.[109] However, after the use of vulgar words by Bono during the 2003 Golden Globe Awards and by Cher and Nicole Richie during the 2002 and 2003 Billboard Music Awards, the FCC announced that it would no longer tolerate even "isolated uses of sexual and excretory words."

Fox Television challenged this new rule, but in 2009 the Supreme Court upheld the FCC's ban on "fleeting expletives" as "entirely rational" under existing law. (Its opinion also took a swipe at the "foul-mouthed glitteratae from Hollywood.")[110] The Court also ruled the following week that the FCC had not acted capriciously in fining CBS $550,000 for Janet Jackson's infamous "wardrobe malfunction" at the 2004 Super Bowl.[111] However, after sending the cases back to the lower courts and another round of appeals, the Supreme Court ruled that the regulations were unconstitutionally vague and the networks could not be fined. The Court also let stand a lower-court ruling that voided the fine against CBS on similar grounds.[112] But the Court did not address the broader constitutional questions, so the regulation still stands; stronger First Amendment protections for broadcast radio and television will have to come from future cases.

Two more recent cases made clear that violence in published material cannot be regulated in the same way as sexual content. In 2010, the Court struck down a federal law that criminalized depictions "in which a living animal is intentionally maimed, mutilated, tortured, wounded, or killed." The law focused on "crush videos," which show the torture and killing of helpless animals, but also included dog fighting and other forms of animal cruelty. In striking down the law, the Court said the First Amendment protected such depictions, even if the underlying behavior itself could be illegal.[113] In 2011, the Court struck down a California law that banned the sale of violent video games to children, saying: "Like the protected books, plays and movies that preceded them, video games communicate ideas—and even social messages—through many familiar literary devices (such as characters, dialogue, plot and music) and through features distinctive to the medium (such as the player's interaction with the virtual world). That suffices to confer First Amendment protection."[114]

Miller test
Established in *Miller v. California*, this three-part test is used by the Supreme Court to determine whether speech meets the criteria for obscenity. If so, it can be restricted by the government.

The right to bear arms

EXPLORE WHY THE SECOND AMENDMENT'S MEANING ON GUN RIGHTS IS OFTEN DEBATED

Until recently, the right to bear arms was the only civil liberty that the Supreme Court had played a relatively minor role in defining. Between 1791 and 2007, the Court issued only four rulings directly pertaining to the Second Amendment. The federal courts had always interpreted the Second Amendment's awkward phrasing—"A well regulated Militia, being necessary to the security of a free State, the right of the people to keep and bear Arms, shall not be infringed"—as a right to bear arms within the context of serving in a militia, rather than as an individual right to own a gun.

Although legal conflict over gun ownership has intensified only recently, battles over guns have always been intense in the broader political realm. Interest groups such as the National Rifle Association have long asserted that the Second Amendment guarantees an individual right to bear arms.[115] Critics of this view emphasize the first clause of the amendment and point to the frequent mention of state militias in congressional debates at the time the Bill of Rights was adopted.[116] They argue that the Second Amendment was adopted to reassure Antifederalist advocates of states' rights that state militias, not a national standing army, would provide national security. In this view, the national armed forces and the National Guard have made the Second Amendment obsolete.

Before the Court's recent entry into this debate, Congress and state and local lawmakers had largely defined gun ownership and gun carrying rights, creating significant variation among the states. Wyoming and Montana have virtually no restrictions on gun ownership, for example, whereas California and Connecticut have many. At the national level, Congress tends to respond to crime waves or high-profile assassinations by passing new gun control laws. The broadest one, the Gun Control Act of 1968, was passed in the wake of the assassinations of Robert F. Kennedy and Martin Luther King Jr. The law sets standards for gun dealers, bans the sale of weapons through the mail, and restricts the sale of new machine guns, among other provisions.

Following the assassination attempt on President Reagan in 1981, the push for stronger gun control laws intensified. Spearheading this effort was Sarah Brady, whose husband, James Brady (Reagan's press secretary), was shot and disabled in the assassination attempt. It took nearly 13 years for the campaign to bear fruit, but in 1993 Congress passed and President Clinton signed the Brady Bill, which mandates a background check and a five-day waiting period for any handgun purchase.

But not all gun tragedies lead to more gun control. There were 417 mass shootings in 2019 and 464 in 2020 (as of September), defined as incidents in which at least four

While the Constitution guarantees the individual right to bear arms (as illustrated here by the woman taking target practice), the shootings at Marjory Stoneman Douglas High School in Parkland, Florida, shocked the nation. In response, students from the school organized the national March for Our Lives to urge the government to pass gun reform.

McDonald v. Chicago
The Supreme Court ruled in 2010 that the Second Amendment's right to keep and bear arms for self-defense in one's home is applicable to the states through the Fourteenth Amendment.

people were killed or injured, not counting the shooter.[117] By the FBI's definition of an "active shooter" there were 277 incidents from 2000 to 2018, including those in Orlando, Florida; San Bernardino, California; Charleston, South Carolina; and Parkland, Florida.[118] In the deadliest mass shooting by a single gunman, 58 people were killed and 546 injured in October 2017 at a country music festival in Las Vegas. While 45 states have passed new gun safety laws since 2013, including "smart gun" laws, laws concerning mental health and gun ownership, laws restricting ownership of assault weapons, and stronger background checks, 30 states now make it relatively easy to get a permit to carry a concealed weapon and 42 states do not require a permit. Many states have also expanded the places in which guns may be carried, including college campuses, and have passed "stand your ground" laws, which allow gun owners to shoot first if they feel threatened.[119]

In 2008, a landmark Supreme Court ruling recognized for the first time an individual right to bear arms for self-defense and hunting.[120] The decision struck down the District of Columbia's ban on handguns, while noting that state and local governments could enforce ownership restrictions, such as preventing felons or the mentally impaired from buying guns. The Court did not apply the Second Amendment to the states in this decision, but it did so two years later in striking down a gun control ordinance in Chicago in *McDonald v. Chicago* (2010) and reaffirming the ownership restrictions noted in the Washington, D.C., case.[121] The dissenters in both strongly divided 5–4 decisions lamented the Court's activism in reopening a legal question considered settled for 70 years (in 32 instances since a 1939 Court ruling, appeals courts had affirmed the focus on a collective right—in the context of a militia—rather than an individual right to bear arms, and recognized an individual right only twice between 1939 and 2007).[122]

There is strong public support for gun ownership in the United States, where there are about 393 million privately owned guns. This accounts for 46 percent of the world's total and is more than twice as high a rate of gun ownership as in the second most heavily armed nation: there are 120.5 guns per 100 people in the United States compared to 52.8 in Yemen. The contrast to our closest allies is even more extreme: there are 34.7 guns per 100 people in Canada, 19.6 in Germany, 4.9 in the United Kingdom, and 0.3 in Japan.[123] The fact that so many Americans support gun ownership, combined with the Supreme Court's endorsement of an individual right to bear arms, means that stronger gun control at the national level is highly unlikely (especially given the unsuccessful pushes after the shootings at Sandy Hook Elementary School in 2012 and in Orlando, Florida, in 2016; Las Vegas in 2017; and Parkland, Florida, in 2018).

However, the president and Congress have taken some limited steps in recent years. Early in 2016, President Obama issued an executive order requiring most gun sales to be through federally licensed dealers who would conduct background checks. The order also required the Social Security Administration to release information about mentally ill recipients of Social Security benefits, which would be considered as part of the background checks. This provision essentially prohibited people with mental illnesses from buying guns.[124] The second part of the order was overturned by Congress early in 2017. After a mass shooting at a Parkland, Florida, high school that killed 17 students in 2018, high school students organized the March for Our Lives, which had 1.2 to 2 million participants in more than 800 cities around the world. In Florida, gun control laws were strengthened by raising the age to buy a gun to 18, banning bump stocks that allow bullets to be fired more rapidly, and introducing a three-day waiting period before buying a long rifle. Congress passed legislation strengthening the National Instant Criminal Background Check System and providing $1 billion to fund initiatives intended to enhance school safety, such as the addition of metal detectors. President Trump also signed an executive order banning bump stocks. However, the ban could be challenged in court because bump stocks appear to be legal under current law. Thus, congressional action would be required for a national ban.

In addition to this limited legislative and executive action, extensive litigation will be necessary to define the acceptable boundaries of gun control and to identify which state and local restrictions will be allowed to stand. Up to this point, the verdicts have been mixed, with some lower courts upholding limitations on gun ownership (such as laws prohibiting felons from owning guns) and other lower courts striking them down. However, 93 percent of challenges to gun control laws have failed and almost all challenges to gun laws in criminal cases have been unsuccessful.[125]

Law, order, and the rights of criminal defendants

Every advanced democracy protects the rights of people who have been accused of a crime. In the United States, the **due process rights** of the Fourth, Fifth, Sixth, and Eighth Amendments include the right to a fair trial, the right to consult a lawyer, freedom from self-incrimination, the right to know what crime you are accused of, the right to confront the accuser in court, and freedom from unreasonable police searches.

It is difficult to apply the abstract principles of due process to concrete situations in a way that protects civil liberties without jeopardizing order. The Fifth and Fourteenth Amendments specify that life, liberty, and property may not be denied "without due process of law." In general, this language refers to *procedural* restrictions on what government can do and is based on the idea of fairness and justice. The difficulty comes in defining what is fair or just.

The difference between abstract principles of due process and their specific application also raises difficult *political* questions. Most people endorse the principle of "due process of law" and general ideas such as requiring that police legally obtain any evidence used in court. However, when the Supreme Court applies these principles to protect the rights of criminal defendants, there is a public outcry that too many suspects are going free on "legal technicalities," such as having to inform a suspect of his or her right to talk to an attorney before being questioned by the police.

DID YOU KNOW?

39,420

people were killed by guns in the United States in 2019. About 61 percent of these deaths were from suicides.

Source: www.gunviolencearchive.org

DESCRIBE THE PROTECTIONS PROVIDED FOR PEOPLE ACCUSED OF A CRIME

due process rights
The idea that laws and legal proceedings must be fair. The Constitution guarantees that the government cannot take away a person's "life, liberty, or property, without due process of law." Other specific due process rights are found in the Fourth, Fifth, Sixth, and Eighth Amendments, such as protection from self-incrimination and freedom from illegal searches.

Elected politicians are very vulnerable to such public pressure and have a strong incentive to be "tough on crime," while the courts are left to decide whether a specific case involves a legal technicality or a fundamental civil liberty.

The Fourth Amendment: unreasonable searches and seizures

The Fourth Amendment says: "The right of the people to be secure in their persons, houses, papers, and effects, against unreasonable searches and seizures, shall not be violated." Defining "unreasonable" puts us back in the familiar position of drawing lines and balancing interests.

Over the years, the Supreme Court has provided strong protections against searches within a person's physical space, typically defined as his or her home. With the introduction of new technology—first telephones and wiretapping, then more sophisticated listening and searching devices—the Court has had to confront a broad array of complicated questions. It has attempted to achieve a balance between privacy and security by requiring the courts to approve search warrants, yet continuing to carve out limited exceptions to this general rule.

Searches and Warrants Under most circumstances, a law-enforcement official seeking a search warrant must provide the court with "personal knowledge" of a "probable cause" of specific criminal activity and must outline the evidence that is the target of the search. Broad, general "fishing expeditions" for evidence are not allowed.

School officials must also balance the constitutional rights of students against the need to maintain discipline. But school searches may be permitted with a weaker "reasonable suspicion"; this is because the courts have viewed the schools as "in loco parentis" (that is, as playing the role of surrogate parents for the students). In 1985, the Court ruled in favor of a school official who discovered two girls smoking in a school bathroom and, in searching the purse of one of the girls for cigarettes, found marijuana, a pipe, rolling papers, plastic bags, and enough cash to suggest that the girl was selling marijuana. Yet, in other cases, the Court ruled that there are limits to searches by school officials and that students have the right to privacy. For example, in 2003 school administrators in Safford, Arizona, responding to a tip that a student was in possession of prescription-strength ibuprofen pills, subjected 13-year-old Savana Redding to a strip search. After searching her backpack and outer clothing and finding nothing, the police told Savana "to pull her bra out and to the side and shake it, and to pull out the elastic on her underpants, thus exposing her breasts and pelvic area to some degree." The Court ruled that this search violated her Fourth Amendment rights because "the content of the suspicion failed to match the degree of intrusion."[126]

Police searches inherently involve a clash between public safety and an individual's private freedom from government intrusions. These issues came to the fore with the passage of the Patriot Act of 2001 after the terrorist attacks of September 11. (The official name of this law is the USA PATRIOT Act, which is an acronym for the "Uniting and Strengthening America by Providing Appropriate Tools Required to Intercept and Obstruct Terrorism Act.") Several of the most controversial parts of the act strengthen police surveillance powers; make it easier to conduct "sneak and peek" searches

The question of whether government officials can compel companies like Apple to assist them in unlocking phones so they can conduct a search remains contentious. This issue became especially prominent after the 2015 shooting in San Bernardino, California, when the FBI ordered Apple to unlock the suspect's phone. The FBI dropped the lawsuit once it unlocked the phone without Apple's help. But in 2018, Apple announced it had changed the iPhone so it couldn't be unlocked.

(the police enter a home with a warrant, look for evidence, and do not inform the suspect that they searched his or her home until months later); broaden Internet surveillance; increase the government's access to individuals' library, banking, and medical records; and permit roving wiretaps for suspected terrorists.

Most police searches conducted without warrants occur because suspects consent to being searched. Officers are not required to tell a suspect that he or she may say no or request a warrant. Here are examples of other instances in which the Court will allow a warrantless search:

- Conducting a search at the time of a legal arrest that "is confined to the immediate vicinity of the arrest."
- Collecting evidence that was not included in the search warrant but is out in the open and in plain view.
- Using a police roadblock to search for information about a crime, to check for illegal immigrants or contraband at borders, or to conduct sobriety checks (but not for random drug searches or license checks), as long as the roadblock stops all drivers.
- Searching containers in cars if the officer has probable cause to suspect criminal activity.
- Searching passengers and the passenger area of a car if the driver has been stopped for a traffic offense (because people in automobiles do not have the same Fourth Amendment protections as people do in their homes).
- Searching an area where the officer thinks there is either a crime in progress or an "armed and dangerous" suspect.
- Searching school lockers, with probable cause.
- Searching for weapons and/or to prevent the destruction of evidence.[127]

Strip searches after an arrest and before the suspect is put in jail were upheld in 2012 by the Supreme Court even when there was no suspicion of illegal substances. The dissenting justices argued that "the humiliation of a visual strip-search" after being "arrested for driving with a noisy muffler, failing to use a turn signal and riding a bicycle without an audible bell" should not be allowed under the Fourth Amendment.[128]

In 2013, the Court ruled that a DNA swab of an arrested suspect is simply for identification and therefore is no more intrusive than a photograph or fingerprint. The late Justice Scalia, a strong defender of privacy rights, wrote in his dissent: "I doubt that the proud men who wrote the charter of our liberties would have been so eager to open their mouths for royal inspection."[129] Scalia argued that DNA evidence could be used to identify the arrestee as a suspect in an unrelated crime and therefore a swab should be taken only if there is probable cause that another crime has also been committed. Another controversial case that deeply divided the Court was the ruling that a warrant was not necessary to draw blood from an unconscious driver (who obviously could not provide consent) under the "exigent-circumstances doctrine" that allows warrantless searches to protect the destruction of evidence.[130]

The Court has generally made it easier for law-enforcement officials to conduct searches without warrants, but two important decisions in the other direction were a 2014 case that required a warrant to search cell phones of people who had been arrested[131] and a 2012 case that required a warrant to place a GPS tracking device on a vehicle. In the latter case, the FBI suspected Antoine Jones of selling cocaine, so agents placed a tracking device on his vehicle without a warrant, monitored his movements for four weeks, and then used the evidence to convict him. Jones was sentenced to life in prison. While the Court required a warrant in this specific case, the basis for the majority's decision was fairly narrow: the placement of the device was a "physical trespass," and the lengthy monitoring of his movement constituted an illegal search.[132] The Court provided additional protection for privacy in 2018 when it ruled that a search warrant is required to access cell phone location records. While the ruling made exceptions for emergencies such as "bomb threats, active shootings, and child abductions," the four dissenting justices feared that law-enforcement officials were losing an important tool in fighting crime.[133]

The Exclusionary Rule Another important concern related to the Fourth Amendment is what to do if the police obtain evidence illegally. Here the need to balance security and privacy becomes concrete. Either the evidence is excluded from a criminal trial to protect privacy rights or it is allowed to support the conviction of the suspect. In 1961, the Fourth Amendment was incorporated (applied to the states through the Fourteenth Amendment) in a case, *Mapp v. Ohio*. This case established for all courts the exclusionary rule, which says that illegally or unconstitutionally obtained evidence cannot be used in a criminal trial. Previously, the rule had applied only at the national level.[134]

In the landmark case, police broke into Dollree Mapp's residence without a warrant, looking for a suspect thought to be hiding in the house. The officers did not find him, but they did find illegal pornographic material, and Mapp was convicted of possessing it. Mapp's lawyer tried to defend her on First Amendment grounds, claiming she had the right to own the pornography, but instead the Court used the opportunity to apply the Fourth Amendment to the states. The Court threw out Mapp's conviction because the police did not have a search warrant, arguing that applying the Fourth Amendment only to the national government and not to the states didn't make any sense: Why should a state's attorney be able to use illegally obtained evidence while a federal prosecutor could not? The justices ruled that for the exclusionary rule to deter illegal searches and seizures, it must apply to law enforcement at both state and national levels.

Subsequently, the Supreme Court began weakening the exclusionary rule. For example, the Court established a "good faith exception" to the exclusionary rule, allowing evidence to be used as long as the officer believed that he or she had conducted a legal search. In this specific case, the officer had a warrant with the wrong address.[135] Yet another case established an "independent source" exception allowing the use of evidence that was initially obtained in an illegal search but subsequently acquired with a valid warrant. A major new exception was established in 2016 when the Court ruled that drugs found during a search in which an officer stopped a person with no probable cause are admissible as evidence if there was an outstanding arrest warrant for the suspect (in this case for a traffic offense) at the time of the search. Justice Sotomayor pointed out in her dissent that there are 7.8 million outstanding warrants, mostly for traffic and parking violations, which means that this new exception has far-reaching consequences: "The mere existence of a warrant not only gives an officer legal cause to arrest and search a person, it also forgives an officer who, with no knowledge of the warrant at all, unlawfully stops that person on a whim or hunch."[136] The bottom line is that the exclusionary rule remains in effect, but in the last several decades the courts have eased the conditions in which prosecutors can use evidence obtained under questionable circumstances.

Drug Testing Another area of Fourth Amendment law concerns drug testing. The clause granting people the right "to be secure in their persons" certainly seems to cover drug testing. However, the courts have long recognized the right of private companies to test their employees for illegal drugs. Moreover, in professional sports testing for

exclusionary rule
The principle that illegally or unconstitutionally acquired evidence cannot be used in a criminal trial.

Can the police search your home without a warrant? After Dollree Mapp was arrested for possession of pornographic material, the case made its way to the Supreme Court and the search was ruled unconstitutional. This case established the exclusionary rule for evidence that is obtained without a warrant.

performance-enhancing drugs is increasingly common. Lance Armstrong was stripped of his seven Tour de France titles after admitting in 2013 to doping, and Major League Baseball has struggled to rein in steroid and human growth hormone use by many of its players, including stars such as Alex Rodriguez, Steven Wright, and Francis Martes, who was suspended for the entire 2020 season for his use of performance-enhancing drugs.

What about drug testing by the state? The Court has upheld random drug testing for high school athletes and mandatory drug testing for any junior high or high school students involved in extracurricular activities.[137] In the case of athletes, proponents of the policy asserted that safety concerns should preclude a 260-pound lineman or a pitcher with a 90-mile-per-hour fastball from using drugs. However, the same arguments could not be made for members of the choir, band, debate club, social dance club, or chess club, so this decision to include all extracurricular activities was a particularly strong endorsement of schools' antidrug policies.

The Court has also upheld drug testing of public employees, with one exception. It struck down a Georgia law that would have required all candidates for state office to pass a drug test within 30 days of announcing a run for office, because candidates are not public employees.[138] Rather than appealing to the courts, former senator Ernest Hollings of South Carolina had a different approach to avoid drug testing. When his opponent challenged him to take a drug test, the senator shot back, "I'll take a drug test if you take an IQ test."[139]

The Post–September 11 Politics of Domestic Surveillance The debate over the trade-off between civil liberties and security intensified in 2005 when a White House–approved domestic surveillance program was revealed. At the center of this controversy is the National Security Agency (NSA), which was created during the Korean War in 1952 by President Harry Truman. The agency was initially kept so secret that for many years the government even denied its existence. Insiders joked that the "NSA" stood for "No Such Agency." Today the NSA is responsible for surveillance to protect national security, whereas the FBI is in charge of spying related to criminal activity and the Central Intelligence Agency (CIA) oversees foreign intelligence gathering. Since the terrorist attacks of September 11, 2001, the NSA has been monitoring the phone calls and Internet usage of many U.S. citizens who have had contact with suspected terrorists overseas. These calls were intercepted without the approval of the Foreign Intelligence Surveillance Court (FISC), which was created by Congress in 1978 under the Foreign Intelligence Surveillance Act (FISA) specifically for approving requests for the interception of calls. The NSA was also found to be creating a database of every phone call made within the borders of the United States. Phone companies AT&T, Verizon, and BellSouth reportedly turned over records of millions of customers' phone calls to the government.[140] In 2013, classified information revealed by Edward Snowden showed that the NSA had been monitoring the phone calls of German chancellor Angela Merkel and other leaders of allied countries, in addition to collecting e-mail traffic in the United States that contained the e-mail address or phone number of a foreign target. In April 2017, the NSA announced that it would no longer collect information on communications that simply mentioned someone rather than being sent to or from that person (so-called "about searches"). It also would discontinue "backdoor" searches in which conversations and Internet data from Americans get swooped up in the course of monitoring foreign targets. However, early in 2018, when Congress reauthorized the foreign surveillance for an additional six years, it opened the door to allowing "about" collection and "backdoor" searches to start up again.[141]

Critics warn that phone surveillance may be the tip of the iceberg, because the government may be monitoring travel, credit card, and banking records more widely than we think. Government agencies have previously skirted the restrictions in the

Privacy Act of 1974 and the Fourth Amendment by purchasing this information from businesses, since the Privacy Act requires disclosure of how the government is using personal information only when the government itself collects the data. The Justice Department spent $19 million in 2005 to purchase commercially gathered data about American citizens, according to a report by the Government Accountability Office. These data are then used to search for suspicious patterns of behavior in a process known as data mining.[142] In 2016, a massive data collection program by AT&T called Project Atmosphere was used by law-enforcement agencies investigating everything from murder to medical fraud.[143]

The debate over domestic surveillance has generated intense disagreement. At one extreme, critics conjure up images of George Orwell's classic novel *1984*, in which Big Brother, a reclusive totalitarian ruler, watches the characters' every move. Critics see the surveillance as a threat to civil liberties and to our system of checks and balances and separation of powers. They believe that when the executive branch refuses to obtain warrants through the FISA court to conduct surveillance, it is taking on too much power without consulting the other branches of government. But supporters of the program argue that getting a court order may take too long, jeopardizing the surveillance necessary to protect the country. Congress tried to strike a balance between these two positions when it enacted the FISA Amendments Act of 2008. This law continued the ban on monitoring the purely domestic communications of Americans without a court order, gave the government authority to intercept international communications, and provided legal immunity to the telecommunications companies that had cooperated in the original wiretapping program. However, the *New York Times* revealed that the NSA had still been engaged in "overcollection" of domestic communication between Americans under the new law, including an attempt to wiretap a member of Congress without a court order. Although the NSA vowed to stop purely domestic surveillance without a court order, technical problems make it difficult to distinguish between communications made within the United States and overseas, and recently declassified information reveals that these searches continued into 2019 without the documentation required by Congress.[144]

The Director of National Intelligence under Barack Obama, James Clapper, testified at a congressional hearing on possible changes to the FISA as protesters in the background called for an end to government surveillance.

The Fifth Amendment

Miranda Rights and Self-Incrimination The familiar phrase "I plead the Fifth" has been part of our criminal justice system since the Bill of Rights was ratified, ensuring that a suspect cannot be compelled to provide court testimony that would cause him or her to be prosecuted for a crime. However, what about outside a court of law? If a police officer coerces a confession out of a suspect, does that amount to self-incrimination?

Coercive police interrogations were allowed until a landmark case in 1966. Ernesto Miranda had been convicted in an Arizona court of kidnapping and rape, on the basis of a confession extracted after two hours of questioning in which he was not read his rights. The Court overturned the conviction, saying that a police interrogation "is inherently intimidating" and in these circumstances "no statement obtained from the defendant can truly be the product of his free choice."[145] To ensure that a confession is truly a free choice, the Court came up with the well-known **Miranda rights**. If police do not read a suspect these rights, nothing the suspect says can be used in court.

Miranda rights
The list of civil liberties described in the Fifth Amendment that must be read to a suspect before anything the suspect says can be used in a trial.

This is a typical example of the Miranda warning card that police officers carry with them and read to every suspect after an arrest.

DEFENDANT	LOCATION

SPECIFIC WARNING REGARDING INTERROGATIONS

1. YOU HAVE THE RIGHT TO REMAIN SILENT.

2. ANYTHING YOU SAY CAN AND WILL BE USED AGAINST YOU IN A COURT OF LAW.

3. YOU HAVE THE RIGHT TO TALK TO A LAWYER AND HAVE HIM PRESENT WITH YOU WHILE YOU ARE BEING QUESTIONED.

4. IF YOU CANNOT AFFORD TO HIRE A LAWYER ONE WILL BE APPOINTED TO REPRESENT YOU BEFORE ANY QUESTIONING, IF YOU WISH ONE.

SIGNATURE OF DEFENDANT	DATE
WITNESS	TIME

☐ REFUSED SIGNATURE   SAN FRANCISCO POLICE DEPARTMENT   PR.9.1.4

The Court has carved out exceptions to the Miranda rights requirement because the public has viewed the practice as "coddling criminals" and letting too many people go free on legal technicalities. In one case, police failed to read a suspect his Miranda rights until after they had frisked him, found an empty holster, and asked him where his gun was. The suspect led police to a gun. The lower court dismissed the charges because the gun had been used as incriminating evidence in the trial, but the Supreme Court reinstated the conviction because "concern for public safety must be paramount to adherence to the literal language of the *Miranda* rule."[146]

Although the Court has been willing to carve out limited exceptions to the Miranda rule, in 2000 the Court rejected Congress's attempt to overturn *Miranda* by designating all voluntary confessions as legally admissible evidence. The Court ruled that it, and not Congress, has the power to determine constitutional protections for criminal defendants. The justices also affirmed their intent to protect the Miranda rule, saying: "*Miranda* has become embedded in routine police practice to the point where the warnings have become part of our national culture."[147]

double jeopardy
Being tried twice for the same crime. This is prevented by the Fifth Amendment.

Double Jeopardy Another Fifth Amendment right for defendants is protection against being tried more than once for a particular crime. This is known as double jeopardy because the suspect is "twice put in jeopardy of life or limb" for a single offense. This prohibition was extended to the states in 1969.[148] But prosecutors can exploit two loopholes in this civil liberty: (1) a suspect may be tried in federal court and state court for the same crime,[149] and (2) if a suspect is found innocent of one set of *criminal* charges brought by the state, he or she may still be found guilty of the same or closely related offenses based on *civil* charges brought by a private individual.

Usually these loopholes are exploited only in high-profile cases in which there is public or political pressure to get a conviction. For example, in 1992 four Los Angeles police officers were acquitted of beating Rodney King, a driver they had chased for speeding. Before the trial, a bystander's video of the beating had been widely broadcast; subsequently, when people heard the news of the police officers' acquittal, massive and destructive riots broke out that lasted three days. Responding to political pressure, President George H. W. Bush urged federal prosecutors to retry the officers not for the *criminal* use of excessive force but for violating Rodney King's *civil* rights. (Two were ultimately found guilty, and two were acquitted.)

Property Rights and Eminent Domain The final part of the Fifth Amendment is at the heart of a hot legal debate over property rights. The clause says, "nor shall private property be taken for public use, without just compensation." For most of American history, this civil liberty has been noncontroversial. When the government needs private property for a public use such as building a highway or a park, it may force a property owner to sell at a fair market value in a practice known as eminent domain.

A new, controversial interpretation of the Fifth Amendment's "takings" clause, however, has attempted to expand the principle of just compensation to cover not only "physical takings" but also "regulatory takings." For example, if the Endangered Species Act protects an animal whose habitat is on your land, you would not be able to develop that property. Thus, its market value would probably be lower than if the endangered species did not live on your land. Therefore, the argument goes, because of this law the government has "taken" some of the value of your land by legally protecting the species, so it should compensate you for your loss.

This issue became even more controversial after a case involving a development project in New London, Connecticut. A working-class neighborhood was sold to a private developer to build a waterfront hotel, office space, and higher-end housing, but a homeowner sued the city to stop the development. The Court supported the local government, saying that "promoting economic development is a traditional and long accepted function of government," so a "plausible public use" is satisfied. Justice O'Connor wrote a strong dissent, saying that the "specter of condemnation hangs over all property. Nothing is to prevent the State from replacing any Motel 6 with a Ritz-Carlton, any home with a shopping mall, or any farm with a factory."[150] In reaction to this decision, legislation or constitutional amendments have been passed in 42 states restricting the use of eminent domain for economic development.[151] This is an evolving area of the law, with several recent cases restoring property rights and an important 2017 case providing another setback for property owners.[152] However, in 2019 the Court ruled that property owners who believe their property has been unfairly taken by local governments can sue for compensation directly in federal court without having to first bring the case in state court. This ruling overturned a 1985 precedent and was seen as a major victory for property owners.[153]

The Sixth Amendment: the right to legal counsel and a jury trial ९

The right to an attorney is one of the civil liberties key to criminal law, because the legal system is too complicated for a layperson to navigate. However, at one time, poor people accused of a state felony were forced to defend themselves in court if they could not afford a lawyer (except in cases involving the death penalty, for which the state would provide a lawyer).[154] This changed in 1963 with the celebrated case of *Gideon v. Wainwright*. Clarence Gideon was accused of breaking into a pool hall and stealing beer, wine, and money. He could not afford an attorney, so he tried to defend himself. He did a pretty good job—calling witnesses, cross-examining the prosecutor's witnesses, and providing a good summary argument. However, he was convicted and sentenced to five years in jail, based largely on the testimony of the person who turned out to be the guilty party. The Court unanimously overturned Gideon's conviction, saying: "In our adversary system of criminal justice, any person hauled into court who is too poor to hire a lawyer cannot be assured a fair trial unless counsel is provided for him."[155]

Unlike the exclusionary rule and the protection against self-incrimination, the right to an attorney has been strengthened over time, through both legislation and subsequent Court rulings. One year after *Gideon*, Congress passed the Criminal Justice Act, which provided better legal representation for criminal defendants in federal court; within two years, 23 states had taken similar action. The Court has defined a general right to *effective* counsel (although the bar is set considerably low in terms of defining "effective") and more recently mandated that defense attorneys must conduct any reasonable investigation into possible lines of defense when presenting evidence that could help the defendant.[156]

The Sixth Amendment also protects an individual's right to a speedy and public trial by an impartial jury in criminal cases. The Court affirmed the right to a speedy trial in 1967,[157] and today under the Federal Speedy Trial Act a trial must begin within 70 days of the defendant's arrest or first appearance in court. This law was strengthened by a 2006 Court decision stating that a defendant may not waive the right to a speedy trial.[158]

The most important legal disputes over the "impartial jury" issue concern the process of jury selection and peremptory challenges, in which lawyers from each side may eliminate certain people from the jury pool without providing any reason. The Court has ruled that race and gender may not be the basis for a peremptory challenge.[159] The Court has also made clear that racial bias during jury deliberation is not allowed. Although jury deliberations are normally secret, in a 2017 case in which Miguel Peña-Rodriguez was convicted of misdemeanor sexual assault, two jurors told the judge that one of the jurors had demonstrated a bias against Mexican Americans, saying things like "nine times out of ten Mexican men [are] guilty of being aggressive toward women and young girls." In the majority opinion Justice Kennedy argued that "racial bias in the justice system must be addressed—including, in some instances, after the verdict has been entered" in order to "prevent a systemic loss of confidence in jury verdicts, a confidence that is a central premise of the Sixth Amendment trial right."[160]

The Eighth Amendment: cruel and ९ unusual punishment

The Founders would be surprised by the intense debates over whether the Eighth Amendment prohibition against "cruel and unusual punishments" applies to the death penalty. Clearly, the death penalty was accepted in their time (even stealing a

Gideon v. Wainwright
The 1963 Supreme Court case that guaranteed the right to an attorney for the poor or indigent for felony offenses.

The fight against terrorism has raised controversial questions about due process rights. After the United States killed Anwar al-Awlaki—an Al Qaeda leader living in Yemen, and a U.S. citizen—critics argued that his due process rights, such as the right to a fair trial, had been violated.

horse was a capital offense!), and the language of the Constitution reflects that. Both the Fifth and Fourteenth Amendments say that a person may not be deprived of "life, liberty, or property, without due process of law," which implies that someone *could* be deprived of life as long as the state followed due process. The death penalty continues to be supported by many people in the United States, with 28 states allowing capital punishment. However, there is a clear overall trend away from the death penalty. Eight U.S. states have abolished the death penalty since 2007 (and four more states have moratoriums on the death penalty imposed by their governors, although Nebraska reinstated the death penalty by state referendum in 2016), and dozens of other countries have done so in recent years. There were 22 executions in the United States in 2019, which is the third-lowest number since 1991 and well below the peak of 98 in 1999.[161] A botched execution in Oklahoma in 2014, in which Clayton Lockett writhed and gasped for nearly 30 minutes when one of the lines filled with the lethal drugs failed, led to renewed calls for abolishing the death penalty.[162]

Supreme Court Rulings on the Death Penalty The Supreme Court remained silent on the issue of the death penalty for nearly two centuries. But in 1972 the Court ruled that the death penalty was unconstitutional because the process of applying it was too inconsistent. Congress and 35 states rushed to make their laws compliant with the Court decision. The typical fix was to say more explicitly which crimes were punishable by death and to make capital sentencing a two-step process: first, the determination of guilt or innocence, and second, a sentencing phase if the suspect is found guilty. Four years later, the Court approved these changes and allowed states to bring back the death penalty.[163]

While never again challenging the constitutionality of the death penalty, the Supreme Court has been chipping away at its edges for two decades. The Court has struck down state laws that mandated the death penalty in murder cases and a law requiring a death sentence for rape. It has also prohibited the execution of insane prisoners and abolished the death penalty for the "mentally retarded"—although the Court left it to the states to define who is "mentally retarded," it has since struck down standards in Florida and Texas that it found to be inappropriate indicators of intellectual capacity.[164] The Court has also prohibited the death penalty for juveniles under the age of 18 and for child rapists.[165]

These death-penalty cases have shown that the Court responds to public opinion and political change. (This is sometimes called the living Constitution perspective, as discussed in Chapters 2 and 6.) In his opinion in the juvenile death-penalty case, Justice Anthony Kennedy noted that 30 states forbid the death penalty for offenders younger than age 18, which was an increase of 5 states from 1989, when the Court had upheld the juvenile death penalty. Similarly, the number of states banning the death penalty for the mentally impaired grew from 14 in 1989 (when the practice was upheld) to 25 in 2002 (when it was struck down).

EXPLAIN WHY THE RIGHTS ASSOCIATED WITH PRIVACY ARE OFTEN CONTROVERSIAL

Privacy rights

You may be surprised to learn that the word "privacy" does not appear in the Constitution. Privacy rights were first developed in a 1965 case that questioned the constitutionality of an 1879 Connecticut law against using birth control. Estelle Griswold, the director of Planned Parenthood in Connecticut, was arrested nine days after opening a clinic that dispensed contraceptives. She was fined $100 and appealed her conviction. Although she lost in state court, she appealed all the way to the Supreme Court, which overturned her conviction.[166]

In a very fractured decision (there were six different opinions), the Court agreed that the law was outdated, but the justices agreed on little else. Even the justices who based their opinions on an implied constitutional right to privacy cited various constitutional roots. Justice William O. Douglas found privacy implicit in the First Amendment right of association, the Third Amendment's protection against the quartering of troops, the Fourth Amendment's prohibition against unreasonable searches and seizures, the Fifth Amendment's protection against self-incrimination, and the Ninth Amendment's catchall statement "The enumeration in the Constitution, of certain rights, shall not be construed to deny or disparage others retained by the people." These all seem like reasonable grounds for implicit privacy rights except the First Amendment right of association—since the Founders clearly meant political association, not an association with your spouse in bed.

The _Griswold v. Connecticut_ case was significant for establishing the constitutional basis for a right to privacy, but the dissenters in the case were concerned about where this right would lead. Justice Black warned that privacy "is a broad, abstract and ambiguous concept" that can be shrunk or expanded in subsequent decisions. He said that Douglas's argument "require[d] judges to determine what is or is not constitutional on the basis of their own appraisal of what laws are unwise or unnecessary. The power to make such decisions is of course that of a legislative body. Surely it has to be admitted that no provision of the Constitution specifically gives such blanket power to courts to exercise such a supervisory veto over the wisdom and value of legislative policies and to hold unconstitutional those laws which they believe to be unwise or dangerous."[167]

Abortion rights

Justice Black's prediction came true eight years later in _Roe v. Wade_, the landmark ruling that struck down laws in 46 states that limited abortion. Twelve of those states allowed abortions for pregnancies due to rape or incest, to protect the life of the mother, and in cases of severe fetal abnormalities. The much-criticized trimester analysis in the _Roe_ ruling said that in the first trimester, states could not limit abortions; in the second trimester, states could regulate abortions in the interests of the health of the mother; and in the third trimester, states could forbid all abortions except those necessary to protect the health or life of the mother. The justices cited a constitutional basis for abortion rights in the general right to privacy outlined in _Griswold_; the concept of "personal liberty" in the Fourteenth Amendment's due process clause; and the "rights reserved to the people" in the Ninth Amendment.[168]

Subsequent decisions have upheld _Roe_ but endorsed state restrictions on abortion, such as requiring parental consent, a waiting period, or counseling sessions aimed at convincing the woman not to have an abortion (see the What Do the Facts Say? feature for more on restrictions currently in effect). Most significantly, _Roe_'s trimester analysis has been replaced by a focus on the viability of the fetus. When the fetus would be viable (generally at 22 or 23 weeks), states can ban abortions "except where it is necessary, in appropriate medical judgment, for the preservation of the life or health of the mother."[169] Laws passed in 2013 by Arkansas and North Dakota limiting abortions as soon as a fetal heartbeat can be detected (as early as 6 weeks) were struck down by federal courts, but laws in 19 states now ban abortions at 20 weeks, in apparent contradiction with _Roe v. Wade_.

privacy rights
Liberties protected by several amendments in the Bill of Rights that shield certain personal aspects of citizens' lives from governmental interference, such as the Fourth Amendment's protection against unreasonable searches and seizures.

AP®
SUPREME
COURT CASE

Roe v. Wade
This 1973 Supreme Court case extended the right of privacy, through the application of the Fourteenth Amendment's due process clause, to a woman's decision to have an abortion while recognizing legitimate state interests in potential life and maternal health. The Court noted that the "relative weight of each of these interests varies over the course of pregnancy, and the law must account for this variability."

Since *Roe*, most political action concerning abortion has been in the courts, but that could change if the Supreme Court overturns the decision. Opponents of abortion are hoping that *Roe* will be overturned, which would shift the politics of abortion back to state legislatures and make it an even more contested political issue. One effort to challenge *Roe* was a "personhood amendment" to the Mississippi constitution that defined life as beginning at conception. But the amendment was soundly defeated in a statewide vote in 2011.[170] The pace of state restrictions on abortions accelerated from 2011 to 2013, with more than 200 limitations on abortion services. In 2013, 22 states enacted 70 new restrictions, including a requirement that abortion doctors have admitting privileges at local hospitals—which would close up to one-third of abortion clinics in affected states.[171] In 2016, the Supreme Court struck down the latter as an "undue burden" on the right to an abortion.[172] In June 2020, the Supreme Court also struck down a Louisiana law that would have limited the number of abortion providers in the state to just one. In his deciding vote, Chief Justice Roberts cited precedent in his decision, pointing to the fact that the Court struck down a similar law in Texas in its 2016 decision. When Justice Ruth Bader Ginsburg died shortly before the 2020 elections and was replaced by Amy Coney Barrett, abortion opponents believed they might have the fifth vote needed to overturn *Roe v. Wade*.

Gay rights

Tyron Garner and John Geddes Lawrence after the Supreme Court decision in *Lawrence v. Texas* in 2003 established broad privacy rights for sexual behavior (including homosexual behavior).

Gay rights have typically been thought of more as a civil right (that is, freedom from discrimination) than a civil liberty, so these issues will be discussed in the next chapter. However, several important cases involving sexual relations are rooted in privacy rights. In 1986, the Court had ruled in *Bowers v. Hardwick* that there was no privacy protection or fundamental right for consenting adults to engage in "homosexual sodomy."[173] But in 2003, in *Lawrence v. Texas*, the Court established very broad privacy rights for sexual behavior. The case involved two Houston men, John Geddes Lawrence and Tyron Garner, who were prosecuted for same-sex sodomy after police entered Lawrence's apartment—upon receiving a false tip about an armed man—and found the two having sex. Under Texas law, sodomy was illegal for gays but not for heterosexuals. In a landmark 6–3 ruling, the Supreme Court said that the liberty guaranteed by the Fourteenth Amendment's due process clause allows homosexuals to have sexual relations: "Freedom presumes an autonomy of self that includes freedom of thought, belief, expression, and certain intimate conduct."[174] The decision explicitly overturned *Bowers v. Hardwick* and five members of the majority signed onto the broad "due process" reasoning of the decision, while Justice O'Connor wrote a concurring opinion in which she agreed that the Texas law was unconstitutional but on narrower grounds. With the broader due process logic, a total of 13 state laws that banned sodomy were struck down.

"Why Should I Care?"

Privacy might not seem important. You may think you'll never be accused of a crime or have your privacy invaded or questioned by the government. Indeed, many people think, "I have nothing to hide, so it is fine if the NSA monitors e-mail and Internet traffic to keep tabs on suspected terrorists." What if your e-mail revealed that you had a serious medical or mental health condition? What if the NSA paid special attention to you because of tweets you posted criticizing a government policy? Knowing your rights and how those rights apply to everyone—both criminals and innocent people—will help you make informed decisions about which policies to support.

Parental Consent Laws for Abortions for Minors

- ■ No parental notification or consent laws
- ■ One or both parents must consent
- ■ One or both parents must be informed
- ■ Both parental consent and notification required
- ■ Parental consent or notification laws blocked

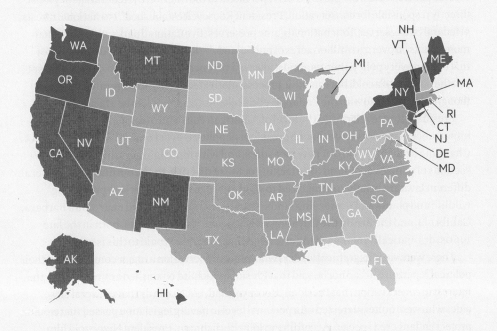

Pre-Abortion Mandatory Waiting Period Laws

- ■ No mandatory waiting period
- ■ Waiting period of less than 24 hours
- ■ Waiting period of 24 hours or more
- ■ Waiting period law blocked

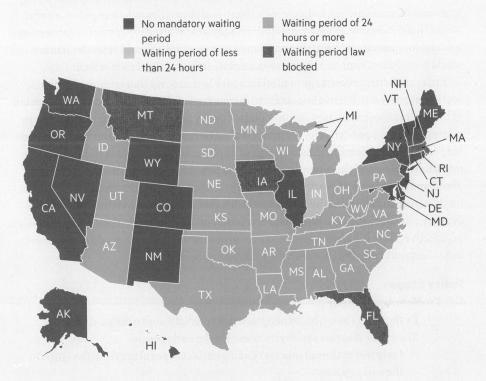

Abortion Rights Today

The Court's 1973 decision in *Roe v. Wade* made abortion legal throughout the United States. How do abortion rights look today? What do the numbers say?

Source: Guttmacher Institute, "An Overview of Abortion Laws," January 6, 2020, www.guttmacher.org/state-policy/explore/overview-abortion-laws (accessed 1/31/20).

Think about it

- **Which states have the most** restrictive policies concerning access to abortions?
- **How do you think waiting periods** and parental notification affect the number of abortions in a state? What about the number of abortions nationwide?

The Endangered Species Act

Environmentalism has been on the political agenda for a very long time, dating most prominently from the presidency of Theodore Roosevelt (1901–1909), a lifelong outdoorsman who took a personal interest in many different aspects of preserving the environment. When he became president, he was able to transform his love of nature into various policies. According to the U.S. Department of the Interior, the federal agency most directly responsible for conservation, President Roosevelt established "150 national forests, 51 federal bird reserves, four national game preserves, five national parks and 18 national monuments on over 230 million acres of public land."[175] Roosevelt's legacy demonstrates that behind every policy, there is almost always a very personal dimension. Policies are not just the product of a cold, bureaucratic process, motivated by political aggrandizement, though as you will see with the Endangered Species Act, that can also be a factor.

President Roosevelt raised the level of American consciousness regarding the importance of conservation, but no president or policy is ever the final word on a subject. Changing times often call for new measures, and with hindsight certain policies or sections of policies are found to be lacking or too restrictive. In the outline below, several different laws are briefly summarized to show the increasing interest in protecting wildlife and plants and preserving lands. Events, such as the oil spill near Santa Barbara, California, and the fire on the Cuyahoga River near Cleveland, Ohio, both in the late 1960s, dramatically increased the attention that Americans paid to this issue.

There were various political leaders who made conservation a major component of their political repertoire. It cannot be said that President Richard Nixon had anywhere near the interest in conservation that President Roosevelt had, but Nixon did have several close aides who were quite interested on a personal level in having legislation passed that would protect endangered species. According to John Ehrlichman, President Nixon told him, "In a flat choice between smoke and jobs, we're for jobs, but just keep me out of trouble on environmental issues."[176] With that warning in mind, aides convinced the president that it would benefit him and the Republican Party politically if he took up the charge of trying to prevent the extinction of endangered animals and plants. Senator George McGovern, whom Nixon correctly anticipated would run against him in the 1972 presidential election, was a major sponsor of several pieces of conservation legislation, and aides thought it would boost Nixon's image if he was associated with similar legislation as well.

In the implementation stage of this landmark legislation a short summary of its sections is provided. It is not important to memorize or fully understand every provision of the law, but these synopses are provided to convey the careful thought that goes into putting together a policy. Careful attention must be paid especially to terminology and language so that those agencies in charge of implementation carry out the legislators' intentions. Like good chess players, effective policy makers have to think several steps ahead and try to think of every possible interpretation and misinterpretation that others might perceive now and in the future for the lifespan of the law. Even then, no policy is ever entirely successful on this front. Fortunately or unfortunately, depending on one's perspective, there are always more chances to pass new legislation or add amendments, as has certainly been the case with the Endangered Species Act.

Policy Stages

1. Problem Recognition
   - By the early 1900s, bison and passenger pigeons were nearly extinct.
   - The extinction rate rapidly increased in the early 1900s.
     - Only two mammal species became extinct per century from the 1500s to the early 1900s.
     - By the 1960s and 1970s, the number of extinct species increased to at least 475.

- The Lacey Act (1900)
  - It banned the illegal trafficking of protected wildlife across state and international borders.
  - It was amended in 2008 to include a wide variety of plants and other vegetation, such as different woods and wood products.
- The Convention for the Protection of Migratory Birds (1916) between the United States and Canada
  - It covered over 800 species of birds. It led to the Migratory Birds Convention Act (1917) in Canada and to the Migratory Birds Treaty Act (1918) in the United States.
  - Similar treaties were also later made with Mexico, Japan, and Russia.
- The Bald and Gold Eagle Protection Act of 1940
  - It prohibited "taking" anything associated with these particular types of eagles.
  - "Taking" was defined as acts intended to "pursue, shoot, shoot at, poison, wound, kill, capture, trap, collect, molest or disturb."
- The Species Preservation Act of 1966
  - It was inspired by dwindling numbers of whooping cranes and bald eagles.
  - It covered only fish and vertebrate wildlife.
- The oil spill in Santa Barbara, California, took place on January 28, 1969.
  - President Nixon visited the site but was slow to respond.
- The Cuyahoga River in Ohio caught fire on June 22, 1969.
  - The fire was due to the river's high concentration of pollution, especially oil.
  - A fire on this river had happened 13 times in 100 years.
- The Endangered Species Conservation Act of 1969
  - It amended the Species Preservation Act of 1966.
  - It extended the types of animals that could be protected to include invertebrates, such as crustaceans and mollusks.
- The national Earth Day movement was started by Senator Gaylord Nelson (D-WI) in 1970.
  - The initial impetus was the Santa Barbara oil spill.
  - Senator Nelson was inspired by Vietnam student protests and thought this type of student activism could also be used for environmental issues, including the extinction of animals.

2. Agenda Setting
- Senators Edmund Muskie (D-ME) and Henry "Scoop" Jackson (D-WA) were vocal advocates for more legislation and stronger regulations to conserve the environment during President Nixon's first term in office (1969–1973).
- Top Nixon officials, John Ehrlichman (White House Domestic Affairs advisor), Russell E. Train (chairman of the Council on Environmental Quality), and John Whitaker (environmental policy aide) were personally interested in environmental conservation.
  - They convinced President Nixon to promote legislation of this type to improve his popularity, increase his political capital, and make protecting the environment a Republican issue as well as a Democratic one.
  - Nixon discussed conservation in his 1970 State of the Union speech and later that year to Congress again.
  - Nixon signed other environmentally friendly acts, including these:
    - The Endangered Species Conservation Act (1969)
    - The National Environmental Policy Act (1970)
    - The Water Quality Improvement Act (1970)

- Nixon created the Environmental Protection Agency (EPA) in 1970.
- Nixon thought Muskie might be a presidential candidate so he wanted to make sure he had a formidable environmental record before his reelection campaign.

3. Deliberation and Formulation
   - The White House commissioned scientists and lawyers, led by Train, to write up the bill that was eventually submitted to Congress.
   - The bill was introduced in the Senate by Harrison A. Williams (D-NJ) on June 12, 1973.
   - The Senate passed its version of the bill on July 24, 1973: **92 YEAs:** 53 Democrats, 37 Republicans, 2 others; **0 NAYs; 8 Not Voting:** 3 Democrats, 5 Republicans, 0 others.
   - The bill was introduced in the House of Representatives by John Dingell (D-MI) on January 3, 1973.
   - The House of Representatives passed its version of the bill on September 18, 1973: **390 YEAs:** 219 Democrats, 170 Republicans, 1 other; **12 NAYs:** 3 Democrats, 9 Republicans, 0 others; **1 Present:** 0 Democrats, 1 Republican, 0 others; **37 Not Voting:** 23 Democrats, 14 Republicans, 0 others.

4. Enactment
   - The Senate passed a compromise bill on December 19, 1973.
   - The House of Representatives passed a compromise bill on December 20, 1973: **355 YEAs:** 194 Democrats, 160 Republicans, 1 other; **4 NAYs:** 0 Democrats, 4 Republicans, 0 others; **79 Not Voting:** 51 Democrats, 28 Republicans, 0 others.
   - The Endangered Species Act of 1973 was signed into law by President Nixon on December 28, 1973.

5. Implementation
   - The act was administered by the Fish and Wildlife Service and the National Marine Fisheries Service.
   - It provided protection from logging, drilling, and other human activities.
   - It protects more than 1,600 plant and animal species.
   - **Section 2 (there is no Section 1):** Findings, Purposes, and Policy: This section provided a summary of the main threats against fish, wildlife, and plants and a general outline of how the federal government and states can address and reverse these problems.
   - **Section 3:** Definitions: This section defined various terms, such as "critical habitat," "endangered," and "threatened." But the most significant term because of its wide-ranging implications is "take," which is defined as follows: "to harass, harm, pursue, hunt, shoot, wound, kill, trap, capture, or collect or to attempt to engage in any such conduct."
   - **Section 4:** Determination of Endangered Species and Threatened Species
     - This section classified wildlife and plants according to how close they are to extinction.
     - It considered how the ecosystem ("critical habitat") of these species contributes to their probability of extinction.
   - **Section 5:** Land Acquisition: This section allowed the federal government to acquire land that will improve the living conditions for particular species.
   - **Section 6:** Cooperation with the States: This section called for the federal government to work with the states as much as possible in addressing problems and solutions and providing funds to the states.

- **Section 7:** Interagency Cooperation: This section required different government agencies to communicate and coordinate with one another to ensure that they were not working at cross-purposes and that the goal of protecting wildlife and plant life was always a priority.
- **Section 8:** International Cooperation: This section required the United States to work with other countries and encourage them to engage in more conservation strategies to preserve endangered and threatened species.
- **Section 8A:** Convention Implementation: This section detailed logistical procedures for carrying out international cooperation.
- **Section 9:** Prohibited Acts: This section provided more detail about the term "taking" and the illegality of the selling, exporting, and importing of endangered and threatened species.
- **Section 10:** Exceptions: This section clarified that under certain circumstances the rules outlined in this policy would not apply, especially when the benefits have to be weighed against the economic impact of protecting different species and when they threaten the livelihood of particular groups of people, such as Native Americans and Eskimos.
- **Section 11:** Penalties and Enforcements: This section detailed the punishments—fines, imprisonment, or seizure of property—and who is authorized to enforce this law.
- **Section 12:** Endangered Plants: This section broadened the scope of protection to include plants and vegetation.
- **Section 13:** Conforming Amendments: This section incorporated and updated provisions made in previous, related legislation.
- **Section 14:** Repealer: This section repealed certain sections of the Endangered Species Conservation Act of 1969.
- **Section 15:** Authorization of Appropriations: This section designated how much money Congress will allocate to carry out many of the functions described in this law.
- **Section 16:** Effective Date: This section explained the provisions of the policy will go into effect as soon as it is enacted.
- **Section 17:** Marine Mammal Protection Act of 1972: This section noted the Endangered Species Act will not supersede or contradict any more stringent provision of the 1972 act.
- **Section 18:** Annual Cost Analysis by the Fish and Wildlife Service: This section required the Secretary of the Interior to provide to Congress a yearly financial report of how much has been spent on protecting each of the designated species.

6. Evaluation
   - The law ignored its economic impact.
     - For example, protecting the snail darter (a small fish) delayed the completion of the $120 million Tellico Dam project in Tennessee.
   - If the economic impact had been considered, then more species would have become extinct.
   - The law has saved 99 percent of more than 1,600 species.
   - Most species never leave the list: only 47 out of 1,650 species have been removed.
   - The law should have been written to cover more species.
   - The bureaucratic process for getting a species on the list is too long and difficult.

- This process increased the likelihood of overlooked species becoming extinct.
- The law promotes biodiversity, which has created a more vibrant and robust ecosystem that benefits all species, endangered or not.
- A pragmatic perspective sees saved species as a possible source for future medicines.
- An ethical/religious perspective sees all of nature's/God's creatures as worthy of protection.

7. Possible Modifications, Expansion, or Termination of Policy
   - 1978 amendment
     - This amendment established the Endangered Species Committee ("God Squad") consisting of seven cabinet members who could vote to exempt a species from protection if potential economic benefits were greater than saving the species.
   - 1982 amendment
     - This amendment stipulated that scientific evidence and not economic considerations would be used for determining if a species should be included on the endangered list.
   - 1988 amendment
     - This amendment increased the overall budget as well as individual fines for violations.
     - Spending was devoted to protecting elephants.
     - Efforts were made to streamline the process so species do not go extinct before getting on the list.
   - 2019 rule changes
     - It will now be easier to remove species from the endangered list.
     - Species on the threatened list will no longer automatically receive the same protections as endangered species.
     - Economic costs and benefits are factors that can be considered when deciding to add a species to the endangered list.
     - Climate change's probable effect on harming the existence of a species is not included in the cost/benefit analysis.

Questions for Discussion

1. President Nixon was reported to have said to an aide, "In a flat choice between smoke and jobs, we're for jobs, but just keep me out of trouble on environmental issues." Do you agree that there is always a trade-off between pollution and jobs? Explain your answer.

2. Until the twenty-first century, environmentalism was a bipartisan concern. Why has it become more of a divisive issue between Democrats and Republicans in recent years?

3. Do you think it is important if the United States is involved in international environmental agreements, such as the Paris Agreement on climate change? Why or why not?

Unpacking the Conflict

Considering all that we've discussed in this chapter, let's apply what we know about how civil liberties work to the example of free speech on college campuses introduced at the beginning of this chapter. Can controversial speech on college campuses be limited? How can we explain this conflict?

The issue of free speech on campus raises difficult questions of balancing interests and drawing lines. Speakers' interests in making their voices and opinions heard must be balanced against the universities' interest in public safety and students' interest in protecting other students from hate speech. The First Amendment is applicable in these instances because the speakers in question are lecturing at public—that is, state government—institutions.

This puts many universities in a difficult spot—they would rather not allow these controversial speakers, especially because of the high cost of providing security. However, the First Amendment protects political speech, and the Supreme Court has established that it cannot be prevented unless there is a direct incitement to imminent violence. Even association with previous acts of violence, as in the case of Richard Spencer, is not sufficient grounds to prevent speech.

You exercise your civil liberties every day, whether speaking in public, going to church, being searched at an airport, participating in a political demonstration, writing or reading an article in your school newspaper, or being free from illegal police searches in your home. Because civil liberties are defined as those things the government *cannot* do to you, defining civil liberties is a political process. Often this process is confined to the courts, but for many issues—including free speech, freedom of the press, pornography, criminal rights, abortion, and gun control—it takes place in the broader political world, where defining civil liberties involves balancing competing ideals and interests and drawing lines by interpreting and applying the law. For example, debates over how to balance national security and civil liberties—whether newspapers should publish stories about classified government programs that may threaten civil liberties, or whether government surveillance powers should be strengthened to fight terrorism—will rage for years.

Other cases, such as the protests at military funerals or the protection of the due process rights of suspected criminals and terrorists, illustrate how difficult and politically unpopular it can be to protect our freedoms and liberty. Nearly everyone would agree that the behavior of the members of Westboro Baptist Church is completely outrageous. But protecting the freedom of speech is easy if you agree with what is being spoken. It becomes much more difficult if the freedom protects the rights of Nazis to march in Skokie, defends a person accused of a heinous crime, or gives a White supremacist like Richard Spencer a platform.

"What's Your Take?"

Should speakers with controversial, sometimes hateful opinions be allowed to speak on college campuses?

Or do universities' and students' interests outweigh their right to free speech?

AP® STUDY GUIDE

Summary

Civil liberties are the protections that individuals receive from the government. These are not absolute rights, however, as individual freedoms can be at odds with the public good and government interests. The courts often play the deciding role in determining where to draw the line between individual rights and public safety.

The Bill of Rights, the first ten amendments to the Constitution, lists individual protections from the federal government and was included in the Constitution in response to demands from the Antifederalists, who feared a strong national government. For most of the nineteenth century, these individual freedoms were guaranteed only from the federal government and did not extend to protections from state governments. With the ratification of the Fourteenth Amendment and the process of selective incorporation, federal freedoms have been gradually extended to the state level.

Religious freedoms are defined by two clauses in the First Amendment: the establishment clause, as represented by cases such as *Engel v. Vitale* (1962), and the free exercise clause, as represented by cases such as *Wisconsin v. Yoder* (1972). Together, they do not allow the government to do anything to benefit any particular religion, nor do they allow the government to hinder religious practice without adequate justification. As is often the case, the Court has struggled to define exactly what constitutes "excessive government entanglement" in religion.

The Supreme Court's attempt to balance individual freedoms and the public good is reflected in the scope of protections guaranteed by the First Amendment. The Court generally prioritizes protecting individual rights to political speech, hate speech, and symbolic speech, as represented by *Tinker v. Des Moines School District* (1969). The Court also protects the freedom to assemble and the freedom of the press, giving the press freedom by establishing a "heavy presumption against prior restraint," even in cases involving national security. However,

Key Terms

civil liberties (p. 316)

Civil War amendments (p. 322)

clear and present danger test (p. 332)

commercial speech (p. 341)

direct incitement test (p. 332)

double jeopardy (p. 352)

due process clause (p. 322)

due process rights (p. 345)

Engel v. Vitale (p. 327)

establishment clause (p. 326)

exclusionary rule (p. 348)

fighting words (p. 339)

free exercise clause (p. 326)

Gideon v. Wainwright (p. 353)

Gitlow v. New York (p. 322)

hate speech (p. 335)

intermediate scrutiny (p. 331)

Lemon test (p. 327)

libel (p. 339)

McDonald v. Chicago (p. 344)

Miller test (p. 342)

Miranda rights (p. 351)

New York Times Co. v. United States (p. 338)

prior restraint (p. 338)

privacy rights (p. 355)

Roe v. Wade (p. 355)

Schenck v. United States (p. 332)

selective incorporation (p. 322)

slander (p. 339)

strict scrutiny (p. 331)

symbolic speech (p. 333)

"time, manner, and place" restrictions (p. 329)

Tinker v. Des Moines School District (p. 333)

Wisconsin v. Yoder (p. 317)

under extreme circumstances—such as speech that directly incites violence or creates a "clear and present danger" as seen in *Schenck v. United States* (1919)—these rights can be limited. Additionally, the Court regularly places a lower priority on, and affords less protection to, fighting words, slander, libel, commercial speech, and offensive or obscene statements and gestures. The Court has also created "time, manner, and place" regulations regarding the protection of free speech.

The Supreme Court has done little to define what freedoms are established in the Second Amendment, largely preferring to allow the national, state, and local governments to make their own laws. One exception is the incorporation of the Second Amendment's right to bear arms for self-defense in one's home, as represented by *McDonald v. Chicago* (2010). The majority of public sentiment appears to be in favor of continued gun ownership, and limitations on Second Amendment rights appear unlikely.

The Fourth, Fifth, Sixth, and Eighth Amendments provide protections—known as due process rights—for individuals accused of a crime. These rights, including the right to legal counsel as represented by *Gideon v. Wainwright* (1963) and the Mirada rule, have been incorporated using the Fourteenth Amendment to apply to not just the federal government but states as well. However, interpreting these general due process rights in specific cases is difficult because specific standards of fairness and justice are very hard to define.

The term "privacy rights" is not found in the Constitution—rather, it was established in a 1965 Supreme Court case—but it may be implied in several amendments in the Bill of Rights. The right to privacy is controversial because of the lack of explicit language in the Constitution and the lack of consensus on exactly what the right to privacy means. It has remained a hot-button issue because recognition of the right to privacy is an important facet of the contemporary debate on abortion, as represented by the landmark case of *Roe v. Wade* (1973).

Enduring Understandings

LOR-2: "Provisions of the U.S. Constitution's Bill of Rights are continually being interpreted to balance the power of government and the civil liberties of individuals." (AP® U.S. Government and Politics Course and Exam Description)

LOR-3: "Protections of the Bill of Rights have been selectively incorporated by way of the Fourteenth Amendment's due process clause to prevent state infringement of basic liberties." (AP® U.S. Government and Politics Course and Exam Description)

Multiple-Choice Questions (Arranged by Topic)

Topic 3.1: The Bill of Rights (LOR-2)

1. **Which of the following scenarios describes a situation that would be protected by the Bill of Rights?**

    (A) A city orders the demolition of a private home in order to build a freeway but does not provide any type of compensation.

    (B) A state requires a voter to pay a tax in order to cast a vote in the upcoming presidential election.

    (C) A suspect that was acquitted of robbing a bank is tried for a second time when new evidence is found.

    (D) A group of protestors gather outside of the state capital to protest the "shelter at home" order during COVID-19.

Topic 3.2: First Amendment: Freedom of Religion (LOR-2)

2. Which of the following is an accurate comparison of the establishment clause and the free exercise clause as used by the Supreme Court when making a decision about the action described in the scenario?

	Establishment Clause	Free Exercise Clause
(A)	a cake shop owner who refuses to bake a cake for the wedding of a same-sex couple	being fired, and then being denied unemployment benefits, for using peyote as part of a religious ceremony
(B)	a daily prayer written by the state recited at the start of each school day	Amish parents who are forced to send their children to school beyond the eighth grade
(C)	the practice of observing a one-minute moment of silence for "meditation or voluntary prayer" in a public school	a 40-foot cross that is part of a World War I Memorial, which is built on state property
(D)	a private corporation that is forced to provide contraception to women under the Affordable Care Act (ACA)	allowing state tax credits for contributions to organizations that provide tuition for religious schools

Topic 3.3: First Amendment: Freedom of Speech (LOR-2)

3. In which of the following scenarios would the Supreme Court most likely use *Tinker v. Des Moines School District* (1969) as a precedent when making its decision?

   (A) A group of students is suspended for protesting a series of recent police shootings by wearing Black Lives Matter T-shirts to school.

   (B) A suspect arrested for robbing a grocery store is denied a court-appointed attorney even though he cannot afford to hire an attorney on his own.

   (C) A man is arrested for burning an American flag to protest the involvement of U.S. troops abroad.

   (D) A student, whose locker was searched without a warrant, is suspended for possession of an illegal substance.

Topic 3.4: First Amendment: Freedom of the Press (LOR-2)

4. Which of the following best describes the issue of prior restraint?

   (A) spoken false statements that damage a person's reputation and that can be regulated by the government

   (B) written false statements that damage a person's reputation and that can be regulated by the government

   (C) the government's ability to limit the press by prohibiting the media from publishing certain materials

   (D) forms of expression that can be regulated by the government because "by their very utterance" they can incite violence

Topic 3.5: Second Amendment: Right to Bear Arms (LOR-2)

5. Which of the following best describes the current position of the Supreme Court concerning the Second Amendment?

   (A) The Court has refused to take a general position on the individual right to bear arms.

   (B) The Court has upheld most gun control laws, both at the state and national levels, arguing that there is no individual right to own guns.

   (C) The Court has upheld most gun control laws at the state level but struck down federal gun control laws, arguing that the Second Amendment applies only to Congress.

   (D) The Court has struck down some state and national limitations on gun ownership, arguing that the Second Amendment protects an individual liberty.

Topic 3.6: Amendments: Balancing Individual Freedom with Public Order and Safety (LOR-2)

6. The Supreme Court's decisions defining cruel and unusual punishment involve interpretations of which of the following amendments?

   (A) Third Amendment

   (B) Sixth Amendment

   (C) Eighth Amendment

   (D) Ninth Amendment

Topic 3.7: Selective Incorporation (LOR-3)

7. Which of the following is a likely consequence of how the application of the doctrine of selective incorporation affects the balance of power between the different levels of government?

   (A) The local government gains more power.

   (B) The federal government gains more power.

   (C) The state government gains more power.

   (D) The distribution of power between the different levels of government is not affected.

Topic 3.8: Amendments: Due Process and the Rights of the Accused (LOR-3)

8. The Fourth Amendment provides protection from which of the following?

   (A) unreasonable searches and seizures

   (B) self-incrimination

   (C) a slow and private trial

   (D) a biased jury in criminal cases

Topic 3.9: Amendments: Due Process and the Right to Privacy (LOR-3)

Questions 9–10 refer to the maps.

Abortion Rights Today

Parental Consent Laws for Abortions for Minors

- No parental notification or consent laws
- One or both parents must be informed
- Parental consent or notification laws blocked
- One or both parents must consent
- Both parental consent and notification required

Pre-Abortion Mandatory Waiting Period Laws

- No mandatory waiting period
- Waiting period of 24 hours or more
- Waiting period of less than 24 hours
- Waiting period law blocked

Source: Guttmacher Institute, "An Overview of Abortion Laws," January 6, 2020, www.guttmacher.org/state-policy/explore/over-view-abortion-laws (accessed 1/31/20).

9. **Based on the information in the maps, which of the following is true about parental consent laws for abortions for minors and pre-abortion mandatory waiting laws?**

    (A)   Michigan (MI) does not require parental consent for a minor to get an abortion but does require a waiting period of at least 24 hours.

    (B)   The majority of states have blocked both parental consent and notification laws for abortions for minors, as well as pre-abortion mandatory waiting laws.

    (C)   More states are in agreement about pre-abortion mandatory waiting periods than about parental consent or notification for a minor to get an abortion.

    (D)   Both Montana (MT) and Florida (FL) have blocked both parental consent and notification laws as well as waiting period laws.

10. **Which of the following best describes the relationship between how the Supreme Court ruled in *Roe v. Wade* (1973) and the information provided in the maps?**

    (A)   While states are limited by the due process clause from infringing upon individual rights, those limits are not absolute.

    (B)   While states are limited by the equal protection clause from infringing upon individual rights, those limits are not absolute.

    (C)   The establishment clause allows the federal government through the Supreme Court to override state laws.

    (D)   The establishment clause allows states to create their own laws, but the Court can place restrictions on those laws.

Free-Response Questions

Concept Application

Since 2005, members of the Westboro Baptist Church (WBC) have protested at hundreds of funerals of members of the armed services who were killed in Iraq and Afghanistan. However, these are not typical antiwar protests. Instead, the protesters claim that the troops' deaths were God's punishment for "the homosexual lifestyle of soul-damning, nation-destroying filth." The church and its members have drawn strong reactions and counterprotests for their confrontational approach at the military funerals, including their use of signs that say "Thank God for Dead Soldiers," "God Killed Your Sons," and "God Hates America." Critics, including many veterans groups and attorneys general from 48 states, argue that the protests should not be allowed. The Veterans of Foreign Wars issued a statement saying, "In a time of profound grief and emotional vulnerability, these personal attacks are an affront of the most egregious kind."

After reading the scenario, respond to A, B, and C below:

    (A)   Referencing the scenario, describe the civil liberty, other than freedom of assembly, that is being discussed in the scenario.

    (B)   In the context of the scenario, explain how the interpretation of the civil liberty described in Part A may make it challenging to achieve a balance between liberty and order.

    (C)   In 2011, the Supreme Court ruled 8–1 that the WBC's protests were protected by the Constitution. Explain how Congress could use its powers to try to prevent the actions of the WBC.

SCOTUS Comparison

This question requires you to compare a Supreme Court case you studied in class with one you have not studied in class. A summary of the Supreme Court case you did not study in class is presented below and provides all of the information you need to know about this case to answer the prompt.

The city of Highland Park, Illinois, passed a series of ordinances banning AK-47s, AR-15s, and other large-capacity magazines that can accept more than 10 rounds. The ordinances followed the school shooting at Sandy Hook Elementary School in Newtown, Connecticut. Many residents of Highland

Park supported the ordinances in light of the tragedy. Arie Friedman, who lives in Highland Park, owned a banned rifle and several large-capacity magazines before the ordinances took effect. The city gave anyone who legally possessed assault weapons or large-capacity magazines 60 days to move them outside city limits, disable them, or surrender them for destruction. Mr. Friedman brought suit against the city, stating that it was violating his protected rights. The U.S. Seventh Circuit Court of Appeals upheld the ban on assault weapons and high-capacity magazines, citing that these weapons did not exist at the writing of the Constitution and therefore were not constitutionally protected.

In the ensuing case, *Friedman v. City of Highland Park, Illinois* (2015), the Supreme Court denied Mr. Friedman a writ of certiorari (refused to hear the case) and remanded the case to the decision of the lower court.

Based on the information above, respond to the following questions.

(A) Identify the amendment of the U.S. Constitution that addresses the main issue in both *McDonald v. Chicago* (2010) and *Friedman v. City of Highland Park, Illinois* (2015).

(B) Explain how the facts in *McDonald v. Chicago* led to a different holding than in *Friedman v. City of Highland Park, Illinois*.

(C) Explain how the Supreme Court's decision in *Friedman v. City of Highland Park, Illinois* affected the balance of power between state and federal governments.

9

Civil Rights

You can't discriminate against me ... right?

» **"No one should live in fear of being stopped whenever he leaves his home to go about the activities of daily life."**
Shira A. Scheindlin, former federal judge

« **"Well, I think profiling is something that we're going to have to start thinking about as a country. And other countries do it. . . . And they do it successfully. And I hate the concept of profiling. But we have to start using common sense, and we have to use our heads."**
President Donald Trump

» **"I don't even talk about whether or not racial profiling is legal. I just don't think racial profiling is a particularly good law enforcement tool."**
Eric Holder, former attorney general

Our civil rights protect us from discrimination by the government and our fellow Americans. This issue came to the fore in 2020 when the killing of an unarmed Black man, George Floyd, by the police set off mass protests across the country against police brutality and racial injustice. Most everyone would agree that selective enforcement of laws depending on the color of one's skin constitutes discrimination—and is unacceptable. However, opinions on discrimination become less clear-cut in the realm of law enforcement, particularly when it comes to strategies that involve racial profiling. Not surprisingly, racial profiling is illegal as a general tool for screening suspects. As Shira Scheindlin, the federal judge who struck down New York City's controversial "stop-and-frisk" policy has made clear, Americans should not be singled out for scrutiny by law-enforcement officers just because of the color of their skin.[1] Under this policy, police officers stopped people based on the "reasonable suspicion" that they were engaged in criminal activity. At its peak in 2011, more than 685,000 New Yorkers were stopped by police; 88 percent were entirely innocent, just over half were between 14 and 24 years old, and 87 percent were African American or Latino. In 2019, 13,459 people were questioned and frisked by police in New York.[2] Stop and frisk became an issue in the 2020 Democratic presidential primary campaign when Mike Bloomberg, the former mayor of New York who expanded the policy, reversed his position and admitted it was a mistake.

Opponents of policing tactics such as "stop-and-frisk" and the use of excessive force have argued that these practices encourage illegal racial profiling. This issue was brought to the fore in 2020 when the killing of an unarmed Black man, George Floyd, by the police set off mass protests across the country against police brutality and racial injustice.

CHAPTER GOALS

Describe the historical struggles groups have faced in winning civil rights. pages 372–381

Analyze inequality among racial, ethnic, and social groups today. pages 381–388

Explain the approaches used to bring about change in civil rights policies. pages 389–411

Examine affirmative action and other ongoing civil rights issues. pages 411–417

However, President Donald Trump and others have called for a "commonsense" approach to profiling when it comes to both matters of local and national security, which would include more intense scrutiny of people who fit a certain profile imagined to be more likely to commit crimes.[3] People who take this position argue that it may be necessary to sacrifice some of our civil rights to more effectively keep neighborhoods safe from crime or secure our borders against terrorism. Many, including former attorney general Eric Holder, disagree with this perspective on purely practical grounds and say that racial profiling is simply not an effective tool of law enforcement.[4]

You probably have experience with questions of profiling and discrimination in your own life, beyond the realm of law enforcement. In fact, civil rights are one of the best examples of the idea that politics is everywhere: policies concerning discrimination in the workplace and in housing and against women, minorities, the LGBTQ community, and disabled people affect millions of Americans every day. Consider the following scenarios:

- Scenario 1: You are driving home one night with a few of your friends after a party. It is late at night, but you have not had anything to drink and you are following all traffic laws. Your heart sinks as you see the flashing lights of a squad car signaling you to pull over. As the police officer approaches your car, you wonder if you have been pulled over because you and your friends are African Americans driving in an all-White neighborhood. Have your civil rights been violated? Change the scene to a car full of White teenagers with all the other facts the same. Can an officer pull them over just because he or she thinks that teenagers are more likely than older people to be engaging in criminal activity?
- Scenario 2: You are a 21-year-old Asian-American woman applying for your first job out of college. After being turned down for a job at an engineering firm, you suspect that you didn't get the job because you are a woman and because management thought that you would not fit in with the "good ol' boy" atmosphere of the firm. Have your civil rights been violated?
- Scenario 3: You and your gay partner are told that "your kind" are not welcome in the apartment complex that you want to live in. Should you call a lawyer?
- Scenario 4: You are a White male graduating from high school. You have just received a letter of rejection from the college that was first on your list. You are very disappointed, but then you get angry when a friend tells you that one of your classmates got into the same school even though he had virtually the same grades as you and his SAT scores were a bit lower. Your friend says that it is probably because of the school's affirmative action policy—the classmate who was accepted is Latino. Are you a victim of "reverse discrimination"? Have your civil rights been violated?

All of these scenarios would seem to be civil rights violations. However, some are, some are not, and some depend on additional considerations (we will return to these examples in the chapter's conclusion). Is it ever acceptable to treat people differently based on the color of their skin, their ethnic status, their gender, or their sexual orientation, in a situation of racial profiling or otherwise? More broadly, when is discrimination legal, and when isn't it? How are civil rights in the United States defined today?

civil rights
Rights that guarantee individuals freedom from discrimination. These rights are generally grounded in the equal protection clause of the Fourteenth Amendment and more specifically laid out in laws passed by Congress, such as the 1964 Civil Rights Act.

DESCRIBE THE HISTORICAL STRUGGLES GROUPS HAVE FACED IN WINNING CIVIL RIGHTS

The context of civil rights

In general, civil rights are rights that guarantee individuals freedom from discrimination. In the United States, individuals' civil rights are monitored by the U.S. Commission on Civil Rights, a bipartisan, independent federal commission that was established by the 1957 Civil Rights Act.[5] The commission's mission is to "appraise federal laws and policies," investigate complaints, and collect information regarding citizens who are "being deprived of their right to vote" or who are being discriminated against or denied the "equal protection of the laws under the Constitution because of race, color, religion, sex, age, disability, or national origin." It investigates government actions, such as allegations of racial discrimination in elections, and discriminatory actions of individuals in the workplace, commerce, housing, and education.

This definition seems straightforward enough, but confusion may arise when comparing the terms "civil rights" and "civil liberties." They are often used interchangeably, but there are important differences. "Civil liberties" refers to the freedoms guaranteed in the Bill of Rights, such as the freedom of speech, religious expression, and the press, as well as the due process protection of the Fourteenth Amendment. In contrast, civil rights protect all persons from discrimination and are rooted in laws and the equal protection clause of the Fourteenth Amendment. Moreover, civil liberties primarily limit what the government can do to you ("*Congress* shall make no law . . . abridging the freedom of speech," for example), whereas civil rights protect you from discrimination both by the government and by individuals. As noted in the previous chapter, to oversimplify, civil liberties are about freedom and civil rights are about equality.

Neither civil liberties nor civil rights figured prominently at the Constitutional Convention. Equality is not even mentioned in the Constitution or the Bill of Rights. However, equality was very much on the Founders' minds, as is evident in this ringing passage from the Declaration of Independence: "We hold these truths to be self-evident, that all men are created equal, that they are endowed by their Creator with certain unalienable Rights, that among these are Life, Liberty, and the pursuit of Happiness." Despite the broad language, this was a limited conception of equality. The reference to "men" was intentional: women had no political or economic rights in the late eighteenth century. Similarly, equality did not apply to enslaved people or to Native Americans. Even propertyless White men did not have full political rights until several decades after the Constitution was ratified. Equality and civil rights in the United States have been a continually evolving work in progress.

AP®
FOUNDATIONAL
DOCUMENT

AP®
FOUNDATIONAL
DOCUMENT

AP®
FOUNDATIONAL
DOCUMENT

African Americans

From the early nineteenth century and the movement for the abolition of slavery until the mid-twentieth century and the civil rights movement, the central focus of civil rights was on the experiences of African Americans. Other groups received attention more gradually. Starting in the mid-nineteenth century women began their fight for equal rights, and over the next century the civil rights movement expanded to include other groups such as Native Americans, Latinos, and Asian Americans. Most recently, attention has turned to the elderly, disabled people, and the LGBTQ community (lesbian, gay, bisexual, transgender, queer/questioning people). The most divisive civil rights issue with the greatest long-term impact, however, has been slavery and its legacy.

Slavery and Its Impact Slavery was part of the American economy from nearly the beginning of the nation's history. Dutch traders brought 20 enslaved people to Jamestown, Virginia, in 1619, a year before the Puritans landed at Plymouth Rock. It is impossible to overstate the importance of enslaved people to the southern economy. The 1860 census shows that there were 2.3 million enslaved people in the Deep South (including Georgia, Alabama, South Carolina, Mississippi, and Louisiana), constituting 47 percent of its population, and there were nearly 4 million enslaved people in the South overall. The economic benefits for owners of enslaved people were clear. By 1860, the per capita income for

Slavery was part of the American economy from the 1600s until it was abolished by the Thirteenth Amendment in 1865. The system of slavery in the South created a highly unequal society in which African Americans were denied virtually all rights. Abolitionists worked to undermine and abolish slavery. Harriet Tubman was instrumental in the success of the Underground Railroad, which brought countless enslaved people to freedom.

99

A house divided against itself cannot stand. I believe this government cannot endure permanently half-slave and half-free.

—President Abraham Lincoln

Whites in the South was $3,978; in the North, it was $2,040. The South had only 30 percent of the nation's free population, but it had 60 percent of the wealthiest men.[6]

Abolitionists worked to rid the nation of slavery as its importance to the South grew, setting the nation on a collision course that would not be resolved until the Civil War. Despite the work of some early abolitionists, the Founders largely ducked the issue (see Chapter 2), and subsequent legislatures and courts did not come any closer to resolving the impasse between the North and South over slavery. The Missouri Compromise of 1820, which limited the expansion of slavery and kept the overall balance between slave states and free states, eased tensions for a while, but the issue persisted. By the 1830s, the abolitionist movement gained considerable strength. Owners of enslaved people became increasingly frustrated with the success of the Underground Railroad, which helped some enslaved people escape to freedom in the North. In 1850, the debate over admitting California as a free state or a slave state (or making it half-free and half-slave) threatened to split the nation once again. As part of the Compromise of 1850, southern states agreed to admit California as a free state, but only if Congress passed the Fugitive Slave Act, which required northern states to treat people who had escaped from slavery as property and return them to their owners. The Compromise also established Utah and New Mexico as territories that could decide for themselves if they would permit slavery. This idea of "popular sovereignty" concerning slavery in new states was fully embraced in the Kansas-Nebraska Act of 1854, thus overturning that central part of the Missouri Compromise.[7]

All possibility of further compromise on the issue ended with the misguided *Dred Scott v. Sandford* decision in 1857. The Supreme Court ruled that at the time of the drafting of the Constitution enslaved people were "considered as a subordinate and inferior class of beings who had been subjugated by the dominant race." Therefore, enslaved people were property rather than citizens and, as such, had no legal rights. The Court also used its power of judicial review for only the second time, ruling that it was unconstitutional for Congress to limit the property rights of owners of enslaved people in the territories. In 1860, believing that slavery was in jeopardy after Abraham Lincoln won the presidency, the southern states seceded from the Union and formed the Confederacy.

When the Civil War ended, national unity was restored and slavery ended, but the price was very high. About 528,000 Americans died in the war, with an astonishingly high casualty rate (25 percent).[8] After the war, Republicans moved quickly to ensure that the changes accomplished by the war could not easily be undone: they promptly adopted the Civil War amendments to the Constitution. The Thirteenth Amendment banned slavery, the Fourteenth guaranteed that states could not deny newly freed people the equal protection of the laws and provided citizenship to anyone born in the United States, and the Fifteenth gave African-American men the right to vote. These amendments were ratified within five years of the war, although southern states resisted giving freed people and their descendants "equal protection of the laws" over the next 100 years.

Voting Rights and Obstacles During Reconstruction (1866–1877), Blacks in the South gained political power through institutions such as the Freedmen's Bureau and the Union League. With the protection of the occupying northern army, Blacks were able to vote and even hold public office. When federal troops withdrew and the Republican Party abandoned the South, however, Blacks were almost completely **disenfranchised** (denied the right to vote) through the imposition of residency requirements, poll taxes, literacy tests, physical intimidation, and other forms of disqualification. Later the practice known as the "white primary" allowed only Whites to vote in Democratic primary elections and, given that the Republican Party did not exist in most southern states, Blacks were effectively disenfranchised. Although most of these provisions were claimed to be race neutral, their impact fell disproportionately on Black voters. For example, the **grandfather clause**, which permitted those who had voted before the war and their descendants to vote even if they did not meet current voting requirements, enabled illiterate Whites (but not illiterate Blacks) to avoid the literacy test.[9] Many states also had "understanding" or "good character" exceptions to the literacy tests, which gave election officials substantial discretion over who would be allowed to vote.

The collective impact of these obstacles virtually eliminated Black voting. For example, only 6 percent of Blacks were registered to vote in Mississippi in 1890 and only 2 percent were registered in Alabama in 1906. After the last post-Reconstruction Black congressman left the House in 1901, 72 years passed before another African American represented a southern district in Congress. In one Mississippi county in 1947, only 6 out of 13,000 eligible Blacks were actually registered to vote. Despite the constitutional guarantees of the Fourteenth and Fifteenth Amendments, Blacks had little access to the political system in the South and they had little success in winning office at any level in the rest of the nation.[10]

Jim Crow The social and economic position of Blacks in the South followed a path similar to their political fortunes. Soon after the Civil War ended, sympathetic Republicans passed the Civil Rights Acts of 1866 and 1875, which aimed to outlaw segregation and provide equal opportunity for Blacks. However, there were no enforcement provisions, and when Reconstruction ended in 1877 the southern states enacted "black codes," or **Jim Crow laws**, that led to complete segregation of the races. Then, in 1883, the Supreme Court ruled that the 1875 Civil Rights Act was unconstitutional because Congress did not have the power to forbid racial discrimination in private businesses. Southern states interpreted this decision as a signal that the national government was unconcerned about protecting the rights of Blacks.

Jim Crow laws forbade interracial marriage and mandated the complete separation of the races for neighborhoods, hotels, apartments, hospitals, schools, restrooms, drinking fountains, restaurants, elevators, and even cemetery plots. In cases where it would have been inconvenient to completely separate the races, as in public transportation, Blacks had to sit in the back of the bus or in separate cars on the train and give up their seats to Whites if asked. The Supreme Court validated these practices in *Plessy v. Ferguson* (1896) by establishing the **"separate but equal" doctrine**, officially permitting segregation as long as Blacks had facilities equal to those of Whites.

disenfranchised
To have been denied the ability to exercise a right, such as the right to vote.

grandfather clause
A type of law enacted in several southern states to allow those who were permitted to vote before the Civil War, and their descendants, to bypass literacy tests and other obstacles to voting, thereby exempting Whites from these tests while continuing to disenfranchise African Americans and other people of color.

Senator Hiram Revels, the first African American to serve in the U.S. Congress, represented Mississippi in 1870 and 1871.

Jim Crow laws
State and local laws that mandated racial segregation in all public facilities in the South, many border states, and some northern communities between 1876 and 1964.

Plessy v. Ferguson
The 1896 Supreme Court ruling that state-imposed racial segregation did not violate the Fourteenth Amendment as long as the public facilities were "separate but equal."

"separate but equal" doctrine
The idea that racial segregation was acceptable as long as the separate facilities were of equal quality; supported by *Plessy v. Ferguson* and struck down by *Brown v. Board of Education*.

In the first several decades after Reconstruction, the rest of the nation mostly ignored the status of Blacks, because 90 percent of all African Americans lived in the South. The subjugation of Blacks in the South went well beyond the separations of the races. A racist criminal justice system ignored widespread lynchings, church burnings, and general intimidation. The Equal Justice Initiative has documented 4,084 "racial terror lynchings" in 12 southern states between the end of Reconstruction in 1877 and 1950.[11] But Blacks' northward migration to urban areas throughout the first half of the twentieth century transformed the nation's demographic profile and its racial politics. America's "race problem" was no longer just a southern problem. Although conditions for Blacks were generally better outside the South, they still faced discrimination and lived largely segregated lives throughout the nation. In World Wars I and II, Black soldiers fought and died for their country in segregated units. Professional sports teams were segregated, and Black musicians and artists could not perform in many of the nation's leading theaters. Moreover, Blacks largely were hired for the lowest-paying menial jobs.

Progress began in the 1940s. The Supreme Court struck down the white primary in 1944, Jackie Robinson broke the color line in Major League Baseball in 1947, and President Harry Truman issued an executive order integrating the U.S. armed services in 1948. Then came the landmark decision *Brown v. Board of Education* (1954), which rejected the "separate but equal" doctrine and declared that race-based school segregation violates the Fourteenth Amendment's equal protection clause, followed by *Brown II* (1955), which ordered that public schools be desegregated "with all deliberate speed." These events set the stage for the growing success of the civil rights movement, discussed later in this chapter.

Native Americans

The legacy of slavery and racial segregation in the South has been the dominant focus of U.S. civil rights policies, but many other groups have also fought for equal rights. Native Americans were the first group to come in contact with the European immigrants. Although initial relations between the Native Americans and the European settlers were good in many places, the settlers' appetite for more land and their insensitivity to Native-American culture soon led to a state of continual conflict. Native Americans were systematically pushed from their land and placed on reservations. The most infamous example was the removal of 60,000 members of the "Five Civilized Tribes" from the southeastern United States following the enactment of the Indian Removal Act in 1830. Thousands of Native Americans died on the Trail of Tears on their way to reservations in Oklahoma.[12]

Native Americans had no political rights; indeed, through much of the nineteenth century the U.S. government considered them "savages" to be eliminated. The American Indian Wars involved about 1,500 different campaigns authorized by the American government between 1622 and the late nineteenth century.[13] By the end of the nineteenth century, the Native-American population had shrunk to 250,000 from at least eight times that many before the Europeans arrived (estimates range from a low of 2.1 million to a high of 18 million).[14] While thousands were killed by the military campaigns, most deaths were caused by European diseases for which the Native Americans did not have immunity, with smallpox being the most deadly.

Native Americans did not gain the universal right to vote until 1924, just after women and well after Black men. Although the U.S. government signed treaties with Native-American tribes that recognized them as sovereign nations (not as foreign nations but as "domestic dependent nations"),[15] in practice the government ignored most of the agreements. Only in recent decades has the government started to uphold

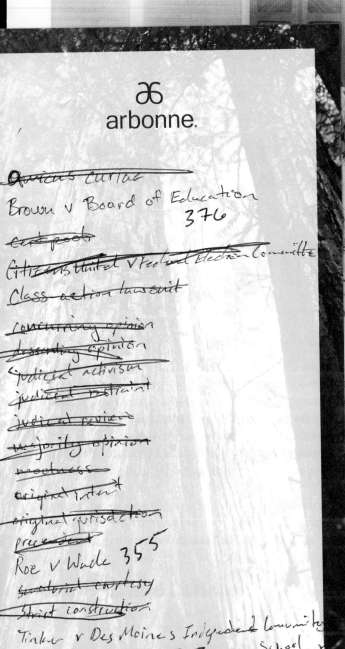

On the overlaid handwritten note (Arbonne notepad):

Amicus Curiae (crossed out)
Brown v Board of Education 376
ex post (crossed out)
Citizens United v Federal Election Committee
Class action lawsuit
concurring opinion
dissenting opinion
judicial activism
judicial restraint
judicial review
majority opinion
mootness
original Intent
original jurisdiction
precedent
Roe v Wade 355
senatorial courtesy
strict construction
Tinker v Des Moines Independent Community School District 333

WATCH ME FLOURISH

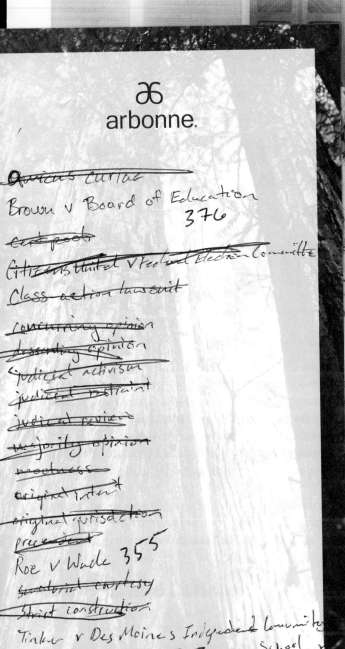

The Carlisle Indian Industrial School in Carlisle, Pennsylvania, was open from 1879 to 1918. The school's Native-American students were forced to cut their hair and change their names.

...tive Americans have struggled ...ce of widespread poverty and ...orce assimilation. The most ...from their families to attend ...ion. Founded shortly after ...late twentieth century, with ...in 1973. Although Christian ...dian Affairs took over the ...apter in American history has

...ality. The early history ...erican War (1846–1848) ...oday makes up most of the ...d in large numbers in the ...ce and discrimination, one of ...rt to organize farmworkers in ...kers Union and forced growers ...rkers in California and Florida. ...back hundreds of years, ...s than two generations.

Consequently, they have become a political force only recently, although they are now the nation's largest minority. Latinos' relative lack of political clout when compared with that of African Americans can be explained by two factors. First, Latinos vote at a much lower rate than African Americans, in part because many have language barriers. In addition, about one-third of Latinos cannot vote in national elections because they are not U.S. citizens. Second, unlike African Americans, Latinos are a relatively diverse group politically, composed of people from many Latin American nations. Most Latino voters are loyal to the Democratic Party, but a majority of Cuban Americans are Republicans. Although this diversity means that Latino voters do not speak with one voice, it brings opportunity for increased political clout in the future. The diversity of partisan attachments among Latinos and their relatively low levels of political involvement mean that both parties are eager to attract them as new voters. In 2016, Donald Trump surprised many experts by winning a higher percentage of the Latino vote (29 percent) than Mitt Romney did in 2012 (27 percent). Trump defied expectations again in 2020, as this percentage increased to 32 percent despite his immigration policies.

Asian Americans

Asian Americans experienced discrimination beginning with their arrival in the United States in the nineteenth century. The first wave of Chinese immigrants came with the 1848 California gold rush. Initially, foreign miners, including the Chinese, were able to stake out their claims along with Americans. But by 1850, when the easy-to-find gold was gone, Americans tried to drive out the Chinese through violence and the Foreign Miners Tax. Subsequently, Chinese immigrants played a crucial role in building the intercontinental railroad between 1865 and 1869. Yet, because they were given the most dangerous jobs, many lost their lives. After the railroad was completed, Chinese workers returned to the West Coast, where they experienced increasing discrimination and violence. Following several race riots, Congress passed the Chinese Exclusion Act of 1882, which prevented Chinese already in the United States from becoming U.S. citizens—although the Supreme Court later granted their American-born children automatic citizenship under the Fourteenth Amendment.[17] The Chinese Exclusion Act also barred virtually all immigration from China—the first time in U.S. history that a specific ethnic group was singled out in this way. During World War II, more

During World War II, tens of thousands of Japanese Americans were forced to relocate to internment camps. Nearly two-thirds were American citizens, and most lost their homes and jobs.

The Carlisle Indian Industrial School in Carlisle, Pennsylvania, was open from 1879 to 1918. The school's Native-American students were forced to cut their hair and change their names.

its obligations, although compliance remains spotty. Native Americans have struggled to maintain their cultural history and autonomy in the face of widespread poverty and unemployment and a sustained and concerted effort to force assimilation. The most notorious of these practices was the removal of children from their families to attend Native-American boarding schools that forced assimilation. Founded shortly after the Civil War, these schools continued to operate into the late twentieth century, with a peak attendance of 60,000 Native-American children in 1973. Although Christian missionaries originally ran the schools, the Bureau of Indian Affairs took over the operation of many in the twentieth century. This dark chapter in American history has been referred to by its critics as "cultural genocide."[16]

Latinos and Latinas

Latinos have also struggled for political and economic equality. The early history of Latinos in the United States is rooted in the Mexican-American War (1846–1848) and the conquest by the United States of the territory that today makes up most of the southwestern states. Since that time, Mexicans have resided in large numbers in the Southwest. Although Latinos had long experienced prejudice and discrimination, one of their first major political successes was Cesar Chavez's effort to organize farmworkers in the 1960s and 1970s. He established the United Farm Workers Union and forced growers to bargain with 50,000 mostly Mexican-American fieldworkers in California and Florida.

Although many Mexican Americans have roots that go back hundreds of years, a majority of Latinos have been in the United States for less than two generations. Consequently, they have become a political force only recently, although they are now the nation's largest minority. Latinos' relative lack of political clout when compared with that of African Americans can be explained by two factors. First, Latinos vote at a much lower rate than African Americans, in part because many have language barriers. In addition, about one-third of Latinos cannot vote in national elections because they are not U.S. citizens. Second, unlike African Americans, Latinos are a relatively diverse group politically, composed of people from many Latin American nations. Most Latino voters are loyal to the Democratic Party, but a majority of Cuban Americans are Republicans. Although this diversity means that Latino voters do not speak with one voice, it brings opportunity for increased political clout in the future. The diversity of partisan attachments among Latinos and their relatively low levels of political involvement mean that both parties are eager to attract them as new voters. In 2016, Donald Trump surprised many experts by winning a higher percentage of the Latino vote (29 percent) than Mitt Romney did in 2012 (27 percent). Trump defied expectations again in 2020, as this percentage increased to 32 percent despite his immigration policies.

Asian Americans

Asian Americans experienced discrimination beginning with their arrival in the United States in the nineteenth century. The first wave of Chinese immigrants came with the 1848 California gold rush. Initially, foreign miners, including the Chinese, were able to stake out their claims along with Americans. But by 1850, when the easy-to-find gold was gone, Americans tried to drive out the Chinese through violence and the Foreign Miners Tax. Subsequently, Chinese immigrants played a crucial role in building the intercontinental railroad between 1865 and 1869. Yet, because they were given the most dangerous jobs, many lost their lives. After the railroad was completed, Chinese workers returned to the West Coast, where they experienced increasing discrimination and violence. Following several race riots, Congress passed the Chinese Exclusion Act of 1882, which prevented Chinese already in the United States from becoming U.S. citizens—although the Supreme Court later granted their American-born children automatic citizenship under the Fourteenth Amendment.[17] The Chinese Exclusion Act also barred virtually all immigration from China—the first time in U.S. history that a specific ethnic group was singled out in this way. During World War II, more

During World War II, tens of thousands of Japanese Americans were forced to relocate to internment camps. Nearly two-thirds were American citizens, and most lost their homes and jobs.

than 110,000 Japanese were placed in internment camps for fear that they were enemy supporters. Although the internment was upheld by the Supreme Court at the time, a 1980 congressional commission determined that it was a "grave injustice" motivated by "racial prejudice, war hysteria and the failure of political leadership." Eight years later, President Ronald Reagan signed into law the Civil Liberties Act, which paid more than $1.6 billion in reparations to the survivors of the camps and their heirs.[18] In 2018, the Court explicitly overturned the 1944 decision that approved the internment, saying, "The forcible relocation of U.S. citizens to concentration camps, solely and explicitly on the basis of race, is objectively unlawful and outside the scope of presidential authority."[19] In recent decades, a much broader range of Asians have emigrated to the United States, including Koreans, Filipinos, Hmong, Vietnamese, and Asian Indians. This variation in national heritage, culture, and language means that Asian Americans are quite diverse in their political views, partisan affiliation, and voting patterns.

Women and civil rights

On the eve of the United States' declaration of independence in 1776, John Adams's wife, Abigail, advised him not to "put such unlimited power in the hands of the husbands. Remember, all men would be tyrants if they could. . . . If particular care and attention is not paid to the ladies, we . . . will not hold ourselves bound by any laws in which we have no voice or representation."[20] John Adams did not listen to his wife. The Constitution did not give women the right to vote, and they were not guaranteed that civil right until the Nineteenth Amendment was ratified in 1920—although 16 states had allowed women to vote before then. Until the early twentieth century, women in most parts of the country could not hold office, serve on juries, bring lawsuits in their own name, own property, or serve as legal guardians for their children. A woman's identity was so closely tied to her husband's that if she married a noncitizen she automatically gave up her citizenship.

The rationale for these policies was called **protectionism**. The argument was that women were too frail to compete in the business world and needed to be protected by men. This reasoning served in many court cases to deny women equal rights. For example, in 1869 Myra Bradwell requested admission to the Illinois bar to practice law. She was the first woman to graduate from law school in Illinois and the editor of *Chicago Legal News*, and she held all the qualifications to be a lawyer in the state except for one—she was a woman. Her request was denied, and she sued all the way to the Supreme Court. In 1873, the Court ruled that the prohibition against women lawyers did not violate the Fourteenth Amendment's privileges and immunities clause because there was no constitutional right to be an attorney. If the Court had stopped there, the decision would have been unremarkable for its time. But Justice Joseph Bradley went on to provide a classic example of protectionism:

> *The civil law as well as nature itself has always recognized a wide difference in the respective spheres and destinies to man and woman. Man is, or should be, woman's protector and defender. The natural and proper timidity and delicacy which belongs to the female sex evidently unfits it for many of the occupations of civil life. The constitution of the family organization which is founded in the divine ordinance, as well as the nature of things, indicates the domestic sphere as that which properly belongs to the domains and functions of womanhood.*[21]

While protectionist sentiment on the Court had waned by the mid-twentieth century, as recently as 1961 the Court upheld a Florida law that automatically exempted women but not men from compulsory jury duty. The case involved a woman who killed her husband with a baseball bat after he admitted that he was having an affair and wanted to end the marriage. The woman argued that her conviction by an all-male jury violated

protectionism
The idea under which some people have tried to rationalize discriminatory policies by claiming that some groups, like women or African Americans, should be denied certain rights for their own safety or well-being.

her Fourteenth Amendment guarantee of "equal protection of the laws" and that a jury panel containing some women would have been more sympathetic to her "temporary insanity" defense. The Court rejected this argument, ruling that the Florida law excluding women from jury duty was reasonable because "despite the enlightened emancipation of women from the restrictions and protections of bygone years, and their entry into many parts of community life formerly considered to be reserved to men, woman still is regarded as the center of home and family life."[22] Apparently, it was unthinkable to the all-male Court that a man might have to stay home from work and take care of the kids while his wife served on a jury (a related point is that businesses at that time would have been unwilling to give men time off from work so their wives could serve on juries). Later in this chapter, we will describe how the Supreme Court has moved away from this discriminatory position and rejected protectionist thinking.

The LGBTQ community

The most recent group to engage in the struggle for civil rights is the LGBTQ community. For most of American history, gays and lesbians lived secret lives and were subject to abuse and discrimination if they openly acknowledged their sexual orientation. The critical moment that spurred the gay rights movement occurred on June 28, 1969, during a routine police raid on the Stonewall Inn in New York City.[23] (Police often raided gay bars to harass patrons and selectively enforce liquor laws.) This time, rather than submitting to the arrests, the customers fought back, throwing stones and beer bottles, breaking windows, and starting small fires. A crowd of several hundred people gathered, and the fighting raged for three nights. The Stonewall rebellion galvanized the gay community by demonstrating the power of collective action.

Since Stonewall, the gay rights movement has made steady progress through a combination of political mobilization and protest, legislative action, and legal action. Public support for gay rights has increased dramatically in recent years. Between

In 2016, President Obama designated the historic site of the Stonewall uprising in New York City as a national monument to honor the LGBTQ equality movement.

two-thirds and three-fourths of Americans (depending on the poll) agree with the national policy established in 2011 that gays may openly serve in the military, whereas a majority of Americans opposed this policy when it was first proposed by President Clinton in 1993. Between 60 and 64 percent of Americans support same-sex marriage according to recent polls, whereas only 35–40 percent held that view in 2009. Seventy-five percent believe that same-sex couples should be able to adopt children (compared to only 14 percent in 1977), 89 percent think that businesses should not be able to discriminate against gays and lesbians, and 63 percent believe that same-sex couples should be entitled to the same benefits as heterosexual couples (whereas only 32 percent think they should not).[24] In May 2012, President Obama endorsed same-sex marriage for the first time (and was the first president to take that position), completing his gradual shift on the issue. In 2015, the Supreme Court ruled that same-sex marriage is legal in all 50 states (we will discuss this and other issues concerning gay and lesbian rights later in the chapter).[25] In the 2016 presidential campaign Donald Trump said, "I will do everything in my power to protect our LGBTQ citizens from the violence and oppression of a hateful foreign ideology. Believe me." But his record on LGBTQ issues has been criticized by civil rights supporters.[26] In 2019, the Trump administration banned transgender people from joining the military and prohibited anyone currently in the military from transitioning genders. This policy was challenged in federal court, and the Supreme Court in 2019 let the ban stand. However, the Court's June 2020 landmark civil rights decision protecting gay and transgender people from discrimination in the workplace complicates the ban. While it remains in effect, a federal court planned to hear the case later in the year.

Why does this history matter for politics today? First, the effects of slavery and Jim Crow laws are still quite evident: legal racial segregation ended 50 years ago, but its legacy—especially evident in the difference that exists in the relative quality of education available to most Whites and Blacks—remains. Second, knowing about this history helps us understand where the inequalities (that we discuss in the next section) in our society come from. Finally, active discrimination based on race, gender, and sexual orientation is still evident in our society. Given the importance of race in the everyday lives of millions of Americans and in gaining an understanding of American politics, a grasp of the history that got us to where we are today is an important starting point.

"Why Should I Care?"

ANALYZE INEQUALITY AMONG RACIAL, ETHNIC, AND SOCIAL GROUPS TODAY

The racial divide today

The racial divide today begins with the unequal treatment of racial minorities, women, gays, and lesbians and is rooted in the gulf that remains between minorities and Whites, in terms of their objective condition as well as their political views. Although substantial progress has been made in bridging that gulf, political, social, and economic inequalities remain.

Discriminatory treatment

Discrimination is much more common today than many people realize. The Equal Employment Opportunity Commission (EEOC) filed an average of 83,000 charges of employment discrimination each year in the past five years,[27] while the National Fair Housing Alliance reports an average of 29,000 cases of housing discrimination a year.[28] The Justice Department has won dozens of lawsuits against banks and mortgage lenders who engage in discriminatory practices, winning settlements totaling several hundred million dollars in the past three years.[29]

The experience of a former graduate student in our department who is White and whose wife is Black puts a human face on these statistics. The couple wanted to rent a bigger apartment, so they searched the want ads and made appointments to see some apartments. One landlord told them to meet him in front of the apartment at a specific time. They waited where they were told, but the landlord didn't show up. Later they remembered seeing a car that slowed down and almost stopped but then sped away. They wondered if this was a case of a "drive-by landlord"—one who checks out potential tenants' race from a distance; if they are not White, he or she skips the appointment and tells them it is rented if they ask. This is exactly what happened. This couple called the landlord, asked what had happened, and were told that the apartment was already rented. To check their suspicions, they had some friends ask about the apartment, and the friends were told it was available. Their friends (both White) made an appointment to meet the landlord, and this time the same car pulled up and stopped. The landlord showed them the apartment and was very friendly. The next day, the graduate student filed a racial discrimination lawsuit.

These types of stories, ranging from irritating and demeaning to serious violations of the law, are familiar to nearly every racial minority, woman, and LGBTQ person in the United States. Consider the well-dressed businessman who cannot get a cab in a major city because he is Black, the woman who is sexually harassed by her boss but hesitates to say anything for fear of losing her job, the teenage Latino who is shadowed in the clothing store by a clerk, the Arab American who endures taunts about her head covering, or the lesbian couple who cannot find an apartment. Such personal experiences, as well as extensive government data and academic research, indicate continuing discrimination in our society, despite significant progress in the past generation.

Differences in voting access

The United States has a long history of discriminating against racial and ethnic minorities in the election process. Although African Americans voted at a rate that was quite similar to that of Whites in presidential elections from 2008 to 2020, their turnout in midterm elections has been somewhat lower than that of Whites, and other racial and ethnic minorities have generally lower turnouts (see Figure 9.1). Much of the difference in voter turnout can be accounted for by education and income, but there still are practices and institutions that specifically depress minority-voter turnout. And many of these deterrents are intentional. The National Association for the Advancement of Colored People (NAACP), the U.S. Commission on Civil Rights, and the Brennan Center for Justice have all documented such practices in elections going back to 2000, including moving and reducing the number of polling places in areas with predominantly minority voters, changing from district-based to at-large elections (citywide or countywide elections in which there is often a mix of minority and White voters), using voter challenges to target minority voters, redistricting to dilute minority voting power, withholding information about registration and voting procedures from Blacks, and "causing or taking advantage of Election Day irregularities."[30]

There are other state practices that are not specifically aimed at minority voters but that have a disproportionate impact on them. Examples have included removing voters' names from the voting rolls if there wasn't an identical match between the

**FIGURE
9.1**

Turnout in Presidential Elections by Race

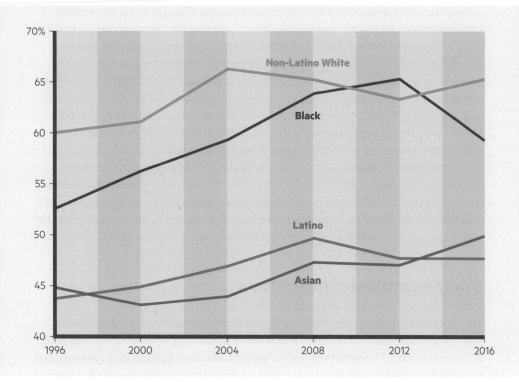

Turnout among African Americans has risen steadily over the last 20 years (with a dip in 2016), while turnout of other groups has remained relatively flat. What do you think accounts for these trends? What could state governments do to increase voter turnout?

Source: United States Elections Project, "Voter Turnout Demographics," www. electproject.org/home/voter-turnout/demographics (accessed 5/13/20).

name the voter used when registering to vote and the name as it appeared in another state database (often the database of driver's license information); purging the names of people who had committed felonies from the voting registration lists, which often produced false matches to people with the same names who had not committed a crime; and engaging in voter intimidation and deceptive practices. Moreover, several states use technical barriers to voter registration and voting, limit access to voter registration services at social services offices (even though such access is required by federal law), and use poorly designed ballots that are especially confusing to less educated or older voters.[31]

Despite the removal of most formal barriers to voting, since 2014 Latinos have been less likely to vote and participate in politics than Whites, Blacks, and Asian Americans. Latino advocacy groups like Mi Familia Vota work to engage and register voters in their local communities.

In recent years many states have restricted access to voting by requiring a photo ID to vote (which has a disproportionate impact on minorities because they are less likely to have a photo ID), requiring proof of citizenship to vote, cutting back on early voting days and times, and making it more difficult for people to register to vote.[32] In addition, as we will discuss later, in 2013 the Supreme Court struck down an important part of the **Voting Rights Act (VRA) of 1965**, making it easier for the nine states that had been covered by this provision of the law to implement discriminatory practices. However, legal challenges in many states pushed back against these changes in voting laws. Those supporting voting rights won at least partial victories in eight states against voter ID laws and restrictions on early voting that had a racial impact. Other states also restored the right to vote for those with past criminal convictions.[33] Also, partly in response to the COVID-19 pandemic, which required restrictions on social gatherings and interactions, many states passed laws to make voting easier, such as automatically registering voters and imposing fewer restrictions on early voting and voting by mail.

Socioeconomic indicators

The racial divide is also evident in social and economic terms. Nearly twice as many Black families are below the poverty line as White families: 18.8 percent compared with 9.1 percent in 2019. The poverty rate of 15.7 percent for Latino families in 2019 was similar to that of Black families. (Poverty thresholds are determined by the amount of money an individual or family earns each year. This figure varies by state, by the composition of the household, and by year, to account for inflation in the cost of living expenses. For 2020, an individual living on an income of less than $12,760, or a family of four living on less than $26,200, would be considered as living in poverty and eligible for certain programs as a result.[34]) While White median household income (that is, income from wages, salaries, interest, and disability and unemployment payments) was $72,204 in 2019, Black median household income was $45,438 (62.9 percent of White family income) and Latino median household income was $56,113 (77.7 percent of White family income).[35] Moreover, the gap in overall wealth is much more dramatic. The average White household has more than six times the assets of the typical non-White family. In 2019, the median household net worth (that is, the sum of all assets, including houses, cars, and stock) was $189,000 for Whites, $24,000 for African Americans, and $36,000 for Latinos.[36] Poverty is not distributed equally throughout the United States but rather is concentrated in areas where the minority population is the highest (see Figure 9.2).

Other indicators show similar patterns. The rate of Black adult male unemployment has been about twice as high as that of White adult male unemployment for the past 45 years. In July 2020, the unemployment rate among Blacks was 16.1 percent, compared with 12 percent for Whites and 16.7 percent for Latinos.[37] Moreover, 38 percent of Black children lived in two-parent households in 2019, compared with 71 percent of White children and 61 percent of Latino children.[38] Also, Blacks are significantly more likely than Whites to be victimized by crime. African Americans are nearly seven times as likely to be murdered as Whites.[39]

On every measure of health—life expectancy, infectious diseases, infant mortality, cancer rates, heart disease, and strokes—the gaps between Whites and Blacks are large and, in some cases, increasing. For example, life expectancy for Blacks is three and a half years shorter than for Whites (75.3 years for Blacks compared with 78.9 years for Whites), the infant mortality rate is more than double for Blacks (11.4 deaths per 1,000 live births compared with 4.9 deaths per 1,000 live births for Whites and 5.0 for Latinos), and maternal mortality is more than triple for Blacks (43.5 deaths per 100,000 births for Black women compared with 12.7 deaths per 100,000 births for White women). Similar gaps also exist for incidences of cancer, Type 2 diabetes, strokes, and heart attacks in Blacks and Whites.[40]

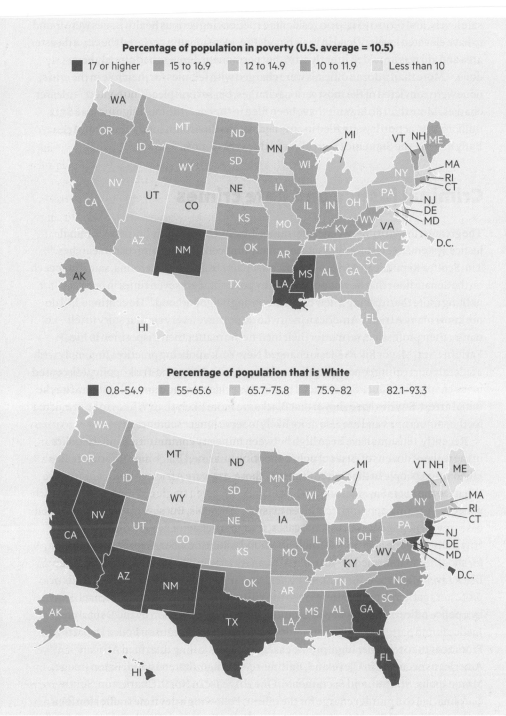

Percentage of population in poverty (U.S. average = 10.5)

■ 17 or higher   ■ 15 to 16.9   ■ 12 to 14.9   ■ 10 to 11.9   ■ Less than 10

Percentage of population that is White

■ 0.8–54.9   ■ 55–65.6   ■ 65.7–75.8   ■ 75.9–82   ■ 82.1–93.3

📊 **FIGURE 9.2**

Poverty and Race, 2020

Carefully examine these maps. What is the relationship between poverty and the minority population? How do you think these patterns might affect the politics of civil rights policies aimed at reducing discrimination in the workplace or housing?

Sources: Poverty data from U.S. Census Bureau, 2019 American Community Survey, www.census.gov/acs; race data from U.S. Census Bureau, Quickfacts, www.census.gov/quickfacts/fact/map (both accessed 9/23/20).

While social scientists continue to debate the causes of the racial disparities in health outcomes, an increasing body of evidence indicates that at least some of the gap is caused by government policies and business-related decisions. Broadly labeled "environmental racism," these practices mean that minority groups are much more likely to live in areas affected by pollution, toxic waste, and hazardous chemical sites.[41] One of the most extreme examples of this, uncovered in late 2015 and early 2016, involved the public water supply in Flint, Michigan. In 2014, to save money, the city switched its water supply from Lake Huron to the Flint River. Residents of the poor, majority-Black city soon reported discolored, foul-looking water, but their complaints were ignored by city and state officials. Researchers demonstrated that levels of lead in the water far exceeded safe levels, and 6,000 to 12,000 residents experiencing serious health issues were found to have elevated levels of lead in their blood. President Obama declared the city a disaster area and aid was provided in early 2016, but permanent damage had already been done.[42] More than a dozen officials were charged with felonies for their role in the crisis; none were convicted of the most serious charges, but several plead "no contest" to lesser charges. More than 80 lawsuits have been filed in the case, the most significant a $722 million class-action lawsuit filed in 2017 against the Environmental Protection Agency. Early in 2020, the Supreme Court allowed that case to move forward.[43]

Criminal justice and hate crimes

There are very few African-American men in this country who haven't had the experience of being followed when they were shopping in a department store. That includes me.

—President Barack Obama

The greatest disparity between racial minorities and Whites may be in the criminal justice system. Racial profiling subjects many innocent Blacks to intrusive searches.[44] Tim Scott, a Republican African-American senator from South Carolina, said in a speech on the Senate floor that he was pulled over by police officers seven times in one year "for nothing more than driving a new car in the wrong neighborhood." He continued, "I do not know many African-American men who do not have a very similar story to tell—no matter their profession, no matter their income, no matter their disposition in life."[45] Early in 2014, Mayor Bill de Blasio changed New York's policing practices to comply with a federal court ruling concerning the city's aggressive "stop-and-frisk" policy (discussed in the chapter introduction).[46] Racial bias is also evident in the criminal system after the initial arrest. Studies have shown that Blacks are more likely than Whites to be convicted for the same crimes and are also more likely to serve longer sentences.[47]

Recently, tensions have been high between minority communities and the police in the wake of dozens of cases of police shooting unarmed Black men. In 2019, police killed 1,004 people in the United States; of those, 235 were African Americans (see the What Do the Facts Say? feature).[48] Most of these involved tragic circumstances in which police were acting appropriately given existing protocols. But several highly publicized cases reveal negligent and, in some cases, criminal behavior by police officers. In 2013, following the acquittal of a neighborhood watch member, George Zimmerman, for shooting an unarmed 17-year-old African American, Trayvon Martin, the group Black Lives Matter was formed.[49] The next year in Ferguson, Missouri, thousands of protesters gathered to call attention to the killing of an unarmed man, Michael Brown, by a police officer. The officer was acquitted, but an investigation by the Department of Justice found patterns of discriminatory behavior by the Ferguson Police Department. From 2015 to 2020, other high-profile cases of officers killing unarmed African Americans occurred in Cleveland, Baltimore, Chicago, Staten Island, Baton Rouge, Minneapolis–St. Paul, and Sacramento. One 2015 case in North Charleston, South Carolina, led to a murder charge for the officer. Following a daytime traffic stop for a broken taillight, Officer Michael Slager shot Walter Scott in the back eight times from a distance of 15 to 20 feet as Scott was running away, and lied about what happened to cover up his crime. A bystander's video showed the murder and led to Slager's arrest. State first-degree murder charges were dismissed, however, as part of a plea deal. Slager ultimately plead guilty to a federal civil rights charge of using excessive force and was sentenced to 20 years in prison.[50] Overall, convictions in these cases are rare. One study found that of the roughly 14,000 police shootings from 2005 to 2019, there were 98 officers arrested for murder or manslaughter and just over one-third were convicted of a crime, but only three for murder.[51] There has also been intensive research on the topic of racial bias in police shootings, with more than 50 studies since 2015. Some of the studies have found that African Americans are more than twice as likely to be killed by police as Whites are, while other studies have found no significant differences.[52]

Racial Inequality in Law Enforcement

In 2020, national protests set off by the killing of an unarmed Black man, George Floyd, in Minneapolis, Minnesota, raised the issue of racial inequality in law enforcement and underscored similar killings in Ferguson, Missouri, Baltimore, Maryland, and Staten Island, New York. These graphs show both the total number and the relative number (expressed as a percentage), by race, of people killed by police. Do racial inequalities exist in law enforcement? What do the facts say?

U.S. population

Black	Hispanic	White	Other
13%	17%	63%	7%

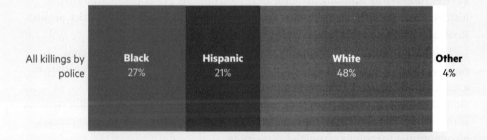

All killings by police

Black	Hispanic	White	Other
27%	21%	48%	4%

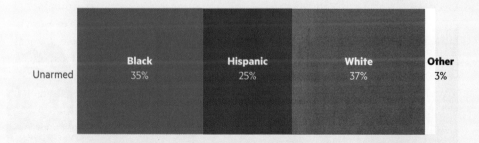

Unarmed

Black	Hispanic	White	Other
35%	25%	37%	3%

Unarmed and not attacking

Black	Hispanic	White	Other
34%	32%	32%	2%

Source: "2017 Police Violence Report," Mapping Police Violence, https://policeviolencereport.org (accessed 9/23/20).

WHAT DO THE FACTS SAY?

Think about it

- **For all victims (total and unarmed),** what racial category had the highest percentage of deaths? What racial category had the highest percentage of victims unarmed and not attacking? What do you think accounts for this difference?
- **Is there a greater racial disparity** in the second chart (which shows all people killed by police) or the third chart (which shows unarmed people)?
- **What, if anything, surprises you** about these numbers? Why?

There have been dozens of high-profile cases in recent years of police shooting unarmed Black men. Walter Scott was killed by North Charleston, South Carolina, police officer Michael Slager following a traffic stop for a broken brake light, inspiring protests throughout the city.

African Americans and other minorities are also subjected to hate crimes much more frequently than Whites.[53] According to FBI statistics, in 2018 nearly half of race-related hate crimes in the United States were "anti-Black" (48 percent), while only 19 percent were "anti-White" (57 percent of all hate crimes are race based). This means that the rate of anti-Black hate crimes is nearly four times what would be expected based on the percentage of African Americans in the United States, while the rate of anti-White hate crimes is less than one-third as high as would be expected. One of the most extreme hate crimes in recent years happened in 2015 when Dylann Roof, a 21-year-old White supremacist, shot and killed nine people at a Bible study in the historic Emanuel African Methodist Episcopal Church in Charleston, South Carolina. Roof later confessed that he was trying to ignite a race war.

This backdrop of racial inequality, discrimination, and violence drives civil rights activists to push their agenda in the three branches of government: legislative, executive, and judicial. In some instances, activists work in several arenas simultaneously; in others, they seek redress in one arena after exhausting alternatives in the others. The civil rights movement, which was crucial in early policy successes, also continues to mobilize from the grass roots.

Mourners outside the Emanuel AME Church in Charleston, South Carolina, pray at the memorial for the nine people shot and killed by White supremacist Dylann Roof during a prayer service.

Key players in the conflict over civil rights

Our civil rights policies are produced by several key players. First, the public becomes involved through social movements to put pressure on the political system to change. But Congress, the president, and the courts all also exert their own influence on policies that define civil rights.

Social movements

From the early women's rights movement and abolitionists of the nineteenth century to the gay rights and civil rights movements of the mid-twentieth century, activists have pressured the political system to change civil rights policies. Through collective action, these social movements have made sure that protecting equal rights remained on the policy agenda.

Women started to push for the right to vote at a convention in 1848 in Seneca Falls, New York. Subsequently, a constitutional amendment to give women the right to vote was regularly introduced in Congress between 1878 and 1913 but never was passed, despite the efforts of women such as Sojourner Truth, Ida B. Wells, Susan B. Anthony, and Elizabeth Cady Stanton. After a parallel movement at the state level had some success, the Nineteenth Amendment, giving women the right to vote, was finally passed in 1919 and ratified in 1920 (see Figure 9.3).

The civil rights movement of the 1950s and 1960s, aimed at ending segregation and guaranteeing equal political and social rights for Blacks, is the most famous example of a successful social movement (see Figure 9.4). Although the *Brown v. Board of Education* decision, which struck down segregation in public schools, gave the movement a boost, most southern Blacks saw little change in their daily lives. As White school boards and local governments resisted integration, Black leaders became convinced that the courts would not effect change because of resistance to their decisions. The only way to change the laws was to get the public, both Black and White, to demand change.

The spark came on December 1, 1955, in Montgomery, Alabama, when a woman named Rosa Parks refused to give up her seat on a bus to a White person, as she was required to do by law. Chroniclers often describe Parks as a seamstress who was tired after a long day's work and simply did not want to give up her seat, in order to cast her not as a pioneering activist in a social movement but as an "everyday hero." This is true, but there is more to the story. Local civil rights leaders had been waiting for years for an opportunity to boycott the local bus company because of its segregation policy. They needed a perfect test case—someone who would help draw attention to the cause.

Rosa Parks was just that person. She was a well-educated, law-abiding citizen who had been active in local civil rights organizations. In her book *My Story*, Parks says: "I was … no more tired than I usually was at the end of a working day. … No, the only tired I was, was tired of giving in."[54] When she was arrested for refusing to give up her seat, local civil rights leaders organized a boycott of the bus company that lasted more than a year. Whites in Montgomery tried to stop the boycott. The police arrested and fined Blacks who had arranged a car pool system to get to work: people waiting for a car to pick them up were arrested for loitering, and car pool drivers were arrested for lacking appropriate insurance or having too many people in their car. Martin Luther King Jr. was elected leader of the bus boycott, and he was subjected to harassment and violence—his house was firebombed, and he was arrested several times. Finally, a federal district court ruled that Montgomery's segregation policy was unconstitutional and the Supreme Court upheld the ruling.

As part of the Montgomery Bus Boycott, many African Americans organized car pools or walked to work.

FIGURE 9.3 **Women's Rights Time Line**

First women's rights convention held in Seneca Falls, New York.	Territory of Wyoming gives women the right to vote.	Congress requires equal pay for equal work for federal employees (but not for private sector workers).	The Nineteenth Amendment gives women the right to vote (however, this largely only benefits White women, as women of color still face significant barriers to voting, including voter suppression and intimidation at the polls).	Equal Pay Act requires equal pay for equal work.	Title VII of the Civil Rights Act bars employment discrimination based on race, sex, and other grounds.
1848	**1869**	**1872**	**1920**	**1963**	**1964**

Source: Compiled by the authors.

Nonviolent Protest On February 1, 1960, four Black students in Greensboro, North Carolina, went to a segregated lunch counter at a local Woolworth's and asked to be served. They sat there for an hour without being served and had to leave when the store closed. When 20 students returned the next day, national wire services picked up the story. Within two weeks, the sit-ins had spread to 11 cities. In some cases, the students were met with violence; in others, they were simply arrested. However, the students continued to respond with passive resistance, and new waves of protesters replaced those who had been arrested. The Student Nonviolent Coordinating Committee (SNCC) was created to coordinate the protests. The Greensboro Woolworth's was integrated on July 26, 1961, but the protests continued in other cities. By August 1961, the sit-ins had 70,000 participants and there had been 3,000 arrests.[55] The sit-ins marked an important shift in the tactics of the civil rights movement: away from the court-based approach, exemplified by the fight against the "separate but equal" doctrine (as we will discuss next), and toward the nonviolent civil disobedience approach that had been successful in Montgomery.

Also during this period, the Freedom Riders were working to get President Kennedy to enforce two Supreme Court decisions that banned segregation in interstate travel, including at bus terminals, in waiting rooms, in restaurants, and in other public facilities related to interstate travel.[56] On May 4, 1961, a group of Whites and Blacks boarded two buses in Washington, D.C., headed for New Orleans. The Whites and Blacks sat together and went into segregated areas of bus stations together. The trip was uneventful until Rock Hill, South Carolina, where several Freedom Riders were beaten. Then, in Anniston, Alabama, one bus had its tires slashed and was firebombed. The Freedom Riders were beaten as they fled the burning bus. A second group encountered an angry mob at the bus station in Birmingham and was severely beaten with baseball bats and iron pipes. When it became clear that police protection would not be forthcoming, the Freedom Riders abandoned the trip and regrouped in Nashville. After much internal debate, they decided to continue the rides.

Following more violence in Montgomery, President Kennedy intervened and his brother Robert Kennedy, the attorney general, worked out a deal: the Freedom Riders would receive police protection, federal troops would not intervene, and they would face the local courts upon their arrest for "disturbing the peace." The Freedom Rides

Griswold v. Connecticut legalizes the use of contraceptives by married couples.	Federal affirmative action policies are extended to women by an executive order.	Title IX of the Education Amendments of 1972 requires equal access to programs for men and women in higher education.	Roe v. Wade establishes a constitutional right to abortion.	Thirty-five states ratify the Equal Rights Amendment, passed by Congress in 1971–1972, falling three states short of the number needed to add the amendment to the Constitution. (As of 2020, three additional states ratified the amendment; however, because their approval occurred after the deadline, they don't legally count toward the three-fourths of the states required.)	Lilly Ledbetter Fair Pay Act makes it easier to sue for gender-based pay discrimination.	The social media campaign #MeToo calls attention to sexual violence against women.
1965	1967	1972	1973	1982	2009	2017

continued throughout the summer. Their actions successfully drew national attention to the continuing resistance in the South to desegregation rulings, forced the Kennedy administration to take a stand on this issue, and led to a stronger Interstate Commerce Commission ruling banning segregation in interstate travel.[57]

The next significant events occurred in Birmingham, Alabama, in 1963. Birmingham had more racial violence than any southern city, with 18 unsolved bombings of Black churches and homes in a six-year period. The city had closed its parks and golf courses rather than integrate them, and there was no progress on integrating the local schools. A leading supporter of integration had been castrated to intimidate other Blacks who might advocate integration. The city's police chief, "Bull" Connor, was a strong segregationist who had allowed the attacks on the Freedom Riders. During a peaceful protest in April 1963, Martin Luther King Jr. and many others were arrested. While in solitary confinement, King wrote his now-famous **"Letter from Birmingham Jail,"** an eloquent statement of the principles of nonviolent civil disobedience.

The letter was a response to White religious leaders who had told King in a newspaper ad that his actions were "unwise and untimely" and that "when rights are consistently denied, a cause should be pressed in the courts and in negotiations among local leaders, and not in the streets." King responded with a justification for civil disobedience, writing that everyone had an obligation to follow just laws but an equal obligation to break unjust laws.

King also laid out the four steps of nonviolent campaigns: (1) collection of the facts to determine whether injustices are alive; (2) negotiation with White leaders to change the injustices; (3) self-purification, which involved training to make sure that the civil rights protesters would be able to endure the abuse that they would receive; and (4) direct action (for example, sit-ins and marches) to create the environment in which change could occur, but always in a nonviolent manner. By following these steps, civil rights protesters ensured that their social movement would draw attention to their cause while turning public opinion against their opponents' violent tactics.

Following King's release from jail, the situation escalated. The protest leaders decided to use children in the next round of demonstrations. After more than 1,000 children were arrested and the jails were overflowing, the police turned fire hoses and police dogs on children who were trying to continue their march. Media coverage of the incident turned the tide of public opinion in favor of the marchers as

**AP®
FOUNDATIONAL
DOCUMENT**

"Letter from Birmingham Jail"
A letter written by Martin Luther King Jr. in 1963 from his jail cell in Alabama as a response to a newspaper ad by White religious leaders telling King that the issue of civil rights should be argued in the courts and not in the streets. King's letter justified civil disobedience, saying that everyone has an obligation to follow just laws but also an equal obligation to break unjust laws.

FIGURE 9.4   African-American Civil Rights Time Line

May 17
U.S. Supreme Court
rules segregated schools
are unconstitutional in
the *Brown v. Board of
Education* decision.

September 9
The Federal Civil Rights Act prohibits
discrimination.

September 23
President Eisenhower sends troops to escort
Black students into a White high school in Little
Rock, Arkansas.

Government Action

1954   1957

December 1
Rosa Parks is arrested
for refusing to move to
the back of a bus in
Montgomery, Alabama.

February 1
Black college students,
refused service at a lunch
counter in Greensboro,
North Carolina, launch
a sit-in.

May 4
Freedom Riders
test a Supreme
Court decision
that integrated
interstate bus
travel, sparking
violence.

Social Movement

1955   1960   1961

Source: Adapted from "Civil Rights Movement Timeline," History.com, www.history.com/topics/civil-rights-movement-timeline (accessed 5/13/20).

Left, a 15-year-old civil rights demonstrator, defying an anti-parade ordinance, is attacked by a police dog in Birmingham, Alabama, on May 3, 1963. Reactions against this police brutality helped spur Congress and the president to enact civil rights legislation. Three months later, civil rights leader Martin Luther King Jr. (right) waves to supporters from the steps of the Lincoln Memorial in Washington, D.C. The March on Washington drew an estimated 250,000 people, who heard King deliver his famous "I Have a Dream" speech.

July 2
President Johnson signs the Civil Rights Act.

August 6
The Federal Voting Rights Act prohibits denying anyone the vote on the basis of color or race.

April 11
Fair Housing Act protects against discrimination in housing.

1964

1965

1968

April 16
Martin Luther King Jr. writes his "Letter from Birmingham Jail," defending nonviolent civil disobedience against unjust laws.

August 28
Martin Luther King Jr. delivers his "I Have a Dream" speech at the March on Washington.

September 15
Four girls are killed when a Baptist church in Birmingham, Alabama, is bombed.

June 21
Three civil rights workers are murdered outside Philadelphia, Mississippi.

February 21
Malcolm X is shot and killed in New York.

March 7
Six hundred voting rights marchers are attacked by police with clubs and whips on the Edmund Pettus Bridge outside Selma, Alabama. On March 21, about 3,200 marchers head out again on a four-day march to Montgomery in support of voting rights.

April 4
Martin Luther King Jr. is slain in Memphis, Tennessee.

1963

1964

1965

1968

the country expressed outrage over the violence in Birmingham. Similar protests occurred throughout the South, with more than 1,000 actions in over 100 different southern cities and more than 20,000 people arrested throughout the summer. The demonstration culminated in August 1963, when 250,000 people participated in the March on Washington. King delivered his famous "I Have a Dream" speech and civil rights leaders pressured congressional leaders to pass civil rights legislation.

Protest Today After King's and others' nonviolent protests produced significant successes, mass protest became the preferred tool of many social movements for civil rights and other causes. Vietnam War protesters marched on Washington by the hundreds of thousands in the late 1960s and early 1970s. The women's rights, gay rights, and environmental movements have staged many mass demonstrations in Washington and other major cities. The largest single day of protest in the United States was the Women's March on January 21, 2017, which drew an estimated 4.2 million people in 654 American cities and another 300,000 in 261 cities around the world to protest the election of Donald Trump and call attention to issues concerning women's rights, health care, and immigration reform.[58]

Social movements may also use direct action, rather than mass protests, to advance their causes, as was the case with the protests against the Dakota Access Pipeline in 2016–2017. When an oil pipeline was approved stretching from North

Native Americans' struggles to maintain the security of their cultural lands were at the forefront of controversy over the construction of the Dakota Access Pipeline. In 2016 and 2017, the Standing Rock Sioux tribe led protests against the oil pipeline and its proposed route, which threatened their ancestral lands and clean water supply.

Dakota to southern Illinois, Native Americans from the nearby Standing Rock Indian Reservation objected on the grounds that the pipeline's route under the Missouri River posed a threat to their sources of clean water and to their ancient burial grounds. Thousands of protesters occupied the construction site for months in an effort to stop the pipeline, but ultimately law-enforcement officers cleared the protesters with water cannons, tear gas, and rubber bullets. In December 2016, President Obama issued an executive order requiring an environmental impact statement for the part of the pipeline that was to go under the river. However, President Trump overturned that order, and the pipeline was completed in May 2017.[59]

The tools of social movements have evolved in recent years to combine the power of social media with mass protest. #BlackLivesMatter started in 2013 on social media but has since expanded to organize mass protests against police killings in many cities across the country. Black Lives Matter is a large, decentralized movement that is not organized under a traditional hierarchy or national leadership. Black Lives Matter activists have thus used a broad range of tactics to raise awareness and put pressure on police departments to change their policies, including marches, "die-ins" (protests in which participants block traffic by lying in the street), and social media campaigns. Many police departments have responded to the organization's concerns about excessive police violence and a lack of accountability by adopting new policies, such as requiring police officers to wear body cameras and complete bias-reduction training programs.[60] The cause received a boost in 2017 when many NFL players kneeled during the playing of the national anthem before games to call attention to racially biased policing and police violence. President Trump pressured NFL owners to force the players to stand, saying that their actions disrespected the flag and the military personnel who serve the country. However, some players continued their protest throughout the season.[61] Protesters intensified their call for changes to police practices during the summer of 2020 after police killed George Floyd in Minneapolis and Breonna Taylor in Louisville and shot Jacob Blake in Kenosha.

The legacy of the civil rights movement has been not only to help change unjust laws but also to provide a new tool for political action across a broad range of policy areas. By putting pressure on political leaders through direct, nonviolent protest, millions of Americans have had their voices heard.

After King's and others' nonviolent protests produced significant successes, mass protests became the preferred tool of many social movements, such as the Women's March on Washington (left) and Black Lives Matter (right).

The courts

The Supreme Court has played an important role in defining civil rights, including those pushed for by the social movements just discussed. In the mid-twentieth century, the justices moved away from the "separate but equal" doctrine, required the desegregation of public schools, and upheld landmark civil rights legislation passed by Congress. More recently, they have expanded civil rights for women and the LGBTQ community, but they also have endorsed a color-blind position that some see as a movement away from protecting civil rights.

Challenging "Separate but Equal" in Education In the 1930s, the NAACP, which was established to fight for equal rights for Black people, started a concerted effort to nibble away at the "separate but equal" doctrine. Rather than tackling segregation head-on, the NAACP first challenged an aspect of segregation that would be familiar to the Supreme Court justices: the ways in which states kept Blacks out of all-White law schools. Another strategy was to challenge admissions practices in law schools outside the Deep South to demonstrate that segregation was not just a "southern problem" and to raise the chances for compliance with favorable Court decisions. A young NAACP attorney named Thurgood Marshall (who later became the first African-American Supreme Court justice) argued that the University of Maryland's practice of sending Black students to out-of-state law schools rather than admitting them to the university's all-White law school violated the Black students' civil rights. (The state gave Black students a $200 scholarship, which did not cover the costs of tuition and travel and was not available to all Black students who wanted to attend law school.) In 1936, the circuit court and subsequently the Maryland appeals court rejected this arrangement and ordered that Black students be admitted to the University of Maryland law school.[62]

Over the next 15 years, a series of successful lawsuits slowly chipped away at the idea of "separate but equal." After these victories, there was a debate within the NAACP over whether to continue the case-by-case approach against the "separate but equal" doctrine or to directly challenge the principle itself. The latter approach was risky because it was unclear if the Court was ready to take this bold step, and defeat in the Court would set back the movement. However, the signals increasingly indicated that the Supreme Court was ready to strike down the "separate but equal" doctrine. In addition to the law school cases, in 1948 the Court ruled that "restrictive covenants"—clauses in real estate contracts that prevented a property owner from selling to an African American—could not be enforced by state or local courts because the Fourteenth Amendment prohibited the states from denying Blacks the "equal protection of the laws."[63]

This application of the Fourteenth Amendment was expanded in the landmark ruling *Brown v. Board of Education*. The case arrived on the Court's docket in 1951, was postponed for argument until after the 1952 election, and then was re-argued in December 1953. The ruling was postponed for so long because the Court was keenly aware of the firestorm that would ensue. In its unanimous decision, the Court ruled: "In the field of public education, the doctrine of separate but equal has no place. Separate educational facilities are inherently unequal, depriving the plaintiffs of the equal protection of the laws. Segregated facilities may generate in Black children a feeling of inferiority that may affect their hearts and minds in a way unlikely ever to be undone."[64] The case was significant not only because it required all public schools in the United States to desegregate but also because it used the equal protection clause of the Fourteenth Amendment in a way that had potentially far-reaching consequences.

Nonetheless, the decision was limited because it focused on segregation in schools rather than segregation more generally and it focused on the psychological damage done to Black schoolchildren through segregation rather than on the broader claim that racial classification itself was not allowed by the Constitution. Chief Justice Earl Warren wanted a unanimous vote and knew that two justices would not support a broader ruling that would overturn *Plessy v. Ferguson* and rule segregation unconstitutional in all contexts. Even if segregation in other public places still was legal, the *Brown* ruling provided an important boost to the civil rights movement.

The Push to Desegregate Schools In 1955, *Brown v. Board of Education II* addressed the implementation of desegregation and required the states to "desegregate with all deliberate speed."[65] The odd choice of words, "all deliberate speed," was read as a signal by southerners that they could take their time with desegregation. The phrase does seem to be contradictory: being deliberate does not usually involve being speedy. Southern states engaged in "massive resistance" to the desegregation order, as articulated by Harry F. Byrd, the segregationist senator from Virginia. In some cases, they even closed public schools rather than integrate them—and then reopened the schools as "private" segregated schools for which the White students received government vouchers. However, Maryland, Kentucky, Tennessee, Missouri, and the District of Columbia desegregated their schools within two years.

Eight years after *Brown I*, little had changed in the Deep South: fewer than 1 percent of Black children attended school with White children.[66] Through the 1960s, the courts had to battle against continued resistance to integration. In 1971, the Court shifted its focus from **de jure** segregation (segregation mandated by law) to **de facto** segregation (segregation that existed because of segregated housing patterns) and approved school busing as a tool to integrate schools.[67] This approach was extremely controversial. The Court almost immediately limited the application of busing by ruling in a Detroit case that busing could not go beyond the boundaries of a city's school district—that is, students did not have to be bused from suburbs to cities—unless it could be shown that the school district's lines were drawn in an intentionally discriminatory way.[68] This rule encouraged "White flight" from the cities to the suburbs in response to court-ordered busing.

In 2007, in perhaps the most important decision on race in education since *Brown*, the Court invalidated voluntary desegregation plans implemented by public school districts in Seattle and Louisville. Both districts set goals for racial diversity and denied school assignment requests if they tipped the racial balance above or below certain thresholds. In a ringing endorsement of the color-blind approach, the majority opinion

DID YOU KNOW?

75%

of African-American students and 79 percent of Latino students attend schools that are majority minority.

Source: *U.S. News & World Report*

de jure
Relating to actions or circumstances that occur "by law," such as the legally enforced segregation of schools in the American South before the 1960s.

de facto
Relating to actions or circumstances that occur outside the law or "by fact," such as the segregation of schools that resulted from housing patterns and other factors rather than from laws.

said: "The way to stop discrimination on the basis of race is to stop discriminating on the basis of race." In this case, the discrimination was against White students who wanted to be in schools with few minority students, rather than Black students who wanted to be in integrated schools.[69]

Expanding Civil Rights for African Americans Other significant rulings in the 1960s struck down state laws that forbade interracial marriages (16 states had such laws), upheld all significant parts of the Civil Rights Act, and upheld and expanded the scope of the Voting Rights Act (VRA; these important laws will be discussed in the next section). In central cases, the justices ruled that Congress had the power to eliminate segregation in public places, such as restaurants and hotels, under the commerce clause of the Constitution.

The first case involved a hotel in Atlanta that was close to an interstate highway, advertised extensively on the highway, and had a clientele that was about 75 percent from out of state. The Court ruled that this establishment was clearly engaging in interstate commerce, so Congress had the right to regulate it.[70] In the second case, "almost all, if not all," of the patrons of Ollie's Barbecue in Birmingham, Alabama, were local. However, the Court pointed out that meat purchased for the restaurant came from out of state and this constituted 46 percent of the total amount spent on supplies. Therefore, the practice of segregation would place significant burdens on "the interstate flow of food and upon the movement of products generally."[71]

The next important area of cases was in employment law. In 1971, the Court ruled that employment tests, such as written exams or general aptitude tests, that are not related to job performance and that discriminate against Blacks violate the 1964 Civil Rights Act.[72] This **disparate impact standard** of discrimination means that if the employment practice has a bad *effect* on a racial group, it doesn't matter whether or not the discrimination is *intended*. The Supreme Court and Congress have gone back and forth in defining this concept, but it is still important in workplace discrimination suits. (See Nuts & Bolts 9.1 for the legal definition of race-based workplace discrimination.)

The Color-Blind Court and Judicial Activism Recently, the Supreme Court has been gradually imposing a "color-blind jurisprudence" over a range of issues—that is, the Court has reasoned that race should not be considered in determining the outcome

Civil Rights Act of 1964
A federal law that outlawed discrimination based on race, color, religion, or national origin in hotels, motels, restaurants, theaters, and all other public accommodations engaged in interstate commerce; banned discrimination in employment based on race, color, religion, sex, or national origin; encouraged the desegregation of public schools; and struck down unequal application of voter registration requirements.

disparate impact standard
The idea that discrimination exists if a practice has a negative effect on a specific group, whether or not this effect was intentional.

Race-Related Discrimination as Defined by the Equal Employment Opportunity Commission

Race/Color Discrimination

Race discrimination involves treating someone (an applicant or employee) unfavorably because he/she is of a certain race or because of personal characteristics associated with race (such as hair texture, skin color, or certain facial features). Color discrimination involves treating someone unfavorably because of skin color complexion. . . . Discrimination can occur when the victim and the person who inflicted the discrimination are the same race or color.

Race/Color Discrimination and Work Situations

The law forbids discrimination when it comes to any aspect of employment, including hiring, firing, pay, job assignments, promotions, layoff, training, fringe benefits, and any other term or condition of employment.

Race/Color Discrimination and Harassment

It is unlawful to harass a person because of that person's race or color. Harassment can include, for example, racial slurs, offensive or derogatory remarks about a person's race or color, or the display of racially offensive symbols. Although the law doesn't prohibit simple teasing, offhand comments, or isolated incidents that are not very serious, harassment is illegal when it is so frequent or severe that it creates a hostile or offensive work environment or when it results in an adverse employment decision (such as the victim being fired or demoted). The harasser can be the victim's supervisor, a supervisor in another area, a coworker, or someone who is not an employee of the employer, such as a client or customer.

Race/Color Discrimination and Employment Policies/Practices

An employment policy or practice that applies to everyone, regardless of race or color, can be illegal if it has a negative impact on the employment of people of a particular race or color and is not job-related and necessary to the operation of the business.

Source: U.S. Equal Employment Opportunity Commission, "Race/Color Discrimination," www.eeoc.gov (accessed 3/20/20).

"Why Should I Care?"

As a job applicant, it is essential to know your rights. These guidelines forbid discrimination when it comes to any aspect of employment, including hiring, firing, pay, job assignments, promotions, layoff, training, fringe benefits, and any other term or condition of employment. They also prohibit retaliation against people who complain of discrimination. Everyone is protected from race and color discrimination: Whites, Blacks, Asians, Latinos, persons of more than one race, and all other persons, whatever their race, color, or ethnicity.

**AP®
SUPREME
COURT CASE**

of certain kinds of cases. One significant area was the 1992 racial redistricting in which 15 new U.S. House districts were drawn to help elect African Americans and 10 new districts were drawn to help elect Latino members. The resulting dramatic change in the number of minorities in Congress (an increase greater than 50 percent) was rooted in the 1982 amendments to the VRA. Instead of mandating a fair *process*, this law and subsequent interpretation by the Supreme Court mandated that minorities have an "equal opportunity" to "elect representatives of their choice" when their numbers and configuration permit. As a result, the legislative redistricting process now had to avoid discriminatory *results* rather than being concerned only with discriminatory *intent*.

However, in a series of decisions starting with the 1993 landmark case *Shaw v. Reno*, the Supreme Court's adherence to a color-blind jurisprudence has thrown the constitutionality of Black-majority districts into doubt. The Court has ruled that Black-majority districts are legal as long as they are "done right."[73] But it has consistently held that if race is the predominant factor in drawing district lines, the districts are unconstitutional because they violate the equal protection clause of the Fourteenth Amendment for the White plaintiffs in these cases. Based on this reasoning, Black-majority districts in North Carolina, Georgia, Louisiana, Virginia, Texas, and Florida have been found to be unconstitutional. In 2001, the Court upheld the re-drawn 12th District in North Carolina, which no longer was a Black-majority district, arguing that when race and partisanship are so intertwined—as they are when 90 percent of African Americans vote for a Democratic candidate—plaintiffs cannot assume that African Americans were placed together for racial reasons. This ruling opens the door for a greater consideration of race than had been allowed in the previous cases.[74]

In 2017, the Court struck down districting plans in North Carolina and Virginia for packing African Americans into districts, thus diluting their ability to have an equal opportunity to elect candidates of their choice.[75] However, racial redistricting remains an unsettled area of the law. According to election law expert Richard Hasen, the Supreme Court's decision in 2019 to no longer decide cases concerning partisan gerrymandering will "force courts to make logically impossible determinations about whether racial reasons or partisan motives predominate when a party gerrymanders for political advantage." That is, a state could redraw districts on racial grounds (which would not be OK), but claim it was for partisan reasons (which now *is* OK, at least in federal court), and there would be no way for the courts to sort this out.[76]

The Court also struck down an important part of the 1965 VRA in a 2013 ruling. This case concerned the "coverage formula" that determines which states have to get approval from the Justice Department before implementing changes in an election law or practice (such as redistricting or closing a polling place). This "preclearance" provision of the law was viewed as one of the best ways to stop discriminatory voting practices because it could prevent them before they were implemented, rather than forcing voters to wait until they went into effect to challenge them. The Court ruled that the coverage formula was an unconstitutional burden on the covered states and was a violation of the Tenth Amendment.[77]

The racial redistricting and voting rights cases illustrate that the Supreme Court is increasingly activist in issues involving civil rights: it is generally unwilling to defer to the other branches of government and will assert its view of discrimination and equal protection regardless of what the other branches think (see Chapter 6 for a broader discussion of judicial activism). In some periods, like the 1950s and 1960s, judicial activism has served to further civil rights. More recently, it has served to limit them.

Women's Rights The Supreme Court has also been central in shaping women's civil rights. Until relatively recently, the Court did not apply the Constitution to protect women's rights, despite the Fourteenth Amendment's language that states may not deny any *person* the equal protection of the laws. Apparently, women were not regarded as people when it came to political and economic rights in the nineteenth and early twentieth centuries. These protectionist notions were finally rejected in three cases between 1971 and 1976, when the Court made it much more difficult for states to treat men and women differently.

The first case involved an Idaho state law that gave a man priority over a woman when they were otherwise equally entitled to execute a person's estate. This law was justified on the "reasonable" grounds that it reduced the state courts' workload by having an automatic rule that would limit challenges. But the Court ruled that the law was arbitrary, did not meet the "reasonableness" test, and therefore violated the woman's equal protection rights under the Fourteenth Amendment.[78] The second case involved a female air force officer who wanted to count her husband as a dependent

rational basis test
The use of evidence to suggest that differences in the behavior of two groups can rationalize unequal treatment of these groups.

for purposes of health and housing benefits. Under the law at the time, a military man could automatically count his wife as a dependent, but a woman could claim her husband only if she brought in more than half the family income. The Court struck down this practice, saying protectionist laws, "in practical effect, put women not on a pedestal, but in a cage."[79]

These two cases relied on the **rational basis test** for discrimination between men and women (which evolved from the reasonableness test). Along with the strict scrutiny test (see Chapter 8), it allows the Fourteenth Amendment to be applied differently to particular categories of people. Under the rational basis test, states can discriminate against a group of people as long as there is a "rational basis" for the state law in question. Today, for example, states can pass drinking laws that allow only those who are 21 and older to drink on the grounds that traffic fatalities will be lower with that drinking age rather than under a law that allows 18-year-olds to drink.

The strict scrutiny test gives racial minorities the strongest protection as the "suspect classification" under the Fourteenth Amendment, but it has not been applied to women. This test stipulates that there must be a "compelling state interest" to discriminate among people if race is involved. The idea of a suspect classification was first used in a case involving the internment of Japanese Americans during World War II. In a controversial ruling, the Court said that the internment camps were justified on national security grounds, making it one of the few instances in which racial classification has survived strict scrutiny.[80] However, the Supreme Court overturned this ruling in a 2018 case involving President Trump's travel ban.[81]

In 1976, the Court established a third test, the intermediate scrutiny test (see Chapter 8), in a case involving the drinking age. In the early 1970s, some states had a lower drinking age for women than for men on the "rational basis" that 18- to 20-year-old women are more mature than men of that age. (States argued that women were less likely to be drunk drivers and less likely to abuse alcohol than men were.) The new intermediate scrutiny standard meant that the government's policy must be "substantially related" to an "important government objective" to justify the unequal treatment of men and women, so the law was struck down.[82]

The intermediate scrutiny test gives women stronger protections than the rational basis test, but it is not as strong as strict scrutiny (see How It Works: Civil Rights). To use the legal jargon, the gender distinction would have to serve an "important government objective," but not a "compelling state interest," in order to withstand intermediate scrutiny.

In many instances, as with the Idaho case, the rights of women were strengthened by this new standard of equal protection. However, in other instances women may actually be more restricted by being treated the same as men. For example, in the drinking age case, instead of dropping the drinking age for men to 18, states raised the age for women to 21. Similarly, the Court struck down an Alabama divorce law in which husbands but not wives could be ordered to pay alimony.[83] Arguably, women would have been better off in these two specific instances under the old discriminatory laws (because they could drink at 18 instead of 21 and did not have to pay alimony in some states). However, the more aggressive application of the Fourteenth Amendment for women was an important step in providing them with the equal protection of the laws, as clearly shown in a Court decision that struck down the male-only admission policy at the Virginia Military Institute (VMI). The majority opinion stated that VMI violated the Fourteenth Amendment's equal protection clause because it failed to show an "exceedingly persuasive justification" for its sex-biased admissions policy.[84]

An important gender-equality case in 2017 concerned the law for determining the citizenship of children born overseas to an unmarried couple when one parent is a citizen and the other is not. Federal law requires a single father to have resided in the

United States for five years prior to his child's birth in order for that child to have U.S. citizenship, while a child born overseas to a single American mother would be granted U.S. citizenship if the mother had lived continuously in the United States for just one year prior to the child's birth. The Court ruled that this gender-based distinction was unconstitutional. As with earlier cases involving the drinking age and alimony, the remedy in this case was to make things worse for women in the short term—that is, rather than reducing the residency requirement for men from five years to one, the Court increased it for women to match the longer period for men. However, supporters of women's rights applauded the decision for what it means for gender equality in the long term. One expert on women's rights noted that the gender difference in this law was rooted in outdated notions of parental responsibilities, and argued, "Romantic ideals about the uniqueness of motherhood perpetuate the notion that women, rather than men, should assume responsibility for children. They also contribute to negative stereotypes that diminish women as workers, wage earners, and participants in public life."[85]

Two other areas where the Supreme Court has helped advance women's rights are affirmative action and protection against sexual harassment. In 1987, the Court approved **affirmative action** in a case involving a woman who was promoted over a man despite the fact that he had scored slightly higher than she did on a test. The Court ruled that the promotion was acceptable to make up for past discrimination.[86] And in 1993 the Court made it easier to sue employers for sexual harassment, saying that a woman did not have to reach the point of a nervous breakdown before claiming that she was being harassed; it was enough to demonstrate a pattern of "repeated and unwanted" behavior that created a "hostile workplace environment."[87] Later rulings stated that if a single act is flagrant, the conduct does not have to be repeated to create a hostile environment.

The issues of sexual harassment exploded on the national scene in October 2017 when Ashley Judd, Angelina Jolie, Gwyneth Paltrow, and Rose McGowan alleged that Hollywood mogul Harvey Weinstein sexually assaulted them. Ten days later, actress Alyssa Milano encouraged other women to share their stories with the hashtag #MeToo, building on the movement started by activist Tarana Burke to raise awareness of sexual assault. Within 24 hours, the messages had been retweeted 500,000 times and shared in 12 million posts on Facebook. In 2020, Weinstein was convicted in New York court and sentenced to 23 years in prison; he faces additional charges in California court.[88] Allegations of sexual harassment or assault have ended the careers of Fox News anchor Bill O'Reilly, Senator Al Franken, comedian Bill Cosby, Representative John Conyers, Alabama Senate nominee Roy Moore, morning show anchors Matt Lauer and Charlie Rose, Olympic gymnast doctor Lawrence G. Nassar, public radio star Garrison Keillor, celebrity chef Mario Batali, conductor James Levine, actor Kevin Spacey, and many more. *Time* magazine named "The Silence Breakers" their "person of the year" for 2017 for their courage in bringing attention to this problem.[89]

While the court of public opinion and the actual courts have played a central role in bringing justice to the victims of sexual assault and harassment, the Supreme Court has been less sympathetic to plaintiffs in cases involving pay discrimination. Lilly Ledbetter sued Goodyear Tire & Rubber Company because she had received lower pay than men doing the same work over a 20-year period, which she claimed was gender discrimination. The Court rejected her claim, saying that she did not meet the time limit required by law, as the discrimination must have occurred within 180 days of the claim.[90] (This overturned the long-standing policy of the EEOC, which held that each new paycheck restarted the 180-day clock as a new act of discrimination.) Dissenters pointed out that pay discrimination usually occurs in small increments over long periods, so it would be impossible to recognize unequal pay within 180 days of an initial paycheck. Furthermore, workers do not have access to information about fellow workers' pay, so it would be almost impossible to meet the standard set by the Court.

At the fourth annual Washington, D.C., Women's March in 2020, demonstrators gathered to show their support for women's rights.

affirmative action
Policies to help people who have been historically excluded or underrepresented, such as women and minorities, have better access to higher education and employment.

DID YOU KNOW?

Women working full-time earn

$0.81

compared to every dollar earned by men.
Source: payscale.com

Civil Rights

Cases Involving "Suspect Classification"
(race, ethnicity, creed, or national origin)

Strict Scrutiny Test

1. Is unequal treatment justified by a **"compelling state interest"**?

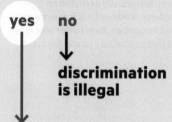

yes **no**

↓

discrimination is illegal

2. Is unequal treatment the **"least restrictive"** option?

yes **no**

↓

discrimination is illegal

Very few cases meet this standard.

Cases Involving Sex or Gender Equality

Intermediate Scrutiny Test

1. Is the discriminatory policy **"substantially related"** to an **"important government objective"**?

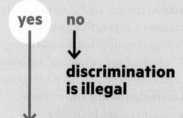

yes **no**

↓

discrimination is illegal

2. Is the discrimination **not substantially broader** than it needs to be to protect the important government interest?

yes **no**

↓

discrimination is illegal

Some discrimination based on gender is permitted, but this test is harder to pass than the rational basis test applied to gender cases in the past.

Cases Involving Age, Economic Status, or Other Criteria

Rational Basis Test

1. Is the law **rationally related to furthering** a legitimate government interest?

yes **no**

↓

discrimination is illegal

2. Does the policy avoid **"arbitrary, capricious, or deliberate"** discrimination?

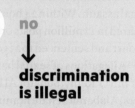

yes **no**

↓

discrimination is illegal

This is the easiest hurdle for a law or policy to pass.

→ **discrimination is legal** ←

Evaluating Discrimination Cases

Strict Scrutiny Test

Case 1:

The University of Michigan Law School's "holistic" race-conscious admissions policy is designed to promote diversity.

Case 2:

The University of Michigan's more rigid race-conscious undergraduate admissions policy was designed to promote diversity.

The Court asked...

1. Is unequal treatment justified by a "compelling state interest"?
2. Is unequal treatment the "least restrictive" option?

The Court said...

In Case 1, discrimination is OK. In *Grutter v. Bollinger* (2003), the Court ruled that the state's interest in **racial diversity in higher education was compelling**, and that this specific admissions policy was narrowly tailored. This was affirmed in *Fisher v. Univ. of Texas* (2016).

In Case 2, discrimination is not OK. In *Gratz v. Bollinger* (2003), the Court **struck down Michigan's undergraduate admissions policy** for not being narrowly tailored.

Intermediate Scrutiny Test

Case 1:

A California state law says that men—but not women—can be guilty of statutory rape.

Case 2:

The Virginia Military Institute maintained a male-only admissions policy.

The Court asked...

1. Is the discriminatory policy "substantially related" to an "important government objective"?
2. Is the discrimination not substantially broader than it needs to be to protect the important government interest?

The Court said...

In Case 1, discrimination is OK. In *Michael M. v. Superior Court* (1981), the Court found that the state had a **strong interest in preventing illegitimate pregnancy** and in punishing only the participant who, by nature, suffers few of the consequences of his conduct.

In Case 2, discrimination is not OK. In *United States v. Virginia* (1996), the Court **struck down the Virginia Military Institute's policy** as a violation of the equal protection clause of the Fourteenth Amendment.

Rational Basis Test

Case 1:

States have a 21-year-old drinking age that applies equally to men and women.

Case 2:

An Oklahoma law allowed 18- to 20-year-old women—but not men—to buy 3.2% ABV ("nonintoxicating") beer.

The Court asked...

1. Is the law rationally related to furthering a legitimate government interest?
2. Does the policy avoid "arbitrary, capricious, or deliberate" discrimination?

The Court said...

In Case 1, discrimination is OK. Various state supreme courts have upheld these laws on the rational basis that **the laws may prevent drunk driving among those younger than 21**.

In Case 2, discrimination is not OK. In *Craig v. Boren* (1976), the Court **struck down this law**, rejecting the rational basis that Oklahoma had claimed and instead applying intermediate scrutiny.

Critical Thinking

1. **Is it easier for the government to discriminate against** someone based on age or race? Why?

2. **What is the standard used by the Court if the state wants** to make distinctions between people based on race? Under what circumstances and in what scenarios is discrimination based on race legal?

FIGURE 9.5

Lifetime Wage Gap for Women as Compared to Men

There is a substantial difference between women's and men's earnings in the United States. What could account for this variation? How much do you think it has to do with levels of discrimination, and how much with differences in the nature of the jobs that men and women hold?

Source: National Women's Law Center, "Lifetime Wage Gap Losses for Women: 2019 State Rankings," based on U.S. Census 2019 American Community Survey Data, March 2019, https://nwlc-ciw49tixgw5lbab. stackpathdns.com/wp-content/uploads/ 2019/03/Women-Lifetime-Losses-State-by-State-2019.pdf (accessed 3/22/20).

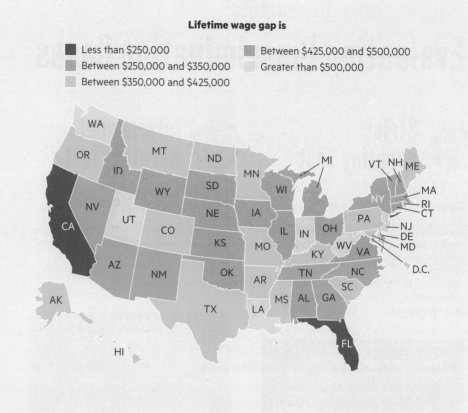

Lifetime wage gap is

- Less than $250,000
- Between $250,000 and $350,000
- Between $350,000 and $425,000
- Between $425,000 and $500,000
- Greater than $500,000

Congress restored the old standard in January 2009 by passing the Lilly Ledbetter Fair Pay Act. But as Figure 9.5 shows, significant pay disparities between men and women remain throughout much of the United States. Early in 2016, President Obama issued an executive order requiring companies with more than 100 employees to report to the federal government what they pay employees by race, gender, and ethnicity. He said, "Women are not getting the fair shot that we believe every single American deserves."[91] However, in 2017 President Trump overturned this order.[92]

The largest sexual discrimination lawsuit in the nation's history was filed in 2001 against Walmart on behalf of 1.5 million women who had worked at Walmart since 1998. Among other things, the plaintiffs alleged the following:

- Over objections from a female executive, senior management regularly referred to female store employees as "little Janie Qs" and "girls."
- A Sam's Club (Walmart's warehouse retail chain) manager in California told another woman that she should "doll up" to get promoted.
- Managers have repeatedly told female employees that men "need to be paid more than women because they have families to support."
- A male manager in South Carolina told a female employee that "God made Adam first, so women would always be second to men."
- A female personnel manager in Florida was told by her manager that men were paid more than women because "men are here to make a career and women aren't. Retail is for housewives who just need to earn extra money."[93]

But in 2011 the Court ruled that the class-action lawsuit was not valid because there was no "convincing proof of a companywide discriminatory pay and promotion policy." That is, women would have to prove discrimination individually, not as a group.

Civil rights experts said this was the "death knell" for class-action lawsuits seeking monetary damages for discrimination.[94] However, the Court did not rule on the merits of the case and in 2019 more than 100 current and former female Walmart employees sued for a persistent pattern of discrimination.[95]

Gay Rights The Supreme Court has a similarly mixed record on gay rights. The Court's decisions in early cases were not supportive of gay rights. One of the first cases concerned Georgia's law banning sodomy. As we discussed in Chapter 8, the Supreme Court ruled in *Bowers v. Hardwick* (1986) that "homosexual behavior" was not protected by the Constitution and that state laws banning it could be justified under the most lenient rational basis test.[96]

After cases in which it sidestepped the issue, the Court first endorsed civil rights for gays in 1996. Here the Court struck down an amendment to the Colorado state constitution that would have prevented gays from suing for discrimination in employment or housing. The Court said that the state amendment violated gays' equal protection rights because it "withdrew from homosexuals, but no others, specific legal protection from the injuries caused by discrimination."[97] The Court rejected the state's "rational basis" arguments and came close to putting gays in the "suspect classification" that had been reserved for racial and ethnic minorities.

An important ruling came in 2003 in a case involving two Houston men. As we discussed in Chapter 8, John Geddes Lawrence and Tyron Garner were prosecuted for same-sex sodomy (which was illegal in Texas) after police found them having sex in Lawrence's apartment. The Supreme Court ruled in a historic 6–3 decision that the due process clause of the Fourteenth Amendment guarantees freedom of not only thought, belief, and expression but also certain intimate conduct (including same-sex relations). This reasoning is rooted in the substantive due process doctrine that underlies constitutional protections for birth control, abortion, and decisions about how to raise one's children.

The decision overturned *Bowers v. Hardwick*, and the majority opinion had harsh words for that decision, saying it "was not correct when it was decided, and it is not correct today." Five members of the majority signed on to the broad "due process" reasoning of the decision, rather than the narrower reasoning in Justice O'Connor's concurring opinion, in which she said that the decision should apply only to the four states that treated gays differently (that is, banning sodomy for homosexuals but not for heterosexuals). With the broader due process logic, a total of 13 state laws that banned sodomy were struck down. Justice Scalia wrote a strong dissent, saying that the decision was "the product of a court that has largely signed on to the so-called homosexual agenda" and warned that the ruling "will have far-reaching implications beyond this case." He predicted that the ruling would serve as the basis for constitutional protections for same-sex marriage.[98]

The Supreme Court issued two important rulings on same-sex marriage in 2013. The first case was a narrow ruling that reinstated same-sex marriage in California but did not affect any other state. The second case was a more far-reaching decision that struck down part of the Defense of Marriage Act (DOMA) as a violation of the Fifth Amendment's due process clause. The majority opinion said that the federal government cannot deny benefits to same-sex couples who are legally married under state law. The gradual movement toward endorsing same-sex marriage culminated in 2015 in the landmark ruling *Obergefell v. Hodges*, which legalized same-sex marriage in all 50 states.[99] The 5–4 ruling said that the fundamental right to marry is guaranteed by both the due process clause and the equal protection clause of the Fourteenth Amendment.

In 2020, there was another landmark ruling in protection of the rights of gay and transgender people. In a 6–3 ruling on *Bostock v. Clayton County*, the Court said that

substantive due process doctrine
One interpretation of the due process clause of the Fourteenth Amendment; in this view the Supreme Court has the power to overturn laws that infringe on individual liberties.

The Constitution promises liberty to all within its reach … [and] extend[s] to certain personal choices central to individual dignity and autonomy, including intimate choices that define personal identity and beliefs.

—Supreme Court's majority opinion in *Obergefell v. Hodges*

the language of the Civil Rights Act of 1964 applies to discrimination based on sexual orientation and gender identity. As such, it protects gay and transgender individuals from discrimination in the workforce.[100] The plaintiff, Gerald Bostock, had been fired from his job for expressing interest in forming a gay softball league at work. The Supreme Court consolidated the case with two other similar cases of workplace discrimination: *Altitude Express Inc. v. Zarda* and *R.G. & G.R. Harris Funeral Homes Inc. v. Equal Employment Opportunity Commission.*[101]

Writing for the majority, Justice Neil Gorsuch said, "An employer who fires an individual merely for being gay or transgender defies the law." Prior to this decision, it had been legal in almost half the states to fire an employee for being gay, bisexual, or transgender.

This section demonstrates that the courts can be both a strong advocate of and an impediment to civil rights. In general, however, the courts have a limited *independent* impact on policy. That is, as the school desegregation cases clearly demonstrate, the courts must rely on the other branches of government to carry out their decisions.

Congress

Congress has provided the basis for today's protection of civil rights through a series of laws that were enacted starting in the 1960s. Applying to racial and ethnic minorities and to women, these laws attempted to ensure that there is a "level playing field" of equal opportunity.

Key Early Legislation The bedrock of equal protection that exists today stems from landmark legislation passed by Congress in the 1960s—the 1964 Civil Rights Act, the 1965 VRA, and the 1968 Fair Housing Act. President Kennedy was slow to seek civil rights legislation for fear of alienating southern Democrats. The events in Birmingham prompted him to act, but he was assassinated before the legislation was passed. President Lyndon Johnson, a former segregationist, helped push through the Civil Rights Act when he became president. The act barred discrimination in employment based on race, sex, religion, or national origin; banned segregation in public places; and established the EEOC as the enforcement agency for the legislation. One of the southern opponents of the legislation inserted the language referring to sex, thinking that it would defeat the bill (assuming, perhaps, that there would be a majority coalition of male chauvinists and segregationists), but it became law anyway.

The VRA of 1965 eliminated direct obstacles to minority voting in the South, such as discriminatory literacy tests and other voter registration tests, and also provided the means to enforce the law: federal marshals were charged with overseeing elections in the South. After its passage, President Johnson hailed the VRA as a "triumph for freedom as huge as any ever won on any battlefield."[102] The VRA, which is often cited as one of the most significant pieces of civil rights legislation in our nation's history,[103] precipitated an explosion in Black political participation in the South. The most dramatic gains came in Mississippi, where Black registration increased from 6.7 percent before the VRA to 59.8 percent in 1967. As one political scientist noted, "The act simply overwhelmed the major bulwarks of the disenfranchising system. In the seven states originally covered, Black registration increased from 29.3 percent in March 1965, to 56.6 percent in 1971–1972; the gap between Black and White registration rates narrowed from 44.1 percentage points to 11.2."[104]

The last piece of landmark legislation, the Fair Housing Act of 1968, barred discrimination in the rental or sale of a home based on race, sex, religion, and national origin. Important amendments to the law enacted in 1988 added disability and familial status (having children under age 18) to the list of protected categories, provided new administrative enforcement mechanisms, and expanded Justice Department jurisdiction to bring suit on behalf of victims in federal district courts.[105]

There have been many other important amendments to civil rights laws since the 1960s. The 1975 amendments to the VRA extended coverage of many of the law's provisions to language minorities, guaranteeing that registration and voting materials are made available to voters in their native language in certain districts with large numbers of citizens who are not proficient in English. The 1982 VRA amendments extended important provisions of the law for 25 years and made it easier to bring a lawsuit under the act. The 1991 Civil Rights Act overruled or altered parts of 12 Supreme Court decisions that had eroded the initial intent of the 1964 civil rights legislation. It also expanded earlier legislation and increased the costs to employers for intentional, illegal discrimination. In 2006, Congress voted to extend the VRA for another 25 years.

Protections for Women Women have also received extensive protection through legislation. As noted, the section of the Civil Rights Act that bars discrimination based on gender, Title VII, was almost an accidental part of the bill (it was included by an opponent to the legislation). Indeed, the first executive director of the EEOC would not enforce the gender part of the law because it was a "fluke." In 1966, the National Organization for Women (NOW) was formed to push for enforcement of the law. Its members convinced President Johnson to sign an executive order that eliminated sex discrimination in federal agencies and among federal contractors, but the order was difficult to enforce. Finally, in 1970, the EEOC started enforcing the law. Before long, one-third of all civil rights cases involved sex discrimination, and those numbers have remained high in recent years (see Figure 9.6).

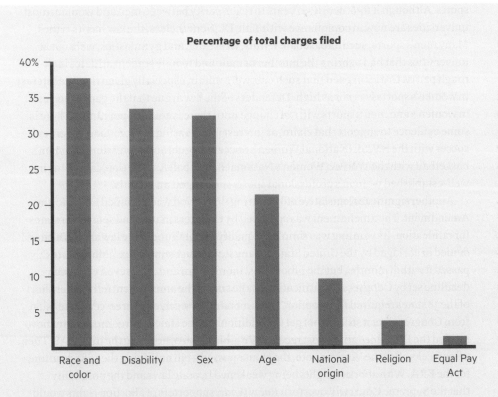

Percentage of total charges filed

Source: "Charge Statistics (Charges Filed with EEOC), FY 1997 through FY 2019," U.S. Equal Employment Opportunity Commission, www.eeoc.gov/eeoc/statistics/enforcement/charges.cfm (accessed 3/22/20).

FIGURE 9.6

Discrimination Cases Filed with the Equal Employment Opportunity Commission, 2019

Discrimination based on race and color, and discrimination based on sex, are the two types most frequently reported, but there is a significant amount of discrimination based on age and disability as well. What types of discrimination do you think would be most likely to go unreported?

Note: Percentages do not sum to 100 because complaints may be filed in more than one category.

While many people imagine Title IX as primarily affecting equal funding for college women's sports teams, it also provides important protections for survivors of sexual violence on college campuses. Here, students protest the Education Department's efforts to revise these provisions in February 2017.

Title IX of the Education Amendments
A federal law that prohibits discrimination on the basis of sex in any federally funded education program or activity. One of the most visible effects of the law was to equalize intercollegiate sports by creating more opportunities for women and eliminating some men's teams in order to achieve parity.

No person in the United States shall, on the basis of sex, be excluded from participation in, be denied the benefits of, or be subjected to discrimination under any educational program or activity receiving Federal financial assistance.

—Full text of Title IX

**AP®
SUPREME
COURT CASE**

Congress passed the next piece of important legislation for women in 1972: **Title IX of the Education Amendments**, which prohibits sex discrimination in institutions that receive federal funds. The law has had the greatest impact in women's sports. In the 1960s and 1970s, opportunities for women to play sports in college or high school were extremely limited. Very few women's scholarships were available at the college level, and budgets for women's sports were tiny compared with the budgets for men's sports. Although it took nearly 30 years to reach parity between men and women, most universities are now in compliance with Title IX. Nonetheless, the law has its critics. Many men's sports, such as baseball, tennis, wrestling, and gymnastics, were cut at universities that had to bring the number of male and female student athletes into rough parity. Critics argued that such cuts were unfair, especially given that the interest in women's sports was not as high. Defenders of the law argue that the gap in interest in women's and men's sports will not change until there is equal opportunity. There is some evidence to support that claim, as interest is increasing in professional women's soccer with the NWSL (National Women's Soccer League) and professional women's basketball with the WNBA (Women's National Basketball Association), as well as in well-established women's professional sports such as golf and tennis.

Another significant legislative effort during this period was the failed Equal Rights Amendment. The amendment was approved by Congress in 1972 and sent to the states for ratification. Its wording was simple: "Equality of rights under the law shall not be denied or abridged by the United States or any state on account of sex." Many states passed it within months, but the process lost momentum and after seven years (the deadline set by Congress for ratification by the states) the amendment fell 3 states short of the 38 states required for adoption. The amendment received a three-year extension from Congress, but it still did not get the additional three states. Three more states have ratified the ERA since 2017, most recently Virginia in 2020, bringing the total to 38. Then, a few weeks after the Virginia vote, the House passed a bill nullifying the 1982 deadline for the ERA. With abortion rights being weakened by state laws and the possibility that the Supreme Court will overturn *Roe v. Wade*, supporters of abortion rights would like to provide constitutional protection.[106] However, five other states rescinded their ratifications back in the late 1970s and the Senate is unlikely to take up the bill. Therefore, the only way to adopt the ERA would be to start the entire process over again.

In 1994, Congress passed the Violence against Women Act, which allowed women who were the victims of physical abuse and violence to sue in federal court and provided funding for investigating and prosecuting violent crimes against women, for helping the victims of such crimes, and for prevention programs. In 2000, part of the law was overturned by the Supreme Court, which ruled that Congress had exceeded its powers under the commerce clause.[107] Nonetheless, the funding provisions of the act were reauthorized and expanded by Congress in 2000, 2005, and 2013.

Protections for Disabled People and for Gay Rights Yet another important piece of civil rights legislation was the 1990 Americans with Disabilities Act, which provided strong federal protections for the 45 million disabled Americans to prevent workplace discrimination and to provide access to public facilities. This law produced curb cuts in sidewalks, access for wheelchairs on public buses and trains, special seating in sports stadiums, and many other changes that make the daily lives of disabled people a little easier and that provide them with an opportunity to participate more fully in society.[108]

Congress's track record in protecting gay rights has not been as strong. In fact, most of the steps taken by Congress have been to restrict rather than expand gay rights. In 1996, Congress passed DOMA to avert the possibility that some liberal states such as Hawaii would allow gay marriage. This act defined marriage as only between a man and woman and barred couples in same-sex marriages from receiving federal insurance or Social Security spousal benefits and from filing joint federal tax returns. Nonetheless, as we have noted, the part of the law depriving same-sex spouses of federal benefits was struck down by the Supreme Court in 2013 and the entire law was overturned in 2015.

In what may represent a change of course, in October 2009 Congress passed the Matthew Shepard and James Byrd Jr. Hate Crimes Prevention Act. This legislation expanded the previous hate-crime laws based on race, color, religion, or national origin to include attacks based on a victim's sexual orientation, gender identity, or intellectual or physical disability. The law also lifted a requirement that a victim had to be attacked while engaged in a federally protected activity, such as attending school, for it to be a federal hate crime. In signing the bill, President Obama said, "After more than a decade of opposition and delay, we've passed inclusive hate-crimes legislation to help protect our citizens from violence based on what they look like, who they love, how they pray or who they are."[109] The law commemorates the horrific murders of James Byrd Jr., a Black man who in 1998 was dragged behind a pickup truck by White supremacists for three miles until his head and right arm were severed, and Matthew Shepard, a gay teenager who in 1998 was beaten by two men, tied to a fence, and left to die. Also, the Employment Non-Discrimination Act, which would prohibit discrimination in employment based on sexual orientation, has been proposed in nearly every Congress since 1994. A version of the bill passed the House in 2007 but died in the Senate.

The president

The mid-century civil rights movement benefited greatly from presidential action. President Truman integrated the armed services in 1948, and President Eisenhower used the National Guard to enforce a court order to integrate Central High School in Little Rock, Arkansas, in 1957. Executive orders by President Kennedy in 1961 and President Johnson in 1965 established affirmative action, and in 1969 Richard Nixon expanded the "goals and numerical ranges" for hiring minorities in the federal government.

You do not take a person who, for years, has been hobbled by chains and liberate him, bring him up to the starting line of a race and then say "you are free to compete with all the others," and still just believe that you have been completely fair.

—**President Lyndon Johnson** on affirmative action

In a landmark civil rights decision in 2020, the Supreme Court ruled that employers cannot discriminate against employees because of their sexual orientation or gender identity. This has renewed questions about President Trump's reversal of the Obama-era policy of allowing transgender people to serve in the military, which is currently being challenged in court.

The most significant unilateral action taken by a president in the area of civil rights for gays and lesbians was President Clinton's effort to end the ban on gays in the military. Clinton was surprised by the strength of the opposition to his plan, so he ended up crafting a compromise policy of "don't ask, don't tell," which pleased no one. Under this policy, the military would stop actively searching for and discharging gays from the military ranks, and recruits would not need to reveal their sexual orientation. But if the military did find out (without conducting an investigation) that a person was gay, he or she still could be disciplined or discharged.

During the 2008 campaign, President Obama promised to repeal "don't ask, don't tell." Republican filibusters stopped several attempts to change the policy in 2010, but Congress finally passed the Don't Ask, Don't Tell Repeal Act in December 2010 and it went into effect on September 20, 2011. Minutes after the new policy was in place, navy lieutenant Gary Ross and his longtime partner were married in Vermont and Ross became the first openly gay married person in the military.[110] President Obama extended the policy to include transgender service members, but President Trump reversed that policy, tweeting that "the United States Government will not accept or allow transgender individuals to serve in any capacity in the U.S. Military." However, an injunction against the ban was ordered by a federal judge, who said that lawsuits against the ban have a strong chance of prevailing and that the ban "does not appear to be supported by any facts."[111] In March 2018, Trump issued a new executive order with essentially the same ban (but with a version of "don't ask, don't tell"), and the Supreme Court allowed the ban to go into effect in 2019 (without ruling on the constitutionality of the ban) while four lawsuits in federal court challenging the policy play out.[112]

Recent presidential candidates have generally made civil rights policy a low priority, which means that it is less likely that significant and dramatic change will come from unilateral action by the president. Instead, attention to civil rights concerns in the executive branch in the past few decades has primarily been in two areas: racial diversity in presidential appointments and use of the bully pulpit to promote racial concerns and interests.

President Bill Clinton was active in both areas. In 1992, as a candidate, Clinton promised a government that "looks like America." His cabinet, subcabinet, and judicial appointments achieved the greatest gender and racial balance of any in history. Clinton also used the bully pulpit to advocate a civil rights agenda. Most significant was his effort to promote a "national conversation on race," which helped focus national attention on many of the problems faced by minorities. President George W. Bush did not achieve the same level of diversity in his appointments as Clinton did, but his administration was more diverse than those of other Republican presidents. Bush also made serious overtures to minorities, especially Latinos, in his effort to expand the Republican Party base.

While the long-term impact of the Obama presidency on the civil rights movement remains to be seen, the historical significance of his successful campaign as a minority candidate is clear. At the 2008 Democratic National Convention, some African-American delegates openly wept as Obama accepted the party's nomination. Many delegates had not expected that they would live to see an African American become a strong contender for the presidency. Obama's nominations for his cabinet and cabinet-level offices consisted of a diverse group of 14 men and 7 women, with 7 of them members of racial minorities. Eric Holder was the first African American to serve as attorney general, and Sonia Sotomayor is the first Latina on the Supreme Court. Obama also nominated Elena Kagan to the Supreme Court, putting three women on the Court for the first time. Obama's second-term team was similar, consisting of 14 men and 8 women, 6 of them racial minorities.

In his first term, Obama tried to downplay race and diversity concerns. Indeed, some observers argue that Obama's presidency signaled the beginning of a "post-racial politics" that places less emphasis on race and devotes more attention to issues that concern all Americans, such as the economy, education, and health care. However, Obama himself rejected this view. In Obama's second term, he used the bully pulpit to draw more attention to women's issues, such as rape on college campuses and equal pay; used executive action on immigration policy to limit deportations of young adults who were brought to the United States as children; called attention to racial disparities in the criminal justice system; and saw the Supreme Court recognize same-sex marriage as a fundamental right.

Donald Trump was elected with racially divisive positions, such as his promises to build a wall between the United States and Mexico and deport 12 million undocumented residents. In his election-night victory speech, he emphasized the importance of representing all Americans and uniting the country. As president, Trump has tended to express polarizing opinions on civil rights issues, rather than unifying themes. He failed to condemn the attacks by White supremacists on counterprotesters in Charlottesville, Virginia, instead blaming "both sides" for the violence and saying that some of the White supremacists were "very fine people." He also said that any NFL player who knelt during the national anthem in protest of racial bias in policing was a "son of a bitch," attempted to ban immigration to the United States from several dominantly Muslim countries, said the immigrants from Africa were from "shithole countries," told four House members who are women of color to go back to the "crime infested places from which they came" (three of the four were born in the United States), and banned transgender service members from the military.

EXAMINE AFFIRMATIVE ACTION AND OTHER ONGOING CIVIL RIGHTS ISSUES

Civil rights issues today

Today, there is vigorous debate among proponents of three main perspectives on the likely direction of the civil rights movement in the twenty-first century. The first group, whose views are articulated by such scholars as Stephan Thernstrom of Harvard University and Abigail Thernstrom of the Manhattan Institute, has suggested that our nation must "move beyond race." This group argues that on many social and economic indicators the gap between Blacks and Whites has narrowed and that public opposition to race-based policies indicates the need for a new approach. The Supreme Court has largely endorsed this view by implementing a color-blind jurisprudence over a broad range of issues. The second group is represented by traditional civil rights activists and organizations such as the Congressional Black Caucus and the NAACP; it argues that the civil rights movement must continue to fight for equal opportunity by enforcing existing law and pushing for equality of outcomes through protecting and expanding affirmative action programs and other policies that address racial inequality. Black Lives Matter, while not a traditional civil rights organization because of its decentralized structure, fits into this category with its fight for racial equality in the criminal justice system. These first two groups share the goal of racial equality and integration but differ on how much progress we have made and how to make further progress. The third group does not support the goal of integration; instead, activists such as Louis Farrakhan and the Nation of Islam argue for African-American self-sufficiency and separation. They believe that African Americans can never gain equality within what they see as the repressive, White-dominated economic and political system.

Most civil rights advocates endorse the second view. They argue that it would be a mistake to conclude that the work of the civil rights movement is complete. They point to the resegregation of public schools, persistent gaps between Whites and racial minorities in health and economic status, racial profiling, hate crimes, a backlash against immigrant groups, and continuing discrimination in employment and housing. At the same time, this group rejects calls for racial separation as shortsighted and self-defeating.

The other two groups would argue that although the traditional civil rights agenda made important contributions to racial equality, further progress will require a different approach. Advocates of the color-blind approach prefer to stop making distinctions between people based on race. They want to use government policies to make sure there is no overt discrimination and to provide equal opportunity for all, and then let merit decide outcomes. The segregationists have given up on the civil rights agenda and believe that minorities can achieve success only on their own. Debates among advocates of these three views play out over a broad range of issues, several of which are outlined in the last section of this chapter.

Affirmative action or reverse discrimination

The Civil Rights Act of 1964 ensured that, at least on paper, all Americans would enjoy equality of opportunity. But even after the act was passed, Blacks continued to lag behind Whites in socioeconomic status; there was still a substantial gap between the equality of opportunity and the equality of outcomes. In an important speech at Howard University in 1965, President Johnson outlined his argument for affirmative action, saying, "This is the next and the more profound stage of the battle for civil rights. . . . We seek not just legal equity but human ability, not just equality as a right and a theory but equality as a fact and equality as a result. . . . To this end equal opportunity is essential, but not enough, not enough."[113] Later that year, Johnson attempted to move closer to equality of outcomes by issuing an executive order requiring all federal agencies and government contractors to submit written proposals to provide an equal opportunity for employment of Blacks, women, Asian Americans, and Native Americans within various job categories and to outline programs to achieve those goals. The policy was expanded under President Nixon, and throughout the 1970s and 1980s affirmative action programs grew in the private sector, higher education, and government contracting. Through such programs, employers and universities gave special opportunities to minorities and women, either to make up for past discrimination or to pursue the general goals of diversity.

Affirmative action takes many forms. The most passive type involves extra effort to recruit women and minorities for employment or college admission by placing ads in newspapers and magazines, visiting schools with diverse student populations, or sending out targeted mailings. A more active form involves including race or gender as a "plus factor" in admissions or hiring decisions. That is, in a pool of qualified candidates a minority applicant may receive an advantage over White applicants. Women generally do not receive special consideration in admissions decisions, but gender may be a "plus factor" in some employment decisions, especially in professions in which women are underrepresented, such as engineering, architecture, the building trades, and computer programming. (In fact, many selective schools have been quietly applying affirmative action for men because more highly qualified women apply than men.) The strongest form of affirmative action is the use of quotas—strict numerical targets to hire or admit a specific number of applicants from underrepresented groups.

Affirmative action has been a controversial policy. Polls indicate that minorities are much more supportive of the practice than Whites are. Many Whites view it as "preferential treatment" and "reverse discrimination." Two-thirds of Whites support affirmative action in general terms to "increase the number of Black and minority students on college campuses," but when asked specifically about race-based admissions or merit-based admissions, only 22 percent said that college admissions should "take race/ethnicity into account" while 76 percent said that admissions should be based "solely on merit" (the comparable numbers for Black respondents were 44 percent and 50 percent).[114] This backlash has spilled over into state politics. California passed Proposition 209 in 1996, which banned the consideration of "race, sex, color, ethnicity or national origin" in public employment, public education, or public contracting.[115] Nine other states have similar laws.

The Supreme Court has helped define the boundaries of this policy debate. The earliest cases concerning affirmative action in employment upheld preferential treatment and rigid quotas when the policies were necessary to make up for past discrimination. The cases involved a worker training program that set aside 50 percent of the positions for Blacks, a labor union that was required to hire enough minorities to get its non-White membership to 29.23 percent, and a state police force that was required to promote one Black officer for every White even if there was a smaller pool of Blacks who were eligible for promotion.[116] In each instance, there had been a previous pattern of discrimination and exclusion.

The Court moved in a more color-blind direction in an important reverse-discrimination employment case in 2009. In that case, 17 White firefighters and 1 Latino firefighter sued the city of New Haven, Connecticut, for throwing out the results of a test that would have been used to promote them. The city tried to ignore the results of the test because no African-American firefighters would have qualified for promotion and the city feared a "disparate impact" lawsuit. However, the Court ruled that the exam did appear to be "job related and consistent with business necessity" (as required by Section VII of the Civil Rights Act) and that unless the city could provide a "strong basis in evidence" that it would have been sued, it had to consider the results of the exam.[117]

The landmark decision for affirmative action in higher education was *Regents of the University of California v. Bakke* (1978).[118] Allan Bakke, a White student, sued when he was denied admission to medical school at the University of California, Davis, in successive years. Bakke's test scores and GPA were significantly higher than those of some minority students who were admitted under the school's affirmative action program. Under that program, 16 of the 100 slots in the entering class were reserved for minority or disadvantaged students. The Supreme Court agreed with Bakke that rigid racial quotas were unconstitutional but allowed race to be used in admissions decisions as a "plus factor" to promote diversity in the student body. This standard was largely unquestioned until 1996, when the Fifth Circuit Court of Appeals held that it was unconstitutional to consider race in law school admissions at the University of Texas.[119] In 2000, the Ninth Circuit Court of Appeals in Seattle, however, reached the opposite conclusion and ruled that race could be considered in admissions to promote educational diversity.[120]

In 2003, the Court affirmed *Bakke*, saying that the University of Michigan law school's "holistic approach," which considered race as one of the factors in the admission decision, was acceptable. However, the more rigid approach for undergraduate admissions at Michigan, which automatically gave minority students 20 of the 100 points needed to guarantee admission, was unacceptable.[121] This was the first time that a majority of the Court clearly stated that "student body diversity is a compelling state interest that can justify the use of race in university admissions."[122] In 2006, voters in Michigan passed Proposal 2, an initiative to make it illegal for state bodies to consider race in admissions and hiring decisions; this policy was upheld by the Supreme Court in 2014.[123] In 2019, voters in Washington State narrowly voted down an affirmative action referendum, 50.6–49.4 percent. This means that states will be able to decide on an individual basis whether to consider affirmative action in higher education, because the policy is neither prohibited nor required by the Constitution.

In 2008, a White student, Abigail Fisher, claimed she was a victim of reverse discrimination and sued the University of Texas at Austin. Texas had achieved a racially diverse student body by extending offers of admission to the top 10 percent of every graduating high school class in the state (in recent years, this policy was changed to the top 7 percent). This approach worked because most high schools in Texas were still segregated. In June 2016, the Court upheld Texas's affirmative action policy by a 4–3 vote.[124] Despite this ruling, documents leaked in August 2017 revealed that the Justice Department was going to "investigate, and potentially sue, colleges and universities over admissions decisions that are perceived as discriminating against White applicants."[125] For more on affirmative action in college admissions, see the Take a Stand feature.

Demonstrators protested against an allegedly discriminatory affirmative action policy at Harvard University that disadvantages Asian-American students.

Multicultural issues and immigration policy

A host of issues involving the multicultural, multiracial nature of American society will become more important as Whites cease to constitute the majority of the population by mid-century. At their cores, these issues are rooted in the fact that the United States is a nation of immigrants. Will that history continue, and if so, what shape will it take? Is our country a "melting pot," focused on the assimilation of new groups, or is it more like a "tossed salad," in which each immigrant group maintains its cultural identity but creates a new, better collective whole? Groups who favor one or the other of these conceptions of American society often clash over issues such as whether English should be our official language (31 states have such laws) and whether bilingual education should be offered in public schools. But the biggest area for debate on this topic in recent years concerns immigration reform and border security.

Following the September 11 terrorist attacks, some people saw immigration as a threat that must be curtailed. The government made it clear that it would not engage in racial profiling of Arab Americans—for example, subjecting them to stricter screening at airports—but many commentators argued that such profiling would be justified, and there was at least anecdotal evidence of an increase in discrimination against people of Middle Eastern descent. After the terrorist attacks in Paris and San Bernardino, California, in 2016, the debate in the presidential campaign shifted to a strongly anti-immigrant tone. During the campaign, Donald Trump proposed preventing all Muslims from entering the United States until the government could make sure they did not pose a terrorist

Affirmative Action in College Admissions

Since 1978, the Supreme Court has endorsed the idea of race as a "plus factor" in college admissions while rejecting the idea of strict quotas or point systems. This approach was affirmed in a 2003 case involving the University of Michigan's law school, but many Court-watchers believed that affirmative action would be struck down in the 2016 case *Fisher v. University of Texas, Austin*.[a] Instead, swing vote Justice Kennedy sided with the liberal justices, and the Court upheld the practice.

UT Austin's college admissions process has two parts. First, anyone in the top 10 percent of a Texas public high school is guaranteed admission to UT (in recent years this has been closer to the top 7 percent). Because most high schools in Texas are somewhat segregated by race, the 10 percent plan automatically creates diversity for the entering class. Seventy-five percent of in-state students are admitted via the 10 percent plan. Second, the remaining 25 percent of in-state students are admitted by a "holistic" program that evaluates their entire record and includes race as a "plus factor." It was this second part that Abigail Fisher challenged after being denied admission to UT. The legal question that the Court had to decide was whether the university's affirmative action program violated the equal protection clause of the Fourteenth Amendment and civil rights laws barring discrimination on the basis of race, or whether the program could be justified as serving a "compelling state interest" under the strict scrutiny standard.

Diversity deserves consideration. Advocates of affirmative action argue that a diverse student body promotes viewpoint diversity that is essential to learning. Having racial diversity in the student body is likely to produce more viewpoint diversity in classroom discussions than would occur with a mostly White student body. The majority opinion in the Texas case also argued that a more diverse student body leads to "the destruction of stereotypes," promotes "cross-racial understanding," and prepares students "for an increasingly diverse work force and society." Furthermore, proponents argue, the courts are not the proper place to decide these issues. Instead, as with the complex and highly charged topic of racial redistricting, the political branches of government are where these decisions should be made. The Court endorsed this position of judicial restraint in a 2014 case involving a ban on affirmative action in Michigan.[b]

The Court argued that the Texas approach was "narrowly tailored" to serve the compelling state interest of viewpoint diversity because the 10 percent plan, by itself, did not produce the desired level of diversity and would create perverse incentives. Justice Kennedy wrote, "Percentage plans encourage parents to keep their children in low-performing segregated schools, and discourage students from taking challenging classes that might lower their grade point averages."

Affirmative action is just another kind of discrimination. Opponents reply that supporters of affirmative action have not provided convincing evidence that racial diversity in colleges has any beneficial effects. They also argue that "viewpoint diversity" arguments assume that members of all racial minorities think alike, drawing a comparison to racial profiling in law enforcement. It is just as offensive, they say, that an admissions committee thinks that one Black student has the same views as another Black student as it is that a police officer may pull over a Black teenage male just because he fits a certain criminal profile.

Opponents also argue that affirmative action amounts to "reverse discrimination" and that any racial classification is harmful. Justice Alito's scathing dissent in the Texas case said, "U.T. has never provided any coherent explanation for its asserted need to discriminate on the basis of race, and . . . U.T.'s position relies on a series of unsupported and noxious racial assumptions." Alito also argued that concepts such as viewpoint diversity and "cross-cultural understanding" are "slippery" and difficult to analyze systematically.

The Texas case will not be the end of the debate concerning affirmative action in higher education. A federal appeals court ruled that Harvard University's affirmative action program did not discriminate against Asian Americans, but that decision is being appealed to the Supreme Court. If you had to rule on the Texas case, how would you have decided? Take a stand.

Students protest outside the Supreme Court in support of diversity at the University of Texas.

take a stand

1. To what extent should race be used as a "plus factor" to promote racial diversity and viewpoint diversity, if at all? Is the "top 10 percent" plan a better approach?

2. Think of your own experiences in high school and college. Has racial diversity contributed to viewpoint diversity?

When President Trump announced his original travel ban preventing individuals from select Muslim-majority countries from entering the United States, people flooded airports across the country in protest.

threat. As president he issued an executive order narrowly targeting Muslim countries that was struck down by a federal court. A second version was also struck down, but in 2018 the Supreme Court upheld the third version of the travel ban. The Court deferred to the president's ability to define national security, saying that his executive power was not undermined by his political comments about the possible intent of the travel ban.[126]

Over the past two decades, immigration has been central in many political debates. The intensity of that debate increased in 2010 when Arizona enacted an anti-immigration law that requires local law-enforcement officials to check the immigration status of a person in a "lawful stop, detention, or arrest" if there is a "reasonable suspicion" that the person is an undocumented immigrant. The law also requires immigrants to always carry papers verifying their immigration status and bans people without proper documents from seeking work in public places. Many civil rights violations occurred when local law-enforcement officials started enforcing this law. States with similar laws include South Carolina, Alabama, Utah, Georgia, and Indiana. Arizona governor Jan Brewer said, "Decades of federal inaction and misguided policy have created a dangerous and unacceptable situation, and states deserve clarity from the Court in terms of what role they have in fighting illegal immigration."[127] Opponents of the law argue that it requires illegal racial profiling and that the federal government has the sole responsibility for deciding immigration law.

In 2012, the Supreme Court struck down three of the four main provisions of the law, citing the supremacy clause of the Constitution. This decision meant that Congress, not the states, determines immigration law when the two laws conflict. The Court upheld the controversial "show me your papers" part of the law, saying that the state was simply enforcing the federal law. However, the Court indicated that the law must be applied in a race-neutral way and could be struck down if there was clear evidence of racial profiling.[128] Several months later, a federal district court judge cleared the way for implementation of the "show me your papers" law, saying that the Supreme Court wanted to see actual evidence of discrimination rather than speculation that the law could have a discriminatory effect.[129]

The immigration system is widely viewed as broken and in need of reform, but neither President Bush nor President Obama was able to get Congress to approve his proposal to provide a "path to citizenship" for undocumented immigrants. In 2019, a Pew poll showed strong support for reform, with 67 percent of those

Despite President Trump's threats of deportation, hundreds of thousands of undocumented immigrants continue to cross into the United States each year. They come seeking better economic opportunities or fleeing crime, war, or other life-threatening situations in their native country. Here, a border control agent detains migrants from Central America seeking asylum.

surveyed saying that the government should "establish a way for most immigrants in the country illegally to remain here legally." A nearly identical percentage supported "increasing security along the U.S.-Mexico border."[130] In 2015, President Obama used executive orders to implement part of his immigration policy (concerning the deportation of young adults who were brought to the United States illegally by their parents and the deportation of the parents of children who are citizens). The Supreme Court deadlocked 4–4 in a June 2016 case, upholding the lower court's ruling that struck down the executive order. More than 4 million immigrants had to await the results of the election. President Trump revoked Obama's executive order and, while Congress deadlocked on the issue, the courts allowed the program to continue for those already enrolled. President Trump also instituted a "zero tolerance" policy that led to the separation of thousands of children and parents at the border. The policy violated a federal court order and was reversed, though about 2,500 children remained in detention centers in late 2019.[131]

The debates over affirmative action, English as the country's official language, and immigration reform clearly illustrate the conflictual nature of civil rights policy. However, history has shown that when public opinion strongly supports a given application of civil rights—for example, the integration of African Americans in the South in the 1960s and, more recently, allowing gays to openly serve in the military and recognizing same-sex marriage—public policy soon reflects those views. Although it is impossible to say when there will be comprehensive immigration reform that includes a path to citizenship, it is likely to eventually happen given the trends in public opinion. However, the Trump administration's efforts to move immigration policy in the opposite direction mean that comprehensive immigration reform is probably off the table until at least 2021.

The Americans with Disabilities Act

The civil rights movement of the 1960s had far-reaching consequences beyond the initial intentions of ending racial discrimination and gaining equal rights for African Americans. One unintended consequence of that movement centered around disabled people who felt they, too, had long suffered from unequal treatment in the workplace and in society at-large. Many proponents, who became more and more vocal during the

**AP®
POLICY IN
PRACTICE**

1970s and 1980s, felt that disabled people should also have their own version of the Civil Rights Act of 1964. The Americans with Disabilities Act of 1990 (ADA) is considered a piece of legislation of that caliber and arguably a direct result of that initiative.

There are economic costs and incentives associated with giving disabled people equal access at the workplace, places of commerce, and recreational venues, to name a few of the types of establishments affected. By and large, economic factors were not a consideration in the original civil rights movement. An argument made at the time when the ADA was being debated is that there would be high costs for retrofitting existing private and government buildings and of course added costs for constructing new buildings as well. For private firms, these costs would mean lower profits and could be the tipping point for going out of business. For government agencies at the state and local levels, these costs would mean that money and other resources would be diverted from other important public goods and services. Economists call these sacrifices opportunity costs. The ADA was also used as a prime example of the unfair costs of what political scientists call unfunded mandates: federal laws that require the states to do certain things but do not provide state governments with funding to implement these policies. State and local governments have contended that the federal government should provide money for such important accommodations affecting so many American citizens. A compromise of sorts, not just related to the ADA, was finally reached with the Unfunded Mandates Reform Act of 1995, which forces the federal government to work more closely with state and local governments to identify cases of unfunded mandates, work to lower these costs, and try whenever possible to remove these types of mandates altogether.

As is apparent in the vote tallies in the Deliberation and Formulation and Enactment stages, there was overwhelming bipartisan support for passing this type of legislation on the part of Congress and by President George H. W. Bush. As with any policy, though, the best laid plans are not without their unforeseen problems, which is why the ADA Amendment of 2008 was later signed by President George W. Bush. Several Supreme Court cases had highlighted some problems with the wording of the original law that the bill's writers had not anticipated, and this amendment sought to correct these oversights.

As with any policy, even one as popular as the ADA, it has not been without its detractors. Costs continue to be a major part of the criticism, and President Trump made an attempt with the failed ADA Education and Reform Act of 2017 to rein in the number of lawsuits, many of which the critics thought were frivolous, lodged against employers and stores who were not ADA compliant. Although he was not successful in getting this legislation passed, it does not mean that future presidents and Congresses might not try again, particularly in economic downturns when reducing costs might take priority over expensive accommodations for a minority of the U.S. population.

Policy Stages
1. Problem Recognition
   - The overarching consensus was that people with disabilities—including, but not limited to, blindness, deafness, and physical and mental impairment from birth defects, chronic diseases, or accidents—should no longer be discriminated against.
   - The 1960s civil rights movement was a major influence.
   - Many believed a law should be passed similar to the Civil Rights Act (1964), which outlawed discrimination based on race, religion, ethnicity, and gender.
   - Prior to the bill's passing in 1990, over 43 million Americans had some type of physical or mental disability.
   - Historically, disabled people have had very few legal options at their disposal when faced with possible discrimination.

2. Agenda Setting
   - The Rehabilitation Act (1973) prohibited people with disabilities from being discriminated against in federal jobs or in jobs or programs that were federally funded.
   - Prominent proponents of rights for the disabled include the following:
     - Justin Dart, "Godfather of the ADA," was a multimillionaire businessman and lifelong advocate who served in many different lobbying groups and governmental agencies that dealt with assisting the disabled.
     - Patrisha Wright, "the General," is co-founder of the Disability Rights Education and Defense Fund and is considered the major lobbyist behind the ADA.
   - The National Council on Disability is an independent federal agency established in 1978.
     - It was originally called the National Council on the Handicapped.
     - In 1986, it published a report, *Toward Independence*, which included a legal blueprint for the legislation later submitted to Congress.
   - Americans Disabled for Attendant Programs Today (ADAPT) is a grassroots organization established in 1983.
     - It was originally called Americans Disabled for Accessible Public Transit.
     - It protested the inaccessibility of buses by blocking them with wheelchairs and then having someone crawl up the steps.
   - The National Council of Disabilities recommended and drafted the first version of the ADA in 1986.

3. Deliberation and Formulation
   - The ADA was originally introduced in the 100th Congress (1987–1989) but very late in the session, and it was overshadowed by the 1988 presidential campaign.
   - It was introduced in the Senate by Tom Harkin (D-IA) on May 9, 1989.
   - The Senate passed its version of the bill on September 7, 1989: **76 YEAs**: 44 Democrats, 32 Republicans, 0 others; **8 NAYs**: 0 Democrats, 8 Republicans, 0 others; **16 Not Voting**: 11 Democrats, 5 Republicans, 0 others.
   - It was introduced in the House of Representatives by Anthony Coelho (D-CA) on May 9, 1989.
   - Several organizations opposed the law because of the increased costs it would cause.
     - The National Association of Evangelicals testified that religious liberty would be impeded by the higher costs.
     - Greyhound Lines Inc. would have to spend a significant amount of money to retrofit its bus fleet.
     - Telephone companies cited an ongoing increase in costs to accommodate the deaf and hard of hearing.
     - State and local governments would have to spend a lot of money to update their public transport systems.
     - The United States Chamber of Commerce spoke on behalf of many businesses.
   - Several amendments were defeated.
     - Victims of workplace discrimination based on a disability would have had a more difficult time getting monetary compensation.
     - Commuter trains would not have had to make all cars accessible to the disabled—only one car per run.
     - Smaller cities would not have had to modernize newer vehicles if they offered alternative means of transportation.

- Several amendments were successfully added.
  - Owners could move food handlers to other jobs if they had communicable diseases, such as AIDS.
  - Depending on their size, smaller businesses would have more time—six months to a year—to be compliant.
- "Capitol Crawl" on March 12, 1990, convinced some legislators to vote in favor of the bill.
  - Many physically disabled people crawled up the 100 Capitol steps at the end of a rally staged to protest the delay of the bill's passage.
- The House of Representatives passed its version of the bill on May 22, 1990: **403 YEAs**: 248 Democrats, 155 Republicans, 0 others; **20 NAYs**: 3 Democrats, 17 Republicans, 0 others; **9 Not Voting**: 5 Democrats, 4 Republicans, 0 others.

4. Enactment
   - The House passed a compromise bill on July 12, 1990: **377 YEAs**: 232 Democrats, 145 Republicans, 0 others; **28 NAYs**: 5 Democrats, 23 Republicans, 0 others; **27 Not Voting**: 19 Democrats, 8 Republicans, 0 others.
   - The Senate passed a compromise bill on July 13, 1990: **91 YEAs**: 54 Democrats, 37 Republicans, 0 others; **6 NAYs**: 0 Democrats, 6 Republicans, 0 others; **3 Not Voting**: 1 Democrat, 2 Republicans, 0 others.
   - The ADA was signed into law by President George H. W. Bush on July 26, 1990.

5. Implementation
   - **Title I: Employment**
     - Qualified persons or persons who need some accommodations to perform their tasks will not be discriminated against in any aspect of the employment process from hiring, doing their job, and being released from employment.
   - **Title II: Public Services**
     - State and local governments or any of their subsidiaries, such as school districts, public transportation, or public housing, cannot discriminate against disabled people.
   - **Title III: Public Accommodations and Services Operated by Private Entities**
     - This applies to almost any type of business that provides goods or services including, but not limited to, hotels, laundromats, theaters, clothing stores, supermarkets, zoos, schools, exercise facilities, and doctors' offices.
   - **Title IV: Telecommunications**
     - These accommodations are directed specifically at deaf people using telephones (telecommunications device for the deaf, or TDD) and watching television (closed captioning, or CC).
   - **Title V: Miscellaneous Provisions**
     - Some historic buildings and sites are exempt if it would be unreasonable for them to make the necessary accommodations.
     - States cannot use the Eleventh Amendment to shield themselves from lawsuits if they are found to be in violation of provisions of the law.
     - This law does not supersede any existing laws which set higher standards for provisions, accommodations, or penalties.
     - Mental conditions that might be construed as disabilities but that society deems to be negative (such as compulsive gambling, drug addiction, pedophilia, kleptomania, and pyromania), are not covered under this law.

6. Evaluation
   - Costs for businesses increased, putting small businesses in particular at risk.
   - Small business owners, especially, found it difficult to understand and to comply with all of the regulations.
   - ADA regulations are generally unfunded mandates.
   - *Board of Trustees of the University of Alabama v. Garrett* (2001)

- The ADA was seen as a violation of states' sovereign immunity (based on the Eleventh Amendment).
- State employees could not sue their employers due to the Eleventh Amendment even though the law specifically states that this amendment does not apply.
  - *Access Now v. Southwest Airlines* (2002)
    - Cyberspace is not covered by the ADA legislation, which was drafted before the proliferation of the Internet.
- Employment had decreased for disabled workers due to employers' fears of higher costs according to some economists, although others disagree.
- According to some studies, wages for disabled workers had not decreased, but they also have not increased and are still well below the wage level of non-disabled workers in comparable jobs.
- Some opponents believe that it is too easy to file frivolous lawsuits.

7. Possible Modifications, Expansion, or Termination of Policy
- The ADA Amendment
  - It was signed by President George W. Bush on September 25, 2008.
  - It broadened the definition of what constitutes a disability to address and essentially to overturn problems raised by two unfavorable Supreme Court cases:
    - *Sutton v. United Air Lines, Inc.* (1999)
      - If one's disability is corrected (in this case, glasses for severe myopia), then it is no longer considered a disability.
      - One's disability does not necessarily exclude one from pursuing other jobs to which one is better suited.
    - *Toyota Motor Manufacturing, Kentucky, Inc. v. Williams* (2002)
      - A disability has to be permanent and not temporary, such as carpal tunnel syndrome, as in this case.
      - This case provided the main impetus for this amendment.
      - It provided an extensive (though not exhaustive) list of specific examples of "major life activities" that might possibly be impaired to be considered a disability.
      - The law does not apply to past cases and possible infractions.
- The ADA Education and Reform Act of 2017
  - Compliance through Education: This section of the act created a program that state and local governments could use to inform property owners how they can comply with the rules laid out in the ADA and how mediators can be trained to deal with possible infractions.
  - Notice and Cure Period: This provision slowed down the process for filing lawsuits to give more time to allow for compliance and to provide mediation before a potential lawsuit goes through the court system.
  - The act did not become a law.

Questions for Discussion

1. Why might the federal government be justified in using unfunded mandates?
2. Should the government—whether local, state, or federal—subsidize businesses to help them pay the costs associated with complying with the ADA? Explain your answer.
3. The Eleventh Amendment stipulates that states cannot be sued without their permission. Do you agree with the Supreme Court's ruling in *Board of Trustees of the University of Alabama v. Garrett* (2001) that state employees cannot sue their employers? Why or why not?

Unpacking the Conflict

Considering all that we've discussed in this chapter, let's apply what we know about how civil rights work to the examples of profiling introduced at the beginning of this chapter. Is it ever acceptable to treat people differently based on the color of their skin, their ethnic status, their gender, or their sexual orientation, in a situation of racial profiling or otherwise?

Enforcing civil rights means providing equal protection of the law to individuals and groups that are discriminated against, which may include noncitizens and illegal immigrants. But figuring out exactly when an individual's civil rights have been violated can be tricky. When does a routine traffic stop by a police officer turn into racial profiling?

To help figure that out, we now can answer the questions about possible civil rights violations that introduced this chapter:

- Scenario 1: On the one hand, the African-American teenagers who were pulled over by the police may or may not have had their civil rights violated, depending on the laws in their state. In Massachusetts, for example, it is prohibited to consider the "race, gender, national or ethnic origin of members of the public in deciding to detain a person or stop a motor vehicle" except in "suspect specific incidents."[132] On the other hand, in the scenario in which the police pulled over White teenagers, the traffic stop would have been acceptable as long as there had been "probable cause" to justify the stop.

- Scenario 2: The Asian-American woman who did not get the job could certainly talk to a lawyer about filing a "disparate impact" discrimination suit. Under the 1991 Civil Rights Act, the employer would have the burden of proof to show that she was not a victim of the good ol' boy network.

- Scenario 3: The gay couple who could not rent the apartment because of their sexual orientation might have a basis for a civil rights lawsuit based on the Fourteenth Amendment. But this would depend on where they lived, given that there is no federal protection against discrimination against gay men and lesbians (and the Supreme Court has not applied the Fourteenth Amendment in this context).

- Scenario 4: Court decisions concerning affirmative action at the University of Michigan and the University of Texas show that the White student who was not admitted to the university of his choice would just have to take his lumps, as long as the affirmative action program considered race as a general "plus factor" rather than assigning more or fewer points for it (and the practice was allowed by his state).

This review of civil rights in the United States has highlighted only some of the most important issues, but a significant agenda remains. The civil rights movement will continue to use the multiple avenues of the legislative, executive, and judicial branches to secure equal rights for all Americans. Although this process may take many years, history demonstrates that when public opinion becomes more supportive of diversity and stronger civil rights, our political institutions support the views of the people.

"What's Your Take?"

Should distinctions between people based on race, ethnic status, gender, or sexual orientation be uniformly prohibited? **Or are they OK** under some circumstances?

AP® STUDY GUIDE

Summary

Civil rights are protections from discrimination, based on characteristics such as race, national origin, religion, and sex, both by the government and by individuals and are rooted in laws and the equal protection clause of the Fourteenth Amendment. The concept of equality has evolved over time with the passage of key laws, such as the Civil Rights Act of 1964, Title IX of the Education Amendments, and the Voting Rights Act (VRA) of 1965, and decisions made by the Supreme Court, such as *Brown v. Board of Education* (1954). These laws and decisions have provided protections for the LGBTQ community, women, African Americans, Native Americans, Asian Americans, and Latinos. Despite our attempts to live in a color-blind society, awareness of race still influences many people's opinions and behavior.

Beyond the unequal treatment of racial minorities, women, and LGBTQ individuals, inequalities in political, social, and economic conditions also persist. Whites are able to participate in politics at a higher rate, enjoy a better standard of living, and avoid prejudice in the criminal justice system. The equal protection clause of the Fourteenth Amendment can support movements to help address these inequalities, as seen in Martin Luther King Jr.'s "Letter from Birmingham Jail" and the civil rights movement of the 1960s as well as the National Organization for Women (NOW), the women's rights movement, and the pro-life (anti-abortion) movement.

Depending on the political context, each branch of government has played a role in the expansion of civil rights. Moreover, federalism has played a role in this process. Although the state governments often lagged behind the federal government in African-American civil rights, they have been on the forefront in protecting the rights of gays and lesbians. At times the Supreme Court has allowed states to restrict the civil rights of minority groups and at other times the Court has provided protection to those groups.

The public is divided on the appropriateness of civil rights policies, with some groups preferring a "color-blind" approach and some groups preferring a "color-conscious" approach. Furthermore, the debates over issues such as affirmative action, immigration reform, and establishing English as the official language in many states indicate the level of conflict over civil rights policy. Nonetheless, when public opinion does strongly support the application of civil rights in a particular arena, policy makers generally respond to these views.

Key Terms

affirmative action (p. 401)

Brown v. Board of Education (p. 376)

civil rights (p. 372)

Civil Rights Act of 1964 (p. 397)

de facto (p. 396)

de jure (p. 396)

disenfranchised (p. 375)

disparate impact standard (p. 397)

grandfather clause (p. 375)

Jim Crow laws (p. 375)

"Letter from Birmingham Jail" (p. 391)

Plessy v. Ferguson (p. 375)

protectionism (p. 379)

rational basis test (p. 400)

"separate but equal" doctrine (p. 375)

Shaw v. Reno (p. 149)

substantive due process doctrine (p. 405)

Title IX of the Education Amendments (p. 408)

Voting Rights Act (VRA) of 1965 (p. 384)

Enduring Understandings

PRD-1: "The Fourteenth Amendment's equal protection clause as well as other constitutional provisions have often been used to support the advancement of equality." (AP® U.S. Government and Politics Course and Exam Description)

PMI-3: "Public policy promoting civil rights is influenced by citizen-state interactions and constitutional interpretation over time." (AP® U.S. Government and Politics Course and Exam Description)

CON-6: "The Court's interpretation of the U.S. Constitution is influenced by the composition of the Court and citizen-state interactions. At times, it has restricted minority rights and, at others, protected them." (AP® U.S. Government and Politics Course and Exam Description)

Multiple-Choice Questions (Arranged by Topic)

Topic 3.10: Social Movements and Equal Protection (PRD-1)

1. **Which of the following is an accurate comparison of civil liberties and civil rights?**

	Civil Liberties	Civil Rights
(A)	*Brown v. Board of Education* (1954)	rooted in the equal protection clause of the Fourteenth Amendment
(B)	rooted in the due process clause of the Fourteenth Amendment	*Gideon v. Wainwright* (1963)
(C)	primarily restrict what the government can do to individuals	protect individuals from discrimination by other people
(D)	concern the issue of equality	concern the issue of freedom

2. **Which of the following best describes the central argument in Martin Luther King Jr.'s "Letter from Birmingham Jail"?**

   (A) When rights are consistently denied, a cause should be pressed in the courts and in negotiations among local leaders, not in the streets.

   (B) Everyone has an obligation to follow just laws but an equal obligation to break unjust laws.

   (C) Even with a compelling state interest for children to attend school, that interest does not supersede an individual's free exercise rights.

   (D) Congress has the power and responsibility to prevent speech that approaches creating a clear and present danger.

Topic 3.11: Government Responses to Social Movements (PMI-3)

3. **Which of the following best describes the decision in *Brown v. Board of Education* (1954)?**

   (A) Race-based school segregation violates the Fourteenth Amendment's equal protection clause.

   (B) Race-based school segregation violates the Fourteenth Amendment's due process clause.

   (C) Using race-based quotas for college admission violates the Fourteenth Amendment's equal protection clause.

   (D) Using race-based quotas for college admission violates the Fourteenth Amendment's due process clause.

Questions 4–5 refer to the map.

Lifetime Wage Gap for Women as Compared to Men

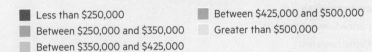

Lifetime wage gap is

■ Less than $250,000

■ Between $250,000 and $350,000

■ Between $350,000 and $425,000

■ Between $425,000 and $500,000

□ Greater than $500,000

Source: National Women's Law Center, "Lifetime Wage Gap Losses for Women: 2019 State Rankings," based on U.S. Census 2019 American Community Survey data, March 2019, https://nwlc-ciw49tixgw5lbab.stackpathdns.com/wp-content/uploads/2019/03/Women-Lifetime-Losses-State-byState-2019.pdf (accessed 3/22/20).

4. **Based on the information in the map, which of the following is true about the lifetime wage gap between men and women?**

    (A) California (CA) and Florida (FL) have the largest wage gap of any state.

    (B) The majority of states have a gap of less than $250,000.

    (C) A lifetime wage gap of greater than $500,000 is more common than one less than $250,000.

    (D) States with the highest wage gaps also tend to have the highest rates of unemployment.

5. **Which of the following laws passed by Congress best relates to the topic of the map?**

    (A) the Kansas-Nebraska Act of 1854

    (B) the Voting Rights Act (VRA) of 1965

    (C) Title IX of the Education Amendments of 1972

    (D) the Defense of Marriage Act (DOMA) of 1996

Topic 3.12: Balancing Majority and Minority Rights (CON-6)

6. **The Supreme Court's decisions in *Plessy v. Ferguson* (1896) and *Brown v. Board of Education* (1954) best reflect which of the following?**

    (A) The Court has consistently upheld the civil rights of minority groups.

    (B) The Court continues to uphold congressional law that limits the civil rights of minority groups.

    (C) The "separate but equal" doctrine is the current standard used by the Court to judge cases related to minority rights.

    (D) At times the Court has allowed the restriction of minority rights and at other times has protected those rights.

7. **Which of the following best describes the effect of state laws, passed using the "separate but equal" doctrine for support, that restricted African-American access to the same establishments (such as restaurants, hotels, and schools) that the majority White population had access to?**

   (A) de jure segregation

   (B) de facto segregation

   (C) the intermediate scrutiny test

   (D) the rational basis test

8. **Which of the following decisions of the Supreme Court upheld the rights of the majority by using the equal protection clause to prohibit redistricting where race was the predominant factor in drawing district lines?**

   (A) *Reed v. Reed* (1971)

   (B) *Roe v. Wade* (1973)

   (C) *Shaw v. Reno* (1993)

   (D) *Gratz v. Bollinger* (2003)

Topic 3.13: Affirmative Action (CON-6)

Questions 9–10 refer to the excerpt.

Racial and ethnic classifications of any sort are inherently suspect and call for the most exacting judicial scrutiny. While the goal of achieving a diverse student body is sufficiently compelling to justify consideration of race in admissions decisions under some circumstances, petitioner's special admissions program, which forecloses consideration to persons like respondent, is unnecessary to the achievement of this compelling goal, and therefore invalid under the Equal Protection Clause.[a]

—Majority Decision by Justice Lewis F. Powell Jr. in *Regents of the University of California v. Bakke* (1978)

9. **Which of the following best describes the opinion of Justice Powell concerning the college admission process?**

   (A) Race cannot play a role.

   (B) Race can be used as a factor.

   (C) Gender cannot play a role.

   (D) Gender can be used as a factor.

10. **Which of the following best describes a viewpoint that disagrees with Justice Powell and that sees the Constitution as color blind?**

    (A) The gap between Blacks and Whites has narrowed.

    (B) The civil rights movement needs to continue to fight for equal opportunity.

    (C) Equality of outcomes is important.

    (D) A diverse student body prepares students for an increasingly diverse workforce.

Free-Response Questions

Quantitative Analysis

Discrimination Cases Filed with the Equal Employment Opportunity Commission, 2019

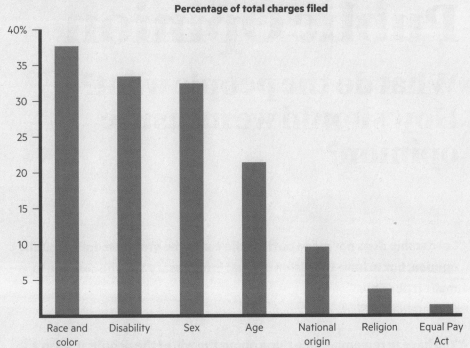

Percentage of total charges filed

Note: Percentages do not sum to 100 because complaints may be filed in more than one category.
Source: U.S. Equal Employment Opportunity Commission, "Charge Statistics (Charges Filed with EEOC), FY 1997 through FY 2019," www.eeoc.gov/statistics/charge-statistics-charges-filed-eeoc-fy-1997-through-fy-2019 (accessed 3/22/20).

Use the bar graph to answer the questions.

(A) Identify the percentage of total charges filed that involved sex discrimination.

(B) Describe a difference between the charges filed with the Equal Employment Opportunity Commission (EEOC) by religion and sex, as illustrated in the bar graph.

(C) Explain a possible limitation of the data in the bar graph.

(D) Explain how the data in the graph might be used to support Congress's continued funding of Title IX of the Education Amendments.

Argument Essay

Develop an argument about which branch of government best provides civil rights protections for individuals or groups.

Use at least one piece of evidence from one of the following foundational documents:

- Article I of the U.S. Constitution
- Amendments to the U.S. Constitution
- "Letter from Birmingham Jail"

In your response, you should do the following:

✓ Respond to the prompt with a defensible claim or thesis that establishes a line of reasoning.

✓ Support your claim with at least *two* pieces of specific and relevant evidence.

- One piece of evidence must come from one of the foundational documents listed above.
- A second piece of evidence can come from any other foundational document not used as your first piece of evidence, or it may be from your knowledge of course concepts.

✓ Use reasoning to explain why your evidence supports your claim or thesis.

✓ Respond to an opposing or alternative perspective using refutation, concession, or rebuttal.

10

Public Opinion

What do the people want? How should we measure opinion?

 "Leadership does not mean putting the ear to the ground to follow public opinion, but to have the vision of what is necessary and the courage to make it possible."[1]

Representative Shirley Chisholm

"You have to remember one thing about the will of the people: it wasn't that long ago that we were swept away by the Macarena."[2]

Jon Stewart, comedian

One of the foundations of democracy is the belief that public opinion matters: while in office, elected officials act in accordance with their constituents' demands or else face the possibility of being defeated in the next election. Every election season, candidates, political parties, journalists, and political scientists take thousands of polls in an attempt to determine who is likely to vote, who they are planning to vote for, and what sorts of arguments, slogans, and platforms might change their minds.

According to political scientist V. O. Key, basing policy and election strategy on public opinion makes sense because "[i]n the large, the electorate behaves about as rationally and responsibly as we should expect, given the clarity and the alternatives presented to it and the character of the information available to it."[3] The expectation is that citizens' evaluations of what government is, their ideas of what they would like done differently, and their thoughts about what they like and don't like more broadly all have some basis in reality. The only way to assess whether government follows the wishes of the people is to have some idea of what people really want—to actually develop surveys, measure public opinion, and compare it to the policy choices made in Washington.

However, a look at the results of some mass surveys might lead you to comedian and political commentator Jon Stewart's concern that public opinion is fickle and only loosely connected to reality. Even as Republicans doubted President Obama's

Significant percentages of Americans hold politically consequential beliefs that are factually untrue. For example, even after Barack Obama had been president for eight years and released copies of his birth certificate showing he was born in Hawaii, large numbers of Republicans believed that he was not a U.S. citizen and therefore not eligible to be president. Can we trust public opinion?

CHAPTER GOALS

Define *public opinion* and explain why it matters in American politics. pages 430–432

Explain how people form political attitudes and opinions. pages 433–441

Describe basic survey methods and potential issues affecting accuracy. pages 442–451

Present findings on what Americans think about government and why it matters. pages 451–459

citizenship,[4] a significant percentage of Democrats believed that the government had advance knowledge of the attacks on September 11, 2001. (Needless to say, both claims are false.[5]) And while most Americans would agree with the late Representative Shirley Chisholm that politicians should not blindly respond to public opinion, the persistence of blatantly false beliefs about Obama's citizenship and the September 11 attacks raises questions about whether public opinion is based in reality at all.

Before we blame Americans for believing in conspiracy theories—or take pollsters to task for mismeasuring public opinion—we need to determine how opinions are formed and how they are expressed. What does it mean when someone reveals an opinion, such as support for a conspiracy theory, a desire for change in some policy, or support for a president? Answering this question requires an understanding of how opinions are formed and what goes into them. We also need to determine whether opinions are real, in the sense that they are considered judgments that shape behavior, and what problems arise when we ask people what they think about politics. Do Americans really hold the bizarre beliefs that are sometimes expressed in polling results? Can we take polls seriously, if they produce results like these? Where does public opinion come from? Can politicians trust public opinion as a guide to what Americans want—and can we use opinions to measure the quality of American democracy?

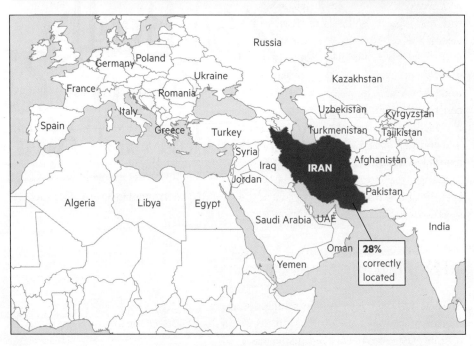

Are Americans poorly informed about political topics? During the height of America's confrontation with Iran in January 2020, only 28 percent of survey respondents could correctly locate Iran on an unlabeled map of the Middle East.[6]

★

DEFINE *PUBLIC OPINION* AND EXPLAIN WHY IT MATTERS IN AMERICAN POLITICS

public opinion
Citizens' views on politics and government actions.

What is public opinion?

Public opinion describes what the population thinks about politics and government— what government should be doing, evaluations of what government *is* doing, and judgments about elected officials and others who participate in the political process, as well as the wider set of beliefs that shape these opinions.

Public opinion matters for three reasons. First, citizens' political actions—including voting, contributing to campaigns, writing letters to senators, and other kinds of activism—are driven by their opinions.[7] For example, as we discuss in more detail in Chapter 11, party identification shapes voting decisions. A voter who thinks of himself or herself as a Democrat is more likely to vote for Democratic candidates than a voter

Politicians read public-opinion polls closely to gauge whether their behavior will anger or please constituents. Few politicians always follow survey results—but virtually none would agree with Calvin's father that polls should be ignored entirely.

who identifies as a Republican.[8] Therefore, if we want to understand an individual's behavior or analyze broader political outcomes, such as who wins an election or the fate of a legislative proposal, we need good data on public opinion.

Second, examining public opinion helps explain the behavior of candidates, political parties, and other political actors. Later chapters (particularly Chapters 12 and 13) show a strong link between citizens' opinions and candidates' campaign strategies and their actions in office. Politicians look to public opinion to determine what citizens want them to do and how satisfied citizens are with their behavior in office. For example, in Chapter 4 we saw how congressional representatives are reluctant to cast votes that are inconsistent with their constituents' preferences (particularly those who share the representative's party identification), especially on issues that constituents consider important. Therefore, to explain a legislator's votes, you need to begin with some measurement of his or her constituents' opinions.

Third, because public opinion is a key to understanding what motivates both citizens and political officials, it can shed light on the reasons for specific policy outcomes. For example, changes in the policy mood—the public's demand for new policies—are linked to changes in government spending.[9] When people want government to do more, spending increases more rapidly; when people want government to do less, spending goes down (or increases more slowly).

> **Whoever can change public opinion can change the government.**
>
> **—President Abraham Lincoln**

Different kinds of opinion

Modern theories of public opinion distinguish between two types of opinions: opinions that are preformed and opinions that are formed on the spot as needed. The first kind of opinions are broad expressions, such as how a person thinks about politics, what a citizen wants from government, or principles that apply across a range of issues. These kinds of beliefs typically form early in life and remain stable over time. Some of these beliefs are obviously political, such as party identification, **liberal or conservative ideology**, and judgments about society's responsibility to those in need. Liberal or conservative ideology is a good example of a stable opinion: the best way to predict an American's ideology at age 40 is to assume it will match his or her ideology at age 20. The same is true for party identification.

The most important thing to understand about public opinion is that although ideology and party identification are largely consistent over time, these particular kinds of opinions are exceptions to the rule.[10] The average person does not maintain a set of fully formed opinions on all political topics, such as evaluations of all the candidates for state or local office or assessments of the entire range of government programs. Instead, most Americans' political judgments are **latent opinions**: they are constructed only as needed, such as when answering a survey question or deciding on Election Day how to vote. For example, when most people are asked about the oppression of the Rohingya people in Myanmar, they probably do not have a specific

liberal or conservative ideology
A way of describing political beliefs in terms of a position on the spectrum running from liberal to moderate to conservative.

latent opinion
An opinion formed on the spot, when it is needed (as distinct from a deeply held opinion that is stable over time).

A person's ideological perspective is relatively stable over time. People who subscribe to a conservative ideology generally support small government and decreased spending.

Images of confrontation between pro–gun control and anti–gun control protesters may conceal the more nuanced considerations that underlie most Americans' opinions about the issue.

response in mind simply because they have not thought much about the question. They might have, at best, some vague ideas about the situation and what should be done about it. Their opinions become concrete only when they are asked about them.

People who follow politics closely have more preformed opinions than the average American, whose interest in politics is relatively low. But very few people are so well informed that they have ready opinions on a wide range of political and policy questions. Moreover, even when people do form opinions in advance, they may not remember every factor that influenced their opinions. Thus, an individual may identify as a liberal or a conservative or as a supporter of a particular party but may be unable to explain the reasons behind these ideological leanings.[11]

Opinions also vary in intensity. For example, one individual might strongly favor policies that allow handgun ownership and open carry in public, while another might oppose both policies but with less intensity. Intensity matters because it shapes whether and how people act on their opinions. The strongly pro-gun individual would be more likely to consider a candidate's gun rights policy when deciding how to vote, while the individual who opposes gun ownership (but less intensely) would likely base his or her vote on other issues. Variation in intensity is one reason why government policies sometimes reflect minority opinions. In the case of gun rights, members of Congress are well aware of polls showing that a majority of people support restrictions on gun ownership. However, polls also show that most supporters of restrictions do not feel strongly about this issue, while people who oppose restrictions are more likely to be intense in their opposition. Thus, when responding to public opinion about gun control, members of Congress reflect the intense minority opinion, not the weaker opinions held by the majority.

"Why Should I Care?"

In a democracy, elected officials stay in office by keeping their constituents happy. As a result, knowing what public opinion looks like—what citizens believe, what they want government to do—helps us understand the choices elected officials make. New policy initiatives such as stricter gun control laws are unlikely to be enacted in the absence of strong, sustained public support. Conversely, even controversial proposals such as Obamacare can be enacted over strong opposition, as long as there are enough enthusiastic supporters. In both ways, public opinion both motivates and constrains elected officials.

Where do opinions come from?

This section describes the sources that people draw from to inform their opinions, and the ways that these different sources interact to determine both individual opinions and collective public opinions. Some opinions are influenced by early life experiences, such as exposure to the beliefs of parents, relatives, or teachers; others result from later life events or from informal conversations with friends. Politicians also play a critical role in the opinion-formation process.

Socialization: families, communities, and networks

Theories of **political socialization** show that children develop a liberal or conservative ideology; a level of trust in others; their own class, racial, and ethnic identity; and other political opinions based on what they learn from their parents.[12] For example, one of the best predictors of a college student's party identification is the party ID of his or her parents. Opinions formed through socialization are not necessarily permanent; in fact, people often respond to events by modifying their opinions, even those developed early in life. Thus, an individual who originally identified as a Democrat because her parents were Democrats might move away from the party later in life because she did not like the party's candidates, because she thought Democrats did a poor job running the country, or because she disagreed with the party's platform. Even so, for many people, ideas learned during childhood continue to shape their political opinions throughout their lives.[13]

Beyond these influences, research finds broader aspects of socialization that shape political opinions. People are socialized by their communities, the people they interact with while growing up, such as neighbors, teachers, clergy, and others.[14] Support for democracy as a system of government and for American political institutions is higher for individuals who take a civics class in high school.[15] Growing up in a homogeneous community, one where many people share the same cultural, ethnic, or political beliefs, increases adults' sense of civic duty—their belief that voting or other forms of political participation are important social obligations.[16] Volunteering in community organizations as a child also shapes political beliefs and participation in later life.[17] Engaging in political activity as a teenager, such as volunteering in a presidential campaign, generates higher levels of political interest as an adult; it also strengthens the belief that people should care about politics and participate in political activities.[18]

Individuals' opinions are also shaped by their network: the people they interact with on a regular basis. For many people, these interactions are an important source of information about political events as well as how these events should be interpreted. Put another way, you might not think that meeting for coffee with a friend would affect your opinions about climate change, but suppose during the conversation your friend mentioned how much hotter this year had been compared to last year. While such casual conversations are unlikely to have a permanent impact, they might well influence your thinking in the short run—for example, if a week after having coffee, you have to decide how to vote in an election where climate change is an issue.

political socialization
The process by which an individual's political opinions are shaped by other people and the surrounding culture.

Events

Although socialization often influences individuals' fairly stable core beliefs, this does not mean that these beliefs or opinions are fixed. All kinds of events—from everyday interactions to traumatic, life-changing disasters—can capture people's attention and force them to revise their understanding of politics and the role of government.

Some events that shape beliefs are specific, individual experiences. For example, individuals' support for same-sex marriage is strongly influenced by the number of people they know who are gay or lesbian.[19] Major national or world events may also shape beliefs. For example, support for restrictions on gun ownership—such as background checks, bans on certain weapons, or confiscation of weapons from individuals with mental health issues—typically increases after a mass shooting event (although it generally returns to prior levels after a few weeks or months). And political scientists Bethany Albertson and Shana Kushner Gadarian show that feelings of anxiety generated by events (such as the COVID-19 pandemic) can also influence opinion formation by de-emphasizing considerations like partisanship and emphasizing others, such as the opinions of political elites.

Some events have a greater impact on public opinion than others, and some people are more likely than others to change their views. Political scientist John Zaller has shown that opinion changes generated by an event or some other new information are more likely when an individual is unfamiliar with the event or information yet considers it to be important. In such cases, the individual does not have a set of preexisting principles or other considerations with which to interpret the event or information. People who do not have strong beliefs are also more likely to change their opinions than are people who hold strong opinions.[20]

Group identity

In the United States, opinions on many issues are correlated with the state or region where a person grew up or lives. For example, until the 1970s relatively few native White southerners identified with the Republican Party.[21] Even today, native White southerners tend to have different attitudes (such as less support for affirmative action) compared to similar people from other regions of the country.[22] People who live in the same area might have common beliefs because they experienced the same historical events at similar points in their lives or learned political viewpoints from one another. Political scientist Katherine Cramer has shown that rural resentment in contemporary American politics stems from the belief that elected officials at the state and national levels do not share the values held by rural residents and will thus shortchange rural communities in the policy process.

In some cases, group identity is a function of age. Changes in attitudes about same-sex marriage over the last decade illustrate this phenomenon (see Figure 10.1). The figure shows that overall support for allowing gay and lesbian couples to marry (or allowing civil unions) has more than doubled in the last 16 years. Moreover, while opinions have shifted in all age cohorts, younger Americans are much more likely to express support than are older Americans—in part because they are much more likely to know someone who is gay or lesbian and in part because they are likely to have other characteristics that predispose them to favor same-sex marriage, such as not being regular churchgoers.

Individuals also may rely on others who "look like" them as a source of opinions. Political scientists Donald Green, Bradley Palmquist, and Eric Schickler, for example, argue that group identities shape partisanship: when people are trying to decide between being a Republican or a Democrat, they think about which demographic groups are associated with each party and pick the party that has more members from the groups they identify with.[23]

Attitudes about Same-Sex Marriage

FIGURE
10.1

Over the last 16 years, support for same-sex marriage has grown. What do these graphs tell us about the influence of group identity on public opinion? Is support for same-sex marriage likely to increase or decrease in the future? Why?

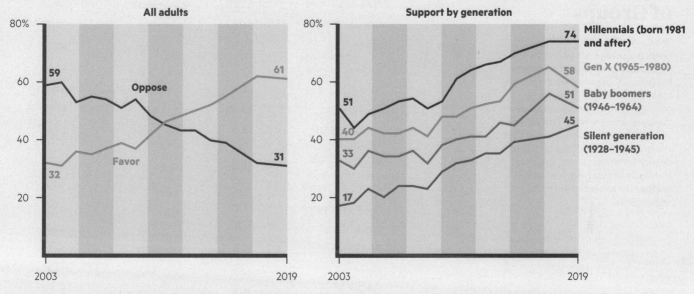

All adults

80%
60 59
Oppose 61
40 Favor 31
32
20

2003 2019

Support by generation

80%
74 Millennials (born 1981 and after)
60 58 Gen X (1965–1980)
51 51 Baby boomers (1946–1964)
40 40 45 Silent generation (1928–1945)
33
20 17

2003 2019

Source: Pew Research Center, "Majority of Public Favors Same-Sex Marriage, but Divisions Persist," May 14, 2019, www.people-press.org/2019/05/14/majority-of-public-favors-same-sex-marriage-but-divisions-persist/ (accessed 12/30/19).

It is important to examine group variations in public opinion because candidates and political consultants often formulate their campaign strategies in terms of groups. For example, analyses of the three previous presidential elections show that the electoral strategies of Democratic candidates are shaped by the goal of attracting support from young Americans, African Americans, Latinos, and women. In contrast, Republican presidential candidates targeted regular churchgoers, as well as older voters and people living in rural areas.

Although events such as wars, economic upheavals, and major policy changes certainly influence public opinion, research shows that most Americans acquire some political opinions early in life from parents, friends, teachers, and others in their community.

TABLE
10.1

The Importance of Groups

The General Social Survey (GSS) has been conducted since 1972 to assess the opinions of Americans on certain key issues. Those who take the surveys are asked to indicate if they agree or disagree with statements such as those shown in the table. The percentages indicate those who agree with the statements. Group differences based on such factors as gender, age, race, and family income have been shown to affect the answers given by the respondents.

Source: 2018 data from General Social Survey 1972–2018, Cumulative Datafile, Survey Documentation and Analysis (SDA) at UC Berkeley, http://sda.berkeley.edu (accessed 12/30/19).

		"Favor preferences in hiring Blacks" (percentage who strongly support or support)	"Abortions OK if woman wants one for any reason" (percentage who agree)	"OK to allow anti-American Muslim cleric to speak" (percentage who agree)
Gender	Male	15.8%	50.3%	49.2%
	Female	15.6	49.6	37.7
Age	18–30	17.5	56.6	41.1
	31–40	17.8	53.5	44.6
	41–55	15.9	48.5	46.5
	56–89	13.8	43.2	40.3
Education	Less than high school	24.8	30.1	19.4
	High school	15.6	46.3	38.2
	Bachelor's degree	13.2	61.1	59.8
	Advanced degree	16.8	67.5	63.3
Race	White	10.7	51.4	48.8
	African-American	34.9	47.0	34.9
	Latino	16.6	44.9	26.6
	Other	25.5	56.6	36.2
Family Income	Low	18.7	43.0	32.6
	Lower middle	17.7	49.7	40.4
	Higher middle	14.0	47.0	44.9
	High	12.1	59.2	57.2

Table 10.1 includes data on the variation in opinions across different groups of Americans, as measured in the General Social Survey (GSS). The table shows group differences on three broad questions: hiring preferences for African Americans, access to abortions, and free speech. There are sharp differences among groups on some questions. For example, people of different education levels respond very differently to both questions about abortion and free speech—however, education has little to do with opinions about affirmative action.

These data indicate that group characteristics can be important predictors of some of an individual's opinions, but they are not the whole story.[24] Because Americans' opinions are also a product of their socialization and life experiences, their group characteristics may tell us something about their opinions on some issues but reveal little about their thoughts on other issues.

Politicians and other political actors

Opinions and changes in opinion are also subject to influence by politicians and other political actors, including political parties and party leaders; interest groups; and leaders of religious, civic, and other large organizations. In part, this link exists because Americans look to these individuals for information based on their presumed expertise. For example, if you do not know what to think about immigration reform or gun control, you might seek out someone who appears to know more about the issues than you do. Insofar as the person's opinions seem reasonable, you might adopt them as your own.[25] Of course, people do not search haphazardly for advice; they take account of an expert's opinions only when they generally agree with the expert, perhaps because they are both conservatives or Democrats or because the individual has some other basis for thinking their preferences are alike. For example, Donald Trump's claims about a "deep state" of individuals in the federal bureaucracy who were working to thwart his policy agenda probably reinforced his supporters' high levels of distrust of government.

Politicians on both sides of the debate tried to influence public opinion about health care reform. While Democrats sought to convince Americans that maintaining Obamacare was necessary, opponents played up the possible disadvantages, with references to costs and bureaucratic incompetence.

Politicians and other political actors also actively work to shape public opinion. Political scientist Jane Mansbridge argues that representation involves tapping public opinion in ways that build support for policy initiatives.[26] That said, because politicians are generally seen as advocates for a particular point of view, it is relatively difficult for them to change opinions of people not already sympathetic to their views. For example, although President Trump and his allies in Congress expended much time and effort in summer 2020 to convince Americans that lockdowns, masks, and social distancing were not needed to combat COVID-19, only Trump's strongest supporters accepted this view. If anything, perhaps because of the dire news about caseloads and deaths in much of the country, public opinion moved against Trump, and increased support for his Democratic opponent in the election, Joe Biden.

Considerations: the process of forming opinions

When people form opinions on the spot (which is true for most opinions), they are based on *considerations*: pieces of relevant information from sources like the ones we've just discussed—such as ideology, party identification, the influence of family and community members, personal and national events, group identification, or opinions and actions of politicians—that come to mind when the opinion is requested.[27] The process of forming an opinion usually is not thorough or systematic, since most people don't take into account everything they know about the issue in question.[28] Rather, they use only considerations that come to mind immediately.[29] Highly informed people who follow politics use this process, as do those with low levels of political interest and knowledge.[30]

In some cases, opinions are formed from very little information. For example, suppose right before the 2020 presidential election you were asked whether you approved of President Trump's performance in office. There are many considerations you might have used, from your evaluations of Trump's response to COVID-19 or the Black Lives Matter protests, news coverage of Trump's tariff war with China or a profile of one of his staffers, how Trump's tax reform affected your personal well-being (or that of your parents)—or even what Trump had tweeted that day. Your opinions might have reflected things that have no connection to Trump, such as whether you just received a pay raise, whether you recently watched a video of politicians arguing with each other, or even whether you were just having a bad day. However, if you are like many Americans, your opinion would have centered on Trump's party affiliation: if you are a Republican, you approved, and if you're a Democrat, you disapproved. In fact, in modern American politics, party affiliation is used to form a wide range of political judgments. For example, when Barack Obama (a Democrat) was president, Republicans were much more likely than Democrats to say that economic conditions were poor. This pattern reversed when Donald Trump (a Republican) took office in 2017. There is also evidence that people use partisanship to form broader judgments about people from the other party: if, for example, you are a Republican, you may dislike Democrats simply because they are Democrats, not because of the policy positions you believe they hold.[31]

Basing decisions about presidential approval on party affiliation may seem simplistic, but in an era when the parties disagree on most things, a Republican voter is likely to agree with most decisions made by a Republican president and disagree with most decisions made by a Democrat. In that sense, considerations are a useful shortcut for people who need to make judgments about a president but don't want to spend too much time gathering or evaluating information. In other situations, considerations may lead to inaccurate judgments; this can happen, for example, when individuals decide what they think about the state of the economy based on the party affiliation of the president. But even here, if the goal is to vote for the candidate who is most likely to share your interests, using partisanship to evaluate the economy and then voting based on this evaluation is an easy way to increase the chances that you vote for the right candidate.

That said, as we discussed earlier, partisanship is not the only consideration people use to form political opinions. A generation ago, when differences between the parties were not as strong, evaluations of presidential performance were often shaped by perceptions of economic conditions, which in turn were based on some combination of personal financial well-being and judgments about the state of the economy. The impact of a candidate's personal characteristics has varied over time as well. For example, one of the author's parents reported that in her first presidential election (1952), she could not vote for the Democrat, Adlai Stevenson, because Stevenson was divorced. In the modern era, when the divorce rate is around 50 percent and many politicians are on their second or third marriage, absent unusual circumstances, divorce is unlikely to be a factor many voters think about when forming opinions about candidates. Even in the debate over Trump's performance in office, in which partisanship played an important role, some citizens may have focused on economic conditions, Trump's golf game, or even his preference for well-done steak. So, if we look at individuals, opinions can sometimes be hard to predict or understand, because we don't know which considerations will come to mind when we ask them what they think.

Individual Considerations and Mass Public Opinion While public opinion may be difficult to predict on a person-to-person basis, at the aggregate level (where opinions are averaged across the population of a community, state, or nation) opinions are easier to predict. Over a large group of people, unique differences in how individuals form beliefs largely cancel each other out, leaving common factors that are important for most people, such as (in the case of presidential approval in the modern era) party identification.

As an example of how considerations work on an aggregate level, consider Figure 10.2, which shows the trend in presidential approval during Donald Trump's four years in office and during the first four years of his two predecessors, Barack Obama and George W. Bush. One important difference is that approval for Bush moved up and down during his first term, while there was no identifiable trend for Obama, and Trump's popularity remained relatively stable until the COVID-19 pandemic reached America in spring 2020, causing his approval to decline. In part, this difference reflects the increasing importance of partisanship in modern American politics. The two sharp upticks in Bush's popularity occurred in November 2001 (after the September 11 attacks) and after the initial successes in the Iraq War in March 2003.

Similarly, Trump's popularity until the pandemic showed no increases in reaction to favorable economic conditions or declines after his impeachment in late 2019. The best explanation is that in the current era, approval ratings are driven by partisanship—for the most part, Americans base their evaluations on whether they share the president's party identification, with other factors, such as evaluations of the man's character or the details of his foreign and domestic policy, playing a much smaller role. There is no guarantee that the predominance of party identification in presidential approval will continue into the future, but until it changes, presidential approval will only modestly reflect other factors such as economic conditions, international crises, or even the president's background or personal characteristics.

How Considerations Interact Considerations can also interact with each other in the opinion-formation process. One of the most common and important interactions is the impact of partisanship, which acts as a kind of filter that shapes how people assess other events and information. As noted earlier, if you share the president's party affiliation, you are more likely to think that economic conditions are good and (assuming your judgments about the economy are constant) more likely to approve of the president's performance. Other potential filters include race, gender, sexual orientation, and age.

Opinions are often influenced by considerations that compete or contradict. In the case of abortion laws, many people believe in protecting human life but also in allowing women to make their own medical decisions.[32] When a survey asks people who hold both beliefs for their opinion about abortion laws, their response will depend on which consideration comes to mind and seems most relevant when they are answering the question.

When considerations compete, opinions can change rapidly for seemingly unrelated reasons. Consider Figure 10.3, which charts Republican and Democratic respondents' evaluations of whether the United States made the right decision to use force in Iraq. As you see, Republicans were always more likely to say that military action was the right choice, although the percentage declined for both parties as casualties mounted during 2003–2008. However, in 2009 a new trend emerged: Democrats became increasingly more likely to say that military force was the right choice, a shift that probably had more to do with Republican George Bush being replaced by Democrat Barack Obama.

Studies of public opinion confirm the opinion-formation strategies that we've just discussed: most people form the bulk of their opinions on the spot using a wide range of considerations. Consider the following findings: Attitudes about immigration are

FIGURE 10.2

First-Term Presidential Approval Ratings

Compared to President Bush's approval ratings, which moved up and down over time, both President Obama's and President Trump's approval ratings were relatively stable. What factors account for the differences in these plots?

Source: FiveThirtyEight, "How Popular Is Donald Trump?," https://projects.fivethirtyeight.com/trump-approval-ratings (accessed 11/2/20).

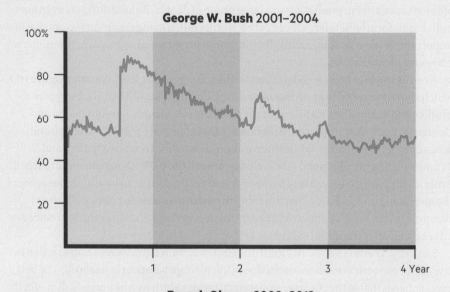

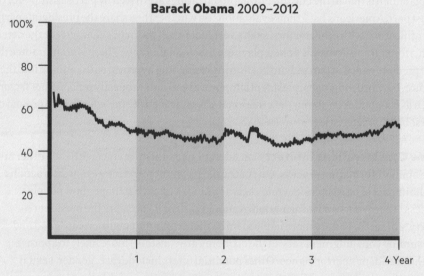

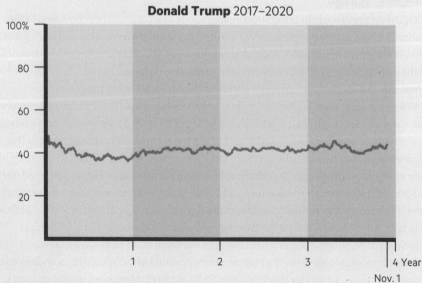

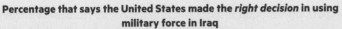

Percentage that says the United States made the *right decision* in using military force in Iraq

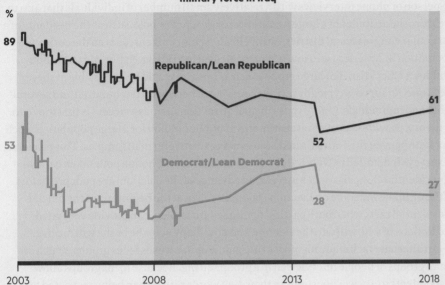

FIGURE 10.3

Evaluations of Military Force in Iraq

The graph shows how Democratic and Republican evaluations of the war in Iraq changed over the last 15 years. What factors might have shaped the observed partisan differences? Why do you think beliefs have largely stayed the same in recent years?

Source: Pew Research Center, "The Iraq War Continues to Divide the U.S. Public, 15 Years after It Began," March 19, 2018, www.people-press.org (accessed 12/30/19).

shaped by evaluations of the state of the economy.[33] People judge government spending proposals differently depending on whether a Republican or a Democrat made the proposal, using their own party identification as a consideration.[34] Evaluations of affirmative action programs vary depending on whether the survey question reminds respondents that their own personal economic well-being may be hurt by these programs.[35] Individuals' willingness to allow protests and other expressions of opinions they disagree with depends on their belief in tolerance.[36] And if people feel obligated to help others in need, they are more likely to support government programs that benefit the poor.[37]

In sum, public opinion at the individual level is largely formed when needed, and is driven by a variety of considerations. In the case of gun control, for example, beliefs are likely to depend on individuals' backgrounds—whether they own a gun, hunt, or know someone who does; their political beliefs, including their tolerance for government regulation of individual behavior and even their partisanship; and horrific events involving guns. Thus, although public opinion may shift somewhat in response to events such as a mass shooting or domestic terror attack, such events are only one factor that shapes opinion. As a result, even if an event is momentous, the shift in opinion may be quite small and transitory.

How people form opinions matters because understanding what people say about politics on the news, or in the classroom, or around the dinner table depends on where they are coming from. Perhaps an important event has shaped their opinion, maybe their parents or connection to a social or generational group has influenced them, or maybe a combination of all of these and more has affected them. Knowing what's behind someone's opinions and arguments on an issue can help you decide how you feel about that issue and whether or not the other person's argument carries weight.

"Why Should I Care?"

mass survey
A way to measure public opinion by interviewing a relatively small sample of a large population.

population
The group of people whom a researcher or pollster wants to study, such as evangelicals, senior citizens, or Americans.

sample
Within a population, the group of people surveyed in order to gauge the whole population's opinion. Researchers use samples because it would be impossible to interview the entire population.

DID YOU KNOW?

The probability that you will be contacted to participate in a typical national poll is

.00001

Source: Calculated by author

On average, people should be more skeptical when they see numbers. They should be more willing to play around with the data themselves.

—Nate Silver, FiveThirtyEight.com

Measuring public opinion

For the most part, information about public opinion comes from **mass surveys**—in-person or phone interviews with a relatively small number of individuals that aim to measure the attitudes of a large **population** or group of people, such as the residents of a particular congressional district, evangelicals, senior citizens, or even the entire adult population in America (see How It Works: Measuring What a Nation of 330 Million Thinks: A Checklist). For large groups such as these, it would be impossible to survey everyone. So surveys typically involve **samples** of between a few hundred and several thousand individuals. One of the principal attractions of mass surveys is that they can, in theory, provide very accurate estimates of public opinion for a large population (such as a state or even the entire United States) using relatively small samples. This property of surveys is detailed in Nuts & Bolts 10.1. For example, although polls taken early in a presidential campaign (such as a year in advance of the election) are poor predictors of the ultimate outcome on Election Day, polls taken at the beginning of the official presidential race, when both parties' nominees are known, can provide very good predictions of who will win the election and how many votes he or she will receive.[38]

An alternate technique for measuring public opinion uses focus groups, which are small groups of people interviewed in a group setting. Because focus groups allow respondents to answer questions in their own words rather than being restricted to a few options in a survey question, they can provide deep insights into why people hold the opinions they do. Candidates sometimes use focus groups to test campaign appeals or fine-tune their messages. However, because of their small size, focus groups cannot be used to draw conclusions about public opinion across the entire country. For example, in December 2019, a polling firm assembled a focus group consisting of 10 individuals who lived in Michigan and had voted for Obama in 2012 but Trump in 2016. One of its principal findings was that all 10 remained committed to Trump, with no signs that they would vote for a Democrat in 2020. While the firm's report provides some insight into which issues were considered relevant by the participants (for example, they opposed Trump's impeachment), it provides little information about the 2020 election, or even about the intentions of Obama-Trump voters nationwide, partly because the sample is so small, and partly because the group discussion may have led participants to form and express opinions that they might not otherwise have held.[39]

Large-scale surveys such as the American National Election Study (ANES) or the Cooperative Congressional Election Survey (CCES), which are conducted every election year (sometimes both before and after the general election), use various types of questions to measure citizens' opinions. In presidential election years, participants in the ANES are first asked whether they voted for president. If they say they did, they are asked which candidate they voted for: a major-party candidate (for example, Donald Trump or Joe Biden in 2020), an Independent candidate, or some other candidate.

Another kind of survey question measures people's preferences using an *issue scale*. For a range of topics, two opposing statements are given and respondents are asked to pick the statement, or one of the choices between the two extremes, that comes closest to their views. As we discuss later, on questions such as these, most Americans pick positions in the middle of these scales.

A typical survey like the GSS, ANES, or CCES will ask several hundred questions related to issues and candidates, along with additional questions that elicit personal information such as a respondent's age, education, marital status, and other factors. Some surveys conducted by media sources, candidates, or political parties are shorter, focusing on voter evaluations of the candidates and the reasons for these evaluations. In the main, the length of a survey reflects the fact that people have limited attention spans, so there is a

Sampling Error in Mass Surveys

The **sampling error** in a survey (the predicted difference between the average opinion expressed by survey respondents and the average opinion in the population, sometimes called the *margin of error*) using a random sample depends on the sample size. Sampling error is large for small samples of around 200 or fewer but decreases rapidly as sample size increases.

The graph shows how the sampling error for a random sample decreases as sample size increases. For example, in surveys with 1,000 respondents the sampling error is about 3 percent, meaning that 95 percent of the time the results of a 1,000-person survey will fall within the range of 3 percentage points above or below the actual percentage of the population who hold a particular opinion. If the sample size was increased to 5,000 people, the sampling error would decline to 1.4 percent. Mass surveys typically interview around 1,000 people. As the figure shows, this is the point where adding interviewees provides relatively little improvement in accuracy.

Sampling errors need to be taken into account when interpreting what a poll says about public opinion. For example, suppose a poll of 1,300 Americans found that 66 percent gave an unfavorable rating of Donald Trump's performance in office and 33 percent rated him favorably. Because the difference between the percentages (33 points) exceeds the sampling error (about 2.5 points), it is reasonable to conclude that, at the time the poll was conducted, more Americans saw Trump unfavorably than favorably.

In contrast, suppose the poll found a narrow 51–49 percent split slightly favoring approval. Because the difference in support is smaller than the sampling error, it would be a mistake to conclude that the majority of Americans had a favorable opinion of Trump. Even though more people in the sample expressed this opinion, there is a good chance that the opposite was true in the overall population.

You don't need to calculate sampling errors to make sense of political polls—just keep two things in mind. First, large samples (1,000 or more) are much more likely to provide accurate information about population opinions than small ones (fewer than 500). Second, be cautious when you read about small differences in survey responses, as these patterns are unlikely to hold true in the entire population.

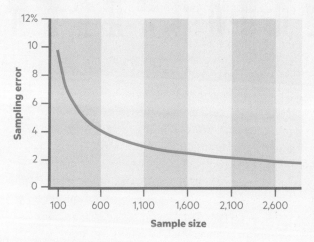

X-axis: Sample size — 100, 600, 1,100, 1,600, 2,100, 2,600. Y-axis: Sampling error — 0, 2, 4, 6, 8, 10, 12%.

"Why Should I Care?" Not all data are equal! Statistical errors that occur when researchers don't select a sample that represents the entire population can significantly affect the accuracy of the conclusions they draw from that survey. When looking at survey data, you need to think critically about the size of the sample, as well as the small differences in results.

trade-off between learning more about each respondent's opinions and getting him or her to agree to be surveyed in the first place.

An important development in recent years is the use of techniques to combine different surveys into a more powerful measure of public opinion. These techniques weigh data from different polls based on their accuracy in previous elections and combine state- and national-level results to generate predictions—thus, if a poll finds that candidate A is ahead in state 1 and polls have found that the winner in state 1 will also win state 2, then the results from state 1 will be used to predict the result in state 2. These techniques generate powerful predictions of election returns. Even in 2020, when high voter turnout and large numbers of mail-in ballots complicated the prediction process, most pollsters correctly forecasted Joe Biden's victory, although they did underpredict support for Donald Trump by a few percentage points in states such as Florida.

sampling error
The predicted difference between the average opinion expressed by survey respondents and the average opinion in the population, sometimes called the *margin of error*. Increasing the number of respondents lowers the sampling error.

Measuring What a Nation of 330 Million Thinks: A Checklist

✓ A Random Sample:
Were the people who participated in the survey selected randomly, such that any member of the population had an equal chance of being selected?

✓ Sample Size:
How many people do researchers need to survey to know what 330 million Americans think? Major national surveys usually use a sample of 1,000–2,000 respondents.

± 3%

✓ Sampling Error:
For a group of any size (even 330 million), 95 percent of the time a survey of 1,000 randomly selected respondents will measure the average opinion in a population within 3 percentage points. Reputable surveys will usually give the sampling error (sometimes also called "margin of error").

✓ Question Wording:
Did the way the question was worded influence the results? Scientific surveys try to phrase questions in a neutral way, but even in reputable polls, differences in question wording can influence answers.

✓ Reliable Respondents: Respondents often give socially acceptable answers rather than truthful ones—or invent opinions on the spot. Is there a reason to think people may not have answered a survey honestly and thoughtfully?

Surveying the 2020 Elections: Two Approaches

To illustrate how these requirements for good survey design play out in real life, we examine how two well-known polling organizations, the Pew Research Center and Rasmussen Reports, designed polls to measure presidential preference during the 2020 campaign.

Rasmussen Reports

Use land-lines... mostly.

A partially random sample: Contact people who have **land-line phones** and use a **nonrandom online panel** to sample groups that tend not to have land-lines.

Respondent selection: Survey the **first person who answers the phone**.

Make robo-calls.

Computer-controlled: Use an automated script to survey respondents; do the survey in a **short time period (hours)**.

One-shot: **Don't call back** people who you miss on the first try.

Adjust the results.

Weighting the responses: If there are more Democrats (or Republicans) in your sample than you expect, **adjust your results** to account for the difference.

Pew Research Center

Include cell phones.

A random sample: Generate a **sample of all Americans**, including people who have only cell phones.

Respondent selection: When you call, **talk only to the person who is in your sample**.

Use a person to call.

Live interviewer: Use a live interviewer who can **help respondents who are unsure what a question means**.

Multiple tries: Implement the survey over several days, and **call people back if you missed them**.

Don't adjust results.

Surprises are interesting: If the partisan divide in your sample is not what you expect, **treat it as a finding**—people may be changing their party ID.

Outcome

Rasmussen data are incomplete (at best)...

A random sample: Rasmussen misses many people who use only cell phones (many of whom are younger and are Democrats).

Sample size: Rasmussen is also **biased toward people who are likely to answer the phone**. These people tend to be older and include a higher proportion of men than in the population.

and assume nothing has changed.

Sampling error: Adjusting for partisanship **assumes that no changes in party ID have occurred** since the last election.

Reliable respondents: Rasmussen tactic **lowers response rate**. Rasmussen tactic makes poll results sensitive to short-term events.

Pew is more reliable.

Pew's results were generally regarded as more reliable than Rasmussen's—and generally **made more accurate predictions about results**. Furthermore, Rasmussen kept its data largely private, while Pew released its questionnaire and data. This made Pew's survey verifiable and provided an opportunity for further analysis.

❓ Critical Thinking

1. **When evaluating these two polling organizations**, how would you respond to someone who said he still preferred Rasmussen's polls because they correctly predicted the outcome of a Senate race in his state in 2018?

2. **Which kinds of respondents are likely to be put off by polls** that the computer scripts? How might this affect the findings of the survey?

Problems in measuring public opinion

Polling is an imperfect science. Many pollsters failed to predict Trump's victory in 2016. In 2020, most underpredicted support for Trump in states such as Florida and overestimated support for Democratic congressional candidates. While the COVID-19 pandemic increased the difficulty of collecting and interpreting survey data, the fact is that measuring public opinion is hard to do. The problems begin with gathering an appropriate, representative sample of subjects. These difficulties are compounded by issues pertaining to the wording of the questions and further complicated by the very nature of public opinion itself. Consequently, survey results must be read carefully, taking into account who is being surveyed, when they are being surveyed, what opinions are being asked about, and what mechanism is used to ask survey questions.

Issues with Survey Methods Building a **random sample** of individuals is not an easy task. One tactic is to choose households at random from census data and send interviewers out for face-to-face meetings. Another is to contact people by telephone using random digit dialing, which allows surveyors to find people who have unlisted phone numbers or who use only a cell phone. In theory, each of these techniques produces a random sample, but in practice, they both may deviate from this ideal. Face-to-face interviews of people in their homes during work hours won't include adults who work during the day and are not home, and is very expensive. Even with phone surveys, many people refuse to participate. Pollsters must adjust their survey results to account for these and other potential biases. Sometimes these adjustments successfully predict results, and sometimes they don't. For example, in the 2016 presidential race, pollsters did a relatively poor job (compared to recent elections) of predicting who was likely to vote. As a result of this error, polls taken close to the election predicted Clinton victories in Wisconsin, Michigan, and Pennsylvania—states that were actually won by Trump. In the 2020 race, pollsters were unprepared for the sharp increase in turnout by both Republican and Democratic supporters. The net effect of these turnout assumptions was to underpredict support for Republican candidates by a few percentage points— enough to cause prediction errors in close races, including the Senate contests in Maine, Michigan, and South Carolina.

To keep costs down, many organizations use Internet polling, in which volunteer respondents log on to a website to participate in a survey, or robo-polls, in which an automated system phones people and interviews them. Although these techniques are less expensive, there are often doubts about the quality of the samples they produce. (*Push polls*, in which a campaign uses biased survey questions as a way of driving support away from an opponent, are not legitimate polls because they are not designed to measure opinion—they are designed to shape it and are a form of negative campaigning; see Chapter 13.)

The wording of questions can also influence survey results. Table 10.2 shows different questions asked to measure opinions about President Trump's executive order banning travel to the United States from seven predominantly Muslim countries. As you can see, support depends on how the question is asked: whether Trump's name is mentioned, the specific countries, and the rationale for the ban. These issues shouldn't make you suspicious that pollsters are trying to skew their findings—rather, they show just how hard it is to accurately measure opinions.

Unreliable Respondents Another problem with surveys is that people are sometimes reluctant to reveal their opinions. Rather than speaking truthfully, they often give socially acceptable answers or answers that they believe the interviewers

random sample
A subsection of a population chosen to participate in a survey through a selection process in which every member of the population has an equal chance of being chosen. This kind of sampling improves the accuracy of public-opinion data.

TABLE
10.2

% Support or Favor	Question	Pollster
57	Do you favor or oppose a temporary ban on refugees from Syria, Iraq, Iran, Libya, Somalia, Sudan and Yemen **until the federal government improves its ability to screen out potential terrorists from coming here**?	Rasmussen
55	Do you approve or disapprove of [President Trump's] executive order prohibiting citizens from seven predominantly Muslim countries **from being able to enter the United States for 90 days and halting processing of refugees for 120 days**?	Politico
46	Do you support or oppose **suspending all travel by citizens of Iraq, Syria, Iran, Libya, Somalia, Sudan and Yemen to the U.S. for 90 days**?	Quinnipiac
42	**Thinking now about some of the specific actions Donald Trump has taken since he has been in office**, would you say you approve or disapprove of ordering a temporary ban on entry into U.S. for most people from seven predominantly Muslim countries?	Gallup

Sources: Rasmussen Reports, "Most Support Temporary Ban on Newcomers from Terrorist Havens," January 30, 2017, www.rasmussenreports.com/public_content/politics/current_events/immigration/january_2017/most_support_temporary_ban_on_newcomers_from_terrorist_havens; Jake Sherman, "Poll: Democrats Want Leaders to Block Trump," Politico, February 7, 2017, www.politico.com/story/2017/02/trump-democrats-poll-234778; Quinnipiac Poll, "American Voters Oppose Trump Immigration Ban, Quinnipiac University National Poll Finds," February 7, 2017, https://poll.qu.edu/national/release-detail?ReleaseID=2427; Frank Newport, "About Half of Americans Say Trump Moving Too Fast," Gallup, February 7, 2017, https://news.gallup.com/poll/203264/half-americans-say-trump-moving-fast.aspx (all accessed 1/2/20).

The Impact of Question Wording on Opinions

How questions are worded can affect survey results. These surveys (all taken in January to February 2017) ask about President Trump's 2017 executive order banning citizens from certain countries from traveling to the United States, but differ in how they describe the details of the ban as well as the supposed goal. In light of how the responses to survey questions are shaped by the precise wording of these questions, what sort of question would you ask if your goal was to show that Americans favored the travel ban? What if you wanted to show high levels of opposition?

want to hear. In the case of voter turnout in elections, in most surveys up to one-third of respondents who say they voted when surveyed actually did not vote at all. Political scientists refer to this behavior as the social desirability bias, meaning that people answering survey questions are less willing to admit to actions or express opinions that they believe their neighbors or society at large would disapprove of, such as racial prejudice.[40]

Pollsters use various techniques to address this problem. One approach is to ask questions in multiple ways; another is to verify answers whenever possible, such as checking with county boards of elections to see if respondents who said they voted actually went to the polls. When there is concern that respondents will try to hide their prejudices, pollsters sometimes frame a question in terms of the entire country rather than the respondent's own beliefs. For example, during the 2008 and 2016 presidential primaries, rather than asking respondents whether they were willing to vote for a woman candidate (such as Democrat Hillary Clinton), some pollsters posed the question indirectly, asking whether a respondent believed that the country was ready for a woman president. Another tactic is to ask respondents for a different kind of evaluation—rather than asking whether they like or dislike candidates, pollsters ask whether they would sit down for a beer (or coffee) with them.

Of course, attempts to account for the social desirability bias by rephrasing a question can introduce new biases. For example, a survey question designed to ask about a sensitive topic might begin with "Some people have argued that…" However, in some cases adding this phrase to a question can produce higher levels of respondent agreement regardless of what is being asked. Again, the problem is not that pollsters are dishonest or inept—the problem is that public opinion is often difficult to measure.

The Accuracy of Public Opinion Because poll results play such an important role in media coverage and public discussions about politics, questions are often raised about the assumptions and corrections that pollsters use to account for the inevitable ambiguities related to poll results. During the 2020 presidential campaign, many Republican politicians and observers argued that polls showing a significant lead for Democrat Joe Biden over Republican Donald Trump were the product of inaccurate polling questions and assumptions about turnout. Some even argued that pollsters were deliberately skewing their findings so as to bolster support for Biden. Of course, Biden won the election, although it appears that pollsters did misestimate turnout of some groups. However, this outcome does not imply that pollsters altered their surveys to hurt Trump's chances. The same models that yielded polling errors in 2020 have proved reliable in many other elections; that's why pollsters used them. Their mistake highlights the difficulty of accurately surveying the American people and shows why we should be reluctant to overinterpret survey results.

In some cases, inaccurate or outlandish survey results are generated because some respondents don't take surveys seriously. They agree to participate but are not interested in explaining their beliefs to a stranger. Faced with a long list of questions, they give quick, thoughtless responses so as to end the interview as quickly as possible. Misperceptions may also result when respondents form opinions on the basis of whatever considerations come to mind. And most importantly, people may reach for considerations that are easy to use but not very informative. Consider claims about Obamacare. A 2015 poll asked people whether health care spending by the federal government was higher or lower than estimates made at the time the program was enacted in 2010. Forty-two percent said spending was higher, 40 percent did not know—and only 5 percent of respondents gave the correct answer, that spending was less than expected.[41] Other surveys were highly correlated with party identification, with Republicans much more likely to say the program cost more than expected and Democrats less likely.

How can these findings be squared with our earlier statement that Americans generally hold opinions that have some basis in reality? For one thing, many respondents probably had not thought about these questions in detail—and it's likely that only very few knew anything about health care costs in the first place. When asked for an opinion as part of a survey, respondents had no time to do research or think things through. One possibility is that people used partisan considerations: Obama supporters (Democrats) said they didn't know, while Obama opponents (Republicans) said costs were higher than expected. If so, the responses say more about partisanship and attitudes toward President Obama than about the cost of Obamacare.

Misinformation may also result from politicians making polarizing or extreme statements about an issue. Over the last ten years, Republicans have tried to repeal Obamacare nearly 50 times and Republican pundits have described the program in highly negative terms. Donald Trump made repeal of Obamacare a central plank in his campaign platform, and attempts to repeal the program occupied Congress for much of 2017. It's no wonder, then, that Republican survey respondents select negative responses when asked about Obamacare—after all, that's all they've been hearing from the political figures they listen to and generally agree with.

Finally, many supposed facts are actually "contested truths," meaning that even if people move beyond considerations and take into account multiple, nuanced sources of information, they may nevertheless arrive at different conclusions about complex questions.[42] For example, it is a fact that the unemployment rate fell by over a third during President Obama's eight years in office and while the numbers improved during the first few years of Trump's presidency as the economy rebounded, the coronavirus pandemic in 2020 led to a steep decline in employment from which the country has not yet recovered.[43] Do these changes mean that Obama was a better steward of the economy than Trump? Obama took office during the most severe economic downturn since the Great Depression, while Trump inherited a stable, growing economy. People can easily arrive at different evaluations of Trump and Obama depending on how they account for these starting points.

Such problems do not arise in all areas of public opinion. Studies show that respondents' ability to express specific opinions, as well as the accuracy of their opinions, rises if the survey questions have something to do with their everyday life.[44] Thus, average Americans would be more likely to have an accurate sense of the state of the economy or their personal economic condition than of the military situation in Syria. Everyday life gives us information about the economy; we learn about Syria only if we take time to gather information. These effects are magnified insofar as the respondent considers the economy the more salient issue of the two.

How useful are surveys?

By now, CNN's disclaimer about the limits of mass surveys should not be much of a surprise. Survey results are most likely to be accurate when they are based on a simple, easily understood question about a topic familiar to the people being surveyed—such as the choice between two candidates, measured close to an election—and when the survey designers have worked to account for all the problems discussed here. Under these conditions, with samples of 1,000 voters or more, poll results are generally within about 3 percentage points of the true population values.[45] You can be even more confident if multiple surveys addressing the same topic in different ways and at different times produce similar findings. However, if a single survey asks about a complex, unfamiliar topic—replacing the income tax with a national sales tax or determining whom to blame for a policy failure—then the results may not provide much insight into public opinion.

The timing of surveys may also affect how useful the results are. Surveys taken immediately after an event—for example, a survey on gun control taken immediately after a school shooting—are generally not good guides to public opinion. The problem is not that people are being insincere or thoughtless. Rather, it is that respondents' opinions are colored by the recent tragedy—but only in the short term. Over the next days, weeks, or months, opinions are likely to return to what they were before the event. Thus, polls taken in the wake of a powerful event may not be a good guide to what people might demand from government in light of what has happened, nor may they reflect how people might react a year later. The same is true of polls taken well in advance of the time when the public actually has to act on their preferences—for example, a poll about the 2022 midterm election taken two years before the election, when most people know almost nothing about the candidates and have not even begun to think about their choice. Under these conditions, poll results tell us almost nothing about what people will ultimately do. On the other hand, polls taken right before an election are generally good predictors of election results.

Beyond all of these factors, the ability of preelection polls to predict election outcomes also depends on the closeness of the race. Many critiques of survey methods focus on the failure of most pollsters to predict Donald Trump's victory in 2016. This failure needs to be placed in context: while giving Democrat Hillary Clinton a slight edge, most pollsters acknowledged that the race was close and that the outcome depended on who turned out to vote. In this sense, the polls got the underlying dynamic

As always, keep in mind that the poll does not, and cannot, predict the outcome of the election in November.

—Disclaimer on CNN preelection poll

Should Politicians Follow the Polls?

Elected officials in America work hard to cast votes and take other actions that their constituents will like. At first glance, this behavior seems easy. All a politician needs to do is take a poll, measure public opinion in his or her state or district, and comply with the demands expressed in the survey responses. The problem is, poll results need interpretation. As we saw for President Trump's travel ban in Table 10.2, small differences in question wording can produce very different responses, or public opinion can remain vague, despite the polls. As a result, even if representatives want to follow constituent opinion, they may decide that they don't really know enough about these opinions to decide what they should do.

Imagine that a survey on immigration was conducted in your congressional district, asking voters if they favored allowing undocumented immigrants to stay in the country or if people here without documentation should be deported as soon as possible. Suppose that the poll results indicate strong support for one of the two options and that you yourself have no strong feelings about undocumented immigrants. The decision you face is: Should you demand that Congress enact immigration reform consistent with the poll results, or should you quietly ask that immigration reform be kept off the agenda?

Follow the poll. Elected officials often have strong incentives to do what constituents demand—in this case, to push for immigration reform measures that are consistent with the demands expressed in the poll. By this logic, if most constituents want immigrants to gain legal status, then you'd ask for a reform proposal that made legal status possible. Conversely, if the poll indicated that most constituents favored deportation, you would push for legislation that funded a program to achieve this goal. Doing so would allow you to claim some credit for the specifics of the bill, as well as for your vote, which in theory would please most of your constituents and increase your chances of reelection.

Stay quiet. As we discuss throughout the chapter, poll results are highly sensitive to question wording, timing, and other factors, making it hard to interpret even seemingly clear findings. Suppose, for example, the poll indicates support for allowing undocumented immigrants to gain legal status.

However, the survey did not ask about any of the details of legalization: whether legal status would require learning English, holding a stable job, paying back taxes, or other conditions. Even though none of these conditions were in the question, most of your constituents probably had some of them in mind when they thought about how they wanted to answer the question. In other words, your constituents' support of immigration reform depends on what the reforms look like. Even if you want to act in accordance with their demands, the survey may not tell you much about what exactly they want.

The situation is no easier if your poll indicates support for deportation. Would government officials search for undocumented immigrants to deport or just deport people they happen to find? What would happen to children whose parents entered the country without documentation but who were born in the United States and are therefore citizens? For some respondents, the solution is a nationwide house-to-house search, with children deported with their parents. But others would reject a deportation process that did either of these things. So here again, the poll results, one-sided as they are, don't provide you with foolproof guidance about how to vote.

 Americans in both parties agree on the need for immigration reform but differ as to what they think the new immigration policies should be.

take a stand

1. Suppose you are a politician who feels that changes in immigration policy are needed but is faced with the quandary described above. Would you do nothing, so as to avoid alienating your constituency, or would you force a policy change and accept the political consequence—possible removal from office?

2. What poll questions would you use to get a clearer picture of public opinion on immigration?

of the 2016 election right. Based on the polls, the best guess was a Clinton victory, even though it would have been more accurate to add that the outcome was in doubt and that the result could change if assumptions about turnout were even slightly off (which they were). The problem was not how polls were taken but the media's desire to simplify a complex situation. We will discuss these issues further in Chapter 14.

New technologies have made surveys cheaper and easier, allowing groups to poll more often and ask a much wider range of questions. However, polls are not infallible. Believing in survey results without some skepticism can lead to fundamental misunderstandings of public opinion, as exemplified by claims that pollsters failed to predict support for Trump and other Republicans in 2020.

"Why Should I Care?"

PRESENT FINDINGS ON WHAT AMERICANS THINK ABOUT GOVERNMENT AND WHY IT MATTERS

What Americans think about politics

In this section, we describe American public opinion, including people's ideological beliefs and what they think of the federal government. These opinions drive overall support for government action and serve as the basis for opinions on more specific policy questions. To understand what America's national government does and why, we have to determine what Americans ask of it.

Ideological polarization

We begin by examining liberal and conservative ideology and party identification to see whether historical data show evidence of **ideological polarization**: sharp differences in Americans' overall ideas of the size and scope of government. Many commentators argue that government's inaction on issues like gun control or immigration reform, as well as continued conflict over issues like Obamacare, reflects increased polarization among the American public. The What Do the Facts Say? feature shows two kinds of survey data that can help us evaluate levels of polarization: responses to a question measuring ideology (liberal-moderate-conservative) and a question that taps a respondent's party identification (Republican-Independent-Democrat). The ideological data show no evidence of increased polarization; in the case of partisanship, a substantial percentage of Americans in 2019 described themselves as Independents. (For more details on partisanship, see Chapter 11.)

Looking more closely at opinion polarization, the third part of the What Do the Facts Say? feature divides the electorate into nine groups based on answers to questions that tap important principles, from foreign policy to domestic issues, civil liberties, and morality. Principles such as these are a kind of consideration—they form the basis for opinions that people express in surveys or act on when they vote or engage in other political behavior. The figure shows, first, that only about one-fifth of the electorate (Solid Liberals and Country-First Conservatives) hold consistent ideological beliefs—meaning that they generally give one kind of answer (conservative or liberal) when asked questions that tap their underlying principles. Moreover, most people fall

ideological polarization
Sharp differences in Americans' overall ideas of the size and scope of government.

WHAT DO THE FACTS SAY?

Are the American People Polarized?

Many commentators describe politics in America as highly conflictual, with most Americans holding either liberal or conservative points of view and identifying with one of the two major parties. Is polarization as strong as these commentators think?

Sources: Data from General Social Survey 1972–2018, Cumulative Datafile, Survey Documentation and Analysis (SDA) at UC Berkeley, https://sda.berkeley.edu/sdaweb/analysis/; jsessionid=E9829C77CA98B226C5A8AEAFD-3031D92?dataset=gss18; Gallup, "Party Affiliation," June 4, 2020, https://news.gallup.com/poll/15370/party-affiliation.aspx; Pew Research Center, "Political Typology Reveals Deep Fissures on the Right and Left," October 26, 2017, www.people-press.org/2017/10/24/political-typology-reveals-deep-fissures-on-the-right-and-left/ (all accessed 6/30/20).

Think about it

- **According to the top figure,** how have levels of polarization changed since the 1990s?
- **What does the political typology** reveal about divisions within each political party?

Liberal or Conservative Ideology in America

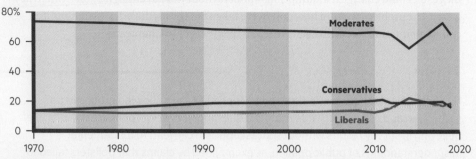

Party Identification in America

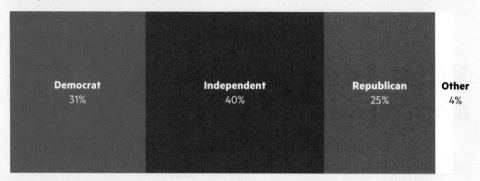

Democrat 31% | Independent 40% | Republican 25% | Other 4%

Political Typology in the General Public

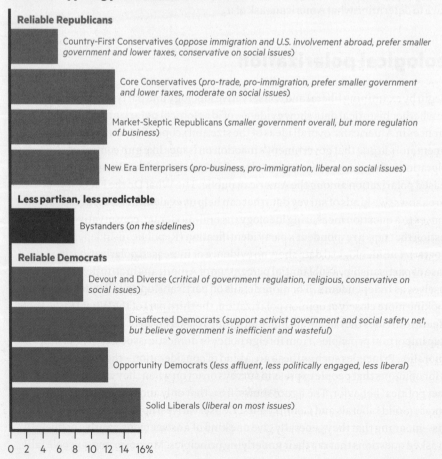

Reliable Republicans

Country-First Conservatives (*oppose immigration and U.S. involvement abroad, prefer smaller government and lower taxes, conservative on social issues*)

Core Conservatives (*pro-trade, pro-immigration, prefer smaller government and lower taxes, moderate on social issues*)

Market-Skeptic Republicans (*smaller government overall, but more regulation of business*)

New Era Enterprisers (*pro-business, pro-immigration, liberal on social issues*)

Less partisan, less predictable

Bystanders (*on the sidelines*)

Reliable Democrats

Devout and Diverse (*critical of government regulation, religious, conservative on social issues*)

Disaffected Democrats (*support activist government and social safety net, but believe government is inefficient and wasteful*)

Opportunity Democrats (*less affluent, less politically engaged, less liberal*)

Solid Liberals (*liberal on most issues*)

0 2 4 6 8 10 12 14 16%

into one of the intermediate groups, meaning that they express a mix of liberal and conservative issue positions. It's also important to remember that typologies like these are designed to identify differences and disagreements—there are many other issues on which there is consensus among the American public.[46]

While these data confirm that Americans disagree on important policy questions, they argue against the conception of a polarized America, with a large group of secular liberals opposing another large group of religious conservatives, and few people in the middle. Public opinion is much more complex. Most people could be labeled as liberals or as conservatives, secular or religious, depending on which issues they are asked about. Thus, even though people say they are liberals (or conservatives), this response does not mean that they hold liberal (or conservative) preferences on all issues. In addition, self-professed moderates may hold relatively extreme preferences on certain policy questions. Thus, understanding what Americans think and what they want from government often requires data on specific policy questions rather than broad judgments about the liberal or conservative nature of American public opinion. (Whether elected officials themselves are more polarized than their constituents is a different story, which we discussed in Chapter 4.)

Given this data, why do political scientists talk so much about high levels of polarization in contemporary America? For the most part, these comments refer to the fact that in contemporary American politics, most of the policy conflicts divide Americans along party lines. These disagreements are magnified by a phenomenon known as negative partisanship, which we discuss in Chapter 11. So the difference between America now and a generation ago is not that we disagree more but that most of our disagreements have Democrats on one side and Republicans on the other. As we have already discussed, presidential approval and beliefs about the state of the economy are highly correlated with partisanship. In Chapter 13, we will show how partisanship drives voter decisions. Data presented throughout this book show partisan and ideological differences on many other political questions. In addition, the opinion data presented in other chapters show sharp partisan and ideological differences on questions about specific public policies. Finally, these partisan differences translate into higher levels of distrust by partisans from one party toward politicians and citizens from the other.[47]

Evaluations of government and officeholders

Another set of politically significant opinions addresses how people view their government: How well or poorly do they think the government is doing? Do they trust the government? How do they evaluate individual politicians? These opinions matter for several reasons. Citizens' judgments about the government's overall performance may shape their evaluations of specific policies, especially if they do not know much about the policies.[48] Evaluations of specific policies may also be shaped by how much a citizen trusts the government; greater trust brings more positive evaluations.[49] Trust in government and overall evaluations might also influence a citizen's willingness to vote for incumbent congressional representatives or for a president seeking reelection.[50]

The top graph in Figure 10.4 reveals that the average American is fairly disenchanted with the government. As of 2019, a majority believes that government is not run for the benefit of all the people and that government programs are usually wasteful and inefficient. These beliefs have not changed much over the last generation, nor in light of COVID-19.

This impression of a disenchanted and disapproving public is reinforced by the second graph, which generally shows declining levels of trust in government since

Trust in government reached a low point during the mid-1970s. The decline partly reflected the economic downturn and conflict over the Vietnam War, but opinions were also shaped by the discovery that President Richard Nixon had lied about the Watergate scandal. Here, Nixon resigns from office to avoid impeachment.

FIGURE 10.4

What Do Americans Think about Government?

A significant percentage of Americans have always been distrustful and disparaging of the federal government—and the percentage of people holding such views has increased markedly in the last generation. Does the perception that government is wasteful and inefficient make it easier or harder to enact new policies? How might the decline in trust explain the rise of the Tea Party organization and candidates like Donald Trump and Bernie Sanders?

Sources: Pew Research Center, "In a Politically Polarized Era, Sharp Divides in Both Partisan Coalitions," December 17, 2019, www.people-press.org/2019/12/17/in-a-politically-polarized-era-sharp-divides-in-both-partisan-coalitions/ (accessed 4/7/20); Pew Research Center, "Public Trust in Government, 1958–2019," April 11, 2019, www.pewresearch.org/politics/2019/04/11/public-trust-in-government-1958-2019/ (accessed 5/3/20).

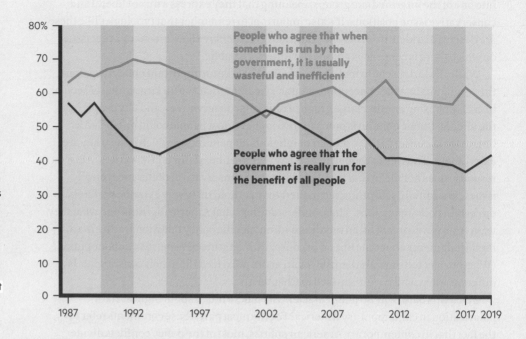

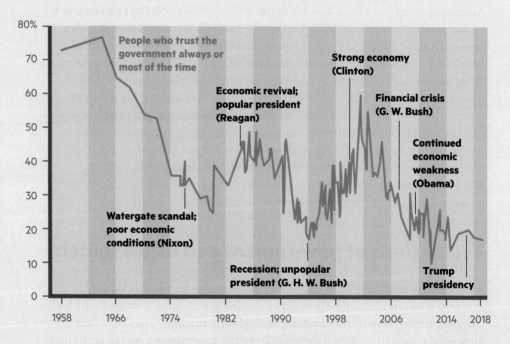

the 1960s. Within this overall trend, trust generally increases given a strong economy (the mid-1980s and late 1990s) and declines during economic hard times (the mid-2000s to now). As noted earlier, many scholars have argued that low levels of trust make it harder for elected officials to enact new policies, especially those that require large expenditures.[51] On a more profound level, some scholars argue that low levels of trust raise questions about the future of democracy in America.[52] How can we say that American democracy is a good or popular form of government when so many people are unhappy with the performance of elected officials and bureaucrats and so few people trust the government? Finally, trust in government also has a partisan

FIGURE 10.5

Measuring American Public Opinion: Is the Government Doing a Good Job?

How is it that Americans disapprove of government overall but give relatively high ratings in many specific areas?

Source: Pew Research Center, "Beyond Distrust: How Americans View Their Government," November 23, 2015, www.people-press.org (accessed 12/5/15).

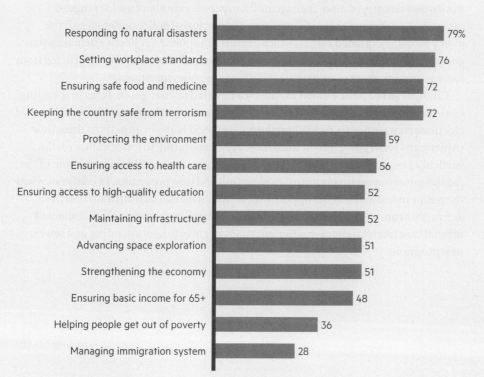

Percentage that says the government is doing a good job . . .

Responding to natural disasters	79%
Setting workplace standards	76
Ensuring safe food and medicine	72
Keeping the country safe from terrorism	72
Protecting the environment	59
Ensuring access to health care	56
Ensuring access to high-quality education	52
Maintaining infrastructure	52
Advancing space exploration	51
Strengthening the economy	51
Ensuring basic income for 65+	48
Helping people get out of poverty	36
Managing immigration system	28

cast—people are more likely to express trust in the government when someone from their party is serving as president.

Interestingly, one response to this question is that low trust in government does not preclude people from approving of specific government programs and activities. Figure 10.5 shows that a majority of Americans give positive evaluations of a wide range of government programs, suggesting that the downward trend in trust is not the result of people being increasingly unhappy with what government actually does.

A second response is that although Americans don't like the government in general, they tend to be far more satisfied with their own representatives in Washington (see Chapter 4). One possibility is that putting a human face on government by asking about specific individuals in office improves respondents' opinions because it calls to mind different considerations. Asking about "the government" may call to mind a vast room of bureaucrats pushing paperwork from one desk to another, whereas asking about "your representative" may lead people to think of someone working on their behalf.

Survey respondents may also be responding to trust questions in ways we do not expect. In particular, in an era when citizens and political organizations are polarized to some degree, high levels of distrust are almost a given, as citizens whose partisan affiliation or leaning differs from the president's party ID are unlikely to report high levels of trust. Moreover, the data shown earlier suggest that even within the president's party, a significant percentage of people may report low trust because they disagree with the president's policy positions. If so, the decline in trust may say more about the nature of contemporary politics than it does about citizens' confidence in their government.

Policy preferences

policy mood
The level of public support for expanding the government's role in society; whether the public wants government action on a specific issue.

In a diverse country of more than 330 million, people care about a wide range of government policies. One useful measure of Americans' policy preferences is the **policy mood**, mentioned earlier, which captures the public's collective demands for government action on domestic policies.[53] Policy mood measures are constructed from surveys that ask about opinions on a wide range of policy questions.[54]

Changes in the policy mood in America have led to changes in defense spending, environmental policy, and civil rights policies, among others—and have influenced elections (see Figure 10.6).[55] When the policy mood leans in an activist direction (Americans want government to do more, corresponding to lower values on the vertical axis), such as in the early 1960s, conditions are ripe for an expansion of the federal government involving more spending and new programs. In contrast, when the policy mood leans in the opposite direction (Americans want a smaller, less-active government, corresponding to higher values on the vertical axis), elected officials are likely to enact smaller increases in government spending and fewer new programs.

FIGURE 10.6

Policy Mood

Surveys assess the public's policy mood by asking questions about specific policy issues such as levels of taxation and government spending and the role of government. The level of conservatism (for example, support for smaller, less-active government) was at a high in 1952 and 1980. Could you have used the policy mood prior to the election to predict the outcomes of the 2020 elections?

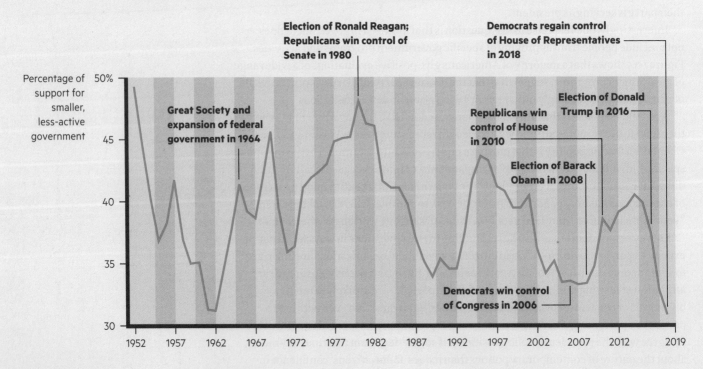

Source: Policy mood data available at http://stimson.web.unc.edu/data (accessed 1/15/20).

Regarding more specific policy preferences, everything we have said in this chapter reinforces the idea that public opinion is often a moving target. While some beliefs and preferences are stable over time, opinions about specific policies can change from year to year, month to month, or even day to day. One of the best ways to take a snapshot of these beliefs is to ask citizens what they see as the top policy priorities facing the nation. Figure 10.7 shows responses to a 2019 survey, which of course does not reflect opinions in the wake of the COVID-19 pandemic or the Black Lives Matter protests of 2020.

The top priorities—the economy, education, and health care—have not changed very much over the last several decades. It is no exaggeration to say that Americans are always worried about the economy. Even when other pressing issues, such as terrorism, surpass the economy as the most important problem to Americans, the economy is typically listed second or third. In general, as the state of the economy declines, more and more people rate the economy as their greatest concern. Moreover, the percentage of people who make reference to their personal economic concerns—for example, unemployment or worries about retirement—also increases.

One important change in recent years is that concerns about terrorism and international conflict are no longer at the top of the list. In the wake of the September 11 attacks and the U.S. invasion of Iraq in 2003, many Americans saw protecting the

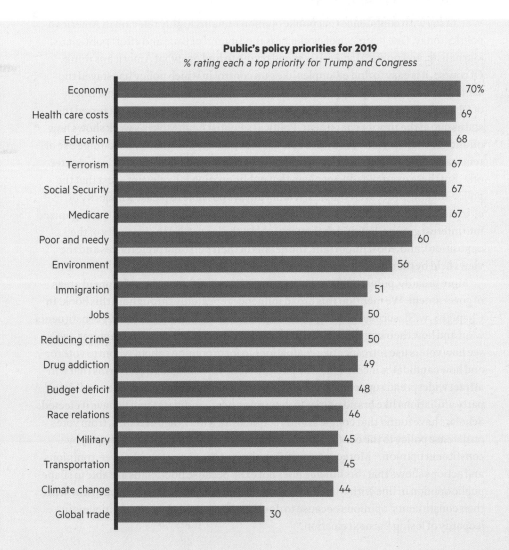

Public's policy priorities for 2019
% rating each a top priority for Trump and Congress

Economy	70%
Health care costs	69
Education	68
Terrorism	67
Social Security	67
Medicare	67
Poor and needy	60
Environment	56
Immigration	51
Jobs	50
Reducing crime	50
Drug addiction	49
Budget deficit	48
Race relations	46
Military	45
Transportation	45
Climate change	44
Global trade	30

FIGURE 10.7

The American Public's Policy Priorities, 2019

Given this data on policy priorities, what issues would you have expected to be prominent in the 2020 election campaign?

Source: Pew Research Center, "Public's Policy Priorities for 2019," January 24, 2019, www.people-press.org (accessed 5/3/20).

country against attack as the top priority. Now, even though U.S. forces are still engaged in fighting groups such as Al Qaeda, the Taliban, and ISIS, Americans see fighting terrorism as less of a priority than domestic policy issues.

These policy priorities frame contemporary political debates and divide the political parties. Think about what Republicans and Democrats in Washington argue about: how best to fight terrorism and secure the United States from attack, how to increase economic growth and reduce the unemployment rate, and what the government's role should be in providing health care and making sure that Americans have secure retirements. In fact, there are sharp partisan disagreements on many of these issues; 67 percent of Democrats see climate change as an important problem, while only 21 percent of Republicans give the same response. Similar differences exist for economic inequality, racism, and illegal immigration. However, in other areas, such as concerns over jobs and social security, responses do not vary much by party.

The list of policy priorities also explains government inaction on some issues. For example, gun control doesn't even appear on the list. Thus, the fact that Congress has not legislated on either of these issues in recent years is actually consistent with public opinion. For better or worse, the average American has other priorities for government action.[56]

Does public opinion matter?

We can say with confidence that public opinion remains highly relevant in American politics today. One key piece of evidence is the amount of time and effort politicians, journalists, and political scientists spend trying to find out what Americans think. Of course, it is easy to find examples like gun control in which policy has stayed the same despite a majority supporting change. In other cases, such as the enactment of Obamacare, new policies have been passed even though a majority preferred the status quo at the time of enactment. Political scientist Leah Stokes's work shows how oil and gas industry lobbyists were able to block policies designed to encourage use of renewable energy technologies—technologies that would make most citizens better off.[57] But these examples do not mean that public opinion is irrelevant—just that the policy-making process is complex. It is not always possible to please a majority of citizens. Politicians' willingness to do so depends on whether the majority is organized into interest groups, how much they care about the issue (and the intensity of the opposition), and, most important, the details of their personal preferences and the views held by their constituents.

More broadly, public opinion exerts a conspicuous influence in widespread areas of government. We mention this broad influence repeatedly throughout this book. In Chapter 4, we described how legislators endeavor to determine what their constituents want and how their constituents will respond to different actions. In Chapter 13, we see how voters use retrospective evaluations to form opinions about whom to vote for and how candidates incorporate the public's views into campaign platforms that will attract widespread support. And in Chapter 11, we discuss how voters use candidates' party affiliations like brand names to determine how candidates will behave if elected. Scholars have found that congressional actions on a wide range of issues, from votes on defense policy to the confirmation of Supreme Court nominees, are shaped by constituent opinion.[58] Moreover, careful analysis of the connection between opinions and actions shows that this linkage does not exist because politicians are able to shape public opinion in line with what they want to do; rather, politicians behave in line with their constituents' opinions because to do otherwise would place the politicians in jeopardy of losing the next election.[59]

Recent events also speak to the influence of public opinion. Think about the failure of elected officials over the last few years to repeal Obamacare, enact immigration reform, or pass new limits on the ownership of handguns and assault rifles. In all of these cases, a significant portion of Americans wanted policy change, but a substantial percentage were opposed, and even the supporters disagreed on what kinds of changes were best. Congressional inaction on these measures does not reflect a willful ignorance of public opinion. Rather, it reflects the lack of a public consensus about what government should do. Inaction on these issues is exactly what we should expect if public opinion is real and relevant to what happens in politics.

Public opinion influences government at election time, when voters' opinions about incumbent politicians and the party in power affect their decisions at the polls. In 2020, voters' evaluations of President Trump were an important factor in the election outcome.

Political scientists and pollsters spend so much time trying to measure public opinion because it shapes election outcomes and policy changes in Washington. If you want to know what the federal government is going to do (or why it's not doing what you think it should be doing), spend some time trying to determine where your own policy opinions fit in with the policy opinions of the country as a whole.

"Why Should I Care?"

**AP®
POLICY IN
PRACTICE**

Deferred Action for Childhood Arrivals

While it is fair to say that all policies are a source of debate, it seems that immigration policy, especially in recent years, takes this debate to another level. Depending on what side one takes on the issue, immigration has been one of America's greatest sources of strength or its most vulnerable Achilles' heel. Any U.S. history book will attest to the fact that the United States was built—literally and figuratively—by immigrants. Governments often look at immigration like a water faucet, something it can turn off and on to regulate the flow in and out. While this is true on paper, even if the legislation can be passed or the president can issue an executive order, it is much more difficult to carry out in practice. When times are good and the economy is expanding, immigrants are a welcome source of additional labor if it is felt that the domestic population is not able to fill the demand. When the economy is on the decline, many politicians seek to slow the flow of immigration. One problem with this view has to do with lags. It is difficult to know or to evaluate when the economy has slowed down until it has already happened. People disagree about the state of the economy all the time. And by the time it is agreed upon by most economists, political leaders have to play catch-up to reverse the immigration flow. By the time political leaders and the public realize there is too much immigration, it has already happened, and there is also a lag in formulating and executing policy to deal with this issue.

In theory, there are two kinds of migration. Pull migration occurs when people leave their home countries because they are attracted to the economic opportunities that are available in the host countries. On the other hand, push migration happens when people feel they have to move from their countries because of the undesirable conditions they have experienced, whether social, economic, and/or political. In practice, migration is often a combination of both pull and push factors. With respect to migration to the United States, the predominant factor has usually been pull because of the economic opportunities this country has to offer. Political refugees, people who are being persecuted in their home countries, as opposed to economic migrants, are motivated by push factors to find a more hospitable place to live. Most of the people discussed here are not political refugees, as their parents came to the United States to seek employment.

The discussion up to now has been about the legal and formal aspects of immigration, but there is also an informal aspect that every nation experiences, and this is the main focus of the Deferred Action for Childhood Arrivals (DACA) policy. This flow is much more difficult to control, but the will to get it under control varies depending on the economic and political circumstances at the time. Unregulated, illegal immigration from Mexico and several Central American countries produces the overwhelming majority of DACA recipients in the United States. This migration has been mutually beneficial for both the immigrants and the citizens of the host country. Migrants were able to make a better living, and American employers often were able to hire workers at reduced or under-the-table wages, which also benefited American consumers with lower prices. On the negative side, some feel that they are taking jobs from Americans and that they have unfairly received money and services from government programs, such as welfare, education, and health care.

A driving motivation behind formulating the DACA program was that no matter what side one fell on regarding the illegal immigration issue, the children of illegal immigrants are not responsible for the actions of their parents. It was not their choice to move to the United States. They should not be punished by being deported back to a country where they might never have lived or had only stayed for a brief time. They have contributed positively to their adopted country by working hard and being law-abiding members of their communities. Those opposed to the DACA program believe that a policy that allows illegal immigrants to stay in the United States, go to college, and get jobs is not fair to American citizens and those who have moved to the United States through normal, legal channels. Furthermore, opponents believe a policy like this will only encourage more illegal immigration in the future.

Another factor that compounds the situation is that children of illegal immigrants who are born on American soil are automatically American citizens regardless of their parents' status ("jus soli," or right of soil). Most countries grant citizenship based on the citizenship of one or both parents ("jus sanguinis," or right of blood), but since the United States practices jus soli, if families are flagged for deportation, only the illegal members would be deported. Families therefore can be split apart. Parents would have to make the very difficult choice between taking all the members back or leaving some of their children behind in the United States, assuming there are relatives or friends who are willing to take the minor children in.

President Barack Obama was clearly on the side of those wanting to support the children of illegal immigrants—so-called Dreamers named after the DREAM

(Development, Relief, and Education for Alien Minors) Act, a law that Congress had tried without success to pass several times. Obama was frustrated that Congress had not passed the Dream Act after several attempts, so he finally issued an executive memorandum, DACA, to stop the deportation of illegal immigrants. Executive memorandums are similar to executive orders in that they unilaterally change government policy without subsequent congressional consent and have the force of law, but they are not recorded in the *Federal Register* so they are much more difficult to track than executive orders, which are recorded. In this case, the advantages of using an executive memorandum were the same as using an executive order: the president was able to enact a policy exactly as he envisioned it, and he could do it relatively quickly. A disadvantage is that it did not go through the typical legislative process. Another disadvantage, as seen in the Possible Modifications, Expansion, or Termination of Policy stage, is that a future president can possibly repeal the act. Until a law is passed by Congress either in support of or against this group of people it is likely that their status in the United States will continue to be in flux.

Policy Stages

1. Problem Recognition
    -   Over the years, many minors (children under the age of 18) have entered the United States illegally with their parents, mostly from Latin American countries with the majority from Mexico.
    -   Although their entry was illegal, they had no choice since they were minors.
    -   These children, many of whom are now adults, have spent most of their lives in the United States and are contributing members of society.
    -   The Mexican population in the United States doubled between 1990 and 2000 (growing from 4.3 to 8.8 million).
        -   The Immigration Reform and Control Act (1986)
            -   It made it illegal for firms to knowingly hire illegal immigrants.
            -   It was not enforced, so immigration from Mexico continued.
        -   Added U.S. border security made many Mexicans afraid they would not be able to cross back and forth easily, so they remained in the United States.
    -   Border control became even stronger after the September 11 attacks.
    -   Moral dilemma: Should the United States
        -   Grant immigrants citizenship?
        -   Grant them legal residency?
        -   Send them back to their birth countries?
2. Agenda Setting
    -   The Dream Act
        -   It gave legal status to young immigrants who came to the United States as children.
        -   It was introduced in 2009.
        -   Different versions were reintroduced in 2010, 2011, and 2012.
        -   Bills were sponsored by Democrats and Republicans.
        -   It was never passed.
3. Deliberation and Formulation
    -   The Dream Act was discussed and debated over many Congresses during President Obama's time in office.
    -   The president encouraged Congress to pass the Dream Act without success due to a lack of cooperation from enough Republicans.

4. Enactment
   - President Obama announced this policy on June 15, 2012, in a speech in the Rose Garden.
     - It would halt the deportation of Dreamers.
     - This memorandum was issued due to the failure of Congress to pass the Dream Act.
   - "Exercising Prosecutorial Discretion with Respect to Individuals Who Came to the United States as Children"
     - This executive branch memorandum was issued by the Secretary of Homeland Security on June 15, 2012.
     - An executive branch memorandum is similar to an executive order in that it is issued by the president and has the force of law, but it can be rescinded by later memorandums or executive orders.
   - It was enacted on the 30th anniversary of the Supreme Court case *Plyler v. Doe* (1982), which ruled that public schools could not charge tuition to undocumented children.

5. Implementation
   - Undocumented people could begin applying to the U.S. Citizenship and Immigration Services (USCIS) on August 15, 2012.
   - Recipients could delay deportation for two years.
   - Recipients could apply for renewal at the end of each two-year period.
   - This was not a pathway for citizenship.
   - Recipients would be allowed to work legally and get health insurance from their employers.
   - Recipients could go to college and pay in-state tuition.

6. Evaluation
   - By the middle of 2016, 88 percent of applicants were approved, 7 percent were denied, and 5 percent were still pending.
   - Most registrants were in their 20s and 80 percent arrived in the United States at the age of 10 or younger.
   - The presence of DACA recipients increased aggregate demand and therefore increased America's gross domestic product (GDP).
   - The American Community Survey conducted by the U.S. Census Bureau found that, for most recipients (of the over 400 surveyed), DACA
     - Increased the number of recipients who received high school diplomas or GEDs
     - Increased their wages and employment
     - Decreased the number living in poverty
     - Increased their chances of
       - Getting any job
       - Getting a better job
       - Working better hours
     - Did not significantly change
       - Employment difficulties
       - Worries about being deported
       - Insufficient health care coverage
   - Other studies show that DACA improved the mental health of recipients.
   - Critics questioned the findings of these studies because of the sample size, selectivity bias, and how quickly many were conducted after the order's implementation.
   - Opponents felt that the president abused his executive power by circumventing Congress by issuing an executive memorandum.
   - Opponents feared that DACA would encourage more illegal immigration.

7. Possible Modifications, Expansion, or Termination of Policy

- Obama issued an executive action to extend the reach of DACA in November 2014.
  - It was called Deferred Action for Parents of Americans and Lawful Permanent Residents (DAPA), also known as Deferred Action for Parental Accountability.
  - It would stop deporting parents of children who are citizens or legal residents.
  - Children who entered the United States illegally with their parents would have the right to work after passing a background check and paying a fee.
  - Immigration officials would be directed to refocus their resources on deporting criminals.
  - Some states sued to block it.
  - The Supreme Court was divided 4–4, and the block against it stayed in place.
  - DAPA was rescinded on June 15, 2017.
- Candidate Trump promised to revoke DACA and DAPA.
- The Department of Homeland Security stopped allowing DACA individuals from traveling outside the United States on June 16, 2017.
- The Trump administration tried to repeal the DACA program on September 5, 2017.
- No new applications have been accepted since the repeal announcement, but those already in the program are still qualified and can continue to renew.
- The Dream Act was reintroduced on July 20, 2017, but not passed.
- The Supreme Court decided on July 2, 2020, that DACA could not be repealed, but a future administration could try again if it came up with better reasons for ending it.
- On December 4, 2020, a federal judge ruled that the Trump administration had not fully complied with the Supreme Court's July decision and ordered that the government comply immediately.
- On January 20, 2021, newly inaugurated President Joe Biden signed an executive order that restored DACA to its original status, further reinforcing the Supreme Court decision and the orders by the federal judge.

Questions for Discussion

1. Should the children of illegal immigrants be held accountable for the actions of their parents and be deported? Why or why not?

2. Should the children of illegal immigrants in the United States be allowed to get a job or go to college? Explain your answer.

3. In what ways has migration to the United States been a source of strength and a source of weakness?

Unpacking the Conflict

Considering all that we've discussed in this chapter, let's apply what we know about how public opinion works to the examples from the beginning of the chapter. Do Americans really hold the bizarre beliefs that are sometimes expressed in polling results? Can we take polls seriously, if they produce results like these? Where does public opinion come from? Can politicians trust public opinion as a guide to what Americans want—and can we use opinions to measure the quality of American democracy?

Given how people form opinions, it's easy to see what Jon Stewart was talking about: at least some of the time, public opinion will be incomplete at best and wildly inaccurate at worst. But that's not surprising. For most people, politics is not the most important thing in their lives, and they don't spend much time worrying about it, learning the details, or forming judgments until they need to. This logic also explains why people are sometimes unable to answer seemingly easy questions, as in the survey mentioned alongside the image at the beginning of this chapter in which respondents were asked to find Iran on a map of the Middle East. Most of the time, there's no reason to know where Iran is. Even if the United States and Iran came close to armed conflict, as they did in early 2020, it is unclear whether knowledge of geography would help average citizens decide how they felt about the matter.

When we ask how "good" opinions are, or whether the electorate acts "rationally and responsibly," as V. O. Key argued, the most important thing to remember is that there is no absolute standard of accuracy. One of the fundamental tenets of a democracy is that people are free to hold whatever opinions they want, and to base these opinions on whatever factors they want to consider. If someone says she approves of Trump's performance in office, and we determine that her judgment is based on Trump's being a Republican, this opinion is as legitimate as that of someone whose evaluation is based on a detailed study of multiple factors. Moreover, making sense of politics requires people to make some pretty sophisticated judgments, and it would be no surprise to find that they make mistakes some of the time, particularly given the shortcuts they use to form their opinions. Nevertheless, the model of opinion formation described in this chapter provides observers of American politics with a guide for interpreting public opinion, including how opinions will change given events.

Should we take polls seriously? Yes, but not too much. Given all the potential problems with mass surveys, we should be suspicious about surprising results such as the support for conspiracy theories cited at the beginning of this chapter. Respondents may not have taken the question seriously, they may have focused on subtle details of the question—or their reply may have been driven by considerations that have nothing to do with the question at hand. Republican suspicions about Barack Obama's citizenship probably reflected the fact that several of their party's leaders, as well as prominent spokespeople including Donald Trump, had repeatedly voiced their suspicions. And Democratic concerns about the government's foreknowledge of the September 11 attacks were colored by the identity of the president at the time, Republican George W. Bush. More generally, we should take poll results seriously to the extent that they are based on multiple surveys, with differently worded questions; are conducted by reputable pollsters; and are conducted at a time when respondents are aware of the issues they are being asked about. One poll on its own doesn't tell us very much.

In sum, while you can't take every poll result you see at face value, public opinion is real, and it matters. Americans have ideas about what they want government to do, and they use these ideas to guide their political choices. Polls showing deep disagreement between Americans on some issues describe the policy landscape on which elections will be contested and the subsequent debates in Washington. While very few Americans are policy experts, their views on policy are the ultimate driver of our government's policy choices.

"What's Your Take?"

Is public opinion important enough that politicians should follow it? Or is public opinion too unreliable and unpredictable to trust?

And if public opinion cannot be trusted, whose wishes should government follow, if not the people's?

Summary

What the population thinks about politics and government matters for three reasons: people's political actions are driven by their opinions; there is a strong linkage between people's opinions and political actors' behavior; and public opinion helps us understand how specific policy outcomes are achieved. Although early research was skeptical that people held meaningful opinions, current research shows that people do have real and meaningful policy positions.

Americans say they believe in a set of core values: equality of opportunity (an equal opportunity for all people to advance in society), free enterprise (a free market with limited government involvement), individualism (valuing individual rights over government rights), limited government (protecting an individual's rights by restricting government power), and rule of law (laws apply to everyone equally). However, Americans have different interpretations of their core values and these differences affect their attitudes toward the role of government.

Political opinions are influenced by a number of factors. The belief systems of parents and relatives influence our opinions early on, and our social groups influence our perspectives later in life. Personal events such as attending college or moving to a new city may also influence how we think about politics, as do national events such as the attacks on September 11, 2001. Even debates among political elites and party leaders shape our political attitudes.

While most information on public opinion comes from mass surveys in which thousands of people respond, some information comes from focus groups in which small numbers of people are interviewed together. Despite a number of limitations, most research on public opinion focuses on mass surveys, as they can be used to draw broad conclusions about the country and impact policy debates. These mass surveys are conducted using scientific polling methods, which include appropriate sampling techniques, neutral questions, and a low sampling error.

As a whole, the American electorate is ideologically moderate, with relatively little ideological polarization. Paradoxically, although trust in the government has declined steadily since the 1960s, people are still generally happy with their own representatives in Washington, D.C., and low trust in government does not preclude Americans from approving specific government programs and activities. While it can be difficult to determine exactly what the American public wants, public

core values
Basic beliefs that shape the way Americans behave and view the role of government in their lives.

equality of opportunity
The equal chance for all people to realize their potential.

free enterprise
An economic system based on competition among businesses with limited government involvement.

individualism
The autonomy of individuals to manage the course of their own lives without government interference.

limited government
A political system in which the powers of the government are restricted to prevent tyranny by protecting property and individual rights.

rule of law
The authority of law to restrict people's behavior equally for the common good.

Key Terms

core values (p. 465)

equality of opportunity (p. 465)

free enterprise (p. 465)

ideological polarization (p. 451)

individualism (p. 465)

latent opinion (p. 431)

liberal or conservative ideology (p. 431)

limited government (p. 465)

mass survey (p. 442)

policy mood (p. 456)

political socialization (p. 433)

population (p. 442)

public opinion (p. 430)

random sample (p. 446)

rule of law (p. 465)

sample (p. 442)

sampling error (p. 443)

opinion is still quite relevant in American politics. Government policy and congressional outcomes are responsive to changes in public mood, and most policy decisions (and arguments) reflect the priorities of a majority of Americans.

Enduring Understandings

MPA-1: "Citizen beliefs about government are shaped by the intersection of demographics, political culture, and dynamic social change." (AP® U.S. Government and Politics Course and Exam Description)

MPA-2: "Public opinion is measured through scientific polling, and the results of public opinion polls influence public policies and institutions." (AP® U.S. Government and Politics Course and Exam Description)

PMI-4: "Widely held political ideologies shape policy debates and choices in American policies." (AP® U.S. Government and Politics Course and Exam Description)

Multiple-Choice Questions (Arranged by Topic)

Topic 4.1: American Attitudes about Government and Politics (MPA-1) and Topic 4.8: Ideology and Policy Making (PMI-4)

1. **Which of the following public policies is the best example of the tension between the competing values of individualism and the rule of law?**

    (A) creating a living wage of $15 per hour

    (B) decreasing funding for the military in order to provide more funding for domestic issues

    (C) states' mandating that masks be worn in public places during the COVID-19 pandemic

    (D) increasing funding for Planned Parenthood

Topic 4.2: Political Socialization (MPA-1)

2. **Which of the following best describes the concept of political socialization?**

    (A) a member of the House of Representatives being elected to a fourth term because she resides in a safe seat

    (B) a first-time voter casting a vote for the party that is often supported by her family and her surrounding community

    (C) polling data results showing that the overall level of public support for expanding the government's role in society is increasing

    (D) the growing tendency of Americans to have sharp differences in what should be the overall size and scope of government

Topic 4.3: Changes in Ideology (MPA-1)

Questions 3–4 refer to the table.

The Importance of Groups

The General Social Survey (GSS) has been conducted since 1972 to assess the opinions of Americans on certain key issues. Those who take the surveys are asked to indicate if they agree or disagree with statements such as those shown in the table. The percentages indicate those who agree with the statements.

		"Favor preferences in hiring Blacks" (percentage who strongly support or support)	"Abortions OK if woman wants one for any reason" (percentage who agree)	"OK to allow anti-American Muslim cleric to speak" (percentage who agree)
Gender	Male	15.8%	50.3%	49.2%
	Female	15.6	49.6	37.7
Age	18–30	17.5	56.6	41.1
	31–40	17.8	53.5	44.6
	41–55	15.9	48.5	46.5
	56–89	13.8	43.2	40.3
Education	Less than high school	24.8	30.1	19.4
	High school	15.6	46.3	38.2
	Bachelor's degree	13.2	61.1	59.8
	Advanced degree	16.8	67.5	63.3
Race	White	10.7	51.4	48.8
	African-American	34.9	47.0	34.9
	Latino	16.6	44.9	26.6
	Other	25.5	56.6	36.2
Family Income	Low	18.7	43.0	32.6
	Lower middle	17.7	49.7	40.4
	Higher middle	14.0	47.0	44.9
	High	12.1	59.2	57.2

Source: 2018 data from General Social Survey 1972–2018, Cumulative Datafile, Survey Documentation and Analysis (SDA) at UC Berkeley, http://sda.berkeley.edu (accessed 12/30/19).

3. **Using the information in the table, which of the following statements is the most accurate?**

   (A) The majority of people in the United States agree that abortion is okay if a woman wants one for any reason.

   (B) The younger generation is more likely to strongly support affirmative action than the older generation.

   (C) The older generation would be more likely to support the Supreme Court's decision in *Roe v. Wade* (1973) than the younger generation.

   (D) The eighteen- to thirty-year-old age group has similar views to those with less than a high school education on the issue of affirmative action.

4. **Which of the following conclusions can be drawn from the data in the table?**

   (A) Generational and life-cycle effects contribute to the political socialization that influences an individual's political attitudes.

   (B) An individual's political socialization occurs during the primary years and rarely changes.

   (C) Race is a group characteristic that is the primary mechanism for determining an individual's views and is rarely influenced by other factors.

   (D) As individuals age, they tend to become more liberal in their views.

Topic 4.4: Influence of Political Events on Ideology (MPA-1)

5. An event or some other new information is most likely to change an individual's opinion when the individual _____ .

   (A) is highly informed about an issue

   (B) holds strong opinions about an issue

   (C) does not have a set of preexisting principles to interpret the information

   (D) does not watch the news but rather focuses on social media coverage of the information

Topic 4.5: Measuring Public Opinion (MPA-2)

Questions 6–7 refer to the infographic.

Public Opinion and Polling

Rasmussen Reports

Use land-lines... mostly.	**Make robo-calls.**	**Adjust the results.**

A partially random sample: Contact people who have **land-line phones** and use a **nonrandom online panel** to sample groups that tend not to have land-lines.

Respondent selection: Survey the **first person who answers the phone**.

Computer-controlled: Use an automated script to survey respondents; do the survey in a **short time period (hours)**.

One-shot: Don't call back people who you miss on the first try.

Weighting the responses: If there are more Democrats (or Republicans) in your sample than you expect, **adjust your results** to account for the difference.

Pew Research Center

Include cell phones.	**Use a person to call.**	**Don't adjust results.**

A random sample: Generate a **sample of all Americans**, including people who have only cell phones.

Respondent selection: When you call, **talk only to the person who is in your sample**.

Live interviewer: Use a live interviewer who can **help respondents who are unsure what a question means**.

Multiple tries: Implement the survey over several days, and **call people back if you missed them**.

Surprises are interesting: If the partisan divide in your sample is not what you expect, **treat it as a finding**—people may be changing their party ID.

6. **Based on the information provided in the infographic, which of the following is a likely limitation of the Rasmussen Reports' use of only land-lines to conduct a poll?**

   (A) Since younger people often only use cell phones, their views are less likely to be represented in the public-opinion survey.

   (B) Through the use of live interviews, respondents can get clarification on the meaning of a question.

   (C) Trying to ask everyone in a nationwide survey causes a long delay in the gathering of the results of the poll.

   (D) Calling people back over several days can lead to a duplication of results in the poll.

7. **Which of the following best explains why the results from a survey conducted by different polling organizations, as demonstrated in the infographic, about Americans' attitudes concerning the deployment of Department of Homeland Security agents in cities with protests might vary depending on how the questions are phrased?**

   (A) Changes in the wording of questions make people suspicious.

   (B) People do not take surveys very seriously.

   (C) Surveys only use automated scripts to avoid issues with question wording.

   (D) Changes in the wording of questions call to mind different considerations.

8. **Which of the following is an accurate comparison of scientific and non-scientific polling types and methods?**

	Scientific	Non-Scientific
(A)	A randomly selected group of 1,000 respondents will measure the average opinion in a population within 3 percentage points.	The survey uses a live interviewer who will be implemented over several days.
(B)	The questions are available online to make it easier for anyone to take the poll at any time.	The sampling error, or margin of error, is around 10 percent.
(C)	Participants are randomly selected, such that any member of the population has an equal chance of being selected.	In order to be accurate, a national survey would need approximately half of the population surveyed.
(D)	The questions are worded to elicit emotion in order to encourage more people to participate.	The questions are worded in a neutral manner in order to not influence the results.

Topic 4.6: Evaluating Public Opinion Data (MPA-2)

Questions 9–10 refer to the excerpt.

On average, people should be more skeptical when they see numbers. They should be more willing to play around with the data themselves.

—Nate Silver, FiveThirtyEight.com

9. **Which of the following titles for an online article would best describe the author's point of view in the excerpt?**

   (A) Data Makes a Comeback

   (B) Statistics Don't Lie, but Liars Use Statistics

   (C) Slander Is the New Norm in Elections

   (D) Elections Have Consequences

10. **If members of Congress view their role as delegates, in terms of representation, which of the following best explains how they would respond to the author's point of view in the excerpt?**

(A) Since the public does not have access to full information to make a decision, public-opinion data is not as important.

(B) Most decisions are made by a small group of wealthy individuals, and having those connections is more important than public opinion.

(C) Public-opinion data need to be reliable in order to effectively represent the needs of constituents.

(D) Polls taken at a national convention are more likely to be scientific, so data manipulation is less of a problem.

Free-Response Questions

Quantitative Analysis

What Do Americans Think about the Trustworthiness of the Government?

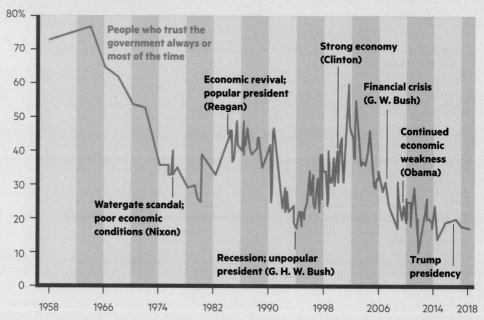

Source: Pew Research Center, "Public Trust in Government, 1958–2019," April 11, 2019, www.pewresearch.org/politics/2019/04/11/public-trust-in-government-1958-2019/ (accessed 5/3/20).

Use the graph to answer the questions.

(A) Identify the year in which Americans had a low level of trust in the government due to a recession and an unpopular president.

(B) Describe the relationship between the country's economic conditions and the percentage of people who trust the government always or most of the time, as shown in the graph.

(C) Draw a conclusion about that relationship between the country's economic conditions and the percentage of people who trust the government always or most of the time, as shown in the graph.

(D) Explain how the wording of the questions in a public opinion survey can affect the reliability of the poll.

Argument Essay

Develop an argument that explains whether or not members of Congress should follow polling results when passing legislation.

Use at least one piece of evidence from one of the following foundational documents:

- Article I of the U.S. Constitution
- Brutus 1
- *Federalist 10*

In your response, you should do the following:

✓ Respond to the prompt with a defensible claim or thesis that establishes a line of reasoning.

✓ Support your claim with at least *two* pieces of specific and relevant evidence.

- One piece of evidence must come from one of the foundational documents listed above.
- A second piece of evidence can come from any other foundational document not used as your first piece of evidence, or it may be from your knowledge of course concepts.

✓ Use reasoning to explain why your evidence supports your claim or thesis.

✓ Respond to an opposing or alternate perspective using refutation, concession, or rebuttal.

11

Political Parties

How do political parties organize American politics?

 "Our diversity is our strength, our unity is our power."[1]
Speaker of the House Nancy Pelosi (D-CA)

 "I've got news for the Republican establishment. I've got news for the Democratic establishment. They can't stop us."
Senator Bernie Sanders (I-VT)

The power and limits of American political parties are best illustrated by the 2020 Democratic presidential nomination contest. Over a dozen candidates ran serious, well-funded campaigns, beginning over a year before the first caucus in Iowa. None of them, not even billionaire Mike Bloomberg, seriously considered running as an Independent. The rules of the contest were set by the Democratic National Committee, which even decided which candidates would appear in DNC-sponsored debates. There was extensive live coverage of the party's presidential nomination convention in August 2020, including the acceptance speech by the winner of the contest, former vice president Joe Biden. At the same time, many critics argued that the nomination process was drawn out and highlighted divisions between liberals and moderates in the party that will complicate Democratic policy initiatives over the next two years.

The 2020 Democratic nomination contest is an example of what political scientist Julia Azari calls "strong partisanship, weak parties."[2] On the one hand, decades of research have shown that most Americans have a long-term attachment to one of the major parties and that this attachment shapes their political behavior— even if they say they are voting for the better candidate rather than according to their party identification. Parties organize elections: although President Trump campaigned in 2016 as a political outsider, he won the presidency as the candidate of the Republican Party. And once candidates are elected to office, parties are also players in the legislative process. Congressional party leaders, such as Senate Majority Leader Mitch McConnell or House Minority Leader Nancy Pelosi during the 115th Congress, are important spokespeople and dealmakers. In these ways, parties unify and mobilize disparate groups, simplify the choices that voters face, and bring efficiency and coherence to government policy making.

During the 2020 Democratic primary, the field was initially crowded with several candidates from a variety of backgrounds. Ultimately, Joe Biden won the nomination and defeated incumbent president Donald Trump.

CHAPTER GOALS

Define *political parties* and show how American political parties and party systems have evolved over time. pages 474–479

Describe the main characteristics of American parties as organizations, in the government, and in the electorate. pages 479–489

Explain the important functions that parties perform in the political system. pages 489–500

Evaluate whether the American party system enhances or hinders democracy. pages 501–503

At the same time, American political parties seem unable to carry through on their promises. While Joe Biden won the nomination, there were doubts about whether he would be able to reach policy compromises and gain the support of the more progressive side of the party that had been excited about the policy proposals championed by Bernie Sanders, including Medicare for All, a Green New Deal, and free higher education. (And as Sanders's quote indicates, he made no secret of his opposition to both party organizations.[3]) But Biden is not the first nominee to receive these criticisms. Many Democrats had doubts about Senator Hillary Clinton's electability in 2016. And even though Donald Trump ran that year on promises to fully repeal Obamacare, build a wall at the Mexican border, and reform federal welfare programs, he was largely unsuccessful—even with Republican control of the presidency and both houses of Congress after his election in 2016. Congressional Democrats were similarly unable to deliver on their pledge to remove President Trump from office through impeachment, despite winning majority control of the House of Representatives in the 2018 midterms. Given the diversity of House Democrats, party leaders face a daunting task in trying to build unity around controversial policy initiatives. Many Americans report that they dislike both major parties—even the one they identify with.

Our task in this chapter is to understand that American political parties can simultaneously be strong and weak, or influential yet disliked and irrelevant. Why is it impossible to describe American politics without talking about Republicans and Democrats? At the same time, why do the parties seem like bystanders as nominees are chosen and policies are debated?

DEFINE *POLITICAL PARTIES* AND SHOW HOW AMERICAN POLITICAL PARTIES AND PARTY SYSTEMS HAVE EVOLVED OVER TIME

What are political parties and where did today's parties come from?

Political parties are organizations that run candidates for political office and coordinate the actions of officials elected under the party banner. Looking around the world, we find many different kinds of parties. In many western European countries, the major political parties have millions of dues-paying members and party leaders control what their elected officials do. These countries typically have several major parties competing for office. In contrast, candidates in many new democracies run as representatives of a party, but party leaders have no control over what candidates say during the campaign or how they act in office.

America's two major political parties, the Republican Party and the Democratic Party, lie somewhere between these extremes. Rather than being unified organizations with party leaders at the top, candidates and party workers in the middle, and citizen-members at the bottom, American political parties are decentralized, each one a loose network of organizations, groups, and individuals who share a party label but are under no obligation to work together.[4] The **party organization** is the structure of national, state, and local parties, including party leaders and workers. The **party in government** is made up of the politicians who are elected as candidates of the party. And the **party in the electorate** includes all the citizens who identify with the party. For example, the Republican Party's national organization, the RNC, functions independently of Republican leaders in government like Senate Majority Leader Mitch McConnell during the 116th Congress; neither one is in charge of the other. In fact, McConnell

party organization
A specific political party's leaders and workers at the national, state, and local levels.

party in government
The group of officeholders who belong to a specific political party and were elected as candidates of that party.

party in the electorate
The group of citizens who identify with a specific political party.

American political parties have three largely separate components: the party organization, represented here by Tom Perez, chair of the DNC; the party in government, represented here by Speaker of the House Nancy Pelosi and Senate Minority Leader Chuck Schumer during the 116th Congress; and the party in the electorate, exemplified here by the crowd at a rally for Representative Alexandria Ocasio-Cortez (D-NY) and New York attorney general candidate Zephyr Teachout.

waited until just before the Republican National Convention in 2016 to endorse the party's nominee for president, Donald Trump, although McConnell strongly supported Trump during the president's term and during his campaign for a second term in 2020. Similarly, although McConnell is the leader of Republican senators, he cannot tell them what to do. While McConnell's colleagues may be somewhat sympathetic to his arguments, there is no political compulsion to do what he asks. For example, McConnell was unable to prevent Republican defections on several of President Trump's Cabinet nominations—although McConnell did assemble a Republican majority to approve Trump's tax cut proposals and Supreme Court nominees, and persuaded almost all Republican senators to vote against removing Trump from office during the impeachment proceedings in 2020. Moreover, while many Americans think of themselves as members of a political party, someone who identifies with the Republican Party is not obligated to work for or give money to the party or to vote for its candidates. As you will see, organization matters: the fact that American political parties are split into three parts has important implications for what they do and for their impact on the nation's politics.

History of American political parties

The Republican and Democratic parties have existed for a long time—the Republicans since 1854 and the Democrats since the early 1800s. Over this time, the parties have been transformed in every respect except their names. These changes are the first important clue about the nature of American political parties: there is nothing inevitable about what the parties stand for, the types of candidates who run under each party's banner, and the groups that support each party. The sharply polarized parties in today's America did not exist a generation ago. American political parties may look very different in the future.

The Republican and Democratic parties have survived throughout most of American history even though they often have not been very popular, even among their supporters. Their survival is partly due to state and local laws that make it easier for candidates to get on the ballot if they run as a major-party candidate. Both parties also work to find good candidates and raise money for their campaigns. In addition, as we discuss later, the fact that America elects officeholders from states or geographic districts makes it harder for new parties to form, keeping the two existing parties in place, a result known as Duverger's Law.[5]

Political scientists use the term **party system** to describe periods of time when the major parties' names, their groups of supporters, and the issues dividing them have all been constant (the beginning and end years that we use throughout this section are approximate). As Table 11.1 shows, there have been six party systems in America.[6] For each party system, the table gives the names of the two major parties, indicates which

party system
Periods in which the names of the major political parties, their supporters, and the issues dividing them have remained relatively stable.

TABLE
11.1

American Party Systems

There have been six party systems in the United States since 1789.

Party System	Major Parties (dominant party in boldface)	Key Issues
First (1789–1828)	Federalists, Democratic-Republicans (neither party was dominant)	Location of the capital, financial issues (e.g., national bank)
Second (1829–1856)	**Democrats**, Whigs	Tariffs (farmers vs. merchants), slavery
Third (1857–1896)	Democrats, **Republicans**	Slavery (pre–Civil War), Reconstruction (post–Civil War), industrialization
Fourth (1897–1932)	Democrats, **Republicans**	Industrialization, immigration
Fifth (1933–1968)	**Democrats**, Republicans	Size and scope of the federal government
Sixth (1969–present)	Democrats, Republicans (neither party is dominant)	Size and scope of the federal government, civil rights, social issues, foreign policy

Source: Compiled by the authors.

party dominated (won the most presidential elections or controlled Congress), and describes the principal issues dividing the parties.

There's no evidence from decades of Pew Research surveys that public opinion, in the aggregate, is more extreme now than in the past. But what has changed—and pretty dramatically—is the growing tendency of people to sort themselves into political parties based on their ideological differences.

—Pew Research Center

party principle
The idea that a political party exists as an organization distinct from its elected officials or party leaders.

spoils system
The practice of rewarding party supporters with benefits like federal government positions.

The Evolution of American Political Parties While most of the Founders held a dim view of political parties, many of them participated in the formation of such parties soon after the Founding of the United States. The Federalists and the Democratic-Republicans were primarily parties in government that consisted of like-minded legislators: Federalists wanted a strong central government and a national bank; Democratic-Republicans took the opposite positions. These political parties were quite different from their modern counterparts. In particular, there were no national party organizations, few citizens thought of themselves as party members, and candidates for office did not campaign as representatives of a party. Even so, the goals of those who developed these parties were similar to the goals of party leaders today: like-minded individuals banded together to help enact their preferred policies and defeat their opponents.

For two decades, the two parties were more or less evenly matched in Congress, although the Federalists did not win a presidential contest after 1800. However, in the 1814 elections Federalist legislators, who had opposed the War of 1812 and supported a politically unpopular pay raise for members of Congress, lost most of their congressional seats.[7] These defeats led to the demise of the Federalist Party and the start of the Era of Good Feelings, when there was only one political party: the Democratic-Republican Party. Following the election of President Andrew Jackson in 1828, this party became known as the Democratic Party. At the same time, another new party, the Whig Party, was formed in opposition to Democratic policy priorities, beginning the second party system.

The new Democratic Party cultivated electoral support by building organizations to mobilize citizens and bind them to the party. The operations of the party reflected two new concepts: the **party principle**, the idea that a party is not just a group of elected officials but an organization that exists apart from its candidates, and the **spoils system**, whereby party workers were rewarded with benefits such as federal jobs.[8]

In the 1840s, the issue of slavery split the second party system. Most Democratic politicians either supported slavery outright or wanted to avoid debating the issue.[9] The Whig Party was split between abolitionists, who wanted to end slavery, and politicians who agreed with the Democrats. Ultimately, antislavery Whigs left the party and formed the Republican Party, which also attracted antislavery Democrats, and the Whig Party soon ceased to exist. These changes initiated the third party system, in which the country was divided into a largely Republican Northeast, a largely Democratic South, and politically split midwestern and border states.[10] These developments illustrate that political parties exist not because the Constitution or laws say they must, but because elites, politicians, party leaders, and activists want them to. The Republican Party was created by people who wanted to abolish slavery, and many other politicians subsequently joined the party because of their ambition: these politicians believed that their chances of winning political office were higher as Republicans than as Whigs or Democrats.

After the Civil War, the Republicans and Democrats remained the two prominent national parties. They were divided over whether the federal government should help farmers and rural residents or inhabitants of rapidly expanding cities and whether it should regulate America's rapidly growing industrial base. Democrats built a coalition of rural and urban voters by proposing a larger, more active federal government, as well as other policies that would help both groups.

This strategy is one example of how American political parties have adapted their issue positions to societal changes and consequently reflect the basic political divisions between Americans. A similar shift occurred during the transition to the fourth party system, in which the parties were divided on the government's response to industrialization and restrictions on immigration. There were also significant moves during this time in expanding who was eligible to vote, although women did not gain this right until the early twentieth century, and minorities were generally barred by a combination of laws and practices until the 1960s.[11]

The fifth party system was born out of the Great Depression: the worldwide economic collapse that led to the unemployment of millions of people. Many Republicans argued that conditions would improve over time and that government intervention would do little good, whereas Democrats proposed new programs that would help people in need and spur economic growth. The Democratic landslide in the 1932 election led to the New Deal, a series of federal programs proposed by President Franklin Delano Roosevelt and enacted by Congress to stimulate the national economy, help needy people, and impose a variety of new regulations. Debate over the New Deal brought together the New Deal coalition of African Americans, Catholics, Jews, union members, and White southerners, who became strong supporters of Democratic candidates over the next generation.[12] This transformation established the basic division between the parties that exists to the present day: Democrats generally favor a large federal government that takes an active role in managing the economy and regulating behavior, and Republicans generally believe that many such programs should be provided by state and local governments or not provided at all.

The move from the fifth to the sixth party system was marked by the introduction of new political questions and debates that divided the parties.[13] Beginning in the late 1940s, many Democratic candidates and party leaders, particularly outside the South, came out against the "separate but equal" system of racial discrimination in southern states and in favor of programs designed to ensure equal opportunity for minority citizens. Then, during the 1960s, many Democratic politicians argued for expanding the role of the federal government in health care, antipoverty programs, and education. Most Republicans opposed such initiatives, although a significant portion did not.

At the same time, these new issues also began to divide American citizens and organized groups, leading to a gradual but significant shift in the groups that identified with each party.[14] White southerners and some Catholics moved to the Republican Party,

"THAT'S WHAT'S THE MATTER."

Boss Tweed. "As long as I count the Votes, what are you going to do about it? say

The Tammany Hall political machine, depicted here as a rotund version of one of its leaders, William "Boss" Tweed, controlled New York City politics for most of the nineteenth and early twentieth centuries. Its strategy was "honest graft," rewarding party workers, contributors, and voters for their efforts to keep the machine's candidates in office.

Debate over Roosevelt's New Deal programs established the basic divide between Democrats and Republicans that continues to this day: in the main, Democrats favor a larger federal government that takes an active role in managing the economy; Republicans prefer a smaller federal government and fewer programs and regulations.

realignment
A change in the size or composition of the party coalitions or in the nature of the issues that divide the parties. Realignments typically occur within an election cycle or two, but they can also occur gradually over the course of a decade or longer.

and minorities, particularly African Americans, started identifying more strongly as Democrats. Democrats also gained supporters in New England and West Coast states. By the late 1980s, all three elements of the Republican and Democratic parties (organization, government, and electorate) were much more like-minded than they had been a generation earlier, a trend that continues to the present day.

Broadly speaking, Democrats tend to favor a larger government that provides more benefits to citizens and regulates corporate and individual behavior, while Republicans advocate for a small government that does less. However, there are exceptions to these rules. On many social issues such as abortion and LGBTQ rights, most Democrats favor individual choice and equality, while most Republicans favor limits on abortion and oppose equality for same-sex couples on issues such as marriage and adoption.[15] Moreover, as the 2020 Democratic presidential nomination contest demonstrates, issues such as expanding government-provided health care divide candidates and their supporters within each party.

The sixth party system also brought changes in party organizations. Both the Republican and Democratic parties increased their involvement in recruiting, training, conducting fund-raising, and campaigning for their party's congressional and presidential candidates in an effort to elect like-minded colleagues who would vote with them to enact their preferred policies.[16] At the same time, disagreements between congressional Republicans and Democrats increased, making it harder to find common ground in many policy areas.

Realignments Each party system is separated from the next by a **realignment**, a change in one or more of the factors that define a party system, including the issues that divide the parties, the nature and function of the party organizations, the composition of the party coalitions, and the specifics of government policy. Early work on realignments argued that realignments began with the emergence of a new question or issue debate that captured the attention of large numbers of ordinary citizens, activists, and politicians.[17] To spur a realignment, the issue had to be *crosscutting*, meaning that within each party coalition there were people who disagreed on what government should do about this new issue. These pressures culminated in a high-turnout election in which the parties took clear stands on the new issues (or a new party emerged) and voters switched parties based on which stand they liked best. Scholars also believed that realignments developed about a generation apart, as citizens who came of age as a past realignment occurred were replaced by new voters.

More recent work, particularly by political scientist David Mayhew, has shown that none of these conditions are necessary for a realignment.[18] Realignments don't happen once in a generation like clockwork, don't always involve a single crosscutting issue, and don't always occur all at once. It may be impossible to know that a realignment is happening until it has already occurred. A good example of what Mayhew is talking about is the change between the fifth (1933–1968) and the sixth (1969–present) party system.[19] Parties in the fifth party system were primarily divided by their positions on the appropriate size of the federal government. In the sixth party system, new issues such as civil rights and social issues as well as gender equality and abortion became more important markers of division between the parties and their supporters. However, these changes only became apparent in the 1990s, as Republicans gained House and Senate seats in southern states, and Democrats gained seats in the Northeast, West, and Southwest.[20] After the 2018 elections, Republicans controlled only one Senate seat in New England, while there were only three Democratic senators in the South (two in Virginia).

Trump's election in 2016, along with Joe Biden's victory in 2020, suggest that America may be beginning to develop a new party system. Other evidence for this possibility includes emerging Democratic support in coastal states and the Southwest, Republican gains in the Midwest, and new splits within each party coalition on issues such as trade, immigration, and a more aggressive role for government in providing health care and other benefits to citizens. It is too soon to tell, however, whether these changes will be significant enough to realign the parties, or even to replace one party with a new organization, particularly given the large and unexpected role that the COVID-19 pandemic played in the 2020 election.

Looking at American political parties today, you might think that Democratic and Republican parties have been around forever, that they are evenly split in party identifiers and officeholders, and that their main disagreement has always concerned the size and scope of government. None of these ideas is true. Moreover, the changes over time in the Republican and Democratic parties illustrate how these organizations adapt to shifts in public opinion. Thus, American political parties may look very different 10 years from now than they do today.

American political parties today

DESCRIBE THE MAIN CHARACTERISTICS OF AMERICAN PARTIES AS ORGANIZATIONS, IN THE GOVERNMENT, AND IN THE ELECTORATE

We've seen that, almost from the beginning, political parties have been a central feature of American politics. The next steps are to examine the different aspects (the party organization, the party in government, and the party in the electorate) of American political parties, describe the role they play in elections and in government, and understand how their organization and operations shape American democracy.

The party organization

The principal body in each party organization is the **national committee** (the Democratic National Committee or the Republican National Committee), which consists of representatives from state party organizations, usually one man and one woman per state. The state party organizations in turn are made up of professional staff plus thousands of party organizations at the county, city, and town levels. The job of these organizations is to run the party's day-to-day operations, recruit candidates and supporters, raise money for future campaigns, and work to build a consensus on major issues. (Of course, other groups in the party, as well as individual politicians, carry out similar tasks at the same time and not always in agreement with the national or state committees.)

Both national party committees include a number of *constituency groups* (the Democrats' term) or *teams* (the Republicans' term). These organizations within the party work to attract the support of demographic groups—such as African Americans, Latinos, people with strong religious beliefs, senior citizens, women, and many others—who are considered likely to share the party's issue concerns and to assist in fund-raising. In some cases, these organizations also attempt to win over groups typically identified with the other party. For example, African Americans have long been strong supporters of Democratic candidates. Accordingly, the Democratic Party has a constituency group that informs African Americans about the party's candidates

national committee
An American political party's principal organization, comprising party representatives from each state.

and works to convince these citizens to vote on Election Day. The group also gives African-American leaders a formal voice in party deliberations.

Each party organization also includes groups designed to build support for, or coordinate the efforts of, particular individuals or politicians. These groups include the Democratic and the Republican Governors' Associations, the Young Democrats, the Young Republicans, and more specialized groups such as the Republican Lawyers' Organization or the Democratic Leadership Council (DLC), an organization of moderate Democratic politicians.[21] The parties use their college and youth organizations to motivate politically minded students to work for the party and its candidates. Groups such as the Governors' Associations and the DLC hold meetings where elected officials discuss solutions to common problems and try to formulate joint strategies. People who work for a party organization perform a wide range of tasks, from recruiting candidates and formulating political strategies to mobilizing citizens, conducting fund-raising, filling out campaign finance reports, researching opposing candidates and parties, and developing websites for the party and its candidates.

Other Allied Groups Many other groups, such as **political action committees (PACs)** or **527 organizations**, labor unions, and other interest groups and organizations, are loosely affiliated with one of the major parties. For example, the organization MoveOn.org typically supports Democratic candidates. Similar organizations on the Republican side include the Club for Growth, Americans for Prosperity, Crossroads GPS, and many evangelical groups. Many of these organizations take advantage of a loophole in a provision of the IRS code to legally solicit large, anonymous donations from corporate and individual contributors. Although these groups often favor one party over the other, they are not part of the party organization and do not always agree with the party's positions or support its candidates—in fact, many have to operate independently of the parties and their candidates to preserve their tax-exempt status. (For more details on campaign finance, see Chapters 12 and 13.)

As this description suggests, the party organization has a fluid structure rather than a rigid hierarchy.[22] Individuals and groups work with a party's leaders and candidates when they share the same goals, but unless they are paid party employees, they are

political action committee (PAC)
An interest group or a division of an interest group that can raise money to contribute to campaigns or to spend on ads in support of candidates. The amount a PAC can receive from each of its donors and the amount it can spend on federal electioneering are strictly limited.

527 organization
A tax-exempt group formed primarily to influence elections through voter mobilization efforts and to issue ads that do not directly endorse or oppose a candidate. Unlike PACs, 527 organizations are not subject to contribution limits and spending caps.

Both parties include internal organizations that attempt to attract the support of certain demographic groups, even ones that are typically identified with the opposite party. Women, for example, tend to vote more for Democrats on average.

under no obligation to do so. (Even paid party workers can, of course, quit rather than work for a candidate or a cause they oppose. The strong support for President Trump from within the Republican party organization was partly due to departures—both voluntary and forced—of party workers and officials who opposed Trump's nomination and his policies.)

Party Brand Names The Republican and Democratic party organizations have well-established "brand names." Because the parties stand for different things, in terms of both their preferred government policies and their ideological leanings, the party names themselves become a shorthand way of providing information to voters about the parties' candidates.[23] Hearing the term "Democrat" or "Republican" calls to mind ideas about what kinds of positions the members of each party support, what kinds of candidates each party runs, and how these candidates will probably vote if they are elected to office. Citizens can use these brand names as a cue to decide whom to vote for in an election. (See Chapter 13 for more information on voting cues.)

Differences in the details of party brand names also create opportunities for **issue ownership**: candidates from a party tend to concentrate their campaigns on issues that are part of their party's brand name and ignore issues that belong to the other party. Figure 11.1 shows one way to measure issue ownership: by surveying citizens who identify with each party about their policy priorities.

Limits of the Party Organization The critical thing to understand about the Democratic and Republican party organizations is that they are not hierarchies. No one person or group in charge determines what either organization does—which often makes them look disorganized. Because the RNC and DNC are organized in the same way, we can consider the example of Tom Perez, the chair of the DNC. He has some influence over who works at the DNC. However, the party organization's issue positions are set not by Perez's employees but by DNC members from all 50 states. The individual committee members are appointed by their state party organizations, so they do not owe their jobs to Perez—in fact, they can remove *him* from office if they like. If Perez and the committee disagree, he can't force the committee members to do what he wants.

The national party organization is also unable to force state and local parties to share its positions on issues or comply with other requests. State and local parties make their own decisions about state- and local-level candidates and issue positions. The national committee can ask nicely, cajole, or even threaten to withhold funds. But if a state party organization, an independent group, or even an individual candidate disagrees with the national committee, there's little the national committee can do to force compliance. For example, Republican leaders could not discourage challengers from running in primaries against their preferred Senate candidates in 2020. Nor could they stop Donald Trump from winning the presidential nomination in 2016—much less control his behavior in office.

Party organizations at the local level, such as the Ohio county Democratic Party meeting shown here, coordinate support for the party's candidates, but they don't necessarily have to follow the lead of the national party organization.

issue ownership
The theory that voters associate certain issues or issue positions with certain parties (like Democrats and support for government-provided health insurance).

I am not a member of an organized political party. I am a Democrat.

—Will Rogers, American actor

The party in government

The party in government consists of elected officials holding national, state, and local offices who took office as candidates of a particular party. They are the public face of the party, somewhat like the players on a sports team. Although players

FIGURE 11.1

Democrats' and Republicans' Top Priorities

The Republican and Democratic party coalitions have different priorities on many issues, ranging from environmental protection to deficit reduction—and their differences are small on a few issues, such as fighting drug addiction and reducing the crime rate. Do these differences make sense in light of each party's "brand name"?

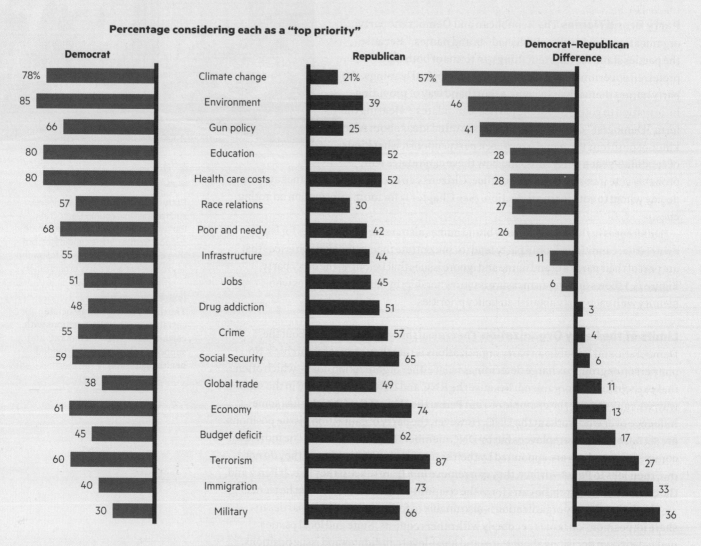

Percentage considering each as a "top priority"

	Democrat		Republican	Democrat–Republican Difference
Climate change	78%		21%	57%
Environment	85		39	46
Gun policy	66		25	41
Education	80		52	28
Health care costs	80		52	28
Race relations	57		30	27
Poor and needy	68		42	26
Infrastructure	55		44	11
Jobs	51		45	6
Drug addiction	48		51	3
Crime	55		57	4
Social Security	59		65	6
Global trade	38		49	11
Economy	61		74	13
Budget deficit	45		62	17
Terrorism	60		87	27
Immigration	40		73	33
Military	30		66	36

Note: Chart reflects priorities prior to the COVID-19 pandemic.

Source: Pew Research Center, "As Economic Concerns Recede, Environmental Protection Rises on the Public's Policy Agenda," February 13, 2020, www.people-press.org (accessed 3/18/20).

are only one part of a sports franchise—along with owners, coaches, trainers, and support staff—the players' identities are what most people call to mind when they think of the team. Because the party in government is made up of officeholders, it has a direct impact on government policy. Members of the party organization can recruit candidates, write platforms, and pay for campaign ads, but only those who win elections—the party in government—serve as members of Congress or as executive officials and actually propose, debate, vote on, and sign the legislation that determines what government does.

Caucuses and Conferences In the House and Senate, the Democratic and Republican parties are organized around working groups called a **caucus** (Democrats) and a **conference** (Republicans). The party caucus or conference serves as a forum for debate, compromise, and strategizing among a party's elected officials. Under **unified government** (in which the same party controls Congress and the presidency) these discussions focus on finding common ground within the party, as in the negotiations that led to the Republican tax cut legislation in 2016, which was enacted without Democratic support. Under **divided government** (in which one party controls at least one house of Congress and the other party controls the presidency, as in 2019-2020), the focus changes to finding opportunities to work with the other party or strategizing on how to block the other party's initiatives. Divided government was relatively rare before the 1960s but has become increasingly common since then. Particularly when control is divided, partisan differences can yield policy gridlock, as neither side is willing to compromise and neither side has the votes to push its preferred package through. Measures such as the economic stimulus legislation enacted rapidly in response to the COVID-19 pandemic in March 2020 are very much the exception to the rule.

Each party's caucus or conference meets to decide on legislative committee assignments, leadership positions on committees, and leadership positions within the caucus or conference.[24] Caucus or conference leaders also serve as spokespeople for their respective parties, particularly when the president is from the other party. The party in government also contains groups that recruit and support candidates for political office: the Democratic Congressional Campaign Committee (DCCC), the Democratic Senatorial Campaign Committee (DSCC), the National Republican Congressional Committee (NRCC), and the National Republican Senatorial Committee (NRSC).

Polarization and Ideological Diversity The modern Congress is polarized: in both the House and the Senate, Republicans and Democrats hold different views on government policy. The graph in the What Do the Facts Say? feature tells us that over the last 60 years the magnitude of ideological differences between the parties in Congress has increased. Up until the 1980s there was some overlap between the positions of Democrats and Republicans, but this overlap has disappeared in recent years. However, if we expanded the figure to look at the ideologies of individual members, we'd find a mixture of ideologies, not a uniform consensus opinion. In the contemporary Congress, Democrats vary from the relatively liberal left end of the axis to the moderate (middle) and even somewhat conservative right end. The same is true for Republican members of Congress: while most are conservative, there are some moderates, as well as a range of conservative opinions.

The ideological diversity within each party in government can create situations in which a caucus or conference is divided on a policy question. Compromise within a party's working group is not inevitable—even though legislators share a party label, they may not be able to find common ground. In the last few years, congressional Democrats have been largely united on most issues, while divisions on the Republican side arose on issues of immigration policy as well as health care, taxation and spending levels, and the federal budget deficit.[25] Differences between the parties are present on virtually all major issues—with the response to COVID-19 being a rare exception.

The party in the electorate

The party in the electorate consists of citizens who identify with a particular political party. Most Americans say they are either Democrats or Republicans, although the percentage has declined slightly over the last two generations. **Party identification (party ID)** is a critical variable in understanding votes and other forms of political participation.

caucus (congressional)
The organization of Democrats within the House and Senate that meets to discuss and debate the party's positions on various issues in order to reach a consensus and to assign leadership positions.

conference
The organization of Republicans within the House and Senate that meets to discuss and debate the party's positions on various issues in order to reach a consensus and to assign leadership positions.

unified government
A situation in which one party holds a majority of seats in the House and Senate and the president is a member of that same party.

divided government
A situation in which the House, Senate, and presidency are not controlled by the same party—for example, when Democrats hold the majority of House and Senate seats and the president is a Republican.

party identification (party ID)
A citizen's loyalty to a specific political party.

Are the Parties More Polarized than Ever?

For the last 20 years, it seems as though all the news about political parties has been about conflict and stalemate. It seems like political campaigns are increasingly negative, bipartisan compromise is rare, and Republicans and Democrats have divided into camps that never agree on anything. Is this trend new? What do the facts say?

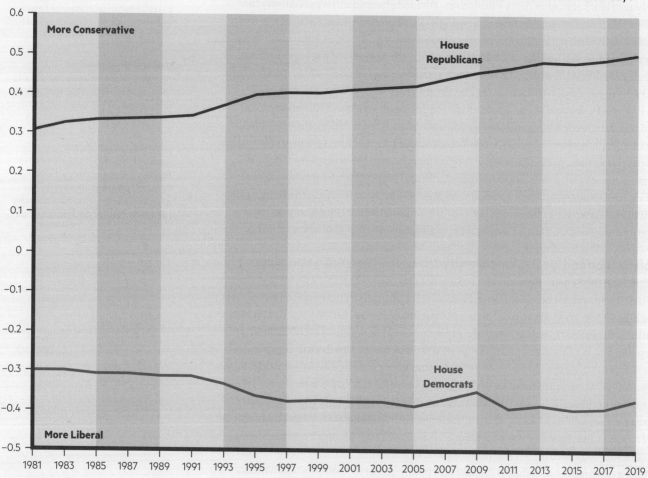

Source: Jeffrey B. Lewis et al., Voteview (congressional roll call votes database), https://voteview.com/ (accessed 3/19/20).

Think about it

- **This graph uses voting behavior to measure** the average ideology (liberal–conservative) of House Democrats and Republicans. Scores near 1 indicate a conservative ideology, while scores near −1 indicate a liberal ideology. Since the 1980s, have Republicans gotten more conservative, have Democrats become more liberal, or both? Has one party moved more than the other?

- **How might these changes make it harder** for members of the contemporary Congress to enact major changes in government policy? What is more likely: compromise or gridlock?

Party ID To say you identify with a party is a personal orientation or decision that does not commit you to anything, nor does it give you any control over a party's actions. Although the Republicans and the Democrats have websites where people can sign up to receive e-mail alerts and to contribute online to party causes, joining a party does not give a citizen any direct influence over what the party does. Rather, the party leaders and the candidates themselves make the day-to-day decisions. These individuals often heed citizens' demands, but there is no requirement that they do so. Real participation in party operations is open to citizens who become activists by working for a party organization or one of its candidates. Activists' contributions vary widely and may include stuffing envelopes, helping out with a phone bank, being a delegate to a party convention, attending campaign rallies, or campaigning door-to-door.

Early theories of party ID described it as a deep attachment to a party that was acquired early in life from parents, friends, and political events and was generally unaffected by subsequent events.[26] Further work showed that party ID does not necessarily remain the same but rather involves continuing evaluation that takes account of new information.[27] Thus, when people say they identify with the Republican Party, they are saying that, based on what they have seen in American politics, they prefer the positions suggested by the Republicans' brand name and how Republicans behave in office. At the same time, party ID shapes how people think about politics and react to new information. Thus, when Republicans argue for managing the entry of undocumented individuals by building a border wall, while Democrats support expanding guest worker programs and providing a path to citizenship, the difference is not what they know but how they react to the same pieces of information—a response that is shaped by their party affiliation. Strong partisans are also more likely to use looser standards to evaluate members or officeholders from their own party, avoid contact with those who identify with the other party, and want preferential treatment for members of their party.[28]

There is also some evidence in recent years of **negative partisanship**, in which party identification is based less on what you like about a party and more about what you dislike about the other party.[29] For example, voters might identify as Republicans even though they disapprove of President Trump and Republicans in Congress, because their feelings about the Democratic Party and its supporters are even more negative. Such negative partisanship could drive lower evaluations of policy debates in Washington—regardless of who wins, someone motivated by negative partisanship will be disappointed by the outcome.

Figure 11.2 gives data on party ID in America from 1992 to 2019, measured when respondents were given the option to say whether they were a Democrat, a Republican, or an Independent. Over this time period, the parties have been nearly evenly split. At various times in the past, one party has opened some advantage over the other (as the Democrats did in the early 2000s), but there is no consistent trend.

Independents Some early analyses concluded that Independents were unaffiliated with a party because they were in the process of shifting their identification from one party to the other.[30] Others saw Independents as evidence that more and more people regarded the parties as irrelevant to their view of politics and their voting decisions.[31] The rise in the number of Independents was also seen as an indication that Americans were becoming more politically savvy—learning more about candidates and not always blindly voting for the same party.[32]

More recent work has modified these findings. Most Independents actually have some weak attachment to one of the major political parties—in fact, some scholars refer to Independents as "closet partisans": people who have party ties but who simply

negative partisanship
Identification with a political party that is based on dislike of the other party rather than positive feelings about the party identified with.

DID YOU KNOW?

5%

of Americans say they worked for a political candidate or issue campaign during the last presidential election.
Source: Pew Research Center

FIGURE 11.2

Party ID Trends among American Voters

In terms of party ID, the parties have moved from rough parity in the 1990s to a slight Democratic advantage in the early twenty-first century, although this change has eroded in recent years. What events might have caused these changes in party ID?

Sources: 1992–2003 data from Pew Research Center, "Party Identification Trends, 1992–2017," March 20, 2018, www.people-press.org (accessed 6/15/20); 2004–2020 data from Gallup, "Party Affiliation," May 2020, https://news.gallup.com/poll/15370/party-affiliation.aspx (accessed 5/30/20).

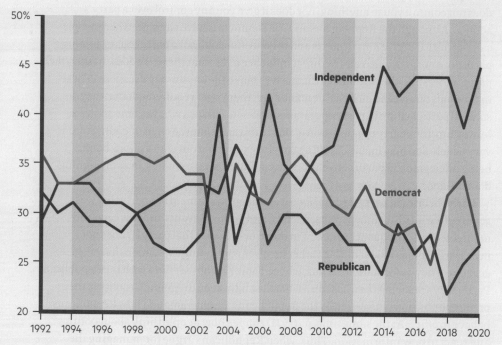

don't admit that they do.[33] In Figure 11.2, for example, over a third of the electorate says it does not identify with a party. However, the percentage of true Independents is much smaller: if we asked these so-called Independents if they leaned toward one party or the other, about two-thirds would claim they do have a slight affiliation, and they would be split evenly between Republicans and Democrats. Independents are not necessarily better informed about candidates, parties, or government policy than are party identifiers. However, they are much less likely to get involved in political activity beyond voting, such as contributing to or working for a candidate or party.[34]

Activist volunteers, such as these two canvassing in the crucial swing state of Ohio, undertake most of the one-on-one efforts to mobilize support for a party and its candidates.

FIGURE
11.3

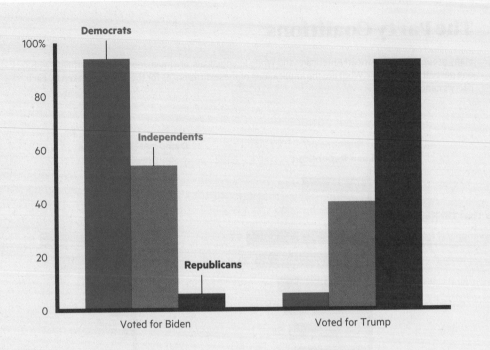

The Impact of Party ID on Voting Decisions in the 2020 Presidential Election

Americans are much more likely to vote for candidates who share their party affiliation. What does this relationship tell us about the impact of campaign events (including speeches, debates, and gaffes) on voting decisions?

Source: Data compiled from CNN Exit Poll, www.cnn.com/election/2020/exit-polls/president/national-results (accessed 11/5/20).

With a closer look at voting decisions, Figure 11.3 shows how Democrats, Republicans, and Independents voted in the 2020 presidential election ("closet partisan" Independents are grouped with the party they actually affiliate with). This figure shows that if you are trying to predict how someone will vote, the most important thing to know is his or her party ID.[35] Over 90 percent of Democrats voted for Joe Biden, the Democratic nominee, and about the same percentage of Republicans voted for Donald Trump.

Party Coalitions Data on party ID enable scholars to study **party coalitions**—that is, groups of citizens who identify with each party. Figure 11.4 shows the contemporary Democratic and Republican party coalitions. As you can see, some groups are disproportionately likely to identify as Democrats (African Americans), some are disproportionately likely to identify as Republicans (White evangelicals), and other groups have no clear party favorite (women born before 1945). Again, these coalitions have shifted over time, often evolving during periods of realignment and changing from one party system to the next. For example, the Republican advantage among White southerners and White evangelical Protestants has existed only since the 1980s.[36]

The Republican and Democratic party coalitions differ systematically in terms of their policy preferences—what they want government to do—as shown in Figure 11.1 on p. 482. This indicates the extent to which they disagree about the relative importance of issues like providing health insurance to the uninsured, dealing with global warming, and strengthening the military. On only a few issues—for example, fighting drug addiction or dealing with crime—are the percentages of those in both parties who consider the matter a priority nearly the same. These data demonstrate that party labels are meaningful: if you know someone is a Republican (or a Democrat), this

party coalitions
The groups that identify with a political party, usually described in demographic terms such as African-American Democrats or evangelical Republicans.

FIGURE 11.4

The Party Coalitions

Many groups, such as African Americans and White evangelicals, are much more likely to affiliate with one party than the other. What are the implications of these differences for the positions taken by each party's candidates?

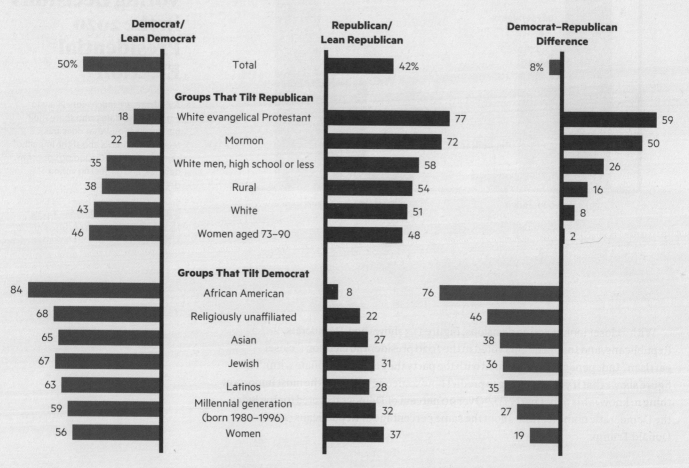

	Democrat/ Lean Democrat	Republican/ Lean Republican	Democrat–Republican Difference
Total	50%	42%	8%
Groups That Tilt Republican			
White evangelical Protestant	18	77	59
Mormon	22	72	50
White men, high school or less	35	58	26
Rural	38	54	16
White	43	51	8
Women aged 73–90	46	48	2
Groups That Tilt Democrat			
African American	84	8	76
Religiously unaffiliated	68	22	46
Asian	65	27	38
Jewish	67	31	36
Latinos	63	28	35
Millennial generation (born 1980–1996)	59	32	27
Women	56	37	19

Source: Pew Research Center, "Wide Gender Gap, Growing Educational Divide in Voters' Party Identification," March 20, 2018, www.people-press.org (accessed 3/20/20).

information tells you something about what that person probably wants government to do, and how he or she will likely vote in the next election.

Figure 11.5 shows the most fundamental difference in Democratic and Republican identifiers: in accordance with the parties' brand names and their positions on specific issues, Democrats are more liberal, while Republicans are more conservative. As you can see, the Democratic Party distribution is dominated by liberal identifiers, while the Republican distribution is dominated by conservatives—although there is still some overlap in the middle, meaning that both parties claim some moderates. Moreover, the current parties are much more homogeneous than a generation ago, with liberals much more likely to be Democrats and conservatives more likely to be Republicans.

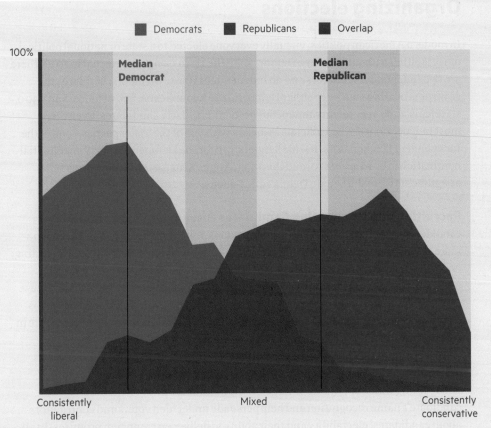

Democrats ■ Republicans ■ Overlap

FIGURE 11.5

The Parties in the Electorate

This graph shows the ideological differences between Democratic and Republican identifiers. The blue area shows the distribution of Democrats, and the red plot shows the distribution of Republicans. This confirms that modern American political parties are ideologically polarized (the median Democrat is a liberal, while the median Republican is a conservative) and homogeneous (most Democrats are liberal or liberal-leaning, while most Republicans are conservative or conservative-leaning). How might these differences affect the kinds of candidates who compete for each party's nomination and the positions they take during campaigns?

Source: Jocelyn Kiley, "In Polarized Era, Fewer Americans Hold a Mix of Conservative and Liberal Views," Pew Research Center, October 3, 2017, www.pewresearch.org/ fact-tank/2017/10/23/in-polarized-era-fewer-americans-hold-a-mix-of-conservative-and-liberal-views/ (accessed 5/30/20).

Knowing that someone is a Democrat or a Republican tells you a lot about the issues he or she cares about, whether he or she will like or dislike different candidates, and whom he or she will vote for in an election. Taken together, information about the kinds of people who identify with each party tells you a lot about the kinds of candidates who will run under the party banner and the platforms they will campaign on.

"Why Should I Care?"

The role of political parties in American politics

EXPLAIN THE IMPORTANT FUNCTIONS THAT PARTIES PERFORM IN THE POLITICAL SYSTEM

Political parties play an important role in American politics, from helping to organize elections to building consensus across branches of government. But these activities are not necessarily coordinated. Candidates and groups at different levels of a party organization may work together, refuse to cooperate, or even actively oppose one another's efforts.

Organizing elections

In modern American politics, virtually everyone elected to a state or national political office is either a Republican or a Democrat. In the 117th Congress, elected in 2020, there are two Independent senators and no Independent House members. Similarly, the governors of all 50 states are either Democrats or Republicans, and of more than 7,300 state legislators very few are Independents or minor-party candidates. Even then, most Independent elected officials associate with one of the major parties—one of the Independent U.S. senators, Bernie Sanders, ran for the Democratic Party presidential nomination in 2016 and 2020, and the other, Angus King, gets his committee assignments from the Senate Democratic Caucus.

Recruiting and Nominating Candidates Historically, the recruitment of candidates was left up to local party organizations. But the process has become much more systematic, with state and national party leaders playing a central role in recruiting, endorsing, and funding candidates—and often promising those candidates help in assembling a staff, organizing a campaign, and raising more money.[37] Actions like these can have a profound impact on congressional elections; years in which one party gains significant congressional seats (such as Republicans in 2010 or Democrats in 2018) are in part the result of one party's disproportionate success in its recruiting efforts.

In fact, one of the most well-known theories of presidential nomination contests argues that endorsements by party leaders and elected officials play a key role in determining which candidate emerges as the nominee.[38] Endorsements enhance a candidate's name recognition and help persuade undecided voters and contributors about candidates' electability and their ability to deliver on campaign promises. In all recent presidential nomination contests except 2016, the winning candidate was the one who gathered the most endorsements from party leaders, elected officials, and other notables. This theory was one of the main reasons why most political scientists thought that Donald Trump was unlikely to be the Republican nominee in 2016. While he led in the polls for several months, he received almost no endorsements from party leaders or elected officials. Conversely, one reason why Joe Biden was seen as the inevitable Democratic nominee in 2020 was the relatively large number of endorsements he garnered from Democratic Party leaders.[39]

Party leaders also play an active role in recruiting candidates for House and Senate seats. When a Senate seat opened up in Utah in 2018 because of Senator Orrin Hatch's retirement, many Republican national and state leaders encouraged former Republican presidential nominee Mitt Romney to enter the race and discouraged other potential candidates. These decisions reflected a simple political logic: party leaders believed that Romney would have a good chance of winning the general election given his reputation (including running the 2002 Winter Olympics in Utah) and Utah's large Mormon population. In addition, party leaders, many of whom opposed President Trump in the 2016 election, wanted to discourage the election of a pro-Trump candidate, such as State Auditor John Dougall.

Despite all of these efforts, however, parties and their leaders do not control who runs in House, Senate, or presidential races (see the Take a Stand feature). In most states, candidates for these offices are selected in a **primary election** or a **caucus**, in which they compete for a particular party's spot on the ballot. About two-thirds of the states use some type of primary election, while the rest use caucuses to select candidates (see Nuts & Bolts 11.1). Most notably, Donald Trump won the 2016 Republican presidential nomination by virtue of his victories in the party's primaries and caucuses over the objections of many party leaders. Trump's victory demonstrates that party endorsements, while significant, are not the only factor in shaping nomination contests.

primary election
A ballot vote in which citizens select a party's nominee for the general election.

caucus (electoral)
A local meeting in which party members select a party's nominee for the general election.

Should Parties Choose Their Candidates?

One of the facts of life for the leaders of the Democratic and Republican parties is that they cannot determine who runs as their party's candidate for political office. They can encourage some candidates to run and attempt to discourage others by endorsing their favorites and funneling money, staff support, and other forms of assistance to the candidates they prefer. But in the end, congressional candidates get on the ballot by winning a primary or a vote at a state party convention; presidential candidates compete in a series of primaries and caucuses. Is this system a good one?

Let the party decide. Many scholars have argued that letting parties choose their candidates increases the chances of getting experienced, talented candidates on the ballot.[a] After all, party leaders probably know more than the average voter about who would make a good candidate or elected official. Plus, party leaders have a strong incentive to find good candidates and convince them to run: their party's influence over government policy increases with the number of people they can elect to political office. And finally, in states that have no party registration or day-of-election registration, giving the nomination power to party leaders would ensure that a group of outsiders could not hijack a party primary to nominate a candidate who disagreed with a party's platform or who was unqualified to serve in office.

While cases of outright hijacking of party nominations are fairly rare, political parties don't always get the nominees their leaders want and party leaders cannot force candidates out of a race. In the 2016 election cycle, for example, many Republican Party leaders believed that Donald Trump was not the party's strongest nominee. Trump gained the nomination over their objections by winning the party's caucus and primary contests. You can judge whether his performance in office refutes or justifies their concerns.

Let the people decide. One argument in favor of giving the nomination power to the people is that party leaders have not always shown good judgment in picking either electable or qualified candidates. Many of the same Republican leaders who opposed Trump had supported party nominees John McCain in 2008 and Mitt Romney in 2012, both of whom went on to lose their general-election contest. This track record suggests that party leaders are far from infallible. In 2020, most Democratic leaders believed that Joe Biden was more electable than the alternatives. While the COVID-19 pandemic complicates judgments about the 2020 election, the party leaders were probably right: Biden was best suited to win back White, less educated, midwestern voters who had defected to Trump in 2016.

The second argument for letting the people decide hinges on a judgment about whose wishes should prevail in nomination contests: the people who make up the party in the electorate or the people in the party organization. What right does the party organization have to select nominees, given that support for the party from the electorate (its contributions and votes in elections) is essential for electoral success? Moreover, shouldn't voters have a say in determining what their electoral choices look like? If party leaders choose, voters may not like any of the options put before them.

Why, then, do voters in America get to pick party nominees in primaries? Direct primaries were introduced in American politics during the late 1800s and early 1900s.[b] The goal was explicit: reform-minded party activists wanted to take the choice of nominees out of the hands of party leaders and give it to the electorate, with the assumption that voters should be able to influence the choice of candidates for the general election. Moreover, reformers believed that this goal outweighed the expertise held by party leaders.

Here is the trade-off: If party leaders select nominees, they will likely (but not inevitably) choose electable candidates who share the policy goals held by party leaders. If voters choose nominees, they can pick whomever they want, using whatever criteria they like—but there is no guarantee that these candidates will be skilled general-election campaigners or effective in office.

In the end, some groups must be given control over the selection of a party's nominees. Should this power be given to party leaders or to the people?

Both political parties organize a series of candidate debates during their presidential contests, giving candidates a chance to present themselves before a national audience.

take a stand

1. One reform proposal would increase the importance of the parties as sources of campaign funds. Would this change have made much of a difference in the 2020 Democratic presidential contest?

2. What kind of nomination procedure would be favored by insurgent groups?

Types of Primaries and Caucuses

Primary Election	An election in which voters choose the major-party nominees for political office, who subsequently compete in a general election.
Closed primary	A primary election system in which only registered party members can vote in their party's primary.
Nonpartisan primary	A primary election system in which candidates from both parties are listed on the same primary ballot. Following a nonpartisan primary, the two candidates who receive the most votes in the primary compete in the general election, even if they are from the same party.
Open primary	A primary election system in which any registered voter can participate in either party's primary, regardless of the voter's party affiliation.
Semi-closed primary	A primary election system in which voters registered as party members must vote in their party's primary, but registered Independents can vote in either party's primary.
Caucus Election	A series of local meetings at which registered voters select a particular candidate's supporters as delegates who will vote for the candidate in a later, state-level convention. (In national elections, the state-convention delegates select delegates to the national convention.) Caucuses are used in some states to select delegates to the major parties' presidential nominating conventions. Some states' caucuses are open to members of any party, while others are closed.

Source: Compiled by the authors.

"Why Should I Care?" People often wonder if their vote really counts. Primaries give citizens the opportunity to select the candidates who will run in the upcoming election, but each format has its own advantages and disadvantages. Even the time of the year in which a primary occurs can matter. We saw this in play during the 2020 Democratic primary. Voters in states with primaries earlier in the year had many candidates on the ballot to choose from, while those whose primaries fell later in the year had far fewer options, as many of the original candidates had long since dropped out.

Running as a major party's nominee, as opposed to running as an Independent, is almost always the easiest way to get on the general-election ballot. Even Vermont senator Bernie Sanders, who won his Senate seat by running as an Independent, ran for the Democratic presidential nomination in 2016 and 2020. Some states give the Republican and Democratic nominees an automatic spot on the ballot. Even in states that don't automatically allocate ballot slots this way, the requirements for the major parties to get a candidate on the ballot are much less onerous than those for minor parties and Independents. For example, in California a party and its candidates automatically qualify for a position on the ballot if any of the party's candidates for statewide office received more than 2 percent of the vote in the previous election. In contrast, Independent candidates need to file petitions with more than 150,000 signatures to get on the ballot without a major-party label—an expensive, time-consuming task.[40] These advantages help explain why virtually all prominent candidates for Congress and the presidency run as Democrats or Republicans.

Even billionaires Mike Bloomberg and Tom Steyer, who could have easily self-financed Independent campaigns for the presidency, chose to run as Democrats in 2020.

National parties also manage the nomination process for presidential candidates. This process involves a series of primaries and caucuses held over a six-month period beginning in January of a presidential election year. The type of election (primary or caucus) and its date are determined by state legislatures, although national party committees can limit the allowable dates, using their control over seating delegates at the party conventions to motivate compliance. Voters in these primaries and caucuses don't directly select the parties' nominees. Instead, citizens' votes are used to determine how many of each candidate's supporters become delegates to the party's national **nominating convention**, where delegates vote to choose the party's presidential and vice-presidential nominees. The national party organizations determine how many delegates each state sends to the convention based on factors such as state population, the number of votes the party's candidate received in each state in the last presidential election, and the number of House members and senators from the party that each state elected (see How It Works: Nominating Presidential Candidates).

Campaign Assistance One of the most visible ways that the political parties support candidates is by contributing to and spending money on campaign activities. By and large, federal law mandates that these funds be spent by the organization that raised them—the national party, for example, is limited in the amount of money it can directly contribute to congressional and presidential candidates or to state party organizations. As we will discuss in Chapter 12, however, party organizations can use the campaign funds they raise to help candidates in other ways, for example, through independent expenditures—running their own ads in a candidate's district or state.

Figure 11.6 shows the amount of money raised by the top groups within the Republican and Democratic parties for the 2020 election (through November 3).

nominating convention
A meeting held by each party every four years at which states' delegates select the party's presidential and vice-presidential nominees and approve the party platform.

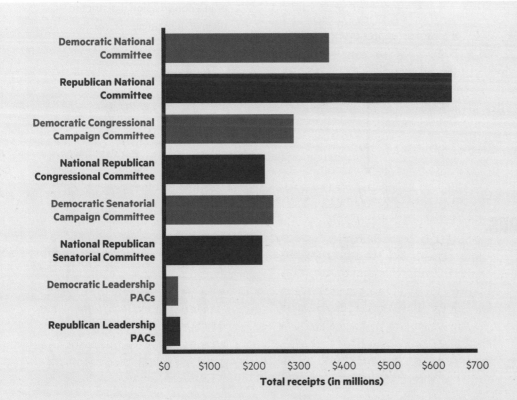

FIGURE 11.6

Democratic and Republican Fund-Raising in the 2019–2020 Election Cycle

In the 2019–2020 election cycle, party and leadership committees raised more than $2 billion in campaign funds. Although most of this money was raised by the national committees, the state, local, and candidate committees also raised significant sums. To what extent might these funds allow the national committees to force candidates to run on the party platform?

Source: The Center for Responsive Politics, www.opensecrets.org (accessed 11/4/20).

Total receipts (in millions)

- Democratic National Committee
- Republican National Committee
- Democratic Congressional Campaign Committee
- National Republican Congressional Committee
- Democratic Senatorial Campaign Committee
- National Republican Senatorial Committee
- Democratic Leadership PACs
- Republican Leadership PACs

$0 $100 $200 $300 $400 $500 $600 $700

Nominating Presidential Candidates

Primaries and caucuses . . .

Closed Primaries
Only voters registered with party vote

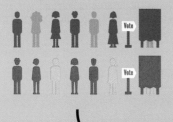

Open Primaries
Open to voters from any political party and Independents

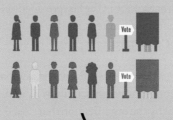

Caucus or Local Convention
Party members meet in groups to select delegates

are used to select delegates . . .

Republican Party
States can award all delegates to the winning candidate

or award delegates proportionally.

Democratic Party
The state's delegates are divided proportionally. A candidate must receive at least 15 percent of the vote either statewide or in a congressional district to receive delegates.

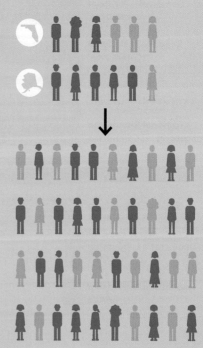

who attend national nominating conventions.

Delegates from all states attend the national convention, where they vote for the party's presidential and vice-presidential nominees based on the primary and caucus results. Superdelegates—important party leaders—also vote at the convention.

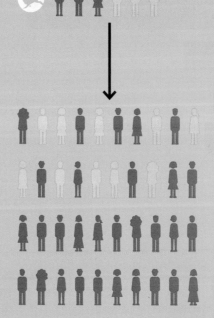

The Nomination of Joe Biden for President, 2020

While Joe Biden was the clear winner in the 2020 Democratic presidential nomination contest, his campaign benefited from the 15 percent threshold rule and the fact that many of the early contests were in states with high percentages of African-American voters, who were strong Biden supporters.

% Percentage of popular vote won
ℹ Delegates allocated
† Caucus

Note: For the contests in which allocated delegates do not add up to the number available or for which the popular vote percentages do not total 100 percent, other candidates omitted here also received delegates or votes. If a candidate drops out of the race before the national convention, any delegates he or she has earned may be reallocated.

Source: Table compiled by the authors from press accounts and U.S. Census data.

❓ Critical Thinking

1. **What would have happened to Biden's candidacy** if more of the early states had lower percentages of African-American voters?

2. **One argument about caucuses is that they allow** lesser-known candidates to build support. Did this work for any candidates in 2020?

	Contest (Delegates)	Biden	Sanders	Warren	Buttigieg	Klobuchar	% African-American*
Feb. 3	Iowa (41)†	15.8%	26.1%	18%	26.2%	12.3%	3%
Feb. 11	New Hampshire (24)	8.4%	25.7%	9.2%	24.4%	19.8%	1%
Feb. 22	Nevada (36)†	20.2%	46.8%	9.7%	14.3%	4.2%	9%
Feb. 29	South Carolina (54)	48.6%	19.8%	7.1%	8.2%	3.1%	27%
Mar. 3	Alabama (52)	63.3%	16.5%	5.7%	0.3%	0.2%	26%
	American Samoa (6)†	8.8%	10.5%	1.4%	0%	0%	0%
	Arkansas (31)	40.5%	22.4%	10%	3.4%	3.1%	16%
	California (415)	28%	35.5%	13.3%	4.4%	2.2%	7%
	Colorado (67)	24.7%	37%	17.6%	0%	0%	4%
	Maine (24)	34.1%	32.9%	15.7%	2.1%	1.4%	1%
	Massachusetts (91)	33.6%	26.7%	21.4%	2.7%	1.2%	8%
	Minnesota (75)	38.6%	29.9%	15.4%	1%	5.6%	5%
	North Carolina (110)	43%	24.1%	10.5%	3.3%	2.3%	22%
	Oklahoma (37)	38.7%	25.4%	13.4%	1.7%	2.2%	8%
	Tennessee (64)	41.7%	25%	10.4%	3.3%	2.1%	17%
	Texas (228)	34.5%	30%	11.4%	4%	2.1%	12%
	Utah (29)	18.4%	36.1%	16.2%	8.5%	3.4%	1%
	Vermont (16)	22%	50.8%	12.6%	2.4%	1.3%	1%
	Virginia (99)	53.2%	23.1%	10.7%	0.8%	0.6%	20%
	Total delegates	**742**	**614**	**63**	**21**	**7**	* Of 2020 Democratic primary and caucus voters

The final figures show that the parties and their various committees raised over $2 billion. The DNC and RNC raised the most money, but the congressional campaign committees also raised significant sums. Congressional Democratic committees outraised their Republican counterparts. And congressional leaders raised over $60 million for the campaigns of their colleagues. [41]

Along with supplying campaign funds, party organizations give candidates other assistance, ranging from offering campaign advice (including which issues to emphasize, how to deal with the press, and the like) to conducting polls. Party organizations at all levels also undertake get-out-the-vote activities, encouraging supporters to get to the polls. In the 2020 election, both campaigns had much less direct contact with voters because of COVID-19, relying more on social media, phone banks, and advertising. In contrast to the 2016 election, Democrats were successful in turning out their core supporters, especially minority voters.

Party Platforms The **party platform** is a set of promises explaining what candidates from the party will do if elected. The most visible party platform is the one approved at each party's presidential nominating convention, but the party organizations in the House and Senate also release platforms, as do other major-party groups. Party platforms generally reflect the brand name differences between the parties. For example, the 2020 Democratic presidential platform expressed support for a woman's right to choose, meaning that abortion would be legal under a wide range of conditions. While the Republican platform would typically take a strong anti-abortion stand, in 2020 that party did not issue a platform, instead pledging to support President Trump and his policies. This wholehearted backing of the president hurt some Republican congressional candidates in the election as voters cast straight-ticket votes against Republicans.

In theory, party platforms describe differences between the major parties, capture each party's diagnosis of the problems facing the country, and give the party's plan for solving those problems. In this way, party platforms give citizens an easy way to evaluate candidates. However, candidates are not obligated to support their party's platform and many take divergent stances on some issues. For example, notwithstanding the consistently strong pro-choice position on abortion in the Democratic Party's presidential platforms over the last generation, some Democratic members of Congress, such as Illinois representative Dan Lipinski, have promised to vote to restrict abortions—a position closer to the traditional Republican platform. [42] (Lipinski, however, was defeated in the 2020 Democratic primary for his House seat.) For some of these candidates, their position reflects personal or religious beliefs; for others, it is driven by the desire to reflect the opinion of voters in their district or state.

Despite these exceptions, party platforms are important documents and it is unlikely that future parties will emulate the Republicans' 2020 strategy. Political scientist John Gerring's research shows that platforms provide a general guide for voters about the issues and issue positions that separate the major parties. Platforms indicate what sorts of policies winning candidates are likely to vote for if elected. While some candidates may ignore or run against their party's platform, most candidates will support the platform because they agree with it or because they believe it is popular with their constituents. [43]

Cooperation in government

As Republicans and Democrats in Congress have become more polarized, particularly in recent years, the majority- and minority-party legislative caucuses have taken on larger roles in efforts to set legislative priorities, formulate compromise proposals, and work to enact these proposals on the floor of the House and Senate.

party platform
A set of objectives outlining the party's issue positions and priorities. Candidates are not required to support their party's platform.

One of the most important ways parties help candidates is by raising funds. Here, volunteers work the phones in a Republican Party field office in Colorado ahead of the 2018 midterm elections.

Within the government, politicians from the same party work together to develop an agenda and try to get it enacted. Here, President Trump meets with Republican leaders at Camp David.

Agenda-Setting Throughout the year, the parties in government meet to devise strategies for legislative action—that is, to set agendas. What proposals should they offer, and in what order should these proposals be considered? Should the parties try to make a deal with the president or with legislators from the other party? For example, after the 2020 election, Democratic congressional leaders met with President-elect Joe Biden and his staff to discuss priorities for the 2021–2022 legislative term, including new health care programs, changes to immigration law, new climate change policies, increased funding for infrastructure projects, and efforts to address the COVID-19 pandemic. At the same time, Republican congressional leaders made their own plans, including how to respond to Democratic initiatives.

Yet the party in government can act collectively this way only when its members can agree on what they want. Such agreement is not always possible or may require extensive negotiation and compromise. Even with unified Republican control of Congress in the 2017–2018 legislative term, legislators were unable to agree on immigration reform, Obamacare repeal, or infrastructure spending. Part of the problem was the narrow Republican majority in the Senate, yet the deeper issue was splits in Republican ranks that would have made compromise difficult even if Republicans had held a larger majority.

Coordination Political parties play an important role in coordinating the actions taken in different branches of government. Such coordination is extremely important for enacting new laws, because, unless supporters in Congress can amass a two-thirds majority to override a veto, they need the president's support. Similarly, the president needs congressional support to enact the proposals he or she favors. To these ends, the president routinely meets with congressional leaders from his or her party and occasionally meets with the entire caucus or conference. Various members of the president's staff also meet with House and Senate members to present the president's proposals and to hear what members of Congress from both parties want to enact.

During 2019 and 2020, President Trump held many meetings with Republican members of Congress to lobby them to support his policy proposals and to persuade them to oppose efforts to impeach him. Trump was successful on impeachment,

Parties don't exert total control over their members. Republican Party leaders could not stop then–freshman senator Ted Cruz (R-TX) from filibustering for 23 hours in an attempt to stop a budget compromise.

in that virtually all Republicans voted against impeachment. But in other areas, including cuts to some federal programs and a plan to enact substantial reductions in legal immigration to the United States, Trump had little success. These two examples illustrate the limits of presidential persuasion: presidential victories have more to do with proposing something that members of Congress are inclined to support (in the case of impeachment, because most Republican voters approve of Trump) than with pressuring them to support a proposal they oppose.

Coordination can also occur between caucuses or conferences in the House and Senate. During the COVID-19 pandemic in 2020, for example, unified Democratic opposition to Republican-proposed economic stimulus legislation forced Senate Republicans to include many Democratic provisions in the final version. Similarly, the need for party unity partly explains Trump's September 2020 nomination of Amy Coney Barrett to the Supreme Court, as other short-listed candidates raised more opposition among Senate Republicans. Such coordination efforts require real compromise since party leaders in Congress do not have authority over each other or the elected members of their party. Nor can the president order a House member or senator to do anything, even if the legislator is from the president's own party. In 2017, for example, President Trump and congressional leaders needed the votes of several moderate Republicans, including Senator Susan Collins of Maine, to pass tax cut legislation in the Senate. The congressional leaders and the president held repeated meetings with Collins and her allies, offering various promises and enticements to secure their votes. Ultimately, these legislators voted for the proposal, but neither the president nor party leaders could have forced them to support it.

Accountability One of the most important functions political parties play in a democracy is to give citizens identifiable groups to reward or punish for government action or inaction. Using the ballot box, voters will reward and punish elected officials, often based on their party affiliation and on the behavior of that party's members in office. In this way, the party system gives the electorate a mechanism that can be used to hold officials accountable for outcomes such as the state of the economy or America's relations with other nations. This mechanism is most clear during periods of unified government, when one party holds majorities in both the House and the Senate *and* controls the presidency, meaning that party has enough votes to enact policies in Congress and a good chance of having them signed into law by the president. Arguments along these lines were one of the central themes of the Democratic campaigns during the 2018 midterms—that majority control of the House or Senate would enable Democratic legislators to limit the regulatory changes, judicial appointments, and budget cuts favored by congressional Republicans and the Trump administration. Republicans made a similar argument in the 2020 campaign, calling for Trump's reelection and a return to Republican control of the House.

In contrast, during times of divided government, when one party controls Congress but not the presidency or when different parties control the House and Senate (such as during most of Obama's presidency as well as the second half of Trump's), it is not clear which party should be held accountable for the state of the nation. While Republicans argued in 2020 that Democrats should be punished for the relatively poor state of the American economy and the government's insufficient response to the COVID-19 pandemic, these arguments did not resonate with the electorate, who believed that Republican control of the presidency and Senate made that party responsible for those conditions.

Focusing on parties makes it easy for citizens to issue rewards and punishments. For example, if the economy is doing well, people can reward the party in power by voting for its candidates. But if the economy is doing poorly, or if people feel that government is wasting tax money or enacting bad policies, voters can punish the party in power by supporting candidates from the party that is currently out of power. When citizens behave this way, they strengthen the incentive for elected officials from the party in power to work together to develop policies that address voters' concerns—on the premise that if they do, voters will reward them with another term in office. Consider the 2020 elections. Although Democrats lost about nine seats in the House and Senate, most Democratic incumbents were reelected. Why? Some were elected from states or districts dominated by Democratic identifiers. But many others were reelected because they campaigned on a platform of promoting Democratic party ideals or because of their efforts to help local constituents; in effect, these candidates said, "Instead of punishing me for my party affiliation, reward me for working on your behalf."

In the end, reelecting members of the party in power despite a poor economy or other troubles makes sense given how American political parties are organized and their lack of control over individual officeholders. Of course, insofar as incumbent members of the party in power present themselves as loyal party members and cast votes in accordance with the wishes of party leaders, they will increase the chances that their constituents will take account of their party label when casting their votes—which will help them get reelected in good times but will increase their chances of defeat when conditions turn against their party.

Minor parties

So far, this chapter has focused on the major American political parties, the Republicans and the Democrats, and paid less attention to other party organizations. The reason is that minor political parties in America are *so* minor that they are generally not significant players on the political stage. Many such parties exist, but few run candidates in more than a handful of races and very few minor-party candidates win political office. Few Americans identify with minor parties, and most of these parties exist for only a relatively short period.

Even so, you may think we are giving minor parties too little attention. Consider Howie Hawkins and Jo Jorgensen, who ran as the Green and Libertarian party candidates for president in 2020. If the votes they received had gone to Donald Trump instead, he might have prevailed in close states and thereby won reelection. In this sense, you might think of minor parties and their supporters as the kingmakers in modern American politics. However, the size of the minor-party vote in 2020 doesn't so much highlight the importance of minor parties as it illustrates the closeness of elections in some states. If Hawkins and Jorgensen had not run, Trump might have received enough additional support to win. But given that Biden's margin of victory in several states was so small, any number of seemingly minor events (rain in some areas and sunshine in others, or some small number of additional pro-Trump ads) could have had the same effect.

Even in terms of lower offices, minor-party candidates typically attract only meager support. While the Libertarian Party claims to have over 200 officeholders, many of these officials hold unelected positions such as seats on county planning boards or ran unopposed for relatively minor offices.[44] In 2020, Justin Amash, who was elected as a Republican representative for the state of Michigan, changed his party affiliation to become a Libertarian and in doing so became the party's first member to serve in Congress, though he chose not to seek reelection.

Looking back in history, we see that some minor-party candidates for president have attracted a substantial percentage of citizens' votes. George Wallace (governor

Minor-party presidential candidates, such as Libertarian Jo Jorgensen in 2020, sometimes attract considerable press attention because of their distinctive policy preferences, but they rarely effect election outcomes.

of Alabama at the time) ran as the candidate of the American Independent Party in 1968, receiving about 13 percent of the popular vote nationwide. Texas millionaire Ross Perot, the Reform Party candidate for president in 1996, won 8.4 percent of the popular vote. Perot also ran as an Independent in 1992, winning 18.2 percent of the popular vote. And environmental and consumer activist Ralph Nader received about 5 percent of the popular vote in 2000.

Unique Issues Facing Minor Parties The differences between major and minor political parties in contemporary American politics grow even more substantial when considered in terms other than election outcomes. For most minor parties, the party in government does not exist, as few of their candidates win office. Many minor parties have virtually no organization beyond a small party headquarters and a website. Some minor parties, such as the Green Party, the Libertarian Party, and the Reform Party, have local chapters that meet on a regular basis. But these modest efforts pale in comparison with the nationwide network of offices, thousands of workers, and hundreds of millions of dollars deployed by Republican and Democratic party organizations.

The most significant factor working against minor parties is the basic structure of the American political system. This principle is summed up by Duverger's Law, which states that in a democracy that has **single-member districts** and **plurality voting**, there will be only two political parties that are able to elect a significant number of candidates to political office, which is the case in contemporary America. Given these electoral institutions (see Chapter 13), many people consider a vote for a minor-party candidate to be a wasted vote, as there is no chance that the candidate will win office.[45] As a result, well-qualified candidates are driven to affiliate with one of the major political parties because they know that running as a minor-party nominee will put them at a considerable disadvantage. These decisions reinforce citizens' expectations that minor-party candidates have no chance of winning elections and that a vote for them is a wasted vote. Although there is no evidence that the Founders wanted to choose electoral institutions that made it hard for minor parties and their candidates, there is no doubt that the rules of the American electoral game have these effects.

A second problem is that the issues and issue positions taken by minor parties and their candidates are almost always very different from those espoused by the major parties. The Constitution Party, for example, advocates ending government civil service regulations; banning compulsory school attendance laws; withdrawing from the UN and all international trade agreements; abolishing foreign aid, the income tax, the Internal Revenue Service, and all federal welfare programs; and repealing all campaign finance legislation, the Endangered Species Act, and federal firearms regulations. These positions are extreme, not in the sense of being silly or dangerous but in the sense that relatively few Americans agree with them. Even in the 2020 presidential contest, Libertarian Jo Jorgensen proposed major cuts in defense spending and domestic programs—positions that attract support from only a relatively small minority of Americans.

Duverger's Law
The principle that in a democracy with single-member districts and plurality voting, only two parties' candidates will have a realistic chance of winning political office, as in the United States.

single-member district
An electoral system in which every elected official represents a geographically defined area, such as a state or congressional district, and each area elects one representative.

plurality voting
A voting system in which the candidate who receives the most votes within a geographic area wins the election, regardless of whether that candidate wins a majority (more than half) of the votes.

"Why Should I Care?"

You may dislike political parties or party leaders in Congress, but the fact is, the parties are key players in congressional policy making and in negotiations between Congress and the president. If you are trying to decide whether a new program (or nominee) has a chance of being approved, one of the first things you need to consider is whether the party caucuses in the House and Senate (particularly the majority-party caucuses) are in favor or opposed.

How well do parties operate?

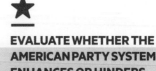
We have argued throughout this chapter that political parties can make democracy operate more smoothly by simplifying and improving the choices that citizens face in elections, and by providing mechanisms that make it easier for elected officials to formulate and enact compromise proposals. However, these arguments are about what parties *can* do, not what they *actually* do. There is no assurance that party leaders, activists, candidates, and citizens who identify with parties will take the actions needed to turn these possibilities into reality. The problem is that the people who make up American political parties are not primarily interested in democracy; they are interested in their own careers, policy goals, and winning political office. These goals often lead them away from actions that would improve American democracy. In this section, we consider when and why American political parties might fall short of our highest expectations for them.

Recruiting good candidates

One of the most important things that American political parties can do for democracy is to recruit candidates who can run effective campaigns and uphold their elected positions. After all, a voter's choices are limited to the people on the ballot. If good candidates decide against running or are prevented from doing so, citizens will be dissatisfied no matter who wins the election.

However, parties have limited influence over candidacy decisions: the potential candidates have to decide for themselves whether their chances of winning justify the enormous investment of time and money needed to run a campaign. When a party is unpopular, the best potential candidates may decide to wait until the next election to run, leaving the already disadvantaged party with a less competitive set of candidates.[46] Even when recruitment is not a problem, party leaders have only limited control over the nomination process—in some states, they cannot even restrict voting in primaries to citizens who are registered with the party. As Donald Trump's 2016 candidacy illustrates, party leaders cannot always prevent a candidate they do not favor from running; from dominating press coverage at the expense of other, more viable candidates; and from saying things that drive some important groups away from the party and its candidates. Of course, Trump won the 2016 election, indicating that party leaders underestimated his electability. Even so, insofar as party leaders are experienced politicians with deep knowledge of public opinion and political institutions, their lack of control over the nomination process can lead to unfavorable outcomes.

Working together in campaigns

Parties can improve the working of democracy by simplifying the choices voters face, most notably by getting their candidates to emphasize the same issues or to take similar issue positions. That way, citizens know that when they vote for, say, a Democrat, they are getting someone whose policy positions are likely to differ from those held by a Republican. As we've noted, however, even in modern America, where the differences between the parties are quite large, there are often disagreements within the party, either among elected officials or in the party organization. Suppose, for example, you want to vote in an election for the candidate who comes closest to your position on immigration policy. It's relatively easy to place Democratic candidates on the spectrum of positions on immigration, as most favor current limits on legal immigration and some form of legal status for undocumented individuals in the United States. It's much harder to determine a Republican candidate's position, as candidates from that party have a wide range of opinions and preferred immigration policies. Some favor policies close to the Democratic Party norm, while others advocate sharp reductions in legal immigration and aggressive deportation efforts against the undocumented. Moreover, immigration is not the exception. The simple fact is that on most issues, political parties in America speak with many voices, not one.

Why don't party leaders simply order their candidates to support the party platform or to work together in campaigns? As we have discussed, party leaders actually have very little power over candidates.[47] They can't kick a candidate off the ballot, because candidates win the nomination in a primary election or caucus, not through party appointment. Even though parties have a lot of campaign money to dispense, their contributions typically make up only a fraction of what a candidate spends on a campaign. And incumbent candidates, who generally hold an advantage over challengers when seeking reelection, are even less beholden to party leaders. Even if party leaders could somehow prevent an incumbent from running for reelection, they would have to find another candidate to take the incumbent's place, which would mean losing the incumbent's popularity and reputation and reducing the party's chances of holding the seat.

Working together in office

After the election, political parties can improve democracy by helping officeholders to find compromise policy proposals that attract broad support, and to select debate and voting procedures that speed enactment of these proposals. Sometimes, finding consensus both within and between parties is easy: for example, congressional Republicans and Democrats united in March 2020 to pass economic stimulus legislation in response to the COVID-19 pandemic. However, there are also many examples of issues that can split a party wide open, such as immigration reform for Republicans. Sometimes party members can compromise their differences, but there is no guarantee, as illustrated by the Democratic House majority's failure to find consensus on their Green New Deal proposal. And of course, even if the members of a party can find common ground, they may fail at building the bipartisan coalitions that are often necessary to enact major legislation, as was the case for many proposals considered during Donald Trump's first two years in office, including immigration reform, infrastructure funding, and cuts to entitlement programs. Even when compromise is reached, the time spent negotiating means that members have less time to scrutinize the details of budgets and policy proposals. For this reason, one recent study argued that the party caucuses are "too weak to govern."[48] Party leaders may do a good job in determining what their colleagues want but be unable to persuade them to support a proposal that they are inclined to oppose.

The fact that American political parties are ideologically diverse means that elected members of the party may not agree on spending, policy, or anything else. And even when senators and House members from a party find a way to bridge their differences, there is no guarantee that the president, even if he or she is from the same party, will agree to the compromise. In that sense, voters can't expect that putting one party in power will result in specific policy changes. Instead, policy outcomes depend on how (and whether) individual officeholders from the party can resolve their differences. Institutions such as the party caucuses or conferences provide a forum in which elected officials can meet and seek common ground, but there is no guarantee that they will find acceptable compromises.

Moreover, concerted action by members of a party in government may be aimed at political rather than policy goals. In recent years, both Democrats and Republicans have decided against bipartisan compromises, believing that standing their ground

The most important part of a Senate majority leader's education is over by the third grade, when he has learned to count.

—**Howard Baker,** former Senate Majority Leader

would help them gain seats in the next elections. This strategy was, at the time, one factor behind the Democratic resurgence in the 2018 midterms. In 2020, however, the same arguments did not help Democrats win enough close Senate races to gain majority control of the chamber. Democrats also lost about eight House seats, although they stayed in firm majority control. In this way, the electoral imperatives faced by American political parties can work against the enactment of effective responses to public problems and increase, rather than decrease, the amount of conflict in American politics.

Providing accountability

Finally, parties can improve American democracy by acting as an accountability mechanism that gives citizens an identifiable group to reward when policies work well and to punish when policies fail. However, while individual legislators are happy to take advantage of party labels when being held accountable works in their favor, they will do everything they can to avoid being tied to an unpopular party. Republican legislators, for example, highlighted their party label in the 2010 election, as the party was much more popular than the Democratic Party at that time.[49] But in 2018, when the party brand was much less popular, many Republican incumbents emphasized their work as individual members of Congress on behalf of constituents and tried to stay as far away as possible from their party's unpopular image. Similarly, some Democratic House members elected in 2018 from traditional Republican strongholds avoided discussing President Trump's impeachment for as long as they could, although virtually all voted for impeachment in the end.

When politicians work to secure their own political future by de-emphasizing their party affiliation, they make it harder for voters to use party labels to decide who should be rewarded and who should be punished for government performance. The result is that legislators are held accountable for their own performance in office, such as how they voted—but no one in Congress is accountable for large-scale outcomes such as the state of the economy or for foreign policy. Of course, attempts by officeholders to disassociate themselves from their party are not always successful, which is why Republicans lost their House majority in 2018. Even so, most Republicans and Democrats in Congress managed to survive these elections, suggesting that party-based accountability is rather weak in contemporary American politics.

Democrats framed the 2020 election as a referendum on President Trump's performance in office, particularly his mismanagement of the COVID-19 pandemic. While this strategy did not lead to as many Senate pickups as the party had hoped, it did help some candidates, including former astronaut Mark Kelly, who defeated incumbent Martha McSally (R-AZ) by arguing that McSally had been an uncritical supporter of Trump's policies. Following Kyrsten Sinema's (D-AZ) election to the Senate in 2018, Arizona is now represented by two Democratic senators for the first time since 1952.

The Federal Election Campaign Act

The Federal Election Campaign Act of 1971 (FECA) was, at the time, just the latest in a series of laws to try to get election spending under control. There has always been a segment of society that has been suspicious of the abuse of power by unchecked politicians. In fact, one might argue that this suspicion is the very basis of the U.S. Constitution given all the checks and balances that it incorporated, but the Constitution, for all of its foresight, did not anticipate the level of campaign spending that would take hold of elections, especially in the twentieth and twenty-first centuries. Given the select laws highlighted in the policy outline below, politicians have wrestled with this problem starting in the early 1900s with the Tillman Act of 1905 and the Federal Corrupt Practices Act of 1910. While the former was fairly limited in scope by banning corporate contributions, the latter was very reminiscent of later bills, especially the FECA. A good question is why subsequent laws are deemed necessary when laws already exist on a topic. Some obvious reasons have already been discussed in Policy in Practice sections in other chapters. For example, after a law has been implemented, loopholes might be discovered that legislators would want to close up or unintended interpretations might arise that lawmakers want to clarify. Sometimes the law might become outdated because of changing technology, as we will see in the discussion of the Federal Communications Commission (FCC) fairness doctrine.

Though technology certainly has changed since the beginning of the twentieth century, and there were also loopholes in the early pieces of legislation dealing with campaign finance, another related problem was that the law was very often just ignored or not enforced. The legislative branch makes laws, and the executive branch is supposed to carry them out, so the effectiveness of any legislation depends on both branches working together. There are various reasons why laws are not carried out. Sometimes a law is so complicated and difficult to understand that well-intentioned administrators simply do not understand what the law is asking them to enforce. Cost might also be a consideration. As one can see in the discussion of unfunded mandates and the Americans with Disabilities Act, complying with the law involved very high costs that state and local governments or private firms had difficulty paying and to which the federal government was not willing to contribute. Also, the president may not agree with the law and may not be willing to carry it out or may be willing to carry out only certain aspects of the law. An example of this relates to the Budget Impoundment Act of 1974, which was passed because President Richard M. Nixon had withheld almost $12 billion in funding that Congress had appropriated. He said he did this to get the deficit (caused by greater government spending versus the tax revenues in a given year) under control, but nevertheless Congress said that he was overstepping his authority and not carrying out his duties to execute laws.

People often mistakenly believe that FECA was passed in response to the Watergate scandal, in which sitting President Nixon orchestrated the break-in at the Democratic National Committee's headquarters at the Watergate Office Building and the subsequent cover-up of the crime. This event took place in 1972 and was related to Nixon's reelection campaign, which he won. The criminal investigation surrounding Watergate started immediately and the Senate hearings started in early 1973, ultimately resulting in Nixon's resignation on August 9, 1974. Many FECA amendments were added in 1974 and caused confusion regarding the original legislation due to Watergate and other problems pertaining to the 1972 presidential election that FECA failed to anticipate. Consequently, it is usually these 1974 changes that are referred to when discussing FECA. As you will see in the discussion of the Bipartisan Campaign Reform Act (BCRA) in the Elections chapter (Chapter 13), the 1979 amendments also implemented significant changes to the original legislation.

The policy outline below focuses on the 1971 legislation because this is the landmark piece of legislation, but it also does discuss the amendments that follow since the policy-making process is always fluid and dynamic.

Policy Stages

1. Problem Recognition
   - The Tillman Act of 1905 banned corporation contributions to election campaigns.
   - The Federal Corrupt Practices Act of 1910
     - It set spending limits on campaign races in the House of Representatives.
     - It required financial disclosures of expenses after elections.
     - It was amended in 1911 to include the Senate.
     - It was amended again in 1925 to strengthen the original law and impose additional disclosure requirements.
   - The Hatch Act of 1939
     - Federal employees could not engage in certain political activities, such as running for office, giving political speeches, and asking for campaign contributions.
     - Federal funds intended for other purposes could not be diverted for financing elections.
     - The 1940 amendment limited individual campaign contributions.
   - The Taft-Hartley Act of 1947 prohibited unions from making direct campaign contributions to federal elections.
   - The Revenue Act of 1971
     - Presidential candidates could spend a certain amount of money only if they received public financing and could not accept private contributions.
     - Individual taxpayers could allocate $1 to a Presidential Election Campaign Fund simply by checking a box on their tax returns.

2. Agenda Setting
   - The Federal Corrupt Practices Act of 1925 was considered very weak and in need of reform.
     - It did not limit federal campaign contributions.
     - It provided no transparency regarding the sources of campaign contributions.
     - It was not enforced.
   - President Nixon vetoed a revision to the Communications Act of 1934, which would have limited campaign spending on radio and television.
     - He wanted a more comprehensive electoral reform bill instead.
   - The National Committee for an Effective Congress, a left-wing political action committee (PAC) founded by Eleanor Roosevelt, was a major proponent of an electoral reform bill.
   - Prominent members of Congress thought that campaign spending had increased significantly in recent years, especially during the 1968 presidential election.

3. Deliberation and Formulation
   - The bill was introduced in the Senate by John O. Pastore (D-RI) on May 6, 1971.
   - The Senate passed its version of the bill on August 5, 1971: **88 YEAs**: 50 Democrats, 36 Republicans, 2 others; **2 NAYs**: 0 Democrats, 2 Republicans, 0 others; **9 Not Voting**: 4 Democrats, 5 Republicans, 0 others.
   - The House of Representatives passed its own version of the bill on November 30, 1971: **372 YEAs**: 220 Democrats, 152 Republicans, 0 others; **23 NAYs**: 10 Democrats, 13 Republicans, 0 others; **35 Not Voting**: 23 Democrats, 12 Republicans, 0 others.

4. Enactment
    - The Senate passed a compromise bill on December 14, 1971.
    - The House of Representatives passed a compromise bill on January 19, 1972: **334 YEAs**: 197 Democrats, 137 Republicans, 0 others; **20 NAYs**: 9 Democrats, 11 Republicans, 0 others; **77 Not Voting**: 47 Democrats, 30 Republicans, 0 others.
    - FECA was signed into law by President Nixon on February 7, 1972.
5. Implementation
    - Disclosure requirements were delayed 60 days before going into effect.
    - Expanded disclosure contribution requirements affected more entities and demanded the inclusion of more detail.
    - The law was first applied to the 1972 presidential election.
    - It set maximum amounts that candidates could contribute to their own campaigns and that could be spent on advertising in all forms of media (including television, radio, newspapers, and magazines).
    - It required radio and television stations to charge normal (not increased) rates for campaign advertising slots.
    - Corporations and unions had to establish PACs to contribute to political campaigns.
    - PACs were required to register and report their spending activities.
    - The General Accounting Office (GAO), renamed the Government Accountability Office in 2004, had major responsibility for enforcing provisions of FECA.
        - It established the Office of Federal Elections to oversee the administration of the law.
        - It intended to work on seeking compliance rather than trying to punish violators, but it did publish a list of violators and their infractions as a way of informing the public.
        - It mailed thousands of packets to state and local officials informing them of the new rules and regulations eight months prior to the 1972 elections.
6. Evaluation
    - Hundreds of the initial 8,000 informational mailings by the GAO came back because of wrong or out-of-date addresses, indicating how inefficient the current system was for disseminating information about the new law.
    - Flagrant noncompliance with FECA during the 1972 election highlighted weaknesses in the 1971 law.
    - Limits on campaign contributions and spending are considered limits on freedom of speech by some critics.
    - Opponents believed a single, independent organization, rather than the GAO, should monitor and enforce the provisions of the law.
    - It was very difficult to understand and to comply with all of the law's rules and regulations.
    - The initial 60-day delay on the law's implementation caused an increase in spending to beat the enforcement date.
    - The 60-day delay created bookkeeping problems for states that had primaries around the time of the enforcement date.
    - Disclosure requirements were so strict that campaigns would circumvent them by using cash to avoid reporting contributions and spending.
7. Possible Modifications, Expansion, or Termination of Policy
    - 1974 amendment to FECA
        - It was signed by President Gerald Ford on October 15, 1974.
        - It set a maximum amount for each election an individual could contribute to any federal election campaign.

- It set a maximum amount an individual could contribute to a political party or political committee.
- It set a maximum amount PACs could contribute to a candidate for each election.
- It set a maximum amount candidates could spend on their own campaigns.
- The Federal Election Commission (FEC) was formed to oversee the proper running of elections, enforce rules, and impose penalties.
- Candidates could receive matching funds up to a certain limit on individual contributions provided the candidates did not spend over a certain maximum amount in the general election.
- All committees connected to the campaigns had to file regular disclosure reports accounting for their expenses.
- 1976 amendment to FECA
  - It was signed into law by President Ford on May 11, 1976.
  - It was enacted due to the Supreme Court decision *Buckley v. Valeo* (1976).
    - It upheld contribution limits by individuals and political committees.
    - It allowed candidates to contribute unlimited amounts to their own campaigns.
- 1979 amendment to FECA
  - It was signed by President Jimmy Carter on January 8, 1980.
  - It simplified disclosure forms and processes.
  - It reduced the number of entities that have to file disclosure forms.
  - It increased the amount of public funding for general election finance.
  - It increased the spending limits for state and local parties.
  - It allowed state and local parties to spend unlimited amounts on campaign-building activities, such as get-out-the-vote and voter registration drives, as long as the money was not directed toward any specific candidate (soft money).
- BCRA (2002) amended FECA.
  - It is also known as the McCain-Feingold Act.
  - It banned legal loopholes to FECA, specifically soft money contributions.
  - It allowed only hard money, donations that are used to help elect or defeat a specific candidate.
  - It was struck down by *Citizens United v. Federal Election Commission* (2010).
- The Senate Campaign Disclosure Parity Act (2018) required Senate candidates to file quarterly reports electronically, like House candidates were already doing, rather than by paper in order to reduce costs and increase efficiency.

AP®
SUPREME
COURT CASE

Questions for Discussion

1. Do limits placed on campaign spending restrict freedom of speech or allow more voices to be heard? Explain your answer.
2. In the UK, the campaigning period before a general election is 25 working days. Should the United States adopt a similar, limited time frame for campaigning? Why or why not?
3. Is money a necessary evil in political campaigns? What are some of the benefits and drawbacks of money in politics?

Unpacking the Conflict

Considering all that we've discussed in this chapter, let's apply what we know about how political parties work to the examples of party dysfunction from the beginning of this chapter. Why is it impossible to describe American politics without talking about Republicans and Democrats? At the same time, why do the parties seem like bystanders as nominees are chosen and policies are debated?

The answer is that we have strong partisanship, but weak parties. Party identification organizes how we think about politics as well as our political behavior as much as or more than it ever has in the past. However, at the same time Americans generally dislike political parties, even the one they identify with. And the laws governing elections allow candidates to claim a party label without having to support or even talk about their party's platform.

As a result, while America's political system gives enormous opportunities to political parties, from organizing elections to working inside Congress to build coalitions behind policy proposals, the fact that these opportunities exist does not ensure that political parties will be able to follow through on them. As we have seen, American political parties are often beset by internal conflicts over who should run for office and what their campaign platforms should look like. The party organization has little control over the party in government (or vice versa). And neither group can order party members in the electorate to work for the party, support its candidates, or do anything they don't want to do.

As a result of these organizational features, there is no guarantee that officeholders and election winners of the same party affiliation will have the same policy priorities or be able to compromise over their differences. This has been true even in recent years, when differences between Republicans and Democrats have been as large as ever. It will be just as hard for Democrats to agree amongst themselves about policy priorities as it will be to gain support for these proposals from Republicans. Republicans will face the same problem even if they gain unified control of government in the future. At the same time, while Americans may not approve of these outcomes, they show no signs of totally abandoning the Republicans or the Democrats in favor of new party organizations.

"What's Your Take?"

Are American political parties too dysfunctional to be useful?

Or do the benefits they provide outweigh their drawbacks?

AP® STUDY GUIDE

Summary

Linkage institutions consist of an actor or a group of actors in American politics that informs citizens about government actions or helps them exercise control over policy. Political parties are one example. Political parties are organizations that run candidates for political office and coordinate the actions of officials elected under the party banner. Here in the United States, parties are relatively decentralized, putting forth a loose configuration of candidates who share a party label but do not necessarily work together. The parties are composed of three semiautonomous units: the party organization, the party in government, and the party in the electorate. Political parties are a central feature of American politics, although they look and act very differently today than they have in the past. Political scientists use the term "party system" to refer to a period of party stability; in all, there have been six different party systems in the country's history. Party systems are broken up by realignments, which occur when some of the defining factors of the party system are changed or specified and rifts in the group develop because of these changes.

Political parties serve two major roles in the political system. First, they compete in elections by recruiting and nominating candidates and supporting candidate campaigns. Second, they facilitate cooperation in government by providing a framework for agenda-setting, coordination, and accountability among members of the same party. There are many different minor political parties, and while they rarely make a significant impact on the political stage, they do occasionally influence election outcomes. The two big issues facing minor parties are that their platforms do not appeal to a large portion of Americans and that the electoral system makes it hard for minor parties to win elections.

Political parties do a number of things that are important to facilitate good democracy: they generally recruit good candidates, simplify voters' choices, encourage candidates to work together in office, and provide a mechanism for holding politicians accountable. Nonetheless, there are limits to the extent to which parties are able to achieve these goals, partially due to the fact that the people who make up the parties are primarily interested in their own careers.

linkage institutions
Institutions such as political parties, interest groups, the media, and elections that are channels through which individuals can communicate their preferences to policy makers.

Key Terms

caucus (congressional) (p. 483)

caucus (electoral) (p. 490)

conference (p. 483)

divided government (p. 483)

Duverger's Law (p. 500)

527 organization (p. 480)

issue ownership (p. 481)

linkage institutions (p. 509)

national committee (p. 479)

negative partisanship (p. 485)

nominating convention (p. 493)

party coalitions (p. 487)

party identification (party ID) (p. 483)

party in government (p. 474)

party in the electorate (p. 474)

party organization (p. 474)

party platform (p. 496)

party principle (p. 476)

party system (p. 475)

plurality voting (p. 500)

political action committee (PAC) (p. 480)

primary election (p. 490)

realignment (p. 478)

single-member district (p. 500)

spoils system (p. 476)

unified government (p. 483)

Enduring Understandings

PMI-4: "Widely held political ideologies shape policy debates and choices in American policies." (AP® U.S. Government and Politics Course and Exam Description)

PMI-5: "Political parties, interest groups, and social movements provide opportunities for participation and influence how people relate to government and policy-makers." (AP® U.S. Government and Politics Course and Exam Description)

Multiple-Choice Questions (Arranged by Topic)

Topic 4.7: Ideologies of Political Parties (PMI-4)

Questions 1–3 refer to the graph.

Are the Parties More Polarized than Ever?

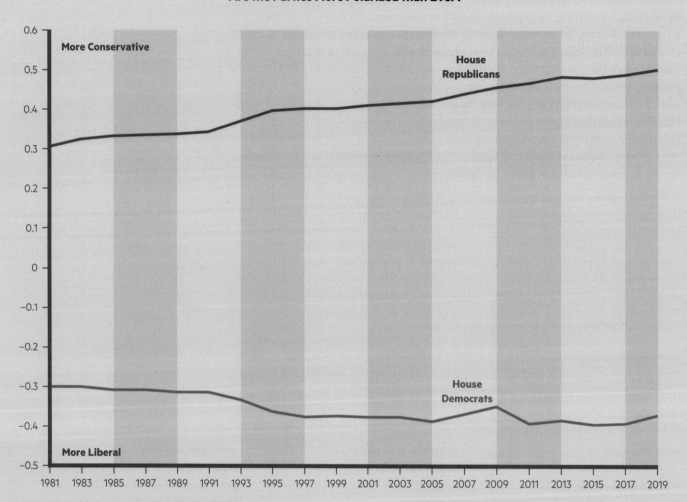

Source: Jeffrey B. Lewis et al., Voteview (congressional roll call votes database), https://voteview.com/ (accessed 3/19/20).

1. **Which of the following statements best reflects a trend in the line graph?**

   (A) House Democrats have become increasingly more conservative.

   (B) House Republicans have become increasingly more liberal.

   (C) Neither party has shifted toward aligning with a more liberal ideology.

   (D) Both parties have become more polarized.

2. **Which of the following is a limitation of the data presented in the line graph?**

   (A) The data would have to be gathered through a survey as it is not possible to see how representatives have voted on bills presented on the House floor.

   (B) Bills that are filibustered in the House are never voted on and that information is not included in the data.

   (C) Representatives may vote against a bill even if they align with the bill ideologically because of an amendment to the bill that they do not support.

   (D) Representatives can use a hold to prevent the bill from going to a vote; thus, that information would not be included in the data.

3. **Which of the following is a likely implication of the data presented in the line graph?**

   (A) It will become increasingly difficult to enact major policy changes due to gridlock in Congress.

   (B) Republicans are more likely to be elected to office because they support increased marketplace regulations.

   (C) Democrats are less likely to vote along party lines because of inconsistencies within the party that prevent alignment on different issues.

   (D) Social policy is more likely to be a focus, as that is an area where both Democrats and Republicans can find agreement.

Topic 4.9: Ideology and Economic Policy (PMI-4)

Questions 4–5 refer to the political cartoon.

4. **Which of the following best conveys the cartoon's message about President Roosevelt's New Deal programs?**

   (A) The only way to fix the economy is through the use of magic.

   (B) Government spending is a dependable way to fix the economy.

   (C) Selling rabbits is what brought the economy out of the Great Depression.

   (D) Overspending is what led to the Great Depression in the first place.

5. **Which of the following political ideologies is best represented by the message in the political cartoon?**

   (A) liberal

   (B) libertarian

   (C) conservative

   (D) Republican

Topic 4.10: Ideology and Social Policy (PMI-4)

6. **Which of the following is an accurate comparison of the different priorities that the Democratic and Republican party coalitions have on social issues?**

	Democrats	Republicans
(A)	improving race relations	tightening environmental regulations
(B)	supporting free trade	supporting the military
(C)	decreasing the budget deficit	reining in health care costs
(D)	controlling climate change	regulating immigration

Topic 5.3: Political Parties (PMI-5)

7. **Which of the following best describes the institutions—such as parties, interest groups, elections, and the media—that allow individuals to communicate their preferences to policy makers?**

   (A) political participants

   (B) linkage institutions

   (C) party platforms

   (D) institutional agenda setters

8. **Which of the following best explains why most candidates support their party platforms?**

   (A) Candidates are required to support the platform in order to run for office.

   (B) Candidates vote on the platform before it is adopted.

   (C) Most candidates and their constituents generally agree with the platform.

   (D) There is very little difference between the platforms of both major parties.

Topic 5.4: How and Why Political Parties Change and Adapt (PMI-5)

9. **In addition to the use of candidate-centered campaigns, which of the following has led to a decrease in the role of the political party in nominating candidates for office?**

   (A) open primaries

   (B) closed primaries

   (C) caucus

   (D) nominating conventions

Topic 5.5: Third-Party Politics (PMI-5)

10. **The United States' use of the single-member district system tends to benefit which of the following?**

    (A) individuals running without a party affiliation or as Independents

    (B) senators running for reelection, regardless of party affiliation

    (C) candidates running under a third party

    (D) candidates running as either Republicans or Democrats

Free-Response Questions

Concept Application

On Monday, March 16, 2020, the day before the primary election, Dr. Amy Acton, director of the Ohio Department of Health, ordered the polls closed the next day due to the COVID-19 pandemic. After a proposed date of June 2 for the primary election by Governor Mike DeWine, the Ohio legislature moved the new primary to April 28. Postmarked ballots would be accepted until April 27, and in-person voting would be available, on a limited basis, at the county election boards on Election Day. As with the previous primary election, voters would be allowed to choose if they wanted a Republican, Democrat, or Independent ballot.[a]

After reading the scenario, respond to A, B, and C below:

    (A) Referencing the scenario, describe the type of primary—open or closed—that is used in Ohio.

    (B) In the context of the scenario, explain how the type of primary described in Part A affects the power of the political party relative to holding a caucus.

    (C) Given the added costs of this type of election, imagine that Ohio instituted a fee to vote in order to cover the added resources needed by the U.S. Post Office to conduct the election. Explain how the Supreme Court might rule if that fee were challenged by a voter.

SCOTUS Comparison

This question requires you to compare a Supreme Court case you studied in class with one you have not studied in class. A summary of the Supreme Court case you did not study in class is presented below and provides all of the information you need to know about this case to answer the prompt.

In the late 1980s, the Pennsylvania legislature added new provisions to the law on abortion. The new law required that a minor seeking an abortion had to have the consent of at least one parent, or a wavier by a judge, prior to the procedure. The law also added a 24-hour waiting period and spousal notification prior to aborting the fetus. These provisions were challenged in the lower courts and upheld, with the exception of the spousal notification, by a federal appeals court.

    In the ensuing case, *Planned Parenthood v. Casey* (1992), the Supreme Court in a 5–4 decision imposed a new standard to determine the validity of laws restricting abortions. The new standard is based on whether or not the state is causing an "undue burden," which is defined as a "substantial obstacle in the path of a woman seeking an abortion before the fetus attains viability."[b] Using this standard, the Court agreed with the federal appeals court and did not consider the parental notification or 24-hour waiting period an "undue burden."

Based on the information above, respond to the following questions.

    (A) Identify the implied right in the U.S. Constitution that addresses the main issue in both *Roe v. Wade* (2010) and *Planned Parenthood v. Casey* (1992).

    (B) Explain how the holding in *Roe v. Wade* was different than the holding in *Planned Parenthood v. Casey*.

    (C) Explain how the Supreme Court's decision in *Planned Parenthood v. Casey* reflects a conservative ideological belief.

12

Interest Groups

Do interest groups serve the needs of the many, or the privileged few?

> "This provision isn't about coronavirus, working families or small businesses struggling to stay afloat. It is just more insider politics to get millions to those who have millions, especially real estate investors and hedge fund managers."[1]
>
> *Representative Lloyd Doggett (D-TX)*

> "The attempt to paint this tax provision as a boon for real estate and hedge fund investors completely misses the mark.... This misleading talking point ignores the unimaginable economic losses that are painfully occurring across my state of Iowa and the rest of America."[2]
>
> *Senator Chuck Grassley (R-IA)*

When a staggering number of Americans lost their jobs in 2020 as the coronavirus pandemic crossed the United States, it was clear Congress needed to act. In quick succession, it passed four relief bills that pumped trillions of dollars into the economy. The largest of these, the Coronavirus Aid, Relief, and Economic Security (CARES) Act, provided $2.2 trillion for direct payments to individuals, forgivable loans to small businesses, and assistance to state and local governments and hospitals. There were huge logistical problems with quickly distributing that much money and there were some significant glitches: millions of people didn't receive their $1,200 checks for several months, and more than 200 large businesses engaged in the time-honored tradition of "feeding at the public trough" by taking billions of dollars that were intended for small businesses. Chastened by the public scrutiny and a stern warning from Treasury Secretary Steven Mnuchin that large companies would face "severe consequences" if they took money they weren't entitled to, dozens of businesses returned the taxpayers' money, including Potbelly, Shake Shack, Ruth's Chris Steak House, and the Los Angeles Lakers basketball team.[3]

While these problems made headlines, a much more significant misuse of taxpayers' funds initially slid through with little attention: a set of changes to the 2017 tax cuts,

Donald Trump signed the CARES Act into law on March 27, 2020. The historic $2.2 trillion bill was passed as part of the emergency response to the 2020 COVID-19 pandemic.

CHAPTER GOALS

Define *interest groups* and describe the characteristics of different types of groups. pages 516–527

Explain how successful interest groups overcome collective action problems. pages 527–529

Explore the ways interest groups try to influence government policies. pages 530–540

Evaluate interest group influence. pages 540–545

which had been a key legislative success of the Trump administration and a fulfillment of a campaign promise to reduce the tax burden on businesses. These changes, when integrated into the coronavirus legislation, illustrate the power of interest groups in the political system. In the 2017 tax cut legislation, Congress placed income limits on some of the more generous tax cuts to reduce the loss of revenue, but in the CARES Act it repealed those limits, which could result in a staggering loss of $135 billion in tax revenue over the next 10 years. The details get a little complicated, which is probably why this didn't get as much attention. After all, it is easier for people to understand why the L.A. Lakers, one of the most highly valued teams in the world (at $3.7 billion), shouldn't get a $4.6 million loan that was intended for small businesses than it is to understand arcane details of tax policy.

We don't need to get into the details here to understand the broad issues at play.[4] These income limit rollbacks affect how business owners can use losses from their businesses to cancel out other nonbusiness income. Another provision rolls back the restrictions on how much debt some companies can deduct from their taxes. How did this happen? Well, large corporations had lobbied hard to change these restrictions since they were enacted in 2017, and in an example that illustrates the power of these corporations' lobbying efforts, Congress snuck the provisions into the massive bill.

Once these changes in the tax law came to light shortly after the CARES bill was signed, an analysis by the nonpartisan Joint Committee on Taxation revealed that 80 percent of the tax cuts included in the bill went to business owners making more than $1 million (because only couples with $500,000 of nonbusiness income benefited from the policy change). And 43,000 business owners received a tax cut of an average of $1.6 million each, which means they received more total dollars than the 47 *million* people earning less than $20,000, who got $1,200 each. The $135 billion for the tax credits is three times more than the CARES Act is spending on safety-net programs like food and housing aid ($42 billion) and is more than is being spent on hospitals and other public health services ($100 billion).[5] Perhaps the most outrageous part of the policy is that wealthy business owners can exploit losses unrelated to the pandemic because the law allows them to retroactively write off losses from 2018 and 2019, well before we even knew about the virus.

This chapter surveys the wide range of interest groups in American politics—from large, powerful groups such as the National Rifle Association (NRA) to small organizations that lobby on issues that concern only a few Americans. Our aim is to get to the bottom of examples in which the lobbyists lose and understand examples in which it seems like the lobbyists always win, as with the CARES Act tax cuts. Some people, such as Senator Chuck Grassley, argue that such policies are good for the overall economy and *are* in the public's interest. However, many others always root for lobbyists, with their perceived insider connections and undue influence, to lose their battles. Is it fair to characterize all interest groups as self-interested organizations that undermine the public good? Are interest groups really too-powerful manipulators of the American policy process?

DEFINE *INTEREST GROUPS* AND DESCRIBE THE CHARACTERISTICS OF DIFFERENT TYPES OF GROUPS

What are interest groups?

Interest groups are organizations that seek to influence government policy. Interest groups may represent very specific or more general interests and they use a variety of tactics, such as lobbying elected officials and bureaucrats, helping draft legislation, mobilizing members and the public to apply pressure on and work with legislators and government agencies, and helping to elect candidates who support the organizations' policy goals. In its most basic form, **lobbying** involves persuasion and monitoring policy development by using reports, protests, informal meetings, or other techniques to convince an elected official or bureaucrat to help enact a law, craft a regulation, or do something else that a group wants. In this way, interest groups serve as a **linkage institution** between the people and their elected representatives. The members of an interest group can be individual citizens, local governments, businesses, foundations or nonprofit organizations, churches, or virtually any other entity. An interest group's employees or members may lobby on the group's behalf, or a group may hire a lobbyist or lobbying firm to do the work for it. Groups may lobby on their own or work with other groups to enact compromise proposals. Many organizations also have lobbying operations or hire lobbyists to work on their behalf. (See Nuts & Bolts 12.1 for some examples of the types of interest groups found in contemporary American politics.)

Single-issue groups, ideological groups, and protest movements form with the goal of influencing society and policy making. One such group is Public Citizen, which conducts research projects, lobbies legislators and bureaucrats, and tries to rally public opinion on a range of environmental, health, and energy issues. In other cases, lobbying is only one part of what an organization does. The NRA, for example, endorses candidates, contributes to campaigns, and lobbies elected officials, but it also runs gun safety classes, holds competitions, and sells gun accessories to its members. Interest

interest group
An organization of people who share common political interests and aim to influence public policy by electioneering and lobbying.

lobbying
Efforts to influence public policy through contact with public officials on behalf of an interest group.

linkage institutions
Institutions such as political parties, interest groups, the media, and elections that are channels through which individuals can communicate their preferences to policy makers.

NUTS & BOLTS 12.1

Types of Interest Groups

Scholars often divide interest groups into categories based on who their members are or the number or kinds of things they lobby for.

- *Institutional interest groups* are formed by nonprofits such as universities, think tanks, or museums. For example, the Big Ten Academic Alliance is a group of universities that prepares research to help individual universities make the case for continued federal support.
- *Businesses* are for-profit enterprises that aim to influence policy in ways that will increase profits or satisfy other goals. Many corporations, such as Google, Exxon Mobil, Boeing, Facebook, Citibank, and Sallie Mae, have lobbying operations that petition government for contracts or favorable regulations of their firm or industry.
- *Trade or peak associations* are groups of businesses (often in the same industry) that band together to lobby for policies that benefit all of them. For example, the National Beer Wholesalers Association, a nationwide group of local businesses that buy beer from brewers and resell it to stores and restaurants, lobbies to require intermediaries between beer producers and the stores, bars, and restaurants that sell beer to consumers.

- *Professional associations* represent individuals who have a common interest in a profession; examples include the American Society of Civil Engineers, National Education Association, American Medical Association, and American Bar Association.
- *Labor organizations* lobby for regulations that make it easy for workers to form labor unions, as well as for a range of other policies. The largest of these is the American Federation of Labor and Congress of Industrial Organizations (AFL-CIO).
- *Citizen groups* range from those with mass membership (such as the Sierra Club) to those that have no members but claim to speak for particular segments of the population. One such group is the Family Research Council (FRC), which describes itself as "promoting the Judeo-Christian worldview as the basis for a just, free, and stable society." FRC Action (the lobbying arm of the organization) promotes a range of policies, from legislation that defines marriage as between a man and a woman to legislation that would eliminate estate taxes.

Source: Compiled by the authors.

Categorizing interest groups can help you see which groups are working for collective interests and which groups are working for more particular or special interests. Which of the types above do you think fall into each category?

group activity is almost hidden within other organizations. For example, most drivers know that AAA (formerly the American Automobile Association) provides emergency roadside service and maps, but many people are not aware that AAA is also an interest group that lobbies for policies such as limiting new drivers to daylight-only hours.

As these descriptions suggest, interest groups and lobbying are ubiquitous in American politics. You may think that you don't belong to a group that lobbies the federal government, but the odds are that you do. In fact, one important view of American politics, *pluralism*, identifies interest groups as America's fundamental political actors.[6] Pluralists argue that most Americans participate in politics through their membership in interest groups like Public Citizen, the NRA, or even AAA. These groups lobby, try to elect candidates who share their views, and negotiate among themselves to encourage legislators to pursue policies that benefit their members. Pluralists see interest groups as important and appropriate participants in the democratic process. Others see interest groups in a more negative light, describing America as an **interest group state**, meaning that these groups are involved whenever policy is made, but in a self-interested way that can undermine the collective good.[7] More recent perspectives on interest group pluralism, such as Frank Baumgartner and coauthors' study of lobbying,[8] note that interest groups' influence is contextual and depends on a number of factors, but their importance in the political system is clear.

interest group state
A government in which most policy decisions are determined by the influence of interest groups.

The business of lobbying

Interest group lobbying is regulated. Lobbying firms must file quarterly reports identifying their clients, specifying how much each client paid, and the issues they lobbied on. Similarly, interest groups and corporations must file reports listing staff members who spent more than 20 percent of their time lobbying Congress, and total expenditures to lobbying firms.[9] Also, most executive or legislative branch employees who take lobbying jobs are legally required to refrain from lobbying people in their former office or agency for one year; elected officials who become lobbyists must wait two years.

Today lobbying involves billions of dollars a year. Figure 12.1 (top) presents annual lobbying expenditures for 2000 through 2019. As the figure shows, a total of $3.51 billion was spent on lobbying in 2019. The amount spent, as well as the number of groups lobbying government, increased significantly from 2000 to 2010 and has held steady since then.

Why are there so many interest groups and registered lobbyists, and why are their numbers increasing? Figure 12.1 (bottom) suggests that this proliferation is related to the large size and widespread influence of the federal government. Simply put, the federal government does so many things and spends so much money that many individuals, organizations, and corporations have strong incentives for lobbying: corporations may lobby for a government contract or for regulations that favor their business sector. Corporations may also lobby to prevent new regulations or reverse existing rules that hurt their profits: in the first two months of the Trump administration, Congress reversed 14 regulations that were passed at the end of Obama's presidency, and 100 environmental rules were overturned by 2020.[10] Energy companies lobbied hard on the Keystone XL pipeline, offshore drilling in the Atlantic and Arctic Oceans, and calculations of the social cost of carbon, and they won. The Environmental Protection Agency (EPA) also replaced the Obama-era emissions rules for power plants and vehicles, weakened protections for more than half the nation's wetlands, and eased restrictions on mercury emissions from power plants. While business dominates lobbying spending, individuals may lobby the government to place limits on what citizens can do or to relax restrictions on behavior—or to change corporate behavior. Trade unions and single-issue groups also spend millions of dollars on lobbying.

Growth in Spending on Lobbying and Total Federal Spending, 2000–2019

FIGURE 12.1

These data show that in recent years interest groups have spent several billion dollars lobbying the federal government. Does this amount seem surprisingly large or surprisingly small, given what lobbyists do and given the total federal outlays of money?

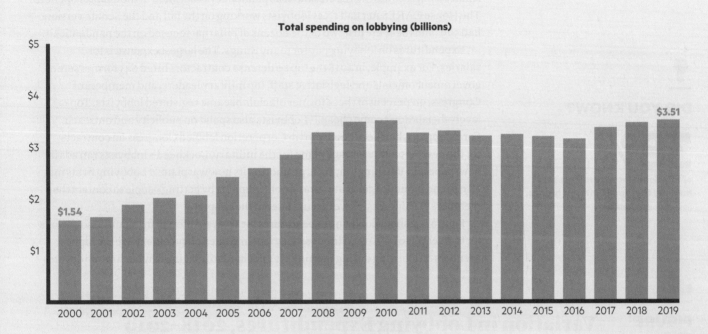

Total spending on lobbying (billions)

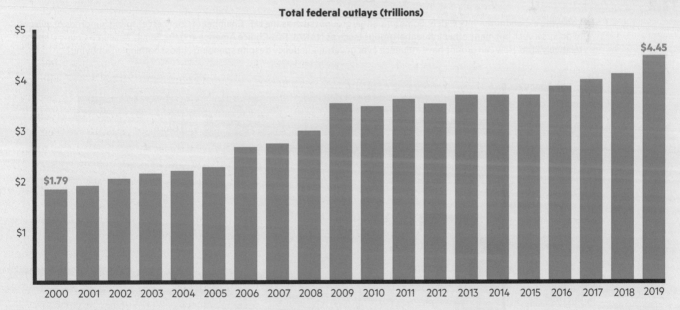

Total federal outlays (trillions)

Sources: Lobbying data available at Center for Responsive Politics, "Lobbying Database," www.opensecrets.org/federal-lobbying; federal spending from Congressional Budget Office, Historical Budget Data, August 2019, www.cbo.gov/about/products/budget-economic-data#2 (both accessed 5/11/20).

Studies of Washington-based lobbying operations confirm this: interest groups are more likely to form around issues that have high levels of government involvement or when new programs or changes in government policy are likely.[11] Moreover, as groups form on one side of a policy question and start to lobby, people who oppose them may form their own interest groups and start lobbying as well, either separately or in concert.[12] The pressure of lobbying is especially strong when new policies are under consideration, such as the government's plan to provide more than $500 billion in aid to small businesses during the coronavirus pandemic, as outlined in the chapter opener. The House CARES Act had 1,545 lobbyists working on the bill and the Senate version had 599 (and these are just two of the dozens of bills that focused on the pandemic).[13]

Expenditures on lobbying pay for many things. The largest expense is for salaries. For example, in 2018 the top 20 defense contractors hired 645 former senior government officials and legislative staff, top military leaders, and members of Congress; 90 percent of these former officials became registered lobbyists. Top-level officials don't come cheap.[14] Lobbyists also spend on publicity and outreach. For example, when Lockheed Martin Corporation lobbied Congress on contracts for the new F-35 fighter-attack plane for the military, Lockheed's lobbyists ran ads in newspapers in Washington, D.C., promoting its new warplane.[15] Lobbying firms may also spend money to generate "grassroots" support by getting people to contact their members of Congress, as we discuss later in the chapter.

Figure 12.2 shows lobbying expenditures for several different firms and associations for two years (2018–2019). Three associations and one policy center were the highest spenders on lobbying during this time. It's not hard to imagine why each group devotes

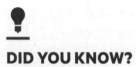

DID YOU KNOW?

38%

of total lobbying expenditures are made by the top 100 interest groups.
Source: OpenSecrets.org

FIGURE 12.2

Variation in Lobbying Expenditures, 2018–2019

Lobbying expenditures vary widely. Some influential groups (such as the U.S. Chamber of Commerce) spend hundreds of millions of dollars a year, but many other influential groups (such as NARAL Pro-Choice America and the Family Research Council) spend relatively little. How can groups have influence over government policy despite spending almost nothing on lobbying?

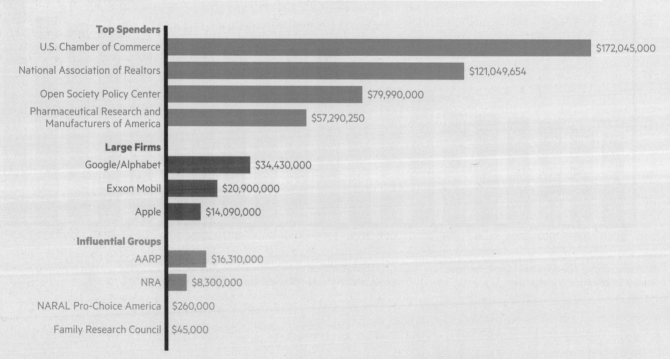

Top Spenders

U.S. Chamber of Commerce	$172,045,000
National Association of Realtors	$121,049,654
Open Society Policy Center	$79,990,000
Pharmaceutical Research and Manufacturers of America	$57,290,250

Large Firms

Google/Alphabet	$34,430,000
Exxon Mobil	$20,900,000
Apple	$14,090,000

Influential Groups

AARP	$16,310,000
NRA	$8,300,000
NARAL Pro-Choice America	$260,000
Family Research Council	$45,000

Source: Data available at Center for Responsive Politics, "Lobbying Data Summary," www.opensecrets.org/federal-lobbying (accessed 5/12/20).

so much effort to lobbying: realtors, for example, might be concerned about maintaining government policies that make it almost essential to hire a realtor to help buy or sell a home. While the $121 million the National Association of Realtors spent on lobbying may sound like a lot, it really isn't that much.[16] After all, over a million people work in real estate, generating billions of dollars in profits every year. The surprise is that real estate brokers are willing to spend only a tiny fraction of their profits to keep their near monopoly in place. The same is true for the large firms listed in Figure 12.2. Apple, for example, is one of the largest firms in the United States, but it spends only about $7 million per year on lobbying ($14.1 million over two years). And only one of the influential interest groups in Figure 12.2 (the AARP) spends more than $10 million per year on lobbying. Clearly, the big spenders on lobbying are exceptions to the rule, and most interest groups and firms spend relatively little on lobbying.[17] For example, the group that sends a turkey to the White House for a ceremonial pardon every year at Thanksgiving, the National Turkey Federation, spends $140,000 a year to lobby the federal government on a relatively small range of issues. Many other groups spend even less, barely scraping together enough cash to send someone to plead their case in Washington. In fact, a few groups account for a substantial fraction of total lobbying expenditures.

That concentration of spending is evident in another way as well: a large proportion of lobbying is done by the business sector and relatively little by political or public interests. According to the Center for Responsive Politics, the top six sectors in 2018–2019 were all business interests (health, finance, miscellaneous business, communication, energy, and transportation), with 77 percent of the total spending on lobbying, while education, nonprofits, and public officials (categorized as "Other") and ideological/single-issue political groups came in seventh and eighth, spending 7.4 and 4.4 percent respectively.[18]

Although the amount of money spent on lobbying by interest groups may seem like a lot (and often leads to calls for restrictions on lobbying, as discussed in the Take a Stand feature), it is small compared with how much is at stake.[19] The federal government now spends more than $4 trillion every year (with spending more than double that in 2020 because of the extraordinary response to the COVID-19 pandemic and economic recession). In recent years, spending by interest groups and by the lobbying arms of organizations and corporations has amounted to $3.5 billion every year. That's a lot of money, but it's still less than one-tenth of 1 percent of total federal spending. This difference raises a critical question: If interest groups can control policy choices by spending money on lobbying, why aren't they spending more?

Organizational structures

There are two main models of interest group structure. Most large, well-known organizations like the AARP and the NRA are centralized groups, which means the organization's leadership is concentrated in its headquarters. These national organizations typically have headquarters in Washington, D.C., field offices in large state capitals, and members nationwide. Their leaders have the responsibility to determine the group's lobbying goals and tactics. The other structural model is a confederation, which is composed of largely independent, local organizations. For example, the National Independent Automobile Dealers Association (NIADA) is made up of 50 state-level organizations that provide membership benefits to car dealers who join the organization and that raise much of the money that NIADA contributes to candidates running for political office (several million dollars in recent elections).

Both organizational structures have advantages and disadvantages. A centralized organization controls all of the group's resources and can deploy them efficiently, but it can be challenging for these groups to find out what their members want.

centralized groups
Interest groups that have a headquarters, usually in Washington, D.C., as well as members and field offices throughout the country. In general, these groups' lobbying decisions are made at headquarters by the group leaders.

confederations
Interest groups made up of several independent, local organizations that provide much of their funding and hold most of the power.

Restrictions on Interest Group Lobbying

Under current rules, members of Congress and their staffs are severely limited in the size of gifts they can receive from lobbyists. These restrictions were tightened in the mid-2000s after it was revealed that former-congressional-staffer-turned-lobbyist Jack Abramoff had used "golf junkets, free meals at the restaurant he owned, seats at sporting events, and, in some cases, old-fashioned cash" to lobby members of Congress.[a] The current restrictions limit members and their staffs to accepting gifts only if they are valued at less than $50—moreover, the total worth of the gifts that any lobbyist can give to a particular member of Congress or staffer is limited to $100 per year. In addition, "cooling off" rules, which prevent staffers and former members of Congress from lobbying for one year after leaving their government job, were instituted in an attempt to limit the revolving door between government and lobbying firms. President Trump vowed to "drain the swamp" of lobbyist influence in Washington, but lobbyists have gained even more access in his administration. Are current restrictions fair? Do they help or hurt the political process? Are even stronger limitations needed?

Keep the rules, and maybe tighten them. Supporting this option seems like a no-brainer. These regulations are based on a sensible intuition that laws are needed to prevent well-funded, unscrupulous lobbyists from offering inducements to members of Congress and their staffs in return for policy change. Simply put, groups that can send people to Washington to wine and dine members of Congress, congressional staff, and bureaucrats might gain a significant advantage over those who are unable to do so. Even if a fancy lunch doesn't buy a legislator's vote, it might help with access—that is, it might give the group a chance to make its arguments and perhaps change some minds. In this way, rules that allow even small gifts create an advantage for interest groups that have a Washington office or hire lobbyists and a disadvantage for those that do not. As a result, many reform proposals should go further, preventing lobbyists from giving anything to a member of Congress, legislative staffer, or bureaucrat—even a cup of coffee.

Relax the rules (a little). Some argue that worries about interest group influence seem a little overstated. Congressional staff and the legislators they work for are going to support a group's proposals only if they help the member's constituents or if they move policy in a way the member favors, not just because of an interest group's free lunch.

When scandals surrounding Jack Abramoff came to light in 2005, many Americans considered him a typical lobbyist. Abramoff's actions were illegal, but the question remains: Are his tactics common in Washington, or was he a rare exception?

There are also downsides to tight controls on these gifts and perks. The current rules on lobbyists' gifts create a lot of paperwork for members and their staffs, who have to file reports on just about anything they receive from a lobbyist, even if that individual is a former colleague, neighbor, or friend. The rules are also extremely complicated—for example, legislators are allowed to eat the hors d'oeuvres provided at a reception, but they cannot sit down to a full meal without violating the gift restrictions. The disclosure requirements are also a burden to smaller interest groups and firms, which have to document everything they do on complex forms. As a result, members of Congress, their staff, interest groups, and lobbying firms spend considerable time and effort on documenting small gifts that are unlikely to have any effect on policy outcomes.

Do both. Another approach would be to relax some of the rules and strengthen others. For example, one suggestion is to get rid of the "cooling off" periods, but have better disclosure of who is lobbying so constituents will be able to hold their elected officials accountable. Many lobbyists skirt current disclosure rules by generously interpreting the 20 percent rule mentioned earlier in the chapter to exclude what most would consider lobbying activity. These "shadow lobbyists" would be exposed by stricter disclosure rules.[b]

take a stand

1. To what extent do you think current congressional rules limiting the size of gifts that members of Congress and their staffers can receive from lobbyists have curbed illegal behavior by interest groups?

2. Are these rules aimed at exceptional cases or average interest groups?

Centralized interest groups typically have headquarters close to Washington, D.C., such as the NRA's offices shown here in Fairfax, Virginia. These offices serve as a hub for the organization's leaders, and the close proximity to the capitol facilitates their lobbying goals.

Confederations have the advantage of maintaining independent chapters at the state and local levels, so it is easier for the national headquarters to learn what their members want—all they have to do is contact their local groups. But this strength is closely related to a weakness: confederated groups are often beset with conflict. Since state and local chapters attract members and raise money largely on their own, they mostly function independently of the national headquarters. However, the national headquarters depends on the local organizations for funds to pay its staff and make campaign contributions. In return, it allows the locals to direct contributions to their preferred candidates, and different local chapters may disagree over what to lobby for and which candidates to support.

Some organizations are hard to categorize, such as the Indivisible grassroots progressive movement that started in 2016 in reaction to the election of Donald Trump. The organizations that make up this movement are very diverse. Some hold meetings or public protests, some endorse candidates, and some simply consist of a website run by one or two people. The issues that motivate each Indivisible organization also vary widely, from opposition to President Trump's policies to calls for radical changes in government. Virtually all the groups lack formal dues-paying members, a headquarters, and a formal organizational structure, and few engage in the wide range of lobbying activities that we describe later in this chapter. For all these reasons, very few of the organizations that identify themselves as part of Indivisible are interest groups as we describe them here, although some may evolve into formal interest groups in the future.

Staff

Interest group staff fall into two categories: experts on the group's main policy areas and people with useful government connections and knowledge of procedures. The first group includes scientists, engineers, and others with advanced degrees; the second is dominated by people who have worked inside government as elected officials, bureaucrats, or legislative staff.[20] Sometimes these former members of government are also policy experts, but their unique contribution is their knowledge of how government works and their relationships with officeholders and other former coworkers in government.

revolving door
The movement of individuals from government positions to jobs with interest groups or lobbying firms, and vice versa.

💡

DID YOU KNOW?

446

former members of Congress had been registered lobbyists as of 2020 (and 356 were currently lobbyists).

Source: OpenSecrets.org

iron triangle
Informal alliance of elected officials, bureaucrats, and interest groups designed to let these groups and individuals dominate the policy-making process in a given area.

issue network
Informal organization of interest groups and individuals who work together to lobby government for policy change. These collaborations are usually short-term efforts focused on specific proposals, issues, or regulations.

The practice of moving from a government position to a job with an interest group or lobbying firm, or of transitioning from a lobbyist to an officeholder, is often called the **revolving door**.[21] For example, as of 2020, more than half the members of Congress who retired at the end of the 115th Congress and were employed had moved to lobbying jobs.[22] The percentages are similar for congressional staff and bureaucrats. Many observers view this dynamic as potentially sowing seeds of corruption; they fear that past government employees might capitalize on personal ties with their former colleagues to negotiate favorable deals for their interest groups—or that people working in government may give special treatment to a corporation or interest group that might hire them as a lobbyist in the future. These concerns have led to proposed restrictions on the revolving door, including banning former elected officials, staff, and bureaucrats from working as lobbyists for some time period after they have left government service, as well as banning former lobbyists in government positions from administering programs that they previously lobbied for.

President Trump's vow to "drain the swamp" was centered on these proposals to limit the revolving door. Of the five specific promises to tighten restrictions on lobbying that he made during the 2016 campaign, only one has been fulfilled (an executive order that bans executive branch officials from lobbying for foreign governments and overseas political parties after they leave the administration).[23] In fact, Trump quickly filled the swamp. In his first three years in office, one out of every 14 political appointees was a former lobbyist, with a total of 281 former lobbyists, including Secretary of Defense Mark Esper (former top lobbyist for Raytheon, one of the leading defense contractors), Secretary of the Interior David Bernhardt (a former oil industry lobbyist), and Trump's second head of the Environmental Protection Agency, Andrew Wheeler (a former coal industry lobbyist). In comparison, President Obama had only 65 former lobbyists among his political appointees in his first *five* years. The Trump administration weakened lobbying restrictions, including removing an Obama-era policy that prevented registered lobbyists from seeking or accepting employment with any executive agency that they lobbied the two years prior.[24] The Pentagon has recently attempted to undo a law authored by the late senator John McCain (R-AZ) that required retired Defense Department officials to wait for two years before lobbying on behalf of defense contractors.[25]

Such restrictions have costs as well as benefits. On the one hand, people who have worked in an industry or as lobbyists know a particular field and the relevant laws very well, making them well qualified to work in the corresponding area of the executive branch. Thus, a ban on hiring lobbyists may lead to a shortage of experienced candidates for government positions. Similarly, former officeholders, congressional staff, and bureaucrats are attractive candidates for lobbying jobs because they have firsthand knowledge of how policies are made and enjoy established relationships with people in government. On the other hand, these restrictions would help lower the potential for corruption mentioned earlier. It is very hard to craft restrictions that avoid these problems.

The revolving door also contributes to another feature of interest group lobbying, **iron triangles**, which refers to informal alliances between elected officials and their staff, bureaucrats, and interest groups. These alliances help these individuals dominate policy making on a set of issues, shutting everyone else out of the process. For example, the agriculture iron triangle would include representatives from farm states, bureaucrats from the Department of Agriculture, and interest groups representing farmers and companies that sell products for farmers. The revolving door helps iron triangles to form, as people in different organizations are likely to know each other because of their prior service. Some see "iron triangles" as an overly restrictive term for these relationships and prefer to use the term "**issue networks**" to characterize a more fluid set of issue-based relationships that may include the same actors in the iron triangle but also may include the media, think tanks, policy experts, and social media.

Membership

Interest groups can be categorized in terms of the size of their membership and the members' role in the group's activities. **Mass associations**, with many dues-paying members, tend to be citizens' groups and labor organizations. One example is the Sierra Club, which has over 3 million members. Besides keeping its members informed about the implementation of environmental policy in Washington, D.C., the Sierra Club endorses judicial nominees and candidates for elected positions, files lawsuits to increase environmental protection on government projects, and works with members of Congress to develop legislative proposals. The group's members elect the organization's board of directors.

Yet not all mass associations give members a say in selecting their leaders or determining their mission. To join the AARP, which has nearly 38 million members, one must be at least 50 years old and pay dues of $16 per year. Members get discounts on insurance, car rentals, and hotels, as well as driver safety courses and help doing their taxes. The AARP claims to lobby for policies its members favor, but members actually have no control over which legislative causes the group chooses. Moreover, the AARP does not poll members to determine its issue positions, nor do members elect AARP leadership.

The members of **peak associations** are businesses or other organizations rather than individuals.[26] Individuals cannot join peak associations—they may work for member companies or organizations, but they cannot become dues-paying members on their own. The Business–Industry Political Action Committee (BIPAC), an association of several hundred businesses and trade associations that aims to elect "pro-business individuals" to Congress, is a good example of a peak association.[27]

Resources and challenges

Interest groups use three key resources to support their lobbying efforts: people, money, and expertise. The resources that a group has at its disposal significantly influence its available lobbying strategies. (We will examine some of these strategies in more detail in a later section.) Some large groups have sufficient funding and staff to pursue a wide range of strategies, whereas some smaller groups with fewer resources face more significant challenges when it comes to the lobbying options they have at their disposal.

People A crucial resource for most interest groups is their membership. Group members can write to or meet with elected officials, travel to Washington for demonstrations, and even offer expertise or advice to their leaders. When the "members" of a group are corporations, as is the case with trade associations, CEOs and other corporate staff can help with the group's lobbying efforts.

Many mass organizations try to get their members involved in the lobbying process through links on their website that encourage members to contact their members of Congress. One organization opposed to President Trump's agenda has developed a service, Resistbot, whose *exclusive* purpose is to make it easier for people to have their voices heard. Resistbot allows users to contact their elected officials by texting "RESIST" to the number 50409 (or by messaging the bot on Facebook). The bot asks for information, like name and zip code, so that it can identify the appropriate senators and House member to contact for each person. After getting information about the user's concerns, the bot faxes or e-mails the politician's office with a personalized message from the user. The first version of Resistbot only sent faxes, but the volume (5 million faxes in six months) overwhelmed congressional offices. Now, the bot first tries to communicate with congressional offices electronically, and if that doesn't work,

Many interest groups speak for large numbers of Americans, while others lobby for changes that would benefit only a few people. Mass associations, such as the Sierra Club, have large numbers of dues-paying members. Here, members in Michigan gather at the Detroit March for Justice to promote environmental issues.

Interest groups use a variety of tactics to draw attention to their concerns, including events designed to generate media coverage. People for the Ethical Treatment of Animals (PETA) stationed a life-size mechanical elephant outside the Ringling Bros. circus to protest the company's treatment of its elephants. Campaigns such as this were credited with reducing the public's support for the circus, which eventually closed in 2017.

it will send a fax or make a phone call. In its first six months, the bot sent and received 91,421,000 text messages from more than 1.3 million unique users.[28] Use of this technique was widely credited with helping stop the repeal of Obamacare.

Interest groups' ability to use people as a resource faces two major challenges. First, it requires having members in the first place, and recruiting new members can be difficult and expensive. The second challenge is motivating members to participate. As we discuss later, although some interest groups have managed to change government policy by persuading their members to write to and visit elected officials, interest groups more often receive little response when they ask for members' help.[29]

Money Virtually everything interest groups do can be purchased as services: groups can spend money on hiring people to meet with elected officials and to fight for what they want in court. Money can also go toward campaign contributions or developing and running campaign ads. And, of course, money is necessary to fund interest groups' everyday operations. The importance of money for interest group operations is evident in their funding appeals to members. For example, the donations page from the Sierra Club's website shows that supporters can give a membership as a gift, join as a life member, or pay dues monthly. They can make commemorative or memorial gifts, set up a planned giving scheme, or donate stock. The group even offers gift-giving plans for non-U.S. residents and a Spanish-language version of its donations page.

Well-funded interest groups and firms have a considerable advantage in the lobbying process. If they need an expert, a lobbyist, or a lawyer, they can simply hire one or open a Washington office to increase contacts with legislators and bureaucrats. They can pay for campaign ads and make contributions to candidates and parties. Groups with less cash, however, cannot use these strategies. Smaller firms might join a trade association that will lobby for policies that benefit all of the association's members.

Still, groups can be effective without spending much. They can rely on members to lobby for them, hire staff willing to work for low pay because they share the group's goals, or cite published research rather than funding their own studies to bolster their case for policy change. Moreover, the fact that a group spends the most money is no guarantee that its lobbying efforts will succeed. For example, in the third quarter of 2019 Amazon spent $4 million on heavy lobbying efforts for a $10 billion cloud computing contract that the Pentagon ended up awarding to Microsoft (which spent $2.3 million lobbying for the contract).[30]

Expertise Expertise takes many forms. Groups can employ staff (or can hire experts) to conduct research or develop policy proposals related to their interests. A firm's in-house lobbyists can provide information about how a change in government policy will affect the firm's profits and employment. Some lobbying firms (especially those that employ former members of Congress or congressional staff) may also have inside information on the kinds of policies that are likely to be enacted in the House or Senate. Interest groups with dues-paying members (such as the Sierra Club) can poll them to find out what they would like government to do. All of this information can be deployed to persuade elected officials or bureaucrats about the merits of a group's or a firm's demands (as well as the political consequences of inaction) and offer ready-made policy solutions to the problems the group has identified.

Consider the AARP, whose website offers a vast array of research and analyses, including information about seniors' part-time employment, how people invest their 401(k) retirement accounts, age discrimination, and dealing with the coronavirus pandemic.[31] The AARP's lobbyists use this research when arguing for policy changes in their public testimony and in private meetings with members of Congress and congressional staff. And they hire former members of Congress and bureaucrats so they are well informed about the preferences of those inside government. However, only a few interest groups can match the AARP's wealth of expertise and resources.

Individual lobbyists also vary in what they offer to a group or corporation. Former members of Congress might know a lot about policy options and the preferences of their former colleagues but be less informed about public opinion or the business challenges faced by the firm that hires them to lobby. In-house lobbyists might know a lot about the firm they work for but much less about congressional preferences. And an interest group's policy expert might know everything there is to know about current government policies in some areas but know nothing about how to sell new proposals to a skeptical member of Congress.

When you think of a lobbyist, don't imagine a person in an expensive suit carrying a briefcase of cash (or a campaign contribution). More often, people become lobbyists because they believe in the goals of the group they represent. And they generally don't wear expensive suits. Understanding who lobbyists really are, and the boundaries of what they can really do, is key to evaluating whether or not they have too much influence in American politics.

"Why Should I Care?"

Getting organized

EXPLAIN HOW SUCCESSFUL INTEREST GROUPS OVERCOME COLLECTIVE ACTION PROBLEMS

A new interest group's first priority is to get organized, which involves formulating policy goals and a lobbying strategy and raising the money needed to hire staff, rent an office, and set up a website. In some cases, a lobbying firm is hired to perform these jobs. Once organized, the group must continue to attract funds for ongoing operations. These tasks are not easy. Even if a group of people (or corporations) shares the same goals, it may be challenging to persuade them to donate time or money to the lobbying operation.

The logic of collective action

collective action problem
A situation in which the members of a group would benefit by working together to produce some outcome, but each individual is better off refusing to cooperate and reaping benefits from those who do the work.

Research has found that **collective action problems** arise when a group of individuals (or corporations) has an opportunity to make itself better off through the cooperative provision of public goods. For interest groups, the public good in question would be a change in government policy desired by group members. Scholars refer to these situations as involving collective action. Even when all members of a group agree on the desirability of a public good and the costs of producing the good are negligible, cooperation is neither easy nor automatic (see Nuts & Bolts 12.2).

The logic of collective action provides insights into how interest groups are organized and how they make lobbying decisions. First, the logic of collective action tells us that group formation is not automatic. Even when a number of citizens want the same things from government, their common interest may not lead them to organize. Society is full of groups of like-minded people who do not organize to lobby or who choose to engage in **free riding** and thus enjoy the benefits of organizations without participating. This tendency explains why certain debates in Washington feature well-organized groups on one side of the issue but few on the other.

free riding
Relying on others to contribute to a collective effort while failing to participate on one's own behalf, yet still benefiting from the group's successes.

selective incentives
Benefits that can motivate participation in a group effort because they are available only to those who participate, such as member services offered by interest groups.

Unless people can easily see benefits from participating, which does not happen often, group leaders must worry about finding the right strategies to get people to join. Thus, given the logic of collective action, motivating people to join and participate is just as important for a group's success as its lobbying strategy. Most organizations develop mechanisms to make cooperation and participation in an interest group's efforts worthwhile. These **selective incentives** fall into three categories: benefits from participation, coercion, and material goods.

NUTS & BOLTS 12.2

Collective Action Problems

What is collective action?
"Collective action" refers to situations in which a group of individuals can work together to provide public goods. For example, working to help change certain government policies can result in public goods: if the government changes policy, such as strengthening environmental laws, everyone benefits from the cleaner air and water.

What are the problems?
Situations like those described above make it hard to motivate people to contribute to collective efforts to change a law, because each would-be group member can see that his or her contribution would be only a minuscule portion of what the group needs to succeed. Regardless of how many other people join, an individual is better off free riding—refusing to join but still being able to enjoy the benefits of any successes the group might have.

Why are collective action problems important?
Groups of like-minded citizens who seek changes in government policy may be unable to lobby effectively because they cannot solve their collective action problem. And organization matters. Groups that remain unorganized are less likely to get what they want from government.

How do interest groups solve collective action problems?
Interest groups solve collective action problems in three ways: (1) like some labor unions, they force people to join; (2) they are small enough so that every member's voice matters and free rider problems are lessened; and (3) they encourage a larger, engaged membership by offering incentives for people to join and participate.

"Why Should I Care?" Collective action problems explain why it is difficult to provide public goods. They explain the tendency for the dirty dishes to pile up in the kitchen: in this case, the public good is a clean kitchen, but each roommate's self-interest is to free ride and let someone else wash the dishes. They also help explain the difficulty of interest group formation.

AAA (formerly the American Automobile Association) is a well-known provider of emergency road service, yet few people are aware of its role as an interest group that lobbies for a wide range of policy changes and builds awareness of key transportation issues.

Studies of political parties and interest groups find that some individuals volunteer out of a sense of duty or because they enjoy working together toward a common goal. Scholars refer to these benefits of participation as either **solidary benefits**, which come from working with like-minded people, or **purposive benefits**, which come from working to achieve a desired policy goal.[32] If most people were spurred to political action because of participation benefits, the free rider problem wouldn't exist.

When solidary or purposive benefits are not enough to solve the free rider problem, groups may require participation through **coercion**. Consider labor unions. They provide public goods to workers by negotiating with management on behalf of worker-members over pay and work requirements. Why don't union members free ride? Because in many cases they have to join the union: union shop laws require them to pay union dues as a condition of their employment. These laws are critical to unions; states with laws that make union membership optional typically have weak unions—if any.

Finally, **material benefits** are benefits given only to the members of an interest group. These incentives are not public goods; an individual can receive a material benefit only by joining the group. Thus, interest groups offer material benefits in the hope of providing people with new reasons to participate. One of the most interesting cases of material benefits provided by an interest group involves AAA. Members with car trouble can call AAA at any time for emergency service. AAA also provides its members with annotated maps and travel guides, a travel agency, a car-buying service, discounts at hotels and restaurants, and other benefits. These services mask the interest group role of AAA. For example, its Foundation for Traffic Safety delivers research reports to legislators on topics ranging from lowering the blood alcohol level threshold that legally defines drunk driving to increasing the restrictions on driving for senior citizens.[33] It's unlikely that many AAA members—who join for the selective incentives—are aware of the organization's lobbying efforts. The incentives drive membership, which funds the organization's lobbying operation.

solidary benefits
Satisfaction derived from the experience of working with like-minded people, even if the group's efforts do not achieve the desired impact.

purposive benefits
Satisfaction derived from the experience of working toward a desired policy goal, even if the goal is not achieved.

coercion
A method of eliminating nonparticipation or free riding by potential group members by requiring participation, as in many labor unions.

material benefits
Benefits that are provided to individuals for joining a group, such as a coffee mug or a T-shirt, that are distinct from the collective benefits provided by the group.

The logic of collective action says that organization is neither automatic nor easy. Rather than complaining about how many lobbyists there are or how much they spend, we should consider whether some groups in society are ignored because they are never able to organize themselves and lobby for their concerns. Are you free riding off of any groups' efforts right now? What would it take to get you involved?

"Why Should I Care?"

inside strategies
The tactics employed within
Washington, D.C., by interest groups
seeking to achieve their policy goals.

outside strategies
The tactics employed outside
Washington, D.C., by interest groups
seeking to achieve their policy goals.

direct lobbying
Attempts by interest group staff to
influence policy by speaking with
elected officials or bureaucrats.

Interest group strategies

Once a group has organized and determined its goals, the next step is to decide how to lobby. There are two types of possible tactics: inside strategies, which are actions taken inside government (whether federal, state, or local), and outside strategies, which are actions taken outside government (see How It Works: Lobbying the Federal Government).[34] The type of strategy is sometimes dictated by the policy in question. In the example of the tax breaks for wealthy individuals and companies hidden in the CARES Act discussed in the chapter opener, an insider strategy was essential because the public would have been opposed had it known about these tax breaks. In other cases, such as the AARP's lobbying effort to help save the Affordable Care Act, an outside strategy is effective to help put pressure on members of Congress. In general, these strategies are undertaken by a single group working on its own, sometimes in opposition to another group or groups. However, as we discuss later, interest groups sometimes work together toward common legislative goals.

Inside strategies

Inside strategies involve some form of contact with elected officials or bureaucrats. Thus, inside strategies require a group to establish an office in Washington, D.C., or to hire a lobbying firm to act on its behalf.

Direct Lobbying When interest group staff meet with officeholders or bureaucrats, they plead their case through direct lobbying, asking government officials to change policy in line with the group's goals.[35] Such contacts are very common—on any given day, each congressional or administrative office gets phone calls, visits, or e-mails from dozens of lobbyists.

Direct lobbying is generally aimed at officials and bureaucrats who are sympathetic to the group's goals.[36] Through these efforts, interest groups and their representatives do not try to convert opponents into supporters; rather, these efforts are a way of helping legislators enact policies that they already prefer—and that the group prefers as well.[37] Groups can assist in a number of ways, from sharing information about proposed changes, to providing lists of other legislators who might be persuadable, to drafting legislative proposals or regulations. These efforts usually do not involve a trade in which the group expects legislative action in return for its help. In fact, legislators and their staff are often happy to meet with a like-minded group's representatives, as the information the group can provide may be vital to the legislators' efforts to enact legislation, manage the bureaucracy, or keep the support of constituents back home in their districts.[38] For example, corporations that stood to lose business if the government moved to direct student loans lobbied legislators whose districts included the companies' call centers and headquarters. For these legislators, helping these companies might have been good public policy, but it was also a way of preserving their constituents' jobs.

Interest groups also contact "fence-sitters" who neither support nor oppose them, with the goal of converting them into supporters. These efforts are less extensive than the lobbying of supporters, however, because opponents are unlikely to change their minds unless a group can provide new information that causes them to rethink their position. However, lobbying opponents may be useful if it forces opposing interest groups to counterlobby, using their limited resources to make sure that their allied legislators do not change their positions.[39]

As these descriptions indicate, interest groups place a high priority on maintaining access to their lobbying targets and being able to present their arguments, regardless of whether they expect to get what they want. Of course, interest groups want to achieve their policy goals, but access is the necessary first step that makes persuasion possible. Therefore, many interest groups try to keep their efforts low-key, providing information to friends and opponents alike and avoiding threats or harsh words, in the hope that they will leave a favorable impression and be able to gain access the next time they want to lobby their opponents. After all, people who are opposed to a group's current priorities one day may agree with the group on some future issue.

Whom do these groups contact for direct lobbying? Analysis of lobbyists' annual disclosure forms shows that they contact people throughout the federal government, including elected officials, members of the president's staff, and bureaucrats in the executive branch. They seek this wide range of contacts because different officials play distinct roles in the policy-making process and thus have various types of influence. Members of Congress shape legislation and budgets; members of the president's staff influence the formation of new policies and obtain presidential consent for new laws; and executive branch bureaucrats change the ways regulations are written and policies are implemented.

Drafting Legislation and Regulations Interest groups sometimes draft legislative proposals and regulations, which they deliver to legislators and bureaucrats as part of their lobbying efforts.[40] Surveys of interest groups found that more than three-quarters reported drafting proposals for members of Congress.[41] In recent years, the role of lobbyists in drafting legislation has become more prominent because Congress has less internal capacity to write the laws due to cuts in committee staff.[42]

Interest groups do not give proposals to just anyone: they seek out legislators who already support their cause and who have significant influence within Congress. A lobbying effort aimed at cutting interest rates on student loans would target supporters of this change who are also members of the congressional committee with jurisdiction over student loan programs—preferably someone who chairs the committee or one of its subcommittees.[43] Interest groups also lobby bureaucrats to influence the details of new regulations.[44] If the types of regulations involved can go into effect without congressional approval, then lobbying the bureaucracy can result in groups' getting exactly what they want. But even if new regulations require approval by Congress or White House staff, interest groups can increase their chances of success by getting involved in the initial drafting of policy.

Research Interest groups often prepare research reports on topics of interest to the group. For example, Public Citizen features on its website a series of research reports on topics such as protecting democracy, making government work, consumer and worker safety, globalization and trade, climate and energy, health care, and justice and the courts.[45] Such reports serve multiple purposes. They may sway public opinion, help persuade elected officials or bureaucrats, or directly influence the industry that is the subject of the report. They also help interest group staff claim expertise on some aspect of public policy. Members of Congress are more likely to accept a group's legislative proposal if they think that the group's staff has research to back up its claims. Journalists are also more likely to respond to an interest group's requests for publicity if they think that the group's staff has supporting evidence.

Hearings Interest group staff often testify before congressional committees. In part, this activity is aimed at informing members of Congress about issues that matter to the interest group. For example, the NRA's website shows that its staff has testified in state

Lobbying the Federal Government: Inside and Outside Strategies

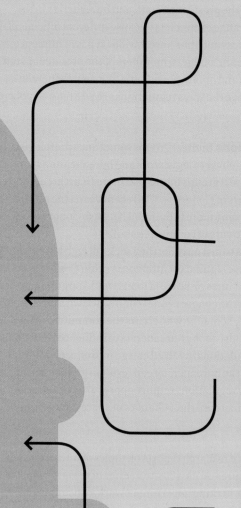

Inside Strategies

Groups **lobby government officials directly** in Washington, D.C.

Examples:

meeting with lawmakers

drafting legislation

providing research and testimony

taking the government to court

Outside Strategies

Groups use **public pressure, elections, and the media** to influence government.

Examples:

grassroots e-mail, letter, or phone campaigns

contributing to election campaigns

getting media coverage of their cause

AIPAC and the Iran Nuclear Deal

Throughout negotiations between Iran and the United States and its allies over limiting Iran's nuclear research program, the American Israel Public Affairs Committee (AIPAC)—an influential pro-Israel interest group—strongly opposed the deal. AIPAC engaged in a diverse set of lobbying activities with the goal of persuading members of Congress to disapprove the deal before a crucial deadline passed and the deal was enacted.

 Inside strategies

 Outside strategies

❓ Critical Thinking

1. **Despite its lobbying efforts, AIPAC's** side initially did not prevail in this situation. It wasn't until they had a more sympathetic ear in the White House that the policy was changed. If you were advising them, what strategy would you suggest they spend time on: inside or outside? Why?

2. **Suppose you are the head of AIPAC.** How could you use the Iran agreement to illustrate AIPAC's power and influence in Washington, despite the fact that the group's position did not prevail in Congress? Given the ultimate outcome, would you change how your group allocates its time and resources?

Do we have a deal?

July 14, 2015
The United States and its negotiation partners announce details of their **nuclear agreement with Iran**.

And they're off!

July 15, 2015
AIPAC announces its opposition to the Iran deal and **forms a new advocacy group to lobby** against the agreement.

Gathering forces.

July 2015
AIPAC organizes a series of **speeches and town hall meetings** in congressional districts and states of undecided legislators.

Making introductions.

July 28–29, 2015
AIPAC arranges a "Washington fly-in"—a series of **meetings between lawmakers and hundreds of constituents** who are opposed to the deal.

Running ads.

August 2015
AIPAC spends over **$20 million running television ads** opposing the deal in 23 states.

Funding trips.

August 2015
AIPAC organizes a **trip to Israel for 58 members of Congress** to meet with Israeli citizens and officials.

Going right to the source.

August 2015
AIPAC representatives **lobby undecided senators** to oppose the agreement.

No luck for AIPAC.

September 2, 2015
Deadline for Congress to disapprove the deal **passes without action**.

But there's a new sheriff in town!

May 8, 2018
Despite initially extending the deal, **President Trump withdraws from the agreement**, saying, "This was a horrible one-sided deal that should have never, ever been made."

While AIPAC's efforts were ultimately unsuccessful, they illustrate the many ways interest groups can work to influence the policy process.

legislatures and the U.S. Congress in favor of right-to-carry laws as well as laws that would grant immunity to gun manufacturers for harm committed with weapons they produced, and against universal background checks and federal funding for research on gun violence.[46]

Litigation Another inside strategy involves taking the government to court. In bringing their case, interest groups can argue that the government's actions are not consistent with the Constitution or that the government has misinterpreted existing law.[47] Interest groups can bring these actions via lawyers on their staff, a hired law firm, or lawyers who will work for no fees. Interest groups can also become involved in an existing case by filing amicus curiae ("friend of the court") briefs, documents that offer judges the group's rationale for how the case should be decided. The drawback of litigation is that it is costly and time-consuming—cases can take years to work through the federal court system. At a minimum, groups that use the litigation strategy generally combine it with direct lobbying or other strategies.

AP®
FOUNDATIONAL
DOCUMENT

The American Civil Liberties Union is an interest group that often uses litigation strategies in its efforts to change government policy. Here, members of the ACLU chapter in Washington State announce their filing of an abortion rights lawsuit against several local hospitals.

Working Together To increase their chances for success, interest groups can work together in their lobbying efforts, formulating a common strategy and future plans. In general, these coalitions of groups are short-term efforts focused on achieving a specific outcome, like supporting or opposing the confirmation of judicial and cabinet nominees.[48] The tax giveaway discussed in the chapter opener had unlikely allies such as Coca-Cola, Hewlett Packard Enterprise, Morgan Stanley, and the National Association of Manufacturers (whose members include companies such as Exxon Mobil, Raytheon, and Caterpillar), which would all gain billions of dollars from the change in the tax law.[49]

Why do groups work together? The most obvious reason lies in the power of large numbers: legislators are more likely to respond, or at least provide access, when many groups with large or diverse memberships are all asking for the same thing.[50]

The problem with working together is that groups may agree on general goals but disagree on specifics, thereby requiring negotiation. If differences cannot be bridged, groups may undertake separate and possibly conflicting lobbying efforts or decide against lobbying entirely. For example, although there are many groups pressing for climate change legislation, they have not developed a unified lobbying effort. The problem? The groups disagree on which policies should be implemented, who should pay for them, and whether the government should aid companies that would be forced to purchase new antipollution equipment. In the absence of agreement, working alone seems a better strategy.[51]

Outside strategies

Outside strategies involve things that groups do across the country rather than in Washington. Again, these activities can be orchestrated by the group or be organized by a firm hired by the group.

Grassroots Lobbying Directly involving interest group members in lobbying efforts is called grassroots lobbying. Members may send letters, make telephone calls, participate in a protest, or express their demands in other ways. Many groups encourage grassroots lobbying. For example, the AARP's website has a page where members can find contact information for their elected leaders in Washington.[52] Other links allow members to e-mail or to fax their representatives letters that are prewritten by the AARP to express the group's positions on various proposals, such as pension protection legislation and proposals to curb identity theft. The AARP also organizes district meetings with elected officials and encourages its members to attend.

Mass protests are another form of grassroots lobbying. In addition to trying to capture the attention of government officials, mass protests also seek to draw media attention, with the idea of publicizing the group's goals and perhaps gaining new members or financial support. For example, after the election of Donald Trump, hundreds of groups partnered with the organizers of the Women's March on January 21, 2017, in 673 marches on all seven continents (yes, there was one in Antarctica!), including 408 marches in the United States. There were more than 5 million participants worldwide (the estimates for the United States range from 3.3 to 5.2 million).[53] The marches were aimed at drawing attention to a range of progressive issues connected with women's rights. The lead sponsors were Planned Parenthood and the Natural Resources Defense Council; more than 550 organizations were listed as "partners" on the Women's March website.[54]

Grassroots strategies are useful because elected officials are loath to act against a large group of citizens who care enough about an issue to express their position.[55] These officials may not agree with the group's goals, but they are likely to at least arrange a meeting with its staff, so that they appear willing to learn about their constituents' demands.[56] However, these member-based strategies work only for a small set of interest groups. To take advantage of these strategies, groups first need a large number of members. Legislators begin to pay attention to a letter-writing campaign only when they receive several thousand pieces of mail.

In addition, for grassroots lobbying to be effective, the letters or other efforts have to come from a Congress member's own constituents. The effectiveness of grassroots lobbying also depends on perceptions of how much a group has done to motivate participation. Suppose a representative gets 10,000 e-mails demanding an increase in federal student aid. However, virtually all the messages contain the same appeal because they were generated and sent from a group's website. Congressional staff refer to these efforts as Astroturf lobbying.[57] Given the similarity of the letters, the representative may discount the effort, believing that it says more about the group's ability to make campaign participation accessible than it does about the number of district residents who strongly support an increase in federal student aid. Even so,

grassroots lobbying
A lobbying strategy that relies on participation by group members, such as a protest or a letter-writing campaign.

The Black Lives Matter movement, formed in 2013 in support of issues of racial justice and police reform, utilizes protests for grassroots lobbying. In 2020, after the killing by police of George Floyd, an unarmed Black man in Minneapolis, Minnesota, mass protests across the country brought increased attention to and support for the group's goals, including ending police brutality and systemic racism.

Astroturf lobbying
Any lobbying method initiated by an interest group that is designed to look like the spontaneous, independent participation of many individuals.

politicians are sometimes reluctant to completely dismiss Astroturf efforts—the fact that so many people participated, even with facilitation by an interest group, means that their demands must at least be considered.

Mobilizing Public Opinion One strategy related to grassroots lobbying involves trying to change what the public thinks about an issue in the hope that elected officials will see this change and respond by enacting (or opposing) new laws or regulations to keep their constituents happy.

Virtually all groups try to influence opinion. Most maintain a website that presents their message, and they write press releases to get media coverage. Most groups are also very active on social media, using Facebook, Twitter, and Instagram to keep in touch with members and let them know about issues that the group is working on. Any contact with citizens, whether to encourage them to join the group, contribute money, or engage in grassroots lobbying, also involves elements of persuasion—trying to transform citizens into supporters and supporters into true believers and even activists. In the case of gun control, for example, the NRA has an aggressive campaign to encourage members to contact their elected officials and to express their opinions.

A focused mobilization effort involves contacting large numbers of potential supporters (beyond just members) through e-mail, phone calls, direct mail, television advertising, print media, social media, and websites. In order to get legislators to respond, a group has to persuade large numbers of people to get involved. One example of mobilization occurs during congressional hearings on nominees to the Supreme Court or other federal judgeships. One study found that about one-third of the groups that lobbied for or against these nominees also deployed direct mail and leaflets and ran phone banks as a way to influence public opinion.[58]

Electioneering Interest groups get involved in elections by making contributions to candidates, mobilizing people (including their own staff) to help in a campaign, endorsing candidates, funding campaign ads, or mobilizing a candidate's or party's supporters. All these efforts seek to influence who gets elected, with the expectation that changing who gets elected will affect what government does.

Federal laws limit groups' electioneering and lobbying efforts (see Nuts & Bolts 12.3). For example, most private organizations and associations in America are organized as 501(c)(3) organizations, a designation based on their Internal Revenue Service classification, which means that donations to the group are tax deductible. However, 501(c)(3) organizations are not allowed to advocate for or against political candidates, and lobbying must not constitute more than 20 percent of the group's total expenditures (certain public-education programs or voter-registration drives that are conducted in a nonpartisan manner do not count toward that 20 percent), although some groups are always looking for loopholes in these restrictions. Groups that want to engage in lobbying or electioneering without looking for exceptions can incorporate under other IRS designations and operate as a **political action committee (PAC)**, a **527 organization**, or a 501(c)(4). Although contributions to these organizations are not tax deductible, such organizations have fewer restrictions on the size of the contributions they can make and on how their money is spent—for example, 527 organizations have no contribution or spending limits.

Two new options for electioneering by interest groups emerged in recent elections: Super PACs and 501(c)(4) organizations. The former was a consequence of the *Citizens United* Supreme Court decision that authorized unlimited independent spending by corporations and labor unions in federal elections.[59] Many groups set up new PACs to take advantage of these latest rules—the "Super" label reflects the fact that these groups take in and spend much more money than the typical PAC.

political action committee (PAC)

An interest group or a division of an interest group that can raise money to contribute to campaigns or to spend on ads in support of candidates. The amount a PAC can receive from each of its donors and the amount it can spend on federal campaigning are strictly limited.

527 organization

A tax-exempt group formed primarily to influence elections through voter mobilization efforts and issue ads that do not directly endorse or oppose a candidate. Unlike PACs, 527s are not subject to contribution limits and spending caps.

**AP®
SUPREME
COURT CASE**

Interest Groups and Electioneering: Types of Organizations

An interest group's ability to engage in electioneering depends on how it is organized—specifically, what section of the IRS code applies to the organization. The following table gives details on four common organizations: 501(c) organizations, 527 organizations, PACs, and so-called Super PACs. Many individuals choose to contribute money to nonprofits organized as 501(c)(4) groups, which can lobby and engage in electioneering as long as their "primary activity" (at least half of their overall activity) is not political.

Type of Organization	Advantages	Disadvantages
501(c)(3)	Contributions tax deductible	Cannot engage in political activities, and lobbying can be no more than 20 percent of spending (but voter education and mobilization are permitted)
527	Can spend unlimited amounts on issue advocacy and voter mobilization	Cannot make contributions to candidates or coordinate efforts with candidates or parties
501(c)(4)	Can spend unlimited amounts on electioneering; does not have to disclose contributors	At least half of its activities must be nonpolitical; cannot coordinate efforts with candidates or parties
PACs	Can contribute directly to candidates and parties	Strict limits on direct contributions
Super PACs	Can spend unlimited amounts on electioneering; can support or oppose specific candidates	Cannot make contributions to candidates or coordinate efforts with candidates or parties

Source: Compiled by the authors.

"Why Should I Care?" This may seem a little deep in the weeds, but understanding the different types of interest groups is important for understanding how they influence elections. Some types of groups have to disclose their donors and others don't. It is more difficult for voters to hold their leaders accountable if voters don't know who is supporting candidates' campaigns.

All the major 2020 presidential candidates had an independent Super PAC running ad campaigns on their behalf.

In 2020, federally focused PACs and Super PACS spent more than $7 billion for electioneering and contributions to candidates and parties, of which ActBlue raised a staggering $3.45 billion and WinRed raised $1.35 billion.[60] However, these large numbers mask some important details. To begin with, some of the largest firms in America (Google, Walmart, and Exxon Mobil, for example) have PACs that spend only a million or so on contributions. Another large firm, Apple, has no PAC. The PAC for the Pharmaceutical Research and Manufacturers of America is also small, and the other influential interest groups mentioned earlier in Figure 12.2 (the AARP, NARAL Pro-Choice America, and the Family Research Council) spend even less or don't have a PAC or a 527. These numbers suggest that money doesn't buy elections or policy outcomes—if it did, these organizations would probably spend a lot more on campaign donations and television ads.

Spending totals can also be deceptive. The National Association of Realtors, for example, made about $3.5 million in contributions in 2020—but spread out the funds over

500 candidates, with slightly more going to Democrats than Republicans. The PAC for EMILY's List collected over $72 million but only $16.9 million went to contributions to candidates and parties, with the rest for fundraising and overhead. Another large spender, NextGen Climate Action, was funded largely by a single wealthy donor but did not make any contributions to federal candidates in the 2020 cycle—their spending was on issue ads. (The founder, billionaire entrepreneur Tom Steyer, ran as a candidate for president during the 2020 Democratic primary.) And some groups used most of their money against candidates they opposed: the conservative Super PAC America First Action spent almost all of its $134 million against Democratic contenders.

Finally, while the $7 billion that these groups raised together seems large, only about two-thirds was spent on behalf of or as contributions to candidates. Most PACs contributed to only a few candidates. And while more than a thousand Super PACs were active in the 2020 election, most were small, and the average group spent just over $500,000. These data highlight a sharp difference in electioneering strategies between the very few large, well-funded interest groups and everyone else. A few 527s, Super PACs, 501(c)(4)s, and PACs have the money to deploy massive advertising and mobilization efforts for candidates or issues they like or against those they don't like. There are also some very large associations that can persuade large numbers of members to work for and vote for candidates whom the group supports or against candidates that the group wants to defeat. And just a few rich individuals can make outsized contributions to a candidate they favor.

But these strategies are not available to the vast majority of interest groups, which simply don't have the resources. Most interest groups hope to give modest help to a few candidates who are sympathetic to their goals. These contributions are generally made in the hope that, once elected, the officeholder will remember their contribution when their group asks for a meeting. It is important to remember that electioneering is only one strategy available to interest groups. Some groups do no electioneering at all, possibly because they lack sufficient funds, because they want to avoid making enemies based on whom they support or don't support, or because other strategies are more promising given the resources that are available to them. Many groups opt for quiet lobbying efforts that use their expertise, or they undertake grassroots efforts to build public support for their policy goals. Massive electioneering operations by interest groups are relatively rare.

Cultivating Media Contacts Media coverage helps a group publicize its concerns without spending any money. Thus, most interest group leaders talk often with journalists to pursue favorable coverage of news stories that pertain to the group's issues.

Conservative Super PACs, such as the Conservative Political Action Conference (CPAC), hold conventions that give candidates a venue to present themselves to conservative activists and donors.

Such attention may mobilize public opinion indirectly, by getting people to join the group, contribute money, or demand that elected officials support the group's agenda. Favorable media coverage also helps a group's leaders assure members that they are actively working on members' concerns.

Journalists listen when interest groups call if they feel that the group's story will catch their readers' attention or address their concerns. Smart interest group leaders make it easy for journalists to cover their cause, holding events that produce intriguing news stories. These stories may not change anyone's mind, but the media coverage provides free publicity for the groups' policy agendas.

Bypassing Government: The Initiative Process A final outside strategy for interest groups bypasses government entirely: a group can work to get its proposed policy change voted on by the public in a general election through an initiative or a referendum. Referenda and initiatives allow citizens to vote on specific proposed changes in policy. The difference between these procedures lies in the source of the proposal. In a **referendum** the legislature or another government body proposes the question that is put to a vote, whereas in an **initiative** citizens put questions on the ballot, typically after gathering signatures of registered voters on a petition.

Initiatives can occur only in states and municipalities that have the appropriate procedures in place; there is no mechanism for a nationwide vote on an interest group's proposal. So if a group wants to use this process to effect national change, it has to get its measure on the ballot in one state at a time. Moreover, only some states allow initiatives and some permit this kind of vote only on a narrow range of issues. The champion state for initiatives is California, whose citizens often vote on dozens of initiatives in each general election, ranging from funding for stem-cell research to limits on taxation and spending.[61]

There are many examples of groups using the initiative process to change government policy. Most notably, advocates of term limits for state legislators have used the initiative process to establish such limits in 21 states, although in 6 states the limits have since been overturned by legislative action or subsequent initiatives (so 15 states currently have term limits for state legislators).[62] Also, 30 states have approved legal use of marijuana in some form through statewide ballot measures.[63] Five of those states legalized its use, to varying degrees, in 2020.[64] Research shows that states with more active interest groups have more initiatives on the ballot, so groups are taking advantage of this mechanism for influencing policy.[65]

One of the principal concerns about the initiative process is that it favors well-funded groups that can advertise heavily in support of their proposals and can mobilize their supporters to vote on Election Day.[66] But spending a lot of money often is not enough: even groups with substantial resources have sometimes been unable to reform policy or stop policy change through the initiative process.[67] For example, in 2016 large tobacco companies spent $71.3 million dollars to try to defeat Proposition 56, which increased the tax on a pack of cigarettes by $2. Supporters of the proposition spent only half that amount ($35.5 million), but voters approved the measure 64–36 percent.[68]

Choosing strategies

Most groups give testimony, do research, contact elected officials and bureaucrats, talk with journalists, and develop legislative and regulatory proposals.[69] A particular group's decisions about which strategies to use depend partly on its resources and partly on what approach the group believes will be most effective in promoting its particular issues. Some strategies that work well for one group's agenda might not be appropriate

referendum
A direct vote by citizens on a policy change proposed by a legislature or another government body. Referenda are common in state and local elections, but there is no mechanism for a national-level referendum.

initiative
A direct vote by citizens on a policy change proposed by fellow citizens or organized groups outside government. Getting a question on the ballot typically requires collecting a set number of signatures from registered voters in support of the proposal. There is no mechanism for a national-level initiative.

for another's. The Humane Society of the United States is an organization that lobbies to prevent the abuse and neglect of animals. It had a $201 million annual budget in 2019 but only a small Washington office. Its lobbying expenses for 2019 were $600,000.[70] Rather than lobbying members of Congress, the group's focus is on investigations and grassroots organizing, highlighting situations in which corporations and countries are not behaving according to existing laws against animal cruelty.

Other interest groups advance their causes in ways that don't look like lobbying. For example, as NASA begins to formulate plans for sending humans to Mars in the 2030s, the Boeing Company has released a series of films and videos about these plans. At one level, Boeing's efforts are all about highlighting the many important discoveries that a voyage to Mars might generate—but they are also a way to increase the chances that NASA's plans will attract public support and be funded by Congress, which, if it happens, will likely generate a series of very lucrative contracts for Boeing to build and help operate exploration hardware.

"Why Should I Care?"

At first glance, lobbying victories should go to the groups that can spend a lot on contributions to candidates or on direct lobbying. But there are many other ways to succeed in the battle to shape public policy, from organizing American citizens to preparing new proposals or doing background research. Policy influence isn't as much about the size of a group's budget as it is about factors such as the size of the group's membership or the perception of its expertise. Even poorly funded groups can find ways to win. If there's an issue that you believe in, you can find a group that supports it, large or small, and get involved in any number of ways.

★

EVALUATE INTEREST GROUP INFLUENCE

99

I will Make Our Government Honest Again—believe me. But First, I'm going to have to #DrainTheSwamp in DC.

—President Donald Trump

How much power do interest groups have?

Two 2020 presidential candidates, Democrats Bernie Sanders and Elizabeth Warren, focused much of their campaigns on the need to reduce the power of large corporations and special interests over policy making in Washington. While neither Sanders nor Warren gained the nomination, their campaigns spoke for the widely held belief about how Washington works: that interest groups have too much power and something drastic must be done to end their domination over policy making in Washington. Donald Trump capitalized on this same sentiment with his pledge to "drain the swamp" in 2016.

As we discuss in the What Do the Facts Say? feature, some studies of interest group influence support Sanders and Warren's claims—but others tell a very different story, one in which a group's chances of getting what it wants depend on whether there is organized opposition to their demand. In other words, as one analysis put it, "the solution to lobbying is more lobbying."[71]

Scholarly research also reveals four reasons why it is so hard to measure interest group influence. First, we know that interest groups usually lobby their friends in government rather than their enemies and moderate their demands in the face of resistance.[72] As a result, what looks like success may in fact be a signal of something else. For example, the NRA leadership would probably favor a new federal law that

Interest Group Power

Conventional wisdom says that business interest groups have too much power over policy outcomes in Washington. But what do the facts say?

To address this question, a group of political scientists tracked a series of issues through years of lobbying, congressional debate, legislative action, and implementation by the bureaucracy. Their goal was to determine whether business groups were successful in getting what they want from Congress, particularly when their efforts were opposed by citizen groups or government officials. This figure shows what they found.

WHAT DO THE FACTS SAY?

Think about it

- **Many people believe that business groups** always succeed in their lobbying efforts. Does this figure confirm or deny these suspicions?
- **After looking at these data,** do you think business groups have too much power? How do these data help us understand the winners and losers in the tax benefits in the CARES Act discussed at the beginning of this chapter?

Which Interest Groups Win . . . and When?

After four years ...

■ Business Groups Win   ■ Other Side Wins   ■ Both/Neither Win

Business groups vs. citizen groups or unions

40%   40%   20%

Business groups vs. government (executive branch, members of Congress)

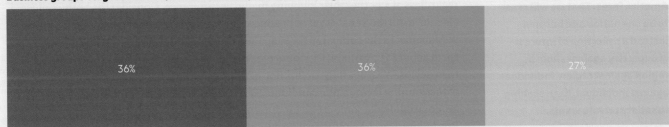

36%   36%   27%

Business groups unopposed

89%   11%

Source: Marie Hojnacki, Kathleen Marchetti, Frank Baumgartner, Jeffrey M. Berry, David C. Kimball, and Beth L. Leech, "Assessing Business Advantage in Washington Lobbying," *Interest Groups and Advocacy* 4 (2015): 206–24.

While many observers credit lobbying by the pharmaceutical industry for policies such as the Medicare Prescription Drug Benefit (and its ban on importing medicines), favorable public opinion, the efforts of the AARP, and bureaucrats' independent judgments probably had greater influence on passing the Drug Benefit Act.

But this is the great danger America faces. That we will cease to be one nation and become instead a collection of interest groups: city against suburb, region against region, individual against individual. Each seeking to satisfy private wants.

—**Barbara Jordan,** civil rights leader and former member of Congress

made it legal to carry a concealed handgun throughout the nation. Why doesn't the NRA demand enactment of this legislation? Because there is no sign that Congress would comply. A more limited proposal that would force states to honor concealed carry permits issued by other states passed the House late in 2017 with the strong support of the NRA,[73] but the bill died in the Senate. Thus, the NRA's decision to not push for national concealed carry legislation and its inability to get the more limited bill through the Senate show the limits of the organization's power.

Second, some complaints about the power of interest groups come from the losing side in the political process. Consider the "net neutrality" rule that was recently overturned by the Federal Communications Commission. The rule "prohibited internet service providers (ISPs) from blocking, slowing or speeding up web content or charging customers additional fees to access certain web services," so corporations like AT&T, Verizon, and Comcast were strongly in favor of eliminating the regulation. The losing side of this debate, which included Microsoft, Google, and Netflix, complained that the large ISPs influenced the outcome with tens of millions of dollars in lobbying and contributions. However, lobbying was intense on both sides.[74]

Third, many interest groups claim responsibility for policies and election outcomes regardless of whether their lobbying made the difference. Consider the hotly contested election to fill the Senate seat of President Trump's first attorney general, Jeff Sessions, in Alabama. In the campaign for or against the two candidates, 45 outside groups spent about $13.7 million, which surpassed the $13.5 million spent by the candidates themselves. With nearly $10.3 million of the outside money being spent on behalf of the winning Democratic candidate, Doug Jones, it is not surprising that interest groups would take some credit for the win. However, the losing Republican candidate, Roy Moore, was a deeply flawed candidate who was shunned by the Republican leadership in the Senate (but endorsed by Donald Trump). He was accused of sexually assaulting a 14-year-old when he was an attorney in his 30s, said that the United States was better off under slavery, and had been kicked off the state supreme court for refusing to follow the order of a federal court. Clearly these factors were central in Moore's defeat.[75] Yet the leaders of interest groups have a considerable incentive to make strong claims about their group's influence and impact, as these claims help them attract members and keep their jobs.[76]

Fourth, arguments about the impact of interest groups on election outcomes, such as Moore's defeat in 2017, ignore the fact that interest groups are almost always active on both sides of an election campaign. Although Moore was the target of attack ads funded by interest groups and many groups gave contributions to his opponent, he also received support from interest groups in the form of campaign contributions and independent ads. Thus, it doesn't make sense to attribute Moore's defeat to actions taken by one set of groups without asking why similar efforts on his behalf had no effect. You can't conclude that interest groups are all-powerful without explaining why Moore's supporters were unable to help him win the election in an overwhelmingly Republican state.

In sum, dire claims about the overwhelming influence of interest groups and lobbying on Washington policy making are probably wrong. Rather than making a blanket claim about interest group influence, a better response is to ask, What are the conditions that enhance a group's influence over policy, and what are the conditions that reduce it? That is, what determines when interest groups succeed?

What determines when interest groups succeed?

Three factors shape interest group influence. The first is the group's goal: Does it want to change a policy (including enacting a new policy) or to prevent change? The second is salience: How many Americans care about what a group is trying to do? The third is conflict: To what extent do other groups or the public oppose the policy change?

Change versus Preventing Change In general, groups are going to have an easier time preventing a change than working to implement one. As we discuss in Chapter 2, enacting a new policy requires the approval of both houses of Congress, the president's signature (or a veto override), and implementation from the appropriate bureaucratic agency. Each of these steps provides an opportunity for interest groups to lobby members of government to do nothing. So if the groups are successful, change will not occur. Studies show that groups are much more likely to be successful when their goals involve this kind of negative lobbying that seeks to block changes in policy.[77] Most of the NRA's legislative victories in recent years fit this description: the NRA has successfully lobbied against a new ban on assault weapons, against reforms to the system of national background checks for handgun purchases, and against new limits on ownership of guns by mentally ill people.

While the success of the NRA's negative lobbying attracts considerable attention, its failures in lobbying for policy change do not. Consider the NRA's advocacy of concealed carry laws. As noted earlier, there is little doubt that the NRA's leaders and most of its members favor the passage of such laws nationwide, but efforts to lobby Congress in favor of such laws are unlikely to be successful given public opposition and well-funded interest groups that are against concealed carry. These groups could respond with negative lobbying against any effort the NRA might make. As a result, while the NRA lobbies for concealed carry, it has failed to help enact national legislation; the limits on its power over legislation do not get much publicity.

Salience Interest groups are more likely to succeed when their request has low salience or attracts little public attention.[78] When the average voter does not know or care about a group's request, legislators and bureaucrats do not have to worry about the political consequences of giving the group what it wants. The only question is whether the officials themselves favor the request or can be convinced that the group's desired change is worthwhile. In contrast, when salience is high, legislators' response to lobbying will hinge on their judgment of constituent opinion: Do voters favor what the group wants? After all, the average legislator has a strong interest in reelection and is unlikely to act against his or her constituents' wishes. As a result, lobbying may count for nothing in the face of public opposition or may be superfluous when the group's position already has public support.[79]

salience
The level of familiarity with an interest group's goals in the general population

If you have ever heard of the National Turkey Federation, it's probably because of its participation in the annual presidential "pardoning" of a turkey before Thanksgiving. The federation's relative anonymity has been beneficial: its effort to increase the amount of turkey served in federally funded school lunches was aided by most Americans' lack of awareness of the proposal.

While the idea of interest group lobbying probably brings to mind titanic struggles on controversial issues, such as gun control, abortion rights, or judicial nominations, low-salience issues are surprisingly common. Many groups are indeed active for or against these high-profile issues and try to capture public attention as a way of pressuring people in government. However, the typical issue attracts much less activity. One analysis of lobbying disclosure forms found that 5 percent of issues attracted more than 50 percent of lobbying activity and 50 percent of issues attracted less than 3 percent.[80] Thus, the typical issue debated by members of Congress may involve relatively little interest group activity, and a group's request may generate little or no opposition from other groups. Remember the National Turkey Federation—the people who give the president a turkey every Thanksgiving? In the winter of 2014, the federation successfully lobbied federal bureaucrats to increase propane supplies to Midwest states facing record cold temperatures, including areas where the federation's members use propane to heat their barns. The policy change resulting from the federation's lobbying efforts attracted no publicity, which is precisely the point. When few people know or care about a policy change, interest groups are able to dominate the policy-making process. Sometimes the public *would* care about an issue, as with the $135 billion in tax credits in the CARES Act, but people don't find out about the issue until it is too late. Then when opponents of the move try to undo it, they fail, illustrating the principle that preventing change is easier than change.

Conflict Interest group influence is much less apparent on conflictual issues—those for which public opinion is split and groups are typically active on both sides of the issue. Consider a high-salience issue such as gun control. The ongoing debate over gun control attracts many well-funded interest groups and coalitions, which support different versions of gun control or want no change to current policy. There is no consensus among members of Congress, interest groups, or the American public about which policy changes are needed. Under these conditions, access doesn't count for very much; legislators have a keen sense of the political costs of accommodating a group's demands. As a result, stalemate is the likely result, which is exactly what has happened over the last few years: gun control laws have not been strengthened, but other than an increase in concealed carry laws, there have not been significant changes in the other direction. After the 2017 massacre in Las Vegas, in which 58 people were killed and 546 injured, the NRA said it would favor additional regulation of "bump stocks," which allow 90 rounds to be fired in 10 seconds. President Trump started the process of banning bump stocks through an executive order in March 2018 (the final rule went into effect on March 26, 2019). If policy change occurs at all, it is likely to reflect a complex process of bargaining and compromise, with no groups getting exactly what they want. In such cases, it is hard to say whether a particular group has won or lost or to attribute any aspect of the final bargain to a particular group's efforts.

The case of gun control illustrates that the fact that a group is large or well funded does not mean government officials will always comply with its requests. As mentioned earlier, many people worry that well-funded interest groups will use their financial resources to dominate the policy-making process, even if public opinion is against them, but these fears are largely unfounded. The conditions that are ripe for well-funded interest groups to become involved in a policy debate typically ensure that there will be well-funded groups on all sides of a question. Under these conditions, no group is likely to get everything it wants and no group's lobbying efforts are likely to be decisive. Some groups may not get anything.

However, gun control is not a typical case. Most cases of interest group influence look a lot like the Turkey Federation's request for more propane: a group asks for something, there is relatively little opposition, and Congress or the bureaucracy responds with appropriate policy changes. The situation might have been very different if another group had lobbied on the other side against the Turkey Federation. If so, satisfying one group would have required displeasing at least one other group. Faced with this no-win situation, bureaucrats or legislators would be less likely to give the group what it wanted. At a minimum, they would have had to measure the Turkey Federation's arguments against those made by the other groups.

Suppose you want to change some federal government policy—you want more funding for a program or an end to some regulation. Does having enough money guarantee a win? Generally speaking, the answer is no. What matters more is the salience of the policy or regulation you're trying to change and whether there is organized opposition on the other side. If your group is the only one lobbying, chances are good that you'll win. But if the issue is highly salient and you have opposition, your prospects aren't good, regardless of the size of your bankroll.

"Why Should I Care?"

AP® POLICY IN PRACTICE

The Honest Leadership and Open Government Act

There is a saying in politics: "He who pays the piper calls the tunes." It is often used when describing the federal expenditures at the state and local levels and the strings the federal government attaches to the money. In general it means that politicians pay special attention to the interests and demands of those who give them money, and that attention increases as the money or other in-kind contributions increase. In the latter part of the twentieth century this problem seemed to be getting more problematic and the monetary contributions to campaigns as well as personal gifts to members of Congresses and their families were increasing and becoming more outlandish. Since these figures were not always recorded and sometimes difficult to quantify or collect, it might be fairer to say that interest group contributions were more on everyone's radar especially after the Watergate scandal (beginning in 1972) during the Nixon presidency (1969–1974). Though there have certainly been enough political scandals in American history to make Americans suspicious of the motives of politicians, the early 1970s seemed to be a major turning point for distrusting politicians, given the scope of the Watergate scandal and that it resulted in the first resignation of a U.S. president. Remarkably, it took 20 years for the Lobbying Disclosure Act of 1995 to be passed, which replaced the Lobbying Act of 1946 and was the predecessor to the Honest Leadership and Open Government Act of 2007.

While you might wonder why it took so long for the anti-lobbying bill of 1995 to be formulated, an equally important question is why the next iteration of this bill was passed only 12 years later. The trigger point for the next bill was the Jack Abramoff Native American lobbying scandal. Though this might have been an extreme example of how lobbyists were wining and dining members of Congress, to the public it was emblematic of how easily politicians could be influenced. It also reinforced the public's perception of members of Congress, which was further damaged by revolving door lobbying that occurs when politicians retire and then immediately join the lobbying organizations they formerly worked with.

It is important to point out that lobbyists do serve an important role in policy making. Members of Congress are expected to deliberate and decide on a wide variety of policy areas, but they cannot be expected to have expertise in all the areas they vote on, so they rely in part on lobbyists, who are specialists for the groups they represent, to provide information that is essential for the politicians to make informed decisions. Lobbyists are not the only source of information for politicians, but as mentioned in the Evaluation stage below, stifling or excluding this group of people would leave a large knowledge gap that would have a detrimental effect on the quality of the policies that are produced. Making it too difficult for lobbyists to do their jobs might also go against democratic principles, especially the right to free speech. While you read through the outline below, notice the balance that has to be struck in the relationship between lobbyists and the politicians whom they are influencing and how giving one group precedence over the other can negatively affect the free exchange of ideas that are integral to a well-functioning democracy.

Policy Stages

1. Problem Recognition
   - The Federal Regulation of Lobbying Act of 1946
     - Lobbyists had to register with the House of Representatives and the Senate.
     - Financial disclosure of expenses was required.
     - An explanation of the purposes and goals of lobbying efforts was required.
     - *United States v. Harriss* (1954)
       - It narrowed the definition of lobbying to encompass only direct contact with members of Congress and not their staff.
       - It was also considered lobbying only if the main purpose was to have a direct impact on legislation.
   - The Lobbying Disclosure Act of 1995 (major sections)

- It replaced the Federal Regulation of Lobbying Act of 1946.
- Section 3: Definitions: Lobbying contact (from the bill) "means any oral or written communication (including an electronic communication) to a covered executive branch official or a covered legislative branch official that is made on behalf of a client with regard to
  - the formulation, modification, or adoption of Federal legislation (including legislative proposals);
  - the formulation, modification, or adoption of a Federal rule, regulation, Executive order, or any other program, policy, or position of the United States Government"
- Section 4: Registration of Lobbyists: All lobbyists had to register with the House of Representative and the Senate.
- Section 5: Reports by Registered Lobbyists: Lobbyists had to submit an account of expenses and activities.
- Section 6: Disclosure and Enforcement: Congress made reports public and ensured lobbyists complied.
- Section 7: Penalties: Congress levied fines for noncompliance.
- Significant shortcomings of the Lobbying Disclosure Act of 1995 have arisen over the years.
  - Lobbyists, regardless of their income or level of influence, did not have to register if they did not work with any one client for more than 20 percent of their time.
  - Lobbyists did not have to register if they did not meet face-to-face with members of Congress or other federal officials.
  - Understaffing made it difficult to investigate or convict those lobbyists suspected of wrongdoing.

2. Agenda Setting
   - The Jack Abramoff Native American lobbying scandal (2005) rocked Washington, D.C., and was the tipping point for the public and many members of Congress to push for meaningful lobbying reform.
     - Abramoff, a major lobbyist, pleaded guilty to fraud, bribery, and tax evasion.
     - Abramoff took millions of dollars from Native-American tribes ostensibly to influence members of Congress to open up gambling casinos on Native American reservations.
     - He used a lot of the money to bribe members of Congress.
     - He cheated his clients by overcharging them and using some of their money to support politicians and groups opposed to gaming.
     - Congressman Bob Ney was convicted of corruption for accepting bribes.
     - The investigation led to the conviction of many aides and other government officials.

3. Deliberation and Formulation
   - The bill was introduced in the Senate by Harry Reid (D-NV) on January 4, 2007.
   - The Senate passed its version of the bill on January 18, 2007: **96 YEAs**: 48 Democrats, 46 Republicans, 2 others; **2 NAYs**: 0 Democrats, 2 Republicans, 0 others; **2 Not Voting**: 1 Democrat, 1 Republican, 0 others.
   - The House of Representatives passed the Senate version of the bill with amendment on July 31, 2007: **411 YEAs**: 221 Democrats, 190 Republicans, 0 others; **8 NAYs**: 6 Democrats, 2 Republicans, 0 others; **13 Not Voting**: 3 Democrats, 10 Republicans, 0 others.

4. Enactment
  - The House of Representatives had no further votes, and the Senate passed the bill with the House of Representatives amendment on August 2, 2007: **83 YEAs**: 47 Democrats, 34 Republicans, 2 others; **14 NAYs**: 0 Democrats, 14 Republicans, 0 others; **3 Not Voting**: 2 Democrats, 1 Republican, 0 others.
  - The Honest Leadership and Government Act was signed into law by President George W. Bush on September 14, 2007.
5. Implementation
  - It amended the Lobbying Disclosure Act of 1995.
  - **Title I: Closing the Revolving Door**
    - It extended the length of time before former members of Congress and their former staff members could lobby Congress.
  - **Title II: Full Public Disclosure of Lobbying**
    - It increased the frequency of filing reports to four times a year.
    - Reports were made available to the public.
    - Fines and jail time increased for noncompliance.
    - Members of Congress and their staffs could not accept gifts and travel by lobbyists.
    - Lobbyists who are immediate family members of congressional members should not take advantage of their relationship to gain an edge over other lobbyists.
  - **Title III: Matters Relating to the House of Representatives**
    - Members and their staffs had to wait until replacements were found before negotiating for future employment.
    - House members could not be lobbied by their spouses.
  - **Title IV: Congressional Pension Accountability**
    - Members who abused the public trust by committing crimes would lose their pensions.
  - **Title V: Senate Legislative Transparency and Accountability**
    - The power of one senator to stop a motion from being voted on, also known as a hold, had to be made public.
    - Committee and subcommittee meetings had to be made available to the public on the Internet.
    - Lobbying restrictions and disclosures required of the House also applied to the Senate.
    - Former members no longer had parking or gym access.
    - Senators and their staffs had to receive ethics training.
  - **Title VI: Prohibited Use of Private Aircraft**
    - Members had to pay fair market value when taking flights.
6. Evaluation
  - Loopholes weakened the effectiveness of the law.
    - Instead of giving gifts to members of Congress, lobbyists could legally make campaign contributions.
    - Lobbyists could not take members of Congress to dinner, but they could buy them food not considered a meal (such as hors d'oeuvres and drinks).
  - Tighter regulations on lobbying
    - were an infringement on the First Amendment right to petition the government.
    - could weaken the relationship between legitimate lobbyists and politicians.
    - could make it more difficult for lobbyists to provide useful information to members of Congress, who cannot possibly be experts in all matters on which they have to legislate.

- could discourage people from contributing to lobbyists if they knew their names would be made public.
- Some felt that more regulations would decrease lobbying activity, but lobbying has actually increased since the law's passage.
- Members of the House of Representatives and their staffs were not required to do ethics training.

7. Possible Modifications, Expansion, or Termination of Policy
   - *National Association of Manufacturers (NAM) v. Taylor* (2008)
     - The case ruled that public disclosure of which individuals or groups hire lobbyists is unconstitutional, as it might result in people boycotting the products or services of firms that have hired certain lobbyists, even though the court said there was no evidence supporting this in NAM's particular situation.
     - The D.C. Circuit Court upheld the law.
   - Different states have come up with different ways of controlling lobbyists.
     - They can make contributions to campaigns only when the legislature is not in session.
     - They cannot make any campaign contributions.
     - They are limited in how much money they can contribute to campaigns.
     - They can contribute to campaigns only in the districts in which they live.
   - The Ensuring Trust and Honorability in Congressional Standards (ETHICS) Act was introduced by David Cicilline (D-RI) and Scott Rigell (R-VA) in 2014.
     - It required members of the House of Representatives to receive yearly ethics training.
     - The bill did not pass and has been introduced several more times without success.

Questions for Discussion

1. How do the activities of lobbyists contribute to a well-functioning democracy?
2. What are the advantages and disadvantages of former members of Congress working as lobbyists?
3. In what ways might term limits for members of Congress either increase or decrease the influence of lobbyists?

Unpacking the Conflict

Considering all that we've discussed in this chapter, let's apply what we know about how interest groups work to the example of the tax credits discussed at the beginning of this chapter. Is it fair to characterize all interest groups as self-interested organizations that undermine the public good? Are interest groups really too-powerful manipulators of the American policy process?

Many Americans think that interest groups are powerful manipulators of the American policy process and that they are able to get what they want regardless of the impact on everyone else. Sometimes it seems like "Heads they win. Tails we lose." While the chapter opener's example of income limit repeals in the CARES Act would support this view, there are countless counterexamples of laws that have been passed over the objections of corporations, including environmental protections, worker safety laws, consumer product and food safety regulations, and minimum wages laws.

So the truth is much more complex. Interest groups represent many different Americans, many of whom are unaware that lobbying occurs on their behalf. Moreover, for many groups the challenge is to get organized in the first place or to scrape together enough resources to start lobbying. These efforts don't always succeed because of the collective action problem. Interest groups are more likely to get what they want when their demands attract little public attention and no opposition from other groups. When a group asks for a large or controversial policy change, it stands little chance of success, even if the group has many members, a large lobbying budget, or an influential leader directing its operation.

The CARES Act also reflects this complexity. While lobbyists were able to sneak in the tax provisions that benefited their clients to the tune of $135 billion over 10 years, the bill also did a lot of good for millions of Americans who were in desperate need. Small businesses, hospitals, state and local governments, and researchers rushing to make a vaccine all received necessary aid. Most Americans received a $1,200 check just in time to help them make their next rent payment, and millions of people who lost their jobs benefited from the extension of unemployment compensation. So the special interests had their big chunk of the pie, but the American people received more of what they needed to try to get back on their feet.

In sum, while individual lobbying efforts often reflect the efforts of small groups to achieve favored policy outcomes at the expense of the majority, when we look across the entire range of interest group activities, a different picture emerges: in the main, interest groups reflect the conflictual nature of American politics and the resulting drive of individuals, groups, and corporations to shape American public policy in line with their policy goals. The average citizen benefits as well as loses from lobbying activities.

"What's Your Take?"

Are interest groups really too-powerful manipulators of the American policy process?

Or do groups play an important role in helping all citizens' voices be heard?

AP® STUDY GUIDE

Summary

Interest groups are organizations that seek to influence government policy by helping elect candidates who support their policy goals and by lobbying elected officials and bureaucrats. Although they are generally viewed with disdain, interest groups are ubiquitous—most organizations have lobbyists working on their behalf—and, under the theory of pluralism, are regarded as fundamental actors in American politics.

A primary challenge in operating an interest group is getting members to coordinate with one another. Interest groups have a number of different ways of overcoming the problem of collective action, with varying degrees of success.

Interest groups have two types of tactics for lobbying elected officials. They can attempt to influence politics by taking action in Washington or they can take action elsewhere. The decision to pursue an inside or outside strategy comes down to the interest group's resources and which strategy members think will be most effective.

It is commonly argued that elected officials are letting interest groups define their agenda. However, the evidence on interest groups does not support these claims: there is no correlation between the amount of money spent on lobbying and a group's success, nor is there conclusive evidence that group lobbying influences policy. Groups are generally most influential when the issues attract little public attention and when an issue does not have organized opposition.

Enduring Understanding

PMI-5: "Political parties, interest groups, and social movements provide opportunities for participation and influence how people relate to government and policy-makers." (AP® U.S. Government and Politics Course and Exam Description)

Key Terms

Astroturf lobbying (p. 535)
centralized groups (p. 521)
coercion (p. 529)
collective action problem (p. 528)
confederations (p. 521)
direct lobbying (p. 530)
527 organization (p. 536)
free riding (p. 528)

grassroots lobbying (p. 535)
initiative (p. 539)
inside strategies (p. 530)
interest group (p. 517)
interest group state (p. 518)
iron triangle (p. 524)
issue network (p. 524)
linkage institutions (p. 517)
lobbying (p. 517)
mass associations (p. 525)

material benefits (p. 529)
outside strategies (p. 530)
peak associations (p. 525)
political action committee (PAC) (p. 536)
purposive benefits (p. 529)
referendum (p. 539)
revolving door (p. 524)
salience (p. 543)
selective incentives (p. 528)
solidary benefits (p. 529)

Multiple-Choice Questions (Arranged by Topic)

Topic 5.6: Interest Groups Influencing Policy Making (PMI-5)

1. Which of the following best describes the main purpose of an interest group?

    (A) running candidates for office

    (B) implementing laws passed by Congress

    (C) determining the constitutionality of an executive order

    (D) influencing public policy on behalf of people with common interests

Questions 2–3 refer to the excerpt.

By a faction, I understand a number of citizens, whether amounting to a majority or a minority of the whole, who are united and actuated by some common impulse of passion, or of interest, adverse to the rights of other citizens, or to the permanent and aggregate interests of the community.

There are two methods of curing the mischiefs of faction: the one, by removing its causes; the other, by controlling its effects.

There are again two methods of removing the causes of faction: the one, by destroying the liberty which is essential to its existence; the other, by giving to every citizen the same opinions, the same passions, and the same interests.

It could never be more truly said than of the first remedy, that it was worse than the disease. Liberty is to faction what air is to fire, an aliment without which it instantly expires. But it could not be less folly to abolish liberty, which is essential to political life, because it nourishes faction, than it would be to wish the annihilation of air, which is essential to animal life, because it imparts to fire its destructive agency.

The second expedient is as impracticable as the first would be unwise. As long as the reason of man continues fallible, and he is at liberty to exercise it, different opinions will be formed. As long as the connection subsists between his reason and his self-love, his opinions and his passions will have a reciprocal influence on each other; and the former will be objects to which the latter will attach themselves. The diversity in the faculties of men, from which the rights of property originate, is not less an insuperable obstacle to a uniformity of interests. The protection of these faculties is the first object of government. From the protection of different and unequal faculties of acquiring property, the possession of different degrees and kinds of property immediately results; and from the influence of these on the sentiments and views of the respective proprietors, ensues a division of the society into different interests and parties.

—James Madison, *Federalist 10*, November 22, 1787

2. Which of the following best describes Madison's view on the purpose of government?

    (A) to cure the mischiefs of factions by removing the causes and controlling their effects

    (B) to protect the diversity in the faculties of men—opinions, passions, and interests—that are unlikely to be in harmony with others

    (C) to enable all citizens to have the same passions, interests, and opinions

    (D) to create a pure democracy with a small number of citizens who can administer the government in person to reduce conflict

3. Which of the following best illustrates how Madison's view on factions is evident in the United States today?

    (A) the vast diversity of interest groups

    (B) the vast number of political parties

    (C) the role of the elite model in policy making

    (D) the creation of a direct democracy

4. **Which of the following is an accurate comparison of the views of interest groups and political parties?**

	Interest Groups	Political Parties
(A)	donate money to PACs	require all members to pay dues
(B)	nominate candidates for office	donate money to PACs
(C)	run candidates for office	help draft legislation
(D)	help draft legislation	run candidates for office

5. **Which of the following best exemplifies an iron triangle?**

   (A) Senate Committee on Agriculture, Nutrition, and Forestry; United States Department of Agriculture (USDA); American Farm Bureau Federation

   (B) Senate Judiciary Committee; Department of Justice; Ninth Circuit Court

   (C) Department of Homeland Security; Transportation Security Administration; United States Secret Service

   (D) Mothers Against Drunk Driving (MADD); National Beer Wholesalers Association; National Highway Traffic Safety Administration

6. **The AARP (formerly called the American Association of Retired Persons) is lobbying Congress to pass a bill that would allow prescription drugs to be imported from Canada, in turn reducing the prices to Americans. Which of the following best describes a free rider problem in this scenario?**

   (A) The AARP will cause tension between the United States and Canada, which will affect future foreign relations.

   (B) Passing the bill would allow members of Congress to claim all the credit and, in the long run, weaken the AARP.

   (C) By taking action, the AARP is allowing other interest groups to focus on other issues.

   (D) Passing this law would benefit everyone, whether they are members of the AARP or not.

Topic 5.7: Groups Influencing Policy Outcomes (PMI-5)

7. **Which of the following terms best describes the process in which an organized nongovernmental group that wants to influence a public policy outcome can collect a set number of signatures from registered voters to get a question on the ballot that can be directly voted on by citizens?**

   (A) referendum

   (B) initiative

   (C) revolving door

   (D) free riding

8. **Which of the following best explains how an interest group would influence public policy by filing an amicus curiae brief?**

   (A) providing information to the bureaucracy to help with the creation of regulations

   (B) giving testimony to Congress at a committee hearing

   (C) presenting information to the Supreme Court prior to a case being heard

   (D) drafting laws that are assigned to committees in the House and Senate

Interest Groups and Electioneering: Types of Organizations

Type of Organization	Advantages	Disadvantages
501(c)(3)	Contributions tax deductible	Cannot engage in political activities, and lobbying can be no more than 20 percent of spending (but voter education and mobilization are permitted)
527	Can spend unlimited amounts on issue advocacy and voter mobilization	Cannot make contributions to candidates or coordinate efforts with candidates or parties
501(c)(4)	Can spend unlimited amounts on electioneering; does not have to disclose contributors	At least half of its activities must be nonpolitical; cannot coordinate efforts with candidates or parties
PACs	Can contribute directly to candidates and parties	Strict limits on direct contributions
Super PACs	Can spend unlimited amounts on electioneering; can support or oppose specific candidates	Cannot make contributions to candidates or coordinate efforts with candidates or parties

9. **A political action committee (PAC) has which of the following advantages that is restricted to the other types of organizations in the visual?**

    (A)   Contributions are tax deductible.

    (B)   A PAC can make unlimited direct contributions to candidates.

    (C)   Contributions given directly to candidates are allowed.

    (D)   Contributions do not have to be disclosed.

10. **Which of the following best explains how the information in the visual relates to the Supreme Court's decision in *Citizens United v. Federal Election Commission* (2010)?**

    (A)   Since political speech is indispensable to a democracy, corporations' spending unlimited amounts of money to support a specific candidate is protected by the First Amendment.

    (B)   Since unions represent a group that may have diverse views, unlimited contributions to support a specific candidate violates the Constitution's implied right to privacy.

    (C)   Due to the "magic words test," only individuals can make unlimited contributions to Super PACs, thus decreasing the power of interest groups.

    (D)   When a 501(c)(3) participates in a GOTV (get out the vote) campaign, the group loses its tax-deductible status.

Free-Response Questions

Quantitative Analysis

Variation in Lobbying Expenditures, 2018–2019

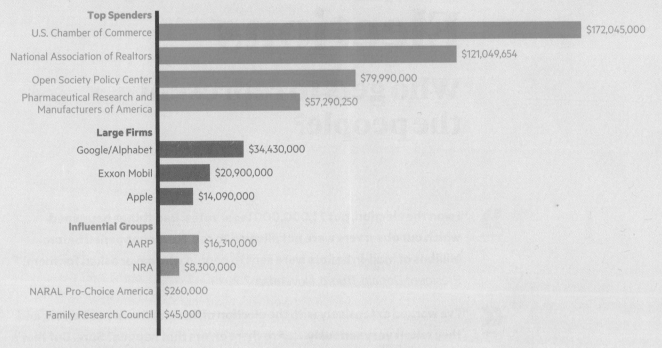

Source: Data available at Center for Responsive Politics, "Lobbying Data Summary," www.opensecrets.org/federal-lobbying (accessed 5/12/20).

Use the graph to answer the questions.

(A) Identify the amount of money that the National Association of Realtors spent on lobbying.

(B) Describe a difference between expenditures on lobbying by large firms and influential groups, as illustrated in the graph.

(C) Draw a conclusion about the difference described in Part B.

(D) Explain how groups like NARAL Pro-Choice America and the Family Research Council can have influence over government policy despite the data presented in the graph.

Argument Essay

Develop an argument that explains whether interest groups or social movements best protect individuals living in a republic.

Use at least one piece of evidence from one of the following foundational documents:

- *Federalist 10*
- "Letter from Birmingham Jail"

In your response, you should do the following:

✓ Respond to the prompt with a defensible claim or thesis that establishes a line of reasoning.

✓ Support your claim with at least two pieces of specific and relevant evidence.

- One piece of evidence must come from one of the foundational documents listed above.
- A second piece of evidence can come from any other foundational document not used as your first piece of evidence, or it may be from your knowledge of course concepts.

✓ Use reasoning to explain why your evidence supports your claim or thesis.

✓ Respond to an opposing or alternate perspective using refutation, concession, or rebuttal.

13
Elections

Who gets to represent the people?

» **"I won the election, got 71,000,000 legal votes. Bad things happened which our observers were not allowed to see. Never happened before. Millions of mail-in ballots were sent to people who never asked for them!"**[1]
President Donald Trump, November 7, 2020

« **"I've worked extensively with the election officials in the city of Detroit, and they take it very seriously. . . . Are there errors that happen? Sure. But that's not fraud. . . . I never saw any sort of fraud. . . . It never happens. Because you can't get away with it. It's way easier to just try and win the election."**[2]
Josh Venable, Michigan Republican political operative

Every two years, Americans elect 435 House members and 33 or so senators; every four years (as in 2020), we also elect a president. The outcomes of these elections are scrutinized because they provide insights into what voters are thinking, because they reveal the usefulness of different campaign strategies, or simply because of what's at stake.

One example in 2020 was the Senate election in Maine between Republican incumbent Susan Collins and her Democratic challenger, Speaker of the Maine House of Representatives Sara Gideon. One reason this election was important was that Democrats needed to flip only four Senate seats to gain control of the chamber, and Maine was one of the few states in 2020 where a Democratic challenger had a good chance of unseating an incumbent. Another was that Collins was one of the few remaining moderate Republicans in the Senate, as well as an occasional supporter of Democratic initiatives. But Collins had also supported many of President Trump's policy initiatives, although she did not vote for Trump's last-minute Supreme Court nominee, Amy Coney Barrett.

Ultimately, Collins won reelection, a surprise to observers who had predicted a Gideon win based on her popularity, her well-funded campaign, and discontent with Collins. Collins's victory illustrates an important truth: even though most Americans are thoroughly disgusted with politicians and politics, most congressional incumbents are reelected. Our task is to understand this outcome. Did Mainers support Collins because she was a Republican, or because of Donald Trump? What role did the campaign play, or the challenger's record? Did Maine's use of a ranked-choice voting system help or hurt Gideon? Answers to these questions help explain whether Collins's victory is a one-off, idiosyncratic win or an indication of how U.S. elections will play out in 2022 and beyond.

The 2020 senate race in Maine between Democrat Sara Gideon and Republican incumbent Susan Collins (shown here) captured the country's attention. Was Collins's surprise victory a result of smart campaigning, approval of her record as a senator, widespread dissatisfaction with Gideon or the Democratic Party, or something else?

CHAPTER GOALS

Present the major rules and procedures of American elections. pages 558–569

Describe the features, strategies, and funding of campaigns for federal office. pages 570–587

Explain the key factors that influence voters' choices. pages 588–592

Analyze the issues and outcomes in the 2018 and 2020 elections. pages 593–600

The 2020 Senate election in Maine is also a good example of the central themes of this text. Elections matter: no one watching the Maine race would think that Collins and Gideon would support the same policies if elected. Candidates competing for political office offer the people distinct, competing visions of what the federal government should do—from what the tax code should look like to what regulations the government should impose on individuals and corporations. In a very real sense, elections are how Americans resolve conflict over whose vision of government policy should prevail—at least until the next election.

American elections are structured by rules. Maine is somewhat unique in using ranked-choice voting, a system wherein voters rank all the candidates running for a given office instead of choosing just one. If no candidate wins a majority of first-place votes, the candidate with the lowest number of first-place votes is eliminated, and that candidate's votes are redistributed according to his or her supporter's second-place votes. In other states, an outcome where neither candidate wins an outright majority leads to a runoff between the two top finishers. These rules matter—runoff elections often produce surprising outcomes because they occur a month or more after Election Day, allowing candidates to refine their message, but also forcing them to motivate supporters to return to the polls a second time. And in 2020, party control of the Senate hinged on the results of two runoffs in Georgia.

The 2020 Senate contest in Maine highlights fundamental facts about American elections. Candidates run for different offices and represent different constituents. Locally set rules determine who runs, who votes, and how money is raised and spent. Even ballot layouts and how votes are cast and counted vary across states. Who wins is up to ordinary citizens. After his defeat, Donald Trump alleged that American elections were rigged, but there is no evidence to support his claims. Rather, as Republican operative Josh Venable asserts, the only way to win is to convince voters that you are the best person for the job. In this chapter, we show how elections are run, how they are decided, and how they affect policy making. Ultimately, how meaningful was Susan Collins's victory in Maine in 2020—or Democrats' victories in the Georgia runoffs that gave them a narrow Senate majority? What do election results tell us about why some candidates win and others lose? Why do these outcomes matter in American politics?

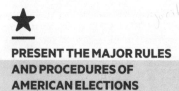

DID YOU KNOW?

There are a total of

510,000

federal, state, and local elected offices in the United States.

Source: Jennifer Lawless, *Becoming a Candidate*

How do American elections work?

The American political system is a representative democracy: Americans do not make policy choices themselves, but they vote for individuals who make these choices on their behalf. This section describes the rules and procedures that define American national elections.

Functions of elections

Our working assumption for explaining the rules and processes of elections as well as the behavior of candidates and voters is that they are tied directly to what elections do: select representatives, give citizens the ability to influence the direction of government policy, and provide citizens with the opportunity to reward and punish officeholders seeking reelection.

Selecting Representatives The most visible function of American elections is the selection of officeholders, including, at the national level, members of the House and Senate and the president and vice president. Candidates can be **incumbents**, running for reelection to their current office, or challengers, running for the office for the first time. Because America is a representative democracy, by voting in elections, Americans have an indirect effect on government policy. Although citizens do not make policy choices themselves, they determine which individuals get to make these choices. In this way, elections are supposed to connect citizen preferences and government actions.

Shaping Policy Although the fundamental choice in an election is between two or more candidates running for some political office, elections also involve a choice between candidates' policy platforms: the set of things they promise to do if elected. By investigating candidates' platforms, citizens learn about the range of options for government policy. Moreover, their voting decisions determine who gets to make choices about future government policy, and thereby shape government policy itself. For example, in the 2020 elections, Democrats wanted to ensure they kept their House majority, which would allow them to block Republican policy initiatives and investigate the Trump administration's actions if Trump was reelected. They also wanted to gain a Senate majority and win the presidency, which would allow them to formulate and enact new policies rather than responding to Republican initiatives.

Promoting Accountability The election process also creates a way to hold incumbents accountable. When citizens choose between voting for an incumbent or a challenger, they can make a retrospective evaluation. They consider the incumbent's performance over his or her previous terms in office and ask, "Has he [or she] done a good job on the issues I care about?"[3] Citizens who answer yes typically vote for the incumbent, and those who answer no typically vote for the challenger. (Of course, as we discussed in Chapters 10 and 11, these judgments are often shaped by party affiliation, so in the case of President Trump in 2020, most Republicans concluded Trump had done a good job in office, while most Democrats made the opposite judgment.)

Retrospective evaluations are significant because they make incumbents responsive to their constituents' demands.[4] If elected officials anticipate that some constituents will make retrospective evaluations objectively (rather than simply reflecting their partisanship), they will try to take actions that these constituents will look back upon favorably when they're in the voting booth. If incumbents ignore the possibility of voters' retrospective evaluations, they run the risk of being voted out of office in the next election. Retrospective evaluations can also form the basis for prospective judgments: voters' beliefs about how the country will fare if different candidates win. This provides an additional reason for incumbents to be responsive to citizens' demands.

Two stages of elections

Candidates running for federal office (House, Senate, or president) face a two-step procedure. First, if the prospective candidates want to run on behalf of a political party, they must win the party's nomination in a **primary** election. If the would-be candidates want to run as Independents, they need to gather signatures on a petition to secure a spot on the ballot. Different states hold either **open primaries**, **semi-closed primaries**, or **closed primaries**, and state law sets the timing of these elections. For House and Senate seats, a few states hold single primaries, in which there is one election involving candidates from both parties, with the top two finalists (regardless of party) receiving nominations to the general election.

incumbent
A politician running for reelection to the office he or she currently holds.

Though incumbents generally fared well in the 2020 congressional elections, some, such as Representative Dan Lipinski (D-IN), a former political science professor and eight-term member of Congress, lost in the primaries.

primary
A ballot vote in which citizens select a party's nominee for the general election.

open primary
A primary election in which any registered voter can participate in the contest, regardless of party affiliation.

semi-closed primary
A primary in which anyone who is a registered member of the party or registered as an Independent can vote.

closed primary
A primary election in which only registered members of a particular political party can vote.

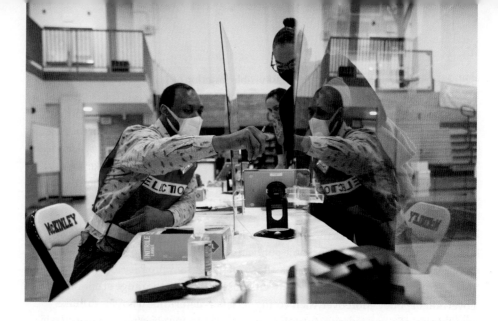

A voter wearing a protective mask checks in before voting during the primary election at a polling location in a high school in Washington, D.C. Americans vote in all sorts of places, including libraries, fire stations, schools, and private homes, all of which had to be configured to protect voters and volunteers during the coronavirus pandemic.

general election
The election in which voters cast ballots for House members, senators, and (every four years) a president and vice president.

**AP®
FOUNDATIONAL
DOCUMENT**

The second step in the election process is the **general election**, which is held throughout the nation on the first Tuesday after the first Monday in November. Federal law designates this day as Election Day. General elections determine who wins elected positions in government. The offices at stake vary depending on the year. Presidential elections occur every four years (2012, 2016, 2020, …). In a presidential election year, Americans elect the entire House of Representatives, one-third of the Senate, and a president and vice president. During midterm elections (2014, 2018, 2022, …), there is no presidential contest, but the entire House and a third of the Senate are up for election.

One implication of this two-step process of primary and general elections is that sometimes the winner of a primary is not a party's best candidate for the general election. For example, in the 2020 presidential race, one of the principal arguments for choosing someone other than Joe Biden as the Democratic nominee (such as Senator Bernie Sanders, Senator Amy Klobuchar, or Senator Elizabeth Warren) was that this candidate would have had a better chance of winning the general election. While Biden had many enthusiastic supporters, a first-rate campaign organization, and considerable Washington experience as senator and vice president, he was also strongly disliked by a sizable fraction of the American electorate—because of his age, his moderately liberal policy stances, and his career in politics. In the end, Biden was a good fit for the unique circumstances of the 2020 election, as he attracted support from working-class White midwestern voters who had supported Donald Trump in 2016, while increasing turnout from minority voters in crucial swing states.

Mechanics of elections

The Constitution limits voting rights to American citizens who are at least 18 years old. There are also numerous restrictions on voter eligibility that vary across states, including residency requirements (usually 30 days) and prohibitions for people convicted of a major crime. A recent development in American elections is an increase in the practice of automatic absentee voting, in which someone can request an absentee ballot without having to provide a reason, such as being out of town on election day. Most states also allow early voting in the weeks prior to Election Day and some allow voters to send in ballots by mail.[5] In 2020, the COVID-19 pandemic led additional states to allow voting by mail in an attempt to minimize large crowds at polling stations. This decision was one reason why turnout was noticeably higher in 2020 than in recent years. Mail-in ballots in most states generally favored

Democrats, although this outcome reflects Donald Trump's encouragement of his supporters to vote in person.

The most fundamental feature of American elections is that officeholders are elected in single-member districts in which only the winner of the most votes takes office. (Although both of each state's senators represent the whole state, they are elected separately, usually in different years.) Senate candidates compete statewide; House candidates compete in congressional districts. In most states, congressional district lines are drawn by state legislatures. In some states, nonpartisan commissions perform this function. Redistricting can happen at any time, but in general, district lines are revised after each census to make sure the boundary lines reflect shifts in population across and within states. (For details on redistricting, see Chapter 4.)

Because members of the House and Senate are elected from specific geographic areas, they often represent very different kinds of people. Their constituents differ in terms of age, race, income level, occupation, and political leaning, including party affiliation and ideology. Therefore, legislators from different areas of the country face highly diverse demands from their constituents, which often leads them to pursue very dissimilar kinds of policies.

For example, Democratic senator Charles Schumer represents the fairly liberal state of New York, where most people take some sort of pro-choice position on abortion rights, while Republican senator Richard Shelby represents the conservative state of Alabama, where most voters have long been opposed to abortions. Suppose the Senate votes on a proposal to ban all abortions after the twelfth week of pregnancy. Shelby knows that most of his constituents would probably want him to vote for the proposal, and Schumer knows that most of his constituents would probably want him to vote against it. This example illustrates that congressional conflicts over policy often reflect differences in constituents' demands. Schumer and Shelby themselves may hold different views on abortion rights, but even if they agreed, their constituents' distinct demands would make it likely that as legislators they would vote differently.

Most House and Senate contests involve **plurality voting**: the candidate who gets the most votes wins. However, some states use **majority voting**, meaning that a candidate needs a majority (more than 50 percent of the vote) to win. If no candidate has a majority, a **runoff election** takes place between the top two finishers. Some candidates have lost runoff elections even though they received the most votes in the first contest.

Ballots and Vote Counting Americans vote using a variety of machines and ballot structures based on where they live. States either use electronic touch screen voting machines, usually with some sort of paper receipt to allow manual recounts, or have voters fill out paper ballots that are then scanned and recorded. When the polls close, workers transcribe vote totals from the various machines, then hand-carry the totals and individual ballots or receipts to county boards of election, where totals are aggregated and sent to state agencies, which certify the results. The process is largely run by volunteers, with both major parties having participants or observers at all stages. One of the motivations for voting by mail in 2020 was to protect these volunteer poll workers from exposure to COVID-19.

Most states have laws that allow vote recounts if a race is sufficiently close (typically within 1 percent or less). Even when a recount occurs, it may be impossible to definitively determine who won a particular election, as the rules that determine which ballots are valid are often open to interpretation. More significant is that when an election is close the question of which candidate wins may depend on how ballots are structured and votes are counted. The problem is not that election officials are dishonest; rather, close elections inherently tend to produce ambiguous outcomes.

plurality voting
A voting system in which the candidate who receives the most votes within a geographic area wins the election, regardless of whether that candidate wins a majority (more than half) of the votes.

majority voting
A voting system in which a candidate must win more than 50 percent of votes to win the election. If no candidate wins enough votes to take office, a runoff election is held between the top two vote-getters.

runoff election
Under a majority voting system, a second election is held only if no candidate wins a majority of the votes in the first general election. Only the top two vote-getters in the first election compete in the runoff.

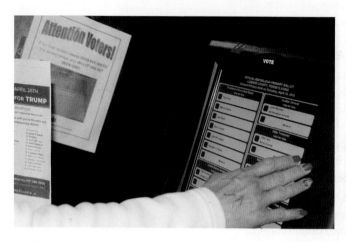
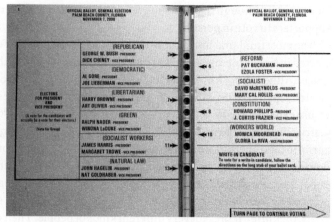

Many different mechanisms are used to record votes in American elections, including paper keypunch ballots and touch screens (left). The design of the infamous butterfly ballot (right), which was used in the 2000 presidential election to vote in Palm Beach County, Florida, inadvertently led some people who intended to vote for Democrat Al Gore to select Reform Party candidate Patrick Buchanan.

Claims are often made that officials manipulate election rules to guarantee wins for their favored candidates. In some states, Republican officials have enacted laws that require voters to verify their identity with an official form of identification such as a driver's license or a passport. The purported goal is to prevent voter fraud—one person voting under another's name, casting multiple votes for the same candidate, voting in multiple places at once, voting in a district where he or she is not a resident, or voting as a noncitizen. However, no reputable study has found significant voter fraud. Many claims are based on simplistic ideas of what constitutes evidence of it. For example, an investigation of possible vote fraud conducted by the New Hampshire secretary of state initially identified several thousand possible fraudulent votes in 2016, including cases in which an individual who voted in New Hampshire had the same name and birthdate as a voter in another state, and claims that Massachusetts residents had been bused to New Hampshire to vote. Virtually all the cross-state matches turned out to be separate people, the alleged Massachusetts voters were young adults who were attending school in New Hampshire and had legally registered to vote—and no cases of actual vote fraud were identified.[6] Donald Trump and his supporters made similar allegations in 2020, focusing on supposedly fraudulent mail-in ballots. They never had evidence to back up these claims, which were dismissed by state and federal courts.

In sum, voter ID laws solve a problem that does not exist. Moreover, voter ID laws create barriers to voting for individuals who lack an official ID—these individuals are generally poor and non-White and disproportionately vote Democratic. While some supporters of voter ID laws may be sincerely concerned about preventing fraud, research shows that enacting these laws hurts Democratic candidates by lowering turnout from groups that are likely to support them.[7]

Presidential elections

Many of the rules governing elections, such as who is eligible to vote, are the same for both presidential and congressional elections. But presidential contests have several unique rules regarding how nominees are determined and how votes are counted. Moreover, the constitutional requirements for presidential candidates are also somewhat stricter than those for congressional candidates (see Nuts & Bolts 13.1).

The Nomination: Primaries and Caucuses Presidential nominees from the Democratic and Republican parties are determined by the outcomes of state-level primaries and **caucuses** held over a five-month period beginning in January of an election year.[8] Primary and caucus voters select a candidate, but their votes do not

caucus
A local meeting in which party members select a party's nominee for the general election.

Constitutional Requirements for Candidates

Office	Minimum Age	Residency Requirement
President	35	Natural-born citizen (born in the United States or on U.S. territory, or child of citizen parent)
Senator	30	Resident of state; U.S. citizen for at least nine years
Representative	25	Resident of state; U.S. citizen for at least seven years

Source: U.S. Constitution.

"Why Should I Care?" These age and citizenship requirements are the most fundamental limits on who can run for political office. They are one explanation for why there are no college-age people elected to Congress—they are prevented from running in the first place.

count directly toward the election of that candidate; their votes instead count toward the selection of **delegates** who have pledged to support the candidate, who then go on to attend the party nominating conventions. There, the delegates cast votes that determine their party's presidential and vice-presidential nominees. The format of these elections, including their timing and the number of delegates selected per state, is determined on a state-by-state basis by the state and national party organizations.[9] In some states, each candidate preselects a list of delegates who will attend the convention if the candidate wins sufficient votes in the primary or caucus. In other states, delegates are chosen by party leaders after the actual primary or caucus takes place. In both cases, a candidate's principal goal is to win as many delegates as possible—and to select delegates who will be reliable supporters at the convention. Some states require delegates to vote for the candidate they are pledged to—at least for the first ballot at the party nominating convention. However, these laws have never been tested and it is not clear that they are enforceable.

The details of translating primary and caucus votes into convention delegates vary from state to state, but some general rules apply. All Democratic primaries and caucuses use **proportional allocation** to divide each state's delegate seats among the candidates; thus, if a candidate receives 40 percent of the votes in a state's primary, the candidate gets roughly 40 percent of the convention delegates from that state. (In the Democratic 2020 primaries, a candidate also needed to gain at least 15 percent of the vote statewide or in a congressional district in order to receive a share of delegates.) Some Republican contests use proportional allocation, but others use a **winner-take-all** system. In these states, the candidate who receives the most votes gets all the convention delegates. These rules can have a significant effect on candidates' campaign strategies and the outcome of the nomination process (see How It Works: Nominating Presidential Candidates in Chapter 11).

The order in which the primaries and caucuses in different states take place is important because many candidacies do not survive beyond the early contests.[10] Most presidential candidates pour everything they have into the first few elections. Candidates who do well attract financial contributions, campaign workers, endorsements, and additional media coverage, all of which enable them to move on to subsequent primaries or caucuses. For candidates who do poorly in the first contests,

delegates
Individuals who are selected in a presidential primary or caucus to attend the party's nomination convention to vote on the party's platform and select the party's presidential and vice-presidential nominees.

proportional allocation
During the presidential primaries, the practice of determining the number of convention delegates allotted to each candidate based on the percentage of the popular vote cast for each candidate. All Democratic primaries and caucuses use this system, as do some states' Republican primaries and caucuses.

winner-take-all
During the presidential primaries, the practice of assigning all of a given state's delegates to the candidate who receives the most popular votes. Some states' Republican primaries and caucuses use this system.

contributions and coverage dry up, leaving these candidates with no alternative but to drop out of the race. For example, more than 20 candidates entered the race for the 2020 Democratic presidential nomination. Several withdrew before any convention delegates were selected. By mid-March, two months into the process and five months before the convention where the nominee would actually be selected, the race was down to only two serious candidates, Sanders and Biden. Thus, the candidate who leads after the first several primaries and caucuses generally wins the nomination.[11] However, when the first few contests do not yield a clear favorite, the race can continue until the last states have voted or even until the convention.

When a sitting president runs for reelection, as Donald Trump did in 2020, he or she typically faces little opposition for the party's general-election nomination—not because challengers defer to the president but because most presidents are popular enough among their own party's faithful supporters that they can win the nomination without too much trouble. Only presidents with particularly low approval ratings have faced serious opposition in their nomination bids.

Among the states, the presidential nomination process is always changing.[12] In 2020, many southern states held their primaries on the same day in early March (Super Tuesday). Others moved the date of their primary (California), moved from a primary to a caucus (Maine), or, on the Democratic side, added a minimum percentage of votes a candidate needed to win any delegates. For many years, Iowa and New Hampshire have held the first presidential nomination contests, with the Iowa Caucuses held a week before the New Hampshire primary. These states' position at the beginning of the process is largely a historical accident, but it is controversial. State party officials from other states often complain about the media attention given to these contests and their disproportionate influence in winnowing the candidate pool, but there is no consensus on an alternate schedule. As a result, the initial 2020 nomination process was roughly the same as in previous years (with the exception of California's move to March), with Iowa and New Hampshire holding the initial contests in early February 2020, followed by a primary in South Carolina and a caucus in Nevada later in the month and the remaining contests beginning in March and continuing through June, although some were delayed due to COVID-19.

One rule that distinguishes the parties' candidate selection processes is that about one-fifth of the delegates to the Democratic convention are not supporters of a particular candidate, nor have they been chosen to attend the convention based on primary and caucus results. Rather, they are superdelegates, elected officials and party officials whom their colleagues select to participate in the convention. Most are automatically seated at the convention regardless of primary and caucus results, and they are free to support any candidate for the nomination, although for the 2020 contest, they were forbidden from participating in the first round of voting at the convention. By forcing candidates to court support from superdelegates, the party aims to ensure that the nominee is someone who these officials believe can win the general election and whom they can work with if he or she is elected.[13] Republicans give state party leaders automatic delegate slots at their convention, but the number of such delegates is a much smaller percentage than for Democrats.

The National Convention Presidential nominating conventions happen late in the summer of an election year. Their main task is to select the party's presidential nominee, although usually the vote at the convention is a formality; in most recent presidential contests, one candidate has emerged from the nomination process leading up to the convention with a clear majority of delegates and has been able to win the nomination on the first ballot. To get the nomination, a candidate needs the support of

Senate campaign appearances almost always involve extensive print and electronic media coverage. Here, Shelley Moore Capito, a West Virginia Republican senator who ran for reelection in 2020, speaks to the media. They helped get out her message and policy agenda, and as a result, she won her contest.

a majority of the delegates. If no candidate receives a majority after the first round of voting at the convention, the voting continues until someone does. In 2020 during the COVID-19 pandemic, the Democratic party held its convention virtually and delegate votes were cast online, while the Republican party held a more traditional convention.

After the convention delegates nominate a presidential candidate, they nominate a vice-presidential candidate. The presidential nominee gets to choose his or her running mate (generally shortly before the convention), and the delegates almost always ratify this choice without much debate. Delegates also vote on the party platform, which describes what the party stands for and what kinds of policies its candidates will supposedly seek to enact if they are elected.

The final purpose of a convention is to attract public attention to the party and its nominees. Public figures give speeches during the evening sessions when all major television networks have live coverage. At some recent conventions, both parties have drawn press attention by recruiting speakers who support their political goals despite being associated with the opposing party. At the 2020 Democratic convention, Republicans John Kasich (former governor of Ohio) and Colin Powell (secretary of state under George W. Bush) gave televised primetime speeches voicing their support for Joe Biden.

Once presidential candidates are nominated, the general-election campaign officially begins—although it often unofficially starts much earlier, as soon as the presumptive nominees are known. We will say more about presidential campaigns in a later section.

Counting Presidential Votes Let's assume for a moment that the campaigning is over and that Election Day has arrived. Even though in the voting booth people choose between the candidates by name, a choice that constitutes the **popular vote**, this vote is not directly for a presidential candidate. Rather, when you select your preferred candidate's name, you are choosing that person's slate of pledged supporters from your state to serve as electors, who will then vote to elect the president.

The number of electors for each state equals the state's number of House members (which varies by state population) plus the state's number of senators (two per state). Altogether, the electors chosen by the citizens of each state constitute the **Electoral College**, the body that casts **electoral votes** to formally select the president. Small-population states, therefore, have few electoral votes—Delaware and Montana, for example, each have only 3—while the highest-population state, California, has 55 (see How It Works: The Electoral College). In most states, electoral votes are allocated on a winner-take-all basis: the candidate who receives the most votes from a given state's citizens gets all of that state's electoral votes. But two states, Maine and Nebraska, allocate most of their electoral votes at the congressional district level: in those states, the candidate who wins the most votes in each congressional district wins that district's single electoral vote. Then the remaining 2 electoral votes go to the candidate who gets the most votes statewide.[14]

The winner-take-all method of allocating most states' electoral votes makes candidates focus their attention on two kinds of states: high-population states with lots of electoral votes and so-called swing states where the contest is relatively close. It's better for a candidate to spend a day campaigning in California (55 electoral votes) than in Montana (3 electoral votes). However, if one candidate is sure to win a particular state, both candidates will direct their efforts elsewhere. For example, during the final weeks of the 2020 campaign, the Trump team was on defense, trying to hold Florida and key Rust Belt states (following the strategy described in the How It Works feature), while the Biden campaign was targeting former Republican strongholds Georgia, Texas, and Arizona.

You win some, you lose some. And then there's that little-known third category.

—**Al Gore,** who lost the 2000 presidential vote in the Electoral College despite winning the most votes on Election Day

popular vote
The votes cast by citizens in an election.

Electoral College
The body that votes to select America's president and vice president based on the popular vote in each state. Each candidate nominates a slate of electors who are selected to attend the meeting of the college if their candidate wins the most votes in a state or district.

electoral votes
Votes cast by members of the Electoral College; after a presidential candidate wins the popular vote in a given state, that candidate's slate of electors casts electoral votes for the candidate on behalf of that state.

The Electoral College

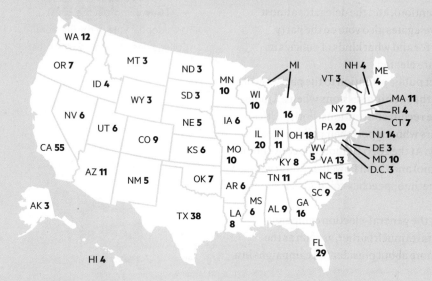

WA 12
OR 7
MT 3
ND 3
MN 10
MI
NH 4
ME 4
VT 3
ID 4
WY 3
SD 3
WI 10
MA 11
NY 29
RI 4
CT 7
NV 6
UT 6
NE 5
IA 6
PA 20
CA 55
CO 9
KS 6
IL 20
IN 11
OH 18
NJ 14
DE 3
MD 10
D.C. 3
WV 5
VA 13
AZ 11
NM 5
OK 7
MO 10
KY 8
NC 15
AK 3
AR 6
TN 11
SC 9
TX 38
MS 6
LA 8
AL 9
GA 16
HI 4
FL 29
16

Electoral Votes per State

The number of electors from each state equals the state's number of House members (which varies based on state population) plus the number of senators (two per state). Each elector has one vote in the Electoral College.

Who Are the Electors?

Candidates to be electors are nominated by their political parties. They pledge to support a certain candidate if they are elected to the Electoral College. When you cast your vote for a presidential candidate, you are in fact voting for the slate of potential electors who support that candidate.

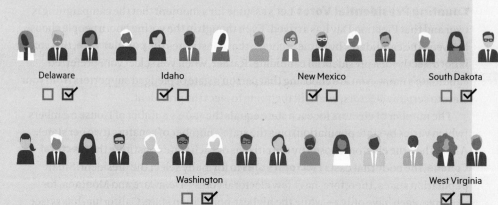

Delaware ☐ ☑
Idaho ☑ ☐
New Mexico ☑ ☐
South Dakota ☐ ☑

Washington ☐ ☑
West Virginia ☑ ☐

Winning a State

Most states give all of their Electoral College votes to the candidate who wins the most votes in that state. So, even if a candidate only gets 51 percent of the vote in the state, his or her entire slate of electors is elected, and he or she gets all of the state's votes in the Electoral College.

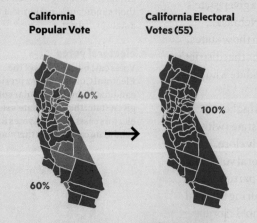

California Popular Vote

40%

60%

California Electoral Votes (55)

100%

100%
of electoral votes go to winner

Donald Trump's Electoral College Strategy, 2020

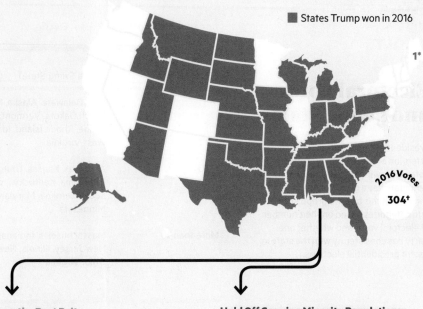

■ States Trump won in 2016

2016 Votes
304†

Trump's campaign started with the electoral map that produced its 2016 victory with 304 electoral votes. It focused on two groups of states—Rust Belt states where it won narrow victories in 2016 (Michigan, Pennsylvania, and Wisconsin) and states where increasing minority populations might swing the outcome toward Democrat Joe Biden (Arizona, Georgia, North Carolina, and Texas)—in an attempt to amass at least 270 electoral votes, the threshold required to win the election.

Keep the Rust Belt:
Michigan, Pennsylvania, and Wisconsin
Trump won these states by small margins in 2016.

WI **10**
MI **16** 1
PA **20**

260+46

306

Hold Off Growing Minority Populations:
Arizona, Georgia, North Carolina, Texas
Growing minority populations in these states were a significant worry for the Trump campaign.

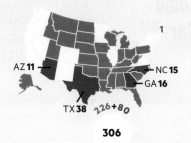

1

AZ **11**
NC **15**
GA **16**
TX **38**   226+80

306

4§

1*

Total Votes
232

2020 Results

This strategy did not succeed for Trump in 2020 like it did in 2016. While he did manage to hold on to Texas and North Carolina, **higher overall turnout and growing Democratic support among minority populations and in the suburbs** helped Biden secure victories across the Rust Belt and in Arizona and Georgia, which ultimately won Biden the election.

Trump's Final Electoral College Map

AL **9**	KS **6**	NE **4**	TN **11**
AK **3**	KY **8**	NC **15**	TX **38**
AR **6**	LA **8**	ND **3**	UT **6**
FL **29**	ME **1**	OH **18**	WV **5**
ID **4**	MS **6**	OK **7**	WY **3**
IN **11**	MO **10**	SC **9**	
IA **6**	MT **3**	SD **3**	

Critical Thinking

1. **Why didn't the Trump campaign** focus on some delegate-rich states like California and New York?

2. **In what state do you think the Trump campaign** spent the most money? Where do you think Trump made the most personal appearances? Why?

---

* Maine splits its electoral votes: in 2016, Trump received 1, Clinton 3; in 2020, Trump received 1, Biden 3.

† Two electors in Texas did not cast their electoral votes for Trump in 2016.

§ Nebraska splits its electoral votes: in 2020, Trump received 4, Biden 1.

Electoral Votes and Swing States

Presidential campaigns focus their attention on states with high electoral votes and swing states where each candidate has a good chance of winning. In this box, we group states into categories based on their number of electoral votes and whether one party has consistently won the state in recent presidential elections.

Source: Compiled by the authors.

One Party Dominates in Recent Elections?

Number of Electoral Votes	Yes (Not a Swing State)	No (Swing State)
3–5	D.C., Delaware, Alaska, Montana, North Dakota, South Dakota, Vermont, Wyoming, Hawaii, Maine, Rhode Island, Idaho, Nebraska, West Virginia	New Hampshire, New Mexico
6–10	Arkansas, Kansas, Utah, Connecticut, Oregon, Oklahoma, Kentucky, Louisiana, Alabama, South Carolina, Maryland, Mississippi, Missouri, Minnesota	Iowa, Nevada, Colorado, Wisconsin
More than 10	Massachusetts, Indiana, Tennessee, Washington, New Jersey, Illinois, New York, Texas, California, Ohio, Virginia	Arizona, North Carolina, Florida, Michigan, Pennsylvania, Georgia

"Why Should I Care?" Data on a state's electoral votes and status as a swing state tell us why presidential candidates campaign in some states more than in others. For the most part, the crucial factor is whether both presidential candidates see a state as winnable—if they do, they will campaign there aggressively.

After the 2020 presidential election, President Trump's campaign demanded recounts in several states, including Wisconsin, Michigan, Georgia, and Pennsylvania. The recounts yielded only small changes in vote totals, and there was no evidence of fraud as the campaign repeatedly alleged.

Nuts & Bolts 13.2 divides states based on their electoral vote and whether they are swing states—defined as states that each party won at least once in recent elections. The table explains why both campaigns in 2020 spent so much time and campaign funds on states such as Pennsylvania and Florida (swing states with a large number of electoral votes)—and why they largely ignored states such as Delaware (small state, one-party-dominates category).

After citizens' votes are counted, each state's slate of electors meets in December in the state capitals. At their meetings, the electors almost always vote for the presidential candidate they have pledged to support. After the votes are certified by a joint session of Congress, the candidate who wins a majority of the nation's electoral votes (at least 270) is the new president. One peculiarity of the Electoral College is that in most states it is legal for an elector to either (1) vote for a candidate he or she is not pledged to support or (2) abstain from voting.[15] Such events are uncommon for the simple reason that electors are selected by the presidential candidates with an eye toward reliable support.

If no candidate receives a majority of the Electoral College votes, the members of the House of Representatives choose the winner. They follow a procedure in which the members from each state decide which candidate to support and then cast one collective vote per state, with the winner needing a majority of these state-level votes to win. This procedure has not been used since 1824, although it might be required if a third-party candidate wins a significant number of electoral votes or if a state's electors refuse to cast their votes.[16]

A presidential candidate can win the Electoral College vote, and thus the election, without receiving a majority of the votes cast by citizens (see Figure 13.1). In 2016,

Popular Vote versus Electoral Vote Percentages, 2000–2020

FIGURE 13.1

Political scientists argue that the Electoral College system tends to magnify the winning candidate's margin of victory. Do the data presented here support this view?

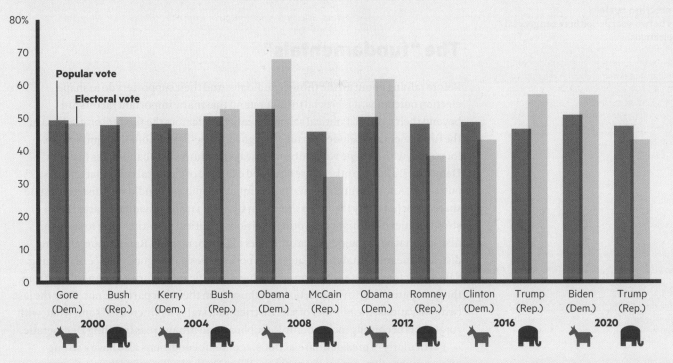

Source: 2000–2016 data from U.S. National Archives and Records Administration, www.archives.gov/federal-register/electoral-college/historical.html (accessed 5/11/18); 2020 data calculated by the authors from election results as of 11/12/20.

Democrat Hillary Clinton received several million more votes than Donald Trump because of large majorities in states such as California and New York, but Trump won a majority in the Electoral College because of narrow victories in states such as Wisconsin and Pennsylvania. A similar outcome occurred in 2000, leading to Republican George W. Bush's victory over Democrat Al Gore. Other presidents who won the Electoral College vote but lost the popular vote were John Quincy Adams in 1824, Rutherford B. Hayes in 1876, and Benjamin Harrison in 1888.

American elections incorporate a complex set of laws, rules, and procedures. And these rules matter—the candidates who win under current rules might lose given other reasonable ways to conduct elections. For example, in 2016, Democrat Hillary Clinton won the popular vote but lost the electoral vote (and the election) due to close losses in Florida, Michigan, Pennsylvania, and Wisconsin. Even small changes in voter registration, voter ID regulations, and other laws in these states might have given Clinton victories in these states—and the presidency.

"Why Should I Care?"

election cycle
The two-year period between general elections.

Electoral campaigns

This section explores the campaign process and what candidates do to convince people to vote for them on Election Day. Our emphasis is on things that candidates do, regardless of the office they are running for, across the entire **election cycle**: the two-year period between general elections.

The "fundamentals"

Before talking about all the things candidates and their supporters do to shape election outcomes, it is crucial to understand that many important factors are beyond their control. Political scientists call these factors the *fundamentals*. In part, the fundamentals include the rules that govern elections. Photo ID requirements for voting, which shape voter turnout in ways that hurt some candidates (usually Democrats) and help others, are one good example of electoral rules that affect outcomes. Another fundamental is how many people in a candidate's district or state share his or her party ID. As we showed in Chapter 11, an individual's party ID is a strong influence on his or her voting decisions. Political scientists refer to states or districts that have roughly equal numbers of Democrats and Republicans as swing districts, meaning that candidates from both parties have a good chance of winning. Safe districts are those where one party has a significant majority, so candidates from that party are likely to win election and those from the other party are not. Over the last two generations, the number of safe districts and states has increased somewhat, with rural areas becoming more solidly Republican and urban areas trending Democratic.

Particularly in presidential elections, economic conditions also have a strong effect on who wins. As you can see in the What Do the Facts Say? feature on p. 571, a stronger economy benefits incumbent presidents running for reelection (for example, Obama in 2012), while a weak economy hurts incumbents (Jimmy Carter in 1980) and their successors (John McCain in 2008). Of course, fundamentals have to be taken in context. Big one-time shocks have unique effects. For example, the COVID-19 pandemic caused a drop in second-quarter GDP that was so big we can't even include it in the figure (that's why there's an asterisk next to the 2020 data point). As we discuss later, while most voters gave Trump low marks for his management of the pandemic and the economic downturn, his approval ratings did not change very much. That said, Trump's ratings were already low prior to the pandemic, and the social and economic turmoil limited his ability to attract the additional support he needed to get reelected.

Candidates might like to think that they can convince people to vote for them regardless of circumstances. But the fundamentals like party ID and economic conditions tell us which candidates face an uphill fight or an easy ride—either because voters are well aware of these factors before the campaign begins or because campaigns are mechanisms by which voters become informed about them.[17] It may not be fair to reward or blame candidates for the state of the economy, as even presidents have only limited control over economic growth or unemployment levels. For better or worse, however, a significant fraction of American voters behave this way.[18] Similarly, for some challengers, defeat is a foregone conclusion because they are running in a state or district that is safe for the other party—no matter what they do, most of the electorate is unlikely to support them.

It's important to remember, though, that the fundamentals are not the final word in an election. The backgrounds of the candidates, their qualifications for office, and the decisions they make about their campaigns sometimes have significant, even decisive effects. For example, Democrat Conor Lamb won a 2018 special election in a strongly

Vote Share for President's Party vs. Economic Growth

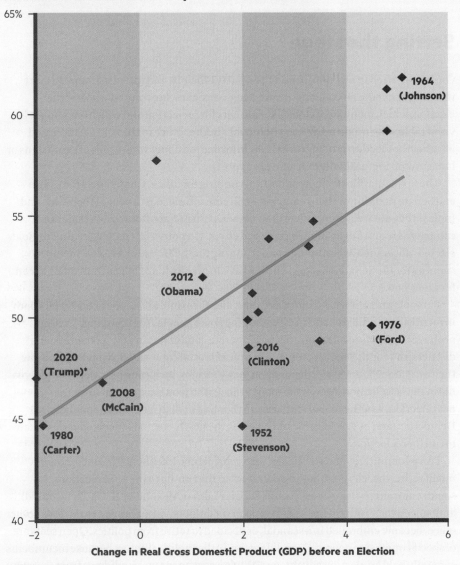

*In 2020 the change in real GDP was −31.4% due to the COVID-19 pandemic.
Source: Data calculated by the authors.

Think about it

- **Why do incumbent presidents do better** when the economy is strong than when it is weak?

- **Candidates who lose, such as Clinton in 2016 or Romney in 2012, are criticized** for running poor campaigns. Look at the data points that describe economic conditions in these elections and the percentage of the popular vote received by Obama in 2012 and Clinton in 2016. Given the state of the economy in these years, is there any evidence that Romney or Clinton did worse than you would expect?

- **What signs are there in the graph** that other factors besides "the fundamentals" might influence presidential election outcomes?

"The Fundamentals" and Presidential Elections

Political scientists argue that "the fundamentals" play a key role in American elections. For example, the state of the economy is thought to influence voter decisions in presidential elections—a strong economy benefits incumbent presidents or their successors. However, most candidates (and journalists) argue that the things candidates say and do during the campaign determine who wins and who loses. What do the facts say?

To answer this question, let's examine this figure, which shows the relationship between presidential election outcomes (vote share for the incumbent president or the candidate from the president's party) and economic conditions (the growth in real gross domestic product [GDP] in the year before the election, controlling for inflation). The blue line gives the predicted relationship between economic conditions and the popular vote, showing that on average, as economic conditions improve, the president or candidate from the president's party receives more votes.

Republican Pennsylvania congressional district—although President Trump won there in 2016 by a 20-point margin. At least part of Lamb's victory was due to a decline in Trump's popularity and the resignation of the district's Republican incumbent due to scandal. But Lamb, who took moderate positions on issues such as gun control, was widely regarded as the stronger, more energetic candidate. Under these conditions, Republican voters appear to have seen Lamb as someone who would do a better job protecting their district's interests, and supported him on that basis.

Setting the stage

On the day after an election, candidates, party officials, and interest groups all start thinking about the next election cycle. They consider who won and who lost the election, which incumbents look like safe bets for reelection and which ones might be vulnerable, who might retire soon or run for another office in the next election, and whether the election returns reveal new information about what kinds of campaigns or issues might increase voter turnout or support.

These calculations reflect the costs of running for office. Challengers for House and Senate seats know that a campaign will consume at least a year of their time and (unless they are wealthy) deplete their personal financial resources. Presidential campaigns require even more money and effort. If a potential challenger already holds elected office, such as a state legislator running for the House or a House member running for the Senate, that person may have to give up his or her current office to run for a new one.[19]

Party organizations and interest groups also face time and money constraints both in recruiting candidates and in discouraging some people from running. They do not have the funds to offer significant support to candidates in all 435 congressional districts, in 33 or 34 Senate races, and in a presidential contest.[20] So which races draw their attention? The answer depends on many factors, including how well incumbents did in the last election, how much money those who won have available for the next election, whether party affiliation in the state or district favors Republicans or Democrats (and by how much), and whether the newly elected officeholders are likely to run for reelection.

Party committees and candidates also consider the likelihood that incumbents might retire, thereby creating an open seat. In the run-up to the 2020 elections, some senior citizen legislators such as Senator Lamar Alexander (R-TN, 80 years old) announced their retirement, as did younger incumbents who planned to run for another office, became embroiled in a scandal, or decided to retire from politics. Open seats are of special interest to potential candidates and other political actors because incumbents generally hold an election advantage.[21] When a seat opens up, candidates from the party that does not control the seat know that they may have a better chance to win because they will not have to run against an incumbent. The incumbent's party leaders, in turn, have to recruit an especially strong candidate in order to hold the seat. Thus, in an election in which a relatively large number of members of Congress choose to retire (as did Republicans in 2018 and 2020), the party with fewer retirements is in the better position because it has fewer open seats to defend.

Presidential campaigns also take incumbency into account. Virtually all first-term presidents run for reelection. Potential challengers in the opposing party study the results of the last election to see how many votes the president received and how this support was distributed across the states to determine their own chances of winning against the incumbent. Candidates in the president's party make the same calculations, although no sitting president in the twentieth century was denied renomination.

open seat
An elected position for which there is no incumbent.

Nonetheless, some presidents (Harry Truman in 1952, Lyndon Johnson in 1968) retired because their chances of being renominated were not good, while others (Gerald Ford in 1976, Jimmy Carter in 1980) barely won tough primary contests.[22]

Before the campaign

While in Office Most sitting House members, senators, and presidents work throughout the election cycle to secure their reelection. Political scientists describe this activity as the permanent campaign.[23] To stay in office, incumbents have to do two things: keep their constituents happy and raise money for their campaign. As we saw in Chapter 4, congressional incumbents pursue the first goal by taking actions that reflect the demands of their constituents. This, in turn, boosts voters' retrospective evaluations of the incumbents at election time.[24] Incumbent presidents make the same kinds of calculations. For example, during the COVID-19 pandemic, Donald Trump faced the decision of when to relax social distancing advisories and allow the economy to reopen. Part of Trump's calculation was to balance safety (preventing the spread of the virus) with the goal of preventing a prolonged economic downturn. But Trump's calculations undoubtedly included the goal of ensuring that voters would remember his actions in a positive way when they returned to the polls in November 2020. Of course, many presidential actions are taken in response to events rather than initiated to gain voter support. Particularly in the case of wars and pandemics, it is far-fetched to say that presidents take actions for political gain. Even so, presidents, just like other politicians, are keenly aware of the political consequences of their actions and the need to build a record they can run on in the next election.

Presidents can also use the federal bureaucracy both to their own advantage and to help members of their party. For example, some scholars have argued that presidents take measures to try to increase economic growth in the months prior to elections, with the aim of increasing support for their own candidacies (if they are eligible to run for reelection) and for their party's candidates.[25] Given the size and complexity of the U.S. economy and the fact that the independent Federal Reserve System controls monetary policy, it is unlikely that such efforts could have much success. Even so, it seems clear that out of a desire to stay in office and help their party's candidates, presidents would want to be seen as having a positive impact on the economy.

Fund-Raising Candidates for all offices, incumbents and challengers alike, also devote considerable time before the campaign to raising campaign funds. Fund-raising helps an incumbent in two ways.[26] First, it ensures that if the incumbent faces a strong opponent, he or she will have enough money to run an aggressive campaign. Second, successful fund-raising deters opposition. Potential challengers are less likely to run against an incumbent if that individual is well funded with a sizable campaign war chest.[27] We'll discuss campaign fund-raising in more detail later in the chapter.

Promises and Party Positions Candidates also spend time before (and sometimes during) a campaign developing or refining their campaign platform, which includes stances on issues and promises about how the candidate will act in office. Given that few voters are well informed about public policy or inclined to learn, candidates do not win elections by trying to educate the electorate or making complex promises. What works is making promises and taking positions that are simple and consistent with what the average voter believes, even if these beliefs are inconsistent with reality. For example, many people believe that interest groups have too much power in Washington, although their influence is far less powerful than most Americans think (see Chapter 12). Even so, many candidates accuse their opponents of being beholden to interest groups. These claims may be far-fetched, but they work well politically because they play into citizens' perceptions.

In writing their platforms, candidates may be constrained by positions they have taken in the past or by their party affiliation. For one thing, candidates whose positions vary from one election to another or between the primary and general elections often lose support from voters who see the changes as a sign of manipulation.[28] Also, as we saw in Chapter 11, the parties have strong brand identities that lead many citizens to associate Democrats with liberal policies and Republicans with conservative ones. As a result, candidates often find it difficult to make campaign promises that contradict these perceptions. For example, during the 2020 presidential campaign, Donald Trump pledged to expand Medicare and Social Security benefits. However, in light of past attempts by Republican officeholders to cut these programs, voters might have doubted that Trump—the Republican nominee—would carry out this pledge if elected. A candidate's positions are also influenced by demands from potential supporters. In a state or district with many conservative or Republican voters, opposition to Obamacare or to amnesty for undocumented immigrants might be a winning electoral strategy— just as support for these proposals would generally be helpful for candidates running in states or districts where most voters are moderate to liberal or Democrats.

The two-step electoral process in American elections also influences candidate positions. To win office, candidates have to campaign three times: first to build a staff and gain contributors and volunteers (the so-called silent primary or money primary), then in a primary to get on the ballot, and then in a general election. This process gives candidates an incentive to take relatively extreme policy positions—and encourages the entry of relatively extreme candidates—because party activists, contributors, and primary voters (the people whose support candidates need to attract in the first two steps) hold more extreme positions than voters in the general election. Thus, in the typical congressional district, Republican candidates win primaries by taking conservative positions, while Democratic candidates win primaries by upholding liberal views.

However, a position or promise that attracts votes in a primary election might not work so well in the general election, or vice versa. For example, during the 2020 Democratic presidential nomination campaign, challenger Bernie Sanders attracted support by promising to expand government health insurance programs. While this promise was popular among Democratic activists, contributors, and primary voters and helped Sanders compete in a close race against Joe Biden for the nomination, it would likely have cost Sanders (or any Democratic candidate) considerable support in the general election.

Table 13.1 lists part of the campaign platforms of the 2020 presidential candidates and shows their similarities and differences in eight issue areas that received considerable attention during the campaign. (As discussed later, Trump's platform was identical to the one he ran on in 2016.) In all these areas, Biden and Trump offered sharply different ideas of what government should do, although in some cases one or both platforms did not offer policy details. The sharp differences between the platforms on most of the issues are somewhat uncommon—in most elections, there are a few areas where parties offer similar proposals, differing only in details.

A candidate's issue positions as described in his or her platform help mobilize supporters and attract volunteers, activists, interest-group endorsements, and contributions. Issue positions also define what government will do differently depending on who gets elected. And as we will see later in this chapter, some people vote based on candidates' issue positions. Even so, there is considerable evidence that many voters do not know much about candidates' issue positions, particularly in House and Senate races. As a result, when a candidate wins a race or a party wins seats across the country, it is risky to read the outcome as a sign that the winners had the most popular set of issue positions.

Campaign Staff Finally, candidates spend time before the campaign building their organization.[29] As with fund-raising, the success or failure of these efforts is a signal

TABLE
13.1

Presidential Candidates' Issue Positions (Selected), 2020

The table indicates where Joe Biden and Donald Trump stood on eight key issues in 2020 as the presidential election approached in November: immigration, health care, gun control, trade, climate change, Iran, international relations, and LGBTQ rights.

Source: Compiled by the authors from news coverage and candidate websites.

Issue	Joe Biden	Donald Trump
Immigration	Comprehensive reform with path to citizenship for undocumented immigrants	Build wall between United States and Mexico, increase deportations, ban refugees
Health care	Improve Obamacare	Repeal Obamacare
Gun control	Expand background check system	Repeal limits on gun ownership
Trade	Generally supportive of free trade	Renegotiate agreements, limit trade
Climate change	Address climate change, stress renewable energy	No action on climate change, stay withdrawn from Paris Agreement on climate change
Iran	Re-implement Iran nuclear agreement	Increase sanctions on Iran
Relations with international allies	Prioritize consultation and cooperation with allies	Demand allies expand defense spending and defer to U.S.
LGBTQ rights	End discrimination against LGBTQ individuals	Support law giving businesses right to refuse service to LGBTQ individuals

Most officeholders are always campaigning—traveling around their states or districts, talking with constituents, and explaining their actions in office—all in the hope of winning and keeping support for the next election. Here, Representative Nanette Diaz Barragán (D-CA) meets with service members.

American presidential campaigns depend on thousands of paid and volunteer staff. Here Joe Biden makes phone calls to potential supporters before the Iowa Caucuses from a campaign office in Cedar Rapids in January 2020.

of a candidate's prospects. If experienced, well-respected people agree to work for a candidate's campaign, observers conclude that the candidate's prospects for being elected are probably good.

Skilled campaign consultants are among the most sought-after campaign staff. These consultants plan strategies, run public-opinion polls, assemble ads and buy television time, and talk with members of the media on the candidate's behalf, among other things. For many consultants, electioneering is a full-time, year-round position. Many concentrate on electing candidates from one party, although some work for whoever will hire them.

Almost all campaigns have paid and volunteer staff, ranging from the dozen or so people who work for a typical House candidate to the thousands needed to run a major-party candidate's presidential campaign. Some campaign staff work full-time for an incumbent's campaign committee or are on the incumbent's congressional or presidential staff. With some exceptions for senior presidential staff, federal law prohibits government employees from engaging in campaign activities during work hours or with congressional resources.[30] As a result, many congressional or presidential staffers take a leave of absence from their government jobs to work on their bosses' reelection campaigns during the last few months of the election cycle, then return to working for the government after the election—assuming the incumbent is reelected.

It's hard to separate what candidates do at election time from what they do between elections—incumbents are *always* campaigning, always making promises and taking positions, and always raising campaign funds—which is part of the reason they are so likely to win reelection. In many cases, incumbent House members and senators wind up running against poorly funded, inexperienced candidates because stronger challengers—seeing that the incumbent has been working hard to solidify a hold on the constituency—decide to wait until the incumbent retires, when they can run for the open seat. Thus, though incumbents are not automatically favored for reelection, they often win by large margins because of all the things they do while holding office in between elections.[31]

Primaries and the general election

Congressional primary elections occur throughout the spring and summer. For congressional candidates, winning the primary allows them to plan for the general election in November and gives them access to party resources including contributions, workers, and assistance with polling and other logistics. As we discussed earlier, presidential primaries and caucuses begin in early January and extend into June, culminating in the party nominating conventions held during the summer. Officially, the general-election campaigns begin in early September. By then, both parties have chosen their presidential nominees and their congressional candidates. Interest groups, candidates, and party committees have raised most of the funds they will use or donate in the campaign. The race is on.

For presidential candidates, the move from primaries to the general election involves a sharp shift in campaign strategies. Unlike in the early primary states, where candidates engage in "retail politics" by meeting more directly with voters on a small, individual scale, the presidential general-election campaigns emphasize "wholesale politics," a style of campaigning in which candidates contact voters indirectly, such as through media coverage and campaign advertising. At this point, presidential campaign events generally involve large numbers of citizens, and if they are smaller events or one-on-one encounters, they are designed to generate media coverage and thereby reach a larger audience.

In contrast, some general-election campaigns for the House and even a few Senate races are more likely to practice retail politics, stressing direct contact with voters. Even so, the start of these general-election campaigns is usually when congressional candidates and groups supporting and opposing them go "on the air" with campaign advertising. (In contrast, all presidential campaigns run ads throughout the primary and general-election campaigns.)

Name Recognition One of the most fundamental campaign strategies, particularly in congressional campaigns, is to build name recognition. Since many citizens know fairly little about congressional candidates, efforts to increase a candidate's name recognition in these races can deliver a few extra percentage points of support—enough to turn a close defeat into a victory. If the only thing a citizen knows is the name of one of the candidates,

Candidates may gain media attention and (if they are not incumbents) name recognition by hosting campaign events. During the 2020 presidential race, this became challenging due to the need for social distancing. While Biden scheduled town halls online, Trump held in-person events throughout the summer, including this one in Tulsa, Oklahoma, which was ultimately poorly attended.

that citizen will almost surely vote for that candidate on Election Day. The importance of name recognition is one reason why campaigns invest in buttons, bumper stickers, and yard signs—all of which help ensure that voters know a candidate's name.

Getting Out the Vote A second basic strategy is mobilization. Turnout is not automatic: just because a citizen supports a candidate does not mean that he or she will actually vote. Candidates have to make sure that their supporters go to the polls on Election Day. Moreover, focusing on getting supporters to the polls (or making sure they have an absentee ballot) is a relatively efficient use of candidates' resources. Given that most people don't pay much attention to politics, it's much easier to get a supporter to go to the polls than it is to convert an opponent into a supporter.

Campaign professionals refer to voter mobilization efforts as **GOTV ("get out the vote")** or the **ground game**.[32] Most campaigns for Congress or the presidency use extensive door-to-door canvassing, in which volunteers knock on doors and present their candidate's message to voters one at a time. Campaigns also commonly use phone banks, e-mail campaigns, and social media to reach out to potential supporters. To determine how best to contact these people and convince them to vote, both Republican and Democratic campaigns use sophisticated databases, combining voter registration data with demographics.[33] Sometimes these contacts are made through social media, but many campaigns still use volunteers to knock on doors and present their candidate's message to voters one at a time.

Sometimes candidates also try to decrease support and turnout for their opponent. One tactic is push polling, in which a candidate or a group that supports a candidate conducts a voter "survey," typically by phone, that isn't actually designed to measure opinions so much as to influence them. Campaigns use these so-called polls to spread false or misleading information about another candidate by including this (mis)information in questions posed to large numbers of citizens.

Going Positive or Negative? Candidates and other organizations also need to determine the tenor of their campaign—whether they emphasize their own (or their preferred candidates') qualifications and platform and refrain from critiquing their opponents (positive campaigning), or focus on criticizing their opponent's positions, experience, and lack of qualifications (negative campaigning). For example, when Senator Elizabeth Warren, who campaigned for the Democratic presidential nomination in 2020, talked about her life growing up or her work on reforming bankruptcy law, this was an example of positive campaigning. But when Warren attacked President Trump for not releasing his tax returns or mentioned allegations of sexual harassment against Trump, that was negative campaigning. Candidates and their supporters often try to raise doubts about their opponents by citing politically damaging statements or unpopular past behavior. In conducting opposition research, candidates and interest groups dig into an opponent's past for embarrassing incidents or personal indiscretions, either by the candidate or by a member of the candidate's family or staff.

The positive or negative tone of a campaign may not be driven completely by the candidates themselves. The Internet, for example, facilitates efforts to popularize damaging information. For example, in early October 2016, various media organizations released video of Donald Trump describing his pursuit of women in vulgar, disturbing terms—ending with the phrase "and when you're a star, they let you do it." While Trump later apologized and tried to explain his comments as "locker room talk," the availability of the video made it difficult for Trump to put the issue to rest. Trump's victory was even more notable in light of the negative publicity generated by media coverage of the video and its aftermath.

Candidates who are behind in the polls (or the organizations that support them) sometimes resort to attack ads: campaign ads that criticize the opponent. While all

GOTV ("get out the vote") or the **ground game**
A campaign's efforts to "get out the vote" or make sure its supporters vote on Election Day.

critical ads are categorized as negative campaigning, campaign experts distinguish between ads that criticize a candidate but at the same time accurately describe his or her action or position, and ads that stretch the truth (or break it outright). In this sense, Warren's criticisms of Trump were negative but factually correct; Trump has not released his taxes, and there were multiple harassment allegations made against Trump. On the other hand, an ad run during the 2017 special House election in Georgia falsely suggested that the Democratic candidate had ties to terrorist organizations, simply because the Middle Eastern news service Al Jazeera had run a story about the candidate and the race. Of course, attack ads often fail because they are too outlandish. However, some succeed in changing votes, while others force the opposing candidate to spend time and money denying the ads' claims.

Debates Candidates often contrast their own records or positions with those of opposing candidates or make claims designed to lower citizens' opinions of their opponents. Sometimes these interactions occur during a formal debate. Most congressional campaigns involve debates in front of an audience of likely voters, a group of reporters, or the editorial board of a local newspaper. Typically candidates take questions from reporters or a debate moderator, although sometimes candidates question each other or answer questions from the audience.

Presidential campaigns involve multiple debates during the primary and caucus season. Throughout the months before the first primaries and caucuses, each party's candidates gather for many single-party debates using a variety of formats. During the general election, the Republican and Democratic nominees meet for several debates. The number and format are negotiated by the campaigns and the Commission on Presidential Debates, a nonpartisan organization that coordinates the debates.[34] The 2020 presidential campaign featured two debates between the presidential nominees and one between the vice-presidential nominees. The debates not only give candidates a chance to present themselves to the electorate but also offer valuable free exposure. Given a relatively uninterested electorate, candidates must figure out how to present themselves to voters in a way that captures their attention and gains their support. Thus, during the 2016 and 2020 presidential election debates Republican Donald Trump positioned himself as a successful businessman who had managed the economy and the response to the COVID-19 pandemic—a good fit for Trump's status as a political outsider (despite being the incumbent president), a good match to voters' concerns about the economy, and a good way to turn his personal wealth into a campaign asset.

Campaign advertising: getting the word out

One of the realities of modern American electoral campaigns is that they are, for the most part, conducted indirectly—through social media, through news coverage of events, and (most important) through paid campaign advertising. Candidates, party committees, and interest groups spend more than several billion dollars during each election cycle on campaign-related activities by all candidates for federal office. Most of that money is spent on 30-second television spots. Campaign advertising is critical because, as we will discuss in Chapter 14, candidates cannot assume that citizens will take the time to learn from other sources about the candidates, their qualifications, and their issue positions.

What Do the Ads Involve? Campaign advertising has evolved considerably over the last generation.[35] During the early years of television, many campaign ads consisted of speeches by candidates or endorsements from supporters and they ran several minutes in length. In the 1964 presidential race, Lyndon Johnson's campaign ran a five-minute ad titled "Confessions of a Republican" that featured an actor talking about why he

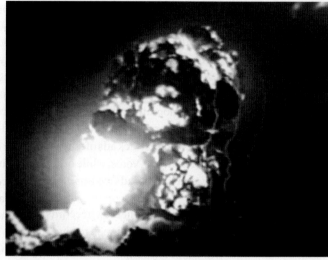

The "Daisy" ad from the 1964 presidential campaign interspersed images of a child in a field of flowers and footage of a nuclear detonation. It was broadcast only once but caused much controversy—and helped crystallize doubts about Republican candidate Barry Goldwater.

didn't want to vote for Republican presidential candidate Barry Goldwater.[36] Johnson's campaign also ran a one-minute ad titled "Peace Little Girl" (nicknamed "Daisy"), which featured a child holding a daisy and pulling its petals off as she counted them aloud one by one. In the background, a voice provided a parallel countdown to the detonation of a nuclear bomb. The ad ended as the television screen filled with the image of the mushroom cloud produced by the nuclear explosion.[37] The implication was that electing Goldwater would increase the chances of a future conflict involving nuclear weapons. The ad remains one of the most iconic pieces of campaign advertising.

Much like the "Daisy" ad, modern campaign ads are short, with arresting images that often use photomontages and bold text to engage a distracted citizenry. Content varies depending on who is running the ads. Table 13.2 provides data from

TABLE 13.2

Campaign Advertising by Major Spenders in the 2020 Presidential Election

The table shows total spending and the total number of ads, as well as the tone of those ads, as paid for directly by the candidates, their parties, and Republican PACs and Democratic PACs.

	Organization	Spending (Millions)	Number of Ads	Slant of Ads
Candidates	Biden campaign	$356.3	356,336	Mixed
	Trump campaign	31.8	261,633	Mostly positive
Parties	Republican National Committee	6.1	6,982	Mostly negative
	Democratic National Committee	6	7,525	Mostly negative
Republican Groups	America First Action	55.6	73,300	Mostly negative
	Preserve America PAC	57.8	30,963	Mostly negative
	Restoration PAC	9.7	6,991	Mostly negative
Democratic Groups	Future Forward	68.8	57,813	Mostly negative
	Independence USA PAC	21.7	19,063	Mostly negative
	Priorities USA Action	35.9	44,800	Mostly negative

Source: Calculated by the authors from data available at Wesleyan Media Project, mediaproject.wesleyan.edu (accessed 11/9/20).

campaign ads in the 2020 presidential general-election campaign from candidates, parties, and interest groups (the top three from each side are listed). These data show that the Biden campaign had a sizable financial advantage over the Trump campaign. Trump also spent less in 2016 than Clinton did. The table also shows a striking difference in ad content: while the candidates ran a mix of positive and negative ads, ads run by political parties and interest groups were uniformly negative.

Do Campaign Ads Work? One critical question about campaign advertising is whether the ads work—whether they shape what people know or influence their voting decisions or other forms of participation. Some observers have complained that campaign ads (particularly negative ads) depress voter turnout and reinforce citizens' negative perceptions of government, although political science research has uncovered no evidence for either effect.[38] Many of these arguments focus on attack ads or negative campaigning. Ads have portrayed candidates as evil blimps hovering over Washington, D.C., or even "demon sheep."[39]

Whether positive or negative, and regardless of whether they feature evil blimps or something else, campaign ads seek to catch voters' attention, to get them to focus on a race long enough to consider the candidates and their real messages. Nonetheless, studies of campaign advertising have shown that most of the time campaign ads fail at this task. Most citizens ignore the ads or remain unconvinced of their messages. For example, during the 2020 presidential nomination campaign Democrat Mike Bloomberg spent hundreds of millions of dollars on campaign ads, only to find that citizens simply did not want to vote for him regardless of how many ads his campaign ran. In the 2016 general election, Hillary Clinton lost despite vastly outspending Donald Trump on campaign ads. And while President Trump campaigned in 2020 on a theme of effective management of the economy and the response to COVID-19, polls showed that Republicans responded favorably to Trump's message, but most Democrats and Independents did not believe it.

Insofar as ads matter and Americans pay attention to politics, studies of campaign advertising suggest that Americans are reasonably thoughtful when assessing campaign ads. Evidence suggests that campaign advertising has several beneficial effects. Researchers have found that people who are exposed to campaign ads tend to be more interested in the campaign and to know more about the candidates.[40] Moreover, many campaign ads highlight real differences between the candidates and the parties.[41] Nonetheless, average citizens know that they cannot believe everything they see on television, so campaign advertising, if it does anything at all, captures their attention without necessarily changing their minds.[42] (See the What Do the Facts Say? feature on p. 582 for more on evaluating facts in the media.) This is particularly true for negative campaign ads, which sometimes drive support away from the candidate running them. As a result, candidates often rely on party committees and interest groups to run negative ads. Then the candidates themselves can run more positive ads (recall Table 13.2) and can try to disassociate themselves from the negative ads run by others.

In the end, despite all the money and effort poured into campaign advertising, these messages must be designed to capture the attention of citizens whose interest in politics is minimal, delivering a message that can be understood without too much interpretation. In this way, campaign advertising reflects an old political belief, that most things candidates do in campaigns are wasted efforts that have little impact on the election—this is why political scientists stress the importance of the fundamentals when trying to predict election outcomes.

In the 2020 presidential race, many of the ads aired by the Trump campaign and Republican groups criticized Joe Biden for his son Hunter's business dealings in Ukraine. As you can see in this ad, these groups questioned whether the Bidens asked for money in return for political favors—a quid pro quo arrangement.

Think about it

- **What techniques could you use** to check a map or figure to ensure the data presented represent "just the facts" and not the author's opinions?
- **What are several sources** of reliable political information or data?

Do Maps Offer "Just the Facts"?

When reading media coverage of politics, it's important to consider the source—the author of the story. In many cases, stories that ostensibly offer "just the facts" are cherry-picking data to support a particular point of view. When a story is written by an overtly partisan individual or publication, a closer look often reveals that the story's facts have been misreported or interpreted in an incorrect or limited way.

One example is the "try to impeach this" map that was featured on Fox News host Sean Hannity's Web page and other conservative, pro-Trump media outlets in fall 2019 during the House impeachment hearings.[a] Counties where Trump received a majority of votes in 2016 were shown in red, while counties Hillary Clinton won were shown in blue. As you see, most of the country is red, with some blue counties on the coasts—supporting Hannity's argument that the Democratic move to impeach Trump amounted to undoing Trump's 2016 electoral victory.

Should we take this map as a serious, fair depiction of political reality? One reason to be suspicious is that Hannity makes no secret of his conservative ideology or the fact that his audience consists mostly of conservative Republicans. This is not to say that Hannity intentionally lies or misrepresents the facts, but simply to point out that his website is hardly the place to look for dispassionate analysis. In fact, the Fox TV network, which broadcasts Hannity's show, classifies it as opinion rather than news.

It also turns out that the map is both incorrect and misleading.[b] For one thing, it mistakenly classifies some counties in the middle of the country as red that should be blue. The bigger problem is that the red/blue classification doesn't consider population density—most of Trump's wins were in low-population rural counties, while Clinton won many high-population urban centers. Even though Trump won more counties than Clinton, Clinton received over 3 million more votes.

Campaign finance

"Campaign finance" refers to money collected for and spent on campaigns and elections by candidates, political parties, and other organizations and individuals. The **Federal Election Commission (FEC)** is in charge of administering election laws, including the complex regulations pertaining to how campaigns can spend money. Changes in campaign finance rules, which were passed as the **Bipartisan Campaign Reform Act (BCRA)**, took effect after the 2002 elections and have been modified by subsequent Supreme Court decisions, most notably *Citizens United v. Federal Election Commission* (2010) and *McCutcheon v. Federal Election Commission* (2014), which we describe later.

While campaign finance law is complex, most Americans believe the effects of campaign finance are simple: candidates cannot win without spending money, victory goes to the candidate with the larger budget, and, as a result, candidates listen to large donors and ignore average citizens. They also believe that elections cost too much. The reality is much more complex. Candidates need money to run effective campaigns (particularly to pay for campaign ads), but spending does not guarantee victory. And while candidates court large donors, they are even more obsessed with winning the support of ordinary citizens, because in the end elections are about votes, not money.

Types of Contributions and Funding Organizations The limits on campaign contributions in the BCRA—also known as the McCain-Feingold Act—vary depending on whether contributions are made by an individual or a group and by the type of group, as shown in Table 13.3. These limits were modified in April 2014 by a 5-4 ruling in *McCutcheon v. Federal Election Commission*, in which the Supreme Court struck down limits on overall campaign contributions to candidates and PACs. A second Supreme Court decision, *Citizens United v. Federal Election Commission*, also eliminated restrictions on campaign advertising by corporations, organizations, and labor unions within 30 days of a primary or 60 days of a general election, which had led to large increases in spending by these groups.

Federal Election Commission (FEC)
The government agency that enforces and regulates election laws; made up of six presidential appointees, of whom no more than three can be members of the same party.

AP®
SUPREME
COURT CASE

Bipartisan Campaign Reform Act (BCRA)
An act passed in 2002 that amended the Federal Election Campaign Act of 1971 to change campaign finance rules.

Citizens United v. Federal Election Commission
A 2010 Supreme Court case that decided that independent spending in campaigns by corporations and labor unions is a form of protected speech under the First Amendment. This overturned a provision of the Bipartisan Campaign Reform Act that restricted corporations and unions from spending money to advocate for the election or defeat of a candidate.

Contribution Limits in the 2020 Elections

TABLE
13.3

The BCRA of 2002 put into effect limits on how much individuals, organizations, and corporations could contribute to candidates' primary and general-election campaigns. The limits were changed based on Supreme Court decisions in 2010 and 2014. At present, although there are still limits on contributions that individuals and PACs can make to each individual candidate, there are no limits on total overall contributions to multiple candidates by individuals and PACs.

	Individual Candidates	National Party Committees	State, District, and Local Parties	PACs	Limit on Total Contributions
Individuals	$2,800	$35,500	$10,000 (combined limit)	$5,000	No limit
PACs	$5,000	$15,000	$5,000 (combined limit)	$5,000	No limit
National Party Committees	$5,000	No limit	No limit	$5,000	$49,600 to Senate candidate per campaign
State, District, and Local Party Committees	$5,000 (combined limit)	No limit	No limit	$5,000 (combined limit)	No limit

Source: Federal Election Commission, "Contribution Limits for 2019–2020," www.fec.gov/resources/cms-content/documents/contribution_limits_chart_2019-2020.pdf (accessed 3/1/20).

DID YOU KNOW?

Candidates, parties, and organizations spent a total of

$11 billion

during the 2019–2020 election cycle.
Source: OpenSecrets.org

Political action committees spend millions on campaign advertising. Often, their ads are highly negative. This one attacks Donald Trump for being homophobic in his rhetoric.

Current law distinguishes between independent expenditures, in which a party or group spends money to advocate for a candidate but the candidate or the campaign does not control, direct, or approve the activity, and coordinated expenditures, in which the candidate has some control. Independent expenditures are not limited, but coordinated expenditures are. For example, in Senate races, there is a cap on coordinated expenditures by political parties, ranging from several hundred thousand dollars in small states like Delaware to several million dollars in California.

A second distinction in campaign finance laws is between hard money, meaning contributions to a candidate, party organization, or other group that are intended to help elect or defeat a specific candidate, and soft money, meaning funds that are used for other activities and are not subject to the limits imposed on hard money. Groups defined by IRS regulations as 527 organizations, for example, can raise unlimited soft money from individuals or corporations for voter mobilization and for issue advocacy, but these expenditures must not be coordinated with a candidate or a party. Ads by 527s cannot advocate the election or defeat of a particular candidate or political party.[43] Another type of organization, again described using the IRS code, is the 501(c)(4), which often collects and spends soft money. The principal difference between 527s and 501(c)(4)s is that the latter type of organization does not have to disclose the names of its contributors.

A third type of organization, the political action committee (PAC), is a group that aims to elect or defeat particular candidates or a particular political party. A company or an organization can form a PAC and solicit contributions from employees or group members. As Table 13.3 shows, the amount PACs can give to each candidate in an election is limited, but these limits pertain only to hard money. PACs can also form 527s, which can then accept unlimited amounts of soft money. So-called Super PACs are PACs that do not donate to candidates but use soft money to make unlimited independent expenditures in campaigns. Chapter 12 looked more closely at PACs, 527s, and 501(c)(4)s.

As discussed in Chapter 11, political party committees are entities within the Republican and Democratic parties. Both major parties have a national committee and a campaign committee in each house of Congress. Party committees are limited in the amount of hard money they can give to any given candidate's campaign and in the amount they can spend on behalf of the candidate as a coordinated expenditure. But a party committee (and, after *Citizens United*, organizations, corporations, and labor unions) can spend an unlimited amount in independent expenditures to elect a candidate or candidates.

Current law gives presidential candidates the ability to receive federal campaign funds for the primary and general-election campaign (in the primary, these are matching funds; in the general election, they are a block grant). These federal funds are generated, in part, by money that taxpayers voluntarily allocate out of the taxes they pay to the federal government by checking off a particular box on their federal tax return form. Funds are also given to minor political parties if their candidate received more than 5 percent of the vote in the previous election. However, in order to accept federal funds, presidential candidates must abide by overall spending limits (and, during the nomination process, by state-by-state spending caps). During the last two presidential campaigns, all the major candidates decided against accepting these funds during the nomination and general-election campaign, which meant that they were not bound by the spending caps (although individual contributors were still limited to the amounts shown in Table 13.3).

The Effects of Money in Politics Campaign finance regulations reflect two simple truths. First, any limits on campaign activities involve balancing the right to free speech about candidates and issues with the idea that rich people or well-funded

TABLE
13.4

Candidate, Party, and Interest-Group Election Fund-Raising, 2018–2020

	2018	2020
Presidential Candidates		
Republican	—	$595,630,157
Democrat	—	$937,673,077
Congressional Candidates		
House incumbents	$711,117,909	$1,007,981,450
House challengers	$438,927,947	$427,837,316
House open-seat candidates	$384,890,754	$274,002,516
Senate incumbents	$539,389,767	$627,228,374
Senate challengers	$350,187,926	$765,656,874
Senate open-seat candidates	$82,890,927	$80,371,448
Political Parties		
Republicans	$859,438,792	$2,303,011,274
Democrats	$802,172,215	$1,022,879,060
Independent Expenditures	$1,110,325,920	$2,973,234,720
Totals	$5,279,342,217	$11,015,506,266

Candidates and political parties raise and spend a great deal of money in their campaigns. Do these numbers help explain the high reelection rates for members of Congress?

Source: Calculated by the authors from data at www.opensecrets.org (accessed 11/11/20).

organizations should not be allowed to dominate what voters hear during the campaign. Second, an enormous amount of money is spent on American elections. Table 13.4 shows the amounts raised by candidates, political parties, and others in 2018 and 2020. More than $11 billion was raised during 2020, a presidential election year, and more than $5 billion was raised for the 2018 midterms. Moreover, campaign spending is concentrated among a relatively small number of organizations with sizable electioneering budgets. In each of the last several election cycles, the largest organizations have spent hundreds of millions of dollars on contesting the election.

The principal concern about all this campaign cash is that the amount of money spent on candidates' campaigns might matter more than the candidates' qualifications or issue positions. That is, candidates—in particular, wealthy candidates who could self-fund their campaigns—could get elected regardless of how good a job they would do, simply because they had more money than competing candidates to pay for campaign ads, polls, a large staff, and mobilization efforts. Another concern is that individuals and organizations or corporations that can afford to make large contributions (or to fund their own electioneering efforts) might be able to dictate election outcomes or, by funding certain candidates' campaigns, garner a disproportionate amount of influence over the subsequent behavior of elected officials. In the main, these concerns affect soft money contributions and independent expenditures because the current law places no limits on how much soft money a party can collect, or on the size of a group's independent expenditures (see the Take a Stand feature).

Is There Too Much Money in Politics?

Campaign finance regulations place restrictions on what Americans can do to influence election outcomes—but should they? Suppose you are a wealthy individual who wants to help elected candidates who agree with your worldview. Under current law, you can make relatively small direct contributions to these candidates, but you can also form one of several types of organizations that can spend unlimited money to run campaign ads, or you can donate to an existing organization that will do the same thing. Clearly, having money gives you options for participation in American elections that are not open to the average citizen. (This is the chief criticism of the *Citizens United* decision that struck down limits on independent spending.) Is that a good thing?

It's a free country, and spending money on politics is part of that freedom. Limits on campaign spending conflict with fundamental tenets of American democracy. The Bill of Rights states that Congress cannot abridge "freedom of speech, or of the press; or the right of the people peaceably to assemble, and to petition the Government for a redress of grievances." One interpretation of the First Amendment that has shaped recent Supreme Court decisions on campaign finance is that people should be free to spend whatever they want on contesting elections—excluding bribes, threats, and other illegal actions, of course.

Another argument for eliminating limits on political activities is that with one exception—donations to 501(c)(4) organizations—donors and political activists are required to file quarterly reports on their campaign activities. Therefore, other activists and even ordinary citizens would quickly learn of any large-scale attempts to manipulate election outcomes and could decide to work for the other side or simply vote against a big donor's preferred candidates.

And ultimately, given that campaign spending is no guarantee of electoral success, it is not clear that eliminating spending limits would give big donors control over election outcomes.

Campaign contributions need to be constrained. Even if there's no evidence that money buys elections, there is also no guarantee that under the right circumstances a big donation or ad campaign would not make the difference for one or more candidates. Because money for ads is a necessary component of a political campaign, the possibility remains that a rich donor could change election outcomes by giving large sums to challengers in congressional elections. And in close races, giving a candidate extra funds to increase his or her GOTV efforts or to run additional campaign ads might be enough to change the outcome.

With this possibility in mind, it makes sense to place broad limits on campaign contributions and independent expenditures to level the playing field between ordinary citizens and political activists with deep pockets. The fact that someone is rich shouldn't give him or her additional ways to influence election outcomes.

Moreover, while it is true that limiting campaign activities requires imposing limits on speech rights, limitations on civil liberties are nothing new. All the individual rights set out in the Bill of Rights are limited in one way or the other. Even freedom of speech is limited in areas such as hate speech and statements that pose a clear and present danger. Imposing limits on campaign activities could be justified on the grounds that maintaining free and fair elections is important enough to justify a modest limitation on what individuals and organizations can do to influence election outcomes.

Does money equal speech or should campaign contributions be limited?

Does the risk of allowing rich donors disproportionate power over elections outweigh the dangers associated with restricting their speech rights?

take a stand

1. Limits on individual campaign contributions guard against allowing wealthy people to dominate elections. What are some of the possible drawbacks of such regulations?

2. Under current law, corporations and unions (not just individuals) are allowed unlimited political expenditures as long as they are independent of a candidate's campaign organization. Why do you think independent expenditures are less regulated than direct contributions to campaigns?

When you look at campaign finance data, the first thing you will see is that it is easy to find which individuals or organizations gave money to a candidate, political party, or other organization.[44] Thus, if you are worried that a particular organization is using campaign contributions to influence elected officials, you can learn which officeholders have received the group's donations. In fact, campaign finance records are so readily available that it is generally easy to identify fraudulent organizations.

However, the raw data do not always tell the whole story. For example, while total spending is often quite high, it is important to remember that a large percentage of campaign expenditures are for advertising. A 30-second ad on a major television network can cost tens or hundreds of thousands of dollars.[45] Given that even House campaigns may run hundreds of ads and presidential campaigns generally run tens of thousands of ads, it is easy to see why campaign costs pile up so quickly.

There is little evidence that campaign contributions alter legislators' behavior or that contributors are rewarded with votes supporting their causes or favorable policies. Research suggests that most contributions are intended to help elect politicians whom contributors already like, with no expectation that these officials will do anything differently because they received a contribution.[46] On the other hand, contributions may help with access, getting the donor an appointment to present arguments to a politician or his or her staff.[47] And yet people and organizations that generally contribute are already friendly with the politicians they support, so the politicians would likely hear their arguments in any case.

It's also clear that having a lot of campaign cash doesn't make a candidate a winner—and winners don't always outspend their opponents. The poster-children for this argument are billionaires Tom Steyer and Mike Bloomberg, who both ran for the Democratic presidential nomination in 2020. Both candidates spent millions on their campaigns, running thousands of ads, opening field offices, and hiring large staffs. Even so, both failed to attract much support. And in the 2016 general election, Hillary Clinton's campaign outspent Trump's by nearly $200 million. The Democratic Party and allied outside groups also outspent the Republican Party and its groups by a similar amount. Even so, Trump won. Of course, Trump entered the campaign with high levels of name recognition and his campaign message resonated with Republican primary voters. But that is exactly the point: victories aren't bought with campaign cash. Candidates need a base level of funding to hire staff, travel, and run some campaign ads. Beyond that point, success is a function of what candidates say and do, not the dollar amount of contributions they receive or the number of ads run on their behalf.[48]

"Why Should I Care?"

When you follow the news about political campaigns, pay attention to the money candidates raise (and spend), where they campaign (and to whom they appeal), the tone and message of their campaigns, and larger fundamentals, such as the strength of the economy. These factors can provide strong clues about who is likely to win (or lose). Remember, though, that politicians don't win elections just by spending a lot of money. Sometimes candidates win despite lower budgets. The other factors listed here and examined in this chapter often have stronger effects on the outcome than money alone.

How do voters decide?

All the electoral activities we have considered so far are directed at citizens: making sure they are registered to vote, influencing their voting decisions, and getting them to the polls. In this section, we examine how citizens respond to these influences. The first thing to understand is that the high level of attention, commitment, and energy exhibited by candidates and other campaign actors is not matched by ordinary citizens. We have seen throughout this chapter and others that although politics is everywhere and elections are the primary mechanism citizens have to control the federal government, only a minority of citizens report high levels of interest in campaigns, many people know little about the candidates or the issues, and many people do not vote.[49]

Who votes, and why?

Politics is everywhere, but getting involved is your choice. Voting and other forms of political participation are optional. Surprisingly, even a strong preference between two candidates may not drive citizens to the polls. They may not be motivated to vote because they feel that their vote is just one of many.[50] And it's true that the only time a vote "counts," in the sense that it changes the outcome, is when the other votes are split evenly so that one vote breaks the tie. Moreover, voting involves costs. Even if citizens don't learn about the candidates but want to vote anyway, they still have to get to the polls on Election Day. Thus, the **paradox of voting** is this: Why does anyone vote, given that voting is costly and the chances of affecting the outcome are small?

Figure 13.2 shows that among Americans the percentage of registered voters who actually voted in recent presidential elections has been around 60 percent, although actual turnout (votes as a percentage of the total adult population) has been closer

After registering and informing themselves about the election, voters have to take the time to go to the polls and possibly wait in line. Voting is costly in terms of time and effort. In 2020, during the coronavirus pandemic, it became a calculated health risk too, as people struggled to socially distance while waiting.

paradox of voting
The question of why citizens vote even though their individual votes stand little chance of changing the election outcome.

FIGURE 13.2

Turnout in Presidential and Midterm Elections, 2000–2020

The figure shows how turnout of registered voters varies both over time and between presidential and midterm elections. Why don't more people vote in midterm election years? Why don't more people vote in any given year?

Source: United States Election Project, www.electproject.org (accessed 11/9/20).

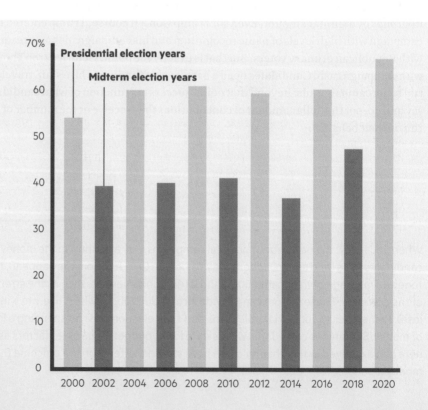

to 50 percent.[51] Turnout is significantly higher in presidential elections than in midterms—in 2020, turnout hit new highs despite the pandemic, largely due to widespread mail-in voting. Turnout is much lower in primaries and caucuses: in the 2020 presidential primaries, some states reported unusually high turnout exceeding 30 percent, although in cases like the Wisconsin primary held in April 2020 during the COVID-19 lockdown, most of the voters cast absentee ballots. Turnout for caucuses is generally only a few percentage points.

In the main, turnout is higher for Whites than for non-Whites (African Americans were an exception in 2008 and 2012, when Barack Obama was on the ballot), for older Americans than for younger Americans, and for college graduates than for people with a high school education or less. Men and women, however, say they vote at roughly the same rate. Many factors explain variation in turnout. Turnout is also affected by structural factors, such as state laws that prohibit convicted felons from voting, laws that require citizens to be registered to vote a set number of days before an election, variation in early-voting and voting-by-mail laws, laws requiring a photo ID to vote, and laws that make it easier or harder to obtain an absentee ballot.

However, turnout is far below 100 percent, even in areas of the country where all of these factors are set to make it easy for people to vote. Analysis shows that turnout is much higher among people who consider going to the polls an obligation of citizenship, feel guilty when they do not vote, or think that the elections matter. Turnout is much lower among those who are angry with the government, think that government actions do not affect them, or think that voting will have no impact on government policy. Citizens who hold these beliefs are unlikely to care about the outcome of the election, are unlikely to feel guilty for abstaining, and are unlikely to see voting as an obligation.[52] Thus, while it is possible to increase turnout somewhat by changing laws, the biggest gains come from convincing individual Americans that voting is something they should feel obligated to do.

These findings demonstrate the importance of mobilization in elections. As we discussed earlier, many candidates for political office spend at least as much time trying to convince their supporters to vote as they do trying to persuade others to become supporters in the first place. Because many Americans either do not vote or vote only sporadically, mobilization is a vital strategy for winning elections.

How do people vote?

Some people are highly interested in politics, collect all the information they can about the candidates, and vote based on this information; they are known as **issue voters**.[53] But most citizens are not interested enough in politics to spend their time that way, and they don't care enough about the details of politics to find out which candidates come closest to their preferences. Reliable information about candidates is also often difficult to find. Although candidates, parties, and other organizations produce a blizzard of endorsements, reports, and press releases throughout the campaign, much of this information may be difficult to interpret. It is a daunting task, even for the rare, highly motivated voter.

Voting Cues This combination of a lack of interest and the relatively complex task of seeking information leads the majority of American voters to base their voting decision on easily interpretable pieces of information, or **voting cues**.[54] Voters in American national elections use many kinds of cues, such as party ID (voting for the candidate who shares your party identification, as we discussed in Chapter 11), the personal vote (voting for a candidate who has helped you get assistance from a government agency or has helped your community benefit from desirable government projects), personal

During campaigns, candidates often seek to strengthen the perception that they share (or at least are sympathetic to) average Americans' beliefs and interests. Here, Senator Kamala Harris (D-CA, center), who became the vice presidential candidate on the Democratic ticket, meets with constituents at the Martin Luther King Jr. Kingdom Day Parade in Los Angeles.

issue voters
People who are well informed about their own policy preferences and knowledgeable about the candidates, and who use all of this information when they decide how to vote.

voting cues
Pieces of information about a candidate that are readily available, easy to interpret, and lead a citizen to decide to vote for a particular candidate.

characteristics (voting for the candidate whose personal characteristics such as age, race, gender, ethnicity, religious beliefs, or background match your own), or pocketbook voting (voting for the incumbent if the economy is strong and for the challenger otherwise). Voters can also use multiple cues. Cues give people a low-cost way to cast what political scientist and campaign consultant Samuel Popkin called a reasonable vote—a vote that, more likely than not, is consistent with the voter's true preference among candidates.[55] Studies have found that citizens who use cues and are politically well informed are more likely to cast a reasonable vote than those who use cues but are otherwise relatively politically ignorant. In essence, knowing something about the candidates and the issues at stake in an election helps people select the right cue on which to base their vote.[56]

On the one hand, the role that cues play in voting decisions is one reason why "the fundamentals matter" in American elections. Because some people vote based on the state of the economy, incumbent presidents are good bets to win reelection when economic conditions are good and poor bets when the economy is in trouble. Similarly, because party ID is often used as a cue, candidates are more likely to win if their party affiliation is shared by the bulk of voters in their state or district. On the other hand, the use of cues also implies that candidates (and campaigns) matter. For example, citizens may use a candidate's record in office to guide their vote decision, especially if the candidate makes this record a central theme in his or her campaign speeches and advertising. In fact, many campaign events and communications are designed to reinforce the impression that candidates share voters' concerns and values. For example, at several points during the 2016 campaign, Donald Trump tweeted pictures of his fast-food dinner on the campaign plane.

Moreover, because personal characteristics are used as a cue, some candidates have a better chance of winning than others, because they have one or more cues that citizens see as desirable. For example, some people voted for Joe Biden in 2020 because of his political career, because of his perceived ideological moderation, or simply because he was a Democrat. Equally, some people voted for Donald Trump because of his career as a businessman or because he was a Republican. Table 13.5 offers some details on what kind of candidate characteristics attract voter support.

TABLE 13.5

Candidate Traits and Voter Choice

Many Americans cast votes based on candidates' personal characteristics and background. What sorts of candidates are advantaged by this practice—and what sorts are disadvantaged?

Source: Pew Research Center, "Faith and the 2016 Campaign," www.pewforum.org/2016/01/27/faith-and-the-2016-campaign/ (accessed 6/18/20).

Likelihood of Supporting a Candidate Who . . .	More Likely	Less Likely	Wouldn't Matter
Has served in the military	50%	4%	45%
Attended a prestigious university	20	6	74
Is Catholic	16	8	75
Has Washington experience	22	31	46
Is an Evangelical Christian	22	20	55
Is Mormon	5	23	69
Has used marijuana in the past	6	20	74
Had personal financial troubles	8	41	49
Is an atheist	6	51	41
Is gay or lesbian	4	26	69
Had an extramarital affair in the past	3	37	58

Note: Categories do not total 100 percent because "don't know"/refused responses are not captured here.

Many voters consider a candidate's military service as an asset, while Americans are less likely to support a candidate who is a known atheist, has had an extramarital affair, or has had personal financial troubles. Of course, candidate information is only one of the things a voter considers and some cues override others—businessman Donald Trump won the presidency despite having never been elected to political office, being 70 years old, and admitting to past extramarital affairs.

Who (usually) wins?

All the strategies discussed so far are used to some extent in every election. In normal elections, when congressional reelection rates are high, voters generally use cues that focus on the candidates themselves, such as incumbency, partisanship, a personal connection to a candidate, the candidate's personal characteristics, or retrospective evaluations. This behavior is consistent with what Tip O'Neill, Speaker of the House from 1977 to 1987, meant when he said that "all politics is local": many congressional elections are independent, local contests in which a candidate's chances of winning depend on what voters think of the candidate in particular—not the president, Congress, or national issues. It also explains why electoral coattails are typically very weak in American elections and why so many Americans cast split tickets rather than straight tickets. In the main, voting decisions in presidential and congressional elections are made independently of each other.

"Wave" elections generally occur when a large number of voters vote against incumbents because of poor economic conditions, political scandal, or a costly, unpopular war. In 2010, many Americans were concerned about the state of the economy, the size of corporate bailouts, the apparent ineffectiveness of economic stimulus legislation, and the enactment of health care reform, and they blamed the party in power (Democrats) for all of these outcomes. As a result, a significant percentage of Americans voted against Democratic congressional candidates, either as a protest vote, because they disapproved of their performance, or as an effort to put different individuals in charge in the hope that new members would bring about improved conditions. Ultimately, Republicans gained several seats in the Senate and regained majority control of the House with a nearly 80-seat gain. In contrast, 2020 was not a wave election: while Democrats won the presidency, Republicans captured House seats and only narrowly lost gaining majority control of the Senate.

Even in wave elections, reelection rates for members of Congress (the percentage of incumbents who successfully run for reelection) are generally high, as Figure 13.3 shows. Over the last generation, neither party has had a House reelection rate less than 80 percent; even in 2006, when 100 percent of Democratic House incumbents running for reelection won, the reelection rate for House Republican incumbents was almost 90 percent. In wave elections such as the one in 2010, one party's House reelection rate is significantly higher than that of the other party's; in normal elections such as the one in 2020, the House reelection rates are similar and approach 100 percent. Reelection rates for Senate incumbents are somewhat lower but show the same patterns.

Reelection rates for members of Congress are so high because the members work to insulate themselves from electoral challenges through tactics we discussed in this chapter and in and Chapter 4. They raise large sums of campaign cash well in advance of upcoming elections, use redistricting to give themselves a safe district populated by supporters, and enact pork-barrel legislation that provides government benefits and programs to their constituents. Even so, congressional incumbents are not necessarily safe from electoral defeat. Rather, their high reelection rates result from the actions

coattails
The ability of a popular president to generate additional support for candidates affiliated with his or her party. Coattails are weak or nonexistent in most American elections.

split ticket
A ballot on which a voter selects candidates from more than one political party.

straight ticket
A ballot on which a voter selects candidates from only one political party.

FIGURE 13.3

Percentage of House Incumbents Reelected, 2000–2020

The figure shows that, despite public dissatisfaction with Congress, incumbents still tend to be reelected in their respective districts. According to the chart, which congressional elections were wave elections? Which were normal elections?

Source: Calculated by the authors from election results.

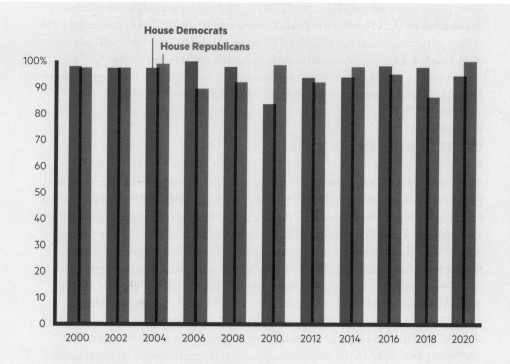

they take every day, which are calculated to win favor with their constituents. In normal elections, these strategies are generally enough to ensure reelection. In nationalized elections, however, they are not enough to guarantee reelection for some legislators from the disadvantaged party, such as Democrats in 2010.

Wave elections are somewhat rare—once a decade or less. Most of the time, not many citizens are highly concerned about national issues or hold strong opinions about the president, Congress, or the overall state of the nation. Congressional incumbents also work hard to focus attention during their campaigns on the good things they have done for their constituents. Plus, they generally run in states or districts where the majority shares their partisanship. And it is important to remember that even in wave elections some voters still use the incumbent-centered cues described earlier. In a wave election, voters don't suddenly become better informed about politics. Rather, some of them just switch to a different set of voting cues depending on the circumstances of the election.

"Why Should I Care?"

After each election, people look at the results and try to figure out what the election was about—why some candidates won and others lost. Before each election, would-be candidates wonder whether this is "the year" to run for office (you may be one of these candidates someday). The most important thing to understand is that there are no easy explanations and no guarantees. The problem is not that voters are fickle or clueless or that the rules are too complex. Rather, elections boil down to voters and the many different ways they decide how to vote. Knowing what is likely to influence voters can help you make predictions about who will win elections and thus what policies and issues government will tackle.

Understanding the 2018 and 2020 elections

In recent years, every election has been described as "the most important election in American history." And in truth, elections always matter because they determine who exercises power in Washington—who sets government policy. During the 2016 campaign, for example, it seemed likely that America's next president would appoint several Supreme Court justices, leading to significant policy changes on issues like abortion and affirmative action. Republican control of the presidency would make it easier to change President Obama's health care and financial reforms, as well as his executive orders. As we discuss throughout this book, the election of Donald Trump in 2016 has brought many of these outcomes to pass.

At one level, the essential question in 2020 was whether voters would support the Trump-Republican policy agenda of tax cuts, reductions in domestic spending and increases in military spending, loosening of business and environmental regulations, reestablishment of tariffs, further restrictions on immigration, and selection of conservatives to the federal judiciary. All of these issues were overshadowed by the debate over how to address the ongoing COVID-19 pandemic and its damage to America's economy and society, and who to blame for missteps in federal policy.

In political terms, the 2020 elections were scrutinized to see if the patterns seen in the 2018 elections would prove lasting or transitory. Would Democrats retain gains in rural and suburban areas, and among Republicans disenchanted with President Trump? Would the gender gap widen or narrow? Would minority turnout, which dropped in 2016 and bounced back somewhat in 2018, increase to earlier levels or grow even more, buoyed by nationwide protests demanding systemic changes in government and policing after the killing of George Floyd? How would the pandemic that still threatened the country impact voter turnout rates, especially for those groups particularly at risk for COVID-19—including the elderly, who are typically one of the most reliable voting blocs? The answers would determine which party held majorities in the House and Senate, and thereby shape the trajectory of government policy over the next two years.

The path to 2020: the 2018 elections

The 2018 elections involved campaigns for all 435 seats in the House of Representatives, as well as 35 Senate elections. At first glance, electoral forces favored Republicans in 2018, with a strong economy and no major international conflicts. However, sustained partisan polarization meant that economic factors were relatively less important than in previous elections. For many Americans, vote decisions were driven by party identification and their approval or disapproval of President Trump's performance in office.

The most important structural feature of 2018 was the partisan division of Senate seats: of the 35 seats contested, Democrats controlled 26 and the Republicans only 9. Moreover, of the dozen or so seats that were truly in play, 10 were Democratic, many of them in strongly Republican states such as North Dakota. Because Democrats had to divide campaign resources among a much larger number of seats than Republicans did, the odds favored Republican rather than Democratic gains.

In contrast, Democrats had notable opportunities in House contests. Democrats needed 23 seats to regain majority control—a number smaller than the average number of seats (about 30) gained by the party out of power in midterm House elections. Moreover, an abnormally high number of Republican incumbents retired rather than pursue another term. Some left because the party's rules forced them to step down

The 2018 midterms favored Republicans in the Senate because they had fewer seats to defend. However, Dean Heller (R-NV), the only Republican senator up for reelection in a state Hillary Clinton won in 2016, lost despite support from President Trump.

from committee chairs, some departed to pursue other offices, some retired because of scandals, and some left because they feared losing a primary or general election. These retirements raised Democratic hopes for gains in Republican-held suburban districts.

A final fundamental factor was a Democratic advantage in enthusiasm—national polls consistently showed higher levels of interest among Democrats compared to Republicans, as well as a Democratic advantage in polls asking which party respondents would like to control Congress.

The Campaign The early months of the election cycle set the tone for the entire campaign. In House campaigns, Democrats fielded many well-funded, politically experienced candidates, while Republicans struggled to find good replacements for retiring incumbents or as challengers against Democrats. And while Senate Republicans reinforced their structural advantage by nominating a slate of well-qualified candidates (including several House members and governors), Democratic incumbents such as Jon Tester (D-MT) and Joe Manchin (D-WV) ran effective campaigns that highlighted their attention to local concerns and willingness to vote with President Trump on issues vital to their states. Democrats also outraised their Republican opponents in many races. In the closing weeks of the campaign, most national-level predictions were close to expectations at the beginning of the election cycle: Democrats were likely to win a House majority, while Republicans would hold the Senate.

Within the parties, however, the campaign revealed important disagreements on policy. In several Democratic primaries, liberal challengers unseated long-time incumbent House members, including Joe Crowley (D-NY), who was chair of the Democratic Caucus. Many other Democratic challengers refused to commit to voting for Minority Leader Nancy Pelosi as Speaker if Democrats regained the majority. On the Republican side, several incumbents, including Senators Jeff Flake (R-AZ) and Bob Corker (R-TN), retired in the face of strong conservative opposition.

The Election During the final weeks of the campaign, polls revealed that many House and Senate seats were still in play, as President Trump also crisscrossed the country, holding rallies in strongly Republican areas. In the end, the 2018 election met expectations: Democrats gained a House majority by capturing Republican suburban districts and capitalizing on Republican open seats. In Senate elections, Democrats captured two seats (Nevada and Arizona) but lost other races, allowing Republicans to retain their Senate majority.

Exit polls that asked respondents about their vote in House elections showed that, for the most part, vote decisions reflected partisanship and opinions about President Trump. The 2018 results also showed a strong gender gap, with higher rates of Democratic voting among women, as well as a strong correlation of Democratic voting with race and with education. Moreover, voters in lower income brackets were much more likely to vote Democratic, while voters in higher income brackets showed similarly high rates of voting for Republicans (though interestingly, the gap between Democratic and Republican voters narrowed for those making over $100,000 per year).

The 2020 elections

The Nomination Process When Joe Biden entered the race for the Democratic presidential nomination in the summer of 2019, many people (and some political scientists) argued that he would have little chance of winning. Biden was a career politician who had held elected office for 47 years, running at a time when trust in government was near all-time lows. He had run two disorganized, unsuccessful presidential nomination campaigns. If elected, he would be 78 years old on Inauguration Day, making him the oldest person to begin a presidency by more than seven years.

In retrospect, however, Biden was a perfect fit for the political moment. His reputation as a centrist Democrat helped secure votes from moderate voters (especially White voters in the Midwest who were not college educated) who had defected to Trump in 2016. At the same time, his willingness to listen and respond to demands from liberal Democratic groups helped unify the party. Biden also had strong support from Black voters (a key Democratic constituency) in part because of his service as Barack Obama's vice president.

Biden faced strong opposition for the nomination from Senators Kamala Harris, Bernie Sanders, and Elizabeth Warren, as well as former mayor of South Bend, Indiana, Pete Buttigieg (the first openly gay candidate for a major-party presidential nomination), former New York City mayor (and billionaire) Michael Bloomberg, and a number of other candidates. While Biden did not do well in the early nomination contests, he scored a decisive win in the South Carolina primary in late February and won the most delegates in the Super Tuesday contests on March 3. By mid-March, as other candidates dropped out of the contest, Biden emerged as the clear favorite for the nomination. He spent the months until the Democratic National Convention in August 2020 building party unity. He further cemented his position by choosing Kamala Harris, a daughter of Indian and Jamaican immigrants, as his vice-presidential nominee.

The COVID-19 pandemic also worked against President Trump's reelection chances. A strong majority of Americans believed that Trump had mismanaged the pandemic, from failing to stockpile medical supplies or order early lockdowns, to discouraging mask wearing and frequently claiming that the end of the pandemic was almost in sight, only to be contradicted by increasing virus caseloads and fatalities.[57] These perceptions were reinforced after Trump, First Lady Melania Trump, and many senior aides caught the coronavirus after a public event in September 2020—an event at which most participants did not wear masks or socially distance. The shutdown of large parts of the economy as a result of the virus led to the loss of 22 million jobs from February through April; just over half of those jobs had been restored by Election Day, presenting an additional hurdle for Trump's reelection. While the pandemic and economic collapse did not cause a sharp decline in Trump's approval rating, they presented a strong, visible counterargument to his attempts to convince Americans that he deserved another term.

President Trump did not face significant opposition in the Republican nomination process. In fact, the entire process demonstrated his control over the party. He received a unanimous endorsement from the Republican National Committee in February 2020. Several states canceled their primaries and caucuses because Trump was the only candidate, and others used winner-take-all voting to ensure that only Trump would receive convention delegates. Finally, national committee members decided against producing a new party platform, instead endorsing the president and the platform adopted at the 2016 convention.

The 2020 General Election Campaign The 2020 general election campaign played out in the middle of the COVID-19 pandemic. In addition to being a major campaign issue, the pandemic transformed the campaign itself. To minimize risks to campaign workers and voters, the Biden campaign did almost no door-to-door canvassing, although Democratic-affiliated groups and the Trump campaign had modest operations. Joe Biden campaigned largely from the basement of his home via Zoom, holding only small, socially distanced events. The Trump campaign relied on large rallies as in 2016. While the Trump campaign began the nomination campaign with a significant financial advantage, it spent much of this cushion on early ads and field

After promising to choose a woman as his running mate, Joe Biden selected California senator Kamala Harris as the Democratic vice-presidential nominee in the 2020 presidential election. With the success of the Biden-Harris ticket, Harris made history as the first woman, the first Black American, and the first South Asian American to serve as vice president of the United States.

offices, forcing it to curb advertising during the general election campaign. In contrast, the Biden campaign raised unprecedented amounts of funds, allowing it to dominate the airwaves during the last few months of the election.

The campaign revolved around two sets of issues. The first involved the candidates themselves. Trump claimed that Biden was a moderate in name only, or that he would defer to the more liberal Harris. On this point, Biden's extensive career in office gave him an effective counter, as it demonstrated his relatively moderate leanings. Trump also argued that Biden lacked the energy and the mental acuity to serve as president, calling him "Sleepy Joe." Here again, Biden's campaign performance, including two national debates, effectively countered these attacks. At the same time, Trump was himself an issue. After four years of outrageous tweets, threats, and blustering against political opponents, and his apparent lack of interest in the details of governing (as exemplified by his perceived mismanagement of the COVID-19 pandemic), Trump's approval ratings were stuck in the low 40s.

The second set of campaign issues reflected the enduring split between the parties. In essence, Trump promised to continue tax cuts, limits on immigration, nominations of conservative judges, and rollbacks of government regulations. The Biden-Harris campaign promised to expand the size and scope of government, including new health care programs, more efforts to combat climate change, fewer limits on immigration (and a path to citizenship for undocumented individuals), and new efforts to limit police brutality against minority citizens.

Because COVID-19 had reduced the amount of campaigning by both candidates and generated uncertainty about turnout, both sides focused on the potential for an "October surprise"—an event that would cause citizens to reconsider their judgments about the candidates. The Trump campaign held high hopes for the first televised debate, believing that Trump could demonstrate that Biden was not up to the job. However, Trump's constant interruptions, muttered asides, and abrupt attacks on Biden only reinforced existing impressions of both candidates. Trump moderated his behavior in the second (and final) debate but was unable to make a convincing attack on Biden or his record. Late in October, the *New York Post* ran a story about a laptop owned by Biden's son Hunter that allegedly contained compromising e-mails. This story collapsed after a few days when it became clear that Trump supporters (including Trump's personal lawyer, former New York mayor Rudy Giuliani) had been involved in bringing the story to the *Post* and that there was no evidence that the laptop actually belonged to Hunter Biden.

The General Election Throughout the general election campaign, polls showed Biden with a significant national lead and smaller but consistent advantages in swing states. Biden's lead widened in early October, after Trump's poor performance in the first debate and his hospitalization for the coronavirus, then contracted slightly as the election approached. There was also uncertainty about who would actually cast votes, as most states expanded early voting and allowed no-excuse absentee (mail-in) voting in order to reduce the risks of holding an election during the pandemic. These concerns were magnified after President Trump repeatedly claimed during the campaign that mail-in voting would encourage fraud and urged his supporters to vote in person.

On Election Day, many observers were surprised by the strength of Trump's support in early returns. He outperformed the polls in several swing states, including Florida and Iowa. Democrats were unsuccessful in capturing Texas, although Biden did much better than other recent Democratic nominees. However, it soon became apparent that Trump's support was overstated by early returns, as several key states had not yet counted the large number of mail-in ballots, which were expected to favor Biden.

In the days after the election, county election boards processed the remaining ballots, giving Biden victories in Wisconsin, Michigan, and Pennsylvania (the "blue

**FIGURE
13.4**

Groups and Votes in the 2020 Elections

This figure shows variation in group support for Democrats and Republicans in the 2020 elections. How did the positions and issues emphasized by candidates in the two parties create or strengthen these differences?

Note: Percentages may not total 100 due to rounding. "Don't know" responses are not represented. Data are current as of 11/5/20.

Source: 2020 CNN Exit Polls, www.cnn.com /election/2020/exit-polls/president/ national-results (accessed 11/5/20).

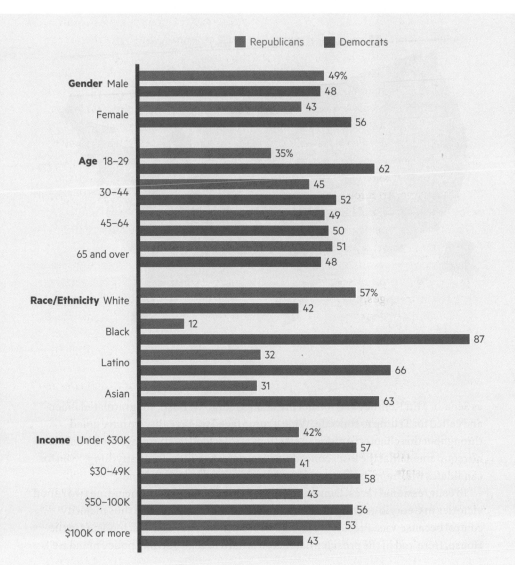

Legend: ■ Republicans ■ Democrats

		Republicans	Democrats
Gender	Male	49%	48
	Female	43	56
Age	18–29	35%	62
	30–44	45	52
	45–64	49	50
	65 and over	51	48
Race/Ethnicity	White	57%	42
	Black	12	87
	Latino	32	66
	Asian	31	63
Income	Under $30K	42%	57
	$30–49K	41	58
	$50–100K	43	56
	$100K or more	53	43

wall" of Democratic midwestern support that Trump won in 2016) as well as victories in Nevada, Arizona, and Georgia. Turnout was almost 67 percent, the highest in 120 years.[58] As Figure 13.4 shows, Biden had strong support from young voters, women, and minorities. In all, Biden received 306 electoral votes (see Figure 13.5).

During the few days it took to determine a clear winner in Pennsylvania, Nevada, and Georgia, President Trump issued numerous tweets and campaign press releases claiming that the extended vote count was fraudulent and that local election officials were stealing the election from him. While Trump was right in claiming that a high percentage of mail-in ballots favored Joe Biden, there was no evidence of misconduct at any level.[59] Biden's strength in the mail-in vote reflected the fact that Trump had discouraged his supporters from voting in this way, and that many mail-in ballots came from urban counties where many voters supported Biden.

After the major networks declared Biden the winner, Trump refused to concede the election or call Biden to congratulate him, and his campaign pursued legal challenges in some states. However, the courts did not sustain these claims, as the Trump campaign had no evidence to back them up. While some Republicans, including Senators Ted Cruz and Lindsey Graham, supported Trump's attacks, others, such

**FIGURE
13.5**

The 2020 Presidential Election: State by State

Note: 2020 Electoral map represents the authors' estimates as of 11/13/20. Two states split their electoral votes: in Maine, Trump received 1 vote and Biden 3; in Nebraska, Trump received 4 votes and Biden 1.

Source: Compiled by the authors.

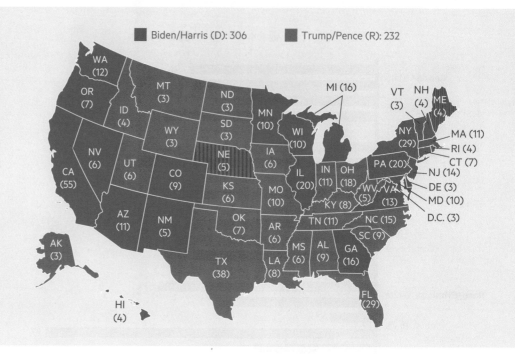

as Senator Mitt Romney and former president George W. Bush, congratulated Biden and called for Trump to concede. What Trump faced was a reality we have noted throughout this chapter: American elections are decided by counting votes. There is no requirement that the loser concede, accept defeat, or literally do anything. Even for candidates who happen to be president, elections are out of their hands.

In congressional races, Democrats netted three Senate seats (including two runoff victories in Georgia), giving them a 50-50 split in the chamber and thus majority control because Vice President Harris can break ties. They also lost ten seats in the House. Here and in the presidential race, it is hard to read a strong policy mandate

The 2020 presidential race was called for Joe Biden by all the major media outlets on November 7, four days after Election Day. Biden and his running mate, Kamala Harris, addressed the nation that night from Biden's hometown of Wilmington, Delaware, vowing to serve all Americans and unite the country—strong promises given the ongoing conflicts in American politics.

TABLE
13.6

		Biden	Trump
Approval of President Trump	Approve (47%)	9%	90%
	Disapprove (51%)	96	3
Most important issue	Racial inequality (20%)	91	8
	Coronavirus pandemic (17%)	82	14
	Economy (35%)	17	82
	Health care (11%)	63	36
Gender	Male (47%)	48	49
	Female (53%)	56	43
Race	White (65%)	42	57
	Non-White (35%)	72	26
Education	College graduate (44%)	55	42
	Not college graduate (56%)	49	49
Partisanship	Democrats (37%)	94	6
	Republicans (35%)	6	93
	Independents (28%)	54	40

Exit Polls in the 2020 Elections

Source: 2020 CNN Exit Polls, www.cnn.com/election/2020/exit-polls/president/national-results (accessed 11/5/20).

Note: Data may not always add up to 100 percent due to rounding.

into the election results. Table 13.6 shows clear policy differences between Biden voters and Trump voters—but given Democrats' narrow majorities in the House and Senate, it is unclear whether Biden can capitalize on his victory to pursue an aggressive policy agenda.

Consequences of the 2020 Election It is easy to imagine that Joe Biden's victory will lead to significant policy changes. Biden has reassembled the Democratic coalition that elected Barack Obama twice and regained control of the House of Representatives in 2018. Biden received millions more votes than Hillary Clinton did in 2016.[60] He leads a Democratic party that unified behind his candidacy, achieving record turnout despite the COVID-19 pandemic, including large numbers of new minority voters.

To be sure, Biden can accomplish a great deal using executive orders and personal action, such as rejoining the World Health Organization and the Paris Agreement on climate change, deprioritizing federal pursuit of undocumented individuals, increasing admissions of refugees, and rebuilding America's relations with other countries. But policies that require legislative action will occur only if Biden can hold together his narrow majorities in the House and Senate. At the same time, Senate Republicans are unlikely to agree to institutional changes that would help Biden, such as eliminating the filibuster or increasing the size of the Supreme Court. There are also deep splits among Democratic officeholders over policy priorities, including hot-button issues of climate change and renewable energy, police reform, immigration, and health care.

Biden also inherits the COVID-19 pandemic, and much of his first few years in office will be focused on deploying an effective vaccine and on returning the country to something approaching normal politics. Indeed, one of his first actions as president-elect was to appoint an informal task force to review current policies and make recommendations for new initiatives.

Finally, Biden leads a country that is as divided as ever. Biden's clear victory in the popular vote and the Electoral College is overshadowed by his razor-thin victories in Georgia, Michigan, Pennsylvania, and Wisconsin and the fact that over 70 million people voted for Donald Trump. Given that Trump vigorously contested the legitimacy of Biden's win, claiming without evidence that the election was stolen from him, many of his supporters are unlikely to ever accept Biden's presidency. Achieving policy victories under these conditions is certainly not guaranteed. What we know for sure is that politics matters, so the fight to win elections and shape government policy will continue unabated.

The Bipartisan Campaign Reform Act of 2002

A theme running throughout the discussions of different policies in this textbook has been their dynamic and changing nature. With some exceptions, most policies never really end. Often when political scientists say that one policy has replaced another, they really mean that the original policy was modified, some to a greater extent than others. When a new policy is adopted, it often includes some elements of the former policy. The Bipartisan Campaign Reform Act (BCRA) of 2002 is definitely the sequel to the Federal Election Campaign Act of 1971 (FECA).

Some might also say it is the new and improved version of FECA, but beside the inevitable opposition that any policy faces, unintended consequences always seem to arise. In fact, one of these unintended consequences occurred when the Federal Election Commission (FEC) allowed unlimited spending for party-building and get-out-the-vote campaigns, which Congress addressed in an amendment to FECA in 1979. Since they were supposed to be party-building activities, the ads were not supposed to be used to directly talk about the candidates or to influence the outcome of the elections, but over the years the line between party-building and influencing elections became hazier and hazier. The 2000 presidential election set a record for the amount of contributions to the two major parties, and this sparked many legislators to push for further electoral reform to end the loophole caused by the 1979 amendment to FECA.

It should come as no surprise that BCRA, while temporarily solving the issue of unlimited soft money spending, perhaps unintentionally opened new loopholes that were quickly exploited. The legislation allowed exemptions on contributions from nonprofit groups called 527 organizations. As a result, the number of these groups increased dramatically, and they now pose similar problems in terms of spending that soft money did before. As seen in the Possible Modifications, Expansion, or Termination of Policy stage, many spending limits and restrictions have been removed by Supreme Court decisions mostly on the basis of the First Amendment's right to free speech. Individuals and groups cannot have their freedom of speech curtailed simply because they have more money and therefore more resources to express their views. No policy on this subject has been able to fully reconcile the limitation on spending and the limitation on the right to free speech. Perhaps the feedback policy makers have received over the years means that they are not meant to be balanced and that members of Congress will have to come up with another approach.

Policy Stages

1. Problem Recognition
   - FECA was signed into law by President Richard M. Nixon on February 7, 1972.
   - The 1974 amendment to FECA was signed into law by President Gerald Ford on October 15, 1974.
   - The 1976 amendment to FECA was signed into law by President Ford on May 11, 1976.
   - The 1979 amendment to FECA was signed by President Jimmy Carter on January 8, 1980.
   - The use of soft money has increased since the 1974 amendment to FECA.
     - Soft money is not directly spent on candidates and is not subject to the limitations of hard money, which is spending used to help elect or defeat a specific candidate.
     - Over time the definition of "soft money" broadened so much that it became a practically meaningless term.

2. Agenda Setting
   - President George H. W. Bush vetoed the Congressional Campaign Spending Limit and Election Reform Act of 1992 on May 9, 1992.
   - Candidate Bill Clinton campaigned on electoral reform, especially limiting soft money, in the 1992 election.
   - President Clinton called for electoral reform during both of his terms, but his two campaigns benefited greatly from soft money.
   - In 1995 Senators Russell Feingold (D-WI) and John McCain (R-AZ) wrote an op-ed article in *Roll Call*, a D.C. newspaper covering Congress and the White House, arguing that limits should be placed on soft money.
   - McCain made campaign election reform a major campaign promise in his 2000 bid for the presidency, but he did not win the Republican primary.
   - Almost half a billion dollars was spent in the 2000 presidential election, which caused many members of Congress to push for more campaign finance reform.
   - The corporate scandals of Enron, Global Crossing, and Tyco in 2001 and 2002 made the public more amenable to financial reform in general.
   - Senators McCain and Feingold and Representatives Marty Meehan (D-MA) and Christopher Shays (R-CT) held a press conference on January 22, 2001, announcing a campaign finance reform bill.

3. Deliberation and Formulation
   - Representative Shays introduced the bill in the House of Representatives on June 28, 2001.
   - Numerous amendments were introduced in the House of Representatives, some of which passed and some of which failed.
   - The House of Representatives passed its version of the bill on February 14, 2002: **240 YEAs**: 198 Democrats, 41 Republicans, 1 other; **189 NAYs**: 12 Democrats, 176 Republicans, 1 other; **6 Not Voting**: 1 Democrat, 5 Republicans, 0 others.

4. Enactment
   - The House of Representatives had no further votes, and the Senate passed the House version of the bill on March 20, 2002: **60 YEAs**: 48 Democrats, 11 Republicans, 1 other; **40 NAYs**: 2 Democrats, 38 Republicans, 0 others; **0 Not Voting**.
   - BCRA was signed into law by President George W. Bush on March 27, 2002.

5. Implementation
   - BCRA went into effect on January 1, 2003.
   - **Title I: Reduction of Special Interest Influence**
     - It ended soft money contributions.
     - Political parties at the state level were able to receive more contributions.
     - Limits were imposed on how much money federal candidates could raise.
     - Formed primarily to influence elections through voter mobilization efforts and to issue ads that do not directly endorse or oppose a candidate, 527 organizations were exempt from contribution and spending restrictions.
   - **Title II: Noncandidate Campaign Expenditures**
     - Corporations and labor organizations could not pay for issue ads, which are supposed to deal with issues and not with specific candidates.
     - Issue ads are now considered electioneering communications.
     - Issue ads could not be aired 30 days before primaries and 60 days before general elections.
     - If costs for producing these ads exceeded a certain amount, reports had to be filed disclosing the costs and source(s) of the funds.
     - Individual contribution limits were increased for candidates, parties, and party committees at the local, state, and national levels.
     - Limits were imposed on how much individuals could contribute to candidates over a two-year period, indexed to inflation.
   - **Title III: Miscellaneous**
     - The ban on donations and contributions from foreign nationals was strengthened.
     - The "Millionaires' Amendment" raised the limit on contributions opposing candidates could receive if a candidate self-funded by more than a certain amount.
     - In an attempt to reduce the number of negative ads, the "Stand by Your Ad" provision required candidates to appear in campaign ads saying that they have approved of the message conveyed.
6. Evaluation
   - The law protects freedom of speech because the voices of lower- and middle-class people are not drowned out by the spending of the rich.
   - *McConnell v. Federal Election Commission* (2003)
     - Plaintiffs argued that banning soft money was beyond the scope of Congress's constitutional powers since it is a violation of freedom of speech to prevent people from using their own money as they see fit to express their political opinions.
     - Plaintiffs also argued that it was a violation of freedom of speech to regulate when political ads could be aired.
     - The Supreme Court essentially supported the major tenets of the law.
     - In his dissent, Justice Clarence Thomas argued that it is an infringement of the right of association to hinder people from contributing to political parties or candidates.
   - *Federal Election Commission v. Wisconsin Right to Life Inc.* (2007)
     - The plaintiff wanted to air ads trying to convince two senators to vote against using filibusters when considering judicial nominees.
     - The FEC contended that the ads were political ads and violated BCRA's rule about airing ads within the 60-day period before a general election.
     - The plaintiff claimed the ads were issue ads since they did not advocate for any particular candidate.

- The Supreme Court ruled that genuine issue ads were exempted from the 30- and 60-day blackout periods before primaries and general elections, respectively.
  - *Davis v. Federal Election Commission* (2008)
    - The plaintiff, a wealthy office seeker, contended that the "Millionaires' Amendment" violated the First Amendment's freedom of speech clause and the Fifth Amendment's implied equal protection principle that no person "shall be deprived of life, liberty, or property, without due process of law" because different competitors were subjected to different contribution limits.
    - The Supreme Court ruled that the "Millionaires' Amendment" violated the First Amendment but did not rule on the Fifth Amendment issue.
  - *McCutcheon v. Federal Election Commission* (2014)
    - The plaintiff contended that individual and overall contribution limits are a violation of freedom of speech and force contributors to make choices about whom to support.
    - The Supreme Court ruled that overall spending limits were unconstitutional but upheld individual contribution limits.
  - *Citizens United v. Federal Election Commission* (2010)
    - The conservative nonprofit organization wanted to show an anti-Hillary Clinton film before the Democratic primaries in 2008.
    - Screening this film violated the law's electioneering section.
    - Citizens United contended the law violated its freedom of speech.
    - The Supreme Court ruled on the following issues:
      - BCRA could not infringe upon the free speech of unions, corporations, or nonprofit organizations by forbidding them from spending money on advertising (that is, electioneering).
      - These groups must file disclosure reports.
      - These groups could still not directly contribute to candidates.

7. Possible Modifications, Expansion, or Termination of Policy
   - The Supreme Court rulings above changed portions of the law:
     - Genuine issue ads were exempted from the 30- and 60-day blackout periods before primaries and general elections, respectively.
     - The "Millionaires' Amendment" was eliminated because it violated the First Amendment.
     - Overall spending limits were considered unconstitutional, but individual contribution limits were upheld.
     - Unions, corporations, and nonprofit organizations were allowed to spend money on electioneering.

Questions for Discussion

1. How does the "Millionaires' Amendment" contribute to either the solution or the problem of increased campaign spending?
2. Should soft money be excluded from election campaigns? Why or why not?
3. Do you think candidates should be allowed to spend their own money on their campaigns? Explain your answer.

Unpacking the Conflict

Considering all that we've discussed in this chapter, let's apply what we know about how elections work to the example of Sara Gideon's loss in the 2020 Maine Senate election introduced at the beginning of this chapter. Ultimately, how meaningful was Susan Collins's victory in Maine in 2020—or Democrats' win of a Senate majority? What do election results tell us about why some candidates win and others lose? Why do these outcomes matter in American politics?

Candidates in American national elections compete for different offices using a variety of rules that determine who can run for office, who can vote, and how ballots are counted and winners determined. Election outcomes are shaped not only by who runs for office and how they campaign, who decides to vote, and how they decide whom to support, but also by the rules that govern electoral competition. By taking these factors into account for the 2020 election, we can explain why Susan Collins beat Sara Gideon, why Joe Biden defeated Donald Trump—and why Republicans lost the Senate and failed to recapture the House.

It is easy to complain about American elections. Citizens are not experts on public policy. They often know little about the candidates running for office. Candidates sensationalize, attack, and dissemble rather than giving details about what they would do if elected. Even so, however candidates campaign and voters vote, elections matter: there are clear, systematic differences between Democratic and Republican candidates that translate into different government policies depending on who holds office. Government policy will be different as a result of Biden's victory in 2020, but complicated by the Democrats' narrow majorities in both houses of Congress.

Campaigns and election outcomes would surely be different if more Americans were well informed about candidates and campaign platforms, if turnout was higher, if campaigns always focused on important issues facing the country, and if attack ads never worked. Even so, despite all their limitations, elections are how we decide who gets to run the government. And as we have discussed, election outcomes are somewhat predictable—they are the product of national and local rules and regulations; the fundamentals of district factors and national forces; candidates' campaign strategies; and citizens' decisions about whether to vote and whom to vote for. The outcome of every election is the result of all these individual-level choices added together. In that sense, election outcomes reflect the preferences of the American people.

"What's Your Take?"

Do the campaigns that candidates run significantly affect election outcomes, or are the outcomes out of the candidates' control?

Are individual election outcomes representative of larger trends?

AP® STUDY GUIDE

Summary

Expansion of opportunities for political participation has transpired through legislation (the Voting Rights Act) and through the suffrage amendments: Fifteenth (Black males), Nineteenth (women), and Twenty-Sixth (eighteen- to twenty-year-olds).

Elections in America generally have two steps. Primary elections select candidates for each party, and general elections determine who wins the office. Some of the rules for presidential elections differ from those for other elections; notably, the Electoral College system determines the winner of the general election.

Party organizations and candidates begin preparing for the next election the day after the last election ends. They focus on fund-raising and determining which races are likely to be competitive. Changes in campaign finance rules, which were passed as the Bipartisan Campaign Reform Act (BCRA), have been modified by subsequent Supreme Court decisions, most notably *Citizens United v. Federal Election Commission* (2010). Incumbents work throughout the election cycle to maintain their good standing among the voters and secure their reelection bids. During a campaign, candidates work hard, particularly through the use of advertisements, to increase their name recognition and mobilize their supporters. Although politics is everywhere, ordinary voters do not pay much attention to politics. Turnout rates are modest, and people know relatively little about the candidates and their positions. While some voters are highly interested in politics and collect all the information they can about the candidates, most voters make their decision based on voting cues. When it comes to voter behavior, political scientists have attempted to define the four most common types: **rational choice theory** (voting in one's own best interest), **retrospective voting** (voting based on the past voting record of a candidate or political party), **prospective voting** (voting based on what people think a candidate will do if elected to office), and **party-line voting** (voting consistently for the same political party at all levels of government). Most elections are determined by local-level politics, but occasionally national issues come to the fore. The 2020 campaign played out amidst the COVID-19 pandemic and revolved around two sets of issues: the first involved

rational choice theory
The behavioral theory that people vote in line with their own best interests.

retrospective voting
Voting based on the past voting record of a candidate or political party.

prospective voting
Voting based on what people think a candidate will do if elected to office.

party-line voting
Voting consistently for the same political party at all levels of government.

Key Terms

Bipartisan Campaign Reform Act (BCRA) (p. 583)

caucus (p. 562)

Citizens United v. Federal Election Commission (p. 583)

closed primary (p. 559)

coattails (p. 591)

delegates (p. 563)

election cycle (p. 570)

Electoral College (p. 565)

electoral votes (p. 565)

Federal Election Commission (FEC) (p. 583)

general election (p. 560)

GOTV ("get out the vote") or the **ground game** (p. 578)

hard money (p. 584)

incumbent (p. 559)

issue voters (p. 589)

majority voting (p. 561)

open primary (p. 559)

open seat (p. 572)

paradox of voting (p. 588)

party-line voting (p. 605)

plurality voting (p. 561)

popular vote (p. 565)

primary (p. 559)

proportional allocation (p. 563)

prospective voting (p. 605)

rational choice theory (p. 605)

retrospective voting (p. 605)

runoff election (p. 561)

semi-closed primary (p. 559)

soft money (p. 584)

split ticket (p. 591)

straight ticket (p. 591)

voting cues (p. 589)

winner-take-all (p. 563)

the candidates themselves and the second reflected the enduring split between the parties. Trump promised to continue tax cuts, limits on immigration, nomination of conservative judges, and rollbacks of government regulations. The Biden-Harris campaign promised new health care programs, more policies to combat climate change, fewer limits on immigration, and new efforts to reduce police brutality against minority citizens.

Enduring Understandings

MPA-3: "Factors associated with political ideology, efficacy, structural barriers, and demographics influence the nature and degree of political participation." (AP® U.S. Government and Politics Course and Exam Description)

PRD-2: "The impact of federal policies on campaigning and electoral rules continues to be contested by both sides of the political spectrum." (AP® U.S. Government and Politics Course and Exam Description)

Multiple-Choice Questions (Arranged by Topic)

Topic 5.1: Voting Rights and Models of Voting Behavior (MPA-3)

1. **Which of the following amendments led to an expansion of opportunities for political participation for young adults?**
   (A) Fifteenth Amendment
   (B) Nineteenth Amendment
   (C) Twenty-Fourth Amendment
   (D) Twenty-Sixth Amendment

2. **Which of the following quotes best describes the political voting behavior model of retrospective voting?**
   (A) "Campaigns don't end—they run out of money." —Richard Gephardt, former Speaker of the House and presidential candidate
   (B) "Are you better off than you were four years ago?" —Ronald Reagan, running for president against incumbent Jimmy Carter
   (C) "The blue wave is not a weather event. . . . It's made. You have to go out and knock on doors and make phone calls and do the work. That's how it happens—you've got to make the wave happen." —Jason Kander, founder of Let America Vote
   (D) "You win some, you lose some. And then there's that little-known third category." —Al Gore, who lost the 2000 presidential vote in the Electoral College despite winning the most votes on Election Day

Topic 5.2: Voter Turnout (MPA-3)

3. **Who among the following is most likely to vote?**
   (A) a 19-year-old Latino college student
   (B) a 50-year-old White college-educated woman
   (C) a 50-year-old White male high school graduate
   (D) a 40-year-old Black person with an associate's degree

Topic 5.8: Electing a President (PRD-2)

4. In a presidential election, the Republican candidate receives 48 percent of a state's electoral vote, the Democratic candidate receives 46 percent of the vote, and the Independent candidate receives 6 percent of the vote. If the state has 16 electoral votes and is similar to most other states, which of the following ways explains how the electoral votes will be allocated?

(A) The Republican candidate will receive eight electoral votes, the Democratic will receive seven, and the Independent will receive one.

(B) The Democratic candidate will receive nine electoral votes and the Republican will receive seven.

(C) The Republican candidate will receive all sixteen electoral votes.

(D) The House of Representatives will determine the allocation of the electoral votes.

Topic 5.9: Congressional Elections (PRD-2) and Topic 5.10 – Modern Campaigns (PRD-2)

5. Which of the following is an accurate comparison of open primaries and closed primaries?

	Open Primaries	Closed Primaries
(A)	State law sets the timing of these elections.	Federal law sets the timing of these elections.
(B)	They strengthen the power of the political party.	They weaken the power of the political party.
(C)	They involve candidates from both parties, with the top two finalists receiving nominations.	Registered Independents are allowed to vote.
(D)	Any registered voter can participate regardless of party affiliation.	Only registered members of a political party can vote.

Questions 6–7 refer to the graph.

Turnout in Presidential and Midterm Elections, 2000–2020

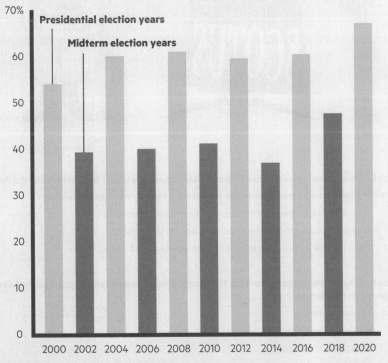

Source: United States Election Project, www.election-project.org (accessed 11/9/20).

6. **Which of the following statements best describes the trend in the data shown in the graph?**

   (A) In 2018 voter turnout during the midterm election was very similar to voter turnout in 2000 during the presidential election.

   (B) Voter turnout is higher in presidential election years than in midterm election years.

   (C) Voter turnout in midterm election years has consistently increased.

   (D) Voter turnout in midterm election years is generally greater than 50 percent.

7. **Which of the following best explains the trend in the graph?**

   (A) Voters view presidential elections as more important than midterm elections and are therefore more likely to turnout to vote.

   (B) During presidential elections the entire Senate is up for election, whereas during midterm elections only a third is up for election.

   (C) Elections for members of the House of Representatives are only held during midterm elections.

   (D) The winner-take-all system in the Electoral College encourages people to vote because they feel as if their individual votes make more of a difference than in a midterm election.

Topic 5.11: Campaign Finance (PRD-2)

Questions 8–10 refer to the political cartoon.

8. **Which of the following best conveys the cartoon's message about the *Citizens United* decision?**

   (A) It allowed the bureaucracy to use amicus curiae briefs to influence the Court.

   (B) It kept decisions made by the Supreme Court out of public view.

   (C) It allowed money to have too much influence in U.S. politics.

   (D) It is a portrayal of citizens who gave their money away to a bad cause.

9. **Which of the following best provides the constitutional basis of the Supreme Court decision depicted in the cartoon?**

   (A) First Amendment

   (B) Second Amendment

   (C) Fourth Amendment

   (D) Eighth Amendment

10. **Which of the following best represents the liberal critique of the Supreme Court's decision alluded to in the cartoon?**

(A) The *Citizens United* decision has made the election process more open by allowing greater participation.

(B) The *Citizens United* decision is healthy for democracy because it has allowed more candidates to seek office.

(C) The *Citizens United* decision distorts the electoral process by allowing corporations undue influence.

(D) The *Citizens United* decision hurts Democratic candidates because they generally raise less money than their Republican opponents.

Free-Response Questions

SCOTUS Comparison

This question requires you to compare a Supreme Court case you studied in class with one you have not studied in class. A summary of the Supreme Court case you did not study in class is presented below and provides all of the information you need to know about this case to answer the prompt.

In 1971 Congress passed the Federal Elections Campaign Act (FECA), designed to regulate and restrict the amount of spending that went into all federal elections. The act also created the Federal Election Commission (FEC), a nonpartisan independent regulatory commission charged with enforcing the provisions of the FECA. A group headed by Senator James L. Buckley of New York sued the federal government, claiming that FECA overstepped the bounds of the federal government's power.

In a per curiam decision, the Supreme Court held in *Buckley v. Valeo* (1976) that parts of FECA were constitutional while other parts were not. The existence of the FEC and its regulatory powers remained in place. The limitations that FECA put on candidates' spending on their own campaigns were struck down. Additionally, limitations could not be placed on "independent expenditures" by outside groups, excluding corporations and unions, as long as they did not violate the "magic words" test.

Based on the information above, respond to the following questions.

(A) Identify the civil liberty that is common in both *Buckley v. Valeo* (1976) and *Citizens United v. Federal Election Commission* (2010).

(B) Explain how the Supreme Court's holding in *Buckley v. Valeo* would later impact its ruling in *Citizens United v. Federal Election Commission*.

(C) Explain how the decision in *Buckley v. Valeo* affected the balance between governmental power and individual rights in the area of campaigns.

Argument Essay

Develop an argument that explains which level of government—state or federal—should have the ability to conduct elections for positions at the federal level.

Use at least one piece of evidence from one of the following foundational documents:

- The Bill of Rights of the U.S. Constitution
- Other amendments to the U.S. Constitution

In your response, you should do the following:

✓ Respond to the prompt with a defensible claim or thesis that establishes a line of reasoning.

✓ Support your claim with at least *two* pieces of specific and relevant evidence.

- One piece of evidence must come from one of the foundational documents listed above.
- A second piece of evidence can come from any other foundational document not used as your first piece of evidence, or it may be from your knowledge of course concepts.

✓ Use reasoning to explain why your evidence supports your claim or thesis.

✓ Respond to an opposing or alternate perspective using refutation, concession, or rebuttal.

14

The Media

Do the media make us more informed?

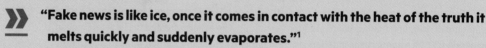

» **"Fake news is like ice, once it comes in contact with the heat of the truth it melts quickly and suddenly evaporates."**[1]
Oche Otorkpa, author

« **"Leaders who play by the rules are having trouble staying ahead of a relentless news cycle and must devote too much effort trying to disprove stories that seem to come out of nowhere and have been invented solely to do them in."**[2]
Madeleine Albright, former secretary of state

For democracy to work well, citizens need information about what government is doing or could do. The media, in their role as watchdog, are supposed to provide this information so that people can decide whether they approve or disapprove, as well as develop their own ideas about what they would like to see happen.

Looking at contemporary American politics, we can easily conclude that the media are failing at this basic job. Consider the question of whether some foreign government (or governments) intervened in the 2016 presidential election. Over the last four years, many mainstream media outlets have used intelligence agency reports as well as their own investigations to show how the Russian government used attack ads and posts on social media outlets to plant false information about Democratic presidential candidate Hillary Clinton's campaign. At the same time, other reports from largely fringe media outlets have argued that the Ukrainian government intervened in the election and targeted Republican Donald Trump. While there is no credible evidence to support this theory, polls show that it is believed by a significant portion of the American public.

This sort of disagreement on basic facts was not supposed to happen. Over the last generation, the rise of the Internet and social media has radically increased the amount of information available to the average citizen. For example, social media makes it easier to research colleges and identify the one that best fits your needs and constraints, particularly by talking directly with people who have firsthand knowledge of different options. Social media does the same in politics: you can use it to find more information in any number of ways, from identifying candidates who share your views to learning about basic facts concerning recent events. A generation ago, many observers argued

Leading up to the 2016 presidential election, fake social media accounts run by Russian operatives pushed out controversial content as a means of sowing tension and discord among American citizens, with the ultimate goal of helping Donald Trump win the election.

The following text appears within the collage of social media images:

Stand for Freedom
Sponsored

up for Freedom. Stand up for America!

Stand for Freedom
Community

👍 Like Page

afraid that the 2016 general election will be "rigged" against
doubt he has reasons to think so.
has already committed voter fraud during the Democrat Iowa
e same time, she has already demonstrated that she prefers
he nation than losing election. She pledged not to deport illegal
ugees, if she is president.
oover, it's known that Hillary is going to take in about one million
ng you, Nov. 8, we'd better be careful, because that election is going
ged," Mr. Trump said. "And I hope the Republicans are watching
or it's going to be taken away from us."

LIKE IF YOU ARE A PART OF
THE 68% OF AMERICANS WHO
DON'T TRUST HILLARY

843 Shares

BM
Sponsored ·

Join us in the streets! Stop Trump and his bigoted agenda!
Meet you at Union Sq. at 12pm and march to Trump Tower (725 5th Ave) at
3pm.
Divided is the reason we just fell. We must unite despite our differences to
stop HATE from ruling the land.... See More

TRUMP IS
MY PRESIDENT.
MARCH
AGAINST TRUMP

12 P.M.

👍 Like Page

BM
Sponsored ·

Your voices matter!
We are looking for the authors. Your opinions will be published!
In our work we have discovered that many Kings and Queens were silenc
and had no opportunity to voice their concerns and opinions. But today, w
want to give you this opportunity. We want America to know what bothers
you as a member of the Black community. We are ready to publish your
articles and your opinions. Plus, it's a good chance for you to be a part of
our team that is interested in... See More

YOUR VOICES MATTER

KING

Clinton FRAUDation
Community
517 people like this.

Clinton Fraudation

Based on scientific literature, sk
indicate they were Negroid people with features very s
modern Black Nubians and people of East Africa.
Remember who you are and know your ancestors.

WHOEVER THINKS WE
COME A LONG WAY

Angry Ea
Community
4,157 peor

👍 Like Page

Army of Jesus
Sponsored ·

At the Last Supper Jesus says:
He said to them, "But now if you have a purse, take it, and also a bag; and if
you don't have a sword, sell your cloak and buy one."
— Luke 22:36 ... See More

SAY A
PRAYE
AND
LO
YOU

28 Reactions 8 Shares

**CHAPTER
GOALS**

**Describe the role of the media in American politics
and how people get political information.**
pages 612–619

**Explain how politicians use the media to achieve
their goals.** pages 619–623

**Explain how the media influence how people think
about politics.** pages 623–631

**Assess whether the media fulfill their role in
American democracy.** pages 631–636

that the Internet and social media would improve the quality of American politics by making it easier for people to become well informed.

Arguments about whether foreign countries intervened in the 2016 election illustrate that these grand hopes have not been realized. There is little evidence that the rise of social media and other changes in media coverage of politics have produced a better-informed or more politically active citizenry. Regardless of whether you think fake news comes from Republican, Democratic, or other sources, there is a lot of it around. In part, the problem is us: as we discussed in Chapter 10, most citizens do not take the time to conscientiously consult different sources or reconcile conflicting information. Yet as we will show in this chapter, media coverage of politics often falls short of providing necessary information on the important stories of the day. If Americans choose to believe in conspiracy theories or to remain poorly informed, at least part of the blame lies with the individuals, groups, and companies that we look to for information.

The disconnect between expectations about social media and the actual effects that social media has had on American politics highlights a larger question about the role of the media in American politics. Social media was supposed to inform us and bring us together—what went wrong? Why don't Americans trust the media as a watchdog? And why do the media fall short of this ideal?

Political media today

This section describes the **mass media**, the many sources of political information available to Americans, and how people use (or don't use) this information. The media are an example in this book of a **linkage institution**—an actor or group of actors in American politics that informs citizens about government actions or helps them exercise control over policy. The development of the Internet and the expansion of social media over the last generation has dramatically increased the number of media sources and the range of information available to the average American. This changing media landscape means that it is less important than it was in the past to describe each media source and what kinds of information it can (and cannot) provide. In contemporary America, there are so many sources and so much information that Americans can become experts on virtually any aspect of politics or public policy—if they are willing to search for information and assess the value of what they find.

Historical overview: how did we get here?

The role of the media as an information source and the controversy over how the media report about politics are nothing new. Since the Founding, politicians have understood that Americans learn about politics largely from the media, have complained about coverage, and have sought to influence both the stories the media select and the way they report on them.

The Media as Watchdog and Business From the beginnings of the United States, mass media has served as a reporter of political events and as a watchdog, keeping track of what politicians are doing and offering insight about their policy successes and failures. Many newspapers chronicled the conflicts of the Revolutionary War; after the war, while politicians negotiated over the size and scope of the new federal

DESCRIBE THE ROLE OF THE MEDIA IN AMERICAN POLITICS AND HOW PEOPLE GET POLITICAL INFORMATION

mass media
Sources that provide information to the average citizen, such as newspapers, television networks, radio stations, podcasts, and websites.

linkage institutions
Institutions such as political parties, interest groups, the media, and elections that are channels through which individuals can communicate their preferences to policy makers.

government, newspapers became a venue for debates over different plans.[3] While the media cover politics, politicians have always tried to shape this coverage to their advantage. During the ratification of the Constitution, for instance, Alexander Hamilton, John Jay, and James Madison supported pro-ratification forces in New York by publishing (under a pseudonym) a series of articles that came to be known as the *Federalist Papers* in local newspapers.[4] And in 1798 Congress and President John Adams enacted the Alien and Sedition Acts, which made it a crime to publish articles that criticized the president or Congress.[5] While these press restrictions were later repealed or allowed to expire, they serve as a reminder that the American media have never been free of government regulation or of the conflictual relationship between politicians and reporters.

Long before the Internet, changes in technology expanded the media's role as information provider, entertainment, and watchdog. In 1833, the *New York Sun* began selling papers for a penny a copy rather than the standard price of six cents. The price reduction, which was facilitated by cheaper, faster printing presses, made the newspaper available to the mass public for the first time, and this increase in circulation made it possible, even with the lower price, to hire more reporters.[6] The development of the telegraph also aided newspapers by enabling reporters on assignment throughout the country to quickly send stories back home for publication. Many of the new publications were unabashedly partisan. For example, the *New York Tribune* was strongly antislavery. By 1860, the *Tribune*'s circulation was larger than that of any other newspaper in the world and its articles "helped to add fuel to the fires of slavery and sectionalism that divided North and South."[7] At the other extreme, the *New York Times* was transformed in the 1800s into a nonpartisan paper with the goals of journalistic impartiality, accuracy, and complete coverage of events—its motto to the present day is "All the News That's Fit to Print."[8]

The media's role as a watchdog has always been constrained by the need to attract a paying audience in order to stay in business and turn a profit. The period after the Civil War saw the beginning of **yellow journalism**, reporting that drew in customers by using bold headlines, illustrations, and sensational stories (the name came from the yellow paper these newspapers were printed on). And during the 1920s hundreds of small, local radio stations appeared, along with some larger stations that could broadcast nationwide. The proliferation of stations eventually led to the development of networks, that is, groups of local radio (and, later, television) stations owned by one company that broadcast a common set of programs. While these new electronic sources made more information available to Americans, many of them were developed not as watchdogs but as highly profitable enterprises that delivered entertainment as well as news to citizens and monetized their audience by selling radio or television time to advertisers.[9]

Regulating the Media Until 1930 or so, there was only minimal federal regulation of the media, reflecting the Constitution's guarantee of freedom of the press—and the fact that newspapers were the only media source that existed. With the rise of the **broadcast media**, including radio and television, and the formation of the **Federal Communications Commission (FCC)** to allocate broadcast frequencies, a new position emerged: if broadcasters were going to make money off their use of the government's broadcast frequencies, the government could place conditions on how this business operated. In recent years, new technologies (cable TV, the Internet) have changed the calculation; the emphasis is now on encouraging competition among media sources rather than regulating a few providers.

Federal regulation of broadcast media was driven by the concern that one company or organization might buy enough stations to dominate the airwaves in a given area and

Yellow journalism emphasized sensational stories and bold headlines, but also made information about contemporary politics available to a wider audience.

yellow journalism
A style of newspaper reporting popular in the late 1800s that featured sensationalized stories, bold headlines, and illustrations to increase readership.

broadcast media
Communications technologies, such as television and radio, that transmit information over airwaves.

Federal Communications Commission (FCC)
A government agency created in 1934 to regulate American radio stations and later expanded to regulate television, wireless communications technologies, and other broadcast media.

President Trump has argued that he should receive "equal time" under the FCC's equal time regulations due to the negative coverage he often receives from late-night television hosts like Stephen Colbert and Trevor Noah. Trump tweeted: "Late Night host [sic] are dealing with the Democrats for their very 'unfunny' & repetitive material, always anti-Trump! Should we get Equal Time?"

equal time provision
An FCC regulation requiring broadcast media to provide equal air time on any non-news programming to all candidates running for an office.

media conglomerates
Companies that control a large number of media sources across several types of media outlets.

become a monopoly, offering only one set of programs or point of view. For many years, FCC regulations limited the number of radio and television stations a company could own in a community and the total nationwide audience that a company's television stations could reach. The FCC also created the **equal time provision**, which says that if a radio or television station gives air time to a candidate outside its routine news coverage—such as during an entertainment show or a cooking program—it has to give an equivalent amount of time to other candidates running for the same office. For example, when then–presidential candidate Donald Trump hosted *Saturday Night Live* in November 2015, the television network (NBC) that broadcast the program had to give free television time (in the form of free advertising slots) to other presidential candidates. The FCC also established a fairness doctrine, whereby broadcasters had to present opposing points of view as part of their coverage of important events; usually this was done by broadcasting editorials during news programs that presented both sides of an issue.

Deregulation The FCC's limits on ownership and content as well as the fairness doctrine have been eliminated because of the development of new communications technologies. The logic is that with so many sources of information, if one broadcaster ignores a candidate, an issue, or a viewpoint, citizens can still find out what they want to know from another source. Pressure for deregulation also came from the owners of media companies, who wanted to buy more television, radio, and cable stations, as well as from book and magazine publishers, Internet service providers, and newspapers.[10]

These regulatory changes have shaped the current media landscape in two ways. First, they have allowed for concentration: many media companies own multiple media sources in a town or community. For example, iHeartMedia owns over 850 AM and FM radio stations, including multiple stations in more than 30 cities. Similarly, Facebook, which is a major source of news for many Americans, also owns Instagram. Second, the changes have allowed for cross-ownership, in which one company owns several different kinds of media outlets, often in the same community. For example, Nexstar owns various Chicago media outlets, including the WGN radio station, the WGN television station, and the *Chicago Tribune* daily newspaper. These trends have given rise to **media conglomerates**, companies that control a wide range of news sources.[11] Nuts & Bolts 14.1 shows the diverse holdings of one such company, the Walt Disney Company. You may think of Disney in terms of theme parks, cruises, and *Avengers* or *Star Wars* movies and TV shows, but the company owns a wide range of media companies, including the ABC broadcast network, Hulu, ESPN, and the political information site FiveThirtyEight.

Media sources in the twenty-first century

Over the last two decades, the Internet has become a major and often dominant information source for information about American politics. Virtually all U.S. newspapers, magazines, television networks, radio stations, and cable stations offer free or (increasingly) paid access to all their content via websites and mobile apps. Many Internet-only sites offer a combination of rumor, inside information, and deep analysis of American politics. Some, such as Politico, Vox, and FiveThirtyEight, have

Holdings of the Walt Disney Company

Broadcast Stations		Film Companies	
ABC broadcast network (owns 8 stations, over 200 affiliates)		20th Century Studios	
KRDC-AM (Los Angeles)		Lucasfilm	
Radio Disney (available through Internet platforms)		Marvel Studios	
		Pixar	
		20th Century Fox Television	
		Walt Disney Studios	

Cable Channels		Other Media	
A&E	Lifetime	Vice Media	
ESPN	National Geographic	FiveThirtyEight	
Freeform	Four Disney-branded channels	Hulu	
FX		Disney+	

Source: Compiled by the authors.

The Walt Disney Company is an example of a media conglomerate, a company that controls a variety of media outlets throughout the world. It owns cable television networks, television and radio stations, cable channels, movie-production companies, subscription programming sites, and websites; this table provides just a few examples of its many holdings. This structure allows the company to rebroadcast or reprint stories in different outlets and thus operate more efficiently, but opponents are concerned that conglomerates might expand to control most—or even all—of the sources that are available to the average citizen, making it impossible to access alternate points of view.

"Why Should I Care?" Think about where you get your news. If all your top sources for political information were owned by the same company, how might that affect the diversity of stories you see or the perspectives you hear? While conglomerates might help make the process of reporting and distributing the news more efficient, it's important to understand how the owners might influence what you ultimately read.

paid staff and report on a wide range of topics. Others have a narrower focus: the Monkey Cage (now affiliated with the *Washington Post*) and the Mischiefs of Faction use political science research to explain contemporary American politics.[12] And many websites, some run by ordinary citizens, provide their own insights and information about American politics. Finally, Facebook, Twitter, and other social media sites provide users with links to coverage written by others; people also use these sites to report and comment on political events themselves.

These changes have dramatically increased the amount of information about politics that is available to the average American. Imagine yourself in the late 1940s. Suppose you wanted to learn about President Truman's State of the Union address. If you couldn't go to Washington to hear it in person, where could you have gotten information about the speech? If you lived in a big city, the speech would probably be covered in the next day's newspaper. If you lived in a small town, your local paper might or might not run the story. If it didn't, you would need a subscription to either a big-city paper (which would arrive a week after the fact) or a weekly or monthly news magazine, or you would need to have access to a radio that could pick up a station broadcasting the speech.

Now consider the modern era, in which major political events saturate the media and a virtually unlimited amount of information is available on the Internet. Suppose you want to know about the president's State of the Union message. You can tune in to one of the four major television networks, numerous cable news channels, public television stations, or radio stations. Most television stations will feature pundits' commentaries on the speech and will interview prominent politicians and commentators. Jimmy Fallon and other late-night hosts will probably make jokes about

DID YOU KNOW?

Newspaper circulation per capita has declined

66%

since 1970.

Source: Pew Research Center

DID YOU KNOW?

67%

of American adults report they get at least some of their news from social media.

Source: Pew Research Center

From protesters covering their marches to refugees filming their journeys, the Internet makes it easy for ordinary people to share political information and report on political events as they happen.

it on television, and John Oliver will skewer the speech on his Sunday show. Tomorrow it will be front-page news and larger papers will publish the full text of the speech online. Countless websites will offer analyses. And you will be able to watch a video of the speech on YouTube and many other sites. Some of your friends (perhaps even you) might offer commentary on social media. The point is, there are many places to get information; you would have to work to avoid them.

The Internet has also made new kinds of political information available to the average citizen. For example, the Center for Responsive Politics offers a searchable database of contributions to candidates and political organizations. Many sites, including FiveThirtyEight and Huffpost Pollster, collect and analyze public opinion surveys, including presidential election polls. Increasingly, podcasts such as the left-leaning *Pod Save America* or the right-leaning *Federalist Radio Hour* are used to deliver analysis and interviews. The Internet also creates new opportunities for interaction between citizens, reporters, and government officials. Many reporters host live online chat sessions, allowing people to ask follow-up questions about published stories, or interact with their audience through a variety of social media sites.

The Internet has also facilitated some entirely new kinds of media sources. People who know something about political events (or think they do) now have a variety of ways, from blogs to Twitter, to contribute to the commentary on political news stories and put information before a wide audience. In 2018, the *New York Post* published an article detailing how "blue-collar voters" in Pittsburgh reacted to President Trump's State of the Union speech—until some individuals with Twitter accounts did some searching and posted that a parent of one of the interviewees was chief of surgery at a local hospital (not exactly "blue-collar"). The *Post* then updated its story to reflect this information.[13] Other sources publish inside information about agency decisions, such as the revelations published by the website Ars Technica in early 2020 about problems revealed in the test flight of Boeing's new crewed spacecraft for NASA.[14]

At the same time, the rise of the Internet has exacerbated the trend toward shorter stories in major news sources, with fewer details and less background information. In theory, the elimination of space limitations should have produced longer, more in-depth reporting on the Internet, but in fact the opposite has occurred. Many popular Internet sources, such as Axios, are designed to present information in short, easy-to-digest form. Similarly, news accounts that individuals may post on social media sites are often light on details—most notably, posts on Twitter are limited to 280 characters, although links are allowed. Major news sources such as the *New York Times* and the *Washington Post* are also shifting both what they report and how they report in favor of stories that can gain the attention of an easily distracted public—and reporters are being evaluated in terms of the number of times their stories are viewed.

While there is much more information available today than there was a generation ago, media sources are constantly in flux. Websites and Web pages come and go. Individuals who post detailed analyses of one political event may be too busy to comment on another. Even well-established media sources can quickly change. For example, in recent years companies that once owned newspapers in Chicago, Philadelphia, and Minneapolis have gone bankrupt, whereas several major U.S. cities, including Seattle, Birmingham, and New Orleans, have a hometown daily newspaper that appears only in digital form. Other newspapers have cut foreign bureaus, reduced their staff, and thinned the amount of news in every edition. (One exception is the *Washington Post*, which expanded its newsroom by over a third under the ownership of Jeff Bezos, the founder of Amazon.) At the same time, the major television networks and cable television sources have seen declines in budgets and viewership.

The increase in sources has also led to a blurring of fact and opinion in some news coverage. Most mainstream media distinguish between news coverage, where the goal is to present facts and analysis without an ideological agenda, and opinion pieces, which have a clear point of view.[15] In print media, the latter stories are usually reserved for a special op-ed (opinions and editorials) section. Newer media sources, especially solo Web-only operations, may not follow these conventions, meaning that casual readers might assume they are reading a factual account when in fact they are not.

At one level, these declines do not present a fundamental barrier to viewers and readers who seek to become well informed about major events, since there are so many alternative news sources to consult. However, information about past events is often difficult to find because it is not archived or because the source of the information goes out of business (this is particularly true for Internet-only sources such as podcasts). And as the budgets for media sources become tighter and tighter, stories that require extensive research (particularly investigative journalism) are less likely to be reported in the first place.

Moreover, as we discussed earlier, the quality of information available on the Internet varies considerably—probably more than it did for the relatively small number of media sources that were available a generation ago. For example, it is easy to find fake photographs of all kinds on the Internet, including Barack Obama shaking hands with Osama bin Laden, House Speaker Nancy Pelosi wearing a hijab (a headscarf worn by Muslim women that leaves only the face exposed), or Donald Trump carrying two cats to safety during relief operations for Hurricane Harvey in 2017. As the quote (falsely) attributed to Abraham Lincoln says, you can't believe something just because it's on the Internet. Even if fake Lincoln quotes are easy to spot, in a world where websites come and go and where citizens often do not take the time to investigate what they see or read, false information may easily be accepted as true, especially if it fits the preconceptions of whoever reads it.

A related problem is that the Internet has made it easier for partisan groups to publish biased or inaccurate information under the guise of investigative journalism, with the supposed goal of informing the public. For example, the conservative group Project Veritas recorded undercover encounters with employees of organizations ranging from Planned Parenthood to the *Washington Post*, using leading questions, hidden video cameras, and selective editing to portray these individuals in politically embarrassing situations. These efforts can backfire: during the 2017 Alabama Senate special election, in which Republican candidate Roy Moore was accused by multiple women of past sexual harassment, a Project Veritas worker tried to convince a *Washington Post* reporter that she had had an affair with Moore. Rather than exposing the *Post*'s supposed bias and corrupt motives in reporting on the Moore story (which was Project Veritas's goal), the operation ended when the *Post* investigated her claim, discovered her link to Project Veritas, and published several stories on the organization's attempt to deceive and entrap the *Post*.

Don't believe everything you read on the Internet—quotes about media literacy have been humorously attributed to President Lincoln to satirize the prevalence of misinformation online.

"DON'T BELIEVE EVERYTHING YOU READ ON THE INTERNET."

—ABRAHAM LINCOLN

Where do people get political information?

While there is a vast amount of information available about politics, very few Americans make it a priority to be well informed about politics—which would require them to systematically consult, evaluate, and integrate information from a range of different sources. Rather, most Americans acquire political information accidentally through a process known as the **by-product theory**.[16] As an example, in 2020 you may have logged in to Facebook or some other social media site to see what your friends were doing, and happened to take a look at a political story or video that appeared in your News Feed. Perhaps the story was a profile of former Massachusetts governor William Weld, who ran against President Donald Trump in the 2020 Republican primaries. Though you hadn't planned to read about Weld, you wound up doing so just because the story came up in your feed—perhaps you were a Massachusetts resident or a Democrat who wanted Republicans to stand up against Trump. However, when people receive information as a by-product, they don't evaluate it in the same way that they evaluate information gained through a careful search, such as the investigation you might have done if you wanted to check out Weld's background and issue positions. Suppose the story criticized Weld's position on legalizing marijuana. If you came upon this information after searching on your own, you would probably have thought about whether the source was credible or whether you cared about marijuana legalization in the first place. Because you are not consciously searching for information, you are much less likely to be skeptical when you acquire information as a by-product.[17]

Whether people seek out political information deliberately or acquire it as a by-product, there are some systematic differences in media use depending on their partisanship and ideological beliefs. Table 14.1 shows data from an early-2020 survey on the most-trusted news sources for Democrats and Republicans. Clearly, there are some sharp differences: by a large margin, the most important source for Republicans voters was Fox News, while Democrats reported high trust for several sources, with CNN at the top. Conservative Republicans included two talk radio hosts as trustworthy sources, Sean Hannity and Rush Limbaugh, while all other groups (both Democratic groups plus moderate/liberal Republicans) reported trusting some or all of the network news programs. A final difference is that Republicans report lower levels of trust in news sources than Democrats do.

by-product theory
The idea that many Americans acquire political information unintentionally rather than by seeking it out.

All I know is just what I read in the papers, and that's an alibi for my ignorance.

—**Will Rogers,** actor

DID YOU KNOW?

The weekly audience for Rush Limbaugh's program, the top conservative talk radio show, was

13 million.

The top liberal program has an audience of only 2 million.

Source: Politico.com

TABLE 14.1

Trust in News Sources among Democrats and Republicans

Democrats				Republicans			
Liberal		**Moderate/Conservative**		**Moderate/Liberal**		**Conservative**	
CNN	70%	CNN	65%	Fox News	51%	Fox News	75%
New York Times	66%	ABC News	63%	ABC News	47%	Hannity (radio)	43%
PBS	66%	NBC News	61%	CBS News	42%	Limbaugh (radio)	38%
NPR	63%	CBS News	60%	NBC News	41%	ABC News	24%
NBC News	61%	PBS	48%	CNN	36%	CBS News	23%

Source: Mark Jurkowitz et al., "U.S. Media Polarization and the 2020 Election: A Nation Divided," Pew Research Center, January 24, 2020, www.journalism.org/2020/01/24/u-s-media-polarization-and-the-2020-election-a-nation-divided/ (accessed 3/7/20).

The question raised by Table 14.1 is whether the differences in issue positions and policy demands of Republicans and Democrats are driven by the differences in the media sources they consume. Do some people demand liberal policies because they listen to CNN, while others demand conservative policies because they listen to Fox News? The answer is almost surely no. As we discussed in Chapter 10, people aren't liberal or conservative because of the stories they listen to, watch, or read—their beliefs run much deeper than that. It's probably more accurate to say that ideological beliefs drive the selection of media sources, rather than media sources driving ideological beliefs. Even so, insofar as different sources report different information, the choice of which media to consume will shape what a person knows about politics—about the candidates, their policy proposals, and the government's performance overall.

★

EXPLAIN HOW POLITICIANS USE THE MEDIA TO ACHIEVE THEIR GOALS

How do politicians use the media? How do the media use politicians?

While the media and politicians are often thought of as adversaries, with a watchdog press working to make sure the public knows what politicians are doing, the fact is that each side has something to offer the other. Reporters want to write stories that attract public attention, so they need information from politicians on what is happening inside the government, preferably information that is given only to them. Politicians in turn want media coverage that highlights their achievements, which ideally will build public support and secure their election (or reelection). Bureaucrats want favorable attention for their programs, and interest groups want publicity to further their causes. Thus, coverage of American politics reflects trade-offs between reporters who want complete, accurate information and sources who want favorable coverage.

Politicians' media strategies

Politicians and others in government try to influence coverage by providing select information to reporters. Sometimes they hold press conferences where they take questions from the media. Other times they speak to single reporters or to a group **on background** or **off the record**, meaning that reporters can use the information but cannot attribute it to the politician by name. These efforts are sometimes trial balloons, where politicians release details of a new proposal to gauge public reaction without committing themselves to any particular policy. Other times politicians might reveal

on background or **off the record**
Describes comments a politician makes to the press on the condition that they can be reported only if they are not attributed to that politician.

You don't tell us how to stage the news, and we won't tell you how to cover it.

—**Larry Speakes,** press secretary to President Ronald Reagan

some details of a negotiation or conflict with the hope of producing media coverage that puts their contributions in a favorable light.

Some scholars argue that elected officials try to use the media to shape public opinion in their favor by doling out information to reward reporters who write stories that support the officials' points of view.[18] To some extent this argument is true: much of the information reporters use to write their stories comes from political appointees, bureaucrats, elected officials, and party leaders.[19] Reporters who are known to be writing stories that are critical of a government program or a political leader may find that some people refuse to talk to them. However, while there is no doubt that elected officials would like to receive sympathetic media coverage and are sometimes successful, news reports on American politics reflect a multitude of sources and information. One politician's attempt to shape coverage by talking or remaining silent may be negated by another's efforts to promote a different point of view, with the same reporter or a different one.

President Trump's behavior was consistent with this strategy. Trump's staff invited the media to events that placed Trump in a favorable light (such as Trump's trips to Afghanistan and Iraq to visit U.S. troops). And like most other politicians, Trump selectively released information to reporters whom he believed would write favorable coverage—for example, he regularly called in to *Fox & Friends* for extended interviews with the hosts. The difference is that Trump used Twitter to speak directly to his supporters and the public at large—with a guarantee that the press would report on his tweets, simply because Trump was president. In this way, Trump's tweeting served as free advertising, as well as a way for Trump to shape press coverage.

Besides talking with the media, politicians also hold events specifically designed to secure favorable press coverage, or appear at an event that the press is likely to cover. This strategy is particularly common among candidates campaigning for office. For example, during the summer of 2019, six months before the Iowa Caucuses met to begin selecting presidential nominees, Joe Biden and the other Democratic candidates for president in 2020 made a point of visiting the Iowa State Fair, where they shook hands, ate some local specialties (from pork chops on sticks to fried Snickers bars), and in general tried to attract as much media attention as they could. By attending the fair, candidates were trying to get their names and their pictures in local newspapers and on local television and thereby increase their name recognition. Such coverage might have also helped persuade Iowa voters that a candidate shared their views on the issues.

Another way politicians, especially candidates, try to shape citizen perceptions is to run campaign ads on television, in newspapers, and on websites. Candidates running for federal office generally spend about 80–90 percent of their budget on advertising. Candidates target these ads to reach groups of likely supporters. A conservative Republican might try to buy advertising slots during a broadcast of a NASCAR event, knowing that people who are interested in NASCAR tend to vote Republican. These ads are an example of the by-product theory in action; people don't watch NASCAR to learn about politicians, but watching the broadcast means they will be exposed to the candidate's messages.

Potential presidential candidates also often appear on television talk shows or allow reporters to shadow them on the campaign trail as a way of increasing name recognition and gaining some free advertising. Studies have shown that viewing a candidate in such a relaxed, nonconfrontational setting can help persuade opponents that a candidate is worth a second look.[20] Like all campaign strategies, however, candidates' attempts to shape media coverage work only some of the time. Candidates have even lost support through misguided attempts to appreciate local cuisine, including biting into an unshucked tamale, ordering Swiss on a Philly cheesesteak, asking for Dijon mustard on a cheeseburger, eating pizza with a fork, or claiming that a taco salad is authentic Mexican food. In the modern era, when everyone has a cell phone, these gaffes are captured on video and used to advantage by the opposition.

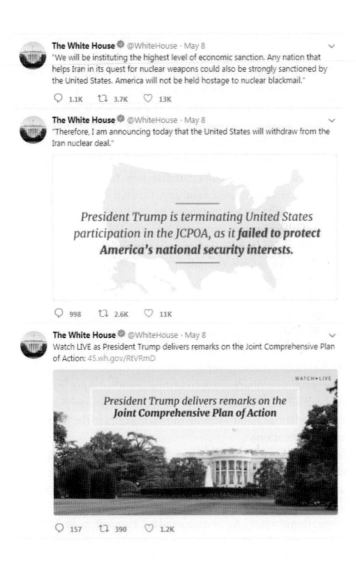

Campaign strategies can also backfire when candidates attack opponents. One instance occurred when the campaign of 2018 Republican Senate incumbent Ted Cruz released a radio ad that claimed his opponent, Beto O'Rourke, had started using a nickname rather than his first name (Robert) in order to appeal to Hispanic Texas voters.[21] The O'Rourke campaign responded by releasing a childhood photo of the candidate that showed him wearing a shirt with the nickname printed on it.[22] At other points in the campaign, the Cruz organization released a 20-year-old photo of O'Rourke playing in a punk rock band and argued that if elected, O'Rourke would try to ban consumption of barbecue (for the record, the candidate had not mentioned doing so). In all three cases, press coverage benefited O'Rourke, who narrowly lost to Cruz in the general election.

The pressures and legal limits on reporters

The proliferation of media sources has increased competition among reporters to find and report on interesting stories. Reporters who refuse to use information that a politician has provided may find that the politician refuses to talk with them in the future, so reporters must carefully consider whether they want to use information provided, to keep their channel of communication with the politician open. Moreover, the Internet has increased the demand for new stories and updates of old ones. Even if reporters covering Congress think that nothing important is happening on a given day, they may be forced to write a story just to have something new on their

**AP®
FOUNDATIONAL
DOCUMENT**

Leaks coming out of the Trump administration raised questions about what the role of the press should be in holding government accountable. In 2019, a senior official in the Trump administration anonymously published a tell-all book, titled *A Warning*, giving an inside look at the inner workings of the White House during Donald Trump's presidency.

newspaper's website. Similarly, an up-and-coming news or commentary site might use a politician's offerings as a way of building its audience.

Because of these demands, reporters rely heavily on their sources—people inside government who provide them with documents, inside information, and the details of negotiations—to supply them with material for new stories. When sources reveal information that is not supposed to be public knowledge, it is often referred to as leaking. Reporters covering important or controversial stories often promise their sources that they will remain anonymous in any coverage based on the information they provide. These assurances are an important factor in the decision to leak information, especially classified information. However, these assurances are not absolute. Reporters and their editors can, under certain circumstances, be compelled by a court to reveal the sources for their stories. Although some states have shield laws that allow reporters to refuse to name their sources, there is no such law at the federal level. As a result, federal prosecutors can ask a judge to force journalists to name their sources, on the grounds that the source's identity is fundamental to the prosecutor's case. If the judge agrees, reporters can be jailed for contempt indefinitely unless they name their sources.

To be clear, leaking or the publication of leaked information is not illegal as long as the information is not classified. For example, it was not illegal for former National Security Advisor John Bolton to disclose private conversations with President Trump about efforts to get the Ukrainian government to investigate Joe Biden. While these revelations were certainly embarrassing to Trump, Bolton did not break any law by writing a book about his experiences (in fact, as with other former National Security aides, he was required to—and did—submit the manuscript to the Justice Department for review prior to publication).

Notwithstanding the freedom of the press guaranteed in the Bill of Rights, reporters are subject to legal limitations that present hurdles as they research stories. If the government can convince a judge that publication of a particular story would lead to immediate harm to a person or persons, a judge can halt publication. But this test sets the bar extremely high for stopping publication of a story. As we discussed in Chapter 8, most attempts to prevent publication have been unsuccessful. In addition, it is not clear as a practical matter how the legal system could control the release of information via social media.

To appreciate the issues surrounding classified information and prior restraint, consider the case of Edward Snowden. While working as a contractor for the U.S. National Security Agency (NSA), Snowden downloaded a number of files that documented the NSA's surveillance activities, including the collection of data on Americans' phone calls overseas and the monitoring of foreign politicians' cell phones. In 2012, Snowden approached several major publications across the world, including the *Washington Post*, to offer access to these documents. After several months of negotiation, the *Post* would not agree to all of Snowden's conditions—among other things, he wanted certain documents to be published in their entirety, while the *Post* wanted to hold back some classified information.[23] Snowden then came to an agreement with a British newspaper, the *Guardian*, which gradually made the documents public, although he also allowed the *Post* to publish some of the documents.

The *Post*'s refusal to accept Snowden's demands was the product of several months of discussions with the U.S. government over what information could be released without harming national security or placing confidential sources in jeopardy. Although some government officials mentioned the possibility of invoking the prior restraint prohibition, no attempts were made to do so. In any case, even if the *Post* could have been deterred from publication, the information would have soon appeared in stories published by other outlets.

The Snowden episode illustrates how government officials work to deter leaks or influence the media's coverage of a story without resorting to prior restraint. Laws prohibit government officials' disclosure of classified information in the first place, and recent administrations have been very aggressive about prosecuting leakers. Newspapers can also face prosecution for publishing classified information. In the case of the Snowden documents, the *Post* published its story only when it was rumored that the *Guardian* planned to release its own story. Even then, *Post* reporters and editors agreed to keep certain information out of their stories.

Why do reporters and publishers restrain their stories? Sometimes they agree with the government that keeping secrets is in the national interest. For example, when the president or other administration officials visit dangerous locations such as Iraq or Afghanistan, major media outlets voluntarily agree to not report on the trip until it is officially announced. Other times reporters are rewarded for cooperating—they may get information about another government policy or be promised future access to officials. Alternatively, reporters may be coerced to back down from a story through the threat of losing future access to people in government or even going to jail.

These constraints apply only to mainstream organizations and their reporters. Groups that are anonymous or that operate outside the United States can violate these laws and norms with impunity. For example, when the international WikiLeaks group released e-mails and documents it had obtained from the Democratic National Committee during the 2016 campaign, the Clinton campaign, and the Gmail account of Clinton campaign chair John Podesta, there was no way for the affected groups (or the government) to initiate legal action or otherwise prevent publication.

Thus, both legal constraints and government officials' efforts to shape the news can affect the way that the media report about politics. Politicians will try to depict their opponents as ill-advised and scandal ridden and to shape media coverage in ways that show them winning and their opponents losing. Given the multitude of media sources, it is not hard for a politician to find a reporter who is willing to write exactly what that politician wants. And that reporter may file a story whether or not he or she believes that the information the politician provides is true or important—the reporter may be motivated by other factors, like attracting an audience, gaining the politician's trust, or hitting a deadline.

Understanding the relationship between politicians and the media is critical for evaluating the quality and accuracy of the political news you see and read. Because journalists are constrained in what they can learn about and what they can report, and because politicians may try to influence what reporters say, there is no guarantee that any one media source will be able to publish a full and complete account of a political event or outcome. Under these conditions, the only way to be well informed about politics is to consult multiple sources and remember that politicians and media members both have agendas. Sometimes those agendas are similar, but often politicians and the media want different things.

How do the media influence their audience?

The study of media effects explores whether exposure to media coverage of politics changes what people think or do (see How It Works: How News Makes It to the Public). There is considerable evidence that media coverage influences its audience—in simple terms, much of what Americans know about politics comes from stories they read, watch, or listen to. In part, **media effects** arise because

How News Makes It to the Public

Editor assigns reporter to cover a particular story or event.

Filtering
Editor decides which stories are important and will attract an audience.

Reporter gathers information and prepares a story.

Framing
Reporter's story includes the overall argument and other information that shapes what the audience learns.

Priming
By describing events using some words or phrases and omitting others, the reporter has additional influence over what the audience learns.

The people have a point!

Chaos in the streets!

Editor revises story, decides on length, content, and placement.

Filtering, Framing, and Priming
Decision about where, when, and how to carry the story gives an additional opportunity for filtering. In addition, the editor can make changes to a story that involve framing, and priming.

The Media's Coverage of the Green New Deal

During the last two years, many news outlets have reported on the Green New Deal, a Democratic proposal to address climate change. Rather than setting out specific policies, the proposal outlined broad goals as a way of setting the agenda for subsequent congressional hearings and debates. Even so, the Green New Deal was the first attempt to build congressional majorities behind a comprehensive legislative solution to climate change.

Filtering
It's a story...

Initial stories cited the Green New Deal as an example of how **Democratic victories in the 2018 midterms would change Washington politics**.

Or is it?

Other sources described the Green New Deal as dead on arrival, particularly after Senate Republicans brought the proposal to a vote and **defeated it by a vote of 0–57**.

Framing
It's a call to action.

Over the succeeding months, the Green New Deal was used to **illustrate the profound policy changes needed** to address climate change.

Maybe not.

Other analyses pointed out that the Green New Deal **contained many nonclimate proposals**, such as a commitment to provide living wages and health care to all Americans.

Priming
It's impossible.

After a year of inaction, end-of-year roundup stories explained how the House's failure to vote on the Green New Deal illustrated the **partisan deadlock in Washington**.

No, there's hope.

In January 2020, Republicans began to develop **their own climate change legislation**.

Filtering, Framing, and Priming

Follow-up stories reported on how Democrats were planning to add climate change proposals to COVID-19 economic stimulus legislation.

?

Critical Thinking

1. **Of the three media effects** (filtering, framing, and priming), which is the easiest one for citizens to detect? Which one is the hardest?

2. **Do a Web search** for "Green New Deal." In the first two articles you see, find all the instances of filtering, framing, and priming. Do you think these articles provide a balanced picture of the proposal? Why or why not?

people exposed to stories that describe a particular event learn new facts as a result of their exposure. However, some of the impact of media coverage stems not from what such stories contain but from how they present information or even whether a story is reported at all.[24]

Media bias and partisanship

Many studies have found that exposure to political coverage changes what citizens know: at the most basic level, people who watch, read, or listen to more coverage about politics know more than people who are exposed to less of this coverage.[25] What people learn from the media, in turn, can shape the demands they place on politicians.[26] However, at least part of the media's effect on people's knowledge level arises because of underlying interest: people who are interested in politics know more in the first place and, because of their interest, watch more media coverage of events as they happen. Moreover, because people can pick and choose which coverage to watch, read, or listen to, what they learn from the media tends to reinforce their preexisting beliefs. That is, a conservative might listen to Sean Hannity, while a liberal might watch MSNBC. Both people may learn something from the coverage, but the most likely result is that they will only grow more certain in the opinions that they already have.[27]

Given this evidence on media effects, one of the central questions is whether reporters and editors have a discernable bias: That is, do their decisions about which events to report on and how they report on them reflect a conscious effort to shape public opinion in a liberal, conservative, or other direction? Surveys of the American electorate have found a **hostile media effect**: regardless of respondents' partisan leanings, they believe that the media favor candidates and ideas from the other party.[28] Conservative critics of the media point to surveys that show that most reporters identify themselves as liberals. Liberal critics respond that most pundits, especially on talk radio, offer conservative points of view—and that many media sources are owned by large corporations, which could lead to underreporting of some stories, such as those offering a favorable portrayal of labor unions.[29]

Questions about media bias have become more urgent since the election of Donald Trump, who criticized the media for reporting what he termed "fake news." Trump even claimed, several times, that the press was "the enemy of the American people."[30] Sometimes Trump used the "fake news" label for stories he found misleading or inaccurate, such as polls that show public disapproval of his actions in office. The deeper message of the "fake news" label is that Trump believed that media coverage of his presidency could not be trusted because reporters and their editors simply dislike him and his supporters.

It is easy to find examples of outright mistakes by reporters and their editors that suggest some sort of overt bias in coverage. For example, in December 2017 the *Washington Post* reporter Dave Weigel posted pictures on Twitter showing large numbers of empty seats at a Trump rally. However, the pictures were taken before the start of the rally; by the time it actually began, the stadium was full. After Trump complained on Twitter, Weigel apologized and published pictures showing that all the seats were taken. Similarly, as we describe in Chapter 13, most polls taken during the 2016 campaign failed to predict Donald Trump's victory. However, while Trump and others may have seen this as evidence of a bias against him, the polls were actually largely accurate. These same polls accurately predicted the popular vote totals; where they went wrong was in predicting turnout in a small number of rural counties in Wisconsin, Michigan, and Pennsylvania—minor differences that were enough to produce an Electoral College victory for Trump. There is no evidence that pollsters

hostile media effect
The tendency of people to see neutral media coverage of an event as biased against their point of view.

were biasing their results to hurt Trump. If anything, each pollster had a strong interest in making correct predictions—any pollster would have been gratified to have been the only one to predict that Trump would win.

Many journalists and commentators admit that they take an ideological or partisan perspective. Talk show hosts Sean Hannity and Glenn Beck, for example, describe themselves as strong conservatives. And many commentators on Fox News make no secret of their conservative viewpoint—just as commentators on MSNBC make no secret of their liberal leanings. Similarly, the political news magazine *The Nation* describes itself as "a weekly journal of left/liberal opinion, covering national and international affairs as well as the arts."[31] These journalists' and organizations' points of view are well known and easy to identify. Some people might even find the bias useful. A liberal, for example, could use *The Nation*'s endorsements as a guide for which candidates to support, and a conservative might have listened to Rush Limbaugh to get similar information.

It is also no surprise that politicians complain that media coverage is biased against them: the stakes for them are very high. For example, during the final weeks of the 2020 election, Donald Trump's campaign wanted more coverage of its claims that Joe Biden was a corrupt politician whose son and other family members had used connections to enrich themselves, and less attention paid to the COVID-19 pandemic and the weak American economy. The Biden campaign in turn complained that the media were focusing too much on rumors about Biden's health or conflicts within the Democratic party, and not enough on Trump's missteps. Thus, while both campaigns complained about bias, the simple explanation for their complaints is that they wanted to win the election and therefore wanted media coverage that exposed their opponent's flaws rather than their candidate's flaws.

In fact, while it is easy to find media coverage of politics that is incomplete or sloppily reported, cases in which reporters made predictions that later turned out to be false, or stories that candidates wish had not been reported, it is hard to find cases of systematic bias in media coverage. President Trump often complained that reporters were spending too much time searching for inconsistencies and exaggerations in his descriptions of past events, arguing that they did not scrutinize President Obama or other Democrats in the same way. Yet it is easy to find exhaustive media coverage of similar issues in Obama's past, including his use of illegal drugs and his mediocre grades during his first years in college. You may think that the media were making too much of Trump's past—but it is hard to say that they gave a free pass to Obama or other Democrats.

Moreover, while some academic studies have found evidence of press coverage favoring one type of candidate or issue position over another, an equally large body of work has produced important critiques of these studies. For one thing, a finding that most reporters are liberal (or Democrats) and few are conservative (Republicans) does not imply that political coverage must necessarily favor liberal positions or Democratic candidates. Reporters may prioritize being as objective as possible, fear that favoring one side will cause their audience to decline, or be subject to review by editors who are on guard against bias. Similarly, the fact that a reporter criticizes a politician or party is not evidence of his or her lack of objectivity. Critiques do not in themselves suggest that a reporter is being unfair—the question is, what would a fair analysis look like? Many analyses of President Trump's time in office (before COVID-19) acknowledged the strong American economy but gave little credit to Trump for this outcome. Were these reporters biased against Trump, or had they read the literature on political control of the economy, which shows that presidential actions have little impact on economic conditions, particularly in the short run? Untangling these effects is difficult, and if media bias were as pronounced as some critics claim, it would likely be easier to measure.

Filtering and framing

Compared with overt bias, filtering and framing may produce subtler but stronger impacts on public opinion. **Filtering** (also called *agenda-setting*) refers to the ways in which journalists' and editors' decisions about which stories to report influence which stories people think about. **Framing** refers to how the description or presentation of a story, including the details, explanations, and context, changes the ways people react to and interpret the information. Space and time limitations mean that some filtering is inevitable as reporters and editors decide which of many potential news stories to cover. Similar decisions about what to report and how to present the information lead to framing effects. Even if everyone in the political media adhered to the highest standards of accuracy, these influences would still exist.

The concept of filtering is illustrated by Project Censored's annual list of Top Censored Stories.[32] The group's list for 2019 includes stories about health concerns raised by new 5G cellular networks and efforts within the Department of Defense to increase surveillance of social media.[33] The group's point is not that the government forces reporters to keep quiet; rather, it claims that reporters and their editors decide against covering these stories, sometimes for self-serving reasons, such as beliefs about what their audience wants to see or read.

The impact of filtering is also apparent in cases of government inaction. Figure 14.1 shows media coverage (as a percentage of total stories from 63,000 publications) of gun control–related stories following the 2018 shooting at Marjory Stoneman Douglas High School in Parkland, Florida. As you can see, the percentage of gun-related stories spiked upward initially, with additional spikes following student walkouts and protests, but returned to its former low level after 12 weeks. The pattern in the graph illustrates what happens when an event grabs public attention: media coverage increases in the days afterward, but the effect soon fades. Put another way, as Americans move on from thinking about a mass shooting or other event, media attention shifts with them. Whether sustained media attention would have galvanized public opinion behind stricter gun control laws is an open question. But if one effect of media coverage is to raise public awareness of an issue, people are not going to be aware of an issue the media ignore.

Reporting on violent crime in America shows clear framing effects. Over the last few years, many stories in major publications have reported sharp increases in homicide rates

filtering
The influence on public opinion that results from journalists' and editors' decisions about which of many potential news stories to report.

framing
The influence on public opinion caused by the way a story is presented or covered, including the details, explanations, and context offered in the report.

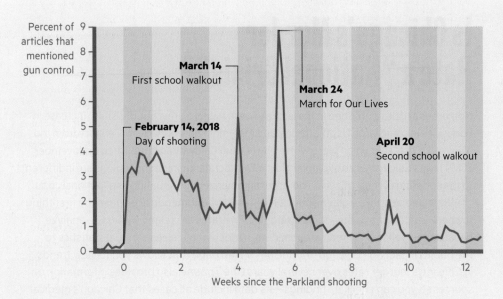

Percent of articles that mentioned gun control

February 14, 2018
Day of shooting

March 14
First school walkout

March 24
March for Our Lives

April 20
Second school walkout

Weeks since the Parkland shooting

Source: Daniel Nass, "Parkland Generated Dramatically More News Coverage Than Most Mass Shootings," The Trace, May 17, 2018, www.thetrace.org/2018/05/parkland-media-coverage-analysis-mass-shooting/ (accessed 1/27/20).

FIGURE 14.1

Gun Control Stories per Week, February 2018 to May 2018

Press attention to gun control spikes upward after a mass shooting, then fades as reporters move on to other stories. How does this pattern help opponents of gun control legislation preserve the status quo?

in cities such as Chicago, St. Louis, and Baltimore, suggesting a nationwide problem.[34] However, other cities saw homicide rates decline—in fact, the average murder rate for the top 50 cities has risen only slightly in the last few years and is far below the peak that it reached in the 1990s (see the What Do the Facts Say? feature). Adding data on nationwide crime rates to a story on murders in three cities doesn't change the facts of what's happening there, but it does suggest that these events are not proof of a larger national trend.

In sum, reporting on politics requires reporters to move beyond "just the facts." They must choose what to report on, how to describe the news, whether to reveal secrets, and

The way a story is reported—which information is included in an article or which images are used—makes a big difference in what people learn from it. Stories that focus on cases of violent crime suggest an epidemic of murders, rapes, and assault, but actual data on crime rates paint a very different picture.

> In my reporting for Fox News, the people I have spoken with feel so under siege by the gun violence that this tiny drop doesn't even register to them, and any talk from a politician who mentions the reduction in murders is a smack in their face because going on their front porch could be a death sentence.

—**Gianno Caldwell,** *New York Post*[a]

Is Chicago's Murder Rate a "National Crisis"?

Numerous articles published in the last few years raised alarms about a sharp increase in homicides in some large U.S. metropolitan areas, most notably Chicago. A story from the *New York Post* (an opinion piece written by Gianno Caldwell and published in November 2019) treats Chicago as an exemplar of how Democratic city administrations are indifferent to the suffering of their citizens. The writer summarized the situation as a "national crisis."

When people make a claim about a real-world phenomenon like crime, the first thing to check is if they have their facts straight. Crime rates are relatively easy to analyze because the police and medical examiners in most areas release annual statistics to the public. In fact, the *Chicago Tribune* has a Web page that allows you to view trends in Chicago's murder rates over several years (the *Tribune* also provides information on sources so you can check its findings—its data include all cases that Chicago's medical examiner classified as homicides).[b] These *Tribune* data tell a different story: rather than being out of control, murder rates in Chicago have been declining for several years following a spike in 2016.

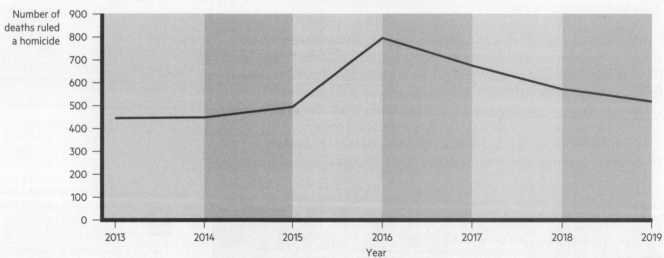

Chicago Murder Rate, 2013–2019

Number of deaths ruled a homicide (y-axis, 0 to 900); Year (x-axis, 2013 to 2019).

Source: "Tracking Chicago Homicide Victims," *Chicago Tribune,* www.chicagotribune.com/news/breaking/ct-chicago-homicides-data-tracker-htmlstory.html (accessed 1/29/20).

Think about it

- **What additional information** might help put Chicago's murder rate as cited in this *New York Post* article in context? Can you think of any comparative data points that might help make better sense of the numbers?

- **What are the dangers** of spreading misleading or incorrect information about public safety? How might these errors lead people to make uninformed decisions?

Additional analysis by *The Economist* places murders in Chicago in a broader context.[c] Homicide rates in any city can vary sharply from year to year simply because homicide is a fairly rare crime. Several cities in *The Economist*'s analysis had the same pattern as in Chicago of sharp increases followed by declines.

The *Post*'s article fails one of the key criteria we discussed in Chapter 1: the claims it makes about Chicago's murder rates are very different from those developed by other researchers. Because the story is so anomalous, we should be very skeptical about its conclusions. Remember to always corroborate the report.

which sources to rely on. Moreover, events do not always speak for themselves—they require interpretation. The fact that Democrats and Republicans consult very different media sources (as shown in Table 14.1 on p. 618) suggests that people see different media sources as trustworthy based on their partisanship, and that they are well aware of framing, filtering, and potential bias and choose their media sources accordingly. Given the vast array of political coverage in modern America, even if we take potential biases as well as filtering and framing into account, virtually all of us can find several sources that we consider reliable, if we take the time to search for those sources.[35]

Americans often demand that journalists give "just the facts and all the facts" about politics and public policy. Most of the time, however, what looks like biased reporting is a journalist trying to make sense of a complex world. The act of reporting requires decisions on which stories matter, which facts deserve mention, and how events should be interpreted. To say that you don't like how a journalist resolves these decisions doesn't mean that he or she is pushing a particular political agenda.

"Why Should I Care?"

Do the media work?

ASSESS WHETHER THE MEDIA FULFILL THEIR ROLE IN AMERICAN DEMOCRACY

In a democracy, the media's role is to provide citizens with information about politicians, government actions, and policy debates. It is easy to argue that the media are falling down on the job: surveys taken in recent years show that substantial percentages of Americans believe that voter fraud is a major problem, that a third of the federal budget is spent on foreign aid, that America is no longer the preeminent military power, and that undocumented immigration is on the rise. In fact, all of these statements are false (actually, foreign aid spending is only about 2 percent of the federal budget).

Claims of ideological bias do not explain these shortcomings. The central finding of the political science literature on media effects is that systematic bias is hard to find. In President Trump's term, the press gave considerable attention to anonymous comments from people working inside the Trump administration that highlighted the president's supposed inattention to detail and unwillingness to spend time studying briefing documents. But these stories did not appear because reporters and editors are hard-core liberals (or Democrats) who wanted to destroy Trump's chances of getting reelected. Rather, coverage was driven by leaks from administration officials and by reporters' belief that Trump's work habits have a measurable effect on the quality of decisions made in the administration. The media have been similarly critical of past presidents, Democrats and Republicans alike—for example, media critiques of the Obama presidency noted Obama's failure to enact gun control and climate legislation, as well as his reliance on a small group of advisers for policy guidance.[36]

You also have to recognize the difficulty of the task being assigned to the media. It's easy to say that the media should be objective, should give us "just the facts," and should report on both sides of an issue. But what if one side makes no sense? Some of the more bizarre QAnon theories posit that the world is being ruled by a small international cabal (led by former president John F. Kennedy, who allegedly faked his death) and that the Black Lives Matter movement and the COVID-19 pandemic were carefully orchestrated to ensure Trump's defeat in the 2020 election. Clearly, these theories do not deserve much attention—but what should reporters do when they believe that elected officials are misrepresenting the truth? Being objective may require them to advise readers that the truth lies on one side rather than in between.

Lack of citizen interest

In part, the media's apparent failure to create a well-informed citizenry is driven by a lack of citizen interest. As we discussed in Chapter 10, the average American has a fairly low interest in politics, and only a small percentage of Americans care enough to take the time and effort to become well informed. Everyone else learns about politics as a by-product of other things he or she does throughout the day.

The lack of citizen interest is one reason why the increased amount of information available on the Internet has not produced a better-informed citizenry: while information is available, average Americans make little attempt to find and understand it. As political scientist Markus Prior noted, the expansion of the Internet has increased the availability of all kinds of information, not just information about politics.[37] Not surprisingly, people gravitate to the topics they are interested in, which for most people is not politics. As a result, putting more information about politics on the Web does not make everyone better informed; rather, it widens the gap between the small percentage of Americans who care about politics and the vast majority whose interest level is much lower.

Even for people who are motivated to learn more about politics, finding information, sifting through conflicting sources, and assessing the credibility of different accounts is a difficult task, even for experts. Surveys by the Pew Research Center show that even highly interested, well-informed individuals can find it difficult to distinguish between factual and opinion statements in the news.[38] Even finding sources in the first place can be difficult. For example, suppose you want to learn more about the Black Lives Matter movement. A Google search in late 2020 of the term returned millions of Web pages, including press reports, blog entries by participants in the protests as well as supporters and opponents, and tweets by President Trump. Thus, the problem is not finding information but deciding which of the millions of pages available will help you learn about the movement.

In short, despite the Internet's wealth of information, there is no guarantee that people will sit down, search for what they want or need to know, distinguish truth from falsehood, and assemble their findings into coherent conclusions. In fact, rather than creating a uniformly well-informed citizenry, the availability of information on the Internet may exacerbate the pattern we saw in Chapter 10, in which a small percentage of Americans are extremely well informed about politics, while the vast majority of the public may simply throw up their hands and make no attempt to become better informed.[39]

Market forces

Another influence on media coverage is competition for an audience. Mass media sources have always tried to get as large an audience as possible in order to generate profits and stay in business, but the expansion of the Internet and the increased availability of free information have increased competitive pressures.[40] In part, these pressures have had positive effects for consumers: newspapers, for example, have put their content online and moved from publishing once per day to continually producing new stories and updates. Television stations have placed their video content online as well, including footage that was never used in broadcasts, so that people can watch at any time.

Many Americans, attracted by clickbait headlines and dramatic storylines, now get the bulk of their political news from nontraditional online sources like BuzzFeed.

One downside of audience pressures is that they lead reporters to search for stories—any stories—to have something new to offer their audience, who otherwise might get its news from somewhere else. For example, although most theories of elections show that polls taken during the early days of a political campaign are almost irrelevant, the media still cover poll results. Early on most people know very little about the candidates, so a well-known figure, such as Donald Trump in 2016 or Joe Biden during the early stages of the 2020 campaign, may attract support simply because people know his or her name. Because reporters need something to write about, they may focus on a new poll even though they are well aware that the poll's findings are almost meaningless. The mere fact that reporters focus so much on each new poll may lead some readers to pay more attention to the findings than they actually deserve.

This quest for an audience also favors coverage of new, breaking issues, particularly if they involve some sort of controversy and feature well-known individuals. Political scientist Amber Boydstun has shown that this practice often leads reporters to sideline important issues in favor of newer, fresher events.[41] For example, the United States has had substantial numbers of ground troops in Afghanistan since late 2001, but this conflict has long since disappeared from the front pages of major news outlets in favor of stories on climate change, the economy, coronavirus, and whatever else happened yesterday. The conflict will not reappear on the front page unless something major happens, such as significant U.S. casualties. And if the conflict is not on the front page, only the few Americans who are political junkies or armchair military strategists will even be aware that the war is still going on.

More generally, audience pressures lead reporters to focus on making their stories simple and dramatic in order to catch the attention of a distracted audience. Stories that say "nothing important happened today in the presidential campaign" or "today's events are hard to explain but almost surely will not affect who wins the election" will lose out to reports that cast events in simple, life-and-death terms. Consider media coverage of the early stages of the Democratic presidential nomination campaign, particularly the Iowa Caucuses held in February 2020. In the months before the caucuses, each debate or campaign appearance was framed in a way that made it seem significant, and thus more interesting to media audiences, as though it would provide deep insights about the candidates and their chances of winning the nomination and defeating Donald Trump. The fact is that a candidate's success in Iowa, a largely rural,

News right now is like a flock of speeded-up sheep running off the side of a cliff.

—**Ali Smith,** author

attack journalism

A type of increasingly popular media coverage focused on political scandals and controversies, which causes a negative public opinion of political figures.

horse race

A description of the type of election coverage that focuses more on poll results and speculation about a likely winner than on substantive differences between the candidates.

soft news

Media coverage that aims to entertain or shock, often through sensationalized reporting or by focusing on a candidate or politician's personality.

hard news

Media coverage focused on facts and important issues surrounding a campaign.

racially homogenous state, does not tell us much about their prospects in other states—Joe Biden, who ultimately won the nomination, came in fourth place in this contest.

The media's efforts to spin a story to attract an audience are nothing new.[42] For decades, scholars have documented the rise of attack journalism, in which journalists focus on scandal, government failures, and politicians' personal failings.[43] Other researchers have argued that campaign coverage overemphasizes the horse race aspects, such as which candidates are ahead and which are falling behind, rather than offering a complete description of each candidate's promises and an analysis of how he or she is likely to behave in office.[44] Similarly, coverage of debates over public policy often focuses on personalities and predictions about who is likely to achieve his or her goals, not the details of what the policies include. Media coverage of politics also emphasizes soft news (stories that are sensational or entertaining) over hard news (stories that focus on important issues and emphasize facts and figures).[45] The media also often give disproportionate coverage to events that are more likely to be recognized by the average American. For example, media coverage of Hurricane Harvey, which hit land in Texas in 2017, was much more extensive than coverage of Hurricane Maria, which devastated Puerto Rico only a month later—and both of these disasters were covered far more aggressively than the far more deadly monsoon storms in Bangladesh that occurred at the same time.[46]

The pressure on journalists to publish as quickly as possible also leads to major mistakes—in January 2019, initial stories on a confrontation involving high school students who attended an anti-abortion rally in Washington, D.C., and an American Indian elder who was a counterprotester at the event alleged that the students had harassed the elder and used racial slurs. After several days of coverage, video of the incident showed that these claims were false. Some major outlets (including the *Washington Post*) had to issue major clarifications of their reporting, and at least one outlet (CNN) settled a lawsuit brought by one of the students.

Why do journalists ignore details and emphasize scandal? Describing the media as an information source for citizens makes sense in terms of how American politics works, but this description does not capture the sometimes contradictory incentives that journalists face. They may feel the need to demonstrate their independence from politicians and government interests and perhaps counter or prevent claims of media bias. And this may lead to aggressive questioning of elected officials and cynical stories about the political process.[47] But again, reporters and their editors are in a competitive business to attract a paying audience.[48] Most American media outlets are for-profit enterprises. Because they need to produce coverage that attracts an audience, they often seek to create stories that consumers want. So if the media focus on something that seems frivolous, like Joe Biden's favorite food (ice cream) or First Lady Jill Biden's fashion choices, it is because these stories find a ready audience.

Even if reporters for major news outlets tried to explain how our democratic government works or the complexity of most policy questions, it is unlikely that citizens would respond favorably. There are sources available that work this way. The nightly television program *PBS NewsHour* has a reputation for producing thoughtful, in-depth stories about politics and policy. The magazine *Congressional Quarterly* is well-known among Congress scholars for its analysis of House and Senate proceedings. But the audience for these sources is minuscule, which is another indication that most people would prefer soft news, cynicism, and scandals to hard news, policy details, and sober analysis (see the Take a Stand feature for the debate over Facebook's plan to allow users to "grade" the news).

Thus, complaints about how the media cover American politics are to a large extent misdirected. The media give Americans the coverage they want. If the average citizen wants to become an expert on politics and public policy, the necessary information is

TAKE A STAND

Should Facebook Grade the News?

As we have discussed in this chapter, most Americans are exposed to only a small fraction of the media's coverage of American politics. Because people read or watch only a limited number of stories, it is especially important for them to judge the reliability of the sources they consult. Do the stories include the right facts? Are the facts being presented fairly? Is the coverage shaped by the authors' conscious or unconscious biases? These are not easy questions to resolve, especially for the typical American who is not highly interested in politics and who has other demands on his or her time.

Facebook, one of the most common channels through which people get their news, has suggested a solution to this problem. It proposes to ask a sample of Facebook users two questions: Do you recognize a particular media source, and how trustworthy do you rate that source? Facebook would use the results of the survey to determine which stories are promoted in News Feeds. Users looking at their News Feeds would then be able to focus on stories from sources that were rated as highly trustworthy and would not be exposed to stories from sources that received low trust scores. Facebook hopes that by filtering the news stories it promotes in this way, it can help users become more informed about politics.

It's a great idea. By asking a random sample of users, Facebook is letting the mass public express its feelings about which information sources it would like to see. While some people might be biased in favor of one source or another, the hope is that these biases will average out over a large sample, ultimately highlighting more neutral sources. Presumably, the survey results would also favor sources that produce simple, easy-to-understand stories. Conversely, if a panel of experts were consulted to pick the "best" sources for news, it might choose sources that generate overly complicated political analyses that the average Facebook user might ignore entirely or misinterpret. Thus, the mass survey is more likely to identify a set of sources that people will actually use if put in front of them. Of course, it would be great if seeing a political story on Facebook prompted a user to investigate further by going to other sites that offer more details and deeper analysis. But Facebook's trustworthiness surveys will increase the chances that people receive accurate information about politics, even if the amount is relatively small.

 Many people have blamed Facebook for facilitating the circulation of "fake news" from untrustworthy sources.

It could make things worse. Facebook's survey strategy assumes that the biggest problem with individuals' assessments of media sources is that they favor sources that support their preferred candidates or policy proposals. Its hope is that these biases will cancel each other out in a large survey. However, the average American's media consumption is shaped by a variety of conscious and unconscious biases. People tend to trust the sources they regularly consult and distrust sources they have never heard of or have only seen a few times. They favor sources that simplify complex stories and deliver information in easy-to-read graphics. And most fundamentally, people like sources that reinforce their beliefs and dislike sources that challenge what they think or force them to learn new ways of thinking about an issue. Facebook's solution may not account for all of these additional biases. Rating sources by their perceived trustworthiness might well lead to a situation in which people think they are better informed, when in fact they are just as uninformed as they were before Facebook's efforts.

take a stand

1. Why do you think Americans are uninformed about political events? Will Facebook's trustworthiness ratings address this problem?
2. Suppose Facebook chose you to participate in its survey. Which media sources would you rate as trustworthy? Which would you rate as untrustworthy? How many would you have no opinion about?
3. What do you think motivated Facebook to begin its media evaluation initiative? Do you think Facebook is likely to succeed?

surely available. But few people are interested in seeking that degree of understanding. For most Americans, the media's coverage of politics as a sports event is enough to keep them satisfied, even as they complain about a lack of details and an emphasis on scandal.

Reporters compete for an audience—that's how they stay in business. That means that stories you consider important (or that really are important) may not get media attention because they're too hard to explain or because people aren't interested. The only way to get more detailed, thoughtful political coverage is for Americans to start demanding it.

The FCC Fairness Doctrine

Policy making has often had a difficult time keeping up with technology. The ways in which people get their news, for example, have changed dramatically since the early 1900s. Before radio became popular in the 1920s, newspapers had been the main news source for several centuries. Even though newspapers in big cities were often printed several times a day, radio was able to offer an unrivaled sense of immediacy. It could deliver breaking news, extended reports, and interviews with the added advantage that the audience could hear what the presenters or interviewees were saying. Newsreels, which are short news pieces or mini-documentaries, appeared in movie theaters since 1910, but they took a while to produce, and customers had to go to theaters to see them—and see them is all they could do until talkies came on the scene in the late 1920s. Radio and movies were primarily for entertainment, but radio also became an important news vehicle, and early legislation recognized its influence and the need for stations to present different views and also remain essentially neutral.

Television, which became popular in the 1950s, offered the best of all worlds: audio, video, immediacy, and easy availability. This combination made it even more influential than radio, and politicians took note. Television might have eclipsed other forms of media in some ways, but it did not replace newspapers and radio as a news source; it supplemented them. By the late 1950s, the Federal Communications Commission (FCC), which had been formed initially to regulate only radio, was dealing with more and more cases of radio and television stations suspected of violating their neutrality. There were also persistent questions about the validity of the neutrality requirement imposed on stations. Broadcast stations were also afraid that it would be impossible to cover the news at all without possibly violating the FCC regulations. The fairness doctrine was implemented to clarify the regulations and to assure broadcasters that they were actually in compliance with the FCC by presenting important issues of the day as long as they presented all points of view. The broadcast stations also had to comply with the equal-time rule, which required them to provide the same amount of time to all political candidates and at the same rates if they are paid advertisements. This FCC rule, along with an early version of the fairness doctrine, came out of the Radio Act of 1927.

As with most policies, the fairness doctrine continued to be debated after it was put in place. It finally met its end most fittingly during the presidency of Ronald Reagan (1981–1989), who previously appeared as a radio, film, and television actor. A theme running through his candidacy and presidency was that when it comes to the federal level, the government that governs least governs best. Probably partly because of some of his experiences on radio and television, he made it known quite early in his first term that he thought the fairness doctrine should go away. His first appointed like-minded

FCC director started the process of dismantling it, which was completed by Reagan's second FCC director in 1987. It was during this time period that radio and television stations started becoming more and more partisan, a trend that continues today. This is the reason why a policy that ended in the 1980s is still taught years later.

Up to now, the policies discussed have focused on the events leading up to their implementation and their effects, both positive and negative. Also keep in mind that the absence of a policy is often a policy itself. The revocation of the fairness doctrine created the vacuum effect of a de facto policy that has led to the proliferation of mostly conservative but also liberal broadcast stations. The Political Parties chapter (Chapter 11) discussed how party polarization started to increase just about the time of the Reagan presidency. Though there are certainly many factors that have increased the divide between Democrats and Republicans, the ending of the fairness doctrine certainly contributed to it. As pointed out in the Possible Modifications, Expansion, or Termination of Policy stage, even though the doctrine is now dead, events inevitably arise, such as the Arizona shootings in 2011, which put the issue back on the political agenda, at least briefly.

Policy Stages

1. Problem Recognition
   - Yellow journalism in the late 1880s was characterized by newspapers that tended to sensationalize the news and did not always present facts in their stories, often using bold headlines and illustrations to increase readership.
   - Under a new owner in 1896, the *New York Times* strived for journalistic objectivity, impartiality, accuracy, and complete coverage of events.
     - The newspaper's motto was "All the News That's Fit to Print."
   - Radio stations proliferated in the 1920s.
     - Many were small stations.
     - Some larger stations could broadcast nationwide.
     - Networks, each owned by one company, developed and broadcast a common set of programs across their stations.
   - The Radio Act of 1927
     - Radio stations had to act in the public interest and remain politically neutral.
     - The equal-time rule stipulated that different sides of political issues must be presented.
     - Four significant court cases in the late 1920s and early 1930s highlighted violations of this law.
   - The Communications Act of 1934
     - It created the FCC.
       - A five-person committee was appointed by the president and confirmed by the Senate.
       - It regulated radio communications and monitored for infractions.
       - It awarded licenses to allow radio stations to operate.
     - All qualified candidates running for political office were given the opportunity for equal air time if at least one candidate was given air time outside normal news coverage.
     - Every candidate was charged the same rate.
     - Broadcasting stations could not increase rates to candidates within a certain period of time before elections.

2. Agenda Setting
   - The FCC Mayflower doctrine (1941–1949)
     - Radio stations were not supposed to champion a particular political position (that is, editorialize).
     - Opponents saw it as censorship and an attack on free speech.

- The FCC held hearings in 1948 and produced the *Report on Editorializing by Broadcast Licensees* (1949) to clarify its expectations of broadcasters:
  - It established the fairness doctrine, which replaced the Mayflower doctrine and which Congress incorporated into law in 1959 by amending the Communications Act of 1934.
  - Broadcasters had to cover important issues of the day.
  - Broadcasters could editorialize but also had to present other viewpoints somewhere in their programming.
  - Broadcasters had to give air time for rebuttal by listeners.
  - Guidelines were broad (and vague, according to many).

3. Deliberation and Formulation
   - Television became very popular during the 1950s.
   - Television's reach and influence were even more extensive than radio's.
   - 1959 FCC case
     - A mayoral candidate claimed that a Chicago television station's reporting of the current mayor's activities demanded that he also receive equal time.
     - The FCC agreed.
     - Television stations worried this would mean they would have to stop covering any political candidate during a campaign.
     - Senate hearings were held in June 1959 to discuss the issue.
       - The Senate issued a report reestablishing the duty of broadcasting stations to present the news in a fair way.
       - Senator William Proxmire (D-WI) thought an existing amendment would make a stronger statement than just producing a report.
   - In 1959, Proxmire introduced an amendment to the Communications Act of 1934 in the Senate.

4. Enactment
   - The House of Representatives and the Senate agreed to a compromise draft of the 1959 amendment to the Communications Act of 1934.
     - They rewrote Chapter 315(a): "A broadcast licensee shall afford reasonable opportunity for discussion of conflicting views on matters of public importance."
     - It enshrined FCC's 1949 fairness doctrine into law.

5. Implementation
   - The fairness doctrine reinforced and clarified rules that had been in place since the repeal of the Mayflower doctrine in 1949.
   - It required broadcasters to present controversial issues of the day, but they had to do so in a "fair and balanced" way.
   - Exceptions were made to equal air time for newscast stories, interviews, and documentaries.
   - Stations could lose their license if they violated this rule.

6. Evaluation
   - The fairness doctrine violated broadcasters' First Amendment free speech rights.
   - Many in the broadcasting industry mistakenly thought every specific program dealing with political or social issues had to be balanced within the program.
   - The cigarette industry was opposed to the doctrine's implications that allowed the anti-smoking lobby, which was in favor of the doctrine, to get equal time for airing its advertisements.
   - *Red Lion Broadcasting Company vs. FCC* (1969)
     - A person who felt he was wrongfully attacked on a radio show was denied an opportunity for air time to respond.
     - The FCC ruled in his favor and the radio station appealed to the Supreme Court.

- The Supreme Court decision
  - supported the FCC and lower court decisions.
  - upheld the fairness doctrine.
  - justified the government's authority to regulate broadcasting stations and require equal time for responses because the "scarcity of broadcast frequencies" does not allow all citizens the ability to express their views themselves.
- The Media Access Project (MAP), a law firm specializing in telecommunications, stated that the doctrine preserved freedom of speech because the public had the right to know different viewpoints of issues of the day.
- Some people in the media thought the doctrine prevented ideologically based (especially conservative) talk shows.
- Others have pointed out that conservative talk shows thrived even before it was repealed.
- Over the years there have been many violations, and the doctrine was difficult to enforce.
- The FCC was getting overwhelmed with lawsuits filed by broadcasting stations.

7. Possible Modifications, Expansion, or Termination of Policy
- The FCC had to provide an exception to allow the 1960 televised presidential debates since this type of situation had been overlooked in the 1959 amendment.
- The FCC issued a fairness doctrine primer in 1964 to clarify its expectations.
- The FCC reinforced the doctrine in 1967 by ensuring that candidates, individuals, and groups have a right to air time to reply to statements made against them.
- President Ronald Reagan heralded a deregulation era from 1981 to 1989.
  - *Telecommunications Research Action v. FCC* (1986): The D.C. District Court decided that because of the amendment's wording, the FCC was not required by law to enforce the fairness doctrine.
  - Reagan-appointed FCC chair from 1981 to 1987, Mark Fowler was against the doctrine and stopped enforcing it in the mid-1980s.
  - The Fairness in Broadcasting Act of 1987
    - It was passed by both houses of Congress to codify the fairness doctrine into law.
    - Reagan vetoed the bill on June 22, 1987.
  - Reagan-appointed FCC chair from 1987 to 1989, Dennis R. Patrick repealed the fairness doctrine on August 5, 1987.
- Congress attempted to reinstate the doctrine in 1991, but President George H. W. Bush's ongoing threat to veto it from 1989 to 1993 caused the bill never to be considered for a vote.
- The Fairness and Accountability in Broadcasting bill was introduced in 2005.
  - It cut in half the length of a station's license from eight years to four.
  - It required broadcasters to cover different sides of important issues.
  - It increased transparency by holding public hearings every six months and reporting to the FCC about its coverage.
  - The bill died in committee.
- Norm Coleman (R-MN) tried to stop any further attempts to introduce another fairness doctrine by introducing an amendment to a bill in the Senate on July 13, 2007.
  - Democrats in the Senate blocked the amendment.
- On August 22, 2011, the FCC formally removed the fairness doctrine rule from the *Federal Register*, "the official daily publication for rules, proposed rules, and notices of Federal agencies and organizations, as well as executive orders and other presidential documents."

- Shootings on January 8, 2011, in Tucson, Arizona, injured U.S. Representative Gabrielle Giffords (D-AZ) among 18 others.
  - James Clyburn (D-SC), Louise Slaughter (D-NY), and other Democrat members of Congress linked the violence to conservative political rhetoric on talk radio.
  - Some wanted to bring back the fairness doctrine, but no real attempts were made.

Questions for Discussion

1. Should the FCC fairness doctrine be reintroduced? Why or why not?
2. An increasing number of people, especially the young, get most of their news from social media sites. Do these sites have an obligation to delete posts and messages that are factually not true or should users be responsible for determining their value? Explain your answer.
3. Why was the ending of the FCC fairness doctrine both a cause and an effect of growing political polarization in the United States?

Unpacking the Conflict

Did the Russian government use fake social media posts and Facebook ads to intervene in the 2016 presidential election? Based on analyses from American intelligence agencies, corroborating evidence from foreign intelligence agencies, and investigations by respected journalists, the answer is that they did. But if you are typical in terms of how much time you spend following politics and the sources you consult, you could be forgiven for having your doubts, or even believing a false narrative that pinned blame on the Ukrainian government—it would all depend on which stories you happened to read, watch, or listen to. Social media was supposed to inform us and bring us together—what went wrong?

The idea that the rise of the Internet would help create a better-informed population also assumed that the producers of media content, from mainstream sources like the *New York Times* to anonymous Twitter users who post insider information about government agency decisions, would all work toward the goal of empowering the American public. The reality is that the media are businesses, in which the goal of attracting an audience often conflicts with the more idealistic goals of telling people what they need to know to make good decisions and acting as a watchdog to monitor government actions. Americans might be better informed if the media ignored sensational stories and focused on the details of public policy, but lurid stories help attract and keep an audience that media companies need to stay in business. Americans will get different media coverage only if they value sources that emphasize details and complexity over scandals and drama.

Social media advocates were right about the ways the media would change—but they were wrong about how citizens would react. Even now, most Americans behave as they always have, consulting a few trusted sources for information about politics. The fact that much more information is available now has not changed our consumption habits. The value of gathering additional information is simply not worth the trouble, especially given the need to reconcile different sources.

For all of these reasons, America's news media often fall short of the goal of acting as a watchdog, making sure people have the information they need to bring government policy in line with their interests. Though social media has changed many aspects of our lives, it has not changed this fundamental truth about American politics: we cannot blame people for refusing to take advantage of what the media offer them, but at the same time we cannot blame the media for citizens' ignorance and misinformation.

"What's Your Take?"

Should social media be judged based on the wealth of information it provides or on its failure to increase citizens' political knowledge?

Should Americans put more trust in the media?

AP® STUDY GUIDE

Summary

The media have been the primary sources of political information in America since the Founding, though the forms of media have changed considerably over time. While the term "media" traditionally referred only to print sources, technological advances have allowed political information to be spread through radio, television, and the Internet. The creation of the Internet and the proliferation of media sources more generally have drastically increased the amount of information about politics that is available to the average American.

Coverage of politics requires that reporters, on the one hand, make a trade-off between cultivating sources with favorable stories and providing complete and accurate information. Politicians, on the other hand, want favorable media coverage that highlights their achievements. One of the best ways reporters can cover political events is to get information "off the record." To maintain this information resource, the confidentiality of sources must be protected, although reporters can be compelled to reveal them in court.

Much of what Americans know about politics comes not only from the stories that they are exposed to in the news but also from the way these stories are presented (if the stories are reported at all). Potential media bias, filtering, and framing all may influence the type and scope of information that reporters choose to disseminate. In particular, the effects of filtering and framing are simply unavoidable given limited resources.

In a democracy, the media's job is to provide citizens with information about politicians, government action, and policy debates. Although the media often fall short of this ideal, there are many reasons for this failure, including market forces and lack of citizen interest.

Enduring Understanding

PRD-3: "The various forms of media provide citizens with political information and influence the ways in which they participate politically." (AP® U.S. Government and Politics Course and Exam Description)

Key Terms

attack journalism (p. 634)

broadcast media (p. 613)

by-product theory (p. 618)

equal time provision (p. 614)

Federal Communications Commission (FCC) (p. 613)

filtering (p. 628)

framing (p. 628)

hard news (p. 634)

horse race (p. 634)

hostile media effect (p. 626)

leaking (p. 622)

linkage institutions (p. 612)

mass media (p. 612)

media conglomerates (p. 614)

media effects (p. 623)

on background or off the record (p. 619)

soft news (p. 634)

yellow journalism (p. 613)

Multiple-Choice Questions (Arranged by Topic)

Topic 5.12: The Media (PRD-3)

1. Which of the following best describes the filtering, or agenda-setting, role of the media?

    (A) attempts by the media to frame public opinion

    (B) newspaper editors determining which stories to report

    (C) politicians attempting to influence coverage by providing select information

    (D) sources trying to remain confidential

Questions 2–3 refer to the table.

Trust in News Sources among Democrats and Republicans

Democrats				Republicans			
Liberal		**Moderate/ Conservative**		**Moderate/Liberal**		**Conservative**	
CNN	70%	CNN	65%	Fox News	51%	Fox News	75%
New York Times	66%	ABC News	63%	ABC News	47%	Hannity (radio)	43%
PBS	66%	NBC News	61%	CBS News	42%	Limbaugh (radio)	38%
NPR	63%	CBS News	60%	NBC News	41%	ABC News	24%
NBC News	61%	PBS	48%	CNN	36%	CBS News	23%

Source: Mark Jurkowitz et al., "U.S. Media Polarization and the 2020 Election: A Nation Divided," Pew Research Center, January 24, 2020, www.journalism.org/2020/01/24/u-s-media-polarization-and-the-2020-election-a-nation-divided/ (accessed 3/7/20).

2. Which of the following is an accurate comparison of trust in news sources between Democrats and Republicans?

	Democrats	**Republicans**
(A)	The most trusted news source is CNN.	The most trusted news source is NPR.
(B)	Radio is included as a source of trusted news.	Newspapers are included as a source of trusted news.
(C)	The majority of liberal Democrats trust PBS.	ABC News is more trusted than CBS News.
(D)	Fewer than half of moderate/ conservative Democrats trust the *New York Times*.	The majority of moderate/liberal Republicans trust Fox News.

3. Which of the following scenarios is most likely given the information in the table?

    (A) Since ideological beliefs drive the selection of media sources, the coverage on CNN is likely to be liberal-leaning.

    (B) Since media sources drive ideological beliefs, an individual will demand conservative policies because they listen to Fox News.

    (C) Since Democrats report lower levels of trust in news sources than Republicans do, Democrats are less likely to follow the news.

    (D) Since radio stations must follow the equal time provision, Hannity and PBS must have approximately the same number of listeners to comply with the law.

4. **Which of the following best describes the Federal Communications Commission (FCC)?**

   (A) a federal court agency that publicizes the decisions of the Supreme Court

   (B) a subcommittee in Congress that enforces the equal time provision

   (C) an interest group that focuses on First Amendment issues

   (D) an independent regulatory agency that regulates broadcast media

5. **When entrepreneur Elon Musk said, "We can't have, like, willy-nilly proliferation of fake news. That's crazy. You can't have more types of fake news than real news. That's allowing public deception to go unchecked. That's crazy," he was most likely criticizing the media for not fulfilling which of the following roles?**

   (A) watchdog

   (B) gatekeeper

   (C) yellow journalist

   (D) horse race journalist

6. **Which of the following best describes the concept of horse race journalism?**

   (A) disproportionate coverage of events that are more likely to be recognized by the average American

   (B) election coverage that focuses more on poll results and speculation about a likely winner

   (C) media coverage that focuses on political scandals and controversies

   (D) election coverage that focuses on important issues and emphasizes facts and figures

7. **Which of the following is a possible consequence of the use of horse race journalism?**

   (A) Being in constant competition with other media outlets leads to tension and the proliferation of fake news.

   (B) The focus on providing in-depth coverage often leads voters to feel overwhelmed and less likely to turnout to vote.

   (C) The absence of coverage of each candidate's promises and lack of analysis of how he or she is likely to behave in office may lead voters to make a less informed choice.

   (D) Since most media outlets are a part of a large conglomerate, there is an increase in ideologically oriented programming.

Topic 5.13: Changing Media (PRD-3)

8. **Which of the following best explains the effect that new communication technologies and advances in social media have had on the media's role as a linkage institution?**

   (A) Fewer opportunities exist for citizens to interact with reporters or government officials, so citizens are less involved.

   (B) People with no official connection to politics can contribute to the commentary and reach a wide audience.

   (C) Due to the diversity of news sources, like-minded political supporters have difficulty organizing and staying informed on issues.

   (D) The accuracy of available political information has improved.

9. **Which of the following best explains why elected officials are often able to successfully demand that journalists give favorable coverage of events and actions?**

   (A) The fairness doctrine requires that journalists publish exactly what elected officials tell them.

   (B) Media consolidation has increased the power of elected officials.

   (C) Journalists defer to elected officials because they need the information that elected officials can provide.

   (D) The equal time provision, included in federal law, provides boundaries on what journalists can print.

10. **Which of the following best explains how the holding in *New York Times Co. v. United States* (1971) had an impact on the power of the media?**

(A) It established a heavy presumption against allowing prior restraint even in cases involving national security.

(B) It allowed companies to control a large number of media sources across several types of media outlets.

(C) It enabled politicians to speak to single reporters or to a group off the record, meaning that reporters can use the information but cannot attribute it to the politician by name.

(D) It required broadcast media to provide equal air time on any non-news programming to all candidates running for office.

Free-Response Questions

Concept Application

While working as a contractor for the U.S. National Security Agency (NSA), Edward Snowden downloaded a number of files that documented the NSA's surveillance activities, including the collection of data on Americans' phone calls overseas and the monitoring of foreign politicians' cell phones. In 2012, Snowden approached several major publications across the world, including the *Washington Post*, to offer access to these documents. After several months of negotiation, the *Post* would not agree to all of Snowden's conditions—among other things, he wanted certain documents to be published in their entirety, while the *Post* wanted to hold back some classified information. Snowden then came to an agreement with a British newspaper, the *Guardian*, which gradually made the documents public, although he also allowed the *Post* to publish some of the documents. The *Post*'s refusal to accept Snowden's demands was the product of several months of discussions with the U.S. government over what information could be released without harming national security or placing confidential sources in jeopardy. In any case, even if the *Post* could have been deterred from publication, the information would have soon appeared in stories published by other outlets. The Snowden episode illustrates how government officials work to deter leaks or influence the media's coverage of a story without resorting to legal action.

After reading the scenario, respond to A, B, and C below:

(A) Referencing the scenario, describe the civil liberty that is being discussed in the scenario.

(B) In the context of the scenario, explain how the civil liberty described in Part A may be limited by the Supreme Court's decision in *Schenck v. United States* (1919).

(C) In the case of the Snowden documents, the *Post* published its story only when it was rumored that the *Guardian* planned to release its own story. Even then, *Post* reporters and editors agreed to keep certain information out of their stories. Explain why reporters and publishers might restrain their own stories even when they are not being threatened with legal action.

Quantitative Analysis

Where Do Americans Get Their Political and Election News?

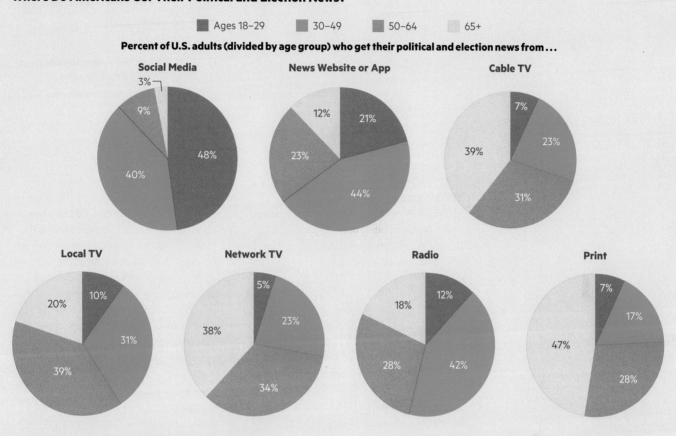

■ Ages 18–29 ■ 30–49 ■ 50–64 ■ 65+

Percent of U.S. adults (divided by age group) who get their political and election news from ...

Social Media
3%
9%
48%
40%

News Website or App
12%
21%
23%
44%

Cable TV
7%
23%
39%
31%

Local TV
10%
20%
31%
39%

Network TV
5%
23%
38%
34%

Radio
12%
18%
28%
42%

Print
7%
17%
47%
28%

Note: Data may not total 100 percent due to rounding.

Source: Pew Research Center, "Americans Who Mainly Get Their News on Social Media Are Less Engaged, Less Knowledgeable," July 30, 2020, www.journalism.org/2020/07/30/americans-who-mainly-get-their-news-on-social-media-are-less-engaged-less-knowledgeable/pj_2020-07-30_social-media-news_00-02/ (accessed 8/20/20).

Use the charts to answer the questions.

(A) Identify the age group that uses network TV most often to get the news.

(B) Describe a difference between how often those 18–29 and those 50+ get their news online (social media and news websites or apps) versus on television (cable, local, and network), as illustrated in the charts.

(C) Draw a conclusion about the difference described in Part B.

(D) Explain how candidates would use the information in the charts to decide if they should concentrate their campaign efforts using either online ads or television ads in order to reach the most potential voters.

Foundational Document: Declaration of Independence

Enduring Understanding

LOR-1: "A balance between governmental power and individual rights has been a hallmark of American political development." (AP® U.S. Government and Politics Course and Exam Description)

Introduction

The Declaration of Independence, drafted by Thomas Jefferson and others, announced the 13 colonies' separation from Great Britain. Borrowing from the ideas of Enlightenment thinkers like John Locke, Jefferson laid out the reasons for rebellion based on natural rights, limited government, and the social contract. These principles expressed in the Declaration became the cornerstones of American democracy embodied in other foundational documents like the Articles of Confederation and the U.S. Constitution. The Declaration of Independence—with its ideas of self-governance and the assertion of human rights—has also inspired social, political, and economic movements around the world.

Full Text of the Declaration of Independence

In Congress, July 4, 1776

The unanimous Declaration of the thirteen united States of America,

When in the Course of human events, it becomes necessary for one people to dissolve the political bands which have connected them with another, and to assume among the powers of the earth, the separate and equal station to which the Laws of Nature and of Nature's God entitle them, a decent respect to the opinions of mankind requires that they should declare the causes which impel them to the separation.

We hold these truths to be self-evident, that all men are created equal, that they are endowed by their Creator with certain <u>unalienable Rights</u>, that among these are <u>Life, Liberty and the pursuit of Happiness</u>.—That to secure these rights, Governments are instituted among Men, deriving their just powers from the consent of the governed, —That whenever any Form of Government becomes destructive of these ends, it is the Right of the People to alter or to abolish it, and to institute new Government, laying its foundation on such principles and organizing its powers in such form, as to them shall seem most likely to effect their Safety and Happiness. Prudence, indeed, will dictate that Governments long established should not be changed for light and transient causes; and accordingly all experience hath **shewn**, that mankind are more disposed to suffer, while evils are sufferable, than to right themselves by abolishing the forms to which they are accustomed. But when a long train of abuses and **usurpations**, pursuing invariably the same Object evinces a design to reduce them under **absolute Despotism**, it is their right, it is their duty, to throw off such Government, and to provide new Guards for their future security.—Such has been the patient sufferance of these Colonies; and such is now the necessity which constrains them to alter their former Systems of Government. The history of the present King of Great Britain is a history of repeated injuries and

> Rights that cannot be taken away by the government | Natural rights not granted by the government but inherently possessed by human beings

> This passage implies that there is a social contract between the government and the people and that the government's power is limited and constrained.

> Shown

> Wrongful infringements or seizures | Tyranny under a single, unjust ruler

usurpations, all having in direct object the establishment of an absolute Tyranny over these States. To prove this, let Facts be submitted to a candid world.

He has refused his Assent to Laws, the most wholesome and necessary for the public good.

He has forbidden his Governors to pass Laws of immediate and pressing importance, unless suspended in their operation till his Assent should be obtained; and when so suspended, he has utterly neglected to attend to them.

He has refused to pass other Laws for the accommodation of large districts of people, unless those people would relinquish the right of Representation in the Legislature, a right inestimable to them and formidable to tyrants only.

He has called together legislative bodies at places unusual, uncomfortable, and distant from the depository of their public Records, for the sole purpose of fatiguing them into compliance with his measures.

He has dissolved Representative Houses repeatedly, for opposing with manly firmness his invasions on the rights of the people.

He has refused for a long time, after such dissolutions, to cause others to be elected; whereby the Legislative powers, incapable of Annihilation, have returned to the People at large for their exercise; the State remaining in the mean time exposed to all the dangers of invasion from without, and convulsions within.

He has endeavoured to prevent the population of these States; for that purpose obstructing the **Laws for Naturalization of Foreigners**; refusing to pass others to encourage their migrations hither, and raising the conditions of new Appropriations of Lands.

He has obstructed the Administration of Justice, by refusing his Assent to Laws for establishing Judiciary powers.

He has made Judges dependent on his Will alone, for the tenure of their offices, and the amount and payment of their salaries.

He has erected a multitude of New Offices, and sent hither swarms of Officers to harass our people, and eat out their substance.

He has kept among us, in times of peace, Standing Armies without the Consent of our legislatures.

He has affected to render the Military independent of and superior to the Civil power.

He has combined with others to subject us to a jurisdiction foreign to our constitution, and unacknowledged by our laws; giving his Assent to their Acts of pretended Legislation:

For Quartering large bodies of armed troops among us:

For protecting them, by a mock Trial, from punishment for any Murders which they should commit on the Inhabitants of these States:

For cutting off our Trade with all parts of the world:

For imposing Taxes on us without our Consent:

For depriving us in many cases, of the benefits of Trial by Jury:

For transporting us beyond Seas to be tried for pretended offences

For abolishing the free System of English Laws in a neighbouring Province, establishing therein an Arbitrary government, and enlarging its Boundaries so as to render it at once an example and fit instrument for introducing the same absolute rule into these Colonies:

For taking away our Charters, abolishing our most valuable Laws, and altering fundamentally the Forms of our Governments:

For suspending our own Legislatures, and declaring themselves invested with power to legislate for us in all cases whatsoever.

He has abdicated Government here, by declaring us out of his Protection and waging War against us.

He has plundered our seas, ravaged our Coasts, burnt our towns, and destroyed the lives of our people.

An effect of the king's dissolving of colonial legislatures inhibited the colonists' right to self-govern.

Several colonial laws that encouraged immigration to the colonies

He is at this time transporting large Armies of foreign Mercenaries to **compleat** the works of death, desolation and tyranny, already begun with circumstances of Cruelty & **perfidy** scarcely paralleled in the most barbarous ages, and totally unworthy the Head of a civilized nation.

He has constrained our fellow Citizens taken Captive on the high Seas to bear Arms against their Country, to become the executioners of their friends and Brethren, or to fall themselves by their Hands.

He has excited domestic **insurrections** amongst us, and has endeavoured to bring on the inhabitants of our frontiers, the merciless Indian Savages, whose known rule of warfare, is an undistinguished destruction of all ages, sexes and conditions.

In every stage of these Oppressions We have **Petitioned for Redress** in the most humble terms: Our repeated Petitions have been answered only by repeated injury. A Prince whose character is thus marked by every act which may define a Tyrant, is unfit to be the ruler of a free people.

Nor have We been wanting in attentions to our Brittish brethren. We have warned them from time to time of attempts by their legislature to extend an **unwarrantable jurisdiction** over us. We have reminded them of the circumstances of our emigration and settlement here. We have appealed to their native justice and magnanimity, and we have conjured them by the ties of our common kindred to disavow these usurpations, which, would inevitably interrupt our connections and correspondence. They too have been deaf to the voice of justice and of **consanguinity**. We must, therefore, acquiesce in the necessity, which denounces our Separation, and hold them, as we hold the rest of mankind, Enemies in War, in Peace Friends.

We, therefore, the Representatives of the united States of America, in General Congress, Assembled, appealing to the Supreme Judge of the world for the rectitude of our intentions, do, in the Name, and by Authority of the good People of these Colonies, solemnly publish and declare, **That these United Colonies are, and of Right ought to be Free and Independent States; that they are Absolved from all Allegiance to the British Crown, and that all political connection between them and the State of Great Britain, is and ought to be totally dissolved; and that as Free and Independent States, they have full Power to levy War, conclude Peace, contract Alliances, establish Commerce, and to do all other Acts and Things which Independent States may of right do**. And for the support of this Declaration, with a firm reliance on the protection of **divine Providence**, we mutually pledge to each other our Lives, our Fortunes and our sacred Honor.

The foregoing Declaration was, by order of Congress, engrossed, and signed by the following members:

John Hancock

New Hampshire
Josiah Bartlett
William Whipple
Matthew Thornton

Massachusetts Bay
Samuel Adams
John Adams
Robert Treat Paine
Elbridge Gerry

Rhode Island
Stephen Hopkins
William Ellery

Connecticut
Roger Sherman
Samuel Huntington
William Williams
Oliver Wolcott

New York
William Floyd
Philip Livingston
Francis Lewis
Lewis Morris

New Jersey
Richard Stockton
John Witherspoon

Francis Hopkinson
John Hart
Abraham Clark

Pennsylvania
Robert Morris
Benjamin Rush
Benjamin Franklin
John Morton
George Clymer
James Smith
George Taylor
James Wilson
George Ross

Sidebar glosses:

Complete or carry out

Deceitfulness; untrustworthiness

Revolts or uprisings

Made complaints to the government about grievances

Unjustified authority

Kinship; family relationship

This resolution proclaims not only the complete separation from the British Empire but also the creation of a new country with its own sovereign powers.

God's intervention

Delaware	**Virginia**	**South Carolina**
Caesar Rodney	*George Wythe*	*Edward Rutledge*
George Read	*Richard Henry Lee*	*Thomas Heyward, Jr.*
Thomas M'Kean	*Thomas Jefferson*	*Thomas Lynch, Jr.*
	Benjamin Harrison	*Arthur Middleton*
Maryland	*Thomas Nelson, Jr.*	
Samuel Chase	*Francis Lightfoot Lee*	**Georgia**
William Paca	*Carter Braxton*	*Button Gwinnett*
Thomas Stone		*Lyman Hall*
Charles Carroll, of	**North Carolina**	*George Walton*
Carrollton	*William Hooper*	
	Joseph Hewes	
	John Penn	

Resolved, That copies of the Declaration be sent to the several assemblies, conventions, and committees, or councils of safety, and to the several commanding officers of the continental troops; that it be proclaimed in each of the United States, at the head of the army.

Making Connections

1. Describe the Founders' main argument articulated in the Declaration of Independence.

2. Besides King George III, identify the intended audiences of the Declaration. That is, whom did the signers want to influence with this document? Explain why.

3. Jefferson expressed basic human rights in the Declaration that men are "endowed by their Creator with certain unalienable Rights, that among these are Life, Liberty and the pursuit of Happiness." What do you think the Founders in 1776 meant by the phrase, "Life, Liberty and the pursuit of Happiness"? In what ways has the meaning of that key phrase changed over time? What does "Life, Liberty and the pursuit of Happiness" mean to you?

4. The authors of the Declaration of Independence contended that governments derive their power from the "consent of the governed." Translate the meaning of "consent of the governed." In American constitutional democracy, describe several ways that citizens can demonstrate their consent or disagreement with government actions or inactions.

5. Notions of equality, and the very interpretation of the foundational idea that "all men are created equal," have evolved over time. To whom did the Founders intend that the phrase "all men are created equal" applied in the late eighteenth century? What groups were excluded from the rights and protections of equality? How do we interpret "all men are created equal" today?

6. Many founding principles written in the Declaration of Independence were incorporated into the U.S. Constitution. Drawing upon the Preamble, the original Constitution, and its amendments, identify several specific examples from the Declaration that were adapted into the U.S. Constitution.

7. The Declaration of Independence exemplifies the ideal principles of American democracy, yet the government has at times over the course of American history failed to carry out these principles in practice. Describe several historical or current examples that show how the principles of ideal democracy embodied in the Declaration conflict with the reality experienced by some groups or individuals in American society.

8. Significant changes in public policy often take time, sometimes decades, in American constitutional democracy. Describe several historical or current examples of how the ideals embodied in the Declaration of Independence became adopted policy by the government.

Foundational Document: Articles of Confederation

Enduring Understanding

CON-1: "The Constitution emerged from the debate about the weaknesses in the Articles of Confederation as a blueprint for limited government." (AP® U.S. Government and Politics Course and Exam Description)

Introduction

The Articles of Confederation were adopted by the Continental Congress on November 15, 1777, and served as the United States' first constitution from 1781 until 1787, when the Constitution went into effect. These Articles tried to balance the necessity for national government during the American Revolution with fears of too much centralized authority. As such, they were a blueprint for failure, taking the concept of limited government to such an extreme that the United States was not united enough to function. The Articles served as a bridge during the United States' transition from a colonial government to a large republic; it is important to understand the powers that the Articles lacked and the Constitution embodied. Because the most important features of the Articles are what they don't contain, pay attention to what important governmental powers are missing.

Full Text of the Articles of Confederation

To all to whom these Presents shall come, we the undersigned Delegates of the States affixed to our Names send greeting. Whereas the Delegates of the United States of America, in Congress assembled, did, on the fifteenth day of November, in the year of our Lord One Thousand Seven Hundred and Seventy seven, and in the Second Year of the Independence of America, agree to certain articles of Confederation and perpetual Union between the states of New Hampshire, Massachusetts-bay, Rhode Island and Providence Plantations, Connecticut, New York, New Jersey, Pennsylvania, Delaware, Maryland, Virginia, North Carolina, South Carolina and Georgia.

I. The **Stile** of this Confederacy shall be "The United States of America."

> Name

II. Each state retains its sovereignty, freedom, and independence, and every power, jurisdiction, and right, which is not by this Confederation expressly delegated to the United States, in Congress assembled.

III. The said States hereby severally enter into a **firm league of friendship** with each other, for their common defense, the security of their liberties, and their mutual and general welfare, binding themselves to assist each other, against all force offered to, or attacks made upon them, or any of them, on account of religion, sovereignty, trade, or any other pretense whatever.

> An alliance to defend one another

IV. The better to secure and perpetuate mutual friendship and intercourse among the people of the different States in this Union, the free inhabitants of each of these States, **paupers, vagabonds, and fugitives** from justice excepted, shall be entitled to all privileges and immunities of free citizens in the several States; and the people of each State shall have free **ingress and regress** to and from any other State, and shall enjoy therein all the privileges of trade and commerce, subject to the same duties,

> A state must help return runaway criminals to the state where the crime was committed. | Travel between the states

Taxes or levies

impositions, and restrictions as the inhabitants thereof respectively, provided that such restrictions shall not extend so far as to prevent the removal of property imported into any State, to any other State, of which the owner is an inhabitant; provided also that no imposition, duties or restriction shall be laid by any State, on the property of the United States, or either of them.

This is known as extradition.

If any person guilty of, or charged with, treason, felony, or other high misdemeanor in any State, shall flee from justice, and be found in any of the United States, **he shall, upon demand of the Governor or executive power of the State from which he fled, be delivered up and removed to the State having jurisdiction of his offense.**

Full faith and credit shall be given in each of these States to the records, acts, and judicial proceedings of the courts and magistrates of every other State.

V. For the most convenient management of the general interests of the United States, delegates shall be annually appointed in such manner as the legislatures of each State shall direct, to meet in Congress on the first Monday in November, in every year, with a power reserved to each State to recall its delegates, or any of them, at any time within the year, and to send others in their stead for the remainder of the year.

No State shall be represented in Congress by less than two, nor more than seven members; and no person shall be capable of being a delegate for more than three years in any term of six years; nor shall any person, being a delegate, be capable of holding any office under the United States, for which he, or another for his benefit, receives any salary, fees or **emolument** of any kind.

Compensation

Each State shall maintain its own delegates in a meeting of the States, and while they act as members of the committee of the States.

In determining questions in the United States in Congress assembled, each State shall have one vote.

Charged with a crime or misdemeanor

Freedom of speech and debate in Congress shall not be **impeached** or questioned in any court or place out of Congress, and the members of Congress shall be protected in their persons from arrests or imprisonments, during the time of their going to and from, and attendance on Congress, except for treason, felony, or breach of the peace.

VI. No State, without the consent of the United States in Congress assembled, shall send any embassy to, or receive any embassy from, or enter into any conference, agreement, alliance or treaty with any King, Prince or State; nor shall any person holding any office of profit or trust under the United States, or any of them, accept any present, emolument, office or title of any kind whatever from any King, Prince or foreign State; nor shall the United States in Congress assembled, or any of them, grant any title of nobility.

No two or more States shall enter into any treaty, confederation or alliance whatever between them, without the consent of the United States in Congress assembled, specifying accurately the purposes for which the same is to be entered into, and how long it shall continue.

Taxes or tributes

No State shall lay any **imposts** or duties, which may interfere with any stipulations in treaties, entered into by the United States in Congress assembled, with any King, Prince or State, in pursuance of any treaties already proposed by Congress, to the courts of France and Spain.

No vessel of war shall be kept up in time of peace by any State, except such number only, as shall be deemed necessary by the United States in Congress assembled, for the defense of such State, or its trade; nor shall any body of forces be kept up by any State in time of peace, except such number only, as in the judgement of the United States in Congress assembled, shall be deemed requisite to garrison the forts necessary for the defense of such State; but every State shall always keep up a well-regulated and disciplined militia, sufficiently armed and **accoutered**, and shall provide and constantly have ready for use, in public stores, a due number of filed pieces and tents, and a proper quantity of arms, ammunition and camp equipage.

Provided with necessary articles of equipment

No State shall engage in any war without the consent of the United States in Congress assembled, unless such State be actually invaded by enemies, or shall have received certain advice of a resolution being formed by some nation of Indians to invade such State, and the danger is so imminent as not to admit of a delay till the United States in Congress assembled can be consulted; nor shall any State grant commissions to any ships or vessels of war, nor **letters of marque or reprisal**, except it be after a declaration of war by the United States in Congress assembled, and then only against the Kingdom or State and the subjects thereof, against which war has been so declared, and under such regulations as shall be established by the United States in Congress assembled, unless such State be infested by pirates, in which case vessels of war may be fitted out for that occasion, and kept so long as the danger shall continue, or until the United States in Congress assembled shall determine otherwise.

These were government licenses that authorized a private person, known as a privateer, to attack and capture vessels of a nation at war with the issuer.

VII. When land forces are raised by any State for the common defense, all officers of or under the rank of colonel, shall be appointed by the legislature of each State respectively, by whom such forces shall be raised, or in such manner as such State shall direct, and all vacancies shall be filled up by the State which first made the appointment.

VIII. All charges of war, and all other expenses that shall be incurred for the common defense or general welfare, and allowed by the United States in Congress assembled, shall be **defrayed** out of a common treasury, which shall be supplied by the several States in proportion to the value of all land within each State, granted or surveyed for any person, as such land and the buildings and improvements thereon shall be estimated according to such mode as the United States in Congress assembled, shall from time to time direct and appoint.

Spent

The taxes for paying that proportion shall be laid and levied by the authority and direction of the legislatures of the several States within the time agreed upon by the United States in Congress assembled.

IX. The United States in Congress assembled, shall have the sole and exclusive right and power of determining on peace and war, except in the cases mentioned in the sixth article—of sending and receiving ambassadors—entering into treaties and alliances, provided that no treaty of commerce shall be made whereby the legislative power of the respective States shall be restrained from imposing such imposts and duties on foreigners, as their own people are subjected to, or from prohibiting the exportation or importation of any species of goods or commodities whatsoever—of establishing rules for deciding in all cases, what captures on land or water shall be legal, and in what manner prizes taken by land or naval forces in the service of the United States shall be divided or appropriated—of granting letters of marque and reprisal in times of peace—appointing courts for the trial of piracies and felonies committed on the high seas and establishing courts for receiving and determining finally appeals in all cases of captures, provided that no member of Congress shall be appointed a judge of any of the said courts.

The United States in Congress assembled shall also be the last resort on appeal in all disputes and differences now subsisting or that hereafter may arise between two or more States concerning boundary, jurisdiction or any other causes whatever; which authority shall always be exercised in the manner following. Whenever the legislative or executive authority or lawful agent of any State in controversy with another shall present a petition to Congress stating the matter in question and praying for a hearing, notice thereof shall be given by order of Congress to the legislative or executive authority of the other State in controversy, and a day assigned for the appearance of the parties by their lawful agents, who shall then be directed to appoint by joint consent, commissioners or judges to constitute a court for hearing and determining the matter in question: but if they cannot agree, Congress shall name three persons out of each of the United States, and from the list of such persons each party shall alternately strike out one, the petitioners beginning, until the number shall be reduced to thirteen; and from that number not less than seven, nor more than nine names as Congress shall direct, shall in the presence of Congress be drawn out by lot, and the persons whose names shall be so drawn or any five of them, shall be commissioners or judges, to hear and finally determine the controversy, so always as a major part of the judges who shall hear the cause shall agree in the determination: and if either party shall neglect to attend at the day appointed, without showing reasons, which Congress shall judge sufficient, or being present shall refuse to strike, the Congress shall proceed to nominate three persons out of each State, and the secretary of Congress shall strike in behalf of such party absent or refusing; and the judgement and sentence of the court to be appointed, in the manner before prescribed, shall be final and conclusive; and if any of the parties shall refuse to submit to the authority of such court, or to appear or defend their claim or cause, the court shall nevertheless proceed to pronounce sentence, or judgement, which shall in like manner be final and decisive, the judgement or sentence and other proceedings being in either case transmitted to Congress, and lodged among the acts of Congress for the security of the parties concerned: provided that every commissioner, before he sits in judgement, shall take an oath to be administered by one of the judges of the supreme or superior court of the State, where the cause shall be tried, "well and truly to hear and determine the matter in question, according to the best of his judgement, without favor, affection or hope of reward:" provided also, that no State shall be deprived of territory for the benefit of the United States.

All controversies concerning the private right of soil claimed under different grants of two or more States, whose jurisdictions as they may respect such lands, and the States which passed such grants are adjusted, the said grants or either of them being at the same time claimed to have originated **antecedent** to such settlement of jurisdiction, shall on the petition of either party to the Congress of the United States, be finally determined as near as may be in the same manner as is before prescribed for deciding disputes respecting territorial jurisdiction between different States.

The United States in Congress assembled shall also have the sole and exclusive right and power of regulating the **alloy** and value of coin struck by their own authority, or by that of the respective States—fixing the standard of weights and measures throughout the United States—regulating the trade and managing all affairs with the Indians, not members of any of the States, provided that the legislative right of any State within its own limits be not infringed or violated—establishing or regulating post offices from one State to another, throughout all the United States, and exacting such postage on the papers passing through the same as may be requisite to defray the expenses of the said office—appointing all officers of the land forces, in the service of the United States, excepting regimental officers—appointing all the officers of the naval forces, and commissioning all officers whatever in the service of the United States— making rules for the government and regulation of the said land and naval forces, and directing their operations.

The United States in Congress assembled shall have authority to appoint a committee, to sit in the recess of Congress, to be denominated "A Committee of the States," and to consist of one delegate from each State; and to appoint such other committees and civil officers as may be necessary for managing the general affairs of the United States under their direction—to appoint one of their members to preside, provided that no person be allowed to serve in the office of president more than one year in any term of three years; to ascertain the necessary sums of money to be raised for the service of the United States, and to appropriate and apply the same for **defraying** the public expenses—to borrow money, or **emit** bills on the credit of the United States, transmitting every half-year to the respective States an account of the sums of money so borrowed or emitted—to build and equip a navy—to agree upon the number of land forces, and to make requisitions from each State for its quota, in proportion to the number of white

Before

Mixture of metals

Providing payment for | Give or send out

inhabitants in such State; which requisition shall be binding, and thereupon the legislature of each State shall appoint the regimental officers, raise the men and cloath, arm and equip them in a solid-like manner, at the expense of the United States; and the officers and men so cloathed, armed and equipped shall march to the place appointed, and within the time agreed on by the United States in Congress assembled. But if the United States in Congress assembled shall, on consideration of circumstances judge proper that any State should not raise men, or should raise a smaller number of men than the quota thereof, such extra number shall be raised, officered, cloathed, armed and equipped in the same manner as the quota of each State, unless the legislature of such State shall judge that such extra number cannot be safely spread out in the same, in which case they shall raise, officer, cloath, arm and equip as many of such extra number as they judge can be safely spared. And the officers and men so cloathed, armed, and equipped, shall march to the place appointed, and within the time agreed on by the United States in Congress assembled.

The United States in Congress assembled shall never engage in a war, nor grant letters of marque or reprisal in time of peace, nor enter into any treaties or alliances, nor coin money, nor regulate the value thereof, nor **ascertain** the sums and expenses necessary for the defense and welfare of the United States, or any of them, nor emit bills, nor borrow money on the credit of the United States, nor appropriate money, nor agree upon the number of vessels of war, to be built or purchased, or the number of land or sea forces to be raised, nor appoint a commander in chief of the army or navy, unless nine States assent to the same: nor shall a question on any other point, except for **adjourning** from day to day be determined, unless by the votes of the majority of the United States in Congress assembled.

Define

Suspending a meeting to a future time

The Congress of the United States shall have power to adjourn to any time within the year, and to any place within the United States, so that no period of adjournment be for a longer duration than the space of six months, and shall publish the journal of their proceedings monthly, except such parts thereof relating to treaties, alliances or military operations, as in their judgement require secrecy; and the yeas and nays of the delegates of each State on any question shall be entered on the journal, when it is desired by any delegates of a State, or any of them, at his or their request shall be furnished with a transcript of the said journal, except such parts as are above excepted, to lay before the legislatures of the several States.

X. The Committee of the States, or any nine of them, shall be authorized to execute, in the recess of Congress, such of the powers of Congress as the United States in Congress assembled, by the consent of the nine States, shall from time to time think expedient to vest them with; provided that no power be delegated to the said Committee, for the exercise of which, by the Articles of Confederation, the voice of nine States in the Congress of the United States assembled be requisite.

XI. Canada acceding to this confederation, and adjoining in the measures of the United States, shall be admitted into, and entitled to all the advantages of this Union; but no other colony shall be admitted into the same, unless such admission be agreed to by nine States.

XII. All bills of credit emitted, monies borrowed, and debts contracted by, or under the authority of Congress, before the assembling of the United States, in pursuance of the present confederation, shall be deemed and considered as a charge against the United States, for payment and satisfaction whereof the said United States, and the public faith are hereby solemnly pledged.

XIII. Every State shall abide by the determination of the United States in Congress assembled, on all questions which by this confederation are submitted to them. And the Articles of this Confederation shall be **inviolably** observed by every State, and the Union shall be perpetual; nor shall any alteration at any time hereafter be made in any

Securely (as from assault or trespass)

God

of them; unless such alteration be agreed to in a Congress of the United States, and be afterwards confirmed by the legislatures of every State.

And Whereas it hath pleased the **Great Governor of the World** to incline the hearts of the legislatures we respectively represent in Congress, to approve of, and to authorize us to ratify the said Articles of Confederation and perpetual Union. Know Ye that we the undersigned delegates, by virtue of the power and authority to us given for that purpose, do by these presents, in the name and in behalf of our respective constituents, fully and entirely ratify and confirm each and every of the said Articles of Confederation and perpetual Union, and all and singular the matters and things therein contained: And we do further solemnly plight and engage the faith of our respective constituents, that they shall abide by the determinations of the United States in Congress assembled, on all questions, which by the said Confederation are submitted to them. And that the Articles thereof shall be inviolably observed by the States we respectively represent, and that the Union shall be perpetual.

In Witness whereof we have hereunto set our hands in Congress. Done at Philadelphia in the State of Pennsylvania the ninth day of July in the Year of our Lord One Thousand Seven Hundred and Seventy-Eight, and in the Third Year of the independence of America.

Agreed to by Congress November 15, 1777; ratified and in force March 1, 1781

Making Connections

1. According to the Articles of Confederation, where is most power supposed to be located? With the states or the federal government?

2. What is the meaning and purpose of "league of friendship"? Does it seem like a nation or a union of separate nations?

3. Identify several inherent weaknesses of the central government under the Articles of Confederation that contributed to its failure by 1787.

4. In what ways did the authors of the Articles of Confederation incorporate the ideas embodied in the Declaration of Independence?

5. Compare and contrast the power and authority vested in the legislature as stated in this document with those of Congress under the Constitution.

6. The Articles of Confederation represent the first national attempt to install a limited government based on the will of the people. In what ways did it succeed given the context of the times? Why were the Articles of Confederation a necessary step toward a constitutional republic?

Foundational Document:
Federalist 10

Enduring Understanding

LOR-1: "A balance between governmental power and individual rights has been a hallmark of American political development." (AP® U.S. Government and Politics Course and Exam Description)

Introduction

The ratification of the U.S. Constitution in 1787–1788 sparked fierce debate over the power, size, and scope of the new federal government relative to the states. Two distinct factions emerged: Federalists, who supported the formation of a republic with a strong federal government, and Antifederalists, who favored a smaller national government with more power left to the states. The *Federalist Papers*, penned by James Madison, Alexander Hamilton, and John Jay, are a series of essays published in newspapers in support of the ratification of the Constitution. The *Federalist Papers* were intended to address citizens' concerns about the new, more powerful federal government. *Federalist 10*, written by James Madison, addressed criticism that the federal government established by the U.S. Constitution was too powerful and too removed to be responsive to the people. Madison countered that a large republic, as designed in the U.S. Constitution, best limits the negative effects of factions.

Full Text of *Federalist 10* (James Madison)

The Same Subject Continued: The Utility of the Union as a Safeguard against Domestic Faction and Insurrection

Among the numerous advantages promised by a well constructed Union, none deserves to be more accurately developed than its tendency to break and control the violence of faction. The friend of popular governments never finds himself so much alarmed for their character and fate, as when he contemplates their **propensity** to this dangerous vice. He will not fail therefore to set a due value on any plan which, without violating the principles to which he is attached, provides a proper cure for it. The instability, injustice, and confusion introduced into the public councils have, in truth, been the mortal diseases under which popular governments have everywhere perished, as they continue to be the favorite and fruitful topics from which the adversaries to liberty derive their most **specious declamations**. The valuable improvements made by the American constitutions on the popular models, both ancient and modern, cannot certainly be too much admired; but it would be an unwarrantable partiality to contend that they have as effectually **obviated** the danger on this side, as was wished and expected. Complaints are everywhere heard from our most considerate and virtuous citizens, equally the friends of public and private faith and of public and personal liberty, that our governments are too unstable, that the public good is disregarded in the conflicts of rival parties, and that measures are too often decided, not according to the rules of justice and the rights of the minor party, but by the superior force of an interested and overbearing majority. However anxiously we may wish that these complaints had no foundation, the evidence of known facts will not permit us to deny that they are in some

> **propensity**
> Natural inclination or bias

> **specious declamations**
> Public statements that are plausible but lacking real merit

> **obviated**
> Took measures to prevent from happening

degree true. It will be found, indeed, on a candid review of our situation, that some of the distresses under which we labor have been erroneously charged on the operation of our governments; but it will be found, at the same time, that other causes will not alone account for many of our heaviest misfortunes; and, particularly, for that prevailing and increasing distrust of public engagements and alarm for private rights which are echoed from one end of the continent to the other. These must be chiefly, if not wholly, effects of the unsteadiness and injustice with which a **factious** spirit has tainted our public administration.

By a faction I understand a number of citizens, whether amounting to a majority or minority of the whole, who are united and **actuated** by some common impulse of passion, or of interest, adverse to the rights of other citizens, or to the permanent and **aggregate** interests of the community.

There are two methods of curing the mischiefs of faction: the one, by removing its causes; the other, by controlling its effects.

There are again two methods of removing the causes of faction: the one, by destroying the liberty which is essential to its existence; the other, by giving to every citizen the same opinions, the same passions, and the same interests.

It could never be more truly said than of the first remedy, that it is worse than the disease. Liberty is to faction what air is to fire, an aliment without which it instantly expires. But it could not be a less folly to abolish liberty, which is essential to political life, because it nourishes faction, than it would be to wish the annihilation of air, which is essential to animal life, because it imparts to fire its destructive agency.

The second **expedient** is as impracticable, as the first would be unwise. As long as the reason of man continues fallible, and he is at liberty to exercise it, different opinions will be formed. As long as the connection subsists between his reason and his self-love, his opinions and his passions will have a reciprocal influence on each other; and the former will be objects to which the latter will attach themselves. The diversity in the faculties of men, from which the rights of property originate, is not less an **insuperable** obstacle to a uniformity of interests. The protection of these faculties is the first object of Government. From the protection of different and unequal faculties of acquiring property, the possession of different degrees and kinds of property immediately results; and from the influence of these on the sentiments and views of the respective proprietors, ensues a division of the society into different interests and parties.

The **latent** causes of faction are thus sown in the nature of man; and we see them everywhere brought into different degrees of activity, according to the different circumstances of civil society. A zeal for different opinions concerning religion, concerning Government, and many other points, as well of speculation as of practice; an attachment to different leaders ambitiously contending for pre-eminence and power; or to persons of other descriptions whose fortunes have been interesting to the human passions, have in turn divided mankind into parties, inflamed them with mutual animosity, and rendered them much more disposed to **vex** and oppress each other, than to co-operate for their common good. So strong is this propensity of mankind to fall into mutual animosities, that where no substantial occasion presents itself, the most frivolous and fanciful distinctions have been sufficient to kindle their unfriendly passions, and excite their most violent conflicts. But the most common and durable source of factions has been the various and unequal distribution of property. Those who hold and those who are without property have ever formed distinct interests in society. Those who are creditors, and those who are debtors, fall under a like discrimination. A landed interest, a manufacturing interest, a **mercantile interest**, a moneyed interest, with many lesser interests, grow up of necessity in civilized nations, and divide them into different classes, actuated by different sentiments and views. The regulation

Quarrelsome; disagreeing with the majority

Motivated; impelled to action

Combined

Means to an end; optional course of action

Insurmountable; impossible

Present but not visible

Agitate

Financial interest; profitmaking goal

of these various and interfering interests forms the principal task of modern Legislation, and involves the spirit of party and faction in the necessary and ordinary operations of Government. No man is allowed to be judge in his own cause, because his interest would certainly bias his judgment and, not improbably, corrupt his integrity. With equal, nay with greater reason, a body of men are unfit to be both judges and parties at the same time; yet what are many of the most important acts of legislation but so many judicial determinations, not indeed concerning the rights of single persons, but concerning the rights of large bodies of citizens; and what are the different classes of legislators but advocates and parties to the causes which they determine? Is a law proposed concerning private debts? It is a question to which the creditors are parties on one side and the debtors on the other. Justice ought to hold the balance between them. Yet the parties are, and must be, themselves the judges; and the most numerous party, or in other words, the most powerful faction must be expected to prevail. Shall domestic manufacturers be encouraged, and in what degree, by restrictions on foreign manufacturers? are questions which would be differently decided by the landed and the manufacturing classes, and probably by neither with a sole regard to justice and the public good. The apportionment of taxes on the various descriptions of property is an act which seems to require the most exact impartiality; yet there is, perhaps, no legislative act in which greater opportunity and temptation are given to a predominant party to trample on the rules of justice. Every shilling with which they overburden the inferior number is a shilling saved to their own pockets.

It is in vain to say that enlightened statesmen will be able to adjust these clashing interests and render them all subservient to the public good. Enlightened statesmen will not always be at the helm. Nor, in many cases, can such an adjustment be made at all without taking into view indirect and remote considerations, which will rarely prevail over the immediate interest which one party may find in disregarding the rights of another or the good of the whole.

The inference to which we are brought is that the causes of faction cannot be removed and that relief is only to be sought in the means of controlling its effects.

If a faction consists of less than a majority, relief is supplied by the republican principle, which enables the majority to defeat its sinister views by regular vote. It may clog the administration, it may convulse the society; but it will be unable to execute and mask its violence under the forms of the Constitution. When a majority is included in a faction, the form of popular government, on the other hand, enables it to sacrifice to its ruling passion or interest both the public good and the rights of other citizens. To secure the public good and private rights against the danger of such a faction, and at the same time to preserve the spirit and the form of popular government, is then the great object to which our enquiries are directed. Let me add that it is the great **desideratum** by which alone this form of government can be rescued from the **opprobrium** under which it has so long labored and be recommended to the esteem and adoption of mankind.

By what means is this object attainable? Evidently by one of two only. Either the existence of the same passion or interest in a majority at the same time must be prevented, or the majority, having such co-existent passion or interest, must be rendered, by their number and local situation, unable to concert and carry into effect schemes of oppression. If the impulse and the opportunity be suffered to coincide, we well know that neither moral nor religious motives can be relied on as an adequate control. They are not found to be such on the injustice and violence of individuals, and lose their **efficacy** in proportion to the number combined together, that is, in proportion as their efficacy becomes needful.

From this view of the subject it may be concluded that a pure Democracy, by which I mean a Society consisting of a small number of citizens, who assemble and administer

This passage expresses concern about tyranny of the majority, in which a majority faction could subvert the public good and individual rights.

Requirement or imperative | State of dishonor

Effectiveness

the Government in person, can admit of no cure for the mischiefs of faction. A common passion or interest will, in almost every case, be felt by a majority of the whole; a communication and concert results from the form of Government itself; and there is nothing to check the inducements to sacrifice the weaker party or an obnoxious individual. Hence it is that such Democracies have ever been spectacles of turbulence and contention; have ever been found incompatible with personal security or the rights of property; and have in general been as short in their lives as they have been violent in their deaths. Theoretic politicians, who have **patronized** this species of Government, have erroneously supposed that by reducing mankind to a perfect equality in their political rights, they would at the same time be perfectly equalized and assimilated in their possessions, their opinions, and their passions.

A Republic, by which I mean a Government in which the scheme of representation takes place, opens a different prospect and promises the cure for which we are seeking. Let us examine the points in which it varies from pure Democracy, and we shall comprehend both the nature of the cure and the efficacy which it must derive from the Union.

The two great points of difference between a Democracy and a Republic are: first, the delegation of the Government, in the latter, to a small number of citizens elected by the rest; secondly, the greater number of citizens and greater sphere of country over which the latter may be extended. The effect of the first difference is, on the one hand, to refine and enlarge the public views by passing them through the medium of a chosen body of citizens, whose wisdom may best discern the true interest of their country and whose patriotism and love of justice will be least likely to sacrifice it to temporary or partial considerations. Under such a regulation it may well happen that the public voice, pronounced by the representatives of the people, will be more **consonant** to the public good than if pronounced by the people themselves, convened for the purpose. On the other hand, the effect may be inverted. Men of factious tempers, of local prejudices, or of sinister designs, may, by intrigue, by corruption, or by other means, first obtain the **suffrages**, and then betray the interests of the people. The question resulting is, whether small or extensive Republics are most favorable to the election of proper guardians of the **public weal**; and it is clearly decided in favor of the latter by two obvious considerations.

In the first place it is to be remarked that however small the Republic may be, the Representatives must be raised to a certain number in order to guard against the **cabals** of a few; and that however large it may be they must be limited to a certain number in order to guard against the confusion of a multitude. Hence, the number of Representatives in the two cases not being in proportion to that of the Constituents, and being proportionally greatest in the small Republic, it follows that if the proportion of fit characters be not less in the large than in the small Republic, the former will present a greater option, and consequently a greater probability of a fit choice.

In the next place, as each Representative will be chosen by a greater number of citizens in the large than in the small Republic, it will be more difficult for unworthy candidates to practise with success the vicious arts by which elections are too often carried; and the suffrages of the people being more free, will be more likely to centre on men who possess the most attractive merit and the most diffusive and established characters.

It must be confessed that in this, as in most other cases, there is a mean, on both sides of which inconveniencies will be found to lie. By enlarging too much the number of electors, you render the representative too little acquainted with all their local circumstances and lesser interests; as by reducing it too much, you render him unduly attached to these, and too little fit to comprehend and pursue great and national objects. The Federal Constitution forms a happy combination in this respect; the great

Supported

In agreement

Right to vote

Public good

Secret groups of political plotters or conspirators

and aggregate interests being referred to the national, the local and particular to the State legislatures.

The other point of difference is the greater number of citizens and extent of territory which may be brought within the compass of Republican than of Democratic Government; and it is this circumstance principally which renders factious combinations less to be dreaded in the former than in the latter. The smaller the society, the fewer probably will be the distinct parties and interests composing it; the fewer the distinct parties and interests, the more frequently will a majority be found of the same party; and the smaller the number of individuals composing a majority, and the smaller the compass within which they are placed, the more easily will they concert and execute their plans of oppression. Extend the sphere and you take in a greater variety of parties and interests; you make it less probable that a majority of the whole will have a common motive to invade the rights of other citizens; or if such a common motive exists, it will be more difficult for all who feel it to discover their own strength and to act in unison with each other. Besides other **impediments**, it may be remarked, that where there is a consciousness of unjust or dishonorable purposes, communication is always checked by distrust in proportion to the number whose concurrence is necessary.

> Obstacles

Hence, it clearly appears that the same advantage which a Republic has over a Democracy in controlling the effects of faction is enjoyed by a large over a small republic—is enjoyed by the Union over the States composing it. Does this advantage consist in the substitution of representatives whose enlightened views and virtuous sentiments render them superior to local prejudices and to schemes of injustice? It will not be denied that the representation of the Union will be most likely to possess these **requisite endowments**. Does it consist in the greater security afforded by a greater variety of parties, against the event of any one party being able to outnumber and oppress the rest? In an equal degree does the increased variety of parties comprised within the Union increase this security? Does it, in fine, consist in the greater obstacles opposed to the concert and accomplishment of the secret wishes of an unjust and interested majority? Here again the extent of the Union gives it the most **palpable** advantage.

> Necessary qualities or abilities

> Obvious or plainly seen

The influence of factious leaders may kindle a flame within their particular States but will be unable to spread a general **conflagration** through the other States: a religious sect may degenerate into a political faction in a part of the Confederacy; but the variety of sects dispersed over the entire face of it must secure the national Councils against any danger from that source: a rage for paper money, for an abolition of debts, for an equal division of property, or for any other improper or wicked project, will be less apt to **pervade** the whole body of the Union than a particular member of it; in the same proportion as such a **malady** is more likely to taint a particular county or district than an entire State.

> Destructive or uncontrollable fire

> Spread throughout | Disease

In the extent and proper structure of the Union, therefore, we behold a republican remedy for the diseases most incident to Republican Government. And according to the degree of pleasure and pride we feel in being republicans ought to be our zeal in cherishing the spirit and supporting the character of Federalists.

PUBLIUS

Making Connections

1. What is Madison's thesis or main argument in *Federalist 10*?

2. How did Madison define a faction? Why did Madison believe that factions present a threat to liberty and the stability of the government?

3. Madison argued that "the *causes* of faction cannot be removed; and that relief is only to be sought in the means of controlling its *effects*." Interpret the quote

and explain why Madison believed that pure democracy is not the answer to controlling the disruptive nature of factions.

4. Why did Madison believe a large republic as created according to the Constitution provides the best means to limit the negative effects of factions? What do you think?

5. In what ways did Madison's *Federalist 10* promote elite democracy? How did Madison's ideas in *Federalist 10* also promote pluralist democracy? Provide specific evidence from *Federalist 10* to support your answers.

6. Compare and contrast the government established under the Articles of Confederation with the political system advocated by Madison in *Federalist 10*.

7. How are factions in Madison's day similar to political parties and special interest groups today? Drawing upon his statements in *Federalist 10*, what do you think Madison might say about the power and influence of modern political parties and interest groups?

Foundational Document: Brutus 1

Enduring Understanding

LOR-1: "A balance between governmental power and individual rights has been a hallmark of American political development." (AP® U.S. Government and Politics Course and Exam Description)

Introduction

Two factions emerged—Federalists and Antifederalists—after the Constitutional Convention, each promoting a differing vision for the future of the American political system. Both factions took to the media of their day, newspapers, to influence public opinion to ratify or reject the new Constitution. The *Federalist Papers* were a series of essays meant to promote the adoption of the new government under the Constitution. The Brutus essays, also known as the *Antifederalist Papers*, articulated why the Constitution should not be ratified. Though the Brutus essays were anonymous, many historians believe that Brutus 1 was penned by New York Antifederalist Thomas Yates, a delegate to the Constitutional Convention. The Antifederalist position represented in Brutus 1 voiced concerns about the creation of a strong national government under the Constitution that would undermine state authority and endanger individual liberties. Brutus 1 further argued that a large republic, whose representatives were distanced from their constituents, could not justly represent the will of the people nor adequately reflect state and local interests. It is important to note that Brutus 1 was published in October 1787, a few weeks before the *Federalist Papers*. The *Federalist Papers*, written by James Madison, Alexander Hamilton, and John Jay under the pseudonym Publius, were initially published in part to refute the Antifederalist arguments raised in the Brutus essays.

Full Text of Brutus 1

To the Citizens of the State of New-York.

When the public is called to investigate and decide upon a question in which not only the present members of the community are deeply interested, but upon which the happiness and misery of generations yet unborn is in great measure suspended, the benevolent mind cannot help feeling itself peculiarly interested in the result.

> Refers to the decision of whether or not to ratify the new Constitution

In this situation, I trust the feeble efforts of an individual, to lead the minds of the people to a wise and **prudent** determination, cannot fail of being acceptable to the candid and dispassionate part of the community. Encouraged by this consideration, I have been induced to offer my thoughts upon the present important crisis of our public affairs.

> Caring; concerned

> Sensible

Perhaps this country never saw so critical a period in their political concerns. We have felt the feebleness of the ties by which these United States are held together, and the want of sufficient energy in our present confederation, to manage, in some instances, our general concerns. Various expedients have been proposed to remedy these evils, but none have succeeded. At length a Convention of the states has been assembled, they have formed a constitution which will

> This passage acknowledges the ineffectual government existing under the Articles of Confederation and recognizes the need to reform the national government.

> Means or measures

now, probably, be submitted to the people to ratify or reject, who are the fountain of all power, to whom alone it of right belongs to make or unmake constitutions, or forms of government, at their pleasure. The most important question that was ever proposed to your decision, or to the decision of any people under heaven, is before you, and you are to decide upon it by men of your own election, chosen specially for this purpose. If the constitution, offered to [your acceptance], be a wise one, calculated to preserve the invaluable blessings of liberty, to secure the inestimable rights of mankind, and promote human happiness, then, if you accept it, you will lay a lasting foundation of happiness for millions yet unborn; generations to come will rise up and call you blessed. You may rejoice in the prospects of this vast extended continent becoming filled with freemen, who will assert the dignity of human nature. You may **solace** yourselves with the idea, that society, in this favored land, will fast advance to the highest point of perfection; the human mind will expand in knowledge and virtue, and the golden age be, in some measure, realized. But if, on the other hand, this form of government contains principles that will lead to the subversion of liberty—if it tends to establish a **despotism**, or, what is worse, a **tyrannic aristocracy**; then, if you adopt it, this only remaining asylum for liberty will be [shut] up, and posterity will **execrate** your memory. . . .

With these few introductory remarks I shall proceed to a consideration of this constitution:

The first question that presents itself on the subject is, whether a **confederated government** be the best for the United States or not? Or in other words, whether the thirteen United States should be reduced to one great republic, governed by one legislature, and under the direction of one executive and judicial; or whether they should continue thirteen confederated republics, under the direction and control of a supreme federal head for certain defined national purposes only?

This inquiry is important, because, although the government reported by the convention does not go to a perfect and entire **consolidation**, yet it approaches so near to it, that it must, if executed, certainly and infallibly terminate in it.

This government is to possess absolute and uncontrollable power, legislative, executive and judicial, with respect to every object to which it extends, for by the **last clause of section 8th, article 1st, it is declared "that the Congress shall have power to make all laws which shall be necessary and proper for carrying into execution the foregoing powers, and all other powers vested by this constitution, in the government of the United States; or in any department or office thereof." And by the 6th article, it is declared "that this constitution, and the laws of the United States, which shall be made in pursuance thereof, and the treaties made, or which shall be made, under the authority of the United States, shall be the supreme law of the land; and the judges in every state shall be bound thereby, any thing in the constitution, or law of any state to the contrary notwithstanding."** It appears from these articles that there is no need of any intervention of the state governments, between the Congress and the people, to execute any one power vested in the general government, and that the constitution and laws of every state are **nullified** and declared void, so far as they are or shall be inconsistent with this constitution, or the laws made in pursuance of it, or with treaties made under the authority of the United States.—The government then, so far as it extends, is a complete one, and not a confederation. It is as much one complete government as that of New-York or Massachusetts, has as absolute and perfect powers to make and execute all laws, to appoint officers, institute courts, declare offences, and annex penalties, with respect to every object to which it extends, as any other in the world. So far therefore as its powers reach, all ideas of confederation are given up and lost. It is true this government is limited to certain objects, or to speak more properly, some small degree of power is still left to the states, but a little attention to the powers vested in the general government, will convince every candid man, that

Comfort

Authoritarianism | Upper-class elite with absolute power

Condemn; despise

Union of sovereign states held together by a limited central government

Union

Refers to the necessary and proper clause, also known as the elastic clause

Refers to the national supremacy clause

Invalidated

if it is capable of being executed, all that is reserved for the individual states must very soon be annihilated, except so far as they are barely necessary to the organization of the general government. The powers of the **general legislature** extend to every case that is of the least importance—there is nothing valuable to human nature, nothing dear to freemen, but what is within its power. It has authority to make laws which will affect the lives, the liberty, and property of every man in the United States; nor can the constitution or laws of any state, in any way prevent or impede the full and complete execution of every power given. The legislative power is competent to lay taxes, duties, imposts, and excises;—there is no limitation to this power, unless it be said that the clause which directs the use to which those taxes, and duties shall be applied, may be said to be a limitation; but this is no restriction of the power at all, for by this clause they are to be applied to pay the debts and provide for the common defense and general welfare of the United States; but the legislature have authority to contract debts at their discretion; they are the sole judges of what is necessary to provide for the common defense, and they only are to determine what is for the general welfare: **this power therefore is neither more nor less, than a power to lay and collect taxes, imposts, and excises, at their pleasure; not only the power to lay taxes unlimited, as to the amount they may require, but it is perfect and absolute to raise them in any mode they please.** No state legislature, or any power in the state governments, have any more to do in carrying this into effect, than the authority of one state has to do with that of another. In the business therefore of laying and collecting taxes, the idea of confederation is totally lost, and that of one entire republic is embraced. It is proper here to remark, that the authority to lay and collect taxes is the most important of any power that can be granted; it connects with it almost all other powers, or at least will in process of time draw all other after it; it is the great mean of protection, security, and defense, in a good government, and the great engine of oppression and tyranny in a bad one. This cannot fail of being the case, if we consider the contracted limits which are set by this constitution, to the late governments, on this article of raising money. No state can **emit** paper money—lay any duties, or imposts, on imports, or exports, but by consent of the Congress; and then the net produce shall be for the benefit of the United States. The only mean therefore left, for any state to support its government and discharge its debts, is by direct taxation; and the United States have also power to lay and collect taxes, in any way they please. Every one who has thought on the subject, must be convinced that but small sums of money can be collected in any country, by direct taxes[; hence,] when the federal government begins to exercise the right of taxation in all its parts, the legislatures of the several states will find it impossible to raise monies to support their governments. Without money they cannot be supported, and they must dwindle away, and, as before observed, their powers [will be] absorbed in that of the general government.

It might be here shown, that the power in the federal legislative, to raise and support armies at pleasure, as well in peace as in war, and their control over the militia, tend, not only to a **consolidation** of the government, but the destruction of liberty.—I shall not, however, dwell upon these, as a few observations upon the judicial power of this government, in addition to the preceding, will fully evince the truth of the position.

The judicial power of the United States is to be vested in a supreme court, and in such inferior courts as Congress may from time to time ordain and establish. The powers of these courts are very extensive; their jurisdiction comprehends all civil causes, except such as arise between citizens of the same state; and it extends to all cases in law and equity arising under the constitution. One **inferior court** must be established, I presume, in each state at least, with the necessary executive officers **appendant** thereto. It is easy to see, that in the common course of things, these courts will eclipse the dignity, and take away from the respectability, of the state courts. These courts will be, in themselves, totally independent of the states, deriving their authority

Congress

This passage reflects the concern that Congress and the federal government have too much economic power relative to the states.

Produce

Strengthening

Powers of the judicial branch are enumerated primarily in Article III of the Constitution.

Federal or state court that is subordinate to the U.S. Supreme Court

Attached or added

from the United States, and receiving from them fixed salaries; and in the course of human events it is to be expected, that they will swallow up all the powers of the courts in the respective states.

Necessary and proper clause

How far the **clause in the 8th section of the 1st article** may operate to do away all idea of confederated states, and to effect an entire consolidation of the whole into one general government, it is impossible to say. The powers given by this article are very general and comprehensive, and it may receive a construction to justify the passing almost any law. A power to make all laws, which shall be necessary and proper, for carrying into execution, all powers vested by the constitution in the government of the United States, or any department or officer thereof, is a power very comprehensive and definite, and may, for ought I know, be exercised in a such manner as entirely to abolish the state legislatures. Suppose the legislature of a state should pass a law to raise money to support their government and pay the state debt, may the Congress repeal this law, because it may prevent the collection of a tax which they may think proper and necessary to lay, to provide for the general welfare of the United States? For all laws made, in pursuance of this constitution, are the supreme law of the land, and the judges in every state shall be bound thereby, any thing in the constitution or laws of the different states to the contrary notwithstanding.—By such a law, the government of a particular state might be overturned at one stroke, and thereby be deprived of every means of its support.

It is not meant, by stating this case, to insinuate that the constitution would warrant a law of this kind; or unnecessarily to alarm the fears of the people, by suggesting, that the federal legislature would be more likely to pass the limits assigned them by the constitution, than that of an individual state, further than they are less responsible to the people. **But what is meant is, that the legislature of the United States are vested with the great and uncontrollable powers, of laying and collecting taxes, duties, imposts, and excises; of regulating trade, raising and supporting armies, organizing, arming, and disciplining the militia, instituting courts, and other general powers.** And are by this clause invested with the power of making all laws, proper and necessary, for carrying all these into execution; and they may so exercise this power as entirely to annihilate all the state governments, and reduce this country to one single government. And if they may do it, it is pretty certain they will; for it will be found that the power retained by individual states, small as it is, will be a clog upon the wheels of the government of the United States; the latter therefore will be naturally inclined to remove it out of the way. Besides, it is a truth confirmed by the unerring experience of ages, that every man, and every body of men, invested with power, are ever disposed to increase it, and to acquire a superiority over every thing that stands in their way. This disposition, which is implanted in human nature, will operate in the federal legislature to lessen and ultimately to subvert the state authority, and having such advantages, will most certainly succeed, if the federal government succeeds at all. It must be very evident then, that what this constitution wants of being a complete consolidation of the several parts of the union into one complete government, possessed of perfect legislative, judicial, and executive powers, to all intents and purposes, it will necessarily acquire in its exercise and operation.

This sentence refers to the enumerated powers of Congress listed in Article I of the Constitution.

Let us now proceed to inquire, as I at first proposed, whether it be best the thirteen United States should be reduced to one great republic, or not? It is here taken for granted, that all agree in this, that whatever government we adopt, it ought to be a free one; that it should be so framed as to secure the liberty of the citizens of America, and such an one as to admit of a full, fair, and equal representation of the people. The question then will be, whether a government thus constituted, and founded on such principles, is **practicable**, and can be exercised over the whole United States, reduced into one state?

Feasible; possible

If respect is to be paid to the opinion of the greatest and wisest men who have ever thought or wrote on the science of government, we shall be constrained to conclude, that a free republic cannot succeed over a country of such immense extent, containing such a number of inhabitants, and these increasing in such rapid progression as that of the whole United States. Among the many illustrious authorities which might be produced to this point, I shall content myself with quoting only two.

The one is the **Baron de Montesquieu**, *Spirit of the Laws*, Chap. xvi. Vol. I [Book VIII]. "It is natural to a republic to have only a small territory, otherwise it cannot long subsist. In a large republic there are men of large fortunes, and consequently of less moderation; there are trusts too great to be placed in any single subject; he has interest of his own; he soon begins to think that he may be happy, great and glorious, by oppressing his fellow citizens; and that he may raise himself to grandeur on the ruins of his country. In a large republic, the public good is sacrificed to a thousand views; it is subordinate to exceptions, and depends on accidents. In a small one, the interest of the public is easier perceived, better understood, and more within the reach of every citizen; abuses are of less extent, and of course are less protected." Of the same opinion is the Marquis Beccarari.

History furnishes no example of a free republic, anything like the extent of the United States. The Grecian republics were of small extent; so also was that of the Romans. Both of these, it is true, in process of time, extended their conquests over large territories of country; and the consequence was, that their governments were changed from that of free governments to those of the most tyrannical that ever existed in the world.

Not only the opinion of the greatest men, and the experience of mankind, are against the idea of an extensive republic, but a variety of reasons may be drawn from the reason and nature of things, against it. In every government, the will of the sovereign is the law. In despotic governments, the supreme authority being lodged in one, his will is law, and can be as easily expressed to a large extensive territory as to a small one. In a pure democracy the people are the sovereign, and their will is declared by themselves; for this purpose they must all come together to deliberate, and decide.

This kind of government cannot be exercised, therefore, over a country of any considerable extent; it must be confined to a single city, or at least limited to such bounds as that the people can conveniently assemble, be able to debate, understand the subject submitted to them, and declare their opinion concerning it.

In a free republic, although all laws are derived from the consent of the people, yet the people do not declare their consent by themselves in person, but by representatives, chosen by them, who are supposed to know the minds of their constituents, and to be possessed of integrity to declare this mind.

In every free government, the people must give their assent to the laws by which they are governed. This is the true criterion between a free government and an arbitrary one. The former are ruled by the will of the whole, expressed in any manner they may agree upon; the latter by the will of one, or a few. If the people are to give their assent to the laws, by persons chosen and appointed by them, the manner of the choice and the number chosen, must be such, as to possess, be disposed, and consequently qualified to declare the **sentiments** of the people; for if they do not know, or are not disposed to speak the sentiments of the people, the people do not govern, but the **sovereignty** is in a few. Now, in a large extended country, it is impossible to have a representation, possessing the sentiments, and of integrity, to declare the minds of the people, without having it so numerous and unwieldy, as to be subject in great measure to the inconveniency of a democratic government.

The territory of the United States is of vast extent; it now contains near three millions of souls, and is capable of containing much more than ten times that number.

Renowned French political philosopher of the Enlightenment, Montesquieu argued that the most effective means to avoid despotism was government based on a separation of powers.

Opinions | Power of authority

Is it practicable for a country, so large and so numerous as they will soon become, to elect a representation, that will speak their sentiments, without their becoming so numerous as to be incapable of transacting public business? It certainly is not.

In a republic, the manners, sentiments, and interests of the people should be similar. If this be not the case, there will be a constant clashing of opinions; and the representatives of one part will be continually striving against those of the other. This will **retard** the operations of government, and prevent such conclusions as will promote the public good. If we apply this remark to the condition of the United States, we shall be convinced that it forbids that we should be one government. The United States includes a variety of climates. The productions of the different parts of the union are very variant, and their interests, of consequence, diverse. Their manners and habits differ as much as their climates and productions; and their sentiments are by no means coincident. The laws and customs of the several states are, in many respects, very diverse, and in some opposite; each would be in favor of its own interests and customs, and, of consequence, a legislature, formed of representatives from the respective parts, would not only be too numerous to act with any care or decision, but would be composed of such heterogeneous and **discordant** principles, as would constantly be contending with each other.

The laws cannot be executed in a republic, of an extent equal to that of the United States, with **promptitude**.

The **magistrates** in every government must be supported in the execution of the laws, either by an armed force, maintained at the public expense for that purpose; or by the people turning out to aid the magistrate upon his command, in case of resistance.

In despotic governments, as well as in all the monarchies of Europe, standing armies are kept up to execute the commands of the prince or the magistrate, and are employed for this purpose when occasion requires: But they have always proved the destruction of liberty, and [are] abhorrent to the spirit of a free republic. In England, where they depend upon the parliament for their annual support, they have always been complained of as oppressive and unconstitutional, and are seldom employed in executing of the laws; never except on extraordinary occasions, and then under the direction of a civil magistrate.

A free republic will never keep a standing army to execute its laws. It must depend upon the support of its citizens. But when a government is to receive its support from the aid of the citizens, it must be so constructed as to have the confidence, respect, and affection of the people. Men who, upon the call of the magistrate, offer themselves to execute the laws, are influenced to do it either by affection to the government, or from fear; where a standing army is at hand to punish offenders, every man is **actuated** by the latter principle, and therefore, when the magistrate calls, will obey: but, where this is not the case, the government must rest for its support upon the confidence and respect which the people have for their government and laws. The body of the people being attached, the government will always be sufficient to support and execute its laws, and to operate upon the fears of any faction which may be opposed to it, not only to prevent an opposition to the execution of the laws themselves, but also to compel the most of them to aid the magistrate; but the people will not be likely to have such confidence in their rulers, in a republic so extensive as the United States, as necessary for these purposes. The confidence which the people have in their rulers, in a free republic, arises from their knowing them, from their being responsible to them for their conduct, and from the power they have of displacing them when they misbehave: but in a republic of the extent of this continent, the people in general would be acquainted with very few of their rulers: the people at large would know little of their proceedings, and it would be extremely difficult to change them. The people in Georgia and New-Hampshire would not know one another's mind, and therefore could not act in concert to enable them to

Hinder or hold back

Disagreeing

Promptness | Minor judicial officers like justices of the peace

Motivated

effect a general change of representatives. The different parts of so extensive a country could not possibly be made acquainted with the conduct of their representatives, nor be informed of the reasons upon which measures were founded. The consequence will be, they will have no confidence in their legislature, suspect them of ambitious views, be jealous of every measure they adopt, and will not support the laws they pass. Hence the government will be nerveless and inefficient, and no way will be left to render it otherwise, but by establishing an armed force to execute the laws at the point of the bayonet—a government of all others the most to be dreaded.

In a republic of such vast extent as the United-States, the legislature cannot attend to the various concerns and wants of its different parts. It cannot be sufficiently numerous to be acquainted with the local condition and wants of the different districts, and if it could, it is impossible it should have sufficient time to attend to and provide for all the variety of cases of this nature, that would be continually arising.

In so extensive a republic, the great officers of government would soon become above the control of the people, and abuse their power to the purpose of **aggrandizing** themselves, and oppressing them. The trust committed to the executive offices, in a country of the extent of the United-States, must be various and of magnitude. **The command of all the troops and navy of the republic, the appointment of officers, the power of pardoning offences, the collecting of all the public revenues, and the power of expending them, with a number of other powers, must be lodged and exercised in every state, in the hands of a few.** When these are attended with great honor and **emolument**, as they always will be in large states, so as greatly to interest men to pursue them, and to be proper objects for ambitious and designing men, such men will be ever restless in their pursuit after them. They will use the power, when they have acquired it, to the purposes of gratifying their own interest and ambition, and it is scarcely possible, in a very large republic, to call them to account for their misconduct, or to prevent their abuse of power.

These are some of the reasons by which it appears, that a free republic cannot long subsist over a country of the great extent of these states. If then this new constitution is calculated to consolidate the thirteen states into one, as it evidently is, it ought not to be adopted.

Though I am of opinion, that it is a sufficient objection to this government, to reject it, that it creates the whole union into one government, under the form of a republic, yet if this objection was **obviated**, there are exceptions to it, which are so material and fundamental, that they ought to determine every man, who is a friend to the liberty and happiness of mankind, not to adopt it. I beg the candid and dispassionate attention of my countrymen while I state these objections—they are such as have obtruded themselves upon my mind upon a careful attention to the matter, and such as I sincerely believe are well founded. There are many objections, of small moment, of which I shall take no notice—perfection is not to be expected in any thing that is the production of man—and if I did not in my conscience believe that this scheme was defective in the fundamental principles—in the foundation upon which a free and equal government must rest—I would hold my peace.

| Glorifying |
| Refers to the enumerated powers of the president in Article II of the Constitution |
| Profit |
| Rendered unnecessary |

Making Connections

1. Describe Brutus's arguments against the kind of large republic established by the U.S. Constitution. Provide examples of specific concerns about the new government raised in Brutus 1.

2. Brutus stated that "a constitution . . . will . . . be submitted to the people to ratify or reject, who are the fountain of all power, to whom alone it of right belongs

to make or unmake constitutions, or forms of government, at their pleasure." Explain the meaning of the quotation. How does Brutus's statement reflect the ideas embodied in the Declaration of Independence?

3. Why did Brutus believe that the federal government created by the Constitution threatens the liberties of its citizens?

4. According to Brutus 1, how does the federal government under the Constitution have too much economic power relative to state and local interests?

5. In what ways did Brutus 1 support participatory democracy? How did Brutus 1 limit elite democracy?

6. Compare and contrast the arguments regarding a large republic in *Federalist 10* with those of Brutus 1. Think about areas of agreement as well as differences between the two documents.

7. Drawing upon historical and current examples, do you think that the concerns raised by Antifederalists in Brutus 1 about the dangers inherent in a large republic are justified? Explain why or why not.

Foundational Document: The Constitution of the United States of America

Enduring Understanding

CON-1: "The Constitution emerged from the debate about the weaknesses in the Articles of Confederation as a blueprint for limited government." (AP® U.S. Government and Politics Course and Exam Description)

Introduction

The 55 delegates representing 12 of the 13 states met in Philadelphia in the summer of 1787 amid a growing economic and political crisis under the Articles of Confederation. The document the framers created is remarkable for its longevity as the world's oldest continuing constitution but also for its audacity in founding a government based upon the enlightenment principle of popular sovereignty. The preamble of the Constitution begins with three simple words: "We the People." These words establish a constitutional republic whose legitimacy is based upon the collective will of the people. The fierce debate between Federalists and Antifederalists over the ratification of the Constitution in 1788 in many ways echoes continuing conflict within American government and politics today. How powerful should the federal government be in relation to the states? How can a government based on majority rule also protect minority rights? How does government under the Constitution best ensure individual liberty while safeguarding the security of the many? What is the meaning of equality and equal justice under the laws? For over two centuries, the Constitution has provided a framework of government and remains the cornerstone of American representative democracy.

Full Text of the Constitution of the United States of America

[PREAMBLE]

We the People of the United States, in Order to form a more perfect Union, establish Justice, insure domestic Tranquility, provide for the common defence, promote the general Welfare, and secure the Blessings of Liberty to ourselves and our Posterity, do ordain and establish this Constitution for the United States of America.

> The preamble begins with the words, "We the People," demonstrating the intent of the framers that the power of the government resides with the people. Though it has no lawful effect, the preamble establishes the purpose of the government.

Article I

[POWERS, QUALIFICATIONS, AND RESPONSIBILITIES OF THE LEGISLATURE]

SECTION 1

[LEGISLATIVE POWERS]

All legislative Powers herein granted shall be vested in a Congress of the United States, which shall consist of a **Senate and House of Representatives**.

SECTION 2

[HOUSE OF REPRESENTATIVES, HOW CONSTITUTED, POWER OF IMPEACHMENT]

The House of Representatives shall be composed of Members chosen every second Year by the People of the several States, and the Electors in each State shall have the Qualifications requisite for Electors of the most numerous Branch of the State Legislature.

> Unlike the unitary government created under the Articles of Confederation, a bicameral legislature is established in Section 1.

No Person shall be a Representative who shall not have attained to the Age of twenty five Years, and been seven Years a Citizen of the United States, and who shall not, when elected, be an Inhabitant of that State in which he shall be chosen.

Refers to enslaved persons

Representatives and *direct Taxes*[1] shall be apportioned among the several States which may be included within this Union, according to their respective Numbers, *which shall be determined by adding to the whole Number of free Persons, including those bound to Service for a Term of Years, and excluding Indians not taxed, three fifths of **all other Persons.**[2]* The actual Enumeration shall be made within three Years after the first Meeting of the Congress of the United States, and within every subsequent Term of ten Years, in such Manner as they shall by Law direct. The Number of Representatives shall not exceed one for every thirty Thousand, but each State shall have at Least one Representative; *and until such enumeration shall be made, the State of New Hampshire shall be entitled to chuse three, Massachusetts eight, Rhode-Island and Providence Plantations one, Connecticut five, New-York six, New Jersey four, Pennsylvania eight, Delaware one, Maryland six, Virginia ten, North Carolina five, South Carolina five, and Georgia three.*[3]

When a member of the House dies in or resigns from office, the governor of the state will call for a special election to fill the vacancy. | The House investigates and brings charges of impeachment, which are similar to an indictment in criminal law.

When vacancies happen in the Representation from any State, the Executive Authority thereof shall issue Writs of Election to fill such Vacancies.

The House of Representatives shall chuse their Speaker and other Officers; and shall have the sole **Power of Impeachment.**

SECTION 3

[THE SENATE, HOW CONSTITUTED, IMPEACHMENT TRIALS]

The Senate of the United States shall be composed of two Senators from each State, *chosen by the Legislature thereof,*[4] **for six Years; and each Senator shall have one Vote.**

In the original Constitution, U.S. senators were chosen by state legislatures, and the terms were staggered so that only one-third of the Senate was up for election at one time.

Immediately after they shall be assembled in Consequence of the first Election, they shall be divided as equally as may be into three Classes. The Seats of the Senators of the first Class shall be vacated at the Expiration of the second Year, of the second Class at the Expiration of the fourth Year, and of the third Class at the Expiration of the sixth Year, so that one third may be chosen every second Year; *and if Vacancies happen by Resignation, or otherwise, during the Recess of the Legislature of any State, the Executive thereof may make temporary Appointments until the next Meeting of the Legislature, which shall then fill such Vacancies.*[5]

No Person shall be a Senator who shall not have attained to the Age of thirty Years, and been nine Years a Citizen of the United States, and who shall not, when elected, be an Inhabitant of that State for which he shall be chosen.

The Vice President of the United States shall be President of the Senate, but shall have no Vote, unless they be equally divided.

The vice president votes in the Senate only to break a tie.

The Senate shall chuse their other Officers, and also a President pro tempore, in the Absence of the Vice President, or when he shall exercise the Office of President of the United States.

The impeachment process is divided between the House and Senate, and the Senate holds the trial of impeachment.

The Senate shall have the sole Power to try all Impeachments. When sitting for that Purpose, they shall be on Oath or Affirmation. When the President of the United States is tried, the Chief Justice shall preside: And no Person shall be convicted without the Concurrence of two thirds of the Members present.

Judgment in Cases of Impeachment shall not extend further than to removal from Office, and disqualification to hold and enjoy any Office of honor, Trust or Profit under

1. Modified by the Sixteenth Amendment.
2. Modified by the Fourteenth Amendment.
3. Temporary provision.
4. Modified by the Seventeenth Amendment.
5. Modified by the Seventeenth Amendment.

the United States: but the Party convicted shall nevertheless be liable and subject to Indictment, Trial, Judgment and Punishment, according to Law.

SECTION 4

[ELECTION OF SENATORS AND REPRESENTATIVES]

The Times, Places and Manner of holding Elections for Senators and Representatives, shall be prescribed in each State by the Legislature thereof; but the Congress may at any time by Law make or alter such Regulations, except as to the Places of chusing Senators.

The Congress shall assemble at least once in every Year, and such Meeting shall be on the first Monday in December, unless they shall by Law appoint a different Day.[6]

SECTION 5

[QUORUM, JOURNALS, MEETINGS, ADJOURNMENTS]

Each House shall be the Judge of the Elections, Returns and Qualifications of its own Members, and a Majority of each shall constitute a **Quorum** to do Business; but a smaller Number may adjourn from day to day, and may be authorized to compel the Attendance of absent Members, in such Manner, and under such Penalties as each House may provide.

Minimum number present, in this case a majority, to conduct business in each house

Each House may determine the Rules of its Proceedings, punish its Members for disorderly Behaviour, and, with the Concurrence of two thirds, expel a Member.

Each House shall keep a **Journal of its Proceedings**, and from time to time publish the same, excepting such Parts as may in their Judgment require Secrecy; and the Yeas and Nays of the Members of either House on any questions shall, at the Desire of one fifth of those Present, be entered on the Journal.

Meaning a public record, unless secrecy is required, such as in an instance of national security

Neither House, during the Session of Congress, shall, without the Consent of the other, adjourn for more than three days, nor to any other Place than that in which the two Houses shall be sitting.

SECTION 6

[COMPENSATION, PRIVILEGES, DISABILITIES]

The Senators and Representatives shall receive a Compensation for their Services, to be ascertained by Law, and paid out of the Treasury of the United States. They shall in all Cases, except Treason, Felony and Breach of the Peace, be privileged from Arrest during their Attendance at the Session of their respective Houses, and in going to and returning from the same; **and for any Speech or Debate in either House, they shall not be questioned in any other Place.**

This ensures freedom of debate in Congress.

No Senator or Representative shall, during the Time for which he was elected, be appointed to any civil Office under the Authority of the United States, which shall have been created, or the Emoluments whereof shall have been encreased during such time; and no Person holding any Office under the United States, shall be a Member of either House during his Continuance in Office.

This provision forbids a member of the House or Senate from serving in civil government in a different capacity.

SECTION 7

[PROCEDURE IN PASSING BILLS AND RESOLUTIONS]

All Bills for raising Revenue shall originate in the House of Representatives; but the Senate may propose or concur with Amendments as on other Bills.

The framers intended that only the House, directly elected by the people, could raise taxes or revenue.

Every Bill which shall have passed the House of Representatives and the Senate, shall, before it become a Law, be presented to the President of the United States: If he approve he shall sign it, but if not he shall return it, with his Objections to that House in which it shall have originated, who shall enter the Objections at large on their Journal, and proceed to reconsider it. If after such Reconsideration

6. Modified by the Twentieth Amendment.

This provision requires that a bill passed by both houses of Congress must be presented to the president for signature or veto.

If the president does not sign a bill within 10 days, the bill becomes law, except 10 days before an adjournment known as the pocket veto.

The process to become a U.S. citizen if born in a foreign country | Financial failures

Refers to copyrights and patents

Congress has the power to establish all lower or "inferior" federal courts under the Supreme Court. | Robbery or illegal violence on the high seas

Authorization to a private party to seize an enemy vessel

Citizen soldiers known today as the National Guard | Domestic uprisings against the government

two thirds of that House shall agree to pass the Bill, it shall be sent, together with the Objections, to the other House, by which it shall likewise be reconsidered, and if approved by two thirds of that House, it shall become a Law. But in all such Cases the Votes of both Houses shall be determined by yeas and Nays, and the Names of the Persons voting for and against the Bill shall be entered on the Journal of each House respectively. **If any Bill shall not be returned by the President within ten Days (Sundays excepted) after it shall have been presented to him, the Same shall be a Law, in like Manner as if he had signed it, unless the Congress by their Adjournment prevent its Return, in which Case it shall not be a Law.**

Every Order, Resolution, or Vote to which the Concurrence of the Senate and House of Representatives may be necessary (except on a question of Adjournment) shall be presented to the President of the United States; and before the Same shall take Effect, shall be approved by him, or being disapproved by him, shall be repassed by two thirds of the Senate and House of Representatives, according to the Rules and Limitations prescribed in the Case of a Bill.

SECTION 8

[POWERS OF CONGRESS]

The Congress shall have Power

To lay and collect Taxes, Duties, Imposts and Excises, to pay the Debts and provide for the common Defence and general Welfare of the United States; but all Duties, Imposts and Excises shall be uniform throughout the United States;

To borrow Money on the credit of the United States;

To regulate Commerce with foreign Nations, and among the several States, and with the Indian Tribes;

To establish an uniform Rule of **Naturalization**, and uniform Laws on the subject of **Bankruptcies** throughout the United States;

To coin Money, regulate the Value thereof, and of foreign Coin, and fix the Standard of Weights and Measures;

To provide for the Punishment of counterfeiting the Securities and current Coin of the United States;

To establish Post Offices and post Roads;

To promote the Progress of Science and useful Arts, by securing for limited Times to Authors and Inventors the exclusive Right to their respective Writings and Discoveries;

To constitute Tribunals inferior to the supreme Court;

To define and punish **Piracies** and Felonies committed on the high Seas, and Offences against the Law of Nations;

To declare War, grant **Letters of Marque and Reprisal**, and make Rules concerning Captures on Land and Water;

To raise and support Armies, but no Appropriation of Money to that Use shall be for a longer Term than two Years;

To provide and maintain a Navy;

To make Rules for the Government and Regulation of the land and naval Forces;

To provide for calling forth the **Militia** to execute the Laws of the Union, suppress **Insurrections** and repel Invasions;

To provide for organizing, arming, and disciplining, the Militia, and for governing such Part of them as may be employed in the Service of the United States, reserving to the States respectively, the Appointment of the Officers, and the Authority of training the Militia according to the discipline prescribed by Congress;

To exercise exclusive Legislation in all Cases whatsoever, over such District (not exceeding ten Miles square) as may, by Cession of particular States, and the Acceptance of Congress, become the Seat of the Government of the United States, and to exercise like Authority over all Places purchased by the Consent of the Legislature of the State in which the Same shall be, for the Erection of Forts, Magazines, Arsenals, dock-Yards, and other needful Buildings;—And

To make all Laws which shall be necessary and proper for carrying into Execution the foregoing Powers, and all other Powers vested by this Constitution in the Government of the United States, or in any Department or Officer thereof.

SECTION 9

[SOME RESTRICTIONS ON FEDERAL POWER]

The Migration or Importation of such Persons as any of the States now existing shall think proper to admit, shall not be prohibited by the Congress prior to the Year one thousand eight hundred and eight, but a Tax or duty may be imposed on such Importation, not exceeding ten dollars for each Person.[7]

The Privilege of the **Writ of Habeas Corpus** shall not be suspended, unless when in Cases of Rebellion or Invasion the public Safety may require it.

No **Bill of Attainder** or **ex post facto Law** shall be passed.

No Capitation, or other direct, Tax shall be laid, unless in Proportion to the Census or Enumeration herein before directed to be taken.[8]

No Tax or Duty shall be laid on Articles exported from any State.

No Preference shall be given by any Regulation of Commerce or Revenue to the Ports of one State over those of another; nor shall Vessels bound to, or from, one State, be obliged to enter, clear, or pay Duties in another.

No Money shall be drawn from the Treasury, but in Consequence of Appropriations made by Law; and a regular Statement and Account of the Receipts and Expenditures of all public Money shall be published from time to time.

No Title of Nobility shall be granted by the United States: And no Person holding any Office of Profit or Trust under them, shall, without the Consent of the Congress, accept of any present, Emolument, Office, or Title, of any kind whatever, from any King, Prince, or foreign State.

SECTION 10

[RESTRICTIONS UPON POWERS OF STATES]

No State shall enter into any Treaty, Alliance, or Confederation; grant Letters of Marque and Reprisal; coin Money; emit Bills of Credit; make any Thing but gold and silver Coin a Tender in Payment of Debts; pass any Bill of Attainder, ex post facto Law, or Law impairing the Obligation of Contracts, or grant any Title of Nobility.

No State shall, without the Consent of the Congress, lay any Imposts or Duties on Imports or Exports, except what may be absolutely necessary for executing its inspection Laws: and the net Produce of all Duties and Imposts, laid by any State on Imports or Exports, shall be for the Use of the Treasury of the United States; and all such Laws shall be subject to the Revision and Control of the Congress.

No State shall, without the Consent of Congress, lay any Duty of Tonnage, keep Troops, or Ships of War in time of Peace, enter into any Agreement or Compact with another State, or with a foreign Power, or engage in War, unless actually invaded, or in such imminent Danger as will not admit of delay.

Article II

SECTION 1

[EXECUTIVE POWER, ELECTION, QUALIFICATIONS OF THE PRESIDENT]

The executive Power shall be vested in a President of the United States of America. *He shall hold his Office during the Term of four Years, and, together with the Vice President, chosen for the same Term, be elected, as follows[9]*

---

7. Temporary provision.
8. Modified by the Sixteenth Amendment.
9. Number of terms limited to two by the Twenty-Second Amendment.

Known as the necessary and proper clause or the elastic clause, this grants Congress additional implied powers needed to carry out its enumerated powers.

Also known as denied powers

Order to bring an individual before a court to show just cause for detainment

A law declaring a person guilty without a trial | A law that makes an act illegal that was legal at the time it was committed

Known as the emolument clause, this prohibits federal office holders from receiving payment or compensation from a foreign state while in office.

Each State shall appoint, in such Manner as the Legislature thereof may direct, a Number of Electors, equal to the whole Number of Senators and Representatives to which the State may be entitled in the Congress: but no Senator or Representative, or Person holding an Office of Trust or Profit under the United States, shall be appointed an Elector.

The electors shall meet in their respective States, and vote by ballot for two Persons, of whom one at least shall not be an Inhabitant of the same State with themselves. And they shall make a List of all the Persons voted for, and of the Number of Votes for each; which List they shall sign and certify, and transmit sealed to the Seat of the Government of the United States, directed to the President of the Senate. The President of the Senate shall, in the Presence of the Senate and House of Representatives, open all the Certificates, and the Votes shall then be counted. The Person having the greatest Number of Votes shall be the President, if such Number be a Majority of the whole Number of Electors appointed; and if there be more than one who have such Majority, and have an equal Number of Votes, then the House of Representatives shall immediately chuse by Ballot one of them for President; and if no Person have a Majority, then from the five highest on the List the said House shall in like Manner chuse the President. But in chusing the President, the Votes shall be taken by States, the Representation from each State having one Vote; A quorum for this Purpose shall consist of a Member or Members from two thirds of the States, and a Majority of all the States shall be necessary to a Choice. In every Case, after the Choice of the President, the person having the greatest Number of Votes of the Electors shall be the Vice President. But if there should remain two or more who have equal Votes, the Senate shall chuse from them by Ballot the Vice President.[10]

The Congress may determine the Time of chusing the Electors, and the Day on which they shall give their Votes; which Day shall be the same throughout the United States.

No Person except a **natural born Citizen**, or a Citizen of the United States, at the time of the Adoption of this Constitution, shall be eligible to the Office of President; neither shall any Person be eligible to that Office who shall not have attained to the Age of thirty five Years, and been fourteen Years a Resident within the United States.

In Case of the Removal of the President from Office, or his Death, Resignation, or Inability to discharge the Powers and Duties of the said Office, the Same shall devolve on the Vice President, and the Congress may by Law provide for the Case of Removal, Death, Resignation or Inability, both of the President and Vice President, declaring what Officer shall then act as President, and such Officer shall act accordingly, until the Disability be removed, or a President shall be elected.

The President shall, at stated Times, receive for his Services, a Compensation, which shall neither be increased nor diminished during the Period for which he shall have been elected, and he shall not receive within that Period any other Emolument from the United States, or any of them.

Before he enter on the Execution of his Office, he shall take the following Oath or Affirmation:—"I do solemnly swear (or affirm) that I will faithfully execute the Office of President of the United States, and will to the best of my Ability, preserve, protect and defend the Constitution of the United States."

SECTION 2

[POWERS OF THE PRESIDENT]

The President shall be Commander in Chief of the Army and Navy of the United States, and of the Militia of the several States, when called into the actual Service of the United States; he may require the Opinion, in writing, of the principal Officer in each of the executive Departments, upon any Subject relating to the Duties of

10. Modified by the Twelfth and Twentieth Amendments.

their respective Offices, and he shall have **Power to grant Reprieves and Pardons for Offences against the United States**, except in Cases of Impeachment.

He shall have Power, by and with the Advice and Consent of the Senate, to make Treaties, provided two thirds of the Senators present concur; and he shall nominate, and by and with the Advice and Consent of the Senate, shall appoint Ambassadors, **other public Ministers and Consuls**, Judges of the supreme Court, and all other Officers of the United States, whose Appointments are not herein otherwise provided for, and which shall be established by Law: but the Congress may by Law vest the Appointment of such inferior Officers, as they think proper, in the President alone, in the Courts of Law, or in the Heads of Departments.

The President shall have Power to fill up all Vacancies that may happen during the Recess of the Senate, by granting Commissions which shall expire at the End of their next Session.

SECTION 3

[POWERS AND DUTIES OF THE PRESIDENT]

He shall from time to time give to the Congress Information of the State of the Union, and recommend to their Consideration such Measures as he shall judge necessary and expedient; he may, on extraordinary Occasions, convene both Houses, or either of them, and in Case of Disagreement between them, with Respect to the Time of Adjournment, he may adjourn them to such Time as he shall think proper; he shall receive Ambassadors and other public Ministers; he shall take Care that the Laws be faithfully executed, and shall Commission all the Officers of the United States.

SECTION 4

[IMPEACHMENT]

The President, Vice President and all civil Officers of the United States, shall be removed from Office on Impeachment for, and Conviction of, Treason, Bribery, or other high Crimes and Misdemeanors.

Article III

SECTION 1

[JUDICIAL POWER, TENURE OF OFFICE]

The judicial Power of the United States, shall be vested in one supreme Court, and in such inferior Courts as the Congress may from time to time ordain and establish. The Judges, both of the supreme and inferior Courts, shall hold their Offices during good Behaviour, and shall, at stated Times, receive for their Services, a Compensation, which shall not be diminished during their Continuance in Office.

SECTION 2

[JURISDICTION]

The judicial Power shall extend to all Cases, in Law and **Equity**, arising under this Constitution, the Laws of the United States, and Treaties made, or which shall be made, under their Authority;—to all Cases affecting Ambassadors, other public Ministers and Consuls;—to all Cases of admiralty and maritime Jurisdiction;—to Controversies to which the United States shall be a Party;—to Controversies between two or more States;— *between a State and Citizens of another State;*—between Citizens of different States,— between Citizens of the same State claiming Lands under Grants of different States, *and between a State,* or the Citizens thereof, *and foreign States, Citizens or Subjects.*[11]

In all Cases affecting Ambassadors, other public Ministers and Consuls, and those in which a State shall be Party, the supreme Court shall have **original Jurisdiction.**

11. Modified by the Eleventh Amendment.

The president can pardon (grant legal forgiveness to) individuals for federal crimes only. Those pardoned are still accountable to violations of state laws.

Refers to the appointment of cabinet officials

This requires the president to deliver a State of the Union address to Congress but does not specify whether it should be delivered in writing or in the form of a speech.

Article I, Section 4, identifies four impeachable offenses, though "high Crimes and Misdemeanors" offenses are not specified.

Justice

Trial court that hears a case for the first time

In all the other Cases before mentioned, the supreme Court shall have **appellate Jurisdiction**, both as to Law and Fact, with such Exceptions, and under such Regulations as the Congress shall make.

The Trial of all Crimes, except in Cases of Impeachment, shall be by Jury; and such Trial shall be held in the State where the said Crimes shall have been committed; but when not committed within any State, the Trial shall be at such Place or Places as the Congress may by Law have directed.

SECTION 3

[TREASON, PROOF, AND PUNISHMENT]

Treason against the United States, shall consist only in levying War against them, or in adhering to their Enemies, giving them Aid and Comfort. No Person shall be convicted of Treason unless on the Testimony of two Witnesses to the same overt Act, or on Confession in open Court.

The Congress shall have Power to declare the Punishment of Treason, but no Attainder of Treason shall work Corruption of Blood, or Forfeiture except during the Life of the Person attainted.

Article IV

SECTION 1

[FAITH AND CREDIT AMONG STATES]

Full Faith and Credit shall be given in each State to the public Acts, Records, and judicial Proceedings of every other State. And the Congress may by general Laws prescribe the Manner in which such Acts, Records and Proceedings shall be proved, and the Effect thereof.

SECTION 2

[PRIVILEGES AND IMMUNITIES, FUGITIVES]

The Citizens of each State shall be entitled to all **Privileges and Immunities** of Citizens in the several States.

A Person charged in any State with Treason, Felony or other Crime, who shall flee from Justice, and be found in another State, shall on Demand of the executive Authority of the State from which he fled, be delivered up, to be removed to the State having Jurisdiction of the Crime.

No person held to Service or Labour in one State, under the Laws thereof, escaping into another, shall, in Consequence of any Law or Regulation therein, be discharged from such Service or Labour, but shall be delivered up on Claim of the Party to whom such Service or Labour may be due.[12]

SECTION 3

[ADMISSION OF NEW STATES]

New States may be admitted by the Congress into this Union; but no new State shall be formed or erected within the Jurisdiction of any other State; nor any State be formed by the Junction of two or more States, or Parts of States, without the Consent of the Legislatures of the States concerned as well as of the Congress.

The Congress shall have Power to dispose of and make all needful Rules and Regulations respecting the Territory or other Property belonging to the United States; and nothing in this Constitution shall be so construed as to Prejudice any Claims of the United States, or of any particular State.

The power to hear cases on appeal from lower courts

This is the only offense that is specifically defined in the Constitution. Most probably, the framers wanted to guard against overzealous prosecution by government to repress political opposition.

Article IV establishes the relationship of states to one another and their mutual responsibilities.

The full faith and credit clause requires states to respect laws and recognize legal documents from other states. Contemporary examples include driver's licenses and child custody agreements.

The privileges and immunities clause of Article IV prevents states from discriminating against citizens from other states.

12. Repealed by the Thirteenth Amendment.

SECTION 4

[GUARANTEE OF REPUBLICAN GOVERNMENT]

The United States shall guarantee to every State in this Union a Republican Form of Government, and shall protect each of them against Invasion; and on Application of the Legislature, or of the Executive (when the Legislature cannot be convened), against domestic Violence.

Requires that state governments are based upon representative democracy

Article V

[AMENDMENT OF THE CONSTITUTION]

The Congress, whenever two thirds of both Houses shall deem it necessary, shall propose Amendments to this Constitution, or, on the Application of the Legislatures of two thirds of the several States, shall call a Convention for proposing Amendments, which, in either Case, shall be valid to all Intents and Purposes, as Part of this Constitution, when ratified by the Legislatures of three fourths of the several States, or by Conventions in three fourths thereof, as the one or the other Mode of Ratification may be proposed by the Congress; *Provided that no Amendment which may be made prior to the Year One thousand eight hundred and eight shall in any Manner affect the first and fourth Clauses in the Ninth Section of the first Article;* and that no State, without its Consent, shall be deprived of its equal Suffrage in the Senate.

Article VI

[DEBTS, SUPREMACY, OATH]

All Debts contracted and Engagements entered into, before the Adoption of this Constitution, shall be as valid against the United States under this Constitution, as under the Confederation.

This Constitution, and the Laws of the United States which shall be made in Pursuance thereof; and all Treaties made, or which shall be made, under the Authority of the United States, shall be the supreme Law of the Land; and the Judges in every State shall be bound thereby, any Thing in the Constitution or Laws of any State to the Contrary notwithstanding.

The national supremacy clause proclaims the Constitution and federal law to take precedence over state laws and prevents states from interfering with the federal government's discharging of its constitutional duties.

The Senators and Representatives before mentioned, and the Members of the several State Legislatures, and all executive and judicial Officers, both of the United States and of the several States, shall be bound by Oath or Affirmation, to support this Constitution; but no religious Test shall be required as a Qualification to any Office or public Trust under the United States.

Article VII

[RATIFICATION AND ESTABLISHMENT]

The Ratification of the Conventions of nine States, shall be sufficient for the Establishment of this Constitution between the States so ratifying the Same.

Done in Convention by the Unanimous Consent of the States present the Seventeenth Day of September in the Year of our Lord one thousand seven hundred and Eighty seven and of the Independence of the United States of America the Twelfth. *In Witness* whereof We have hereunto subscribed our Names,

Nine of the thirteen states were required to ratify the Constitution.

G:º WASHINGTON—
Presidt. and deputy from Virginia

New Hampshire	**Massachusetts**	**Connecticut**
John Langdon	*Nathaniel Gorham*	*Wm. Saml. Johnson*
Nicholas Gilman	*Rufus King*	*Roger Sherman*

New York	Delaware	North Carolina
Alexander Hamilton	*Geo: Read*	*Wm. Blount*
	Gunning Bedford jun	*Richd. Dobbs Spaight*
New Jersey	*John Dickinson*	*Hu Williamson*
Wil: Livingston	*Richard Bassett*	
David Brearley	*Jaco: Broom*	**South Carolina**
Wm. Paterson		*J. Rutledge*
Jona: Dayton	**Maryland**	*Charles Cotesworth*
	James McHenry	*Pinckney*
Pennsylvania	*Dan of St Thos. Jenifer*	*Charles Pinckney*
B Franklin	*Danl. Carroll*	*Pierce Butler*
Thomas Mifflin		
Robt. Morris	**Virginia**	**Georgia**
Geo. Clymer	*John Blair—*	*William Few*
Thos. FitzSimons	*James Madison Jr.*	*Abr Baldwin*
Jared Ingersoll		
James Wilson		
Gouv Morris		

Full Text of the Amendments to the Constitution

Proposed by Congress and Ratified by the Legislatures of the Several States, Pursuant to Article V of the Original Constitution.

Amendments I–X, known as the Bill of Rights, were proposed by Congress on September 25, 1789, and ratified on December 15, 1791.

[PREAMBLE TO THE BILL OF RIGHTS]

The Conventions of a number of the States, having at the time of their adopting the Constitution, expressed a desire, in order to prevent misconstruction or abuse of its powers, that further declaratory and restrictive clauses should be added: And as extending the ground of public confidence in the Government, will best ensure the beneficent ends of its institution.

The first 10 amendments of the Constitution, known as the Bill of Rights, were added in 1791. During the ratification debate, Antifederalists voiced concerns that the Constitution did not provide sufficient protections to individual rights from the abuse of government power. The rights enumerated and reserved in the Bill of Rights not only protect individual liberty but also help to ensure due process under the law.

Depriving

Amendment I

[FREEDOM OF RELIGION, OF SPEECH, AND OF THE PRESS]

Congress shall make no law respecting an establishment of religion, or prohibiting the free exercise thereof; or **abridging** the freedom of speech, or of the press; or the right of the people peaceably to assemble, and to petition the Government for a redress of grievances.

Amendment II

[RIGHT TO KEEP AND BEAR ARMS]

A well regulated Militia, being necessary to the security of a free State, the right of the people to keep and bear Arms, shall not be infringed.

Amendment III

[QUARTERING OF SOLDIERS]

No Soldier shall, in time of peace be quartered in any house, without the consent of the Owner, nor in time of war, but in a manner to be prescribed by law.

Amendment IV

[SECURITY FROM UNWARRANTABLE SEARCH AND SEIZURE]

The right of the people to be secure in their persons, houses, papers, and effects, against unreasonable searches and seizures, shall not be violated, and no **Warrants** shall issue, but upon **probable cause**, supported by Oath or affirmation, and particularly describing the place to be searched, and the persons or things to be seized.

> Documents issued by a judge or magistrate authorizing a search of a person or property | Legal standard that law enforcement must demonstrate a reasonable belief of a commission of a crime

Amendment V

[RIGHTS OF ACCUSED PERSONS IN CRIMINAL PROCEEDINGS]

No person shall be held to answer for a **capital**, or otherwise infamous crime, unless on a presentment or **indictment of a Grand Jury**, except in cases arising in the land or naval forces, or in the Militia, when in actual service in time of War or in public danger; nor shall any person be subject for the **same offence to be twice put in jeopardy of life or limb**; nor shall be compelled in any **criminal case to be a witness against himself**, nor be deprived of life, liberty, or property, without **due process of law**; nor shall private property be taken for public use, without just compensation.

> Carries the possibility of the death penalty | Informs the accused in a criminal case of the charges against him or her

> The double jeopardy clause prohibits a person from being prosecuted twice for the same crime. | Refers to self-incrimination | Fair treatment under the law to which a citizen is entitled

Amendment VI

[RIGHT TO SPEEDY TRIAL, WITNESSES, ETC.]

In all criminal prosecutions, the accused shall enjoy the right to a speedy and public trial, by an impartial jury of the State and district wherein the crime shall have been committed, which district shall have been previously ascertained by law, and to be informed of the nature and cause of the accusation; to be confronted with the witnesses against him; to have **compulsory process** for obtaining witnesses in his favor, and to have the Assistance of Counsel for his defence.

> The defendant may compel witnesses to testify in his or her favor through a court-ordered subpoena.

Amendment VII

[TRIAL BY JURY IN CIVIL CASES]

In suits at **common law**, where the value in controversy shall exceed twenty dollars, the right of trial by jury shall be preserved, and no fact tried by a jury, shall be otherwise reexamined in any Court of the United States, than according to the rules of the common law.

> Refers in this case to civil jury trials in the federal court

Amendment VIII

[BAILS, FINES, PUNISHMENTS]

Excessive bail shall not be required, nor excessive fines imposed, nor **cruel and unusual punishments** inflicted.

> This generally means that federal courts cannot impose unduly harsh punishment to a person convicted of a crime. However, the phrase is relatively vague and has been open to interpretation.

Amendment IX

[RESERVATION OF RIGHTS OF PEOPLE]

The enumeration in the Constitution, of certain rights, shall not be construed to deny or disparage others retained by the people.

> The Ninth Amendment allows for additional rights, such as the right to privacy, given to the people but not specifically written in the Constitution.

Amendment X

[POWERS RESERVED TO STATES OR PEOPLE]

The powers not delegated to the United States by the Constitution, nor prohibited by it to the States, are reserved to the States respectively, or to the people.

> These powers, known as the reserved powers, have often been used in court to defend states' rights.

Amendment XI

[Proposed by Congress on March 4, 1794; declared ratified on January 8, 1798.]
[RESTRICTION OF JUDICIAL POWER]

The Judicial power of the United States shall not be construed to extend to any suit in law or equity, commenced or prosecuted against one of the United States by Citizens of another State, or by Citizens or Subjects of any Foreign State.

Amendment XII

[Proposed by Congress on December 9, 1803; declared ratified on September 25, 1804.]
[ELECTION OF PRESIDENT AND VICE PRESIDENT]

The Electors shall meet in their respective states and vote by ballot for President and Vice-President, one of whom, at least, shall not be an inhabitant of the same state with themselves; they shall name in their ballots the person voted for as President, and in distinct ballots the person voted for as Vice-President, and they shall make distinct lists of all persons voted for as President, and of all persons voted for as Vice-President, and of the number of votes for each, which lists they shall sign and certify, and transmit sealed to the seat of the government of the United States, directed to the President of the Senate;—the President of the Senate shall, in presence of the Senate and House of Representatives, open all the certificates and the votes shall then be counted;—The person having the greatest number of votes for President, shall be the President, if such number be a majority of the whole number of Electors appointed; and if no person have such majority, then from the persons having the highest numbers not exceeding three on the list of those voted for as President, the House of Representatives shall choose immediately, by ballot, the President. But in choosing the President, the votes shall be taken by states, the representation from each state having one vote; a quorum for this purpose shall consist of a member or members from two-thirds of the states, and a majority of all the states shall be necessary to a choice. And if the House of Representatives shall not choose a President whenever the right of choice shall devolve upon them, before the fourth day of March next following, then the Vice-President shall act as President, as in the case of the death or other constitutional disability of the President.—The person having the greatest number of votes as Vice-President, shall be the Vice-President, if such number be a majority of the whole number of Electors appointed, and if no person have a majority, then from the two highest numbers on the list, the Senate shall choose the Vice-President; a quorum for the purpose shall consist of two-thirds of the whole number of Senators, and a majority of the whole number shall be necessary to a choice. But no person constitutionally ineligible to the office of President shall be eligible to that of Vice-President of the United States.

Amendment XIII

[Proposed by Congress on January 31, 1865; declared ratified on December 18, 1865.]

SECTION 1

[ABOLITION OF SLAVERY]

Neither slavery nor **involuntary servitude**, except as a punishment for crime whereof the party shall have been duly convicted, shall exist within the United States, or any place subject to their jurisdiction.

SECTION 2

[POWER TO ENFORCE THIS ARTICLE]

Congress shall have power to enforce this article by appropriate legislation.

Amendment XIV

[Proposed by Congress on June 13, 1866; declared ratified on July 28, 1868.]

SECTION 1

[CITIZENSHIP RIGHTS NOT TO BE ABRIDGED BY STATES]

All persons born or naturalized in the United States, and subject to the jurisdiction thereof, are citizens of the United States and of the State wherein they reside. No State shall make or enforce any law which shall abridge the privileges or immunities of citizens of the United States; nor shall any State deprive any person of life, liberty, or property, without due process of law; nor deny to any person within its jurisdiction the equal protection of the laws.

SECTION 2

[APPORTIONMENT OF REPRESENTATIVES IN CONGRESS]

Representatives shall be apportioned among the several States according to their respective numbers, counting the whole number of persons in each State, excluding Indians not taxed. But when the right to vote at any election for the choice of electors for President and Vice-President of the United States, Representatives in Congress, the Executive and Judicial officers of a State, or the members of the Legislature thereof, is denied to any of the male inhabitants of such State, being twenty-one years of age, and citizens of the United States, or in any way abridged, except for participation in rebellion, or other crime, the basis of representation therein shall be reduced in the proportion which the number of such male citizens shall bear to the whole number of male citizens twenty-one years of age in such State.

SECTION 3

[PERSONS DISQUALIFIED FROM HOLDING OFFICE]

No person shall be a Senator or Representative in Congress, or elector of President and Vice-President, or hold any office, civil or military, under the United States, or under any State, who, having previously taken an oath, as a member of Congress, or as an officer of the United States, or as a member of any State legislature, or as an executive or judicial officer of any State, to support the Constitution of the United States, shall have engaged in insurrection or rebellion against the same, or given aid or comfort to the enemies thereof. But Congress may by a vote of two-thirds of each House, remove such disability.

SECTION 4

[WHAT PUBLIC DEBTS ARE VALID]

The validity of the public debt of the United States, authorized by law, including debts incurred for payment of pensions and bounties for services in suppressing insurrection or rebellion, shall not be questioned. But neither the United States nor any State shall assume or pay any debt or obligation incurred in aid of insurrection or rebellion against the United States, or any claim for the loss or emancipation of any slave; but all such debts, obligations and claims shall be held illegal and void.

SECTION 5

[POWER TO ENFORCE THIS ARTICLE]

The Congress shall have power to enforce, by appropriate legislation, the provisions of this article.

The Fourteenth Amendment, Section 1, is often referred to as the second Bill of Rights because it eventually incorporated freedoms and protections of the Bill of Rights to apply to the states. The citizenship clause grants citizenship to former enslaved persons and overturns the Supreme Court decision in *Dred Scott v. Sandford* (1857). The privileges and immunities clause prevents states from limiting legal protections given to citizens of the United States. The due process clause has been interpreted by the courts to mean that states cannot take away a person's property or life without providing fair and impartial process. The equal protection clause limits a state's ability to discriminate against people based on their race, gender, or other status.

Amendment XV

[*Proposed by Congress on February 26, 1869; declared ratified on March 30, 1870.*]

SECTION 1

[BLACK SUFFRAGE]

The right of citizens of the United States to vote shall not be denied or abridged by the United States or by any State on account of race, color, or previous condition of servitude.

This amendment granted voting rights to former enslaved persons.

SECTION 2

[POWER TO ENFORCE THIS ARTICLE]

The Congress shall have power to enforce this article by appropriate legislation.

Amendment XVI

[*Proposed by Congress on July 2, 1909; declared ratified on February 25, 1913.*]

[AUTHORIZING FEDERAL INCOME TAXES]

The Congress shall have power to lay and collect taxes on incomes, from whatever source derived, without apportionment among the several States, and without regard to any census or enumeration.

Amendment XVII

[*Proposed by Congress on May 13, 1912; declared ratified on May 31, 1913.*]

[POPULAR ELECTION OF SENATORS]

The Senate of the United States shall be composed of two Senators from each State, elected by the people thereof, for six years; and each Senator shall have one vote. The electors in each State shall have the qualifications requisite for electors of the most numerous branch of the State legislatures.

This amendment changed Article I, Section 3, in which senators were chosen by state legislatures, to election by the people.

When vacancies happen in the representation of any State in the Senate, the executive authority of such State shall issue writs of election to fill such vacancies: *Provided,* That the legislature of any State may empower the executive thereof to make temporary appointments until the people fill the vacancies by election as the legislature may direct.

This amendment shall not be so construed as to affect the election or term of any Senator chosen before it becomes valid as part of the Constitution.

Amendment XVIII

[*Proposed by Congress December 18, 1917; declared ratified on January 29, 1919.*]

SECTION 1

[NATIONAL LIQUOR PROHIBITION]

After one year from the ratification of this article the manufacture, sale, or transportation of intoxicating liquors within, the importation thereof into, or the exportation thereof from the United States and all territory subject to the jurisdiction thereof for beverage purposes is hereby prohibited.

SECTION 2

[POWER TO ENFORCE THIS ARTICLE]

The Congress and the several States shall have concurrent power to enforce this article by appropriate legislation.

SECTION 3

[RATIFICATION WITHIN SEVEN YEARS]

This article shall be inoperative unless it shall have been ratified as an amendment to the Constitution by the legislatures of the several States, as provided in the Constitution, within seven years from the date of the submission hereof to the States by the Congress.[13]

13. Repealed by the Twenty-First Amendment.

Amendment XIX

[*Proposed by Congress on June 4, 1919; declared ratified on August 26, 1920.*]

[WOMAN SUFFRAGE]

The right of citizens of the United States to vote shall not be denied or abridged by the United States or by any State on account of sex.

Congress shall have power to enforce this article by appropriate legislation.

Amendment XX

[*Proposed by Congress on March 2, 1932; declared ratified on February 6, 1933.*]

SECTION 1

[TERMS OF OFFICE]

The terms of the President and Vice President shall end at noon on the 20th day of January, and the terms of Senators and Representatives at noon on the 3d day of January, of the years in which such terms would have ended if this article had not been ratified; and the terms of their successors shall then begin.

SECTION 2

[TIME OF CONVENING CONGRESS]

The Congress shall assemble at least once in every year, and such meeting shall begin at noon on the 3d day of January, unless they shall by law appoint a different day.

SECTION 3

[PRESIDENTIAL SUCCESSION UPON DEATH OF PRESIDENT-ELECT]

If, at the time fixed for the beginning of the term of the President, the President elect shall have died, the Vice President elect shall become President. If a President shall not have been chosen before the time fixed for the beginning of his term, or if the President elect shall have failed to qualify, then the Vice President elect shall act as President until a President shall have qualified; and the Congress may by law provide for the case wherein neither a President elect nor a Vice President elect shall have qualified, declaring who shall then act as President, or the manner in which one who is to act shall be selected, and such person shall act accordingly until a President or Vice President shall have qualified.

SECTION 4

[ELECTION OF THE PRESIDENT]

The Congress may by law provide for the case of the death of any of the persons from whom the House of Representatives may choose a President whenever the right of choice shall have devolved upon them, and for the case of the death of any of the persons from whom the Senate may choose a Vice President whenever the right of choice shall have devolved upon them.

SECTION 5

[AMENDMENT TAKES EFFECT]

Sections 1 and 2 shall take effect on the 15th day of October following the ratification of this article.

SECTION 6

[RATIFICATION WITHIN SEVEN YEARS]

This article shall be inoperative unless it shall have been ratified as an amendment to the Constitution by the legislatures of three-fourths of the several States within seven years from the date of its submission.

Amendment XXI

[*Proposed by Congress on February 20, 1933; declared ratified on December 5, 1933.*]

SECTION 1

[NATIONAL LIQUOR PROHIBITION REPEALED]

The eighteenth article of amendment to the Constitution of the United States is hereby repealed.

SECTION 2

[TRANSPORTATION OF LIQUOR INTO "DRY" STATES]

The transportation or importation into any State, Territory, or Possession of the United States for delivery or use therein of intoxicating liquors, in violation of the laws thereof, is hereby prohibited.

SECTION 3

[RATIFICATION WITHIN SEVEN YEARS]

This article shall be inoperative unless it shall have been ratified as an amendment to the Constitution by conventions in the several States, as provided in the Constitution, within seven years from the date of the submission hereof to the States by the Congress.

Amendment XXII

[*Proposed by Congress on March 21, 1947; declared ratified on February 27, 1951.*]

SECTION 1

[TENURE OF PRESIDENT LIMITED]

No person shall be elected to the office of President more than twice, and no person who has held the office of President or acted as President, for more than two years of a term to which some other person was elected President shall be elected to the office of the President more than once. But this Article shall not apply to any person holding the office of President when this Article was proposed by the Congress, and shall not prevent any person who may be holding the office of President, or acting as President, during the term within which this Article becomes operative from holding the office of President or acting as President during the remainder of such term.

George Washington established the precedent for presidents serving only two terms. This amendment was passed after Franklin Roosevelt was elected to four terms.

SECTION 2

[RATIFICATION WITHIN SEVEN YEARS]

This article shall be inoperative unless it shall have been ratified as an amendment to the Constitution by the legislatures of three-fourths of the several States within seven years from the date of its submission to the States by the Congress.

Amendment XXIII

[*Proposed by Congress on June 16, 1960; declared ratified on March 29, 1961.*]

SECTION 1

[ELECTORAL COLLEGE VOTES FOR THE DISTRICT OF COLUMBIA]

The District constituting the seat of Government of the United States shall appoint in such manner as the Congress may direct:

A number of electors of President and Vice President equal to the whole number of Senators and Representatives in Congress to which the District would be entitled if it were a State, but in no event more than the least populous State; they shall be in addition to those appointed by the States, but they shall be considered, for the purposes of the election of President and Vice President, to be electors appointed by a State; and they shall meet in the District and perform such duties as provided by the twelfth article of amendment.

Though Washington, D.C., is not a state and has no voting representation in Congress, this amendment grants citizens of the District of Columbia three electors and a say in the election of the president of the United States.

SECTION 2

[POWER TO ENFORCE THIS ARTICLE]

The Congress shall have power to enforce this article by appropriate legislation.

Amendment XXIV

[*Proposed by Congress on August 27, 1962; declared ratified on January 23, 1964.*]

SECTION 1

[ELMINATES POLL TAXES]

The right of citizens of the United States to vote in any primary or other election for President or Vice President, for electors for President or Vice President, or for Senator or Representative of Congress, shall not be denied or abridged by the United States or any State by reason of failure to pay any poll tax or other tax.

Instituting a polls tax was a discriminatory method after Reconstruction to prevent African Americans from voting.

SECTION 2

[POWER TO ENFORCE THIS ARTICLE]

The Congress shall have power to enforce this article by appropriate legislation.

Amendment XXV

[*Proposed by Congress on July 6, 1965; declared ratified on February 10, 1967.*]

SECTION 1

[VICE PRESIDENT TO BECOME PRESIDENT]

In case of the removal of the President from office or his death or resignation, the Vice President shall become President.

SECTION 2

[CHOICE OF A NEW VICE PRESIDENT]

Whenever there is a vacancy in the office of the Vice President, the President shall nominate a Vice President who shall take the office upon confirmation by a majority vote of both houses of Congress.

SECTION 3

[PRESIDENT MAY DECLARE OWN DISABILITY]

Whenever the President transmits to the President pro tempore of the Senate and the Speaker of the House of Representatives his written declaration that he is unable to discharge the powers and duties of his office, and until he transmits to them a written declaration to the contrary, such powers and duties shall be discharged by the Vice President as Acting President.

SECTION 4

[ALTERNATE PROCEDURES TO DECLARE AND TO END PRESIDENTIAL DISABILITY]

Whenever the Vice President and a majority of either the principal officers of the executive departments, or of such other body as Congress may by law provide, transmit to the President pro tempore of the Senate and the Speaker of the House of Representatives their written declaration that the President is unable to discharge the powers and duties of his office, the Vice President shall immediately assume the powers and duties of the office as Acting President.

Thereafter, when the President transmits to the President pro tempore of the Senate and the Speaker of the House of Representatives his written declaration that no inability exists, he shall resume the powers and duties of his office unless the Vice

President and a majority of either the principal officers of the executive department, or of such other body as Congress may by law provide, transmit within four days to the President pro tempore of the Senate and the Speaker of the House of Representatives their written declaration that the President is unable to discharge the powers and duties of his office. Thereupon Congress shall decide the issue, assembling within forty eight hours for that purpose if not in session. If the Congress, within twenty one days after receipt of the latter written declaration, or, if Congress is not in session, within twenty one days after Congress is required to assemble, determines by two-thirds vote of both Houses that the President is unable to discharge the powers and duties of his office, the Vice President shall continue to discharge the same as Acting President; otherwise, the President shall resume the powers and duties of his office.

Amendment XXVI

[*Proposed by Congress on March 23, 1971; declared ratified on July 1, 1971.*]

SECTION 1

[EIGHTEEN-YEAR-OLD VOTE]

The right of citizens of the United States, who are eighteen years of age or older, to vote shall not be denied or abridged by the United States or by any State on account of age.

SECTION 2

[POWER TO ENFORCE THIS ARTICLE]

The Congress shall have power to enforce this article by appropriate legislation.

Amendment XXVII

[*Proposed by Congress on September 25, 1789; declared ratified on May 8, 1992.*]
[CONGRESS CANNOT RAISE ITS OWN PAY]

No law varying the compensation for the services of the Senators and Representatives, shall take effect, until an election of representatives shall have intervened.

Making Connections

1. Ratified in 1788, the U.S. Constitution is the longest surviving government charter in the world today. Why is the Constitution so important to American democracy? Why is the continuing existence of the Constitution significant to the international community?

2. The framers of the Constitution drew upon ideas of freedom and popular sovereignty embodied in earlier documents like the Declaration of Independence. Describe several examples in the Constitution that exemplify government by the people.

3. Compare and contrast the structure of the national government established in the Constitution with that of the central government created in the Articles of Confederation. Be sure to note both similarities and differences between the two.

4. Article I of the Constitution that establishes the legislative branch of the federal government is by far the longest article in the Constitution.

   · Explain why the framers made the legislative branch the most prominent of the three branches of the federal government.
   · The framers were also concerned about the legislative branch becoming too powerful. Drawing upon the text itself as well as other foundational documents

like *Federalist 51*, explain ways in which the framers limited a concentration of power in the legislative branch.

5. The Constitution creates a relatively powerful chief executive. What do you think are the president's most important constitutional powers? Explain why.

6. Article III, which created the federal judiciary, is relatively brief, and the U.S. Supreme Court is the only national court identified specifically. Yet the most important power of the court—judicial review, or the power to decide the constitutionality of federal law and government actions—is not written in the Constitution at all. Why is it important to have a national court with judicial review in a constitutional system?

7. Article VI of the Constitution, also known as the national supremacy clause, states, "This Constitution, and the Laws of the United States . . . and all Treaties made . . . shall be the supreme Law of the Land; and the Judges in every State shall be bound thereby, any Thing in the Constitution or Laws of any State to the Contrary notwithstanding."

   · Interpret the meaning of the national supremacy clause as it relates to the relationship between the national government and the states.
   · Describe several historical or current examples that demonstrate a conflict between the Constitution and federal law, and state laws or actions.

8. Devising the amendment process spelled out in Article V, the framers understood the necessity for the Constitution to adapt to changing times and circumstances. Yet, since its ratification in 1788, only 27 amendments have been added to the Constitution. Explain several reasons why it is difficult to pass constitutional amendments. Why do you think the framers intended the amendment process to be so arduous?

9. Draft a proposed constitutional amendment to be presented to Congress that addresses an issue or topic you think is important. How would you convince members of Congress, the states, and the American people to adopt your Twenty-Eighth Amendment?

Foundational Document: *Federalist 51*

Enduring Understanding

PMI-1: "The Constitution created a competitive policy-making process to ensure the people's will is accurately represented and that freedom is preserved." (AP® U.S. Government and Politics Course and Exam Description)

Introduction

The *Federalist Papers* are a series of essays published in several newspapers between October 1787 and April 1788. These essays, written by James Madison, Alexander Hamilton, and John Jay under the pseudonym Publius, advocated the ratification of the Constitution. The *Federalist Papers* also addressed concerns raised by Antifederalists in the Brutus essays, also known as the *Antifederalist Papers*, that the federal government created by the Constitution threatens states' rights and individual liberties. *Federalist 51*, written by James Madison, demonstrated how the Constitution created several mechanisms through the separation of powers, checks and balances, and federalism that would constrain federal power and mitigate the negative effects of majority factions. Madison believed wise leaders would not necessarily emerge in every generation, so the government itself must be constructed so that "[a]mbition . . . counteract[s] ambition."

Full Text of *Federalist 51* (James Madison)

The Structure of the Government Must Furnish the Proper Checks and Balances between the Different Departments

To the People of the State of New York:

TO WHAT **expedient**, then, shall we finally resort, **for maintaining in practice the necessary partition of power among the several departments, as laid down in the Constitution?** The only answer that can be given is, that as all these exterior provisions are found to be inadequate, the defect must be supplied, by so contriving **the interior structure of the government as that its several constituent parts may, by their mutual relations, be the means of keeping each other in their proper places.** Without presuming to undertake a full development of this important idea, I will hazard a few general observations, which may perhaps place it in a clearer light, and enable us to form a more correct judgment of the principles and structure of the government planned by the convention. In order to lay a due foundation for that separate and distinct exercise of the different powers of government, which to a certain extent is admitted on all hands to be essential to the preservation of liberty, it is evident that each department should have a will of its own; and consequently should be **so constituted that the members of each should have as little agency as possible in the appointment of the members of the others.** Were this principle rigorously adhered to, it would require that all the appointments for the supreme executive, legislative, and judiciary **magistracies** should be drawn from the same fountain of authority, the people, through channels having no communication whatever with one another. Perhaps such a plan of constructing the several departments

Means to an end | This refers to the separation of powers in which the Constitution grants authority to each of the three branches of the federal government.

This expresses approval for a constitutional system of checks and balances in which each branch is given the means to oversee the other two.

This expresses the idea that the members of each branch should have minimal influence over the selection of members of the other branches.

Judicial officers

would be less difficult in practice than it may in contemplation appear. Some difficulties, however, and some additional expense would attend the execution of it. Some deviations, therefore, from the principle must be admitted. In the constitution of the judiciary department in particular, it might be **inexpedient** to insist rigorously on the principle: first, because peculiar qualifications being essential in the members, the primary consideration ought to be to select that mode of choice which best secures these qualifications; secondly, because the **permanent tenure** by which the appointments are held in that department, must soon destroy all sense of dependence on the authority conferring them.

It is equally evident, that the members of each department should be as little dependent as possible on those of the others, for the **emoluments** annexed to their offices. Were the executive magistrate, or the judges, not independent of the legislature in this particular, their independence in every other would be merely nominal. But the great security against a gradual concentration of the several powers in the same department, consists in giving to those who administer each department the necessary constitutional means and personal motives to resist **encroachments** of the others. The provision for defense must in this, as in all other cases, be made commensurate to the danger of attack. Ambition must be made to counteract ambition. The interest of the man must be connected with the constitutional rights of the place. It may be a reflection on human nature, that such **devices** should be necessary to control the abuses of government. But what is government itself, but the greatest of all reflections on human nature? If men were angels, no government would be necessary. If angels were to govern men, neither external nor internal controls on government would be necessary. In framing a government which is to be administered by men over men, the great difficulty lies in this: you must first enable the government to control the governed; and in the next place oblige it to control itself. A dependence on the people is, no doubt, the primary control on the government; but experience has taught mankind the necessity of **auxiliary** precautions. This policy of supplying, by opposite and rival interests, the defect of better motives, might be traced through the whole system of human affairs, private as well as public. We see it particularly displayed in all the subordinate distributions of power, where the constant aim is to divide and arrange the several offices in such a manner as that each may be a check on the other that the private interest of every individual may be a sentinel over the public rights. These inventions of **prudence** cannot be less **requisite** in the distribution of the supreme powers of the State. But it is not possible to give to each department an equal power of self-defense. **In republican government, the legislative authority necessarily predominates. The remedy for this inconveniency is to divide the legislature into different branches; and to render them, by different modes of election and different principles of action, as little connected with each other as the nature of their common functions and their common dependence on the society will admit.** It may even be necessary to guard against dangerous encroachments by still further precautions. As the weight of the legislative authority requires that it should be thus divided, the weakness of the executive may require, on the other hand, that it should be fortified.

An absolute negative on the legislature appears, at first view, to be the natural defense with which the executive magistrate should be armed. But perhaps it would be neither altogether safe nor alone sufficient. On ordinary occasions it might not be exerted with the requisite firmness, and on extraordinary occasions it might be **perfidiously** abused. May not this defect of an absolute negative be supplied by some qualified connection between this weaker department and the weaker branch of the stronger department, by which the latter may be led to support the constitutional rights of the former, without being too much detached from the rights of its own department?

Inadvisable

According to the Constitution, members of the federal judiciary including Supreme Court justices serve life terms.

Compensation

Intrusions

Mechanisms

Backup or supplementary

Caution | Required or necessary

The Constitution employs bicameralism, a two-house legislature, as an internal check to prevent the dominant legislative branch from becoming too powerful.

This refers to the presidential veto as a means to bolster the chief executive to provide a check on the legislative branch.

Dangerously; deceitfully

If the principles on which these observations are founded be just, as I persuade myself they are, and they be applied as a criterion to the several State constitutions, and to the federal Constitution it will be found that if the latter does not perfectly correspond with them, the former are infinitely less able to bear such a test.

There are, moreover, two considerations particularly applicable to the federal system of America, which place that system in a very interesting point of view. First. In a **single republic**, all the power surrendered by the people is submitted to the administration of a single government; and the **usurpations** are guarded against by a division of the government into distinct and separate departments. **In the compound republic of America, the power surrendered by the people is first divided between two distinct governments, and then the portion allotted to each subdivided among distinct and separate departments. Hence a double security arises to the rights of the people. The different governments will control each other, at the same time that each will be controlled by itself.** Second. It is of great importance in a republic not only to guard the society against the oppression of its rulers, but to guard one part of the society against the injustice of the other part. Different interests necessarily exist in different classes of citizens. If a majority be united by a common interest, the rights of the minority will be insecure.

There are but two methods of providing against this evil: the one by creating a will in the community independent of the majority that is, of the society itself; the other, by comprehending in the society so many separate descriptions of citizens as will render an unjust combination of a majority of the whole very improbable, if not impracticable. The first method prevails in all governments possessing an hereditary or self-appointed authority. This, at best, is but a precarious security; because a power independent of the society may as well **espouse** the unjust views of the major, as the rightful interests of the minor party, and may possibly be turned against both parties. The second method will be exemplified in the federal republic of the United States. Whilst all authority in it will be derived from and dependent on the society, the society itself will be broken into so many parts, interests, and classes of citizens, that the rights of individuals, or of the minority, will be in little danger from interested combinations of the majority.

In a free government the security for civil rights must be the same as that for religious rights. It consists in the one case in the **multiplicity of interests**, and in the other in the multiplicity of sects. The degree of security in both cases will depend on the number of interests and sects; and this may be presumed to depend on the extent of country and number of people comprehended under the same government. This view of the subject must particularly recommend a proper federal system to all the sincere and considerate friends of republican government, since it shows that in exact proportion as the territory of the Union may be formed into more circumscribed Confederacies, or States oppressive combinations of a majority will be facilitated: the best security, under the republican forms, for the rights of every class of citizens, will be diminished: and consequently the stability and independence of some member of the government, the only other security, must be proportionately increased. Justice is the end of government. It is the end of civil society. It ever has been and ever will be pursued until it be obtained, or until liberty be lost in the pursuit. In a society under the forms of which the stronger faction can readily unite and oppress the weaker, anarchy may as truly be said to reign as in a state of nature, where the weaker individual is not secured against the violence of the stronger; and as, in the latter state, even the stronger individuals are prompted, by the uncertainty of their condition, to submit to a government which may protect the weak as well as themselves; so, in the former state, will the more powerful factions or parties be gradnally induced, by a like motive, to wish for a government which will protect all parties, the weaker as well as the more powerful.

This responds to criticism levied by Antifederalists of the danger of a large, "single republic," which amounts to a powerful unitary system. | Illegal seizures of power

This passage suggests that a "compound republic," based on the principle of federalism in which the national government shares power with the states, provides another check against the concentration of power.

Advocate

This claims that a federal republic is the best mechanism to counteract tyranny of the majority because there will be many different factions competing for power.

It can be little doubted that if the State of Rhode Island was separated from the Confederacy and left to itself, the insecurity of rights under the popular form of government within such narrow limits would be displayed by such reiterated oppressions of factious majorities that some power altogether independent of the people would soon be called for by the voice of the very factions whose misrule had proved the necessity of it. In the extended republic of the United States, and among the great variety of interests, parties, and sects which it embraces, a coalition of a majority of the whole society could seldom take place on any other principles than those of justice and the general good; whilst there being thus less danger to a minor from the will of a major party, there must be less pretext, also, to provide for the security of the former, by introducing into the government a will not dependent on the latter, or, in other words, a will independent of the society itself. It is no less certain than it is important, notwithstanding the contrary opinions which have been entertained, that the larger the society, provided it lie within a practical sphere, the more duly capable it will be of self-government. And happily for the REPUBLICAN CAUSE, the practicable sphere may be carried to a very great extent, by a judicious modification and mixture of the **FEDERAL PRINCIPLE**.

PUBLIUS.

<aside>Rhode Island supported the continuance of the government under the Articles of Confederation, boycotted the Constitutional Convention, and initially opposed the ratification of the Constitution.</aside>

<aside>This refers to the constitutional system of federalism, in which the national and state governments share power.</aside>

Making Connections

1. Describe Madison's main argument in *Federalist 51*, which defends the "federal republic" established in the U.S. Constitution.

2. In *Federalist 51*, Madison asserted that the top priority of government should be the "preservation of liberty." Do you agree with Madison's statement? Explain why or why not.

3. Advocating the system of government devised by the Constitution, Madison stated, "Ambition must be made to counteract ambition. . . . But what is government itself, but the greatest of all reflections on human nature? If men were angels, no government would be necessary."

   · How does this quotation support the importance of constitutional checks and balances?
   · What does this quotation tell us about Madison's view of human nature? What do you think?

4. Madison asserted that the principle of federalism in which power is "divided between two distinct governments" (federal and state) will best protect against tyranny of the majority. Explain how the division of power between the national government and the states helps to protect minority rights and limit majority rule.

5. Drawing upon evidence in the document, how does *Federalist 51* support elite democracy?

6. Brutus 1, representing the Antifederalist perspective, warned of the concentration of power granted to the federal government by the Constitution as a threat to liberty. How effectively do you think Madison addressed these concerns in *Federalist 51*? Provide specific evidence from the document to support your position.

Foundational Document: *Federalist 70*

Enduring Understanding

CON-4: "The presidency has been enhanced beyond its expressed constitutional powers." (AP® U.S. Government and Politics Course and Exam Description)

Introduction

The *Federalist Papers* are a series of essays published in several newspapers between October 1787 and April 1788. These treatises, penned by James Madison, Alexander Hamilton, and John Jay under the pseudonym Publius, advocated for the ratification of the Constitution. *Federalist 70*, written by Alexander Hamilton, argued for the creation of a unitary executive branch featuring a strong, energetic executive leader. During the Constitutional Convention in 1787, fierce debate erupted over the structure and authority of the executive branch. In *Federalist 70*, Hamilton responded to a multi-executive structure proposed by Antifederalist supporters. Hamilton countered that the creation of a unitary executive branch under the Constitution, featuring a strong, energetic executive leader, best promoted security and stability.

Full Text of *Federalist 70* (Alexander Hamilton)

The Executive Department Further Considered

To the People of the State of New York:

The Antifederalists were suspicious of a powerful chief executive.

THERE is an idea, which is not without its advocates, that a vigorous Executive is inconsistent with the genius of republican government. The enlightened well-wishers to this species of government must at least hope that the supposition is destitute of foundation; since they can never admit its truth, without at the same time admitting the condemnation of their own principles. Energy in the Executive is a leading character in the definition of good government. It is essential to the protection of the community against foreign attacks; it is not less essential to the steady administration of the laws; to the **protection of property against those irregular and high-handed combinations which sometimes interrupt the ordinary course of justice;**

Refers to dangerous factions that could form to subvert justice

to the security of liberty against the enterprises and assaults of ambition, of faction, and of anarchy. **Every man the least conversant in Roman story, knows how often that republic was obliged to take refuge in the absolute power of a single man**, under the formidable title of Dictator, as well against the

Refers to powerful Roman emperors

intrigues of ambitious individuals who aspired to the **tyranny**, and the **seditions** of

Oppression | Insurgence

whole classes of the community whose conduct threatened the existence of all government, as against the **invasions of external enemies** who menaced the conquest and

Refers to threats of foreign countries | Hamilton means that a weak executive leadership would make it difficult to carry out enacted laws or policies.

destruction of Rome.

There can be no need, however, to multiply arguments or examples on this head. A feeble Executive implies a feeble **execution of the government**. A feeble execution is but another phrase for a bad execution; and a government ill executed, whatever it may be in theory, must be, in practice, a bad government.

Taking it for granted, therefore, that all men of sense will agree in the necessity of an energetic Executive, it will only remain to inquire, what are the ingredients which constitute this energy? How far can they be combined with those other ingredients which constitute safety in the republican sense? And how far does this combination characterize the plan which has been reported by the **convention**?

The ingredients which constitute energy in the Executive are, first, **unity**; secondly, duration; thirdly, an adequate provision for its support; fourthly, **competent powers**.

The ingredients which constitute safety in the republican sense are, first, a due dependence on the people, secondly, a due responsibility.

Those politicians and statesmen who have been the most celebrated for the soundness of their principles and for the justice of their views, have declared in favor of a single Executive and a numerous legislature. They have with **great propriety**, considered energy as the most necessary qualification of the former, and have regarded this as most applicable to power in a single hand, while they have, with equal propriety, considered the latter as best adapted to deliberation and wisdom, and best calculated to **conciliate** the confidence of the people and to **secure their privileges and interests**.

That unity is conducive to energy will not be disputed. Decision, activity, secrecy, and despatch will generally characterize the proceedings of one man in a much more eminent degree than the proceedings of any greater number; and in proportion as the number is increased, these qualities will be diminished.

This unity may be destroyed in two ways: either by vesting the power in two or more magistrates of equal dignity and authority; or by vesting it **ostensibly** in one man, subject, in whole or in part, to the control and co-operation of others, in the capacity of counsellors to him. Of the first, the two Consuls of Rome may serve as an example; of the last, we shall find examples in the constitutions of several of the States. New York and New Jersey, if I recollect right, are the only States which have intrusted the executive authority wholly to single men. Both these methods of destroying the unity of the Executive have their **partisans**; but the **votaries** of an executive council are the most numerous. They are both liable, if not to equal, to similar objections, and may in most lights be examined in conjunction.

The experience of other nations will afford little instruction on this head. As far, however, as it teaches any thing, it teaches us not to be enamoured of **plurality** in the Executive. We have seen that the Achaeans, on an experiment of two Praetors, were induced to abolish one. The Roman history records many instances of mischiefs to the republic from the dissensions between the Consuls, and between the military Tribunes, who were at times substituted for the Consuls. But it gives us no **specimens** of any peculiar advantages derived to the state from the circumstance of the plurality of those magistrates. That the dissensions between them were not more frequent or more fatal, is a matter of astonishment, until we advert to the singular position in which the republic was almost continually placed, and to the prudent policy pointed out by the circumstances of the state, and pursued by the Consuls, of making a division of the government between them. The **patricians** engaged in a perpetual struggle with the **plebeians** for the preservation of their ancient authorities and dignities; the Consuls, who were generally chosen out of the former body, were commonly united by the personal interest they had in the defense of the privileges of their order. In addition to this motive of union, after the arms of the republic had considerably expanded the bounds of its empire, it became an established custom with the Consuls to divide the administration between themselves by lot—one of them remaining at Rome to govern the city and its environs, the other taking the command in the more distant provinces. This **expedient** must, no doubt, have had great influence in preventing those collisions and rivalships which might otherwise have embroiled the peace of the republic.

Refers to the Constitutional Convention | Single chief executive | Refers to delegated powers given to the chief executive

Careful consideration

Gain | Means to represent the common good or the will of the people

Primarily

Supporters | Devotees

Multiple executives

Examples

Aristocracy; upper class | Common people

Advantage

Venture

Jealous rivalry

Attack

Input

Compassionate; generous

Impulses

Malicious

Beneficial | Caution

Relieve | Make up

Safeguard

Group or faction | Agreement

But quitting the dim light of historical research, attaching ourselves purely to the dictates of reason and good sense, we shall discover much greater cause to reject than to approve the idea of plurality in the Executive, under any modification whatever.

Wherever two or more persons are engaged in any common **enterprise** or pursuit, there is always danger of difference of opinion. If it be a public trust or office, in which they are clothed with equal dignity and authority, there is peculiar danger of personal **emulation** and even animosity. From either, and especially from all these causes, the most bitter dissensions are apt to spring. Whenever these happen, they lessen the respectability, weaken the authority, and distract the plans and operation of those whom they divide. If they should unfortunately **assail** the supreme executive magistracy of a country, consisting of a plurality of persons, they might impede or frustrate the most important measures of the government, in the most critical emergencies of the state. And what is still worse, they might split the community into the most violent and irreconcilable factions, adhering differently to the different individuals who composed the magistracy.

Men often oppose a thing, merely because they have had no **agency** in planning it, or because it may have been planned by those whom they dislike. But if they have been consulted, and have happened to disapprove, opposition then becomes, in their estimation, an indispensable duty of self-love. They seem to think themselves bound in honor, and by all the motives of personal infallibility, to defeat the success of what has been resolved upon contrary to their sentiments. Men of upright, **benevolent** tempers have too many opportunities of remarking, with horror, to what desperate lengths this disposition is sometimes carried, and how often the great interests of society are sacrificed to the vanity, to the conceit, and to the obstinacy of individuals, who have credit enough to make their passions and their **caprices** interesting to mankind. Perhaps the question now before the public may, in its consequences, afford melancholy proofs of the effects of this despicable frailty, or rather detestable vice, in the human character.

Upon the principles of a free government, inconveniences from the source just mentioned must necessarily be submitted to in the formation of the legislature; but it is unnecessary, and therefore unwise, to introduce them into the constitution of the Executive. It is here too that they may be most **pernicious**. In the legislature, promptitude of decision is oftener an evil than a benefit. The differences of opinion, and the jarrings of parties in that department of the government, though they may sometimes obstruct **salutary** plans, yet often promote deliberation and **circumspection**, and serve to check excesses in the majority. When a resolution too is once taken, the opposition must be at an end. That resolution is a law, and resistance to it punishable. But no favorable circumstances **palliate** or **atone** for the disadvantages of dissension in the executive department. Here, they are pure and unmixed. There is no point at which they cease to operate. They serve to embarrass and weaken the execution of the plan or measure to which they relate, from the first step to the final conclusion of it. They constantly counteract those qualities in the Executive which are the most necessary ingredients in its composition—vigor and expedition, and this without any counterbalancing good. In the conduct of war, in which the energy of the Executive is the **bulwark** of the national security, every thing would be to be apprehended from its plurality.

It must be confessed that these observations apply with principal weight to the first case supposed—that is, to a plurality of magistrates of equal dignity and authority a scheme, the advocates for which are not likely to form a numerous **sect**; but they apply, though not with equal, yet with considerable weight to the project of a council, whose **concurrence** is made constitutionally necessary to the operations of the ostensible Executive. An artful **cabal** in that council would be able to distract and to **enervate** the whole system of administration. If no such cabal should exist, the mere diversity of views and opinions would alone be sufficient to tincture the exercise of the executive authority with a spirit of habitual feebleness and **dilatoriness**.

But one of the weightiest objections to a plurality in the Executive, and which lies as much against the last as the first plan, is, that it tends to conceal faults and destroy responsibility.

Responsibility is of two kinds—to censure and to punishment. The first is the more important of the two, especially in an elective office. Man, in public trust, will much oftener act in such a manner as to render him unworthy of being any longer trusted, than in such a manner as to make him obnoxious to legal punishment. But the multiplication of the Executive adds to the difficulty of detection in either case. It often becomes impossible, amidst mutual accusations, to determine on whom the blame or the punishment of a pernicious measure, or series of pernicious measures, ought really to fall. It is shifted from one to another with so much dexterity, and under such plausible appearances, that the public opinion is left in suspense about the real author. The circumstances which may have led to any national miscarriage or misfortune are sometimes so complicated that, where there are a number of actors who may have had different degrees and kinds of agency, though we may clearly see upon the whole that there has been mismanagement, yet it may be impracticable to pronounce to whose account the evil which may have been incurred is truly chargeable.

"I was overruled by my council. The council were so divided in their opinions that it was impossible to obtain any better resolution on the point." These and similar **pretexts** are constantly at hand, whether true or false. And who is there that will either take the trouble or incur the **odium**, of a strict scrunity into the secret springs of the transaction? Should there be found a citizen zealous enough to undertake the unpromising task, if there happen to be collusion between the parties concerned, how easy it is to clothe the circumstances with so much ambiguity, as to render it uncertain what was the precise conduct of any of those parties?

In the single instance in which the governor of this State is coupled with a council—that is, in the appointment to offices, we have seen the mischiefs of it in the view now under consideration. Scandalous appointments to important offices have been made. Some cases, indeed, have been so flagrant that *all parties* have agreed in the impropriety of the thing. When inquiry has been made, the blame has been laid by the governor on the members of the council, who, on their part, have charged it upon his nomination; while the people remain altogether at a loss to determine, by whose influence their interests have been committed to hands so unqualified and so manifestly improper. In tenderness to individuals, I forbear to descend to particulars.

It is evident from these considerations, that the plurality of the Executive tends to deprive the people of the two greatest securities they can have for the faithful exercise of any **delegated power**, first, the restraints of public opinion, which lose their efficacy, as well on account of the division of the censure attendant on bad measures among a number, as on account of the uncertainty on whom it ought to fall; and, **second, the opportunity of discovering with facility and clearness the misconduct of the persons they trust, in order either to their removal from office or to their actual punishment in cases which admit of it.**

In England, the king is a perpetual magistrate; and it is a maxim which has obtained for the sake of the public peace, that he is unaccountable for his administration, and his person sacred. Nothing, therefore, can be wiser in that kingdom, than to annex to the king a constitutional council, who may be responsible to the nation for the advice they give. Without this, there would be no responsibility whatever in the executive department—an idea inadmissible in a free government. But even there the

Small group of secret plotters | Weaken or debilitate

Delay

Excuses

Loathing

Power granted by law or constitution

This problem is addressed in the Constitution through the impeachment process.

Refers to the divine right of the monarch

king is not bound by the resolutions of his council, though they are answerable for the advice they give. He is the absolute master of his own conduct in the exercise of his office, and may observe or disregard the counsel given to him at his sole discretion.

But in a republic, where every magistrate ought to be personally responsible for his behavior in office the reason which in the British Constitution dictates the propriety of a council, not only ceases to apply, but turns against the institution. In the monarchy of Great Britain, it furnishes a substitute for the prohibited responsibility of the chief magistrate, which serves in some degree as a hostage to the national justice for his good behavior. In the American republic, it would serve to destroy, or would greatly diminish, the intended and necessary responsibility of the Chief Magistrate himself.

The idea of a council to the Executive, which has so generally obtained in the State constitutions, has been derived from that maxim of republican jealousy which considers power as safer in the hands of a number of men than of a single man. If the maxim should be admitted to be applicable to the case, I should contend that the advantage on that side would not counterbalance the numerous disadvantages on the opposite side. But I do not think the rule at all applicable to the executive power. I clearly concur in opinion, in this particular, with a writer whom the celebrated Junius pronounces to be "deep, solid, and ingenious," that "the executive power is more easily confined when it is *one*"; that it is far more safe there should be a single object for the jealousy and watchfulness of the people; and, in a word, that all multiplication of the Executive is rather dangerous than friendly to liberty.

A little consideration will satisfy us, that the species of security sought for in the multiplication of the Executive, is unattainable. Numbers must be so great as to render combination difficult, or they are rather a source of danger than of security. The united credit and influence of several individuals must be more formidable to liberty, than the credit and influence of either of them separately. When power, therefore, is placed in the hands of so small a number of men, as to admit of their interests and views being easily combined in a common enterprise, by an artful leader, it becomes more liable to abuse, and more dangerous when abused, than if it be lodged in the hands of one man; who, from the very circumstance of his being alone, will be more narrowly watched and more readily suspected, and who cannot unite so great a mass of influence as when he is associated with others. **The Decemvirs of Rome**, whose name denotes their number, 3 were more to be dreaded in their **usurpation** than any *one* of them would have been. No person would think of proposing an Executive much more numerous than that body; from six to a dozen have been suggested for the number of the council. The extreme of these numbers, is not too great for an easy combination; and from such a combination America would have more to fear, than from the ambition of any single individual. A council to a magistrate, who is himself responsible for what he does, are generally nothing better than a clog upon his good intentions, are often the instruments and accomplices of his bad and are almost always a cloak to his faults.

I **forbear** to dwell upon the subject of expense; though it be evident that if the council should be numerous enough to answer the principal end aimed at by the institution, the salaries of the members, who must be drawn from their homes to reside at the seat of government, would form an item in the catalogue of public expenditures too serious to be incurred for an object of **equivocal** utility. I will only add that, prior to the appearance of the Constitution, I rarely met with an intelligent man from any of the States, who did not admit, as the result of experience, that the *unity* of the executive of this State was one of the best of the distinguishing features of our constitution.

PUBLIUS.

Refers to the 10-member commission who created the first Roman code of law | Wrongful or illegal encroachment

Refrain

Questionable

Making Connections

1. Hamilton states in *Federalist 70*, "Energy in the Executive is a leading character in the definition of good government." According to Hamilton, why is an "energetic Executive" essential to effective republican government?

2. What does Hamilton mean by "good government"? In the context of twenty-first century government and politics, how would you define "good government"?

3. Identify Hamilton's four "ingredients" which constitute an "energetic Executive." Explain why each "ingredient" is important.

4. What evidence does Hamilton provide to demonstrate the weaknesses of a multi-executive system or an executive council?

5. How does the vigorous chief executive supported by Hamilton in the Constitution conflict with the Antifederalist idea of limited government proposed in Brutus 1?

6. Compare and contrast Hamilton's view of the chief executive expressed in *Federalist 70* with modern-day expectations for the American presidency.

Foundational Document: *Federalist 78*

Enduring Understanding

CON-5: "The design of the judicial branch protects the Supreme Court's independence as a branch of government, and the emergence and use of judicial review remains a powerful judicial practice." (AP® U.S. Government and Politics Course and Exam Description)

Introduction

The *Federalist Papers* are a series of essays published in several newspapers October 1787 through April 1788. These essays, penned by James Madison, Alexander Hamilton, and John Jay, advocated for the ratification of the Constitution. Under the Articles of Confederation, no national courts existed to arbitrate disputes between states, interpret laws, or protect individual liberties. Antifederalist supporters at the Constitutional Convention voiced strong opposition to an independent federal judiciary, which insulated unelected judges from the will of the people. In *Federalist 78*, Hamilton countered that, though judges were given lifetime appointments under the Constitution, these were conditional on "good behavior." Hamilton further argued that an independent judiciary was necessary to interpret the laws, resolve disputes, protect individual rights, and provide a check on legislative power.

Full Text of *Federalist 78* (Alexander Hamilton)

The Judiciary Department

We proceed now to an examination of the judiciary department of the proposed government.

In unfolding the defects of the existing Confederation, the utility and necessity of a federal judicature have been clearly pointed out. It is the less necessary to recapitulate the considerations there urged as the propriety of the institution in the abstract is not disputed; the only questions which have been raised being relative to the manner of constituting it, and to its extent. To these points, therefore, our observations shall be confined.

The manner of constituting it seems to embrace these several objects: 1st. The mode of appointing the judges. 2nd. The tenure by which they are to hold their places. 3d. The partition of the judiciary authority between different courts and their relations to each other.

First. As to the mode of appointing the judges: this is the same with that of appointing the officers of the Union in general and has been so fully discussed in the two last numbers that nothing can be said here which would not be useless repetition.

Second. As to the tenure by which the judges are to hold their places: this chiefly concerns their duration in office; the provisions for their support, and the precautions for their responsibility.

According to the plan of the convention, all the judges who may be appointed by the United States are to hold their offices during good behavior; which is

The government structure under the Articles of Confederation lacked a national judicial branch.

Under Article II of the Constitution, the president nominates federal judges with the "advice and consent" of the Senate.

Article III of the Constitution stipulates that all federal judges serve lifetime appointments subject to "good behavior."

conformable to the most approved of the State constitutions, and among the rest, to that of this State. Its propriety having been drawn into question by the adversaries of that plan is no light symptom of the rage for objection which disorders their imaginations and judgments. The standard of good behavior for the continuance in office of the judicial magistracy is certainly one of the most valuable of the modern improvements in the practice of government. In a monarchy it is an excellent barrier to the **despotism** of the prince; in a republic it is a no less excellent barrier to the **encroachments** and oppressions of the representative body. And it is the best **expedient** which can be devised in any government to secure a steady, upright and impartial administration of the laws.

Tyranny | Infringements | Suitable means

Whoever attentively considers the different departments of power must perceive that, in a government in which they are separated from each other, the judiciary, from the nature of its functions, will always be the least dangerous to the political rights of the Constitution; because it will be least in a capacity to annoy or injure them. **The executive not only dispenses the honors but holds the sword of the community.** The legislature not only commands the purse but prescribes the rules by which the duties and rights of every citizen are to be regulated. The judiciary, on the contrary, has no influence over either the sword or the purse; no direction either of the strength or of the wealth of the society, and can take no active resolution whatever. It may truly be said to have neither *force* nor *will* but merely judgment; **and must ultimately depend upon the aid of the executive arm even for the efficacy of its judgments**.

This refers to the constitutional separation of powers in which each branch is given delegated powers.

Under the Constitution, the president not only appoints federal judges but also wields the power, or the "sword," to execute the laws.

Federal courts must depend on the chief executive to carry out its judgments.

This simple view of the matter suggests several important consequences. It proves incontestably that the judiciary is beyond comparison the weakest of the three departments of power; that it can never attack with success either of the other two; and that all possible care is **requisite** to enable it to defend itself against their attacks. It equally proves that though individual oppression may now and then proceed from the courts of justice, the general liberty of the people can never be endangered from that quarter: I mean, so long as the judiciary remains truly distinct from both the legislative and executive. For I agree that "there is no liberty if the power of judging be not separated from the legislative and executive powers." And it proves, in the last place, that as liberty can have nothing to fear from the judiciary alone, but would have everything to fear from its union with either of the other departments; that as all the effects of such a union must ensue from a dependence of the former on the latter, notwithstanding a nominal and apparent separation; that as, from the natural feebleness of the judiciary, it is in continual jeopardy of being overpowered, awed or influenced by its coordinate branches; and that as nothing can contribute so much to its firmness and independence as **permanency in office**, this quality may therefore be justly regarded as an indispensable ingredient in its constitution, and in a great measure as the **citadel** of the public justice and the public security.

Necessary

Refers to lifetime appointment | Stronghold

The complete independence of the courts of justice is peculiarly essential in a limited Constitution. By a limited Constitution, I understand one which contains certain specified exceptions to the legislative authority; such, for instance, as that **it shall pass no bills of attainder, no ex post facto laws, and the like. Limitations of this kind can be preserved in practice no other way than through the medium of the courts of justice, whose duty it must be to declare all acts contrary to the manifest tenor of the Constitution void**. Without this, all the reservations of particular rights or privileges would amount to nothing.

Congress may not pass laws that punish a group or individual without a trial, or change legal consequences of an action already committed. Implicitly, this defends the Court's power to declare legislative acts contrary to the Constitution void. *Marbury v. Madison* (1803) established the official precedent for judicial review.

Some **perplexity** respecting the right of the courts to pronounce legislative acts void, because contrary to the Constitution, has arisen from an imagination that the doctrine would imply a superiority of the judiciary to the legislative power. It is urged

Confusion

Assigned | Meaning

that the authority which can declare the acts of another void must necessarily be superior to the one whose acts may be declared void. As this doctrine is of great importance in all the American constitutions, a brief discussion of the grounds on which it rests cannot be unacceptable.

There is no position which depends on clearer principles than that every act of a **delegated** authority, contrary to the **tenor** of the commission under which it is exercised, is void. No legislative act therefore contrary to the constitution can be valid. To deny this would be to affirm that the deputy is greater than his principal; that the servant is above his master; that the representatives of the people are superior to the people themselves; that men acting by virtue of powers may do not only what their powers do not authorize, but what they forbid.

Determine

If it be said that the legislative body are themselves the constitutional judges of their own powers and that the construction they put upon them is conclusive upon the other departments it may be answered that this cannot be the natural presumption where it is not to be collected from any particular provisions in the Constitution. It is not otherwise to be supposed that the Constitution could intend to enable the representatives of the people to substitute their will to that of their constituents. It is far more rational to suppose that the courts were designed to be an intermediate body between the people and the legislature in order, among other things, to keep the latter within the limits assigned to their authority. The interpretation of the laws is the proper and peculiar province of the courts. A constitution is in fact, and must be regarded by the judges as, a fundamental law. It therefore belongs to them to **ascertain** its meaning as well as the meaning of any particular act proceeding from the legislative body. **If there should happen to be an irreconcilable variance between the two, that which has the superior obligation and validity ought, of course; to be preferred; or, in other words, the Constitution ought to be preferred to the statute**, the intention of the people to the intention of their agents.

Hamilton defends the supremacy of the Constitution over a conflicting legislative action.

Nor does this conclusion by any means suppose a superiority of the judicial to the legislative power. It only supposes that the power of the people is superior to both, and that where the will of the legislature, declared in its statutes, stands in opposition to that of the people, declared in the Constitution, the judges ought to be governed by the latter rather than the former. They ought to regulate their decisions by the fundamental laws rather than by those which are not fundamental.

This refers to the possibility of a state law conflicting with a federal law or the existence of conflicting state laws.

This exercise of judicial discretion in determining between two contradictory laws is exemplified in a familiar instance. **It not uncommonly happens that there are two statutes existing at one time, clashing in whole or in part with each other, and neither of them containing any repealing clause or expression. In such a case, it is the province of the courts to liquidate and fix their meaning and operation**. So far as they can, by any fair construction, be **reconciled** to each other, reason and law conspire to dictate that this should be done; where this is impracticable, it becomes a matter of necessity to give effect to one in exclusion of the other. The rule which has obtained in the courts for determining their relative **validity** is that the last in order of time shall be preferred to the first. But this is mere rule of construction, not derived from any positive law but from the nature and reason of the thing. It is a rule not **enjoined upon** the courts by legislative provision but adopted by themselves, as **consonant to** truth and propriety, for the direction of their conduct as interpreters of the law. They thought it reasonable that between the interfering acts of an equal authority that which was the last indication of its will, should have the preference.

Brought into agreement

Legality

Ordered by | In agreement with

But in regard to the interfering acts of a superior and subordinate authority of an original and **derivative** power, the nature and reason of the thing indicate the converse of that rule as proper to be followed. They teach us that the prior act of a superior ought to be preferred to the subsequent act of an inferior and subordinate authority; and that,

Secondary

accordingly, whenever a particular statute contravenes the Constitution, it will be the duty of the judicial tribunals to adhere to the latter and disregard the former.

It can be of no weight to say that the courts, on the pretense of a **repugnancy**, may substitute their own pleasure to the constitutional intentions of the legislature. This might as well happen in the case of two contradictory statutes; or it might as well happen in every **adjudication** upon any single statute. The courts must declare the sense of the law; and if they should be **disposed** to exercise *will* instead of *judgment* the consequence would equally be the substitution of their pleasure to that of the legislative body. The observation, if it proved any thing, would prove that there ought to be no judges distinct from that body.

If, then, the courts of justice are to be considered as the **bulwarks** of a limited Constitution against legislative **encroachments**, this consideration will afford a strong argument for the permanent tenure of judicial offices, since nothing will contribute so much as this to that independent spirit in the judges which must be essential to the faithful performance of so arduous a duty.

This independence of the judges is equally requisite to guard the Constitution and the rights of individuals from the effects of those ill humors which the arts of designing men, or the influence of particular **conjunctures**, sometimes disseminate among the people themselves, and which, though they speedily give place to better information, and more deliberate reflection, have a tendency, in the meantime, to occasion dangerous innovations in the government, and **serious oppressions of the minor party in the community**. Though I trust the friends of the proposed Constitution will never concur with its enemies in questioning that fundamental principle of republican government which admits the right of the people to alter or abolish the established Constitution whenever they find it inconsistent with their happiness; **yet it is not to be inferred from this principle that the representatives of the people, whenever a momentary inclination happens to lay hold of a majority of their constituents incompatible with the provisions in the existing Constitution would, on that account, be justifiable in a violation of those provisions; or that the courts would be under a greater obligation to connive at infractions in this shape than when they had proceeded wholly from the <u>cabals</u> of the representative body**. Until the people have, by some solemn and authoritative act, **annulled** or changed the established form, it is binding upon themselves collectively, as well as individually; and no presumption, or even knowledge of their sentiments, can warrant their representatives in a departure from it prior to such an act. But it is easy to see that it would require an uncommon portion of fortitude in the judges to do their duty as faithful guardians of the Constitution, where legislative invasions of it had been instigated by the major voice of the community.

But it is not with a view to infractions of the Constitution only that the independence of the judges may be an essential safeguard against the effects of occasional ill humors in the society. These sometimes extend no farther than to the injury of the private rights of particular classes of citizens, by unjust and partial laws. Here also the firmness of the judicial magistracy is of vast importance in **mitigating** the severity and confining the operation of such laws. It not only serves to moderate the immediate mischiefs of those which may have been passed but it operates as a check upon the legislative body in passing them; who, perceiving that obstacles to the success of an **iniquitous** intention are to be expected from the scruples of the courts, are in a manner compelled, by the very motives of the injustice they meditate, to qualify their attempts. This is a circumstance calculated to have more influence upon the character of our governments than but few may be aware of. The benefits of the integrity and moderation of the judiciary have already been felt in more states than one; and though they may have displeased those whose sinister expectations they may have disappointed, they must have commanded

Distastefulness; objectionableness

Act of the court | Inclined

Safeguards | Infringements or intrusions

Circumstances

Refers to the threat of a powerful, minority faction to the good of the nation as a whole

Hamilton argues that the Court must also provide a check on a majority faction, especially in the legislature, if it acts in violation of the Constitution.

Groups of plotters and schemers | Made void

Alleviating or moderating

Wicked

Hamilton contends that in order to attract the most qualified individuals to the federal judiciary, permanent appointment to the Court is necessary. Likewise, judges should not be elected by the people in order to insulate judges from politics.

Compliance

Large

the esteem and applause of all the virtuous and disinterested. Considerate men of every description ought to prize whatever will tend to **beget** or fortify that temper in the courts; as no man can be sure that he may not be tomorrow the victim of a spirit of injustice, by which he may be a gainer today. And every man must now feel that the inevitable tendency of such a spirit is to sap the foundations of public and private confidence and to introduce in its stead universal distrust and distress.

That inflexible and uniform adherence to the rights of the Constitution, and of individuals, which we perceive to be indispensable in the courts of justice, can certainly not be expected from judges who hold their offices by a temporary commission. Periodical appointments, however regulated, or by whomsoever made, would in some way or other, be fatal to their necessary independence. If the power of making them was committed either to the executive or legislature there would be danger of an improper <u>complaisance</u> to the branch which possessed it; if to both, there would be an unwillingness to hazard the displeasure of either; if to the people, or to persons chosen by them for the special purpose, there would be too great a disposition to consult popularity to justify a reliance that nothing would be consulted but the Constitution and the laws.

There is yet a further and a weighty reason for the permanency of the judicial offices which is deducible from the nature of the qualifications they require. It has been frequently remarked with great propriety that a **voluminous** code of laws is one of the inconveniences necessarily connected with the advantages of a free government. To avoid an arbitrary discretion in the courts, it is indispensable that they should be bound down by strict rules and precedents which serve to define and point out their duty in every particular case that comes before them; and it will readily be conceived from the variety of controversies which grow out of the folly and wickedness of mankind that the records of those precedents must unavoidably swell to a very considerable bulk and must demand long and laborious study to acquire a competent knowledge of them. Hence it is that there can be but few men in the society who will have sufficient skill in the laws to qualify them for the stations of judges. And making the proper deductions for the ordinary depravity of human nature, the number must be still smaller of those who unite the requisite integrity with the requisite knowledge. These considerations apprise us that the government can have no great option between fit characters; and that a temporary duration in office which would naturally discourage such characters from quitting a lucrative line of practice to accept a seat on the bench would have a tendency to throw the administration of justice into hands less able and less well qualified to conduct it with utility and dignity. In the present circumstances of this country and in those in which it is likely to be for a long time to come, the disadvantages on this score would be greater than they may at first sight appear; but it must be confessed that they are far inferior to those which present themselves under the other aspects of the subject.

Upon the whole, there can be no room to doubt that the convention acted wisely in copying from the models of those constitutions which have established good behavior as the tenure of their judicial offices, in point of duration; and that so far from being blamable on this account, their plan would have been inexcusably defective if it had wanted this important feature of good government. The experience of Great Britain affords an illustrious comment on the excellence of the institution.

PUBLIUS

Making Connections

1. In *Federalist 78*, Hamilton addresses criticism that under the Constitution, the federal judiciary wields too much power by arguing that "in a government in which . . . [the branches of government] are separated from each other, the

judiciary, from the nature of its functions, will always be the least dangerous to the political rights of the Constitution . . . ." What evidence does Hamilton provide that the judiciary is the weakest of the three branches of the federal government under the Constitution?

2. How does the relatively weak Supreme Court envisioned by Hamilton in the eighteenth century compare with the influence of the Supreme Court in modern American government and politics? You may use relevant Supreme Court decisions to support your answer.

3. Explain why Hamilton believes that the "complete independence of the courts of justice is peculiarly essential in a limited Constitution."

4. How does a strong and independent judiciary advocated by Hamilton conflict with the Antifederalist opinions expressed in Brutus 1?

5. Though it is not explicitly enumerated in Article III, Hamilton provides an early defense of judicial review, stating that it is "the right of the courts to pronounce legislative acts void" if contrary to the Constitution. Explain why Hamilton believes judicial review is essential to the function and influence of the Court.

6. Hamilton contends that federal judges should be appointed with lifetime tenure upon "good behavior." Do you agree with Hamilton's position, or should federal judges be subject to term limits? Support your argument with specific evidence and examples.

Foundational Document: Letter from Birmingham Jail

Enduring Understanding

PRD-1: "The Fourteenth Amendment's equal protection clause as well as other constitutional provisions have often been used to support the advancement of equality." (AP® U.S. Government and Politics Course and Exam Description)

Introduction

In the spring of 1963, Martin Luther King Jr. led a campaign in Birmingham, Alabama, to end segregation in the city's stores, lunch counters, and hiring practices. The Birmingham Campaign sought to bring national attention to the brutality of southern racism and the injustices suffered by Black Americans under segregation. On April 12, 1963, King was arrested along with other civil rights protestors while boycotting White-owned businesses. While in solitary confinement, King received a copy of a Birmingham newspaper containing an open letter written by eight local White clergy critical of the timing and tactics used in the civil rights march. The clergy also referred to King himself as an "outside agitator." King responded by writing an eloquent letter defending the philosophy of nonviolent, direct action while demanding equal justice under the laws. King's letter, smuggled out on scraps of newspaper by his lawyer, was later widely published and drew moral attention to the cause of African Americans struggling to end segregation. As a pastor himself, King drew upon theological references as well as connections to American political traditions and doctrine. "Letter from Birmingham Jail" not only stoked the American moral consciousness in its time to end segregation but also continues to inform and inspire movements for racial justice today.

Full Text of "Letter from Birmingham Jail" (Martin Luther King Jr.)

April 16, 1963

My Dear Fellow Clergymen:

While confined here in the Birmingham city jail, I came across your recent statement calling my present activities "unwise and untimely." Seldom do I pause to answer criticism of my work and ideas. If I sought to answer all the criticisms that cross my desk, my secretaries would have little time for anything other than such correspondence in the course of the day, and I would have no time for constructive work. But since I feel that you are men of genuine good will and that your criticisms are sincerely set forth, I want to try to answer your statement in what I hope will be patient and reasonable terms.

I think I should indicate why I am here in Birmingham, since you have been influenced by the view which argues against "outsiders coming in." I have the honor of serving as president of the **Southern Christian Leadership Conference**, an organization operating in every southern state, with headquarters in Atlanta, Georgia. We have some eighty five affiliated organizations across the South, and one of them is the **Alabama Christian Movement for Human Rights**. Frequently we share staff, educational and financial resources with our affiliates. Several months ago the affiliate here in Birmingham asked us to be on call to engage in a nonviolent direct action program if

King is referring to "A Call for Unity," an open letter written by White clergy in Alabama responding to civil rights demonstrations in Birmingham.

Civil rights organization founded by King and others during the Montgomery bus boycott in 1955

Civil rights organization based in Birmingham, Alabama, that organized boycotts and sponsored federal lawsuits challenging segregation laws

such were deemed necessary. We readily consented, and when the hour came we lived up to our promise. So I, along with several members of my staff, am here because I was invited here. I am here because I have organizational ties here.

But more basically, I am in Birmingham because injustice is here. Just as the prophets of the eighth century B.C. left their villages and carried their "thus saith the Lord" far beyond the boundaries of their home towns, and just as the Apostle Paul left his village of Tarsus and carried the gospel of Jesus Christ to the far corners of the Greco Roman world, so am I compelled to carry the gospel of freedom beyond my own home town. Like Paul, I must constantly respond to the Macedonian call for aid.

As a pastor writing to fellow clergy, King frequently refers to biblical text in the letter.

Moreover, I am cognizant of the interrelatedness of all communities and states. I cannot sit idly by in Atlanta and not be concerned about what happens in Birmingham. Injustice anywhere is a threat to justice everywhere. We are caught in an inescapable network of mutuality, tied in a single garment of destiny. Whatever affects one directly, affects all indirectly. Never again can we afford to live with the narrow, provincial "outside agitator" idea. Anyone who lives inside the United States can never be considered an outsider anywhere within its bounds.

You deplore the demonstrations taking place in Birmingham. But your statement, I am sorry to say, fails to express a similar concern for the conditions that brought about the demonstrations. I am sure that none of you would want to rest content with the superficial kind of social analysis that deals merely with effects and does not grapple with underlying causes. It is unfortunate that demonstrations are taking place in Birmingham, but it is even more unfortunate that the city's white power structure left the Negro community with no alternative.

In any nonviolent campaign there are four basic steps: collection of the facts to determine whether injustices exist; negotiation; **self purification**; and direct action. We have gone through all these steps in Birmingham. There can be no **gainsaying** the fact that racial injustice engulfs this community. Birmingham is probably the most thoroughly segregated city in the United States. Its ugly record of brutality is widely known. Negroes have experienced grossly unjust treatment in the courts. There have been more unsolved bombings of Negro homes and churches in Birmingham than in any other city in the nation. These are the hard, brutal facts of the case. On the basis of these conditions, Negro leaders sought to negotiate with the city fathers. But the latter consistently refused to engage in good faith negotiation.

Then, last September, came the opportunity to talk with leaders of Birmingham's economic community. In the course of the negotiations, certain promises were made by the merchants—for example, to remove the stores' humiliating racial signs. On the basis of these promises, the Reverend Fred Shuttlesworth and the leaders of the Alabama Christian Movement for Human Rights agreed to a **moratorium** on all demonstrations. As the weeks and months went by, we realized that we were the victims of a broken promise. A few signs, briefly removed, returned; the others remained. As in so many past experiences, our hopes had been blasted, and the shadow of deep disappointment settled upon us. We had no alternative except to prepare for direct action, whereby we would present our very bodies as a means of laying our case before the conscience of the local and the national community. Mindful of the difficulties involved, we decided to undertake a process of self purification. We began a series of workshops on nonviolence, and we repeatedly asked ourselves: "Are you able to accept blows without retaliating?" "Are you able to endure the ordeal of jail?" We decided to schedule our direct action program for the Easter season, realizing that except for Christmas, this is the main shopping period of the year. Knowing that a strong economic-withdrawal program would be the by product of direct action, we felt that this would be the best time to bring pressure to bear on the merchants for the needed change.

Self-cleansing | Contradicting

Suspension

Connor was a staunch segregationist and ardent White supremacist who served as Commissioner of Public Safety in Birmingham for 22 years. His aggressive approach to enforcing segregation laws drew national attention to the brutality of segregation in the South.

Greek philosopher acclaimed as the first moral philosopher of Western political thought

People who provoke others with criticism and demands

King refers to the organized opposition to desegregation of many White southern leaders after the *Brown* decision in 1954.

Unfortunately

American theologian who spoke about the intersection of religion and politics

Then it occurred to us that Birmingham's mayoral election was coming up in March, and we speedily decided to postpone action until after election day. When we discovered that the **Commissioner of Public Safety, Eugene "Bull" Connor**, had piled up enough votes to be in the run off, we decided again to postpone action until the day after the run off so that the demonstrations could not be used to cloud the issues. Like many others, we waited to see Mr. Connor defeated, and to this end we endured postponement after postponement. Having aided in this community need, we felt that our direct action program could be delayed no longer.

You may well ask: "Why direct action? Why sit ins, marches and so forth? Isn't negotiation a better path?" You are quite right in calling for negotiation. Indeed, this is the very purpose of direct action. Nonviolent direct action seeks to create such a crisis and foster such a tension that a community which has constantly refused to negotiate is forced to confront the issue. It seeks so to dramatize the issue that it can no longer be ignored. My citing the creation of tension as part of the work of the nonviolent resister may sound rather shocking. But I must confess that I am not afraid of the word "tension." I have earnestly opposed violent tension, but there is a type of constructive, nonviolent tension which is necessary for growth. Just as **Socrates** felt that it was necessary to create a tension in the mind so that individuals could rise from the bondage of myths and half truths to the unfettered realm of creative analysis and objective appraisal, so must we see the need for nonviolent **gadflies** to create the kind of tension in society that will help men rise from the dark depths of prejudice and racism to the majestic heights of understanding and brotherhood. The purpose of our direct action program is to create a situation so crisis packed that it will inevitably open the door to negotiation. I therefore concur with you in your call for negotiation. Too long has our beloved Southland been bogged down in a tragic effort to live in monologue rather than dialogue.

One of the basic points in your statement is that the action that I and my associates have taken in Birmingham is untimely. Some have asked: "Why didn't you give the new city administration time to act?" The only answer that I can give to this query is that the new Birmingham administration must be prodded about as much as the outgoing one, before it will act. We are sadly mistaken if we feel that the election of Albert Boutwell as mayor will bring the millennium to Birmingham. While Mr. Boutwell is a much more gentle person than Mr. Connor, they are both segregationists, dedicated to maintenance of the status quo. I have hope that Mr. Boutwell will be reasonable enough to see the futility of **massive resistance** to desegregation. But he will not see this without pressure from devotees of civil rights. My friends, I must say to you that we have not made a single gain in civil rights without determined legal and nonviolent pressure. **Lamentably**, it is an historical fact that privileged groups seldom give up their privileges voluntarily. Individuals may see the moral light and voluntarily give up their unjust posture; but, as **Reinhold Niebuhr** has reminded us, groups tend to be more immoral than individuals.

We know through painful experience that freedom is never voluntarily given by the oppressor; it must be demanded by the oppressed. Frankly, I have yet to engage in a direct action campaign that was "well timed" in the view of those who have not suffered unduly from the disease of segregation. For years now I have heard the word "Wait!" It rings in the ear of every Negro with piercing familiarity. This "Wait" has almost always meant "Never." We must come to see, with one of our distinguished jurists, that "justice too long delayed is justice denied."

We have waited for more than 340 years for our constitutional and God given rights. The nations of Asia and Africa are moving with jetlike speed toward gaining political independence, but we still creep at horse and buggy pace toward gaining a cup of coffee at a lunch counter. Perhaps it is easy for those who have never felt the stinging darts of segregation to say, "Wait." But when you have seen vicious mobs lynch your mothers and fathers at will and drown your sisters and brothers at whim; when you have seen hate filled policemen curse, kick and even kill your black brothers and sisters; when you see the vast majority of your twenty million Negro brothers smothering in an airtight cage of poverty in the midst of an affluent society; when you suddenly find your tongue twisted and your speech stammering as you seek to explain to your six year old daughter why she can't go to the public amusement park that has just been advertised on television, and see tears welling up in her eyes when she is told that Funtown is closed to colored children, and see ominous clouds of inferiority beginning to form in her little mental sky, and see her beginning to distort her personality by developing an unconscious bitterness toward white people; when you have to concoct an answer for a five year old son who is asking: "Daddy, why do white people treat colored people so mean?"; when you take a cross county drive and find it necessary to sleep night after night in the uncomfortable corners of your automobile because no motel will accept you; when you are humiliated day in and day out by nagging signs reading "white" and "colored"; when your first name becomes "nigger," your middle name becomes "boy" (however old you are) and your last name becomes "John," and your wife and mother are never given the respected title "Mrs."; when you are harried by day and haunted by night by the fact that you are a Negro, living constantly at tiptoe stance, never quite knowing what to expect next, and are plagued with inner fears and outer resentments; when you are forever fighting a degenerating sense of "nobodiness"—then you will understand why we find it difficult to wait. There comes a time when the cup of endurance runs over, and men are no longer willing to be plunged into the abyss of despair. I hope, sirs, you can understand our legitimate and unavoidable impatience. You express a great deal of anxiety over our willingness to break laws. This is certainly a legitimate concern. Since we so diligently urge people to obey the Supreme Court's decision of 1954 outlawing segregation in the public schools, at first glance it may seem rather paradoxical for us consciously to break laws. One may well ask: "How can you advocate breaking some laws and obeying others?" The answer lies in the fact that there are two types of laws: just and unjust. I would be the first to advocate obeying just laws. One has not only a legal but a moral responsibility to obey just laws. Conversely, one has a moral responsibility to disobey unjust laws. I would agree with **St. Augustine** that "an unjust law is no law at all."

Now, what is the difference between the two? How does one determine whether a law is just or unjust? A just law is a man made code that squares with the moral law or the law of God. An unjust law is a code that is out of harmony with the moral law. To put it in the terms of St. Thomas Aquinas: An unjust law is a human law that is not rooted in eternal law and natural law. Any law that uplifts human personality is just. Any law that degrades human personality is unjust. All segregation statutes are unjust because segregation distorts the soul and damages the personality. It gives the segregator a false sense of superiority and the segregated a false sense of inferiority. Segregation, to use the terminology of the Jewish philosopher **Martin Buber**, substitutes an "I it" relationship for an "I thou" relationship and ends up relegating persons to the status of things. Hence segregation is not only politically, economically and sociologically unsound, it is morally wrong and sinful. **Paul Tillich** has said that sin is separation. Is not segregation an existential expression of man's tragic separation, his awful estrangement, his terrible sinfulness? Thus it is that I can urge men to obey the 1954 decision of the Supreme Court, for it is morally right; and I can urge them to disobey segregation ordinances, for they are morally wrong.

Let us consider a more concrete example of just and unjust laws. An unjust law is a code that a numerical or power majority group compels a minority group to obey but does not make binding on itself. This is difference made legal. By the same token, a just

Early Christian theologian and philosopher who assumed that people enjoyed natural law

Here King invokes ideas of natural law in which human beings are given inherent rights by their creator also espoused by the Catholic theologian and philosopher St. Thomas Aquinas.

Buber espoused the philosophy of dialogue in his book *I and Thou*.

Protestant theologian and philosopher who believed God and faith could be illuminated in both modern culture and Christianity

law is a code that a majority compels a minority to follow and that it is willing to follow itself. This is sameness made legal. Let me give another explanation. A law is unjust if it is inflicted on a minority that, as a result of being denied the right to vote, had no part in enacting or devising the law. Who can say that the legislature of Alabama which set up that state's segregation laws was democratically elected? Throughout Alabama all sorts of devious methods are used to prevent Negroes from becoming registered voters, and there are some counties in which, even though Negroes constitute a majority of the population, not a single Negro is registered. Can any law enacted under such circumstances be considered democratically structured?

Sometimes a law is just on its face and unjust in its application. For instance, I have been arrested on a charge of parading without a permit. Now, there is nothing wrong in having an ordinance which requires a permit for a parade. But such an ordinance becomes unjust when it is used to maintain segregation and to deny citizens the First-Amendment privilege of peaceful assembly and protest.

I hope you are able to see the distinction I am trying to point out. In no sense do I advocate evading or defying the law, as would the rabid segregationist. That would lead to **anarchy**. One who breaks an unjust law must do so openly, lovingly, and with a willingness to accept the penalty. I submit that an individual who breaks a law that conscience tells him is unjust, and who willingly accepts the penalty of imprisonment in order to arouse the conscience of the community over its injustice, is in reality expressing the highest respect for law.

Of course, there is nothing new about this kind of **civil disobedience**. It was evidenced sublimely in the refusal of Shadrach, Meshach and Abednego to obey the laws of Nebuchadnezzar, on the ground that a higher moral law was at stake. It was practiced superbly by the early Christians, who were willing to face hungry lions and the excruciating pain of chopping blocks rather than submit to certain unjust laws of the Roman Empire. To a degree, academic freedom is a reality today because Socrates practiced civil disobedience. In our own nation, the Boston Tea Party represented a massive act of civil disobedience.

We should never forget that everything Adolf Hitler did in Germany was "legal" and everything the Hungarian freedom fighters did in Hungary was "illegal." It was "illegal" to aid and comfort a Jew in Hitler's Germany. Even so, I am sure that, had I lived in Germany at the time, I would have aided and comforted my Jewish brothers. If today I lived in a Communist country where certain principles dear to the Christian faith are suppressed, I would openly advocate disobeying that country's antireligious laws.

I must make two honest confessions to you, my Christian and Jewish brothers. First, I must confess that over the past few years I have been gravely disappointed with the white moderate. I have almost reached the regrettable conclusion that the Negro's great stumbling block in his stride toward freedom is not the **White Citizen's Counciler or the Ku Klux Klanner**, but the white moderate, who is more devoted to "order" than to justice; who prefers a negative peace which is the absence of tension to a positive peace which is the presence of justice; who constantly says: "I agree with you in the goal you seek, but I cannot agree with your methods of direct action"; who paternalistically believes he can set the timetable for another man's freedom; who lives by a mythical concept of time and who constantly advises the Negro to wait for a "more convenient season." Shallow understanding from people of good will is more frustrating than absolute misunderstanding from people of ill will. Lukewarm acceptance is much more bewildering than outright rejection.

I had hoped that the white moderate would understand that law and order exist for the purpose of establishing justice and that when they fail in this purpose they become the dangerously structured dams that block the flow of social progress. I had hoped that

State of lawlessness

A form of peaceful protest by refusing to abide by perceived unjust laws

A member of White supremacist organizations who frequently used violence and intimidation to oppress African Americans and their White supporters.

the white moderate would understand that the present tension in the South is a necessary phase of the transition from an obnoxious negative peace, in which the Negro passively accepted his unjust plight, to a substantive and positive peace, in which all men will respect the dignity and worth of human personality. Actually, we who engage in nonviolent direct action are not the creators of tension. We merely bring to the surface the hidden tension that is already alive. We bring it out in the open, where it can be seen and dealt with. Like a boil that can never be cured so long as it is covered up but must be opened with all its ugliness to the natural medicines of air and light, injustice must be exposed, with all the tension its exposure creates, to the light of human conscience and the air of national opinion before it can be cured.

In your statement you assert that our actions, even though peaceful, must be condemned because they precipitate violence. But is this a logical assertion? Isn't this like condemning a robbed man because his possession of money precipitated the evil act of robbery? Isn't this like condemning Socrates because his unswerving commitment to truth and his philosophical inquiries precipitated the act by the misguided **populace**

General public

in which they made him drink hemlock? Isn't this like condemning Jesus because his unique God consciousness and never ceasing devotion to God's will precipitated the evil act of crucifixion? We must come to see that, as the federal courts have consistently affirmed, it is wrong to urge an individual to cease his efforts to gain his basic constitutional rights because the quest may precipitate violence. Society must protect the robbed and punish the robber. I had also hoped that the white moderate would reject the myth concerning time in relation to the struggle for freedom. I have just received a letter from a white brother in Texas. He writes: "All Christians know that the colored people will receive equal rights eventually, but it is possible that you are in too great a religious hurry. It has taken Christianity almost two thousand years to accomplish what it has. The teachings of Christ take time to come to earth." Such an attitude stems from a tragic misconception of time, from the strangely irrational notion that there is something in the very flow of time that will inevitably cure all ills. Actually, time itself is neutral; it can be used either destructively or constructively. More and more I feel that the people of ill will have used time much more effectively than have the people of good will. We will have to repent in this generation not merely for the hateful words and actions of the bad people but for the appalling silence of the good people. Human progress never rolls in on wheels of inevitability; it comes through the tireless efforts of men willing to be co workers with God, and without this hard work, time itself becomes an ally of the forces of social stagnation. We must use time creatively, in the knowledge that the time is always ripe to do right. Now is the time to make real the promise of democracy and transform our pending national **elegy** into a creative psalm of brother-

Mournful poem

hood. Now is the time to lift our national policy from the quicksand of racial injustice to the solid rock of human dignity.

You speak of our activity in Birmingham as extreme. At first I was rather disappointed that fellow clergymen would see my nonviolent efforts as those of an extremist. I began thinking about the fact that I stand in the middle of two opposing forces in the Negro community. One is a force of complacency, made up in part of Negroes who, as a result of long years of oppression, are so drained of self respect and a sense of "somebodiness" that they have adjusted to segregation; and in part of a few middle-class Negroes who, because of a degree of academic and economic security and because in some ways they profit by segregation, have become insensitive to the problems of the masses. The other force is one of bitterness and hatred, and it comes perilously close to advocating violence. It is expressed in the various **black nationalist groups** that are

This refers to organizations like the Nation of Islam and later the Black Panther Party who were influenced by the early twentieth-century teachings of Marcus Garvey.

springing up across the nation, the largest and best known being Elijah Muhammad's Muslim movement. Nourished by the Negro's frustration over the continued existence of racial discrimination, this movement is made up of people who have lost faith in

Irredeemable

The spirit of the time

America, who have absolutely repudiated Christianity, and who have concluded that the white man is an **incorrigible** "devil."

I have tried to stand between these two forces, saying that we need emulate neither the "do nothingism" of the complacent nor the hatred and despair of the black nationalist. For there is the more excellent way of love and nonviolent protest. I am grateful to God that, through the influence of the Negro church, the way of nonviolence became an integral part of our struggle. If this philosophy had not emerged, by now many streets of the South would, I am convinced, be flowing with blood. And I am further convinced that if our white brothers dismiss as "rabble rousers" and "outside agitators" those of us who employ nonviolent direct action, and if they refuse to support our nonviolent efforts, millions of Negroes will, out of frustration and despair, seek solace and security in black nationalist ideologies—a development that would inevitably lead to a frightening racial nightmare.

Oppressed people cannot remain oppressed forever. The yearning for freedom eventually manifests itself, and that is what has happened to the American Negro. Something within has reminded him of his birthright of freedom, and something without has reminded him that it can be gained. Consciously or unconsciously, he has been caught up by the **Zeitgeist**, and with his black brothers of Africa and his brown and yellow brothers of Asia, South America and the Caribbean, the United States Negro is moving with a sense of great urgency toward the promised land of racial justice. If one recognizes this vital urge that has engulfed the Negro community, one should readily understand why public demonstrations are taking place. The Negro has many pent up resentments and latent frustrations, and he must release them. So let him march; let him make prayer pilgrimages to the city hall; let him go on freedom rides—and try to understand why he must do so. If his repressed emotions are not released in nonviolent ways, they will seek expression through violence; this is not a threat but a fact of history. So I have not said to my people: "Get rid of your discontent." Rather, I have tried to say that this normal and healthy discontent can be channeled into the creative outlet of nonviolent direct action. And now this approach is being termed extremist. But though I was initially disappointed at being categorized as an extremist, as I continued to think about the matter I gradually gained a measure of satisfaction from the label. Was not Jesus an extremist for love: "Love your enemies, bless them that curse you, do good to them that hate you, and pray for them which despitefully use you, and persecute you." Was not Amos an extremist for justice: "Let justice roll down like waters and righteousness like an ever flowing stream." Was not Paul an extremist for the Christian gospel: "I bear in my body the marks of the Lord Jesus." Was not Martin Luther an extremist: "Here I stand; I cannot do otherwise, so help me God." And John Bunyan: "I will stay in jail to the end of my days before I make a butchery of my conscience." And Abraham Lincoln: "This nation cannot survive half slave and half free." And Thomas Jefferson: "We hold these truths to be self evident, that all men are created equal . . ." So the question is not whether we will be extremists, but what kind of extremists we will be. Will we be extremists for hate or for love? Will we be extremists for the preservation of injustice or for the extension of justice? In that dramatic scene on Calvary's hill three men were crucified. We must never forget that all three were crucified for the same crime—the crime of extremism. Two were extremists for immorality, and thus fell below their environment. The other, Jesus Christ, was an extremist for love, truth and goodness, and thereby rose above his environment. Perhaps the South, the nation and the world are in dire need of creative extremists.

I had hoped that the white moderate would see this need. Perhaps I was too optimistic; perhaps I expected too much. I suppose I should have realized that few members of the oppressor race can understand the deep groans and passionate yearnings of the oppressed race, and still fewer have the vision to see that injustice must be rooted out by strong, persistent and determined action. I am thankful, however, that some of our white brothers in the South have grasped the meaning of this social revolution and committed themselves to it. They are still all too few in quantity, but they are big in quality. Some—such as **Ralph McGill, Lillian Smith, Harry Golden, James McBride Dabbs, Ann Braden and Sarah Patton Boyle**—have written about our struggle in eloquent and prophetic terms. Others have marched with us down nameless streets of the South. They have languished in filthy, roach infested jails, suffering the abuse and brutality of policemen who view them as "dirty nigger-lovers." Unlike so many of their moderate brothers and sisters, they have recognized the urgency of the moment and sensed the need for powerful "action" antidotes to combat the disease of segregation. Let me take note of my other major disappointment. I have been so greatly disappointed with the white church and its leadership. Of course, there are some notable exceptions. I am not unmindful of the fact that each of you has taken some significant stands on this issue. I commend you, Reverend Stallings, for your Christian stand on this past Sunday, in welcoming Negroes to your worship service on a nonsegregated basis. I commend the Catholic leaders of this state for integrating Spring Hill College several years ago.

King identifies six White journalists and activists who chronicled events of the movement and participated in civil rights demonstrations.

But despite these notable exceptions, I must honestly reiterate that I have been disappointed with the church. I do not say this as one of those negative critics who can always find something wrong with the church. I say this as a minister of the gospel, who loves the church; who was nurtured in its bosom; who has been sustained by its spiritual blessings and who will remain true to it as long as the cord of life shall lengthen.

When I was suddenly catapulted into the leadership of the bus protest in Montgomery, Alabama, a few years ago, I felt we would be supported by the white church. I felt that the white ministers, priests and rabbis of the South would be among our strongest allies. Instead, some have been outright opponents, refusing to understand the freedom movement and misrepresenting its leaders; all too many others have been more cautious than courageous and have remained silent behind the anesthetizing security of stained glass windows.

In spite of my shattered dreams, I came to Birmingham with the hope that the white religious leadership of this community would see the justice of our cause and, with deep moral concern, would serve as the channel through which our just grievances could reach the power structure. I had hoped that each of you would understand. But again I have been disappointed.

I have heard numerous southern religious leaders admonish their worshipers to comply with a desegregation decision because it is the law, but I have longed to hear white ministers declare: "Follow this decree because integration is morally right and because the Negro is your brother." In the midst of blatant injustices inflicted upon the Negro, I have watched white churchmen stand on the sideline and mouth pious irrelevancies and **sanctimonious** trivialities. In the midst of a mighty struggle to rid our nation of racial and economic injustice, I have heard many ministers say: "Those are social issues, with which the gospel has no real concern." And I have watched many churches commit themselves to a completely other worldly religion which makes a strange, un-Biblical distinction between body and soul, between the sacred and the secular.

Self-righteous

I have traveled the length and breadth of Alabama, Mississippi and all the other southern states. On sweltering summer days and crisp autumn mornings I have looked at the South's beautiful churches with their lofty spires pointing heavenward. I have beheld the impressive outlines of her massive religious education buildings. Over and over I have found myself asking: "What kind of people worship here? Who is their God? Where were their voices when the lips of **Governor Barnett** dripped with words of interposition and nullification? Where were they when **Governor Wallace** gave a clarion call for defiance and hatred? Where were their voices of support when bruised and

Ross Barnett was the segregationist governor of Mississippi who organized the arrests of Freedom Riders in 1961 and refused admission to James Meredith, the first African American to enroll at the University of Mississippi.

George Wallace was the segregationist governor of Alabama who tried to prevent the racial integration of the University of Alabama.

weary Negro men and women decided to rise from the dark dungeons of complacency to the bright hills of creative protest?"

Yes, these questions are still in my mind. In deep disappointment I have wept over the laxity of the church. But be assured that my tears have been tears of love. There can be no deep disappointment where there is not deep love. Yes, I love the church. How could I do otherwise? I am in the rather unique position of being the son, the grandson and the great grandson of preachers. Yes, I see the church as the body of Christ. But, oh! How we have blemished and scarred that body through social neglect and through fear of being nonconformists.

There was a time when the church was very powerful—in the time when the early Christians rejoiced at being deemed worthy to suffer for what they believed. In those days the church was not merely a thermometer that recorded the ideas and principles of popular opinion; it was a thermostat that transformed the mores of society. Whenever the early Christians entered a town, the people in power became disturbed and immediately sought to convict the Christians for being "disturbers of the peace" and "outside agitators." But the Christians pressed on, in the conviction that they were "a colony of heaven," called to obey God rather than man. Small in number, they were big in commitment. They were too God-intoxicated to be "astronomically intimidated." By their effort and example they brought an end to such ancient evils as infanticide and gladiatorial contests. Things are different now. So often the contemporary church is a weak, ineffectual voice with an uncertain sound. So often it is an archdefender of the status quo. Far from being disturbed by the presence of the church, the power structure of the average community is consoled by the church's silent—and often even vocal—sanction of things as they are.

But the judgment of God is upon the church as never before. If today's church does not recapture the sacrificial spirit of the early church, it will lose its authenticity, forfeit the loyalty of millions, and be dismissed as an irrelevant social club with no meaning for the twentieth century. Every day I meet young people whose disappointment with the church has turned into outright disgust.

Perhaps I have once again been too optimistic. Is organized religion too inextricably bound to the status quo to save our nation and the world? Perhaps I must turn my faith to the inner spiritual church, the church within the church, as the true **ekklesia** and the hope of the world. But again I am thankful to God that some noble souls from the ranks of organized religion have broken loose from the paralyzing chains of conformity and joined us as active partners in the struggle for freedom. They have left their secure congregations and walked the streets of Albany, Georgia, with us. They have gone down the highways of the South on tortuous rides for freedom. Yes, they have gone to jail with us. Some have been dismissed from their churches, have lost the support of their bishops and fellow ministers. But they have acted in the faith that right defeated is stronger than evil triumphant. Their witness has been the spiritual salt that has preserved the true meaning of the gospel in these troubled times. They have carved a tunnel of hope through the dark mountain of disappointment. I hope the church as a whole will meet the challenge of this decisive hour. But even if the church does not come to the aid of justice, I have no despair about the future. I have no fear about the outcome of our struggle in Birmingham, even if our motives are at present misunderstood. We will reach the goal of freedom in Birmingham and all over the nation, because the goal of America is freedom. Abused and scorned though we may be, our destiny is tied up with America's destiny. Before the pilgrims landed at Plymouth, we were here. Before the pen of Jefferson etched the majestic words of the Declaration of Independence across the pages of history, we were here. For more than two centuries our forebears labored in this country without wages; they made cotton king; they built the homes of their masters while suffering gross injustice and shameful humiliation—and yet out of a bottomless

Democratic assemblies of citizens in Greek city-states

vitality they continued to thrive and develop. If the inexpressible cruelties of slavery could not stop us, the opposition we now face will surely fail. We will win our freedom because the sacred heritage of our nation and the eternal will of God are embodied in our echoing demands. Before closing I feel impelled to mention one other point in your statement that has troubled me profoundly. You warmly commended the Birmingham police force for keeping "order" and "preventing violence." I doubt that you would have so warmly commended the police force if you had seen its dogs sinking their teeth into unarmed, nonviolent Negroes. I doubt that you would so quickly commend the policemen if you were to observe their ugly and inhumane treatment of Negroes here in the city jail; if you were to watch them push and curse old Negro women and young Negro girls; if you were to see them slap and kick old Negro men and young boys; if you were to observe them, as they did on two occasions, refuse to give us food because we wanted to sing our grace together. I cannot join you in your praise of the Birmingham police department.

It is true that the police have exercised a degree of discipline in handling the demonstrators. In this sense they have conducted themselves rather "nonviolently" in public. But for what purpose? To preserve the evil system of segregation. Over the past few years I have consistently preached that nonviolence demands that the means we use must be as pure as the ends we seek. I have tried to make clear that it is wrong to use immoral means to attain moral ends. But now I must affirm that it is just as wrong, or perhaps even more so, to use moral means to preserve immoral ends. Perhaps Mr. Connor and his policemen have been rather nonviolent in public, as was Chief Pritchett in Albany, Georgia, but they have used the moral means of nonviolence to maintain the immoral end of racial injustice. As T. S. Eliot has said: "The last temptation is the greatest treason: To do the right deed for the wrong reason."

I wish you had commended the Negro sit inners and demonstrators of Birmingham for their sublime courage, their willingness to suffer and their amazing discipline in the midst of great provocation. One day the South will recognize its real heroes. They will be the James Merediths, with the noble sense of purpose that enables them to face jeering and hostile mobs, and with the agonizing loneliness that characterizes the life of the pioneer. They will be old, oppressed, battered Negro women, symbolized in a seventy two year old woman in Montgomery, Alabama, who rose up with a sense of dignity and with her people decided not to ride segregated buses, and who responded with ungrammatical **profundity** to one who inquired about her weariness: "My feets is tired, but my soul is at rest." They will be the young high school and college students, the young ministers of the gospel and a host of their elders, courageously and nonviolently sitting in at lunch counters and willingly going to jail for conscience' sake. One day the South will know that when these disinherited children of God sat down at lunch counters, they were in reality standing up for what is best in the American dream and for the most sacred values in our Judaeo Christian heritage, thereby bringing our nation back to those great wells of democracy which were dug deep by the founding fathers in their formulation of the Constitution and the Declaration of Independence.

Never before have I written so long a letter. I'm afraid it is much too long to take your precious time. I can assure you that it would have been much shorter if I had been writing from a comfortable desk, but what else can one do when he is alone in a narrow jail cell, other than write long letters, think long thoughts and pray long prayers?

If I have said anything in this letter that overstates the truth and indicates an unreasonable impatience, I beg you to forgive me. If I have said anything that understates the truth and indicates my having a patience that allows me to settle for anything less than brotherhood, I beg God to forgive me.

I hope this letter finds you strong in the faith. I also hope that circumstances will soon make it possible for me to meet each of you, not as an integrationist or a civil-rights

Wisdom

leader but as a fellow clergyman and a Christian brother. Let us all hope that the dark clouds of racial prejudice will soon pass away and the deep fog of misunderstanding will be lifted from our fear drenched communities, and in some not too distant tomorrow the radiant stars of love and brotherhood will shine over our great nation with all their scintillating beauty.

Yours for the cause of Peace and Brotherhood,
MARTIN LUTHER KING, JR.

Making Connections

1. Identify the audiences whom Martin Luther King Jr. intends to influence or persuade in "Letter from Birmingham Jail." What is his purpose in writing the letter?

2. Drawing upon examples in "Letter from Birmingham Jail," explain the objectives and strategies employed by King and civil rights organizations to end segregation in the South.

3. Explain why King is particularly critical of "white moderates," especially White clergy, in "Letter from Birmingham Jail."

4. King makes a distinction between "just and unjust laws." How does King contrast the Supreme Court's decision in *Brown v. Board of Education* with segregation laws in Birmingham?

5. King makes numerous references to American political traditions and texts. Describe several examples of his connections to the plight of African Americans and their struggle for civil rights with the Declaration of Independence and the U.S. Constitution.

6. King writes, "I am cognizant of the interrelatedness of all communities and states. I cannot sit idly by in Atlanta and not be concerned about what happens in Birmingham. Injustice anywhere is a threat to justice everywhere. We are caught in an inescapable network of mutuality, tied in a single garment of destiny. Whatever affects one directly, affects all indirectly."

   · Translate the meaning of the quotation and explain its significance to the civil rights movement.
   · Explain the relevance of the ideas espoused in the quotation to the struggle for racial justice in America today.

7. Describe current examples of protest movements in the United States. How are the objectives and tactics of these movements today both similar to and different from the civil rights movement in the 1960s?

Supreme Court Case Clusters

Bob Baker

Needham High School, MA

Cluster 1: Balance of Power between State and National Governments

*McCulloch v. Maryland (1819)

*United States v. Lopez (1995)

United States v. Morrison (2000)

Cluster 2: Judicial Review

*Marbury v. Madison (1803)

United States v. Nixon (1974)

Swann v. Charlotte-Mecklenburg Board of Education (1971)

Cluster 3: Freedom of Speech and Press

*Schenck v. United States (1919)

*Tinker v. Des Moines Independent Community School District (1969)

*New York Times Co. v. United States (1971)

Cluster 4: Freedom of Religion

West Virginia State Board of Education v. Barnette (1943)

*Engel v. Vitale (1962)

*Wisconsin v. Yoder (1972)

Greece v. Galloway (2014)

Cluster 5: The Doctrine of Selective Incorporation

Mapp v. Ohio (1961)

*Gideon v. Wainwright (1963)

Miranda v. Arizona (1966)

*McDonald v. Chicago (2010)

Cluster 6: Privacy and Due Process

*Roe v. Wade (1973)

Board of Education of Independent School District No. 92 of Pottawatomie County v. Earls (2002)

Riley v. California (2014)

Cluster 7: Equal Protection

Reed v. Reed (1971)

*Brown v. Board of Education (1954)

Milliken v. Bradley (1974)

Cluster 8: Affirmative Action and Equal Protection

Regents of the University of California v. Bakke (1978)

Gratz v. Bollinger and *Grutter v. Bollinger* (2003)

Parents Involved in Community Schools v. Seattle School District No. 1 (2007)

Cluster 9: Ideological Movements and the High Court

Planned Parenthood of Southeastern Pennsylvania v. Casey (1992)

Zelman v. Simmons-Harris (2002)

Obergefell v. Hodges (2015)

Cluster 10: Election Processes, Partisanship, and Divided Government

*Baker v. Carr (1962)

*Shaw v. Reno (1993)

*Citizens United v. Federal Election Commission (2010)

Cluster 11: Equal Protection, Marriage, Gender, and Sexual Orientation

Loving v. Virginia (1967)

United States v. Virginia (1996)

Lawrence v. Texas (2003)

Cluster 12: The Powers of Congress

Heart of Atlanta Motel v. United States (1964)

National Federation of Independent Business v. Sebelius (2012)

Shelby County v. Holder (2013)

Cases with an asterisk are landmark Supreme Court cases noted in the AP® U.S. Government and Politics Curriculum Framework.

Using the Supreme Court Case Clusters

The 39 cases that are profiled here include the 15 core cases identified in the College Board's 2020 course description for U.S. Government and Politics, and 24 others that are closely related to the "Essential Knowledge Statements" in the course description.

The goal of this material is to help students become conversant in constitutional principles and to be able to respond to new situations with constitutional theory. The cases are best thought of as unfolding stories, not as massive amounts of facts to be memorized.

The story of these 39 cases not only gives students an overview of civil rights, civil liberties, and the judiciary but also provides valuable information about other parts of the U.S. Government and Politics curriculum. The cases demonstrate important issues at play in both Congress and the executive and between the states and the national government, and they cover a wide range of significant policy issues.

The landmark decisions in this appendix are organized into 12 clusters of three to four cases. The clusters provide a structure for effective lesson planning, but the cases can be organized in different manners according to teacher discretion. The cases can also be selected for study individually as a means to cover areas that have been missed or as reinforcement of other learning activities.

Included in each student cluster

- Background information for each case
- Portions of the Constitution that are being contested
- Summary of significant facts for each case
- Key constitutional question(s) for each case
- Summary and quotations from majority and dissenting opinions
- Implications of the case with subsequent decisions and policy connections
- References to specific Enduring Understandings from the College Board's course outline
- Summary of main points with ongoing constitutional issues
- Timeline of events
- Three questions to assess student understanding
- Three questions for discussion and debate
- Two Free-Response Questions modeled after the "SCOTUS Comparison Question" in the new testing format
- Instructor notes and sample answers are available in Instructor Resources. Please speak to your sales representative to gain access.

Cluster 1: Balance of Power between State and National Governments

The Big Issues

One of the major themes in the study of both American government and American history has been the ongoing struggle over power between the state and national governments. This multifaceted, two-century-long policy battle makes up part of the broader topic of federalism, which includes issues of national and state cooperation. Thirteen of the fifteen cases that the College Board has required in the study of U.S. government deal with the clash of federal and state policies. The cases in this grouping include the first landmark decision that involved federalism (*McCulloch v. Maryland* [1819]) and two cases from the Rehnquist Court at the end of the twentieth century that appeared to create limits to national power.

McCulloch v. Maryland questioned whether Congress has the power to do something that is not specifically listed in the delegated powers of Article I, Section 8. When Congress created the Second Bank of the United States, it claimed to do so to help fulfill other delegated constitutional powers such as coining money and regulating its value. Furthermore, Congress justified its actions by citing the final clause of Article I, Section 8, the necessary and proper, or elastic, clause. It says that Congress has the power "to make all Laws which shall be necessary and proper for carrying into Execution the foregoing Powers, and all other Powers vested by this Constitution in the Government of the United States, or in any Department or Officer thereof."

Today, the Federal Reserve Bank operates in all 50 states. It is an important part of national policies that attempts to stabilize the economy, and it is not subject to state regulation. Democrats and Republicans clash over the direction of macroeconomic policy, but the constitutional basis of national control over banking and finance has been firmly established.

Following the ruling in *McCulloch v. Maryland*, a great deal of the constitutional clash between state and national governments shifted to four words in the third clause of Article I, Section 8, which states that Congress controls commerce "among the several states." This is known as the commerce clause, and it has been interpreted to mean that Congress controls interstate commerce and not intrastate commerce.

As our economy has grown more complex, the difference between interstate and intrastate commerce has become harder to gauge. Almost all of the products and services in our daily lives are the result of labor taking place in many states and nations. Citing the commerce clause, the federal government has increased its power over the economy. In *Heart of Atlanta Motel v. United States* (1964), the commerce clause was used as the constitutional basis to force a motel owner to abide by the Civil Rights Act of 1964 and to end discriminatory practices against African Americans.

The final two cases in this grouping are significant because they are the first major decisions that limit congressional power under the commerce clause. These two 5-4 decisions are often cited as evidence of a new form of federalism called "devolution," the return of some powers to the states.

Police powers are traditional examples of reserved powers, or powers that rest with the states alone. The term "police" does not refer to the men and women in blue. It means sovereignty over policies that deal with the health, safety, and morals of the people. As we will see in the many cases ahead, a great deal of this power has shifted to being shared with or dominated by national policy.

How significant are the limits that were placed on national policy by *United States v. Lopez* (1995) and *United States v. Morrison* (2000)? At this juncture, their impact is hard to assess. What we can be sure of is that this fundamental constitutional clash will continue to appear in new ways as our economy and culture change.

Constitutional Connections

Article I, Section 8

The Congress shall have Power To lay and collect Taxes, Duties, Imposts and Excises, to pay the Debts and provide for the common Defense and general Welfare of the United States; but all Duties, Imposts and Excises shall be uniform throughout the United States; To borrow Money on the credit of the United States; To regulate Commerce with foreign Nations, and among the several states, and with the Indian Tribes; To establish an uniform Rule of Naturalization, and uniform Laws on the subject of Bankruptcies throughout the United States; To coin Money, regulate the Value thereof, and of foreign Coin, and fix the Standard of Weights and Measures; To provide for the Punishment of counterfeiting the Securities and current Coin of the United States; To establish Post Offices and post Roads; To promote the Progress of Science and useful Arts, by securing for limited Times to Authors and Inventors the exclusive Right to their respective Writings and Discoveries; To constitute Tribunals inferior to the supreme Court; To define and punish Piracies and Felonies committed on the high Seas, and Offences against the Law of Nations; To declare War, grant Letters of Marque and Reprisal, and make Rules concerning Captures on Land and Water; To raise and support Armies, but no Appropriation of Money to that Use shall be for a longer Term than two Years; To provide and maintain a Navy; To make Rules for the Government and Regulation of the land and naval Forces; To provide for calling forth the Militia to execute the Laws of the Union, suppress Insurrections and repel Invasions; To provide for organizing, arming, and disciplining, the Militia, and for governing such Part of them as may be employed in the Service of the United States, reserving to the States respectively, the Appointment of the Officers, and the Authority of training the Militia according to the discipline prescribed by Congress; To exercise exclusive Legislation in all Cases whatsoever, over such District (not exceeding ten Miles square) as may, by Cession of particular States, and the Acceptance of Congress, become the Seat of the Government of the United States, and to exercise like Authority over all Places purchased by the Consent of the Legislature of the State in which the Same shall be, for the Erection of Forts, Magazines, Arsenals, dock-Yards, and other needful Buildings; —And To make all Laws which shall be necessary and proper for carrying into Execution the foregoing Powers, and all other Powers vested by this Constitution in the Government of the United States, or in any Department or Officer thereof.

Article VI, Clause 2 (Supremacy Clause)

This Constitution, and the Laws of the United States which shall be made in Pursuance thereof; and all Treaties made, or which shall be made, under the Authority of the United States, shall be the supreme Law of the Land; and the Judges in every State shall be bound thereby, any Thing in the Constitution or Laws of any State to the Contrary notwithstanding.

Tenth Amendment

The powers not delegated to the United States by the Constitution, nor prohibited by it to the States, are reserved to the States respectively, or to the people.

CORE CASES

McCulloch v. Maryland (1819)

Key Facts of the Case

- The First Bank of the United States was created largely through the efforts of Alexander Hamilton, a Federalist and the first secretary of the Treasury.
- Always opposed by Jeffersonians, who later organized as the Democratic-Republican Party, the bank's charter was allowed to expire in 1811.
- The lack of a central bank was seen as one of several reasons the United States was unable to successfully achieve its stated military aims in the War of 1812.
- Congress established a second national bank in 1816 in Philadelphia, with a branch in Baltimore, Maryland.
- Attempting to impede the operation of the second bank, Maryland passed a law that taxed transactions at the National Bank.

Constitutional Questions

Did Congress have the right to create a national bank under the necessary and proper clause of Article I, Section 8? Did Maryland have the right to interfere with the bank's operation?

Majority Opinion

In a unanimous decision, the Marshall Court found that Congress, under the necessary and proper clause, has the power to create a bank, and, given that "the power to tax involves the power to destroy," the state does not have the right to tax federal activities. The necessary and proper, or elastic, clause is finitely elastic. Powers granted must closely relate to the delegated powers in Article I, Section 8. Congress has the delegated power to tax, borrow, pay debts, and coin money. The creation of a national bank advances goals that are clearly related to these delegated powers.

The Marshall Court also applied the supremacy clause to this case:

> If we apply the principle for which the State of Maryland contends, to the Constitution generally, we shall find it capable of changing totally the character of that instrument. We shall find it capable of arresting all the measures of the Government, and of prostrating it at the foot of the States. The American people have declared their Constitution and the laws made in pursuance thereof to be supreme, but this principle would transfer the supremacy, in fact, to the States.

Dissenting Opinion

There was no dissent in this case, although the application of the necessary and proper clause in extending Congress's control of interstate commerce has remained highly controversial.

Implications of the Case

- The high court reaffirmed the powers granted to Congress in Article I, Section 8, a few years later in *Gibbons v. Ogden* (1824). In that case, a New York law that attempted to license steamships from New Jersey was found to be unconstitutional because it conflicted with laws passed by Congress. This was the first case that used the commerce clause. Marshall's definition of commerce was slowly expanded over the next two centuries. *Gibbons v. Ogden* also reaffirmed the validity of the supremacy clause (Article VI, Clause 2).
- In *Barron v. Baltimore* (1833), the Marshall Court clearly affirmed state rights. The plaintiff in this case sued the city of Baltimore for abridging his Fifth Amendment

property rights. In a unanimous decision, the Court ruled that the Bill of Rights only limited the actions of the federal government. Bill of Rights protections extended to all government actions after the passage of the Fourteenth Amendment in 1868.

· Although Congress's right to establish a national bank under the necessary and proper clause of Article I, Section 8, has not been in doubt since *McCulloch v. Maryland*, the bank and its policies have been controversial at many points in U.S. history. Its charter was allowed to expire by Congress during President Jackson's term, but Congress re-created it under President Wilson.

United States v. Lopez (1995)

Key Facts of the Case

· In 1990, Congress passed and President George H. W. Bush signed the Crime Control Act of 1990. It was a bill that had many parts including the Gun-Free School Zones Act of 1990.

· The Gun-Free School Zones Act made it a federal crime to bring firearms into a school or a school zone.

· In 1995, twelfth grader Alfonso D. Lopez Jr. was caught with a handgun and bullets at a high school in San Antonio, Texas. The state dropped charges when it learned that federal prosecutors had taken the case. The student was found guilty in federal court and sentenced to six months of imprisonment and two years of probation.

Constitutional Question

Did the Gun-Free School Zones Act exceed Congress's authority under the interstate commerce clause?

Majority Opinion

In a 5–4 decision, the high court ruled that Congress did not have authority under the commerce clause to ban firearms from school zones. Chief Justice Rehnquist wrote, "The Act neither regulates a commercial activity nor contains a requirement that the possession be connected in any way to interstate commerce. We hold that the Act exceeds the authority of Congress to regulate Commerce."

Rehnquist argued that to side with the United States in this case would have been to give Congress infinitely expandable powers under the commerce clause, a situation that the framers clearly sought to avoid. To demonstrate this, he quoted Madison's *Federalist Paper 45*, "The powers delegated by the proposed Constitution to the federal government are few and defined. Those which are to remain in the State governments are numerous and indefinite."

Rehnquist's ruling demanded that Congress demonstrate a more tangible link to interstate commerce. "To uphold the Government's contentions here, we would have to pile inference upon inference in a manner that would bid fair to convert congressional authority under the Commerce Clause to a general police power of the sort retained by the States."

Dissenting Opinion

The government argued that there were clear connections between guns in school and commercial activity. Justice Breyer wrote, "Guns are both articles of commerce and articles that can be used to restrain commerce. Their possession is the consequence, either directly or indirectly, of commercial activity."

The presence of firearms in schools is a major impediment to the learning environment. This can negatively impact the economic activity of a local area and its ability to compete against other regions in the country and other nations both in the short and in the long run. "Indeed, Congress has said, when writing other statutes, that 'functionally or technologically illiterate' Americans in the work force 'erode our economic' standing in the international marketplace."

Implications of the Case

- The courts have always struggled with the applicability of the commerce clause. Both the majority and dissenting opinions in this case examined a wide variety of case law going all the way back to *Ogden*. They also wrote about cases from the New Deal and cases that tested federal civil rights legislation.
- Congress rewrote the legislation, changing the language to state, "It shall be unlawful for any individual knowingly to possess a firearm that has moved in or that otherwise affects interstate or foreign commerce at a place that the individual knows, or has reasonable cause to believe, is a school zone." Courts have found that the law is now constitutional. However, the vast majority of weapons charges in school zones are still prosecuted by states.
- Historians view this case as the most important example of devolution (the movement to return powers to the states under the constitutional system of federalism). The judicial branch is not the only actor in this trend; Congress, the executive branch, the states, and international economic and security developments also impact the devolution movement.

United States v. Morrison (2000)

Key Facts of the Case

- Drafted by Senator Joe Biden after at least a 15-year lobbying effort by victim's rights advocates, the Violence Against Women Act of 1994 (VAWA) provided a wide array of protections and programs for victims of gender-based violence (protections for men as well as women).
- The law included provisions for victims to sue their attackers in federal court.
- Congress included language in the law that claimed powers under the commerce clause and the Fourteenth Amendment.
- A female student at Virginia Tech was raped by two football players. One of the football players was found guilty by the university and faced punishment. Eventually, the university withdrew the attacker's punishment, and the victim sued her attackers in federal court using the VAWA.

Constitutional Question

Does Congress have the right to extend civil law protections to victims of gender-based violence under the commerce clause or the Fourteenth Amendment?

Majority Opinion

In a 5–4 decision, the Court ruled that the provision in the VAWA that allowed victims to sue their attackers in federal court was unconstitutional. All other parts of the law were left intact.

The majority ruled that the commerce clause did not extend to requiring this type of civil law remedy. In his majority decision, Chief Justice Rehnquist wrote the following:

> *If accepted, this reasoning would allow Congress to regulate any crime whose nationwide, aggregated impact has substantial effects on employment, production, transit, or consumption. Moreover, such reasoning will not limit Congress to regulating violence, but may be applied equally as well to family law and other areas of state regulation since the aggregate effect of marriage, divorce, and childrearing on the national economy*

is undoubtedly significant. The Constitution requires a distinction between what is truly national and what is truly local, and there is no better example of the police power, which the Founders undeniably left reposed in the States and denied the central Government, than the suppression of violent crime and vindication of its victims.

Also, the court ruled that the Fourteenth Amendment's due process and equal protection clauses could only apply to an individual seeking redress against the state, not against another individual. Rehnquist wrote, "The Fourteenth Amendment places limitations on the manner in which Congress may attack discriminatory conduct. Foremost among them is the principle that the Amendment prohibits only state action, not private conduct."

Dissenting Opinion

The same four justices dissented in this case that had dissented in *United States v. Lopez*, and they used many of the same arguments. Justice Souter believed that Congress, not the courts, should determine the connections to interstate commerce:

By passing legislation, Congress indicates its conclusion, whether explicitly or not, that facts support its exercise of the commerce power. The business of the courts is to review the congressional assessment, not for soundness but simply for the rationality of concluding that a jurisdictional basis exists in fact.

Justice Souter also cited the substantial evidence that Congress had assembled in demonstrating the impact gender-based violence had on commerce.

Implications of the Case

- Together with *United States v. Lopez*, this case marks a dramatic departure from the trend of expanding federal powers. Critics of the VAWA, especially the part of the law tested in this case, viewed this decision as reaffirmation of the police powers traditionally reserved for the states.
- Congress reauthorized the VAWA in 2000, 2005, and 2013. The law requires states to extend many protections to victims of gender-based violence. For example, state laws requiring rape victims to take lie detector tests have been banned. The law provides funding and guidelines for communities to develop integrated services for victims of gender-based violence. The VAWA, combined with Title IX in educational settings, has created a large federal footprint in local policies regarding gender-based violence. In 2013, Congress extended protections in the law to same-sex couples.

Balance of Power between State and National Governments Case Timeline

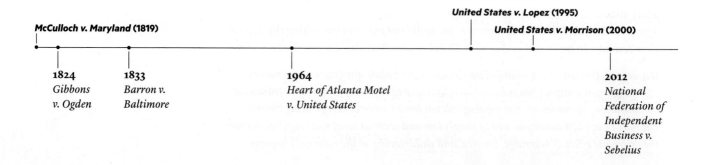

Summary of Main Points

LOR-2: Provisions of the U.S. Constitution's Bill of Rights are continually being interpreted to balance the power of government and the civil liberties of individuals.

Before becoming president, Woodrow Wilson was a constitutional scholar and a prolific writer on the theory and practice of American government. He wrote that the problem of federalism cannot be solved by any one generation. Changing economic and social conditions would require new solutions. The federal judiciary, as well as the other branches and the states, will always advocate for different interpretations, as constitutional applications of federalism evolve.

Yet, the cases in this group represent clear outer limits in our judicial history. *McCulloch v. Maryland* demonstrates that Article I, Section 8, does not represent a finite list of delegated powers. The courts recognized that Congress's right to establish a bank was clearly connected to its delegated powers to support the nation's financial well-being. Similarly, the commerce power has been extended to cover a wide variety of laws governing wages, workplace issues, environmental regulations, and many other areas of policy. Also, combined with the Fourteenth Amendment, it has required government and businesses to end discriminatory practices against women and minorities.

Both *United States v. Lopez* and *United States v. Morrison* are precedents that have significantly strengthened the state's reserve powers. These cases build on a long history of decisions and practices that have reinvigorated state powers. They demonstrate that although almost all activities impact commerce in some manner, this does not mean that the federal government can always usurp state policies.

The recent history of Supreme Court cases regarding federalism is both fascinating and maddeningly unclear. Some Americans with Disabilities Act protections have been denied to state and local workers because of the Eleventh Amendment's sovereign immunity protections. In a 5-4 decision in *National Federation of Independent Business v. Sebelius* (2012), the high court ruled that the Affordable Care Act (Obamacare) was constitutional under the taxing provisions of the Sixteenth Amendment, not under the commerce clause. At the same time, it ruled that the federal government did not have the right to withhold all Medicaid funding if states chose not to expand Medicaid. This type of "condition of aid" had been used in many areas as a financial incentive to convince states to adopt policies that Congress favored. For example, Congress eventually convinced all states to raise their drinking age by threatening to withhold highway funds.

Clearly, cases about federalism will last as long as the Republic itself. For example, many states have recently legalized medical and recreational marijuana; this issue has been tested and will be tested again in the courts. Does the use of marijuana impact interstate commerce in a significant way?

Looking beyond judicial issues, we can see that policy in the United States represents "marble cake federalism." Federal and local policies coexist in education, guns, health care, water, electricity, and so many other policy areas. We may identify as Americans first, but we are also the loyal citizens of a region or perhaps many regions. Our historical approach to federalism reflects our unanimity and our regional diversity.

Assessing Student Understanding

1. Explain how both the commerce clause and the necessary and proper clause have been used to expand federal power.

2. Decisions made by the Rehnquist Court ushered in a new era of federalism known as "devolution." Explain the concept of devolution and how it has limited the applicability of the commerce clause.

3. Identify and explain two parts of the Constitution that have been used to strengthen state powers.

Questions for Class Discussion and Debate

1. What are the dangers and advantages of too much federal power? What are the dangers and advantages of too much state power?

2. Since the *Lopez* decision in 1995, has more power devolved to the states or has it continued to centralize with the federal government? Support your opinion with specific policy examples.

3. What is the proper dividing line between interstate commerce and police powers? In other words, where should federal control of laws governing the general welfare of citizens end and state sovereignty begin?

Cluster 2: Judicial Review

The Big Issues

The cases in this group represent the varied powers of the Supreme Court. In *Marbury v. Madison* (1803), judicial review was established when a law passed by Congress was declared unconstitutional. In *United States v. Nixon* (1974), a sitting president was ordered to obey a subpoena and to deliver taped recordings to the Court, and *Swann v. Charlotte-Mecklenburg Board of Education* (1971) set the basis for direct federal judicial control of integration efforts being carried out by school boards around the nation.

All three cases presented below were unanimous decisions, but they were also highly controversial. Does this type of power represent a contradiction of Hamilton's claim in *Federalist 78* that the judiciary is the weakest branch and should not be feared? The courts have no army, no regulators, and no means to enforce their decisions other than popular will and the belief in constitutional government.

The Court's powers stem from the brief and somewhat vague passages of Article III, which at 377 words is less than one-sixth the size of Article I. From its humble origins in Article III, the courts have come to play an essential role in the U.S. balance of power. For example, when the Court found large parts of Franklin Delano Roosevelt's New Deal unconstitutional, the public supported its president in his outrage, but not in his court-packing scheme that would have weakened the power of the Supreme Court.

These cases represent important milestones in recognizing the judiciary's role in the balance of power between the branches and between the states and the national government.

Constitutional Connections

Article III, Section 1

The judicial Power of the United States shall be vested in one Supreme Court, and in such inferior Courts as the Congress may from time to time ordain and establish. The Judges, both of the supreme and inferior Courts, shall hold their Offices during good Behaviour, and shall, at stated Times, receive for their Services, a Compensation, which shall not be diminished during their Continuance in Office.

from Article VI

This Constitution, and the Laws of the United States which shall be made in Pursuance thereof; and all Treaties made, or which shall be made, under the Authority of the United States, shall be the supreme Law of the Land; and the Judges in every State shall be bound thereby, any Thing in the Constitution or Laws of any State to the Contrary notwithstanding.

CORE CASES

Marbury v. Madison (1803)

Key Facts of the Case

- In the election of 1800, the Federalists lost control of both the executive and legislative branches. In his last day in office, President John Adams appointed and the Senate confirmed many judges and justices of the peace. Among these confirmations was his secretary of state, John Marshall, who was approved as chief justice of the U.S. Supreme Court.

- In its lame duck session, the sixth Congress also passed the Judiciary Act of 1801, an act that modified the Judiciary Act of 1789.
- The Judiciary Act of 1801 reduced the number of justices on the Supreme Court from six to five and added 16 new federal judgeships and over 40 justice of the peace positions in the District of Colombia.
- In the new city of Washington in 1800, federal appointees received official notification of their jobs when the secretary of state delivered their commissions.
- Acting as secretary of state, John Marshall did not finish delivering all of the commissions by the time Thomas Jefferson had taken the oath of office as the nation's third president.
- The incoming secretary of state, James Madison, was ordered by the new president to not deliver any more commissions. William Marbury, who had been confirmed by the Senate as a justice of the peace in the District of Columbia, sued Madison for his commission.

Constitutional Questions

Does Marbury have a right to his commission? Does the Supreme Court have the authority to order the delivery of this commission?

Majority Opinion

Newly minted Chief Justice Marshall wrote for a unanimous Court and said that Marbury did not have a right to his commission but that the Court did have the authority to order its delivery. Marshall accomplished this seemingly contradictory result by striking down part of the Judiciary Act of 1789. He claimed that the part of the act that gave the Court the power to order the commission's delivery changed its Article III powers. In altering the meaning of the Constitution, the Congress had surpassed its authority. This is the first law found unconstitutional by the courts, and this decision confirmed the existence of judicial review as a critical part of the balance of power between the branches.

Dissenting Opinion

There were no dissenting opinions, but the judicial branch is still the subject of great criticism for striking down laws passed by Congress or by state legislatures.

Implications of the Case

- The Court's decision in this case may have saved the Republic in both the long and short run. It avoided a constitutional crisis that could have resulted in all Federalist judges and justices being removed for political causes, a precedent that would have destabilized the United States and lowered the odds that a democratic form of government would endure. In the long run, it enshrined the practice of judicial review, a power inferred but not specified in the Constitution. Judicial review has served an important role in the balance of power between the branches, and between the national and state governments.
- In the first 225 years of the Republic, the courts have struck down 180 acts of Congress (out of more than 60,000 laws passed).
- This case has frustrated students of history and politics for many generations because its logic is so hard to follow. This is because there is a great deal that is not very logical. Today, the section of the Judiciary Act that was struck down probably

would have been found to be constitutional and Marshall would have been pressured to recuse himself from this case because he had been an involved party. The critical thing to remember is, other than saving the nation, it established judicial review.

United States v. Nixon (1974)

Key Facts of the Case

- A grand jury investigating the break-in at the Watergate complex by men associated with Nixon's campaign for reelection became aware that recorded conversations had taken place in the Oval Office about this crime and its aftermath. The grand jury issued a subpoena for the tapes.
- President Nixon claimed executive privilege, the right of the executive to shield internal communications.
- Executive privilege is not mentioned in the Constitution, but its existence is inferred from the separation of powers. To function properly, any organization will, at times, need internal communications that are confidential.

Constitutional Questions

Do the courts have power to subpoena private communication within the executive branch? Does the president's executive privilege take precedence over this request?

Majority Opinion

Chief Justice Burger delivered the opinion of the Court, which was unanimous. The Court ordered that Nixon turn the tapes over to the grand jury; "neither the doctrine of separation of powers nor the generalized need for confidentiality of high-level communications, without more, can sustain an absolute, unqualified Presidential privilege of immunity from judicial process under all circumstances."

The Court did confirm the existence of executive privilege, but other than suggesting it held greater sway in covert foreign involvements, it gave little certainly to how future presidents might be able to use it. "Absent a claim of need to protect military, diplomatic, or sensitive national security secrets, the confidentiality of Presidential communications is not significantly diminished by producing material for a criminal trial . . ."

Dissenting Opinion

There was no dissenting opinion. Justice William Rehnquist, a recent appointee who had worked in Nixon's Justice Department, recused himself.

Implications of the Case

- Almost every president has claimed executive privilege to prevent the release of sensitive or embarrassing material. The battle over executive privilege is often highly partisan. A Democratic Congress demanded shielded documents from George W. Bush and a Republican Congress demanded documents from the Obama Justice Department. Both requests were only partially successful.
- *United States v. Nixon* is unusual because the acts of the president were not just politically controversial but were illegal, and their investigation had bipartisan support. In fact, the material on the subpoenaed tapes would have played an important role in Nixon's impeachment and removal had he not resigned.
- Other than President Jackson's decision to ignore the Supreme Court's decision to halt the Trail of Tears and the Cherokee removal from Georgia, presidents have

generally followed Court orders. In *Clinton v. Jones* (1997), the Supreme Court ruled that presidents were not immune from civil actions, and President Bill Clinton was questioned as part of a lawsuit against him (he was allowed to testify via a remote video feed).

Swann v. Charlotte-Mecklenburg Board of Education (1971)

Key Facts of the Case

- In *Brown v. Board of Education* (1954), Chief Justice Warren ordered that the nation's schools be desegregated "with all deliberate speed." Brown's lead attorney and future Supreme Court Justice Thurgood Marshall spoke for many when he said that "all deliberate speed" had come to mean "slow."
- In fact, in many parts of the nation, integration efforts were not moving forward. After the *Brown* decision, the Charlotte-Mecklenburg school system had adopted neighborhood-based school assignments. This approach left the population of most schools either entirely Black or entirely White.
- When the Supreme Court issues an opinion, it usually includes a summary of case facts, which is known as a syllabus. The syllabus for this case stated, "The Charlotte-Mecklenburg school system, which includes the city of Charlotte, North Carolina, had more than 84,000 students in 107 schools in the 1968–1969 school year. Approximately 29% (24,000) of the pupils were Negro, about 14,000 of whom attended 21 schools that were at least 99% Negro."
- Nine plaintiffs brought action against the Charlotte-Mecklenburg Board of Education in an attempt to force local authorities to create real school integration plan as defined in *Brown*.

Constitutional Question

Do the federal courts have the authority to design and oversee local desegregation plans when it is determined that local authorities are violating the Fourteenth Amendment?

Majority Opinion

In a unanimous decision the Court decided that federal courts had the power and the obligation to direct desegregation efforts around the nation.

Chief Justice Burger's opinion reviews the years that had passed since *Brown* and the dozens of lawsuits that had taken place in an effort to implement *Brown*:

> *Over the 16 years since Brown II, many difficulties were encountered in implementation of the basic constitutional requirement that the State not discriminate between public school children on the basis of their race. Nothing in our national experience prior to 1955 prepared anyone for dealing with changes and adjustments of the magnitude and complexity encountered since then. Deliberate resistance of some to the Court's mandates has impeded the good faith efforts of others to bring school systems into compliance. The detail and nature of these dilatory [delay-causing] tactics have been noted frequently by this Court and other courts.*

Burger's lengthy and detailed opinion set guidelines for integration efforts around the nation and granted extensive powers to federal courts to implement those plans should local authorities fail to act with genuine speed. "Once a right and a violation have been shown, the scope of a district court's equitable powers to remedy past wrongs is broad, for breadth and flexibility are inherent in equitable remedies."

Dissenting Opinion

There was no dissent.

Implications of the Case

- As a result of this case, federal courts took over stalled desegregation efforts around the country. Efforts to desegregate schools were met with resistance in many White neighborhoods. In Boston in 1975, 21 years after *Brown*, desegregation efforts resulted in riots and violence. While President Ford discussed passing an anti-busing constitutional amendment, many local leaders worked to maintain calm and carry out the busing and the desegregation plans. Schools around the nation were finally desegregated.
- A subsequent case, *Milliken v. Bradley* (1974), ruled that federal desegregation orders were limited to the school districts that had practiced segregationist polices. In other words, White suburban towns and cities were excluded from court-ordered plans.
- In many parts of the nation, schools have resegregated, sometimes at levels even higher than before *Brown*. Current segregation reflects residential demographics and is de facto (based on cultural and economic factors) as opposed to de jure (based on law).

Judicial Review Case Timeline

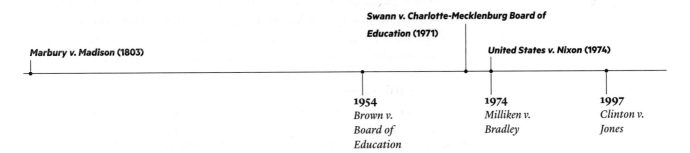

Summary of Main Points

CON-5: The design of the judicial branch protects the Court's independence as a branch of government, and the emergence and use of judicial review remains a powerful judicial practice.

In *Federalist 78*, Alexander Hamilton wrote that the judiciary branch, as formed by the Constitution, poses no threat of tyranny: "Whoever attentively considers the different departments of power must perceive that, in a government in which they are separated from each other, the judiciary, from the nature of its functions, will always be the least dangerous to the political rights of the Constitution; because it will be least in a capacity to annoy or injure them."

Although these cases represent instances when the judiciary claimed powers within the constitutional system, and therefore seem to contradict *Federalist 78*, it should be noted that the courts often defer to the powers of the Congress, the executive, and the states. The courts do not operate as a legislature does. They cannot pick policy issues; they only choose from among the cases that are appealed to them. Their impact on policy is limited by the willingness of the other branches to follow their decrees. Also, the courts depend on the public's trust and respect to enforce their decisions.

It is unlikely that the public would have supported the court in *United States v. Nixon* if the people believed that the president should have dictatorial powers. It is unlikely that there would have been enough public support to enforce the decision in *Swann v. Charlotte-Mecklenburg BOE* if the public was not at least partially prepared for integration. As with the decision a generation later legalizing same-sex marriage across the nation, Court decisions can nudge society forward, but attempts to entirely redirect policy usually fail. The failure of the *Dred Scott* decision and the Court's attempt to stop the Cherokee removal are examples of failed attempts to dictate policy.

In fact, after *Marbury v. Madison*, the next act of Congress struck down by the Court was almost 50 years later in the *Dred Scott* decision, a misguided attempt to lower sectional strife that was widely considered one of the low points of U.S. judicial history. Now, more than a century and half after the Civil War, a substantial amount of precedent has set clear patterns that predict when laws passed by Congress or state legislature will be challenged along constitutional grounds. The cases in this group demonstrate how judicial review operates in general, and how it limits the actions of federal and local policy makers.

Assessing Student Understanding

1. What is judicial review? What role did *Marbury v. Madison* play in establishing judicial review?

2. How does judicial review help to stabilize the balance of power in a democracy? Can it ever be used in a manner that concentrates too much power in the judiciary?

3. What is executive privilege? How did the decision in *United States v. Nixon* limit the concept of executive privilege? When would a presidential claim of executive privilege have the greatest chance of being constitutional?

Questions for Class Discussion and Debate

1. Why is executive privilege needed within the executive branch? How is it similar to other private discussions and correspondences in other instances where individuals are meeting in order to develop sensitive plans? For example, does a type of "executive privilege" exist when parents are discussing their child? When school administrators are discussing a difficult situation at their school?

2. Does the Court use judicial review to the proper degree? In other words, does the judicial branch claim too much, too little, or the proper amount of political power?

3. Other than directly taking over part of the administrative functions of organizations like local school districts, what type of strategies can courts use to see that their decisions are followed?

Cluster 3: Freedom of Speech and Press

The Big Issues

The scope of our civil liberties depends on balancing interests and drawing lines. This is especially true of the First Amendment's freedom of speech, which can be envisioned on a continuum from the most to least protected types of speech based on Supreme Court cases that have tested their limits. Similarly, the balancing of conflicting interests is central to many freedom of the press cases. The general issue here is prior restraint, the government's right to prevent media coverage. Prior restraint is an issue that the Court has never clearly defined, but it has set a high bar for suspending this essential freedom.

Constitutional Connection

First Amendment

Congress shall make no law respecting an establishment of religion or prohibiting the free exercise thereof, or abridging the freedom of speech or of the press, or the right of the people peaceably to assemble and to petition the government for a redress of grievances.

CORE CASES

Schenck v. United States (1919)

Key Facts of the Case

- As a socialist who opposed the capitalist system, Charles T. Schenck also opposed U.S. entry into World War I and distributed political literature urging citizens to resist the draft. The U.S. decision to enter the war that had ravaged Europe for the prior three years was contentious. Shortly after Congress declared war in April 1917, it passed the Espionage Act, which attempted to limit dissent.
- Schenck was charged with violating a clause of the Espionage Act that made it illegal to distribute information that interfered with the success of the U.S. military.
- The Court was uncomfortable with the first prosecutions under this act. In particular, Justice Oliver Wendell Holmes felt that the Court was merely punishing unpopular opinions. With the *Schenck* case, however, Holmes found what he then believed was a constitutional way to suppress speech during wartime and he wrote the opinion for a unanimous Court.

Constitutional Questions

Were Schenck's efforts to distribute information opposing U.S. involvement in World War I protected by the First Amendment? Do the president and the Congress have the power to limit freedoms during wartime?

Majority Opinion

Holmes's majority opinion added two time-honored expressions into U.S. legal writing. He said that the freedom of speech is not absolute. For example, yelling "fire" in a crowded theater that is not on fire is not protected speech. In fact, it creates a "clear and present danger"—something Holmes and the Court claimed that Schenck did by distributing this literature.

Delivering the opinion of the Court, Holmes stated, "The question in every case is whether the words used are used in such circumstances and are of such a nature as to create a clear and present danger that they will bring about the substantive evils that Congress has a right to prevent." During wartime, utterances tolerable in peacetime can be punished.

Dissenting Opinion

There was no dissent, but as time went on, this decision began to stand on less steady ground. The Court has begun to recognize the right to dissent, even during wartime.

Implications of the Case

- Shortly after the *Schenck* case, Holmes dissented in cases that involved this type of prosecution. He returned to the theory that political speech was protected by the First Amendment. The Court's decisions zigzag through the Red Scare of the 1920s and Cold War prosecutions of communists in the 1950s.
- In *Bradenburg v. Ohio* (1969) the Court ruled that Ku Klux Klan and Nazi protesters could not be stopped from marching because of the "clear and present danger" test. Similarly, in *Texas v. Johnson* (1989), the Court ruled that burning a U.S. flag was protected symbolic speech. The clear and present danger test has been abandoned in favor of an "imminent lawless action" test—a much higher standard for prosecutors to reach.
- In general, the Court has expanded free speech applications, even during wartime, but there are still exceptions. In *Holder v. Humanitarian Law Project* (2010), Americans were prosecuted for helping groups officially designated as terrorists even though they were only advising them on how to become involved in the legislative process in their home countries.

Tinker v. Des Moines Independent Community School District (1969)

Key Facts of the Case

- On December 16, 1965, four children from the Tinker family and a friend wore black armbands to their Des Moines, Iowa, public schools as a symbolic protest against the Vietnam War. The two high school students and one junior high student were suspended.
- The Tinkers' father filed suit on his children's behalf, claiming that their First Amendment rights had been violated. Although no disruptions had occurred, Des Moines Independent Community School District argued that the armbands created a potential disturbance. Also, student rights of free expression can be curtailed by school officials in an effort to create the best possible learning environment.

Constitutional Questions

Did the school rule against wearing armbands violate the students' free speech protections in the First Amendment? To what extent do student rights of free expression parallel those of adults?

Majority Opinion

In a 7–2 decision, the Court ruled in favor of John and Mary Beth Tinker. Schools cannot ban speech unless it "materially and substantially interfered" with a school's normal functioning. The armbands were seen as a form of symbolic speech. Justice Fortas wrote, "It can hardly be argued that either students or teachers shed their constitutional rights to freedom of speech or expression at the schoolhouse gate."

Justice Fortas wrote in the majority decision, "First, the Court concludes that the wearing of armbands is 'symbolic speech,' which is 'akin to pure speech,'" and therefore protected by the First and Fourteenth Amendments. Secondly, the Court decides that the public schools are an appropriate place to exercise 'symbolic speech' as long as normal school functions are not 'unreasonably' disrupted."

In a concurring opinion, Justice Stewart noted that there are limits to student speech rights in a school, even when no clear disruption can be proven. "Although I agree with much of what is said in the Court's opinion, and with its judgment in this case, I cannot share the Court's uncritical assumption that, school discipline aside, the First Amendment rights of children are coextensive with those of adults." Subsequent court decisions would clarify Justice Stewart's opinion.

Dissenting Opinion

School officials should be granted wide discretion in creating the proper disciplinary climate in their own schools. Culture and community norms differ widely, and courts should not usurp local autonomy.

Implications of the Case

- The *Tinker* precedent is still used in student free expression cases, but it has been limited by subsequent Supreme Court decisions. In *Hazelwood School District v. Kuhlmeier* (1989), the Court ruled that school officials had virtually complete control over the content of student publications such as newspapers and yearbooks.
- In *Morse v. Frederick* (2007), the Court upheld the suspension of a student who held a sign at an off-campus event that said, "BONG HiTS 4 JESUS." Also, the Court upheld the suspension of a student who made a sexually charged nominating speech during a student election assembly. This case (*Bethel School District No. 403 v. Fraser* [1986]) is significant because if there is such a thing as pure political speech and total First Amendment freedoms in a school setting, it would be during an election.

New York Times Co. v. United States (1971)

Key Facts of the Case

- In 1967, the Defense Department initiated a massive study of the ongoing Vietnam War. The 7,000-page study, called the Pentagon Papers, was completed in early 1969 and labeled "Top Secret—sensitive." The study revealed embarrassing details about the war effort, including the conclusion that it was not winnable.
- For years after its release, U.S. government policy in Vietnam remained committed to a full-scale military effort, resulting in massive casualties on all sides. One of the report's authors, Daniel Ellsberg, leaked the Pentagon Papers to the *New York Times*, which began to publish them. The first publication was on June 13, 1971.
- Within 48 hours of publication, the *New York Times* and the *Washington Post*, which also planned to publish the Pentagon Papers, received an order from a federal judge ordering them to cease publication. The order, which cited powers based on the Espionage Act of 1917, would allow the President to ban publications that could give useful information to the enemy.

Constitutional Question

Did the U.S. government's effort to prevent the publication of documents it alleged were top secret violate the First Amendment's freedom of the press?

Majority Opinion

Thirteen days after the first publication, the Court ruled in a 6–3 decision that the government's case did not meet the high standard needed to usurp the freedom of the press. Concurring, Justices Black and Douglas wrote, "Framers of the First Amendment, able men that they were, wrote in language they earnestly believed could never be misunderstood: 'Congress shall make no law . . . abridging the freedom . . . of the press.'" Preventing publication from occurring is known as prior restraint, an occurrence with almost no precedent in U.S. legal tradition. The six justices in the majority viewed the Pentagon Papers as critical, not top-secret information. Most of the material was historical and did not reveal details about ongoing U.S. military operations. The justices agreed that there could be cases where prior restraint was needed, but this was not one of them.

Dissenting Opinion

Citing other First Amendment cases, Chief Justice Burger argued that this case should have been allowed to evolve in a much longer time span. There was nothing urgent about the newspaper's need to publish this information. Furthermore, the executive branch should be given wide discretion in protecting national security during wartime, as was done in *Schenck v. United States* (1919).

Implications of the Case

- In the era of Wikileaks and the World Wide Web, the government has even less power to attempt prior restraint of the media. However, the government is still able to prosecute and punish the leakers. In the Pentagon Paper's case, however, prosecutions ended when it was learned that the Nixon administration had ordered an illegal break-in at Daniel Ellsberg's psychiatrist's office.

Freedom of Speech and Press Case Timeline

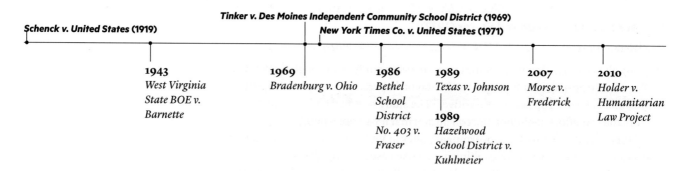

Schenck v. United States (1919)

Tinker v. Des Moines Independent Community School District (1969)
New York Times Co. v. United States (1971)

1943
West Virginia State BOE v. Barnette

1969
Bradenburg v. Ohio

1986
Bethel School District No. 403 v. Fraser

1989
Texas v. Johnson

1989
Hazelwood School District v. Kuhlmeier

2007
Morse v. Frederick

2010
Holder v. Humanitarian Law Project

Summary of Main Points

LOR-2: Provisions of the U.S. Constitution's Bill of Rights are continually being interpreted to balance the power of government and the civil liberties of individuals.

Throughout the over 200-year history of the U.S. Constitution, the freedom of speech has been tested in a wide variety of ways, some anticipated and others that the framers could not have imagined. The freedom of speech got off to a rocky start with the highly unpopular Alien and Sedition Acts, passed by a Federalist Congress and repealed after the Democratic-Republicans took power in 1800. When Congress made its next major attempt to limit political speech during World War I with the Espionage Act, the courts temporarily agreed. The clear and present danger test established in *Schenck v. United States* was almost completely chipped away in the second half of the twentieth century. Today, Americans enjoy an extensive freedom of speech.

In the second half of the twentieth century, freedom of speech rights were also tested in many different settings, such as public schools. The landmark *Tinker* case built on other cases that had supported the civil liberties of students. It also expanded the concept of speech to include symbolic acts, and then acted as precedent for other examples of symbolic political speech.

Unlike the pattern that began after *Schenck v. United States* when speech rights expanded, *Tinker v. Des Moines Independent Community School District* represented a high-water mark of student speech rights. Although administrators must still prove a significant disturbance to limit political speech (sometimes called the Tinker Test), schools have gained more control over student speech and dress in subsequent court decisions.

Meanwhile, there have been relatively few cases testing the freedom of the press. *New York Times Co. v. United States* allowed the publication of sensitive government documents, and no act of Congress or court decision has eroded this liberty. Even slander and libel cases carry such a high burden of proof that the threat of a civil suit has no chilling effect on political speech.

Unlike dictatorships, which control public speech and the press, and unlike democracies with strict hate and defamation laws, the United States is flooded with speech and press from all perspectives and from all types of sources. With these great freedoms come great responsibilities. Our freedoms of speech and press depend on an educated public that understands our government and is well informed about the important issues of our time. We must be able to select the most salient and insightful messages from a babble of competing voices.

Assessing Student Understanding

1. Why did the clear and present danger test fail to create a clear method of identifying protected speech?

2. What is symbolic speech? Give an example of a different type of symbolic speech than the Tinkers used.

3. What is prior restraint? Why is it commonly used in dictatorships?

Questions for Class Discussion and Debate

1. When should the freedom of speech be suppressed because of national security? Give examples of protected and unprotected speech.

2. When should the freedom of press be suppressed because of national security? Give examples of protected and unprotected press coverage.

3. Do students have too many, too few, or the right amount of First Amendment rights in school? In what ways should school rules be changed to better reflect educational goals or the Constitution?

Cluster 4: Freedom of Religion

The Big Issues

Freedom of religion has two very different and sometimes overlapping parts. The first part has been interpreted as a prohibition against the government establishing, supporting, or favoring religion, or of treating one religion more or less favorably than others. The second guarantees that citizens will have freedom to exercise their religion without governmental restrictions. Of course, over the course of our history, there have been many instances when religious freedom conflicts with one of society's secular goals, and then the courts have ruled that this behavior lacks First Amendment protections. For example, both polygamy and using certain drugs are illegal in all states, even though these laws limit the practice of certain religions. Although the two parts of the First Amendment that deal with religion seem straightforward, the cases contested in our court system, especially since the middle of the twentieth century, have been numerous and complex.

Constitutional Connection

First Amendment

Congress shall make no law respecting an establishment of religion or prohibiting the free exercise thereof, or abridging the freedom of speech or of the press, or the right of the people peaceably to assemble and to petition the government for a redress of grievances.

CORE CASES

West Virginia State Board of Education v. Barnette (1943)

Key Facts of the Case

- In 1942, the West Virginia legislature passed a law requiring all school children and teachers to salute the American flag or face expulsion from school for "insubordination."
- At the time, the lawmakers in the Mountain State believed that they were following the decision issued by the Supreme Court in *Minersville School District v. Gobitis* (1940). In *Gobitis*, the Supreme Court ruled that the state had the right to regulate the secular behavior of school children in its pursuit of instilling the values of national cohesion and national unity.
- In *West Virginia State BOE v. Barnette* (1943), students from the Jehovah's Witness faith had been expelled from school, and state officials considered sending them to schools for juvenile delinquents. In the Jehovah's Witness faith, it is forbidden to honor a graven image, and religious leaders considered a flag to be a graven image.
- This case provides a stark example of how world events sometimes creep into the Court's thinking. In 1940, Europe and Asia were engulfed in a brutal world war, and many educational leaders viewed the flag salute as a way to remind children of U.S. independence and pride. Nazi Germany required both a flag salute and a salute to Hitler, and German Jehovah's Witnesses who refused to perform these salutes were some of the first victims of the concentration camps.

Constitutional Question

Does the state have the right to require a flag salute, or is this a violation of First Amendment rights?

Majority Opinion

In a 6–3 decision, the Court ruled that state laws and local rules that require a flag salute are a violation of the First Amendment. A flag salute is symbolic speech; compelling participation is a violation of an individual's free speech rights. According to the majority opinion, "There is no doubt that, in connection with the pledges, the flag salute is a form of utterance. Symbolism is a primitive but effective way of communicating ideas. The use of an emblem or flag to symbolize some system, idea, institution, or personality is a short-cut from mind to mind."

Justice Jackson delivered the opinion of the Court, stating the following:

> *The freedom asserted by these appellees does not bring them into collision with rights asserted by any other individual. It is such conflicts which most frequently require intervention of the State to determine where the rights of one end and those of another begin. But the refusal of these persons to participate in the ceremony does not interfere with or deny rights of others to do so. Nor is there any question in this case that their behavior is peaceable and orderly. The sole conflict is between authority and rights of the individual.*

These freedoms extend to all Americans whether they are religious or not. "Nor does the issue, as we see it, turn on one's possession of particular religious views or the sincerity with which they are held."

Dissenting Opinion

The dissent used a wide variety of arguments, including the power of stare decisis, as the Court had just ruled the other way on this issue only three years earlier. Also, the dissenters argued that this matter was best left for local school officials and legislatures. If citizens didn't support the flag salute policy, they should seek policy change through democratic means such as town meetings and ousting incumbents.

Justice Frankfurter delivered the dissenting opinion:

> *Saluting the flag suppresses no belief, nor curbs it. Children and their parents may believe what they please, avow their belief and practice it. It is not even remotely suggested that the requirement for saluting the flag involves the slightest restriction against the fullest opportunity on the part both of the children and of their parents to disavow, as publicly as they choose to do so, the meaning that others attach to the gesture of salute. All channels of affirmative free expression are open to both children and parents.*

Implications of the Case

- The precedent in *Barnette* endures, although there is strong pressure to participate in the flag salute and the pledge. Although students have a right to not salute or pledge to the flag, and to not stand during these activities, some public schools still discipline students for exercising these constitutional rights.
- Does a teacher have to participate in the pledge? This is an issue that has not been fully adjudicated. In most states, teachers are still required to stand and to teach children how to participate in the flag salute, if that is part of the curriculum.

Engel v. Vitale (1962)

Key Facts of the Case

- New York state officials who worked for the Board of Regents wrote what they believed was a denominationally neutral prayer for school children to recite:

"Almighty God, we acknowledge our dependence upon Thee, and we beg Thy blessings upon us, our parents, our teachers and our Country. Amen."

- The case began in Hyde Park, New York, when a group of parents brought suit against the school board in order to stop the recitation of the prayer.

Constitutional Questions

Does the state have the right to require the reading of a nondenominational prayer in school? Do these actions violate the establishment clause of the First Amendment?

Majority Opinion

The Supreme Court ruled against New York 6–1. Justice Black's majority opinion reviews the long history of the framers' efforts to disentangle government and religion, including Madison and Jefferson's effort to pass the groundbreaking "Virginia Bill of Religious Liberty" in 1786, which served as a model for the freedoms of religion included in the Bill of Rights.

Black writes that the state, in its oral and written arguments, has never denied the religious nature of this prayer. "We think that, by using its public school system to encourage recitation of the Regents' prayer, the State of New York has adopted a practice wholly inconsistent with the Establishment Clause."

The majority opinion anticipated the backlash this ruling would cause and pointed out that it did not inhibit religious practice. It linked the Court's logic with the framers' intent. "These men knew that the First Amendment, which tried to put an end to governmental control of religion and of prayer, was not written to destroy either."

Dissenting Opinion

Justice Stewart's lone dissent focused on the fact that students were not required to participate in reciting the prayer. He also cited the long history of references to God in American history, including inscriptions on our money, the Pledge of Allegiance, and many presidential statements.

Furthermore, Stewart claimed that in the Court's ban of prayer in public school, it quashed other freedoms:

> With all respect, I think the Court has misapplied a great constitutional principle. I cannot see how an "official religion" is established by letting those who want to say a prayer say it. On the contrary, I think that to deny the wish of these school children to join in reciting this prayer is to deny them the opportunity of sharing in the spiritual heritage of our Nation.

Implications of the Case

- Subsequent Supreme Court decisions hardened the ban on governmental involvement in school prayer. *Lee v. Weisman* (1992) banned benedictions from religious officials at public school graduations. *Santa Fe Independent School District v. Doe* (2000) banned student use of the public address system to recite student-chosen prayers at a football game.
- In general, students are allowed to pray in a public school as long as there is no school-sponsored supervision or direction, and as long as it doesn't interfere with the school's educational mission. Voluntary student prayer, such as Christian Bible study groups, or Muslim students being given private spaces to perform their daily prayers, is allowed.
- Some states required a moment of silence, which can be used for prayer. Some school districts dismiss students in the middle of the day for off-campus religious instruction.

- Legislation passed in many states has attempted to overcome these decisions by allowing voluntary prayer in different situations in public schools. *Engel v. Vitale* is a highly contentious decision that is at the heart of the culture war, and we are likely to see this issue return to the high court.

Wisconsin v. Yoder (1972)

Key Facts of the Case

- The state of Wisconsin required children to attend school until the age of 16.
- Following their religious traditions, a group of parents from the Amish faith pulled their children out of school at age 14. The Amish and faiths with similar practices, such as Mennonites and Quakers, had a long history of clashing with local and state officials over issues such as school attendance and pacifism. Because the Amish faith opposed involvement with the court system, their defense was organized by a Lutheran minister. By the time the case reached the Supreme Court, people from a wide variety of religions were contributing to the efforts of the defense team.
- The state believed that requiring school attendance until age 16 was well within its police powers to protect and promote the health, safety, and morals of the community.

Constitutional Question

Does the state have the right to require mandatory school until age 16, or is this a violation of an individual's rights to freely exercise his or her religious beliefs?

Majority Opinion

In a unanimous ruling, the Court held that the state could not require school attendance past age 16 if this violated clearly held religious beliefs. "Respondents have amply supported their claim that enforcement of the compulsory formal education requirement after the eighth grade would gravely endanger if not destroy the free exercise of their religious beliefs."

The state presented no clear evidence that two more years of schooling would make these children more productive members of society or that their welfare would be negatively impacted in any way.

Dissenting Opinion

Justice Douglas agreed with the main decision in this case but partially dissented because he believed that the opinions and the religious freedom of the 14-year-olds should also be considered:

> *I agree with the Court that the religious scruples of the Amish are opposed to the education of their children beyond the grade schools, yet I disagree with the Court's conclusion that the matter is within the dispensation of parents alone. The Court's analysis assumes that the only interests at stake in the case are those of the Amish parents, on the one hand, and those of the State, on the other. The difficulty with this approach is that, despite the Court's claim, the parents are seeking to vindicate not only their own free exercise claims, but also those of their high-school-age children.*

Implications of the Case

- This is one of the few rulings that was a clear victory for those seeking the free exercise of religion. In other rulings regarding polygamy, drug use, and zoning, the high court has allowed state regulations to stand when they impeded religious practice.
- *Wisconsin v. Yoder* opened the door for the homeschooling movement that now exists in all 50 states, and no longer requires parents to demonstrate religious conviction.

- State regulations vary with regard to homeschooling. In some states, parents must meet educational standards and teach required topics. Local school systems are also required to provide some resources to homeschoolers free of charge.

Greece v. Galloway (2014)

Key Facts of the Case

- The town of Greece, New York, invited local clergy to give a prayer at the beginning of monthly board meetings. (Greece is a suburb of Rochester, New York, with a population just under 100,000 inhabitants.)
- The contents of the prayers were selected by the religious officials themselves and often did not attempt to be nondenominational—for example, "We look with anticipation to the celebration of Holy Week and Easter. It is in the solemn events of next week that we find the very heart and center of our Christian faith. We acknowledge the saving sacrifice of Jesus Christ on the cross. We draw strength, vitality, and confidence from his resurrection at Easter."
- The town neither sought out nor denied access to non-Christian clergy.

Constitutional Question

Do religious prayers offered during the official functioning of government violate the establishment clause of the First Amendment when the government has played no role in selecting the wording of the prayer?

Majority Opinion

In a highly partisan 5–4 decision, the Court ruled that Greece did not violate the establishment clause and its practice of prayer before town meetings was constitutional. Justice Kennedy, often the swing vote in cases like this one, wrote the following for the majority:

> It is presumed that the reasonable observer is acquainted with the tradition of legislative prayer and understands that its purposes are to lend gravity to public proceedings and to acknowledge the place religion holds in the lives of many private citizens, not to afford government an opportunity to proselytize or force truant constituents into the pews.

Justice Kennedy found that the board's method of choosing a religious official to begin town meetings did not favor a religion or entangle government with religion:

> The town followed an informal method for selecting prayer givers, all of whom were unpaid volunteers. A town employee would call the congregations listed in a local directory until she found a minister available for that month's meeting. The town eventually compiled a list of willing "board chaplains" who had accepted invitations and agreed to return in the future. The town at no point excluded or denied an opportunity to a would-be prayer giver.

In a concurring opinion, Justice Thomas argued that the establishment clause was only meant to apply to federal actions and should not limit the actions of state or local governments.

Dissenting Opinion

The four dissenters interpreted the town's actions and non-actions as giving preference to Christianity over all other religions. Justice Breyer wrote the following:

> The significance is that, in a context where religious minorities exist and where more could easily have been done to include their participation, the town chose to do nothing.

It could, for example, have posted its policy of permitting anyone to give an invocation on its website, greeceny.gov, which provides dates and times of upcoming town board meetings along with minutes of prior meetings. It could have announced inclusive policies at the beginning of its board meetings, just before introducing the month's prayer giver.

Justice Kagan also believed that Greece's policies favored one religion, and she underscored the importance of public institutions representing all citizens:

I respectfully dissent from the Court's opinion because I think the Town of Greece's prayer practices violate that norm of religious equality—the breathtakingly generous constitutional idea that our public institutions belong no less to the Buddhist or Hindu than to the Methodist or Episcopalian. . . . And I believe that pluralism and inclusion in a town hall can satisfy the constitutional requirement of neutrality; such a forum need not become a religion-free zone.

Implications of the Case

- This case expanded opportunities for religious content to be included more regularly in the public sphere. It differs from the precedent set in *Marsh v. Chambers* (1983) when the Court ruled that a publicly employed chaplain could offer a prayer at the beginning of Nebraska's legislative session. In *Greece v. Galloway*, private citizens offered prayers, but the content was more clearly associated with one religion.
- It is unclear if this ruling will eventually be tested in public schools, where the controlling precedent (*Lee v. Weisman*) banned prayer in public school graduations and other school-wide events.
- This ruling shows how the establishment clause's application has varied widely in courts with conservative and liberal majorities. This schism reflects the deep divisions in America about the proper role of religion in public life.

Freedom of Religion Case Timeline

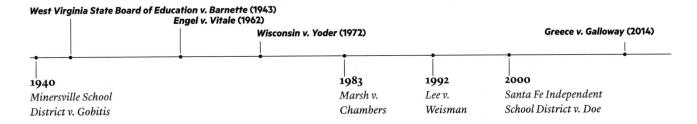

West Virginia State Board of Education v. Barnette (1943)
Engel v. Vitale (1962)
Wisconsin v. Yoder (1972)
Greece v. Galloway (2014)

1940
Minersville School District v. Gobitis

1983
Marsh v. Chambers

1992
Lee v. Weisman

2000
Santa Fe Independent School District v. Doe

Summary of Main Points

LOR-2: Provisions of the U.S. Constitution's Bill of Rights are continually being interpreted to balance the power of government and the civil liberties of individuals.

These cases span 70 years of American history and a wide range of thought in the application of the freedom of religion. Jefferson's "wall of separation" never applied to state and local governments until well after the passage of the Fourteenth Amendment. Many states required all citizens to pay taxes to the dominant church or churches, and overtly religious prayers were included in school curriculums, but these policies were always controversial. Americans remembered the discord caused in Great Britain and other nations by mixing government and religion, and these government sponsorships of religion were rolled back long before the *Engel v. Vitale* case in 1962.

These constitutional clauses set the stage for an inevitable conflict, because when policy makers act to limit the addition of religion in government activities, others see this as a limit on free exercise. Since the *Engel v. Vitale* decision, policy makers have found a variety of ways to bring religion back into the public sphere, culminating with *Greece v. Galloway*.

In terms of free exercise, *Engel v. Vitale* and *Wisconsin v. Yoder* expanded religious freedom in significant ways. Citizens cannot be required to do many things that they believe contradict their religious beliefs, such as saluting a flag or attending school.

One thing is certain in regard to this complicated topic: we have not seen the end of important cases dealing with both establishment and free exercise. The courts will continue to reinterpret how these important freedoms apply to our ever-changing society.

Assessing Student Understanding

1.   Explain the two parts of the First Amendment that deal with religion.

2.   From the cases above, offer one example of governmental behavior regarding religion that is constitutional and one that is unconstitutional.

3.   Why is the free exercise of religion, like other freedoms, not absolute? Give an example of a law that has been found to be constitutional in limiting religious freedom.

Questions for Class Discussion and Debate

1.   What limitations, if any, should be placed on holiday displays on public land?

2.   Why is school prayer such a powerful culture war issue? Are there any compromises that could come closer to satisfying both sides?

3.   After *Greece v. Galloway*, has the Court gone too far in including religion in public life? If so, what is the proper balance? Or has it not gone far enough and other restrictions should be overturned?

Cluster 5: The Doctrine of Selective Incorporation

The Big Issues

The doctrine of selective incorporation is the process by which the states are held responsible to uphold the liberties in the Bill of Rights through the requirements of the Fourteenth Amendment on a case-by-case basis. In 1833, after hearing *Barron v. Baltimore*, the Supreme Court ruled that state governments had no obligation to uphold the liberties in the Bill of Rights. The Bill of Rights was originally written as a form of protections against the abuses of the central government. With the passage of the Fourteenth Amendment in 1868, Congress attempted to extend those liberties to include protections from the actions of all levels of government. Their intent was thwarted for decades as many states, often with the cooperation of national policy makers, continued to deny basic constitutional rights and liberties to many of their citizens. Slowly, the Court began to reverse its view of the Fourteenth Amendment. In the 1960s, during the Warren Court, selective incorporation began to move much more quickly, and citizens gained many new protections against the actions of state and local governments. The most recent act of incorporation was of the Second Amendment in 2010 with the decision in *McDonald v. Chicago* (2010).

The cases in this grouping are examples of important incorporation cases, but they are far from the only ones. Approximately two-thirds of the cases in this booklet and two-thirds of the so-called core cases that the College Board has identified in the U.S. Government and Politics framework hold the states accountable to extend a portion of the Bill of Rights to their citizens. For example, in the previous section on the freedom of religion, all of the cases other than *Greece v. Galloway* (2014) incorporated aspects of either the free exercise or the establishment clause of the First Amendment.

Legal scholars refer to incorporation being "selective," meaning that it has taken place in a piecemeal manner and implying that there are parts that have not been incorporated, but this term is somewhat deceptive. All of the important parts of the Bill of Rights have been incorporated, and the exceptions are not typically part of public policy. For example, the Third Amendment prohibition against the government forcibly stationing troops in the private homes of citizens has never been incorporated because there is no instance of the government attempting to do this.

The cases in this grouping deal with the incorporation of the Second Amendment and of procedural due process in the Fourth, Fifth, and Sixth Amendments.

Constitutional Connections

Second Amendment

A well regulated militia, being necessary to the security of a free state, the right of the people to keep and bear arms, shall not be infringed.

Fourth Amendment

The right of the people to be secure in their persons, houses, papers, and effects, against unreasonable searches and seizures, shall not be violated, and no warrants shall issue, but upon probable cause, supported by oath or affirmation, and particularly describing the place to be searched, and the persons or things to be seized.

Fifth Amendment

No person shall be held to answer for a capital, or otherwise infamous crime, unless on a presentment or indictment of a grand jury, except in cases arising in the land or naval forces, or in the militia, when in actual service in time of war or public danger; nor shall any person be subject for the same offense to be twice put in jeopardy of life or limb; nor shall be compelled in any criminal case to be a witness against himself, nor be deprived of life, liberty, or property, without due process of law; nor shall private property be taken for public use, without just compensation.

Sixth Amendment

In all criminal prosecutions, the accused shall enjoy the right to a speedy and public trial, by an impartial jury of the state and district wherein the crime shall have been committed, which district shall have been previously ascertained by law, and to be informed of the nature and cause of the accusation; to be confronted with the witnesses against him; to have compulsory process for obtaining witnesses in his favor, and to have the assistance of counsel for his defense.

Fourteenth Amendment, Section 1

All persons born or naturalized in the United States, and subject to the jurisdiction thereof, are citizens of the United States and of the State wherein they reside. No State shall make or enforce any law which shall abridge the privileges or immunities of citizens of the United States; nor shall any State deprive any person of life, liberty, or property, without due process of law; nor deny to any person within its jurisdiction the equal protection of the laws.

CORE CASES

Mapp v. Ohio (1961)

Key Facts of the Case

- On May 23, 1957, in Cleveland, Ohio, police officers burst into the home of Dollree Mapp in search of a suspect wanted for questioning. They claimed to have a search warrant, but it was never produced in court.
- The suspect was apprehended and then the police ransacked Mapp's home. While searching small spaces such as drawers and trunks, officers found obscene material and betting slips, which were both illegal.
- Under Ohio law, Mapp was convicted of possessing obscene material. She appealed her decision under her First Amendment freedom of expression rights, but the Court never took up this issue. Instead, the manner of the search and the evidence it produced became the central question in this case.

Constitutional Question

Do prosecutors have the right to use evidence not obtained with a proper search warrant in court?

Majority Opinion

In a 6–3 decision, the Court ruled that evidence from an illegal search cannot be used in court. In his majority opinion, Justice Tom Clark ruled that the time to end the discrepancy between federal and state prosecutorial standards had arrived:

> *Moreover, our holding that the exclusionary rule is an essential part of both the Fourth and Fourteenth Amendments is not only the logical dictate of prior cases, but it also makes*

very good sense. There is no war between the Constitution and common sense. Presently,
a federal prosecutor may make no use of evidence illegally seized, but a State's attorney
across the street may, although he supposedly is operating under the enforceable prohibi-
tions of the same amendment. Thus, the State, by admitting evidence unlawfully seized,
serves to encourage disobedience to the Federal Constitution which it is bound to uphold.

The majority decision also emphasized that police need probable cause in order to obtain a search warrant. Evidence that was obtained illegally must be excluded from court. (This is known as "the exclusionary rule" and "the fruits of the poison tree.")

Dissenting Opinion

In his dissenting opinion, Justice Harlan wrote that the exclusionary rule's applicability to the states had been tried just a few years earlier in *Wolf v. Colorado* (1949) and had been denied. He argued that stare decisis (the primacy of precedent) should be respected. In that case, states were allowed to set their own standards for how to apply some Fourth Amendment requirements:

I would not impose upon the States this federal exclusionary remedy. . . . Our concern
here, as it was in Wolf, is not with the desirability of that rule, but only with the question
whether the States are Constitutionally free to follow it or not as they may themselves
determine, and the relevance of the disparity of views among the States on this point lies
simply in the fact that the judgment involved is a debatable one.

Implications of the Case

- Search warrants must be specific. If police are searching for a person, they may not search drawers, suitcases, and photo albums, as they did in Dollree Mapp's home.
- Eventually, the laws banning the possession of obscene material would be struck down as violating the First Amendment.
- In many situations a search warrant is not needed. For example, police are allowed to gather and prosecutors are allowed to use evidence that was "in plain sight" or that was the result of a "good faith" error.
- In many situations, warrantless searches are allowed of automobile drivers, their passengers, and of the vehicles themselves.
- Case law that produces both exceptions to and reaffirmations of *Mapp v. Ohio* (1961) take place regularly. Obtaining evidence properly is a complex activity, and police officers need a great deal of training in order to do their jobs effectively.
- There are many other sets of Fourth Amendment issues that are still being debated, including the National Security Agency's data collection from phone and internet, and drug testing in schools and at work.

Gideon v. Wainwright (1963)

Key Facts of the Case

- Clarence Earl Gideon was charged with breaking into a poolroom with the intent to commit a misdemeanor.
- He could not afford an attorney and requested a court-appointed attorney. Florida's policy was to provide an attorney to poor defendants only in murder cases and rejected Gideon's request.
- Florida's case against Gideon was based on one unreliable witness, and Gideon did a reasonably good job defending himself, but he was found guilty and was sentenced to five years in prison.
- Gideon continued his legal efforts from prison, including an appeal to the Supreme Court in forma pauperis (the form of a poor person). His pencil-written appeal

was granted certiorari or cert, meaning that the Supreme Court agreed to hear his appeal. He then received legal representation from some of the nation's top constitutional attorneys.

- In *Betts v. Brady* (1942), the Court decided that states were under no obligation to provide attorneys to poor defendants who are competent. Indigent defendants who were illiterate or unable to understand their situation were provided with government-appointed attorneys in state courts, and federal courts were already bound by the Fifth and Sixth Amendments to provide attorneys to all defendants who could not afford to hire their own.

Constitutional Question

Does the Sixth Amendment require states to provide an attorney to indigent defendants in all criminal cases?

Majority Opinion

In a unanimous decision, the Court decided in favor of Gideon and fully incorporated the right to counsel provision of the Sixth Amendment. In the majority and concurring opinions, justices pointed to many of the criminal rights that already had been extended to defendants in state courts through the Fourteenth Amendment, such as the Eighth Amendment's ban on cruel and unusual punishment and the Fifth Amendment's restrictions on the taking of private property. Justice Douglas wrote, "That the Sixth Amendment requires appointment of counsel in 'all criminal prosecutions' is clear both from the language of the Amendment and from this Court's interpretation."

Dissenting Opinion

There was no dissent.

Implications of the Case

- Across the nation, defendants who had been incarcerated without legal assistance were released from prison or retried. Pending and future criminal defendants were guaranteed the right to an attorney.
- Unlike the exclusionary rule, the right to counsel has only been strengthened and affirmed.
- Many issues remain in terms of funding public defender programs. Public defenders are often overworked and underpaid, and politicians are reluctant to seek more funding for programs to defend accused criminals.
- Gideon's case was retried in Florida, and with the help of an attorney, he was acquitted.

Miranda v. Arizona (1966)

Key Facts of the Case

- Ernesto Miranda was arrested for rape, kidnapping, and murder.
- While held at the police station, he was questioned for two hours without being advised of his rights. Miranda confessed to the crime and was sentenced to 20–30 years in prison.

Constitutional Question

Does police questioning of suspects who have not been advised of their right to counsel violate the Fifth Amendment's protections against self-incrimination?

Majority Opinion

In a 5-4 decision, the Court voided Miranda's conviction and set guidelines for arrest that became known as the Miranda rights or Mirandizing a suspect. Upon arrest, suspects must be advised of their right to an attorney and their right to remain silent and that anything they say is admissible evidence.

Unlike the precedents to this case, which stressed the Sixth Amendment right to an attorney, Chief Justice Warren's majority opinion focused on the Fifth Amendment's protections against self-incrimination. He wrote that "the prosecution may not use statements, whether exculpatory or inculpatory, stemming from custodial interrogation of the defendant unless it demonstrates the use of procedural safeguards effective to secure the privilege against self-incrimination."

The majority viewed custodial interrogations, even when force or threats of force were not used, as a source of many false confessions. Chief Justice Warren had read many police training manuals about the use of custodial interrogation. He summarized their approach:

> To highlight the isolation and unfamiliar surroundings, the manuals instruct the police to display an air of confidence in the suspect's guilt and, from outward appearance, to maintain only an interest in confirming certain details. The guilt of the subject is to be posited as a fact. The interrogator should direct his comments toward the reasons why the subject committed the act, rather than court failure by asking the subject whether he did it. Like other men, perhaps the subject has had a bad family life, had an unhappy childhood, had too much to drink, had an unrequited desire for women. The officers are instructed to minimize the moral seriousness of the offense, to cast blame on the victim or on society.

Dissenting Opinion

Four justices believed that the Court had gone too far in maligning the police. Justice Clark wrote the following:

> Moreover, the examples of police brutality mentioned by the Court are rare exceptions to the thousands of cases that appear every year in the law reports. The police agencies— all the way from municipal and state forces to the federal bureaus—are responsible for law enforcement and public safety in this country. I am proud of their efforts, which, in my view, are not fairly characterized by the Court's opinion.

Justice Clark considered the Miranda rules arbitrary and believed that they could result in a higher crime rate. He wrote, "The thrust of the new rules is to negate all pressures, to reinforce the nervous or ignorant suspect, and ultimately to discourage any confession at all."

Implications of the Case

- Miranda was retried, found guilty without using his confession as evidence, and served a prison sentence. A few years after being paroled, he was stabbed to death in a bar fight. His killer was read his Miranda rights upon arrest.
- The courts have made many exceptions to the Miranda rights over the years. For example, incriminating statements made by an individual who is not in custody are admissible in court, as are statements made to police informants and statements made in the process of being arrested. Also, statements made to police during emergencies or while there is a threat to public safety, such as trying to locate a weapon, are admissible.
- When Congress added language to a crime bill that attempted to nullify the Miranda rights, the Court ruled that this legislation was unconstitutional. The Court has

significantly weakened Miranda rights, but it has retained the power to interpret a defendant's constitutional rights.

- False confessions during custodial interrogation still take place on a regular basis. One famous example involved a group of five Black and Hispanic youths who were arrested for a brutal rape in New York's Central Park in 1989. They were held for up to 30 hours of interrogation before making partial confessions in the hope that they would be able to go home. After spending 41 years in prison collectively, they were released and exonerated. DNA evidence and an unforced confession identified the true rapist and murderer, a serial criminal who was already in prison.
- The impact of *Miranda v. Arizona* is still being studied and debated.

McDonald v. Chicago (2010)

Key Facts of the Case

- A Chicago law banned handguns.
- Otis McDonald's home had been broken into multiple times. He owned licensed hunting guns, but he believed that they were too unwieldy for self-defense during a home invasion.
- The city refused his request to license a handgun. With other plaintiffs, he brought suit against the city of Chicago.
- Two years earlier in a highly controversial 5–4 decision, the Court ruled in *D.C. v. Heller* (2008) that there was a Second and Fourteenth Amendment right for an individual to possess a gun. This decision reversed precedent from four earlier cases that had interpreted the Second Amendment as ensuring gun rights to authorized state and local militias, not to individuals. Because the District of Columbia is a federally controlled region, *D.C. v. Heller* did not incorporate the Second Amendment.
- Before hearing *McDonald v. Chicago*, the Court received a high number of amicus curiae briefs, including appeals made by hundreds of members of Congress and dozens of states.

Constitutional Question

Do individuals have a Second and Fourteenth Amendment right to possess firearms?

Majority Opinion

By a 5–4 decision, the Court incorporated the Second Amendment and struck down Chicago's handgun ban. Writing for the majority, Justice Alito saw the incorporation of the Second Amendment as a natural continuation of the long-established trend to prevent states from violating the Bill of Rights:

> *With this framework in mind, we now turn directly to the question whether the Second Amendment right to keep and bear arms is incorporated in the concept of due process. In answering that question, as just explained, we must decide whether the right to keep and bear arms is fundamental to our scheme of ordered liberty . . . or as we have said in a related context, whether this right is "deeply rooted in this Nation's history and tradition."*

Justice Alito cited the need for citizens who live in high-crime areas to be able to defend themselves. He accused the dissenters in this case of being inconsistent in their application of the Fourteenth Amendment:

> *Justice Breyer is correct that incorporation of the Second Amendment right will to some extent limit the legislative freedom of the States, but this is always true when a Bill of Rights provision is incorporated. Incorporation always restricts experimentation and local variations, but that has not stopped the Court from incorporating virtually every other provision of the Bill of Rights.*

Dissenting Opinion

Justice Stevens wrote that gun regulations were the proper domain of state and local government and that the federal judiciary should not reverse established precedent. "Petitioners have given us no reason to believe that the interest in keeping and bearing arms entails any special need for judicial lawmaking, or that federal judges are more qualified to craft appropriate rules than the people's elected representatives."

In a separate dissent, Justice Breyer echoed the opinion of the three other dissenting justices. He believed that the Court had erred in *D.C. v. Heller* and that the mistaken interpretation of the Second Amendment continued in *McDonald v. Chicago*:

> *The Second Amendment says: "A well-regulated Militia, being necessary to the security of a free State, the right of the people to keep and bear Arms, shall not be infringed."*
> *Two years ago, in District of Columbia v. Heller . . . the Court rejected the pre-existing judicial consensus that the Second Amendment was primarily concerned with the need to maintain a "well-regulated Militia."*

Implications of the Case

- There is a wide variety of state and local restrictions on gun ownership that may be subject to challenge in courts or legislatures. For example, can a state that bans concealed carry prohibit an individual from carrying a gun who has a concealed carry permit from a different state?
- In general, blue states continue to pass gun restrictions and red states continue to loosen gun regulations. The last major federal gun regulations were passed in 1994, and many parts of the bill, including a ban on assault weapons, have expired.
- The Court has a mixed record on Second Amendment cases since 2010. For example, the Court upheld a Massachusetts law requiring gunlocks and struck down a Chicago law requiring shooting range practice for gun owners while also banning shooting ranges within city limits.

The Doctrine of Selective Incorporation Case Timeline

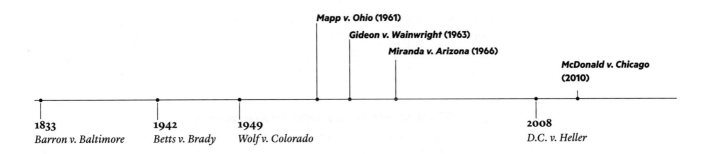

Summary of Main Points

LOR-3: Protections of the Bill of Rights have been selectively incorporated by way of the Fourteenth Amendment's "due process" clause to prevent state infringement of basic liberties.

These four cases represent important examples, but they are not the only examples of selective incorporation. The only amendments that have avoided at least partial incorporation are the Third and the Tenth. The Third Amendment has avoided this application because there have been no instances when the government has forced citizens to house soldiers. The Tenth, or states' rights, Amendment has never been incorporated because it is a statement about state sovereignty.

This one long sentence in the Fourteenth Amendment continues to be a guidepost and flashpoint of U.S. policy, particularly regarding issues related to federalism: "No State shall make or enforce any law which shall abridge the privileges or immunities of citizens of the United States; nor shall any State deprive any person of life, liberty, or property, without due process of law; nor deny to any person within its jurisdiction the equal protection of the laws."

The writers of this amendment intended to extend constitutional rights and liberties to all citizens, even in situations when states were acting as the agents of oppression. During and after Reconstruction, the Supreme Court thwarted the power of the Fourteenth Amendment by interpreting its meaning very narrowly. As a result, states were allowed to continue practices such as segregation, laws limiting the freedom of speech and religion, and laws limiting the due process rights of defendants.

Mapp v. Ohio incorporated parts of the Fourth Amendment. *Gideon v. Wainwright* incorporated the Sixth Amendment's right to counsel. *Miranda v. Arizona* incorporated Fifth Amendment protections against self-incrimination, and *McDonald v. Chicago* incorporated the Second Amendment.

More than incorporating these amendments, these cases expanded and clarified the meaning of the amendments themselves. The Fourth Amendment's prohibition against unreasonable searches became a ban on using evidence in court that was obtained without using proper procedures. The Fifth Amendment's self-incrimination protections became a source of caution for police in conducting interrogations. The Sixth Amendment's right to counsel became a right for poor defendants to acquire legal counsel at the state's expense. The Second Amendment's ambiguous wording about militias and arms became a specific right for individuals to possess guns. Other than the right to an attorney for a criminal defendant, which is an important practice in democracies around the world, all of these changes have been controversial and will, undoubtedly, be further refined with future cases and future legislation.

Assessing Student Understanding

1. What does it mean to incorporate the Bill of Rights? Give two examples of incorporation from the cases above.

2. Explain the exclusionary rule. Explain its reasoning and one reason why it has faced criticism.

3. Give three examples of the rights possessed by accused criminals in the United States that stem from the Fifth and Sixth Amendments that were not addressed by the cases in this group.

Questions for Class Discussion and Debate

1. The police have a right to search an individual who is being arrested. Should that search extend to the contents of a cell phone or does the exclusionary rule apply?

2. Why would innocent people confess to crimes during custodial interrogation? How can custodial interrogation be a form of coercion even when no force or threat of force is used?

3. What do you think the intent of the Second Amendment was? What type of state gun restrictions should be viewed as constitutional?

Cluster 6: Privacy and Due Process

The Big Issues

In crafting the Fourth Amendment, the framers provided protection for citizens against unreasonable searches in "their persons, houses, papers and effects." They did not mention pregnancy, urine, or cell phones, as the following cases do.

The word "privacy" also never appears in the Constitution, but it has come to be recognized as a right in certain situations. The Court has clearly indicated that losing the right to privacy without the due process of law is a violation of the Fourth and Fourteenth Amendments.

The cases in this cluster represent different applications of the right of privacy. The last and most recent case, *Riley v. California* (2014), is the most traditional. It involved a search made by a government agent, the police. The crafters of the Fourth Amendment clearly intended it to be a restraint on the powers of government. In the middle case, *Board of Education of Independent School District No. 92 of Pottawatomie County v. Earls* (2002), a high school is the agent making a search with the goal of student safety. Is that covered by the Fourth Amendment?

The earliest case's relationship to the Fourth Amendment is the most controversial. Some legal scholars have linked a woman's right of privacy in making decisions regarding child birth and contraception to parts of the First, Third, Fourth, Fifth, Ninth, and Fourteenth Amendments. *Roe v. Wade* (1973) was an important continuation in the now well-established belief that the Bill of Rights protects a zone of privacy for Americans. Beyond agreeing there is a zone of privacy, the nation is deeply split on how and where it exists.

It all began in 1965 with *Griswold v. Connecticut*, a case that struck down a state law that had criminalized the distribution of birth control to married couples. In that case, seven justices recognized a marital zone of privacy that existed beyond the power of legislatures. Writing for the majority, Justice Douglas said, "The present case, then, concerns a relationship lying within the zone of privacy created by several fundamental constitutional guarantees. And it concerns a law which, in forbidding the use of contraceptives, rather than regulating their manufacture or sale, seeks to achieve its goals by means having a maximum destructive impact upon that relationship."

Dissenters in *Griswold v. Connecticut* argued that this concept of privacy was too broad, too vague, and would lead to other policy challenges that rightly belonged to legislatures. It didn't take long for this heated culture war battle to get even more contentious. In 1971, the high court began hearing its first blockbuster abortion case, *Roe v. Wade*, which challenged abortion laws in 46 states.

Cases that involve privacy and the Fourth Amendment include areas of settled law and areas that will be impacted by future landmark decisions. As culture and technologies evolve, there are sure to be more cases that test the rights of privacy in ways that the framers could never have envisioned. Justice Alito has asked whether, in a nation where tens of millions of citizens post intimate details of their lives online, is there even an expectation of privacy?

Constitutional Connections

Fourth Amendment

The right of the people to be secure in their persons, houses, papers, and effects, against unreasonable searches and seizures, shall not be violated, and no Warrants shall issue, but upon probable cause, supported by Oath or affirmation, and particularly describing the place to be searched, and the persons or things to be seized.

Fourteenth Amendment, Section 1

All persons born or naturalized in the United States, and subject to the jurisdiction thereof, are citizens of the United States and of the State wherein they reside. No State shall make or enforce any law which shall abridge the privileges or immunities of citizens of the United States; nor shall any State deprive any person of life, liberty, or property, without due process of law; nor deny to any person within its jurisdiction the equal protection of the laws.

CORE CASES

Roe v. Wade (1973)

Key Facts of the Case

- When this case came to the Supreme Court in 1973, legal abortions were only available in four states: Hawaii, Alaska, Washington, and New York.
- State laws against abortion stem from English common law. Forms of abortion were practiced throughout history and, until medical improvements in the twentieth century, were always very dangerous to the health of the mother. Abortion has always been an emotionally charged issue that has sparked religious, ethical, and legal controversy.
- In 1969, at age 21, Norma McCorvey sought both a legal and an illegal abortion in the state of Texas during her third pregnancy. Her request for a legal abortion was based on a false claim that she had been raped. It was rejected by the state because of a lack of evidence. Her search for an illegal abortion failed because Texas had found and closed the illegal clinics. She sought the services of two attorneys who did not resolve her situation, but would eventually argue her case in the Supreme Court. In order to protect McCorvey's identity she was referred to as "Jane Roe." By the time the case was heard, she had given birth and her baby had been adopted.
- Roe's attorneys argued that the Texas laws against abortion violated a woman's constitutional rights.

Constitutional Question

Do rights listed in the Bill of Rights, extended to the states through the Fourteenth Amendment, protect a woman's privacy from state interference when deciding to have an abortion?

Majority Opinion

In a 7–2 decision, the justices struck down the Texas law that prevented Roe's abortion and abortion laws in 45 other states. This decision established a trimester system in determining a state's ability to regulate abortion. During the first trimester, or three months, a woman had complete freedom to choose an abortion. During the next trimester, states could create more regulations, and in the final trimester states could ban almost all abortions.

In a concurring decision, Justice White explained why a women's right to choose an abortion in the first trimester stems from the Fourteenth Amendment's due process clause:

> *This right of privacy, whether it be founded in the Fourteenth Amendment's concept of personal liberty and restrictions upon state action, as we feel it is, or, as the District*

Court determined, in the Ninth Amendment's reservation of rights to the people, is broad enough to encompass a woman's decision whether or not to terminate her pregnancy. The detriment that the State would impose upon the pregnant woman by denying this choice altogether is apparent. Specific and direct harm medically diagnosable even in early pregnancy may be involved. Maternity, or additional offspring, may force upon the woman a distressful life and future. Psychological harm may be imminent. Mental and physical health may be taxed by child care. There is also the distress, for all concerned, associated with the unwanted child, and there is the problem of bringing a child into a family already unable, psychologically and otherwise, to care for it.

Dissenting Opinion

The Court's newest justice and future chief justice, William Rehnquist, wrote the dissenting opinion in which he pointed out all the state laws that banned abortion at the time the Fourteenth Amendment was passed. He also viewed this issue's relationship to the Fourth Amendment as far-fetched:

Even if there were a plaintiff in this case capable of litigating the issue which the Court decides, I would reach a conclusion opposite to that reached by the Court. I have difficulty in concluding, as the Court does, that the right of "privacy" is involved in this case. Texas, by the statute here challenged, bars the performance of a medical abortion by a licensed physician on a plaintiff such as Roe. A transaction resulting in an operation such as this is not "private" in the ordinary usage of that word. Nor is the "privacy" that the Court finds here even a distant relative of the freedom from searches and seizures protected by the Fourth Amendment to the Constitution.

Implications of the Case

- Although the basic logic of *Roe v. Wade* remains intact, conservative states have found many ways to regulate and discourage abortions including mandatory waiting periods, mandatory ultrasounds, and requiring doctors to read prepared scripts to patients that describe a fetus's ability to feel pain. According to the National Institute of Health, states have passed 300 restrictions on abortion since 2010. The rate at which women sought abortions climbed sharply after Roe, but it has now fallen back to levels that are similar to the 1970s before abortion was legalized in all states. This sharp decline is the result of many complex factors including new regulations, the declining number of clinics that perform abortions, the availability of other forms of contraception, and falling rates of teen sexual activity.
- Abortion rights remain one of the most controversial issues in the United States. On the anniversary of the *Roe* decision each January, tens of thousands of Americans come to Washington from all states to participate in the March for Life, a rally seeking to end abortion in all states. State regulations against abortion continue to be passed and the Supreme Court may receive a case with the right fact pattern for the conservative majority that is currently on the Court to overturn *Roe*.
- As medicine has advanced, fetal viability (the time during a pregnancy when the baby can survive outside the womb) comes earlier in the pregnancy. Many consider the trimester system established in *Roe v. Wade* outdated.
- Overturning Roe would cause a constitutional conundrum for movements like March for Life. Now, the pro-life movement argues in favor of the states' right to ban abortion under police powers and against the application of the Fourteenth Amendment to women's liberty in being able to determine the fate of their own pregnancies. If *Roe* is reversed, many blue states will keep abortion legal. Pro-lifers who seek to end abortion in those states may argue against state rights and in favor of the application of the Fourteenth Amendment to fetuses.

Board of Education of Independent School District No. 92 of Pottawatomie County v. Earls (2002)

Key Facts of the Case

- In a 6–3 decision in *Veronia School District v. Acton* (1995), the Court ruled that random drug testing of high school athletes was constitutional. In order to counter drug use and protect students during potentially dangerous activities such as sports, the Court viewed that the school district had a "legitimate governmental interest" and that the collection of urine samples in a public restroom had minimal impacts on student expectations of privacy.
- Tecumseh, Oklahoma, adopted a drug testing policy that included students who participated in all extracurricular activities.
- Lindsay Earls was a 16-year-old junior at Tecumseh High School, about 40 miles southeast of Oklahoma City. A self-admitted "goodie two shoes," she participated in a school choir, the marching band, and the quiz bowl team. She was summoned for drug testing, complied, and passed. After doing so, she brought suit against the school district claiming that her Fourth Amendment rights had been violated.

Constitutional Question

Does the state have the right to require students who participate in extracurricular activities to comply with random drug testing, or is this an unreasonable search?

Majority Opinion

The Court ruled 5–4 that Tecumseh High School's drug testing policy was constitutional. In the majority opinion, Justice Clarence Thomas wrote that the Court's judgment was that drug testing promotes a valid governmental interest with minimal violations of privacy and was therefore not a violation of the Fourth Amendment:

> The Student Activities Drug Testing Policy implemented by the Board of Education of Independent School District No. 92 of Pottawatomie County (School District) requires all students who participate in competitive extracurricular activities to submit to drug testing. Because this Policy reasonably serves the School District's important interest in detecting and preventing drug use among its students, we hold that it is constitutional.

Affirming earlier school law decisions, Thomas pointed out that probable cause is not at issue. "Given that the School District's Policy is not in any way related to the conduct of criminal investigations . . . respondents do not contend that the School District requires probable cause before testing students for drug use."

The Court assessed the constitutionality of the school's practice, not its effectiveness. In a concurring opinion, Justice Breyer wrote, "In upholding the constitutionality of the Policy, we express no opinion as to its wisdom."

Dissenting Opinion

Three of the four dissenting justices saw this case as furthering the incorrect decision in *Veronia School District v. Acton*. The only dissenting justice who was new to the Court since 1995, Ruth Bader Ginsberg, pointed out that the Court had also abandoned its logic in *Veronia* when it had condoned drug testing for student athletes in high-risk sports. The same risk of physical injury is not a factor on the quiz bowl team.

Justice Ginsberg cited precedents that had backed students' constitutional liberties such as *Tinker v. Des Moines Independent Community School District* (1969) and *West Virginia State BOE v. Barnette* (1943). Her disappointment in the direction that the Court took in student constitutional rights cases was accompanied by skepticism that the school district's policy was an effective tool in combating student drug use. She cited a study that said that students who were involved in extracurricular activities were 49 percent less likely to use drugs and "Even if students might be deterred from drug use in order to preserve their extracurricular eligibility, it is at least as likely that other students might forgo their extracurricular involvement in order to avoid detection of their drug use."

She recommended that schools "teach by example" by avoiding symbolic measures that diminish constitutional protections.

Implications of the Case

- This case furthered the trend of diminishing student rights that began before *Veronia School District v. Acton*. In *T.L.O. v. New Jersey* (1984), the Court ruled that the police did not need probable cause to search a student's bag, and in *Hazelwood School District v. Kuhlmeier* (1987), the Court granted schools unlimited power in censoring school-sponsored student publications.
- About 18 percent of public high schools in the United States used some form of student drug testing in 2015. Random drug testing policies range from testing students in high-risk sports to testing all students (even though testing all students is unconstitutional).
- Random drug testing of students has been resisted by most schools for a variety of reasons. It has not been proven to be effective in lowering the overall rate of teen drug use, and it is very costly. Also, skilled teachers and school administrators have many other means of identifying students who use drugs.

Riley v. California (2014)

Key Facts of the Case

- On August 22, 2009, David Leon Riley was pulled over for expired registration tags.
- The arresting officer found that Riley was driving with a suspended license. A routine and permissible vehicle search after arrest revealed two loaded handguns under the hood.
- Police officers are allowed to take all personal possessions from a suspect upon arrest, and they did so when Riley was arrested. His cell phone was taken and searched.
- Police found photographs linking Riley to a gang that had been involved in a shooting and other crimes. Ballistics tests revealed that one of the guns under Riley's hood had been used in the shooting.
- Evidence of gang membership under California law meant that Riley could face a longer prison sentence.

Constitutional Question

Was the admission of evidence from Riley's cell phone a violation of his Fourth Amendment rights to be free from unreasonable searches?

Majority Opinion

Chief Justice Roberts wrote for a unanimous Court in finding that the actions of the police were unconstitutional. He focused on how the large and varied contents of a cell phone resemble the "papers and effects" referred to in the Fourth Amendment:

> *The storage capacity of cell phones has several interrelated consequences for privacy. First, a cell phone collects in one place many distinct types of information—an address, a note, a prescription, a bank statement, a video—that reveal much more in combination than any isolated record. Second, a cell phone's capacity allows even just*

one type of information to convey far more than previously possible. The sum of an individual's private life can be reconstructed through a thousand photographs labeled with dates, locations, and descriptions; the same cannot be said of a photograph or two of loved ones tucked into a wallet.

Also, the contents of a cell phone pose no immediate risk to the police officers making an arrest. A great deal of cell phone data is stored remotely, and the government conceded that to access this information a search warrant would be needed. The Court ruled that police should obtain a search warrant before searching any content on a cell phone.

Dissenting Opinion

There was no dissent.

Implications of the Case

- State courts and appellate courts around the country had come to different conclusions about whether the contents of a cell phone could be searched after arrest without a warrant. This type of discrepancy greatly increases the likelihood that the Supreme Court will hear a case in order to set a national standard.
- In past cases that examined the admissibility of evidence obtained during vehicle stops or after arrests, the Court had been split, often in unusual ways. In *Gant v. Arizona* (2009), a case that tested the admissibility of evidence obtained after a vehicle stop and an arrest, Justice Ginsberg joined Justices Thomas and Scalia in a 5–4 majority. This unusual split in the Court reflects the fact that opinions about governmental searches, like those sanctioned by the USA PATRIOT Act, are not along traditional partisan lines.
- Reaching a 9–0 decision was a major achievement for the Robert's Court.
- Police officers are still allowed to turn off a cell phone after arrest to try to prevent remote wiping. They can search a cell phone case for other contents, and in rare circumstances, when the cell phone is being used to activate weapons and endanger the public, they will still search it without a warrant. Also, they can get a search warrant in as little as 15 minutes.
- For David Leon Riley himself, this decision made no difference. The prosecutors had enough legally obtained evidence linking him to the shooting and other crimes that his 15-year prison sentence continued after his Supreme Court victory.

Privacy and Due Process Case Timeline

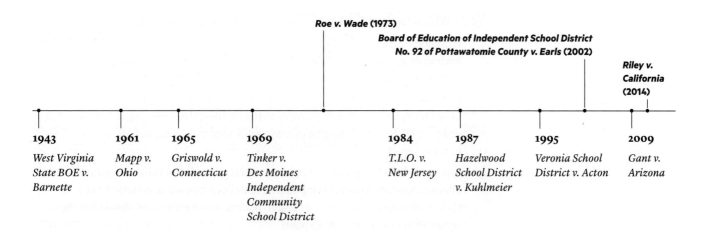

Summary of Main Points

LOR-3: Protections of the Bill of Rights have been selectively incorporated by way of the Fourteenth Amendment's "due process" clause to prevent state infringement of basic liberties.

The incorporation of the Bill of Rights has taken place in a case-by-case, amendment-by-amendment manner. Starting with *Mapp v. Ohio* (1961), the Court incorporated (applied to the states) a prohibition against state courts using evidence that was obtained improperly. Starting with *Griswold v. Connecticut* (1965), the Court began to strike down state laws that invaded their citizens' zones of privacy.

The Fourth Amendment's powerful and brief prohibition against "unreasonable searches" has resulted in reams of legal pleadings, case briefs, and judicial decisions. Furthermore, it is safe to bet that the parameters of what constitutes an unreasonable search will change as the Court examines more situations.

It may seem contradictory that as privacy recedes in so many situations, legal protections against unreasonable searches and legally recognized zones of privacy have solidified. Americans are free to use many types of contraceptives and to engage in a variety of sexual practices without government prosecution. The government must obtain a search warrant to use the content of our electronic files against us in court. However, we are also subject to National Security Agency eavesdropping in certain situations, and cameras record our movements in public. We regularly give up our protection against unreasonable searches when we board airplanes or attend concerts and sporting events, and a great deal of our private information is stored and traded by private companies.

Some would argue that the coexistence of greater freedoms and of more pervasive security measures are evidence of the Constitution's durability and continued applicability in situations that the framers never envisioned. However, most Americans are a lot less philosophical about these trends and, instead, experience them as critical political and legal policy issues.

Assessing Student Understanding

1. How did *Griswold v. Connecticut* establish a right of privacy? How did *Roe v. Wade* further that right?

2. Why are school officials allowed to conduct searches of students that would be considered illegal if the police performed them?

3. If evidence is obtained illegally, can it still be used in court? Explain the relationship between *Mapp v. Ohio* and *Riley v. California*.

Questions for Class Discussion and Debate

1. How does the Constitution protect a right of privacy from unreasonable searches such as drug and genetic testing? Is there a difference between drug and genetic testing? Between being tested by a private employer and by the state?

2. Schools around the nation can legally require students to go through drug testing in order to participate in extracurricular activities. Does this policy help to reduce drug use? What are examples of reasonable searches by school officials? Of unreasonable searches?

3. Is it possible to be against abortion on moral grounds but think it should be allowed constitutionally? Is it possible to believe that women should have the right to choose an abortion but also to believe that a state's legislation has the right to limit or prevent it? Explain.

Cluster 7: Equal Protection

The Big Issues

The concept of equality in the United States received a dramatic introduction in the nation's founding document in 1776. "We hold these truths to be self-evident, that all men are created equal, that they are endowed by their Creator with certain unalienable Rights, that among these are Life, Liberty and the pursuit of Happiness."

Thirteen years after Jefferson penned these words in the Declaration of Independence, the word "equal" appeared in the Constitution only to describe some of the structural elements of the Senate and of the Electoral College. The Bill of Rights added a great deal about liberty, but nothing about equality. In fact, for almost 100 years after the Declaration of Independence was signed, Jefferson's phrase remained, at best, an unfulfilled goal. Enslaved people, women, native peoples, the poor, and others lacked political and legal equality.

As Jefferson and all of the framers knew, slavery was the nation's most significant unresolved issue. After the Civil War, the concept of real equality made its first dramatic appearance in the Constitution in 1868 in the form of the Fourteenth Amendment. It guaranteed all Americans equal protection under the law.

For most of the next century, courts and states found ways to evade providing equality to African Americans, women, and other minority groups. Apart from a case in 1880 that found it was a violation of the Fourteenth Amendment to exclude African Americans from juries, the courts consistently dodged the concept of racial equality. Congress passed the Civil Rights Act of 1875 in order to give real teeth to the Fourteenth Amendment. This act required equality in public accommodations, but it was rendered powerless when the Supreme Court decided it did not apply to the actions of private citizens. The Supreme Court guaranteed the continuation of racially biased policy by governments and private businesses alike with the *Plessy v. Ferguson* (1896) "separate but equal" decision.

"Separate but equal" assured more than another half century of segregation and did nothing to promote equality. Jim Crow, the system of strict racial segregation in the South, hardened and spread. The NAACP estimates that almost 5,000 lynchings took place in the United States between 1882 and 1968. These lynchings represent an extreme lack of equal protection under the law and are exactly the type of vigilante racism that the authors of the Fourteenth Amendment were attempting to prevent.

In the twentieth century, legal pioneers began to pick apart the logic of "separate but equal" and apply the equal protection clause to the issue of race in cases involving transportation to school and admission to graduate programs. Three years after the parents of a kindergarten student from Topeka, Kansas, filed suit against the segregationist policies of the local schools, the Supreme Court heard the case of *Brown v. Board of Education* (1954). This decision reversed *Plessy v. Ferguson* and abandoned the policy of "separate but equal," but there was little immediate change for African-American schoolchildren.

It would take another case—*Brown v. Board of Education II* (1955)—to begin to design remedies and another decade or two for many school districts to put them into practice. Combined with many important laws passed by Congress, including the Civil Rights Act of 1964, equal protection under the law finally extended into many parts of African Americans' daily lives, including employment, lodging, and housing.

As the Fourteenth Amendment's equal protection clause came into play in many legal decisions in the Warren Court, more than half of the persons in the United States saw no benefit from this change. In *Reed v. Reed* (1971), the Court struck down an Idaho law that gave preference to men as administrators of estates. This was the first time the equal protection clause was used to protect women's rights. It would not be the last. In fact, equal protection has become a component of cases involving a wide range of issues, including LGBTQ rights and rights for the disabled.

The Court has also found limits to the equal protection clause. In *Milliken v. Bradley* (1974), the use of busing to integrate schools was limited to urban school districts in many areas of the United States. Also, the equal protection clause has been used successfully by plaintiffs representing the majority in cases that limit affirmative action.

Constitutional Connection

Fourteenth Amendment, Section 1

All persons born or naturalized in the United States, and subject to the jurisdiction thereof, are citizens of the United States and of the State wherein they reside. No State shall make or enforce any law which shall abridge the privileges or immunities of citizens of the United States; nor shall any State deprive any person of life, liberty, or property, without due process of law; nor deny to any person within its jurisdiction the equal protection of the laws.

CORE CASES

Reed v. Reed (1971)

Key Facts of the Case

· The state of Idaho had a law that said, "males must be preferred to females" as administrators of estates (in this context, an estate means the assets of a person who is deceased).
· After Cecil and Sally Reed separated, their son committed suicide. He died without a will and the court appointed his father as the administrator of his estate, which consisted of under $500 and a few personal possessions.
· Sally Reed appealed the decision on the grounds that the Idaho law violated her Fourteenth Amendment rights.

Constitutional Question

Did the Idaho law that gave preference to men over women as administrators of estates violate the equal protection clause of the Fourteenth Amendment?

Majority Opinion

A unanimous Court struck down the Idaho law. It was the first time the equal protection clause was applied to women's rights. Chief Justice Burger's majority opinion rejected the argument that Idaho's law was justified as a means of solving family disputes:

> *To give a mandatory preference to members of either sex over members of the other, merely to accomplish the elimination of hearings on the merits, is to make the very kind of arbitrary legislative choice forbidden by the Equal Protection Clause of the Fourteenth Amendment; and whatever may be said as to the positive values of avoiding intrafamily controversy, the choice in this context may not lawfully be mandated solely on the basis of sex.*

Dissenting Opinion

There was no dissent.

Implications of the Case

- The issue of equality for women had been on the policy agenda at many important junctures before *Reed v. Reed*. For more than 100 years, women fought for the right to vote, which was finally added to the Constitution with the Nineteenth Amendment in 1920. Although women's earnings still lag behind those of men, the Equal Pay Act of 1963 was one of the most significant laws passed during the civil rights movement.
- As a result of *Reed v. Reed*, other laws that discriminated based on sex were also struck down. For example, laws that based welfare benefits on the father's income and not the mother's and laws that gave men more control over marital property were found to violate the equal protection clause. A Social Security rule that gave widows more survivor benefits than widowers was declared unconstitutional, a change that benefited men. In 1996, in the *United States v. Virginia*, the Supreme Court ruled that exclusion of women from Virginia's elite military academy was a violation of the equal protections clause.
- Future Supreme Court justice Ruth Bader Ginsberg worked on Sally Reed's appeal.

Brown v. Board of Education (1954)

Key Facts of the Case

- Third grader Linda Brown of Topeka, Kansas, was thrilled to learn that she would be able to attend the school with many of her playmates from the integrated neighborhood where she lived. When she was rejected from the school on account of her race, her father brought suit against the school board.
- The Supreme Court combined five different cases challenging segregation from a wide variety of areas that included South Carolina, Virginia, Delaware, Washington, D.C., and Kansas. It was a class-action suit because its decision applied to thousands of school districts across the nation not directly involved with these legal actions.
- Not all of the African-American plaintiffs in this lawsuit attended schools that were blatantly unequal.

Constitutional Question

Do schools that are segregated by race violate the Fourteenth Amendment's equal protection clause?

Majority Opinion

A unified Supreme Court declared that racially segregated schools, even in the rare instance when they are provisioned equally to White majority schools, are a violation of the equal protections clause.

The vast majority of Supreme Court cases are heard in one day. Oral argument in *Brown v. Board of Education* took place over six days. The case was first argued from December 9–11, 1952, and seemed to be headed toward a divided and uncertain outcome. Justice Felix Frankfurter, who favored ending "separate but equal," convinced the Court to hear the case again in the Court's next term instead of issuing a ruling that upheld segregation.

Before the Court began its 1953–54 session, Fred Vinson, the chief justice and a supporter of "separate but equal," passed away. President Eisenhower appointed former California governor Earl Warren to replace him. From December 7–9, 1953, the Court heard reargument of the five cases know as *Brown v. Board of Education.* For the next five months, the high court worked behind the scenes to craft its opinions in this highly sensitive and hugely important case.

The legal community waited anxiously to hear the decision and anticipated a divided court. Chief Justice Earl Warren calmly read the decision to a small group of Supreme Court reporters on May 17, 1954. The first part of the decision restated the facts and the history of the cases that had been heard and did not indicate that a critical turning point in national policy had been reached. Near the end of the decision, Warren revealed the dramatic nature of the decision:

> We conclude that, in the field of public education, the doctrine of 'separate but equal' has no place. Separate educational facilities are inherently unequal. Therefore, we hold that the plaintiffs and others similarly situated for whom the actions have been brought are, by reason of the segregation complained of, deprived of the equal protection of the laws guaranteed by the Fourteenth Amendment.

To reach this conclusion, the Warren Court, in part, relied on data that had been examined in the Delaware case on the severe psychological impact of segregation. Warren wrote the following:

> Segregation of white and colored children in public schools has a detrimental effect upon the colored children. The impact is greater when it has the sanction of the law, for the policy of separating the races is usually interpreted as denoting the inferiority of the negro group. A sense of inferiority affects the motivation of a child to learn. Segregation with the sanction of law, therefore, has a tendency to retard the educational and mental development of negro children and to deprive them of some of the benefits they would receive in a racially integrated school system.

Dissenting Opinion

There was no dissent in this case.

Implications of the Case

- A year later, the Supreme Court held additional hearings in order to create guidelines for the integration of schools across the nation. In these hearings, the attorney general of the United States and the attorney generals of the states that had practiced segregation were invited to participate. This case, referred to as *Brown II*, reaffirmed *Brown v. Board of Education* unanimously and turned the details of integration efforts over to local officials who were supervised by federal courts. Warren wrote that integration should take place with "all deliberate speed."
- Many school districts in the North and the South evaded these orders, and this issue returned to the Supreme Court on other occasions. *Swann v. Charlotte-Mecklenburg Board of Education* (1971) was the beginning of the end of a great deal of the resistance to *Brown*, while *Milliken v. Bradley* limited the impact of the *Brown* decision to school districts with a documented history of racist practices.
- Some southern states had promised to build and supply schools for African Americans that were truly equal as long as they were not forced to integrate. When federal courts began issuing desegregation orders, these promises vanished and many communities resisted by shutting down all schools.
- To many students of American history and politics, *Brown v. Board of Education* seems to be a moment of progress that appears from nowhere. Nothing could be further from the truth. Generations of mostly African-American attorneys toiled relentlessly, often sacrificing their own health and safety, to build the legal framework that led to the *Brown* decision and the reversal of *Plessy v. Ferguson*. Charles

Houston, known to many as the man who killed Jim Crow, founded an elite law school at Howard University, one of the nation's most significant historically Black colleges. Although he did not live to see the end of legal segregation, one of his students, Thurgood Marshall, was the lead attorney for Brown and the first African-American justice on the Supreme Court.

Milliken v. Bradley (1974)

Key Facts of the Case

- As the city of Detroit struggled to implement desegregation policies, the city's percentage of African-American schoolchildren skyrocketed. Between 1940 and 1970, half a million African Americans, most emigrants from the Jim Crow South, moved to Detroit. The city's population went from roughly 9 percent to 45 percent African American.
- Partly as a result of this shift, there were not enough White children left in Detroit to integrate the schools.
- Many African-American-majority schools had substandard conditions. Resources and facilities were inferior, class sizes reached 50 students, and some classes were housed in trailers.
- The NAACP brought legal action against Detroit and the state of Michigan, arguing that 53 suburban communities should be required to participate in a massive busing plan that would create integrated schools.
- Plaintiffs argued that the segregation of schools in Michigan was a result of a lot more than just "White flight" (the tendency of middle-class White Americans to move to suburban districts as African-American families moved to the cities). They contended that a complex pattern of new school construction, various housing situations, mortgage restrictions, and real estate practices created all-White and all-Black communities. They argued that the state of Michigan was involved in the policies that created this segregation.
- Lower courts ruled in favor of the NAACP-backed plan.
- This case carried great significance for desegregation efforts in the North. Its decision impacted schools in dozens of major urban areas.

Constitutional Question

Do federal courts have the right to require public schools in towns and cities with no documented history of discrimination to participate in metropolitan desegregation plans?

Majority Opinion

In a 5–4 decision, the Supreme Court ruled that desegregation orders were only valid within the borders of Detroit and that the 53 suburban towns and cities were not required to participate in Detroit's desegregation plan because they had not played a role in creating the unequal conditions that existed within Detroit. "The relief ordered by the District Court and affirmed by the Court of Appeals was based upon erroneous standards, and was unsupported by record evidence that acts of the outlying districts had any impact on the discrimination found to exist in the Detroit schools."

In a concurring opinion, Justice Stewart wrote that all the White suburbs outside of the city were not evidence of a lack of equal protection:

> *Since the mere fact of different racial compositions in contiguous districts does not itself imply or constitute a violation of the equal protection clause in the absence of a showing that such disparity was imposed, fostered, or encouraged by the State or its political subdivisions, it follows that no inter-district violation was shown in this case.*

Speaking for the Court, Chief Justice Burger wrote the following:

The boundaries of the city of Detroit, were established over a century ago by neutral legislation when the city was incorporated; there is no evidence in the record, nor is there any suggestion by the respondents, that either the original boundaries of the Detroit School District, or any other school district in Michigan, were established for the purpose of creating, maintaining, or perpetuating segregation of races.

Dissenting Opinion

Of the four dissenting justices, three wrote opinions. They believed that both Detroit and Michigan state policies played a role in creating unequal schools for African Americans in Detroit and that the Fourteenth Amendment and the *Brown* decision demanded a statewide remedy.

Justice White wrote the following:

Regretfully, and for several reasons, I can join neither the Court's judgment nor its opinion. The core of my disagreement is that deliberate acts of segregation and their consequences will go unremedied not because a remedy would be infeasible or unreasonable in terms of the usual criteria governing school desegregation cases, but because an effective remedy would cause what the Court considers to be undue administrative inconvenience to the State. The result is that the State of Michigan, the entity at which the Fourteenth Amendment is directed, has successfully insulated itself from its duty to provide effective desegregation remedies by vesting sufficient power over its public schools in its local school districts. If this is the case in Michigan, it will be the case in most States.

Justice Marshall saw this case as a dangerous retreat from the principles fought for and gained in the *Brown* decision, writing the following:

The rights at issue in this case are too fundamental to be abridged on grounds as superficial as those relied on by the majority today. We deal here with the right of all of our children, whatever their race, to an equal start in life and to an equal opportunity to reach their full potential as citizens. Those children who have been denied that right in the past deserve better than to see fences thrown up to deny them that right in the future.

Implications of the Case

- For the most part, this decision halted segregation efforts at the borders of the nation's big cities. As minority children became more concentrated in many of the nation's largest and poorest districts, White Americans flocked to the suburbs. A change of one vote on the Supreme Court may have had a huge impact on this developing demographic pattern in the United States.
- Segregation today is not based on discriminatory laws but on housing patterns that are determined by building codes and land values. Some argue that the only way to create a more racially integrated nation is to pass laws that mandate low-income housing in high-income zip codes. Others ask whether it is a violation of equal protection that wealthy communities provide higher funding for education than poor communities within the same state.
- This case, and many other situations in northern cities, demonstrated that racial segregation is a national issue and was not, as many northerners preferred to believe, something that only took place south of the Mason-Dixon line.
- This case also demonstrates a limit to the use of equal protection. In order to procure a legal remedy to discriminatory practices, the issue must clearly stem from a specific government policy.

- Older U.S. cities tend to be physically smaller with close-by suburbs that have separate school systems and governments. For example, you can be 10 miles from downtown Boston and live several school districts away, but if you are 10 miles from downtown Phoenix, you are probably still part of the same school district and subject to its desegregation plans. These "accidents of geography" are not, however, written in stone. There is movement in the southern part of Baton Rouge, which is largely wealthy and White, to secede from the city and create a new city called St. George. Officials estimate that this would create a $53 million yearly deficit for Baton Rouge and further segregate schools.

Equal Protection Case Timeline

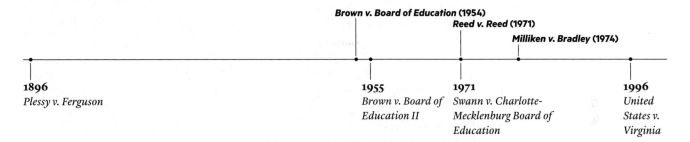

Brown v. Board of Education (1954)
Reed v. Reed (1971)
Milliken v. Bradley (1974)

1896
Plessy v. Ferguson

1955
Brown v. Board of Education II

1971
Swann v. Charlotte-Mecklenburg Board of Education

1996
United States v. Virginia

Summary of Main Points

PRD-1: The Fourteenth Amendment's "equal protection clause" and other constitutional provisions have often been used to support the advancement of equality.

PMI-3: Public policy promoting civil rights is influenced by citizen-state interactions and constitutional interpretation over time.

CON-6: The Court's interpretation of the U.S. Constitution is influenced by the composition of the Court and citizen-state interactions. At times, it has restricted minority rights and, at others, protected them.

A quick glance at the Fourteenth Amendment reveals that there are two significant clauses in its Section 1. States are not allowed to deny any person equal protection of the law, "nor shall any State deprive any person of life, liberty, or property, without due process of law." The due process clause of the Fourteenth Amendment uses the same language found in the Fifth Amendment and it incorporates it. The equal protection clause, however, added something entirely new to the Constitution.

It is not always easy to tell the difference between a situation that involves due process and a situation that involves equal protection. The good news is that, unless you are a judge or a law professor, or you are arguing a fine point of law in court, it is usually not necessary to disentangle the two concepts.

Warren wrote that the *Brown* decision "makes unnecessary any discussion whether such segregation also violates the Due Process Clause of the Fourteenth Amendment." The results of the case and the remedies ordered were the same whether segregated schools also violated the due process clause.

In general, due process shields the rights of individuals, while equal protection prevents discriminatory policies toward a group of people. Similarly, civil liberties belong to an individual and are protected by the Bill of Rights, while civil rights prevent discrimination against groups based on the equal protection clause of the Fourteenth Amendment. Here again, the two categories can overlap. For example, the right of same-sex marriage is considered both a civil liberty and a civil right.

The cases in this cluster, however, clearly lie within the area of equal protection. They examine state policies that impact the rights of a clearly defined group. In *Reed v. Reed*, that group is women. The application of the equal protection clause to women's rights has wiped out almost every legal distinction between the sexes. This change has completed the long legal journey women have undertaken to achieve legal equality.

After two and a half centuries of bondage and another century of often-extreme oppression, African Americans also attained legal equality. In *Brown v. Board of Education*, the Court decreed that racial integration was a critical component of legal equality.

Milliken v. Bradley limited the nation's legal obligation to integrate. In that case, the Court set important limits in its powers of judicial review. White elementary school students in suburban towns were not constitutionally required to board school buses to be transported to many of the same urban neighborhoods that their parents had left. The Court was not taking a stand for or against the desirability of racial integration; it was merely limiting possible remedies and protecting the rights of children and families in the 53 towns outside Detroit and in similarly situated communities across the nation.

Of course, for both African Americans and women, legal equality is not the same as true equality in terms of specific areas of accomplishment such as income and educational levels. African Americans and women still lag behind White men in terms of income, but women now outnumber men on college campuses; this change may, in the long run, reverse gender-based income trends.

Equal protection is a critical legal concept in the United States, and it will reappear many more times in the cases that follow. Cases about marriage, sexual practice, college admissions, voting, and redistricting will all invoke the equal protection clause.

Assessing Student Understanding

1. In what new manner did the Supreme Court use the equal protection clause in *Reed v. Reed*?

2. How does *Milliken v. Bradley* represent a limit to the Court's use of equal protection?

3. For each case in this cluster, explain how the decisions impacted millions of U.S. citizens beyond the parties directly involved in the litigation.

Questions for Class Discussion and Debate

1. Are there ever times when it is justified for laws to be different for males and females? For example, if the draft is brought back, should women also be subject to conscription?

2. Does the current segregation of U.S. schools by race and socioeconomic groups represent a public-policy problem? Why or why not? If it does, what steps should be taken to address this issue?

3. How does American society deal with the concept of equality today? Do we, as many have commented, believe in equality of opportunity but not of results? In what ways do we succeed at providing equality of opportunity? In what ways do we fail to do so?

Cluster 8: Affirmative Action and Equal Protection

The Big Issues

In 1965, Democratic president Lyndon Johnson issued an executive order to all departments asking that they take "affirmative action" to end discrimination. In 1969, Republican president Richard Nixon expanded the concept of affirmative action when he ordered all federal contractors to set goals and timelines for the hiring of minorities. Slowly, affirmative action evolved into a policy that attempted to diversify many of the nation's workplaces and schools.

The 80 words of the Fourteenth Amendment's Section 1 have taken a long journey that included generations of being ignored, then being used for its intended purpose, then being extended into unforeseen areas. The word "race" does not appear in the Fourteenth Amendment, nor does it appear anywhere in the Constitution. The writers and advocates of the Fourteenth Amendment intended to deny states the ability to treat African Americans as second-class citizens. Yet, the amendment itself makes no reference to African Americans. It decrees the equal protection of law for all "persons."

Conservative justices have complained about extending equal protection to gay marriage. Liberals have complained about extending equal protection to White Americans in affirmative action cases. Though both uses have become partially accepted, the Court has struggled with the use of race in programs that are compensatory for past wrongs and as a means of achieving diversity. As these following cases demonstrate, most justices since *Brown v. Board of Education* (1955) have agreed that the integration of races is a compelling government interest, but it is increasingly unclear how government policies can foster integration without running afoul of the Fourteenth Amendment.

In *Regents of the University of California v. Bakke* (1978), a White plaintiff successfully sued the University of California for "reverse discrimination." This was the first in a long series of lawsuits that limited the use of affirmative action.

Today, Americans solidly support the advancements that have been made in civil rights, but the nation is deeply divided about the use of affirmative action. Justice Thomas speaks for many when he has said that all public policy should be completely "color blind" and that all forms of affirmative action are unconstitutional. In 2003, in *Grutter v. Bollinger*, Justice Sandra Day O'Connor cast the vote that saved parts of affirmative action policy, but she did so with deep reservations. Writing for the majority, O'Connor said she expected that "25 years from now," the "use of racial preferences will no longer be necessary." Most of those 25 years are behind us.

Constitutional Connection

Fourteenth Amendment, Section 1

All persons born or naturalized in the United States, and subject to the jurisdiction thereof, are citizens of the United States and of the State wherein they reside. No State shall make or enforce any law which shall abridge the privileges or immunities of citizens of the United States; nor shall any State deprive any person of life, liberty, or property, without due process of law; nor deny to any person within its jurisdiction the equal protection of the laws.

CORE CASES

Regents of the University of California v. Bakke (1978)

Key Facts of the Case

- Allen Bakke served four years in the Marines in Vietnam, trained to become an engineer, and then applied to medical school. He applied for admission to the University of California (UC) at Davis in 1973.
- The University of California Medical School at Davis reserved 16 of 100 spots for minority candidates.
- Bakke's application was rejected. His GPA and admission test scores ranked him ahead of all 16 minority candidates who had been admitted.
- Bakke claimed reverse discrimination and sued for admission.

Constitutional Questions

Did the affirmative action program of the University of California at Davis violate Bakke's Fourteenth Amendment rights of equal protection? Did it also violate part of the Civil Rights Act?

Majority Opinion

The quota or "set aside" system used by UC Davis and all similar affirmative action programs were declared unconstitutional.

All of the justices supported Bakke's admission to medical school, but they also believed that affirmative action programs were constitutional, as long as they avoided strict quota systems. Justice Brennan wrote for the majority, "Government may take race into account when it acts not to demean or insult any racial group, but to remedy disadvantages cast on minorities by past racial prejudice. . . ."

Though the justices found the University of California's affirmative action program unconstitutional, they found one that passed muster on the East Coast:

> *In Harvard College admissions, the Committee has not set target quotas for the number of blacks, or of musicians, football players, physicists or Californians to be admitted in a given year. . . . But that awareness of the necessity of including more than a token number of black students does not mean that the Committee sets a minimum number of blacks or of people from west of the Mississippi who are to be admitted. It means only that, in choosing among thousands of applicants who are not only "admissible" academically but have other strong qualities, the Committee, with a number of criteria in mind, pays some attention to distribution among many types and categories of students.*

Dissenting Opinion

Even though Bakke's cause earned eight of the nine justices' votes, six different opinions were written, many concurring and dissenting in part. The only opinion that was considered fully dissenting was written by Justice White. He did not object to the overall decision. He objected to the use of the Civil Rights Act as a basis for Bakke's litigation. He believed that the violation of the Fourteenth Amendment was sufficient to strike down the University of California's quota system and that the only remedy available by a violation of the Civil Rights Act was a loss of federal funding.

Implications of the Case

- Allan Bakke was admitted to UC Davis Medical School.
- Shedding quotas, affirmative action programs continued.

- One of the main reasons Bakke was originally denied admission was his age. Medical education and training is a long process, and many felt that age 35 was too late to set out to become a doctor. Age discrimination is a complex topic. The Age Discrimination in Employment Act of 1967 protects workers over age 40, and some states have laws that start protections at a younger age, but age discrimination remains hard to prove, and workers who are laid off in midlife continue to have difficulty finding employment.
- The University of California at Davis did not produce a lot of documentation to support its admission program. Subsequent investigations revealed that in addition to setting aside spots for minorities, it also set aside spots for the children of the politically connected. For example, the son of a California assemblyman who hadn't even applied was admitted. This program was eliminated in 1976.

Gratz v. Bollinger and *Grutter v. Bollinger* (2003)

Key Facts of the Cases

- Julie Gratz was an unsuccessful White candidate for admission in the undergraduate program of the University of Michigan. Barbara Grutter was an unsuccessful White candidate for admission at Michigan's law school. Lee Bollinger was the president of the University of Michigan. These cases are sometimes referred to as the University of Michigan cases or as just *Gratz v. Bollinger*, but the two cases rendered two different decisions that today define the parameters of affirmative action.
- The undergraduate college used a point-based system. Candidates for admission needed 100 points to gain admission. Being an underrepresented minority gave a candidate 20 points. In comparison, a perfect SAT score was worth 12 points.
- In comparison for the 20 points automatically awarded for belonging to a disadvantaged racial minority, a fabulous essay earned only 3 points, leadership and service earned only 5 points, and the most astounding personal achievements earned a maximum of only 5 points.
- Julie Gratz was considered "well qualified" by the admissions office, but she did not earn admission to the university. She was told that she could apply to the waiting list, which she did not do. Most White students with admissions profiles similar to Gratz's were admitted from the waiting list. Because she did not enter her name on the waiting list, the university argued that she did not have standing to sue.
- The law school used a more holistic system that examined candidates in depth. Race was used as one of many "plus factors" and the university argued it also paid attention to "critical mass," the concept that minority students should not be isolated or viewed as spokespeople for their race.
- At the age of 43, Barbara Grutter decided to enter the field of law and sought admission to her state's top law school at the University of Michigan. In 1996, when she applied, she was raising two sons, ages 10 and 7, and running a small business in health care technology. Her goal was to become a health care attorney.
- Grutter had an undergraduate GPA of 3.8 and an LSAT score of 161 that put her in the 86th percentile. Grutter sued the University of Michigan for reverse discrimination. In lower court pleadings, her attorneys presented evidence that 100 percent of minority candidates with GPA and LSAT scores similar to Grutter's were admitted.

Constitutional Question

Did the college's and/or the law school's use of race in the admissions process violate the Fourteenth Amendment's equal protection clause?

Gratz v. Bollinger

Majority Opinion

By a 6–2 majority, the Supreme Court declared that the University of Michigan's admission system to its college was, in effect, a quota, and it was declared unconstitutional. Writing for the majority Chief Justice Rehnquist said, "Because the University's use of race in its current freshman admissions policy is not narrowly tailored to achieve respondents' asserted interest in diversity, the policy violates the Equal Protection Clause."

Chief Justice Rehnquist made a detailed study of the many University of Michigan undergraduate admissions policies used during the period. He looked at exam scores such as the SAT and the ACT and something that the undergraduate admissions office called "GPA 2," a recalculated GPA used to compare diverse grading systems from different high schools. He concluded the following:

> [A]pplicants with the same GPA 2 score and ACT/SAT score were subject to different admissions outcomes based upon their racial or ethnic status. For example, as a Caucasian in-state applicant, Gratz's GPA 2 score and ACT score placed her within a cell calling for a postponed decision on her application. An in-state or out-of state minority applicant with Gratz's scores would have fallen within a cell calling for admission.

The college had argued that a separate admissions committee provided detailed review of candidates, but the majority found that the point system, in effect, controlled that admissions process. Justice O'Connor wrote in a concurring opinion, ". . . the procedures employed by the University of Michigan's (University) Office of Undergraduate Admissions do not provide for a meaningful individualized review of applicants."

In a separate concurring opinion, Justice Thomas argued that any consideration of race violates the equal protection clause.

Dissenting Opinion

The dissenting justices believed that the undergraduate college's system did not resemble the one used by UC Davis in *Bakke*. Justices Souter and Ginsburg wrote the following:

> The plan here, in contrast, lets all applicants compete for all places and values an applicant's offering for any place not only on grounds of race, but on grades, test scores, strength of high school, quality of course of study, residence, alumni relationships, leadership, personal character, socioeconomic disadvantage, athletic ability, and quality of a personal essay.

Grutter v. Bollinger

Majority Opinion

In a 5–4 ruling, the Court declared the law school's admission system was constitutional. Justices Breyer and O'Connor were the two justices who had switched sides from the *Gratz* decision.

Writing for the majority, Justice O'Connor described the law school's admission policies:

> The policy does not restrict the types of diversity contributions eligible for "substantial weight" in the admissions process, but instead recognizes "many possible bases for diversity admissions" . . . The policy does, however, reaffirm the Law School's longstanding commitment to "one particular type of diversity," that is, racial and ethnic diversity with special reference to the inclusion of students from groups which have been historically discriminated against, like African-Americans, Hispanics and Native Americans, who without this commitment might not be represented in our student body in meaningful numbers.

Justice O'Connor rejected arguments that the concept of critical mass was merely a disguised quota systems, ". . . the Law School defines its critical mass concept by reference to the substantial, important, and laudable educational benefits that diversity is designed to produce, including cross-racial understanding and the breaking down of racial stereotypes."

Dissenting Opinion

In his dissenting opinion, Chief Justice Rehnquist did an extensive examination of the law school's applicants and admissions over many years and rejected the notion that the law school was only using race as a minor factor. In particular, he found that the concept of critical mass was used inconsistently and did not result in a similar number of admissions for the three targeted groups: African Americans, Hispanics, and Native Americans:

> *I do not believe that the Constitution gives the Law School such free rein in the use of race. The Law School has offered no explanation for its actual admissions practices and, unexplained, we are bound to conclude that the Law School has managed its admissions program, not to achieve a "critical mass," but to extend offers of admission to members of selected minority groups in proportion to their statistical representation in the applicant pool.*

Implications of the Cases

- Colleges and universities around the nation created more complex admissions systems that resemble the techniques used by Michigan Law.
- In 2006, Michigan voters banned the use of affirmative action in state-sponsored institutions by ballot initiative. In 2014, the Supreme Court upheld this ban with a vote of 6–2 in *Schuette v. Coalition to Defend Affirmative Action*. African-American enrollment at Michigan's flagship campus at Ann Arbor dropped from 8.9 percent in 1995 to 4.9 percent in 2014. Graduation rates were even more severely impacted. (According to the U.S. Census, Michigan is 14.2 percent African American.)
- As of 2014, eight states have banned the use of affirmative actions—six by ballot question, one by legislation, and one by executive order.
- In the *Gratz* case, some of the dissenting justices also focused on the issue of standing. Gratz could not demonstrate that she had asked to be wait-listed in Ann Arbor. All of the wait-listed students had been admitted in her year. Also, in the meantime, she graduated from the University of Michigan at Dearborn, majored in math, and found gainful employment.

Parents Involved in Community Schools v. Seattle School District No. 1 (2007)

Key Facts of the Case

- In many large cities, racial desegregation plans have given way to a choice of "magnet" schools with different characteristics. Parents and their children prioritize their choice of high schools, and often do not get their first choice.
- In Seattle, when a high school was oversubscribed, racial identity was used as a tiebreaker in determining admissions. Ideally, according to the city, an individual high school's racial composition reflected that of the city: 41 percent White and 59 percent non-White. In using these percentages as guidelines, both White and non-White Americans were denied admission to certain high schools.
- In the Supreme Court, this case was combined with a similar issue that took place in Louisville, Kentucky.

Constitutional Questions

Does the consideration of race, as used by the public schools in this case, violate the equal protection clause? Is the goal of racial diversity in public schools a compelling government interest?

Majority Opinion

A 5–4 majority ruled that the Seattle and Louisville plans were not "narrowly tailored" and were therefore unconstitutional, although each justice in the majority used differing reasoning to support his or her opinion. Chief Justice John Roberts wrote in the plurality opinion that "[t]he way to stop discrimination on the basis of race is to stop discriminating on the basis of race."

Chief Justice Roberts seemed to edge closer to Justice Thomas's vision of a post-racial legal landscape: "Allowing racial balancing as a compelling end in itself would effectively assure that race will always be relevant in American life, and that the 'ultimate goal' of 'eliminating entirely from governmental decision making such irrelevant factors as a human being's race' will never be achieved."

The Court applied the same standards to both Seattle, a northwestern city that had created its own voluntary desegregation plan, and Louisville, a southern city that once had de jure segregation and had been under court-ordered desegregation until 2000.

There was also a 5–4 majority that stated that high school assignment plans could consider race as a "plus factor" in a manner similar to Michigan Law, but it was unclear how this could be accomplished by public schools.

Dissenting Opinion

In Justice Steven's scathing dissent, he accused Chief Justice Roberts and others of misusing the *Brown* precedent and of ignoring important parts of U.S. history:

> There is a cruel irony in The Chief Justice's reliance on our decision in Brown v. Board of Education. *The first sentence in the concluding paragraph of his opinion states:* "Before Brown, *schoolchildren were told where they could and could not go to school based on the color of their skin.*" This sentence reminds me of Anatole France's observation: "The majestic equality of the law forbids rich and poor alike to sleep under bridges, to beg in the streets, and to steal their bread." The Chief Justice fails to note that it was only black schoolchildren who were so ordered; indeed, the history books do not tell stories of white children struggling to attend black schools. In this and other ways, The Chief Justice rewrites the history of one of this Court's most important decisions . . . It is my firm conviction that no Member of the Court that I joined in 1975 would have agreed with today's decision.

Implications of the Case

- Seattle ceased using race as a factor in high school assignments. Instead, it uses sibling placement, elementary school assignments, and a lottery as factors to determine tiebreakers.
- Louisville, Kentucky, was a southern city that had embraced its 40-year history of integrated schools. Many in the city were stunned by this Supreme Court decision. It devised a system that used diversity of household income as a factor in high school assignments and that worked to maintain nearly the same levels of integration.
- Many other school districts around the nation have found non-race-based means of achieving some integration. In other districts, schools have resegregated. This resegregation is the result of many factors, including an end to forced busing and increased segregation in housing patterns.

- The Obama Justice Department wrote a 14-page memo to school districts after the *Parents Involved in Community Schools v. Seattle School District No. 1* decision offering guidance about permissible methods to keep classrooms and schools racially integrated. Although the memo cites the Court's sentiments that racial diversity in public schools is a compelling government interest, it offers no clear race-based means of achieving that goal.

Affirmative Action and Equal Protection Case Timeline

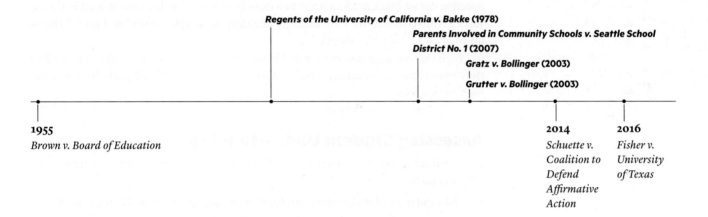

Regents of the University of California v. Bakke (1978)

Parents Involved in Community Schools v. Seattle School District No. 1 (2007)

Gratz v. Bollinger (2003)

Grutter v. Bollinger (2003)

1955
Brown v. Board of Education

2014
Schuette v. Coalition to Defend Affirmative Action

2016
Fisher v. University of Texas

Summary of Main Points

CON-6: The Court's interpretation of the U.S. Constitution is influenced by the composition of the Court and citizen-state interactions. At times, it has restricted minority rights and, at others, protected them.

It appears that the policy of affirmative action in schools is waning. It remains alive, although on life support, in colleges and universities. K–12 school districts have no direct means of considering a child's race in determining the composition of their schools.

As it stands, race can be used as a narrowly tailored factor, among many factors in determining admissions to a college or university. In examining an affirmative action plan, a court must be sure that other non-race-based methods could not have been used to achieve racial diversity. Although legal precedent and admissions offices seem to have reached a workable compromise, the nation and the Court seems more ideologically polarized than ever.

This is reflected in the twice-heard case of Abigail Fisher, a White student who was denied admission to the University of Texas. The University of Texas fills the vast majority of its seats using a system that does not consider race. The top 7–10 percent of each high school class is automatically admitted. Because so many high schools in Texas are racially segregated, this policy has maintained some racial diversity on campus. A small number of spots are reserved for students who did not receive automatic admission. They are evaluated on a wide variety of criteria, and race is one of them. Many worthy candidates, including Fisher, were denied admission. Most admitted under this separate program were White, and many minorities with better board scores and higher GPAs than Fisher's were denied admission.

When *Fisher v. University of Texas* was first heard in 2012, the Court produced a flurry of opinions, but its most important decision was a 7–1 decree to send the case back to the lower court. When reheard in the appellate court with instructions from the

Supreme Court regarding how to apply "strict scrutiny" to policies dealing with racial distinctions, the University of Texas's policies were upheld.

Fisher's legal team decided to relitigate the case. Foes of affirmative action felt that Fisher's case presented the perfect fact pattern and narrative to finally kill off a policy that many believe deny White Americans equal protection of the law. During the intervening years, Fisher had attended and graduated from Louisiana State University. Justice Kennedy surprised Court watchers by switching back to the side that backed admissions policies that used race as a plus factor as outlined in *Grutter v. Bollinger*. *Fisher v. University of Texas* upheld the precedents set in the University of Michigan cases.

The three dissenting justices were dismayed that small vestiges of affirmative action survived. During oral argument, Chief Justice Roberts asked, "What unique perspective does a black student bring to a class in physics?" In his dissent read in Court, Justice Alito characterized the majority decision as "simply wrong" and said, "This is affirmative action gone berserk."

With this complex and convoluted history, we can be sure of two things regarding the issue of affirmative action: it will remain very divisive and it will make its way to the high court again.

Assessing Student Understanding

1. What is reverse discrimination? Explain how it is covered by the Fourteenth Amendment.

2. Why did the Court view the consideration of race constitutional in the case of *Grutter v. Bollinger* and not in *Gratz v. Bollinger*?

3. The Court always applies "strict scrutiny" to policies that distinguish people by race. Give two examples of strict scrutiny used in examining the constitutionality of a policy.

Questions for Class Discussion and Debate

1. Many colleges admit "legacies," the children of important alumnae. Because colleges used to be more exclusively White and upper class, most of these "legacies" are White and upper class. Is this a form of preferential treatment that violates the equal protection clause?

2. Across the United States, many have noted a developing trend where female high school students have higher GPAs and higher test scores than males. Should colleges admit the worthiest candidates without regard to gender? Is the current system that allows males with lower scores to enter ahead of females with higher scores a violation of equal protection?

3. How would you respond to Chief Justice Roberts's questions about the value added by "the perspective of a black student in physics class"? Does diversity have value on its own in a classroom? Or is its value in the diversity of the workforce in highly skilled jobs?

Cluster 9: Ideological Movements and the High Court

The Big Issues

The three cases presented here represent dramatic courtroom moments in ideologically driven social movements from across the political spectrum. The legal actions were only part of the strategies of these movements. The movements also used many other forms of political action, including lobbying at the state and federal levels, grassroots organizing, holding rallies and protests, and endorsing and funding candidates.

The fact that ideology enters judicial proceedings poses a dilemma. After all, constitutional precepts, unlike societal conditions, do not change. Does the change represented by these cases result from the evolving sentiments of sitting justices, the changing personnel of the high court, or the introduction of new legal quandaries? Most likely, these changes represent some combination of all three factors.

In one very important way, these cases demonstrate how judicial principles carry more power than political sentiment in the high court. In the first case, *Planned Parenthood of Southeastern Pennsylvania v. Casey* (1992), the pro-life movement hoped to see the more conservative court, with justices appointed by Ford, Reagan, and H. W. Bush, overturn *Roe v. Wade* (1973), but it didn't. In fact, all five justices that voted to retain the logic of *Roe* were Republican appointees, and one of the dissenters was a Democratic appointee.

The second case, *Zelman v. Simmons-Harris* (2002), tested the constitutionality of using taxpayer funds for school vouchers in private religious schools. This is a practice supported by many Republicans, yet two Republican-appointed justices voted against it. In the final case, *Obergefell v. Hodges* (2015), which legalized same-sex marriage across the nation, Justice Kennedy, a Reagan appointee, cast the deciding vote in favor of gay marriage. We can conclude from these examples that justices often vote against their own political beliefs as they render judicial decisions.

That this check on popular passions survives is something that the framers would be pleased to learn, but it doesn't stop political entrepreneurs from trying to design cases that will bring about the type of political change that they are seeking. All of the cases here began with grassroots social movements that passed pioneering laws at the state level. With the passage of these laws, social activists looked forward to their day in court, hoping for victory and not giving too much thought to the consistency of their constitutional arguments. After all, social activists are likely to see the courts as a means to an end, and they do not have to align their positions with the logic used in dozens of other cases. On the other hand, Supreme Court justices and scholars of American government must be able to place individual cases into a broader context.

The first case in this cluster examines restrictions on abortions by the state of Pennsylvania and addresses violations of the standards set by *Roe v. Wade*. *Zelman v. Simmons-Harris* resulted from laws designed by the state of Ohio that primarily tested the interpretation of the establishment clause. *Obergefell v. Hodges* was preceded by a great deal of same-sex marriage legislation in states across the country. Many states had banned same-sex marriage, and others had legalized it. The case, in part, tested whether states that banned same-sex marriages should be forced to recognize those that had been performed in other states. In all three situations, the Court's decision played an important, but not final, role in these culture war issues.

Constitutional Connections

First Amendment

Congress shall make no law respecting an establishment of religion, or prohibiting the free exercise thereof; or abridging the freedom of speech, or of the press; or the right of the people peaceably to assemble, and to petition the Government for a redress of grievances.

Fourteenth Amendment, Section 1

All persons born or naturalized in the United States, and subject to the jurisdiction thereof, are citizens of the United States and of the State wherein they reside. No State shall make or enforce any law which shall abridge the privileges or immunities of citizens of the United States; nor shall any State deprive any person of life, liberty, or property, without due process of law; nor deny to any person within its jurisdiction the equal protection of the laws.

CORE CASES

Planned Parenthood of Southeastern Pennsylvania v. Casey (1992)

Key Facts of the Case

- The highly controversial decision in *Roe v. Wade* created a backlash and a movement that sought to end legal abortion. The movement used a variety of tactics, including the passage of state laws, that made a legal abortion more difficult to obtain.
- The first state laws to be tested in the high court were passed in the state of Missouri. State legislators had enacted regulations that prohibited the involvement of state employees in carrying out most abortions. Also, counseling that encouraged abortion was outlawed, and physicians were required to test the viability of the fetus starting at 20 weeks into a pregnancy. In a 5-4 decision, when even the majority did not agree on its reasoning, the Court found in *Webster v. Reproductive Health Services* (1989) that all Missouri regulations were constitutional.
- The state of Pennsylvania created a variety of abortion regulations that required women seeking an abortion to perform certain actions during the first trimester of pregnancy, something that many believed *Roe v. Wade* had banned.
- The laws required women to wait 24 hours after requesting an abortion and to sign an informed consent waiver that stated, among other things, that the abortion may cause physical and psychological damage and that the state may provide assistance for the care of newborns.
- The law also required minors to inform their parents and married women to inform their husbands of plans to get an abortion. A woman was allowed to request a judicial bypass for these procedures if she could demonstrate that informing her parents or husband might endanger her safety.

Constitutional Question

Do state abortion regulations that require women to wait 24 hours, sign informed consent waivers, and inform parents (if a minor) or a husband (if married) violate the standards set by *Roe v. Wade*?

Majority Opinion

In a highly contentious 5-4 decision, the Court upheld most of the restrictions put in place by the state of Pennsylvania, and it upheld the original logic of *Roe v. Wade*. The five justices in the majority underscored the importance of *stare decisis*, "Liberty finds no refuge in a jurisprudence of doubt."

This decision introduced the concept of "undue burden" to assess state-imposed regulations on abortion. Delivering the opinion of the Court, Justice O'Connor, Justice Kennedy, and Justice Souter state:

> *Numerous forms of state regulation might have the incidental effect of increasing the cost or decreasing the availability of medical care, whether for abortion or any other medical procedure. The fact that a law which serves a valid purpose, one not designed to strike at the right itself, has the incidental effect of making it more difficult or more expensive to procure an abortion cannot be enough to invalidate it. Only where state regulation imposes an undue burden on a woman's ability to make this decision does the power of the State reach into the heart of the liberty protected by the Due Process Clause.*

The majority only struck down the husband-notification provision, which it found to be reminiscent of bygone gender roles, as it "embodies a view of marriage consonant with the common-law status of married women but repugnant to our present understanding of marriage and of the nature of the rights secured by the Constitution."

This decision was, in part, supported by data on domestic abuse. "These findings are supported by studies of domestic violence. The American Medical Association (AMA) has published a summary of the recent research in this field, which indicates that in an average 12-month period in this country, approximately two million women are the victims of severe assaults by their male partners."

Dissenting Opinion

Chief Justice Rehnquist questioned the majority's inconsistent use of precedent. "The joint opinion [in this case, he is referring to the majority opinion], following its newly minted variation on *stare decisis*, retains the outer shell of *Roe v. Wade*, but beats a wholesale retreat from the substance of that case."

His dissent asserted that all of the provisions of the Pennsylvania laws were constitutional based on the powers of the state legislature:

> *The joint opinion is forthright in admitting that it draws this distinction based on a policy judgment that parents will have the best interests of their children at heart, while the same is not necessarily true of husbands as to their wives. . . . This may or may not be a correct judgment, but it is quintessentially a legislative one. The "undue burden" inquiry does not in any way supply the distinction between parental consent and spousal consent which the joint opinion adopts. Despite the efforts of the joint opinion, the undue burden standard presents nothing more workable than the trimester framework which it discards today. Under the guise of the Constitution, this Court will still impart its own preferences on the States in the form of a complex abortion code.*

Rehnquist's dissent supported all the provisions of Pennsylvania law that were upheld and did so in more emphatic language than the majority opinion, and it also supported the spousal-notification provision. "The question before us is therefore whether the spousal notification requirement rationally furthers any legitimate state interests. We conclude that it does. First, a husband's interests in procreation within marriage and in the potential life of his unborn child are certainly substantial ones."

Implications of the Case

- Several more major abortion rights cases have landed in the Supreme Court since 1992, all of them testing state or federal restrictions of abortion. Although the pro-life movement has won some and lost some, the number of clinics that perform abortions in the United States has fallen precipitously in many red states. In fact, as of 2014, five states had only one facility. Women seeking an abortion often must deal with long travel times and expenses in addition to all of the other hurdles that states have created.

- In *Whole Women's Health v. Hellerstedt* (2016), the Court struck down a Texas law that placed many medical regulations on abortion providers, including that clinics must have the same type of facilities as those used in much more complex medical procedures and that doctors must be associated with a hospital within 30 miles of the clinic. In a 5–3 decision, the majority found that these regulations violated the standards set in *Planned Parenthood of Southeast Pennsylvania v. Casey*. Writing for the majority, Justice Breyer said, "We conclude that neither of these provisions offers medical benefits sufficient to justify the burdens upon access that each imposes."

- At the time that *Whole Women's Health v. Hellerstedt* was heard, the Court had an empty seat as a result of Justice Scalia's death. The Republican Senate refused to hold hearings on Obama's appointee and waited to confirm a new justice until a Republican president took office.

- Future appointees to the high court could shift the balance and either reaffirm or overturn both *Roe* and *Casey*. If the Court decides to reverse these precedents, that is a decision that the pro-life movement will savor and the abortion rights movement will view as a disastrous limitation of women's rights. If the justices who crafted the decision in *Casey* thought that they had reached a workable legal compromise that would allow the Court to move on to other issues, they were mistaken.

Zelman v. Simmons-Harris (2002)

Key Facts of the Case

- School voucher programs have a long and varied history. In rural Vermont, vouchers were first introduced in 1869 and continue today. Towns that are too small to maintain their own schools issue a tax credit or voucher for parents to choose their own school for their children. The vouchers can be used in neighboring towns or private academies, but they cannot be used in religious schools.

- In an 1875 speech, President Ulysses S. Grant advocated a constitutional amendment that would have banned all tax money from going to religious institutions. The proposed amendment, written by Representative James G. Blaine of Maine, failed in the Senate by one vote, but today, 38 states have a similar amendment, referred to as a Blaine Amendment, as part of their constitutions.

- The modern American fight over vouchers intensified after conservative economist Milton Friedman advocated their use in his landmark book and television series "Free to Choose."

- Beginning in the Reagan era, the Republican Party began to advocate vouchers as a means to both give parents a choice and to force public education programs to improve through competition.

- Following the theory of conservative economists, many school districts across the nation have created some variety of a voucher or a school choice plan. Ohio created one for low-income students in Cleveland, a city with a school system that many believed to be failing.

- The pro-voucher movement ran into constitutional complications when it included religious schools as potential recipients of taxpayer money. A group of parents sued Susan Zelman, the superintendent of Ohio schools, to stop public monies from going to religious institutions.

- Ohio has a Blaine Amendment, but the Court did not consider it. Instead, it focused its attention on the establishment clause.

Constitutional Question

Does the transfer of taxpayer money to religious schools violate the establishment clause?

Majority Opinion

In a 5–4 decision, Chief Justice Rehnquist wrote for the majority and said that Ohio's voucher system did not violate the establishment clause because it was religiously neutral. The state handed parents the voucher and parents were free to choose religious or nonreligious schools.

His statement began with a description of Cleveland's public schools:

> There are more than 75,000 children enrolled in the Cleveland City School District. The majority of these children are from low-income and minority families. Few of these families enjoy the means to send their children to any school other than an inner-city public school. For more than a generation, however, Cleveland's public schools have been among the worst performing public schools in the Nation. In 1995, a Federal District Court declared a "crisis of magnitude" and placed the entire Cleveland school district under state control.

The decision to use the voucher in a religious setting is made by a citizen, not by the state. Rehnquist continued with the following:

> We believe that the program challenged here is a program of true private choice . . . and thus constitutional. . . . The program permits the participation of all schools within the district, religious or nonreligious. Adjacent public schools also may participate and have a financial incentive to do so. Program benefits are available to participating families on neutral terms, with no reference to religion. The only preference stated anywhere in the program is a preference for low-income families, who receive greater assistance and are given priority for admission at participating schools.

Dissenting Opinion

Speaking for the four dissenters, Justice Souter reviewed a long history of Court decisions that denied public funding to religious institutions. He questioned the relevance of assumptions about the quality of the public schools in Cleveland to constitutional principles:

> The Court's majority holds that the Establishment Clause is no bar to Ohio's payment of tuition at private religious elementary and middle schools under a scheme that systematically provides tax money to support the schools' religious missions. The occasion for the legislation thus upheld is the condition of public education in the city of Cleveland. The record indicates that the schools are failing to serve their objective, and the vouchers in issue here are said to be needed to provide adequate alternatives to them. If there were an excuse for giving short shrift to the Establishment Clause, it would probably apply here. But there is no excuse. Constitutional limitations are placed on government to preserve constitutional values in hard cases, like these.

Implications of the Case

- The voucher debate continues across the nation, with advocates claiming that it gives low-income parents a choice, and foes, in addition to voicing First Amendment concerns, claim that it subtracts from the budget of already underfunded public schools, thus exacerbating performance issues. Opponents of voucher programs also point to the fact that many private schools only accept the best students, leaving the most academically and emotionally disadvantaged in the same public schools with less funding.

- Conservatives in Florida, California, and Michigan put voter initiatives on the ballot to repeal their state's Blaine Amendments. All of them failed, but efforts to repeal state laws that deny funding to religious school are underway across the nation.
- The state of Missouri recycles scrap rubber from used tires to help soften the surface of children's playgrounds. Trinity Lutheran Church of Columbia, Missouri, operates a preschool program and applied to the state for scrap rubber. Its application was denied because Missouri bans the transfer of public resources to religious institutions. In *Trinity Lutheran Church of Columbia v. Comer* (2017), the high court ruled 7–2 that Missouri's policy violated the free exercise rights of church members. It is unclear whether this decision will open the door to other challenges that will further break down the barrier between public funds and religious institutions.

Obergefell v. Hodges (2015)

Key Facts of the Case

- The fight for and against gay rights has a long and complex history in the United States and in the world. In 1996, Congress passed and President Clinton signed legislation declaring that marriage is a union of one man and one woman. The legislation also denied same-sex couples any federal benefits and declared that states were not obligated to recognize same-sex marriages performed in other states. This act was known as the Defense of Marriage Act (DOMA).
- In 2000, Vermont became the first state to legalize same-sex marriage.
- In 2003, in the case *Lawrence v. Texas* (2003), the Supreme Court struck down all state laws that made consenting sexual activity between adults of the same sex illegal. In the same year, many in Congress considered proposing a constitutional amendment to ban same-sex marriage.
- In *United States v. Windsor* (2013), the Supreme Court declared in a 5–4 decision that the ban on federal benefits for same-sex couples was unconstitutional based on the Fifth Amendment's due process clause. This decision made one of the two clauses of DOMA unconstitutional.
- Partly based on the ruling in *United States v. Windsor*, plaintiffs across the nation began to litigate in pursuit of having same-sex marriages recognized by all states. District courts around the nation came to different conclusions, making it more likely that the Supreme Court would hear a gay-marriage case.
- When *Obergefell v. Hodges* arrived in the Supreme Court, similar to *Brown v. Board of Education* (1954), it was the compilation of many cases. Jim Obergefell and his partner, John Arthur of Ohio, had been together for 20 years and had recently gotten married in Maryland in 2013. When Arthur died, Obergefell wanted to be listed as the surviving spouse on the death certificate. In addition to being a matter of principle, this would entitle Obergefell to traditional survivor benefits for widows and widowers from Social Security or other sources. Richard Hodges was an official in Ohio state government that opposed recognizing same-sex marriages.

Constitutional Question

Does the Fourteenth Amendment require states to license same-sex marriage and to recognize same-sex marriages from other states?

Majority Opinion

In a 5–4 decision, the Court recognized same-sex marriage as a fundamental right guaranteed by the due process clause. Writing for the majority, Justice Kennedy said the following:

> Under the Due Process Clause of the Fourteenth Amendment, no State shall "deprive any person of life, liberty, or property, without due process of law." The fundamental

liberties protected by this Clause include most of the rights enumerated in the Bill of Rights. . . . In addition these liberties extend to certain personal choices central to individual dignity and autonomy, including intimate choices that define personal identity and beliefs.

Kennedy's opinion reminded court watchers of *Loving v. Virginia* (1967), the landmark case that struck down state laws that had banned interracial marriage. It was evidence of the changing applications of fundamental constitutional liberties. He wrote the following:

The nature of injustice is that we may not always see it in our own times. The generations that wrote and ratified the Bill of Rights and the Fourteenth Amendment did not presume to know the extent of freedom in all of its dimensions, and so they entrusted to future generations a charter protecting the right of all persons to enjoy liberty as we learn its meaning. When new insight reveals discord between the Constitution's central protections and a received legal stricture, a claim to liberty must be addressed.

Justice Kennedy also rejected the notion that states could be left to make their own decisions on this issue, which would have allowed a patchwork of policies to continue:

Leaving the current state of affairs in place would maintain and promote instability and uncertainty. For some couples, even an ordinary drive into a neighboring State to visit family or friends risks causing severe hardship in the event of a spouse's hospitalization while across state lines. In light of the fact that many States already allow samesex marriage and hundreds of thousands of these marriages already have occurred the disruption caused by the recognition bans is significant and ever-growing.

Dissenting Opinion

All four dissenting justices wrote opinions. They felt that this decision denied states the right to determine their own marriage laws. Chief Justice Roberts wrote the following:

Today, however, the Court takes the extraordinary step of ordering every State to license and recognize same-sex marriage. Many people will rejoice at this decision, and I begrudge none their celebration. But for those who believe in a government of laws, not of men, the majority's approach is deeply disheartening. Supporters of same-sex marriage have achieved considerable success persuading their fellow citizens—through the democratic process—to adopt their view. That ends today. Five lawyers have closed the debate and enacted their own vision of marriage as a matter of constitutional law. Stealing this issue from the people will for many cast a cloud over same-sex marriage, making a dramatic social change that much more difficult to accept.

Justice Scalia strenuously objected to how far the notion of due process had been extended:

The opinion in these cases is the furthest extension in fact—and the furthest extension one can even imagine—of the Court's claimed power to create "liberties" that the Constitution and its Amendments neglect to mention. This practice of constitutional revision by an unelected committee of nine, always accompanied (as it is today) by extravagant praise of liberty, robs the People of the most important liberty they asserted in the Declaration of Independence and won in the Revolution of 1776: the freedom to govern themselves.

Implications of the Case

- All 50 states were required to perform and recognize gay marriage.
- Some officials who are licensed to perform civil marriages have been forced to perform gay marriages in spite of their religious objections. In offices where there

is more than one justice of the peace, officials have been allowed to shift responsibilities so that employees are not forced to perform marriages that violate their religious beliefs.

· In the case of *Masterpiece Cakeshop Ltd. v. Colorado Anti-Discrimination Commission* (2017), a cake baker asserted his right not to make a wedding cake for a gay couple because it violated his religious beliefs. The Colorado Anti-Discrimination Commission likened this to retailers refusing to serve African Americans prior to the passage and enforcement of civil rights laws.

· With so much attention devoted to the topic of gay marriage, it is often overlooked that there are no federal civil rights laws which protect the LBGT community from discrimination in employment, housing, or other sectors of the economy.

· Although polling reveals a major swing in the attitude of Americans toward approval of gay marriage and gay rights, this is still a major culture war issue with many battles left to fight.

Ideological Movements and the High Court Case Timeline

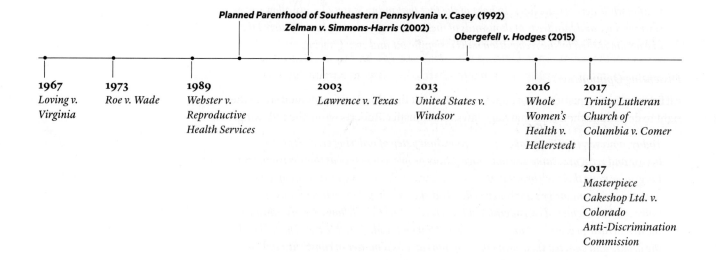

Planned Parenthood of Southeastern Pennsylvania v. Casey (1992)
Zelman v. Simmons-Harris (2002)
Obergefell v. Hodges (2015)

1967 *Loving v. Virginia*

1973 *Roe v. Wade*

1989 *Webster v. Reproductive Health Services*

2003 *Lawrence v. Texas*

2013 *United States v. Windsor*

2016 *Whole Women's Health v. Hellerstedt*

2017 *Trinity Lutheran Church of Columbia v. Comer*

2017 *Masterpiece Cakeshop Ltd. v. Colorado Anti-Discrimination Commission*

Summary of Main Points

PMI-4: Widely held political ideologies shape policy debates and choices in American policies.

In many landmark Supreme Court cases, the Court treads on ground that is already well worn by policy entrepreneurs from the legislative and executive branches. We often question whether the Court oversteps its constitutional role in these instances, but in all the cases in this group, social activists used the federal courts as part of a broader strategy. The Court did not seek out these cases—activists for social change sought that change through the courts.

Furthermore, as the culture war issues in these cases continue to play out in American society, the courts may or may not play a decisive role in their resolution. Shifts in public opinion, major state or federal legislation, or cultural and economic changes will also weigh heavily in determining the future of abortion policy, school vouchers, and same-sex marriage.

These cases demonstrate how the Court is both buffeted by and insulated from the winds of social change. As policy entrepreneurs and average citizens advocate their ideologies relentlessly, the courts pause to consider constitutional principles and precedent.

How and when do ideological shifts reach the high court? This is a question that spurs a variety of answers. If nothing else, ideological shifts reach the courts when members of new generations are appointed to the bench. Clearly, future judges born in the twenty-first century will bring a different sensibility to issues like same-sex marriage than judges born 75 or 100 years earlier.

Cases that touch on social ideology often result in plurality decisions. That is to say the majority of justices may be voting the same way, but they are doing so for very different reasons. Not only are all the cases in this cluster plurality decisions but they are also 5–4 decisions. Citizens may hope for greater clarity from their courts, but the courts are a reflection of the larger society. Culture war issues are highly divisive in all venues, and the courts are no exception.

Assessing Student Understanding

1. Pick one of the cases above and explain the role that social movements played in bringing it into the legal system.

2. What is the voucher movement? How does it intensify the clash between the two clauses that deal with religion in the First Amendment?

3. All three cases in the bundle test a freedom that is desired by some but, in the view of others, imposes an intolerable social cost. For each case, identify that freedom and the political party that is most closely associated with its support.

Questions for Class Discussion and Debate

1. Do ideological movements impact the legal thinking of justices on the Supreme Court? Support your answer with specific information from these cases or others.

2. It has not been argued that providing religious institutions the protection of local fire and police violates the establishment clause, but many aspects of government support for religious institutions are highly controversial, including school vouchers. Where should the line be drawn in terms of the use of public resources in religious schools?

3. Should states have sovereignty in determining their own marriage laws? Are your answers consistent with your opinion about state sovereignty in regard to laws regarding gun regulations, campaign finance restrictions, and the legalization of marijuana? If not, explain the discrepancies.

Cluster 10: Election Processes, Partisanship, and Divided Government

The Big Issues

The control of elections is an area of overlapping state and federal powers. The three cases in this cluster, presented in chronological order, grow increasingly more controversial. *Baker v. Carr* (1962) codified the concept of "one person, one vote." It required that voting districts within a state be equal in population and not be malapportioned.

Although many states and localities conduct their own censuses, after *Baker v. Carr*, states were required to resize their districts at least every 10 years to account for population shifts based on the U.S. Census, a mammoth effort required by the Constitution and carried out by the U.S. Department of Commerce. Before *Baker v. Carr*, the only mandated use of the census was to redistribute seats in the U.S. House of Representatives.

Though *Baker v. Carr* represents settled law, the next two cases expose live issues that continue to manifest themselves at both the state and federal levels. Other than requiring that legislative districts within a state are equal in population, the courts considered gerrymandering to be a purely political question until 1993. That is to say, state legislatures had complete power in drawing district lines.

Shaw v. Reno (1993) brought a highly unusual, gerrymandered district to the docket of the high court. Its decision in this case gave states some guidance about how to deal the issue of race while drawing district lines, but most redistricting questions remain purely political matters and are left to state discretion.

Liberals and conservatives can agree that elections are the lifeblood of a democracy, but there is little agreement today on where the power resides to create the rules that govern an election. Article I, Section 4, says that the "Time, Place and Manner" of elections are to be determined by the states, but it also gives Congress the power to legislate in this vital area. Congress has passed many laws, including the Voting Rights Act, to ensure that the vote is available to all citizens.

Congress has also passed a wide range of campaign finance reform in order to attempt to limit the power of money in dominating an election. One of the most important reforms was struck down as unconstitutional in *Citizens United v. Federal Election Commission* (2010). A 5-4 majority ruled that, in many instances, spending freely in support of a candidate or a cause is a form of free speech.

Since *Citizens United*, the amount of money involved in elections has risen dramatically and it is still rising. States have also passed Clean Elections laws that were abridged by the *Citizens United* decision. When it comes to rules and laws about elections, we can be sure of a bitter and protracted battle. Both major parties want to bend the rules in a manner that will give them an advantage.

Will the role of the Court as arbiter, or will Congress, acting with the high republican ideals that the framers vested in it, act to strengthen the democratic nature of our elections? Court decisions in this area have created as many questions as answers, and Congress's last major legislation in the areas of voting and elections was passed in 2002.

Events are moving more quickly than policy. When the framers crafted the constitutional guidelines for voting and elections, they probably did not anticipate billionaires attempting to buy elections or powerful computer programs suggesting ways to slice a state's population in a manner that will yield the most seats for one political party. *Shaw v. Reno* and *Citizens United v. Federal Election Commission* represent issues that are significant challenges to our democracy. They will continue to be played out in states and in all branches of the federal government. To understand future developments in this field, it is important to understand each of the three following cases.

Constitutional Connections

First Amendment

Congress shall make no law respecting an establishment of religion, or prohibiting the free exercise thereof; or abridging the freedom of speech, or of the press; or the right of the people peaceably to assemble, and to petition the Government for a redress of grievances.

Article 1, Section 4

The Times, Places and Manner of holding Elections for Senators and Representatives, shall be prescribed in each State by the Legislature thereof; but the Congress may at any time by Law make or alter such Regulations, except as to the Places of choosing Senators.

Fourteenth Amendment, Section 1

All persons born or naturalized in the United States, and subject to the jurisdiction thereof, are citizens of the United States and of the State wherein they reside. No State shall make or enforce any law which shall abridge the privileges or immunities of citizens of the United States; nor shall any State deprive any person of life, liberty, or property, without due process of law; nor deny to any person within its jurisdiction the equal protection of the laws.

CORE CASES

Baker v. Carr (1962)

Key Facts of the Case

- In spite of population shifts between 1901 and 1961, Tennessee had not redistricted.
- The state senator from Tennessee's most populous senatorial district represented over five times the number of voters represented by the senator from the least populous district, while the corresponding ratio for most and least populous House districts was more than eighteen to one.
- Redistricting had always been viewed as a political question as opposed to a judicial one. In other words, courts had always deferred to state legislatures in this matter. There was a growing sentiment that this dilution of voter strength in the higher population districts was a violation of the equal protection clause.

Constitutional Questions

Are district lines a purely political question or do plaintiffs have a constitutional right to sue? Do legislative districts that are unequal in population violate the equal protection clause?

Majority Opinion

In a 7–2 decision, the Court found that Tennessee's use of malapportionment in creating its state legislative districts was a violation of the equal protection clause. Justice Brennan, writing for the majority, found that this issue was appropriate for the courts to address: "Article III, 2, of the Federal Constitution provides that 'the judicial Power shall extend to all Cases, in Law and Equity, arising under this Constitution, the Laws of the United States, and Treaties made, or which shall be made, under their Authority. . . .'"

It is clear that the cause of action is one that "arises under" the federal Constitution. The complaint alleges that the 1901 statute effects an apportionment that deprives the appellants of the equal protection of the laws in violation of the Fourteenth Amendment.

The majority opinion agreed with the plaintiff's contention and found that the diluted voting strength of individuals in the higher population districts violated their rights of equal protection. As a result of this decision, the "one person, one vote" principle has been applied throughout the U.S. political system.

Dissenting Opinion

Justice Harlan, one of two dissenters, believed that the federal courts had no authority in this matter:

> Once one cuts through the thicket of discussion devoted to "jurisdiction," "standing," "justiciability," and "political question," there emerges a straightforward issue which, in my view, is determinative of this case. Does the complaint disclose a violation of a federal constitutional right, in other words, a claim over which a United States District Court would have jurisdiction? . . . However, in my opinion, appellants' allegations, accepting all of them as true, do not, parsed down or as a whole, show an infringement by Tennessee of any rights assured by the Fourteenth Amendment. Accordingly, I believe the complaint should have been dismissed for "failure to state a claim upon which relief can be granted."

Implications of the Case

- Many areas of the United States had experienced a similar shift of population from rural to urban areas. The decision in *Baker v. Carr* forced all states that had not redistricted their state legislatures based on their current population distribution to do so.
- Because of the *Baker* decision, when population patterns shifted again in subsequent decades from urban to suburban areas, representation in state legislatures and in Congress shifted as well to mirror this change.
- "One person, one vote" has become a bedrock principle of American democracy. The only exceptions are specified by the U.S. Constitution. In both the Electoral College and the U.S. Senate, lower population states have more power per capita. Because *Baker v. Carr* has become accepted law, the fight over district lines has focused on the concept of gerrymandering.

Shaw v. Reno (1993)

Key Facts of the Case

- Drawing bizarrely shaped political districts to benefit a political party has a long history in the United States and around the world. The term "gerrymander" was first used to describe a Massachusetts state senate district drawn by Governor Elbridge Gerry that resembled the shape of a salamander and intended to benefit the minority Democratic-Republican Party. The gerrymander worked, as Federalists, in spite of an overwhelming victory in the 1812 elections in Massachusetts, could not take control of the gerrymandered Senate seat.
- Until the case of *Shaw v. Reno*, redistricting was largely considered a political question, one outside the scope of judicial remedies.
- In the 1990s, African Americans made up approximately 11 percent of the voting age population and held about 5 percent of the seats in Congress and in state legislatures. The Voting Rights Act encouraged states to draw majority-minority districts to increase the representation of minority groups in legislatures.
- The U.S. attorney general rejected a North Carolina plan that created only one majority-minority district. (Approximately 22 percent of North Carolina was African American.) After the 1990 census, the state received a twelfth seat in Congress and endeavored to create a second African-American majority district.
- The twelfth district attempted to string together far-flung centers of the African-American population. This gerrymander created a bizarre and irregular

shape that at one point was connected by I-85, an interstate highway that housed no residents. The *Wall Street Journal* dubbed it "political pornography."

- White plaintiffs in North Carolina and four other states sued, claiming that the majority-minority districts violated their equal protection rights.

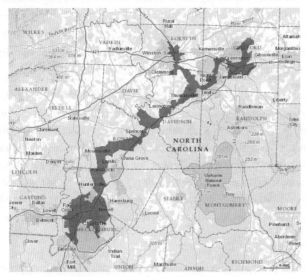

Source: United States Department of the Interior

Constitutional Questions

Can race be used as the sole or primary factor in redistricting? Are there any limits to the lack of compactness a state can employ in gerrymandering its voting districts?

Majority Opinion

In a very complex 5–4 decision, Justice Sandra Day O'Connor applied the strict scrutiny standard to the state's use of race and found that District 12 needed to reexamine:

> *A reapportionment plan that includes in one district individuals who belong to the same race, but who are otherwise widely separated by geographical and political boundaries, and who may have little in common with one another but the color of their skin, bears an uncomfortable resemblance to political apartheid. It reinforces the perception that members of the same racial group—regardless of their age, education, economic status, or the community in which they live—think alike, share the same political interests, and will prefer the same candidates at the polls.*

The majority opinion did not exclude all consideration of race, but it ruled that it cannot be the sole factor:

> *Moreover, redistricting differs from other kinds of state decision making in that the legislature always is aware of race when it draws district lines, just as it is aware of age, economic status, religious and political persuasion, and a variety of other demographic factors. That sort of race consciousness does not lead inevitably to impermissible race discrimination. As Wright demonstrates, when members of a racial group live together in one community, a reapportionment plan that concentrates members of the group in one district and excludes them from others may reflect wholly legitimate purposes.*

The high court remanded the case to the lower court with instructions about how to avoid an unconstitutional racial gerrymander. The 12th district was reshaped in a more compact manner. Litigation regarding North Carolina's congressional districts has continued until today without much of a respite. The district that was broken up as a result of

Shaw v. Reno was one of the first examples of the use of computer modeling in constructing voter districts. Now computer models are used most commonly to "crack and pack" districts in order to win the most possible seats in Congress for the majority party in the state legislature. Litigation today focuses mostly around the dilution of the strength of Democratic voters in states whose legislatures are controlled by Republicans.

Dissenting Opinion

Justice Souter, writing for four dissenting justices, discussed the irony of using the equal protection clause to erode the voting strength of minority voters:

> *Finally, we must ask whether otherwise permissible redistricting to benefit an underrepresented minority group becomes impermissible when the minority group is defined by its race. The Court today answers this question in the affirmative, and its answer is wrong. If it is permissible to draw boundaries to provide adequate representation for rural voters, for union members, for Hasidic Jews, for Polish Americans, or for Republicans, it necessarily follows that it is permissible to do the same thing for members of the very minority group whose history in the United States gave birth to the Equal Protection Clause. . . . A contrary conclusion could only be described as perverse.*

Implications of the Case

- The new frontier of gerrymandering cases may center on something political scientists call the "efficiency gap," or how many votes are wasted by the minority party as compared to the majority party in legislative elections. Although this type of analysis involves complex math, some of the results are plain to see. In the nation as a whole, Democratic candidates received 48 percent of the votes for seats in the U.S. House in 2016 but won only 45 percent of the seats.
- States that have worked their cracking and packing to its maximum extent have more dramatic results. In Texas, Democratic candidates for the U.S. House received 37 percent of the vote in 2016 and 31 percent of the seats in Congress. In North Carolina, Democratic candidates for the U.S. House received 47 percent of the vote in 2016 and 23 percent of the seats in Congress. In Wisconsin in 2016, Democratic candidates for the U.S. House received 50 percent of the vote and 38 percent of the state's seats in Congress.
- In January 2018, the Supreme Court refused to hear an appeal based on this type of cracking and packing from North Carolina.
- Many other cases about redistricting are working their way toward the Supreme Court. The Court appears to be sharply divided between liberal and conservative justices. One claim often made by Republicans is that they are merely doing the same thing that Democrats once did when they controlled Congress and state governments.
- Many red and blue states have decided to remove the state legislature from the redistricting process and have appointed nonpartisan commissions that draw district lines based on geography and on the commonalities of the population. The mechanics of these commissions operate in very different manners, but California, Arizona, Idaho, and Washington have created a nonpartisan redistricting process that excludes the governors and the state legislatures.

Citizens United v. Federal Election Commission (2010)

Key Facts of the Case (including a brief history of major events in campaign finance reform):

- In 1907, the Tillman Act banned corporate contributions to candidates and political parties. (Corporations easily evaded this by giving money to executives who then donated money to candidates or to political parties.)
- In 1947, the provisions of the Tillman Act were extended to labor unions.

- Congress passed the Federal Elections Campaign Act of 1971 (FECA). It required the disclosure of all contributors and it established a new agency with regulatory authority, the Federal Election Commission (FEC).
- In 1974, FECA was amended and set limits for individual donations. Those limits have been raised many times. Wealthy donors often multiply these limits by including all the individuals in their household and friends and relatives (to whom they can currently gift $15,000 a year without tax consequences).
- One method of avoiding FECA limits was to give to the party instead of the candidate who then used the money to support the candidate. (This is called soft money.)
- In a rare act of cooperation between liberals and conservatives, Congress passed the Bipartisan Campaign Reform Act in 2002 (also known as the BCRA or McCain-Feingold Act). It banned soft money and issue or advocacy ads within 30 days of a primary or 60 days of a general election.
- The BCRA was challenged as an unconstitutional impingement on free speech in *McConnell v. FEC* (2003). By a 5–4 vote, the major provisions of the act were found to be constitutional. The majority opinion said that the limits on spending and on issue or advocacy ads had a minimal impact of free speech and that they acted to counter "both the actual corruption threatened by large financial contributions and . . . the appearance of corruption."
- During the 2004 campaign, the FEC ruled that Michael Moore's film, *Fahrenheit 9/11*, which was highly critical of then-presidential candidate George W. Bush, did not violate the BCRA because it was a film produced for normal commercial activity.
- Justice Sandra Day O'Connor retired in 2006 and was replaced with Justice Samuel Alito. With Justice Alito's vote, *McConnell v. FEC* was partially overturned in 2007 in *FEC v. Wisconsin Right to Life*. In this case, the Court ruled 5–4 that the BCRA prohibition against airing an issue-oriented film within 60 days of a general election was unconstitutional. Although the film clearly suggested which candidate was superior, it did not specifically ask viewers to vote for or against anything.
- Citizens United is a conservative 501(c)3 organization, an officially registered charity where contributors can claim a tax deduction. During the 2008 presidential primary season, it produced *Hillary: The Movie*, a movie that was highly critical of candidate Hillary Clinton. Similar to the film in *FEC v. Wisconsin Right to Life*, it did not use the "magic words" vote for or vote against. Citizens United sought to offer the film on on-demand cable television, and the FEC sought to ban it under the BCRA.

Constitutional Question

Did the BCRA deny citizens and corporations their free speech rights in the 30 days before a primary and the 60 days before a general election?

Majority Opinion

In an extremely contentious 5–4 decision, the Supreme Court ruled that BCRA restrictions on political speech that didn't expressly advocate a voting choice or coordinate efforts with a campaign were unconstitutional. In the majority decision Justice Kennedy wrote, "If the First Amendment has any force, it prohibits Congress from fining or jailing citizens, or associations of citizens, for simply engaging in political speech." Kennedy also criticized the aspects of enforcement that targeted large corporations, "Thus, under the Government's reasoning, wealthy media corporations could have their voices diminished to put them on par with other media entities. There is no precedent for permitting this under the First Amendment."

Chief Justice Roberts dismissed arguments that the Court was swiftly overturning recent precedents such as *McConnell v. FEC*:

> *Stare decisis is a doctrine of preservation, not transformation. It counsels deference to past mistakes, but provides no justification for making new ones. There is therefore no*

basis for the Court to give precedential sway to reasoning that it has never accepted, simply because that reasoning happens to support a conclusion reached on different grounds that have since been abandoned or discredited.

Dissenting Opinion

Justice Stevens, in his thirty-fifth and final year on the Court, penned a potent dissent:

The real issue in this case concerns how, not if, the appellant may finance its electioneering. Citizens United is a wealthy nonprofit corporation that runs a political action committee (PAC) with millions of dollars in assets. Under the Bipartisan Campaign Reform Act of 2002 (BCRA), it could have used those assets to televise and promote Hillary: The Movie *wherever and whenever it wanted to. It also could have spent unrestricted sums to broadcast* Hillary *at any time other than the 30 days before the last primary election. Neither Citizens United's nor any other corporation's speech has been "banned," ante, at 1. All that the parties dispute is whether Citizens United had a right to use the funds in its general treasury to pay for broadcasts during the 30-day period. The notion that the First Amendment dictates an affirmative answer to that question is, in my judgment, profoundly misguided.*

He feared that this decision would unleash an avalanche of corporate spending on political campaign:

At bottom, the Court's opinion is thus a rejection of the common sense of the American people, who have recognized a need to prevent corporations from undermining self-government since the founding, and who have fought against the distinctive corrupting potential of corporate electioneering since the days of Theodore Roosevelt. It is a strange time to repudiate that common sense. While American democracy is imperfect, few outside the majority of this Court would have thought its flaws included a dearth [lack] of corporate money in politics.

Implications of the Case

- "Super-PACS" spent over $1 billion on the 2020 campaign and are predicted to spend even more in future elections. About 40 percent of the spending comes from 50 ultra-rich individuals.
- Although independent organization like 501(c)3s and corporations still cannot expressly advocate support for a candidate or donate directly to a candidate or to a party, their independent expenditures during an election are free of regulation.
- Some of this spending comes from 501(c)4s, which are also registered as charitable organizations but ones that can shield the identity of their donors. Many fear that this "dark money" can come from criminals and foreigners attempting to influence the U.S. political system.
- *Citizens United v. Federal Election Commission* remains a controversial decision, with most conservatives supporting it and most liberals blaming it for the increased glut of money in politics. There are exceptions, however, including the usually liberal American Civil Liberties Union, which supported the decision.
- If a majority in Congress and the president or a two-thirds majority in Congress without the president opposed *Citizens United v. Federal Election Commission*, they could legislate in ways that would curb the influence of this decision.
- For example, laws could require stricter donor disclosure requirements and that unions and corporations put all political spending decisions to a vote of shareholders or members; they could also order the IRS to crack down on tax-deductible donations that are really benefiting candidates or parties.

- Others argue that our campaign finance systems have become so complex, the best reform is just to eliminate all restrictions. Even though *Citizens United v. Federal Election Commission* freed independent organizations, restrictions still remain on parties and candidates. A complete elimination of restrictions would level the playing field.

Election Processes, Partisanship, and Divided Government Timeline

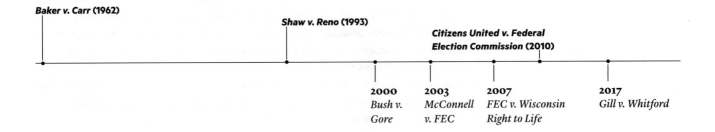

Baker v. Carr (1962)

Shaw v. Reno (1993)

Citizens United v. Federal Election Commission (2010)

2000
Bush v. Gore

2003
McConnell v. FEC

2007
FEC v. Wisconsin Right to Life

2017
Gill v. Whitford

Summary of Main Points

CON-3: The Republican ideal in the United States is manifested in the structure and operation of the legislative branch.

PRD-2: The impact of federal policies on campaigning and electoral rules continues to be contested by both sides of the political spectrum.

These cases demonstrate the highly contentious nature of the rules that govern the U.S. political system. We expect that politics, like our favorite sporting events, will be hard fought, but we expect the battles to be about winning elections or winning major votes in Congress, not about settling the rules of the game. The rules of great American sports like baseball, football, and basketball have been crafted and refined over many years. In the off season, changes in rules are sometimes negotiated and announced. Unlike politics, these rules fights do not take place in the heat of action on the playing field.

With only a few months to go before the 2018 midterm elections, several states were involved in complex legal battles to settle the lines of congressional districts. In Pennsylvania, a plan that cracks and packs Democratic-leaning regions of the state was passed by a Republican-dominated legislature, vetoed by the Democratic governor, replaced by Democratic judges with a plan that will swing seats to the Democrats, and may be revived by the Republican-dominated Supreme Court.

The issues in these cases do not represent all of the rules fights that are pending and that have taken place in recent elections. For example, in *Bush v. Gore* (2000), the Supreme Court shut down Florida's recount effort and, as a result, handed the 2000 presidential election to George W. Bush. In many states across the nation, courts are evaluating if newly passed voter ID laws violate the equal protection clause. In some states, felons are banned from voting for life, but federal law could grant them the right to vote in congressional and presidential elections.

Although the battle over election rules is almost endless, there have been some areas of bipartisan agreement that have endured. After the 2000 election, Congress passed the Help Americans Vote Act (HAVA). The funding attached to this law helped eliminate the infamous punch card ballot with the "hanging chad" that Florida struggled to recount in the weeks before *Bush v. Gore*. Also, *Baker v. Carr* eliminated the possibility of districts that were skewed in population. This settled rule of law has provided clear limits to gerrymandering, and it established the judicial branch as an arbiter of equal protection issues related to voting. Similarly, *Shaw v. Reno* provided guidance on how states should consider race while redistricting. Both of these rulings attempted to boost the integrity of the legislative branch.

Settled points of law quickly become contentious again as events and strategies evolve. In *Baker v. Carr*, states were ordered to redistrict. Forty years later in Texas, Republican Party operatives redistricted in the middle of the decade, an act later sanctioned by a Supreme Court decision. The finely tuned cracking and packing in that plan resulted in six U.S. House seats swinging into GOP control. Many other states followed suit, and now the Court is examining whether this type of systematic underrepresentation of the minority party in a state violates the equal protection clause. The Supreme Court heard oral arguments in the case of *Gill v. Whitford* on October 3, 2017, which tests the constitutionality of Wisconsin's highly gerrymandered voting districts.

A totally different but equally important area of election rules involves campaign finance. Political reformers have long recognized the need to counter the power of money in the political system. In Madisonian terms, campaign finance laws represent ambition counteracting ambition, but the power of money in elections cannot be fully neutralized without eliminating the freedom of speech, a cure that would usher in a new set of constitutional problems.

In *Citizens United v. Federal Election Commission*, the Court eliminated bans on issue advocacy ads before an election, opening the floodgates for massive Super PAC spending. Although limits and restrictions remain in place on candidates, parties, and regular PACs, independent and often anonymous sources flood all media with highly partisan information at all times and especially during election years.

While the Courts are busy arbitrating these election-related rules fights, Congress remains uninterested in crafting new legislation to address either campaign finance or redistricting. Both problems could be addressed through new legislation. Though laws that depoliticize redistricting or that make political spending more transparent may be temporarily disadvantageous to the party in control, they would instill long-term confidence and allow government to spend more time addressing issues other than the rules of political engagement. In the meantime, we will have to look to the Court as it attempts to resolve competing claims about equal protection, the freedom of speech, and the role of federalism in determining election laws.

Assessing Student Understanding

1. Explain one way in which highly gerrymandered districts impact the work of the U.S. House of Representatives.

2. Explain the difference between gerrymandering and malapportionment.

3. After the *Citizens United v. Federal Election Commission* decision, explain one restriction on campaign finance that was eliminated and two that remain in place.

Questions for Class Discussion and Debate

1. What is the best method for redistricting? Should it remain a natural extension of the very partisan politics that takes place in state legislatures, or should it be carried out in a different manner?

2. Is it necessary to enact laws to counter the influence of money in elections? Why or why not? If so, what laws should Congress create?

3. The equal protection clause of the Fourteenth Amendment has come into play in a wide variety of cases that deal with the right to vote. Assess the performance of our electoral system in facilitating voter equality. In your opinion, how do we match up to the ideal of "one person, one vote"?

Cluster 11: Equal Protection, Marriage, Gender, and Sexual Orientation

The Big Issues

If you have read through the 10 preceding clusters of cases, you will find some familiar concepts in the cases that follow. Once again, they display a Court and a society that is grappling with how to apply the concept of equal protection in changing conditions. Also, they demonstrate how the high court often becomes an arbiter in highly charged issues that spring from social movements.

The cases in this cluster also deal with very personal matters, and two of them also involve protections based on the due process as well as the equal protection clause. *Loving v. Virginia* (1967) examines the constitutionality of state laws that ban interracial marriages. By the time this case reached the high court, almost all distinctions based on race had been eliminated from state law through either legislation or court decisions. The Commonwealth of Virginia argued that its laws against interracial marriage did not violate the equal protection clause because they applied equally to White Americans and Black Americans.

United States v. Virginia (1996) is a women's rights case that builds on the precedent established in *Reed v. Reed* (1971). In that case, almost all legal distinctions between males and females were struck down as unconstitutional. Plaintiffs in *United States v. Virginia* challenged the state's operation of a male-only public college. In order to rectify the situation, Virginia proposed establishing an equivalent female college. Unlike the segregation of races, male-only and female-only educational settings have been sometimes viewed as positive formative experiences.

The final case in this cluster examines laws that regulated individual sexual practices. These concerns are at the center of the sphere of privacy that had been recognized in many other cases such as *Griswold v. Connecticut* (1965) and *Roe v. Wade* (1973). We expect laws to protect individuals from unwanted sexual contact, but we also expect liberty from government interference in the freely chosen sexual practices of adults. Yet, that is a recent development. Colonies and most states had "sodomy" laws proscribing certain sexual acts, even between consenting married adults.

In *Lawrence v. Texas* (2003), because these laws were often enforced against gays and not heterosexuals, this appeared to be an equal protection issue. However, the very existence of these laws and their invasive nature brought forward due process concerns.

Constitutional Connection

Fourteenth Amendment, Section 1

All persons born or naturalized in the United States, and subject to the jurisdiction thereof, are citizens of the United States and of the State wherein they reside. No State shall make or enforce any law which shall abridge the privileges or immunities of citizens of the United States; nor shall any State deprive any person of life, liberty, or property, without due process of law; nor deny to any person within its jurisdiction the equal protection of the laws.

CORE CASES

Loving v. Virginia (1967)

Key Facts of the Case

- Mildred Jeter and Richard Loving, residents of Virginia, went to neighboring Washington, D.C., to marry.
- Richard was White and Mildred, who self-identified as Native American, was considered to be African American by Virginia authorities.
- Virginia and 15 other states had laws that made miscegenation, or interracial marriage, illegal.
- The local police arrested them and charged them with miscegenation.
- At first, the Lovings dealt with their legal troubles by living in Washington, D.C., where interracial marriage was legal, but they both missed their homes and their families.
- They returned to Virginia, where they pursued this case with the help of the American Civil Liberties Union.
- The Lovings did not attend oral arguments at the Supreme Court when their landmark case was heard.
- When their attorney asked Richard Loving if he had anything that he wanted the justices to hear, he is reported to have said, "Tell the Court I love my wife, and it is just unfair that I can't live with her in Virginia."

Constitutional Question

Did the state's laws against interracial marriage violate the equal protection clause of the Fourteenth Amendment?

Majority Opinion

A unanimous court ruled that Virginia's laws against interracial marriage violated the equal protection clause and the due process clause of the Fourteenth Amendment. Chief Justice Warren, writing for the whole Court, said the following:

> *There can be no question but that Virginia's miscegenation statutes rest solely upon distinctions drawn according to race. The statutes proscribe generally accepted conduct if engaged in by members of different races. Over the years, this Court has consistently repudiated "distinctions between citizens solely because of their ancestry" as being "odious to a free people whose institutions are founded upon the doctrine of equality."*

The Court also ruled that Virginia's law violated the due process rights of its citizens:

> *These statutes also deprive the Lovings of liberty without due process of law in violation of the due process clause of the Fourteenth Amendment. The freedom to marry has long been recognized as one of the vital personal rights essential to the orderly pursuit of happiness by free men. Marriage is one of the basic civil rights of man, "fundamental to our very existence and survival." Skinner v. Oklahoma (1942). . . . To deny this fundamental freedom on so unsupportable a basis as the racial classifications embodied in these statutes, classifications so directly subversive of the principle of equality at the heart of the Fourteenth Amendment, is surely to deprive all the State's citizens of liberty without due process of law. The Fourteenth Amendment requires that the freedom of choice to marry not be restricted by invidious racial discriminations. Under our Constitution, the freedom to marry, or not marry, a person of another race resides with the individual, and cannot be infringed by the State.*
>
> *These convictions must be reversed.*
>
> *It is so ordered.*

Dissenting Opinion

There was no dissent.

Implications of the Case

- All state laws against miscegenation were declared unconstitutional.
- *Loving v. Virginia* was used as precedent in arguing that laws banning same-sex marriage were unconstitutional.
- Richard died a few years after this case, killed by a drunk driver. Mildred Loving passed away in 2008, never having remarried. They are survived by three generations of offspring.

United States v. Virginia (1996)

Key Facts of the Case

- The Virginia Military Institute (VMI), founded in 1839, was an all-male publicly funded military college.
- At the time an anonymous complaint was filed against VMI in 1989, only two publicly funded colleges or universities excluded women. They were both elite southern military colleges, VMI and The Citadel in South Carolina.
- VMI employs an "adversative" system of education that begins with seven months of extreme physical and psychological challenges. New recruits are called "rats" and forced to run the "rat line," part of a finely honed training process that, in the opinion of most associated with VMI, has played a critical role in creating generations of excellent military leaders, soldiers, and citizens in all lines of work.
- VMI and its supporters claimed that the admission of women would severely degrade its unique educational approach.
- Instead of admitting women to VMI, Virginia proposed creating a similar school for women, the Virginia Women's Institute for Leadership (VWIL).

Constitutional Questions

Does the state's refusal to admit women to VMI violate the equal protection clause? If so, is the creation of a women's school with similar goals and practices a satisfactory remedy?

Majority Opinion

The Court ruled 7–1 that as a publicly funded college, VMI must be open to women. The proposed creation of a woman's military college would not have provided an equal opportunity for women because it would lack VMI's prestige and its graduates would not be afforded the same opportunities. Justice Ruth Bader Ginsburg wrote for the majority, "Neither the goal of producing citizen-soldiers nor VMI's implementing methodology is inherently unsuitable to women. And the school's impressive record in producing leaders has made admission desirable to some women. Nevertheless, Virginia has elected to preserve exclusively for men the advantages and opportunities a VMI education affords."

Ginsberg argued for full application of the equal protection clause to women:

Since Reed, the Court has repeatedly recognized that neither federal nor state government acts compatibly with the equal protection principle when a law or official policy denies to women, simply because they are women, full citizenship stature—equal opportunity to aspire, achieve, participate in and contribute to society based on their individual talents and capacities.

Dissenting Opinion

Justice Thomas recused himself because his son was enrolled at VMI at the time. Therefore, Justice Scalia was the lone dissent. He argued that the Court was trying to instill social value and usurp legislative powers:

> *Much of the Court's opinion is devoted to deprecating the closed mindedness of our forebears with regard to women's education, and even with regard to the treatment of women in areas that have nothing to do with education. Closed minded they were—as every age is, including our own, with regard to matters it cannot guess, because it simply does not consider them debatable. The virtue of a democratic system with a First Amendment is that it readily enables the people, over time, to be persuaded that what they took for granted is not so, and to change their laws accordingly. . . . But in my view the function of this Court is to preserve our society's values regarding (among other things) equal protection, not to revise them . . .*

Justice Scalia did not believe that the state was necessarily obligated to create a parallel college for women, but the fact that it did should have satisfied any equal protection concerns. He wrote "VWIL was carefully designed by professional educators who have long experience in educating young women."

Implications of the Case

- VMI was the last all-male public university in the United States. The VMI Board of Directors considered becoming a private institution so it could remain all male, but they decided that they needed state funding to remain viable. The only other state-sponsored military institute, The Citadel in South Carolina, had admitted women while this case played out. U.S. military academies such as West Point and Annapolis had admitted women 20 years earlier.
- Between 1997 and 2017, 431 women have graduated from VMI with a retention rate of 66 percent (compared to 69 percent for men).
- All publicly funded education programs must be open to males and females.
- The majority opinion still allowed for single-sex private colleges to continue operating. A small number of all-female colleges and an even smaller number of all-male colleges still exist. Students in single-sex colleges receive federal financial aid and benefit from any federal grants that may have been awarded to the school.
- Some believe that even this federal involvement is unconstitutional, but it has not been challenged in court.

Lawrence v. Texas (2003)

Key Facts of the Case

- In a similar case in 1986, the Court ruled 5–4 in *Bowers v. Hardwick* that state laws against sodomy were constitutional. In a legal sense, sodomy included all types of consensual sexual contact that a state deemed to be illegal.
- In *Bowers v. Hardwick,* two gay men were arrested for engaging in consensual sex. Because they were prosecuted under a law that punished both homosexual and heterosexual sodomy, the majority did not consider equal protection issues.
- The four dissenting justices in *Bowers v. Hardwick* pointed out how these laws were only used to prosecute gays and that heterosexuals, whether married or not, had acquired considerable rights of privacy through decisions such as *Griswold v. Connecticut* and *Eisenstadt v. Baird* (1972).
- The fact pattern in *Lawrence v. Texas* was remarkably similar to *Bowers v. Hardwick.* Both cases began with police officers entering homes for other reasons and then arresting gay men who were engaged in consensual sex. Lawrence was held overnight in prison and fined $200.

Constitutional Questions

Did the state's enforcement of its sodomy laws against individuals for homosexual acts and not for heterosexual acts violate the equal protection clause? Do laws that regulate private consensual sex violate the due process clause?

Majority Opinion

Even though the Court had become more conservative on most issues in the 17 years since *Bowers v. Hardwick*, justices voted 6–3 to overturn Lawrence's conviction and to strike down Texas's anti-sodomy laws.

Justice Kennedy wrote the opinion of the Court:

> *Liberty protects the person from unwarranted government intrusions into a dwelling or other private places. In our tradition the State is not omnipresent in the home. And there are other spheres of our lives and existence, outside the home, where the State should not be a dominant presence. Freedom extends beyond spatial bounds. Liberty presumes an autonomy of self that includes freedom of thought, belief, expression, and certain intimate conduct.*

The majority rejected making this decision on the grounds of equal protection, because a state could continue to legislate about private sexual activity as long as the laws applied to everyone. "Were we to hold the statute invalid under the Equal Protection Clause some might question whether a prohibition would be valid if drawn differently, say, to prohibit the conduct both between same-sex and different-sex participants."

Kennedy's opinion was a precedent for *Obergefell v. Hodges* (2015):

> *When homosexual conduct is made criminal by the law of the State, that declaration in and of itself is an invitation to subject homosexual persons to discrimination both in the public and in the private spheres. The central holding of* Bowers *has been brought in question by this case, and it should be addressed. Its continuance as precedent demeans the lives of homosexual persons.*

Dissenting Opinion

The dissent was written by Justice Scalia and joined by Chief Justice Rehnquist and Justice Thomas. Justice Scalia began by accusing the majority of a double standard in reversing *Bowers v. Hardwick* so rapidly while claiming that *Roe v. Wade* created precedent that should endure:

> *"Liberty finds no refuge in a jurisprudence of doubt."* Planned Parenthood of Southeastern Pa. v. Casey *(1992). That was the Court's sententious response, barely more than a decade ago, to those seeking to overrule* Roe v. Wade. *The Court's response today, to those who have engaged in a 17-year crusade to overrule* Bowers v. Hardwick, *is very different. The need for stability and certainty presents no barrier.*

The dissenting justices believed that the states have the right to regulate the moral behavior of their citizens. "Countless judicial decisions and legislative enactments have relied on the ancient proposition that a governing majority's belief that certain sexual behavior is 'immoral and unacceptable' constitutes a rational basis for regulation."

Justice Scalia pointed to the potentially far-reaching impacts of this decision in denying states their traditional police powers:

> *State laws against bigamy, same-sex marriage, adult incest, prostitution, masturbation, adultery, fornication, bestiality, and obscenity are likewise sustainable only in light of* Bowers' *validation of laws based on moral choices. Every single one of these laws is called into question by today's decision; the Court makes no effort to cabin the scope of its decision to exclude them from its holding.*

Implications of the Case

- At the time of the *Lawrence v. Texas* decision, only 13 states still had sodomy laws. All of them were struck down by this decision.
- Kansas's law that punished underage consensual sex between males and females less harshly than underage homosexual contact was struck down.
- The laws against incest in all 50 states and D.C. remain in force and Alabama's law against the sale of "sex toys" has been upheld.
- In 2003, a few months after *Lawrence v. Texas*, the Massachusetts Supreme Court ruled that the state must allow same-sex couples to marry. The majority opinion included a line from *Planned Parenthood of Southeastern Pennsylvania v. Casey* that was also cited in *Lawrence v. Texas*: "Our obligation is to define the liberty of all, not to mandate our own moral code."

Equal Protection, Marriage, Gender, and Sexual Orientation Case Timeline

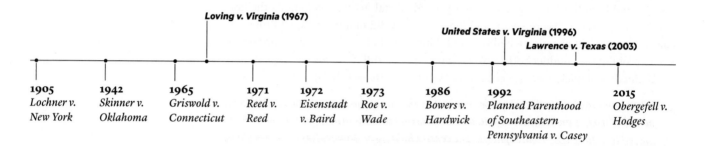

Loving v. Virginia (1967)

United States v. Virginia (1996)

Lawrence v. Texas (2003)

1905	1942	1965	1971	1972	1973	1986	1992	2015
Lochner v. New York	Skinner v. Oklahoma	Griswold v. Connecticut	Reed v. Reed	Eisenstadt v. Baird	Roe v. Wade	Bowers v. Hardwick	Planned Parenthood of Southeastern Pennsylvania v. Casey	Obergefell v. Hodges

Summary of Main Points

PRD-1: The Fourteenth Amendment's "equal protection clause" as well as other constitutional provisions have often been used to support the advancement of equality.

PMI-3: Public policy promoting civil rights is influenced by citizen-state interactions and constitutional interpretation over time.

Two of the three cases in this cluster deal with the sometimes overlapping and critically important main clauses of the Fourteenth Amendment. Thankfully, understanding how to differentiate the equal protection and due process clause is more important to legal scholars than to students of U.S. government. Also, when one clause is violated, the application of the other clause usually becomes a moot or irrelevant point. In *Brown v. Board of Education* (1954), the Court considered questions about due process violations irrelevant, as segregation of schools clearly violated equal protection. In *Lawrence v. Texas*, the majority focused on substantive due process instead of equal protection. The impact was the same and the concept of freedom was expanded.

However, there are some helpful points to keep in mind about the concept of due process. When the term appears in the Fifth Amendment, it says that no person shall "be deprived of life, liberty or property without due process of law." The most common way for a state to strip a citizen of life, liberty, or property is through civil or criminal proceedings. Therefore, the right to an attorney, the right to confront witnesses, the right to be free from unreasonable searches, and all of the other rights in the Bill of Rights that protect citizens during legal proceedings are due process rights. These rights relate to procedural due process because they protect people during court procedures.

Procedural due process is relatively clear and straightforward compared to the type of due process that appears in the cases in this cluster. *Loving v. Virginia* and *Lawrence v. Texas* feature the appearance of substantive due process, a much more abstract and controversial concept. If citizens were prohibited from marrying the partners of their choice or if the government could regulate the private sex lives of consenting adults, significant liberty would be lost without any type of due process.

Substantive due process was first used in *Lochner v. New York* (1905) when it struck down a law that prohibited bakers from working more than a certain number of hours each week. The Court ruled that the law denied bakers the liberty to make their own decisions. In the later part of the twentieth century, the Court moved away from applying the concept of substantive due process to economic matters and began applying it to protect personal rights such as the liberty to use birth control.

Conservatives on the Court such as Justice Thomas and Justice Scalia have objected to the extension of due process rights in these areas of morality that have been traditionally subject to state regulation. They favor extending more power to states to operate in the manner that they see fit and that coincide with choices made by the state legislature. They have largely rejected the Court's role as an agent of social change.

The social movements and the cultural changes that propelled these legal battles sometimes move faster than the laws themselves. Although cases like *United States v. Virginia* are still controversial, that was not evident in 2017 when Justice Ruth Bader Ginsburg, author of the majority decision, made her first visit to VMI. At the time of the decision, the college's superintendent called it "a savage disappointment." More than 20 years later, students, 11 percent of which are female, enthusiastically received the 89-year-old justice. Justice Ginsburg shared her own physical training regimen with students and reminisced about one of her best friends, Justice Antonin Scalia, who wrote the dissent in this case and always challenged her to be better at her profession. "I miss him very much," she said. "I say without him, the court is a paler place, because he brought such zest to our discussions."

Assessing Student Understanding

1. Explain how each of the cases in this cluster impacted traditional state powers.

2. Explain the difference between substantive and procedural due process.

3. Identify the social movement that played a role in each of the cases in this cluster.

Questions for Class Discussion and Debate

1. Combined with Title IX, *United States v. Virginia* challenges all educational activities to be coeducational, especially if there is no parallel activity available for the gender that had been excluded. This has resulted in some unanticipated sights, such as boys competing in girls' swim meets and field hockey games and girls joining high school football teams. Do you agree with the current practice of equal protection of genders in state-supported activities, or do you favor modifications?

2. Should single-sex colleges continue to be able to apply for federal grants and for financial aid for their students? Is this a violation of the equal protection clause?

3. Even after *Loving v. Virginia* and *Obergefell v. Hodges*, differences in state marriage laws remain in effect. For example, states across the nation vary in age and blood test requirements and on the legality of cousins marrying each other. Do these differences violate equal protection, or are they examples of traditional areas of state control?

Cluster 12: The Powers of Congress

The Big Issues

The judiciary's evolving interpretation of the commerce clause is at the heart of the study of American government. Starting with *Gibbons v. Ogden* (1824), the Court has used the commerce clause as the basis for many congressional actions. *Gibbons v. Ogden* provided a clear and easily understood first example of interstate commerce. Steamboats that crossed the Hudson River between New York and New Jersey were, literally, interstate commerce that Congress was empowered to regulate.

All subsequent examples of interstate commerce that came under court rulings are more abstract. The study of cases dealing with the commerce clause could take up the entirety of a college-level history course. The course would include the slowly expanding uses of the commerce clause as a basis for regulation during the age of populism and during the New Deal.

The first case in this cluster, *Heart of Atlanta Motel v. United States* (1964), shows how the commerce clause was used to support legislation that banned discriminatory practices by businesses, and it represents the high-water mark of congressional powers. As we have seen, *United States v. Lopez* (1995) was the beginning of an era when the courts began to chip away at congressional powers. The second case in this cluster, *National Federation of Independent Business v. Sebelius* (2012) demonstrates how congressional powers are in flux.

The final case in this cluster, *Shelby County v. Holder* (2013), raises issues with an article and an amendment that rarely appear in court. The case is about federal control over local voting practices, and it examines state sovereignty provisions in Article IV and federal powers to legislate based on the Fifteenth Amendment, the Civil War–era amendment that attempted to end racial discrimination in voting.

In *Federalist 51*, Madison argues one thing that remains indisputable. He said that our federalist system created a "very interesting point of view." Challenges to Congress's delegated powers in Article I, Section 8, are still exciting and essential to the understanding of our government. All nations have methods to decide upon a proper course of action for a given problem, but the U.S. constitutional system also demands that we also identify the source of the power to take action.

The cases that follow are important examples of Congress and federalism at work. American citizens are understandably agitated about the political issues of the day, but it would be helpful to remember Madison's explanation of the purposeful division of state and national powers from *Federalist 51*:

> *In a single republic, all the power surrendered by the people is submitted to the administration of a single government; and the usurpations are guarded against by a division of the government into distinct and separate departments. In the compound republic of America, the power surrendered by the people is first divided between two distinct governments, and then the portion allotted to each subdivided among distinct and separate departments. Hence a double security arises to the rights of the people.*

Constitutional Connections

Article I, Section 8

The Congress shall have Power To lay and collect Taxes, Duties, Imposts and Excises, to pay the Debts and provide for the common Defence and general Welfare of the United States; but all Duties, Imposts and Excises shall be uniform throughout the United States; To borrow Money on the credit of the United States; To regulate Commerce with foreign Nations, and among the several States, and with the Indian Tribes; To establish an uniform Rule of Naturalization, and uniform Laws on the subject of Bankruptcies throughout the United States; To coin Money, regulate the Value thereof, and of foreign Coin, and fix the Standard of Weights and Measures; To provide for the Punishment of counterfeiting the Securities and current Coin of the United States; To establish Post Offices and post Roads; To promote the Progress of Science and useful Arts, by securing for limited Times to Authors and Inventors the exclusive Right to their respective Writings and Discoveries; To constitute Tribunals inferior to the supreme Court; To define and punish Piracies and Felonies committed on the high Seas, and Offenses against the Law of Nations; To declare War, grant Letters of Marque and Reprisal, and make Rules concerning Captures on Land and Water; To raise and support Armies, but no Appropriation of Money to that Use shall be for a longer Term than two Years; To provide and maintain a Navy; To make Rules for the Government and Regulation of the land and naval Forces; To provide for calling forth the Militia to execute the Laws of the Union, suppress Insurrections and repel Invasions; To provide for organizing, arming, and disciplining, the Militia, and for governing such Part of them as may be employed in the Service of the United States, reserving to the States respectively, the Appointment of the Officers, and the Authority of training the Militia according to the discipline prescribed by Congress; To exercise exclusive Legislation in all Cases whatsoever, over such District (not exceeding ten Miles square) as may, by Cession of particular States, and the Acceptance of Congress, become the Seat of the Government of the United States, and to exercise like Authority over all Places purchased by the Consent of the Legislature of the State in which the Same shall be, for the Erection of Forts, Magazines, Arsenals, dock-Yards and other needful Buildings; And To make all Laws which shall be necessary and proper for carrying into Execution the foregoing Powers, and all other Powers vested by this Constitution in the Government of the United States, or in any Department or Officer thereof.

Article IV, Section 1

Full Faith and Credit shall be given in each State to the public Acts, Records, and judicial Proceedings of every other State. And the Congress may by general Laws prescribe the Manner in which such Acts, Records and Proceedings shall be proved, and the Effect thereof.

Tenth Amendment

The powers not delegated to the United States by the Constitution, nor prohibited by it to the States, are reserved to the States respectively, or to the people.

Fourteenth Amendment, Section 1

All persons born or naturalized in the United States, and subject to the jurisdiction thereof, are citizens of the United States and of the State wherein they reside. No State shall make or enforce any law which shall abridge the privileges or immunities of citizens of the United States; nor shall any State deprive any person of life, liberty, or property, without due process of law; nor deny to any person within its jurisdiction the equal protection of the laws.

Fifteenth Amendment

Section 1

The right of citizens of the United States to vote shall not be denied or abridged by the United States or by any State on account of race, color, or previous condition of servitude.

Section 2

The Congress shall have the power to enforce this article by appropriate legislation.

CORE CASES

Heart of Atlanta Motel v. United States (1964)

Key Facts of the Case

- After President Kennedy's assassination in November 1963, his successor, Lyndon Johnson, fought relentlessly for the passage of a major civil rights act that would, among other things, end racial discrimination by private businesses.
- The bill overcame major hurdles in Congress, including the longest filibuster on record, and was signed into law on July 2, 1964.
- Title two of the act said, "Injunctive Relief Against Discrimination In Places Of Public Accommodation Sec. 201. (a) All persons shall be entitled to the full and equal enjoyment of the goods, services, facilities, and privileges, advantages, and accommodations of any place of public accommodation, as defined in this section, without discrimination or segregation on the ground of race, color, religion, or national origin."
- Moreton Rolleston, owner of the Heart of Atlanta Motel, sued because he believed that Title II of the Civil Rights Act of 1964 violated his Fifth Amendment property rights.

Rolleston believed that he had the constitutional right to use his property as he saw fit, which in this case meant denying rooms to African Americans.

- The complaint also claimed that the Civil Rights Act of 1964 exceeded the constitutional limits of Article I's commerce clause in spite of the fact that Heart of Atlanta was a large motel located on an interstate and 75 percent of its patrons were from out of town.
- Rolleston claimed that the Civil Rights Act of 1964 also violated his Thirteenth Amendment rights because it forced him into "involuntary servitude." The Court quickly dismissed this part of his lawsuit.
- Rolleston's suit was joined by Lester Maddox, owner of the Pickrick Restaurant and a future governor of the state of Georgia. Both business owners claimed that they had a constitutional right to choose their customers and to exclude African Americans.

Constitutional Question

Does Congress have the power under the commerce clause to require public businesses to end discriminatory practices?

Majority Opinion

In this case, the Court moved both swiftly and unanimously. On December 14, 1964, only six months after the passage of the act, the Court declared that Congress's actions were firmly based on the commerce clause and that the owners of private businesses had no right to select their customers free from government regulation.

Justice Clark's majority opinion reviewed Congress's power under the commerce clause dating back to *Gibbons v. Ogden*. "We therefore conclude that the action of the Congress in the adoption of the Act as applied here to a motel which concededly serves interstate travelers is within the power granted it by the commerce clause of the Constitution, as interpreted by this Court for 140 years."

He also rejected the plaintiff's use of the Fifth Amendment:

> *Moreover, it would be highly ironical to use the guarantee of due process—a guarantee which plays so important a part in the Fourteenth Amendment, an amendment adopted with the predominant aim of protecting Negroes from discrimination—in order to strip Congress of power to protect Negroes from discrimination. For the foregoing reasons, I concur in holding that the anti-racial discrimination provisions of Title II of the Civil Rights Act of 1964 are valid as applied to this motel and this restaurant.*

The Court also believed Congress had the power to pass this legislation under the Fourteenth Amendment as well as the commerce clause:

> *A decision based on the Fourteenth Amendment would have a more settling effect, making unnecessary litigation over whether a particular restaurant or inn is within the commerce definitions of the Act or whether a particular customer is an interstate traveler. Under my construction, the Act would apply to all customers in all the enumerated places of public accommodation. And that construction would put an end to all obstructionist strategies, and finally close one door on a bitter chapter in American history.*

Dissenting Opinion

There was no dissent.

Implications of the Case

- Businesses across the United States are banned from using discriminatory practices based on race, color, religion, or national origin. Businesses that continue to discriminate are subject to civil lawsuits and penalties from both governments and private citizens.
- The Civil Rights Act of 1964 also bans discrimination in hiring for all businesses with more than 15 employees.
- Although the battle against racial discrimination continues, many historians consider the Civil Rights Act of 1964 to be one of the nation's most effective policies. Interestingly, almost 90 years earlier, the post–Civil War Congress passed similar civil rights bills. Through the combined efforts of all branches of the federal government and the states, those bills were never enforced.
- Congress followed up this legislation with other critically important acts. For example, the Voting Rights Act of 1965 and the Fair Housing Act of 1968 gave local and federal authorities more tools to combat racial discrimination.
- One often overlooked detail in the passage of the Civil Rights Act of 1964 was that President Johnson pushed for its passage in a presidential election year. Many assumed that its passage would cause a negative backlash for him and for his party in the 1964 elections, but the Democrats scored dramatic victories in both the Electoral College and in Congress. In more recent times, it is rare that major legislation is enacted during an election year.

National Federation of Independent Business v. Sebelius (2012)

Key Facts of the Case

- In 2010, 48 million Americans (about 15 percent of the population) lacked health insurance. When those individuals were forced to go to the emergency room or the hospital, taxpayers, insurers, and the hospitals themselves were forced to pick up the tab.

- Indebtedness as a result of health care bills has been a major factor in causing both severe poverty and homelessness.
- Most developed nations provide health insurance to all citizens through general taxes.
- The reform of health care in the United States has been a deeply divisive political issue for more than a generation.
- Access to health care and its costs were major issues in many recent presidential elections, especially in 2008.
- In March 2010, President Barack Obama, fulfilling a campaign pledge, signed the Affordable Care Act (ACA) into law. Among the many provisions of this complex law, it requires most employers to provide health insurance to their employees, and it requires individuals not covered by an employer to purchase health insurance or pay a tax penalty. This law is most commonly called "Obamacare" in the media.
- The law also attempted to force states to expand their Medicaid programs by including people whose incomes were above the poverty line but who still could not afford health care premiums.
- With the promise of repealing the ACA, the Republicans made dramatic gains in the 2010 midterms and took control of both chambers of Congress.
- Most states with Republican governors refused to expand their Medicaid programs. The ACA gave the federal government authority to end all Medicaid funding in those states.
- Many groups sued to stop implementation of parts of the ACA. The National Federation of Independent Business, a lobby for small businesses, was among them. Kathleen Sebelius, a former governor of Kansas, was Obama's Secretary of Health and Human Services, and it was her job to implement the ACA.

Constitutional Questions

Does the individual mandate exceed Congress's powers under the commerce clause and/or taxing and spending clause of Article I, Section 8? Does the coercion to expand Medicaid violate the principles of federalism?

Majority Opinion

The Court voted 5–4 that the commerce clause does not empower Congress to mandate the purchase of health insurance, but Chief Justice Roberts switched sides and voted to uphold the individual mandate under the taxing and spending clause. If this vote had gone the other way, the ACA would have been inoperable.

The Court also voted 7–2 that the coercion built into the ACA to force states to expand Medicaid was unconstitutional. Based on this ruling, states that did not expand Medicaid continued to receive other Medicaid funds.

Justice Breyer voted with the majority on all three issues and wrote the Court's opinion:

According to the majority, the commerce clause does not empower the Federal Government to order individuals to engage in commerce, and the Government's efforts to cast the individual mandate in a different light were unpersuasive.

ACA UPHELD BY TAXING AND SPENDING CLAUSE:

Put simply, Congress may tax and spend. This grant gives the Federal Government considerable influence even in areas where it cannot directly regulate. The Federal Government may enact a tax on an activity that it cannot authorize, forbid, or otherwise control.

WITHHOLDING FUNDS TO STATES THAT REFUSED THE EXPANSION OF MEDICAID IS UNCONSTITUTIONAL:

The second provision of the Affordable Care Act directly challenged here is the Medicaid expansion. Enacted in 1965, Medicaid offers federal funding to States to assist pregnant women, children, needy families, the blind, the elderly, and the disabled in obtaining medical care. . . . In order to receive that funding, States must comply with federal criteria governing matters such as who receives care and what services are provided at what cost. By 1982 every State had chosen to participate in Medicaid. Federal funds received through the Medicaid program have become a substantial part of state budgets, now constituting over 10 percent of most States' total revenue.

The Affordable Care Act expands the scope of the Medicaid program and increases the number of individuals the States must cover. For example, the Act requires state programs to provide Medicaid coverage to adults with incomes up to 133 percent of the federal poverty level, whereas many States now cover adults with children only if their income is considerably lower, and do not cover childless adults at all. . . .

We have upheld Congress's authority to condition the receipt of funds on the States' complying with restrictions on the use of those funds, because that is the means by which Congress ensures that the funds are spent according to its view of the "general Welfare."

Conditions that do not here govern the use of the funds, however, cannot be justified on that basis. When, for example, such conditions take the form of threats to terminate other significant independent grants, the conditions are properly viewed as a means of pressuring the States to accept policy changes.

Dissenting Opinion

ACA VIOLATES COMMERCE CLAUSE AND TAXING AND SPENDING CLAUSE

Justices Scalia, Thomas, Alito, and Kennedy found no constitutional basis for mandating the purchase of health care:

What is absolutely clear, affirmed by the text of the 1789 Constitution, by the Tenth Amendment ratified in 1791, and by innumerable cases of ours in the 220 years since, is that there are structural limits upon federal power—upon what it can prescribe with respect to private conduct, and upon what it can impose upon the sovereign States. Whatever may be the conceptual limits upon the commerce clause and upon the power to tax and spend, they cannot be such as will enable the Federal Government to regulate all private conduct and to compel the States to function as administrators of federal programs.

FORCED EXPANSION OF MEDICAID IS CONSTITUTIONAL AND THE INDIVIDUAL MANDATE IS ALSO COVERED BY THE COMMERCE CLAUSE

Justice Ginsberg concurred on the issue of taxing and spending powers but dissented on the two other votes on constitutional issues. She argued that health care is critically linked to interstate commerce:

The provision of health care is today a concern of national dimension, just as the provision of old-age and survivors' benefits was in the 1930s. In the Social Security Act, Congress installed a federal system to provide monthly benefits to retired wage earners and, eventually, to their survivors. Beyond question, Congress could have adopted a similar scheme for health care. Congress chose, instead, to preserve a central role for private insurers and state governments. According to The Chief Justice, the commerce clause does not permit that preservation. This rigid reading of the Clause makes scant sense and is stunningly retrogressive.

Justice Ginsberg also wrote that conditions of aid have always been accepted by the Court and that to satisfy the majority's concerns about Medicaid expansion all Congress would have had to do was repeal the entirety of Medicaid and then pass it with the new provisions. Instead, it amended the existing law. Ginsberg wrote the following:

> The question posed by the 2010 Medicaid expansion, then, is essentially this: To cover a notably larger population, must Congress take the repeal/reenact route, or may it achieve the same result by amending existing law? The answer should be that Congress may expand by amendment the classes of needy persons entitled to Medicaid benefits. A ritualistic requirement that Congress repeal and reenact spending legislation in order to enlarge the population served by a federally funded program would advance no constitutional principle and would scarcely serve the interests of federalism.

Implications of the Case

- Under the ACA, 20 million more Americans have health insurance. Most of those who still lack coverage live in states that refused to expand Medicaid.
- President Trump was not able to repeal the ACA, but he worked toward weakening the law in many ways, including not enforcing the mandate, not funding parts of the law, not publicizing enrollment procedures, and cutting back on the essential benefits insurance companies are required to cover.
- Americans overwhelmingly support the concept of guaranteed health care but are wary of the government playing too large a role in its administration.
- Parts of the ACA are widely supported by the public, including requiring insurance companies to cover preexisting conditions and parents being able to include children up to age 26 on their insurance plans.
- Many politicians have promised low-cost, high-quality health care, and though the ACA has improved access, the cost of health care still spirals out of control. America's aging population compounds the problem of cost, and some legislative solutions might be unconstitutional based on the Roberts Court's interpretation of the commerce clause.

Shelby County v. Holder (2013)

Key Facts of the Case

- In 1965, Congress passed the landmark Voting Rights Act. Martin Luther King Jr. had attempted to convince President Johnson to include voting rights protections in the Civil Rights Act of 1964, but Johnson decided to wait until after the 1964 election to tackle the issue of voting rights.
- The main goal of the Voting Rights Act of 1965 was to prevent racial discrimination in voting.
- The law gave the U.S. Department of Justice greater oversight in districts with a history of racial discrimination. The law set guidelines to identify those districts by focusing on voter registration and voter turnout rates.
- Districts that were identified as having a history of racial discrimination were required to get "pre-clearance" from the U.S. Department of Justice if they wanted to change any policies related to voting.
- The law was reauthorized by Congress in 1970, 1975, 1982, 1992, and 2006.
- In 2006, a Republican-controlled Congress reauthorized the law for 25 years.
- President George W. Bush signed the extension of the Voting Right Act on July 27, 2006. During the signing ceremony, he said "Today, we renew a bill that helped bring a community on the margins into the life of American democracy. My administration will vigorously enforce the provisions of this law, and we will defend it in court."

- Shelby County, Alabama, sued the U.S. Department of Justice, claiming that the Voting Rights Act exceeded Congress's Fourteenth and Fifteenth Amendment powers. Furthermore, Shelby County asserted Alabama's right to monitor and make policy for its own elections.

Constitutional Questions

Does the renewal of the Voting Rights Act exceed congressional powers granted under the Fourteenth and Fifteenth Amendments? Do states retain the power to conduct elections without federal interference based on Article IV, Section 1, and the Tenth Amendment?

Majority Opinion

In a highly divisive 5-4 decision, the Supreme Court struck down parts of the Voting Rights Act and ended federal supervision of voting in areas with a history of racial discrimination. Chief Justice Roberts wrote the majority opinion. He stressed the ongoing selection of certain localities for federal monitoring and no longer found any data supporting this policy. "Nearly 50 years later, they are still in effect; indeed, they have been made more stringent, and are now scheduled to last until 2031. There is no denying, however, that the conditions that originally justified these measures no longer characterize voting in the covered jurisdictions."

Roberts ruled that the Voting Rights Act, in effect, discriminated against certain states. "And despite the tradition of equal sovereignty, the Act applies to only nine States (and several additional counties). While one State waits months or years and expends funds to implement a validly enacted law, its neighbor can typically put the same law into effect immediately, through the normal legislative process."

The chief justice was highly critical of Congress for renewing this act with 50-year-old data as part of its justification. The Court found Section 4(b) of the law unconstitutional, which stripped the U.S. Department of Justice of its powers to oversee election policies in areas of the nation with a history of racial discrimination in voting:

> Striking down an Act of Congress is the gravest and most delicate duty that this Court is called on to perform. . . . We do not do so lightly. . . . Congress could have updated the coverage formula at that time, but did not do so. Its failure to act leaves us today with no choice but to declare Section 4(b) unconstitutional. The formula in that section can no longer be used as a basis for subjecting jurisdictions to preclearance.

Dissenting Opinion

Without Section 4(b), Section 5 of the law, which gave the federal government the power to oversee local voting policies, is useless. Justice Ginsberg's dissent stresses how Congress's legislation is well within the guidelines established after the Civil War in both the Fourteenth and Fifteenth Amendments:

> Recognizing that large progress has been made, Congress determined, based on a voluminous record, that the scourge of discrimination was not yet extirpated [destroyed completely]. The question this case presents is who decides whether, as currently operative, Section 5 remains justifiable, this Court, or a Congress charged with the obligation to enforce the post–Civil War Amendments "by appropriate legislation." With overwhelming support in both Houses, Congress concluded that, for two prime reasons, Section 5 should continue in force, unabated. First, continuance would facilitate completion of the impressive gains thus far made; and second, continuance would guard against backsliding. Those assessments were well within Congress' province to make and should elicit this Court's unstinting approbation [approval].

Joined by the three other dissenting justices, Ginsberg outlined some of the ways that these voting districts will now be able to backslide:

> *Second-generation barriers come in various forms. One of the blockages is racial gerrymandering. . . . Another is adoption of a system of at-large voting in lieu of district-by-district voting in a city with a sizable black minority. A similar effect could be achieved if the city engaged in discriminatory annexation by incorporating majority-white areas into city limits, thereby decreasing the effect of VRA-occasioned increases in black voting. Whatever the device employed, this Court has long recognized that vote dilution, when adopted with a discriminatory purpose, cuts down the right to vote as certainly as denial of access to the ballot. . . . Although discrimination today is more subtle than the visible methods used in 1965, the effect and results are the same, namely a diminishing of the minority community's ability to fully participate in the electoral process and to elect their preferred candidates.*

Implications of the Case

- This case represented a new extension of judicial power. It is the first instance that a congressional act in support of voting rights was struck down by the Supreme Court.
- This decision shifts power to the states, but many other areas of voting rights, such as photo ID requirements and highly engineered gerrymanders, remain to be decided.
- After this ruling, many states eliminated provisions that were designed to make access to voting easier, such as same-day registration, and they added voter ID laws.
- After being removed from federal oversight, Alabama drew a new congressional district map that dramatically increased the cracking and packing of its African-American communities.
- Although a great many legislative proposals have been put forward in Congress to increase voter access, such as nationwide online voter registration, none have made any forward progress.

The Powers of Congress Case Timeline

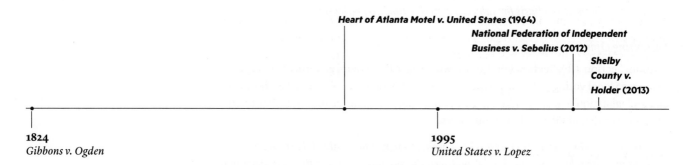

Heart of Atlanta Motel v. United States (1964)

National Federation of Independent Business v. Sebelius (2012)

Shelby County v. Holder (2013)

1824
Gibbons v. Ogden

1995
United States v. Lopez

Summary of Main Points

CON-2: Federalism reflects the dynamic distribution of power between national and state governments.

CON-3: The republican ideal in the United States is manifested in the structure and operation of the legislative branch.

CON-5: The design of the judicial branch protects the Supreme Court's independence as a branch of government, and the emergence and use of judicial review remains a powerful judicial practice.

The Marshall Court's hesitancy to question the laws passed by Congress stands in sharp contrast to the last two decisions in this cluster. The Roberts Court has clipped Congress's power in its ability to base legislation on the commerce clause and the Fourteenth and Fifteenth Amendments. However, Chief Justice Roberts and his fellow conservatives on the Court would argue that it is Congress that has changed. The ACA and the Voting Rights Act, in their view, were laws that trampled state powers and individual liberties.

A determined Congress could have easily bypassed these decisions by redrafting the laws in question. Congress could have added new and supportive data to the Voting Rights Act it reauthorized in 2006. It could have completely repealed Medicaid and then passed it again with the new condition of aid including the ACA-mandated Medicaid expansion. However, there were not majorities in either chamber in Congress that would have voted for these measures in 2012.

In fact, House and Senate Republicans congratulated the Court on its decision not to force Medicaid expansion and to end federal supervision of what were mostly southern voting districts, but they were taken aback by Roberts's vote to save Obamacare. During the 2016 Republican presidential primaries, Roberts's performance as chief justice was harshly criticized because of this one departure from conservative doctrine.

Will Congress, as a result, switch tactics and pass legislation that is based on the taxing and spending clause instead of the commerce clause? The distinction made by the Court in *National Federation of Independent Business v. Sebelius* is clear and concise. The commerce clause empowers Congress to regulate interstate commerce, but it does not give Congress the authority to require individuals to participate in commerce. Individuals cannot be forced to buy health insurance, but they can be taxed if they choose to remain uninsured.

The unanimous decision reached in *Heart of Atlanta Motel v. United States* is still on solid ground, but many of our other assumptions about congressional power are shifting. It is, of course, much more difficult to discern long-term patterns as we come closer to the present time. If it seems like power may be shifting toward the judiciary in ways that the framers did not anticipate, that may have as much to do with Congress's inactivity in passing major legislation as it does with judicial activism.

Assessing Student Understanding

1. Compare and contrast the Court's logic in assessing the constitutionality of the commerce clause in *Heart of Atlanta Motel v. United States* and in *National Federation of Independent Business v. Sebelius*.

2. If legislators in a state sought to lower voter turnout, identify three policy changes they might pursue.

3. Although the United States does not have a single national health care system, the federal government is deeply involved in health care policy. Identify two major national health care programs and explain their purposes.

Questions for Class Discussion and Debate

1. During the peak of the civil rights movement, both laws and attitudes shifted toward greater tolerance and inclusion. Did far-reaching laws like the Civil Rights Act of 1964 lead the way toward change, or were they primarily a reaction to cultural shifts that were already underway?

2. From a legal or an ethical perspective, should all citizens be required to participate in a health care plan?

3. What are the advantages and disadvantages to streamlining a citizen's access to the act of voting? Should it be a public policy goal to increase voter turnout?

Endnotes

Chapter 1

1. John Wagner, "'Very Much Our Friend': Romney Speaks Out Against Trump Calling the Media 'the Enemy of the People,'" *Washington Post*, November 1, 2018, www.washingtonpost.com/politics/very-much-our-friend-romney-speaks-out-against-trump-calling-the-media-the-enemy-of-the-people/2018/11/01/d28b0000-ddf7-11e8-85df-7a6b4d25cfbb_story.html (accessed 2/18/20).

2. "'Spies and Treason': Read a Transcript of Trump's Remarks Related to the Whistle-Blower," *New York Times*, September 26, 2019, www.nytimes.com/2019/09/26/us/politics/trump-treason-spies-whistle-blower.html (accessed 2/18/20).

3. Ben Gilbert, "The 10 Most-Viewed Fake-News Stories on Facebook in 2019 Were Just Revealed in a New Report," *Business Insider*, November 6, 2019, www.businessinsider.com/most-viewed-fake-news-stories-shared-on-facebook-2019-2019-11 (accessed 12/20/19); Mihir Zaveri, Allie Conti, and Sandra E. Garcia, "Fireworks Conspiracy Theories: Why You Should Be Skeptical," *New York Times*, September 1, 2020, www.nytimes.com/2020/06/25/nyregion/fireworks-nyc-conspiracy.html (accessed 9/30/20).

4. Thomas Hobbes, *Leviathan* (1651; repr., Indianapolis, IN: Bobbs, Merrill, 1958).

5. Alexander Hamilton, James Madison, and John Jay, *The Federalist Papers*, ed. Roy P. Fairfield, 2nd ed. (1788; repr., Baltimore, MD: Johns Hopkins University Press, 1981), p. 160.

6. Hamilton, Madison, and Jay, *The Federalist Papers*, p. 18.

7. E. E. Schattschneider, *The Semisovereign People: A Realist's View of Democracy in America* (New York: Holt, Rinehart, and Winston, 1960).

8. Irving L. Janis, *Victims of Groupthink: A Psychological Study of Foreign-Policy Decisions and Fiascoes* (Boston: Houghton Mifflin, 1972).

9. Larry M. Bartels, *Unequal Democracy: The Political Economy of the New Gilded Age*, 2nd ed. (Princeton, NJ: Princeton University Press, 2016); Lawrence Baum, *Ideology in the Supreme Court* (Princeton, NJ: Princeton University Press, 2017).

10. Robert S. Erikson and Kent L. Tedin, *American Public Opinion*, 9th ed. (New York: Routledge, 2015).

11. John R. Hibbing and Elizabeth Theiss-Morse, *Stealth Democracy: Americans' Beliefs about How Government Should Work* (New York: Cambridge University Press, 2002), p. 147. See Diana E. Hess, *Controversy in the Classroom: The Democratic Power of Discussion* (New York: Routledge, 2009), for evidence that diverse viewpoints in the classroom have important effects on discussion.

12. For various surveys on abortion, see www.pollingreport.com/abortion.htm (accessed 1/16/18).

13. Donald Green, Bradley Palmquist, and Eric Schickler, *Partisan Hearts and Minds* (New Haven, CT: Yale University Press, 2004); Christopher Achen, "Parental Socialization and Rational Party Identification," *Political Behavior* 24:2 (2002): 151–70.

14. Robert S. Erikson, Michael B. MacKuen, and James A. Stimson, *The Macro Polity* (New York: Cambridge University Press, 2002); Christopher H. Achen and Larry M. Bartels, *Democracy for Realists: Why Elections Do Not Produce Responsive Government* (Princeton, NJ: Princeton University Press, 2016).

15. Office of Personnel Management, September 2019, www.fedscope.opm.gov/; Congressional Budget Office, November 2019, www.cbo.gov/topics/budget; Code of Federal Regulations, www.govinfo.gov/help/cfr#about (all accessed 12/20/19).

16. Andrew Heywood, *Political Theory: An Introduction*, 4th ed. (New York: Macmillan, 2015).

17. Morris P. Fiorina, with Samuel J. Abrams and Jeremy C. Pope, *Culture War: The Myth of a Polarized America*, 3rd ed. (New York: Pearson, Longman, 2010), pp. 46–7.

18. For more on political culture, see Pippa Norris, *Democratic Deficit: Critical Citizens Revisited* (New York: Cambridge University Press, 2011).

19. Frank M. Bryan, *Real Democracy: The New England Town Meeting and How It Works* (Chicago: University of Chicago Press, 2004).

20. National Archives, "Congress and the New Deal: Social Security," www.archives.gov/exhibits/treasures_of_congress/text/page19_text.html (accessed 8/12/20).

21. Social Security Administration, "Traditional Sources of Economic Security," www.ssa.gov/history/briefhistory3.html (accessed 8/12/20).

AP® Study Guide

a. Wagner, "'Very Much Our Friend.'"

Chapter 2

1. Donald Trump, Twitter, November 10, 2019, 2:43 P.M., https://twitter.com/realDonaldTrump/status/1193615188311912449 (accessed 2/20/20).

2. Nancy Pelosi, Twitter, October 29, 2019, 9:59 A.M., https://twitter.com/speakerpelosi/status/1189179898960715776 (accessed 4/16/20).

3. Alexander Hamilton, John Jay, and James Madison, *The Federalist Papers*, ed. Roy P. Fairfield, 2nd ed. (1788; repr., Baltimore, MD: Johns Hopkins University Press, 1981).

4. For a good overview of the political thought of the American Revolution, see Gordon S. Wood, *The Radicalism of the American Revolution* (New York: Vintage Books, 1993). For an excellent summary of the history, see Wood's *The American Revolution: A History* (New York: Modern Library, 2003).

5. David McCullough, *John Adams* (New York: Simon and Schuster, 2001), p. 90.

6. A classic text on the Founding period is Gordon S. Wood, *The Creation of the American Republic* (New York: W. W. Norton, 1969).

7. J. W. Peltason, *Corwin and Peltason's Understanding the Constitution*, 7th ed. (Hinsdale, IL: Dryden Press, 1976), p. 12.

8. The pamphlet sold 120,000 copies within a few months of publication, a figure that would leave the Harry Potter books

in the dust in terms of the proportion of the literate public that purchased the book.

9. Thomas Hobbes, *Leviathan* (1651; repr., Indianapolis, IN: Bobbs, Merrill, 1958).

10. John Locke, *Second Treatise of Government* (1690; repr., Indianapolis, IN: Bobbs, Merrill, 1952).

11. Robert A. Dahl, *How Democratic Is the American Constitution?* (New Haven, CT: Yale University Press, 2001), p. 12.

12. John Jay to Richard Price, September 27, 1785, in *The Founders' Constitution*, ed. Philip B. Kurland and Ralph Lerner (Chicago: University of Chicago Press, 1987), vol. 1, chap. 15, document 31, http://press-pubs.uchicago.edu/founders/documents/v1ch15s31.html (accessed 12/5/19).

13. Hamilton, Madison, and Jay, *The Federalist Papers*, p. 22.

14. Locke, *Second Treatise of Government*, Section 160.

15. Many delegates probably assumed that the electors would reflect the wishes of the voters in their states, but there is no clear indication of this in Madison's notes. (Hamilton makes this argument in the *Federalist Papers*.) Until the 1820s, many electors were directly chosen by state legislatures rather than by the people. In the first presidential election, George Washington won the unanimous support of the electors, but in only five states were the electors chosen by the people.

16. Richard Beeman, *Plain, Honest Men: The Making of the American Constitution* (New York: Random House, 2009), pp. 66–67.

17. The actual language of the section avoids the term "slavery." Instead, it says: "The Migration or Importation of such Persons as any of the States now existing shall think proper to admit, shall not be prohibited by Congress prior to the Year one thousand eight hundred and eight." The ban on the importation of enslaved people was implemented on the earliest possible date, January 1, 1808.

18. Brutus 1, October 18, 1787, The Constitution Society, www.constitution.org/afp/brutus01.htm (accessed 6/28/18).

19. Patrick Henry, "Shall Liberty or Empire Be Sought?," in *America, 1761–1837*, vol. 8 of *The World's Famous Orations*, ed. William Jennings Bryan (New York: Funk and Wagnalls, 1906), pp. 73, 76.

20. Thomas Jefferson to John Adams, 1787, in *The Writings of Thomas Jefferson*, Memorial Edition, ed. Andrew A. Lipscomb and Albert Ellery Bergh (Washington, DC: Thomas Jefferson Memorial Association of the United States, 1903), vol. 6, p. 370.

21. Sharon LaFraniere, "Court Throws Out Emoluments Case Brought against Trump by Democrats," *New York Times*, February 7, 2020, www.nytimes.com/2020/02/07/us/emoluments-trump-democrats.html (accessed 2/12/20); Byron Tau, "Supreme Court Won't Review Democrats' Emoluments Case Against Trump," *Wall Street Journal*, October 13, 2020, www.wsj.com/articles/supreme-court-wont-review-democrats-emoluments-case-against-trump-11602616606 (accessed 11/5/20).

22. Charlie Savage, "Can Trump Pardon Himself? Explaining Presidential Clemency Powers," *New York Times*, July 21, 2017, www.nytimes.com/2017/07/21/us/politics/trump-pardon-himself-presidential-clemency.html (accessed 8/17/17).

23. Thomas B. Edsall, "The Savage Injustice of Trump's Military Pardons," *New York Times*, December 4, 2019, www.nytimes.com/2019/12/04/opinion/trump-military-pardons.html (accessed 12/6/19).

24. Associated Press, "House Overwhelmingly Votes Bipartisan Condemnation of Trump Withdrawal of U.S. Troops from Syria," October 16, 2019, www.nbcnews.com/politics/congress/house-overwhelmingly-votes-bipartisan-condemnation-trump-withdrawal-u-s-troops-n1067586 (accessed 12/6/19).

25. *Hamdi v. Rumsfeld*, 542 U.S. 507 (2004); *Rasul v. Bush*, 542 U.S. 466 (2004); *Hamdan v. Rumsfeld*, 548 U.S. 557 (2006); *Boumediene v. Bush*, 553 U.S. 723 (2008).

26. Charlie Savage, "Obama's War on Terror May Resemble Bush's in Some Areas," *New York Times*, February 17, 2009, p. A1.

27. Peter M. Shane, *Madison's Nightmare: How Executive Power Threatens American Democracy* (Chicago: University of Chicago Press, 2009).

28. The responses on the three branches are from "Americans' Knowledge of the Branches of Government Is Declining," Annenberg Public Policy Center, September 13, 2016, www.annenbergpublicpolicycenter.org/americans-knowledge-of-the-branches-of-government-is-declining (accessed 7/14/17); the responses on the right to own a pet or home are from "Is There a Constitutional Right to Own a Home or a Pet?," Annenberg Public Policy Center, September 16, 2015, www.annenbergpublicpolicycenter.org/is-there-a-constitutional-right-to-own-a-home-or-a-pet (accessed 9/30/15).

29. NCC staff, "What We Can Learn about the Constitution from *The Simpsons*," National Constitution Center, January 14, 2018, https://constitutioncenter.org/blog/what-we-can-learn-about-the-constitution-from-the-simpsons (accessed 2/12/20).

30. *United States v. Alfonso D. Lopez, Jr.*, 514 U.S. 549 (1995).

31. Thomas Jefferson to James Madison, in *Thomas Jefferson on Democracy*, ed. Saul Padover (New York: Mentor Books, 1953), p. 153.

32. Cass R. Sunstein, "Making Amends," *New Republic*, March 3, 1997, p. 42.

33. *Furman v. Georgia*, 408 U.S. 238 (1972).

34. The case concerning minors was *Roper v. Simmons*, 543 U.S. 551 (2005), and the case concerning the mentally impaired was *Atkins v. Virginia*, 536 U.S. 304 (2002).

35. Valerie Strauss, "In the Age of Trump, a New Surge of Interest in the Constitution," *Washington Post*, August 17, 2017, www.washingtonpost.com/news/answer-sheet/wp/2017/08/17/in-the-age-of-trump-a-new-surge-of-interest-in-the-u-s-constitution/?utm_term=.e3abb53b9976 (accessed 8/18/2017).

36. Walter F. Murphy, "The Nature of the American Constitution," The Edmund Janes James lecture, December 6, 1987 (Department of Political Science, University of Illinois at Urbana-Champaign, 1989), p. 8, http://babel.hathitrust.org/cgi/pt?id=mdp.39015078286518;view=1up;seq=12 (accessed 1/22/20).

Take a Stand

a. Kristen Bialik, "Growing Share of Americans Say Supreme Court Should Base Its Rulings on What Constitution Means Today," Pew Research Center, May 11, 2018, www.pewresearch.org/fact-tank/2018/05/11/growing-share-of-americans-say-supreme-court-should-base-its-rulings-on-what-constitution-means-today/ (accessed 12/6/19).

b. Clarence Thomas, "How to Read the Constitution," *Wall Street Journal*, October 20, 2008.

c. *State of Missouri v. Holland*, 252 U.S. 416 (1920), 252.

d. William Rehnquist, "The Notion of a Living Constitution," *Harvard Journal of Law and Public Policy* 29 (2006): 402.

e. Rehnquist, "The Notion," p. 405.

f. Thurgood Marshall at the Annual Seminar of the San Francisco Patent and Trademark Law Association, Maui, Hawaii, May 6, 1987, www.thurgoodmarshall.com/speeches/constitutional_speech.htm (accessed 12/20/13).

AP® Study Guide

a. GovTrack Insider, "Proposed Constitutional Amendment Would Prevent President from Pardoning Himself, Family, or Administration Officials," January 14, 2019, https://govtrackinsider.com/constitutional-amendment-would-prevent-president-from-pardoning-himself-family-or-administration-e74b31b4ab06 (accessed 7/28/20).

Chapter 3

1. Paul A Einstein, "Trump Axes California's Right to Set Own Auto Emissions Standards," NBC News, September 18, 2019, www.nbcnews.com/business/autos/trump-about-strip-california-its-right-overrule-emissions-regulations-n1055811 (accessed 2/27/20).

2. United States Environmental Protection Agency, "Administrator Wheeler Addresses National Automobile Dealers Association," September 17, 2019, www.epa.gov/newsreleases/administrator-wheeler-addresses-national-automobile-dealers-association (accessed 2/27/20).

3. Slaughterhouse Cases, 83 U.S. 36 (1873). See Ronald M. Labbe and Jonathan Lurie, *The Slaughterhouse Cases: Regulation, Reconstruction, and the Fourteenth Amendment* (Lawrence: University Press of Kansas, 2003).

4. Civil Rights Cases, 109 U.S. 3 (1883).

5. *United States v. E. C. Knight Co.*, 156 U.S. 1 (1895).

6. *Hammer v. Dagenhart*, 247 U.S. 251 (1918).

7. *Schechter Poultry Corporation v. United States*, 295 U.S. 495 (1935).

8. Four key cases are *West Coast Hotel Company v. Parrish* (1937), *Wright v. Vinton Branch* (1937), *Virginia Railway Company v. System Federation* (1937), and *National Labor Relations Board v. Jones and Laughlin Steel Corporation* (1937).

9. Martin Grodzins, *The American System* (New York: Rand McNally, 1966).

10. *Brown v. Board of Education*, 347 U.S. 483 (1954); *Swann v. Charlotte-Mecklenburg Board of Education*, 402 U.S. 1 (1971).

11. *Baker v. Carr*, 369 U.S. 186 (1962); *Reynolds v. Sims*, 377 U.S. 533 (1964); *Wesberry v. Sanders*, 376 U.S. 1 (1964); Martha Derthick, *Keeping the Compound Republic: Essays in American Federalism* (Washington, DC: Brookings Institution, 2001).

12. *Miranda v. Arizona*, 384 U.S. 436 (1966); *Mapp v. Ohio*, 367 U.S. 643 (1961).

13. Barry Rabe, "Environmental Policy and the Bush Era: The Collision between the Administrative Presidency and State Experimentation," *Publius* 37:3 (May 2007): 413–31.

14. Lois Beckett, "Nullification: How States Are Making It a Felony to Enforce Federal Gun Laws," *ProPublica*, May 2, 2013, www.propublica.org/article/nullification-how-states-are-making-it-a-felony-to-enforce-federal-gun-laws (accessed 11/15/13).

15. From a review of Michael S. Greve, *Real Federalism: Why It Matters, How It Could Happen* (Washington, DC: American Enterprise Institute Press, 1999), www.federalismproject.org/publications/books (accessed 10/10/07).

16. *Gregory v. Ashcroft*, 501 U.S. 452 (1991).

17. *City of Boerne v. Flores*, 521 U.S. 507 (1997), 520.

18. *Kimel et al. v. Florida Board of Regents*, 528 U.S. 62 (2000).

19. *United States v. Lopez*, 514 U.S. 549 (1995).

20. *United States v. Morrison*, 529 U.S. 598 (2000); Nia-Malika Henderson, "Obama Signs a Strengthened Violence Against Women Act," *Washington Post*, March 7, 2013, www.washingtonpost.com/politics/obama-signs-a-strengthened-violence-against-women-act/2013/03/07/e50d585e-8740-11e2-98a3-b3db6b9ac586_story.html (accessed 3/21/14).

21. *Romer v. Evans*, 517 U.S. 620 (1996).

22. *National Federation of Independent Business v. Sebelius*, 132 S. Ct. 2566 (2012).

23. *National Federation of Independent Business v. Sebelius*, 132 S. Ct. 2566 (2012), p. 51.

24. David J. Edquist and Jeffrey E. Mark, "Analysis: U.S. Supreme Court Upholds the Affordable Care Act: Roberts Rules?" *National Law Review* 2:181 (June 29, 2012), www.natlawreview.com/article/analysis-us-supreme-court-upholds-affordable-care-act-roberts-rules (accessed 7/11/20).

25. "H.R. 1628, American Health Care Act of 2017," Congressional Budget Office, May 24, 2017, www.cbo.gov/publication/52752 (accessed 7/11/20).

26. Martha Derthick, *Keeping the Compound Republic: Essays on American Federalism* (Washington, DC: Brookings Institution, 2001), pp. 9–32.

What Do the Facts Say?

a. One example is Umair Irfan, "The EPA Refuted Its Own Bizarre Justification for Rolling Back Fuel Efficiency Standards," Vox, August 16, 2018, www.vox.com/2018/4/2/17181476/epa-fuel-economy-standards-tesla (accessed 11/18/19).

Chapter 4

1. Donald J. Trump, Twitter, June 18, 2020, 1:20 P.M., https://twitter.com/realDonaldTrump/status/1273666793362673665 (accessed 6/29/20).

2. Quoted in Morgan Gstalter, "Cruz: No Path to Citizenship for Dreamers," *The Hill*, January 25, 2018, https://thehill.com/latino/370771-cruz-no-path-to-citizenship-for-dreamers (accessed 6/11/20).

3. Quoted in Felicia Sonmez, "House Passes Immigration Bill to Protect 'Dreamers,' Offer a Path to Citizenship," *Washington Post*, June 4, 2019, www.washingtonpost.com/powerpost/house-poised-to-pass-immigration-bill-that-would-protect-dreamers/2019/06/04/bac5cf98-86d7-11e9-a491-25df61c78dc4_story.html (accessed 6/11/20).

4. Katie Reilly, "Here's What President Trump Has Said about DACA in the Past," *Time*, September 5, 2017, http://time.com/4927100/donald-trump-daca-past-statements/ (accessed 2/15/18).

5. Most of the poll questions specified the conditions of the DACA program for becoming a citizen: "To qualify, immigrants had to be under the age of 30 as of 2012, have no criminal record, and be a student, in the military, or have earned a high school diploma." A few only mentioned not having a criminal record. See www.pollingreport.com/immigration.htm for a record of the polls taken early in 2018 (accessed 2/9/18).

6. See Wendy J. Schiller and Charles Stewart III, *Electing the Senate: Indirect Democracy before the Seventeenth Amendment* (Princeton, NJ: Princeton University Press, 2015), for an

analysis of Senate elections before the popular vote. See Paul Gronke, *The Electorate, the Campaign, and the Office: A Unified Approach to Senate and House Elections* (Ann Arbor: University of Michigan Press, 2000), for research showing that the House and Senate elections share many similar characteristics. See Richard F. Fenno, *Senators on the Campaign Trail: The Politics of Representation* (Norman: University of Oklahoma Press, 1996), for a good general discussion of Senate elections.

7. The poll data on Congress's general approval is from PollingReport.com; see www.pollingreport.com/CongJob.htm (accessed 5/23/20). The occupations poll was conducted by Gallup in December 2017; see http://news.gallup.com/poll/1654/honesty-ethics-professions.aspx (accessed 2/15/18). There has not been recent polling on DACA, but for a summary of public sentiment on the issue, see Giovanni Russonello, "The Supreme Court May Let Trump End DACA. Here's What the Public Thinks about It," *New York Times*, November 15, 2019, www.nytimes.com/2019/11/15/us/politics/daca-supreme-court-polls.html (accessed 5/23/20).

8. "Congress Less Popular than Cockroaches, Traffic Jams," Public Policy Polling, January 8, 2013, www.publicpolicypolling.com/pdf/2011/PPP_Release_Natl_010813_.pdf (accessed 4/11/14).

9. Claudine Gay, "Spirals of Trust? The Effect of Descriptive Representation on the Relationship between Citizens and Their Government," *American Journal of Political Science* 46:4 (October 2002): 717–32.

10. In addition to those mentioned in the text, P.B.S. Pinchback was elected by the Louisiana state legislature in 1873, but he was not seated.

11. David T. Canon, *Race, Redistricting, and Representation: The Unintended Consequences of Black Majority Districts* (Chicago: University of Chicago Press, 1999); Katherine Tate, *Concordance: Black Lawmaking in the U.S. Congress from Carter to Obama* (Ann Arbor, MI: University of Michigan Press, 2014); Stella M. Rouse, *Latinos in the Legislative Process: Interests and Influence* (New York: Cambridge University Press, 2013); Michele L. Swers, *Women in the Club: Gender and Policy Making in the Senate* (Chicago: University of Chicago Press, 2013); Michele L. Swers, *The Difference Women Make: The Policy Impact of Women in Congress* (Chicago: University of Chicago Press, 2002).

12. R. Douglas Arnold, *The Logic of Congressional Action* (New Haven, CT: Yale University Press, 1990), pp. 60–71.

13. Richard F. Fenno, *Home Style: House Members in Their Districts* (Boston: Little, Brown, 1978).

14. David R. Mayhew, *Congress: The Electoral Connection* (New Haven, CT: Yale University Press, 1974).

15. Mayhew, *Congress*, p. 17.

16. Mayhew, *Congress*, p. 37.

17. Patrick J. Sellers, "Fiscal Consistency and Federal District Spending in Congressional Elections," *American Journal of Political Science* 41:3 (July 1997): 1024–41.

18. David T. Canon, "History in the Making: The 2nd District in Wisconsin," in *The Battle for Congress: Candidates, Consultants, and Voters*, ed. James A. Thurber (Washington, DC: Brookings Institution Press, 2001), pp. 199–238.

19. Gary C. Jacobson, *The Politics of Congressional Elections*, 5th ed. (New York: Longman, 2001), pp. 24–30.

20. Fenno, *Home Style*.

21. The trend has been an increasing gap between incumbent and challenger spending in the House, peaking at nearly 5–1 in 2016. However, in 2018 Democratic challengers raised almost as much as Republican incumbents ($1.86 million versus $2.26 million), reducing the overall gap to less than 2–1 (Democratic incumbents outspent Republican challengers by more than 7–1 in 2018). See Center for Responsive Politics, "Incumbent Advantage," OpenSecrets.org, www.opensecrets.org/overview/incumbs.php?cycle=2018&type=G&party=S (accessed 5/30/20).

22. Morris Fiorina, *Congress: Keystone of the Washington Establishment*, rev. ed. (New Haven, CT: Yale University Press, 1989).

23. Steve Peoples and Ken Thomas, "Not All GOP Candidates Want Trump to Stump," Associated Press, May 19, 2018, https://apnews.com/80611e33a0d94c6a9889fe77622b48c6/Not-all-GOP-candidates-want-Trump-to-stump (accessed 6/17/18).

24. Ed Kilgore, "Final Pre-census Estimates Show Which States Will Become More Powerful After 2020," *New York*, December 30, 2019, https://nymag.com/intelligencer/2019/12/pre-census-estimates-show-reapportionment-winners-losers.html (accessed 11/9/20).

25. The language used by the Court in 1960 was "one-man, one-vote." The Court ruled in *Baker v. Carr*, 369 U.S. 186 (1962), that state legislative districts that were unequal in population violated the equal protection clause of the Fourteenth Amendment. *Wesberry v. Sanders*, 376 U.S. 1 (1964), applied the same principle to U.S. House districts.

26. *Davis v. Bandemer*, 478 U.S. 109 (1986); *Vieth v. Jubelirer*, 541 U.S. 267 (2004); *League of United Latin American Citizens v. Perry*, 548 U.S. 399 (2006).

27. The North Carolina case is *Rucho v. Common Cause* 558 U.S. _____ (2019); this case was consolidated with the Maryland case, *Lamone v. Benisek* (No. 18-726) and was issued as a single opinion for both cases.

28. *Shelby County v. Holder*, 570 U.S. 529 (2013). The full citation for the North Carolina case is *Shaw v. Reno*, 509 U.S. 630 (1993).

29. See Kenneth R. Mayer and David T. Canon, *The Dysfunctional Congress: The Individual Roots of an Institutional Dilemma* (New York: Routledge, 2019), for an extended discussion of this argument.

30. Richard F. Fenno, "If as Ralph Nader Says, Congress Is the 'Broken Branch,' How Come We Love Our Congressman So Much?," in *Congress in Change: Evolution and Reform*, ed. Norman J. Ornstein (New York: Praeger, 1975), pp. 277–87.

31. Nicole Ogrysko, "Trump Signs Shutdown-Averting Spending Bills, Makes Federal Pay Raise Law," Federal News Service, December 20, 2019, https://federalnewsnetwork.com/budget/2019/12/trump-signs-shutdown-averting-spending-bills-makes-federal-pay-raise-law/ (accessed 6/2/20).

32. Caitlin Emma, "House Swiftly Advances Behemoth $1.4T Spending Deal," Politico, December 17, 2019, www.politico.com/news/2019/12/17/house-passes-massive-deal-to-fund-government-and-avoid-shutdown-086514 (accessed 6/2/20).

33. An important qualification to the norm was imposed by Republicans in 1995 when they set a six-year term limit for committee and subcommittee chairs.

34. Congressional Quarterly, "CQ Federal Congressional Bill Tracker," https://info.cq.com/legislative-tracking/cq-federal/ (accessed 8/1/20).

35. David W. Rohde, *Parties and Leaders in the Post-reform House* (Chicago: University of Chicago Press, 1991).

36. David Rohde and John Aldrich, "The Transition to Republican Rule in the House: Implications for Theories of Congressional Politics," *Political Science Quarterly* 112:4 (Winter 1997–1998): 541–67.

37. Nelson W. Polsby, *Congress and the Presidency*, 4th ed. (Englewood Cliffs, NJ: Prentice Hall, 1986), p. 111.

38. Paul Steinhauser, "Obama 2014 Campaign Role: Fundraiser-in-Chief," CNN Politics, March 20, 2014, http://politicalticker.

blogs.cnn.com/2014/03/20/obama-2014-campaign-role-fundraiser-in-chief (accessed 4/16/14).

39. Kathryn Watson, "Trump Addresses Record-Setting GOP Fundraiser," CBS News, March 20, 2018, www.cbsnews.com/news/trump-addresses-one-of-the-biggest-gop-fundraisers-of-the-year (accessed 6/7/18).

40. Cristina Marcos, "The Republicans Who Didn't Vote for Ryan," *The Hill*, October 28–29, 2015, http://thehill.com/blogs/floor-action/house/258542-the-republicans-who-didnt-vote-for-ryan (accessed 3/19/16).

41. However, recent research shows that members of Congress do not confine their credit claiming to legislative activity that is rooted in committee work. See Justin Grimmer, Sean J. Westwood, and Solomon Messing, *The Impression of Influence: Legislator Communication, Representation, and Democratic Accountability* (Princeton, NJ: Princeton University Press, 2014).

42. Keith Krehbiel, *Information and Legislative Organization* (Ann Arbor: University of Michigan Press, 1992).

43. Richard F. Fenno, *Congressmen in Committees* (Boston: Little, Brown, 1973).

44. Richard L. Hall, *Participation in Congress* (New Haven, CT: Yale University Press, 1996).

45. Grace Segers, Stefan Becket, and Melissa Quinn, "House Committee Approves Rules for Impeachment Vote," CBS News, December 18, 2019, www.cbsnews.com/live-updates/trump-impeachment-house-rules-committee-debate-live-updates-live-stream-2019-12-17/ (accessed 6/3/20).

46. Barbara Sinclair, *Unorthodox Lawmaking* (Washington, DC: CQ Press, 2000), p. xiv.

47. Mike DeBonis, "House Changes Its Rules during Pandemic, Allowing Remote Voting for the First Time in Its 231-Year History," *Washington Post*, May 15, 2020, www.washingtonpost.com/politics/house-poised-to-adopt-historic-changes-allowing-remote-voting-during-pandemic/2020/05/15/b081d9f2-96ab-11ea-91d7-cf4423d47683_story.html (accessed 6/4/20).

48. Edward Epstein, "Dusting Off Deliberation," *CQ Weekly*, June 14, 2010, pp. 1434–42.

49. See Congressional Research Service, Appropriations Status Table, https://crsreports.congress.gov/AppropriationsStatusTable/Index/AppropriationsStatusTable?id=2019 (accessed 6/3/20).

50. USA Patriot Act, Hearing before the Subcommittee on the Constitution, Civil Rights and Civil Liberties, Committee on the Judiciary, House of Representatives, September 22, 2009, www.gpo.gov/fdsys/pkg/CHRG-111hhrg52409/html/CHRG-111hhrg52409.htm (accessed 6/7/18).

51. Mike DeBonis, Ed O'Keefe, and Erica Werner, "Here's What Congress Is Stuffing into Its $1.3 Trillion Spending Bill," *Washington Post*, March 22, 2018, www.washingtonpost.com/news/powerpost/wp/2018/03/22/heres-what-congress-is-stuffing-into-its-1-3-trillion-spending-bill/?utm_term=.cae1f7d276e2 (accessed 6/7/18).

52. Paul Waldman, "A Lot of Bad Things Got into the Rescue Package. Here's a List," *Washington Post*, March 30, 2020, www.washingtonpost.com/opinions/2020/03/30/lot-bad-things-got-into-rescue-package-heres-list/ (accessed 6/3/20).

53. Congressional Record, 46th Congress, 2nd session, April 22, 1880, p. 2661.

54. Howard H. Baker Jr., "Leaders Lecture Series Address to the Senate," July 14, 1998, www.senate.gov/artandhistory/history/common/generic/Leaders_Lecture_Series_Baker.htm (accessed 5/7/08).

55. Paul Kane, "Reid, Democrats Trigger 'Nuclear' Option; Eliminate Most Filibusters on Nominees," *Washington Post*, November 21, 2013, www.washingtonpost.com/politics/senate-poised-to-limit-filibusters-in-party-line-vote-that-would-alter-centuries-of-precedent/2013/11/21/d065cfe8-52b6-11e3-9fe0-fd2ca728e67c_story.html (accessed 6/6/14).

56. Matt Flegenheimer, "Senate Republicans Deploy 'Nuclear Option' to Clear Path for Gorsuch," *New York Times*, April 6, 2017, www.nytimes.com/2017/04/06/us/politics/neil-gorsuch-supreme-court-senate.html (accessed 2/20/18).

57. Michael Thorning, "Congress's Mid-Year Review: Amendment Drought Persists, Committees Off to Slow Start," Bipartisan Policy Center, July 31, 2019, https://bipartisanpolicy.org/blog/congresss-mid-year-review-amendment-drought-persists-committees-off-to-slow-start/ (accessed 6/3/20).

58. Philip Rucker and Robert Costa, "McCarthy's Comments on Benghazi Probe May Be a Political Gift to Clinton," *Washington Post*, October 1, 2015, www.washingtonpost.com/politics/mccarthys-comments-on-benghazi-probe-may-be-a-political-gift-to-clinton/2015/10/01/6ceb6e88-6857-11e5-9223-70cb36460919_story.html. For an account of the Ukraine investigation, see Jerrold Nadler, "Impeachment of Donald J. Trump, President of the United States," Report of the Committee on the Judiciary, House of Representatives, December 2019, https://docs.house.gov/billsthisweek/20191216/CRPT-116hrpt346.pdf (both accessed 6/3/20).

59. House Committee on Oversight and Reform, "Oversight of Trump Administration," https://oversight.house.gov/oversight-of-trump-administration (accessed 6/3/20).

60. Mathew McCubbins and Thomas Schwartz, "Congressional Oversight Overlooked: Police Patrol versus Fire Alarm," *American Journal of Political Science* 28:1 (February 1984): 165–77.

61. House Committee on the Judiciary, Hearing on "Oversight of the Department of Justice: Political Interference and Threats to Prosecutorial Independence," June 24, 2020, https://judiciary.house.gov/calendar/eventsingle.aspx?EventID=3034; House Committee on the Judiciary, Hearing on "Oversight of the Department of Justice," July 28, 2020, https://judiciary.house.gov/calendar/eventsingle.aspx?EventID=3140 (both accessed 8/6/20).

62. Hailey Fuchs, "House Can Sue to Force Testimony From McGahn, Appeals Court Rules," *New York Times*, August 7, 2020, www.nytimes.com/2020/08/07/us/politics/donald-mcgahn-congress-lawsuit.html (accessed 8/10/20).

63. The cases concerning financial records and tax returns are discussed in John Kruzel, "Supreme Court Divided over Fight for Trump's Financial Records," *The Hill*, May 12, 2020, https://thehill.com/regulation/497385-supreme-court-divided-over-fight-for-trumps-financial-records. The McGahn case is discussed in Jennifer Rubin, "What the McGahn Case Means and Does Not Mean," *Washington Post*, March 2, 2020 www.washingtonpost.com/opinions/2020/03/02/what-mcgahn-case-means-does-not-mean/ (both accessed 6/4/20).

64. Nina Totenberg, "Supreme Court Says Trump Not 'Immune' From Records Release, But Hedges On House Case," National Public Radio, July 9, 2020, www.npr.org/2020/07/09/884447882/supreme-court-says-trump-not-immune-from-records-release-pushes-back-on-congress (accessed 8/10/20).

65. Paul Kane, "Democrats Warn Republicans They Will Regret Backing Trump's Defiance of Congressional Oversight," *Washington Post*, May 20, 2020, www.washingtonpost.com/powerpost/democrats-warn-republicans-they-will-regret-backing-trumps-defiance-of-congressional-oversight/2020/05/20/3084f0ac-9ab8-11ea-ac72-3841fcc9b35f_story.html (accessed 6/3/20).

What Do the Facts Say?

a. Glenn Kessler, Meg Kelly, Salvador Rizzo, and Michelle Ye Hee Lee, "In 1,316 days, President Trump Has Made 22,247 False or Misleading Claims," *Washington Post*, August 27, 2020, www.washingtonpost.com/graphics/politics/trump-claims-database/ (accessed 11/8/20).

Take a Stand

a. The warning against entering the "political thicket" comes from *Colegrove v. Green*, 328 U.S. 549 (1946).

AP® Study Guide

a. Adele Peters, "This Candidate for Congress Will Let His Constituents Decide How He Votes," *Fast Company*, January 2, 2018, www.fastcompany.com/40509226/this-candidate-for-congress-will-let-his-constituents-decide-how-he-votes (accessed 10/20/20).

Chapter 5

1. Quoted in Meagan Flynn and Allyson Chiu, "Trump Says His 'Authority Is Total.' Constitutional Experts Have 'No Idea' Where He Got That," *Washington Post*, April 14, 2020, www.washingtonpost.com/nation/2020/04/14/trump-power-constitution-coronavirus/ (accessed 4/26/20).

2. Quoted in Morgan Chalfant and Brett Samuels, "Trump Eases Back on Asserting Power over Governors on Reopening," *The Hill*, April 14, 2020, https://thehill.com/homenews/administration/492837-trump-eases-back-on-asserting-power-over-governors-on-reopening (accessed 4/26/20).

3. Philip Bump, "What Trump Has Undone," *Washington Post*, August 24, 2017, www.washingtonpost.com/news/politics/wp/2017/08/24/what-trump-has-undone/ (accessed 4/24/20).

4. Lori Cox Han and Caroline Heldman, eds., *Madam President? Gender and Politics on the Road to the White House* (Boulder, CO: Lynne Rienner, 2020).

5. John Aldrich, *Why Parties? A Second Look* (Chicago: University of Chicago Press, 2011).

6. Ernest R. May, *The Making of the Monroe Doctrine* (Cambridge, MA: Harvard University Press, 1975).

7. Arthur M. Schlesinger Jr., *The Age of Jackson* (Boston: Little, Brown, 1945).

8. David Greenberg, "Lincoln's Crackdown," *Slate*, November 30, 2001, www.slate.com/id/2059132 (accessed 8/8/16).

9. Stephen Skowronek, *Building a New American State: The Expansion of National Administrative Capacities* (New York: Cambridge University Press, 1982).

10. Theda Skocpol, *Protecting Soldiers and Mothers: The Political Origins of Social Policy in the United States* (Cambridge, MA: Harvard University Press, 1995).

11. Kendrick Clements, *The Presidency of Woodrow Wilson* (Lawrence: University Press of Kansas, 1992).

12. Thomas J. Knock, *To End All Wars: Woodrow Wilson and the Quest for a New World Order* (New York: Oxford University Press, 1992).

13. William E. Leuchtenburg, *FDR Years: On Roosevelt and His Legacy* (New York: Columbia University Press, 1995).

14. Chester Pach and Elmo Richardson, *The Presidency of Dwight D. Eisenhower* (Lawrence: University Press of Kansas, 1991).

15. Richard E. Neustadt, *Presidential Power and the Modern Presidents* (1960; repr., New York: Free Press, 1991).

16. Thomas J. Weko, *The Politicizing Presidency: The White House Personnel Office, 1948–1994* (Lawrence: University Press of Kansas, 1995).

17. Kenneth Mayer, *With the Stroke of a Pen: Executive Orders and Presidential Power* (Princeton, NJ: Princeton University Press, 2001).

18. Brian Hallett, *Declaring War: Congress, the President, and What the Constitution Does Not Say* (New York: Cambridge University Press, 2012).

19. Frederick S. Tipson, "The War Powers Resolution: A Continuing Constitutional Struggle," in *Making Government Work: From White House to Congress*, ed. Robert E. Hunter (New York: Routledge, 2019), pp. 115–51.

20. Lewis Fisher and David G. Adler, "The War Powers Resolution: Time to Say Goodbye," *Political Science Quarterly* 113:1 (1998): 1–20.

21. William G. Howell and Jon C. Pevehouse, *While Dangers Gather: Congressional Checks on Presidential War Powers* (Princeton, NJ: Princeton University Press, 2007).

22. Mark A. Peterson, *Legislating Together: The White House and Capitol Hill from Eisenhower to Reagan* (Cambridge, MA: Harvard University Press, 1990).

23. Andrew Rudalevige, *Managing the President's Program: Presidential Leadership and Legislative Policy Formation* (Princeton, NJ: Princeton University Press, 2002).

24. Charles Cameron and Nolan M. McCarty, "Models of Vetoes and Veto Bargaining," *Annual Review of Political Science* 7 (2004): 409–35.

25. Mark J. Rozell, "The Law: Executive Privilege: Definition and Standards of Application," *Presidential Studies Quarterly* 29:4 (1999): 918–30.

26. For a summary of the case, see Oyez, *United States v. Nixon*, 418 U.S. 683 (1974), www.oyez.org/cases/1973/73-1766 (accessed 6/5/18).

27. Mark J. Rozell, *Executive Privilege: The Dilemma of Secrecy and Democratic Accountability* (Baltimore, MD: Johns Hopkins University Press, 1994).

28. John Hart, *The Presidential Branch: From Washington to Clinton* (Chatham, NY: Chatham House, 1987).

29. Kelly Chang, David Lewis, and Nolan McCarthy, "The Tenure of Political Appointees" (paper presented at the 2003 Midwest Political Science Association Annual Meeting, Chicago, April 4, 2003).

30. David E. Lewis, "Staffing Alone: Unilateral Action and the Politicization of the Executive Office of the President, 1988–2004," *Presidential Studies Quarterly* 35 (2005): 496–514.

31. Jonathan Swan and Alayna Treene, "New White House Personnel Chief Tells Cabinet Liaisons to Target Never Trumpers," Axios, February 21, 2020, www.axios.com/scoop-white-house-personnel-chief-targets-never-trumpers-2ee51bfd-03f9-4971-8308-863c81ace5f0.html (accessed 4/21/20).

32. For a series of articles detailing Cheney's role, see "Angler: The Cheney Vice Presidency," *Washington Post*, June 24–27, 2007, http://voices.washingtonpost.com/cheney/ (accessed 5/8/20).

33. Richard E. Neustart, *Presidential Power and the Modern Presidents* (New York: Simon and Schuster, 1991).

34. Erika Werner and Seung Min Kim, "Senate Passes $484 Billion Bill That Would Expand Small-Business Aid, Boost Money for Hospitals and Testing," *Washington Post*, April 21, 2020, www.washingtonpost.com/us-policy/2020/04/21/congress-coronavirus-small-business/ (accessed 5/8/20).

35. Terry M. Moe and William G. Howell, "The Presidential Power of Unilateral Action," *Journal of Law, Economics, and Organization* 15 (1999): 132–46.

36. These examples appear throughout Moe and Howell, "The Presidential Power of Unilateral Action"; see also William G. Howell, "Unilateral Powers: A Brief Overview," *Presidential Studies Quarterly* 35:3 (2005): 417–39.

37. Andrew Rudalevige, *The New Imperial Presidency: Renewing Presidential Power after Watergate* (Ann Arbor: University of Michigan Press, 2005).

38. Louis Fisher, *Presidential War Power*, 2nd ed. (Lawrence: University Press of Kansas, 2004); James M. Lindsay, "Deference and Defiance: The Shifting Rhythms of Executive-Legislative Relations in Foreign Policy," *Presidential Studies Quarterly* 33:3 (2003): 530–46; Lawrence Margolis, *Executive Agreements and Presidential Power in Foreign Policy* (New York: Praeger, 1985), 209–32.

39. Christopher Deering and Forrest Maltzman, "The Politics of Executive Orders: Legislative Constraints on Presidential Power," *Political Research Quarterly* 52:4 (1999): 767–83.

40. David E. Lewis, *Presidents and the Politics of Agency Design: Political Insulation in the United States Government Bureaucracy, 1946–1997* (Palo Alto, CA: Stanford University Press, 2003).

41. David Epstein and Sharyn O'Halloran, *Delegating Powers* (Cambridge, UK: Cambridge University Press, 1999).

42. Quoted in Danny Hakim, "Army Officer Who Heard Trump's Ukraine Call Reported Concerns," *New York Times*, October 28, 2019, www.nytimes.com/2019/10/28/us/politics/Alexander-Vindman-trump-impeachment.html (accessed 5/8/20).

43. William G. Howell, *Thinking about the Presidency: The Primacy of Power* (Princeton, NJ: Princeton University Press, 2015).

44. George C. Edwards III, *The Public Presidency* (New York: St. Martin's Press, 1983); George C. Edwards III, *On Deaf Ears: The Limits of the Bully Pulpit* (New Haven, CT: Yale University Press, 2003).

45. For evidence, see Edwards, *On Deaf Ears*.

46. George C. Edwards III, *Predicting the Presidency: The Potential of Persuasive Leadership* (Princeton, NJ: Princeton University Press, 2015).

47. Eric Berger, "Email Release Reveals Chaos Sowed by President Trump's Hurricane Tweets," Ars Technica, February 1, 2020, https://arstechnica.com/science/2020/02/email-release-reveals-choas-sowed-by-president-trumps-hurricane-tweets/ (accessed 4/24/20).

48. Stephen Skowronek, *Presidential Leadership in Political Time: Reprise and Reappraisal*, 2nd ed., revised and expanded (Lawrence: University of Kansas Press, 2011).

Chapter 6

1. Donald J. Trump, Twitter, July 13, 2016, 12:54 A.M., https://twitter.com/realDonaldTrump/status/753090242203283457 (accessed 7/10/20).

2. Joan Biskupic, "Justice Ruth Bader Ginsburg Calls Trump a 'Faker,' He Says She Should Resign," July 13, 2016, CNN Politics, www.cnn.com/2016/07/12/politics/justice-ruth-bader-ginsburg-donald-trump-faker/index.html (accessed 3/20/20).

3. Adam Liptak, "Ruth Bader Ginsburg, No Fan of Donald Trump, Critiques Latest Term," *New York Times*, July 11, 2016, www.nytimes.com/2016/07/11/us/politics/ruth-bader-ginsburg-no-fan-of-donald-trump-critiques-latest-term.html (accessed 7/10/20).

4. Editorial Board, "Justice Ginsburg's Inappropriate Comments on Donald Trump," *Washington Post*, July 12, 2016, www.washingtonpost.com/opinions/justice-ginsburgs-inappropriate-comments-on-donald-trump/2016/07/12/981df404-4862-11e6-bdb9-701687974517_story.html?utm_term=.fed5635b0e1a (accessed 3/30/20).

5. Editorial Board, "Donald Trump Is Right about Justice Ruth Bader Ginsburg," *New York Times*, July 13, 2016, www.nytimes.com/2016/07/13/opinion/donald-trump-is-right-about-justice-ruth-bader-ginsburg.html (accessed 3/20/20).

6. Eliza Collins, "Ginsburg on Trump Comments: 'I Regret Making Them,'" *USA Today*, July 14, 2016, www.usatoday.com/story/news/politics/onpolitics/2016/07/14/ginsburg-apologizes-trump-comments/87074576/ (accessed 3/20/20).

7. Debra Cassens Weiss, "Chief Justice Roberts Defends Judicial Independence after Trump's 'Obama Judge' Criticism," *ABA Journal*, November 21, 2018, www.abajournal.com/news/article/chief_justice_roberts_criticizes_trumps_reference_to_obama_judge_in_asylum (accessed 6/15/20).

8. SCOTUSblog, Final Stat Pack for October Term 2019, July 20, 2020, www.scotusblog.com/wp-content/uploads/2020/07/Final-Statpack-7.20.2020.pdf (accessed 11/9/20).

9. Ralph Ketcham, *The Anti-Federalist Papers and the Constitutional Convention Debates* (New York: Penguin Putnam, 2003), p. 304.

10. Lester S. Jayson, ed., *The Constitution of the United States of America: Analysis and Interpretation* (Washington, DC: U.S. Government Printing Office, 1973), p. 585.

11. David G. Savage, *Guide to the U.S. Supreme Court*, 4th ed. (Washington, DC: CQ Press, 2004), p. 7.

12. Savage, *Guide to the U.S. Supreme Court*, pp. 5–7.

13. Winfield H. Rose, "*Marbury v. Madison*: How John Marshall Changed History by Misquoting the Constitution," *Political Science and Politics* 36:2 (April 2003): 209–14. Rose argues that in a key quotation in the case Marshall intentionally left out a clause of the Constitution that suggests that Congress *did* have the power to expand the original jurisdiction of the Court. Other constitutional scholars reject this argument.

14. *Marbury v. Madison*, 5 U.S. 1 Cranch 137 (1803).

15. Revisionist historians, legal scholars, and political scientists have challenged the landmark status of *Marbury v. Madison*. For example, Michael Stokes Paulsen's *Michigan Law Review* article points out that *Marbury* was not cited in subsequent Supreme Court cases as a precedent for judicial review until the late nineteenth century. Legal scholars in the early twentieth century were the first to promote the idea that *Marbury* was a landmark decision. Paulsen also notes that when the opinion was delivered in 1803 it was not controversial. Even the Jeffersonian Democrats, who were at odds with Marshall's Federalists, thought that it was a reasonable decision and not the institutional power grab that is described in modern accounts. Finally, Marshall made a very narrow case for judicial review, arguing that the Supreme Court could declare legislation that was contrary to the Court's interpretation of the Constitution null and void only if it concerned judicial powers. Revisionists argue that what appear to be broad claims of judicial power in *Marbury* (e.g., the Court has the power "to say what the law is") are taken out of the context of a much more narrow claim of power. Michael Stokes Paulsen, "Judging Judicial Review: *Marbury* in the Modern Era: The Irrepressible Myth of *Marbury*," *Michigan Law Review* 101 (August 2003): 2706–43.

16. Bureau of Justice Statistics, "Criminal Cases," www.bjs.gov/index.cfm?ty=tp&tid=23 (accessed 3/20/20).

17. *Wal-Mart v. Dukes*, 564 U.S. (2011). However, in 2011 the Court struck down any class-action claim unless there was "convincing proof of a companywide discriminatory pay and promotion policy"—statistical evidence of pay disparities

would not suffice. David Savage, "Supreme Court Blocks Huge Class-Action Suit against Wal-Mart," *Los Angeles Times*, June 21, 2011, http://articles.latimes.com/2011/jun/21/nation/la-na-court-walmart-20110621 (accessed 3/20/20).

18. Brandon J. Murrill, "The Supreme Court's Overruling of Constitutional Precedent," Congressional Research Service, CRS Report R45319, September 24, 2018, https://fas.org/sgp/crs/misc/R45319.pdf (accessed 6/15/20).

19. *Franchise Tax Board of California v. Hyatt*, 587 U.S. ___ (2019). For a discussion of the implications of this case, see Henry Gass, "Overruled: Is Precedent in Danger at the Supreme Court?," *Christian Science Monitor*, June 25, 2019, www.csmonitor.com/USA/Justice/2019/0625/Overruled-Is-precedent-in-danger-at-the-Supreme-Court (accessed 6/15/20).

20. *Lujan v. Defenders of Wildlife*, 504 U.S. 555 (1992).

21. The case concerning the bombing in Libya was *Kucinich v. Obama*, 821 F.Supp. 2d 110 (Dist. of Columbia 2011). The cases limiting taxpayers' standing to challenge laws they disagree with are *Flast v. Cohen*, 392 U.S. 83 (1968), and *Arizona Christian School Tuition Org. v. Winn*, 131 S.Ct. 1436 (2011).

22. United States Courts, "Authorized Judgeships," www.uscourts.gov/judges-judgeships/authorized-judgeships (accessed 3/20/20).

23. The official name for each appeals court is the "United States Court of Appeals for the Circuit."

24. United States Courts, "Authorized Judgeships."

25. TRAC Reports, "Federal Senior Judges Carry a Growing Workload," Judge Information Center, Syracuse University, July 9, 2015, https://trac.syr.edu/tracreports/judge/395/ (accessed 6/15/20).

26. *Ledbetter v. Goodyear Tire & Rubber Co.*, 550 U.S. 618 (2007).

27. The Eleventh Amendment does not mention lawsuits against a state brought in federal court by citizens of that same state. However, in *Alden v. Maine*, 527 U.S. 706 (1999), the Court extended the logic of sovereign immunity to apply to these cases as well. Then in *Franchise Tax Board of California v. Hyatt*, 587 U.S. ___ (2019), the Court ruled that states cannot be sued by citizens in the courts of another state.

28. Savage, *Guide to the U.S. Supreme Court*, p. 1003.

29. Allyson Escobar, "Why Do Catholics Make Up a Majority of the Supreme Court?," *America Magazine*, October 27, 2020, www.americamagazine.org/politics-society/2018/07/18/why-do-catholics-make-majority-supreme-court (accessed 11/10/20).

30. "President Bush Discusses Judicial Accomplishments and Philosophy," Cincinnati, Ohio, October 6, 2008, https://georgewbush-whitehouse.archives.gov/news/releases/2008/10/20081006-5.html (accessed 3/20/20).

31. Paul Kane, "Reid, Democrats Trigger 'Nuclear' Option; Eliminate Most Filibusters on Nominees," *Washington Post*, November 21, 2013, www.washingtonpost.com/politics/senate-poised-to-limit-filibusters-in-party-line-vote-that-would-alter-centuries-of-precedent/2013/11/21/d065cfe8-52b6-11e3-9fe0-fd2ca728e67c_story.html (accessed 5/2/14).

32. United States Courts, "Judicial Vacancies," www.uscourts.gov/judges-judgeships/judicial-vacancies (accessed 6/16/20).

33. John Roberts, "2019 Year-End Report on the Federal Judiciary," U.S. Supreme Court, December 31, 2019, www.supremecourt.gov/publicinfo/year-end/2019year-endreport.pdf (accessed 6/16/20).

34. Supreme Court of the United States *In Re Frederick W. Bauer*, On Motion for Leave to Proceed in forma pauperis, No. 99-5440, Decided October 18, 1999, per curiam, www.justice.gov/sites/default/files/osg/briefs/1990/01/01/sg900418.txt (accessed 7/10/20).

35. Roberts, "2019 Year-End Report on the Federal Judiciary."

36. *New Jersey v. New York*, No. 120 Orig., 118 S.Ct. 1726 (1998), and *Texas v. New Mexico*, 138 S.Ct. 954 (2018).

37. Henry J. Abraham, *The Judiciary: The Supreme Court in the Governmental Process*, 7th ed. (Boston: Allyn and Bacon, 1987), p. 25, says that original jurisdiction has been invoked "about 150 times." A Lexis search revealed an additional 27 original-jurisdiction cases between 1987 and December 2004. A search of the U.S. Supreme Court's website, www.supremecourt.gov, found 14 more original jurisdiction cases from 2005 to 2020.

38. Amanda L. Tyler, "Setting the Supreme Court's Agenda: Is There a Place for Certification?," *George Washington Law Review Arguendo* 78 (May 2010): 101–18.

39. Savage, *Guide to the U.S. Supreme Court*, p. 848.

40. See Thomas G. Walker and Lee Epstein, *The Supreme Court of the United States: An Introduction* (New York: St. Martin's Press, 1993), pp. 80–85, for a more detailed discussion of these concepts and citations to the relevant court cases.

41. *Shaw v. Reno*, 509 U.S. 630 (1993).

42. *Elk Grove Unified School District v. Newdow*, 542 U.S. 1 (2004).

43. Gregory A. Caldeira and John R. Wright, "The Discuss List: Agenda Building in the Supreme Court," *Law and Society Review* 24 (1990): 813; Benjamin Johnson, "The Supreme Court's Political Docket: How Ideology and the Chief Justice Control the Court's Agenda and Shape Law," *Connecticut Law Review* 50:3 (August 2018): 581–639.

44. Walker and Epstein, *Supreme Court*, p. 89; Ryan C. Black and Ryan J. Owens, *The Solicitor General and the United States Supreme Court: Executive Branch Influence and Judicial Decisions* (New York: Cambridge University Press, 2012).

45. U.S. Supreme Court, "The Court and Its Procedures," www.supremecourt.gov/about/procedures.aspx (accessed 3/21/20).

46. Lee Epstein et al., *The Supreme Court Compendium: Data, Decisions, and Developments*, 6th ed. (Washington, DC: CQ Press, 2015), Table 7-22.

47. Gregory A. Caldeira and John R. Wright, "*Amicus Curiae* before the Supreme Court: Who Participates, When, and How Much?," *Journal of Politics* 52 (August 1990): 803.

48. Richard L. Pacelle Jr. et al., "The Influence of the Solicitor General as Amicus Curiae on the Roberts Court, 2005–2014: A Research Note," *Justice System Journal* 38:2 (2017): 202–8.

49. Andrew Christy, "'Obamacare' Will Rank among the Longest Supreme Court Arguments Ever," National Public Radio, November 15, 2011, www.npr.org/blogs/itsallpolitics/2011/11/15/142363047/obamacare-will-rank-among-the-longest-supreme-court-arguments-ever (accessed 3/21/20).

50. U.S. Supreme Court, *Rules of the Supreme Court of the United States*, adopted April 8, 2019, effective July 1, 2019, www.supremecourt.gov/ctrules/2019RulesoftheCourt.pdf (accessed 3/21/20).

51. Savage, *Guide to the U.S. Supreme Court*, p. 852.

52. U.S. Supreme Court, "Argument Transcripts," www.supremecourt.gov/oral_arguments/argument_transcript/2019 (accessed 3/20/20).

53. Adam Feldman, "Is Oral-Argument Talking Time All It's Cut Out to Be?," SCOTUSblog, October 21, 2019, www.scotusblog.com/2019/10/empirical-scotus-is-oral-argument-talking-time-all-its-cut-out-to-be/; Adam Feldman, "Competition to Speak during 2018 Supreme Court Oral Arguments," SCOTUSblog, May 6, 2019, https://empiricalscotus.com/2019/05/06/competition-to-speak/ (both accessed 6/16/20).

54. Garrett Epps, "Clarence Thomas Breaks His Silence," *The Atlantic*, February 29, 2016, www.theatlantic.com/politics/archive/2016/02/clarence-thomas-supreme-court/471582/ (accessed 5/27/16).

55. For an interesting analysis of oral arguments during the pandemic, see Adam Feldman, "Results from the Court's Experiment with a New Oral Argument Format," SCOTUSblog, May 22, 2020, www.scotusblog.com/2020/05/empirical-scotus-results-from-the-courts-experiment-with-a-new-oral-argument-format/. On a lighter note, in addition to the normal problems of remote meetings, like forgetting to turn on your audio, there was one embarrassing moment when there was a distinct sound of a toilet flushing. See Ariane de Vogue, "Supreme Embarrassment: The Flush Heard around the Country," CNN, May 6, 2020, www.cnn.com/2020/05/06/politics/toilet-flush-supreme-court-oral-arguments/index.html (both accessed 6/16/20).

56. Quoted in Savage, *Guide to the U.S. Supreme Court*, p. 854.

57. Richard J. Lazarus, "Back to 'Business' at the Supreme Court: The 'Administrative Side' of Chief Justice Roberts," *Harvard Law Review Forum* 129:33 (2015): 33–93.

58. Michael A. McCall and Madhavi M. McCall, "Quantifying the Contours of Power: Chief Justice Roberts & Justice Kennedy in Criminal Justice Cases," *Pace Law Review* 37:1 (2016): 115-74.

59. *Smith v. Allwright*, 321 U.S. 649 (1944).

60. Walker and Epstein, *Supreme Court*, p. 110.

61. Linda Greenhouse, "Chief Justice Roberts in His Own Voice: The Chief Justice's Self-Assignment of Majority Opinions," Yale Law School, Public Law Research Paper no. 496, August 15, 2013.

62. Savage, *Guide to the U.S. Supreme Court*, p. 854.

63. Lee Epstein, William M. Landes, and Richard A. Posner, "Are Even Unanimous Decisions in the United States Supreme Court Ideological?," *Northwestern University Law Review* 106:2 (2012): 702.

64. SCOTUSblog, Final Stat Pack for October Term 2019.

65. In cases involving statutory interpretation, the language of the law passed by Congress would be the starting point. The logic of these various perspectives on constitutional interpretation generally applies to statutory interpretation as well.

66. Quoted in Lee Epstein and Thomas G. Walker, *Constitutional Law for a Changing America: Institutional Powers and Constraints*, 5th ed. (Washington, DC: CQ Press, 2004), p. 29.

67. The consolidated cases were *Bostock v. Clayton County, Georgia*, 590 U.S. ___ (2020); *Altitude Express v. Zarda*, 590 U.S. ___ (2020); and *R.G. & G.R. Harris Funeral Homes v. EEOC*, 590 U.S. ___ (2020).

68. Epstein and Walker, *Constitutional Law for a Changing America*, p. 31.

69. Seth Stern and Stephen Wermiel, *Justice Brennan: Liberal Champion* (Boston: Houghton Mifflin Harcourt, 2010).

70. Epstein et al., *Supreme Court Compendium*, Table 6-2.

71. Forrest Maltzman and Paul J. Wahlbeck, "Strategic Policy Considerations and Vote Fluidity on the Burger Court," *American Journal of Political Science* 90 (1996): 581–92; Forrest Maltzman, James F. Spriggs, and Paul J. Wahlbeck, *Crafting Law on the Supreme Court: The Collegial Game* (New York: Cambridge University Press, 2000), p. 33.

72. Finley Peter Dunne, Paul Green, and Jacques Barzun, *Mr. Dooley in Peace and in War* (1898; repr., Champaign-Urbana: University of Illinois Press, 2001).

73. Robert Dahl, "Decision-Making in a Democracy: The Supreme Court as a National Policy-Maker," *Journal of Public Law* 6 (1957): 279–95, is the classic work on this topic. More recent work has challenged Dahl's methods but largely supports the idea that the Court follows the will of the majority.

74. Jeffrey A. Segal, Richard J. Timpone, and Robert M. Howard, "Buyer Beware? Presidential Success through Supreme Court Appointments," *Political Research Quarterly* 53:3 (September 2000): 557–73; Gregory A. Caldeira and Charles E. Smith Jr., "Campaigning for the Supreme Court: The Dynamics of Public Opinion on the Thomas Nomination," *Political Research Quarterly* 58:3 (August 1996): 655–81.

75. William Mishler and Reginald S. Sheehan, "The Supreme Court as a Countermajoritarian Institution? The Impact of Public Opinion on Supreme Court Decisions," *American Political Science Review* 87:1 (March 1993): 87–101.

76. Thomas R. Marshall, *Public Opinion and the Supreme Court* (Boston: Unwin Hyman, 1989), p. 12; as cited in Epstein and Walker, *Constitutional Law for a Changing America*, p. 92.

77. Matthew E. K. Hall, "The Semiconstrained Court: Public Opinion, the Separation of Powers, and the U.S. Supreme Court's Fear of Nonimplementation," *American Journal of Political Science* 58:2 (April 2014): 352–66; Matthew E. K. Hall, *The Nature of Supreme Court Power* (New York: Cambridge University Press, 2011).

78. *Stanford v. Kentucky*, 492 U.S. 361 (1989); *Roper v. Simmons*, 543 U.S. 551 (2005).

79. David O'Brien, *Storm Center: The Supreme Court in American Politics*, 4th ed. (New York: W. W. Norton, 1996), p. 276.

80. Helmut Norpoth and Jeffrey A. Segal, "Popular Influence in Supreme Court Decisions," *American Political Science Review* 88 (1994): 711–16.

81. While it is clear that the Supreme Court is at least somewhat sensitive to public opinion, the reverse does not appear to be true. A survey experiment had half the respondents read Chief Justice Roberts's admonition to President Trump about how there were not "Obama judges and Trump judges" and the other half did not see that statement. Both were shown a story about a federal court's decision on a political asylum case that President Trump was unhappy about to see if the respondents who read Roberts's statement would respond any differently than those who did not. There were absolutely no differences. However, another study by the same authors found that those who saw a speech by Justice Sotomayor were more likely than those who did not see the speech to think that law rather than ideology determined court decisions. See David Fontana and Christopher Krewson, "Can the Supreme Court Learn to Speak Up for Itself?," *Washington Post*, February 26, 2020, washingtonpost.com/magazine/2020/02/26/can-supreme-court-learn-speak-up-itself/?arc404=true (accessed 6/17/20).

82. Thomas M. Keck, *The Most Activist Supreme Court in History: The Road to Modern Judicial Conservatism* (Chicago: University of Chicago Press, 2004).

83. Calculated by the author from data provided by Harold J. Spaeth et al., 2019 Supreme Court Database, Version 2019 Release 01, http://supremecourtdatabase.org (accessed 6/17/20).

84. Jeffrey Rosen, "Has the Supreme Court Gone Too Far?," *Commentary* 116:3 (October 2003): 41–2.

85. *National Federation of Independent Business v. Sebelius*, 567 U.S. 519 (2012).

86. Abby Phillip, Robert Barnes, and Ed O'Keefe, "Supreme Court Nominee Gorsuch Says Trump's Attacks on Judiciary Are 'Demoralizing,'" *Washington Post*, February 9, 2017, www.washingtonpost.com/politics/supreme-court-nominee-gorsuch-says-trumps-attacks-on-judiciary-are-demoralizing/2017/02/08/64e03fe2-ee3f-11e6-9662-6eedf1627882_story.html?utm_term=.ade3f9791d87 (accessed 3/15/18).

87. *Foster v. Neilson*, 27 U.S. 253 (1829).

88. *Charles B. Rangel v. John A. Boehner*, United States District Court for the District of Columbia, Civil Action No. 13-540, December 11, 2013, p. 48, https://ecf.dcd.uscourts.gov/cgi-bin/show_public_doc?2013cv0540-24 (accessed 5/2/14).

89. We thank Dan Smith for raising this point.

90. Ken Rudin, "Gay Marriage, DOMA and the Dramatic Shift in Public Opinion in One Year," National Public Radio, March 18, 2013, www.npr.org/sections/politicaljunkie/2013/03/18/173970922/gay-marriage-doma-and-the-dramatic-shift-in-public-opinion-in-one-year (accessed 9/16/20).

Take a Stand

a. Martin Kady II, "Justice Alito Mouths 'Not True,'" Politico, January 27, 2010, www.politico.com/blogs/politico-now/2010/01/justice-alito-mouths-not-true-024608 (accessed 8/24/18).

b. Donald J. Trump, Twitter, June 28, 2020, 10:08 A.M., https://twitter.com/realDonaldTrump/status/1273633632742191106 (accessed 6/17/20).

AP® Study Guide

a. Oyez, *United States v. Comstock*, 560 U.S. 126 (2010), www.oyez.org/cases/2009/08-1224 (accessed 9/11/20); Public Law 109-248, U.S. Government Printing Office, www.govinfo.gov/content/pkg/PLAW-109publ248/html/PLAW-109publ248.htm (accessed 9/11/20).

Chapter 7

1. Robert A. Heinlein, *Stranger in a Strange Land* (1961; repr., New York: Berkley, 1983), p. 95.

2. Joseph A. Schumpeter, *Capitalism, Socialism and Democracy* (1943; repr., London: Routledge, 2013), p. 206.

3. Dwight Waldo, *The Administrative State: A Study of the Political Theory of American Public Administration* (1948; repr. Piscataway, NJ: Transaction, 2006).

4. For a history of the FDA, see John P. Swann, FDA History Office, "History of the FDA," www.fda.gov/AboutFDA/History/FOrgsHistory/EvolvingPowers/ucm124403.htm (accessed 7/6/18).

5. For details, see Cornelius Kerwin, *Rulemaking: How Government Agencies Write Law and Make Policy* (Washington, DC: CQ Press, 1999).

6. The *Federal Register* is available at www.federalregister.gov/ (accessed 5/18/20).

7. Andrew Pollack, "New Sense of Caution at FDA," *New York Times*, September 29, 2006, www.nytimes.com/2006/09/29/business/29caution.html?_r=0 (accessed 8/29/16).

8. There are two exceptions. A patient can enroll in a clinical trial for a new drug during the approval process, but there is a good chance that the patient will get a placebo or a previously approved treatment rather than the drug being tested. The FDA does allow companies to provide some experimental drugs to patients who cannot participate in a trial, but only those drugs that have passed early screening trials.

9. Susan Okie, "Access before Approval—a Right to Take Experimental Drugs?," *New England Journal of Medicine* 355 (2004): 437-40.

10. Stephen Skowronek, *Building a New American State: The Expansion of National Administrative Capacities, 1877-1920* (New York: Cambridge University Press, 1982).

11. Terry Moe, "An Assessment of the Positive Theory of Congressional Dominance," *Legislative Studies Quarterly* 4 (1987): 475-98.

12. Leon Neyfakh, "The FCC Just Voted to Reduce the Exorbitant Cost of Prison Phone Calls," *Slate*, October 22, 2015, www.slate.com/blogs/the_slatest/2015/10/22/prison_phone_calls_the_fcc_is_finally_making_them_cheaper.html (accessed 5/6/16).

13. Juliet Eilperin and Steven Mufson, "Top Interior Official Who Pushed to Expand Drilling in Alaska to Join Oil Company There," *Washington Post*, September 4, 2019, www.washingtonpost.com/climate-environment/2019/09/04/top-interior-official-who-pushed-expand-drilling-alaska-join-oil-company-there/ (accessed 6/4/20).

14. Frances E. Rourke, "Responsiveness and Neutral Competence in American Bureaucracy," *Public Administration Review* 52 (1992): 539-46; Max Weber, *Essays on Sociology* (New York: Oxford University Press, 1958).

15. Samuel Workman, *The Dynamics of Bureaucracy in the U.S. Government* (New York: Cambridge University Press, 2015).

16. Peter H. Schuck, *Why Government Fails So Often and How It Can Do Better* (Princeton, NJ: Princeton University Press, 2015).

17. Karen Orren and Steven Skowronek, "Regimes and Regime Building in American Government: A Review of the Literature on the 1940s," *Political Science Quarterly* 113 (1998): 689-702.

18. Michael Nelson, "A Short, Ironic History of American National Bureaucracy," *Journal of Politics* 44 (1982): 747-78.

19. Nelson, "A Short, Ironic History of American National Bureaucracy."

20. Nelson, "A Short, Ironic History of American National Bureaucracy."

21. John Aldrich, *Why Parties?* (Chicago: University of Chicago Press, 1995).

22. Nelson, "A Short, Ironic History of American National Bureaucracy."

23. Matthew A. Crenson, *The Federal Machine: Beginnings of Bureaucracy in Jacksonian America* (Baltimore, MD: Johns Hopkins University Press, 1975).

24. James Q. Wilson, "The Rise of the Bureaucratic State," in *The American Commonwealth*, ed. Nathan Glazer and Irving Kristol (New York: Basic Books, 1976).

25. Skowronek, *Building a New American State*.

26. Robert Harrison, *Congress, Progressive Reform, and the New American State* (New York: Cambridge University Press, 2004).

27. The National Archives and Records Administration has an excellent summary of the Pendleton Act at www.ourdocuments.gov/doc.php?flash=false&doc=48 (accessed 7/6/18).

28. Lawrence C. Dodd and Richard L. Schott, *Congress and the Administrative State* (New York: Wiley, 1979).

29. Ira Katznelson and Bruce Pietrykowski, "Rebuilding the American State: Evidence from the 1940s," *Studies in American Political Development* 5:2 (1991): 301-39.

30. David Plotke, *Building a Democratic Political Order: Reshaping American Liberalism in the 1930s and 1940s* (New York: Cambridge University Press, 1996).

31. Theda Skocpol and Kenneth Finegold, "State Capacity and Economic Intervention in the Early New Deal," *Political Science Quarterly* 97 (1999): 255-70.

32. Michael Brown, "State Capacity and Political Choice: Interpreting the Failure of the Third New Deal," *Studies in American Political Development* 9 (1995): 187-212.

33. Ira Katznelson, Kim Geiger, and Daniel Kryder, "Limiting Liberalism: The Southern Veto in Congress, 1933–1950," *Political Science Quarterly* 108 (1993): 283–306.

34. Joseph Califano, "What Was Really Great about the Great Society," *Washington Monthly*, October 1999, https://washingtonmonthly.com/1999/10/01/what-was-really-great-about-the-great-society (accessed 7/16/08).

35. David T. Canon, *Race, Redistricting, and Representation: The Unintended Consequences of Black Majority Districts* (Chicago: University of Chicago Press, 1999).

36. Charles Murray, *Losing Ground: American Social Policy, 1950–1980* (New York: Basic Books, 1984).

37. Henry J. Aaron, *Politics and the Professors: The Great Society in Perspective* (Washington, DC: Brookings Institution Press, 1978).

38. Michael B. Katz, *In the Shadow of the Poorhouse: A Social History of Welfare in America* (New York: Basic Books, 1996).

39. Richard P. Nathan, *The Administrative Presidency* (New York: Wiley, 1983).

40. Andrew Rudalevige, "The Structure of Leadership: Presidents, Hierarchies, and Information Flow," *Presidential Studies Quarterly* 35 (2005): 333–60.

41. David E. Lewis, *Presidents and the Policy of Agency Design* (Palo Alto, CA: Stanford University Press, 2003).

42. Yasmeen Abutaleb and Laurie McGinley, "Ousted Vaccine Official Alleges He Was Demoted for Prioritizing 'Science and Safety,'" *Washington Post*, May 5, 2020, www.washingtonpost.com/health/2020/05/05/rick-bright-hydroxychloroquine-whistleblower-complaint/ (accessed 6/5/20).

43. Terry M. Moe, "An Assessment of the Positive Theory of Congressional Dominance," *Legislative Studies Quarterly* 4 (1987): 475–98.

44. William A. Niskanen, *Bureaucracy and Public Economics* (Washington, DC: Edward Elgar, 1976); Robert Whaples and Jac C. Heckelman, "Public Choice Economics: Where Is There Consensus?," *American Economist* 49 (2005): 66–78.

45. Alan Schick and Felix LoStracco, *The Federal Budget: Politics, Process, Policy* (Washington, DC: Brookings Institution Press, 2000).

46. Joel D. Aberbach, "The Political Significance of the George W. Bush Administration," *Social Policy and Administration* 39:2 (2005): 130–49.

47. David E. Lewis, "The Politics of Agency Termination: Confronting the Myth of Agency Immortality," *Journal of Politics* 64 (2002): 89–107.

48. Ronald A. Wirtz, "Put It on My . . . Er, His Tab: Opinion Polls Show a Big Gap between the Public's Desire for Services and Its Willingness to Pay for These Services," *Fedgazette*, January 2004, www.minneapolisfed.org/publications/fedgazette/put-it-on-my-er-his-tab (accessed 6/25/18).

49. James L. Perry and Annie Hondeghem, *Motivation in Public Management: The Call of Public Service* (Oxford, UK: Oxford University Press, 2008).

50. Paul Light, *A Government Well-Executed: Public Service and Public Performance* (Washington, DC: Brookings Institution Press, 2003).

51. This discussion of the details of the civil service system is based on U.S. Office of Personnel Management General Schedule, www.opm.gov/policy-data-oversight/pay-leave/salaries-wages/2017/general-schedule/ (accessed 7/6/18).

52. Dennis Cauchon, "Some Federal Workers More Likely to Die Than Lose Jobs," *USA Today*, July 19, 2011, p. A1.

53. Ronald N. Johnson and Gary D. Liebcap, *The Federal Civil Service System and the Problem of Bureaucracy* (Chicago: University of Chicago Press, 1993).

54. For the details of the Hatch Act, see Daniel Engber, "Can Karl Rove Plot Campaign Strategy on the Government's Dime?," *Slate*, April 21, 2006, www.slate.com/id/2140418 (accessed 8/29/16).

55. Nicole Ogrysko, "Energy Employee Banned for 3 Years after 'Flagrant' Hatch Act Violation," Federal News Network, January 16, 2020, https://federalnewsnetwork.com/workforce/2020/01/energy-employee-banned-for-3-years-after-flagrant-hatch-act-violation/ (accessed 5/22/20).

56. Timothy Noah, "Low Morale at Homeland Security," *Slate*, September 14, 2005, www.slate.com/id/2126313 (accessed 8/29/16).

57. For details on the SES, see www.opm.gov/policy-data-oversight/senior-executive-service/ (accessed 5/7/18).

58. "Tracking How Many Key Positions Trump Has Filled So Far," *Washington Post*, www.washingtonpost.com/graphics/politics/trump-administration-appointee-tracker/database/?utm_term=.1b5914b69716 (accessed 6/4/20).

59. Lisa Rein and Juliet Eilperin, "White House Installs Political Aides at Cabinet Agencies to Be Trump's Eyes and Ears," *Washington Post*, March 19, 2017, www.washingtonpost.com/powerpost/white-house-installs-political-aides-at-cabinet-agencies-to-be-trumps-eyes-and-ears/2017/03/19/68419f0e-08da-11e7-93dc-00f9bdd74ed1_story.html (accessed 6/5/20).

60. Todd Frankel, "Why the CDC Still Isn't Researching Gun Violence, despite the Ban Being Lifted Two Years Ago," *Washington Post*, January 14, 2015, www.washingtonpost.com/news/storyline/wp/2015/01/14/why-the-cdc-still-isnt-researching-gun-violence-despite-the-ban-being-lifted-two-years-ago/ (accessed 6/5/20).

61. Umair Irfan, "'Climate Change' and 'Global Warming' Are Disappearing from Government Websites," Vox, January 11, 2018, www.vox.com/energy-and-environment/2017/11/9/16619120/trump-administration-removing-climate-change-epa-online-website (accessed 5/18/18).

62. Helena Bottemiller Evich, "Agriculture Department Buries Studies Showing Dangers of Climate Change," Politico, June 23, 2019, www.politico.com/story/2019/06/23/agriculture-department-climate-change-1376413 (accessed 5/27/20).

63. John D. Huber and Charles R. Shipan, *Deliberate Discretion? The Institutional Foundations of Bureaucratic Autonomy* (New York: Cambridge University Press, 2002).

64. David Epstein and Sharyn O'Halloran, *Delegating Powers: A Transaction Cost Politics Approach to Policy Making under Separate Powers* (New York: Cambridge University Press, 1999).

65. Mathew D. McCubbins, Roger G. Noll, and Barry R. Weingast, "Structure and Process as Solutions to the Politician's Principal–Agency Problem," *Virginia Law Review* 74 (1989): 431–82.

66. Barry R. Weingast, "Caught in the Middle: The President, Congress, and the Political–Bureaucratic System," in *Institutions of American Democracy: The Executive Branch*, ed. Joel D. Aberbach and Mark A. Peterson (New York: Oxford University Press, 2006).

67. Keith Whittington and Daniel P. Carpenter, "Executive Power in American Institutional Development," *Perspectives on Politics* 1 (2003): 495–513.

68. Roger Noll, Mathew McCubbins, and Barry Weingast, "Administrative Procedures as Instruments of Political Control," *Journal of Law, Economics, and Organization* 3 (1987): 243-77.

69. Hannah Knowles, "Top Democrats Launch Investigation into Late-Night Firing of State Department Inspector General," *Washington Post*, March 16, 2020, www.washingtonpost.com/politics/2020/05/16/state-department-inspector-general-fired-democrats-decry-dangerous-pattern-retaliation/ (accessed 6/5/20).

70. Mathew McCubbins and Thomas Schwartz, "Congressional Oversight Overlooked: Fire Alarms vs. Police Patrols," *American Journal of Political Science* 28 (1984): 165-79.

71. McCubbins and Schwartz, "Congressional Oversight Overlooked."

72. Steven J. Balla and John R. Wright, "Interest Groups, Advisory Committees, and Congressional Control of the Bureaucracy," *American Journal of Political Science* 45 (2001): 799-812.

73. Daniel P. Carpenter, "The Gatekeeper: Organizational Reputation and Pharmaceutical Regulation at the FDA" (unpublished paper, Harvard University, 2006).

74. Terry M. Moe, "Political Control and the Power of the Agent," *Journal of Law, Economics, and Organization* 22 (2006): 1-29.

75. See David Weil, "OSHA: Beyond the Politics," *Frontline*, January 9, 2003, www.pbs.org/wgbh/pages/frontline/shows/workplace/osha/weil.html (accessed 8/29/16).

76. Evan Lehmann and Nathanael Massey, "Obama Warns Congress to Act on Climate Change, or He Will," *Scientific American*, February 13, 2013, www.scientificamerican.com/article/obama-warns-congress-to-act-on-climate-change-or-he-will/ (accessed 9/16/20).

Chapter 8

1. Donald J. Trump, "Remarks by President Trump at Signing of Executive Order, 'Improving Free Inquiry, Transparency, and Accountability at Colleges and Universities,'" The White House, March 21, 2019, www.whitehouse.gov/briefings-statements/remarks-president-trump-signing-executive-order-improving-free-inquiry-transparency-accountability-colleges-universities/ (accessed 1/29/20).

2. Katherine Timpf, "Biden Is Right and Kasich Is Wrong on Campus Free Speech," *National Review*, October 18, 2017, www.nationalreview.com/2017/10/john-kasich-joe-biden-campus-free-speech-debate/ (accessed 1/29/20).

3. Patrick Strudwick, "Milo Yiannopoulos Calls Abuse Victims 'Whinging, Selfish Brats' in a Newly Emerged Video," BuzzFeed, March 11, 2017, www.buzzfeed.com/patrickstrudwick/milo-yiannopoulos-described-sexual-abuse-victims-as-whinging?utm_term=.sgZNwrBGy#.kmGkJoeZd; Graeme Wood, "His Kampf: Richard Spencer Is a Troll and an Icon for White Supremacists," *The Atlantic*, June 2017, www.theatlantic.com/magazine/archive/2017/06/his-kampf/524505 (both accessed 4/11/18).

4. A partial list of campuses that have protested conservative speakers includes Middlebury College; University of California, Berkeley; University of Florida; DePaul; Harvard; Auburn; Emory; Georgetown; and the University of Washington. For an insightful discussion of the broader debate, see Lee C. Bollinger, "Free Speech on Campus Is Doing Just Fine, Thank You," *The Atlantic*, June 12, 2019, www.theatlantic.com/ideas/archive/2019/06/free-speech-crisis-campus-isnt-real/591394/ (accessed 1/29/20).

5. Michael S. Roth, "Free Speech Wars Miss the Point of College," CNN, September 10, 2019, www.cnn.com/2019/09/10/opinions/free-speech-on-campus-roth/index.html (accessed 1/29/20).

6. Meghan Keneally and Julia Jacobo, "Police: Suspect Shouted 'Heil Hitler' before Shooting Incident after Spencer Event," ABC News, October 20, 2017, http://abcnews.go.com/US/security-ramped-white-nationalist-richard-spencers-florida-event/story?id=50585570 (accessed 10/24/17).

7. Trump, "Remarks by President Trump." President Trump also explained that the federal government would require private institutions that receive federal grants to follow "their own policies on free speech."

8. Yanan Wang, "Obama to Campus Protesters: Don't 'Shut Up' Opposing Viewpoints," *Washington Post*, December 22, 2015, www.washingtonpost.com/news/morning-mix/wp/2015/12/22/obama-to-campus-protesters-dont-shut-up-opposing-viewpoints (accessed 12/30/15).

9. "Speech on Campus," American Civil Liberties Union, www.aclu.org/other/speech-campus (accessed 1/16/20).

10. Bollinger, "Free Speech on Campus."

11. Foundation for Individual Rights in Education (FIRE), Disinvitation Database, www.thefire.org/research/disinvitation-database/#home/?view_2_sort=field_6|desc&view_2_page=7 (accessed 1/29/20).

12. *Arar v. Ashcroft et al.*, WL 346439 (E.D. N.Y. 2006). The case was dismissed because Arar, a Canadian citizen, did not have standing to sue the U.S. government. Supporters of this decision (and the practice more generally) say that it is an essential part of the War on Terror and that the enemy combatants who are arrested have no legal rights. Opponents say that the practice violates international law and our own standards of decency; furthermore, torture almost never produces useful information because people will say anything to get the torture to stop.

13. *State v. Massey et al.*, 51 S.E.2d 179 (N.C. 1949). The case was appealed to the Supreme Court, but the Court declined to hear the case, which means that the state decision stands (*Bunn v. North Carolina*, 336 U.S. 942 [1949]).

14. Alan Blinder, "Tennessee Pastor Disputes a Wildlife Possession Charge by State," *New York Times*, November 15, 2013, www.nytimes.com/2013/11/16/us/tennessee-pastor-disputes-wildlife-possession-charge-by-state.html?_r=0 (accessed 1/24/14).

15. *Pennsylvania v. Miller*, Court of Common Pleas, WL 31426193 (Penn. 2002). However, supreme courts in Minnesota, Wisconsin, and several other states have decided that requiring the Amish to use orange SMV triangles violates their free exercise of religion.

16. *Wisconsin v. Yoder*, 403 U.S. 205 (1972).

17. Jeffrey Rosen, "Lemon Law," *New Republic*, March 29, 1993, p. 17.

18. Max Farrand, ed., *The Records of the Federal Convention of 1787*, rev. ed. (New Haven, CT: Yale University Press, 1937), pp. 587-88, 617-18.

19. *The Papers of Thomas Jefferson*, ed. J. Boyd (Princeton, NJ: Princeton University Press, 1958), pp. 557-83, cited in Lester S. Jayson, ed., *The Constitution of the United States of America: Analysis and Interpretation* (Washington, DC: U.S. Government Printing Office, 1973), p. 900.

20. Ralph Ketcham, *The Anti-Federalist Papers and the Constitutional Convention Debates* (New York: Signet Classic, Penguin Putnam, 2003), p. 247.

21. The two that were not ratified by the states were a complicated amendment on congressional apportionment and the pay raise amendment.

22. *Annals of Congress* 755 (August 17, 1789), cited in Lester S. Jayson, ed., *The Constitution of the United States of America* (Washington, DC: U.S. Government Printing Office, 1973), p. 898.

23. There is an intense scholarly debate on whether the authors of the Fourteenth Amendment intended for it to apply the Bill of Rights to the states. The strongest argument against this position is Raoul Berger's *The Fourteenth Amendment and the Bill of Rights* (Norman: University of Oklahoma Press, 1989), and a good book in support is Akhil Reed Amar's *The Bill of Rights* (New Haven, CT: Yale University Press, 1998).

24. *Barron v. Baltimore* 32 U.S. 243 (1833), 250. The 1873 case was *Slaughter-House Cases*, 83 U.S. 36 (1873). The Supreme Court also declined to apply the Bill of Rights to the states in the *Civil Rights Cases*, 109 U.S. 3 (1883), in which the Court ruled that the Fourteenth Amendment did not give Congress the power to regulate the conduct of private business (thus the Civil Rights Act of 1875 was unconstitutional and private businesses could discriminate on the basis of race).

25. *Chicago, Burlington, and Quincy Railroad v. Chicago*, 166 U.S. 226 (1897); *Twining v. New Jersey*, 211 U.S. 78, 98 (1908).

26. *Gitlow v. New York*, 268 U.S. 652 (1925).

27. James Hutson, "'A Wall of Separation,'" *Library of Congress Information Bulletin* 57:6 (June 1998), www.loc.gov/loc/lcib/9806/danbury.html (accessed 3/3/08).

28. Henry J. Abraham and Barbara A. Perry, *Freedom and the Court: Civil Rights and Civil Liberties in the United States*, 8th ed. (Lawrence: University Press of Kansas, 2003), p. 300.

29. *Engel v. Vitale*, 370 U.S. 421 (1962).

30. *Wallace v. Jaffree*, 482 U.S. 38 (1985).

31. *Lee v. Weisman*, 505 U.S. 577 (1992); *Santa Fe Independent School District v. Doe*, 530 U.S. 290 (2000).

32. *Marsh v. Chambers*, 463 U.S. 783 (1983); *Jones v. Clear Creek Independent School*, 61 LW 3819 (1993); *Town of Greece, N.Y. v. Galloway*, 572 U.S. 565 (2014).

33. *Lemon v. Kurtzman*, 403 U.S. 602 (1971).

34. *Lynch v. Donnelly*, 465 U.S. 668 (1984), 672–73.

35. Jeffrey Rosen, "Big Ten," *New Republic*, March 14, 2004, p. 11.

36. *American Legion v. American Humanist Association*, 588 U.S. ___ (2019).

37. *Zelman v. Simmons-Harris*, 536 U.S. 639 (2002).

38. *Arizona Christian School Tuition Organization v. Winn*, U.S. Supreme Court slip. op. 09-987 and 09-991 (2011).

39. *Mitchell v. Helms*, 530 U.S. 793 (2000).

40. *Zobrest v. Catalina Foothills School District*, 509 U.S. 1 (1993). A similar decision in 1997 allowed a public school teacher to teach in a special program in a parochial school, *Agostini v. Felton*, 521 U.S. 203 (1997).

41. *Espinoza v. Montana Department of Revenue*, 591 U.S. ___ (2020).

42. We will not cite all the cases here. See Abraham and Perry, *Freedom and the Court*, Chapter 6, for a summary of cases on this topic, especially Tables 6.1 and 6.2.

43. *Employment Division, Department of Human Resources of Oregon v. Smith*, 494 U.S. 872 (1990), 878–80. This case is often erroneously reported as having banned the religious use of peyote. In fact, the Court said: "Although it is constitutionally permissible to exempt sacramental peyote use from the operation of drug laws, it is not constitutionally required."

44. *City of Boerne v. Flores*, 521 U.S. 527 (1997); *Cutter v. Wilkinson*, No. 03-9877 (2005); *Gonzales v. O Centro Espirita Beneficente Uniao do Vegetal (UDV) et al.*, 546 U.S. 418 (2006). The Sherbert test requires that whenever the government limits religious expression it must prove a compelling interest that is narrowly tailored to achieve that interest if a person is substantially burdened by the law (*Sherbert v. Verner*, 374 U.S. 398 [1963]).

45. *Burwell v. Hobby Lobby*, 573 U.S. 682 (2014).

46. In *Little Sisters of the Poor Saints Peter and Paul Home v. Pennsylvania*, 591 U.S. ___ (2020), the Supreme Court upheld an administrative rule that overturned an Obama-era rule that had provided a workaround by having insurance pay directly for contraception for employees of private employers who objected to paying for it on religious grounds. The playground case, *Trinity Lutheran Church of Columbia, Inc. v. Comer*, 582 U.S. ___ (2017), would appear to be an establishment clause case (can the state provide direct funds to a church?), but it was decided on free exercise grounds. This opens the door to a broader range of protections for religious activity. See Garrett Epps, "A Major Church-State Ruling That Shouldn't Have Happened," *The Atlantic*, June 27, 2017, www.theatlantic.com/politics/archive/2017/06/a-major-church-state-case-that-shouldnt-have-happened/531789 (accessed 10/18/17).

47. *Masterpiece Cakeshop v. Colorado Civil Rights Commission*, 584 U.S. ___ (2018).

48. *Police Department of Chicago v. Mosley*, 408 U.S. 92 (1972).

49. *United States v. O'Brien*, 391 U.S. 367 (1968); *Ladue v. Gilleo*, 512 U.S. 43 (1994).

50. *Schenck v. United States*, 249 U.S. 47 (1919), 52.

51. Alan Dershowitz, *Shouting Fire: Civil Liberties in a Turbulent Age* (New York: Little, Brown, 2002).

52. *Abrams v. United States*, 250 U.S. 616 (1919), 630–31.

53. *Dennis v. United States*, 341 U.S. 494 (1951).

54. *Brandenburg v. Ohio*, 395 U.S. 444 (1969).

55. *Snyder v. Phelps*, 131 S.Ct. 1207 (2011).

56. *Smith v. Goguen*, 415 U.S. 566 (1974).

57. *Tinker v. Des Moines School District*, 393 U.S. 503 (1969).

58. *Spence v. Washington*, 418 U.S. 405 (1974).

59. *Spence v. Washington*, 418 U.S. 409–10 (1974).

60. *Texas v. Johnson*, 491 U.S. 397 (1989).

61. *United States v. Eichman*, 496 U.S. 310 (1990).

62. David Wright, "Trump: Burn the Flag, Go to Jail," CNN, November 29, 2016, www.cnn.com/2016/11/29/politics/donald-trump-flag-burning-penalty-proposal/index.html (accessed 10/18/17).

63. *United States v. O'Brien*, 391 U.S. 367, 376 (1968).

64. *Walker v. Texas Division, Sons of Confederate Veterans*, 576 U.S. ___ (2015).

65. Southern Poverty Law Center, "Whose Heritage? Public Symbols of the Confederacy," February 1, 2019, www.splcenter.org/20190201/whose-heritage-public-symbols-confederacy (accessed 1/29/20).

66. *Buckley v. Valeo*, 424 U.S. 1 (1976).

67. *Davis v. Federal Election Commission*, 554 U.S. 724 (2008).

68. *Citizens United v. Federal Election Commission*, 558 U.S. 310 (2010); *McCutcheon v. Federal Election Commission*, 572 U.S. ___ (2014).

69. *McConnell v. Federal Election Commission*, 540 U.S. 93 (2003).

70. *Board of Regents of the University of Wisconsin System et al., Petitioners v. Scott Harold Southworth et al.*, 529 U.S. 217 (2000).

71. One example was a speech code adopted at the University of Michigan that prohibited "any behavior, verbal or physical, that stigmatizes or victimizes an individual on the basis of race, ethnicity, religion, sex, sexual orientation, creed, national

origin, ancestry, age, marital status, handicap, or Vietnam veteran status" and "creates an intimidating, hostile, or demeaning environment for educational pursuits, employment or participation in University-sponsored extra-curricular activities." Kermit L. Hall, "Free Speech on Public College Campuses: Overview," www.firstamendmentcenter.org/speech/pubcollege/overview.aspx (accessed 2/10/08).

72. Liam Stack, "Yale's Halloween Advice Stokes a Racially Charged Debate," *New York Times,* November 8, 2015, www.nytimes.com/2015/11/09/nyregion/yale-culturally-insensitive-halloween-costumes-free-speech.html?_r=0 (accessed 12/30/15).

73. Michael D. Regan, "Yale Lecturer Resigns over Halloween Costume Email Controversy," *Christian Science Monitor,* December 8, 2015, www.csmonitor.com/USA/Education/2015/1208/Yale-lecturer-resigns-over-Halloween-costume-email-controversy (accessed 12/30/15).

74. One of the authors of this book took Introduction to American Politics in that lecture hall, and the other has taught many classes in the room. For a description of the controversy, see Dwight Adams and Holly V. Hays, "IU: Room with Mural of KKK Rally Will No Longer Be a Classroom," *Indianapolis Star,* September 29, 2017, www.indystar.com/story/news/2017/09/29/indiana-university-no-longer-use-room-mural-showing-kkk-rally-classroom/717308001 (accessed 10/18/17).

75. *City of St. Paul v. RAV,* 505 U.S. 377 (1992).

76. *Virginia v. Black,* 538 U.S. 343 (2003).

77. The Editorial Board, "Hate Speech on Facebook," *New York Times,* May 30, 2013, www.nytimes.com/2013/05/31/opinion/misogynist-speech-on-facebook.html (accessed 1/28/14).

78. Facebook "community standards" on hate speech, www.facebook.com/communitystandards (accessed 1/28/14).

79. Jeff Rosen, "Who Decides? Civility v. Hate Speech on the Internet," *Insights on Law and Society* 13:2 (Winter 2013): 32–36.

80. Mike Isaac, "Why Everyone Is Angry at Facebook over Its Political Ads Policy," *New York Times,* November 22, 2019, www.nytimes.com/2019/11/22/technology/campaigns-pressure-facebook-political-ads.html (accessed 1/29/20).

81. *Packingham v. North Carolina,* 582 U.S. ____ (2017).

82. *De Jonge v. State of Oregon,* 299 U.S. 353 (1937); *Edwards v. South Carolina,* 372 U.S. 229 (1963).

83. The Supreme Court declined to review the case in *Smith v. Collin,* 439 U.S. 916 (1978), which meant that the lower-court rulings stood (447 F. Supp. 676 [1978], 578 F.2d 1197 [1978]). See Donald A. Downs, *Nazis in Skokie: Freedom, Community and the First Amendment* (Notre Dame, IN: University of Notre Dame Press, 1985), for an excellent analysis of this important case.

84. *Forsyth County v. Nationalist Movement,* 505 U.S. 123 (1992).

85. Keneally and Jacobo, "Police."

86. *Frisby et al. v. Schultz et al.,* 487 U.S. 474 (1988).

87. See https://freespeech.ufl.edu/ for a discussion of all the related issues (accessed 3/7/18).

88. *McCullen v. Coakley,* 573 U.S. 464 (2014).

89. *New York Times Co. v. United States,* 403 U.S. 713 (1971).

90. *New York Times Co. v. United States,* 403 U.S. 713 (1971).

91. Quotation from James Risen, "Reporters Face New Threats from the Governments They Cover," *New York Times,* January 26, 2020, www.nytimes.com/2020/01/26/opinion/greenwald-brazil-reporter.html; also see Alex Emmons, "The Espionage Act Is Again Deployed against a Government Official Leaking to the Media," *The Intercept,* October 9 2019, https://theintercept.com/2019/10/09/the-espionage-act-is-again-deployed-against-a-government-official-leaking-to-the-media/ (both accessed 1/29/20).

92. *Chaplinsky v. State of New Hampshire,* 315 U.S. 568 (1942).

93. *Chaplinsky v. State of New Hampshire,* 315 U.S. 568 (1942).

94. *New York Times v. Sullivan,* 376 U.S. 254 (1964), cited in Abraham and Perry, *Freedom and the Court,* p. 193.

95. *Hustler v. Falwell,* 485 U.S. 46 (1988).

96. Jeffrey Toobin, "Gawker's Demise and the Trump-Era Threat to the First Amendment," *New Yorker,* December 19 and 26, 2016, www.newyorker.com/magazine/2016/12/19/gawkers-demise-and-the-trump-era-threat-to-the-first-amendment (accessed 10/16/2017).

97. "Melania Trump and *Daily Mail* Settle Her Libel Suits," *New York Times,* April 12, 2017, www.nytimes.com/2017/04/12/business/media/melania-trump-daily-mail-libel.html (accessed 10/16/17).

98. Adam Liptak, "Can Trump Change Libel Laws?," *New York Times,* March 30, 2017, www.nytimes.com/2017/03/30/us/politics/can-trump-change-libel-laws.html (accessed 10/16/17).

99. Veronica Stracqualursi and Athena Jones, "Judge Denies Trump's Request to Dismiss Summer Zervos Defamation Case," CNN, November 19, 2019, www.cnn.com/2019/11/19/politics/summer-zervos-trump-defamation-case/index.html (accessed 1/30/20).

100. *Valentine v. Chrestensen,* 316 U.S. 52 (1942).

101. *Virginia State Board of Pharmacy v. Virginia Citizens Consumer Council, Inc.,* 425 U.S. 748 (1976); *City of Cincinnati v. Discovery Network, Inc. et al.,* 507 U.S. 410 (1993).

102. *Central Hudson Gas & Electric Corp. v. Public Service Commission,* 447 U.S. 557 (1980).

103. *Matal v. Tam,* 582 U.S. ____ (2017).

104. *Iancu v. Brunetti,* 588 U.S. ____ (2019).

105. In 1996, Congress passed the Child Pornography Prevention Act. This law makes the possession, production, or distribution of child pornography a criminal offense punishable with up to 15 years in jail and a fine. However, two parts of the law were struck down by the Court for being "overbroad and unconstitutional." *Ashcroft v. Free Speech Coalition,* 353 U.S. 234 (2002).

106. *Jacobellis v. Ohio,* 378 U.S. 184, 197 (1964).

107. *Roth v. United States,* 354 U.S. 476 (1957).

108. *Miller v. California,* 413 U.S. 15 (1973).

109. *Federal Communications Commission v. Pacifica Foundation,* 438 U.S. 726 (1978).

110. *Federal Communications Commission et al. v. Fox Television Stations,* 556 U.S. 502 (2009).

111. *Federal Communications Commission and United States v. CBS Corporation,* 556 U.S. 1218 (2009).

112. *Federal Communications Commission v. Fox Television Stations,* 567 U.S. ____ (2012); *Federal Communications Commission v. CBS Corporation,* no. 11-1240 (2012), writ of *certiorari* denied.

113. *United States v. Stevens,* 559 U.S. 460 (2010).

114. *Brown v. Entertainment Merchants Association,* 564 U.S. (2011).

115. David French, "Of Course the Second Amendment Protects an Individual Right to Keep and Bear Arms," *National Review,* April 13, 2016, www.nationalreview.com/2016/04/second-amendment-protects-individual-right-keep-bear-arms (accessed 3/29/18).

116. Dorothy Samuels, "The Second Amendment Was Never Meant to Protect an Individual's Right to a Gun," *The Nation,* September 23, 2015, www.thenation.com/article/how-the-roberts-court-undermined-sensible-gun-control/; John Paul Stevens, "Repeal the Second Amendment," *New York Times,* March 27, 2018, www.nytimes.com/2018/03/27/opinion/john-paul-stevens-repeal-second-amendment.html (accessed 3/29/18).

117. Gun Violence Archive, www.gunviolencearchive.org (accessed 9/23/20).

118. The FBI defines an active shooter as "an individual actively engaged in killing or attempting to kill people in a confined and populated area." For data on active shooters, see Federal Bureau of Investigation, Office of Partner Engagement, "Quick Look: 277 Active Shooter Incidents in the United States from 2000 to 2018," www.fbi.gov/about/partnerships/office-of-partner-engagement/active-shooter-incidents-graphics (accessed 1/30/20).

119. Giffords Law Center, "Gun Law Trend Watch, 2017 Year-End Review," http://lawcenter.giffords.org/wp-content/uploads/2017/12/Trendwatch-2017-Year-End-12.19.17-pages.pdf; Giffords Law Center, "Concealed Carry," http://lawcenter.giffords.org/gun-laws/policy-areas/guns-in-public/concealed-carry (both accessed 4/9/18).

120. *District of Columbia v. Heller*, 554 U.S. 290 (2008).

121. *McDonald v. Chicago*, 561 U.S. 742 (2010).

122. Robert J. Spitzer, *The Politics of Gun Control* (Chatham, NJ: Chatham House, 1995). Also see www.bradycampaign.org/reforming-gun-industry-practices for a complete list of the cases (accessed 6/27/18). The two cases recognizing the individual right to bear arms were *United States v. Timothy Joe Emerson*, 46 F. Supp. 2d 598 (1999), and the D.C. Circuit Court case that was appealed in the landmark ruling *Parker v. District of Columbia*, 478 F.3d 370 (D.C. Cir. 2007).

123. The second-place country to the United States is actually the Falkland Islands (at 62.1), but there are only 3,000 people in that nation. All data are from the Switzerland-based Small Arms Survey; see especially Aaron Karp, "Estimating Global Civilian-Held Firearms Numbers," June 2018, www.smallarmssurvey.org/fileadmin/docs/T-Briefing-Papers/SAS-BP-Civilian-Firearms-Numbers.pdf; for a complete list of nations, see www.smallarmssurvey.org/fileadmin/docs/Weapons_and_Markets/Tools/Firearms_holdings/SAS-BP-Civilian-held-firearms-annexe.pdf (both accessed 1/31/20).

124. Juliet Eilperin and David Nakamura, "An Emotional Obama Flexes His Executive Muscle on Gun Control," *Washington Post*, January 5, 2016, www.washingtonpost.com/politics/obama-moves-on-guns-with-executive-actions-that-circumvent-congress/2016/01/05/97f23336-b3bc-11e5-a76a-0b5145e8679a_story.html?hpid=hp_hp-top-table-main_obamaguns-1215pm%3Ahomepage%2Fstory (accessed 4/9/18).

125. Giffords Law Center, "Post-*Heller* Litigation Summary," June 2019, https://lawcenter.giffords.org/wp-content/uploads/2019/07/PHLS-June-2019-Update.pdf (accessed 1/31/20).

126. *New Jersey v. T. L. O.*, 469 U.S. 325 (1985); *Safford United School District No. 1 et al. v. Redding*, 557 U.S. 364 (2009).

127. See Abraham and Perry, *Freedom and the Court*, Chapter 4, for a discussion of these cases. The most recent case is *Kentucky v. King*, 563 U.S. 452 (2011).

128. *Florence v. Board of Chosen Freeholders*, 566 U.S. 318 (2012).

129. *Maryland v. King*, 133 S.Ct. 1958 (2013).

130. *Mitchell v. Wisconsin*, 588 U.S. ___ (2019).

131. *Riley v. California*, 573 U.S. 373 (2014).

132. *United States v. Jones*, 565 U.S. 400 (2012).

133. *Carpenter v. United States*, 585 U.S. ___ (2018).

134. *Mapp v. Ohio*, 367 U.S. 643 (1961).

135. *Herring v. United States*, 555 U.S. 135 (2009).

136. *Utah v. Strieff*, 579 U.S. ___ (2016).

137. *Vernonia School District v. Acton*, 515 U.S. 646 (1995); *Board of Education of Pottawatomie County v. Earls*, 536 U.S. 832 (2002).

138. *Chandler v. Miller*, 520 U.S. 305 (1997).

139. National Public Radio, "Political Comebacks: The Art of the Putdown," *Morning Edition*, May 12, 2008, www.npr.org/templates/story/story.php?storyId=90337494 (accessed 5/7/20).

140. Leslie Cauley, "NSA Has Massive Database of Americans' Phone Calls," *USA Today*, May 11, 2006, p. 1.

141. Andrew Crocker and David Ruiz, "How Congress's Extension of Section 702 May Expand the NSA's Warrantless Surveillance Authority," Electronic Frontier Foundation, February 1, 2018, www.eff.org/deeplinks/2018/02/how-congresss-extension-section-702-may-expand-nsas-warrantless-surveillance (accessed 6/14/18).

142. Lorraine Woellert and Dawn Kopecki, "The Snooping Goes beyond Phone Calls," *Business Week*, May 29, 2006, p. 38; "Data Mining: Federal Efforts Cover a Wide Range of Uses," GAO Report 04-548, May 2004, www.gao.gov/assets/250/242241.pdf (accessed 5/13/14).

143. Anthony Cuthbertson, "AT&T Spying Program Is 'Worse than Snowden Revelations,'" *Newsweek*, October 26, 2016, www.newsweek.com/att-spying-program-worse-snowden-revelations-513812 (accessed 10/23/17).

144. Jennifer Stisa Granick and Ashley Gorski, "How to Address Newly Revealed Abuses of Section 702 Surveillance," Just Security, Reiss Center on Law and Security at New York University School of Law, October 18, 2019; www.justsecurity.org/66622/how-to-address-newly-revealed-abuses-of-section-702-surveillance/ (accessed 1/31/20); Eric Lichtblau and James Risen, "Officials Say U.S. Wiretaps Exceeded Law," *New York Times*, April 16, 2009.

145. *Miranda v. Arizona*, 384 U.S. 436 (1966).

146. *New York v. Quarles*, 467 U.S. 649 (1984).

147. *Dickerson v. United States*, 530 U.S. 428 (2000).

148. *Benton v. Maryland*, 395 U.S. 784 (1969).

149. This "separate sovereigns" exception was established in *Abbate v. United States*, 359 U.S. 187 (1959), and recently confirmed in *Gamble v. United States*, 587 U.S. ___ (2019).

150. *Kelo v. City of New London*, 545 U.S. 469 (2005).

151. National Conference of State Legislatures, "Eminent Domain Overview," January 1, 2012, www.ncsl.org/research/environment-and-natural-resources/eminent-domain-overview.aspx (accessed 1/31/14).

152. The 2017 case, *Murr v. Wisconsin*, 582 U.S. ___ (2017), involved a property owner who tried to sell a lot that was contiguous to another lot that he owned; he did not have to be compensated for the value of that lot when it was rendered worthless by a state regulation. The recent cases that ruled in favor of property owners were *Arkansas Game and Fish Commission v. United States*, 568 U.S. 23 (2012); *Koontz v. St. Johns River Water Management District*, 568 U.S. 936 (2013); and *Horne v. United States Department of Agriculture*, 569 U.S. 513 (2013).

153. *Knick v. Township of Scott, Pennsylvania*, 588 U.S. ___ (2019). The overruled precedent was *Williamson County Regional Planning Commission v. Hamilton Bank of Johnson City*, 473 U.S. 172 (1985).

154. *Powell v. Alabama*, 287 U.S. 45 (1932).

155. *Gideon v. Wainwright*, 372 U.S. 335 (1963).

156. *Evitts v. Lucy*, 469 U.S. 387 (1985); *Wiggins v. Smith*, 539 U.S. 510 (2003). See Elizabeth Gable and Tyler Green, "*Wiggins v. Smith*: The Ineffective Assistance of Counsel Standard Applied Twenty

Years after *Strickland*," *Georgetown Journal of Legal Ethics* (Summer 2004): 755–71, for a discussion of many of these issues.

157. *Klopfer v. North Carolina*, 386 U.S. 213 (1967).

158. The law is 18 U.S.C. § 3161(c)(1) and the ruling is *Zedner v. United States*, 47 U.S. 489 (2006).

159. The case concerning African Americans is *Batson v. Kentucky*, 106 S.Ct. 1712 (1986); the case about Latinos is *Hernandez v. New York*, 500 U.S. 352 (1991); and the gender case is *J.E.B. v. Alabama ex rel. T.B.*, 511 U.S. 127 (1994). Three more-recent cases affirming that peremptory challenges cannot be used in a racially discriminatory fashion are *Miller-El v. Dretke*, 545 U.S. 231 (2005); *Snyder v. Louisiana*, 552 U.S. 472 (2008); and *Flowers v. Mississippi*, 588 U.S. ___ (2019).

160. *Peña-Rodriguez v. Colorado*, 580 U.S. ___ (2017).

161. Death Penalty Information Center, "Number of Executions since 1976," www.deathpenaltyinfo.org/executions-year (accessed 3/25/20); *Hall v. Florida*, 572 U.S. 701 (2014).

162. Erik Eckholm, "One Execution Botched, Oklahoma Delays the Next," *New York Times*, April 29, 2014, www.nytimes. com/2014/04/30/us/oklahoma-executions.html (accessed 5/13/14).

163. *Furman v. Georgia*, 408 U.S. 238 (1972); *Gregg v. Georgia*, 428 U.S. 513 (1976).

164. *Moore v. Texas*, 581 U.S. ___ (2017).

165. See Abraham and Perry, *Freedom and the Court*, pp. 72–73, for a discussion of the earlier cases, and Charles Lane, "5–4 Supreme Court Abolishes Juvenile Executions," *Washington Post*, March 2, 2005, p. A1, for a discussion of the 2002 and 2005 cases. The cases were *Atkins v. Virginia*, 536 U.S. 304 (2002); *Roper v. Simmons*, 543 U.S. 551 (2005); and *Kennedy v. Louisiana*, 554 U.S. 407 (2008).

166. *Griswold v. Connecticut*, 381 U.S. 479 (1965), 482–86.

167. *Griswold v. Connecticut*, 381 U.S. 479 (1965), 511–12.

168. *Roe v. Wade*, 410 U.S. 113 (1973), 129.

169. *Planned Parenthood of Southeastern Pennsylvania v. Casey*, 505 U.S. 833 (1992).

170. Katharine Q. Seelye, "Mississippi Voters Reject Anti-abortion Measure," *New York Times*, November 8, 2011, www.nytimes. com/2011/11/09/us/politics/votes-across-the-nation-could-serve-as-a-political-barometer.html (accessed 12/5/11).

171. Erik Eckholm, "Access to Abortion Falling as States Pass Restrictions," *New York Times*, January 3, 2014, www.nytimes. com/2014/01/04/us/women-losing-access-to-abortion-as-opponents-gain-ground-in-state-legislatures.html (accessed 1/31/14).

172. *Whole Woman's Health v. Hellerstedt*, 579 U.S. ___ (2016).

173. *Bowers v. Hardwick*, 478 U.S. 186 (1986).

174. *Lawrence v. Texas*, 539 U.S. 558 (2003).

175. U.S. Department of the Interior, "The Conservation Legacy of Theodore Roosevelt," February 14, 2020, www.doi.gov/blog/conservation-legacy-theodore-roosevelt (accessed 9/16/20).

176. Richard Reeves, *President Nixon: Alone in the White House* (New York: Simon & Schuster, 2002), p. 163.

Take a Stand

a. *Florida v. Jardines*, 569 U.S. 1 (2013), 6–7.

b. Oral arguments in *U.S. v. Jones* (2012), November 8, 2011, www.supremecourt.gov/oral_arguments/argument_transcripts/2011/10-1259.pdf, p. 44 (accessed 4/9/18).

Chapter 9

1. Joseph Goldstein, "Judge Rejects New York's Stop-and-Frisk Policy, *New York Times*, August 12, 2013, www.nytimes. com/2013/08/13/nyregion/stop-and-frisk-practice-violated-rights-judge-rules.html (accessed 11/7/17).

2. Rocco Parascandola and Thomas Tracy, "NYPD Stop-and-Frisk Numbers Jumped by 22% in 2019 from Prior Year: Report," *New York Daily News*, February 10, 2020, www.nydailynews. com/new-york/nyc-crime/ny-stop-question-and-frisk-numbers-jump-20200210-vamjtzdfcvdorot57ajtrhnghu-story. html (accessed 3/4/20).

3. *Face the Nation*, CBS News, June 19, 2016, transcript, www. cbsnews.com/news/face-the-nation-transcripts-june-19-2016-trump-lynch-lapierre-feinstein/ (accessed 11/7/17).

4. *Meet the Press*, NBC News, May 9, 2010, transcript, www. nbcnews.com/id/37024384/ns/meet_the_press/t/meet-press-transcript-may/#.WgIRPXZryiM (accessed 11/7/17).

5. There are eight commissioners on the U.S. Commission on Civil Rights, four appointed by the president and four by Congress. The commissioners serve six-year terms and do not require Senate confirmation, and no more than four members may be of the same political party.

6. Howard Dodson, "How Slavery Helped Build a World Economy," in Schomburg Center for Research in Black Culture of the New York Public Library, *Jubilee: The Emergence of African-American Culture* (Washington, DC: National Geographic Press, 2003).

7. Other provisions of the Compromise of 1850, which was a package of five bills, included creating the current boundaries for Texas as it dropped its claim to land in parts of five current states in exchange for the federal government's assumption of $10 million in debt from the old Texas Republic. Also, the trading of enslaved people, but not slavery itself, was abolished in the District of Columbia. See "The Compromise of 1850," Primary Documents in American History, Library of Congress, www.loc.gov/rr/program/bib/ourdocs/Compromise1850.html (accessed 10/26/17).

8. John W. Wright, ed., *New York Times 2000 Almanac* (New York: Penguin Reference, 1999), p. 165. Estimates from various online sources are quite a bit higher, averaging about 620,000 deaths.

9. V. O. Key Jr., *Southern Politics in State and Nation* (New York: Knopf, 1949), p. 538. For example, the Louisiana grandfather clause read: "No male person who was on January 1, 1867, or at any date prior thereto, entitled to vote under the Constitution of the United States, wherein he then resided, and no son or grandson of any such person not less than twenty-one years of age at the date of the adoption of this Constitution . . . shall be denied the right to register and vote in this State by reason of his failure to possess the educational or property qualifications." Grandfather clauses as they applied to voting were ruled unconstitutional in 1915.

10. Chandler Davidson, "The Voting Rights Act: A Brief History," in *Controversies in Minority Voting: The Voting Rights Act in Perspective*, ed. Bernard Grofman and Chandler Davidson (Washington, DC: Brookings Institution, 1992), p. 21.

11. Equal Justice Initiative, *Lynching in America: Confronting the Legacy of Racial Terror*, 3rd ed. (2017), https://lynchinginamerica.eji.org/report/ (accessed 3/6/20).

12. "Indian Removal: 1814–1848," Public Broadcasting System, www.pbs.org/wgbh/aia/part4/4p2959.html (accessed 1/26/12).

13. Donald L. Fixico, "When Native Americans Were Slaughtered in the Name of 'Civilization,'" August 16, 2019, www.history. com/news/native-americans-genocide-united-states (accessed 3/12/20).

14. Bruce E. Johansen, *The Native Peoples of North America* (New Brunswick, NJ: Rutgers University Press, 2006); Russell Thornton, *American Indian Holocaust and Survival: A Population History since 1492* (Norman: University of Oklahoma Press, 1990), pp. 26–32; Henry F. Dobyns, *Their Number Become Thinned: Native American Population Dynamics in Eastern North America* (Knoxville: University of Tennessee Press, 1983).

15. *Cherokee Nation v. Georgia*, 30 U.S. 1 (1831).

16. Andrea Smith, "Soul Wound: The Legacy of Native American Schools," *Amnesty International Magazine,* posted on News around Indian Country, Lara Trace Hentz, October 9, 2015, https://laratracehentz.wordpress.com/2015/10/09/soul-wound-the-legacy-of-native-american-schools/ (accessed 3/12/20).

17. *United States v. Wong Kim Ark*, 169 U.S. 649 (1898).

18. Bilal Qureshi, "From Wrong to Right: A U.S. Apology for Japanese Internment," National Public Radio, August 9, 2013, www.npr.org/sections/codeswitch/2013/08/09/210138278/japanese-internment-redress (accessed 1/29/16).

19. *Trump v. Hawaii*, 585 U.S. ___ (2018).

20. This Day in History, "Abigail Adams Urges Husband to 'Remember the Ladies,'" Abigail Adams to John Adams, March 31, 1776, www.history.com/this-day-in-history/abigail-adams-urges-husband-to-remember-the-ladies (accessed 4/13/18).

21. *Bradwell v. Illinois*, 83 U.S. 130 (1873).

22. *Hoyt v. Florida*, 368 U.S. 57 (1961).

23. Lucian K. Truscott IV, "The Real Mob at Stonewall," *New York Times,* June 25, 2009, p. A19.

24. "LGBT" (various surveys), www.pollingreport.com/lgbt.htm; Justin McCarthy, "Gallup First Polled on Gay Issues in '77. What Has Changed?," June 6, 2019, https://news.gallup.com/poll/258065/gallup-first-polled-gay-issues-changed.aspx; Justin McCarthy, "U.S. Support for Gay Marriage Stable, at 63%," May 22, 2019, https://news.gallup.com/poll/257705/support-gay-marriage-stable.aspx (all accessed 3/13/20).

25. *Obergefell v. Hodges*, 576 U.S. ___ (2015).

26. Sean Cahill, "Trump Administration Amasses Striking Anti-LGBT Record in First Year," *The Hill,* January 19, 2018, http://thehill.com/opinion/campaign/369790-trump-administration-amasses-striking-anti-lgbt-record-in-first-year (accessed 4/13/18).

27. "Charge Statistics, FY 1997 through FY 2019," U.S. Equal Employment Opportunity Commission, www.eeoc.gov/eeoc/statistics/enforcement/charges.cfm (accessed 4/3/20).

28. "2019 Fair Housing Trends Report: Defending against Unprecedented Attacks on Fair Housing," National Fair Housing Alliance, p. 13, https://nationalfairhousing.org/wp-content/uploads/2019/10/2019-Trends-Report.pdf (accessed 3/21/20).

29. "Recent Accomplishments of the Housing and Civil Enforcement Section," U.S. Department of Justice, March 11, 2020, www.justice.gov/crt/recent-accomplishments-housing-and-civil-enforcement-section (accessed 3/21/20).

30. Davidson, "The Voting Rights Act," p. 22; also see U.S. Department of Justice, Civil Rights Division, "About Section 5 of the Voting Rights Act," www.justice.gov/crt/about-section-5-voting-rights-act (accessed 4/13/18), for a complete list of cases in which the Justice Department has denied "preclearance" of a change in an electoral practice under Section 5 of the Voting Rights Act. Note that in racially homogeneous single-member districts, minority candidates usually win. But in at-large elections, in which representatives are elected citywide or countywide (and which thus may contain a mix of minority and White voters from the districts making up the city or county), the majority-White voters can outvote the minority voters and elect an all-White city council or school board.

31. "The Long Shadow of Jim Crow: Voter Suppression in America," Special Report, People for the American Way Foundation and NAACP, http://archive.fairvote.org/righttovote/PFAW-NAACP.pdf (accessed 4/13/18); "Election 2016: Restrictive Voting Laws by the Numbers," Brennan Center for Justice, September 28, 2016, www.brennancenter.org/analysis/election-2016-restrictive-voting-laws-numbers (accessed 3/21/20).

32. "Voting Laws Roundup 2020," Brennan Center for Justice, February 4, 2020, www.brennancenter.org/our-work/research-reports/voting-laws-roundup-2020 (accessed 3/21/20).

33. *Husted v. A. Philip Randolph Institute*, 584 U.S. ___ (2018).

34. Office of the Assistant Secretary for Planning and Evaluation, "HHS Poverty Guidelines for 2020," U.S. Department of Health and Human Services, January 8, 2020, https://aspe.hhs.gov/poverty-guidelines (accessed 10/2/20).

35. Jessica Semega, Melissa Kollar, Emily A. Shrider, and John F. Creamer, "Income and Poverty in the United States: 2019," U.S. Census Bureau, September 15, 2020, Figure 1, www.census.gov/library/publications/2020/demo/p60-270.html (accessed 9/23/20).

36. Federal Reserve Board, "Survey of Consumer Finances (SCF), 2019," September 28, 2020, www.federalreserve.gov/econres/scf/dataviz/scf/chart/ (accessed 10/21/20).

37. U.S. Bureau of Labor Statistics, "Labor Force Statistics from the Current Population Survey," July 2, 2020, www.bls.gov/web/empsit/cpsee_e16.htm (accessed 7/6/20).

38. "America's Families and Living Arrangements: 2019," U.S. Census, Table C3, www.census.gov/data/tables/2019/demo/families/cps-2019.html (accessed 7/6/20).

39. Federal Bureau of Investigation, "Crime in the United States, 2018, Expanded Homicide Data Tables, Table 6," https://ucr.fbi.gov/crime-in-the-u.s/2018/crime-in-the-u.s.-2018/tables/expanded-homicide-data-table-6.xls (accessed 7/6/20).

40. Life expectancy data are from Elizabeth Arias, Jiaquan Xu, and Kenneth D. Kochanek, "United States Life Tables, 2016," *National Vital Statistics Reports,* Centers for Disease Control and Prevention, May 7, 2019, Table A, p. 3, www.cdc.gov/nchs/data/nvsr/nvsr68/nvsr68_04-508.pdf. Infant mortality numbers are from "Infant Mortality," Centers for Disease Control and Prevention, www.cdc.gov/reproductivehealth/maternalinfanthealth/infantmortality.htm. Maternal mortality rates are from "Pregnancy Mortality Surveillance System," November 9, 2017, Centers for Disease Control and Prevention, www.cdc.gov/reproductivehealth/maternalinfanthealth/pmss.html (all accessed 3/31/20).

41. See the National Resource Defense Council's program on environmental justice, www.nrdc.org/about/environmental-justice, and the Environmental Justice and Health Alliance for Chemical Policy reform's report "Who's in Danger? Race, Poverty, and Chemical Disasters," May 2014, http://comingcleaninc.org/assets/media/images/Reports/Who%27s%20in%20Danger%20Report%20FINAL.pdf (both accessed 4/13/18).

42. Steve Carmody, "5 Years after Flint's Crisis Began, Is the Water Safe?," National Public Radio, April 25, 2019, www.npr.org/2019/04/25/717104335/5-years-after-flints-crisis-began-is-the-water-safe (accessed 3/22/20).

43. Ariane de Vogue and Devan Cole, "Supreme Court Won't Block Lawsuit Brought by Flint Water Crisis Victims," CNN, January 21,

2020, www.cnn.com/2020/01/21/politics/supreme-court-flint-michigan-lawsuit-water-crisis/index.html (accessed 3/22/20).

44. Evelyn Diaz, "Nick Cannon Accuses L.A. Cops of Racial Profiling," BET News, www.bet.com/news/celebrities/2011/11/18/nick-cannon-accuses-la-cops-of-racial-profiling.html (accessed 1/29/12).

45. Cristina Corbin, "Senate's Lone Black GOP Member Says Police Stopped Him 7 Times in a Year," Fox News, July 14, 2016, www.foxnews.com/politics/2016/07/14/senates-lone-black-gop-member-says-police-stopped-him-7-times-in-year.html (accessed 11/2/17).

46. Benjamin Weiser and Joseph Goldstein, "Mayor Says New York City Will Settle Suits on Stop-and-Frisk Tactics," *New York Times*, January 30, 2014, www.nytimes.com/2014/01/31/nyregion/de-blasio-stop-and-frisk.html (accessed 4/6/14).

47. Hundreds of studies have examined these patterns, and, not surprisingly, there are divergent findings. However, most have found differences in sentencing based on race. A 2015 Bureau of Justice Statistics study found that "black men received roughly 5% to 10% longer prison sentences than white men for similar crimes, after accounting for the facts surrounding the case." See "Federal Sentencing Disparity: 2005-2012," Bureau of Justice Statistics, October 2015, www.bjs.gov/content/pub/pdf/fsd0512_sum.pdf. Government statistics on crime may be found on the FBI site at www.fbi.gov. (Both sources accessed 11/2/17.)

48. "Fatal Force," *Washington Post*, March 16, 2020, www.washingtonpost.com/graphics/2019/national/police-shootings-2019/ (accessed 3/22/20).

49. "Herstory," Black Lives Matter, https://blacklivesmatter.com/about/herstory (accessed 4/17/18).

50. Holly Yan, Khushbu Shah, and Emanuella Grinberg, "Ex-officer Michael Slager Pleads Guilty in Shooting Death of Walter Scott," CNN, May 2, 2017, www.cnn.com/2017/05/02/us/michael-slager-federal-plea/ (accessed 2/23/18).

51. Janell Ross, "Police Officers convicted for Fatal Shootings Are the Exception, Not the Rule," NBC News, March 13, 2019, www.nbcnews.com/news/nbcblk/police-officers-convicted-fatal-shootings-are-exception-not-rule-n982741 (accessed 3/22/20).

52. Lynne Peeples, "What the Data Say about Police Shootings: How Do Racial Biases Play into Deadly Encounters with the Police?," *Scientific American*, September 5, 2019, www.scientificamerican.com/article/what-the-data-say-about-police-shootings/ (accessed 3/22/20).

53. "2018 Hate Crime Statistics," U.S. Department of Justice, https://ucr.fbi.gov/hate-crime/2018/topic-pages/tables/table-1.xls (accessed 3/22/20).

54. Rosa Parks with James Haskins, *Rosa Parks: My Story* (New York: Dial Books, 1992), p. 116.

55. Clayborne Carson et al., eds., *The Eyes on the Prize Civil Rights Reader* (New York: Penguin Books, 1997).

56. *Boynton v. Virginia*, 363 U.S. 454 (1960).

57. David Halberstam, *The Children* (New York: Ballantine Books, 1999).

58. Matt Broomfield, "Women's March against Donald Trump Is the Largest Day of Protests in US History, Say Political Scientists," *Independent*, January 23, 2017, www.independent.co.uk/news/world/americas/womens-march-anti-donald-trump-womens-rights-largest-protest-demonstration-us-history-political-a7541081.html (accessed 10/26/17). Jeremy Pressman of the University of Connecticut and Erica Chenoweth of the University of Denver collected data on the Women's March, https://docs.google.com/spreadsheets/d/1xaoiLqYKz8x9Yc_rfhtmSOJQ2EGgeUVjvV4A8LsIaxY/edit#gid=0 (accessed 10/26/17). The low end of their estimate

is 3,267,134, the high end is 5,246,670, and their "best guess" is 4,157,894.

59. "Dakota Access Pipeline in Operation after Months of Resistance," *PBS News Hour*, June 3, 2017, www.pbs.org/newshour/nation/dakota-access-pipeline-operation-months-resistance (accessed 10/26/17).

60. See https://blacklivesmatter.com/ for more information about the movement, including the "Black Lives Matter 4-Year Anniversary Report" and news about recent events (accessed 10/26/17).

61. By the end of the 2019 regular season, only three teams featured at least one player regularly sitting or kneeling on the sidelines for the anthem. See Mark Maske, "NFL Owners Approve New National Anthem Policy with Hope of Ending Protests, *Washington Post*, May 23, 2018, www.washingtonpost.com/news/sports/wp/2018/05/23/nfl-owners-leaning-towards-requiring-players-to-stand-for-national-anthem-or-remain-in-locker-room/?utm_term=.71eed9fa2d60; and Associated Press, "NFL Stops Anthem Policy after Dolphins Criticized for Considering Suspensions for Players Who Protest," NBC News, July 19, 2018, www.nbcnews.com/news/sports/nfl-halts-anthem-policy-after-dolphins-criticized-considering-suspensions-players-n893021 (both accessed 3/22/20).

62. *Pearson v. Murray*, 169 Md. 478 (1936).

63. *Shelley v. Kraemer*, 334 U.S. 1 (1948).

64. *Brown v. Board of Education*, 347 U.S. 483 (1954).

65. *Brown v. Board of Education II*, 349 U.S. 294 (1955).

66. Paul Brest and Sanford Levinson, *Process of Constitutional Decision Making: Cases and Material* (Boston: Little, Brown, 1982), pp. 471-80.

67. *Swann v. Charlotte-Mecklenburg Board of Education*, 402 U.S. 1 (1971).

68. *Milliken v. Bradley*, 418 U.S. 717 (1974).

69. *Parents Involved in Community Schools Inc. v. Seattle School District*, 05-98 (2007); *Meredith v. Jefferson County (Ky.) Board of Education*, 551 U.S. 701 (2007).

70. *Heart of Atlanta Motel, Inc. v. United States*, 379 U.S. 241 (1964).

71. *Katzenbach v. McClung*, 379 U.S. 294 (1964).

72. *Griggs v. Duke Power*, 401 U.S. 424 (1971).

73. *Easley v. Cromartie*, 532 U.S. 234 (2001), rehearing denied, 532 U.S. 1076 (2001).

74. *Easley v. Cromartie*, 532 U.S. 1076 (2001).

75. *Bethune-Hill v. Virginia State Board of Elections*, 580 U.S. ____ (2017); *Cooper v. Harris*, 581 U.S. ____ (2017). In *Alabama Legislative Black Caucus v. Alabama* 575 U.S. ____ (2015), the Court also struck down state legislative districts in Alabama as unconstitutional "packing." In January 2017, a three-judge panel also struck down the state's next attempt to draw the districts, and finally, in October 2017, the third attempt was upheld.

76. Richard L. Hasen, "The Gerrymandering Decision Drags the Supreme Court Further into the Mud: Ignoring the Racial Redistricting Problem Won't Make It Go Away," *New York Times*, June 27, 2019, www.nytimes.com/2019/06/27/opinion/gerrymandering-rucho-supreme-court.html (accessed 3/22/20). The case is *Rucho v. Common Cause*, 588 U.S. ____ (2019).

77. *Shelby County v. Holder*, 570 U.S. 529 (2013).

78. *Reed v. Reed*, 404 U.S. 71 (1971). As a young women's rights attorney, Ruth Bader Ginsburg wrote the plaintiff's brief in this case. She argued more than three hundred gender discrimination cases, including six before the Supreme Court, before becoming a federal judge.

79. *Frontiero v. Richardson*, 411 U.S. 677 (1973).

80. *Korematsu v. United States*, 323 U.S. 214 (1944).

81. *Trump v. Hawaii*, 585 U.S. ____ (2018).

82. *Craig v. Boren*, 429 U.S. 190 (1976).

83. *Orr v. Orr*, 440 U.S. 268 (1979).

84. *United States v. Virginia*, 518 U.S. 515 (1996).

85. Joanna L. Grossman, "Policing Sexism at the Border: The Supreme Court's Decision in *Sessions v. Morales-Santana*," Verdict: Legal Analysis and Commentary from Justia, June 20, 2017, https://verdict.justia.com/2017/06/20/policing-sexism-border-supreme-courts-decision-sessions-v-morales-santana (accessed 11/6/17). The case is *Sessions v. Morales-Santana*, 582 U.S. ____ (2017).

86. *Johnson v. Transportation Agency of Santa Clara*, 480 U.S. 616 (1987).

87. *Harris v. Forklift Systems*, 510 U.S. 17 (1993).

88. Jan Ransom, "Harvey Weinstein's Stunning Downfall: 23 Years in Prison," *New York Times*, March 11, 2020, www.nytimes.com/2020/03/11/nyregion/harvey-weinstein-sentencing.html (accessed 3/22/20).

89. Stephanie Zacharek, Eliana Dockterman and Haley Sweetland Edwards, "Person of the Year 2017: The Silence Breakers," *Time*, http://time.com/time-person-of-the-year-2017-silence-breakers (accessed 4/18/18).

90. *Ledbetter v. Goodyear Tire & Rubber Co.*, 550 U.S. 618 (2007).

91. Julie Hirschfeld Davis, "Obama Moves to Expand Rules Aimed at Closing Gender Pay Gap," *New York Times*, January 29, 2016, www.nytimes.com/2016/01/29/us/politics/obama-moves-to-expand-rules-aimed-at-closing-gender-pay-gap.html (accessed 1/30/16).

92. "Presidential Executive Order on the Revocation of Federal Contracting Executive Orders," The White House, March 27, 2017, www.whitehouse.gov/presidential-actions/presidential-executive-order-revocation-federal-contracting-executive-orders/ (accessed 3/22/20).

93. "Women Present Widespread Discrimination at Wal-Mart," press release, April 28, 2003, www.walmartclass.com/staticdata/press_releases/wmcc.html (accessed 10/4/12).

94. David Savage, "Supreme Court Blocks Huge Class-Action Suit against Wal-Mart," *Los Angeles Times*, June 21, 2011. The case is *Wal-Mart v. Dukes*, 564 U.S. 338 (2011).

95. Michael Sainato, "Walmart Facing Gender Discrimination Lawsuits from Female Employees," *Guardian*, February 18, 2019, www.theguardian.com/us-news/2019/feb/18/walmart-gender-discrimination-supreme-court (accessed 3/22/20).

96. *Bowers v. Hardwick*, 478 U.S. 186 (1986), rehearing denied, 478 U.S. 1039 (1986).

97. *Romer v. Evans*, 517 U.S. 620 (1996).

98. *Lawrence v. Texas*, 539 U.S. 558 (2003). Because the basis for the decision was the due process clause of the Fourteenth Amendment and not the equal protection clause, this ruling upheld a civil liberty rather than a civil right. As such, it applied to all laws regarding sodomy, not just those that applied to gays. However, the decision has been widely regarded as a landmark civil rights case because it provided equal rights for gays.

99. The three cases are *Hollingsworth v. Perry*, 570 U.S. 693 (2013), *United States v. Windsor*, 570 U.S. 744 (2013), and *Obergefell v. Hodges*, 576 U.S. ____ (2015).

100. *Bostock v. Clayton* County, 590 U.S. ____ (2020).

101. *Altitude Express Inc. v. Zarda*, 590 U.S. ____ (2020); *R.G. & G.R. Harris Funeral Homes Inc. v. Equal Employment Opportunity Commission*, 590 U.S. ____ (2020).

102. Quoted in Voting Rights Act Extension: Report of the Subcommittee of the Constitution of the Committee on the Judiciary, U.S. Senate, 97th Congress, 2nd session, May 25, 1982, S. Rept. 97-417, 4.

103. Drew S. Days III, "Section 5 Enforcement and the Justice Department," in *Controversies in Minority Voting: The Voting Rights Act in Perspective*, ed. Bernard Grofman and Chandler Davidson (Washington, DC: Brookings Institution Press, 1992), p. 52; Frank R. Parker, *Black Votes Count* (Chapel Hill: University of North Carolina Press, 1990), p. 1.

104. Davidson, "The Voting Rights Act," p. 21.

105. "Fair Housing: It's Your Right," U.S. Department of Housing and Urban Development, www.hud.gov/program_offices/fair_housing_equal_opp/online-complaint (accessed 4/18/18).

106. Alexandra DeSanctis, "Would the Equal Rights Amendment Enshrine Abortion Rights in the Constitution?," *National Review*, February 17, 2020, www.nationalreview.com/2020/02/would-the-equal-rights-amendment-enshrine-abortion-rights-in-the-constitution/ (accessed 3/22/20).

107. *United States v. Morrison*, 529 U.S. 598 (2000).

108. *Board of Trustees of the University of Alabama v. Garrett*, 531 U.S. 356 (2001). Also, in *State of Tennessee v. George Lane and Beverly Jones*, 541 U.S. 509 (2004), the Court ruled that disabled people must have access to courthouses.

109. The White House, "Remarks by the Reception Commemorating the Enactment of the Matthew Shepard and James Byrd Jr. Hate Crimes Prevention Act," October 28, 2009, https://obamawhitehouse.archives.gov/the-press-office/remarks-president-reception-commemorating-enactment-matthew-shepard-and-james-byrd- (accessed 4/18/18).

110. Tim Mak, "Post-'Don't Ask,' Gay Navy Lt. Marries," Politico, September 20, 2011, www.politico.com/news/stories/0911/63909.html (accessed 1/24/12).

111. Justin Jouvenal, "Federal Judge in D.C. Blocks Part of Trump's Transgender Military Ban," *Washington Post*, October 30, 2017, www.washingtonpost.com/local/public-safety/federal-judge-in-dc-blocks-part-of-trumps-transgender-military-ban/2017/10/30/41d41526-bd94-11e7-959c-fe2b598d8c00_story.html?utm_term=.fe88c4776b62 (accessed 11/6/17).

112. Rebecca Kheel, "Navy Officer Sues Pentagon over Transgender Military Ban," *The Hill*, March 18, 2020, https://thehill.com/policy/defense/488240-navy-officer-sues-pentagon-over-transgender-military-ban (accessed 3/22/20).

113. *Public Papers of the Presidents of the United States: Lyndon B. Johnson, 1965*, vol. 2, entry 301 (Washington, DC: Government Printing Office, 1966), pp. 635-40.

114. The first poll is from the Pew Research Center, October 4, 2017, www.people-press.org/2017/10/05/4-race-immigration-and-discrimination/4_7-6/, and the second from Gallup, July 8, 2016, news.gallup.com/poll/193508/oppose-colleges-considering-race-admissions.aspx (both accessed 4/18/18).

115. State of California, article 1, section 31.

116. The training program case was *United Steel Workers of America v. Weber*, 443 U.S. 193 (1979); the labor union case was *Sheet Metal Workers v. EEOC*, 478 U.S. 421 (1986); and the Alabama state police case was *U.S. v. Paradise*, 480 U.S. 149 (1987).

117. *Ricci v. DeStefano*, 557 U.S. 557 (2009).

118. *Regents of the University of California v. Bakke*, 438 U.S. 265 (1978).

119. *Hopwood v. Texas*, 78 F3d 932 (5th Cir. 1996).

120. *Smith v. University of Washington*, 233 F3d 1188 (9th Cir. 2000).

121. *Grutter v. Bollinger*, 539 U.S. 306 (2003), was the law school case, and *Gratz v. Bollinger*, 539 U.S. 244 (2003), was the undergraduate admissions case.

122. In *Bakke*, Justice Lewis Powell was the only member of the Court who held this position, even though it became the basis for all affirmative action programs over the next 25 years. Four justices in the *Bakke* decision wanted to get rid of race as a factor in admissions, and another four thought that the "strict scrutiny" standard should not even be applied in this instance.

123. *Schuette v. Coalition to Defend Affirmative Action*, 572 U.S. 291 (2014).

124. *Fisher v. University of Texas, Austin*, 579 U.S. ____ (2016).

125. Adam Harris, "In Trump Era, the Use of Race in Admissions Comes under New Scrutiny," *Chronicle of Higher Education*, August 2, 2017, www.chronicle.com/article/In-Trump-Era-the-Use-of-Race/240821?cid=rclink (accessed 11/6/17).

126. *Trump v. Hawaii*, 585 U.S. ____ (2018).

127. James Vicini, "Supreme Court to Decide Arizona Immigration Law," Reuters, December 12, 2011, www.reuters.com/article/2011/12/12/us-usa-immigration-arizona-idUSTRE7BB0XJ20111212 (accessed 2/2/12).

128. *Arizona v. United States*, 567 U.S. 387 (2012).

129. Fernanda Santos, "Arizona Immigration Law Survives Ruling," *New York Times*, September 6, 2012, www.nytimes.com/2012/09/07/us/key-element-of-arizona-immigration-law-survives-ruling.html?r=0 (accessed 10/5/12).

130. Andrew Daniller, "Americans' Immigration Policy Priorities: Divisions between—and within—the Two Parties," Pew Research Center, November 12, 2019, www.pewresearch.org/fact-tank/2019/11/12/americans-immigration-policy-priorities-divisions-between-and-within-the-two-parties/ (accessed 3/22/20).

131. Emily Kassie, "Detained: How the US Built the World's Largest Immigrant Detention System," *Guardian*, September 24, 2019, www.theguardian.com/us-news/2019/sep/24/detained-us-largest-immigrant-detention-trump (accessed 3/22/20).

132. "An Act Providing for the Collection of Data Relative to Traffic Stops," Massachusetts state law, Chapter 228 of the Acts of 2000, www.mass.gov/legis/laws/seslaw00/sl000228.htm (accessed 7/22/08).

Take a Stand

a. *Fisher v. University of Texas, Austin*, 579 U.S. ____ (2016).

b. *Schuette v. Coalition to Defend Affirmative Action*, 572 U.S. 291 (2014).

AP® Study Guide

a. *Regents of the University of California v. Bakke*, 438 U.S. 265 (1978).

Chapter 10

1. Shirley Chisholm, "Vote Chisholm 1972: Unbought and Unbossed," January 25, 1972, 4President.org, www.4president.org/speeches/shirleychisholm1972announcement.htm (accessed 10/27/20).

2. Quoted in Mark Dawidziak, "Jon Stewart Blurs the Lines between Jester and Journalist," *Cleveland Plain Dealer*, March 28, 2019.

3. V. O. Key, *The Responsible Electorate* (Cambridge, MA: Harvard University Press, 1966).

4. Josh Clinton and Carrie Roush, "Poll: Persistent Partisan Divide over 'Birther' Question," NBC News, August 10, 2016, www.nbcnews.com/politics/2016-election/poll-persistent-partisan-divide-over-birther-question-n627446 (accessed 1/28/20).

5. Adam Berinsky, "Telling the Truth about Believing the Lies? Evidence for the Limited Prevalence of Expressive Survey Responding," *Journal of Politics* 80:1 (2018): 211–24.

6. Joanna Piacenza, "Can You Locate Iran? Few Voters Can," Morning Consult, January 8, 2020, https://morningconsult.com/2020/01/08/can-you-locate-iran-few-voters-can/ (accessed 1/28/20).

7. For a review, see Arthur Lupia and Mathew D. McCubbins, *The Democratic Dilemma* (New York: Cambridge University Press, 1998).

8. Larry Bartels, "Partisanship and Voting Behavior, 1952–1996," *American Journal of Political Science* 44 (2000): 35–50.

9. Robert S. Erikson, Michael B. MacKuen, and James A. Stimson, *The Macro Polity* (New York: Cambridge University Press, 2002).

10. John Zaller, "Coming to Grips with V. O. Key's Concept of Latent Opinion" (unpublished paper, University of California, Los Angeles, 1998).

11. Morris Fiorina, *Retrospective Voting in American National Elections* (Cambridge, MA: Harvard University Press, 1981).

12. Virginia Sapiro, "Not Your Parents' Political Socialization: Introduction for a New Generation," *Annual Review of Political Science* 7 (2004): 1–23.

13. M. Kent Jennings and Richard G. Niemi, *Generations and Politics: A Panel Study of Young Adults and Their Parents* (Princeton, NJ: Princeton University Press, 1981).

14. Robert Putnam, *Bowling Alone: The Collapse and Revival of American Community* (New York: Simon and Schuster, 2000).

15. Richard G. Niemi and Mary Hepburn, "The Rebirth of Political Socialization," *Perspectives on Politics* 24 (1995): 7–16.

16. David Campbell, *Why We Vote: How Schools and Communities Shape Our Civic Life* (Princeton, NJ: Princeton University Press, 2006).

17. Sidney Verba, Kay Schlozman, and Henry Brady, *Voice and Equality: Civic Volunteerism in American Politics* (Cambridge, MA: Harvard University Press, 1995).

18. Paul Allen Beck and M. Kent Jennings, "Pathways to Participation," *American Political Science Review* 76 (1982): 94–108.

19. Pew Research Center, "In Gay Marriage Debate, Both Supporters and Opponents See Legal Recognition as 'Inevitable,'" June 6, 2013, www.people-press.org/2013/06/06/in-gay-marriage-debate-both-supporters-and-opponents-see-legal-recognition-as-inevitable (accessed 10/30/15).

20. John Zaller, *The Nature and Origins of Mass Opinion* (New York: Cambridge University Press, 1992).

21. Richard Nadwau et al., "Class, Party, and South–Nonsouth Differences," *American Politics Research* 32 (2004): 52–67.

22. James H. Kuklinski et al., "Racial Prejudice and Attitudes toward Affirmative Action," *American Journal of Political Science* 41 (1997): 402–19.

23. Donald P. Green, Bradley Palmquist, and Eric Schickler, *Partisan Hearts and Minds* (New Haven, CT: Yale University Press, 2002).

24. For elaboration on this point, see William T. Bianco, Richard G. Niemi, and Harold W. Stanley, "Partisanship and Group Support over Time: A Multivariate Analysis," *American Political Science Review* 80 (September 1986): 969–76.

25. Lupia and McCubbins, *The Democratic Dilemma*.

26. Jane Mansbridge, "Rethinking Representation," *American Political Science Review* 97:4 (2003): 515–28.

27. Zaller, *The Nature and Origins of Mass Opinion*.

28. R. Michael Alvarez and John Brehm, *Hard Choices, Easy Answers* (Princeton, NJ: Princeton University Press, 2002).

29. John Zaller and Stanley Feldman, "A Theory of the Survey Response: Revealing Preferences versus Answering Questions," *American Journal of Political Science* 36 (1992): 579–616.

30. Janet M. Box-Steffensmeier and Susan DeBoef, "Macropartisanship and Macroideology in the Sophisticated Electorate," *Journal of Politics* 63:1 (2001): 232–48.

31. Shanto Iyengar, Gaurav Sood, and Yphtach Lelkes, "Affect, Not Ideology: A Social Identity Perspective on Polarization," *Public Opinion Quarterly* 76:3 (2012): 405–31.

32. R. Michael Alvarez and John Brehm, "American Ambivalence towards Abortion Policy: Development of a Heteroskedastic Probit Model of Competing Values," *American Journal of Political Science* 39:4 (1995): 1055–82.

33. Pew Research Center, "Beyond Red vs. Blue: The Political Typology. Section 6: Foreign Affairs, Terrorism and Privacy," June 26, 2014, www.people-press.org/2014/06/26/section-6-foreign-affairs-terrorism-and-privacy (accessed 3/11/16).

34. Richard Wike and Katie Simmons, "Global Support for Principle of Free Expression, but Opposition to Some Forms of Speech: Americans Especially Likely to Embrace Individual Liberties," Pew Research Center, November 18, 2015, www.pewglobal.org/2015/11/18/global-support-for-principle-of-free-expression-but-opposition-to-some-forms-of-speech (accessed 11/18/15).

35. Milton Lodge and Charles Taber, "Three Steps toward a Theory of Motivated Political Reasoning," in *Elements of Reason: Cognition, Choice, and the Bounds of Rationality*, ed. Arthur Lupia, Mathew D. McCubbins, and Samuel L. Popkin (London: Cambridge University Press, 2000); George E. Marcus, W. Russell Neuman, and Michael MacKuen, *Affective Intelligence and Political Judgment* (Chicago: University of Chicago Press, 2000); David Redlawsk, "Hot Cognition or Cool Consideration? Testing the Effects of Motivated Reasoning on Political Decision Making," *Journal of Politics* 64 (2002): 1021–44; David Redlawsk, Andrew Civettini, and Karen Emmerson, "The Affective Tipping Point: Do Motivated Reasoners Ever 'Get It'?" *Political Psychology* 31:4 (2010): 563–93.

36. See Harry Holloway and John George, *Public Opinion* (New York: St. Martin's Press, 1986); Paul R. Abramson, *Political Attitudes in America* (San Francisco: Freeman, 1983).

37. See Paul M. Sniderman and Edward G. Carmines, *Reaching beyond Race* (Cambridge, MA: Harvard University Press, 1997).

38. Christopher Wlezien and Robert S. Erikson, "The Horse Race: What Polls Reveal as the Election Campaign Unfolds," *International Journal of Public Opinion Research* 19:1 (2007): 74–88.

39. Alexi McCammond, "Focus Group: These Obama/Trump Voters Are Just Trump Voters Now," Axios, December 19, 2019, www.axios.com/focus-group-michigan-swing-voters-trump-impeachment-183e4fc7-5ecc-41bd-add1-537ed8a2fd8f.html (accessed 12/31/19).

40. Anton J. Nederhof, "Methods of Coping with Social Desirability Bias: A Review," *European Journal of Social Psychology* 15:3 (2006): 263–80.

41. Sarah Kliff, "Obamacare Is 5 Years Old, and Americans Are Still Worried about Death Panels," Vox, May 23, 2015, www. vox.com/2015/3/23/8273007/obamacare-poll-death-panels (accessed 11/2/15).

42. Michael X. Delli Carpini and Scott Keeter, *What Americans Know about Politics and Why It Matters* (New Haven, CT: Yale University Press, 1997).

43. Dan Diamond, "The Unemployment Rate Doubled under Bush. It's Fallen by More than One-Third under Obama," Vox, November 7, 2015, www.vox.com/2015/11/7/9684780/unemployment-rate-obama (accessed 11/7/15).

44. Delli Carpini and Keeter, *What Americans Know about Politics and Why It Matters*.

45. Nate Silver, "How FiveThirtyEight Calculates Pollster Ratings," September 25, 2014, http://fivethirtyeight.com/features/how-fivethirtyeight-calculates-pollster-ratings (accessed 11/6/15).

46. Lilliana Mason, "'I Disrespectfully Agree': The Differential Effects of Partisan Sorting on Social and Issue Polarization," *American Journal of Political Science* 59:1 (2015): 128–45.

47. Shanto Iyengar and Sean J. Westwood, "Fear and Loathing across Party Lines: New Evidence on Group Polarization," *American Journal of Political Science* 59:3 (2015): 690–707.

48. For a review of the literature on trust in government, see Karen Cook, Russell Hardin, and Margaret Levi, *Cooperation without Trust* (New York: Russell Sage Foundation, 2005), as well as Marc J. Hetherington, *Why Trust Matters: Declining Political Trust and the Demise of American Liberalism* (Princeton, NJ: Princeton University Press, 2004).

49. William T. Bianco, *Trust: Representatives and Constituents* (Ann Arbor: University of Michigan Press, 1994).

50. Sean M. Theriault, *The Power of the People: Congressional Competition, Public Attention, and Voter Retribution* (Columbus: Ohio State University Press, 2005).

51. Thomas Rudolph and Jillian Evans, "Political Trust, Ideology, and Public Support for Government Spending," *American Journal of Political Science* 49 (2005): 660–71.

52. Patricia Moy and Michael Pfau, *With Malice toward All? The Media and Public Confidence in Democratic Institutions* (Boulder, CO: Praeger, 2000).

53. Erikson, MacKuen, and Stimson, *The Macro Polity*.

54. James A. Stimson, *Public Opinion in America: Moods, Swings, and Cycles* (Boulder, CO: Westview Press, 1999).

55. Robert S. Erikson, Michael B. MacKuen, and James A. Stimson, "American Politics: The Model" (unpublished paper, Columbia University, 2000).

56. Pew Research Center, "Public's Policy Priorities for 2019," January 24, 2019, www.people-press.org/2019/01/24/publics-2019-priorities-economy-health-care-education-and-security-all-near-top-of-list/pp_2019-01-24_political-priorities_0-02/ (accessed 5/3/20).

57. Leah Cardamore Stokes, *Short Circuiting Policy: Interest Groups and the Battle Over Clean Energy and Climate Policy in the American States* (New York: Oxford University Press, 2020).

58. Larry Bartels, "Constituency Opinion and Congressional Policy Making: The Reagan Defense Buildup," *American Political Science Review* 85 (June 1991): 457–74; Jonathan Kastellec, Jeffrey R. Lax, and Justin H. Phillips, "Public Opinion and Senate Confirmation of Supreme Court Nominees," *Journal of Politics* 72 (2010): 767–84.

59. Lawrence R. Jacobs and Robert Y. Shapiro, *Politicians Don't Pander: Political Manipulation and the Loss of Democratic Responsiveness* (Chicago: University of Chicago Press, 2000).

Chapter 11

1. Nancy Pelosi, "Transcript of Pelosi Weekly Press Conference Today," May 23, 2019, www.speaker.gov/newsroom/52319 (accessed 10/30/20).

2. Julia Azari, "Weak Parties and Strong Partisanship Are a Bad Combination," Vox, November 3, 2016, www.vox.com/mischiefs-of-faction/2016/11/3/13512362/weak-parties-strong-partisanship-bad-combination (accessed 4/13/20).

3. Bernie Sanders, Twitter, February 25, 2020, 8:02 P.M., https://twitter.com/BernieSanders/status/1231021453270769664 (accessed 4/2/20).

4. Joseph Schlesinger, *Political Parties and the Winning of Office* (Ann Arbor: University of Michigan Press, 1994).

5. Kenneth Benoit, "Duverger's Law and the Study of Electoral Systems," *French Politics* 4:1 (2006): 69–83.

6. William Nesbit Chambers and Walter Dean Burnham, *The American Party Systems: Stages of Political Development* (Oxford, UK: Oxford University Press, 1966).

7. Donald H. Hickey, "Federalist Party Unity and the War of 1812," *Journal of American Studies* 12 (April 1978): 23–39; William T. Bianco, David B. Spence, and John D. Wilkerson, "The Electoral Connection in the Early Congress: The Case of the Compensation Act of 1816," *American Journal of Political Science* 40 (February 1996): 145–71.

8. John Aldrich, *Why Parties?* (Chicago: University of Chicago Press, 2005).

9. James MacPherson, *Battle Cry of Freedom: The Civil War Era* (New York: Oxford University Press, 1988).

10. Michael F. Holt, *The Rise and Fall of the Whig Party: Jacksonian Politics and the Onset of the Civil War* (New York: Oxford University Press, 1999).

11. David A. Bateman, *Disenfranchising Democracy: Constructing the Electorate in the United States, the United Kingdom, and France* (New York: Cambridge University Press, 2018).

12. Harold W. Stanley, William T. Bianco, and Richard G. Niemi, "Partisanship and Group Support over Time: A Multivariate Analysis," *American Political Science Review* 80 (1986): 969–76.

13. Eric Schickler, *Racial Realignment: The Transformation of American Liberalism, 1932–1965* (Princeton, NJ: Princeton University Press, 2016).

14. Hans Noel, *Political Ideologies and Political Parties in America* (New York: Cambridge University Press, 2014)

15. Ben Protess, Danielle Ivory, and Steve Eder, "Where Trump's Hands-Off Approach to Governing Does Not Apply," *New York Times*, September 10, 2017, www.nytimes.com/2017/09/10/business/trump-regulations-religious-conservatives.html (accessed 3/20/20).

16. Aldrich, *Why Parties?*

17. James L. Sundquist, *Dynamics of the Party System*, rev. ed. (Washington, DC: Brookings Institution, 1983).

18. David R. Mayhew, *Electoral Realignments: A Critique of an American Genre* (New Haven, CT: Yale University Press, 2002).

19. John H. Aldrich and Richard G. Niemi, "The Sixth American Party System: Electoral Change, 1952–1992," in *Broken Contract: Changing Relationships between Americans and Their Governments*, ed. Steven Craig (Boulder, CO: Westview Press, 1993).

20. Charles S. Bullock III, Donna R. Hoffman, and Ronald Keith Gaddie, "Regional Variations in the Realignment of American Politics, 1944–2004," *Social Science Quarterly* 87:3 (2006): 494–518.

21. Jon F. Hale, "The Making of the New Democrats," *Political Science Quarterly* 110:2 (1995): 207–32.

22. James Monroe, *The Political Party Matrix* (Albany: SUNY Press, 2001).

23. Gary Cox and Mathew McCubbins, *Legislative Leviathan* (Berkeley: University of California Press, 1993); James M. Snyder and Michael M. Ting, "An Informational Rationale for Political Parties," *American Journal of Political Science* 46 (2002): 90–110.

24. Jason Roberts and Steven Smith, "Procedural Contexts, Party Strategy, and Conditional Party Government," *American Journal of Political Science* 47:2 (2003): 305–17.

25. Catherine Rampell, "Tax Pledge May Scuttle a Deal on Deficit," *New York Times*, November 18, 2011, p. B1.

26. Donald Green, Bradley Palmquist, and Eric Schickler, *Partisan Hearts and Minds* (New Haven, CT: Yale University Press, 2004); Christopher Achen, "Political Socialization and Rational Party Identification," *Political Behavior* 24:2 (2002): 151–70.

27. Morris Fiorina, *Retrospective Voting in American National Elections* (New Haven, CT: Yale University Press, 1981).

28. Yphtach Lelkes and Sean J. Westwood, "The Limits of Partisan Prejudice," *Journal of Politics* 79:2 (2017): 485–501.

29. Alan I. Abramowitz and Steven W. Webster, "Negative Partisanship: Why Americans Dislike Parties but Behave Like Rabid Partisans," *Political Psychology* 39 (2018): 119–35.

30. Walter Dean Burnham, "The Reagan Heritage," in *The Election of 1988: Reports and Interpretations*, ed. Gerald M. Pomper et al. (Chatham, NJ: Chatham House, 1989).

31. Martin P. Wattenberg, *The Decline of American Political Parties: 1952–1994* (Cambridge, MA: Harvard University Press, 1996).

32. David S. Broder, *The Party's Over: The Failure of Partisan Politics in America* (New York: Harper and Row, 1971).

33. Donald P. Green and Bradley Palmquist, "Of Artifacts and Partisan Instability," *American Journal of Political Science* 34:3 (August 1990): 872–902.

34. Samara Kiar and Yanna Krupnikov, *Independent Politics: How American Disdain for Parties Leads to Political Inaction* (New York: Cambridge University Press, 2016).

35. Larry M. Bartels, "Partisanship and Voting Behavior, 1952–1996," *American Journal of Political Science* 44:1 (2000): 35–50.

36. Daniel Schlotzman, *When Movements Anchor Parties: Electoral Alignments in American History* (Princeton, NJ: Princeton University Press, 2015).

37. Jill Lawrence, "Party Recruiters Lead Charge for '06 Vote; Choice of Candidates to Run in Fall May Decide Who Controls the House," *USA Today*, May 25, 2006, p. A5.

38. Marty Cohen et al., *The Party Decides: Presidential Nominations before and after Reform* (Chicago: University of Chicago Press, 2008).

39. Jonathan Bernstein, "Clinton Knows Who's Boss: Her Party," November 18, 2015, www.bloombergview.com/articles/2015-11-18/democratic-party-is-more-important-than-hillary-clinton (accessed 11/20/15).

40. Compiled from information available at www.ballot-access.org (accessed 2/18/18).

41. The Center for Responsive Politics, opensecrets.org (accessed 11/4/20).

42. Heather Caygle, "Anti-abortion Democrat Snubbed by Party for Reelection," Politico, February 26, 2018, www.politico.com/story/2018/02/25/lipinski-democrats-abortion-chicago-illinois-423431 (accessed 5/9/18).

43. John Gerring, *Party Ideologies in America, 1828–1996* (New York: Cambridge University Press, 2001).

44. Libertarian National Committee, "Elected Officials," www.lp.org/elected-officials (accessed 7/14/20).

45. Lee Drutman, *Breaking the Two-Party Doom Loop* (New York: Oxford University Press, 2019).

46. Janet Hook and Peter Wallsten, "GOP Feels Sting of Candidates' Rejection," *Los Angeles Times*, October 10, 2005, p. A1.

47. Gary Cox, *Making Votes Count: Strategic Coordination in the World's Electoral Systems* (Cambridge, UK: Cambridge University Press, 1997).

48. Peter Hanson, *Too Weak to Govern: Majority Party Power and Appropriations in the U.S. Senate* (New York: Cambridge University Press, 2015).

49. Thomas B. Edsall, "GOP Gains Advantage on Key Issues, Polls Say," *Washington Post*, January 27, 2002, p. A4.

Take a Stand

a. Nelson Polsby, *Consequences of Party Reform* (New York: Oxford University Press, 1983).

b. Daniel A. Smith and Caroline J. Tolbert, *Educated by Initiative: The Effects of Direct Democracy on Citizens and Political Organizations in the American States* (Ann Arbor: University of Michigan Press, 2004).

AP® Study Guide

a. Nick Corasaniti and Stephanie Saul, "16 States Have Postponed Primaries During the Pandemic. Here's a List," *New York Times*, August 10, 2020, www.nytimes.com/article/2020-campaign-primary-calendar-coronavirus.html (accessed 8/20/20).

b. Oyez, *Planned Parenthood of Southeastern Pennsylvania v. Casey*, 505 U.S. 833 (1992), www.oyez.org/cases/1991/91-744 (accessed 9/17/20).

Chapter 12

1. Quoted in Naomi Jagoda, "Democrats Offer bill to Undo Business Tax Provisions in Coronavirus Law," *The Hill*, https://thehill.com/policy/finance/494647-democrats-offer-bill-to-undo-business-tax-provisions-in-coronavirus-law (accessed 5/18/20).

2. Chuck Grassley, "Coronavirus-Damaged Businesses Deserve Financial Relief," www.grassley.senate.gov/news/news-releases/grassley-op-ed-coronavirus-damaged-businesses-deserve-financial-relief (accessed 5/18/20).

3. Jim Zarroli, "Even the Los Angeles Lakers Got a PPP Small Business Loan," National Public Radio, April 27, 2020, www.npr.org/sections/coronavirus-live-updates/2020/04/27/846024717/even-the-la-lakers-got-a-ppp-small-business-loan (accessed 5/16/20).

4. For an excellent summary of the details, see Steven M. Rosenthal and Aravind Boddupalli, "Heads I Win, Tails I Win Too: Winners from the Tax Relief for Losses in the CARES Act," Tax Policy Center, April 20, 2020, www.taxpolicycenter.org/taxvox/heads-i-win-tails-i-win-too-winners-tax-relief-losses-cares-act (accessed 5/16/20).

5. Joint Committee on Taxation, "Estimated Revenue Effects of the Revenue Provisions Contained in an Amendment in the Nature of a Substitute to H.R. 748, the 'Coronavirus Aid, Relief, and Economic Security ("CARES")' Act," JCX-11R-20, April 23, 2020, www.jct.gov/publications.html?func=startdown&id=5255 (accessed 5/16/20).

6. Robert A. Dahl, *A Preface to Democratic Theory* (Chicago: University of Chicago Press, 1951) and *Who Governs? Democracy and Power in an American City* (New Haven, CT: Yale University Press, 1961); David Truman, *The Governmental Process* (New York: Harper and Row, 1951).

7. Theodore Lowi, *The End of Liberalism: The Second Republic of the United States* (New York: W. W. Norton, 1979); E. E. Schattschneider, *The Semisovereign People: A Realist's View of Democracy in America* (Hinsdale, IL: Dryden Press, 1975).

8. Frank R. Baumgartner et al., *Lobbying and Policy Change: Who Wins, Who Loses, and Why* (Chicago: University of Chicago Press, 2009).

9. Lobbying regulations are often changed; the discussion here is just a general guide. For a summary of federal law, see "Lobbying Disclosure Act Guidance," Office of the Clerk, U.S. House of Representatives, January 31, 2017, https://lobbyingdisclosure.house.gov/amended_lda_guide.html; for state law, see Lobbying Regulation, National Conference of State Legislatures, www.ncsl.org/research/ethics/lobbyist-regulation.aspx (both accessed May 11, 2020).

10. Nadja Popovich, Livia Albeck-Ripka, and Kendra Pierre-Louis, "The Trump Administration Is Reversing 100 Environmental Rules. Here's the Full List," *New York Times*, July 15, 2020, www.nytimes.com/interactive/2020/climate/trump-environment-rollbacks.html (accessed 8/20/20).

11. Frank Baumgartner and Beth Leech, *Basic Interests: The Importance of Interest Groups in Politics and in Political Science* (Princeton, NJ: Princeton University Press, 1999), p. 109.

12. Beth L. Leech et al., "Drawing Lobbyists to Washington: Government Activity and the Demand for Advocacy," *Political Research Quarterly* 58:1 (March 2005): 19–30.

13. Open Secrets, "Bills," www.opensecrets.org/federal-lobbying/bills (accessed 5/12/20).

14. Project on Government Oversight, "Brass Parachutes: Defense Contractors' Capture of Pentagon Officials through the Revolving Door," November 5, 2018, https://s3.amazonaws.com/docs.pogo.org/report/2018/POGO_Brass_Parachutes_DoD_Revolving_Door_Report_2018-11-05.pdf (accessed 5/12/20).

15. Roxana Tiron, "Lockheed Martin Leads Expanded Lobbying by US Defense Industry," *Washington Post*, January 26, 2012, www.washingtonpost.com/business/economy/lockheedmartin-leads-expanded-lobbying-by-us-defenseindustry/2012/01/26/gIQAlgQtaQ_story.html (accessed 2/4/14).

16. However, the sector of "finance, insurance, and real estate" spent $502,107,659 on lobbying in 2019, which is a lot!

17. Tim LaPira, Lee Drutman, and Matthew Grossmann, "The Interest Group Top Tier: More Groups, Concentrated Clout," paper presented at the 2014 American Political Science Association Annual Meeting.

18. 2018 Ranked Sectors, Center for Responsive Politics, www.opensecrets.org/federal-lobbying/ranked-sectors?cycle=2018; 2019 Ranked Sectors, Center for Responsive Politics, www.opensecrets.org/federal-lobbying/ranked-sectors?cycle=2019 (both accessed 5/12/20).

19. For more on this argument, see Tim Harford, "There's Not Enough Money in Politics," *Slate*, April 1, 2006, www.slate.com/id/2138874 (accessed 7/29/16); and Stephen Ansolabehere, John M. de Figueiredo, and James M. Snyder, "Why Is There So Little Money in American Politics?," *Journal of Economic Perspectives* 17 (2003): 105–30.

20. Scott Ainsworth, *Analyzing Interest Groups: Group Influence on People and Policies* (New York: W. W. Norton, 2002).

21. Timothy LaPira and Hershel F. Thomas III, "Revolving Door Lobbyists and Interest Representation," *Interest Groups and Advocacy* 3 (2013): 4–29.

22. One hundred and six members retired in January 2019; 58 of those were employed by mid-2020, and 31 of those were employed in lobbying jobs. Data available at www.opensecrets.org/revolving/departing.php (accessed 5/13/20).

23. Theodoric Meyer, "Has Trump Drained the Swamp in Washington?," Politico, October 19, 2017, www.politico.com/story/2017/10/19/trump-drain-swamp-promises-243924 (accessed 12/19/17).

24. Paul Waldman, "In Trump's Swamp, the Corporate Lobbyists Are in Charge," *Washington Post*, July 17, 2019, www.washingtonpost.com/opinions/2019/07/17/trumps-swamp-corporate-lobbyists-are-charge/; David Mora, "We Found a 'Staggering' 281 Lobbyists Who've Worked in the Trump Administration," Columbia Journalism Investigations, *ProPublica*, October 15, 2019, www.propublica.org/article/we-found-a-staggering-281-lobbyists-whove-worked-in-the-trump-administration (both accessed 5/13/20).

25. John M. Donnelly, "Pentagon Looks to Undo Parts of McCain Anti-lobbying Law," April 14, 2020, *Roll Call*, www.rollcall.com/2020/04/14/pentagon-looks-to-undo-parts-of-revolving-door-law/ (accessed 7/20/20).

26. Robert H. Salisbury et al., "Who Works with Whom? Interest Group Alliances and Opposition," *American Political Science Review* 81 (1987): 1217–34.

27. Business–Industry Political Action Committee, "About BIPAC," www.bipac.org/about-us (accessed 6/5/18).

28. Becky Peterson, "Citizens Angry over GOP Healthcare Bills Are Overloading the Bot Designed to Help Them Reach Congress," *Business Insider*, September 22, 2017, www.businessinsider.com/resistbot-overloaded-users-fax-congress-about-gop-healthcare-2017-9; Jason Putorti, "Welcome to Resistbot v3," November 9, 2017, https://resistbot.news/welcome-to-resistbot-v3-5fe513aa457a (both accessed 12/19/17).

29. Thomas Holyoke, "Choosing Battlegrounds: Interest Group Lobbying across Multiple Venues," *Political Science Quarterly* 56 (2003): 325–36.

30. Beth Kindig, "Microsoft Fairly and Squarely Beat Amazon in $10 Billion Pentagon Cloud Contract," MarketWatch, December 7, 2019, www.marketwatch.com/story/microsoft-fairly-and-squarely-beat-amazon-in-10-billion-pentagon-cloud-contract-2019-12-03. Amazon has sued in federal court, claiming that President Trump intervened to stop Amazon from getting the contract; see Aaron Gregg, "Microsoft Blasts Amazon's 'Sensationalist and Politicized Rhetoric' in Pentagon Cloud Lawsuit," *Washington Post*, February 11, 2020, www.washingtonpost.com/business/2020/02/11/microsoft-blasts-amazons-sensationalist-politicized-rhetoric-pentagon-cloud-lawsuit/ (both accessed 5/14/20).

31. AARP, "AARP Research," www.aarp.org/research/ (accessed 5/14/20).

32. James Q. Wilson, *Political Organizations* (New York: Basic Books, 1974).

33. AAA, Foundation for Traffic Safety, www.aaafoundation.org/home (accessed 7/29/16).

34. Kenneth Kollman, *Outside Lobbying: Public Opinion and Interest Group Strategies* (Princeton, NJ: Princeton University Press, 1998).

35. Jack Walker, *Mobilizing Interest Groups in America* (Ann Arbor: University of Michigan Press, 1991); Frank R. Baumgartner et al., *Lobbying and Policy Change: Who Wins, Who Loses, and Why* (Chicago: University of Chicago Press, 2009).

36. John P. Heinz, Edward O. Laumann, and Robert Salisbury, *The Hollow Core: Private Interests in National Policymaking* (Cambridge, MA: Harvard University Press, 1993).

37. Richard L. Hall and Alan V. Deardorff, "Lobbying as Legislative Subsidy," *American Political Science Review* 100 (2006): 69–84.

38. Hall and Deardorff, "Lobbying as Legislative Subsidy."

39. David Austen-Smith and John R. Wright, "Counteractive Lobbying," *American Journal of Political Science* 38:1 (1994): 25–44.

40. Key Lehman Schlozman and John T. Tierney, *Organized Interests and American Democracy* (New York: HarperCollins, 1986).

41. Baumgartner and Leech, *Basic Interests*, p. 152.

42. Anthony Madonna and Ian Ostrander, "If Congress Keeps Cutting Its Staff, Who Is Writing Your Laws? You Won't Like the Answer," *Washington Post*, August 20, 2015, www.washingtonpost.com/news/monkey-cage/wp/2015/08/20/if-congress-keeps-cutting-its-staff-who-is-writing-your-laws-you-wont-like-the-answer/?utm_term=.d4773b24c7cf (accessed 12/20/17).

43. Christine A. DeGregorio, *Networks of Champions: Leadership, Access, and Advocacy in the U.S. House of Representatives* (Ann Arbor: University of Michigan Press, 1992).

44. Daniel Carpenter, *The Forging of Bureaucratic Autonomy: Reputations, Networks, and Policy Innovation in Executive Agencies, 1862–1928* (Princeton, NJ: Princeton University Press, 2002).

45. Public Citizen, www.citizen.org (accessed 5/15/20).

46. Derived from a search of the NRA Institute for Legislative Action site, www.nraila.org (accessed 5/15/20).

47. Kim Scheppele and Jack L. Walker, "The Litigation Strategies of Interest Groups," in *Mobilizing Interest Groups in America*, ed. Jack Walker (Ann Arbor: University of Michigan Press, 1991).

48. Lauren Cohen Bell, *Warring Factions: Interest Groups, Money, and the New Politics of Senate Confirmation* (Columbus: Ohio State University Press, 2002).

49. Jesse Drucker, "The Tax-Break Bonanza Inside the Economic Rescue Package," *New York Times*, April 24, 2020, www.nytimes.com/2020/04/24/business/tax-breaks-wealthy-virus.html (accessed 5/15/20).

50. Kevin W. Hula, *Lobbying Together: Interest Group Coalitions in Legislative Politics* (Washington, DC: Georgetown University Press, 1999).

51. Jeanne Cummings, "Word Games Could Threaten Climate Bill," Politico, June 9, 2009, www.politico.com/news/stories/0609/24059.html (accessed 9/19/12).

52. AARP, "A Guide to Your Elected Officials," https://action.aarp.org/site/SPageServer?pagename=electedOfficials (accessed 5/15/20).

53. Erica Chenoweth and Jeremy Pressman, "This Is What We Learned by Counting the Women's Marches," *Washington Post*, February 7, 2017, www.washingtonpost.com/news/monkey-cage/wp/2017/02/07/this-is-what-we-learned-by-counting-the-womens-marches/?utm_term=.4dd6925ad4a6 (accessed 12/20/17).

54. In addition to Planned Parenthood and the Natural Resources Defense Council, other supporting organizations included the AFL-CIO, Amnesty International USA, the Mothers of the Movement, the National Center for Lesbian Rights, the National Organization for Women, MoveOn.org, Human Rights Watch, Code Pink, Black Girls Rock!, the NAACP, the American Indian Movement, EMILY's List, Oxfam, Greenpeace USA, and the League of Women Voters.

55. Richard Fenno, *Home Style: U.S. House Members in Their Districts* (Boston: Little, Brown, 1978). See also Brandice

Caines-Wrone, David W. Brady, and John F. Cogan, "Out of Step, Out of Office: Electoral Accountability and House Members' Voting," *American Political Science Review* 96 (2002): 127–40.

56. Emily Yoffe, "Am I the Next Jack Abramoff?," *Slate*, April 1, 2006, www.slate.com/id/2137886 (accessed 8/28/09).

57. Kollman, *Outside Lobbying*.

58. Gregory Calderia, Marie Hojnacki, and John R. Wright, "The Lobbying Activities of Organized Interests in Federal Judicial Nominations," *Journal of Politics* 62 (2000): 51–69.

59. *Citizens United v. Federal Election Commission*, 558 U.S. 310 (2010).

60. Data from www.opensecrets.org and www.fec.gov (accessed 11/8/20).

61. John G. Matsusaka, "Direct Democracy and Fiscal Gridlock: Have Voter Initiatives Paralyzed the California Budget?," *State Politics and Policy* 5 (2005): 346–62.

62. National Conference of State Legislature, "The Term-Limited States," www.ncsl.org/research/about-state-legislatures/chart-of-term-limits-states.aspx (accessed 5/15/20).

63. "History of Marijuana on the Ballot," Ballotpedia, https://ballotpedia.org/History_of_marijuana_on_the_ballot (accessed 11/8/20).

64. "2020 Marijuana Legalization and Marijuana-Related Ballot Measures," Ballotpedia, https://ballotpedia.org/2020_marijuana_legalization_and_marijuana-related_ballot_measures (accessed 11/8/20).

65. Frederick J. Boehmke, "The Initiative Process and the Dynamics of State Interest Group Populations," *State Politics and Policy Quarterly*, 8:4 (Winter 2008): 362–83.

66. John G. Matsusaka, *For the Many or the Few: The Initiative, Public Policy, and American Democracy* (Chicago: University of Chicago Press, 2004).

67. Elizabeth R. Gerber, *The Populist Paradox: Interest Group Influence and the Promise of Direct Legislation* (Princeton, NJ: Princeton University Press, 1999).

68. "California Proposition 56, Tobacco Tax Increase (2016)," Ballotpedia, https://ballotpedia.org/California_Proposition_56,_Tobacco_Tax_Increase_(2016) (accessed 5/16/20).

69. Baumgartner and Leech, *Basic Interests*, Chapter 8, pp. 147–67.

70. Annual budget from the Humane Society of the United States, Annual Report, 2019, p. 23, www.humanesociety.org/sites/default/files/docs/HSUS_2019_AnnualReport.pdf; lobbying expenses from the Center for Responsive Politics, Open Secrets, www.opensecrets.org/orgs//summary?id=D000026546 (both accessed 5/15/20).

71. Lee Drutman, "The Solution to Lobbying Is More Lobbying," *Washington Post*, April 29, 2015, www.washingtonpost.com/blogs/monkey-cage/wp/2015/04/29/the-solution-to-lobbying-is-more-lobbying (accessed 2/16/16).

72. Keith E. Schnakenberg, "Informational Lobbying and Legislative Voting," *American Journal of Political Science* 61:1 (January 2017): 129–145.

73. Nicholas Fandos, "House Votes to Sharply Expand Concealed-Carry Gun Rights," December 6, 2017, *New York Times*, www.nytimes.com/2017/12/06/us/politics/house-concealed-carry-guns-nra-reciprocity.html (accessed 6/5/18).

74. Emma Leathley, "Net Neutrality," Open Secrets, December 2017, www.opensecrets.org/news/issues/net_neutrality/ (accessed 12/20/17).

75. Eric Bradner, "Alabama Election: Doug Jones Scores Stunning Win, but Moore Won't Concede," CNN, December 13, 2017, www.cnn.com/2017/12/12/politics/alabama-senate-election-mainbar/index.html (accessed 6/5/18).

76. David Lowery, "Why Do Organized Interests Lobby? A Multi-Goal, Multi-Context Theory of Lobbying," *Polity* 39 (2007): 29–54.

77. Amy McKay, "Negative Lobbying and Policy Outcomes," *American Politics Review* 40 (2011): 116–46.

78. Jeffrey M. Berry, *The Interest Group Society* (New York: HarperCollins, 1997); Raymond A. Bauer, Ithiel de Sola Pool, and Lewis Dexter, *American Business and Public Policy* (New York: Atherton Press, 1963).

79. Kollman, *Outside Lobbying*.

80. Frank Baumgartner and Beth Leech, "Interest Niches and Policy Bandwagons: Patterns of Interest Group Involvement in National Politics," *Journal of Politics* 63 (2001): 1191–1213.

Take a Stand

a. Jacob Weisberg, "Three Cities, Three Scandals: What Jack Abramoff, Anthony Pellicano, and Jared Paul Stern Have in Common," *Slate*, April 9, 2006, www.slate.com/id/2140238 (accessed 10/25/12).

b. Herschel F. Thomas and Timothy M. LaPira, "How Many Lobbyists Are in Washington? Shadow Lobbying and the Gray Market for Policy Advocacy," *Interest Groups and Advocacy* 6:3 (2017): 199–214.

Chapter 13

1. Donald Trump, Twitter, November 7, 2020, 4:53 P.M., https://twitter.com/realdonaldtrump/status/1325194709443080192 (accessed 11/17/20).

2. Quoted in Tim Alberta, "The Election That Broke the Republican Party," Politico, November 6, 2020, www.politico.com/news/magazine/2020/11/06/the-election-that-broke-the-republican-party-434797 (accessed 11/17/20).

3. Morris P. Fiorina, *Retrospective Voting in American National Elections* (New Haven, CT: Yale University Press, 1981); V. O. Key, *The Responsible Electorate* (New York: Vintage Books, 1966).

4. David Mayhew, *Congress: The Electoral Connection* (New Haven, CT: Yale University Press, 1973).

5. For details on early voting, see the Early Voting Information Center site at http://earlyvoting.net/resources/ (accessed 5/9/18).

6. John DiStaso, "Exhaustive Investigation Reveals Little Evidence of Possible Voter Fraud in NH," WMUR Manchester, May 29, 2018, www.wmur.com/article/exhaustive-investigation-reveals-little-evidence-of-possible-voter-fraud-in-nh/20955267# (accessed 4/7/20).

7. United States Government Accountability Office, "Issues Related to State Voter Identification Laws," 2014, www.gao.gov/assets/670/665966.pdf (accessed 3/4/16).

8. Minor-party candidates are typically selected during party conventions.

9. Barbara Norrander, "Presidential Nomination Politics in the Post-reform Era," *Political Research Quarterly* 49 (1996): 875–90.

10. Larry Bartels, *Presidential Primaries and the Dynamics of Public Choice* (Princeton, NJ: Princeton University Press, 1988).

11. William G. Mayer, "Forecasting Presidential Nominations or, My Model Worked Just Fine, Thank You," *Political Science and Politics* 36 (2003): 153–59.

12. Marty Cohen et al., "Beating Reform: The Resurgence of Parties in Presidential Nominations, 1980 to 2000" (paper presented at the 2001 American Political Science Association Annual Meeting, San Francisco, CA).

13. Richard Herrera, "Are 'Superdelegates' Super?," *Political Behavior* 16 (1994): 79–93.

14. FairVote, "Maine and Nebraska," www.fairvote.org/maine_nebraska (accessed 5/9/18).

15. Robert Bennett, "The Problem of the Faithless Elector," *Northwestern University Law Review* 100 (2004): 121–30.

16. James Q. Wilson, "Is the Electoral College Worth Saving?," *Slate*, November 3, 2000, www.slate.com/id/92663 (accessed 10/19/12).

17. Robert Erikson and Christopher Wlezien, *The Timeline of Presidential Elections* (Chicago: University of Chicago Press, 2013).

18. Larry M. Bartels and Christopher H. Achen, *Democracy for Realists: Why Elections Do Not Produce Responsive Government* (Princeton, NJ: Princeton University Press, 2016).

19. Linda Fowler and Robert McClure, *Political Ambition: Who Decides to Run for Congress* (Ann Arbor: University of Michigan Press, 1989).

20. Robin Kolodny, *Pursuing Majorities: Congressional Campaign Committees in American Politics* (Norman: University of Oklahoma Press, 1999).

21. Steven Ansolabehere and Alan Gerber, "Incumbency Advantage and the Persistence of Legislative Majorities," *Legislative Studies Quarterly* 22 (1997): 161–80.

22. For a discussion of Johnson's decision, see Robert A. Caro, *The Path to Power* (New York: Knopf, 1983).

23. Thomas Mann and Norman Ornstein, *The Permanent Campaign and Its Future* (Washington, DC: American Enterprise Institute, 2000).

24. Mayhew, *Congress: The Electoral Connection.*

25. Sarah Binder and Mark Spindel, *The Myth of Independence: How Congress Governs the Federal Reserve* (Princeton, NJ: Princeton University Press, 2017).

26. Jonathan Krasno and Donald P. Green, "The Dynamics of Campaign Fundraising in House Elections," *Journal of Politics* 56 (1991): 459–74.

27. Michael J. Goff, *The Money Primary: The New Politics of the Early Presidential Nomination Process* (New York: Rowman & Littlefield, 2007).

28. Michael Babaro, "Candidates Stick to Script, If Not the Truth, in the 2016 Race," *New York Times*, November 7, 2015, p. A1.

29. Chris Cillizza, "Consulting Firms Face Conflict in 2008," *Roll Call*, June 20, 2005, p. 1.

30. For details, see the House Ethics Committee guidelines at https://ethics.house.gov/campaign/campaign-work-house-employees (accessed 5/1/20).

31. Cherie Maestas, Walter Stone, and L. Sandy Maisel, "Quality Counts: Extending the Strategic Politician Model of Incumbent Deterrence," *American Journal of Political Science* 48 (2004): 479–90.

32. Matt Bai, "Turnout Wins Elections," *New York Times Magazine*, December 14, 2003, p. 100.

33. Christopher Drew, "New Telemarketing Ploy Steers Voters on Republican Path," *New York Times*, November 6, 2006.

34. For a history of presidential debates, see the Commission on Presidential Debates site at www.debates.org (accessed 10/19/12).

35. For a video library of presidential campaign ads, see Museum of the Moving Image, "The Living Room Candidate: Presidential Campaign Commercials 1952–2012," http://livingroomcandidate.org (accessed 10/19/12).

36. Museum of the Moving Image, "The Living Room Candidate: 1964: Johnson vs. Goldwater," http://livingroomcandidate.org/commercials/1964/dowager (accessed 10/19/12).

37. Museum of the Moving Image, "The Living Room Candidate: 1964: Johnson vs. Goldwater."

38. Steven E. Finkel and John G. Geer, "A Spot Check: Casting Doubt on the Demobilizing Effect of Attack Advertising," *American Journal of Political Science* 42:2 (1998): 573–95; Richard R. Lau, Lee Sigelman, and Ivy Brown Rovner, "The Effects of Negative Political Campaigns: A Meta-analytic Reassessment," *Journal of Politics* 69:4 (2007): 1176–1209; Yanna Krupnikov, "When Does Negativity Demobilize? Tracing the Conditional Effect of Negative Campaigning on Voter Turnout," *American Journal of Political Science* 55:4 (2011): 797–813.

39. Richard Adams, "US Midterm Elections 2010: The 10 Worst Political Ads," *Guardian*, November 2, 2010, www.theguardian.com/world/richard-adams-blog/2010/nov/02/us-midterm-elections-2010-top-10-worst-political-ads (accessed 10/24/18).

40. Paul Freeman, Michael Franz, and Kenneth Goldstein, "Campaign Advertising and Democratic Citizenship," *American Journal of Political Science* 48 (2004): 723–41.

41. Constantine J. Spilotes and Lynn Vavreck, "Campaign Advertising: Partisan Convergence or Divergence?," *Journal of Politics* 64 (2002): 249–61.

42. Kathleen Hall Jameson, *Packaging the Presidency: A History and Criticism of Presidential Campaign Advertising* (New York: Oxford University Press, 1996).

43. Jonathan Krasno and Frank J. Sorauf, "For the Defense," *Political Science and Politics* 37 (2004): 777–80.

44. Contribution and spending data are available from the Center for Responsive Politics at www.opensecrets.org.

45. Brian Stelter, "The Price of 30 Seconds," *New York Times*, October 1, 2007, http://mediadecoder.blogs.nytimes.com/2007/10/01/the-price-of-30-seconds (accessed 10/19/12).

46. For a review of this literature, see Michael Malbin, *The Election after Reform: Money, Politics, and the Bipartisan Campaign Reform Act* (Washington, DC: Rowman & Littlefield, 2006).

47. Lynda Powell, *The Influence of Campaign Contributions in State Legislatures* (Ann Arbor: University of Michigan Press, 2012).

48. David Karol, "If You Think Super PACs Have Changed Everything about Presidential Primaries, Think Again," September 21, 2015, www.washingtonpost.com/blogs/monkey-cage/wp/2015/09/21/if-you-think-super-pacs-have-changed-everything-about-the-presidential-primary-think-again (accessed 9/21/15).

49. For a discussion, see Thomas Patterson, *The Vanishing Voter* (New York: Knopf, 2002), especially Chapter 1, "The Incredible Shrinking Electorate," pp. 3–22.

50. William H. Riker and Peter Ordeshook, "A Theory of the Calculus of Voting," *American Political Science Review* 62 (1968): 25–39.

51. Michael McDonald, The United States Elections Project, www.electproject.org (accessed 5/11/18).

52. Pew Research Center, "Regular Voters, Intermittent Voters, and Those Who Don't," October 18, 2006, www.pewresearch.

org/wp-content/uploads/sites/4/legacy-pdf/292.pdf (accessed 5/1/20).

53. For a review of the literature on issue voters, see Jon K. Dalager, "Voters, Issues, and Elections: Are Candidates' Messages Getting Through?," *Journal of Politics* 58 (1996): 486–515.

54. Richard P. Lau and David P. Redlawsk, *How Voters Decide: Information Processing during Electoral Campaigns* (New York: Cambridge University Press, 2006).

55. Samuel Popkin, *The Reasoning Voter* (Chicago: University of Chicago Press, 1991).

56. Richard R. Lau and David P. Redlawsk, "Advantages and Disadvantages of Cognitive Heuristics in Political Decision Making," *American Journal of Political Science* 45 (2001): 951–71.

57. Mark Jurkowitz, "Majority of Americans Disapprove of Trump's COVID-19 Messaging, though Large Partisan Gaps Persist," Pew Research Center, September 15, 2020, www.pewresearch.org/fact-tank/2020/09/15/majority-of-americans-disapprove-of-trumps-covid-19-messaging-though-large-partisan-gaps-persist/ (accessed 11/17/20).

58. Kevin Schaul, Kate Rabinowitz, and Ted Mellnik, "2020 Turnout Is the Highest in Over a Century," *Washington Post*, November 5, 2020, www.washingtonpost.com/graphics/2020/elections/voter-turnout/ (accessed 11/17/20).

59. Nick Corasaniti, Reid J. Epstein, and Jim Rutenberg, "The Times Called Officials in Every State: No Evidence of Voter Fraud," *New York Times*, November 10, 2020, www.nytimes.com/2020/11/10/us/politics/voting-fraud.html (accessed 11/17/20).

60. Nicholas Riccardi, "Democrats Keep Winning the Popular Vote. That Worries Them," AP News, November 14, 2020, https://apnews.com/article/democrats-popular-vote-win-d6331f7e8b51d52582bb2d60e2a007ec (accessed 11/17/20).

What Do the Facts Say?

a. See "Trump's Challenge: The President Dares Congress to 'Impeach This,'" Sean Hannity, October 1, 2019, https://hannity.com/media-room/trumps-challenge-the-president-dares-congress-to-impeach-this/ (accessed 4/14/20).

b. Philip Bump, "The Four Simple Reasons Trump's 'Impeach This' Map Doesn't Make Any Sense," *Washington Post*, October 1, 2019, www.washingtonpost.com/politics/2019/10/01/four-simple-reasons-that-trumps-impeach-this-map-doesnt-make-any-sense/ (accessed 4/14/20).

Chapter 14

1. "Quotes," Goodreads, www.goodreads.com/quotes/9676544-fake-news-is-like-ice-once-it-comes-in-contact (accessed 10/5/20).

2. Madeleine Albright, *Fascism: A Warning* (New York: HarperCollins, 2018).

3. William H. Riker, *The Strategy of Rhetoric: Campaigning for the American Constitution* (New Haven, CT: Yale University Press, 1996).

4. Garry Wills, *Explaining America: The Federalist* (New York: Penguin Press, 2001).

5. Geoffrey R. Stone, *Perilous Times: Free Speech in Wartime from the Sedition Act of 1798 to the War on Terrorism* (New York: W. W. Norton, 2004).

6. John D. Stevens, *Sensationalism and the New York Press* (New York: Columbia University Press, 1991).

7. Robert C. Williams, *Horace Greeley: Champion of American Freedom* (New York: New York University Press, 2006).

8. Gay Talese, *The Kingdom and the Power* (New York: Calder and Boyars, 1983).

9. For a detailed history, see United States Early Radio History, www.earlyradiohistory.us (accessed 9/17/12).

10. The Project for Excellence in Journalism, "State of the News Media," www.pewresearch.org/topics/state-of-the-news-media (accessed 5/3/18).

11. The *Columbia Journalism Review* maintains a list of holdings for major media companies at Who Owns What, www.cjr.org/resources (accessed 3/7/20).

12. See www.themonkeycage.org (accessed 1/25/18) and www.vox.com/mischiefs-of-faction (accessed 2/23/18).

13. For the original and revised versions, see "New York Post Goes on Cletus Safari, Finds This Scrappy Blue Collar … Chief of Surgery?," January 21, 2018, https://wonkette.com/629157/new-york-post-goes-on-cletus-safari-finds-this-scrappy-blue-collar-chief-of-surgery (accessed 5/3/18).

14. Eric Berger, "Boeing's Starliner Problems May Be Worse Than We Thought," Ars Technica, February 7, 2020, https://arstechnica.com/science/2020/02/boeings-starliner-problems-may-be-worse-than-we-thought/ (accessed 4/14/20).

15. To see the difference between facts and opinions, take this Pew Research quiz: www.pewresearch.org/quiz/news-statements-quiz/ (accessed 3/7/20).

16. Matthew Baum, "Sex, Lies and War: How Soft News Brings Foreign Policy to the Inattentive Public," *American Political Science Review* 96 (2002): 91–109.

17. Patti M. Valkenburg, Jochen Peter, and Joseph B. Walther, "Media Effects: Theory and research," *Annual Review of Psychology* 67 (2016): 315–38.

18. Lance Bennett, *News: The Politics of Illusion* (New York: Pearson, 2012).

19. Danny Hayes and Matthew Guardino, *Influence from Abroad: Foreign Voices, the Media, and U.S. Public Opinion* (New York: Cambridge University Press, 2013).

20. Matthew Baum, "Talking the Vote: Why Presidential Candidates Hit the Talk Show Circuit," *American Journal of Political Science* 49 (2005): 213–34.

21. Harriet Sinclair, "Ted Cruz Releases Strange Song about Opponent Beto O'Rourke as Pair Win Primaries," *Newsweek*, March 7, 2018, www.newsweek.com/ted-cruz-beto-orourke-texas-834257 (accessed 10/2/18).

22. Tara Golshan, "The Raging Controversy over Beto O'Rourke's Full Name, Explained," Vox, March 8, 2018, www.vox.com/policy-and-politics/2018/3/7/17091094/controversy-beto-orourke-robert-name-ted-cruz (accessed 10/2/18).

23. Barton Gellman, "Code Name 'Verax': Snowden, in Exchanges with *Post* Reporter, Made Clear He Knew Risks," *Washington Post*, June 13, 2012, p. A1.

24. For a discussion of these concepts, see Paul M. Sniderman and Sean M. Theriault, "The Structure of Political Argument and the Logic of Issue Framing," in *Studies in Public Opinion*, ed. William E. Saris and Paul M. Sniderman (Princeton, NJ: Princeton University Press, 2004); and Shanto Iyengar and Donald Kinder, *News That Matters* (Chicago: University of Chicago Press, 1987). See also Maxwell McCombs and Donald L. Shaw, "The Agenda-Setting Functions of Mass Media," *Public Opinion Quarterly* 36 (1972): 176–87; and Amos Tversky and Daniel Kahnemann, "The Framing of Decisions and the Psychology of Choice," *Science* 211 (1981): 453–58.

25. Markus Prior, "Media and Political Polarization," *Annual Review of Political Science* 16 (2013): 101–27.

26. Kevin Arceneaux et al., "The Influence of News Media on Political Elites: Investigating Strategic Responsiveness in Congress," *American Journal of Political Science* 60:1 (2016): 5–29.

27. Matthew S. Levendusky, "Why Do Partisan Media Polarize Viewers?," *American Journal of Political Science* 57:3 (2013): 611–23.

28. Kevin Arceneaux, Martin Johnson, and Chad Murphy, "Polarized Political Communication, Oppositional Media Hostility, and Selective Exposure," *Journal of Politics* 74:1 (2012): 174–86.

29. See Eric Alterman, *What Liberal Media?* (New York: Basic Books, 2003); and Bernard Goldberg, *Bias* (New York: Regnery, 2001).

30. Donald Trump, Twitter, February 17, 2017, 4:48 P.M., https://twitter.com/realDonaldTrump/status/832708293516632065 (accessed 6/2/20).

31. This description runs on the editorial masthead of every issue of *The Nation*.

32. Project Censored, "The Top 25 Censored Stories of 2016–2017," http://projectcensored.org/category/the-top-25-censored-stories-of-2016-2017/ (accessed 1/31/18).

33. Andy Lee Roth, *Censored 2020* (New York: Seven Stories Press, 2020).

34. Carl Bialik, "Scare Headlines Exaggerated the US Crime Wave," September 11, 2015, http://fivethirtyeight.com/features/scare-headlines-exaggerated-the-u-s-crime-wave (accessed 11/20/15).

35. Pew Research Center, "Press Widely Criticized, but Trusted More than Other Information Sources," September 22, 2011, www.people-press.org/2011/09/22/press-widely-criticized-but-trusted-more-than-other-institutions (accessed 9/17/12).

36. Oliver Milman et al., "Obama's Legacy: The Promises, Shortcomings and Fights to Come," *The Guardian*, January 2, 2017, p. 1.

37. Markus Prior, "News vs. Entertainment: How Increasing Media Choice Widens Gaps in Political Knowledge and Turnout," *American Journal of Political Science* 49:3 (2005): 577–92.

38. Amy Mitchell et al., "Distinguishing between Factual and Opinion Statements in the News," Pew Research Center, June 18, 2018, www.journalism.org/2018/06/18/distinguishing-between-factual-and-opinion-statements-in-the-news/ (accessed 1/28/20).

39. Markus Prior, *Post-Broadcast Democracy: How Media Choice Increases Inequality in Political Involvement and Polarizes Elections* (New York: Cambridge University Press, 2007).

40. Pablo Boczkowski, *Imitation in an Age of Information Abundance* (Chicago: University of Chicago Press, 2010).

41. Amber E. Boydstun, *Making the News: Politics, the Media, and Agenda Setting* (Chicago: University of Chicago Press, 2013).

42. Jonathan Ladd, "Four Approaches to Providing Political News Given That So Many People Don't Want It," August 20, 2015, http://mischiefsoffaction.blogspot.com/2015/08/four-approaches-to-providing-political.html (accessed 3/8/20).

43. Thomas Patterson, "Bad News, Period," *Political Science and Politics* 29 (1996): 17–20.

44. Shanto Iyengar, Helmut Norpoth, and Kyu Hahn, "Consumer Demand for Election News: The Horserace Sells," *Journal of Politics* 66 (2004): 157–75.

45. Steve M. Barkin, *American Television News: The Media Marketplace and the Public Interest* (New York: Routledge, 2016).

46. Dhrumil Mehta, "The Media Has Really Neglected Puerto Rico," September 28, 2017, https://fivethirtyeight.com/features/the-media-really-has-neglected-puerto-rico/ (accessed 2/5/18).

47. T. E. Patterson, *The Vanishing Voter* (New York: Knopf, 2002); J. N. Cappella and K. H. Jamieson, *Spiral of Cynicism: The Press and the Public Good* (New York: Oxford University Press, 1997).

48. Robert McChesney, *The Problem of the Media: U.S. Communication Politics in the 21st Century* (New York: Monthly Review Press, 2004).

What Do the Facts Say?

a. Gianno Caldwell, "Violence in Chicago Proves Black Lives Don't Matter to Liberal Politicians," *New York Post*, November 9, 2019, https://nypost.com/2019/11/09/chicagos-crime-proves-black-lives-dont-matter-to-democrats/ (accessed 4/14/20).

b. The data are available at www.chicagotribune.com/news/breaking/ct-chicago-homicides-data-tracker-htmlstory.html (accessed 1/29/20).

c. "Daily Chart: Murder Rates in 50 American Cities," *The Economist*, February 7, 2017, www.economist.com/blogs/graphicdetail/2017/02/daily-chart-3 (accessed 2/3/18).

Credits

Text and Line Art

AP® U.S. Government and Politics Skills Handbook: Excerpts from *AP® U.S. Government and Politics Course and Exam Description* © 2021 The College Board. www.collegeboard.org. Used with permission.

Chapter 1, What Do the Facts Say? (p. 17): Map: "2020 Presidential Election, Purple America," by Robert J. Vanderbei, Princeton University, http://www.princeton.edu/~rvdb/JAVA/election2020/. Reprinted by permission of the author.

Chapter 1 AP® Study Guide Free-Response Questions (p. 39): Graph: "Looking to the Future, Public Sees an America in Decline on Many Fronts," Pew Research Center, Washington, D.C. (March 2019), https://www.pewresearch.org/social-trends/2019/03/21/worries-priorities-and-potential-problem-solvers/.

Figure 4.6 (p. 156): Graph: Liberal-conservative partisan polarization by chamber, from "Polarization in Congress," March 11, 2018, Jeffrey Lewis, Keith T. Poole, and Howard Rosenthal, voteview.com. Reprinted by permission.

Figure 9.5 and Chapter 9 AP® Study Guide (pp. 404, 425): Map: Lifetime Wage Gap for Women Compared with Men, from National Women's Law Center, "The Lifetime Wage Gap, State by State," April 4, 2018. Reprinted by permission.

Figure 10.1 (p. 435): Graphs from "Majority of Public Favors Same-Sex Marriage, but Divisions Persist," Pew Research Center, Washington, D.C. (May 2019), https://www.pewresearch.org/politics/2019/05/14/majority-of-public-favors-same-sex-marriage-but-divisions-persist/.

Figure 10.3 (p. 441): Graph from "The Iraq War continues to divide the U.S. public, 15 years after it began," Pew Research Center Fact Tank, Washington, D.C. (March 2018), https://www.pewresearch.org/fact-tank/2018/03/19/iraq-war-continues-to-divide-u-s-public-15-years-after-it-began/.

Figure 10.7 (p. 457): Graph from "Economic Issues Decline Among Public's Policy Priorities," Pew Research Center, Washington, D.C. (January 2018), http://www.people-press.org/2018/01/25/economic-issues-decline-among-publics-policy-priorities/.

Figure 11.4 (p. 488): Figure from "A Deep Dive Into Party Affiliation," Pew Research Center, Washington, D.C. (April 2015), http://www.people-press.org/2015/04/07/a-deep-dive-into-party-affiliation/.

Figure 11.5 (p. 489): Figure from "Political Polarization in the American Public," Pew Research Center, Washington, D.C. (June 2014), http://www.people-press.org/2014/06/12/political-polarization-in-the-american-public/.

Table 14.1 (pp. 618, 642): Table from "U.S. Media Polarization and the 2020 Election: A Nation Divided," Pew Research Center, Washington, D.C. (January 2020) https://www.journalism.org/2020/01/24/u-s-media-polarization-and-the-2020-election-a-nation-divided/.

Figure 14.1 (p. 629): Graph: "Tracking the Gun Control Conversation," https://www.thetrace.org/2018/05/parkland-media-coverage-analysis-mass-shooting/. Reprinted by permission of The Trace.

Appendix (pp. A60–A70): Martin Luther King, Jr., "Letter from Birmingham Jail." Reprinted by arrangement with The Heirs to the Estate of Martin Luther King Jr., c/o Writers House as agent for the proprietor, New York, NY. Copyright © 1963 Dr. Martin Luther King, Jr., © renewed 1991 Coretta Scott King.

Photographs

Front Matter

ii–iii: Morry Gash/AP/Shutterstock; **v (top):** Paul B.; **v (bottom):** Kolin Goldschmidt, University of Wisconsin-Madison; **vi (top):** Kimberly A. Owens; **vi (center):** Emmanuelle Estelle Logmo-Ngog; **vi (bottom):** Kevin Murphy; **ix:** Robert Alexander/Getty Images; **x (top):** AP Photo/Evan Vucci; **x (bottom):** AP Photo/Andrew Harnik; **xi:** UPI/Alamy Stock Photo; **xii (top):** Hum Images/Alamy Stock Photo; **xii (bottom):** Brendan Smialowski/AFP via Getty Images; **xiii:** Jabin Botsford/The Washington Post via Getty Images; **xiv:** Noah Berger/REUTERS/Newscom; **xv (top):** Marilyn Humphries/Alamy Stock Photo; **xv (bottom):** David McNew/Getty Images; **xvi (top):** SOPA Images Limited/Alamy Stock Photo; **xvi (bottom):** Storms Media Group/Alamy Stock Photo; **xvii:** Jennifer Booher/Alamy Stock Photo; **xviii:** AP Photo/Jon Elswick

Chapter 1

3: Robert Alexander/Getty Images; **5:** Mark Wilson/Getty Images; **8 (left):** US Army Photo/Alamy Stock Photo; **8 (right):** Melvyn Longhurst/Alamy Stock Photo; **10:** Allison Shelley/The Washington Post via Getty Images; **12:** Olivier Douliery/SIPA/Newscom; **13 (right):** Eva Marie Uzcategui T./Anadolu Agency/Getty Images; **15 (left):** Patrick Gorski/NurPhoto/Sipa USA/Newscom; **15 (center):** Williams Paul/Icon Sportswire via Getty Images; **15 (right):** Fox/Photofest; **18 (top):** AP Photo/Odessa American, Courtney Sacco; **18 (bottom):** © Flip Schulke/CORBIS/Corbis via Getty Images; **20:** Chip Somodevilla/Getty Images; **23:** Xinhua/Alamy Stock Photo; **33:** Robert Alexander/Getty Images

Chapter 2

41: AP Photo/Evan Vucci; **43:** North Wind Picture Archives/Alamy Stock Photo; **46:** Ian Dagnall/Alamy Stock Photo; **47:** Imagno/Getty Images; **48:** © North Wind Picture Archives—All rights reserved.; **52:** Bettmann/Getty Images; **56:** Library of Virginia; **58:** Library of Congress/Corbis/VCG via Getty Images; **60:** Library of Congress; **61 (top):** Francis G. Mayer/Corbis/VCG via Getty Images; **61 (bottom):** Library of Congress; **63:** Mandel Ngan/AFP via Getty Images; **65 (top left):** Draper, Eric, 1964-, Photographer/National Archives; **65 (top center):** Spx Chrome/Getty Images; **65 (top right):** ZUMA Press, Inc./Alamy Stock Photo; **65 (center left):** Spx Chrome/Getty Images; **65 (center):** ZUMA Press, Inc./Alamy Stock Photo; **65 (center right):** Dpa Picture Alliance/Alamy Stock Photo; **65 (bottom left):** JStone/Shutterstock; **65 (bottom right):** Spx Chrome/Getty Images; **67:** ZUMA Press, Inc./Alamy Stock Photo; **68:** World History Archive/Alamy Stock Photo; **69:** Jim Watson/AFP via Getty Images; **73:** Porter Gifford/Corbis via Getty Images; **75 (left):** Everett Collection Inc/Alamy Stock Photo; **75 (right):** Everett Collection Inc/Alamy Stock Photo; **76:** Norma Jean Gargasz/Alamy Stock Photo; **81:** AP Photo/Evan Vucci

Chapter 3

89: AP Photo/Andrew Harnik; 91: American Photo Archive/Alamy Stock Photo; 94: AP Photo/Eric Gay; 98: The Metropolitan Museum of Art, New York. The Edward W. C. Arnold Collection of New York; Prints, Maps, and Pictures. Bequest of Edward W. C. Arnold, 1954 (54.90.491); 100: MPI/Getty Images; 101: Bettmann/Getty Images; 103: GRANGER; 107 (top left): J Main/Shutterstock; 107 (top center): Ivana Star/Getty Images; 107 (top right): Space Images/Getty Images; 107 (center left): Food Collection/Getty Images; 107 (center): Sam Edwards/Getty Images; 107 (center right): JStone/Shutterstock; 107 (bottom left, top): Ivana Star/Getty Images; 107 (bottom left, bottom): Food Collection/Getty Images; 107 (bottom center, left): Gado Images/Alamy Stock Photo; 107 (bottom center, right): Sam Edwards/Getty Images; 107 (bottom right): Michael Betts/Getty Images; 109: DOE Photo/Alamy Stock Photo; 110: AP Photo/Andrew Harnik; 113: Joe Raedle/Getty Images; 115: Justin Sullivan/Getty Images; 116: Bill Pugliano/Getty Images; 121: AP Photo/Andrew Harnik

Chapter 4

129: UPI/Alamy Stock Photo; 133: Sarin Images/GRANGER; 136: Heather Ainsworth/AP Images for Boys and Girls Clubs of America; 143: Brian Hill/Daily Herald via AP; 144: ZUMA Press, Inc./Alamy Stock Photo; 148 (left): United States Department of the Interior; 148 (right): United States Department of the Interior; 151: Tom Williams/CQ Roll Call via AP Images; 154: UPI/Alamy Stock Photo; 157: ZUMA Press, Inc./Alamy Stock Photo; 163 (row 1, left): Xinhua/Alamy Stock Photo; 163 (row 1, right): Dpa Picture Alliance/Alamy Stock Photo; 163 (row 2, center): Beneda Miroslav/Shutterstock; 163 (row 2, left): Xinhua/Alamy Stock Photo; 163 (row 2, right): Dpa Picture Alliance/Alamy Stock Photo; 163 (row 3, center): Photomaster/Shutterstock; 163 (row 3, right): Beneda Miroslav/Shutterstock; 163 (row 3, left): SOPA Images Limited/Alamy Stock Photo; 163 (row 4, left): Xinhua/Alamy Stock Photo; 163 (row 4, right): Dpa Picture Alliance/Alamy Stock Photo; 163 (row 5): Xinhua/Alamy Stock Photo; 163 (row 6): JStone/Shutterstock; 171: Toni L. Sandys/The Washington Post via AP, Pool; 175: UPI/Alamy Stock Photo

Chapter 5

183: Hum Images/Alamy Stock Photo; 185: Painting/Alamy Stock Photo; 186 (left): Bettmann/Getty Images; 186 (right): AP Photo/Bob Daugherty; 189: ZUMA Press, Inc./Alamy Stock Photo; 193 (top left): ZUMA Press, Inc./Alamy Stock Photo; 193 (top center): Official White House Photo by Pete Souza/National Archives; 193 (top right): A Katz/Shutterstock; 193 (center left): Dpa Picture Alliance/Alamy Stock Photo; 193 (center): Dpa Picture Alliance/Alamy Stock Photo; 193 (center right): Nazlisart/Shutterstock; 193 (left): JStone/Shutterstock; 193 (right): JStone/Shutterstock; 196 (left): AP Photo/Pablo Martinez Monsivais; 196 (right): Doug Mills/The New York Times/Redux; 200: Sipa USA/Alamy Stock Photo; 201: Al-Mayadeen via AP Video; 203: HO/Jiji Press/Newscom; 204 (left): Al Drago/The New York Times/Redux; 204 (right): Backgrid/Alamy Stock Photo; 207: Mandel Ngan/AFP via Getty Images; 208: Mikhail Klimentyev, Sputnik, Kremlin Pool Photo via AP; 209: AP Photo/Andrew Harnik; 213: UPI/Alamy Stock Photo; 218: Hum Images/Alamy Stock Photo

Chapter 6

225: Brendan Smialowski/AFP via Getty Images; 226: B Christopher/Alamy Stock Photo; 229: North Wind Picture Archives/Alamy Stock Photo; 231: UPI/Alamy Stock Photo; 235 (top): Glow Images/Getty Images; 235 (center left): Alexsandar Nakic/Getty Images; 235 (center right): Spx Chrome/Getty Images; 235 (bottom): United States Department of the Interior; 237: Ken Cedeno/ZUMA Press/Newscom; 240: Perisha Gates/ZUMA Press/Newscom; 243: Janice and Nolan Braud/Alamy Stock Photo; 245: David Hume Kennerly/Getty Images; 247: Dana Verkouteren via AP; 249: Leah Millis/Pool via AP; 253: Bettmann/Getty Images; 257: John Badman/The Telegraph via AP; 258: WDC Photos/Alamy Stock Photo; 260: Alex Wong/Getty Images; 261: Bettmann/Getty Images; 265: Brendan Smialowski/AFP via Getty Images

Chapter 7

273: Jabin Botsford/The Washington Post via Getty Images; 275: American Photo Archive/Alamy Stock Photo; 277 (top left): J Main/Shutterstock; 277 (top center): United States Environmental Protection Agency; 277 (top right): Spx Chrome/Getty Images; 277 (center left): ZUMA Press, Inc./Alamy Stock Photo; 277 (center, center right): United States Environmental Protection Agency; 277 (bottom left): JStone/Shutterstock; 277 (bottom right): Corine van Kapel/Alamy Stock Photo; 278: UPI/Alamy Stock Photo; 282: Dpa Picture Alliance/Alamy Stock Photo; 283: CARLSON © 2005 Milwaukee Journal Sentinel. Reprinted with permission of ANDREWS MCMEEL SYNDICATION. All rights reserved; 284: Bettmann/Getty Images; 287: Justin Lane/EPA/REX/Shutterstock; 296: AP Photo/Andrew Harnik; 299: Andrew Holbrooke/Corbis via Getty Images; 300 (left): CFPB/Alamy Stock Photo; 300 (right): Dpa Picture Alliance/Alamy Stock Photo; 302: Storms Media Group/Alamy Stock Photo; 307: Jabin Botsford/The Washington Post via Getty Images; 311: CARLSON © 2005 Milwaukee Journal Sentinel. Reprinted with permission of ANDREWS MCMEEL SYNDICATION. All rights reserved.

Chapter 8

315: Noah Berger/REUTERS/Newscom; 318 (left): Rick Barbero/The Register-Herald via AP; 318 (right): William Thomas Cain/Getty Images; 319: Johannes Eisele/AFP via Getty Images; 325 (top left): Thinkstock Images/Getty Images; 325 (top center): Spx Chrome/Getty Images; 325 (top right): John Parra/Getty Images; 325 (center left): Spx Chrome/Getty Images; 325 (center): ZUMA Press Inc./Alamy Stock Photo; 325 (center right): Image Navi/Getty Images; 325 (bottom): Stockbyte/Getty Images; 328: Lawrence Hurley/REUTERS/Newscom; 329: Matthew Staver/The New York Times/Redux; 333: Michael S. Williamson/The Washington Post via Getty Images; 334: J. Lawler Duggan/For the Washington Post via Getty Images; 336: Indiana University Campus Art Collection, THB X, Thomas Hart Benton, *Indiana Murals: Parks, the Circus, the Klan, the Press*. Photograph by: Michael Cavanagh and Kevin Montague, Eskenazi Museum of Art at Indiana University; 337: Michael Nigro/Pacific Press/LightRocket via Getty Images; 339: Shawn Thew/EPA-EFE/Shutterstock; 340: Pool/REUTERS/Newscom; 341: Anthony Pidgeon/Redferns/Getty Images; 344 (left): John Wingfield/Alamy Stock Photo; 344 (right): Erin Schaff/The New York Times/Redux; 346: Chip Somodevilla/Getty Images; 348: AP Photo; 350: Jason Reed/Reuters/Newscom; 351: Bettmann/Getty Images; 353: Reuters/Newscom; 356: AP Photo/Michael Stravato; 363: Noah Berger/REUTERS/Newscom

Chapter 9

371: Marilyn Humphries/Alamy Stock Photo; 374 (left): Library of Congress; 374 (right): HB Lindsey/Underwood Archives/Getty Images; 375: Time Life Pictures/Timepix/The LIFE Picture Collection/Getty Images; 377: Alpha Stock/Alamy Stock Photo; 378: Photo by Library of Congress/Corbis/VCG via Getty Images; 380: AP Photo/Julia Weeks; 383: AP Photo/Hillery Smith Shay; 388 (top left): Feidin Santana via AP Images; 388 (top right): Richard Ellis/Getty Images; 388 (bottom): Curtis Compton/Atlanta Journal-Constitution via AP; 389: Don Cravens/The LIFE Images Collection/Getty Images; 392 (left): AP Photo/Bill Hudson; 392 (right): AFP/Getty Images; 394: Robyn Beck/AFP via Getty Images; 395 (left): Bryan Woolston/REUTERS/Newscom;

395 (right): AP Photo/John Minchillo; 397: AP Photo; 401: Kyodo via AP Images; 403 (left): David Schaffer/Getty Images; 403 (right): Tetra Images/Getty Images; 408: Jim Watson/AFP via Getty Images; 410: ZUMA Press, Inc./Alamy Stock Photo; 414: Liu Jie Xinhua News Agency/Newscom; 415: Jose Luis Magana/Reuters/Newscom; 416: ZUMA Press, Inc./Alamy Stock Photo; 417: Rey R. Jauregui/EPA-EFE/Shutterstock; 422: Marilyn Humphries/Alamy Stock Photo

Chapter 10

429: David McNew/Getty Images; 431: CALVIN AND HOBBES © 1994 Watterson. Reprinted with permission of ANDREWS MCMEEL SYNDICATION. All rights reserved.; 432 (top): AP Photo/Rogelio V. Solis; 432 (bottom): Scott Olson/Getty Images; 435 (left): Stephanie Keith/Getty Images; 435 (right): AP Photo/Gene J. Puskar; 437: Alex Wong/Getty Images; 445 (top left): Tetra Images/Getty Images; 445 (top center): Evirgen/Getty Images; 445 (top right): Daniel Grill/Getty Images; 445 (bottom left): John Lamb/Getty Images; 445 (bottom center): Hero Images/Getty Images; 445 (bottom right): Image Navi/Getty Images; 450 (left): Lucy Nicholson/REUTERS/Newscom; 450 (right): AP Photo/David J. Phillip; 453: AP Photo; 459 (left): AP Photo/Mary Altaffer; 459 (right): Tannen Maury/Epa/Shutterstock; 463: David McNew/Getty Images; 468 (top left): Tetra Images/Getty Images; 468 (top center): Evirgen/Getty Images; 468 (top right): Daniel Grill/Getty Images; 468 (bottom left): John Lamb/Getty Images; 468 (bottom center): Hero Images/Getty Images; 468 (bottom right): Image Navi/Getty Images

Chapter 11

473: SOPA Images Limited/Alamy Stock Photo; 475 (left): AP Photo/Patrick Semansky; 475 (center): UPI/Alamy Stock Photo; 475 (right): Pacific Press/Alamy Stock Photo; 477: © CORBIS/Corbis via Getty Images; 478: Sarin Images/GRANGER; 480: Mark Peterson/Redux; 481: Andrew Spear for The Washington Post via Getty Images; 486: Chris Hondros/Getty Images; 491: AP Photo/John Locher; 495 (left): White House Photo/Alamy Stock Photo; 495 (center left): Matt Baron/Shutterstock; 495 (center): Matt Baron/Shutterstock; 495 (center right): Matt Baron/Shutterstock; 495 (right): Michael Brochstein/Alamy Stock Photo; 496: Denver Post via Getty Images; 497: Joyce Boghosian/ZUMA Press/Newscom; 498: AP Photo/Charles Dharapak; 499: SOPA Images Limited/Alamy Stock Photo; 503: ZUMA Press, Inc./Alamy Stock Photo; 508: SOPA Images Limited/Alamy Stock Photo; 511: Sarin Images/GRANGER

Chapter 12

515: Storms Media Group/Alamy Stock Photo; 522: Tom Williams/Roll Call/Newscom; 523: Nicole S Glass/Shutterstock; 525: Jim West/Alamy Stock Photo; 526: Mike Theiler/AFP via Getty Images; 529: JeffG/Alamy Stock Photo; 533 (top left): Pressmaster/Shutterstock;

533 (top right): Yuri Arcurs/Getty Images; 533 (center left): Image Source/Getty Images; 533 (center): Tetra Images/Getty Images; 533 (center right): Greg Bajor/Getty Images; 533 (bottom left): Dpa Picture Alliance/Alamy Stock Photo; 533 (bottom right): JStone/Shutterstock; 534: AP Photo/Elaine Thompson; 535: Janine Wiedel Photolibrary/Alamy Stock Photo; 538: Pacific Press Agency/Alamy Stock Photo; 542 (both): Jim West/Alamy Stock Photo; 544: Xinhua/Alamy Stock Photo; 545: Alex Wong/Getty Images; 549: Storms Media Group/Alamy Stock Photo

Chapter 13

557: Jennifer Booher/Alamy Stock Photo; 559: Bill Clark/CQ Roll Call/Newscom; 560: UPI/Alamy Stock Photo; 562 (left): Ellen F. O'Connell/Hazelton Standard-Speaker via AP; 562 (right): Marc Serota/Reuters/Newscom; 564: UPI/Alamy Stock Photo; 573: AP Photo/Steve Helber; 576 (top): AB Forces News Collection/Alamy Stock Photo; 576 (bottom): ZUMA Press, Inc./Alamy Stock Photo; 577: UPI/Alamy Stock Photo; 580 (both): Democratic National Committee/LBJ Library; 586: Drew Angerer/Getty Images; 588: John Spink/Atlanta Journal-Constitution via AP; 589: ZUMA Press, Inc./Alamy Stock Photo; 594: Bridget Bennett/Bloomberg via Getty Images; 595: Shiiko Alexander/Alamy Stock Photo; 598: Tasos Katopodis/POOL/EPA-EFE/Shutterstock; 604: Jennifer Booher/Alamy Stock Photo; 608: Mike Flinn/CartoonStock.com

Chapter 14

611: AP Photo/Jon Elswick; 613: GRANGER; 614 (left): John Paul Filo/CBS via Getty Images; 614 (right): Evan Agostini/Invision/AP; 616 (left): Scott Olson/Getty Images; 616 (right): Carl Court/Getty Images; 617: National Portrait Gallery, Smithsonian Institution; gift of the James Smithson Society; 622: AP Photo/Julia Weeks; 625 (row 1, left): Photomaster/Shutterstock; 625 (row 1, right): Beneda Miroslav/Shutterstock; 625 (row 2): Klaus Vedfelt/Getty Images; 625 (row 3): Beneda Miroslav/Shutterstock; 625 (row 4): Photomaster/Shutterstock; 627: Official White House Photo by Shealah Craighead; 629: Michael Matthews – Police Images/Alamy Stock Photo; 633: M4OS Photos/Alamy Stock Photo; 635: Stephen Lam/REUTERS/Newscom; 640: AP Photo/Jon Elswick

Icons

70, 76, 97, 112, 145, 149, 228, 246, 249, 253, 256, 317, 327, 332, 333, 338, 345, 353, 355, 376, 398, 408, 507, 583: Luqman Hakiim/Shutterstock

Glossary/Index

by-product theory, 618–19, 620 The idea that many Americans acquire political information unintentionally rather than by seeking it out.

Cabinet, 204, 205, 288, 410 The group of 15 executive department heads who implement the president's agenda in their respective positions.

casework, 140, 175 Assistance provided by members of Congress to their constituents in solving problems with the federal bureaucracy or addressing other specific concerns.

categorical grants, 105, 109 Federal aid to state or local governments that is provided for a specific purpose, such as a mass-transit program within the transportation budget or a school lunch program within the education budget.

caucus, congressional, 4, 154, 483, 490, 498, 500, 502 The organization of Democrats within the House and Senate that meets to discuss and debate the party's positions on various issues in order to reach a consensus and to assign leadership positions.

caucus, electoral, 490–93, 492, 494, 495, 562, 620, 633 A local meeting in which party members select a party's nominee for the general election.
    in presidential elections, 494, 561–64
    voter turnout for, 589

centralized groups, 521–23 Interest groups that have a headquarters, usually in Washington, D.C., as well as members and field offices throughout the country. In general, these groups' lobbying decisions are made at headquarters by the group leaders.

cert pool, 245 A system initiated in the Supreme Court in the 1970s in which law clerks screen cases that come to the Supreme Court and recommend to the justices which cases should be heard.

Clinton, Bill (*Continued*)
   impeachment of, 170, 209
   presidential power of, 187
   vetoes from, *197*
Clinton, Hillary, 184, 254, 446, 449–51, 474,
   571, 581, 594, 603
   electoral votes for, 569, *569*
   e-mail practices of, 169, 623, 627
   fake news on, 610
   popular votes for, 599
   presidential campaign of (2016), *see*
     presidential campaign and election
     of 2016
   public opinion on, 144, 447
Clinton v. Jones, A86, A187

closed primary, 492, 494, 559 A primary
election in which only registered members
of a particular political party can vote.

closed rules, 168 Conditions placed on
a legislative debate by the House Rules
Committee prohibiting amendments to a bill.

cloture, 168 A procedure through which
the Senate can limit the amount of time
spent debating a bill (cutting off a filibuster)
if a supermajority of 60 senators agree.

Club for Growth, 480
Clyburn, James, 640
CNN, 157, 224, 449, 618, 634
coalitions:
   bipartisan, 502
   in political parties, 487–88, *488*
*Coalition to Defend Affirmative Action,
   Schuette v.*, A129, A131
Coastal Zone Management Act, 108

coattails, 591 The ability of a popular
president to generate additional support for
candidates affiliated with his or her party.
Coattails are weak or nonexistent in most
American elections.
Code of Federal Regulations, 15
Coelho, Anthony, 419

coercion, 529 A method of eliminating
nonparticipation or free riding by potential
group members by requiring participation,
as in many labor unions.

Coercive Acts (1774), 43

**coercive federalism, *104*, 105, 106, 108,
121** A form of federalism in which the
federal government pressures the states to
change their policies by using regulations,
mandates, or conditions (often involving
threats to withdraw federal funding).

Colbert, Stephen, *615*
Cold War, 186
Cole, James, 115
Coleman, Norm, 639
Cole Memo, 115

collective action problems, 8, 15, 35, 528–29
Situations in which the members of a group
would benefit by working together to
produce some outcome, but each individual
is better off refusing to cooperate and
reaping benefits from those who do the work.

college:
   affirmative action in admission to, 372,
     412–14, 415, 422
   controversial speech in, 314–16, 363
   student loans for, *see* student loans
Collins, Susan, 498, 556–58, *556*
collusion, 244
Colorado, 115, 330, 405, 495
Colorado, Wolf v., 323, A103, A107
*Colorado Anti-Discrimination Commission,
   Masterpiece Cakeshop Ltd. v.*, A140, *A140*
color-blind jurisprudence, 253, 396–99,
   412, 413
Comcast, 542
*Comer, Trinity Lutheran Church of Columbia
   v.*, A138, A140
Comey, James, 76, 170
commander in chief, presidential power as,
   66–68, 191–93, 205–6

commerce clause, 71, 72, 101, 112–13 The
part of Article I, Section 8, of the Constitution that gives Congress "the power to
regulate Commerce … among the several
States." The Supreme Court's interpretation of this clause has varied, but today it
serves as the basis for much of Congress's
legislation.

Commerce Department, 289, *289*, 291

commercial speech, 341 Public expression
with the aim of making a profit. It has
received greater protection under the First
Amendment in recent years but remains less
protected than political speech.

Commission on Civil Rights, 372–73, 382
Commission on Presidential Debates, 579

Committee of the Whole, 177 The
parliamentary mechanism for the initial
consideration of legislation and expediting
debate and voting on amendments in the
U.S. House. The Committee of the Whole is
comprised of all members of the House but
has a smaller quorum (100 members instead
of 218) and amendments are considered
under a five-minute rule.

committee system in Congress, 158–64, 169,
   175, *175*, 176
   in budget process, 166–67

common law, 232 Law based on the precedent of previous court rulings rather than on
legislation. It is used in all federal courts and
49 of the 50 state courts.

Common Sense (Paine), 46

community, political socialization in, 433
commutations, presidential power in, 199
comparison, xxxiv–xxxv

competitive federalism, 110, 116, 117–18 A
form of federalism in which states compete
to attract businesses and jobs through the
policies they adopt.

compromise in political conflicts, 12–13
   at Constitutional Convention, 50–62
Compromise of 1850, 185
concept application, xxxvi–xxxix, 86, 181,
   265, 368, 513, 644

concurrent powers, 91, 92 Responsibilities
for particular policy areas, such as transportation, that are shared by federal, state, and
local governments.
concurrent resolution, 161

concurring opinion, 249, 356, 405 An
opinion of the court that agrees with the
majority decision but disagrees on at least
part of the rationale for the decision.

concurring opinions, *250*
Confederacy, 334, *337*, 374

confederal government, 9, 93 A form of
government in which states hold power over
a limited national government.

confederations, 521–23 Interest groups
made up of several independent, local
organizations that provide much of their
funding and hold most of the power.

conference, 154, 483, 498 The organization
of Republicans within the House and Senate
that meets to discuss and debate the party's
positions on various issues in order to
reach a consensus and to assign leadership
positions.

conference, of Supreme Court justices, 248

conference committees, 159, 165–66
Temporary committees created to negotiate
differences between the House and Senate
versions of a piece of legislation that has
passed through both chambers.

confessions, Miranda rights in, 351
confidentiality, executive privilege for,
   199–201
conflicts, political, 5, 9, 10–13, 15
   compromise in, 12–13, 50–59
   and Constitution, 42–43, 81–82
   critical analysis of political information
     in, 23–26
   on economic policies, 16
   gridlock in, 150
   on health care, 13
   as human nature, 47–48
   resolution of, 21–24
   sources of, 16–21

de jure, 396 Relating to actions or circumstances that occur "by law," such as the legally enforced segregation of schools in the American South before the 1960s.
Delaware, 57, 565, 568, 584, *598*

delegate, 135–36 A member of Congress who loyally represents constituents' direct interests.

delegates, 563–65, 595 Individuals who are selected in a presidential primary or caucus to attend the party's nomination convention to vote on the party's platform and select the party's presidential and vice-presidential nominees.

demand-side economics, 172

democracy, 9, 21, 24, 35, 37–38 Government by the people. In most contexts, this means representative democracy in which the people elect leaders to enact policies. Democracies must have fair elections with at least two options.
    elite, 35, 37–38
    media in, 631, 640
    participatory, 35, 37–38
    pluralist, 35, 37–38
    political parties in, 498, 500, 501–3
    representative, 21–22, 35, 37–38, 50–52
    republican, 46–47

Democratic Congressional Campaign Committee, 483, *493*
Democratic Governors' Association, 480
Democratic Leadership Council, 480, *493*
Democratic National Committee, 472, *475*, 479, 481, *493, 493*, 623
Democratic National Convention (2020), 472, 564–65, 595
Democratic Party, 474, 508
    in bipartisan compromises, 502–3
    in "blue states," 16, 17
    as brand name, 481
    in campaign financing, 493–96, *493*, *585*, *587*
    coalitions in, 487–88, *488*
    congressional caucuses of, 154, 483, 490
    in congressional elections, 210, 478, 502–3, 556, 558, 559, 591, 593–94, 625
    on Constitution as living document, 73
    in divided government, 498
    economic policies of, 16
    in election process, 490–96
    and federal bureaucracy, 286–87, 293, 301
    on federal government, 477–78
    history of, 475–79, *475*
    identification with, 433, 434, 438, 483–89, *486, 487*
    and ideological polarization, 156–58, *156*, *451, 452, 453*
    Latinos in, 18, 378
    liberal ideology in, 20, 24
    media coverage on, 625

New Deal supported by, 286
    organization of, 478, 479–81, *481*
    party unity in, *155*, 156
    party votes in, *155*, 156
    platform of, 496, *575*
    policy priorities in, *482, 483, 487*, 496, 501–2
    in presidential election (2016), *474*
    in presidential election (2020), 17, *473*, 495, 594–95
    public opinion in, 439–41, 448, 464
    racial, gender, and ethnic identity in, 18, *18*
    in Reconstruction era, 375
    recruiting and nominating candidates from, 490–93, *494*, 495, 563, 564–65
    in redistricting, 146, 147, 148
    reelection of incumbents in, 140–41, 144–45, *591, 592*
    on slavery, 476
    in state and local governments, 55
    on voter ID laws, 562
Democratic primary in 2020, 16, 26, 184, 472–74, *473*, 540, 560, 563–64, 578
Democratic-Republicans, 228, 476
Democratic Senatorial Campaign Committee, 483, *493*
deregulation of media, 614
Dershowitz, Alan, 42
Derthick, Martha, 121–22

descriptive representation, 133–35 Representation in which a member of Congress shares the characteristics (such as gender, race, religion, or ethnicity) of his or her constituents.

desegregation:
    of hotels and restaurants, 397
    of military, 207
    of public schools, 108, 256, 257, *261*, 376, 389, 391, 395–97, 406
Des Moines Independent Community School District, Tinker v., 253, A90–A91, *A92*, A93, A113, *A115*
DeVos, Betsy, *109*, 190
Dingell, John, 14, 360

direct incitement test, 332 Established in *Brandenburg v. Ohio*, this test protects threatening speech under the First Amendment unless that speech aims to and is likely to cause imminent "lawless action."

direct lobbying, 520–31, 539 Attempts by interest group staff to influence policy by speaking with elected officials or bureaucrats.

disabled people, 109, 117, 409
disaster response, 91, 108, 116, 303
    fake news on, 617

discharge petition, 166 A mechanism for forcing a standing committee to report a bill to the floor in the U.S. House (and some state legislatures). A majority of members must sign the petition to force a bill out of committee.

discrimination, 381–82
    against African Americans, 72, *101*, 108, 111–12, 117, 370–72, 375–76, 381–82, 395–99, 406, 422, 477–78
    age, 111, 112, 117
    against Asian Americans, 372, 378–79, 415, 422
    civil rights in protection from, 370–427
    current issues in, 411–17
    against disabled people, 109, 117, 409, 417–21
    disparate impact standard on, 397
    in employment, 111, 112, 381–82, 397, 398, 401–4, *404, 407*, 409
    in housing, 381–82, 406–7
    intermediate scrutiny test in, 400, 402, 403
    investigated by U.S. Commission on Civil Rights, 372–73
    against Latinos, 377, 381–82
    in law enforcement, 370–72, 386–87
    against LGBTQ people, 117, 356, 372, 380–82, 405–6, 409, 422
    liberal policies against, 114
    against Muslims, 70
    political conflicts in, 19
    in protectionism, 379–80, 399
    rational basis test in, 400, 402, 403, 405
    remedial legislation in, 112
    in restaurants, 72, 101, 375, 390
    reverse, 372, 412–14, 415, 422
    separate but equal doctrine in, 375–76, 390, 477
    state laws on, 117
    strict scrutiny test in, 400, 402, 403
    suspect classification in, 400, 402, 405
    viewpoint, 336
    in voting access, 382–84, 397–99, 406
    against women, 236, 372, 379–80, 381–82, 399–405, 407–9, *408*

disenfranchised, 375 To have been denied the ability to exercise a right, such as the right to vote.

disparate impact standard, 397 The idea that discrimination exists if a practice has a negative effect on a specific group, whether or not this effect was intentional.

dissenting opinion, 249 An opinion of the court that disagrees with the majority decision in a case.

dissenting opinions of Supreme Court, 250, *250*

distributive theory, 159 The idea that members of Congress will join committees that best serve the interests of their district and that committee members will support one another's legislation.

presidential, *see* presidential campaigns and elections

presidential support in, 157–58

primary, *see* primary elections

public appearances in, 139

redistricting in, *see* redistricting

runoff, 561

stages of, 559–60

and total number of elected offices, 558

voting in, 588–92; *see also* voting

wave, 144, 591–92

Electoral College, 54–55, 565–69, 597, 600, 626 The body that votes to select America's president and vice president based on the popular vote in each state. Each candidate nominates a slate of electors who are selected to attend the meeting of the college if their candidate wins the most votes in a state or district.

electoral connection, 138–44 The idea that congressional behavior is centrally motivated by members' desire for reelection.

electoral votes, 54–55, 565–69 Votes cast by members of the Electoral College; after a presidential candidate wins the popular vote in a given state, that candidate's slate of electors casts electoral votes for the candidate on behalf of that state.

Elementary and Secondary Education Act (1965), 108

Eleventh Amendment, 74, 112, 237

elite democracy, 35, 37–38 A model of representative democracy in which some citizens (such as the wealthy, the better educated, or certain social groups) have disproportionate influence over government policy.

Ellis Island, 243

Emancipation Proclamation, 190, 207

emergency response in disasters, *91*, 108, 116

fake news on, 617

EMILY's List, 538

eminent domain, 352

emoluments clause, 63, 77, 82, 169

employment:

affirmative action in, 401, 413

discrimination in, 111, 112, 381–82, 397, 398, 401–4, *404*, *407*, 409

hiring preferences for African Americans in, 436, *436*

pay gap for women in, 20, 236, 401–4, *404*

sexual harassment in, 20, 209, 230, 239, 382, 401, 404, 578, 617

and unemployment rate, *see* unemployment rate

Employment Non-Discrimination Act, 409

Endangered Species Act, 108, 233, 304, 352, 358–62

Energy Department, 108, *289*, *291*, 296

***Engel v. Vitale*, 327, A95–A97, A99, A100** The 1962 Supreme Court ruling that prayer in public schools was a violation of the First Amendment's establishment clause.

English language, 19, 414, 417

enumerated powers, 62–66 Powers explicitly granted to Congress, the president, or the Supreme Court in the first three articles of the Constitution. Examples include Congress's power to "raise and support armies" and the president's power as commander in chief.

environmental policies:

and federalism, 108

interest group lobbying on, 518

Paris Agreement on, 13, 110, 193, 195, 305–7, 599

political processes affecting, 13

presidential power in, 88–90, 91, 94, 97, 121, 195, 303–7

regulations in, 88–90, 91, 94, 95, 97, 108, 121, 275, 277, 279

of state governments, 88–90, 91, 94, 95, 97, 108, 110, 114, 121

of Trump, 82, 88–90, 91, 94, 95, 97, 108, 121, 193, 195, 277, 279, 298, 299, 307, 593

Environmental Protection Agency (EPA), 88–90, *89*, 91, 94, 95, 108, 298, 299, 304–7, 360, 386, 524

Clean Power Plan, 277, 279

regulations of, 108, 275, 277, 279

environmental racism, 385–86

Equal Employment Opportunity Commission, 381, 398, 401, 406, *407*

Equal Employment Opportunity Commission, R.G. & G.R. Funeral Home Inc. v., 406

equality, 23, 24, 35 In the context of American politics, "equality" means equality before the law, political equality (one person, one vote), and equality of opportunity (the equal chance for everyone to realize his or her potential), but not material equality (equal income or wealth).

and affirmative action, 412–14, 415

and civil rights, 99–101, 316, 370–427

and conflict resolution, 23–24

Constitution on, 46–47, 373

in income, 16, 23, 48, 384; *see also* income inequality

in law enforcement, 386, 387

of opportunity, 23, 412–14

political, 23, 48

and separate but equal doctrine, 287, 375–76, 390, 395–97, 477

socioeconomic indicators of, 384–86

in voting access, 382–84

equality of opportunity, 23, 412, 465 The equal chance for all people to realize their potential.

equal protection clause of Fourteenth Amendment, 373, 375, 376, 380, 396, 399

and affirmative action policies, 415

and gay rights, 405

and women's rights, 399, 400

Equal Rights Amendment, 408

equal time provision, 614, 636–39 An FCC regulation requiring broadcast media to provide equal air time on any non-news programming to all candidates running for an office.

Era of Good Feelings, 476

Espaillat, Adriano, 128, *129*

Esper, Mark, 524

Espinoza v. Montana Department of Revenue, 328–29

Espionage Act (1917), 332, 338

ESPN, 614, *615*

establishment clause, 325, 326–29 Part of the First Amendment that states, "Congress shall make no law respecting an establishment of religion," which has been interpreted to mean that Congress cannot sponsor or favor any religion.

ethnicity, and party identification, 18–19

European Union, trade with, 196

evangelicals, party identification of, 487

Everson v. Board of Education of Ewing Township, 323

evidence collection:

DNA in, 347, 354

drug testing in, 349–50

exclusionary rule in, 348, *348*

Miranda rights in, 351

search warrants in, 346–48

exclusionary rule, 348 The principle that illegally or unconstitutionally acquired evidence cannot be used in a criminal trial.

exclusive powers, 62–66, 91 Policy-making responsibilities that are exercised only by the national government.

executive agreement, 195 An agreement between the executive branch and a foreign government, which acts as a treaty but does not require Senate approval.

executive branch:

Antifederalist concerns about, 59–60

Articles of Confederation on, 44, *49*

Cabinet in, 204, *205*, 410

checks and balances with other branches, 7, 9, 64, 68–70

Constitutional Convention compromises on, 53–55

Constitution on, 49, *51*

exclusive powers of, 63–64

in parliamentary system, 54

president in, *see* president

and separation of powers, 7, 9

executive branch (*Continued*)
    shared powers of, 66–68
    structure of, 202–5, 288–91, *289*
    vice president in, *see* vice president
executive immunity, 170

Executive Office of the President (EOP),
202–3, 288, 291, 292 The group of
policy-related offices that serve as support
staff to the president.

executive orders, 190–91 Proclamations
made by the president that change
government policy without congressional
approval.
    of Obama, 76, 194, 207, 214–18,
      303–7, 593
    of Trump, 190–91, 194, 207, 217–18, 307

executive powers clause, 71–72 The part
of Article II, Section 1, of the Constitution
that states: "The executive Power shall be
vested in a President of the United States of
America." This broad statement has been
used to justify many assertions of presidential power.

executive privilege, 199–201, *200* The
right of the president to keep executive
branch conversations and correspondence
confidential from the legislative and judicial
branches.

ex post facto laws, 320
Exxon Mobile, *520, 537*

F-35 fighter-attack plane, 274, 520
Facebook, 611, 614, 615, 617–18
    interest group use of, 536
    reliability of news on, 4, *635*, 640
    speech restrictions on, 336
FactCheck.org, 132

factions, 7, 35–36, 47–48, 50–52 Groups of
like-minded people who try to influence the
government. American government is set
up to avoid domination by any one of these
groups.

Fair Housing Act (1968), 406–7
fairness doctrine of FCC, 504, 614, 636–40
fake news, 2–4, 24–28, 95, 610–12, 634,
    635, 640
    doctored photos in, 617
    and Trump, 2–4, 340, 617, 626
Fallon, Jimmy, 615–16
Falwell, Jerry, 340
family, political socialization in, 433
Family Research Council, *520, 537*
Farrakhan, Louis, 412
Fauci, Anthony, *171, 272, 273*
FEC, McConnell v., A147, A149
FEC v. Wisconsin Right to Life, A147
Federal Aviation Administration (FAA),
    278, 289

Federal Bureau of Investigation (FBI), 7,
    80–81, 170, *346*, 348–49

federal civil service, 285 A system created
by the 1883 Pendleton Civil Service Act in
which bureaucrats are hired on the basis of
merit rather than political connections.

Federal Communications Commission
(FCC), 278, 281, 342, 504, 542, 613–14,
636–40 A government agency created in
1934 to regulate American radio stations
and later expanded to regulate television,
wireless communications technologies, and
other broadcast media.

Federal Election Campaign Act (FECA),
    504–7

Federal Election Commission, 335, 507,
583, 600, 602–4 The government agency
that enforces and regulates election laws;
made up of six presidential appointees, of
whom no more than three can be members
of the same party.

Federal Election Commission, Citizens
    United v., 246, 259, 260, *260*, 507,
    536, 583, 584, 603, A142, A146–A149,
    A149, A150
Federal Election Commission, McCutcheon
    v., 583, 603
Federal Emergency Management Agency
    (FEMA), *91*, 116
Federal Employees Political Activities Act
    (1993), 296
Federal Food, Drug, and Cosmetic Act
    (1938), 275
federal government:
    Antifederalist concerns about, 59–60
    autonomy of, 91
    balance of power with state and local
      governments, 7, 9, 48–49, 55, 93–97
    bureaucracy of, 272–313
    checks and balances in, 7, 47, 52
    in cooperative federalism, 102–3
    in daily life, 14–15
    education role of, 108, 109, *109*
    environmental policies of, 108
    evolving concept of, 97–98
    in federalism, 7, 9, 48–49, 54–55, 90, 91,
      92, 93–97
    financial aid to states, 105–8
    forms of, 9
    goals of, 5–8
    historical growth of, 185–86
    lobbying of, 518–21, 531, 545–49
    in media regulation, 613–14
    party views on role of, 477–78
    policy priorities in, 456–58
    public opinion on, 453–55, *453, 454, 455*
    responsibilities of, 91, *92*
    separation of powers in, 7, 9, 47, 52
    size of, 15, 291–94
    spoils system in, 476
    strong role of, 114–18

Supreme Court rulings on, 97–103, *98*
    unfunded mandates of, 105, 418
Federal Highway Administration, 290

federalism, 7, 35, 60–62, 88–122, *104* The
division of power across the local, state, and
national levels of government.
    advantages and disadvantages of, 114–18
    and Antifederalists, 48–49, 59–62
    assessment of, 114–18
    balance of national, state, and local
      power in, 7, 9, 48–49, 54–55, 88–97, *92*
    coercive, *104*, 105, 106, 108
    competitive, 110, 116, 117–18
    concurrent powers in, 91–92, *92*
    cooperative, 102–8, *104*, 116
    dual, 97, 99–100, 102, *104*, 108, 230
    and environmental policies, 108
    evolving concept of, 97–103, *104*, 106
    fiscal, 104–8, *104*
    levels of government and autonomy in,
      91–92
    "marble cake" and "layer cake" models
      of, 102, *104*, 106
    picket fence, 102–3, *104*, 106
    policy implications of, 114
    and recreational marijuana, 115
    states' rights in, 99–101, 110–13
    Supreme Court rulings on, 97–103,
      98, 105

Federalist 10, 48, 50–52, A11–A16 A
foundational document written by James
Madison in 1787 and titled *The Union as a*
Safeguard against Domestic Faction and
Insurrection.

Federalist 51, 7, 47, A44–A47 A
foundational document written by James
Madison in 1788 and titled *The Structure*
of the Government Must Furnish the Proper
Checks and Balances between the Different
Departments.

Federalist 70, 54, 219, A48–A53 A
foundational document written by Alexander Hamilton in 1788 and titled *The Executive*
Department Further Considered.

Federalist 78, 66, 227, 228, 309, A54–A59 A
foundational document written by Alexander
Hamilton in 1788 and titled *The Judiciary*
Department.

Federalist Papers, 47–48, 61, *61*, 66, 131, 227,
    228, 613, A11–A17, A44–A59
    on impeachment, 61
Federalist Radio Hour, 616

Federalists, 48, 49, 50–52, 97–98, 228–29,
476 Those at the Constitutional Convention
who favored a strong national government
and a system of separated powers.
    on judiciary, 227, 228
    on presidential powers, 69
    on proposed Constitution, 60–62

Federalist Society, 61
Federal Meat Inspection Act (1906), 285

federal preemption, 105 Imposition of national priorities on the states through national legislation that is based on the Constitution's supremacy clause.

Federal Register, 275, 278, 461, 639
Federal Reserve System, 8, 288, 290–91
    monetary policies of, 573–74
Federal Speedy Trial Act, 353
Federal Trade Commission (FTC), 278
Feenstra, Randy, 144
Feingold, Russell, 601
FEMA (Federal Emergency Management Agency), *91*, 116
Fenno, Richard F., 136, 150, 159
Ferguson, Mo., *334*, 386
Ferguson, Plessy v., 375, 396, A117, A120, *A123*
Ferreiro, Josefina Vidal, 216
feudalism, 48
Fifteenth Amendment, 74, 99, 322, 375
Fifth Amendment, 99, *321*, 322, *323*, 351–52, 355, 405, 603

fighting words, 339 Forms of expression that "by their very utterance" can incite violence. These can be regulated by the government but are often difficult to define.

filibuster, 167–68, 498, 599 A tactic used by senators to block a bill by continuing to hold the floor and speak—under the Senate rule of unlimited debate—until the bill's supporters back down.

Fillmore, Millard, 185

filtering, 623–31 The influence on public opinion that results from journalists' and editors' decisions about which of many potential news stories to report.

financial crisis (2008), 298
Fiorina, Carly, 184

fire alarm oversight, 169–70, 301 A method of oversight in which members of Congress respond to complaints about the bureaucracy or problems of implementation only as they arise rather than exercising constant vigilance.

First Amendment, 77, 314, 316, 318, 320, *321*, 322–43, 548, 638
    and campaign financing, 586, 600, 602–3
    establishment clause in, 325, 327–29
    on freedom of religion, 322–40
    on freedom of speech, assembly, and press, 331–43, 363
    free exercise clause in, 325, 326, 329–30
    limits to freedoms in, 318
    and privacy rights, 355
    selective incorporation of, *323*
    Supreme Court on, 251–52, *253*, 255, 256
First Circuit Court, 236

fiscal federalism, 104–8 A form of federalism in which federal funds are allocated to the lower levels of government through transfer payments or grants.

Fisher, Abigail, 414, 415
Fisher v. Univ. of Texas, 403, 415, A131–A132, *A131*
501(c)(3) organizations, 536–37, *537*
501(c)(4) organizations, 536–38, *537*, 586

527 organizations, 480, 536–38, 584, 600–602 Tax-exempt groups formed primarily to influence elections through voter mobilization efforts and to issue ads that do not directly endorse or oppose a candidate. Unlike PACs, 527 organizations are not subject to contribution limits and spending caps.

Five Thirty Eight, 25, 442, 614, *615*, 616
flag:
    of Confederacy, 334
    of U.S., and symbolic speech, 333–34, *334*
Flag Protection Act (1989), 333
Flake, Jeff, 594
Flint, Mich., 385–86
Flores, Bill, *151*
Flores, City of Boerne v., 111
Florida:
    death penalty in, 354
    drug-sniffing dogs in, 319
    gun laws in, 344
    Latinos in, 377
    Marjory Stoneman Douglas High School in, *113*, *344*, 628, *629*
    presidential election in (2016), 499
    presidential election in (2020), in, *13*, *562*, 565, 568, 569, 596
    shooting incidents in, 344, *344*
    voting districts in, 399
    women on juries in, 379–80
Florida, Seminole Tribe v., 111
Floyd, George, 370, *371*, 387, 394, *535*, 593
focus groups, 442
Food and Drug Administration (FDA), 8, 278
    drug approval process of, 275, 279, 280–81, 302, *302*, 303
    as independent agency, 289
Ford, Gerald, 187, *211*, 506, 507, 573, 601
Foreign Intelligence Surveillance Act (1978), 349, *350*
Foreign Intelligence Surveillance Court, 349–50
Foreign Miners Tax, 378
foreign policy, 185–86, 195–96, 206–7
    alliances and treaties in, 195–96
    implied powers in, 76
    of Obama, 195–96, 214–18
    presidential power in, 185–86, 195–96
    of Trump, 4–5, 195–96, *196*, 214, 217–18, 438
Founders:
    Articles of Confederation of, 43–46
    on Congress, 131, *133*

at Constitutional Convention, 46–59, *46*
on equality, 23
on goals of government, 7
on human nature, 7, 47–48
on judiciary, 227
on liberty, 22
original intent of, 252
on political parties, 476
on republicanism, 46–47
on separation of church and state, 326–27
on strong national government, 93–94, 96
Fourteenth Amendment, 72, 74, 99–101, 110, 111–12, 113, 322–26, 375, 376, 378
    and abortion rights, 355
    on due process, 99–101, 112, 322, 405
    equal protection clause in, *see* equal protection clause of Fourteenth Amendment
    and gay rights, 113, 356, 405
    and remedial legislation, 112
    and slavery, 375
    Supreme Court on, 230, 253, 322–26
    and women's rights, 379, 399, 400
Fourth Amendment, 318, 319, *321*, *323*, 345–50, 355
Fowler, Mark, 639
Fox & Friends, 620
Fox News, 296, 401, 582, 618, 627, *627*, 630
Fox Television, 342, 615

framing, 628–31, 634–36 The influence on public opinion caused by the way a story is presented or covered, including the details, explanations, and context offered in the report.

France, 9, *43*, 44, 93, 171
    Paris terrorist attacks in (2016), 414
Francis, Pope, 216, 217
Franken, Al, 401
Frankfurter, Felix, 249, 252
Franklin, Benjamin, 50, 58–59, 60
Fraser, Bethel School District No. 403 vs, A91, *A92*
Frederick, Morse v., A91, *A92*
free countries, 9
Freedmen's Bureau, 363
freedom:
    of assembly, 324, 337–38, 343
    of press, 2, 320, 324, 338–39, 343, 610, 613–14, 622
    of religion, 322–40
    of speech, *see* speech, freedom of
Freedom Caucus, 158
Freedom Riders, 390–91

free enterprise, 465 An economic system based on competition among businesses with limited government involvement.

free exercise clause, 325, 326, 329–30 Part of the First Amendment that states that Congress cannot prohibit or interfere with the practice of religion unless there are important secular reasons for doing so.

free market, 16 An economic system based on competition among businesses without government interference.

free-response questions, xliv–xlv
    see also argument essay; concept application; quantitative analysis; SCOTUS comparison

free rider problem, 8, 35, 528–29 The incentive to benefit from others' work without making a contribution, which leads individuals in a collective action situation to refuse to work together.

free riding, 528–29 Relying on others to contribute to a collective effort while failing to participate on one's own behalf, yet still benefiting from the group's successes.

French and Indian War (1754–1763), 42
Fugitive Slave Act, 58, 374

full faith and credit clause, 96 The part of Article IV of the Constitution requiring that each state's laws be honored by the other states. For example, a legal marriage in one state must be recognized across state lines.

fundamental factors in elections, 570–72
Gabbard, Tulsi, 173
Gadarian, Shana Kushner, 434
Galloway, Greece v., A98–A99, *A99*, A100, A101
Gant v. Arizona, A115, *A115*
Garland, Merrick, 66, 190, 239–40, *240*, 254
Garner, Tyron, 356, *356*, 405
Garrett, Alabama v., 111–12
Gawker Media, 340, *340*
gay people, *see* LGBTQ people
gender:
    and Clinton defeat, 26
    and descriptive representation, 133–35
    and equality, 23, 373, 379–80, 389, 390–91, 399–405
    of federal court judges, 238–39, *238*
    and party identification, 18, *480*
    and pay gap, 20, 401–4, *404*, *405*
    and political conflicts, 19–20
    see also women

general election, 560 The election in which voters cast ballots for House members, senators, and (every four years) a president and vice president.
    campaigns in, 577–79
    policy issues in, 575

General Services Administration, 292
General Social Survey, 436, *436*, 442
Georgia:
    at Constitutional Convention, 53
    drug testing in, 349–50
    gay rights in, 405
    immigration policies in, 416
    presidential campaign and election in (2020), 565, 567, 597, 600

    slavery in, 57, 373
    special election in (2017), 578
    voting districts in, 399
Georgia, Chisholm v., 98, 237
Gephardt, Richard, 564
Germany, 93, 344
Gerring, John, 496
Gerry, Elbridge, 60, 146, 320

gerrymandering, 146, 147, 148, 235 Attempting to use the process of re-drawing district boundaries to benefit a political party, protect incumbents, or change the proportion of minority voters in a district.

get out the vote (GOTV), 578, 600 A campaign's efforts to "get out the vote" or make sure its supporters vote on Election Day.

Gibbons v. Ogden, 98, A77, A79, A80, A158, A161, A166
Gideon, Clarence, 353
Gideon, Sara, 556–58

***Gideon v. Wainwright*, 323, 353, A103–A104, A107, A108** The 1963 Supreme Court case that guaranteed the right to an attorney for the poor or indigent for felony offenses.

Giffords, Gabrielle, 640
Gillibrand, Kirsten, 26
Gill v. Whitford, A149, A150
Ginsburg, Ruth Bader, 224, 225, 226, 240, 248, 250, 254, 255, 258, *258*, 260, 265–66, 356
Gitlow, Benjamin, 322

***Gitlow v. New York*, 322, 323** The 1925 Supreme Court ruling that the free speech protections of the First Amendment apply to the states because of the due process clause of the Fourteenth Amendment. However, states could still restrict speech if it had a "dangerous tendency" (that standard is not applied today.)

Giuliani, Rudy, 596
global warming, 110, 121, 298, 625
    see also climate change
Gobitis, Minersville School District v., A94, A99

going public, 212–14 A president's use of speeches and other public communications to appeal directly to citizens about issues the president would like the House and Senate to act on.

Goldwater, Barry, 579–80, *580*
Goodyear Tire & Rubber, Ledbetter v., 236, 401
Google, 336, 520, 537, 542
Gorbachev, Mikhail, *186*
Gore, Al, 562, 565, 569, *569*
Gore, Bush v., 250, 258, A149, *A149*
Gorsuch, Neil, 168, 190, 237, 240, *240*, 249, 252, 254, 255, 258, 259, 328, 406

government, 6, 35 The system for implementing decisions made through the political process.
    bureaucracy of, 272–313
    confederal, 9, 93
    divided, 145, 498
    federal, *see* federal government
    forms of, 9, 43–44, 54, 92–93
    goals of, 5–8
    levels of, 91–92
    local, *see* local government
    in parliamentary system, 54
    president as head of, 188–89
    public opinion on, 453–55, *453*, *454*, *455*
    state, *see* state government
    unified, 69, 214, 218, 498, 559
    unitary, 9, 93

Government Accountability Office, 350
GPS tracking devices, 347
Graham, Lindsey, 597

grandfather clause, 375 A type of law enacted in several southern states to allow those who were permitted to vote before the Civil War, and their descendants, to bypass literacy tests and other obstacles to voting, thereby exempting Whites from these tests while continuing to disenfranchise African Americans and other people of color.

Grass, Alan, 216
Grassley, Chuck, 514, 516

grassroots lobbying, 535–36 A lobbying strategy that relies on participation by group members, such as a protest or a letter-writing campaign.

Gratz v. Bollinger, 403, A127–A129, *A131*
Great Britain, colonial policies of, 42–43

Great Compromise, 52–53 A compromise between the large and small states, proposed by Connecticut, in which Congress would have two houses: a Senate with two legislators per state and a House of Representatives in which each state's representation would be based on population (also known as the Connecticut Compromise).

Great Depression, 102, *102*, 108, 172
    and New Deal programs, 28–33, 285–86
    and political parties, 477
    and presidential power, 186
Great Society, 108, 287, 456
Great Society programs in, 287
Greece v. Galloway, A98–A99, *A99*, A100, A101
Green, Donald, 434
Green New Deal, 474, 502, 625
Green Party, 499, 500
Greensboro, N.C., 390
Gregory v. Ashcroft, 111

gridlock, 150 An inability to enact legislation because of partisan conflict within Congress or between Congress and the president.

hard money, 584, 601 Donations that are used to help elect or defeat a specific candidate.

hard news, 634, 640 Media coverage focused on facts and important issues surrounding a campaign.

hate speech, 315, 335–36 Expression that is offensive or abusive, particularly in terms of race, gender, or sexual orientation. It is currently protected under the First Amendment.

head of government, 188 One role of the president, through which he or she has authority over the executive branch.

head of state, 188 One role of the president, through which he or she represents the country symbolically and politically.

hold, 168 An objection to considering a measure on the Senate floor.

horse race, 634 A description of the type of election coverage that focuses more on poll results and speculation about a likely winner than on substantive differences between the candidates.

hostile media effect, 626 The tendency of people to see neutral media coverage of an event as biased against their point of view.

House Rules Committee, 168 Resolutions (or "rules") governing the amending process and length of debate come from this committee. These rules must be adopted by a majority vote of the entire House.

housing:
    discrimination in, 381–82, 406–7
    mortgages on, *see* mortgages
Housing and Urban Development
    Department, 187, *289*, *291*
Howard, John, *282*
Howell, William G., 206
Hughes, Charles, 249
Hulu, 614, *615*
Humane Society, 540
Humanitarian Law Project, Holder v.,
    A90, A92
human nature, view of Founders on, 7, 47
Humphrey, Hubert, 176
hunting, and right to bear arms, 344
Hurricane Harvey, 116, 617, 634
Hurricane Irma, 116
Hurricane Maria, 116, 634
Hustler, 340

Idaho, 399, 400

ideological polarization, 451–53 Sharp
differences in Americans' overall ideas of
the size and scope of the government.
    of Congress, 156–58, *156*, *483*, *484*
    of political parties, 156–58, 451, *452*, 453,
        483, *484*, 489, 636–40
    social media in, 612
    Trump affecting, 6, 411

ideology, 20–21, 35, 36 A cohesive set
of ideas and beliefs used to organize and
evaluate the political world.
    conservative, 20, 21, 39, 114, 431, *432*
    liberal, 20, 21, 39, 114, 431
    libertarian, 20–21
    and media bias, 582, 627–28
    and media sources, 618–19
    and public opinion, 431, 432, *432*,
        451–53, *452*
    of Supreme Court justices, 239, 249,
        252–55, 258–59, 260, 261

"I Have a Dream" speech of King, 393, *393*
iHeartMedia, 614
Illinois, 115, 147, 337, 344, 379, 629, *630*
immigration, party preferences on, 461, 485
immigration policies, 414–17
    on Chinese, 378
    and DACA program, 128–30, *129*, 132,
        175–76, 459–63
    executive orders on, 190–91
    of Obama, 207, 411, 416–17
    party preferences on, 501–2
    political conflicts on, 4, 5, 18–19, 22
    as presidential election issue (2020), *575*,
        594, 596
    public opinion on, 446, *447*, 450, 458, 459
    state and federal power in enforcement
        of, 109
    of Trump, 5, 82, 109, 128–30, 132, 182,
        190–91, 207, 208–9, *209*, 211, 212,
        411, 414–17, *417*, 497–98, 502, *575*,
        593, 594

**impeachment, 68–69, 170, 199, *200*, 203,
208, 209–10, 259** A negative or checking
power over the other branches that allows
Congress to remove the president, the vice
president, or other "officers of the United
States" (including federal judges) for abuses
of power.
    in *Federalist Papers*, 61
    of Trump, *see* Trump, Donald, impeach-
        ment of

implied powers, 76 Powers supported
by the Constitution that are not expressly
stated in it.

income inequality, 23, 48, 384
    and group identity, *436*
    international comparison of, 16
    in southern states, 48, 373–74
    for women, 20, 236, 401–4, *404*
income taxes, 185

incumbency advantage, 141–45 The
relative infrequency with which members of
Congress are defeated in their attempts for
reelection.

incumbent, 556, 559, 572–73 A politician
running for reelection to the office he or she
currently holds.
    accountability of, 559
    advantage of, 141–45
    campaign staff of, 576
    constituency service of, 141–44
    credit claiming by, 139–40
    redistricting affecting, 146
    reelection of, 136, 138–45, *139*, 158, 556,
        591–92, *592*
    retirement of, 573
    seniority of, 152
    and wave elections, 591–92

independent agencies, 288–91 Government
offices or organizations that provide
government services and are not part of an
executive department.

Independents, 472, 490–93, 500
    identification with, 485–87,
        486, *487*
    nomination of candidates, 492–93
Indiana, 416
Indiana, Timbs v., 323
Indiana University, 335–36, *336*
Indian Removal Act (1830), 376

individualism, 16, 465 The autonomy
of individuals to manage the course of
their own lives without government
interference.

individualism, economic, 16
Indivisible movement, 523
inequality, *see* equality
information, political, *see* political
    information

informational theory, 159 The idea that
having committees in Congress made up of
experts on specific policy areas helps ensure
well-informed policy decisions.
infrastructure repairs, 117

initiative, 539 A direct vote by citizens on
a policy change proposed by fellow citizens
or organized groups outside government.
Getting a question on the ballot typically
requires collecting a set number of signatures from registered voters in support of
the proposal. There is no mechanism for a
national-level initiative.

In re Oliver 333 U.S. 257 (1948), 323

inside strategies, 530–35 The tactics
employed within Washington, D.C., by
interest groups seeking to achieve their
policy goals.

Instagram, 336, 536
institutional interest groups, *517*

interest groups, 480, 514–55, 574 An
organization of people who share common
political interests and aim to influence
public policy by electioneering and
lobbying.
    in campaign financing, 521–23, 536–38,
        542–43, 581
    centralized, 521, *523*
    and collective action problems,
        528–29, *528*
    confederation model, 521–23
    congressional testimony of, 531–34
    direct lobbying by, 530–31, 540
    expertise in, 527
    gifts to Congress from, 522
    grassroots lobbying by, 535–36
    implementing or preventing change, 543
    incentives for participation in, 528–29
    initiatives and referenda of, 539
    inside strategies of, 530–35
    iron triangles in, 524
    legislation and regulations drafted by,
        531
    litigation strategies of, 534, *534*
    media coverage on, 538–39
    membership in, 521–23, 525, *525*, 526
    organizational structure of, 521–23
    outside strategies of, 530, 532, 533,
        535–40
    political action committees, *see* political
        action committees
    power and influence of, 540–42
    research of, 531
    resources of, 525–27
    restrictions on, 522
    revolving door with Congress, 522, 524
    salience of goals, 543–44
    spending by, 518–21, 526, 539–40
    staff of, 523–24, 526–27, 531, 534
    and Supreme Court decisions, 255
    types of, *517*

interest group state, 518 A government in which most policy decisions are determined by the influence of interest groups.

Interior Department, 102, 108, 233, 289, 291, 358, 361
Intermediate-Range Nuclear Forces (INF) Treaty, 66

intermediate scrutiny, 331, 335, 400, 402, 403 The middle level of scrutiny the courts can use when determining whether a law is constitutional. To meet this standard, the law or policy must be "content neutral," must further an important government interest in a way that is "substantially related" to that interest, and must use means that are a close fit to the government's goal and not substantially broader than is necessary to accomplish that goal.

Internal Revenue Service (IRS), 8, 500, 536, 537
International Women's Day, 404
Internet:
    and net neutrality, 542
    news and political information from, 24–25, 612, 614–17, 616, 632, 633
    speech on, 336
    surveillance of activity on, 81, 349–50
internment camps, Japanese Americans in, 378–79, 378, 400
interrogation, Miranda rights in, 351
Interstate Commerce Commission, 185, 285, 391
Intolerable Acts (1774), 43
Iowa, 495, 564, 576, 596, 620, 633
iPhones, 346
Iran, 191, 464
    nuclear program of, 195, 533, 575
    public knowledge of, 430
    theocracy in, 22
Iraq, 196, 623
    air strikes in, 338
    invasion of (2003), 67, 212, 439, 441, 457
    military expenses in, 207
    nuclear program of, 66
    party affiliation and opinions on invasion of, 439, 441
    public opinion on invasion of, 439, 441, 457

iron triangle, 524 Informal alliance of elected officials, bureaucrats, and interest groups designed to let these groups and individuals dominate the policy-making process in a given area.

IRS (Internal Revenue Service), 8, 500, 536, 537
ISIS (Islamic State in Iraq and Syria), 67, 458
    party affiliation and opinions on, 575, 575
    in Syria, 191
Islam, 19, 412
Israel, 93, 203

issue network, 524 Informal organization of interest groups and individuals who work together to lobby government for policy change. These collaborations are usually short-term efforts focused on specific proposals, issues, or regulations.

issue ownership, 481 The theory that voters associate certain issues or issue positions with certain parties (like Democrats and support for government-provided health insurance).

issue scale, 442

issue voters, 589 People who are well informed about their own policy preferences and knowledgeable about the candidates, and who use all of this information when they decide how to vote.

Italy, 93

Jackson, Andrew, 185, 284, 284, 476
Jackson, Henry "Scoop," 359
Jackson, Janet, 342
Jackson, Robert, 249
Jacobs, Lawrence R., 437
Jacobson, Roberta A., 216
January 6, 2021, capitol insurrection, 4, 210
Japan, 9, 67, 93, 344
Japanese Americans in internment camps, 256, 378–79, 378, 400
Jardines, Joelis, 319
Jay, John, 47, 613, A11, A17, A54
Jefferson, Thomas, 22, 47, 50, 55, 60, 97, 320, A1–A4
    on Congress, 131
    on constitutional amendments, 72
    on implied powers, 76
    presidential election, 228–29, 331
    presidential power of, 185
    on separation of church and state, 326–27

Jim Crow laws, *101*, 375–76, 381 State and local laws that mandated racial segregation in all public facilities in the South, many border states, and some northern communities between 1876 and 1964.

Johnson, Andrew, 170, 209
Johnson, Lyndon, 108, 157, 405, 409, 571, 573
    on affirmative action, 409, 412
    approval rating of, 211
    campaign ads of, 579–80, 580
    Great Society programs of, 108, 287, 456
    presidential power of, 186–87
Johnson, Texas v., A90, A92
Johnson Space Center, 301
Joint Committee on Taxation, 516

joint committees, 158–59 Committees that contain members of both the House and Senate but have limited authority.

joint resolution, 161
Jolie, Angelina, 401
Jones, Antoine, 347
Jones, Clinton v., A86, A187
Jones, Doug, 542
Jones and Laughlin Steel Corporation, National Labor Relations Board v., 102
Jordan, 316
Jordan, Barbara, 542
Jorgensen, Jo, 499, 499, 500
journalism:
    attack, 634
    fake news in, 2–4
    investigative, 617
    yellow, 613, 613
Judd, Ashley, 401

judicial activism, 255, 258–59, 261–62, 399 The idea that the Supreme Court should assert its interpretation of the law even if it overrules the elected executive and legislative branches of government.

judicial branch, 224–71
    Articles of Confederation on, 44, 49
    checks and balances with other branches, 7, 9, 64, 68–70, 228–30, 261–62
    congressional advice and consent on nominations to, 76
    Constitution on, 49, 226–27, 228, 229–30, 237, 243, 244
    exclusive powers of, 66
    historical development of, 226–29
    and political processes, 13
    relationship with other branches, 7, 9, 76–77, 258–62
    selection of judges in, 237–41
    and separation of powers, 7
    structure of, 233–41
    see also courts

judicial restraint, 255, 258–59 The idea that the Supreme Court should defer to the democratically elected executive and legislative branches of government rather than contradicting existing laws.

judicial review, 70, 227–30, 261–62 The Supreme Court's power to strike down a law or executive branch action that it finds unconstitutional.
    activism and restraint in, 255, 258–59, 261–62, 399

Judiciary Act (1789), 227, 229 The law in which Congress laid out the organization of the federal judiciary. The law refined and clarified federal court jurisdiction and set the original number of justices at six. It also created the office of the attorney general and established the lower federal courts.

jurisdiction, 233, 234, 243 The sphere of a court's legal authority to hear and decide cases.

latent opinion, 431 An opinion formed on the spot, when it is needed (as distinct from a deeply held opinion that is stable over time).

leaking, 338, 622–23 The practice in which someone in government provides nonpublic information to a reporter, with the aim of generating press coverage favorable to the leaker's aims.

Lemon test, 327, 328 The Supreme Court uses this test, established in *Lemon v. Kurtzman*, to determine whether a practice violates the First Amendment's establishment clause.

"Letter from Birmingham Jail" (King), 391, 393, A60–A70 A letter written by Martin Luther King Jr. in 1963 from his jail cell in Alabama as a response to a newspaper ad by White religious leaders telling King that the issue of civil rights should be argued in the courts and not in the streets. King's letter justified civil disobedience, saying that everyone has an obligation to follow just laws but also an equal obligation to break unjust laws.

as presidential election issue (2020), *575*
privacy rights of, 356
and same-sex marriage, *see* same-sex
marriage
and social movements, 389, 393
and sodomy laws, 258, 356, 405
and Stonewall uprising, 263, 380, *380*

libel, 339–40 Written false statements that
damage a person's reputation. They can be
regulated by the government but are often
difficult to distinguish from permissible
speech.

liberal, 20, 21, 35, 39, 114, 431 The side
of the ideological spectrum defined by
support for stronger government programs
and more market regulation; generally
associated with Democrats.
of Supreme Court justices, 249, 253–55,
258–59, 260, 261

liberal or conservative ideology, 431 A
way of describing political beliefs in terms
of a position on the spectrum running from
liberal to moderate to conservative.
and ideological polarization, 451–53, *452,*
453, 636–40
of Supreme Court justices, 239, 249,
253–55, 258–59, 260, 261

Libertarian Party, 499, *499,* 500

libertarians, 20–21, 35, 499, 500 Those
who prefer very limited government and
therefore tend to be conservative on issues
such as social welfare policy, environmental
policy, and government funding for education but liberal on issues involving personal
liberty such as free speech, abortion, and
the legalization of drugs.

liberty, 22, 24, 35, 47 Political freedom,
such as the freedom of speech, press,
assembly, and religion. These and other
legal and due process rights protecting
individuals from government control are
outlined in the Bill of Rights of the U.S.
Constitution.
Antifederalist concerns about, 59–60
and civil liberties, 314–69
and conflict resolution, 22–23

Libya, 191, 233
life expectancy, 384
Lilly Ledbetter Fair Pay Act, 236, 404
Limbaugh, Rush, 618, 627

limited government, 43, 465 A political
system in which the powers of the
government are restricted to prevent
tyranny by protecting property and
individual rights.

Lincoln, Abraham, 133, 185, 190, 374, 431,
617, *617*
Linick, Steve, 300

linkage institutions, 509, 517, 612 Institutions such as political parties, interest
groups, the media, and elections that are
channels through which individuals can
communicate their preferences to policy
makers.

Lipinski, Dan, 496, *559*
literacy tests for voting, 375
litigation strategies of interest groups,
534, *534*
Little Rock, Ark., 409

living Constitution, 72–77, 252, 256 A way
of interpreting the Constitution that takes
into account evolving national attitudes and
circumstances rather than the text alone.

loans, mortgage, *see* mortgages

lobbying, 514–55 Efforts to influence
public policy through contact with public
officials on behalf of an interest group.
Astroturf, 535–36
and collective action problems, 528–29
direct, 530–31, 539–40
gifts to Congress members in, 522
grassroots, 535–36
influence of, 540–45
inside strategies in, 530–31
iron triangles in, 524
outside strategies in, 530, 531–40
resources used in, 525–27
restrictions on, 522, 545–49
and revolving door, 522, 524
spending on, 518–21, 526, 539–40

local government:
balance of power with national government, 54–55, 93–97
citizen participation in, 114–16, 118
in cooperative federalism, 102–3
in daily life, 15
environmental policies of, 108
federal financial aid to, 105–8
in federalism, 7, 9, 54–55, 90, 91–92,
93–94, 96–97
responsibilities of, 91–92
Lochner v. New York, A156, A157
Locke, John, 47, *47,* 54
Lockett, Clayton, 354
Lockheed Martin Corporation, 274, 520

logrolling, 56–57, 151, 159 A form of
reciprocity in which members of Congress
support bills that they otherwise might not
vote for in exchange for other members'
votes on bills that are very important to them.

Long, Huey, 29, 30
Looking Glass for 1787, The (Doolittle), *60*
Lopez, Alfonso, 112
Lopez, United States v., 111, 112, 113, A76,
A78–A79, A80, A81, A158, A166
Loughlin, Lori, *231*
Louisiana, 232, 373, 399

Louisiana, Duncan v., 323
Louisiana, Ramos v., 323
Loving, Richard, 264
Loving v. Virginia, A139, A140, A151,
A152–A153, A156, A157
Lowey, Nita M., 173

Madison, James, 12, 52, 72, 320
at Annapolis Convention, 45
on Bill of Rights, 320–21
on common good, 131
on congressional power, 65
on constitutional amendments, 74
at Constitutional Convention, 50,
54, 55
on dual federalism, 97
on factions, 47–48, 50–52
Federalist Papers of, 42, 613, A11–A17,
A44–A47, A54
Gerry as vice president under, 146
on human nature, 7, 47–48
on liberty and conflict, 22
and *Marbury* case, 70, 228–29, 229
notes to Constitutional Convention, 42
on republicanism, 46
on role of government, 7, 47–48
on separation of church and state, 327
Madison, Marbury v., 70, 228–29, 229, A55,
A83–A85, *A87,* A88
Maine, 115, 446, 495, 556–58, 564, 565

Majority Leader, 154 The elected head of
the party holding the majority of seats in the
House or Senate.

majority opinion, 249 A court ruling on
which more than half of the members agree.
The ruling will present the decision of the
court and explain the retaking behind the
decision.

majority opinions, *250*
majority rule, 50–52

majority voting, 21, 561 A voting system
in which a candidate must win more than
50 percent of votes to win the election. If no
candidate wins enough votes to take office,
a runoff election is held between the top two
vote-getters.

Malloy v. Hogan, 323
Manchin, Joe, 594
Manning, Chelsea, 199, 338, *339*
Mapp, Dollree, 348, *348*
Mapp v. Ohio, 323, 348, A102–A103, A107,
A108, A115, A116
Marbury, William, 229

Marbury v. Madison, 70, 228–29, 229, A55,
A83–A85, *A87,* A88 The landmark case
in which the Supreme Court for the first
time declared that part of a law passed by
Congress was unconstitutional. This case
helped establish judicial review.

March for Our Lives, *344, 345, 629*
margin of error, 443, 444, 445
Margolies-Mezvinsky, Marjorie, 135
marijuana, 16, 115, 121, 539, *590*, 618
Marjory Stoneman Douglas High School, *113, 344,* 628, *629*
market forces on media coverage, 632–36

markup, 165 One of the steps through which a bill becomes a law, in which the final wording of the bill is determined.

marriage:
    interracial, 21, 375, 397
    same-sex, *see* same-sex marriage
Marshall, John, 70, 71, 73, 97–98, 99, 228–29, 229, 502
Marshall, Thurgood, 73, 248, 254, 395
Marsh v. Chambers, A99, A99
Martes, Francis, 349
Martin, Trayvon, 386
Maryland, 45, 57, 76, 97, 146, 148, 328, 395, 396
Maryland, Benton v., 323
Maryland, McCulloch v., 73, 76, 97, 98, A75, A77–A78, A80, A81
Mason, George, 42, 60, 320, 338
Massachusetts, 338, 618
    at Constitutional Convention, 53, 59
    health care in, 114, 116
    marijuana in, 115
    presidential campaign in (2020), 495
    ratification of Constitution, 61
    Shays's Rebellion in, 45–46
    slavery in, 57

mass associations, 525–26 Interest groups that have a large number of dues-paying individuals as members.

mass media, 612, 619, 632, 646–40
Sources that provide information to the average citizen, such as newspapers, television networks, radio stations, podcasts, and websites.
    see also media

mass protests, grassroots lobbying in, 535, *535*
mass shootings, 298, 343–45, 544
    media coverage of, 628–29, *629*

mass surveys, 71, 442–51 A way to measure public opinion by interviewing a relatively small sample of a large population.
    accuracy of, 25–26, 443, 446, 448–49, 464, 626
    media coverage of, 633–34
    reliability of, 27, 442, 444, 445, 446–48, 464, 626
    sample in, 442–43, 444, 445
    timing of, 449–51
    usefulness of, 428–30, *431*, 432, 449–51
    wording of questions in, 133, 444, 446, *446*, 447, 450, 464, 578

Masterpiece Cakeshop Ltd. v. Colorado Anti-Discrimination Commission, A140, *A140*

material benefits, 529 Benefits that are provided to individuals for joining a group, such as a coffee mug or a T-shirt, that are distinct from the collective benefits provided by the group.

Matthew Shepard and James Byrd Jr. Hate Crimes Prevention Act (2009), 409
Mayhew, David R., 138, 139, 478
McCain, John, 491, 524, 569, 570, 571, 601
McCain-Feingold Act, 246, 507, 583
McCarthy, Joe, 332
McCarthy, Kevin, *154*, 158, 212
McConnell, Mitch, *154*, 157, 163, 170, 173, 212, 307, 472, 474–75
McConnell, Pat Lyn, 263
McConnell v. FEC, A147, A149

McCulloch v. Maryland, 73, 76, 97, 98, A75, A77–A78, A80, A81 A landmark Supreme Court ruling in 1819 that Maryland did not have the power to tax the Second Bank of the United States and that Congress did have the power to create the Bank under the necessary and proper clause and the national supremacy clause.

McCutcheon v. Federal Election Commission, 583, 603
McDaniel, Ronna, 211

McDonald v. Chicago, 323, 344, A101, A106–A107, A107, A108 The Supreme Court ruled in 2010 that the Second Amendment's right to keep and bear arms for self-defense in one's home is applicable to the states through the Fourteenth Amendment.

McGahn, Donald, 170
McGovern, George, 358
McGowan, Rose, 401
McHenry, James, 60
McSally, Martha, *503*
Meadows, Mark, 203
media, 610–45
    advertising in, *see* advertising
    attack journalism in, 634
    broadcast, 613–14
    business of, 612–13, 632–36
    critical analysis of, 24–26
    equal time provision on, 614, *614*
    and fake news, 2–4, 24–28, 340, 612, 617, *617*, 626
    filtering of news in, 582, 624–25, 628–30
    framing of news in, 582, 628–30, 634–36
    and free press, 2, 320, 324, 338–39, 342, 622
    historical overview of, 612–14
    in horse race elections, 634
    influence on audience, 623–31
    interest group coverage in, 538–39
    Internet sources of political information in, 299, 614–17, *616*
    leaks of information in, 338, 622–23, *622*
    market forces on, 632–36

politician strategies on, 619–21
poll results reported in, 634
pressures and legal limits on, 621–23
priming of news in, 624–25
publishing process in, 625
regulation and deregulation of, 613–14
reliability of news in, 582, 635, 640
role in democracy, 631, 640
social, *see* social media
as watchdog, 610–13, 640
Media Checklist for Assessing Reporting on Politics, 27

media conglomerates, 614, 615 Companies that control a large number of media sources across several types of media outlets.

media effects, 623–26 The influence of media coverage on average citizens' opinions and actions.

Medicaid:
    and Affordable Care Act, 109–10, 113, 119, 120
    block grants in, 108
    creation of, 187
    federal funds in, 104, 105–8, 109–10, 113, 257
    and fiscal federalism, 104, 105–8
    state role in, 105–8, 109–10, 113
Medicare, 119, 574
    creation of, 187
    prescription drug benefits in, *283, 542*
    reform of, 474
    spending on, 104
Medicare for All, 474
Meehan, Marty, 601
melting pot image, 18–19
Menendez, Bob, 217
mental impairment, death penalty in, 354
Merkel, Angela, 349
Mexican Americans, 377–78
Mexican-American War, 185, 191, 377
Mexico-U.S. border, 461
    National Guard at, 191
    wall proposed for, 69, 130, 167, 184, 212, 218, 474, 485
Michael M. v. Superior Court, 403
Michigan, 115
    affirmative action in, 414, 415, 422
    presidential election in (2016), 446, 499, 626
    presidential election in (2020), 567, *568*, 596, 600
    senatorial election in (2020), 446
    water supply in, 385–86
Microsoft, 526, 542
Milano, Alyssa, 401
military:
    African Americans in, 376
    bureaucracy role in, 279
    and conscientious objectors, 329
    desegregation of, 207
    drone aircraft in, 200, 201
    in federalism, 94
    as government function, 7, *8*, 94

Nazi marchers, 337, 363
NBC broadcast network, 614
Near v. Minnesota, 323
Nebraska, 354, 565

necessary and proper clause, 63, 71, 94
Part of Article I, Section 8, of the Constitution that grants Congress the power to pass all laws related to its expressed powers; also known as the elastic clause.

negative partisanship, 485 Identification with a political party that is based on dislike of the other party rather than positive feelings about the party identified with.

Neguse, Joe, 128
Nelson, Gaylord, 359
Netflix, 542
net neutrality, 542
Neustadt, Richard, 188
Nevada, 564
    marijuana in, 115
    mass shooting in, 344, 544
    presidential campaign and election in (2020), 495, 564, 597
Nevada Department of Human Resources v. Hibbs, 111
New Deal, 28
    bureaucracy growth in, 285–86, 286
    and federal government power, 103, 108, 133
    and party system, 477, 478
    and presidential power, 186, 186
    and Supreme Court, 69, 72, 77, 230, 238, 256, 258
New Hampshire, 57, 61, 495, 564
New Jersey, 57, 243
New Jersey, T.L.O. v., A114, A115

New Jersey Plan, 52, 53, 74 A plan that was suggested in response to the Virginia Plan; smaller states at the Constitutional Convention proposed that each state should receive equal representation in the national legislature, regardless of size.

news, political information in, *see* political information
newspapers:
    circulation trends, 615
    historical role of, 610
    leaking information to, 622–23
    market forces on, 632–36
    media conglomerates in, 614, 615
    recent changes in, 617
    and yellow journalism, 613
Newtown, Conn., Sandy Hook Elementary School in, 344
New York, 45, 54, 91, 477, 567
    Antifederalists in, 60
    at Constitutional Convention, 59
    Ellis Island dispute with New Jersey, 243
    interstate commerce in, 98, 98
    public prayer in, 327
    ratification of Constitution, 61–62, 61

slavery in, 57
Stonewall uprising in, 380, 380
"stop-and-frisk" policy in, 370, 386
New York, Gitlow v., 322, 323
New York, Lochner v., A156, A157
New York Post, 596, 616, 630
New York Sun, 613
New York Times, 224, 338, 350, 613, 616, 637, 640

New York Times Co. v. United States, 338, A91–A92, A92 The Supreme Court ruled in 1971 that the government could not prevent the publication of the Pentagon Papers, which revealed lies about the progress of the war in Vietnam.

New York Tribune, 613
Nexstar, 614
NextGen Climate Action, 538
Ney, Bob, 547
Nickles, Don, 264
1984 (Orwell), 350
Nineteenth Amendment, 19, 74, 75, 379, 389
Ninth Amendment, 321, 323, 355
Ninth Circuit Court, 236
Nixon, Richard, 257, 304, 504–6, 601
    affirmative action program of, 409, 412
    approval rating of, 211
    court nominations of, 239
    Endangered Species Act and, 358–62
    executive privilege of, 199, 200
    presidential power of, 187
    public opinion on, 453
    resignation of, 209
Nixon, United States v., 199, 200, A83, A85–A86, A87, A87
Noah, Trevor, 614

nominating conventions, 493, 494, 562–64 A meeting held by each party every four years at which states' delegates select the party's presidential and vice-presidential nominees and approve the party platform.

nongovernmental organizations, 196
nonpartisan primary, 477
nonviolent protests, 390–93

norms, 21, 35 Unwritten rules and informal agreements among citizens and elected officials about how government and society should operate.

North American Free Trade Agreement (NAFTA), 187
North Carolina:
    civil rights movement in, 390
    presidential campaign in (2020), 495
    presidential election in (2020), 567
    ratification of Constitution, 61, 62
    slavery in, 57
    social media restrictions for sex offenders in, 336
    voting districts in, 146, 149, 149, 399

North Dakota, 355
Northern Securities Company, 185
North Korea:
    nuclear weapons of, 66
    and Trump, 66, 196, 206

notice-and-comment procedure, 275–78, 283, 300 A step in the rule-making process in which proposed rules are published in the *Federal Register* and made available for debate by the general public.

NSA (National Security Agency), 349–50, 356, 622
nuclear technology:
    campaign ad on, 580, 580
    of Iran, 195, 533, 575
    of North Korea, 66

Obama, Barack, 32
    Affordable Care Act of, *see* Affordable Care Act
    appointments and nominations of, 66, 190, 224, 238, 239–40, 240, 241, 253, 265, 300, 524
    bureaucracy under, 287, 293, 298
    campaign strategies of, 435
    citizenship of, 428, 429, 464
    as commander in chief, 191
    and congressional elections, 157–58
    DACA program of, 128, 132, 459–63
    and Dakota Access Pipeline, 394
    on discriminatory treatment, 386
    and divided government, 69, 498
    and drone attacks, 200, 201
    economy under, 570, 571
    electoral votes for, 569
    environmental policies of, 95, 108, 193, 195, 277, 303–7, 518, 631
    executive orders of, 76, 194, 207, 214–18, 593
    executive privilege of, 200
    fake news on, 3, 617
    and Flint water crisis, 386
    foreign policy of, 195–96, 196, 214–18
    on freedom of speech, 316
    and gay rights, 262–65, 380, 381, 410, 411
    on gender pay disparities, 404
    going public, 212
    and government shutdowns, 158
    and Guantánamo Bay detention center, 65, 70
    and gun laws, 212, 345, 631
    on hate crimes, 409
    historic candidacy of, 184
    immigration policies of, 190, 207, 411, 416–17, 459–63
    and marijuana laws, 115
    media coverage of, 627–28, 631
    and national debt, 167
    pardons by, 199, 338
    presidential power of, 188
    public opinion on, 211, 428, 429, 438, 439, 440, 442, 448–49, 454, 456
    and Republican filibusters, 168

party organization, 474–75, 478, 479–81, 508 A specific political party's leaders and workers at the national, state, and local levels.

party platform, 496, 502, 508, 559, 565, 574–76 A set of objectives outlining the party's issue positions and priorities. Candidates are not required to support their party's platform.

party principle, 476 The idea that a political party exists as an organization distinct from its elected officials or party leaders.

party system, 474–76 Periods in which the names of the major political parties, their supporters, and the issues dividing them have remained relatively stable.
    realignments in, 478–79

party unity, 155, 156 The extent to which members of Congress in the same party vote together on party votes.

party votes, 155, 156 A vote in which the majority of one party opposes the position of the majority of the other party.

Pastore, John O., 505
Patrick, Dennis R., 639
Patriot Act (2001), 77–81, 166, 346–47
pay gap for women, 20, 236, 401–4, *404*
PBS NewsHour, 634
Peace Corps, 207

peak associations, *517, 525* Interest groups whose members are businesses or other organizations rather than individuals.

Pearl Harbor bombing, 67
Pecos River Compact, 243, *243*
Pelosi, Nancy, 4, 40, 119, 152, *154*, 158, 171, *472*, 475, 594, 617
Peña-Rodriguez, Miguel, 353
Pence, Mike, 190, 203–4, *204*, 212
Pendleton Civil Service Act (1883), 285
Pennsylvania, 46, *377*
    at Constitutional Convention, 59, 320
    presidential election of 2016 in, 446, 499, 626
    presidential election of 2020 in, 567, 568, *568*, 569, 596, 597, 600
    redistricting in, 146, 148
    slavery in, 57
    special election in (2018), 570–72
Pentagon Papers, 338
People for the Ethical Treatment of Animals (PETA), *526*
per curiam opinions, *250*
Perez, Jorge Luis Garcia, 217
Perez, Tom, 475, 481
performance-enhancing drugs, 348–49
Pericles, 15

permanent campaign, 133, 573 The continual quest for reelection that is rooted in high-cost professional campaigns that are increasingly reliant on consultants and expensive media campaigns.

Perot, Ross, 500
Perry, James L., 294
Perry, Rick, 110
Persian Gulf War, 187
Pew Research Center, 292, 445, 476, 632
peyote in religious ceremonies, 330
pharmaceutical industry, *520*, 542
Pharmaceutical Research and Manufacturers of America, *520*, 537, 542
Phillips, Jack, *329*
phone use:
    privacy and security in, 79–81, *346*, 347–48
    surveillance of, 79–81, 349–50
Photoshop, 25

picket fence federalism, 96, 102–3, *104*, 108 A more refined and realistic form of cooperative federalism in which policy makers within a particular policy area work together across the levels of government.

Pierce, Franklin, 185
Pinckney, Charles, 320

plaintiff, 231 The person or party who brings a case to court.

Planned Parenthood, 354–55, 535, 617, *617*
Planned Parenthood of Southeastern Pennsylvania v. Casey, A133, A134–A136, A140, A155, A156, *A156*

plea bargains and settlement agreements, 231, 231–32 Agreements between a plaintiff and a defendant to settle a case before it goes to trial or the verdict is decided. In a civil case, this usually involves an admission of guilt and an agreement on monetary damages; in a criminal case, this often involves an admission of guilt in return for a reduced charge or sentence.

Pledge of Allegiance, 244

***Plessy v. Ferguson*, 375, 396, A117, A120, A123** The 1896 Supreme Court ruling that state-imposed racial segregation did not violate the Fourteenth Amendment as long as the public facilities were "separate but equal."

pluralism, 52, 518 The idea that having a variety of parties and interests within a government will strengthen the system, ensuring that no group possesses total control.

pluralist democracy, 35, 37–38 A model of representative democracy in which

organized groups compete with other to influence policy and no single group dominates the political process.

plurality opinions, *250*

plurality voting, 21, 500, 561 A voting system in which the candidate who receives the most votes within a geographic area wins the election, regardless of whether that candidate wins a majority (more than half) of the votes.

pocket veto, 166, 196–97, *197*, 198, A28 The automatic death of a bill passed by the House and Senate when the president fails to sign the bill in the last 10 days of a legislative session.

Podesta, John, 623
Pod Save America, 616
Pointer v. Texas, 323
polarization, ideological, *see* ideological polarization
police, 7, *8*, 108
    brutality against minorities by, 596
    interrogations of, 351
    racial profiling by, 370–72, 386
    reform of, 599
    shooting of African Americans, 4, 386–87, *388*, 394, *535*

police patrol oversight, 170, 300–301 A method of oversight in which members of Congress constantly monitor the bureaucracy to make sure that laws are implemented correctly.

police powers, 91 The power to enforce laws and provide for public safety.

policy making, seven stages of, 26–28

policy mood, 456–58 The level of public support for expanding the government's role in society; whether the public wants government action on a specific issue.

political action committees (PACs), 480, 536–38 An interest group or a division of an interest group that can raise money to contribute to campaigns or to spend on ads in support of candidates. The amount a PAC can receive from each of its donors and the amount it can spend on federal electioneering are strictly limited.
    in campaign financing, 480, 493, 506–7, 536–38, *537*, 583, *583*, 584, *584*
    party affiliation of, 480
    and Super PACs, 536–38, *537*, *538*, 584

political appointees, 274 People selected by an elected leader, such as the president, to hold a government position.

political equality, 23, 48

on original meaning of Constitution, 73
party unity in, *155*, 156
party votes in, *155*, 156
platform of, 496, 574–75, *575*
policy priorities in, *482*, 483, 487, 496,
497, 501–2
in presidential election (2016), 490, 491,
496
in presidential election (2020), 17
public opinion in, 439–41, 448, 464
racial, gender, and ethnic identity in, 18
recruiting and nominating election
candidates from, 490–93, *494*, 564–65
in redistricting, 146, 147, 148
in "red states," 16, 17
reelection of incumbents in, 140–41,
144–45, 591, *592*
on slavery, 476
on state and local power, 55
on unfunded mandates, 105
views on Trump, 4–5
and voter ID laws, 562
research by interest groups, 531

reserved powers, 55, 96, 99, 110, 321 As
defined in the Tenth Amendment, powers
that are not given to the national government by the Constitution, or not prohibited to the states, are reserved by the states or the
people.

residency requirement for citizenship,
400–401
Resistbot, 525–26
resolutions, 161, *164*, 165–66
restraint, judicial, 255, 258–59
retirement, of incumbents, 572–73

retrospective voting, 605 Voting based
on the past voting record of a candidate or
political party.

Revels, Hiram, *375*
reverse discrimination, 372, 412–14,
415, 422
Revolutionary War, 67, 612
and Articles of Confederation, 43, *43*

**revolving door, 282, 522, 524, 546,
548** The movement of individuals from
government positions to jobs with interest
groups or lobbying firms, and vice versa.

*R.G. & G.R. Harris Funeral Home Inc. v.
Equal Employment Opportunity Commission*, 406
Rhode Island, 44, 52, 57, 59, *61*, 62
Richie, Nicole, 342
Rigell, Scott, 549
rights:
Antifederalist concerns about, 59–60
to bear arms, 343–45
Bill of Rights on, *see* Bill of Rights
civil, *see* civil rights
of defendants, 345–54
of minority in majority rule, 50–52

natural, 47
in republicanism, 46–48
of states, 99–101, 102–3, 110–13, 114
voting, *see* voting rights
"rights revolution," 108
Riley v. California, A110, A114–A115, *A115*
Risen, James, 338
roadblocks, warrantless searches in, 347
Roberts, John G., Jr., 170, 224–26, 240, 248,
249, *249*, 254, 255, 258–59, *258*, 261, 265
Robinson, Jackie, 376
Robinson v. California, 323
Rodiles, Antonio, 217
Rodriguez, Alex, 349

***Roe v. Wade*, 249, 257, 258, 355–56, 357,
408, A110, A111–A112, *A115*, A133–A136,
A140, A151, A155, *A156*** This 1973 Supreme
Court case extended the right of privacy,
through the application of the Fourteenth
Amendment's due process clause, to a
woman's decision to have an abortion while
recognizing legitimate state interests in
potential life and maternal health. The
Court noted that the "relative weight of each
of these interests varies over the course of
pregnancy, and the law must account for
this variability."

Rogers, Will, 481, 618
Rohingya people, oppression of, 431

roll call vote, 156 A recorded vote on legislation; members may vote "yes," "no," or
"present," or they may abstain.

Romney, Mitt, 2, 42, 209, 378, 490, 491, 569,
571, 598
Roof, Dylann, 388, *388*
Roosevelt, Eleanor, 505
Roosevelt, Franklin Delano, 28–31, 69, 186,
186, 238, *286*, 477, 478
New Deal programs of, *see* New Deal
Roosevelt, Theodore, 118, 119, 185, 358
Rose, Charlie, 401
Rosen, Jeff, 336
Ross, Gary, 410
Rubio, Marco, 217
Rule of Four, 243

rule of law, 128, 226, 465 The authority of
law to restrict people's behavior equally for
the common good.

rules and procedures in political processes,
11, 14
constitutional, 40–87
Rules Committee, 159, 166, 168
Rumsfeld, Hamdan v., 65

runoff elections, 558, 561 Under a majority
voting system, a second election is held only
if no candidate wins a majority of the votes
in the first general election. Only the top two
vote-getters in the first election compete in
the runoff.

Russia, 93
authoritarian government in, 22
interference in 2016 presidential
election, 2, 169–70, 184, 199–201, 207,
208, *208*
sanctions on, 207–8, *208*, 212
and Trump, 25, 66, 69, 76, 82, 206, 207–8,
208, 212
Rutledge, John, 227
Ryan, Paul, 152, 158

Sagan, Carl, 25

salience, 532–44 The level of familiarity
with an interest group's goals in the general
population.

Sallie Mae, *517*
same-sex marriage, 110, 256, 381, 405,
409, 411
political conflicts on, *10*, 16, 21, 478
public opinion on, 434, *435*
religious opposition to, 325, 329, 330
Supreme Court ruling on, *10*, 94, *94*, 262,
263, 265

sample, 442 Within a population, the
group of people surveyed in order to gauge
the whole population's opinion. Researchers use samples because it would be impossible to interview the entire population.
random, 443, 444, 446
size of, 443, 444, 445

sampling error, 443, 444, 445 The
predicted difference between the average
opinion expressed by survey respondents
and the average opinion in the population,
sometimes called the *margin of error*.
Increasing the number of respondents
lowers the sampling error.

Sanders, Bernie, 472, 474, 540, 564
on health insurance, 575
as presidential candidate (2016), 490,
492, 629
as presidential candidate (2020), 473,
495, 560, 575, 595
Sandford, Dred Scott v., 98, 99–100, *100*,
229, 321, 374, A88
Sandy Hook Elementary School, 344
Santa Fe Independent School District v. Doe,
A96, *A99*
Saturday Night Live, 614
Scalia, Antonin, 230, 239, 240, 248, 254, 255,
347, 405
Schattschneider, E. E., 10
Scheindlin, Shira A., 370
Schenck, Charles, 331–32

***Schenck v. United States*, 331–32, A89–
A90, A92, A93** The 1919 Supreme Court
ruling that Charles Schenck's protests
against World War I were not protected by
the First Amendment because they posed a
"clear and present danger... that Congress
has a right to prevent."

slander, 339–40 Spoken false statements that damage a person's reputation. They can be regulated by the government but are often difficult to distinguish from permissible speech.

Slants (rock band), 341, *341*
Slaughter, Louise, 640
slavery, 23, 103, 373–75, 381
    and Civil War, 58, *58*, 99, 374
    and Civil War amendments, 322, 375
    as Constitutional Convention issue, *51,*
        56–59, *56*
    and *Dred Scott* decision, *98*, 99–100,
        100, 229, 374
    as "original sin," *56*, 57
    political party views on, 476
    and presidential power, 185
    state differences in, *51*, 56–59, 99
    Three-Fifths Compromise on, 55, 56
Smith, Ali, 633
snake handling in religious practice, 317,
    318, 326
SNAP (Supplemental Nutrition Assistance
    Program), 288
SNCC (Student Nonviolent Coordinating
    Committee), 390
Snowden, Edward, 349, 622–23

social contract, 83, A1 A concept developed by political philosophers of the eighteenth century that defined the legitimacy of the state. The people recognize the authority of the state to govern over them, and, in turn, the government protects the rights and freedoms of the people.

socialization, political, 433
social media, 610–12
    fake news on, 2–4, *635*
    interest group use of, 535–36
    political information on, 24–25, 612, 615,
        616–19, 622, 635, 640
    speech restrictions on, 336
social movements on civil rights, 389–94
social networks in political socialization, 433
social policy, in poverty and income
    inequality, 458
Social Security, 4, 8, 28–33, 286, 574
    public opinion on, 458
socioeconomic indicators of inequality,
    384–86
    and affirmative action programs, 412
    and political equality, 48
sodomy laws, 258, 356, 405

soft money, 335, 584, 600–603 Contributions that can be used for voter mobilization or to promote a policy proposal or point of view as long as these efforts are not tied to supporting or opposing a particular candidate.

soft news, 634, 640 Media coverage that aims to entertain or shock, often through sensationalized reporting or by focusing on a candidate or politician's personality.

Soleimani, Qasem, 191

solicitor general, 246, 247 A presidential appointee in the Justice Department who conducts all litigation on behalf of the federal government before the Supreme Court and supervises litigation in the federal appellate courts.

solidary benefits, 529 Satisfaction derived from the experience of working with like-minded people, even if the group's efforts do not achieve the desired impact.

Somalia, 279
Sons of Confederate Veterans, 334
Sotomayor, Sonia, 240, 248, 254, 255, *258*,
    348, 410
source analysis, xxxix–xl, 37
Souter, David, 254, 255
South Carolina, 53
    active shooter incidents in, 344
    civil rights movement in, 390
    hate crimes in, 388, *388*
    immigration policies in, 416
    police shooting of unarmed Blacks in,
        386, *388*
    presidential primary elections in, 495,
        564, 595
    senatorial election in (2020), 446
    slavery in, *57*, 373
Southern Poverty Law Center, 334
southern states:
    civil rights in, 117, 389–93
    group identity in, 434
    Jim Crow laws in, 101, *101*, 375–76
    in New Deal era, 286
    party identification in, 476–79, 487
    school desegregation in, 396
    slavery in, 56–59, 373–75
    voting rights of African Americans in,
        375, 406
    see also specific states
sovereign immunity of states, 112

sovereign power, 90 The supreme power of an independent state to regulate its internal affairs without foreign interference.

Soviet Union, 93
Spacey, Kevin, 401
Spanish-American War, 191

Speaker of the House, 152–54 The elected leader of the House of Representatives.

Speakes, Larry, 620
speech, freedom of, 77, 314–16, 318, 322, 324,
    331–43
    in campaigns, 334–35, 506, 586
    clear and present danger test in, 332
    in commercial speech, 341, *341*
    in controversial speech on college
        campuses, 108–10, 152, 314–16, 363
    direct incitement test in, 332
    and fighting words, 339

    in free press, 338–39
    generally protected expression in,
        331–43
    in hate speech, 314, 335–36
    intermediate scrutiny in, 331, 335
    on Internet, 336
    limits to, 318
    in money as speech, 334–35
    and obscenity, 341–42
    in political speech, 331–33, 334–35
    public opinion on, 436, *436*
    and slander or libel, 339–40
    standards for protection in, 331
    strict scrutiny in, 331
    in symbolic speech, 333–34
    Trump on, 314
speedy trial, right to, 353
Spencer, Richard, 314, 337–38, 363
spending:
    on campaigns, 141, 504–7, 584, 586, 587
    congressional authority over, 63, 68
    in lobbying, 518–21, 526, 539–40
    pork barrel, *see* pork barrel
    public opinion on, 431, 441, 448,
        456, *456*
    state and local, *117*
Spirit of the Laws, The (Montesquieu), 47

split tickets, 591 A ballot on which a voter selects candidates from more than one political party.

splitting the difference, 56–57

spoils system, 284, 285, 476 The practice of rewarding party supporters with benefits like federal government positions.

sports:
    African-American athletes in, 376
    kneeling during national anthem in,
        394, 411
    performance-enhancing drugs in,
        348–49
    Senate resolution honoring team in,
        161, *164*
    Title IX on sex discrimination in, *399*, 408
Stamp Act (1765), 42

standard operating procedures (SOPs), 282, 284, 303 Rules that lower-level bureaucrats must follow when implementing policies.

standing, 233, 244 Legitimate justification for bringing a civil case to court.

standing committees, 158 Committees that are a permanent part of the House or Senate structure, holding more importance and authority than other committees.

Standing Rock Indian Reservation,
    393–94, *394*
"stand your ground" laws, 344
Stanton, Elizabeth Cady, 389

trade policies (*Continued*)
 Constitutional Convention compromises on, *51*
 economic interests in, 48–49
 in federalism, 93–94, 96, 98, *98*
 in intrastate and interstate commerce, 72, 96, 101
 as presidential election issue (2020), 575
 Supreme Court on, 98, *98*, 101
 tariffs in, *see* tariffs
 of Trump, 4–5, 184
Trail of Tears, 376
Train, Russell E., 359, 360
transgender people, 381, 405–6, 410, *410*, 411
 see also LGBTQ people
Trans-Pacific Partnership (TPP), 66
Transportation Department, 289–90, *289*, *291*
Transportation Security Administration, 280
travel ban of Trump, 65, 66, 70, 76, 82, 208–9, *209*, 211, 212, 400, 414–16, 446, *447*
Treasury Department, 189, 207, 284, 289
treaties, 94, 195
Treaty of Paris (1783), 44
trials, 345
 discovery process in, 232
 and double jeopardy, 352
 evidence in, 108, 348, 351
 fair and speedy, 353, *353*
 for illegal immigrants, 191
 by jury, 60, 321, 353, 379–80
 plea bargaining in, 231–32, *231*
 Seventh Amendment on, *321*, *323*
 Sixth Amendment on, *321*, *323*, 338, 353
 for suspected terrorists, 70, *353*
Trinity Lutheran Church of Columbia v. Comer, A138, A140
Troubled Asset Relief Program (TARP), 135
Truman, Harry, 186, 209, 349, 376, 409, 573, 615
Trump, Donald, 5, 32, 33, 163, *183*, 253, 272, 273, *515*, *538*, 559, *577*
 appointments and nominations of, 170, 189–90, 218, 241, *241*, 297, 298, 300, *300*, 301–2
 approval rating of, 25, 211, *211*, *213*, 214, 218, 570, 595, 596
 and athletes kneeling during national anthem, 394
 baseless allegations of election fraud by, 596, 597, 600
 border wall proposal of, 69, 130, 167, 184, 212, 218, 474, 485
 bureaucracy under, 293
 campaigning for congressional candidates, 144, 158, *158*, 542, 556
 on civil rights issues, 411
 as commander in chief, 191
 and Constitution, 40–42, 81–82
 COVID-19 contracted by, 595, 596
 on DACA program, 128–30, 132, 176, 463
 and Dakota Access Pipeline, 394
 debate positions of, 579
 drone attacks deployed by, 201

 economic policies of, 573
 education policies of, *109*
 electoral votes for, *569*
 and emoluments clause, 5, 65, 169
 environmental policies of, 66, 82, 88–90, 91, 94, 95, 97, 108, 121, 182, 193, 195, 277, 279, 298, 299, 303–7, 518, 593
 and equal time provision on media, 614, *614*
 Executive Office staff of, 203, *203*
 executive orders of, 190–91, 194, 207, 214, 217–18
 and fake news, 2–4, 25, 340, 617, 626–27
 and federal bureaucracy, 194–96, 274, 279, 287, 307–8
 federal court nominations of, 239
 on flag protection, 334
 foreign policy of, 66, 195–96, 217–18, 219, 438
 on freedom of speech, 314
 and gender politics, 20
 Ginsburg comments on, 224, 226, 260, 265–66
 going public, 212–14
 and Guantánamo Bay detention center, 65
 and gun laws, 345
 on health insurance, 12–13, 82, 184, 214, 448
 and Hurricane Dorian, 212–14, *213*
 and ideological polarization, 411
 immigration policies of, 82, 109, 128–30, 132, 182, 190–91, 207, 208–9, *209*, 211, 212–14, 411, 414–17, *417*, 463, 474, 497–98, 575, 593, 596
 impeachment of, 4–5, 40–42, *157*, 170, 184, 193, 200, *200*, 203, 208, 209–10, 442, 474, 475, 497–98, 631
 Internet information on, 615–16
 interpretation and implementation of laws by, 207–8
 on Iran nuclear deal, 66, 533
 and Justice Department, 66, 170, 184, 207, 338
 Latino support of, 378
 and leaks to press, 338, 622
 legislative priorities of, 497–98
 on LGBTQ rights, 259, 260, 381, 410
 on libel laws, 340
 lobbying in opposition to, 525–26, 535
 lobbying policies of, 522, 524, 540
 loyalty to, 297
 and marijuana laws, 115
 media coverage on, 25, 578, 627–28, 632, 634
 media strategies of, 132, 620–21, *621*
 midterm congressional elections as referendum on (2018), 503, *503*, 593–94
 negative campaigning against, 578–79
 news sources used by supporters of, 618, *618*
 and North Korea, 66, 196
 pardons granted by, 66, 199
 as party leader, 211–12
 policy agenda of, 55
 political party of, 472, 474, 475, 481, 490, 491, 496

 in presidential campaign and election (2016), *see* presidential campaign and election of 2016
 in presidential campaign and election (2020), *see* presidential campaign and election of 2020
 presidential power of, 40–42, 70, 182–84, 187, 206, 207, 214, 218, 272
 on profiling, 370
 progressive movement in response to, 523
 public opinion on, 25, 144–45, 212–14, *213*, 214, 218, 437, 438, 439, *440*, 442, 443, 446, 448–49, *454*, *459*, 464, 485, 572, 593–94
 rallies of, 212–14, 437, 565, 626
 regulations repealed by, 182, 214, 218, 279, 596
 Republican opposition to, 211–12, 490, 491, 501, 593
 response to COVID-19 pandemic, 171–75, 182–84, *189*, 190, 206, 211, 272, 291, 301, 307–8, 437, 438, *503*, 570, 573, 579, 581, 595, 596
 and Russia, 25, 66, 69, 76, 82, 207–8, *208*, 212
 on Supreme Court decisions, 259, 260
 Supreme Court nominations of, 23–24, *67*, 190, 225, *237*, 240–41, *240*, 260, 556, 593
 and Syria, 66, 68
 tax policies of, 182, 211, 438, 498, 502, 514–16, *514*, 534, 549–50, 593, 596
 tax returns of, 170
 trade policies of, 66, 184, 438, 593
 travel ban of, 65, 66, 70, 76, 82, 208–9, *209*, 211, 212, 400, 414–16, 446, *447*
 Twitter use of, 212, 582, 596, 620–21, *621*
 unified government of, 214, 218
 unilateral actions of, 207, *207*, 208–10, *209*, 211, 212, 214, 218
 vetoes from, *197*, *199*
 on voting by mail, 136
 and Women's March, 393
Trump, Ivanka, 203, *203*
Trump, Melania, 340, 595, 634
Trump University, 239

trustee, 135–36 A member of Congress who represents constituents' interests while also taking into account national, collective, and moral concerns that sometimes cause the member to vote against the preference of a majority of constituents.

Truth, Sojourner, 389
Tubman, Harriet, *374*

turkey farms, 296–97 Agencies to which campaign workers and donors can be appointed in reward for their service because it is unlikely that their lack of qualifications will lead to bad policy.

Twain, Mark, 135
Tweed, William "Boss," 477
Twelfth Amendment, 55, 74
Twenty-First Amendment, 74

Twenty-Second Amendment, 219 "No person shall be elected to the office of the President more than twice, and no person who has held the office of President or acted as President, for more than two years of a term to which some other person was elected President shall be elected to the office of the President more than once. This constitutional amendment limits presidential power.

Twitter, 3, 5, 24, 33, 132, 158, 212, 336, 640
    interest group use of, 536
    political information on, 615, 616
    Trump use of, 212, 582, 596, 620-21, 621
Tyler, John, 185

Ukraine, 40, 170, 200, 208, 209, 581, 610, 622, 640
unalienable rights, 47

unanimous consent agreement, 49, 168, 169, A33 Agreement reached by party leaders in the Senate to limit debate and the consideration of amendments on legislation.

Underground Railroad, 374, 374
Underwood, Lauren, 143
unemployment benefits, 329
unemployment rate, 186, 384, 448-49, 458, 570
    in COVID-19 pandemic, 172-75, 595
    in Great Depression, 186, 477
    of Native Americans, 377
Unfunded Mandate Reform Act (1995), 105, 418

unfunded mandates, 105, 109, 418 Federal laws that require the states to do certain things but do not provide state governments with funding to implement these policies.

unified government, 69, 214, 218, 483, 498, 559 A situation in which one party holds a majority of seats in the House and Senate and the president is a member of that same party.

unilateral action, presidential, 206-7, 207, 214, 218 Any policy decision made and acted upon by the president and presidential staff without the explicit approval or consent of Congress.

Union League, 375

unitary executive theory, 207 The idea that the vesting clause of the Constitution gives the president the authority to issue orders and policy directives that cannot be undone by Congress.

unitary government, 9, 93 A system in which the national, centralized government holds ultimate authority. It is the most common form of government in the world.

United Arab Emirates, 22
United Farm Workers Union, 377
United Kingdom, 9, 92-93, 344
United Nations (UN), 186
United States, Heart of Atlanta Motel v., A75, A80, A158, A160-A161, A166, A167
United States, New York Times Co. v., 338, 338, A91-A92, A92
United States, Schenck v., 331-32, A89-A90, A92, A93
United States v. Bond, 111

***United States v. Lopez*, 111, 112, 113, A76, A78-A79, A80, A81, A158, A166** A 1995 Supreme Court case that struck down a federal law regulating the possession of firearms around schools. It was the first time that the Court had restricted Congress's power to pass legislation under the commerce clause since the New Deal in the 1930s.

United States v. Morrison, 111, A76, A79-A80, A80, A81
United States v. Nixon, 199, 200, A83, A85-A86, A87, A87
United States v. Virginia, 403, A119, A123, A151, A153-A154, A156, A157
United States v. Windsor, 111, A138, A140
"Unite the Right" rally and violence in Virginia, 334, 337
universalism, 151
University of California, 314, 315, 323, 413
University of Florida, 314, 337
University of Maryland, 395
University of Michigan, 255, 403, 414, 415, 422
University of Missouri, 335
University of Texas, 403, 414, 415, 422
University of Texas, Fisher v., 403, 415, A131-A132, A131
University of Wisconsin, 335
Unorthodox Lawmaking (Sinclair), 160
unreasonable searches and seizures, 345-50
USA Patriot Act (2001), 77-81, 166, 346-47
Utah, 416, 490, 495

values, cultural, and political conflicts, 16-18
Van Buren, Martin, 185
Velázquez, Nydia, 128, 129
Venable, Josh, 556
Verizon, 349, 542
Vermont, 57, 115, 495
Vernonia School District v. Acton, A113, A114, A115

vesting clause, 188 Article II, Section 1, of the Constitution, which states: "The executive Power shall be vested in a President of the United States of America," making the president both the head of government and the head of state.

Veterans Affairs Department, 288, 289, 291
Veterans of Foreign Wars, 140, 333

veto, 69, 166, 196-99, 206, 497 The president's rejection of a bill that has been passed by Congress. A veto can be overridden by a two-thirds vote in both the House and Senate.

vice president, 203-4
    election of, 55, 559, 560
    impeachment of, 68, 170, 209
    nomination of candidates for, 493, 494, 565
    as Senate president, 154, 190, 203
Victory Fund, 538
video games, violent, 342, 343
Vietnam War, 67-68, 187, 338, 453
    protests against, 253, 333-34, 393
viewpoint discrimination, 336
Vindman, Alexander, 209
violence:
    in fighting words, 339
    gun-related, 343-45, 640
    in video games, 342, 343
Violence Against Women Act (1994), 112-13, 408
Virginia, 45-46, 58, 61
    cross burning in, 336
    presidential campaign in (2020), 495
    slavery in, 57
    "Unite the Right" rally and violence in, 334, 337, 411
    voting districts in, 399
Virginia, Loving v., A139, A140, A151, A152-A153, A156, A157
Virginia, United States v., 403, A119, A123, A151, A153-A154, A156, A157
Virginia Military Institute, 400, 403

Virginia Plan, 52, 53, 74 A plan proposed by the larger states during the Constitutional Convention that based representation in the national legislature on population. The plan also included a variety of other proposals to strengthen the national government.

Vitale, Engel v., 327, A95-A97, A99, A100
vote counting, 561-62, 565-68
    recounts in, 561-62, 568
voter turnout, 560, 570, 572, 577-78, 588-89, 588, 593
    of African Americans, 382-83, 383, 406, 446, 589, 594
    in midterm congressional elections (2018), 588, 589
    in presidential elections, 382-83, 383, 446, 588-89, 588, 594, 626-27
voting, 588-92
    absentee, 560, 589
    access to, 382-84, 562
    accountability of incumbents in, 559
    by African Americans, 18, 23, 74, 108, 112, 249, 322, 375, 382-84, 406, 446, 589, 594, 595
    ballots and machines in, 561-62, 562
    candidate traits as factor in, 590-91, 590
    counting of votes in, 561-62, 565-68
    cues in, 481, 589-91, 592

voting (*Continued*)
    in democracy, 21–22
    economy affecting, 570, 571, *571*, 573–74, 591, 594
    equality in, 23
    identification required for, 384, 562, 589
    on initiatives and referenda, 539
    by issue voters, 589
    in local and national elections, 116–17
    by mail, 498, 560, 561, 589, 596–97
    majority, 21, 561
    for minor party candidates, 500
    paradox of, 588
    party identification in, 485, 486–87, *486*, *487*, 570
    party platform affecting, 559
    plurality, 21, 500, 561
    polling places for, 382, 399, *560*
    popular vote in, 565, 568–69
    in presidential election (2016), 446, 487, *569*, *571*
    in presidential election (2020), 17
    racial and ethnic differences in, 18, 382–83, *383*
    redistricting in, *see* redistricting
    registration for, 382–84, 406
    reliability of survey answers on, 446–48
    split tickets in, 591
    straight tickets in, 591
    by women, 19, 23, 74, *75*, 379, 389

voting cues, 484, 589–91, *592* Pieces of information about a candidate that are readily available, easy to interpret, and lead a citizen to decide to vote for a particular candidate.

voting machines, 561–62, *562*
voting rights, 77, 232, 382–84, 406, 560
    of African Americans, *18*, 23, 74, 108, 112, 249, 287, 322, 375, 382–84, 406
    grandfather clause on, 375
    of Latinos, 377
    of Native Americans, 376
    Supreme Court on, 247, 249
    of women, 19, 23, 74, *75*, 379, 389
Voting Rights Act (1965), *18*, 112, 147, 149, 384, 406
    amendments to, 406
    Supreme Court on, 247

Voting Rights Act (VRA) of 1965, 384 A federal law that banned racial discrimination in voting. The law provided for federal election examiners to enforce the law, covered certain jurisdictions with a history of voting discrimination to stop illegal voting practices before they were put in place, and prohibited any jurisdiction from requiring a person to comply with any "test or device" to register to vote or cast a ballot.

voucher programs for education, 328
Vox, 95, 614

Wade, Roe v., 249, 257, 258, 355–56, 357, 408, A110, A111–A112, *A115*, A133–A136, A140, A151, A155, *A156*
Wagner, Robert, 30
Wainwright, Gideon v., 323, 353, A103–A104, *A107*, A108
Wallace, George, 499–500
Wall Street bailout, 135
Wall Street Journal, 132
Walmart, 232, 404–5, 537
Walt Disney Company, 614, *615*
War Department, 284
Warning, A (Anonymous), 622
War of 1812, 67, 191, 476
War on Terror, 65, 69, 77–81, 316–17
war powers, 66–68, 191–95, 205–7, *207*
    of Congress, 66–68
War Powers Resolution (1973), 67–68, 191–95, *195*, 206, 207, *207*
warrants, search, 346–48
Warren, Earl, 237–38, 239, 253, 258, 396
Warren, Elizabeth, 16, 26, 184, 298, *300*, 473, 495, 540, 560, 578–79, 595
Washington, D.C., 90, 110, 344, 396, 634
Washington, George, *43*, 44, 62, 67, 68, 97, 132, 241
    on Congress, 131
    on constitutional amendments, 72
    at Constitutional Convention, 50
    foreign policy of, 76
    justices appointed by, 227
    presidential power of, 185, *185*
Washington (state), 115
Washington Post, 40–41, 132, 170, 224, 428, 615, 616, 617, 622, 623, 626
Washington v. Texas, 323
Watergate scandal, 199, 200, *453*, 454, 504, 546
water supply, lead in, 385–86
wave elections, 144, 591–92
Ways and Means Committee, 159
Weber, Max, 282
Webster v. Reproductive Health Services, A134, *A140*
Weigel, Dave, 626
Weinstein, Harvey, 401
Weisman, Lee v., A96, A99, *A99*
Weld, William, 618
welfare, general, promotion of, 7–8
Wells, Ida B., 389
Westboro Baptist Church, 332–33, *333*, 363
West Virginia State BOE v. Barnette, A92, A94–A95, *A99*, A113, *A115*
West Wing of White House, 203
Wheeler, Andrew, 88–90, 95, 524
Whig Party, 476–77

whip system, 154 An organization of House leaders who work to disseminate information and promote party unity in voting on legislation.

Whitaker, John, 359
White population:
    composition of U.S., 19, *19*
    flight from cities, 396
    police shooting of, 387

    reverse discrimination against, 372, 412–14, 415, 422
    socioeconomic indicators on, 384, *385*
    voting by, 18, *18*, 382, *383*, 406
white primary practice, 375
White supremacists, 334, 337–38
    hate crimes by, 388, *388*
    and Trump, 411
Whitford, Gill v., *A149*, A150
Whole Women's Health v. Hellerstedt, A136, *A140*
WikiLeaks, 199, 338, *339*, 623
Wilcox, John A., *133*
Williams, Harrison A., 360
Wilson, Darren, 334
Wilson, James, 50
Wilson, Woodrow, 185, 186
Windsor, United States v., 111, A138, *A140*

winner-take-all, 563, 565, 566 During the presidential primaries, the practice of assigning all of a given state's delegates to the candidate who receives the most popular votes. Some states' Republican primaries and caucuses use this system.

WinRed, 537
Wisconsin, 317, 329, 337
    presidential election in (2016), 446, 499, 626
    presidential election in (2020), 226, 567, *568*, 569, 589, 596, 600
    redistricting in, 146
    student activity fees in, 335
Wisconsin Right to Life, FEC v., A147

Wisconsin v. Yoder, 317, 329, A97–A98, A99, A100 A 1972 case in which the Supreme Court held that compelling Amish students to attend school past the eighth grade violates the free exercise clause. The ruling opened the door to homeschooling, which is a common practice today.

Wolf v. Colorado, 323, A103, *A107*
women, 19–20
    abortion rights of, 355–56, 357
    affirmative action policies for, 401, 412
    civil rights of, 373, 379–80, 389, 390–91, 399–405, 407–9
    in Congress, 20, 134, 135, 140, *143*, 152, 239
    discrimination against, 236, 372, 379–80, 381–82, 399–405, 407–9, *408*
    as federal court judges, *238*
    on intercollegiate athletic teams, *278*
    as jury members, 379–80
    party identification of, 18, *480*
    pay gap for, 20, 236, 401–4, *404*
    presidential appointments of, 410
    sexual harassment of, 20, 209, 230, 239, 382, 401, 404, 578, 617
    on Supreme Court, 135, 240, 410
    voting rights of, 19, 23, 74, *75*, 379, 389
Women's March (2017), 20, 393, *395*, 535
Women's Rights Convention (1848), 19
Woolworth's, 390

workplace, *see* employment
Works Progress Administration, *103*
World Economic Forum, 196
World Health Organization (WHO), 599
World War I, 186, 191, 331, 376
World War II, 191, 376
    internment camps during, 378–79,
        378, 400
    presidential power in, 186
Wright, Patrisha, 419
Wright, Steven, 349

writ of *certiorari*, 243 The most common
way for a case to reach the Supreme Court,
in which at least four of the nine justices
agree to hear a case that has reached them
via an appeal from the losing party in a lower
court's ruling.

Wyoming, 343

Xi Jinping, 206

Yang, Andrew, 173, 184
Yates, Robert, 60
Yates, Thomas, A17–A24

yellow journalism, 613, 637 A style of
newspaper reporting popular in the late
1800s that featured sensationalized stories,
bold headlines, and illustrations to increase
readership.

Yemen, 344, *353*
Yiannopoulos, Milo, 314, *315*

Yoder, Wisconsin v., 317, 329, A97–A98, *A99*,
    A100
Young Democrats, 480
Young Republicans, 480
YouTube, 336, 616

Zaller, John, 434
Zarda, Altitude Express Inc., 406
Zelensky, Volodymyr, 40
Zelman v. Simmons-Harris, A133, A136–A138,
    A140
Zervos, Summer, 340
Zimmerman, George, 386